Fodor's

GERMANY

NINETEEN

SEP 1 3 2016

WELCOME TO GERMANY

From half-timbered medieval towns to cosmopolitan cities, Germany offers a thoroughly engaging mix of tradition and modernity. You can explore Bavaria's magnificent baroque palaces one day, and immerse yourself in Hamburg's cool, redeveloped HafenCity the next. In hip Berlin, historic sites such as the Brandenburg Gate and contemporary art galleries create exciting contrasts. Throughout the country, discovering world-class museums and cutting-edge design is as quintessentially German as grabbing a stein of beer at a centuries-old *biergarten*.

TOP REASONS TO GO

★ **Castles:** Majestic palaces such as Neuschwanstein seem straight out of a fairy tale.

★ **Fun Cities:** You can party all night in Berlin or soak up culture in Munich.

★ **Music:** From Bach to Beethoven to Wagner, Germany is the birthplace of the classics.

★ **Beer and Wine:** The home of Oktoberfest also surprises with top-notch regional wines.

★ **Markets:** Locally made crafts shine, especially during the Christmas season.

★ **Great Drives:** Scenic roads wind through the Alps and past vineyards and villages.

Fodor's GERMANY

Publisher: Amanda D'Acierno, *Senior Vice President*

Editorial: Arabella Bowen, *Editor in Chief*; Linda Cabasin, *Editorial Director*

Design: Tina Malaney, *Associate Art Director*; Chie Ushio, *Senior Designer*; Erica Cuoco, *Production Designer*

Photography: Jennifer Arnow, *Senior Photo Editor*; Mary Robnett, *Photo Researcher*

Production: Linda Schmidt, *Managing Editor*; Evangelos Vasilakis, *Associate Managing Editor*; Angela L. McLean, *Senior Production Manager*

Maps: Rebecca Baer, *Senior Map Editor*; Mark Stroud (Moon Street Cartographers) and David Lindroth, *Cartographers*

Sales: Jacqueline Lebow, *Sales Director*

Marketing & Publicity: Heather Dalton, *Marketing Director*; Katherine Punia, *Publicity Director*

Business & Operations: Susan Livingston, *Vice President, Strategic Business Planning*; Sue Daulton, *Vice President, Operations*

Fodors.com: Megan Bell, *Executive Director, Revenue & Business Development*; Yasmin Marinaro, *Senior Director, Marketing & Partnerships*

Copyright © 2016 by Fodor's Travel, a division of Penguin Random House LLC

Writers: Dan Allen, Christie Dietz, Lee A. Evans, Adam Groffman, Evelyn Kanter, Jeff Kavanagh, Giulia Pines, Clare Richardson, Leonie Schaumann, Juergen Scheunemann, Courtney Tenz, Yasha Wallin, Elizabeth Willoughby

Editors: Salwa Jabado (lead editor), Caroline Trefler (Berlin editor); Bethany Beckerlegge, Penny Phenix (editorial contributors)

Production Editor: Jennifer DePrima

28th Edition

ISBN 978-1-101-87970-2

ISSN 1525-5034

SPECIAL SALES

This book is available at special discounts for bulk purchases for sales promotions or premiums. For more information, e-mail specialmarkets@penguinrandomhouse.com.

PRINTED IN THE UNITED STATES OF AMERICA

10 9 8 7 6 5 4 3 2 1

CONTENTS

CONTENTS

CONTENTS

MAPS

CONTENTS

ABOUT THIS GUIDE

Fodor's Recommendations

Everything in this guide is worth doing—we don't cover what isn't—but exceptional sights, hotels, and restaurants are recognized with additional accolades. Fodor's Choice ★ indicates our top recommendations; and **Best Bets** call attention to notable hotels and restaurants in various categories. Care to nominate a new place? Visit Fodors.com/contact-us.

Trip Costs

We list prices wherever possible to help you budget well. Hotel and restaurant price categories from $ to $$$$ are noted alongside each recommendation. For hotels, we include the lowest cost of a standard double room in high season. For restaurants, we cite the average price of a main course at dinner or, if dinner isn't served, at lunch. For attractions, we always list adult admission fees; discounts are usually available for children, students, and senior citizens.

Hotels

Our local writers vet every hotel to recommend the best overnights in each price category, from budget to expensive. Unless otherwise specified, you can expect private bath, phone, and TV in your room. For expanded hotel reviews, facilities, and deals visit Fodors.com.

Top Picks	Hotels & Restaurants
★ Fodor'sChoice	🏨 Hotel
Listings	⤴ Number of rooms
✉ Address	⑩ Meal plans
✉ Branch address	✕ Restaurant
☎ Telephone	⎙ Reservations
📠 Fax	🏛 Dress code
🌐 Website	▭ No credit cards
✉ E-mail	$ Price
🎫 Admission fee	
⊙ Open/closed times	**Other**
Ⓜ Subway	⇨ See also
✛ Directions or Map coordinates	☞ Take note
	🏌 Golf facilities

Restaurants

Unless we state otherwise, restaurants are open for lunch and dinner daily. We mention dress code only when there's a specific requirement and reservations only when they're essential or not accepted. To make restaurant reservations, visit Fodors.com.

Credit Cards

The hotels and restaurants in this guide typically accept credit cards. If not, we'll say so.

EUGENE FODOR

Hungarian-born Eugene Fodor (1905–91) began his travel career as an interpreter on a French cruise ship. The experience inspired him to write *On the Continent* (1936), the first guidebook to receive annual updates and discuss a country's way of life as well as its sights. Fodor later joined the U.S. Army and worked for the OSS in World War II. After the war, he kept up his intelligence work while expanding his guidebook series. During the Cold War, many guides were written by fellow agents who understood the value of insider information. Today's guides continue Fodor's legacy by providing travelers with timely coverage, insider tips, and cultural context.

EXPERIENCE
GERMANY

GERMANY TODAY

Germany is a country in transition that is constantly looking for new ways to redefine itself. About the size of Montana but home to Western Europe's largest population, Germany has once again taken a leading economic and political role from its position in the heart in Europe, where it often bridges the divide between East and West. The land of "Dichter und Denker" ("poets and thinkers") is also one of the world's leading export countries, specializing in mechanical equipment, vehicles, chemicals, and household goods. Germany is both deeply conservative, valuing tradition, hard work, precision, and fiscal responsibility, and one of the world's most liberal countries, with a generous social welfare state, a strongly held commitment to environmentalism, and a postwar determination to combat xenophobia. Reunited after 45 years of division, Germany maintains an open dialogue about the darkest aspects of its history while simultaneously thinking toward the future.

Integration

In the 1950s and 1960s, West Germany invited migrants to come work on projects to rebuild after the Second World War and fuel the postwar economic boom. "Guest workers" from Italy, Greece, the former Yugoslavia, and above all Turkey provided cheap labor. The Germans assumed these guest workers would only stay temporarily, so they provided little in the way of cultural integration policies. But many of these migrants were manual workers from the countryside with little formal education, and often they did not want to return to their economically depressed home countries. Instead, they brought wives and family members to join them and settled in Germany, often forming parallel societies cut off from mainstream

German life. Today, Berlin is home to the largest Turkish community outside of Turkey itself, and even claims to be the birthplace of the *döner kebab,* the ubiquitous fast-food dish. However, Germany has fumbled somewhat when it comes to successful integration. Germany is historically a land of emigrants, not immigrants, but its demographics are undergoing a radical shift: the country recently became the second-most-popular migration destination after the United States, and one in three children in Germany today is foreign-born or has a parent who is foreign-born. In recent years, anti-immigrant sentiment has given rise to far-right nationalist parties, but their demonstrations are usually wildly outnumbered by much larger counterprotests.

Eurozone Enforcer

Germany, the world's fourth-largest economy, was the world's largest exporter until 2009, when China overtook it. The worldwide recession hit Germany squarely, though thanks to a strong social network, the unemployed and underemployed did not suffer on the level we are used to in the United States. In Germany, losing your job does not mean you lose your health insurance, and the unemployed receive financial help from the state to meet housing payments and other basic expenses. More recently, Germany has been a bastion of economic strength during the eurozone crisis, maintaining a solid economy while countries like Greece, Spain, and Portugal have entered into economic tailspins. By far the most important economy in the European Union, Germany, with its traditional, don't-spend-more-than-you-earn culture, has a strong voice in setting the EU's economic agenda. It took center stage following the euro crisis in its negotiations with Greece over further bailout packages. Germany was seen as taking a hard line against Athens for not repaying its loans, and many noted Berlin's approach was perhaps best understood by the fact that the German word for debt, *Schuld*, is the same word for guilt.

Engineer This

Germany has a well-deserved reputation as a land of engineers. The global leader in numerous high-tech fields, German companies are hugely successful on the world's export markets, thanks to lots of innovation, sophisticated technology, and quality manufacturing. German cars, machinery, and electrical and electronic equipment are all big sellers. But recent years have seen a series of bloopers. Three major building projects in Germany—the Elbphilharmonie concert hall in Hamburg; Stuttgart 21, a new train station in Stuttgart; and the new airport in Berlin—have run way over budget and dragged on for years. Of the three, the airport is the most egregious: originally planned to open in 2010, Berlin Brandenburg Airport has suffered delays due to poor construction planning, management, and execution (in 2012, the airport canceled its grand opening only days before flights were scheduled to begin). No one knows when it will open, and numerous politicians have expressed concern that failures like these will tarnish Germany's reputation as a country of can-do engineers.

Privacy, Please

The Germans are not big fans of Facebook. With good reason: following recent experiences of life in a police state under both the Nazi regime and the East German state, they don't like the idea of anyone collecting personal information about them. Germany has some of the most extensive data privacy laws in the world,

with everything from credit card numbers to medical histories strictly protected.

To the Left, to the Left

By American standards, German politics are distinctly left-leaning. One thing that's important to know is that the Germans don't have a two-party system; rather, they have several important parties, and these must form alliances after elections to pass initiatives. Thus, there's an emphasis on cooperation and deal-making, sometimes (but not always) making for odd bedfellows. A "Red-Green" (or "stoplight") coalition between the Green Party and the socialist SPD held power from 1998 to 2002; since then, there has been a steady move to the center-right in Germany, with recent reforms curtailing some social welfare benefits and ecological reforms. In 2005, Germany elected the first female chancellor, center-right Christian Democratic party member Angela Merkel. A politician from the former East Germany who speaks Russian, Merkel has enjoyed much popularity.

Going Green

In the early 2000s, Germany began moving away from fossil fuels toward renewable energy sources such as solar and wind, a policy known as *Energiewende*—literally, "energy transition." The transformation is a role model for many environmentalists, and thanks to aggressive government legislation over the past few decades, Germany is a leader in green energy technology. In 2014, 26% of the electricity produced nationwide came from renewable sources.

WHAT'S WHERE

1 Munich. Beautiful Munich boasts wonderful opera, theater, museums, and churches—and the city's chic residents dress their best to visit them. This city also has lovely outdoor spaces, from parks, beer gardens, and cafés, to the famous Oktoberfest grounds.

2 The Bavarian Alps. Majestic peaks, lush green pastures, and frescoed houses brightened by flowers make for one of Germany's most photogenic regions. Quaint villages like Mittenwald, Garmisch-Partenkirchen, Oberammergau, and Berchtesgaden have preserved their charming historic architecture. Nature is the prime attraction here, with the country's finest hiking and skiing.

3 The Romantic Road. The Romantische Strasse is more than 355 km (220 miles) of soaring castles, medieval villages, *fachwerk* (half-timber) houses, and imposing churches, all set against a pastoral backdrop. Winding its way from Würzburg to Füssen, it features such top destinations as Rothenburg-ob-der-Tauber and Schloss Neuschwanstein, King Ludwig II's fantastical castle.

4 Franconia and the German Danube. Thanks to the centuries-old success of craftsmanship and trade, Franconia is a proud, independent-minded region in northern Bavaria. Franconia is home to historic Nürnberg, the well-preserved medieval jewel-box town of Bamberg, and Bayreuth, where Wagner lived and composed.

5 The Bodensee. The sunniest region in the country, the Bodensee (Lake Constance) itself is the highlight. The region is surrounded by beautiful mountains, and the dense natural surroundings offer an enchanting contrast to the picture-perfect towns and manicured gardens.

6 The Black Forest. Synonymous with cuckoo clocks and primeval woodland that is great for hiking, the Black Forest includes the historic university town of Freiburg—one of the most colorful and hip student cities in Germany—and proud and elegant Baden-Baden, with its long tradition of spas and casinos.

7 Heidelberg and the Neckar Valley. This medieval town is quintessential Germany, full of cobblestone alleys, half-timber houses, vineyards, castles, wine pubs, and Germany's oldest university.

1

WHAT'S WHERE

8 Frankfurt. Nicknamed "Mainhattan" because it is the only German city with appreciable skyscrapers, Frankfurt is Germany's financial center and transportation hub.

9 The Pfalz and Rhine Terrace. Wine reigns supreme here. Bacchanalian festivals pepper the calendar between May and October, and wineries welcome drop-ins for tastings year-round. Three great cathedrals are found in Worms, Speyer, and Mainz.

10 The Rhineland. The region along the mighty Rhine River is one of the most dynamic in Europe. Fascinating cities such as Köln (Cologne), steeped in Roman and medieval history, offer stunning Gothic architecture, such as the Kölner Dom. Visit during Karneval for boisterous celebrations.

11 The Fairy-Tale Road. The Märchenstrasse, stretching 600 km (370 miles) between Hanau and Bremen, is the Brothers Grimm country. They nourished their dark and magical imaginations as children in Steinau an der Strasse, a beautiful medieval town in this region of misty woodlands and ancient castles.

12 Hamburg. Hamburg, with its long tradition as a powerful and wealthy Hanseatic port city, is quintessentially elegant. World-class museums of modern art; the wild red-light district along the Reeperbahn; and HafenCity, an environmentally and architecturally avant-garde quarter currently under construction, make Hamburg well worth a visit.

13 Schleswig-Holstein and the Baltic Coast. Off the beaten path, this region is scattered with medieval towns, fishing villages, unspoiled beaches, and summer resorts like Sylt, where Germany's jet set go to get away.

14 Berlin. No trip to Germany is complete without a visit to its capital, Europe's hippest urban destination. Cheap rents drew artists from all over the world to this gritty, creative, and broke city. Cutting-edge art exhibits, stage dramas, musicals, and bands compete for your attention with two cities' worth of world-class museums, three opera houses, eight state theaters, and two zoos.

15 Saxony, Saxony-Anhalt, and Thuringia. The southeast is a secret treasure trove of German high culture. Friendly, vibrant cities like Dresden, Leipzig, Weimar, and Eisenach are linked to Schiller, Goethe, Bach, Luther, and the like.

NEED TO KNOW

Berlin ✪

GERMANY

AT A GLANCE

Capital: Berlin

Population: 81,000,000

Currency: Euro

Money: ATMs common; credit cards not widely accepted

Language: German

Country Code: 49

Emergencies: 110

Driving: On the right

Electricity: 220–240v/50 cycles; plugs have two round prongs

Time: Six hours ahead of New York

Documents: Up to 90 days with valid passport; Schengen rules apply

Mobile Phones: GSM (900 and 1800 bands)

Major Mobile Companies: Telekom, Vodafone, o2, E-Plus

WEBSITES

Germany: ⊕ www.germany.travel

Berlin: ⊕ www.visitberlin.de

Bavaria: ⊕ www.bavaria.us

GETTING AROUND

✈ **Air Travel:** Germany's major hubs are Frankfurt and Munich. Berlin is served by two smaller international airports, Tegel and Schönefeld.

🚌 **Bus Travel:** Buses cover major routes at much cheaper prices than trains or planes.

🚗 **Car Travel:** Renting a car is easy in any city and highways are top quality, but gas is expensive.

🚆 **Train Travel:** Germany has an excellent rail network, but trains can be more expensive than flying. Book early for the best deals. High-speed InterCity Express (ICE) trains connect major cities.

PLAN YOUR BUDGET

	HOTEL ROOM	MEAL	ATTRACTIONS
Low Budget	€90	€12	Bier & Oktoberfest Museum, €4
Mid Budget	€160	€25	Neuschwanstein and Hohenschwangau Castles admission, €23
High Budget	€220	€80	Berlin's Staatsoper performance, €80

WAYS TO SAVE

Picnic in the park. Germany has wonderful outdoor markets perfect for gathering picnic provisions. In winter, market halls offer indoor alternatives.

Book a rental apartment. Families and groups can get more space and a kitchen for less with a rental.

Buy train tickets in advance. For the cheapest rail fares, book online up to 90 days before travel. ⊕ www.bahn.de

Look for free museum days. Many museums are free one day a week.

Hassle Factor	Low. Flights to Germany are frequent, and it has a fantastic network of trains, buses, and cheap domestic flights.
3 days	Visit one major city, like Berlin or Munich, and venture out of town on a half- or full-day trip.
1 week	Combine two major destinations, visiting Hamburg, Dresden, or Leipzig along with Berlin, or the Bavarian Alps along with Munich. Enjoy a boat cruise along a scenic German river, like the Rhine, the Elbe, or the Mosel.
2 weeks	Pick a region to explore in depth, combining stops in major cities with a long weekend at the Baltic Sea's beaches and islands or a hiking trip through the legendary Black Forest.

WHEN TO GO

High Season: June through August is the most popular and expensive time to visit. In July and August, many Germans take vacation and leave the cities for the beach (in the north) or mountains and lakes (in the south). Flocks of tourists visit in December for Germany's charming Christmas markets.

Low Season: January to March is cold and dark, and locals may be in sour moods from the seemingly endless string of gray days. Consequently, there are deals on lodging and airfare.

Value Season: September is gorgeous, with temperate weather and saner airfares. Temperatures start to drop by late November. Late April or early May is also a great time to visit, before crowds arrive but when the trees are in bloom and the locals are reveling in the return of spring. However, the weather can be unpredictable and wet.

BIG EVENTS

May: On May Day (May 1), there are street festivals and leftist protests for workers' rights.

June: Musicians perform throughout Berlin during the daylong festival Fête de la Musique. ⊕ www.fetedelamusique.de

September: Oktoberfest, the world's biggest beer festival, actually begins in September. ⊕ www.oktoberfest.de

February: Cologne celebrates Carnival with street parties and parades. ⊕ www.koelnerkarneval.de

READ THIS

■ *Five Germanys I Have Known,* Fritz Stern. Twentieth-century German historical memoir.

■ *Stasiland,* Anna Funder. Personal stories of life under East Germany's secret police.

■ *Germania,* Simon Winder. A satirical account of Germany and its people.

WATCH THIS

■ *The Lives of Others.* A Stasi agent in East Berlin spies on a playwright and his lover.

■ *Wings of Desire.* Angels watch over a divided Berlin.

■ *Cabaret.* An iconic film set in Weimar Germany.

EAT THIS

■ *Currywurst*: sliced sausage drenched in curry powder and ketchup

■ *Schweinshaxe*: Bavarian crispy pork knuckle

■ *Käsespätzle*: Swabian noodles topped with melted cheese and sometimes fried onions

■ *Weisser Spargel*: sweet white asparagus (April/May)

■ *Germknödel*: a dumpling filled with plum sauce and topped with poppy seeds

■ *Stollen*: fruitcake covered in powdered sugar, a favorite at Christmastime

GERMANY
TOP ATTRACTIONS

Berlin, Capital City

(A) Berlin was the capital of Prussia, the German Empire, the Weimar Republic, and the Third Reich before being divided after World War II. The famed Brandenburger Tor (Brandenburg Gate), built in the late 1700s, became a symbol of both the country's division and reunification. The nearby Reichstag (parliament building) was rebuilt with a special glass dome that offers sweeping views of the city and looks directly into the parliament chambers below in a nod to government transparency. In former East Berlin, the soaring TV tower at Alexanderplatz is a reminder of the GDR's political power.

Bodensee

The blue waters of Bodensee (Lake Constance) lap the shores of Switzerland and Austria, framed by a stunning view of the Alps. The beach offers space for sunbathers and lakeside paths are available for cyclists. On the island of Mainau you can stroll through peaceful gardens on the grounds of a baroque palace.

Black Forest

(B) Thousands of miles of hiking and cycling trails guide you through pine and fir trees in these woodlands. The area's many thermal baths provide an opportunity to treat yourself after a long day outdoors.

Frauenkirche, Dresden

(C) Dresden's Church of Our Lady is a masterpiece of baroque architecture. Completed in 1743, the magnificent church was destroyed by an Allied bombing raid in February 1945. The church was finally rebuilt in its original style 60 years later, using much of the rubble.

Heidelberg Castle

(D) Heidelberg's immense ruined fortress is a prime example of Renaissance and Gothic styles. It inspired 19th-century writers, especially the poet Goethe, who

admired its decay amidst the beauty of the Neckar Valley.

Kölner Dom
(E) This breathtaking cathedral in Köln (Cologne) is the first sight that greets you when you step out of the train station. The Gothic marvel took more than 600 years to build and was the tallest structure in the world when it was finished in 1880.

Munich's Oktoberfest
(F) For 15 days spanning the end of September and early October, Munich hosts the world's largest beer festival with tents from traditional German breweries.

Neuschwanstein Castle
(G) Walt Disney modeled the castle in *Sleeping Beauty* and later the Disneyland castle itself on Neuschwanstein. "Mad" King Ludwig II's creation is best admired from the heights of the Marienbrücke, an iron bridge over the deep Pöllat Gorge.

The Berlin Wall
(H) When the wall fell in 1989, Berliners couldn't wait to get rid of it. The longest stretch left standing is the East Side Gallery. In 1990, the city invited artists to paint one side of the nearly mile-long wall in a tribute to peace, resulting in famous works such as the socialistic fraternal kiss. The Berlin Wall Memorial, located along another remaining segment, has a museum and open-air exhibition dedicated to the years of division. At the best-known border crossing, the Checkpoint Charlie Museum highlights ways people tried to escape the GDR.

Weimar: Goethe, Schiller, Bauhaus
(I) Weimar was once home to German luminaries such as Goethe and Schiller, whose homes are now museums. The Bauhaus movement, which gave rise to much of modern architecture and design, was also born here—as you'll learn on a visit to the Bauhaus Museum Weimar.

TOP EXPERIENCES

Imbibe in a Beer Garden

As soon as the sun comes out and temperatures allow, Germans set up tables and chairs under the open skies and offer a "Prost!" to their friends or colleagues. Bavaria is the home of the *Biergarten,* but you can sample local variations of beer and bratwurst at outdoor tables almost anywhere in the country. If it's a beautiful day and you don't see a beer garden nearby, take your own drink to the park: Germany has no open-container laws.

Hike a Mountain

Germany's landscape is ideal for hiking, from leisurely strolls through flat fields to steep climbs up tough terrain. The country has tens of thousands of miles of walking trails, many with views of castles, vineyards, or waterfalls. Pack a bag lunch, strap on your hiking boots, and join the crowd—it's a great way to get a feel for the real Germany.

Eat White Asparagus

If you visit between April and June, you're in for a treat: it's white asparagus season. Germans go crazy for the stuff, which is thicker and larger than green asparagus. Enjoy it with a slice of ham and potatoes with butter or hollandaise sauce.

Visit a Museum

Every major German city has world-class art museums, but it doesn't stop there. From the antique treasures in Berlin's legendary Pergamon Museum, to fascinating objects in the fields of science and technology at Munich's Deutsches Museum, Germany has impressive and informative exhibitions around the country. Open-air museums offer collections of buildings from previous epochs that visitors can walk through to get a sense of daily life in the past.

Take a Bike Tour

Whether you're discovering Munich, Dresden, Cologne, Hamburg, Berlin, or one of Germany's smaller cities, seeing the place from the seat of a bike is the way to do it. Take a guided tour or rent a bike and set off on your own. As you wind your way through Munich's English Garden or along Hamburg's harbor, you'll find that you see much more than you would from a tour bus.

Enjoy a German Breakfast

Breakfast in Germany can be a major affair, especially on the weekend. Show up hungry to indulge in a spread including several types of bread rolls, salami and dry sausage, hard cheeses, butter, honey, jam, sliced tomatoes, sliced cucumber, liver pâté, cold cuts, hard-boiled eggs, and coffee.

Snack at the Bakery

Germany takes its bread seriously. It's a historically important part of the German diet, and the tradition of *Brotkultur,* or bread culture, continues today. Each region has its own delicious variation, so wherever you visit check out a local artisanal *Bäckerei* and sample the various pastries and rolls.

Take a Curative Bath

With more than 300 *Kurorte* (health spas) and *Heilbäder* (spas with healing waters), Germany has a spa tradition dating back to the time of the Kaisers. Visit one by the sea, near mineral-rich mud sources, near salt deposits, or natural springs, and you'll be treated to salt baths, mud baths, saunas, thermal hot springs, and mineral-rich air, depending on the specialties of the region.

Cruise along the Rhine

No trip to Germany is complete without a boat tour of the Rhine. Board in Rudesheim and follow the river to Bingen, or do it in reverse. Along the way, you'll see countless castles rising up from the banks along the river. Keep a lookout for the rock of the Loreley, the beautiful river maiden of legend who lured sailors to their deaths with her song.

Sip Wine at a Vineyard

Germany is internationally renowned for its beer, but it's also an oenologist's dream. Go to a wine tasting to try high-quality Riesling and Pinot Noir on the sloping hills of the Mosel Valley and find new favorites to fill your cellar.

Browse a Christmas Market

Just about every city, town, and village has an outdoor Christmas market (and larger cities have more than one—in Berlin, for example, there are as many as 60 small markets each year). The most famous are the markets in Dresden and Nürnberg, both of which have long traditions. Christmas markets open the last week of November and run through Christmas. Bundle up and shop for handmade gifts like the famous wooden figures carved in the Erzgebirge region as you sip traditional, hot-spiced *Glühwein* to stay warm.

Drive on the Autobahn

Germany is the spiritual home of precision auto engineering, and Germans love their cars. You can rent a Porsche, Mercedes, or BMW for a day to see what it's like to drive on a German highway—some stretches of the autobahn have no speed limit. Take your rental to the Nürburgring, a world-famous racetrack built in the 1920s. There, you can get a day pass to drive your car around the track. Visit the on-site auto museum afterward. Both BMW and Mercedes-Benz have fantastic museums, too.

Take a Dip in a Lake

Germany is dotted with tranquil lakes, and when the weather is warm, locals strip down and jump right in. Don't worry if you don't have your suit: it's perfectly acceptable to swim in the nude. If swimming's not your thing, rent a paddleboat and cruise past the sunbathers.

Watch a Movie Under the Stars

Throughout the summer, many German cities set up huge screens in parks and other public places. Spread out a blanket and enjoy snacks and beer in the open air at a *Freiluftkino*. You can catch a movie in English or German with subtitles—just check the day's program.

Cheer at a Soccer Game

As you might expect of the recent world champions, Germans are nuts for soccer. Even if you aren't a fan, going to a live match is an exciting experience. There's a palpable energy and it's easy to follow the action. You can catch a game just about anywhere, anytime except for June, July, and over the Christmas break.

Go Sledding

In winter, children and adults alike head for the nearest slope, sleds in hand. If you don't have a sled, just stand back and enjoy the spectacle. The children's old-fashioned wooden sleds are truly charming.

QUINTESSENTIAL GERMANY

Culture Vultures

With more theaters, concert halls, and opera houses per capita than any other country in the world, high culture is an important part of German life. Before the formation of the German state, regional courts competed to see who had the best artists, actors, musicians, and stages, resulting in the development of a network of strong cultural centers that exists to this day. For Germans, high culture is not just for the elite. They consider it so important to provide communities with rich cultural life that they use their tax money to do it. As a result, tickets to these publicly funded operas, classical music concerts, ballets, and plays are quite inexpensive, with tickets readily available in the €10 to €40 range. Drop in on a performance or concert—it's one of the best travel bargains around.

Another Beer, Bitte

The German *Kneipekultur,* or pub culture, is an important and long-standing tradition. *Stammgäste,* or regulars, stop by their local pub as often as every evening to drink beer and catch up. In summer, *Kneipe* life moves outdoors to beer gardens. Some, such as the famous Chinese Pavilion in Munich's English Garden, are institutions, and can seat hundreds of guests. Others are more casual, consisting of a café's graveled back garden under soaring chestnut trees. Most beer gardens offer some sort of food: self-serve areas might sell pasta or lamb in addition to grilled sausages and pretzels. Although beer gardens are found all over Germany, the smoky beer-hall experience—with dirndls and oompah bands—is traditionally Bavarian. You'll discover how different various combinations of the three key ingredients—malt, hops, and water—can taste.

If you want to get a sense of contemporary German culture and indulge in some of its pleasures, start by familiarizing yourself with the rituals of daily life.

Easy Being Green

Germany has one of the world's most environmentally conscious societies. Conserving resources, whether electricity or food, is second nature in a country where postwar deprivation has not yet faded from public memory. Recycling is practically a national sport, with separate garbage bins for regular trash, clear glass, green glass, plastics and cans, and organic garbage. Keep your eyes out for the giant brown, green, and yellow pods on the streets—these are used for neighborhood recycling. Many people ride their bikes to work (even in high heels or business suits) much of the year, and there are well-defined bike lanes in most cities. Drivers know to keep an eye out for cyclists, and as a visitor you'll need to be careful not to walk in the bike lanes. Great public transportation is also part of this environmental commitment.

Kaffe und Kuchen

The tradition of afternoon coffee and cake, usually enjoyed around 3 pm, is a serious matter. If you can, finagle an invitation to someone's house to get the real experience, which might involve a simple homemade *Quarkkuchen* (cheesecake), or a spread of creamy cakes topped with apples, rhubarb, strawberries, or cherries and whipped cream. Otherwise, find an old-fashioned *Konditorei,* or pastry shop. Germans bake more than a thousand different kinds of cakes, with even more regional variations. Among the most famous is the *Schwarzwälder Kirschtorte* (Black Forest cake), a chocolate layer cake soaked in *Kirsch* schnapps, with cherries, whipped cream, and chocolate shavings. Another favorite is the *Bienenstich* (bee sting), a layered sponge cake filled with cream and topped with a layer of crunchy honey-caramelized almonds.

IF YOU LIKE

Being Outdoors

The Germans have a long-standing love affair with Mother Nature. The woods, as well as the mountains, rivers, and oceans, surface repeatedly in the works of renowned German poets and thinkers. The idea that nature is key to the mysteries of the soul can be seen in works as varied as those by naturalist Romantic painter Caspar David Friedrich and the 20th-century philosopher Martin Heidegger. Today, Germany has designated large tracts of land as national recreation areas, and cities boast extensive urban parks and gardens.

The Bavarian Alps, where the Winter Olympics town **Garmisch-Partenkirchen** offers cable cars to ascend Germany's highest mountain, the **Zugspitze,** is one of the country's best spots for skiing in winter and hiking in summer.

Lakes such as **Chiemsee** and **Bodensee** dot the area between the Alps and Munich and many hikers and bikers enjoy circling them. Boat rentals are possible, but you'll often need a German-recognized license. In summer, walk a trail around the pure waters of **Lake Königssee,** pausing to hear your voice echo off the surrounding rock faces.

On the island of **Rügen,** the turn-of-the-20th-century resort town **Binz** stands before the gentle (and cold) waters of the Baltic Sea. Even on windy days you can warm up on the beach in a sheltered beach chair for two. Among the Baltic Coast's most dramatic features are Rügen's white chalk cliffs in **Jasmund National Park,** where you can hike, bike, or sign up for nature seminars and tours.

Medieval Towns

The trail of walled towns and half-timber houses known as the **Romantic Road** is a route long marketed by German tourism, and therefore the road more traveled. The towns are lovely, but if you'd prefer fewer tour groups spilling into your photographs, venture into the Harz Mountains in the center of Germany.

Rothenburg-ob-der-Tauber is known for its impressively preserved medieval center, giving visitors the feeling they've stepped back in time. Some 400 km farther north, **Quedlinburg** has been declared a UNESCO World Heritage site. With 1,600 half-timber houses, it has more of these historic, typically northern German buildings than any other town in the country.

A mighty fortress south of the Harz Mountains is the **Wartburg,** in the ancient, half-timber town of **Eisenach.** Frederick the Wise protected Martin Luther from papal proscription within these stout walls in the 16th century.

Options for exploring closer to Munich include **Regensburg** and **Nürnberg.** The former is a beautiful medieval city, relatively unknown even to Germans, and has a soaring French Gothic cathedral that can hold 6,000 people. Nürnberg dates to 1050, and is among the most historic cities in the country. Both emperors and artists convened here, including the Renaissance genius Albrecht Dürer. If you're in Hessen, the birthplace of the Brothers Grimm, you can follow the **Fairy-Tale Road.** Stop off for a day of natural saltwater swimming in the idyllic medieval town of **Bad Sooden-Allendorf.**

The Arts

With as many as 600 galleries, world-class private collections, and ateliers in every *Hinterhof* (back courtyard), **Berlin** is one of Europe's contemporary art capitals. Berlin's **Museumsinsel** (Museum Island), a UNESCO World Heritage site, is its crowning jewel. The small island hosts a complex of five state museums, including the **Altes Museum**, with a permanent collection of classical antiquities; the **Alte Nationalgalerie**, with 18th- to early-20th-century paintings and sculptures from the likes of Cézanne, Rodin, Degas, and Germany's own Max Liebermann; the **Bode-Museum**, containing German and Italian sculptures, Byzantine art, and coins; and the **Pergamonmuseum**, whose highlight is the world-famous Ishtar Gate, an entrance to the ancient city of Babylon in modern-day Iraq.

Leipzig is a rising star in the European art world. The **Museum der Bildenden Künste** (Museum of Fine Arts) is the city's leading gallery, followed closely by the **Grassimuseum** complex. The **Spinnerei** (a former cotton mill) has become Leipzig's prime location for contemporary art, and houses more than 80 artists and galleries, especially those of the New Leipzig School.

Fans of old-master painters must haunt the halls of the **Zwinger** in Dresden, where most works were collected in the first half of the 18th century, and the **Alte Pinakothek** in Munich, which has one of the world's largest collections of Rubens.

Castles and Palaces

Watching over nearly any town with a name ending in "-burg" is a medieval fortress or Renaissance palace. These have often been converted into museums, restaurants, or hotels.

The **Wartburg** in Eisenach is considered "the mother of all castles" and towers over the foothills of the Thuringian Forest. Abundant vineyards surround **Schloss Neuenburg**, which dominates the landscape around the sleepy village of Freyburg (Unstrut). The castle ruins overlooking the Rhine River are the result of constant fighting with the French, but even the remains were picturesque enough to inspire 19th-century Romantics. **Burg Rheinstein** is rich with Gobelin tapestries, stained glass, and frescoes.

Schloss Heidelberg mesmerizes with its Gothic turrets, Renaissance walls, and abandoned gardens. Other fortresses lord over the **Burgenstrasse** (Castle Road) in the neighboring **Neckar Valley**. You can stay the night (or just enjoy an excellent meal) at **Burg Hornberg**, or at any of a number of other castle-hotels in the area.

The medieval **Burg Eltz** in the Mosel Valley looms imposingly, and its high turrets make it look like something straight out of a Grimm fairy tale. The castle has been perfectly preserved and owned by the same family for almost a thousand years.

Louis XIV's Versailles inspired Germany's greatest castle-builder, King Ludwig II, to construct the opulent **Schloss Herrenchiemsee**. One of Ludwig's palaces in turn inspired a latter-day visionary—his **Schloss Neuschwanstein** is the model for Walt Disney's Sleeping Beauty Castle. **Schloss Linderhof**, also in the Bavarian Alps, was Ludwig's favorite retreat.

FLAVORS OF GERMANY

Traditional German cuisine fell out of fashion several decades ago, and was replaced by Italian and Mediterranean food, Asian food, and Middle Eastern food. But there's a growing movement to go back to those roots, and even high-class German chefs are rediscovering old classics, from sauerkraut to *Sauerbraten* (traditional German pot roast). Traditional fruits and vegetables, from parsnips and pumpkins to black salsify, sunchoke, cabbage, yellow carrots, and little-known strawberry and apple varietals, are all making a comeback. That said, "German food" is a bit of a misnomer, as traditional cooking varies greatly from region to region. Look for the "typical" dish, wherever you are, to get the best sense of German cooking.

Generally speaking, regions in the south, like Baden-Württemberg and Bavaria, have held onto their culinary traditions more than states in the north. But with a little effort, you can find good German food just about anywhere you go.

Bavaria: White Sausage and Beer (for Breakfast)

In Bavaria, a traditional farmer's *Zweites Frühstück* (second breakfast) found at any beer hall consists of fat white sausages, called *Weisswurst*, made of veal and eaten with sweet mustard, pretzels, and, yes, a big glass of *Helles* or *Weissbier* (light or wheat beer). Other Bavarian specialties include *Leberkäse* (literally, "liver cheese"), a meat loaf of pork and beef that can be eaten sliced on bread, and tastes a lot better than it sounds. *Knödelgerichte*, or noodle dishes, are also popular.

Swabia: The Sausage Salad

Swabia (the area surrounding Stuttgart) is generally thought to have some of the best traditional food in Germany, having held onto its culinary heritage better than other areas. *Schwäbische Wurstsalat* (Swabian sausage salad), a salad of sliced sausage dressed with onions, vinegar, and oil, is a typical dish, as is *Käsespätzle* (Swabian pasta with cheese), a noodlelike dish made from flour, egg, and water topped with cheese. *Linsen mit Spätzle* (lentils and spätzle) could be considered the Swabian national dish: it consists of egg noodles topped with lentils and, often, a sausage.

Franconia: Nürnberger Bratwürste

Perhaps the most beloved of all *Bratwürste* (sausages) in a country that loves sausages is the small, thin sausage from the city of Nürnberg. Grilled over a beech-wood fire, it is served 6 or 12 at a time with horseradish and sauerkraut or potato salad. Fresh marjoram and ground caraway seeds give the pork-based sausage its distinctive flavor.

Hessen: Apfelwein in Frankfurt

Apfelwein (hard apple cider) is a specialty in and around Frankfurt. Look for an *Apfelweinkneipe* (cider bar), where you can spend a pleasant evening sipping this tasty alcoholic drink. Order *Handkäse*, traditional Hessian curdled milk cheese, to go with it. If you order *Handkäse mit Musik* (Handkäse with music), you'll get it with onions. Another winner is *Frankfurter Rippchen*, spare ribs served with sauerkraut.

Rhineland: Horse Meat and Kölsch

In Köln (Cologne), influenced by nearby Belgium and Holland, there's a traditional taste for horse meat, which they use in their local version of the pot roast, *Rheinische Sauerbraten*. Or try the *Kölsche Kaviar*—blood sausage with onions. Wash these dishes down with the local beer, *Kölsch*.

Northwest Germany: Herring with That?

States near the north coast, like Bremen, Hamburg, Westphalia, and Schleswig-Holstein, all have cuisines that are oriented toward the sea. Cod, crab, herring, and flatfish are all common traditional foods. *Labskaus,* a traditional fisherman's dish of choice, is made from corned beef, however. The salty meal comes with accompaniments such as fried egg, herring, pickle, and red beets. For your fix of vegetables, potatoes, cabbage, and rutabagas are all served stewed or pickled. *Rote Grütze,* a traditional dessert, is a berry pudding often served with whipped cream.

Northeast Germany: Currywurst and More

Berlin is known for its *Eisbein* (pork knuckle), *Kasseler* (smoked pork chop), *Bockwurst* (large sausage), and *Boulette* (a kind of hamburger made of beef and pork), but its most famous dish is *Currywurst,* a Berlin-born snack that consists of sausage cut in pieces and covered in ketchup and curry powder, often served with a side of fries. Brandenburg's idyllic Spreewald is famous for its pickled gherkins.

The East: Da, Soljanka

In former GDR states like Saxony, Saxony-Anhalt, and Thuringia, the Soviet influence can be felt in the popularity of traditionally Russian dishes like *Soljanka* (meat soup). *Rotkäppchen* sparkling wines come from Saxony-Anhalt, Germany's northernmost wine-making region (named for the company's bottles with red tops, Rotkäppchen is also the German name for Little Red Riding Hood). Another local treat is *Baumkuchen,* or tree cake, which is formed by adding layer upon layer of batter on a spit and rotating it over a heat source. When you cut into the cake, it looks like the rings of a tree—hence the name.

The Döner Kebab: It's Fine Anytime

It would be hard to visit Germany without trying this Turkish sandwich, whether for lunch, dinner, or a snack after a night out on the town. Made from some combination of lamb, chicken, pork, or beef roasted on a spit then sliced into pita pockets with lettuce, chopped tomato, yogurt, and spicy sauce, the döner kebab is the indisputable king of snack food. An inexpensive alternative to German fare, they're available on almost any city corner.

Seasonal Favorites

Germans are very much attuned to seasonal fruits and vegetables. Traditional German produce like white asparagus, strawberries, plums, cherries, blueberries, and apples are for sale in supermarkets, farmers' markets, and from sidewalk sellers. When in season, these are delicious items to add to your diet and a healthy way to keep your blood sugar up as you set off to explore Germany.

BEERS OF GERMANY

Beer, or "liquid bread" as it was described by medieval monks who wanted to avoid God's anger, is not just a vital element of German cuisine, but of German culture. The stats say Germans are second only to the Czechs when it comes to per capita beer consumption, though they have been losing their thirst recently—from a peak of 146 liters (about 39 gallons) per head in 1980, each German now only manages 107 liters (roughly 28 gallons) every year. And yet the range of beers has never been wider.

Reinheitsgebot (Purity Law)

There are over 1,300 breweries in Germany, offering more than 5,000 types of beer. Thanks to Germany's ancient "Beer Purity Law," or *Reinheitsgebot*, which allowed only three ingredients (water, malt, and hops), they are all very high quality. The water used in German beer also has to meet certain standards—a recent discussion about introducing fracking in certain parts of Germany was roundly criticized by the German Beer Association because the water in the area would become too dirty to use for making beer.

Germany's Major Beer Varieties

Pils: One effect of the Beer Purity Law was that Germany became dominated by one kind of beer: *Pils*. Invented in Bohemia (now the Czech Republic) in 1842, and aided by Bavarian refrigeration techniques, Pils was the first beer to be chilled and stored, thus allowing bottom fermentation, better clarity, and a longer shelf life. Today, the majority of German beers are brewed in the Pils, or Pilsner, style. German Pils tends to have a drier, more bitter taste than what you might be used to, but a trip to Germany is hardly complete without the grand tour along these lines: Augustiner in Bavaria, Bitburger in the Rhineland, Flensburger in the north.

Helles: *Hell* is German for "light," but when it comes to beer, that refers to the color rather than the alcohol content. *Helles* is a crisp and clear Bavarian pale lager with between 4.5% and 6% alcohol. It was developed in the mid-19th century by a German brewer named Gabriel Sedlmayr, who adopted and adapted some British techniques to create the new beer for his famous Spaten Brewery in Bavaria. Another brewer, Josef Groll, used the same methods to produce one of the first German Pils, Pilsner Urquell. Spaten is still one the best brands for a good Helles, as are Löwenbräu, Weihenstephaner, and Hacker-Pschorr—all classic Bavarian beers.

Dunkelbier: At the other end of the beer rainbow from Helles is dark beer, or *Dunkelbier*. The dark, reddish color is a consequence of the darker malt that is used in the brewing. Despite suspicions aroused by the stronger, maltier taste, Dunkelbier actually contains no more alcohol than Helles. Dunkelbier was common in rural Bavaria in the early 19th century. All the major Bavarian breweries produce a Dunkelbier to complement their Helles.

Bock: Dunkelbier should not be confused with *Bock*, which also has a dark color and a malty taste but is a little stronger. It was first created in the Middle Ages in the northern German town of Einbeck, before it was later adopted by the Bavarian breweries, which had come to regard themselves as the natural home of German beer. In fact, the name Bock comes from the Bavarian interpretation of the word "Einbeck." Bock often has a sweeter flavor, and is traditionally drunk on public holidays. There are also subcategories, like *Eisbock* and *Doppelbock,* which have been refined to make an even stronger beverage.

Kölsch: If you're looking for lighter refreshment, then *Kölsch* is ideal. The traditional beer of Cologne, Kölsch is a mild, carbonated beer that goes down easily. It is usually served in a small, straight glass, called a *Stange,* which is much easier to wrangle than the immense Bavarian *Mass* (liter) glasses. If you're part of a big party, you're likely to get Kölsch served in a *Kranz,* or wreath—a circular wooden rack that holds up to 18 *Stangen.* Kölsch is very specific to Cologne and its immediate environs, so there's little point in asking for it anywhere else. Consequently, the major Kölsch brands are all relatively small; they include Reissdorf, Gaffel, and Früh.

Hefeweizen: Also known as *Weissbier* or *Weizenbier,* *Hefeweizen* is essentially wheat beer, and it was originally brewed in southern Bavaria. It has a very distinctive taste and cloudy color. It's much stronger than standard Pils or Helles, with an alcohol content of more than 8%. On the other hand, that content is slightly compensated for by the fact that wheat beer can be very filling. For a twist, try the clear variety called *Kristallweizen,* which tastes crisper, and is often served with half a slice of lemon. Hefeweizen is available throughout Germany, and the major Bavarian breweries all brew it as part of their range.

Top Brews by Region

Bavaria: Helles, Dunkelbier, Hefeweizen.

The six most famous brands are also the only ones allowed to be sold at Oktoberfest: Löwenbräu, Augustiner, Paulaner, Hacker-Pschorr, Spaten-Franziskanerbräu, and Hofbräu. Tegernseer Hell is also very good.

Rhineland: Kölsch, Pils.

Apart from Kölsch, which is impossible to avoid, look out for Krombacher and Bitburger.

Eastern Germany: Pils.

Radeberger and Hasseröder are two of the few beers in the region to have survived the fall of communism in former East Germany.

Berlin: Pils.

The most famous brands are Berliner Kindl, Schultheiss, and Berliner Pilsner, which are all worth trying.

Hamburg: Pils.

Astra—with its anchor-heart logo—is a cult Pils that is very much identified with Germany's biggest port city.

Northern Germany: Pils, Bock.

The best brands include Flensburger, Jever, and, of course, Beck's, which comes from the northern city of Bremen.

WINES OF GERMANY

Germany produces some of the finest white wines in the world. Although more and more quality red wine is being produced, the majority of German wines are white due to the northern continental climate. Nearly all wine production in Germany takes place by the River Rhine in the southwest. As a result, a single trip to this lovely and relatively compact wine region can give you a good overview of German wines.

German Wines: Then and Now

A Brief History

The Romans first introduced viticulture to the southernmost area of what is present-day Germany about 2,000 years ago. By the time of Charlemagne, wine making centered on monasteries. A 19th-century grape blight necessitated a complete reconstitution of German grape stock, grafted with pest-resistant American vines, and formed the basis for today's German wines. With cold winters, a relatively northern climate, and less sun than other wine regions, the Germans have developed a reputation for technical and innovative panache. The result has traditionally been top-quality sweet Rieslings, though Germany has been making excellent dry and off-dry white wines and Rieslings in the past 30 years.

Today's Wine Scene

For years, German wines were known by their lowest common denominator, the cheap, sweet wine that was exported en masse to the United States, England, and other markets. However, more recently there has been a push to introduce the world to the best of German wines. Exports to the United States, Germany's largest export market, have grown steadily, followed by England, The Netherlands, Sweden, and Russia. Eighty-three percent of its exports are white wines. The export of *Liebfraumilch*, the sugary, low-quality stuff that gave German wine a bad name, has been steadily declining, and now 66% of exports are so-called *Qualitätswein*, or quality wines. Only 15% of exports are destined to be wine-in-a-box. This is a more accurate representation of German wine as it exists in Germany.

Germany's Dominant Varietals

Whites

Müller-Thurgau: Created in the 1880s, this grape is a cross between a Riesling and a Madeleine Royale. Ripening early, it's prone to rot and, as the grape used in most Liebfraumilch, has a less than golden reputation.

Riesling: The most widely planted (and widely famous) of German grapes, the Riesling ripens late. A hardy grape, it's ideal for late-harvest wines. High levels of acidity help wines age well. When young, grapes have a crisp, floral character.

Silvaner: This grape is dying out in most places, with the exception of Franconia, where it is traditionally grown. With low acidity and neutral fruit, it can be crossed with other grapes to produce sweet wines like Kerner, Grauburgunder (Pinot Gris), Weissburgunder (Pinot Blanc), Bacchus, and others.

Reds

Dornfelder: A relatively young varietal. Dornfelder produces wines with a deep color, which distinguishes them from other German reds, which tend to be pale, light, and off-dry.

Spätburgunder (Pinot Noir): This grape is responsible for Germany's full-bodied, fruity wines, and is grown in more southerly vineyards.

Terminology

German wine is a complex topic, even though the wine region is relatively small. Wines are ranked according to the ripeness of the grapes when picked, and instead of harvesting a vineyard all at once, German vineyards are harvested up to five times. The finest wines result from the latest harvests of the season, due to increased sugar content. Under the category of "table wine" fall *Deutscher Tafelwein* (German table wine) and *Landwein* (like the French Vin de Pays). Quality wines are ranked according to when they are harvested. *Kabinett* wines are delicate, light, and fruity. *Spätlese* ("late-harvest" wine) has more-concentrated flavors, sweetness, and body. *Auslese* wines are made from extra-ripe grapes, and are even richer, even sweeter, and even riper. *Beerenauslese* are rare and expensive, made from grapes whose flavor and acid has been enhanced by noble rot. *Eiswein* ("ice" wine) is made of grapes that have been left on the vine to freeze and may be harvested as late as January. They produce a sugary syrup that creates an intense, fruity wine. Finally, *Trockenbeerenauslese* ("dry ice" wine) is made in tiny amounts using grapes that have frozen and shriveled into raisins. These can rank amongst the world's most expensive wines. Other terms to keep in mind include *Trocken* (dry) and *Halbtrocken* (half-dry, or "off-dry").

Wine Regions

Mosel: The Mosel's steep, mineral-rich hillsides produce excellent Rieslings. With flowery rather than fruity top-quality wines, the Mosel is a must-stop for any wine lover. The terraced hillsides rising up along the banks of the River Mosel are as pleasing to the eye as the light-bodied Rieslings are to the palate.

Nahe: Agreeable and uncomplicated: this describes the wines made from Müller-Thurgau and Silvaner grapes of the Nahe region. The earth here is rich not just in grapes, but also in semiprecious stones and minerals, and you might just detect a hint of pineapple in your wine's bouquet.

Rheinhessen: The largest wine-making region of Germany, Rheinhessen's once grand reputation was tarnished in the mid-20th century, when large, substandard vineyards were cultivated and low-quality wine produced. Nonetheless, there's plenty of the very good stuff to be found, still. Stick to the red sandy slopes over the river for the most full-bodied of Germany's Rieslings.

Rheingau: The dark, slatey soil of the Rheingau is particularly suited to the German Riesling, which is the major wine produced in this lovely hill country along the River Rhine. Spicy wines come from the hillsides, while the valley yields wines with body, richness, and concentration.

Pfalz: The second-largest wine region in Germany, the Pfalz stretches north from the French border. Mild winters and warm summers make for some of Germany's best Pinot Noirs and most opulent Rieslings. Wine is served here in a special dimpled glass called the *Dubbeglas*.

Baden: Farther to the south, Baden's warmer climate helps produce ripe, full-bodied wines that may not be well known but certainly taste delicious. The best ones, both red and white, come from Kaiserstuhl-Tuniberg, between Freiburg and the Rhine. But be forewarned: the best things in life do tend to cost a little extra.

GREAT ITINERARIES

Each of Germany's 16 states offers something different: tantalizing gastronomic adventures, medieval churches standing side by side with glassy high-rises, and local traditions kept alive despite being one of the most advanced economies in the world. Enjoy the lush countryside as you travel by train or car. *Below are three suggested itineraries—pick one or two, or combine elements from each.*

GERMANY FOR FIRST TIMERS, 10-DAY ITINERARY

See the best Germany has to offer: stunning landscapes, charming medieval towns, and cosmopolitan cities. Make the most of your trip by taking the train between stops. You'll enjoy views of rolling green countryside, towering wind turbines, and fairy-tale villages as you zip across the country. You'll also skip the hassle of finding parking and paying for high-cost gasoline.

Fly in: Munich Airport (MUC), Munich

Fly out: Tegel Airport (TXL), Berlin

Days 1 and 2: Munich

Fly into **Munich**, where you'll spend the first three nights. Get your bearings in Bavaria's capital city by standing in the center of the **Marienplatz** and watching the charming, twirling figures of the Glockenspiel in the tower of the **Rathaus** (town hall). Visit one of many world-class museums to see masterpieces in art, science, and technology, then wander through the sprawling **Englischer Garten** (English Garden). Throughout the city, you can sit elbow to elbow with genial Bavarians at long tables in sunny beer gardens, savoring a liter of cold Hefeweizen and a salty pretzel.

Day 3: Neuschwanstein

From Munich it's an easy day trip to Germany's fairy-tale castle, **Schloss Neuschwanstein,** in Schwangau. Though the 19th-century castle's fantastic silhouette has made it famous, this creation is more opera set than piece of history—the interior was never completed. A tour reveals why the king of Bavaria who built it earned the nickname "Mad" King Ludwig. Tickets come with a specific admission time and should be booked in advance by phone or online. You must pick them up from the ticket center in Hohenschwangau at least an hour before the tour starts—and before making your way up to the castle. Tours last about half an hour. Across the narrow wooded valley from Schloss Neuschwanstein is the ancient castle of the Bavarian Wittelsbach dynasty, **Schloss Hohenschwangau,** also open for tours. Return to Munich city center in the evening and treat yourself to a hearty meal of *Schweinshaxe* (roasted pork knuckle) and potatoes.

Logistics: Train from Munich's Hauptbahnhof to Füssen, then 15-minute bus ride to Hohenschwangau. From there it's a 30-minute walk to the castle; 4 hours and 30 minutes round-trip.

Day 4: Freiburg

Get an early start to arrive by late morning in **Freiburg,** one of Germany's most beautiful historic towns. Damaged during WWII, it has been rebuilt to preserve its delightful medieval character. Residents love to boast that Freiburg is the country's sunniest city. Its **cathedral** is a masterpiece of Gothic architecture, built over three centuries. Explore on foot, or by bike, and look out for the *Bächle*, or little brooks, that run for kilometers through this bustling university town. Check in

at the **Colombi,** the town's most luxurious hotel, for a stay with views of the old city.

Logistics: Train from Munich's Hauptbahnhof to Freiburg im Breisgau; 4 hours.

Day 5: The Black Forest

Freiburg puts you at the perfect point from which to explore the spruce-covered, low-lying mountains of the **Black Forest.** For a romp around the great outdoors, set out for **Titisee,** a placid glacial lake, passing deep gorges along the way. If your idea of relaxation includes getting off your feet, head toward the northern Black Forest. You can treat yourself to a spa day in tony **Baden-Baden,** relaxing in curative waters. In the evening return to Freiburg and rest up before the next day's train ride to the north.

Logistics: Train from Freiburg im Breisgau to Titisee or Baden-Baden; 1 hour and 20 minutes round-trip.

Days 6 and 7: Hamburg

Hamburg is one of Germany's wealthiest cities and the country's largest port. If you're in Hamburg on Sunday, wake up early to visit the open-air **Fischmarkt** (fish market) and see vendors set up their fresh wares while locals dance to live music as the sun comes up. Then, take a cruise through the city's canals with views of the Speicherstadt historic warehouse district, a UNESCO World Heritage site. Exploring the harbor you'll see the enormous ocean liners that stop in Hamburg before crossing the Atlantic. The city offers exclusive shopping along the **Junfernstieg,** a lakeside promenade. Spend the night at the **Adina Apartment Hotel Hamburg Michel** and enjoy the amenities of your own apartment space.

Logistics: Train from Freiburg im Breisgau to Hamburg Hauptbahnhof; 5 hours and 45 minutes.

Days 8 and 9: Berlin

Start the day at two of the city's most iconic symbols, the **Reichstag** and the nearby **Brandenburg Gate** (note that if you want to visit the Reichstag dome you need to register in advance). Head south to experience the moving silence in the maze of the Holocaust memorial, the **Denkmal für die Ermordeten Juden Europas.** Stop by Potsdamer Platz, which embodies the city's renaissance: once a no-go zone between East and West Berlin, the square now teems with glittering towers of optimism. A bit farther south is the **Topographie des Terrors,** an exhibition telling the story of the Nazi takeover in harrowing detail, built where the Gestapo headquarters used to be. Head back to Potsdamer Platz, where you can hop on the double-decker public Bus 200, which travels down the grand, tree-lined boulevard Unter den Linden to the colossal **Berliner Dom** cathedral. You can then devote the entire afternoon to the stupendous collections of the **Museumsinsel**. The beautifully restored Neues Museum and the majestic Pergamon are standouts—the Pergamon Altar is closed for restoration until 2019 but the rest of the museum, including the stunning Ishtar Gate, remains open—as is the excellently curated Deutsches Historisches Museum (German History Museum).

Spend the second day exploring the young side of Berlin, in Kreuzberg. This is a good time to rent a bicycle. Browse vintage clothing stores and indie boutiques and have lunch at Markthalle IX, home to a bevy of excellent local food stalls, then head south to **Tempelhofer Park**, the historic airfield-turned-park. Exit the park to Neukölln, a working-class neighborhood that has emerged as an epicenter of cool. For lunch, there are many Middle Eastern eateries as well as the popular Italian restaurant **Lavanderia Vecchia**. Continue east and cross the Spree over the red-brick Oberbaum Bridge, which served as a border crossing between East and West Berlin. On the other side of the river is Friedrichshain and the famous **East Side Gallery,** where international artists covered remnants of the Berlin Wall with colorful murals.

Logistics: Train from Hamburg Hauptbahnhof to Berlin Hauptbahnhof; 1 hour and 40 minutes.

Day 10: Potsdam
If you can tear yourself away from Berlin, take a day trip out to **Potsdam** and tour the opulent palaces and manicured gardens of **Sanssouci Park. Schloss Sanssouci**, a palace constructed to resemble Versailles,

was used as a summer getaway for Frederick the Great and is a must-see. Return to Berlin in the evening to explore more of its distinct neighborhoods, like Turkish Kreuzberg or hip Prenzlauer Berg. The next day, fly home from Berlin.

Logistics: Train from Berlin Hauptbahnhof to Potsdam Hauptbahnhof; 1 hour and 20 minutes round-trip.

GERMANY'S NORTHERN PORT CITIES AND BEACH TOWNS, 8-DAY ITINERARY

The North Sea and Baltic Sea lap the north coast of Germany, feeding a sprawling network of waterways that placed the country at the heart of historically important trade routes. Take in brickwork warehouses in old port cities, soak up the sun on sandy white beaches, float in Brandenburg's serene lakes, and cruise down the Rhine as you vacation like a local.

Fly in: Cologne Bonn Airport (CGN), Köln

Fly out: Tegel Airport (TXL), Berlin

Day 1: Köln (Cologne)
Fly into **Köln** and spend your first day in the heart of the Rhineland enjoying the city. Marvel at the **Kölner Dom** (cathedral), a UNESCO World Heritage site and Gothic masterpiece. Take a boat cruise down the River Rhine past the picturesque Altstadt (Old Town), then celebrate your first night in Germany by sipping a Kölsch beer at one of the city's sleek bars before getting some well-earned sleep.

Days 2 and 3: Hamburg
Hamburg is home to more canals than Venice, and is dotted with cafés and bars overlooking the accompanying locks and bridges. Start in front of the **Rathaus** (city

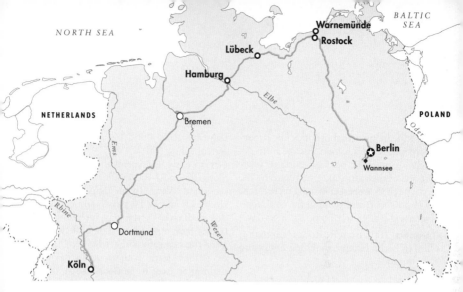

hall), a lavish structure built with the city's riches from its history as one of the most important trading ports in Europe. Stop to eat the traditional seafarer's favorite, *Labskaus*, a dish made of minced meat and served with a fried egg on top. Then head to the Speicherstadt, a UNESCO Heritage site, to see traditional redbrick warehouses, and make a stop at **Miniatur Wunderland,** the world's biggest model railway—it's a must-see, even if you're not a train enthusiast. Spend two nights in the trendy neighborhood of Sternschanze.

Logistics: Train from Köln to Hamburg Hauptbahnhof; 4 hours.

Day 4: Lübeck

Hop on an intercity train the next morning for a quick ride to **Lübeck.** Explore on foot through medieval alleyways in this 12th-century city founded by King Henry the Lion. Check out **Holstentor,** the western gate of the old city center, before making your way into the Altstadt, which boasts more 13th- to 15th-century buildings than the rest of Germany's major northern cities combined. Dine on large servings of seafood specialties from oak tables at **Schiffergesellschaft,** an old mariners' club. Stay the night in Lübeck.

Logistics: Train from Hamburg Hauptbahnhof to Lübeck; 35 minutes.

Days 5 and 6: Rostock and Warnemünde

Head east toward the city of **Rostock,** the former East German state's biggest ship-building center and your base for finding the perfect stretch of sandy white beach on the Baltic Sea. From there it's 9 miles north to the resort town of **Warnemünde,** a popular destination for German tourists. If you're there on the weekend, stop by the **Skybar** at night to watch ship lights under the stars. Stay in a 19th-century mansion in Rostock's Old Town, the **Pental Hotel.**

Logistics: Train from Lübeck to Rostock Hauptbahnhof; 1 hour and 50 minutes.

Days 7 and 8: Berlin

Spend your last days in Germany's capital, **Berlin,** a city with a fascinating history, particularly its recent division and shifting neighborhood dynamics after the fall of the **Berlin Wall** in 1989. Berlin is notorious for its late-night culture. You can even get some touring in in the evening: Sir Norman Foster's glass dome on the **Reichstag** (parliament building), the **TV tower** at Alexanderplatz, and the **Checkpoint Charlie Museum** don't close until 10 pm or later. Grab a beer and sit by the side of the **Spree** river, which winds through the middle of the city, before venturing out to the best nightlife in hip neighborhoods like Kreuzberg and Friedrichshain. Escape from the urban center the next morning to relax at one of the many lakes surrounding the city, such as **Wannsee.** Bring a picnic, rent a paddleboat, and swim in the cool, rejuvenating waters. Fly home the next day.

Logistics: Train from Rostock Hauptbahnhof to Berlin Hauptbahnhof; 2 hours and 40 minutes.

CASTLES IN WINE COUNTRY, 8-DAY ITINERARY

While frothy beers come to mind when you think of Germany, the country also produces a range of outstanding wines. It's best known for Riesling, but take a drive through the winding countryside past ancient fortresses and you'll get a taste of what German vineyards have to offer along with some of its history.

Fly in: Cologne Bonn Airport (CGN), Köln

Fly out: Munich Airport (MUC), Munich

Day 1: Koblenz

Pick up a rental car in Köln and start your tour in **Koblenz,** at the confluence of the Rhine and Mosel rivers. Once you have arrived in the historic downtown area, head straight for the charming little **Hotel Zum weissen Schwanen,** a half-timber inn and mill since 1693. Explore the city on the west bank of the **Rhine River** and then visit Europe's biggest fortress, the impressive **Festung Ehrenbreitstein** on the opposite riverbank.

Logistics: 90 km (60 miles); 1 hour and 10 minutes by car.

Day 2: Koblenz and Surrounding Castles

Get up early and spend the day driving along the most spectacular and historic section of "Vater Rhein." Stay on the left riverbank and you'll pass many mysterious landmarks on the way, including the **Loreley rock,** a 430-foot slate cliff named after the beautiful siren who lured sailors to their deaths with her song. Stay the night at **St. Goar** or **St. Goarshausen,** both lovely river villages.

Logistics: 35 km (22 miles); 40 minutes by car.

Day 3: Eltville and the Eberbach Monastery

The former Cistercian monastery **Kloster Eberbach** in **Eltville** is one of Europe's best-preserved medieval cloisters. Parts of the film *The Name of the Rose,* based on Umberto Eco's novel and starring Sean Connery, were filmed here. Spend the night at the historic wine estate **Schloss Reinhartshausen** and sample the fantastic wines of the region.

Logistics: 70 km (45 miles), 1 hour to Eltville, 15 minutes more to monastery by car.

Day 4: Heidelberg

On Day 4, leave early so you can spend a full day in **Heidelberg.** No other city symbolizes the German spirit and history better than this meticulously restored, historic town. Don't miss the impressive **Schloss Heidelberg,** one of Europe's greatest Gothic-Renaissance fortresses. Then head for the **Romantik Hotel zum Ritter St. Georg,** a charming 16th-century inn with a great traditional German restaurant.

Logistics: 110 km (70 miles); 1 hour and 15 minutes by car.

Days 5 and 6: The Burgenstrasse and the Neckar Valley

Head to the quaint little villages in the **Neckar Valley** just east of Heidelberg for superb food and wine. The predominant grapes here are Riesling (white) and Spätburgunder (red). Try to sample wines from small, private wineries—they tend to have higher-quality vintages. Sightseeing is equally stunning, with a string of castles and ruins along the famous **Burgenstrasse** (Castle Road). Since you have two days for this area, take your time and head to Eberbach and its romantic **Schloss Zwingenberg**, tucked away in the deep forest a 15-minute drive outside the village. In the afternoon, continue on to **Burg Hornberg** at Neckarzimmern, the home to the legendary German knight Götz von Berlichingen. Stay the night here, in the former castle stables.

The next morning, continue on another 20 minutes to **Bad Wimpfen,** the most charming valley town at the confluence of the Neckar and Jagst rivers. Spend half a day in the historic city center and tour the **Staufer Pfalz** (royal palace). Soaring high above the city, the palace was built in 1182, and was a popular retreat for the emperor Barbarossa.

Logistics: 60 km (40 miles); car via the B-37 to Eberbach; 1 hour to Neckarzimmern; 15 km (10 miles), 20 minutes to Bad Wimpfen.

Days 7 and 8: German Wine Route

Devote your last day to the **German Wine Route,** which winds its way through some of the most pleasant landscapes in Germany: the gentle slopes and vineyards of the Pfalz. The starting point for the route is **Bad Dürkheim,** a spa town and proud home of the world's largest wine cask, which holds 1.7 million liters (450,000 gallons). You can enjoy wine with lunch in the many Weinstuben here or wait until you reach **Neustadt** farther south, which is Germany's largest wine-making community. Thirty of the vintages grown here can be sampled (and purchased) at the downtown **Haus des Weines.** If time permits, try to visit **Burg Trifels** in the afternoon. Near Annweiler, the castle is a magnificent Hohenzollern residence, perched dramatically on three sandstone cliffs, and makes for a great photo op. Take it easy in the evening to prepare for the next day's drive to Munich and flight home.

Logistics: Car via A61 and A6 to Neustadt; 75 km (50 miles), 1 hour to Bad Dürkheim, then 20 km (12 miles), 20 minutes to Neustadt, then 40 km (25 miles), 40 minutes to Burg Trifels; from there it's a 4-hour drive to Munich.

Travel Times By Train

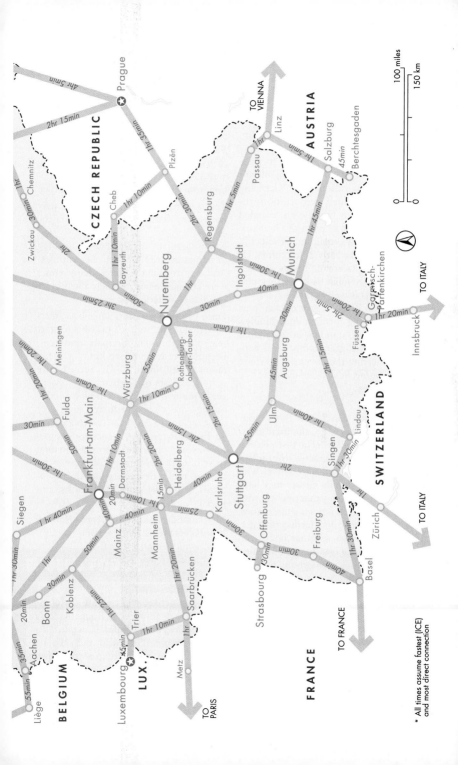

TRACING YOUR GERMAN ROOTS

More than 51 million Americans claim German ancestry, and many of these Americans have a strong desire to trace their long-lost roots. The first significant waves of immigration from Germany came after the failed democratic revolutions of 1848, a time period coupled with potato blight in parts of Germany. The numbers of German immigrants did not let up until the early 20th century. Of course, Jewish Germans fleeing fascism also left much of what had been their cultural heritage (as well as material possessions) behind. If you've ever been curious about wandering through your family's ancestral village, standing in the church where your great-grandmother was baptized, or meeting the cousins who share your last name, it's easier than ever to make it happen.

Before You Go

The more you can learn about your ancestors before you go, the more fruitful your search will be. The first place to seek information is directly from members of your family. Even relatives who don't know any family history may have documents stored away that can help with your sleuthing—old letters, wills, diaries, photo albums, birth and death certificates, and Bibles or other religious books can be great sources of information. The first crucial facts you'll need are the name of your ancestor; his or her date of birth, marriage, or death; town or city of origin in Germany; date of emigration; ship on which he or she emigrated; and where in America he or she settled.

If family resources aren't leading you anywhere, try turning to the **Mormon Church.** The Mormon Church has made it its mission to collect mountains of genealogical information, much of which it makes available free of charge at ⊕ *www. familysearch.org.* The **National Archives** (⊕ *www.nara.gov*) keeps census records, and anyone can, for a fee, get information from the censuses of 1940 and earlier.

The spelling of your family name may not be consistent through time. Over the course of history varying rates of literacy in Germany meant that the spelling of names evolved through the centuries. And on arrival in the States, many names were changed again to make them more familiar to American ears.

Once you've established some basic facts about your ancestor, it's possible to start searching through German resources. Because Germany as we know it today didn't unify until 1871, records are scattered. Lists of German ship passengers—many of which are now available online—are a good next step since they often included a person's "last residence." So if you can target your ancestor's hometown, you'll open the door to a potential trove of records. Many parish registers go back to the 15th century and document births, baptisms, marriages, deaths, and burials.

Check out the links at the **German National Tourist Office's** websites ⊕ *germanoriginality. com, www.germany.travel*, and if you're tracking down living cousins, try the German phone book at ⊕ *DasTelefonbuch.de.*

On the Ground in Germany

Once you arrive, you can use the computerized facilities of Bremerhaven's **German Emigration Center** (⊕ *www.dah-bremerhaven.de*) or enlist the help of an assistant to search the passenger lists of the HAPAG shipping line, at Hamburg's **Family Research Center** (⊕ *www. BallinStadt.de*).

WORLD WAR II SITES

After Adolf Hitler rose to power, he led the country into war in 1939 and perpetrated the darkest crimes against humanity. Nazi Germany systematically murdered 6 million Jews and millions of others deemed undesirable, including Roma and Sinti people, the disabled, and homosexuals. You can visit sites around the country that document and provide perspective on the extent of the horror.

Topography of Terror. This documentation center in Berlin takes a deep look at the political circumstances that led to the rise of the Nazi Party and the terror tactics they used. It stands on the former site of the headquarters for state security groups such as the Gestapo and the SS.

Obersalzburg. Upon his election, Hitler set about turning Obersalzburg into the southern headquarters for the Nazi party and a retreat for its elite. Located in the Bavarian Alps, the compound included luxurious homes for party officials. Today you can walk through the extensive bunker system while learning about the Nazis' takeover of the area.

Kehlsteinhaus. Not far from Obersalzburg you'll find the Kehlsteinhaus, Hitler's private home. Designed as a 50th birthday gift for Hitler by the Nazi party, the house is also known as *Adlerhorst* (Eagle's Nest). It's perched on a cliff, seemingly at the top of the world. The house's precarious location probably saved it from British bombing raids.

Bebelplatz. The Nazis organized mass burnings of books they considered offensive, including one in May 1933 at Bebelplatz in Berlin. Today a glass panel in the square looks down onto an underground room filled with empty shelves. A plaque also memorializes the event with the haunting words of the German poet Heinrich Heine, who wrote over one hundred years earlier that those who burn books will eventually burn people.

Nazi Party Rally Grounds. Masters of propaganda, the Nazis staged colossal rallies intended to impress the German people. Hitler considered Nürnberg so quintessentially German he developed an enormous complex here to host massive parades, military exercises, and major assemblies of the Nazi party. The Congress Hall, meant to outshine Rome's Colosseum, is the largest remaining building from the Nazi era. It houses a **Documentation Center** that explores the Nazis' tyranny.

Nürnberg Trials Memorial. War crimes trials took place here between November 1945 and October 1946. In this courthouse Nazi officials stood before an international military tribunal to answer for their crimes. The Allied victors chose Nürnberg on purpose—it's the place Germany's first anti-Semitic laws passed, decreeing the boycott of Jewish businesses.

KZ-Gedenkstätte Dachau. This is the memorial and site of the former notorious death camp. Hitler created Dachau soon after taking power, and it became the model for all other camps. Tens of thousands of prisoners died here. Today you'll see a few remaining cell blocks and the crematorium, along with shrines and memorials to the dead.

Bergen-Belsen. This is the concentration camp where Anne Frank perished along with more than 52,000 others. A meadow is all that remains of the camp, but it is still a chilling place to visit. The documentation center exhibits photos of the prisoners and interviews with survivors.

Other concentration camps include **Buchenwald, Sachsenhausen,** and **Dora-Mittelbau.**

MUNICH

WELCOME TO MUNICH

TOP REASONS TO GO

★ **Deutsches Museum:** The museum has an impressive collection of science and technology exhibits, and its location on the Isar River is perfect for a relaxing afternoon stroll.

★ **Englischer Garten:** With expansive greens, beautiful lakes, and beer gardens, the English Garden is a great place for a bike ride or a long walk.

★ **Gärtnerplatz:** Gärtnerplatz and the adjoining Glockenbachviertel are the hip hoods of the moment, with trendy bars, restaurants, cafés, and shops.

★ **Marienplatz:** The heart of Munich, everyone passes through this pretty medieval square at the center of everything. Be sure to take in the Glockenspiel's turning knights and musicians on the facade of the Rathaus at midday.

★ **Viktualienmarkt:** Experience farmers'-market-style shopping, where there's fresh produce, finger food, and a beer garden. Dating back to 1823, this market should not be missed.

1 Altstadt. Altstadt (Old Town) is home to Marienplatz, the Rathaus, and Frauen-kirche—Munich's landmark church with two soaring towers—as well as the Residenz and Hofgarten (royal palace and court gardens).

2 Lehel. East of Marienplatz, down toward the Isar River, is a maze of Altstadt's smaller streets. These run seamlessly into Lehel, which gently spreads out across the Isar. A highly sought-after residential neighborhood, Lehel is calm, chic, and self-sufficient.

3 Ludwigsvorstadt and Isarvorstadt. These neighborhoods south and west of Altstadt encompass several smaller quarters, with cafés, bars, restaurants, and nightclubs, as well as the world-famous Deutsches Museum. Ludwigsvorstadt is home to two of Munich's most important landmarks: Hauptbahnhof (main train station) and Theresienwiese,

2

GETTING ORIENTED

In the relaxed and sunnier southern part of Germany, Munich (*München*) is the proud capital of the state of Bavaria. Even Germans come here to vacation, mixing the city's pleasures with the nearby natural surroundings—on clear days, from downtown the Alps appear to be much closer than around 40 miles away. The city bills itself as "Die Weltstadt mit Herz" ("The Cosmopolitan City with Heart"), but in rare bouts of self-deprecatory humor, friendly Bavarians will remind you that it isn't much more than a country town with 1.5 million people. *Münchners* will also tell visitors that the city is special because of its *Gemütlichkeit* (cozy atmosphere). With open-air markets, numerous parks, the lovely Isar River, and loads of beer halls, Munich has a certain charm that few cities can match.

where Oktoberfest takes place each autumn.

4 Schwabing and Maxvorstadt. Maxvorstadt marks the northern boundary of Innenstadt (City Center). On the east side of Maxvorstadt is Ludwigstrasse, a wide avenue flanked by impressive buildings. A block west are Maxvorstadt's smaller streets, lined with shops and restaurants frequented by students. The big museums lie farther west.

Schwabing starts north of the Victory Arch, where Ludwigstrasse becomes Leopoldstrasse. The Englischer Garten extends from Schwabing back down into the northeast part of Altstadt.

5 Au and Haidhausen. Across the Isar are fashionable Au and Haidhausen; these residential neighborhoods are conveniently located to Munich's Altstadt.

6 Outside Innenstadt. Although Ludwigvorstadt and Isarvorstadt begin in the City Center, they extend south and west beyond what is considered the Innenstadt borders. The western part of Munich, outside of the Innenstadt, is Nymphenburg, dominated by Nymphenburg Castle and its glorious grounds.

VIKTUALIENMARKT

Vegetables, fruits, and prepared foods are available at Munich's biggest farmers' market.

It's not just the fascinating array of fruit, vegetables, olives, breads, cheeses, meats, pickles, and honey that make the Viktualienmarkt (victuals market) so attractive. The towering maypole, small *Wirtshäuser* (pub-restaurants), and beer gardens also set the scene for a fascinating trek through Munich's most famous market.

The Viktualienmarkt's history can be traced to the early 19th century, when King Max I Joseph decreed that Marienplatz was too small to house the major city market. In 1807, a bigger version was created a few hundred yards to the south, where it stands today. You are just as likely to find a Münchner buying something here as you are a visitor. Indeed, a number of City Center restaurants proudly proclaim that they get their ingredients "fresh from the market." This is the place to pick up a *Brotzeit*: bread, olives, cheeses, gherkins, and whatever else strikes your fancy, then retreat to a favorite Biergarten to enjoy the bounty.

—Paul Wheatley

MARKET ETIQUETTE

All stalls are open weekdays 10–6 and Saturday 10–3, though some stalls open earlier or close later. It's not kosher to touch the fresh produce but it is to ask to taste a few different olives or cheeses before buying. The quality of the various produce is invariably good; competition is fierce, so it has to be. Therefore, buy the best of what you fancy from a number of stalls, not just one or two.

2

VIKTUALIENMARKT BEST BUYS

BEER AND PREPARED FOOD

If it's just a beer you're after, there are a number of beer stalls not far from the towering maypole. **Biergarten am Viktualienmarkt** is the main location, but there are also small *Imbissstände* (snack bars) where you can pick up roast pork and beer. **Kleiner Ochsenbrater** sells delicious organic roast dishes. **Poseidon** and the nearby **Fisch Witte** rustle up a fine selection of fish dishes, including very good soups and stews. **Luigino's Bio Feinkost,** an organic deli that also has fine cheeses and wines, is the spot for a quick grilled sandwich. And the modest-looking **Münchner Suppenküche** dishes out delightful helpings of soup, including oxtail, chicken, and spicy lentil.

FRUITS AND VEGETABLES

The mainstay of the market is fruit and vegetables, and there are a number of top-quality stalls to choose from. The centrally located **Fruitque** has some of the freshest, most attractive-looking, and ripest produce on display, or try **Frische Kräuter und Gewürze** for the tastiest olives, peppers, garlic, and dips of all kinds. For something a little more exotic, try out **Exoten Müller,** which specializes in unusual fruits and vegetables from around the world.

HONIGHÄUSEL AM MÜNCHNER VIKTUALIENMARKT

Honighäusel means "small honey house" and is an apt description of

this petite honey wonderland. Much of the produce comes from Bavaria, but there's also a selection of honeys from farther afield: Italy, France, even New Zealand. This is also the place to buy honey marmalades and soaps, and beeswax candles. For a chilly evening, pick up a bottle of Bavarian honey schnapps.

SCHENK UND SCHMIDT

There are numerous stalls at the market that serve mouthwatering, freshly pressed fruit drinks, so no matter where you buy, you won't be disappointed. "Schenk's frischgepresste Säfte" is a favorite because the drinks are top-notch and the staff are engaging, speak English, and take the time to explain the ingredients in each drink.

LEBKUCHEN

There is no better Lebkuchen, the ginger Christmas cookies that originated in Nürnberg, available in Munich than from **Lebkuchen-Schmidt.** This little corner store offers their authentic products in attractive tin boxes for any occasion.

A WINE BREAK

For a welcome respite from summer heat or a chilly winter wind, or even from the omnipresent offers of Bavarian beers, nip into **Edle Pfälzer Weine,** and stand around a table with friends for a glass of wine to help you decide which bottle to select for dinner later.

MUNICH'S BEER GARDENS

With a bit of sunshine, a handful of picnic tables, and a few of the finest beers around, you have yourself a *Biergarten* (beer garden). There are beer gardens throughout Germany, and many imitations across the world, but the most traditional, and the best, are still found in and around Munich. The elixir that transforms the traditional Munich beer garden into something special is the unbeatable atmosphere.

Beer gardens formed out of necessity. Brewers in the 18th and 19th centuries struggled to keep beer cool to prevent it from spoiling in warm weather. As early as 1724, Munich brewers dug cellars and began to store beer next to the shady shores of the Isar River. Local residents promptly took along their beer glasses for a cool drink and before long the odd table and bench appeared, and the beer garden tradition was born.

—Paul Wheatley

(above and lower right) It's easy to make friends in the convivial atmosphere of a beer garden. (upper right) The Englischer Garten's Chinese Tower is one of the most famous beer gardens in Munich.

BIERGARTEN ETIQUETTE

Often, a beer garden is separated between where guests can bring food and where they must buy it. Simply ask to avoid confusion, or look for tablecloths—generally these are table-service only. The basis of a beer garden *Brotzeit* is delicious black bread, Obatzda, sausage, gherkin, and radish. As tradition dictates, remember to also order "Ein Mass Bier bitte!" ("A liter of beer please!")

2

MUNICH'S BEST BEER GARDENS

AUGUSTINER KELLER BIERGARTEN

This is perhaps the most popular beer garden in Munich and certainly one of the largest. Located in Maxvorstadt, it is part of the **Augustiner Keller** restaurant, a few hundred yards from Hackerbrücke S-bahn station, or five minutes from the Hauptbahnhof. The main garden is separated in half between where you can bring your own food and where you buy food from the beer garden. The leaves of countless horse chestnut trees provide a canopy covering, which adds to the dreamy atmosphere.

HOFBRÄUKELLER AM WIENER PLATZ

Some of the best beer gardens are found away from the City Center. This one in Haidhausen is a 15-minute walk (or take Tram No. 18 or 19 from the Hauptbahnhof) over the Isar River, past the Maximilianeum, to Wiener Platz, a delightful square well worth visiting. The beer garden attracts Münchners, as well as groups of British, Australian, and American expats. The staple beer garden chicken, fries, roast pork, and spare ribs are better here than most.

KÖNIGLICHER HIRSCHGARTEN

With seating for 8,000, this is the biggest and most family-friendly beer garden in Munich. In a former royal hunting area outside the City Center (in Nymphenburg), it takes a little time and effort

to reach. Your best bet is to take the S-bahn, or rent a bike and cycle there. The rewards are clear: surrounded by trees and green parkland, the tables and benches seem to go on forever. The food and beer is good and there is even a small deer sanctuary, lending the "Deer Park" its name.

PARK CAFÉ

This is where trendsetters head for a more modern and sunny—there isn't as much shade here—take on the traditional beer garden. Set in Maxvorstadt in Munich's old botanical garden, five minutes from the Hauptbahnhof, this medium-size beer garden regularly has live bands on Friday and Saturday evenings, and live jazz often plays during Sunday-morning family breakfasts. It also has a good selection of cakes and a hip indoor bar.

SEEHAUS IM ENGLISCHEN GARTEN

Within Munich's very own oasis, the **Englischer Garten,** it was an inspired decision to build this beer garden next to a boating lake. A leisurely stroll through the garden to the Seehaus takes about an hour, but go early because it's popular after 11:30. Lots of people visit the Englischer Garten in Schwabing to play soccer and other sports, and if you want to join in you might choose to pass on the roast dinner and instead snack on a *Brezn* (pretzel), Obatzda, and salad.

Updated by
Elizabeth
Willoughby

Known today as the city of laptops and lederhosen, modern Munich is a cosmopolitan playground that nevertheless represents what the rest of the world incorrectly sees as "typically German": world-famous Oktoberfest, traditional *Lederhosen* (leather pants), busty Bavarian waitresses in *Dirndls* (traditional dresses), beer steins, and sausages.

Munich's cleanliness, safety, and Mediterranean pace give it a slightly rustic feel. The broad sidewalks, fashionable boutiques and eateries, views of the Alps, a sizable river running through town, and a huge green park make Munich one of Germany's most visited cities. When the first rays of spring sun begin warming the air, follow the locals to their beloved beer gardens, shaded by massive chestnut trees.

The number of electronics and computer firms—Siemens, Microsoft, and SAP, for starters—makes Munich a sort of mini–Silicon Valley of Germany, but for all its business drive, this is still a city with roots in the 12th century, when it began as a market town on the "salt road" between mighty Salzburg and Augsburg.

That Munich was the birthplace of the Nazi movement is a difficult truth that those living here continue to grapple with. To distance the city from its Nazi past, city leaders looked to Munich's long pre-Nazi history to highlight what they decreed was the real Munich: a city of great architecture, high art, and fine music. Many of the Altstadt's architectural gems were rebuilt postwar, including the lavish Cuvilliés-Theater, the Altes Rathaus, and the Frauenkirche.

The city's appreciation of the arts began under the kings and dukes of the Wittelsbach dynasty, which ruled Bavaria for eight centuries, until 1918. The Wittelsbach legacy is alive and well in many of the city's museums and exhibition centers, the Opera House, the philharmonic, and, of course, the Residenz, the city's royal palace. Any walk in the City Center will take you past ravishing baroque decoration and grand 19th-century neoclassical architecture.

PLANNING

WHEN TO GO

It's nicer to walk through the Englischer Garten when the weather's fine in summer. A few post-summer sunny days are usual, but the Oktoberfest is also an indication that fall is here, and the short march to winter has arrived. There are world-class museums and good restaurants to keep you entertained year round, though, and theater and opera fans will especially enjoy winter, when the tour buses and the camera-toting crowds are gone.

FESTIVALS

Munich comes alive during Fasching, Germany's Mardi Gras, the week before Ash Wednesday in the pre-Easter season. The festival of festivals, Oktoberfest, takes place from the end of September to early October.

Die Lange Nacht der Musik (*Long Night of Music*). In late April or May this festival is devoted to live performances through the night by untold numbers of groups, from heavy-metal bands to medieval choirs, at more than 100 locations throughout the city. One ticket covers everything, including transportation on special shuttle buses that run between locations. ⊠ *Munich* ☎ *089/3061–0041* ⊕ *www.muenchner.de/musiknacht* 🎫 *€15.*

GETTING HERE AND AROUND

AIR TRAVEL

Munich's International Airport is 35 km (22 miles) northeast of the City Center and has excellent air service from all corners of the world. An excellent train service links the airport with downtown. The S-1 and S-8 lines operate from a terminal directly beneath the airport's arrival and departure halls. Trains of both S-bahn lines leave at 20-minute intervals, and the journey takes around 40 minutes. Easiest is to buy a *Tageskarte* (day card) for the *Gesamtnetz* (whole network), costing €12, which allows you to travel anywhere on the system until 6 am the next morning. A one-way bus trip costs around €10.50 and takes about 40 minutes to the City Center. A taxi from the airport costs around €70. During rush hours (7 am–10 am and 4 pm–7 pm), allow up to an hour of driving time. If you're driving to the city yourself, take the A-9 and follow the signs for "München Stadtmitte" (downtown). If you're driving to the airport from the City Center, head north through Schwabing, join the A-9 autobahn at the Frankfurter Ring intersection, and follow the signs for the "Flughafen" (airport).

Airport Information Flughafen München. ⊠ *Flughafen München 2* ☎ *089/97500* ⊕ *www.munich-airport.de/en/* Ⓜ *Flughafen.*

BUS TRAVEL

The location of Munich's 2009 Central Bus Terminal (ZOB) means that many excursions and longer trips are now centralized in this futuristic hub five minutes from the main train station. As well as numerous shops and banks, it has travel firms offering bus tickets and destination advice.

Touring Eurolines buses arrive at and depart from the ZOB. Check their website for trips to Neuschwanstein and the Romantic Road.

Bus Information Central Bus Station Munich (*ZOB*). ✉ *Arnulfstr. 21, Ludwigs-vorstadt* ⊕ *www.muenchen-zob.de* Ⓜ *Hackerbrücke*. **Touring Eurolines.** ✉ *DTG-Ticket-Center München* (*ZOB*), *Hackerbrücke 4, Ludwigvorstadt* ☎ *089/8898–9513* ⊕ *www.eurolines.de/en/home* Ⓜ *Hackerbrücke*.

CAR TRAVEL

If you're driving to Munich from the north (Nürnberg or Frankfurt), leave the autobahn at the Schwabing exit. From Stuttgart and the west, the autobahn ends at Obermenzing, one of Munich's most westerly suburbs. The autobahns from Salzburg and the east, Garmisch and the south, and Lindau and the southwest all join the Mittlerer Ring (city beltway). When leaving any autobahn, follow the signs reading "Stadtmitte" for downtown Munich.

PUBLIC TRANSIT

Munich has one of the most efficient and comprehensive public transportation systems in Europe, consisting of the U-bahn (subway), the S-bahn (suburban railway), the Strassenbahn (streetcar, also called "Tram"), and buses. Marienplatz forms the heart of the U-bahn and S-bahn network, which operates regularly from around 5 am to 1 am (intermittently in the very early morning, so check times if you're expecting a long night or early start). The main MVV service counter under Marienplatz sells tickets and gives out information, also in English. The website ⊕ *www.mvv-muenchen.de* has excellent and extensive transportation information, also in English.

A basic *Einzelfahrkarte* (one-way ticket) costs under €2 for a journey of up to four stops (a maximum of two of them using U- or S-bahn), and under €3 for a longer ride in the inner zone. If you're taking a number of trips around the city, save money by buying a *Streifenkarte*, or multiple 10-strip ticket. On a journey of up to four stops validate one stripe, for the inner zone validate two stripes. If you plan to do several trips during one day, buy a *Tageskarte* (day card), which allows you to travel anywhere until 6 am the next morning. For a group of up to five there is a Tageskarte for the inner zone and one for all zones. There is also a three-day card for a single person and one for two people. See the MVV website for current prices and options. All tickets must be validated at one of the blue time-stamping machines at the station, or on buses and trams as soon as you board (don't wait till you've found a seat; if an inspector's around you'll get fined €40 that must be paid on the spot, and they don't care whether you're a tourist or a local). Spot checks for validated tickets are common. All tickets are sold at the blue dispensers at U- and S-bahn stations and at some bus and streetcar stops. Bus drivers have only single tickets (the most expensive kind). ■ TIP➔ **Holders of a EurailPass, a Youth Pass, or an Inter-Rail card can travel free on all suburban railway trains (S-bahn) and regional trains.** Be forewarned: if caught on an U-bahn, tram, or bus without a normal public-transport ticket, you will be fined €40, with no exceptions.

Munich Transport Corporation (*MVG*). Munich Transport Corporation operates the integrated and extensive subway (U-bahn), bus, and streetcar (tram) system. In cooperation with Munich Transport and Tariff Association (MVV) and its partner companies, the transport system extends to urban rail (S-bahn), regional railway, and other bus operators. For the most part, this complex system manages to run like clockwork. Tickets, maps, schedules, and advice in English are available at this service center. ⊠ *Hauptbahnhof (Central Station), Bahnhofpl. 1–3, Ludwigsvorstadt* ✛ *Underground in the mezzanine of the U- and S-bahn by exit to the U1/U2* ☎ *0800/3442–26600 toll-free throughout Germany* ⊕ *www.mvg.de/en* ☉ *Closed Sunday* Ⓜ *Hauptbahnhof.*

TAXI TRAVEL

Munich's cream-color taxis are numerous. Hail them in the street, find them at a taxi stand, download their app, locate the nearest call box online, or phone the call center for one. Rates start at €3.50. Expect to pay around €10 for a 5-km (3-mile) trip within the city. There's a €0.60 charge for each piece of non–hand luggage and an additional charge of €1.20 if you call to order a cab.

Taxi München. This taxi association in Munich is the largest in Germany, with over 3,000 automobiles owned by various companies operating under the Taxi München umbrella. ⊠ *Munich* ☎ *089/21610, 089/21610* ⊕ *www.taxi-muenchen.com.*

TRAIN TRAVEL

All long-distance rail services arrive at and depart from the Hauptbahnhof; trains to and from some destinations in Bavaria use the adjoining Starnberger Bahnhof, which is under the same roof. The high-speed InterCity Express (ICE) trains connect Munich, Stuttgart, and Frankfurt on one line, Munich, Nürnberg, Würzburg, and Hamburg on another. Regensburg can be reached from Munich on Regio trains. You can purchase tickets by credit card at vending machines.

Fodor's Choice ★ **Deutsche Bahn.** For travel information at the main train station, go to the Deutsche Bahn (German Rail) office in the main arrival and departures hall (don't forget to grab a number before you start waiting), or use their website. The office is open daily 7 am to 9 pm. ⊠ *Reisezentrum München Hauptbahnhof, Bahnhofpl. 2, Ludwigsvorstadt* ☎ *180/699–6633* ⊕ *www.bahn.de/p_en/view/index.shtml* Ⓜ *Hauptbahnhof.*

Fodor's Choice ★ **EurAide.** For train travel assistance in English go to the EurAide counter within the Deutsche Bahn office. EurAide is very thorough and, as an agency of the German railroad, knows the systems inside and out, saving travelers a lot of money. Be patient, because they also spend time fixing the mistakes people have made by buying the wrong tickets online. In summer, go in the afternoon (2 pm–7 pm) when EurAide operates two counters. They also offer discounted hop-on, hop-off Munich bus tickets. The counter is open May through October, weekdays 8:30–8, Saturday 8:30–2; March, April, November, and December, weekdays 10–7. It is closed January and February. ⊠ *Reisezentrum, Bahnhofpl. 2, Counter 1, Ludwigsvorstadt* ⊕ *www.euraide.com* Ⓜ *Hauptbahnhof.*

TOURS

There are several ways to experience a guided tour through Munich, on foot or by various modes of transportation, such as bus, rickshaw, octopus bike (an eight-person bicycle) and Segway.

City Segway Tours. Take a 2½-hour group Segway tour for a stop-and-go trek to see the main sights of the city, or a four-hour day tour to learn

Munich's history from its humble beginnings, through tumultuous times and up to the present day. Tours begin with a "driving" lesson. Drivers must be at least 15 years old and have a valid driver's license. ⊠ *Karlspl. 4, Altstadt* ✛ *Look for the shop in the courtyard* ☎ *089/2388–8798* ⊕ *munich.citysegwaytours.com* ⊠ *From €59* Ⓜ *Karlsplatz Stachus.*

FAMILY **Gray Line Sightseeing Munich.** The best way to get a feel for Munich is to board a double-decker sightseeing bus—look for *Stadtrundfahrten* (city sightseeing). These blue buses, run by Autobus Oberbayern, offer a hop-on, hop-off service throughout the City Center, with commentary headphones available in eight languages and a live host who offers commentary in English and German. The tour takes an hour. Buses run every 20 minutes April through October and every 30–60 minutes November through March. ■ TIP➔ Book online for the best price. ⊠ *Hauptbahnhof, Bahnhofpl. 7, Ludwigsvorstadt* ✛ *Wait outside the Karstadt department store* ☎ *089/5490–7560* ⊕ *www.stadtrundfahrten-muenchen.de/ en/* ⊠ *From €15.50* Ⓜ *Hauptbahnhof.*

FAMILY **Mike's Bike Tours.** The oldest bike-tour operation in Munich, Mike's humorous tours last four to seven hours, typically with an hour's break at a beer garden, and cover upward of 6 km (4 miles). From March through mid-November tours start on foot daily at the Altes Rathaus at the east end of Marienplatz, followed by a short walk around the corner to pick up the bikes. A standard tour starts at 11:30 am, and from mid-April through August a second tour starts at 4:30 pm. November–March is by appointment. Reserve to be sure, though you'll probably get a bike if you just show up. Bus Bavaria, part of the same company, also offers day trips by bus to Neuschwanstein castle. ⊠ *Bräuhausstr. 10, Altstadt* ☎ *089/2554–3987* ⊕ *www.mikesbiketours.com* ⊠ *From €30* Ⓜ *Marienplatz, Isartor.*

FAMILY **Munich Tourist Office.** Munich's tourist office offers individual guided Fodor'sChoice tours with certified guides in 29 languages. Tours should be booked at ★ least six days ahead of time and should include all the specifics, such as the desired language, the number of people in your group, meeting place, time, date, and duration, and your address. You can include any specific sights if you have something in particular you want to see. Tours can last up to three hours. ⊠ *Marienpl. 2, Altstadt* ☎ *089/2333–0234* ⊕ *www.muenchen.de/rathaus/home_en/Tourist-Office/Service/Guided-Tours* ⊠ *From €120* Ⓜ *Marienplatz.*

FAMILY **Pedalheroes Munich.** A novel way of seeing the city is to hop on one of the bike-rickshaws with foldable rain canopies. The bike-powered two-seater cabs operate from Marienplatz and, besides the planned tours, you can also let a driver take you to a sight of your choosing. It's best to book a week ahead. Those traveling in a group, large or small, could consider taking an octopus bike tour on a circular tandem bicycle. ⊠ *Müllerstr. 6, Altstadt* ☎ *089/2421–6880* ⊕ *www.pedalhelden. de* ⊠ *From €39* Ⓜ *Marienplatz.*

FAMILY **Radius Tours & Bike Rental.** Theme walks of Munich's highlights, Third Reich Munich, and the Dachau concentration camp are offered here, all departing from the Radius office in Hauptbahnhof. Third Reich tours start daily at 3 pm between April and mid-October and daily at 11:30

am the rest of the year. The Dachau tour starts daily at 9:15 am and 12:15 pm from April to mid-October, with a third tour added daily in June and July at 10:15 am. The rest of the year the Dachau tours run daily at 10:15 am. Advance booking is not necessary for individuals, but it is recommended. ⊠ *Hauptbahnhof, Arnulfstr. 3, Ludwigsvorstadt* ✚ *Office: in Hauptbahnhof opposite platform 31* ☎ *089/5434–8777 20* ⊕ *www.radiustours.com* ✉ *From €13* Ⓜ *Hauptbahnhof.*

Segway Tour Munich. Reserve your Segway online for the Classic Tour that stops at 20 key Bavarian sights around Munich, or the Third Reich Tour for the 22 most important places of the Nazi regime. With several starting times to choose from, standard tours of up to eight people begin at the Altes Rathaus at Marienplatz. Tours take about three hours, including a safety briefing. A valid driver's license is required to operate a Segway in Germany. ⊠ *Marienpl. 15, Altstadt* ✚ *Below the archway of the Altes Rathaus (Old Town Hall)* ☎ *089/2420–3401* ⊕ *www.seg-tour-munich.com* ✉ *€75* Ⓜ *Marienplatz.*

FAMILY **Stadtrundfahrt CitySightseeing.** Yellow Cab's double-decker buses offer hop-on, hop-off service on one-hour tours leaving every 10–20 minutes between 10 am and 5 pm from April through October. From November through March, the red and yellow buses leave between 10 am and 4 pm every 30 to 60 minutes on weekdays, and every 15 to 30 minutes on weekends. Commentary is in German over a loudspeaker and in several other languages with headsets. Tickets ordered online are cheaper. ⊠ *Luisenstr. 4, Ludwigsvorstadt* ✚ *Across the street from Hauptbahnhof Nord* ⊕ *www.citysightseeing-munich.com* ✉ *From €14.90* Ⓜ *Hauptbahnhof.*

PLANNING YOUR TIME

Set aside at least a whole day for the Old Town, hitting Marienplatz with the rest of the spectators when the glockenspiel plays at 11 am, noon, and also 5 pm in summertime. There's a reason why Munich's Kaufingerstrasse has Germany's most expensive shop rents. Munich is Germany's most affluent city and Münchners like to spend. The pedestrian zone can get maddeningly full between noon and 2 pm, when everyone in town seems to be taking a quick shopping break, though it's hardly any better up until around 5 pm. If you've already seen the glockenspiel, try to avoid the area at that time. Avoid the museum crowds in Maxvorstadt by visiting as early in the day as possible. All Munich seems to discover an interest in art on Sunday, when most municipal and state-funded museums are €1 or even free; you might want to take this day off from culture and have a late breakfast or brunch at the Elisabethmarkt or around the Gärtnerplatz-Glockenbach areas. Some beer gardens and taverns have Sunday-morning jazz concerts. Many Schwabing bars have happy hours between 6 pm and 8 pm—a relaxing way to end your day.

VISITOR INFORMATION

The Munich Tourist office has two locations. The Hauptbahnhof (main train station) tourist office is open Monday through Saturday 9–8 and Sunday 10–6. The Tourist office in Neues Rathaus (New Town Hall)

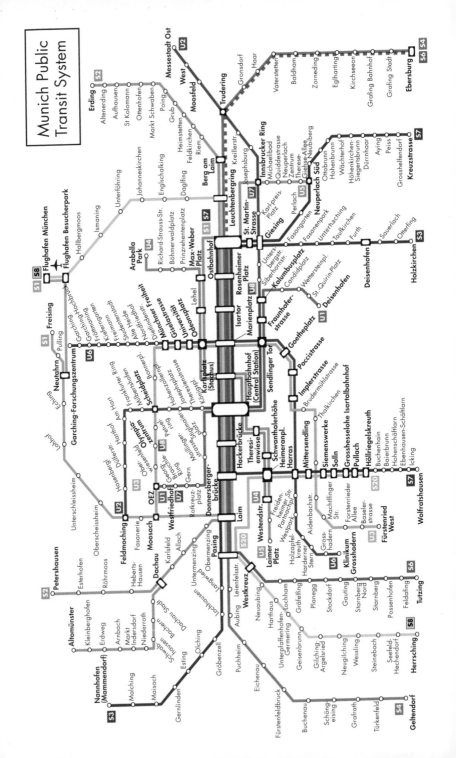

Munich Public Transit System

in Marienplatz is open weekdays 9:30–7:30, Saturday 9–4, and Sunday 10–2.

For information on the Bavarian mountain region south of Munich, contact Bavarian Tourism (⊕ *www.bavaria.us*).

As well as tourist offices, a great way to start your Munich visit is to go to Infopoint in Alterhof's Münchner Kaiserburg, a comprehensive information center for all museums and palaces across Bavaria.

Fodor's Choice ★ **Infopoint Museen Bayern, Münchner Kaiserburg.** In addition to information on Bavarian museums and palaces, you'll find a vaulted cellar where two short films (also in English) play, one about Munich's history, the other about Alter Hof. To get here from Marienplatz, walk 180 yards down attractive Burgstrasse and through Alter Hof's tower. On the right is Infopoint. Another 100 yards will take you to the Münzhof entrance, and another 50 to the Residenz Theater, next to the Residenz. This walk is an incredible introduction to 1,000 years of history. It's open Monday–Saturday 10–6. ⊠ *Alter Hof 1, Altstadt* ☎ *089/2101–4050* ⊕ *www.muenchner-kaiserburg.de* Ⓜ *Marienplatz.*

Munich Tourist Office — Hauptbahnhof. Come here for maps, flyers, event information, tours and sightseeing information, or even to book a hotel. Assistance is available in English. The office is open Monday to Saturday 9 to 8 and Sunday 10 to 6. ⊠ *Hauptbahnhof, Bahnhofpl. 2, Ludwigsvorstadt* ✛ *Entrance is from the street, outside of Hauptbahnhof* ☎ *089/2339–6500* ⊕ *www.muenchen.de* Ⓜ *Hauptbahnhof.*

Fodor's Choice ★ **Munich Tourist Office — Rathaus.** Come here for maps, museum flyers, and information about sightseeing tours. Assistance in English is available. Ticket sales to performances and events have moved around the corner to Dienerstrasse. Still within the Rathaus building, the ticket shop is across the street from Dienerstrasse 20. The office is open weekdays 9:30–7:30, Saturday 9–4, and Sunday 10–2. ⊠ *Marienpl. 2, Altstadt* ☎ *089/2339–6500* ⊕ *www.muenchen.de* Ⓜ *Marienplatz.*

EXPLORING MUNICH

Munich is a wealthy city—and it shows. At times this affluence may come across as conservatism. But what makes Munich so unique is that it's a new city superimposed on the old. The hip neighborhoods that make up the City Center (Innenstadt) are replete with traditional locales, and flashy materialism thrives together with a love of the outdoors.

ALTSTADT

The core of Munich's Innenstadt is Altstadt (Old Town), which has been rebuilt so often over the centuries that it no longer has the homogeneous look of so many other German towns. World War II leveled a good portion of the center, but unlike other cities that adopted more modern architectural styles, much of Munich's Altstadt was rebuilt as it was before the destruction. An amazing job has been done to restore the fairy-tale feel that prevailed here. From the modest palace of the Alter Hof in the Old Town, the Wittelsbachs expanded their quarters northward, away from the jumble of narrow streets. The new palace, the Residenz, is one of the stunning royal landmarks, and abuts the Englischer Garten, a present from the royal family to the locals. Although a few royal-themed sites can be found farther afield, most of the historical treasures are fairly concentrated in the Innenstadt, and mostly in Altstadt, making them easy to visit on foot.

TOP ATTRACTIONS

Feldherrnhalle (*Field Marshals' Hall*). Erected in 1841–44, this open pavilion, fronted with three huge arches, was modeled on the 14th-century Loggia dei Lanzi in Florence. Set on Odeonsplatz, it faces Ludwigstrasse, with Siegestor in the distance, and was built to honor Bavarian military leaders and the Bavarian army. Two huge Bavarian lions are flanked by the larger-than-life statues of Count Johann Tserclaes Tilly, who led Catholic forces in the Thirty Years' War, and Prince Karl Philipp Wrede, hero of the 19th-century Napoleonic Wars.

There's an astonishing photograph in existence of a 25-year-old Adolf Hitler standing in front of the Feldherrnhalle on August 2, 1914, amid a huge crowd gathered to celebrate the beginning of World War I. The imposing Feldherrnhalle structure was turned into a militaristic shrine in the 1930s and '40s by the Nazis, to whom it was significant because it marked the site of Hitler's failed coup, or *putsch,* in 1923, and where they installed a memorial in 1933 to commemorate the Nazis killed that day. During the Third Reich, all who passed the guarded memorial had to give the Nazi salute. Viscardigasse, a passageway behind Feldherrnhalle linking Residenzstrasse and Theatinerstrasse, and now lined with exclusive boutiques, was used as a bypass by those who didn't want to salute the memorial. The alley became nicknamed *Drückebergergassl'* (Shirkers' Lane). The memorial was removed in 1945. ✉ *Residenzstr. 1, Altstadt* ✛ *Odeonspl., between Theatinerkirche and the Residenz* ⊕ *www.schloesser.bayern.de/englisch/palace/objects/mu_feldh.htm* Ⓜ *Odeonsplatz.*

Fodor's Choice
★ **Frauenkirche** (*Church of Our Lady*). Munich's *Dom* (cathedral) is a distinctive late-Gothic brick structure with two huge towers, each 99 meters (325 feet) high (a Munich trademark). The main body of the cathedral was completed in 20 years (1468–88)—a record time in those days, and the distinctive onion-dome-like cupolas were added by 1525. Shortly after the original work was completed in 1488, Jörg von Halspach, the Frauenkirche's architect, died, but he managed to see the project through. In 1944–45, the building suffered severe damage during Allied bombing raids, and was restored between 1947 and 1957. Inside, the church combines most of von Halspach's plans with a stark, clean modernity and simplicity of line. The cathedral houses the elaborate marble tomb of Duke Ludwig IV (1282–1347), who became Holy Roman Emperor Ludwig the Bavarian in 1328. One of the Frauenkirche's great treasures is the collection of wooden busts by Erasmus Grasser. ✉ *Frauenpl. 1, Altstadt* ☎ *089/290–0820* ⊘ *Tower closed until 2017 for renovation* Ⓜ *Marienplatz.*

FAMILY **Hofbräuhaus.** Duke Wilhelm V founded Munich's Hofbräuhaus (court brewery) in 1589; it's been at its present location since 1607, where the golden beer is consumed from 1-liter mugs called *Mass*. If the cavernous ground-floor hall or beer garden is too noisy, there's a quieter restaurant upstairs. Americans, Australians, and Italians far outnumber locals, who regard HBH as a tourist trap. The brass band that performs here most days adds modern pop and American folk music to the traditional German numbers. ⊠ *Platzl 9, Altstadt* ☎ *089/2901–36100* ⊕ *www.hofbraeuhaus.de/en/index_en.html* ☉ *Daily 9 am–11:30 pm* Ⓜ *Marienplatz / Isartor.*

QUICK BITES

Tambosi. Open since 1775, Tambosi is Munich's longest-running café. Its location is superb, partly sitting in full view of Theatinerkirche on Odeonsplatz and partly in the Hofgarten. Watch the hustle and bustle of Munich's street life from an outdoor table on the city side, or retreat through a gate in the Hofgarten's western wall to the café's tree-shaded beer garden. If the weather is cool or rainy, find a corner in the cozy, eclectically furnished interior. ⊠ *Odeonspl. 18, Altstadt* ☎ *089/298–322* ⊕ *www.tambosi.de* ☉ *Daily 8 am–1 am* Ⓜ *Odeonsplatz / Marienplatz.*

Hofgarten (*Court Garden*). The creation of the formal court garden, part of the royal residence, dates back to 1613 when it lay outside the Residenz moat. It's now bordered on two sides by arcades designed in the 19th century by court architect Leo von Klenze. On the east side of the garden is the state chancellery (office of the Bavarian prime minister), built in 1990–93 around the ruins of the 19th-century Army Museum and incorporating the remains of a Renaissance arcade. Bombed during World War II air raids, the museum stood untouched for almost 40 years as a reminder of the war. Critics were horrified that a former army museum building could be used to represent modern, democratic Bavaria, not to mention about the immense cost. In front of the chancellery stands one of Europe's most unusual—some say most effective—war memorials. Instead of looking up at a monument, you are led down to a **sunken crypt** covered by a massive granite block. In the crypt lies a German soldier from World War I. The crypt is a stark contrast to the **memorial** that stands unobtrusively in front of the northern wing of the chancellery: a simple cube of black marble bearing facsimiles of handwritten wartime manifestos by anti-Nazi leaders, including the youthful members of the White Rose resistance movement. As you enter the garden from Odeonsplatz, take a look at the frescoes (drawn by art students 1826–29 and of varying degrees of quality) in the passage of the Hofgartentor with scenes from Bavarian history. ⊠ *Hofgartenstr. 1, Altstadt* ✛ *North of the Residenz.* ⊕ *www.residenz-muenchen.de/ englisch/garden/index.htm* Ⓜ *Odeonsplatz / Marienplatz.*

FAMILY
Fodor's Choice
★

Marienplatz. Bordered by the Neues Rathaus, shops, and cafés, this square is named after the gilded statue of the Virgin Mary that has watched over it for more than three centuries. It was erected in 1638 at the behest of Elector Maximilian I as an act of thanksgiving for the city's survival of the Thirty Years' War, the cataclysmic, partly religious struggle that devastated vast regions of Germany. When the statue was taken down from its marble column for cleaning in 1960, workmen found a small casket in the base containing a splinter of wood said to be from the cross of Christ. On the fifth floor of a building facing the Neues Rathaus is Café Glockenspiel. It overlooks the entire square and provides a perfect view of the glockenspiel. Entrance is around the back. ⊠ *Bounded by Kaufingerstr., Rosenstr., Weinstr., and Dienerstr., Altstadt* ⊕ *www.marienplatz.de* Ⓜ *Marienplatz.*

FAMILY **Michaelskirche** (*St. Michael's Church*). A curious story explains why this hugely impressive Renaissance church, adjoining a former extensive Jesuit college, has no tower. Seven years after the start of construction, in 1583, the main tower collapsed. Its patron, pious Duke Wilhelm V, regarded the disaster as a heavenly sign that the church wasn't big enough, so he ordered a change in the plans—this time without a tower. Completed in 1597, the barrel vaulting of St. Michael's is second in size only to that of St. Peter's in Rome. The duke is buried in the crypt, along with 40 other Wittelsbach family members, including the eccentric King Ludwig II. A severe neoclassical monument in the north transept contains the tomb of Napoléon's stepson, Eugène de Beauharnais, who married a daughter of King Maximilian I and died in Munich in 1824. Once again a Jesuit church, it is the venue for performances of church music. A poster to the right of the front portal gives the dates. ⊠ *Neuhauser Str. 6, Altstadt* ☎ *089/231–7060* ⊕ *www. st-michael-muenchen.de* 🎫 *Crypt: €2. Church: free. Musical performances: mostly free* ☉ *Church: Mon. and Fri. 10–7, Tues. 8–8:15, Wed., Thurs., and Sat. 8–7, Sun. 7–10:15. Crypt: Mon.–Thurs. 9:30–4:30, Fri. 10–4:30, Sat. 9:30–2:30* Ⓜ *Karlsplatz / Marienplatz.*

Fodor's Choice ★ **Neues Rathaus** (*New Town Hall*). Munich's present neo-Gothic town hall was built in three sections and two phases between 1867 and 1905. It was a necessary enlargement on the nearby Old Town Hall, but city fathers also saw it as presenting Munich as a modern city, independent from the waning powers of the Bavarian Wittelsbach royal house. Architectural historians are divided over its merits, although its dramatic scale and lavish detailing are impressive. Perhaps the most serious criticism is that the Dutch and Flemish styles of the building seem out of place amid the baroque and rococo styles of parts of the Altstadt. The main tower's 1908 **glockenspiel** (a chiming clock with mechanical figures), the largest in Germany, plays daily at 11 am and noon, with an additional performance at 5 pm March–October. As chimes peal out over the square, the clock's doors flip open and brightly colored dancers and jousting knights act out two events from Munich's past: a tournament held in Marienplatz in 1568 and the *Schäfflertanz* (Dance of the Coopers), which commemorated the end of the plague of 1515–17. You, too, can travel up there, by elevator, to an observation point near the top of one of the towers. On a clear day the view across the city with the Alps beyond is spectacular. ⊠ *Marienpl. 8, Altstadt* ⊕ *www.muenchen.de/int/en/sights/attractions/new-town-hall-neues-rathaus.html* 🎫 *Tower €2.50* ☉ *Tower: May–Sept., daily 10–7; Oct.–Apr., weekdays 10–5* Ⓜ *Marienplatz.*

Fodor's Choice ★ **Peterskirche** (*Church of St. Peter*). The Altstadt's oldest parish church (called locally Alter Peter, Old Peter) traces its origins to the 11th century, and has been restored in various architectural styles, including Gothic, baroque, and rococo. The rich baroque interior has a magnificent high altar and aisle pillars decorated with exquisite 18th-century figures of the apostles. In clear weather it's well worth the long climb up the approximately 300-foot-high tower, with a panoramic view of the Alps. ✉ *Rindermarkt 1, Altstadt* ☎ *089/2102–37760* ⊕ *www.muenchen.de/ int/en/sights/churches/church-of-st-peter.html* 🎫 *Tower €2* ⊗ *Tower: late Mar.–late Oct., weekdays 9–6:30, weekends 10–6:30; late Oct.–late Mar., weekdays 9–5:30, weekends 10–5:30. Church: daily 7:30–6:30* Ⓜ *Marienplatz.*

FAMILY

Fodor'sChoice

★

Residenz (*Royal Palace*). One of Germany's true treasures, Munich's royal Residenz began in 1363 as the modest Neuveste (New Fortress) on the northeastern city boundary. By the time the Bavarian monarchy fell, in 1918, the palace could compare favorably with the best in Europe. With the Residenz's central location, it was pretty much inevitable that the Allied bombing of 1944–45 would cause immense damage, and subsequent reconstruction took decades. For tourists today, however, it really is a treasure chamber of delight. A wander around the Residenz can last anywhere from three hours to all day. The 16th-century, 70-meter-long arched Antiquarium, built for Duke Albrecht V's collection of antiques and library, is recognized as one of the most impressive Renaissance creations outside Italy (today it's used chiefly for state receptions). ■TIP➜ **All the different rooms, halls, galleries, chapels, and museums within the Residenzmuseum, as well as the Cuvilliés-Theater and Treasury, can be visited with a combination ticket that costs €13.** ✉ *Residenzstr. 1, Altstadt* ✛ *Enter from Max-Joseph-Pl. 3* ☎ *089/290–671* ⊕ *www.residenz-muenchen.de/englisch/residenc/ index.htm* 🎫 *Combination entry to Residenz Museum, Treasury, and Cuvilliés Theater €13. Audio guides free* ⊗ *Museum and Treasury: Apr.–mid-Oct., daily 9–6; mid-Oct.–Mar., daily 10–5* Ⓜ *Odeonsplatz/ Marienplatz.*

Cuvilliés-Theater. This stunning example of a rococo theater was originally built by court architect François Cuvilliés between 1751 and 1753 and it soon became the most famous in Germany. In 1781 it premiered Mozart's *Idomeneo* , commissioned by the Elector of Bavaria, Karl Theodor. The lavish rococo style went out of fashion with the emergence of the less ostentatious, more elegant period of 18th-century classicism. But in 1884 it became the first theater in Germany to be fitted out with electric lighting and in 1896 the first to have a revolving stage. As with so much of the Altstadt, it was destroyed during Allied bombing raids, although some of the original rococo decoration had been removed. A new theater, the Neues Residenz-Theater (now the Bavarian State Drama Theatre Company) was built (1948–51) in a different location. In 1956–58, using some of the original rococo furnishings, Cuvilliés's lavish theater was rebuilt at a corner of the Residenz's Apothekenhof (courtyard). ✉ *Residenzstr. 1, Altstadt* ✛ *Enter from Kapellenhof (Chapel Courtyard)* ⊕ *www.residenz-muenchen.de/englisch/cuv/* 🎫 *From €3.50. Combined ticket with Treasury and Museum €13* ⊗ *Aug.–mid-Sept., daily 9–6; mid-Sept.–mid-Oct. and Apr.–July, Mon.–Sat. 2–6, Sun. 9–6; mid-Oct.–Mar., Mon.–Sat. 2–5, Sun. 10–5. Closed during rehearsals* Ⓜ *Odeonsplatz / Marienplatz.*

Residenzmuseum. The Residenzmuseum comprises everything in the Residenz apart from the Schatzkammer (Treasury) and the Cuvilliés-Theater. Paintings, tapestries, furniture, and porcelain are housed in various rooms and halls. One highlight is the **Grüne Galerie (Green Gallery)**, named after its green silk decoration, and its opulence and outstanding paintings are captivating. Also impressive is the Ahnengalerie (Ancestral Gallery) at the end of the tour, which demonstrates the Wittelsbach royal family lineage. ⊠ *Residenzstr. 1, Altstadt* ⊹ *Enter from Max-Joseph-Pl.* 3 ⊕ *www.residenz-muenchen.de/englisch/museum/index.htm* ⌑ *From €7. Combined ticket with Treasury and Cuvilliés Theater €13. Audio guide free* ⊗ *Apr.–mid-Oct., daily 9–6; mid-Oct.–Mar., daily 10–5* Ⓜ *Odeonsplatz / Marienplatz.*

Schatzkammer (*Treasury*). The Schatzkammer comprises many hundreds of masterworks, including a host of treasures from the Wittelsbach royal crown jewels. A highlight is the crown belonging to Bavaria's first king, Maximilian I Joseph, created in Paris in 1806–07. The Schatzkammer collection has a staggering centerpiece—a renowned 50-cm-high (20-inch-high) Renaissance statue of St. George studded with diamonds, pearls, and rubies. ⊠ *Residenzstr. 1, Altstadt* ⊹ *Enter from Max-Joseph-Pl.* 3 ⊕ *www.residenz-muenchen.de/englisch/treasury/index.htm* ⌑ *€7. Combined ticket with Residenz Museum and Cuvilliés Theater €13. Audio guide free* ⊗ *Apr.–mid-Oct., daily 9–6; mid-Oct.–Mar., daily 10–5* Ⓜ *Odeonsplatz / Marienplatz.*

Staatliche Münzsammlung. More than 300,000 coins, banknotes, medals, and precious stones, some 5,000 years old, star in the Staatliche Münzsammlung. ⊠ *Residenzstr. 1, Altstadt* ⊹ *Enter from Kapellenhof (Chapel Courtyard)* ☎ *089/227–221* ⊕ *www.staatliche-muenzsammlung.de* ⌑ *From €2.50* ⊗ *Tues.–Sun. 10–5* Ⓜ *Odeonsplatz / Marienplatz.*

Theatinerkirche (St. Kajetan). This glorious baroque church owes its Italian appearance to its founder, Princess Henriette Adelaide of Savoy, who commissioned it in gratitude for the long-awaited birth of her son and heir, Max Emanuel, in 1662. A native of Turin, the princess mistrusted Bavarian architects and builders and thus summoned Agostino Barelli, a master builder from Bologna, to construct her church. It is modeled on Rome's Sant'Andrea della Valle. Barelli worked on the building for 12 years, but he was dismissed as too quarrelsome. It was another 100 years before the building was finished in a style similar to today's. Its striking yellow facade stands out, and its two lofty towers, topped by delightful cupolas, frame the entrance, with the central dome at the back. The superb stucco work on the inside has a remarkably light feeling owing to its brilliant white color. The expansive Odeonsplatz in front of the Feldherrnhalle and Theatinerkirche is often used for outdoor stage events. ⊠ *Theatinerstr. 22, Altstadt* ⊹ *Facing Odeonspl.* ☎ *089/210–6960* ⊕ *www.theatinerkirche.de/index.php?cID=1&set_language_id=2* ⊗ *Daily 7 am–7:30 pm* Ⓜ *Odeonsplatz / Marienplatz.*

FAMILY

Fodor's Choice

★

Viktualienmarkt (*Victuals Market*). The city's open-air market really is the beating heart of downtown Munich. It has just about every fresh fruit or vegetable you can imagine, as well as German and international

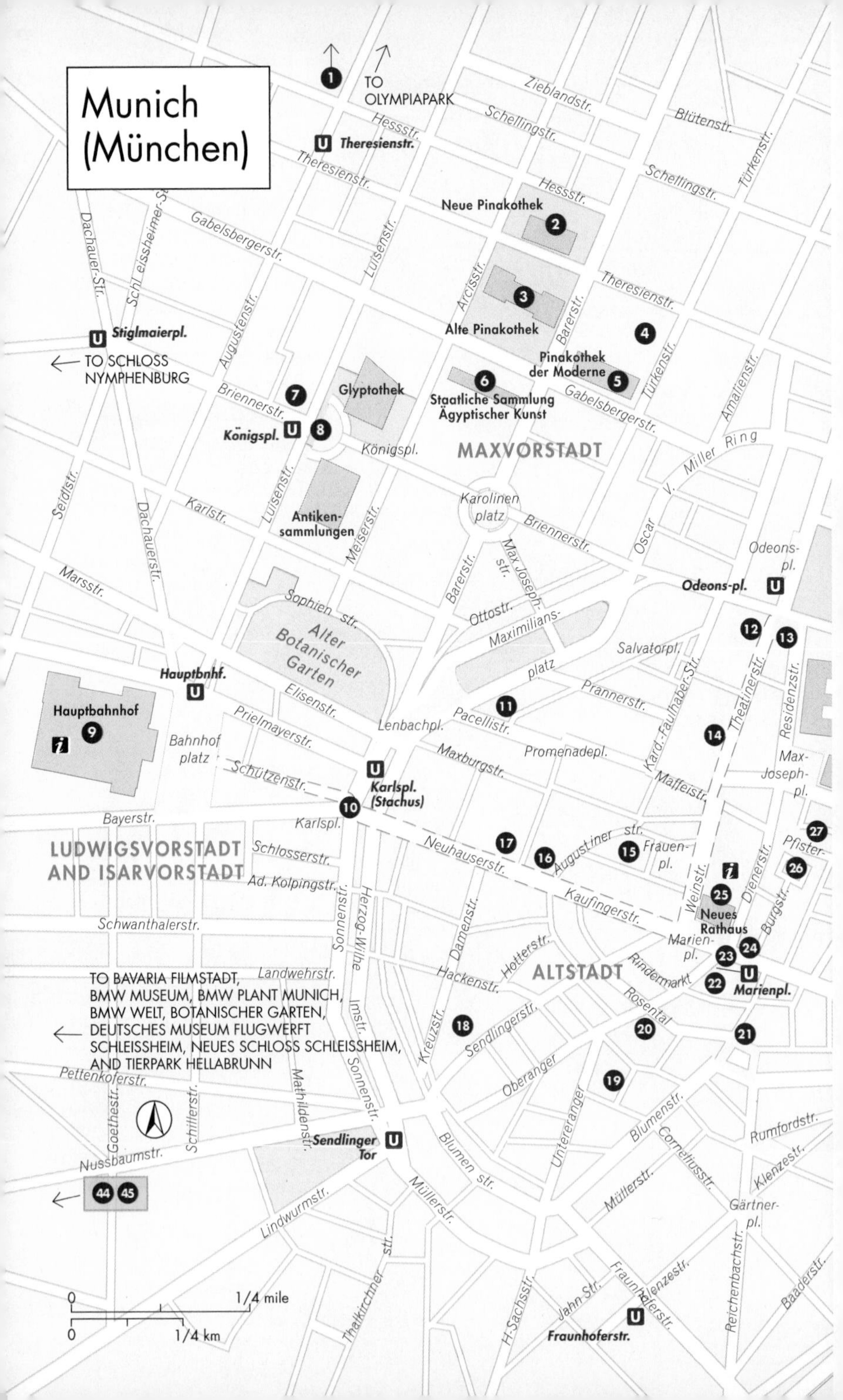

Munich (München)
TO OLYMPIAPARK
Theresienstr.
Zieblandstr.
Schellingstr.
Blütenstr.
Hessstr.
Türkenstr.
Theresienstr.
Neue Pinakothek
Gabelsbergerstr.
Luisenstr.
Dachauer-Str.
Schleissheimer-Str.
Arcisstr.
Barerstr.
Alte Pinakothek
Stiglmaierpl.
Augustenstr.
TO SCHLOSS NYMPHENBURG
Pinakothek der Moderne
Amalienstr.
Briennerstr.
Glyptothek
Staatliche Sammlung Ägyptischer Kunst
Königspl.
MAXVORSTADT
Oscar v. Miller Ring
Seidlstr.
Dachauerstr.
Karlstr.
Antiken-sammlungen
Meiserstr.
Karolinen platz
Max Joseph-str.
Odeons-pl.
Marsstr.
Sophien str.
Alter Botanischer Garten
Ottostr.
Maximilians-platz
Salvatorpl.
Hauptbnhf.
Hauptbahnhof
Elisenstr.
Prannerstr.
Kard.-Faulhaber-Str.
Theatinerstr.
Residenzstr.
Prielmayerstr.
Lenbachpl.
Pacellistr.
Bahnhof platz
Schützenstr.
Maxburgstr.
Promenadepl.
Max-Joseph-pl.
Karlspl. (Stachus)
Maffeistr.
Bayerstr.
Karlspl.
Neuhauserstr.
Augustiner str.
Frauen-pl.
Pfister-
LUDWIGSVORSTADT AND ISARVORSTADT
Schlosserstr.
Ad. Kolpingstr.
Weinstr.
Dienerstr.
Kaufingerstr.
Neues Rathaus
Burgstr.
Schwanthalerstr.
Sonnenstr.
Herzog-Wilhe
Damenstr.
Hotterstr.
Marien-pl.
Rindermarkt
Landwehrstr.
Hackenstr.
ALTSTADT
Marienpl.
Rosental
TO BAVARIA FILMSTADT, BMW MUSEUM, BMW PLANT MUNICH, BMW WELT, BOTANISCHER GARTEN, DEUTSCHES MUSEUM FLUGWERFT SCHLEISSHEIM, NEUES SCHLOSS SCHLEISSHEIM, AND TIERPARK HELLABRUNN
Imstr.
Kreuzstr.
Sendlingerstr.
Pettenkoferstr.
Mathildenstr.
Sonnenstr.
Oberanger
Goethestr.
Schillerstr.
Unteranger
Blumenstr.
Corneliusstr.
Rumfordstr.
Sendlinger Tor
Blumen str.
Nussbaumstr.
Klenzestr.
Müllerstr.
Müllerstr.
Gärtner-pl.
Lindwurmstr.
Thalkirchner str.
H.Sachsstr.
Jahn Str.
Fraunhoferstr.
Klenzestr.
Reichenbachstr.
Baaderstr.
Fraunhoferstr.
0 1/4 mile
0 1/4 km

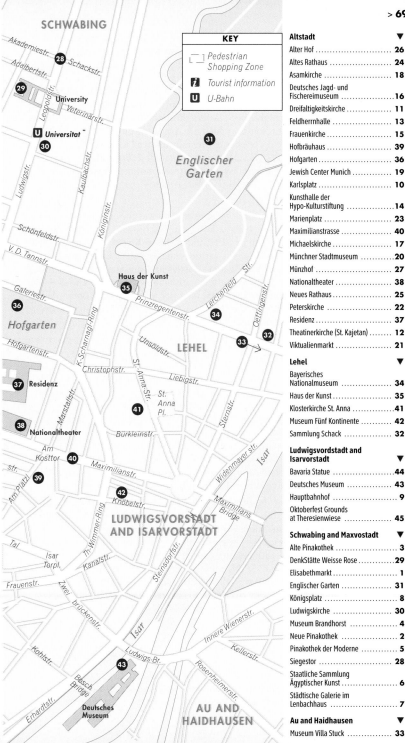

SCHWABING

Englischer Garten

Haus der Kunst

LEHEL

Hofgarten

Residenz

Nationaltheater

LUDWIGSVORSTADT AND ISARVORSTADT

Deutsches Museum

AU AND HAIDHAUSEN

KEY

Pedestrian Shopping Zone

i Tourist information

U U-Bahn

specialties. All kinds of people come here for a quick bite, from well-heeled businesspeople and casual tourists to mortar- and paint-covered workers. It's also the realm of the garrulous, sturdy market women who run the stalls with dictatorial authority. Whether here, or at a bakery, *do not* try to select your pickings by hand. Ask, and let it be served to you. There's a great beer garden (open pretty much whenever the sun is shining).The available beers rotate throughout the year among the six major Munich breweries, which are displayed on the maypole. These are also the only six breweries officially allowed to serve their wares at the Oktoberfest. ✉ *Viktualienmarkt, Altstadt* ✛ *Just south of Marienpl.* ⊕ *www.muenchen.de/int/en/sights/attractions/viktualienmarkt.html* ⊙ *Weekdays 10–6, Sat. 10–3* Ⓜ *Marienplatz.*

WORTH NOTING

Alter Hof (*Münchner Kaiserburg*). Alter Hof was the original home of the Wittelsbach dynasty of Bavaria (not to be confused with the adjacent Residenz). Established in 1180, the **Münchner Kaiserburg** (Imperial Palace) at Alter Hof now serves various functions. Its **Infopoint** is a tourist-information center for Bavaria's castles and museums. In the vaulted hall beneath is a multimedia presentation about the palace's history. The west wing is home to **Restaurant Alter Hof**, offering Franconian delicacies and a wine bar. ✉ *Alter Hof 1, Altstadt* ☎ *089/2101–4050* ⊕ *www.muenchner-kaiserburg.de* ⊙ *Infopoint: Mon.–Sat. 10–6* Ⓜ *Marienplatz.*

Altes Rathaus (*Old Town Hall*). Much of the work on Munich's first town hall was done in the 15th century, though various alterations were made through the centuries. Its great hall—destroyed in 1943–45 but now fully restored—was the work of the renowned architect Jörg von Halspach. Postwar, the tower was rebuilt as it looked in the 15th century and now it's used for official receptions and is not usually open to the public. The tower provides a fairy-tale-like setting for the **Spielzeugmuseum** (Toy Museum), accessible via a winding staircase. Its toys, dolls, and teddy bears are on display, together with a collection of Barbies from the United States. ✉ *Marienpl. 15, Altstadt* ☎ *089/294–001 Spielzeugmuseum* ⊕ *www.muenchen.de/sehenswuerdigkeiten/orte/120398.html* ☜ *Spielzeugmuseum €5* ⊙ *Daily 10–5:30* Ⓜ *Marienplatz.*

Fodor's Choice
★ **Asamkirche** (*St.-Johann-Nepomuk-Kirche*). Perhaps Munich's most ostentatious church, it has a suitably extraordinary entrance, framed by raw rock foundations. The insignificant door, crammed between its craggy shoulders, gives little idea of the opulence and lavish detailing within the small 18th-century church (there are only 12 rows of pews). Above the doorway St. Nepomuk, the 14th-century Bohemian monk and patron saint of Bavaria, who drowned in the Danube, is being led by angels from a rocky riverbank to heaven. The church's official name is Church of St. Johann Nepomuk, but it's known as the Asamkirche for its architects, the brothers Cosmas Damian and Egid Quirin Asam. The interior of the church is a prime example of true southern German late-baroque architecture. Frescoes by Cosmas Damian Asam and rosy marble cover the walls. The sheer wealth of statues and gilding is stunning—there's even a gilt skeleton at the sanctuary's portal. ✉ *Sendlingerstr. 32, Altstadt* ⊕ *www.muenchen.de/sehenswuerdigkeiten/orte/130982.html* ⊙ *Daily 9–6 (from 1 pm Fri.)* Ⓜ *Sendlingertor.*

FAMILY **Deutsches Jagd- und Fischereimuseum** (*German Museum of Hunting and Fishing*). This quirky museum is in the enormous former St. Augustus Church, and it contains a large collection of fishhooks, taxidermy animals (including a 6½-foot-tall brown bear and a grizzly from Alaska), and a 12,000-year-old megaloceros (giant deer) skeleton. You'll even find the *Wolpertinger,* a mythical creature with body parts of various animals. Its newest exhibit contains a forest path that displays animal habitats within Germany to be discovered via a virtual guided tour, and there is a walk-under-water area that showcases the different fish habitats of Germany. ⊠ *Neuhauser Str. 2, Altstadt* ☎ *089/220–522* ⊕ *www.jagd-fischerei-museum.de* 🖃 *From €3.50* ☉ *Daily 9:30–5 (until 9 Thurs.)* Ⓜ *Karlsplatz / Marienplatz.*

Dreifaltigkeitskirche (*Church of the Holy Trinity*). Take a quick look at this characteristic church built to commemorate Bavaria's part in the Spanish War of Succession. A further motivation for its construction was a prophecy from the devout Maria Anna Lindmayr that if the city survived the war intact and a church was not erected in thanks, the city was doomed. The city was saved and a church was built between 1711 and 1718. It has a striking baroque exterior, and its interior is brought to life by frescoes by Cosmas Damian Asam depicting various heroic scenes. Remarkably, it is the only church in the city's Altstadt spared destruction in the war. ⊠ *Pacellistr. 6, Altstadt* ☎ *089/290–0820* ⊕ *www.muenchen.de/sehenswuerdigkeiten/orte/130940.html* ☉ *Daily 7–7 (until 6 Fri.)* Ⓜ *Karlsplatz / Lenbachplatz (Tram).*

FAMILY **Jewish Center Munich** (*Jüdisches Zentrum*). The striking Jewish Center at St.-Jakobs-Platz has transformed a formerly sleepy area into an elegant, busy modern square. The buildings signify the return of the Jewish community to Munich's City Center, six decades after the end of the Third Reich. The center includes a museum focusing on Jewish history in Munich (plus kosher café), and the impressive Ohel Jakob Synagogue, with its rough slabs topped by a latticelike cover, manifesting a thought-provoking sense of permanence. The third building is a community center, which includes the kosher Einstein restaurant (*089/2024–00332, www.einstein-restaurant.de*). Guided tours of the synagogue are in great demand, and must be booked at least two weeks in advance (*089/2024– 00100*). ⊠ *St.-Jakobs-Pl. 16, Altstadt* ☎ *089/2339–6096* ⊕ *www. juedisches-museum-muenchen.de* 🖃 *From €3* ☉ *Museum: Tues.–Sun. 10–6; synagogue by prior arrangement* Ⓜ *Marienplatz / Sendlinger Tor.*

FAMILY **Karlsplatz** (*Stachus*). In 1728, Eustachius Föderl opened an inn and beer garden here, which might be how the square came to be called Stachus—it's still called that by the locals although the beer garden is gone. One of Munich's most popular fountains is here. It's a magnet on hot summer days and makes way for an ice-skating rink in winter. Karlsplatz is a bustling meeting point, even more so because of the underground shopping center. ⊠ *Karlspl., Altstadt* ⊕ *www.stachus-passagen.com* ☉ *General hrs for Stachus Passage shops: Mon.–Sat. 9:30–8* Ⓜ *Karlsplatz.*

FAMILY **Kunsthalle der Hypo-Kulturstiftung** (*Hall of the Hypobank's Cultural Foundation*). Chagall, Giacometti, Picasso, and Gauguin are among the artists that have been featured in the past at this exhibition hall in the middle of the shopping pedestrian zone. It is set within the upscale **Fünf Höfe shopping mall**, designed by the Swiss architect team Herzog and de Meuron, who also designed London's Tate Modern. Exhibitions at the Kunsthalle rarely disappoint, making it one of Germany's most interesting exhibition venues. ✉ *Theatinerstr. 8, Altstadt* ☎ *089/224–412* ⊕ *www.kunsthalle-muc.de/en/* 🎟 *€12* ⊙ *Daily 10–8* Ⓜ *Odeonsplatz / Marienplatz.*

FAMILY **Maximilianstrasse.** Munich's most expensive and exclusive shopping street was named after King Maximilian II, who wanted to break away from the Greek-influenced classical architecture favored by his father, Ludwig I. He thus created this broad boulevard lined with majestic buildings culminating on a rise above the River Isar at the stately **Maximilianeum.** Finished in 1874, this building was conceived as an elite education foundation for the most talented young people across Bavaria, regardless of status or wealth. It is still home to an education foundation, but its principal role is as the grand, if slightly confined, home to the Bavarian state parliament. Rather than take the tram to see the Maximilianeum, the whole walk along Maximilianstrasse (from Max-Joesph-Platz) is rewarding. You'll pass various boutiques, plus the five-star Hotel Vier Jahreszeiten, the Upper Bavarian Parliament, the Museum Fünf Kontinente (State Museum of Ethnology), and cross the picturesque River Isar. Five minutes past the Maximilianeum, on the charming Wiener Platz, is the Hofbräukeller and its excellent beer garden. ✉ *Maximilianstr., Altstadt* Ⓜ *Maximilianeum (Tram).*

FAMILY **Münchner Stadtmuseum** (*City Museum*). This museum is as eclectic inside as the architecture is outside. The buildings facing St.-Jakobs-Platz date to the 15th century, though they were destroyed in WWII and rebuilt. Recent extensive renovation has revitalized the City Museum, exemplified by its fabulous **Typical Munich!** exhibition, charting a riotous history few other cities can match: royal capital, brewery center, capital of art and classical music, and now wealthy, high-tech, and cultural center par excellence. There is also a separate, permanent exhibition dealing with the city's Nazi past. The museum is home to a puppet theater, a film museum showing rarely screened movies, and numerous photo and other temporary exhibitions. Check out the museum shop, servus. heimat, with the great and good of Munich kitsch and souvenirs. If the threat of sunshine makes it difficult to get a table outside at the lively museum café on St.-Jakobs-Platz, try the Stadtmuseum's inner courtyard, which still catches the sun but can be less packed. ✉ *St.-Jakob-spl. 1, Altstadt* ☎ *089/2332–2370* ⊕ *www.muenchner-stadtmuseum.de* 🎟 *€7* ⊙ *Tues.–Sun. 10–6* Ⓜ *Marienplatz / Sendlinger Tor.*

FAMILY **Münzhof** (*Mint*). Originally built between 1563 and 1567, the ground floor was home to Duke Albrecht V's stables, the second floor to living quarters for the servants, and the third to the ducal collection of high art and curiosities (6,000 pieces by 1600). Between 1809 and 1983 it housed the Bavarian mint, and a neoclassical facade, with allegories of copper, silver, and gold, was added in 1808–09. Today, with its slightly garish green exterior on three sides, it can appear to be little more than the somewhat undistinguished home to the Bavarian Land Bureau for the Conservation of Historic Monuments, but step inside the inner arcade to see a jewel of German Renaissance architecture. ⊠ *Hofgraben 4, Altstadt* ✛ *Enter from Pfisterstr.* 🕮 *Free* Ⓜ *Marienplatz.*

FAMILY   **Nationaltheater** (*National Theater*). Bavaria's original National Theater at Max-Joseph-Platz didn't last long. Opened in 1818, it burned to the ground in 1823 before it was completely finished. By 1825 it was rebuilt with its eight-column portico, and went on to premiere Richard Wagner's world-famous *Tristan und Isolde* (1865), *Meistersinger von Nürnberg* (1868), *Rheingold* (1869), and *Walküre* (1870). Allied bombs destroyed much of the interior in 1943, and its facade and elements of its interior were rebuilt as it was prewar. It finally reopened in 1963. Today, it is one of Europe's largest opera houses and contains some of the world's most advanced stage technologies. As the principal home to the Bavarian State Opera, it is considered one of the world's outstanding opera houses. Family opera is also available for children under 16 with an accompanying adult. The Munich Opera Festival takes place each July, including performances, free open-air Opera for All events, and live streaming opera online with Staatsoper TV. ⊠ *Max-Joseph-Pl. 2, Altstadt* ☎ *089/2185–1024* ⊕ *www.bayerische.staatsoper.de* 🕮 *From €15* Ⓜ *Odeonsplatz / Marienplatz.*

LEHEL

Seamlessly extending from Altstadt, Lehel is also home to some of Munich's royal-themed sights. While it mixes and mingles with the Old Town, it's a chic residential neighborhood as well, where locals come to escape from the crowded City Center.

TOP ATTRACTIONS

Haus der Kunst (*House of Art*). This colonnaded, classical-style building is one of Munich's most significant examples of Hitler-era architecture, and was officially opened as House of German Art by the Führer himself. During the Third Reich it only showed work deemed to reflect the Nazi aesthetic. One of its most successful postwar exhibitions was devoted to works banned by the Nazis. It now hosts cutting-edge exhibitions on art, photography, and sculpture, as well as theatrical and musical happenings, and P1 is the hottest bar in town. ⊠ *Prinzregentenstr. 1, Altstadt* ☎ *089/2112–7113* ⊕ *www.hausderkunst.de/en/* 🕮 *€12* ⊙ *Daily 10–8 (Thurs. until 10)* Ⓜ *Odeonsplatz / Lehel / Nationalmuseum/Haus d.Kunst (Tram).*

WORTH NOTING

FAMILY   **Bayerisches Nationalmuseum** (*Bavarian National Museum*). Although the museum places emphasis on Bavarian cultural history, it has art and artifacts of international importance and regular exhibitions that attract worldwide attention. The museum is a journey through time, principally from the early Middle Ages to the 20th century, with medieval and Renaissance wood carvings, works by the great Renaissance sculptor Tilman Riemenschneider, tapestries, arms and armor, a unique collection of Christmas crèches (the *Krippenschau*), Bavarian and German folk art, and a significant *Jugendstil* (art nouveau) collection. ⊠ *Prinzregentenstr. 3, Lehel* ☎ *089/211–2401* ⊕ *www.bayerisches-nationalmuseum.*

de ⊠ *From €7* ⊙ *Tues.–Sun. 10–5 (Thurs. until 8)* Ⓜ *Lehel / National-museum/Haus d.Kunst (Tram).*

OFF THE BEATEN PATH

Klosterkirche St. Anna (*Monastery Church of St. Anne*). This striking example of the two Asam brothers' work in the Lehel district impresses visitors with its sense of movement and heroic scale. The ceiling fresco from 1729 by Cosmas Damian Asam glows in all its original glory. The ornate altar was also designed by the Asam brothers. Towering over the delicate little church, on the opposite side of the street, is the neo-Romanesque bulk of the 19th-century Parish Church of St. Anne. Stop at one of the stylish cafés, restaurants, and patisseries gathered at the junction of St.-Anna-Strasse and Gewürzmühlstrasse, about 250 feet from the churches. ⊠ *St.-Anna-Str. 19, Lehel* ☎ *089/211–260* ⊕ *www.erzbistum-muenchen.de/Pfarrei/Page000453.aspx* ⊙ *Mon.–Sat. 8:30–11:45 and 2–5:45, Sun. 9:30–11:45* Ⓜ *Lehel.*

FAMILY **Museum Fünf Kontinente** (*Five Continents Museum*). Founded in 1862, this museum houses an enormous quantity of ethnographic articles from around the world, including arts, crafts, photographs, and library material. The extensive museum takes a peek into non-European cultures from Africa, America, Asia, Australia, the Near and Middle East, and the South Seas to see how they differ (or not) from Europe with both permanent displays and special exhibits. ⊠ *Maximilianstr. 42, Lehel* ☎ *089/2101–36100* ⊕ *www.museum-fuenf-kontinente.de/services/english-summary.html* ⊠ *€5* ⊙ *Tues.–Sun. 9:30–5:30* Ⓜ *Isartor / Lehel / Maxmonument (Tram).*

FAMILY **Sammlung Schack** (*Schack-Galerie*). Around 180 German 19th-century paintings from the Romantic era up to the periods of Realism and Symbolism make up the collections of the Sammlung Schack, originally the private collection of Count Adolf Friedrich von Schack. ⊠ *Prinzregent-enstr. 9, Lehel* ☎ *089/2380–5224* ⊕ *www.pinakothek.de/sammlung-schack* ⊠ *From €4. Day ticket to the three Pinakotheks, Brandhorst, and Sammlung Schack €12* ⊙ *Wed.–Sun. 10–6 (1st and 3rd Wed. of month until 8)* Ⓜ *Lehel / Nationalmuseum/Haus d.Kunst (Tram).*

LUDWIGSVORSTADT AND ISARVORSTADT

LUDWIGSVORSTADT

Oktoberfest and the Winter Tollwood Festival, not far from Hauptbahnhof, take place at the Theresienwiese meadow, which is located in Ludwigsvorstadt. This neighborhood, which includes the Hauptbahnhof (main train station), runs south from there, and is joined to the east by Isarvorstadt.

FAMILY **Bavaria Statue.** Overlooking the Theresienwiese, home of the Oktoberfest, is a 19th-century hall of fame (Ruhmeshalle) featuring busts of famous Bavarian scientists, artists, engineers, generals, and philosophers, and a monumental bronze statue of the maiden Bavaria. Unsurprisingly, it was commissioned by the art- and architecture-obsessed King Ludwig I, though not finished before his abdication in 1848. The Bavaria is more than 60 feet high and at the time was the largest bronze figure since antiquity. The statue is hollow, and an initial 48 steps take you up to its base. Once inside, there are 66 steps to her knee, and a further 52 all the way into the braided head, the reward being a view of Munich through Bavaria's eyes. ⊠ *Theresienhöhe 16, Ludwigsvorstadt* ⊕ *www.schloesser.bayern.de/englisch/palace/objects/mu_ruhm.htm* 🖅 *€3.50* ⊙ *Bavaria Statue and Ruhmeshalle: Apr.–mid-Oct., daily 9–6. Bavaria Statue open until 8 during Oktoberfest. Ruhmeshalle closed during Oktoberfest* Ⓜ *Theresienwiese / Theresienhöhe (Bus).*

Hauptbahnhof (*Central Station*). The train station isn't a cultural site, but it's a particularly handy starting point for exploring. The city tourist office here has maps and helpful information on events around town. On the underground level are all sorts of shops that remain open even on Sunday and holidays. There are also a number of places to get a late-night snack in and around the station. ⊠ *Bahnhofpl., Ludwigsvorstadt* Ⓜ *Hauptbahnhof.*

FAMILY

Fodor'sChoice

★

Oktoberfest Grounds at Theresienwiese. The Oktoberfest and winter Tollwood music fest grounds are named after Princess Therese von Sachsen-Hildburghausen, who celebrated her marriage to the future King Ludwig I here in 1810 with thousands of Münchners. The event was so successful that it grew into a 16- to 18-day international beer and fair-ride bonanza attracting over 6 million people annually. Oktoberfest originally began in October. As it grew, it extended into September for better weather. Follow the crowds to any of the several points of entry. ⊠ *Theresienwiese, Ludwigsvorstadt* ⊹ *Some entrance points: in the northeast at St.-Pauls-Pl. from Theresienwiese station; from the east at Beethovenstr.; in the southeast at Matthias-Pschorr-Str. from Goetheplatz station* ⊕ *www.oktoberfest.de/en/* ⊙ *Opening night 10 am–midnight, Mon.–Thurs. 10 am–11:30 pm, Fri. 10 am–midnight, Sat. 9 am–midnight, Sun. 10 am–11:30 pm* Ⓜ *Theresienwiese / Goetheplatz.*

ISARVORSTADT

Isarvorstadt, west of Ludwigsvorstadt and south of Altstadt and Lehel, continues eastward until just past the Isar River. Close to Altstadt, this neighborhood has happening restaurants and shops, as well as the world-famous Deutsches Museum.

FAMILY

Fodor'sChoice

★

Deutsches Museum (*German Museum*). Aircraft, vehicles, cutting-edge technology, historic machinery, and even a mine fill this monumental building on an island in the Isar River, which comprises one of the best science and technology museums in the world. The collection is spread out over some 500,000 square feet, with eight floors of exhibits, The Centre for New Technologies includes interactive exhibitions, such as nanotechnology, biotechnology, and robotics. Children have their own "kingdom," the Kinderreich, where they can learn about modern technology and science through numerous interactive displays (parents must accompany their children). One of the most technically advanced planetariums in Europe has two shows daily, at 10 am and 2 pm, albeit in German only. The **Verkehrszentrum** (Center for Transportation), on the former trade fair grounds at the Theresienhöhe, has been completely renovated and houses an amazing collection of the museum's transportation exhibits. The museum's **Flugwerft Schleissheim** airfield is in Oberschleissheim, north of Munich. ⊠ *Museumsinsel 1, Isarvorstadt* ☎ *089/21791* ⊕ *www. deutsches-museum.de* 🖅 *Museum €11* ⊙ *Daily 9–5* Ⓜ *Isartor.*

SCHWABING AND MAXVORSTADT

Some of the finest museums in Europe are in lower Schwabing and Maxvorstadt, particularly in the *Kunstareal* (Art Quarter). Schwabing, the former artists' neighborhood, is no longer quite the bohemian area where such diverse residents as Lenin and Kandinsky were once neighbors, but the cultural foundations of Maxvorstadt are immutable. Where the two areas meet, in the streets behind the university, life hums with a creative vibrancy. The difficult part is having time to see it all.

SCHWABING

Formerly Munich's bohemian quarter, Schwabing is known for the Englischer Garten, one of the world's largest urban parks. Due to the universities that are located in Maxvorstadt to the south, Schwabing also has a healthy selection of bars, clubs, and restaurants which are frequented by students.

Elisabethmarkt (*Elisabeth Market*). Founded in 1903, Schwabing's permanent outdoor market is smaller than the more famous Viktualienmarkt, but hardly less colorful. It has a pocket-size beer garden, where a jazz band performs on Saturdays in summer. ⊠ *Elisabethpl., Arcisstr. and Elisabethstr., Schwabing* ⊕ *www.muenchen.de/int/en/shopping/markets/elisabethmarkt.html* ⊙ *Weekdays 10–6, Sat. 1–3* Ⓜ *Josephsplatz; Elisabethplatz (Tram).*

FAMILY

Fodor's Choice

★

Englischer Garten (*English Garden*). This seemingly endless green space blends into the open countryside at the north of the city. Today's park covers nearly 1,000 acres and has 78 km (48 miles) of paths and more than 100 bridges. The open, informal landscaping—reminiscent of the English-style rolling parklands of the 18th century—gave the park its name. It has a boating lake, five beer gardens, and a series of curious decorative and monumental constructions. In the center of the park's most popular beer garden is a Chinese pagoda, erected in 1790 (reconstructed after World War II). The Englischer Garten is a paradise for joggers, cyclists, musicians, soccer players, sunbathers, and, in winter, cross-country skiers. The park has semi-official areas for nude sunbathing—the Germans have a positively pagan attitude toward the sun—so in some areas don't be surprised to see naked bodies bordering the flower beds and paths. ⊠ *There are various entrance points around the garden, Schwabing* ⊕ *www.muenchen.de/int/en/sights/parks/english-garden.html* Ⓜ *Chinesischer Turm (Bus); Seehaus: Münchner Freiheit (U-bahn); Hirschau: Herzogpark (Bus); Mini-Hofbräuhaus: Herzogpark (Bus); Aumeister: Studentenstadt (U-bahn).*

Siegestor (*Victory Arch*). Built to bookend the Feldherrnhalle and mark the end of Ludwigstrasse, Siegestor nowadays also marks the beginning of Leopoldstrasse. Unsurprisingly, it has Italian origins and was modeled on the Arch of Constantine in Rome. It was built (1843–52) to honor the achievements of the Bavarian army during the Wars of Liberation (1813–15) against Napoléon. It received heavy bomb damage in 1944, and at the end of the war Munich authorities decided it should be torn down for safety reasons. Major Eugene Keller, the head of the U.S. military government in the postwar city, intervened and saved it. Its postwar inscription on the side facing the inner city is best

The Aeronautics Hall of the Deutsches Museum displays aircraft from the early days of flight to jets and helicopters.

translated as: "Dedicated to victory, destroyed by war, a monument to peace." ✉ *Leopoldstr. 2, Schwabing* ✛ *Intersection of Leopoldstr., Ludwigstr., Shackstr., and Akademiestr.* ⊕ *www.siegestor.de* Ⓜ *Universität / Giselastrasse.*

MAXVORSTADT

Just north of Munich's Altstadt, Maxvorstadt is home to Ludwigs-Maximilians-Universität (LMU) and the Technical University (TUM) of Munich, two of Germany's top universities popular with students the world over. Maxvorstadt's Kunstareal is rife with not-to-miss world-class museums and galleries as well.

TOP ATTRACTIONS

Fodor's Choice
★

Alte Pinakothek. With numerous old master paintings from the Netherlands, Italy, France, and Germany, the long redbrick Alte Pinakothek holds one of the most significant art collections in the world. At this writing it is partially closed due to renovations that are scheduled to last until 2018. It was originally constructed by Leo von Klenze between 1826 and 1836 to exhibit the collection of 14th- to 18th-century works (started by Duke Wilhelm IV in the 16th century). The collection comprises about 700 pieces, including masterpieces by Dürer, Titian, Rembrandt, da Vinci, Rubens (the museum has one of the world's largest Rubens collections), and two celebrated Murillos. Most of the picture captions are in German only, so it is best to rent an English audio guide. The Alte Pinakothek forms a central part of Munich's world-class *Kunstareal* (Art Quarter). Museums and collections here are of the highest quality, and are a few hundred yards apart. ✉ *Barer Str. 27, entrance faces Theresienstr., Maxvorstadt* ☎ 089/2380–5216 ⊕ *www.*

alte-pinakothek.de 🎫 *€4 during renovations. Day ticket to the three Pinakotheks, Brandhorst, and Sammlung Schack €12* ⊙ *Tues. 10–8, Wed.–Sun. 10–6* Ⓜ *Königsplatz.*

FAMILY **Königsplatz.** Bavaria's greatest monarch, Ludwig I, was responsible for Munich in the 19th century becoming known as Athens on the Isar, and the impressive buildings designed by Leo von Klenze that line this elegant and expansive square bear testament to his obsession with antiquity. The two temple-like structures facing one another are now the **Staatliche Antikensammlungen** (an acclaimed collection of Greek and Roman antiquities) and the **Glyptothek** (a fine collection of Greek and Roman statues). After WWII, Munich authorities ensured that the square returned to the more dignified appearance intended by Ludwig I, since this was a favorite parade ground for the Nazis, and it was paved over for that purpose in the 1930s. Today, the broad green lawns in front of the museums attract students and tourists in the warmer months, who gather for concerts, films, and other events. The area around here, focused on Briennerstrasse, became the national center of the Nazi Party in the 1930s and '40s, with various buildings taken over or built by the authorities. Nazi HQ, the Brown House, was between Königsplatz and the obelisk at Karolinenplatz. Destroyed in the war, the new **Munich Documentation Centre for the History of National Socialism** opened here in 2015 on Brienner Strasse 34. On Arcisstrasse 12 is the Nazi-era building (now a music school) where in 1938 Britain's prime minister, Neville Chamberlain, infamously thought he had negotiated "peace in our time" with Hitler. ✉ *Königspl. 1, Maxvorstadt* ☎ *089/5998–8830 Staatliche Antikensammlungen, 089/286–100 Glyptothek, 089/2336–7007 NS-Dokumentationszentrum* ⊕ *www.muenchen.de/ sehenswuerdigkeiten/orte/130668.html* 🎫 *From €6, includes Antikensammlungen and Glyptothek. From €5 for NS-Dokumentationszentrum* ⊙ *Antikensammlungen: Tues.–Sun. 10–5 (Wed. until 8); Glyptothek: Tues.–Sun. 10–5 (Thurs. until 8); NS-Dokumentationszentrum: Tues.– Sun. 10–7* Ⓜ *Königsplatz.*

FAMILY **Museum Brandhorst.** This multicolor abstract box is filled with videos, paintings, sculptures, and installations by artists such as Andy Warhol, Damien Hirst, Gerhard Richter, and Joseph Beuys, and is a real treat for contemporary art fans. The location in the middle of the historic Kunstareal art district, although shocking to some less progressive art aficionados, highlights that the city has broken out of the shackles of its postwar conservatism. Königsplatz U-bahn is a simple way to get to the Kunstareal, though it involves a pleasant 15-minute walk. Tram 27 takes you directly from Karlsplatz to the Pinakothek stop, in the heart of the Kunstareal. ✉ *Theresienstr. 35a, Maxvorstadt* ☎ *089/2380–52286* ⊕ *www.museum-brandhorst.de/en.html* 🎫 *€7. Day ticket to the three Pinakotheks, Brandhorst, and Sammlung Schack €12* ⊙ *Tues.–Sun. 10–6 (Thurs. until 8)* Ⓜ *Königsplatz; Pinakotheken (Tram).*

FAMILY

Fodor's Choice

★

Neue Pinakothek. Another museum packed with masters, the fabulous Neue Pinakothek reopened in 1981 to house the royal collection of modern art left homeless and scattered after its original building was destroyed in the war. The exterior of the modern building mimics an older one with Italianate influences. The interior offers a magnificent

The Glyptothek museum on Königsplatz houses Greek and Roman statues.

environment for picture gazing, partly owing to the natural light flooding in from skylights. French impressionists—Monet, Degas, Manet—are all well represented, while the comprehensive collection also includes the great Romantic landscape painters Turner and Caspar David Friedrich, and other artists of the caliber of van Gogh and Cezanne. This is another must-see. ⊠ *Barer Str. 29, Maxvorstadt* ☎ *089/2380–5195* ⊕ *www.pinakothek.de/en/neue-pinakothek* ⊠€7. *Day ticket to the three Pinakotheks, Brandhorst, and Sammlung Schack €12* ⊙ *Wed. 10–8, Thurs.–Mon. 10–6* Ⓜ *Königsplatz / Pinakotheken (Tram).*

FAMILY **Pinakothek der Moderne.** Opened to much fanfare in 2002, this fascinating, light-filled building is home to four outstanding museums under one cupola-topped roof: art, graphic art, architecture, and design. The striking 130,000-square-foot glass-and-concrete complex by Stefan Braunfels has permanent and temporary exhibitions throughout the year in each of the four categories. The design museum is particularly popular, showing permanent exhibitions in vehicle design, computer culture, and other design ideas. ⊠ *Barer Str. 40, Maxvorstadt* ☎ *089/2380–5360* ⊕ *www. pinakothek.de/en/pinakothek-der-moderne* ⊠€10. *Day ticket to the three Pinakotheks, Brandhorst, and Sammlung Schack €12* ⊙ *Tues.–Sun. 10–6 (Thurs. until 8)* Ⓜ *Königsplatz; Pinakotheken (Tram).*

QUICK BITES

Brasserie Tresznjewski. A good spot, especially if you're visiting the neighboring Pinakothek museums, the ever-popular Brasserie Tresznjewski serves an eclectic menu, well into the wee hours. ⊠ *Theresienstr. 72, corner of Barer Str., Maxvorstadt* ☎ *089/282–349* ⊕ *www.tresznjewski.com* ⊙ *Daily 8 am–midnight (Fri. and Sat. until 2 am)* Ⓜ *Pinakotheken (Tram).*

Fodor's Choice **Städtische Galerie im Lenbachhaus.** Art aficionados were waiting in antici-
★ pation for the reopening of this exquisite late-19th-century Florentine-
style villa, the former home and studio of the artist Franz von Lenbach
(1836–1904). In the middle of the 19th century, Munich was one of
the most important art centers in Europe, and in the 1880s, Lenbach
was one of the most famous artists in Germany. He painted Germany's
Chancellor Bismarck around 80 times. Nowadays, Lenbachhaus is
home to the stunning assemblage of art from the early-20th-century *Der
Blaue Reiter* (Blue Rider) group: Kandinsky, Klee, Jawlensky, Macke,
Marc, and Münter. Indeed, only New York's Guggenheim comes close
to holding as many works from a group that was at the forefront in the
development of abstract art. There are also vivid pieces from the New
Objectivity movement, and a variety of local Munich artists are represented here. Renowned British architecture firm Foster+Partners was
commissioned with the renovation work, and crucially to design a new
building on the grounds. Now with the addition of a significant Joseph
Beuys collection, its new gallery and renovated exhibition spaces were
met with great acclaim on the museum's unveiling in spring 2013. The
adjoining **Kunstbau** (art building) within the Königsplatz U-bahn station
hosts changing exhibitions of modern art. ⊠ *Luisenstr. 33, Maxvorstadt*
☎ *089/2333–2000* ⊕ *www.lenbachhaus.de/?L=1* 🖾 *From €10* ⊗ *Tues.
10–9, Wed.–Sun. 10–6* Ⓜ *Königsplatz.*

WORTH NOTING

FAMILY **DenkStätte Weisse Rose** (*Memorial to the White Rose Resistance Group*).
Siblings Hans and Sophie Scholl, fellow students Alexander Schmorell
and Christian Probst, and Kurt Huber, professor of philosophy, were
the key members of the Munich-based resistance movement against the
Nazis in 1942–43 known as the Weisse Rose (White Rose). All were
executed by guillotine. A small exhibition about their work is in the
inner quad of the university, where the Scholls were caught distributing
leaflets and denounced by the janitor. A memorial to White Rose is just
outside the university. ⊠ *Ludwig-Maximilians-Universität, Geschwis-
ter-Scholl-Pl. 1, Maxvorstadt* ☎ *089/2180–3053* ⊕ *www.weisse-rose-
stiftung.de* 🖾 *Permanent exhibition free. Prebooked guided tour €60*
⊗ *Weekdays 10–4, Sat. noon–3* Ⓜ *Universität.*

Ludwigskirche. Planted halfway along the stark, neoclassical Ludwigstrasse is this superb twin-towered Byzantine- and Italian-influenced
church, built between 1829 and 1838 at the behest of King Ludwig
I to provide his newly completed suburb with a parish church. From
across the road, look up to see the splendidly colored, 2009 mosaic
on the church's roof. Inside, see one of the great modern frescoes, the
Last Judgment by Peter von Cornelius, in the choir. At 60 feet by 37
feet, it's also one of the world's largest. ⊠ *Ludwigstr. 22, Maxvorstadt*
☎ *089/287–7990* ⊕ *www.st-ludwig-muenchen.de* ⊗ *Mon. and Fri. 9–
noon, Tues. and Thurs. 2–7* Ⓜ *Universität.*

FAMILY **Staatliche Sammlung Ägyptischer Kunst.** Various Bavarian rulers were fascinated with the ancient world and in the 19th century accumulated
huge quantities of significant Egyptian treasures, part of which make
up the Staatliche Sammlung Ägyptischer Kunst. In 2013 the collection
moved from the Residenz to an impressive new building in Munich's

superb Kunstareal (Art Quarter). ✉ *Gabelsbergerstr. 35, Maxvorstadt*
☎ *089/2892–7630* ⊕ *www.smaek.de/index.php?id=999* ✉ *From €7*
🕐 *Tues. 10–8, Wed.–Sun. 10–6* Ⓜ *Königsplatz.*

AU AND HAIDHAUSEN

On the east side of the River Isar, bordered by Lehel and Isarvorstadt to
the west, lie Au and Haidhausen, calm, green, and pleasant residential
areas punctuated with a few cafés and restaurants, and very conveniently located to Munich's Altstadt.

FAMILY **Museum Villa Stuck.** This dramatic neoclassical villa is the former home
Fodor'sChoice of one of Germany's leading avant-garde artists from the turn of the
★ 20th century, Franz von Stuck (1863–1928). His work, at times haunting, frequently erotic, and occasionally humorous, covers the walls
in many rooms. Stuck was prominent in the Munich art Secession
(1892), though today the museum is famous for its fabulous Jugendstil
(art nouveau) collections. The museum also features special exhibits
of international modern and contemporary art. ✉ *Prinzregentenstr.
60, Haidhausen* ☎ *089/455–5510* ⊕ *www.villastuck.de* ✉ *From €9*
🕐 *Tues.–Sun. 11–6 (1st Fri. of month until 10)* Ⓜ *Prinzregentenplatz.*

OUTSIDE INNENSTADT

TOP ATTRACTIONS

FAMILY **Olympiapark** (*Olympic Park*). Built for the 1972 Olympic Games on the
staggering quantities of rubble delivered from the wartime destruction
of Munich, the Olympiapark was—and still is—considered an architectural and landscape wonder. The jewel in the crown is the **Olympic
Stadium**, former home of Bayern Munich soccer team. With its truly
avant-garde sweeping canopy roof, winding its way across various parts
of the complex, it was an inspired design for the big events of the 1972
Olympic Games. Tragically, a bigger event relegated what was heading
to be the most successful Games to date to the sidelines. It was from
the adjacent accommodation area that a terrorist attack on the Israeli
team began, eventually leaving 17 people dead.

Unlike many former Olympic sites around the world, today the area
is heavily used; it's home to numerous concerts and sporting events,
and is a haven for joggers, swimmers, and people just wishing to relax.
Tours of the park are conducted on a Disneyland-style train throughout the day. For the more adventurous, how about climbing the roof
of the Olympic Stadium and rappelling down? For the best view of the
whole city and the Alps, take the elevator up the 955-foot **Olympiaturm**
(Olympic Tower) or try out the revolving **Restaurant 181** on the same
level. ✉ *Spiridon-Louis-Ring 21, Milbertshofen* ☎ *089/3067–2415
restaurant* ⊕ *www.olympiapark.de/en/olympiapark-munich/* ✉ *Stadium tour €7.50* 🕐 *Tour schedules vary; call ahead for departure times*
Ⓜ *Olympiazentrum.*

FAMILY **Schloss Nymphenburg.** This glorious baroque and rococo palace, the larg-
Fodor'sChoice est in Germany, grew in size and scope over more than 200 years. Begun
★ in 1662 by the Italian architect Agostino Barelli, it was completed by

Continued on page 90

CELEBRATING OKTOBERFEST
By Ben Knight

Oktoberfests are found around the world, but the original Munich Oktoberfest has never been equaled. Six million participants over 16–18 days make this one of Europe's largest and best-attended festivals. It's a glorious celebration of beer, Bavarian culture, beer, folk traditions, and still more beer. So tap a barrel, grab a *Mass*, and join the party with the immortal cry: *O'zapft is!* ("It's tapped!").

You could be forgiven for reducing the world's most famous beer festival to a string of clichés—drunken revelers, deafening brass bands, and red-faced men in leather shorts and feathered hunting hats singing uproariously. But Oktoberfest appeals to a broad range of people—it can be a great day out for families, a fun night for couples, or the scene of a spectacular party for larger groups—and provides enough entertainment to exhaust kids of all ages. Party aside, Oktoberfest is a cultural institution with costumes, parades, and traditions that play an important role in Oktoberfest and are an integral part of local identity.

OKTOBERFEST BY THE NUMBERS
More than 6 million liters (1.58 million gallons) of beer are put away, along with 650,000 sausages, 530,000 roast chickens, and around 110 oxen on the 103-acre Theresienwiese every year.

Left, Theresienwiese fairground. Top, Festival procession band.

OKTOBERFEST 101

HISTORY

The original Oktoberfest was a royal wedding party conceived in 1810 by Major Andreas Michael Dall'Armi, an officer in the Bavarian national guard. The major suggested a horse race to celebrate the wedding of Crown Prince Ludwig I (the future king) and Princess Therese of Saxony-Hildburghausen. The sports event proved popular, and was repeated every year, but in the long–term it did not prove as popular as the barrels of beer and wagons of roasted meat that came from the countryside to feed the onlookers. Out of these catering departments, the Oktoberfest was born.

The Oktoberfest grounds were named *Theresienwiese* after Princess Therese (literally "Therese meadow"), which gave rise to the popular nickname *Wiesn* now used to denote the grounds and sometimes the festival itself.

Above, Opening ceremony.
Opposite. Top, Münchner Kindl. Below, Bavarian couple dancing at Oktoberfest. Far right, Bratwurst sausage with beer and mustard.

TOP EVENTS

Three not-to-miss Oktoberfest events are worth planning your trip around. First, there's the **ceremonial arrival of the brewers and landlords,** which starts at about 10:50 am on the first day of the festival. Setting off from Josephspitalstrasse approximately a mile east of the Theresienwiese, the brewers and beertent landlords arrive at the Oktoberfest grounds on horse-drawn carriages festooned with flowers.

This is followed at noon by the **tapping of the first barrel,** performed by the mayor of Munich with a cry of *"O'zapft is!"* in the Schottenhamel tent.

The first Sunday of the festival sees the **Costume and Rifleman's Procession** (*Trachten- und Schützenzug*). This is Europe's biggest folk parade, consisting of almost 8,000 people promenading through Munich on horse-drawn wagons, in marching bands, or in formation, all in their full folk regalia. It begins between 9 and 10 am at the Maximilianeum and follows a fourmile route to the Oktoberfest grounds.

COSTUMES

Walking to the Theresienwiese, you'll see more and more people wearing the traditional Oktoberfest costumes—*dirndls* (traditional dresses with a fitted bodice, blouse, skirt, and apron) for the ladies, and *lederhosen* (leather breeches) and leather waistcoats for the gentlemen. As a first-time visitor, you might be surprised by how many people of all ages actually wear the traditional Bavarian garb, also known as *Trachten*. Plenty of visitors wear it too; you can buy your Trachten from **Angermaier, Moser,** or more cheaply at department stores like **C&A** and **Galeria Kaufhof.**

NOSTALGIA ZONE

The introduction of a "nostalgia area" in 2010, to mark the 200th anniversary of the first Oktoberfest, showed how well-loved the old sights and sounds remain. It recreated the Oktoberfests of simpler eras, complete with horse-racing, wooden fairground rides, and beer brewed using traditional recipes. It has now become a regular feature of the fest, known as the **Oide Wiesn** (Old Wiesn).

FOOD

The full range of hearty and surprisingly excellent Bavarian cuisine is available by table service in the tents. Tents that specialize in food, rather than beer (although they sell beer too), include sausage-centered **Zur Bratwurst;** fish emporium **Fischer-Vroni; Hochreiters Kalbsbraterei,** where you can try veal in myriad forms, among them the famous *Wiener Schnitzel;* and the **Ochsenbraterei,** which features ox meat.

The wide avenues between the tents are lined with stalls selling roast chicken, sugared almonds, *Lebkuchen* (decorated Bavarian gingerbread), and plenty of other baked or deep-fried treats for those who don't get a seat in a tent.

A main course in a tent can easily cost over €15, while half a chicken from a stall can cost over €10. Purchases are made in cash only, but there are ATMs near the main entrance, at the Theresienwiese U-bahn station, and throughout the Oktoberfest grounds.

GUIDE TO MAJOR BEER TENTS

The spectacular vista inside a beer tent is really what a trip to Oktoberfest is all about. There is something awe-inspiring about the sight of up to 10,000 people raising immense glasses of beer above their heads while a band leads a robust sing-along. This is a setting where the often reserved Germans let their inhibitions go, and since most of the seats are at long, communal tables, it's easy to make new friends. Below are descriptions of five of the 14 major tents. There are also 21 smaller beer tents. Altogether the tents, both large and small, provide some 114,000 seats.

SCHOTTENHAMEL

Scene: This is arguably the center of the Oktoberfest, because the mayor of Munich officially opens the festival here by tapping the first barrel. There's room for 10,000 people and it's considered the central party tent, where the young, single people of Munich gather.

Pros: Extremely lively, uninhibited atmosphere.

Cons: The emphasis is on drinking and dancing. This is not the place for a quiet, cozy chat.

Beer: Spaten-Franziskaner-Bräu has a fresh, malty taste with a clear amber color.

MARSTALL

Scene: New as a big tent since 2014, Marstall (meaning "royal riding school") has equipped their tent with an equestrian theme, evoking traditional horse imagery with carriages and carousels.

Pros: Happy to be in one of the big tents, the Able family's motivation to be a big player at Oktoberfest is palpable through the friendly service, and is a step up in class from some of the other tents.

Cons: With room for only 4,200 people, this is one of the smallest of the big beer tents, making it fairly hard to get a seat. Still, it's worth wandering around.

Beer: Spaten-Franziskaner-Bräu's golden colored Oktoberfest beer is savory and aromatic.

Above, Revelers in the Hacker-Festzelt tent.

ABOUT THE BEER

Only the six Munich breweries (Spaten-Franziskaner-Bräu, Augustiner, Paulaner, Hacker-Pschorr, Hofbräu, and Löwenbräu) are allowed to sell beer at Oktoberfest. Each brews a special beer for the Oktoberfest with a higher alcohol percentage (6%, as opposed to 5%), and runs a major beer tent. Beer has surpassed €10 per *Mass* (liter).

HOFBRÄU-FESTZELT

Scene: This is the official Oktoberfest presence of the Hofbräuhaus, the immense beer hall in central Munich that has become one of the city's main tourist attractions. The proprietors take special pride in their international guests, and the tent has become an Oktoberfest launchpad for many U.S. and Australian revelers, with close to 10,000 seats.

Pros: This is the only main tent with a dance floor in front of the band. So you're spared precariously getting your groove on atop a wooden bench.

Cons: Since it's connected to the Hofbräuhaus, it can feel pretty touristy.

Beer: **Hofbräu München** has a sweet, yeasty flavor with a good frothy head.

LÖWENBRÄU-FESTZELT

Scene: The traditional home tent of Munich's soccer club TSV 1860 München, this 8,500-seat tent is the closest the Oktoberfest comes to a real, working-class Munich feel. Patrons are regaled at the entrance by a giant, beer-swilling plastic lion, who occasionally roars the name of his favorite beer—Löwenbräu—at new arrivals.

Pros: This tent has an unpretentious, what-you-see-is-what-you-get atmosphere.

Cons: Although the food here is good, it is pretty basic fare.

Beer: **Löwenbräu** is a strong beer with a slightly spicy flavor.

HACKER-FESTZELT

Scene: This tent is often nicknamed the "Bavarian heaven," mainly because of the painted clouds and other sky-related decor that hang from the ceiling (installed by Oscar-winning designer Rolf Zehetbauer). It has also become a favorite tent for native Bavarians.

Pros: This tent offers unique features including a rotating bandstand and a partially retractable roof for sunny days.

Cons: Because it's generally considered the most attractive of the tents, it fills up particularly quickly—so get a seat early.

Beer: Copper-colored **Hacker-Pschorr** has a bready taste and is one of the best of the Oktoberfest beers.

PLANNING FOR OKTOBERFEST

ADVANCE PLANNING Oktoberfest is one of Germany's biggest tourist events—it's estimated to contribute over one billion euros to Munich's economy—so you should plan everything at least six months in advance.

WHERE TO STAY Booking in advance is advisable for hotels, although you're unlikely to get a cheap deal anywhere in the immediate vicinity of Oktoberfest. For cheaper city-center options, especially if you're part of a bigger group, check out **Jaeger's Hotel** (⊕ *www.jaegershotel.de*) or **Easy Palace** (⊕ *www.easypalace.de*). Otherwise book a hotel in Munich's outskirts and take public transit in.

RESERVATIONS The tents are free to enter, but if you want to sit and carouse into the evening, you need to reserve a seat at least six months in advance and up to ten months. Reservations are free, but the beer tents require you to buy food and drink vouchers with the reservation. Two liters of beer and half a chicken per seat is the usual standard minimum, and will cost a minimum of €30 per person, though could cost more depending on the tent and the time of day (evenings and weekends are more expensive). The vouchers can either be sent to you by mail (for a small fee), or picked up from special offices in Munich up to two weeks in advance. Reservations are only available through the individual beer tents, not through the Oktoberfest organizers. You can find the websites of the tents, plus addresses of the ticket offices on ⊕ *www.oktoberfest.de*.

WITHOUT RESERVATIONS There is only table service at the major tents, so in order to get served you must have a seat. If you don't have a reservation, come as early as you can; by mid-morning at the latest. One section of the central area of each tent (known as the *Mittelschiff*, or "mid-ship") is always reservation-free and you can snag a seat if you get there early. You can also sit in a reserved seat until its owner arrives.

HOURS Oktoberfest takes place the third weekend in September through the first weekend in October. It is open from 10 am to 11:30 pm every day, although the

Above, Schottenhamel tent.
Opposite, chain carousel at Oktoberfest fairground.

tents open at 9 am on weekends and public holidays. Last call is 10:30 pm.

RESTROOMS You can use the restrooms in any tent even if you're not drinking there. They are generally clean, well lit, and easy to find.

FAMILY DAYS Tuesdays are designated family days when there are discounts on all the fairground rides and food for kids. Rides range from old-fashioned carousels to vertiginous modern roller-coasters and cost under €10. There are also haunted houses, halls of mirrors, a flea circus, and many carnival games. Children are allowed in the beer tents, but kids under 6 years old must exit the tents after 8 pm.

PUBLIC TRANSIT The **Theresienwiese U-Bahn** (subway) stop is right outside Oktoberfest. However, this stop gets extremely crowded, particularly at closing time, so consider walking to either the nearby **Goetheplatz** or **Poccistrasse** stations. The **Hauptbahnhof**, where virtually all public transit lines converge, is just a 10- to 15-minute walk away.

TAXIS There is one taxi stand at the southern end of the Oktoberfest area, and taxis are easy to flag down in the city.

SAFETY Oktoberfest is generally very safe. There are plenty of security personnel in the tents and at the doors, and fights are rare. There is an information center, first aid, and police station behind the Schottenhamel tent. Sexual assault is not unknown at the Oktoberfest, but facilities have been revamped to increase safety, and a security point for women is located below the Bavaria statue in the service center next to the police and Red Cross. See ⊕ *www.sicherewiesn.de* for more safety information for women.

FOR MORE INFORMATION The official Oktoberfest website is ⊕*www.oktoberfest.de*, which includes a useful English guide. The official "Oktoberfest.de" app offers news on upcoming events and a location feature in case you get lost.

his successor, Enrico Zuccalli. It represents a tremendous high point of Italian cultural influence, in what is undoubtedly Germany's most Italian city. Within the original building, now the central axis of the palace complex, is the magnificent **Steinerner Saal** (Great hall), extending over two floors and richly decorated with stucco and grandiose frescoes by masters such as Francois Cuvilliés the Elder and Johann Baptist Zimmermann. One of the surrounding royal chambers houses Ludwig I's famous **Schönheitsgalerie** (Gallery of Beauties), portraits of women who caught his roving eye. The palace park is laid out in formal French style, with low hedges and gravel walks extending into woodland. Among the ancient tree stands are three fascinating pavilions, including the **Amalienburg** hunting lodge by François Cuvilliés. ☒ *Schloss Nymphenburg, Nymphenburg* ☎ *089/179–080* ⊕ *www.schloss-nymphenburg.de/ englisch/palace/index.htm* 💳 *From €4.50. Combination tickets from €8.50* ⊗ *Nymphenburg Palace, Marstallmuseum, and Museum of Nymphenburg Porcelain: Apr.–mid-Oct., daily 9–6; mid-Oct.–Mar., daily 10–4; Amalienburg, Badenburg, Pagodenburg, and Magdalenenklause: Apr.–mid-Oct., daily 9–6* Ⓜ *Schloss Nymphenburg (Tram or Bus).*

Marstallmuseum and Nymphenburger Porzellan (*Museum of Royal Carriages & Porcelain Manufacturer Nymphenburg*). Nymphenburg contains so much of interest that a day hardly provides enough time. Don't leave without visiting the former royal stables, now the **Marstallmuseum**. It houses a fleet of vehicles, including an elaborately decorated sleigh in which King Ludwig II once glided through the Bavarian twilight, flaming torches lighting the way. Also exhibited in the Marstallmuseum's upper rooms are examples of the world-renowned Nymphenburg porcelain, the electoral porcelain factory founded by Max III Joseph in 1747. Nymphenburg porcelain has a flagship store at Odeonsplatz and is also available in numerous other shops around the city. ☒ *Schloss Nymphenburg, Nymphenburg* ☎ *089/179–080 Schloss Nymphenburg* ⊕ *www.schloss-nymphenburg.de/englisch/marstall/ index.htm* 💳 *From €4.50* ⊗ *Apr.–mid-Oct., daily 9–6; mid-Oct.–Mar., daily 10–4* Ⓜ *Schloss Nymphenburg (Tram or Bus).*

Museum Mensch und Natur (*Museum of Man and Nature*). This popular museum in the north wing of Schloss Nymphenburg has nothing to do with the Wittelsbachs but is one of the palace's major attractions. Through interactive exhibits, the Museum Mensch und Natur looks at the variety of life on Earth, the history of humankind, and our place in the environment, as well as genetics and nature conservation. Main exhibits include a huge representation of the human brain and a chunk of Alpine crystal weighing half a ton. ☒ *Schloss Nymphenburg, Nymphenburg* ☎ *089/179–5890* ⊕ *www.mmn-muenchen.de/index.php/en/* 💳 *€3* ⊗ *Tues.–Fri. 9–5 (Thurs. until 8), weekends 10–6* Ⓜ *Schloss Nymphenburg (Tram or Bus).*

WORTH NOTING

FAMILY **Bavaria Filmstadt.** For real movie buffs, Munich has its own Hollywood-like neighborhood, the Geiselgasteig, in the affluent Grünwald district, on the southern outskirts of the city. A number of notable films, such as *Das Boot* (*The Boat*) and *Die Unendliche Geschichte* (*The Neverending Story*), were made here. It was also here that in 1925 British filmmaker

Alfred Hitchcock shot his first film, *The Pleasure Garden*. There are a number of tours and shows, including a 4-D cinema (in English at 1 pm in high season), and extra events for kids. ✉ *Bavaria Filmpl. 7, Geiselgasteig* ☎ *089/6499–2000* ⊕ *www.filmstadt.de* 💰 *From €5.50* ⊙ *Apr.–mid-Nov., daily 9–6; mid-Nov.–Mar., daily 10–5* Ⓜ *Grünwald, Bavariafilmplatz (Tram, Bus).*

FAMILY **BMW Museum.** Munich is the home of the famous BMW car company. The circular tower of its museum is one of the defining icons of Munich's modern cityscape. It contains not only a dazzling collection of BMWs old and new but also items and exhibitions relating to the company's social history and its technical developments. It's a great place to stop in if you're at the Olympiapark already. ✉ *Am Olympiapark 2, Milbertshofen* ☎ *089/1250–16001* ⊕ *www.bmw-welt.com/ en/exhibitions/museum/current/index.html* 💰 *€10* ⊙ *Tues.–Sun. 10–6* Ⓜ *Olympiazentrum.*

FAMILY **BMW Plant Munich.** Come see how a BMW car is made. The BMW factory live production can be toured on weekdays (minimum age to participate is seven). Registration for plant tours, which last a maximum of 2½ hours, is only possible with a reservation. The tours start and finish at the north information counter at BMW Welt. Due to plant reconstruction, there is no wheelchair access at present. Reserve at least two weeks in advance via phone or email; see the website for details. ✉ *BMW Welt, Am Olympiapark 1, Milbertshofen* ☎ *089/1250–16001* ✉ *infowelt@ bmw-welt.com* ⊕ *www.bmw-plant-munich.com/lowband/com/en/index. html* 💰 *From €8* ⊙ *Weekdays 9–4:30* Ⓜ *Olympiazentrum.*

FAMILY **BMW Welt.** Opened in 2007, the cutting-edge design of BMW Welt, with its sweeping, futuristic facade, is one structure helping to overcome the conservative image Munich has had in the realm of architecture since 1945. Even if you have just a passing interest in cars and engines, this showroom is a must—it has averaged 2 million visitors a year since its opening. In addition to tours of the building, there are readings, concerts, and exhibitions. Tours can only be booked via telephone or email.

✉ *Am Olympiapark 1, Milbertshofen* ☎ *089/1250–16001* ⊕ *www. bmw-welt.com/en/index.html* ⊙ *Mon.–Sat. 7:30 am–midnight, Sun. 9 am–midnight* Ⓜ *Olympiazentrum.*

FAMILY **Botanischer Garten** (*Botanical Garden*). On the northern edge of Schloss Nymphenburg, this collection of some 16,000 plants, including orchids, cacti, cycads, alpine flowers, and rhododendrons, makes up one of the most extensive botanical gardens in Europe. It is also used to provide a refuge for bee species, and for scientific research by local university students. ✉ *Menzingerstr. 65, Nymphenburg* ☎ *089/1786–1310* ⊕ *www. botmuc.de* 💰 *€4.50* ⊙ *Nov.–Jan., daily 9–4:30; Feb., Mar., and Oct., daily 9–5; Apr. and Sept., daily 9–6; May–Aug., daily 9–7. Hothouses close 30 mins earlier.*

FAMILY **Deutsches Museum Flugwerft Schleissheim.** Connoisseurs of airplanes and flying machines will appreciate this magnificent offshoot of the Deutsches Museum, some 20 km (12 miles) north of the City Center in Oberschleissheim. These buildings, constructed in the early 20th century by the Königlich-Bayerische Fliegertruppen (Royal Bavarian

Wander the extensive grounds of Schloss Nymphenburg.

Flying corps), tell the story of aviation history. It's an ideal complement to a visit to Schloss Schleissheim. ✉ *Effnerstr. 18, Oberschleissheim* ☎ *089/315–7140* ⊕ *www.deutsches-museum.de/flugwerft* ✆ *€6. Combined ticket with Deutsches Museum and Verkehrszentrum €16.* ⊙ *Daily 9–5* Ⓜ *Oberschleissheim.*

FAMILY **Neues Schloss Schleissheim** (*Schleissheim Palace*). Duke Wilhelm V found the perfect peaceful retreat outside Munich, and in 1598 built what is now known as the **Altes Schloss Schleissheim** (Schleissheim Old Palace). In 1685 Elector Max Emanuel added **Lustheim,** which houses one of Germany's most impressive collections of Meissen porcelain, and at the beginning of the 18th century the **Neues Schloss Schleissheim** (Schleissheim New Palace). This baroque palace's rooms display great works of art and outstanding interior decoration. ✉ *Maximilianshof 1, Oberschleissheim* ☎ *089/315–8720* ⊕ *www.schloesser.bayern.de/englisch/ palace/objects/schl_ns.htm* ✆ *€4.50. Combined ticket with Old Palace and Lustheim Palace €8* ⊙ *Apr.–Sept., Tues.–Sun. 9–6; Oct.–Mar., Tues.–Sun. 10–4* Ⓜ *Oberschleissheim.*

FAMILY **Tierpark Hellabrunn.** On the Isar, just upstream from the city, this attractive zoo has many parklike enclosures but a minimum of cages. Founded in 1911, the zoo is slightly different from most others in that it's a self-styled nature reserve, and it follows a concept called Geo-Zoo, which means care has been taken to group animals according to their natural and geographical habitats. Critics of the concept of zoos won't agree, but supporters appreciate the extra attention to detail. As well as the usual tours, there are also 90-minute nighttime guided tours with special night-vision equipment (register ahead of time at ⊕ *www.hellabrunn.*

de/anmeldeformular). The huge zoo area also includes restaurants and children's areas, and some of the older buildings are in typical art nouveau style. ✉ *Tierparkstr. 30, Harlaching* ✛ *From Marienplatz, take U-bahn 3 to Thalkirchen, at the southern edge of the city* ☎ *089/625–080* ⊕ *www.hellabrunn.de/en/* 🎫 *From €14* 🕑 *Late Mar.–late Oct., daily 9–6; late Oct.–late Mar., daily 9–5* Ⓜ *Thalkirchen (Tierpark) / Tierpark (Alemannenstrasse) (Bus).*

WHERE TO EAT

Munich claims to be Germany's gourmet capital. It certainly has an inordinate number of fine restaurants, but you won't have trouble finding a vast range of options in both price and style.

Typical, more substantial dishes in Munich include *Tellerfleisch,* boiled beef with freshly grated horseradish and boiled potatoes on the side, served on wooden plates. *Schweinebraten* (roast pork) is accompanied by dumplings and sauerkraut. *Hax'n* (ham hocks) are roasted until they're crisp on the outside and juicy on the inside. They are served with sauerkraut and potato puree. Game in season (venison or boar, for instance) and duck are served with potato dumplings and red cabbage. As for fish, the region has not only excellent trout, served either smoked as an hors d'oeuvre or fried or boiled as an entrée, but also the perchlike *Renke* from Lake Starnberg.

You'll also find soups, salads, casseroles, hearty stews, and a variety of baked goods—including *Breze* (pretzels). For dessert, indulge in a bowl of Bavarian cream, apple strudel, or *Dampfnudel,* a fluffy leavened-dough dumpling usually served with vanilla sauce.

The generic term for a snack is *Imbiss,* and thanks to growing internationalism you'll find a huge variety, from the generic *Wiener* (hot dogs) to the Turkish *döner kebab* sandwich (pressed and roasted lamb, beef, or chicken). Almost all butcher shops and bakeries offer some sort of *Brotzeit,* which can range from a modest sandwich to a steaming plate of goulash with potatoes and salad. A classic beer garden Brotzeit is a Breze with Obatzda (a cheese spread made from Camembert and paprika served with freshly sliced rings of onion).

Some edibles come with social etiquette attached. The *Weisswurst,* a tender minced-veal sausage—made fresh daily, steamed, and served with sweet mustard and a crisp pretzel—is a Munich institution and, theoretically, should be eaten before noon with a *Weissbier* (wheat beer), supposedly to counteract the effects of a hangover. Some people use a knife and fork to peel off the skin, while others might indulge in *auszuzeln,* sucking the sausage out of the skin.

Another favorite Bavarian specialty is *Leberkäs*—literally "liver cheese," though neither liver nor cheese is among its ingredients. Rather, it's a sort of meat loaf baked to a crust each morning and served in pink slabs throughout the day. A *Leberkässemmel*—a wedge of the meat loaf between two halves of a bread roll slathered with a slightly spicy mustard—is the favorite Munich on-the-go snack.

Prices in the reviews are the average cost of a main course at dinner, or if dinner is not served, at lunch. Use the coordinates (✛ B3) at the end of each listing to locate a site on the corresponding map.

WHAT IT COSTS IN EUROS				
	$	**$$**	**$$$**	**$$$$**
AT DINNER	under €15	€15–€20	€21–€25	over €25

Price per person for a main course or equivalent combination of smaller dishes at dinner.

ALTSTADT AND LEHEL

$
GERMAN

✕ **Andechser am Dom.** At this Munich mainstay for both locals and visitors, the vaulted, frescoed ceiling and the old stone floor recall the nearby Andechs monastery. As with many smaller Bavarian *Wirtshäuser* (pub-restaurants), it's invariably pretty full, so be prepared to find seats at a table already half full, though this is part of the lively charm of the place. The boldly Bavarian food—blood sausage with potatoes or roast duck—and fine selection of delectable Andechs beers will quickly put you at ease. The covered terrace, steps from the Frauenkirche, is a favorite meeting place, rain or shine, for shoppers, local businesspeople, and even the occasional VIP. Ⓢ *Average main: €12* ✉ *Weinstr. 7, Altstadt* ☎ *089/2429–2920* ⊕ *www.andechser-am-dom.de* Ⓜ *Marienplatz* ✛ *D4.*

$
FRENCH

✕ **Brasserie L'Atelier Art & Vin.** Take a seat by the wall of windows, or at the long blond-wood bar, in this airy, casual brasserie, which specializes in French food and wine. On nice days, tables are also set outside on the sidewalk of the pleasant, relatively quiet street. The light, crisp quiches, in particular, are a delight, and the wine list is a curated selection of French wines. The Bier & Oktoberfestmuseum is right next door, highlighting the wonderful contrasts that are so typical of this city. Ⓢ *Average main: €12* ✉ *Westenriederstr. 43, Altstadt* ☎ *089/2126–6783* ⊕ *www.atelier-artetvin.de* ▬ *No credit cards* ⊗ *Closed Sun. and public holidays* Ⓜ *Marienplatz / Isartor* ✛ *E5.*

$$
EUROPEAN

✕ **Brasserie OskarMaria.** After New York, Munich has more publishing houses than any other city in the world. Literaturhaus is a converted Renaissance-style schoolhouse that, as the name suggests, is now a "literature" center, for authors, publishers, and book fans. The front side of the building is a stylish brasserie, named after Munich writer Oskar Maria Graf, an exile after the Nazis took power in Germany in 1933, and who eventually settled in New York. The brasserie's vaulted high ceiling and plate-glass windows create a light and spacious atmosphere. The range of dishes here is pretty eclectic, from beetroot with garden vegetables and goat's cheese to lobster risotto. It has a sprawling terrace, and it's one of the city's best outdoor eating locations, whether for a main meal or cappuccino and *Kuchen* (cake). About 100 yards away, on Jungfernturmstrasse, is one of the largest remaining remnants of the city wall. Reservations are highly recommended. Ⓢ *Average main: €16* ✉ *Salvatorpl. 1, Altstadt* ☎ *089/2919–6029* ⊕ *www.oskarmaria.com* Ⓜ *Odeonsplatz / Marienplatz* ✛ *D4.*

2

$ ✕ **Bratwurstherzl.** Tucked into a quaint little square off Viktualienmarkt,
GERMAN this delightful Bratwurst joint cooks up specialty sausages right in the
main room over an open grill. For those looking for a bit less meat,
there is also a hearty farmer's salad with veal strips and tasty oyster
mushrooms. They have outdoor seating, perfect for people-watching
when the weather is good. $ *Average main: €9* ✉ *Dreifaltigkeitspl. 1,*
Altstadt ☎ *089/295–113* ⊕ *www.bratwurstherzl.de* ☉ *Closed Sun. and*
public holidays Ⓜ *Marienplatz* ✛ *E5.*

$$$ ✕ **Buffet Kull.** This simple yet comfortable international bistro delivers a
EUROPEAN high-quality dining experience accompanied by a good variety of wines
and friendly service. Dishes range from bouillabaisse halibut with king
prawns and calamari to the excellent New York steak. The daily spe-
cials are creative, portions are generous, and the prices are good value
for the quality. Reservations are recommended (dinner service starts at
6 pm). $ *Average main: €25* ✉ *Marienstr. 4, Altstadt* ☎ *089/221–509*
⊕ *www.buffet-kull.de* Ⓜ *Marienplatz* ✛ *F5.*

$ ✕ **Café Dukatz.** This café has been a popular relatively upmarket eatery
FRENCH on the Munich scene for years. Even with the closure of their city-center
restaurant, it has been a busy time for the owners as they now have two
cafés—one in Maxvorstadt on Klenzestrasse 69 and this one in Lehel.
They specialize in French-style pâtisseries, with the daily home-baked
delights and fine coffees expected of such a renowned name. $ *Aver-*
age main: €4 ✉ *St.-Anna-Str. 11, Lehel* ☎ *089/2303–2444 St.-Anna-*
Str., 089/2006–2893 Klenzestr. ⊕ *www.dukatz.de* ▭ *No credit cards*
Ⓜ *Lehel* ✛ *D6 and G4.*

$$$$ ✕ **City Hotel Lux Restaurant.** The chef here learned his trade at Munich's
INTERNATIONAL much-vaunted Königshof. Much of the meat here is organic; ask the
ever-charming staff for information. The creamy asparagus risotto is a
real treat for lunch, while the duck with ratatouille and potato-celery
gratin is a highlight of the evening menu. Though the restaurant is
small, it deliberately has a front-room feel, with red, velvetlike uphol-
stery complementing the wooden ceiling and walls. The small bar is
also terrific. Hotel Lux is a hotel with 17 rooms (€149), free Wi-Fi,
and simply furnished rooms—except for the top-floor "birdroom,"
designed by Hans Langner, who is famous for his bird depictions. This
extraordinary blue, bird-filled single room is not to everyone's taste,
but good fun for a night or two. $ *Average main: €25.50* ✉ *Ledererstr.*
13, Altstadt ☎ *089/4520–7300* ⊕ *munich.hotel-lux.info/restaurant.php*
Ⓜ *Marienplatz / Isartor* ✛ *F5.*

$ ✕ **Due passi.** So small it's easy to miss, this former dairy shop, now an
ITALIAN Italian specialty shop, offers Italian fare for a quick lunch. There's a
Fodor's Choice small but fine selection of fresh antipasti and pasta. You can eat at
★ the high wooden tables and counters or have your food to go. Menus
change daily. Beat the lunch crowd and arrive by 11:30 for the quieter,
cooler window seat. $ *Average main: €8* ✉ *Ledererstr. 11, Altstadt*
☎ *089/224–271* ⊕ *bistroduepassi.wordpress.com* ▭ *No credit cards*
☉ *Closed Sun. and holidays* Ⓜ *Marienplatz* ✛ *F5.*

$$$ ✕ **Gandl.** This specialty shop, where you can buy various European
FRENCH FUSION staples from French cheese to Belgian chocolate, doubles as a com-
fortable, relaxed restaurant. Their extensive Saturday buffet breakfast

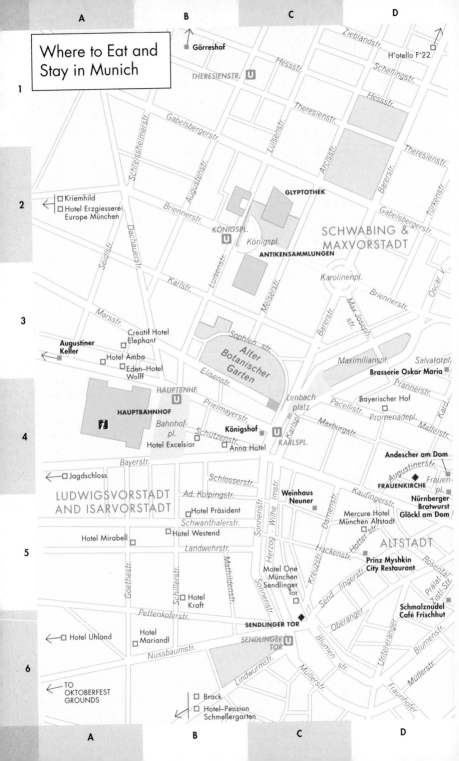

Where to Eat and Stay in Munich

A   B   C   D

1

□ Görreshof

THERESIENSTR. U

Zieblandstr.

H'otello F'22

Schellingstr.

Hessstr.

Theresienstr.

Hessstr.

Gabelsbergerstr.

Luisenstr.

Arcisstr.

Theresienstr.

Barerstr.

Türkenstr.

2

□ Kriemhild

□ Hotel Erzgiesserei
Europe München

Schleissheimerstr.

Augustenstr.

Brennerstr.

GLYPTOTHEK

KÖNIGSPL.
U
Königspl.

ANTIKENSAMMLUNGEN

Dachauerstr.

Seidlstr.

Luisenstr.

Meiserstr.

SCHWABING &
MAXVORSTADT

Karolinenpl.

Barerstr.

Max-Joseph-str.

Brennerstr.

Gabelsbergerstr.

Oscar V.

3

Augustiner
Keller

Marsstr.

Creatif Hotel
Elephant

Hotel Amba

Eden-Hotel
Wolff

Sophien str.

Alter
Botanischer
Garten

Elisenstr.

Maximilianspl.

Salvatorpl.

Brasserie Oskar Maria

Prannerstr.

4

HAUPTBNHF.
U

HAUPTBAHNHOF
ℹ

Bahnhof-
pl.

Prielmayerstr.

Königshof

Hotel Excelsior

Schützenstr.

Anna Hotel

Lenbach
platz

Pacellistr.

Karlspl.

U
KARLSPL.

Maxburgstr.

Bayerischer Hof
□
Promenadepl.

Kard.

Maffeistr.

Andescher am Dom

Augustinerstr.

FRAUENKIRCHE ◆
Frauen-
pl.

Nürnberger
Bratwurst
Glöckl am Dom

5

□ Jagdschloss

Bayerstr.

LUDWIGSVORSTADT
AND ISARVORSTADT

Schlosserstr.

Ad. Kolpingstr.

Hotel Präsident

Schwanthalerstr.

Hotel Mirabell □

Hotel Westend

Landwehrstr.

Sonnenstr.

Amstr.

Wither- Herzog

Weinhaus
Neuner

Damenstr.

Kaufingerstr.

Mercure Hotel
München Altstadt

str.

Hackenstr.

Hotterstr.

Kreuzstr.

Sendlingerstr.

ALTSTADT

Prinz Myshkin
City Restaurant

Rosental

Prälat-Zistl-Str.

Hotel
Kraft

Pettenkoferstr.

Hotel Uhland

Hotel
Mariandl

Goethestr.

Schillerstr.

Mathildenstr.

Nussbaumstr.

Motel One
München
Sendlinger
Tor

Sonnenstr.

SENDLINGER TOR ◆

SENDLINGER
TOR
U

Oberanger

Untereranger

Schmalznudel
Café Frischhut

Blumenstr.

6

TO
OKTOBERFEST
GROUNDS

Lindwurmstr.

□ Brack

□ Hotel-Pension
Schmellergarten

Müllerstr.

Blumen str.

Fraunhofer

Müllerstr.

A   B   C   D

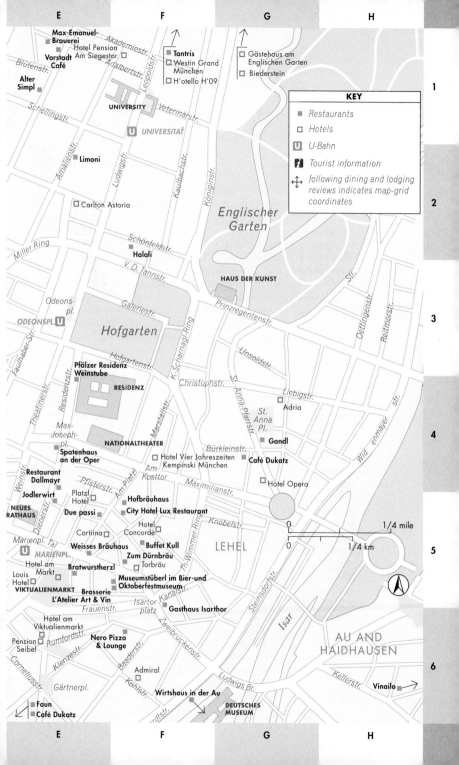

is popular in the neighborhood. Seating can become a little crowded inside, but the excellent service will make up for it and you'll feel right at home. In summertime, however, tables spill out onto St.-Anna-Platz in a charming setting. At lunch Gandl is just the place for a quick pastry or excellent antipasto misto before proceeding with the day's adventures. Dinner is more relaxed, with Mediterranean-influenced cuisine. $ *Average main: €22* ⊠ *St.-Anna-Pl. 1, Lehel* ☎ *089/2916–2525* ⊕ *www. gandl.de* ☉ *Closed Sun.* Ⓜ *Lehel* ✛ *G4.*

$ ✕ **Gasthaus Isarthor.** This old-fashioned *Wirtshaus* is one of the few places
GERMAN   that serve Augustiner beer exclusively from wooden kegs, freshly tapped on a daily basis. Beer simply doesn't get any better than this. The traditional Bavarian fare is good, and the midday menu changes daily. All kinds are drawn to the simple wooden tables of this unspectacular establishment. Antlers and a wild boar look down on actors, government officials, apprentice craftspersons, journalists, and retirees, all sitting side by side. $ *Average main: €11* ⊠ *Kanalstr. 2, Lehel* ☎ *089/227–753* ⊕ *www.gasthaus-isarthor.de* ▭ *No credit cards* Ⓜ *Isartor* ✛ *F5.*

$ ✕ **Hofbräuhaus.** The Hofbräuhaus is simply the most famous beer hall
GERMAN   not just in Munich but in the world. Regulars aside, many Bavarians see it as the biggest tourist trap ever created, and few ever go more than once, but they are still proud that it attracts so many visitors. Yes, it's a little kitschy, but the pounding oompah band draws the curious, and the singing and shouting drinkers contribute to the festive atmosphere (the beer garden provides a bit of an escape from the noise in good weather). This is no place for the fainthearted, and a trip to Munich would be incomplete without at least having a look. Upstairs is a quieter restaurant, where the food is fine, although there are better places for Bavarian cuisine. In March, May, and September ask for one of the special, extra-strong seasonal beers (Starkbier, Maibock, Märzen), which complement the traditional Bavarian fare. $ *Average main: €12* ⊠ *Platzl 9, Altstadt* ☎ *089/2901–3610* ⊕ *www.hofbraeuhaus.de/en/index_en.html* ✍ *Reservations not accepted* Ⓜ *Marienplatz / Isartor* ✛ *F5.*

$ ✕ **Jodlerwirt.** This cozy alpine lodge–style restaurant in a small street
GERMAN   behind the Rathaus is a treat for those craving an old-world tavern, complete with live accordion playing. As its name suggests, yodelers perform most nights, telling jokes and poking fun at their adoring guests in unintelligible Bavarian slang. The food is traditional, including *Käsespätzle* (a hearty German version of macaroni and cheese), goulash, and meal-size salads. The tasty beer is from the Ayinger brewery. The place is small and fills up fast. $ *Average main: €14* ⊠ *Altenhofstr. 4, Altstadt* ☎ *089/221–249* ⊕ *www.jodlerwirt-muenchen.net* ▭ *No credit cards* ☉ *Closed Sun. and Mon. except during Oktoberfest. No lunch* Ⓜ *Marienplatz* ✛ *E5.*

$ ✕ **Museumsstüberl im Bier und Oktoberfestmuseum.** In one of the oldest
GERMAN   buildings in Munich, dating to the 14th century, the beer museum (open Tuesday–Saturday 1–6) takes an imaginative look at the history of this popular elixir, the monasteries that produced it, the purity laws that govern it, and Munich's own long tradition with it. The rustic Museumsstüberl restaurant, consisting of a few heavy wooden tables, accompanies the museum. It serves traditional *Brotzeit* (breads, cheeses, and

cold meats) during the day and hot Bavarian dishes from 6 pm. You can visit the Museumsstüberl restaurant without paying the museum's admission fee and try beer from one of Munich's oldest breweries, the Augustiner Bräu. $ *Average main: €9* ⊠ *Sterneckerstr. 2, Altstadt* ☎ *089/2424–3941* ⊕ *www.museumsstueberl.de* 🍴 *Museum €4* ▭ *No credit cards* ⊘ *Closed Sun.* Ⓜ *Isartor* ✛ *F5.*

$ ✕ **Nero Pizza & Lounge.** The typical Italian thin-crust pizzas and pastas at
ITALIAN this independent restaurant are great; try the diavolo, with spicy Neapolitan salami. They also serve great steaks. On a side street between Gärtnerplatz and Isartor, Nero has high ceilings and large windows that give it an open, spacious feel. You can sit upstairs in the lounge for a cozier experience. Credit-card payment is only accepted for meals over €50. $ *Average main: €11* ⊠ *Rumfordstr. 34, Altstadt* ☎ *089/2101–9060* ⊕ *www.nero-muenchen.de* Ⓜ *Isartor* ✛ *F6.*

$ ✕ **Nürnberger Bratwurst Glöckl am Dom.** One of Munich's most popular
GERMAN beer taverns is dedicated to the delicious *Nürnberger Bratwürste* (finger-sized grilled sausages), a specialty from the rival Bavarian city of Nürnberg. They're served by a busy team of friendly waitresses dressed in Bavarian dirndls who flit between the crowded tables with remarkable agility. There are other options available as well. In warmer months, tables are placed outside, partly under a large awning, beneath the towering Frauenkirche. In winter the mellow, dark-panel dining rooms provide relief from the cold. For a quick, cheaper beer go to the side door where, just inside, there is a little window serving fresh Augustiner from a wooden barrel. You can stand around with the regulars or enjoy the small courtyard if the weather is nice. $ *Average main: €10* ⊠ *Frauenpl. 9, Altstadt* ☎ *089/291–9450* ⊕ *www.bratwurst-gloeckl.de* Ⓜ *Marienplatz* ✛ *D5.*

$ ✕ **Pfälzer Residenz Weinstube.** A huge stone-vaulted room within the
GERMAN Residenz, a few smaller rooms on the side, wooden tables, flickering candles, dirndl-clad waitresses, and a long list of wines add up to a storybook image of a timeless Germany. The wines are mostly from the Pfalz (Palatinate), as are many of the specialties on the limited menu. Beer drinkers, take note—beer is not served here. $ *Average main: €11* ⊠ *Residenzstr. 1, Altstadt* ☎ *089/225–628* ⊕ *www.pfaelzerweinstube. de* Ⓜ *Odeonsplatz / Marienplatz* ✛ *E4.*

$$ ✕ **Prinz Myshkin City Restaurant.** Traditional Bavarian dishes can some-
VEGETARIAN times be heavy affairs, and after a meal or three they can become a bit much. This restaurant is one of the finest in the city, and it's vegetarian to boot, with a selection of vegan dishes. The delightful holiday from meat here brings an eclectic choice of skillfully prepared antipasti, quiche, pizza, gnocchi, tofu, crepes, stir-fried dishes, plus excellent wines. The airy room has a high ceiling, and there's always some art exhibited to feed the eye and mind. $ *Average main: €16* ⊠ *Hackenstr. 2, Altstadt* ☎ *089/265–596* ⊕ *prinzmyshkin.com/en/city/prinz-myshkin-city.html* Ⓜ *Marienplatz* ✛ *D5.*

$$$$ ✕ **Restaurant Dallmayr.** Enter one of Munich's premier delicatessens,
EUROPEAN where rows of specialties tempt your nose. If you can tear yourself
Fodor'sChoice away from the mesmerizing displays of foods, take a carpeted flight of
★ stairs either to the much-vaunted **Restaurant Dallmayr** or the adjoining

elegant-yet-casual **Café-Bistro**. Whether your choice is restaurant or café, this place is a sheer delight, showcasing delicacies from the delicatessen, while the service is friendly and attentive. Few are surprised that Diethard Urbansky, head chef at Restaurant Dallmayr, has won Michelin stars from 2009 onward. Menus change often, but a typical starter might be red king prawns with vegetables and yogurt. For mains, try the Nebraska beef with goose liver, tarragon, and pineapple. [$] *Average main: €130* ✉ *Dienerstr. 14–15, Altstadt* ☎ *089/213–5130* 🌐 *www.dallmayr.com/delicatessen/restaurant-dallmayr/* 🕓 *Restaurant closed Sun. and Mon. No lunch Tues.–Fri.* [M] *Marienplatz* ✥ *E4.*

$ GERMAN 🍴 **Schmalznudel Café Frischhut.** From the deep Bavarian accent to the food on offer, this is as Bavarian as one could get, though it serves neither typical great slabs of meat nor *Knödel*. The fryers are turned on in the early morning for Viktualienmarkt workers, and stay on for those still standing after a night out. At midday, lines of people are waiting for helpings of freshly cooked *Schmalznudel*, a selection of doughnut-type creations, from apple to sugar-coated to plain. It's really no more than a narrow-passage kind of café, located on a busy street between the Stadtmuseum and Viktualienmarkt, and easily missed by those not in the know. Regulars are equally happy whether they manage to find a seat inside or at the handful of tables outside, or there's always the option to take out and eat as you wind your way through the ever-colorful market. [$] *Average main: €2* ✉ *Prälat-Zistl-Str. 8, Altstadt* ☎ *089/2602–3156* 💳 *No credit cards* 🕓 *Closed Sun.* [M] *Marienplatz* ✥ *D6.*

$$$ GERMAN 🍴 **Spatenhaus an der Oper.** The best seats are the window tables on the second floor. The quiet dining-room walls and ceiling are paneled with old hand-painted wood and have a wonderful view of the square and the opera house. Make a reservation if you want to come after a performance. The outdoor tables are a favorite for people-watching. There are few better places for roasted fillet of brook trout, lamb with ratatouille, or duck with apple and red cabbage. And they do the best Wiener schnitzel in the city. Leave room for one of the wonderful desserts featuring fresh fruit. [$] *Average main: €21* ✉ *Residenzstr. 12, Altstadt* ☎ *089/290–7060* 🌐 *www.kuffler.de/de/spatenhaus.php* [M] *Odeonsplatz / Marienplatz* ✥ *E4.*

$$$$ GERMAN 🍴 **Weinhaus Neuner.** Munich's oldest wine tavern serves good food as well as superior wines in its two nooks: the wood-panel restaurant and the Weinstube. The choice of food is remarkable, from roast duck to fish to traditional Bavarian. [$] *Average main: €52* ✉ *Herzogspitalstr. 8, Altstadt* ☎ *089/260–3954* 🌐 *www.weinhaus-neuner.de* 🕓 *Closed Sun. and holidays* [M] *Marienplatz / Karlsplatz (Stachus)* ✥ *C5.*

$ GERMAN 🍴 **Weisses Bräuhaus.** If you've developed a taste for Weissbier, this institution in downtown Munich is the place to indulge. The tasty brew from Schneider, a Bavarian brewery in existence since 1872, is served with hearty Bavarian dishes, mostly variations of pork and dumplings or cabbage. The restaurant itself was beautifully restored in 1993 to something approaching how it would have looked when first opened in the 1870s. The waitresses here are famous in Munich for being a little more straight-talking than visitors might be used to in restaurants back home. But if you're good-natured, the whole thing can be quite funny. There is the possibility to sit outside, though it is quite a busy street. Credit cards are accepted for totals over €20, but with the good beer and food, this isn't difficult to reach. [$] *Average main: €14* ✉ *Tal 7, Altstadt* ☎ *089/290–1380* 🌐 *www.weisses-brauhaus.de* [M] *Marienplatz / Isartor* ✣ *E5.*

$$ GERMAN 🍴 **Zum Dürnbräu.** In existence in one form or another since 1487, this is easily one of the oldest establishments serving food in Munich, and there's little surprise that the food is resolutely traditional: lots of roast meat, potato and bread dumplings, fish, and equally hearty desserts. As the *Bräu* in the name suggests, this was also a brewery centuries ago. The front biergarten is small so get there early in good weather. Inside, the central 21-foot table is a favorite spot and fills up first. It's popular and attracts everyone from businesspeople to students. [$] *Average main: €18* ✉ *Dürnbräug. 2, Altstadt* ✣ *An alleyway from Tal 21 offers convenient access* ☎ *089/222–195* 🌐 *www.zumduernbraeu.de/html/speisekarte_en.html* [M] *Marienplatz / Isartor* ✣ *F5.*

LUDWIGSVORSTADT AND ISARVORSTADT

$ ECLECTIC 🍴 **Faun.** The beloved Faun is on Hans-Sachs-Strasse, one of the city's most interesting streets, with great restaurants and boutique shops—even a century-old cinema. It's a happy combination of Munich tavern and international bistro, with great outdoor seating on a small square. The Thai curries are wonderful, and their juicy Schweinebraten will satisfy any meat cravings. The dishes on the daily changing menu are tasty, filling, and easy on your wallet. The beer served is Augustiner, so you can't go wrong there. Build up your appetite by browsing your way through the neighborhood shops and boutiques, or walk off your meal on a stroll back into the Old Town. [$] *Average main: €9* ✉ *Hans-Sachs-Str. 17, Ludwigsvorstadt* ☎ *089/263–798* 🌐 *www.faun.mycosmos.biz* 💳 *No credit cards* [M] *Frauenhoferstrasse* ✣ *E6.*

$$$$ ECLECTIC 🍴 **Königshof.** Don't be fooled as you cross the threshold of the dour and unremarkable-looking postwar Hotel Königshof. The contrast with the opulent interior is remarkable. From a window table in this elegant and luxurious restaurant in one of Munich's grand hotels, you can watch the hustle and bustle of Munich's busiest square, Karlsplatz, below. You'll forget the outside world, however, when you taste the outstanding French- and Japanese-influenced dishes created by Michelin-starred chef Martin Fauster, former sous-chef at Tantris. Ingredients are fresh and menus change often, but you might see lobster with fennel and candied ginger, or venison with goose liver and celery, and for dessert, flambéed peach with champagne ice cream. Service is expert and personal; let the sommelier help you choose from the fantastic wine selection. Reservations are recommended, especially Fridays and Saturdays. [$] *Average main: €57* ✉ *Karlspl. 25, Ludwigsvorstadt* ☎ *089/551–360* 🌐 *www.koenigshof-hotel.de/en/* ⏲ *Closed Sun. and Mon., and Aug.* 👔 *Jacket and tie* [M] *Karlsplatz* ✣ *C4.*

SCHWABING AND MAXVORSTADT

$ GERMAN 🍴 **Alter Simpl.** Named after Germany's most famous satirical magazine, *Simplicissimus*, this pub-restaurant has been a Munich institution since 1903, when it was a meeting and discussion center for leading writers, comedians, and artists. Today the pictures of those days hang on the dark wood-panel walls. It's quite small inside and far from salubrious, but the beer's good and the equally good food is served until 2 am (beer until 3 am). The menu includes filling options like roast pork, Munich schnitzel, and a bacon-cheeseburger with french fries. Students are at home here and will welcome anyone at their table when the others are all taken. [$] *Average main: €11* ✉ *Türkenstr. 57, Maxvorstadt* ☎ *089/272–3083* 🌐 *www.eggerlokale.de/restaurant-alter-simpl-muenchen.html* 💳 *No credit cards* [M] *Universität* ✣ *E1.*

$ GERMAN 🍴 **Augustiner Keller.** This flagship beer restaurant of one of Munich's oldest breweries opened in about 1812. It is also the location of the unbeatable Augustiner beer garden, which should be at the top of any visitor's beer garden list. The menu offers Bavarian specialties, including half a duck with a good slab of roast suckling pig, dumpling, and blue cabbage. If you're up for it, end your meal with a *Dampfnudel* (yeast dumpling served with custard), though you probably won't feel hungry again for quite a while. [$] *Average main: €13* ✉ *Arnulfstr. 52, Maxvorstadt* ☎ *089/594–393* 🌐 *www.augustinerkeller.de/home/?L=1* [M] *Hauptbahnhof* ✣ *A3.*

$ GERMAN 🍴 **Görreshof.** In 1893 Augustiner, the oldest brewery in Munich, built this sturdy Wirtshaus to sustain travelers on the 12-km (7-mile) trek from Munich to the castles at Schleissheim. This pub-restaurant has been renovated over the years and is today as much a forum for good eating and drinking as it was more than 100 years ago. You'll get hearty food in a dining room festooned with antlers. If you want to relax further, retire to the small Bibliothek (library), or head outside to sit on the covered terrace. [$] *Average main: €14* ✉ *Görresstr. 38, Maxvorstadt* ☎ *089/2020–9550* 🌐 *www.goerreshof.de* [M] *Josephsplatz* ✣ *B1.*

$$$$ GERMAN 🍴 **Halali.** With nearly 100 years of history to its credit, polished wood paneling, and antlers on the walls, the Halali is an old-style Munich restaurant that is *the* place to try traditional dishes of venison, pheasant, partridge, and other game in a quiet and elegant atmosphere. Save room for the crème brûlée and hazelnut ice cream. [$] *Average main: €31* ✉ *Schönfeldstr. 22, Maxvorstadt* ☎ *089/285–909* 🌐 *www.restaurant-halali.de* ⏲ *Closed Sun. and public holidays. No lunch Sat.* ✍ *Reservations essential* 👔 *Jacket and tie* [M] *Odeonsplatz* ✣ *F2.*

$$$ ITALIAN Fodor's Choice ★ 🍴 **Limoni.** It's not just Munich's neoclassical architecture that underpins its playful, centuries-old moniker as Italy's most northern city. There are a number of fine Italian restaurants around the city, but this is certainly one of the best. You'll pay more for meat and fish dishes, but there are also lovely pasta dishes that are a little more budget-friendly. There is a Bavarian professionalism combined with Italian grace and elegance in how the delicacies are served: pea and ginger cream soup, *strozzapreti* with veal ragout, artichokes, thyme, and scarmoza cheese to name just a couple, and then the fantastic chocolate cake with mascarpone cream. Be sure to reserve your table in good weather so you can sit on the

charming patio in the back; note that warm food is only served from 6:30 pm to 11 pm. [$] *Average main: €24* ✉ *Amalienstr. 38, Maxvorstadt* ☎ *089/2880–6029* 🌐 *www.limoni-ristorante.com* 🕒 *Closed Sun. No lunch* [M] *Universität* ✥ *E2.*

$ GERMAN 🍴 **Max-Emanuel-Brauerei.** This historic old brewery tavern, first opened in 1880, offers great value Bavarian dishes. The best part about this place, however, is the cozy, secluded little beer garden with huge chestnut trees, tucked in the back amid the apartment blocks. [$] *Average main: €10* ✉ *Adalbertstr. 33, Schwabing* ☎ *089/271–5158* 🌐 *www.max-emanuel-brauerei.de/en/* 🕒 *No lunch Nov.–Mar.* [M] *Universität / Giselastrasse* ✥ *E1.*

$$$$ EUROPEAN Fodor's Choice ★ 🍴 **Tantris.** Few restaurants in Germany can match the Michelin-starred Tantris. Select the menu of the day and accept the suggestions of the sommelier or choose from the à la carte options and you'll be in for a treat. Try, for example, the variation of char with marinated white asparagus and orange hollandaise, followed by roast lamb fillets with spinach, beans, and fennel-curry puree, superbly complemented by stuffed semolina dumplings with raspberries and curd-cheese ice cream. It surprises few that head chef Hans Haas has kept his restaurant at the top of the critics' charts in Munich for so long. [$] *Average main: €150* ✉ *Johann-Fichte-Str. 7, Schwabing* ☎ *089/361–9590* 🌐 *www.tantris.de/home.php* 🕒 *Closed Sun., Mon., and public holidays* 👔 *Jacket and tie* [M] *Münchener Freiheit / Dietlindenstrasse* ✥ *F1.*

$ GERMAN 🍴 **Vorstadt Café.** Young professionals mix with students at this lively restaurant, a symphony in red and orange in an ode to the 1970s, on the corner of Adalbert- and Türkenstrasse. The 13 different breakfasts are a big draw: the Vorstadt Classic includes bacon and eggs, rolls and several other kinds of bread, with a plate of salami and homemade jam; the Veggie has scrambled eggs with tomatoes, cheese, and spinach, muesli with fresh fruit, and cheese with nuts. Their daily lunch specials, served quickly, are good value. The atmosphere at dinner is relaxed, complete with candlelight. Reservations are recommended on weekends. There is another location in Altstadt at Maximilianstrasse 40. [$] *Average main: €14* ✉ *Türkenstr. 83, Maxvorstadt* ☎ *089/272–0699 Türkenstr., 089/2554–7010 Maximilianstr.* 🌐 *www.vorstadt-cafe.de* 💳 *No credit cards* [M] *Universität* ✥ *E1.*

AU AND HAIDHAUSEN

$$$$ ITALIAN 🍴 **Vinaiolo.** In the setting of an old apothecary, diners can enjoy specialties from Venice and other northern Italian regions, such as spaghetti with sardines or roast goat, prepared to perfection by chef Marco Pizzolato. Service is good-humored and conscientious and the menu changes regularly. [$] *Average main: €28* ✉ *Steinstr. 42, Haidhausen* ☎ *089/4895–0356* 🌐 *www.vinaiolo.de* 🕒 *No lunch Sat.* [M] *Rosenheimer Platz* ✥ *H6.*

$$ GERMAN 🍴 **Wirtshaus in der Au.** *Wirtshaus* is a word that describes a kind of bar-restaurant serving traditional Bavarian food and beer. This has been serving since 1901 and it's one of the best. A stone's throw from the Deutsches Museum, it has a great vaulted room and collections of beer steins, providing one of the best atmospheres around. It has a

combination of fantastic service and outstanding local dishes, and it serves everything from *Hofente* (roast duck) to *Schweinsbraten* (roast pork). But the real specialty, and for which it is renowned, is *Knödel* (dumplings), which, in addition to traditional *Semmel* (bread) and *Kartoffel* (potato) varieties, come in spinach, cheese, and even red-beet flavors. Weather permitting, you can sit in the small beer garden under chestnut trees. Spend a day in the Deutsches Museum followed by an evening here, and experience Munich at its best. $ *Average main: €15* ✉ *Lilienstr. 51, Au* ☎ *089/448–1400* ⊕ *wirtshausinderau.de/en/ startseite/* ⊙ *No lunch weekdays* Ⓜ *Isartor / Rosenheimerplatz* ✛ *F6.*

WHERE TO STAY

Though Munich has a vast number of hotels in all price ranges, booking one can be a challenge, as this is a trade-show city as well as a prime tourist destination. If you're visiting during any of the major trade fairs such as the ISPO (sports, fashion) in January or the IHM (crafts) in February/March, or during Oktoberfest at the end of September, try to make reservations at least a few months in advance. It is acceptable practice in Europe to request to see a room before committing to it, so feel free to ask at check-in once you arrive.

Some of the large, upscale hotels that cater to expense-account business travelers have attractive weekend discount rates—sometimes as much as 50% below normal prices. Conversely, most hotels raise their regular rates by at least 30% during big trade fairs and Oktoberfest. Online booking sites like Hotel Reservation Service (⊕ *www.hrs.com*) often have prices well below the hotel's published prices (i.e., price ranges in this guide) in slow periods and on short notice. Look for the names we suggest here and search online for potential deals.

■ TIP→ **Munich's tourist information office has two outlets that can help you with hotel bookings if you haven't reserved in advance. One is outside Hauptbahnhof, the central station, and the other is at Marienplatz, in the Rathaus information office. Your best bet is to visit in person.**

Prices in the reviews are the lowest cost of a standard double room in high season. For expanded reviews, facilities, and current deals, visit Fodors.com. Use the coordinates (✛ B3) at the end of each listing to locate a site on the corresponding map.

WHAT IT COSTS IN EUROS			
$	$$	$$$	$$$$
under €100	€100–€175	€176–€225	over €225

FOR TWO PEOPLE

Prices reflect the rack rate of a standard double room for two people in high season, including tax. Check online for off-season rates and special deals or discounts.

ALTSTADT AND LEHEL

$$ **Adria.** This modern hotel is near a number of great museums and
HOTEL the English Garden, with large rooms that are tastefully decorated.
Pros: good location; nice lobby. **Cons:** no bar or restaurant. $ *Rooms*
from: €117 ⊠ Liebigstr. 8a, Altstadt ☎ *089/242–1170* ⊕ *www.adria-*
muenchen.de ⤳ *44 rooms* ⊠| *Breakfast* Ⓜ *Lehel* ✛ *G4.*

$$$$ **Bayerischer Hof.** There's the Michelin-starred Atelier, the swanky
HOTEL suites, the rooftop Blue Spa and Lounge with panoramic city views,
Fodor'sChoice fitness studio, pool, private cinema, and to top it all, suites in Pal-
★ ais Montgelas, the adjoining early-19th-century palace. **Pros:** superb
public rooms with valuable oil paintings; the roof garden restaurant
has an impressive view of the Frauenkirche two blocks away; Atelier
restaurant has a habit of garnering Michelin two stars. **Cons:** expensive.
$ *Rooms from: €498* ⊠ *Promenadepl. 2–6, Altstadt* ☎ *089/21200*
⊕ *www.bayerischerhof.de/hbh_intro_flash_en.html* ⤳ *340 rooms, 65*
suites ⊠| *Breakfast* Ⓜ *Karlsplatz / Marienplatz* ✛ *D4.*

$$ **Cortiina.** One of Munich's design hotels, Cortiina follows the mini-
HOTEL malist gospel. **Pros:** welcoming, modern reception and bar; nice, com-
fortable rooms; personalized service. **Cons:** street noise; expensive
breakfast. $ *Rooms from: €169* ⊠ *Ledererstr. 8, Altstadt* ☎ *089/242–*
2490 ⊕ *www.cortiina.com* ⤳ *75 rooms* ⊠| *No meals* Ⓜ *Marienplatz*
✛ *E5.*

$$ **Hotel am Markt.** At this excellent location next to the Viktualienmarkt,
HOTEL you'll find simple rooms and fair prices. **Pros:** friendly and helpful staff;
free Wi-Fi; decent restaurant. **Cons:** rooms are simple; some spots could
use fresh paint; breakfast costs extra. $ *Rooms from: €112* ⊠ *Hei-*
liggeiststr. 6, Altstadt ☎ *089/225–014* ⊕ *www.hotel-am-markt.eu* ⤳ *22*
rooms ⊠| *No meals* Ⓜ *Marienplatz* ✛ *E5.*

$$ **Hotel Concorde.** Although the Concorde is just steps away from the
HOTEL Hofbräuhaus, it has a peaceful location on a side street. **Pros:** quiet;
functional; good location. **Cons:** no restaurant or bar. $ *Rooms from:*
€160 ⊠ *Herrnstr. 38–40, Altstadt* ☎ *089/224–515* ⊕ *www.concorde-*
muenchen.de ⤳ *72 rooms* ⊠| *Breakfast* Ⓜ *Isartor* ✛ *F5.*

$$$ **Hotel Opera.** In the quiet residential district of Lehel, Hotel Opera
HOTEL offers rooms decorated in an elegant style—lots of Empire, some art
Fodor'sChoice deco; some rooms even have glassed-in balconies. **Pros:** free Wi-Fi
★ throughout; elegant; pleasant courtyard; quiet location; special service.
Cons: parking is €18 per day; no restaurant. $ *Rooms from: €210*
⊠ *St.-Anna-Str. 10, Lehel* ☎ *089/210–4940* ⊕ *www.hotel-opera.de/en*
⤳ *25 rooms* ⊠| *Breakfast* Ⓜ *Lehel* ✛ *G4.*

$$$$ **Hotel Vier Jahreszeiten Kempinski München.** Trend and tradition blend
HOTEL throughout this property, especially in the new guest rooms, where
Fodor'sChoice flat-screen TVs hang on the walls alongside original oil paintings and
★ Bose stereos rest on antique cupboards. **Pros:** great location; occasional
special packages that are a good value; free Wi-Fi. **Cons:** expensive.
$ *Rooms from: €490* ⊠ *Maximilianstr. 17, Altstadt* ☎ *089/2125–2799*
⊕ *www.kempinski.com/de/muenchen/hotel-vier-jahreszeiten/welcome/*
⤳ *230 rooms, 67 suites* ⊠| *No meals* Ⓜ *Lehel / Kammerspiele (Tram)*
✛ *F4.*

$$$$ HOTEL Fodor's Choice ★ 🏨 **Louis Hotel.** No other hotel in Munich manages to combine the subdued elegance of a design hotel, first-rate service, and perhaps the best Old Town location, overlooking Viktualienmarkt, as this hotel. **Pros:** brilliant location; attentive service; modern designs; very good restaurant. **Cons:** the bustle of the Viktualienmarkt is not for everyone; parking costs €26 a day. [$] *Rooms from: €289* ✉ *Viktualienmarkt 6, Altstadt* ✥ *Enter from the "Viktualienmarkt passageway" that runs from Rindermarkt street to Viktualienmarkt street* ☎ *089/4111–9080* 🌐 *www.louis-hotel.com* 🛏 *72 rooms* 🍴 *No meals* [M] *Marienplatz* ✥ *E5.*

$$ HOTEL 🏨 **Mercure Hotel München Altstadt.** This straightforward, comfortable hotel is a decent deal for its great location; there are a number of Mercure hotels in Munich, but this location, between Marienplatz and Karlsplatz, is in the Altstadt. **Pros:** central location; moderate price; free mineral water; free Wi-Fi. **Cons:** public parking garage is a bit of a hike. [$] *Rooms from: €121* ✉ *Hotterstr. 4, Altstadt* ☎ *089/232–590* 🌐 *www.mercure-muenchen-altstadt.de* 🛏 *75 rooms* 🍴 *Breakfast* [M] *Marienplatz / Karlsplatz / Sendlinger Tor* ✥ *D5.*

$ HOTEL 🏨 **Motel One München-Sendlinger Tor.** With well-thought-out designs and free Wi-Fi, the Motel One chain jumped ahead of the game with its simple but classy concept that caters to the young, fast-paced professional. **Pros:** great location; decent designs; amiable, attentive service; free breakfast for kids age 1–6; children under 12 stay in parents' room for free. **Cons:** staying in one is like staying in all of them; no restaurant or room service; breakfast, parking, and pets cost extra. [$] *Rooms from: €94* ✉ *Herzog-Wilhelm-Str. 28, Altstadt* ☎ *089/5177–7250* 🌐 *www.motel-one.com/en/* 🛏 *241 rooms* 🍴 *No meals* [M] *Sendlinger Tor* ✥ *C5.*

$$$$ HOTEL Fodor's Choice ★ 🏨 **Platzl Hotel.** The privately owned Platzl has won awards and wide recognition for its ecologically aware management, which uses heat recyclers in the kitchen, environmentally friendly detergents, recyclable materials, waste separation, and other eco-friendly practices. **Pros:** excellent restaurant Pfistermühle; progressive environmental credentials; around the corner from the Hofbräuhaus; free Wi-Fi. **Cons:** rooms facing the Hofbräuhaus get more noise; some rooms are on the small side. [$] *Rooms from: €265* ✉ *Sparkassenstr. 10, Altstadt* ☎ *089/237–030* 🌐 *www.platzl.de* 🛏 *167 rooms* 🍴 *Breakfast* [M] *Marienplatz* ✥ *E5.*

$$$ HOTEL 🏨 **Torbräu.** The welcoming Torbräu has been looking after guests in one form or another since 1490, making it the oldest hotel in Munich, and it has been run by the same family for more than a century. **Pros:** nice rooms, air-conditioned and with free Wi-Fi; central location; good restaurant; very attentive service. **Cons:** underground parking difficult; front rooms a little noisy. [$] *Rooms from: €215* ✉ *Tal 41, Altstadt* ☎ *089/242–340* 🌐 *www.torbraeu.de* 🛏 *90 rooms* 🍴 *Breakfast* [M] *Isartor* ✥ *F5.*

LUDWIGSVORSTADT AND ISARVORSTADT

$$ HOTEL Fodor's Choice ★ 🏨 **Admiral.** The small, privately owned, tradition-rich Admiral enjoys a quiet side-street location and its own garden, close to the River Isar, minutes from the Deutsches Museum. **Pros:** attention to detail; quiet; excellent service. **Cons:** no restaurant. [$] *Rooms from: €149* ✉ *Kohlstr.*

9, Isarvorstadt ☎ 089/216–350 ⊕ *www.hotel-admiral.de/en_index.html* ↩ *33 rooms* ⦿❘ *Breakfast* Ⓜ *Isartor* ✦ *F6.*

$$$$ 🏨 **Anna Hotel.** Modern, slightly minimalist decor and features are char-
HOTEL acteristic of this design hotel. **Pros:** terrific location; fabulous views from the top floor; beds are huge; free Wi-Fi throughout. **Cons:** bar and restaurant get hectic from passersby on the busy street; no single rooms. Ⓢ *Rooms from: €230* ✉ *Schützenstr. 1, Ludwigsvorstadt* ☎ *089/599–940* ⊕ *www.annahotel.de* ↩ *75 rooms* ⦿❘ *Breakfast* Ⓜ *Karlsplatz* ✦ *B4.*

$$ 🏨 **Brack.** A nice, light-filled lobby makes a first good impression,
HOTEL but Oktoberfest revelers value Brack's proximity to the beer-festival grounds, and its location—on a busy, tree-lined thoroughfare just south of the city's center—is handy for city attractions. **Pros:** good location for accessing Oktoberfest and city; breakfast until noon; free use of bicycles; free Wi-Fi. **Cons:** front rooms can be noisy despite sound-proof windows. Ⓢ *Rooms from: €119* ✉ *Lindwurmstr. 153, Ludwigsvorstadt* ☎ *089/747–2550* ⊕ *www.hotel-brack.de/index_e.html* ↩ *50 rooms* ⦿❘ *Breakfast* Ⓜ *Poccistrasse* ✦ *B6.*

$$ 🏨 **Hotel am Viktualienmarkt.** This design-led hotel is perfectly located a
HOTEL few hundred yards from Viktualienmarkt and the Gärtnerplatz quarter. **Pros:** refreshing atmosphere; service attentive but not overbearing; great location. **Cons:** no air-conditioning; no restaurant; no parking on-site. Ⓢ *Rooms from: €149* ✉ *Utzschneiderstr. 14, Isarvorstadt* ☎ *089/231–1090* ⊕ *www.hotel-am-viktualienmarkt.de/EN/index.php* ↩ *26 rooms* ⦿❘ *Breakfast* Ⓜ *Marienplatz / Isartor / Reichenbachplatz (Tram)* ✦ *E6.*

$$ 🏨 **Hotel Excelsior.** Just a short walk along an underpass from the Haupt-
HOTEL bahnhof station, the Excelsior welcomes you with rooms that are spacious and inviting. **Pros:** welcoming reception; spacious rooms; excellent breakfast; free Wi-Fi throughout. **Cons:** Schützenstrasse can get very busy; breakfast is normally not included in room price; fee per night for pet, and additional cleaning service after the stay. Ⓢ *Rooms from: €155* ✉ *Schützenstr. 11, Ludwigsvorstadt* ☎ *089/551–370* ⊕ *www.excelsior-hotel.de/en.html* ◔ *No lunch Sun. in restaurant* ↩ *118 rooms, 9 suites* ⦿❘ *No meals* Ⓜ *Hauptbahnhof / Karlsplatz* ✦ *B4.*

$$ 🏨 **Hotel Kraft.** Conveniently located between the City Center and the
HOTEL Oktoberfest grounds, this hotel has spacious rooms with an armchair, an ample-size writing desk, and natural light from a large window. **Pros:** privately owned; hotel and rooms well cared for; quiet neighborhood; Wi-Fi and breakfast are included in the price. **Cons:** no nightlife. Ⓢ *Rooms from: €110* ✉ *Schillerstr. 49, Ludwigsvorstadt* ☎ *089/550–5940* ⊕ *www.hotel-kraft.com* ↩ *33 rooms* ⦿❘ *Breakfast* Ⓜ *Sendlingertor / Theresienwiese* ✦ *B5.*

$$ 🏨 **Hotel Mariandl.** The American armed forces commandeered this turn-
HOTEL of-the-20th-century neo-Gothic mansion in May 1945 and established Munich's first postwar nightclub, the Femina, on the ground floor. **Pros:** hotel and café are charmingly worn and a bit bohemian. **Cons:** no elevator; no private parking spaces. Ⓢ *Rooms from: €128* ✉ *Goethestr. 51, Ludwigsvorstadt* ☎ *089/552–9100* ⊕ *www.mariandl.com/en/* ↩ *28 rooms* ⦿❘ *Breakfast* Ⓜ *Hauptbahnhof* ✦ *A6.*

$$ 🏨 **Hotel Mirabell.** This family-run hotel is used to American tourists
HOTEL who appreciate the friendly service, central location (between the main

railway station and the Oktoberfest fairgrounds), and reasonable room rates. **Pros:** free Wi-Fi; family run; personalized service. **Cons:** no restaurant; this area of the Hauptbahnhof is not the most salubrious. [$] *Rooms from: €119* ✉ *Landwehrstr. 42, entrance on Goethestr., Ludwigsvorstadt* ☎ *089/549–1740* 🌐 *www.m-privathotels.de* 🛏 *69 rooms* 🍴 *Breakfast* [M] *Hauptbahnhof* ✢ *A5.*

$ B&B/INN 🏨 **Hotel-Pension Schmellergarten.** Popular with young budget travelers, this family-run hotel tries to make everyone feel at home on a quiet street off Lindwurmstrasse, a few minutes' walk from the Theresienwiese (Oktoberfest grounds). **Pros:** good location; good price; free Wi-Fi; all rooms have a fridge and microwave; no extra fee for pet. **Cons:** no elevator. [$] *Rooms from: €92* ✉ *Schmellerstr. 20, Ludwigsvorstadt* ☎ *089/773–157* 🌐 *www.schmellergarten.de* 🛏 *14 rooms* 🍴 *Breakfast* [M] *Poccistrasse* ✢ *B6.*

$ HOTEL 🏨 **Hotel Präsident.** The location—just a block from the main train station—is the biggest draw of this hotel; the second draw is the price. **Pros:** central location; filling breakfast. **Cons:** rooms toward the street are noisy; streets around the hotel are not the most salubrious; parking is 100 yards away, not free. [$] *Rooms from: €98* ✉ *Schwanthalerstr. 20, Ludwigsvorstadt* ☎ *089/549–0060* 🌐 *www.hotel-praesident.de* 🛏 *42 rooms* 🍴 *Breakfast* [M] *Hauptbahnhof / Karlsplatz* ✢ *B5.*

$$ HOTEL Fodor's Choice ★ 🏨 **Hotel Uhland.** This stately villa is a landmark building with pleasant rooms that are quite large and can accommodate three people. **Pros:** a real family atmosphere; care is given to details; free Wi-Fi in most rooms; free on-site parking. **Cons:** no restaurant or bar. [$] *Rooms from: €105* ✉ *Uhlandstr. 1, Ludwigsvorstadt* ☎ *089/543–350* 🌐 *www.hotel-uhland.de/enwelcome.html* 🛏 *29 rooms* 🍴 *Breakfast* [M] *Theresienwiese* ✢ *A6.*

$ HOTEL 🏨 **Hotel Westend.** Visitors have praised the friendly welcome and service they receive at this well-maintained and affordable lodging above the Oktoberfest grounds. **Pros:** good location; good prices; free Wi-Fi, no charge for pets. **Cons:** no restaurant; rooms are simple; it's best to confirm your reservation; breakfast and parking cost extra. [$] *Rooms from: €88* ✉ *Schwanthalerstr. 121, Ludwigsvorstadt* ☎ *089/540–9860* 🌐 *www.westend-hotel.de/en/welcome.html* 🛏 *44 rooms* 🍴 *No meals* [M] *Hackerbrücke / Schwanthalerhöhe* ✢ *B5.*

$ HOTEL 🏨 **Pension Seibel.** If you're looking for an affordable little "pension" a stone's throw from the Viktualienmarkt, this is the place. **Pros:** great location at a great price; pets are welcome. **Cons:** tiny breakfast room; no elevator; Wi-Fi and pets cost extra. [$] *Rooms from: €79* ✉ *Reichenbachstr. 8, Isarvorstadt* ☎ *089/231–9180* 🌐 *www.seibel-hotels-munich.de/en/pension-seibel.html* 🛏 *15 rooms* 🍴 *Breakfast* [M] *Marienplatz / Isartor / Reichenbachplatz (Tram)* ✢ *E6.*

SCHWABING AND MAXVORSTADT

$$ HOTEL 🏨 **Biederstein.** A modern block of a building, but covered with geraniums in summer, the Biederstein seems to want to fit into its old Schwabing surroundings at the edge of the English Garden. **Pros:** wonderfully quiet location; all rooms have balconies; exemplary service; underground parking is available. **Cons:** not the most handsome building;

no restaurant; U-bahn is four blocks away. $ *Rooms from: €135* ✉ *Keferstr. 18, Schwabing* ☎ *089/3302–9390* ⊕ *www.hotel-biederstein.de* ➦ *34 rooms* ❖ *Breakfast* Ⓜ *Münchner Freiheit* ✛ *G1.*

$$ ▦ **Carlton Astoria.** This family-run house, with an atmosphere of simple elegance, is a three- or four-minute walk to Amalienstrasse and Türkenstrasse, two of the most lively places in town, with dozens of restaurants, eateries, and student pubs. Its downtown location, near the Pinakotheken (art museums) and the university, means you can reach many places on foot. **Pros:** well located; fairly priced; free Wi-Fi. **Cons:** rooms on main street can be noisy; limited parking (prearrange with hotel). $ *Rooms from: €140* ✉ *Fürstenstr. 12, Maxvorstadt* ☎ *089/383–9630* ⊕ *www.carlton-astoria.de/seiten/en/hotel.htm* ➦ *49 rooms* ❖ *Breakfast* Ⓜ *Universität / Odeonsplatz* ✛ *E2.*
HOTEL

$ ▦ **Creatif Hotel Elephant.** Tucked away on a quiet street near the train station, this hotel appeals to a wide range of travelers, from businesspeople to tourists on a budget. **Pros:** close to Hauptbahnhof, the main station. **Cons:** no restaurant; modest furnishings. $ *Rooms from: €59* ✉ *Lämmerstr. 6, Maxvorstadt* ☎ *089/555–785* ⊕ *www.creatif-hotel-elephant. de/en/index.html* ➦ *44 rooms* ❖ *Breakfast* Ⓜ *Hauptbahnhof* ✛ *A3.*
HOTEL

$$$ ▦ **Eden-Hotel Wolff.** Beyond a light-filled lobby, a spacious bar with dark-wood paneling beckons, contributing to the old-fashioned elegance of this downtown favorite with rooms that are large, comfortable, and furnished well. **Pros:** all rooms have air-conditioning; some breakfasts included. **Cons:** close to the hustle and bustle of the main station. $ *Rooms from: €194* ✉ *Arnulfstr. 4, Maxvorstadt* ☎ *089/551–150* ⊕ *www.eden-hotel-wolff.de/english/* ➦ *214 rooms* ❖ *Breakfast* Ⓜ *Hauptbahnhof* ✛ *A3.*
HOTEL

$$ ▦ **Gästehaus am Englischen Garten.** Reserve well in advance for a room at this popular converted water mill, more than 300 years old, adjoining the English Garden. **Pros:** quiet location; ideal for walking or cycling; wonderfully cozy rooms; free Wi-Fi. **Cons:** no elevator; no restaurant. $ *Rooms from: €163* ✉ *Liebergesellstr. 8, Schwabing* ☎ *089/383–9410* ⊕ *hotelenglischergarten.de/en/* ➦ *11 rooms, 6 with private bathroom; 20 apartments in the annex* ❖ *Breakfast* Ⓜ *Münchner Freiheit* ✛ *G1.*
B&B/INN
Fodor's Choice
★

$ ▦ **Hotel Amba.** Right across the street from the main train station, Amba provides clean, bright rooms, good service, no expensive frills, and everything you need to plug and play. **Pros:** convenient to train station and sights. **Cons:** breakfast is usually extra; rooms that face the main street and the station are noisy. $ *Rooms from: €98* ✉ *Arnulfstr. 20, Maxvorstadt* ☎ *089/545–140* ⊕ *www.hotel-amba.de/EN/Home.aspx* ➦ *86 rooms* ❖ *No meals* Ⓜ *Hauptbahnhof* ✛ *A3.*
HOTEL

$$ ▦ **Hotel Erzgiesserei Europe München.** Rooms in this modern hotel are bright and decorated in soft pastels. **Pros:** relatively quiet location; nice courtyard; air-conditioning in all rooms. **Cons:** charm of a business hotel; Wi-Fi costs extra. $ *Rooms from: €109* ✉ *Erzgiesserei-istr. 15, Maxvorstadt* ☎ *089/126–820* ⊕ *www.topinternational.com/ hotelinfo-en/tophotelerzgiessereieuropemunich.html* ➦ *106 rooms* ❖ *Breakfast* Ⓜ *Stiglmaierplatz* ✛ *A2.*
HOTEL

$$ ▦ **H'Otello F'22.** This is a high-caliber example of the design- and style-driven nature of the new Munich hotel scene—the style is minimalist,
HOTEL

but with a roomy feel. **Pros:** parking available; well-thought-out design; some rooms have balconies; free Wi-Fi. **Cons:** no restaurant; breakfast costs extra. $ *Rooms from: €129* ✉ *Fallmerayerstr. 22, Schwabing* ☎ *089/4583–1200* ⊕ *www.hotello.de/f22-muenchen/en/* ⟋ *74 rooms* ¡❍¡ *No meals* Ⓜ *Hohenzollernplatz / Kufürstenplatz (Tram)* ✛ *D1.*

$$ 🏨 **H'Otello H'09.** The second in the H'Otello chain to open in Munich,
HOTEL   this high-design hotel is a five-minute walk to the Englischer Garten; the style is minimalist but still luxurious with king-size beds and a breakfast buffet. **Pros:** free Wi-Fi; great location; well-thought-out design; uncomplicated rooms. **Cons:** no restaurant. $ *Rooms from: €159* ✉ *Hohenzollernstr. 9, Schwabing* ☎ *089/4583–1200* ⊕ *www.hotello.de* ⟋ *71 rooms* ¡❍¡ *Breakfast* Ⓜ *Münchner Freiheit / Giselastrasse* ✛ *F1.*

$ 🏨 **Hotel Pension Am Siegestor.** Modest but appealing, the pension—which
B&B/INN takes up three floors of a fin de siècle mansion between the Siegestor monument on Leopoldstrasse, and the university—is a great deal in Germany's most expensive city. **Pros:** a delightful and homey place to stay; very good value stay for the price; not far to walk to the English Garden; free Wi-Fi. **Cons:** if elevators make you nervous, don't use this old one; no restaurant or bar. $ *Rooms from: €98* ✉ *Akademiestr. 5, Maxvorstadt* ☎ *089/399–550* ⊕ *www.siegestor.com* ▭ *No credit cards* ⟋ *20 rooms* ¡❍¡ *Breakfast* Ⓜ *Universität* ✛ *F1.*

OUTSIDE INNENSTADT

$$ 🏨 **Jagdschloss.** This century-old hunting lodge in Munich's leafy Ober-
HOTEL   menzing suburb is a delightful hotel. **Pros:** peaceful location; beer garden; easy parking; free Wi-Fi in rooms. **Cons:** away from the City Center; convenient only with a car; no elevator. $ *Rooms from: €140* ✉ *Alte Allee 21, Pasing-Obermenzing* ☎ *089/820–820* ⊕ *www.jagdschloss.com* ⟋ *36 rooms, 1 apartment* ¡❍¡ *Breakfast* ✛ *A4.*

$$ 🏨 **Kriemhild.** This welcoming, family-run pension is in a quiet western
HOTEL   suburb. **Pros:** quiet location; family-run; free Wi-Fi; close to Nymphen-
FAMILY burg Castle. **Cons:** far from the sights at the city's center; rates don't include breakfast. $ *Rooms from: €108* ✉ *Guntherstr. 16, Nymphenburg* ☎ *089/171–1170* ⊕ *www.kriemhild.de/en/* ⟋ *21 rooms* ¡❍¡ *No meals* Ⓜ *Laim / Kriemhildenstrasse (Tram)* ✛ *A2.*

$$$ 🏨 **Westin Grand München.** The building itself, with 23 floors, may raise
HOTEL   a few eyebrows as it stands on a slight elevation and is not the shapeliest of the Munich skyline. **Pros:** luxurious lobby and restaurant; rooms facing west toward the city have a fabulous view. **Cons:** hotel is difficult to reach via public transportation; €29 breakfast; free Wi-Fi in lobby only. $ *Rooms from: €177* ✉ *Arabellastr. 6, Bogenhausen* ☎ *089/92640* ⊕ *www.westingrandmunich.com/en* ⟋ *627 rooms, 28 suites* ¡❍¡ *No meals* Ⓜ *Arabellapark* ✛ *F1.*

NIGHTLIFE AND PERFORMING ARTS

NIGHTLIFE

Munich has a lively night scene ranging from beer halls to bars to chic clubs. The fun areas for a night out are in Altstadt, Isarvorstadt (Gärtnerplatz and Glockenbachviertel are arguably the best in the city), and Schwabing around Schellingstrasse and Münchner Freiheit. Regardless of their size or style, many bars, especially around Gärtnerplatz, have DJs spinning either mellow background sounds or funky beats.

However many fingers you hold up, just remember the easy-to-pronounce "Bier bitte" ("beer please") when ordering a beer. The tricky part is, Germans don't just produce *one* beverage called beer; they brew more than 5,000 varieties. Germany has about 1,300 breweries, 40% of the world's total.

In Munich you'll find the most famous breweries, the largest beer halls and beer gardens, the biggest and most indulgent beer festival, and the widest selection of brews. Even the beer glasses are bigger: a *Mass* is a 1-liter (almost 2-pint) serving; a *Halbe* is half a liter and the standard size. The Hofbräuhaus is Munich's best-known beer hall, but you are more likely to find locals in one of the English Garden's four beer gardens or in a *Wirtshaus* (tavern).

In summer, last call at the beer gardens is around 11 pm. Most of the traditional places stay open until 1 am or so and are great for a few hours of wining and dining before heading out on the town. Most bars stay open until at least 3 am on weekends; some don't close until 5 or 6 am.

Munich has dozens of beer gardens, ranging from huge establishments that seat several hundred to small terraces tucked behind neighborhood pubs; the rest of the beer gardens are a bit farther afield and can be reached handily by bike or S- and U-bahn. Beer gardens are such an integral part of Munich life that a council proposal to cut down their hours provoked a storm of protest in 1995, culminating in one of the largest demonstrations in the city's history. They open whenever the thermometer creeps above 10°C (50°F) and the sun filters through the chestnut trees that are a necessary part of the scenery.

Everybody in Munich has at least one favorite beer garden, so you're usually in good hands if you ask someone to point you in the right direction. You do not need to reserve. No need to phone either. If the weather says yes, then go. Most—but not all—allow you to bring your own food, but if you do, buy your drinks from the beer garden and don't defile this hallowed territory with something so foreign as pizza or a burger.

There are a few dance clubs in town worth mentioning, but the larger the venue, the more difficult the entry. In general, big nightclubs are giving way to smaller, more laid-back lounge types of places scattered all over town. If you're really hankering for a big club, go to Optimolwerke in the Ostbahnhof area. Otherwise, enjoy the handful of places around the City Center.

Munich also has a decent jazz scene, and some beer gardens have even taken to replacing their brass oompah bands with funky combos. Jazz musicians sometimes accompany Sunday brunch, too.

ALTSTADT AND LEHEL

BARS

Bar Centrale. Around the corner from the Hofbräuhaus, Bar Centrale is very Italian—the waiters don't seem to speak any other language. The coffee is excellent; small fine meals are served as well. They have a retro-looking back room with leather sofas. ⊠ *Ledererstr. 23, Altstadt* ☎ *089/223–762* ⊕ *www.bar-centrale.com* Ⓜ *Marienplatz / Isartor.*

Goldene Bar. Everything glows golden at this aptly named bar within the Haus der Kunst. Despite its 75-year-old wall paintings, it's very hip. ⊠ *Prinzregentenstr. 1, Lehel* ☎ *089/5480–4777* ⊕ *www.goldenebar.de* Ⓜ *Odeonsplatz / Lehel / Nationalmuseum/Haus d.Kunst (Tram).*

Hotel Vier Jahreszeiten Kempinski. The Hotel Vier Jahreszeiten Kempinski's talented bartenders offer sparkling wines, whiskeys, and an entertaining range of cocktails. Live piano plays until 1 am weeknights and 2 am on weekends. ⊠ *Maximilianstr. 17, Altstadt* ☎ *089/2125–2217* ⊕ *www.kempinski.com/en/munich/hotel-vier-jahreszeiten/fine-dining/* Ⓜ *Lehel / Marienplatz / Kammerspiele (Tram).*

Fodor'sChoice ★ **Kilian's Irish Pub and Ned Kelly's Australian Bar.** Just behind the Frauenkirche, Kilian's Irish Pub and Ned Kelly's Australian Bar offer an escape from the German tavern scene. Naturally, they have Guinness and Foster's, but they also serve Munich's lager, Augustiner, and regularly televise international soccer, rugby, and sports in general. ⊠ *Frauenpl. 11, Altstadt* ☎ *089/2421–9899 both bars* ⊕ *www.kiliansirishpub.com; www.nedkellysbar.com* Ⓜ *Marienplatz.*

Night Club Bar. The Bayerischer Hof's Night Club Bar has live music, most famously international stars from the jazz scene, but also reggae to hip-hop and everything in between. ⊠ *Promenadepl. 2–6, Altstadt* ☎ *089/212–0994 table reservation* ⊕ *www.bayerischerhof.de/en/bars* ⊙ *Closed last 2 wks Aug.* Ⓜ *Karlsplatz / Marienplatz.*

Pusser's Bar Munich. At the American-inspired, nautical-style Pusser's Bar Munich, great cocktails and Irish-German black-and-tans (Guinness and strong German beer) are poured to the sounds of live piano music. Try the "Painkiller," a specialty of the house. ⊠ *Falkenturmstr. 9, Altstadt* ☎ *089/220–500* ⊕ *www.pussersbar.de/en/pussers-bar.html* ☞ *Live piano Tues.–Sat. from 9 pm, reservations necessary* Ⓜ *Marienplatz / Lehel.*

Schumann's Les Fleurs du Mal. At Schumann's Les Fleurs du Mal, Munich's most famous bar, the bartenders are busy shaking cocktails after the curtain comes down at the nearby opera house. On the first floor of Schumann's Bar am Hofgarten, Les Fleurs du Mal has one 27-foot-long table for guests to share and converse with the barman. Alternatively, there's Schumann's Bar, which gets going after midnight. ⊠ *Odeonspl. 6–7, Altstadt* ☎ *089/229–060* ⊕ *www.schumanns.de/en/schumanns-bar.html* ⊙ *Les Fleurs du Mal closed Sun.* Ⓜ *Marienplatz / Odeonsplatz.*

2

Trader Vic's. Exotic cocktails are the specialty at Trader Vic's, a smart cellar bar in the Hotel Bayerischer Hof that's as popular among out-of-town visitors as it is with locals. It's open till 3 in the morning. ✉ *Promenadenpl. 2–6, Altstadt* ☎ *089/212–0995* ⊕ *www.bayerischerhof.de/en/bars/trader-vics-bar/index.php* Ⓜ *Karlsplatz / Marienplatz.*

BEER GARDENS

FAMILY

Fodor's Choice

★

Biergarten am Viktualienmarkt. The only true beer garden in the center of the city, and therefore the easiest to find, is the one at Viktualienmarkt. The beer on tap rotates among the six major Munich breweries to keep everyone happy throughout the year. ✉ *Viktualienmarkt, Altstadt* ☎ *089/297–545* ⊕ *www.biergarten-viktualienmarkt.com* Ⓜ *Marienplatz.*

DANCE CLUBS

P1. Bordering the Englischer Garten, in a wing of Haus der Kunst, P1 is definitely one of the most popular clubs in town for the see-and-be-seen crowd. It is chockablock with the rich and the wannabe rich and can be fun if you're in the mood. The bouncers can be choosy about whom they let in, so you'll need to dress in style. ✉ *Prinzregentenstr. 1, Lehel* ⊕ *On west side of Haus der Kunst* ☎ *089/211–1140* ⊕ *www.p1-club.de.*

LUDWIGSVORSTADT AND ISARVORSTADT

Around Gärtnerplatz and Glockenbachviertel are a number of cool bars and clubs for a somewhat younger, hipper crowd.

BARS

Holy Home. For a New York City–style, corner-bar-type experience, check out Holy Home. A hip local crowd frequents this smoky hole-in-the-wall that books great low-key DJs. ✉ *Reichenbachstr. 21, Isarvorstadt* ☎ *089/201–4546* Ⓜ *Fraunhoferstrasse / Isartor.*

Trachtenvogl. Take a seat on Grandma's retro couches at Trachtenvogl, which is more of a daytime bar than a nighttime destination (it closes at 10 pm on weekdays and 3 pm on weekends). The café serves all sorts of tasty treats from good sandwiches to hearty Bavarian meals, which you can top off with a Tegernseer beer—a Munich favorite. ✉ *Reichenbachstr. 47, Isarvorstadt* ☎ *089/201–5160* ⊕ *www.trachtenvogl.de* Ⓜ *Fraunhoferstrasse.*

GAY AND LESBIAN BARS

Munich's well-established gay scene stretches between Sendlingertor-platz and Isartorplatz in the Glockenbach neighborhood. For an overview, check ⊕ *www.munich-cruising.de.*

Ochsengarten. The Ochsengarten is Munich's men-only bar for lovers of leather and rubber. ✉ *Müllerstr. 47, Isarvorstadt* ☎ *089/266–446* ⊕ *www.ochsengarten.de* Ⓜ *Sendlinger Tor / Fraunhoferstrasse.*

Paradiso Tanzbar. Formerly Old Mrs. Henderson, this is still one of the most lively clubs on the scene, combining dance, champagne, all kinds of music, all night long. ✉ *Rumfordstr. 2, Isarvorstadt* ☎ *089/263–469* ⊕ *www.paradiso-tanzbar.de* ☾ *Closed Sun.–Thurs.* Ⓜ *Blumenstrasse (Bus) / Reichenbachplatz (Tram) / Isartor.*

JAZZ

Fodor's Choice
★
Jazzbar Vogler. The Jazzbar Vogler is a nice bar with jam sessions on Monday nights and regular jazz concerts. ⊠ *Rumfordstr. 17, Isarvorstadt* ☏ *089/294–662* ⊕ *www.jazzbar-vogler.com* Ⓜ *Isartor / Reichenbachplatz (Tram).*

Mr. B's. The tiny Mr. B's is a treat. It's run by New Yorker Alex Best, who also mixes great cocktails and, unlike so many other barkeeps, usually wears a welcoming smile. ⊠ *Herzog-Heinrich-Str. 38, Ludwigsvorstadt* ☏ *089/534–901* ⊕ *www.misterbs.eu/index-e.html* ⊗ *Closed Mon.* Ⓜ *Goetheplatz.*

SCHWABING AND MAXVORSTADT

BARS

Alter Simpl. Media types drink Weissbier, Helles, as well as Guinness and Kilkenny, at the square bar at Alter Simpl. More than 100 years old, this establishment serves German food until 2 am (weekends till 3 am). ⊠ *Türkenstr. 57, Maxvorstadt* ☏ *089/272–3083* ⊕ *www.eggerlokale.de/restaurant-alter-simpl-muenchen.html* Ⓜ *Universität.*

Schall und Rauch. Up on Schellingstrasse, this legendary student hangout, whose name literally means "Noise and Smoke," has great music and food. ⊠ *Schellingstr. 22, Schwabing* ☏ *089/2880–9577* Ⓜ *Universität.*

Schelling-Salon. An absolute cornerstone in the neighborhood is the Schelling-Salon. On the corner of Barerstrasse, this sizeable bar has several pool tables and even a secret Ping-Pong room in the basement with an intercom for placing beer orders. The food's not bad and pretty inexpensive. ⊠ *Schellingstr. 54, Schwabing* ☏ *089/272–0788* ⊕ *www.schelling-salon.de* ⊗ *Closed Tues. and Wed., and mid-July–early Sept.* Ⓜ *Universität / Shellingstrasse (Bus and Tram).*

Türkenhof. The Türkenhof is a solid local joint that serves Augustiner and good food. ⊠ *Türkenstr. 78, Schwabing* ☏ *089/280–0235* ⊕ *www.augustiner-braeu.de/augustiners/html/en/gaststaetten/Gaststatte_Turkenhof.html* Ⓜ *Universität / Türkenstrasse (Bus).*

BEER GARDENS

Fodor's Choice
★
Augustiner Keller Biergarten. Among the largest (5,000 seats), and Munich's oldest beer garden, Augustiner Keller is one of the more authentic beer gardens, with excellent food, beautiful chestnut shade trees, a mixed local crowd, and Munich Augustiner beer. It's a few minutes from the Hauptbahnhof and Hackerbrücke. ⊠ *Arnulfstr. 52, Maxvorstadt* ☏ *089/594–393* ⊕ *www.augustinerkeller.de* Ⓜ *Hackerbrücke / Hauptbahnhof.*

Biergarten am Chinesischen Turm. The famous Biergarten am Chinesischen Turm is at the five-story Chinese Tower in the Englischer Garten. Enjoy your beer to the strains of oompah music played by traditionally dressed musicians. ⊠ *Englischer Garten 3, Schwabing* ☏ *089/383–8730* ⊕ *www.chinaturm.de* Ⓜ *Chinesischer Turm (Bus).*

Hirschau. The Hirschau, pleasantly located in the Englischer Garten, has room for 2,500 guests, and it's about 10 minutes north of the Kleinhesseloher See. ⊠ *Gysslingstr. 15, Englischer Garten, Schwabing* ☏ *089/3609–0490* ⊕ *www.hirschau-muenchen.de* Ⓜ *Herzogpark (Bus).*

Park Café. This is one of Munich's hippest cafés, restaurants, night-clubs, and beer gardens. It often draws a younger crowd, attracted by a thriving music scene in the café itself, which ranges from DJs to live bands, and the occasional celebrity spotting. There's a great atmosphere to go with the good food and drinks, even better when the sun is shining and the beer garden is open. ⊠ *Sophienstr. 7, Maxvorstadt* ☎ *089/5161–7980* ⊕ *www.parkcafe089.de/en/home* Ⓜ *Hauptbahnhof.*

Fodor'sChoice ★ **Seehaus im Englischen Garten.** The Seehaus im Englischen Garten is on the banks of the artificial lake Kleinhesseloher See, where all of Munich converges on hot summer days. Take Bus 59 and exit at Osterwald-strasse or U-bahn 3/6 to Münchner Freiheit and stroll through the park. ⊠ *Kleinhesselohe 3, Schwabing* ☎ *089/381–6130* ⊕ *www.kuffler.de/en/seehaus.php* Ⓜ *Münchner Freiheit.*

JAZZ

Alfonso's Live-Music Club. At tiny Alfonso's, the nightly live music redefines the concept of intimacy. ⊠ *Franzstr. 5, Schwabing* ☎ *089/338–835* ⊕ *www.alfonsos.de* Ⓜ *Münchner Freiheit.*

AU AND HAIDHAUSEN

BEER GARDENS

FAMILY
Fodor'sChoice ★ **Hofbräukeller am Wiener Platz.** This is one of the city's midsize beer gardens but undoubtedly one of the best. Its location off Wiener Platz makes it attractive enough, plus the food's good, and it serves the same beer as the Hofbräuhaus. Inside, the restaurant is well worth a look. There is a play area for the little'uns, sometimes with babysitter (best to reserve), and as usual a play area for children outdoors as well. There's also a lounge area with sand and sun loungers. ⊠ *Innere Wiener Str. 19, Haidhausen* ☎ *089/459–9250* ⊕ *www.hofbraeukeller.de* Ⓜ *Max-Weber-Platz.*

DANCE CLUBS

Muffathalle. One of the best live venues in the city, this club housed inside a historic power station puts on up-and-coming bands as well as ones on their second or third or more appearances after making it big. Many leading acts from the U.K. and U.S. scenes have played here. The café-bar here has different DJs nearly every night of the week, and the modest beer garden serves organic food. ⊠ *Muffatwerk, Zellstr. 4, behind Müllersches Volksbad near the river, Haidhausen* ☎ *089/4587–5010* ⊕ *www.muffatwerk.de/en/* Ⓜ *Isartor / Deutsches Museum (Tram) / Gasteig (Tram).*

Optimolwerke. A former factory premises hosts the city's largest late-night party scene. The Optimolwerke has no fewer than eight clubs (the number changes) including a Brazil bar, the self-styled "party bar" Die Burg, and Theaterfabrik, a venue for concerts and more parties. ⊠ *Friedenstr. 10, Haidhausen* ☎ *089/450–6920* ⊕ *www.optimolwerke. de* Ⓜ *Ostbahnhof.*

JAZZ

Fodor'sChoice ★ **Jazzclub Unterfahrt.** Unterfahrt is the place for the serious jazzologist, though hip-hop is making heavy inroads into the scene. ⊠ *Einsteinstr. 42, Haidhausen* ☎ *089/448–2794* ⊕ *www.unterfahrt.de* Ⓜ *Max-Weber-Platz.*

OUTSIDE INNENSTADT
BEER GARDENS

Fodor'sChoice ★ **Königlicher Hirschgarten.** Out in the district of Nymphenburg is the huge Königlicher Hirschgarten, Munich's largest beer garden, with 8,000 seats. It's also a family-oriented beer garden; it even has a deer reserve. To get there, rent bikes and make a day of it in the park and beer garden, or take the S-bahn to Hirschgarten, then walk for 10 to 15 minutes. No matter how you get there, it'll be worth it. ⊠ *Hirschgarten 1, Nymphenburg* ☎ *089/1799–9119* ⊕ *www.hirschgarten.de* Ⓜ *Hirschgarten.*

Taxisgarten. The crowd at Neuhausen's Taxisgarten, with 1,500 seats, is fairly white-collar and tame, but the food here is excellent, not to mention the beer. While parents refresh themselves, children exhaust themselves at the playground. ⊠ *Taxisstr. 12, Neuhausen-Nymphenburg* ☎ *089/156–827* ⊕ *www.taxisgarten.de* Ⓜ *Gern.*

DANCE CLUBS

Backstage. The Backstage is mostly a live-music venue for alternative music of all kinds, but there's also a chilled-out club and a beer garden. Purchase tickets at various websites, including **München Ticket** (*www.muenchenticket.de*). ⊠ *Reitknechtstr. 6, Neuhausen-Nymphenburg* ☎ *089/126–6100* ⊕ *www.backstage.eu* Ⓜ *Hirschgarten.*

JAZZ

The Big Easy. This classy New Orleans–style restaurant features jazz-accompanied Sunday brunch. It's pricey, but it's good. ⊠ *Frundsbergstr. 46, Neuhausen-Nymphenburg* ⊕ *At the corner of Ruffinistr.* ☎ *089/1589–0253* ⊕ *www.thebigeasy.de/muenchen* Ⓜ *Rotkreuzplatz.*

PERFORMING ARTS

Bavaria's capital has an enviable reputation as an artistic hot spot. Details of concerts and theater performances are listed in *in münchen* (free) and *Monatsprogramm,* booklets available at most hotel reception desks, newsstands, and tourist offices. *Prinz* magazine lists almost everything happening in the city, as do a host of other city magazines, while the superb and official city website (⊕ *www.muenchen.de*) has listings. Otherwise, just keep your eye open for advertising pillars and posters.

Box Office of the Bavarian State Theaters. Tickets for performances at the Bavarian State Theater, Nationaltheater, Staatstheater am Gärtnerplatz (scheduled to reopen in October 2016), plus many other locations, are sold at the central box office. It's open Monday to Saturday 10 am–7 pm. ⊠ *Marstallpl. 5, Altstadt* ☎ *089/2185–1920* ⊕ *www.staatstheater-tickets.bayern.de/willkommen.html/language=en* Ⓜ *Marienplatz / Lehel / Odesonsplatz.*

München Ticket. This ticket agency has a German-language website where tickets for most Munich venues can be booked. ⊠ *Munich* ☎ *089/5481–8181* ⊕ *www.muenchenticket.de.*

Zentraler Kartenvorverkauf. Two Zentraler Kartenvorverkauf ticket kiosks are in the underground concourse: one at Marienplatz, and one at Karlsplatz (Stachus). ⊠ *Altstadt-Lehel* ☎ *089/292–540 Marienplatz,*

089/5450–6060 Karlsplatz (Stachus) ⊕ *www.zkv-muenchen.de* Ⓜ *Marienplatz / Karlsplatz.*

CONCERTS

Munich and music go together. The city has two world-renowned orchestras. The Philharmonic was directed by Lorin Maazel, formerly of the New York Philharmonic, from the 2012 season until his death in 2014. Valery Gergiev filled the position in 2015. The Bavarian State Opera Company is managed by Russian conductor Kirill Petrenko, who will leave in 2018 for the equivalent position in Berlin. The leading choral ensembles are the Munich Bach Choir, the Munich Motettenchor, and Musica Viva, the last specializing in contemporary music. The choirs perform mostly in city churches.

Bayerischer Rundfunk Ticket. The Bavarian Radio Symphony Orchestra sometimes performs at the Bayerischer Rundfunk and other city venues, such as Gasteig. The box office is open weekdays 9–5:30. ☒ *Arnulfstr. 42, Maxvorstadt* ☎ *089/5900–10880 tickets* ⊕ *www.info. br-klassikticket.de/?l=en* Ⓜ *Hauptbahnhof.*

Gasteig Culture Center. Hugely expensive to build and not particularly beautiful, this brick complex stands high above the Isar River, east of downtown. Its Philharmonic Hall is the permanent home of the Munich Philharmonic Orchestra and the largest concert hall in Munich. Gasteig also hosts the occasional English-language work. It hosts the annual book fair and numerous other events and celebrations. The sizeable open-kitchen Gast (*www.gast-muenchen.de*), part of the Gasteig complex, is a good option for a range of quick foods, from Thai curries to pizzas. There are also several smaller concert and event spaces in Gasteig, as well as the public library. ☒ *Rosenheimerstr. 5, Haidhausen* ☎ *089/480–980* ⊕ *www.gasteig.de* Ⓜ *Rosenheimerplatz.*

Herkulessaal in der Residenz. This highly regarded orchestral and recital venue is in the former throne room of King Ludwig I. ☒ *Residenzstr. 1, Altstadt* ☎ *089/5481–8181 München Ticket* ⊕ *www.muenchenticket. de* Ⓜ *Odeonsplatz / Marienplatz.*

Hochschule für Musik. Free concerts featuring conservatory students are given at the Hochschule für Musik. ☒ *Arcisstr. 12, Maxvorstadt* ☎ *089/28903* ⊕ *www.musikhochschule-muenchen.de* Ⓜ *Königsplatz.*

Fodor'sChoice ★ **Nationaltheater** (*Bayerische Staatsoper*). The Bavarian State Orchestra is based at the Nationaltheater. ☒ *Max-Joseph-Pl. 2, Altstadt* ☎ *089/218–501* ⊕ *www.staatsoper.de/en/index.html* Ⓜ *Odeonsplatz / Marienplatz.*

Fodor'sChoice ★ **Olympiahalle.** One of Munich's major pop-rock concert venues is the Olympiahalle, and the official ticket seller is München Ticket. ☒ *Spiridon-Louis-Ring 21, Milbertshofen* ⊕ *www.olympiapark.de/en/ olympiapark-munich/* Ⓜ *Olympiazentrum.*

Staatstheater am Gärtnerplatz. At this writing, the theater was under extensive renovation, but expected to be finished for the 2016/2017 season. The romantic art nouveau Staatstheater am Gärtnerplatz has a variety of performances including opera, ballet, and musicals. Tickets can be purchased at the theater on weekdays 10–6, Saturday until 1 pm, or at Zentraler Kartenvorverkauf in Marienplatz, and Karlsplatz

(Stachus). ✉ *Gärtnerpl. 3, Isarvorstadt* ☎ *089/2185–1960 tickets* ⊕ *www.gaertnerplatztheater.de/&language=en* Ⓜ *Fraunhoferstrasse.*

OPERA, BALLET, AND MUSICALS

Nationaltheater. Munich's Bavarian State Opera Company and its ballet ensemble perform at the Nationaltheater. ✉ *Max-Joseph-Pl. 2, Altstadt* ☎ *089/218–501* ⊕ *www.staatsoper.de/en/index.html* Ⓜ *Odeonsplatz / Marienplatz.*

THEATER

Munich has scores of theaters and variety-show venues, although most productions will be largely impenetrable if your German is shaky. Listed here are all the better-known theaters, as well as some of the smaller and more progressive spots. Note that most theaters close during July and August.

Bayerisches Staatsschauspiel (*Bavarian State Theater*). Bayerisches Staatsschauspiel is Munich's leading ensemble for classic playwrights such as Goethe, Schiller, Lessing, Shakespeare, and Chekhov. Its main home is the Residenz Theater, but it also plays at the Cuvilliés-Theater and at Marstall. ✉ *Max-Joseph-Pl. 1, Altstadt* ☎ *089/2185–2020* ⊕ *www.bayerischesstaatsschauspiel.de* Ⓜ *Odeonsplatz / Marienplatz.*

Fodor'sChoice
★
Cuvilliés-Theater. This is an incredible historic, rococo venue particularly famous for its Mozart productions. ✉ *Residenzstr. 1, Altstadt* ✢ *Enter from Kapellenhof (Chapel Courtyard)* ☎ *089/2185–1940 tickets* ⊕ *www.residenztheater.de* Ⓜ *Odeonsplatz / Marienplatz.*

Deutsches Theater. After years of renovation work, the Deutsches Theater has reopened and is again the premier spot for musicals, revues, balls, and big-band shows. ✉ *Schwanthalerstr. 13, Ludwigsvorstadt* ☎ *089/5523–4444 tickets* ⊕ *www.deutsches-theater.de* Ⓜ *Hauptbahnhof.*

Münchner Kammerspiele. A city-funded rival to the nearby state-backed Bayerisches Staatschauspiel, Münchner Kammerspiele-Schauspielhaus presents the classics as well as new works by contemporary playwrights in a beautiful art nouveau setting. ✉ *Maximilianstr. 28, Altstadt* ☎ *089/2339–6600* ⊕ *www.muenchner-kammerspiele.de* Ⓜ *Marienplatz / Isartor / Kammerspiele (Tram).*

SPORTS AND THE OUTDOORS

BICYCLING

A bike is hands-down the best way to experience this flat, pedal-friendly city. There are loads of bike lanes and paths that wind through its parks and along the Isar River. The rental shop will give you maps and tips, or you can get a map at any city tourist office.

Weather permitting, here is a route to try: go past the Isar Tor to the Isar River and head north to the Englischer Garten. Ride around the park and have lunch at a beer garden. Exit the park and go across Leopoldstrasse, making your way back down toward the museum quarter via the adorable Elisabethmarkt. Check out one or two of the galleries then pass through Königsplatz as you head back to the Old Town via Odeonsplatz.

You can also take your bike on the S-bahn, U-bahn, and certain regional trains (except during rush hours Monday to Friday from 6 am to 9 am and from 4 pm to 6 pm), which take you out to the many lakes and attractions outside town. Bicycles on public transportation cost €2.60 for a day ticket.

RENTALS

Mike's Bike Tours. Besides offering guided tours, Mike's Bike Tours also rents bikes. You can book your tour at the office around the corner from the rear entrance of the Hofbräuhaus, at Bräuhausstrasse 10, but the bike-rental location is a few hundred yards away, on the other side of the Isar Tor. Return time is 8 pm mid-April–August, earlier in other seasons. ⊠ *Thomas-Wimmer-Ring 16, Lehel* ☎ *089/2554–3987* ⊕ *www. mikesbiketours.com* ⌁ *Bikes from €16/day, €75/ week* Ⓜ *Isartor.*

Radius Tours and Bikes. Based at the central station, Radius Tours and Bikes rents bikes. Choose from seven/eight-gear bikes to 24/27 gears to e-bikes. Helmets, child bikes, and child seats are also available. ⊠ *Hauptbahnhof, Arnulfstr. 3, Ludwigsvorstadt* ✛ *Office: in Hauptbahnhof opposite platform 31* ☎ *089/5434–877720* ⊕ *www.radiustours.com* ⌁ *Bikes from €3/hour, €14.50/day, and €75/week* Ⓜ *Hauptbahnhof.*

ICE-SKATING

Climate changes permitting, there's outdoor skating on the lake in the Englischer Garten and on the Nymphenburger Canal in winter. Watch out for signs reading "*gefahr*" (danger), warning you of thin ice.

FAMILY
Fodor'sChoice
★

Karlsplatz. In winter the fountain on Karlsplatz is turned into a public rink with music and an outdoor bar. ⊠ *Karlspl., Altstadt* ⊕ *www. muenchnereiszauber.de/index.htm* ▢ *From €4.50* Ⓜ *Karlsplatz.*

JOGGING

Fodor'sChoice
★

Englischer Garten. The best place to jog is in the Englischer Garten, which is 11 km (7 miles) around and has dirt and asphalt paths throughout. ⊠ *Schwabing* ⊕ *www.muenchen.de/int/en/sights/parks/english-garden. html* Ⓜ *Odeonsplatz / Universität / Giselastrasse / Münchner Freiheit.*

Isar River. The banks of the Isar River are a favorite route for local runners. ⊠ *Lehel* Ⓜ *Isartor.*

Olympiapark. The 500-acre park of Schloss Nymphenburg is ideal for running, as is the Olympiapark, if you're in that area. Olympiapark also has four Nordic walking routes. ⊠ *Milbertshofen* ⊕ *www. olympiapark.de/en/sport-leisure/outdoor/running-nordic-walking/* Ⓜ *Olympiazentrum.*

SHOPPING

Munich has three of Germany's most exclusive shopping streets as well as flea markets to rival those of any other European city. In between are department stores, where acute German-style competition assures reasonable prices and often produces outstanding bargains. Artisans bring their wares of beauty and originality to the Christmas markets. Collect their business cards—in summer you're sure to want to order another of those little gold baubles that were on sale in December.

Munich has an immense central shopping area, a 2-km (1-mile) *Fussgängerzone* (pedestrian zone) stretching from Karlsplatz to Marienplatz along Neuhauser Strasse and Kaufingerstrasse, where most of the major department stores are, and then north to Odeonsplatz. For upscale shopping, Maximilianstrasse, Residenzstrasse, and Theatinerstrasse are unbeatable. Schwabing, north of the university, has more offbeat shopping streets—Schellingstrasse and Hohenzollernstrasse are two to try. ■TIP→ The neighborhood around Gärtnerplatz also has lots of new boutiques.

A few small shops around Viktualienmarkt sell Bavarian antiques, though their numbers are dwindling under the pressure of high rents. Antiques shoppers should also try the area north of the university—Türkenstrasse, Theresienstrasse, and Barerstrasse are all filled with antiques stores.

If you're looking for something really rare and special and money's no object, try the exclusive shops lining Prannerstrasse, at the rear of the Hotel Bayerischer Hof. Interesting and inexpensive antiques and assorted junk from all over Europe are laid out at the Friday and Saturday flea markets at Olympiapark (7 am–4 pm), not far from the Olympic Stadium, with hundreds of sellers.

If you want to deck yourself out in *Lederhosen* or a *Dirndl,* or acquire a green loden coat and little pointed hat with feathers, you have a wide choice in the Bavarian capital. ■TIP→ There are a couple of other shops along Tal street that have new and used lederhosen and dirndls at good prices in case you want to spontaneously get into the spirit of the 'Fest.

Munich is a city of beer, and items related to its consumption are obvious choices for souvenirs and gifts. Munich is also the home of the famous Nymphenburg Porcelain factory. Between Karlsplatz and Viktualienmarkt there are loads of shops for memorabilia and trinkets.

ALTSTADT

ANTIQUES

Antike Uhren Eder. In Antike Uhren Eder, the silence is broken only by the ticking of dozens of highly valuable German antique clocks and by discreet negotiation over the high prices. ⊠ *Prannerstr. 4, Altstadt ✛ Behind Fünf Höfe* ☏ *089/220–305* ⊕ *www.uhreneder.ch/index_en.php* ⊗ *Weekdays 10:30–6:30, Sat. 11–3* Ⓜ *Karlsplatz / Odeonsplatz.*

Roman Odesser. Antique German silver is the specialty at Roman Odesser. ⊠ *Westenriederstr. 21, Altstadt* ☏ *089/226–388* ⊕ *roman-odesser-muenchen.mux.de* ⊗ *Weekdays 10–6, Sat. 10–2* Ⓜ *Marienplatz.*

BOOKS

FodorśChoice
★
Hugendubel. There is a good selection of novels in English on the fifth floor of Hugendubel. ⊠ *Marienpl. 22, Altstadt* ☎ *089/3075–7575* ⊕ *www. hugendubel.de/de/branch?branchId=9809* ☉ *Mon.–Sat. 9–8* Ⓜ *Marienplatz* ⊠ *Karlspl. 12, Altstadt* ☎ *089/3075–7575* ⊕ *www.hugendubel.de/ de/branch?branchId=9808* ☉ *Mon.–Sat. 9–8* Ⓜ *Karlsplatz.*

CERAMICS AND GLASS

Kunstring. For Dresden and Meissen porcelain wares, go to Kunstring near Odeonsplatz. ⊠ *Briennerstr. 4, Altstadt* ⊕ *www.meissen. com/de/geschaefte/de/kunstring* ☉ *Weekdays 10–6:30, Sat. 10–6* Ⓜ *Odeonsplatz.*

Porzellan Manufaktur Nymphenburg. Nymphenburg's flaship store, this opulent space resembles a drawing room in the Munich palace of the same name. It has delicate, expensive porcelain safely locked away in bowfront cabinets. ⊠ *Odeonspl. 1, Altstadt* ☎ *089/282–428* ⊕ *www.nymphenburg.com/en/home/* ☉ *Weekdays 10–6:30, Sat. 10–6* Ⓜ *Odeonsplatz.*

CRAFTS

FodorśChoice
★
Bayerischer Kunstgewerbe–Verein. Bavarian craftspeople have a showplace of their own, the Bayerischer Kunstgewerbe–Verein. Here you'll find every kind of handicraft, from glass and pottery to textiles. ⊠ *Pacellistr. 6, Altstadt* ☎ *089/290–1470* ⊕ *www.bayerischer-kunstgewerbeverein. de* ☉ *Mon.–Sat. 10–6* Ⓜ *Karlsplatz / Odeonsplatz.*

Max Krug. If you've been to the Black Forest and forgot to acquire a clock, or if you need a good Bavarian souvenir, like a *Krug* (stein) try Max Krug in the pedestrian zone. ⊠ *Neuhauser Str. 2, Altstadt* ☎ *089/224–501* ⊕ *www.max-krug.com* ☉ *Mon.–Sat. 8:30–8* Ⓜ *Karlsplatz / Marienplatz.*

FOOD AND BEER

Chocolate & More. Opened in 2001, this tiny shop, located in the Viktualienmarkt, specializes in all things chocolate. ⊠ *Westenrieder Str. 15, Altstadt* ☎ *089/2554–4905* ⊕ *www.chocolate-and-more-munich. de* ☉ *Mon.–Sat. 10–6* Ⓜ *Marienplatz.*

Dallmayr. Dallmayr is the city's most elegant and famous gourmet food store, with delights that range from exotic fruits and English jams to a multitude of fish and meats, all served by efficient Munich matrons in smart blue-and-white-linen uniforms. The store's famous specialty is coffee, with more than 50 varieties to blend as you wish. It even has its own chocolate factory. This is the place to prepare a high-class— if pricey—picnic. ⊠ *Dienerstr. 14–15, Altstadt* ☎ *089/21350* ⊕ *www. dallmayr.com* ☉ *Mon.–Sat. 9:30–7* Ⓜ *Marienplatz.*

GIFTS AND SOUVENIRS

Sebastian Wesely. Besides a great variety of religious trinkets, Sebastian Wesely is the place to come for beer-related vessels and schnapps glasses (*Stampferl*), walking sticks, scarves, and napkins with the famous Bavarian blue-and-white lozenges. ⊠ *Rindermarkt 1, at Peterspl.,*

Altstadt ☎ *089/264–519* ⊕ *www.wesely-schnitzereien.de* ⊗ *Weekdays 9–6:30, Sat. 9–6* Ⓜ *Marienplatz.*

MARKETS

Fodor's Choice ★ **Christkindlmarkt.** From the end of November until December 24, the open-air stalls of the Christkindlmarkt are a great place to find gifts and warm up with mulled wine. Two other perennial Christmas-market favorites are those in Schwabing (Münchner-Freiheit Square) and at the Chinese Tower, in the middle of the Englischer Garten. ⊠ *Marienpl., Altstadt* ⊕ *www.muenchen.de/rathaus/home_en/Tourist-Office/Events/Christmas* ⊗ *Mon.–Sat. 10–9 (Sun. until 8, Dec. 24 until 2)* Ⓜ *Marienplatz.*

Fodor's Choice ★ **Viktualienmarkt.** Munich's Viktualienmarkt is *the* place to shop and to eat. Just south of Marienplatz, it's home to an array of colorful stands that sell everything from cheese to sausages, flowers to wine. A visit here is more than just an opportunity to find picnic makings; it provides an opening into Müncheners' robust—though friendly—nature, especially at the Viktualienmarkt's Bavarian Biergarten (beer garden). ⊠ *Viktualienmarkt, Altstadt* ⊕ *www.muenchen.de/int/en/shopping/markets/viktualienmarkt.html* ⊗ *Weekdays 10–6, Sat. 10–3* Ⓜ *Marienplatz.*

SHOPPING MALLS AND DEPARTMENT STORES

Breiter. For a classic selection of German clothing and hats, including some with a folk touch, try Munich's traditional family-run Breiter, with one of its stores on Altstadt's Kaufingerstrasse. ⊠ *Kaufingerstr. 26, Altstadt* ☎ *089/8905–8401* ⊕ *www.hutbreiter.de* ⊗ *Mon.–Sat. 9:30–8* Ⓜ *Marienplatz.*

Fünf Höfe. For a more upscale shopping experience, visit the many stores, boutiques, galleries, and cafés of the Fünf Höfe, a modern arcade carved into the block of houses between Theatinerstrasse and Kardinal-Faulhaber-Strasse. The architecture of the passages and courtyards is cool and elegant, in sharp contrast to the facades of the buildings. There's a decent Thai restaurant in there as well, not to mention the Kunsthalle, one of Germany's leading art exhibition venues. ⊠ *Theatinerstr. 15, Altstadt* ✛ *Other entrances from Salvatorstr., Kardinal-Faulhaber-Str., and Maffeistr.* ⊕ *www.fuenfhoefe.de* ⊗ *Weekdays 10–7, Sat. 10–6* Ⓜ *Marienplatz / Odeonsplatz.*

Galeria Kaufhof. With eight floors of offerings in this department store, you'll find midprice goods from cosmetics, fashion, and jewelry to greeting cards, office supplies, household items, and culinary delicacies. The end-of-season sales are bargains. ⊠ *Kaufingerstr. 1–5, Marienpl., Altstadt* ☎ *089/231–851* ⊕ *www.galeria-kaufhof.de/filialen/muenchen-marienplatz/Language/Englisch/* ⊗ *Mon.–Sat. 9–8* Ⓜ *Marienplatz.*

Hirmer. Hirmer has Munich's most comprehensive collection of German-made men's clothes, with a markedly friendly and knowledgeable staff. International brands are also here, such as Polo, Diesel, and Levi's. ⊠ *Kaufingerstr. 28, Altstadt* ☎ *089/236–830* ⊕ *www.hirmer-muenchen.de* ⊗ *Weekdays 9:30–8, Sat. 9–8* Ⓜ *Marienplatz / Karlsplatz.*

Kaufinger Tor. Kaufinger Tor has several floors of boutiques and cafés packed neatly together along a passageway under a high glass roof.

✉ *Kaufingerstr. 117, Altstadt* ⊕ *kaufingertor.de/en/home/* ⊗ *Mon.–Sat. 10–8* Ⓜ *Marienplatz / Karlsplatz.*

Ludwig Beck. Ludwig Beck is considered a step above other department stores by Müncheners. It's packed from top to bottom with highly original wares and satisfies even the pickiest of shoppers. ✉ *Marienpl. 11, Altstadt* ☎ *089/236–910* ⊕ *kaufhaus.ludwigbeck.de/english/* ⊗ *Mon.–Sat. 9:30–8* Ⓜ *Marienplatz.*

Oberpollinger. The more-than-100-year-old Oberpollinger—one of Germany's finest upscale department stores—was renovated in 2008. Its seven floors are packed with pricey and glamorous fashion, furniture, and beauty items. The large, open-plan self-service restaurant on the top floor, with an outdoor patio for the warm and sunny days, is well worth a visit, and isn't expensive. ✉ *Neuhauser Str. 18, Altstadt* ☎ *089/290–230* ⊕ *www.oberpollinger.de* ⊗ *Closed Sun.* Ⓜ *Karlsplatz.*

Pool. Pool is a hip shop on the upscale Maximilianstrasse, with fashion, music, and accessories for house and home. It's a shopping experience for the senses. ✉ *Maximilianstr. 11, Altstadt* ☎ *089/266–035* ⊕ *www.verypoolish.com* ⊗ *Closed Sun.* Ⓜ *Marienplatz / Nationaltheater (Tram).*

TEXTILES

Johanna Daimer Filze aller Art. In an arcade of the Neues Rathaus is tiny Johanna Daimer Filze aller Art, a shop founded in 1883 that sells every kind and color of felt imaginable. ✉ *Dienerstr., Altstadt* ⊹ *In the Rathaus building a few steps up from Marienpl.* ☎ *089/776–984* ⊕ *www. daimer-filze.com* ⊗ *Closed Sun.* Ⓜ *Marienplatz.*

TRADITIONAL CLOTHING

C&A. For a more affordable option on loden (water-resistant woolen material used for traditional coats and hats) and general fashion, try the department store C&A in the pedestrian zone. ✉ *Kaufingerstr. 13, Altstadt* ☎ *089/231–930* ⊗ *Mon.–Sat. 9–8* Ⓜ *Marienplatz / Karlsplatz.*

Lederhosen Wagner. The tiny Lederhosen Wagner, right up against the Heiliggeist Church, carries Lederhosen, woolen sweaters called *Walk* (not loden), and children's clothing. ✉ *Tal 2, Altstadt* ☎ *089/225–697* Ⓜ *Marienplatz / Isartor.*

Loden-Frey. Much of the fine loden clothing on sale at Loden-Frey is made at the company's own factory, on the edge of the Englischer Garten. ✉ *Maffeistr. 7, Altstadt* ☎ *089/210–390* ⊕ *www.lodenfrey.com* ⊗ *Closed Sun.* Ⓜ *Marienplatz / Odeonsplatz.*

TOYS

Fodor's Choice ★ **Spielwaren Obletters.** In the corner shop beside Hugendubel, Spielwaren Obletters has two extensive floors of toys, with the usual favorites plus many handmade playthings of great charm and quality. ✉ *Karlspl. 12, Altstadt* ☎ *089/5508–9510* ⊕ *www.mueller.de/sortiment/spielwaren/ obletter.html* ⊗ *Closed Sun.* Ⓜ *Karlsplatz.*

LUDWIGSVORSTADT AND ISARVORSTADT

BOOKS

Internationale Presse. Various locations in the train stations have magazines and novels. ⊠ *Opposite track 23, Hauptbahnhof, Ludwigsvorstadt* ☎ *089/5511-7170* ⊕ *www.einkaufsbahnhof.de/muenchen-hauptbahnhof/k-presse-buch-querbahnsteig-s6750* Ⓜ *Hauptbahnhof.*

Karstadt. Karstadt commands an entire city block between the main train station, Hauptbahnhof, and Karlsplatz. It is the largest and one of the best department stores in the city. On the fourth floor is a cafeteria with a great selection of excellent and inexpensive dishes. ⊠ *Bahnhofpl. 7, Ludwigsvorstadt* ☎ *089/55120* ⊕ *www.karstadt.de* ⊘ *Closed Sun.* Ⓜ *Hauptbahnhof / Karlsplatz.*

FOOD AND BEER

GötterSpeise. GötterSpeise is across the street from the restaurant Faun in Glockenbachviertel. The name of this delectable chocolate shop means "ambrosia," a fitting name for their gifts, delights, and hot drinks. ⊠ *Jahnstr. 30, Isarvorstadt* ☎ *089/2388-7374* ⊕ *www.goetterspeise-muenchen.de* ⊘ *Closed Sun.* Ⓜ *Fraunhoferstrasse.*

SHOPPING MALLS AND DEPARTMENT STORES

Slips. Slips, a beautiful shop on Gärtnerplatz, has a wide range of dresses, jeans, shoes, and accessories. Prices are a bit outrageous. ⊠ *Gärtnerpl. 2, Isarvorstadt* ☎ *089/202-2500* ⊕ *www.slipsfashion.com* ⊘ *Closed Sun.* Ⓜ *Fraunhoferstrasse / Isartor.*

SCHWABING AND MAXVORSTADT

ANTIQUES

Die Puppenstube. For Munich's largest selection of dolls and marionettes, head to Die Puppenstube. ⊠ *Luisenstr. 68, Maxvorstadt* ☎ *089/272-3267* ⊘ *Closed weekends* Ⓜ *Theresienstrasse / Josephsplatz.*

BOOKS

Lehmkuhl. Lehmkuhl is Munich's oldest and one of its finest bookshops; it also sells beautiful cards. ⊠ *Leopoldstr. 45, Schwabing* ☎ *089/380-1500* ⊕ *www.lehmkuhl.net* ⊘ *Closed Sun.* Ⓜ *Münchner Freiheit.*

FOOD AND BEER

Ludwig Mory. This pewter handcraft shop has everything from dinner plates and veal sausage to mugs and beer. Mugs come in all shapes and sizes, and are also available in ceramic. ⊠ *Amalienstr. 16, Maxvorstadt* ☎ *089/224-542* ⊕ *www.zinn-mory.de.*

MARKETS

FAMILY **Elisabethplatz.** If you're in the Schwabing area, the daily market at Elisabethplatz is worth a visit—it's much smaller than the Victualienmarkt but the range and quality of produce are comparable. Whereas at Viktualienmarkt you have visitors from many lands pushing past the stands, here life is more peaceful and local. There is a nicely shaded beer garden here as well. ⊠ *Elisabethpl., Schwabing* ⊕ *www.muenchen.de/rathaus/*

Stadtverwaltung/Kommunalreferat/markthallen/elisabethmarkt.html ⊙ *Closed Sun.* Ⓜ *Elisabethplatz (Tram).*

OUTSIDE INNENSTADT

Schloss Nymphenburg. You can buy porcelain directly from the factory called Porzellanmanufaktur Nymphenburg on the grounds of Schloss Nymphenburg. ⊠ *Nördliches Schlossrondell 8, Nymphenburg* ⚓ *Take tram 17 from Karlsplatz Stachus to stop Schloss Nymphenburg (direction Amalienburgstrasse)* ☎ *089/179–1970* ⊕ *www.nymphenburg.com/en/home* ⊙ *Closed weekends* Ⓜ *Schloss Nymphenburg (Tram and Bus).*

SIDE TRIPS FROM MUNICH

Munich's excellent suburban railway network, the S-bahn, brings several quaint towns and attractive rural areas within easy reach for a day's excursion. The two nearest lakes, Starnberger See and the Ammersee, are popular year-round. Dachau attracts overseas visitors mostly because of its concentration-camp memorial site, but it's a picturesque and historic town in its own right. Landshut, north of Munich, is way off the tourist track, but if it were the same distance south of Munich, this jewel of a Bavarian market town would be overrun. All these destinations have a wide selection of restaurants and hotels, and you can bring a bike on any S-bahn train. German Railways, DB, often has weekend specials that allow a family or group of five to travel inexpensively. (Inquire at the main train station for a Bayern ticket, a cheap way for up to five people to travel in Bavaria for a day, and the *Wochenendticket* (weekend ticket), which is also at a reduced price. You can also opt for a *Tageskarte* (day ticket), in the ticket machines in the subway stations.

■TIP→ Keep in mind that there are quite a few options for day trips to the famous castles built by King Ludwig, which are only a couple of hours away. Mike's Bike Tours organizes trips, or ask at your hotel for bus-tour excursions. A train out to Füssen and Schloss Neuschwanstein takes two hours. *For more information on this fairy-tale castle and others, see Chapter 4, The Romantic Road.*

AMMERSEE

40 km (25 miles) southwest of Munich.

Ammersee, known as "Peasants' Lake," is the country cousin of the better-known, more cosmopolitan Starnberger See (the "Princes' Lake"), and, accordingly, many Bavarians (and tourists, too) like it all the more. Munich cosmopolites of centuries past thought it too distant for an excursion, not to mention too rustic, so the shores remained relatively free of villas and parks. Though some upscale holiday homes claim some stretches of the eastern shore, Ammersee still offers more open areas for bathing and boating than the larger lake to the east. Bicyclists circle the 19-km-long (12-mile-long) lake (it's nearly 6 km [4 miles] across at its widest point) on a path that rarely loses sight of the water.

Hikers can spread out the tour for two or three days, staying over-night in any of the comfortable inns along the way. Dinghy sailors and windsurfers zip across in minutes with the help of the alpine winds that swoop down from the mountains. A ferry cruises the lake at regular intervals in summer, stopping at several piers. Board it at Herrsching.

Herrsching has a delightful promenade, part of which winds through the town's park. The 100-year-old villa that sits so comfortably there is a romantic and fanciful mixture of medieval turrets and Renaissance-style facades. It was actually built for the artist Ludwig Scheuermann in the late 19th century, and became a favorite meeting place for Bavarian artists. It's now a municipal cultural center and the setting for chamber-music concerts on some summer weekends.

GETTING HERE AND AROUND

Take A-96, follow the signs towards Lindau, and after about 20 km (12 miles) take the exit for Herrsching, the lake's principal town.

Herrsching is also the end of S-bahn Line 8, a 53-minute ride from Munich's Marienplatz. From the Herrsching train station, Bus No. 950 goes to Starnberg in a 40-minute journey.

Getting around by boat is the best way to visit. Each town on the lake has an *Anlegestelle* (pier).

EXPLORING

Fodor's Choice **Andechs Monastery.** The Benedictine monastery Andechs, one of south-
★ ern Bavaria's most famous pilgrimage sites, lies 5 km (3 miles) south of Herrsching. You can reach it on Bus 951 from the S-bahn station (the bus also connects Ammersee and Starnberger See), but you can easily walk there too, as most people do. This extraordinary ensemble, sur-mounted by an octagonal tower and onion dome with a pointed helmet, has a busy history going back more than 1,000 years. The church, origi-nally built in the 15th century, was entirely redone in baroque style in the early 18th century. The **Heilige Kapelle** contains the remains of the old treasure of the Benedictines in Andechs, including Charlemagne's "Vic-tory Cross" and a monstrance containing the three sacred hosts brought back from the crusades by the original rulers of the area, the Counts of Diessen-Andechs. One of the attached chapels contains the remains of composer Carl Orff, and one of the buildings on the grounds has been refurbished as a concert stage for the performance of his works.

Admittedly, however, the crowds of pilgrims are drawn not just by the beauty of the hilltop monastery but primarily by the beer brewed here and the stunning views. The monastery makes its own cheese as well, and serves hearty Bavarian food, an excellent accompaniment to the rich, almost black beer. You can enjoy both at large wooden tables in the monastery tavern or on the terrace outside. ⊠ *Bergstr. 2, 5 km (3 miles) south of Herrsching, Herrsching* ☎ *08152/3760* ⊕ *andechs.de/ no_cache/en/* ⊙ *Church daily 9–7; restaurant daily 10–8.*

Diessen am Ammersee. The little town of Diessen am Ammersee at the southwest corner of the lake has one of the most magnificent religious buildings of the whole region: the **Augustine abbey church of St. Mary.** No lesser figure than the great Munich architect Johann Michael Fischer designed this airy, early rococo structure. François Cuvilliés the Elder, whose work can be seen all over Munich, did the sumptuous gilt-and-marble high altar. Visit in late afternoon, when the light falls sharply on its crisp gray, white, and gold facade, etching the pencil-like tower and spire against the darkening sky over the lake. Don't leave without at least peeping into neighboring St. Stephen's courtyard, its cloisters smothered in wild roses.

Diessen has also attracted artists and craftspeople since the early 20th century. Among the most famous who made their home here was the composer Carl Orff. ✉ *Bahnhofstr. 15, Diessen* 🌐 *www.tourist-info-diessen.de* ⏲ *Tourism Office: Mar., Apr., and Oct., Mon.–Sat. 9–noon; May–Sept., weekdays 9–noon and 3:30–6, Sat. 9–noon; Nov.–Feb., Mon., Wed., and Fri. 10–noon.*

Carl-Orff-Museum. Among the most famous artists who made their home here was the composer Carl Orff, author of numerous works inspired by medieval material, including the famous *Carmina Burana*. His life and work—notably the pedagogical Schulwerk instruments—are exhibited in the Carl-Orff-Museum. ✉ *Hofmark 3, Diessen* ☎ *08807/91981* 🌐 *www.orff.de* 🎟 *From €3* ⏲ *Weekends 2–5* ☞ *Guided tours by appointment.*

WHERE TO STAY

$$ HOTEL 🏨 **Ammersee Hotel.** This very comfortable, modern resort hotel is located on the Ammersee. **Pros:** prime location (request a room with balcony); good restaurant. **Cons:** rooms facing the street are noisy; limited balcony rooms. [$] *Rooms from: €112* ✉ *Summerstr. 32, Herrsching* ☎ *08152/96870* 🌐 *www.ammersee-hotel.de* 🛏 *40 rooms* 🍴 *All meals* [M] *Herrsching.*

$$ HOTEL 🏨 **Landhotel Piushof.** In a parklike garden, the family-run Piushof has elegant Bavarian guest rooms, with oak and hand-carved cupboards. **Pros:** great views and location; great place for a business gathering. **Cons:** no restaurant. [$] *Rooms from: €128* ✉ *Schönbichlstr. 18, Herrsching* ☎ *08152/96820* 🌐 *www.piushof.de* 🛏 *24 rooms* 🍴 *Breakfast* [M] *Herrsching.*

$$ HOTEL 🏨 **Seehof Herrsching.** The hotel's long lakefront turns into a huge beer garden in summer. **Pros:** great views; food in the restaurant is good. **Cons:** restaurant gets packed in summer. [$] *Rooms from: €146* ✉ *Seestr. 58, Herrsching* ☎ *08152/9350* 🌐 *www.seehof-ammersee.de/en/* 🛏 *43 rooms* 🍴 *Breakfast* [M] *Herrsching.*

DACHAU

20 km (12 miles) northwest of Munich.

Dachau predates Munich, with records going back to the time of Charlemagne. It's a handsome town, too, built on a hilltop with views of Munich and the Alps, which was why it became such a favorite for numerous artists. A guided tour of the town, including the castle and palace, leaves from the Rathaus (Konrad-Adenauer-Strasse 2–6) on Saturdays at 11 am from May through October, in German, or rent an audio guide from the Tourist Information office. Dachau is infamous worldwide as the site of the "model" Nazi concentration camp, which was built just outside it. Dachau preserves the memory of the camp and the horrors perpetrated there with deep contrition while trying, with commendable discretion, to signal that the town has other points of interest.

GETTING HERE AND AROUND

From Munich take the Stuttgart autobahn (A8) to the Dachau-Fürsten-feldbruck exit, or the Nuremberg autobahn (A9) to the Oberschleis-sheim-Dachau exit. Dachau is also on S-bahn Line 2, a 25-minute ride from Munich's Marienplatz.

ESSENTIALS

Visitor Information Tourist Information Dachau. ⊠ *Konrad-Adenauer-Str. 1* ☏ *08131/75286* ⊕ *www.dachau.de/tourism.html?L=1* Ⓜ *Dachau Rathaus (Bus) from the Dachau train station.*

EXPLORING

Bezirksmuseum. To get a sense of the town's history, visit the Bezirks-museum (district museum), which displays historical artifacts, furniture, and traditional costumes from Dachau and its surroundings. ⊠ *Augsburger Str. 3* ☏ *08131/56750* ⊕ *www.dachauer-galerien-museen. de* 🎟 *From €5* 🕐 *Tues.–Fri. 11–5, weekends 1–5* Ⓜ *Dachau Rathaus (Bus) from Dachau train station.*

FAMILY
Fodor's Choice
★

Dachau Concentration Camp Memorial Site (*KZ—Gedenkstätte Dachau*). The site of the infamous camp, now the KZ-Gedenkstätte Dachau, is just outside town. Photographs, contemporary documents, the few cell blocks, and the grim crematorium create a somber and moving picture of the camp, where more than 41,000 of the 200,000-plus prisoners lost their lives. A documentary film in English is shown daily at 11:30, 12:30, and 3. The former camp has become more than just a grisly memorial: it's now a place where people of all nations meet to reflect upon the past and on the present. By public transport take the S-2 from Marienplatz or Hauptbahnhof in the direction of Petershausen, and get off at Dachau. From there, take the clearly marked bus from right outside the Dachau S-bahn station (No. 726 toward Saubachsiedlung; it leaves about every 20 minutes). If you are driving from Munich, take the autobahn toward Stuttgart, get off at Dachau, and follow the signs. ⊠ *Alte Römerstr. 75* ☏ *08131/6699–7135* ⊕ *www.kz-gedenkstaette-dachau.de* 🕐 *Daily 9–5* ☞ *English guided tours daily at 11 and 1* Ⓜ *Dachau, KZ-Gedenkstätte (Bus) from Dachau train station.*

Gemäldegalerie. An artists' colony formed here during the 19th century, and the tradition lives on. Picturesque houses line Hermann-Stock-mann-Strasse and part of Münchner Strasse, and many of them are still the homes of successful artists. The Gemäldegalerie displays the works of many of the town's 19th-century artists. ⊠ *Konrad-Adenauer-Str. 3* ☏ *08131/56750* ⊕ *www.dachauer-galerien-museen.de/index.php/en/ aktuelle-ausstellung-gemaeldegalerie* 🎟 *From €5* 🕐 *Tues.–Fri. 11–5, weekends 1–5* Ⓜ *Dachau Rathaus (Bus) from Dachau train station.*

St. Jakob. St. Jakob, Dachau's parish church, was built in 1624–25 in late-Renaissance style on the foundations of a 13th-century Gothic structure. Baroque features and a characteristic onion dome were added in 1676–78. On the south wall you can admire a very fine sundial from 1699, which displays the month, the zodiac, and the time. ⊠ *Pfarrstr.*

7 ☎ 08131/36380 ⊕ *www.pv-dachau-st-jakob.de/st-jakob* ☉ *Summer, daily 8–7; winter, daily 8–6* Ⓜ *Dachau Rathaus (Bus).*

FAMILY   **Schloss Dachau.** Schloss Dachau, the hilltop castle, dominates the town. What you'll see is the one remaining wing of a palace built by the Munich architect Josef Effner for the Wittelsbach ruler Max Emanuel in 1715. During the Napoleonic Wars the palace served as a field hospital and then was partially destroyed. King Max Joseph lacked the money to rebuild it, so all that's left is a handsome cream-and-white building, with an elegant pillared and lantern-hung café on the ground floor and a former ballroom above. About once a month the grand Renaissance hall, with a richly decorated and carved ceiling, covered with painted panels depicting figures from ancient mythology, is used for chamber concerts. The east terrace affords panoramic views of Munich and, on fine days, the distant Alps. There's also a 250-year-old *Schlossbrauerei* (castle brewery), which hosts the town's beer and music festival each year in the first two weeks of August. The Schloss restaurant serves good Bavarian food with regional ingredients, as well as great home-made cakes. ⊠ *Schlossstr. 7* ☎ *08131/87923* ⊕ *www.schloesser.bayern. de/englisch/palace/objects/dachau.htm* ☜ *€2* ☉ *Tues.–Sun. 10–7.*

WHERE TO STAY

$$ ☐ **Hotel Fischer.** You can see this hotel across the square from the S-bahn
HOTEL   station. **Pros:** free Wi-Fi; prime location; good restaurant. **Cons:** on nice evenings, noise from the patio may filter up to your room. $ *Rooms from: €125* ⊠ *Bahnhofstr. 4* ☎ *08131/612–200* ⊕ *www.protutti.com/ firmen/Weitere/Hotel-Fischer/en/index.php* ⇅ *29 rooms* ⊙| *All meals* Ⓜ *Dachau.*

THE BAVARIAN ALPS

WELCOME TO
THE BAVARIAN ALPS

TOP REASONS
TO GO

★ **Herrenchiemsee:** Take the old steam-driven ferry to the island in Chiemsee to visit the last and most glorious castle of Bavaria's King Ludwig II.

★ **Great nature:** From the crystalline waters of the Königssee to the grandiose Karwendel Mountains and the powdery snow atop the Zugspitze, it's everything a nature lover needs.

★ **Meditating in Ettal monastery:** Baroque ornamentation, a riot of frescoes, the fluid sound of the ancient organ that puts you in a deep, relaxing trance. A great brewery and distillery round out a deeply religious experience.

★ **Rejuvenation in Reichenhall:** A salt mine beneath the city feeds into the Rupertus Therme, a modern spa in Bad Reichenhall where you can soak in saltwater baths year-round.

★ **Berchtesgaden:** A national park attracts hikers and bikers; history buffs can explore the darkest chapter of German history at Obersalzberg, Hitler's mountain retreat.

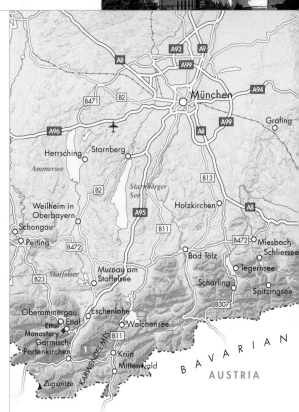

1 Werdenfelser Land and Wetterstein Mountains. Like villages lost in time, Mittenwald and Oberammergau are both famous for their half-timber houses covered in *Lüftlmalerei* frescoes. The entire region sits serenely in the shadow of Germany's highest point: the Zugspitze. The Wetterstein Mountains offer fantastic skiing and hiking.

2 Upper Bavarian Lake District. Bavaria's Lake District is almost undiscovered by foreign tourists but has long been a secret destination for Germans. Several fine, hidden lakes dot the area. The Chiemsee dominates the Chiemgau, with one of the most impressive German palaces and great water sports. Residents, or Chiemgauer,

GETTING ORIENTED

3

Ask a Bavarian about the "Bavarian Alps" and he'll probably shake his head in confusion. To Bavarians "the Alps" consist of several adjoining mountain ranges spanning the Ammergau, Wetterstein, and Karwendel Alps in the west to the Chiemgauer and Berchtesgadener Alpen in the east. Each region has its die-hard fans. The constants, however, are the incredible scenery, clean air, and a sense of Bavarian *Gemütlichkeit* (coziness) omnipresent in every *Hütte* (cottage), *Gasthof* (guesthouse), and beer garden. The area is an outdoor recreation paradise, and almost completely lacks the high-culture institutions that dominate German urban life.

often wear traditional *Trachten*, elaborate lederhosen and dirndl dresses, as an expression of their proud cultural heritage.

3 Berchtesgadener Land. Home to the second-highest mountain peak in the country, Berchtesgaden is one of the most ruggedly beautiful regions. Hundreds of miles of hiking trails with serene Alpine cottages and

the odd cow make the area a hiking and mountaineering paradise. Berchtesgaden and Bad Reichenhall are famous for the salt trade, and the salt mines provide the visitor with a unique and entertaining insight into the history and wealth of the region. The Königssee is the most photographed place in the country, and for good reason.

OUTDOORS IN THE BAVARIAN ALPS

Bursting up from the lowlands of southern Germany, the Bavarian Alps form both an awe-inspiring border with Austria and a superb natural playground for outdoors enthusiasts.

(above) Mountain bikers in the Bavarian foothills. (upper right) Bavarian Alps. (lower right) Backcountry skiers.

Visible from Munich on a clear day, the northern front of the Alps stretches over 300 km (186 miles) from Lake Constance in the west to Berchtesgaden in the east, and acts as a threshold to the towering mountain ranges that lie farther south. Lower in altitude than their Austrian, Swiss, and French cousins, the Bavarian Alps have the advantage of shorter distances between their summits and the valleys below, forming an ideal environment for casual hikers and serious mountaineers alike.

In spring and summer cowbells tinkle and wild flowers blanket meadows beside trails that course up and down the mountainsides. In winter, snow engulfs the region, turning trails into paths for cross-country skiers and the mountainsides into pistes for snowboarders and downhill skiers to carve their way down.

—Updated by Courtney Tenz

LEDERHOSEN

Along with sausages and enormous mugs of frothy beer, lederhosen form the holy trinity of what many foreigners believe to be stereotypically "German." The reality, however, is that the embroidered leather breeches are traditionally worn only in Bavaria, particularly the southern Alpine areas, where the durability and protection of leather are advantageous for those working as carpenters or farmers in the region. Handmade, tailored versions are worn on Sundays and on special occasions.

BEST WAYS TO EXPLORE

BY FOOT

It's not without good reason that wanderlust is a German word. The desire to travel and explore has been strong for hundreds of years in Germany, especially in places like the Alps where strenuous strolls are rewarded with breathtaking vistas. There are more than 7,000 km (4,350 miles) of walking trails in the Allgäu region alone to wander, conveniently divided into valley walks, mid-altitude trails, and summit hikes reflecting the varying altitude and difficulty. Hikes can be undertaken as day trips or as weeks-long endeavors, and there are campsites, mountain huts, farmhouses, and hotels to overnight in along the way, as well as a decent infrastructure of buses, trains, and cable cars to get you to your starting point. The Bavaria Tourism Office (⊕ *www.bavaria.by*) has more information on hiking trails.

BY BIKE

You don't need to venture onto their slopes to appreciate the Alps' beauty; cycling through the foothills at their base affords stunning views of the mountains combined with the luxury of refreshing stop-offs in beer gardens and dips in beautiful lakes like the Tegernsee. There's plenty of accommodation tailored to cyclists throughout the region and local trains are normally equipped with a bicycle carriage or two to transport you to more remote locations. The Alps also have thousands of miles of mountain-bike-friendly trails and a number of special bike parks serviced by cable cars.

BY SKIS

Neither as high nor famous as their neighbors, the Bavarian Alps are frequently overlooked as a winter-sports destination. Resorts on the German side of the border may have shorter seasons than places like Zermatt and Chamonix, but they're also generally less expensive in terms of food and accommodations, and many, including Zugspitze, are easily accessed from Munich for day trips.

BEST PHOTO OPS

No matter where you are around the Alps you'll be inundated with sights worth snapping. Here are a few:

■ **Neuschwanstein Castle** sits theatrically on the side of a mountain, its grand towers set against a background of tree- and snow-covered peaks.

■ The panoramic view from close to 10,000 feet at the peak of Germany's highest mountain, the **Zugspitze,** takes in 400 peaks in four countries.

■ Reputedly the cleanest lake in Germany, **Königs-see** is also endowed with steep rock formations that soar thousands of meters up above the lake, beautifully framing its crystalline waters.

■ From **Tegernsee's** lovely Benedictine monastery, you can wander down to the lake for spectacular vistas of its glittering surface and the Alps beyond.

Updated by
Courtney Tenz

Fir-clad mountains, rocky peaks, lederhosen, and geranium-covered houses: the Bavarian Alps come closest to what many of us envision as "Germany." Quaint towns full of frescoed half-timber houses covered in snow pop up among the mountain peaks and shimmering hidden lakes, as do the creations of King Ludwig II, one of the last kings of Bavaria. The entire area has plenty of sporting opportunities year-round.

Upper Bavaria (Oberbayern) stretches south and east from Munich to the Austrian border. Leaving the city, you'll soon find yourself on a gently rolling plain leading to lakes surrounded by ancient forests. The plain merges into foothills, which suddenly give way to jagged Alpine peaks, and in Berchtesgadener Land, snowcapped mountains rise straight up from the gemlike lakes.

Continuing south, you'll encounter cheerful villages with richly painted houses, churches, and monasteries filled with the especially sensuous Bavarian baroque and rococo styles, and several salt deposits in the area have created a spa culture where you can relax as you "take the waters." Some of the best sport in Germany can be enjoyed here: downhill and cross-country skiing, snowboarding, and ice-skating in winter; tennis, swimming, sailing, golf, and, above all (sometimes literally), hiking, paragliding, and ballooning in summer.

PLANNING

WHEN TO GO

This mountainous region is a year-round holiday destination. Snow is promised by most resorts from December through March, although there's year-round skiing on the glacier slopes at the top of the Zugspitze. Spring and autumn are ideal times for leisurely hikes on the many mountain trails. November is a between-seasons time, when many hotels and restaurants close down or attend to renovations. Note, too, that many locals take a vacation after January 6, and in smaller towns, businesses may be closed for anywhere up to a month. The lakes are extremely popular with European visitors, who flood the Alps in July and August.

GETTING HERE AND AROUND

AIR TRAVEL

Munich, 95 km (59 miles) northwest of Garmisch-Partenkirchen, is the gateway to the Bavarian Alps. If you're staying in Berchtesgaden, consider the closer airport in Salzburg, Austria—it has fewer international flights, but it is a budget-airline and charter hub.

Airport Information Salzburg Airport (*SZG*). ✉ *Innsbrucker Bundesstr., Salzburg* ☎ *0662/85800* ⊕ *www.salzburg-airport.com.*

CAR TRAVEL

The Bavarian Alps are well connected to Munich by train, and an extensive network of buses links even the most remote villages. Since bus schedules can be unreliable and are timed for commuters, those in a hurry may want to visit the area by car. Three autobahns reach into the Bavarian Alps: A-7 comes in from the northwest (Frankfurt, Stuttgart, Ulm) and ends near Füssen in the western Bavarian Alps; A-95 runs from Munich to Garmisch-Partenkirchen; take A-8 from Munich for Tegernsee, Chiemsee, and Berchtesgaden. ■ TIP➜ **The A-8 is statistically the most dangerous autobahn in the country, partially due to it simultaneously being the most heavily traveled highway and the road most in need of repair.** The driving style is fast, and tailgating is common, although illegal. The recommended speed on the A-8 is 110 kph (68 mph); if an accident occurs at higher speeds, your insurance may not cover it. It is a good idea to pick a town like Garmisch-Partenkirchen, Bad Tölz, or Berchtesgaden as a base and explore the area from there.

TRAIN TRAVEL

Most Alpine resorts are connected with Munich by regular express and slower service trains. Due to the rugged terrain, train travel in the region can be challenging, but with some careful planning—see ⊕ *www.bahn. de* for schedules and to buy tickets—you can visit this region without a car. The Bavarian Alps are furnished with cable cars, steam trains, and cog railroads that whisk you to the tops of Alpine peaks, allowing you to see the spectacular views without hours of mountain climbing.

RESTAURANTS

Restaurants in Bavaria run the gamut from the casual and *gemütlich* (cozy) Gasthof to formal gourmet offerings. More upscale establishments try to maintain a feeling of casual familiarity, but you will probably feel more comfortable at the truly upscale restaurants if you dress up a bit. Note that many restaurants take a break between 2:30 and 6 pm. If you want to eat during these hours, look for the magic words *Durchgehend warme Küche*, indicating warm food is served throughout the day, possibly snacks during the off-hours. Most restaurants in the region don't accept credit cards.

Prices in the reviews are the average cost of a main course at dinner, or if dinner is not served, at lunch.

HOTELS

With few exceptions, a hotel or *Gasthof* in the Bavarian Alps and lower Alpine regions has high standards and is traditional in style, with balconies, pine woodwork, and gently angled roofs on which the snow sits and insulates. Many in the larger resort towns offer special packages, including spa or "wellness" packages online. Private homes all through the region offer Germany's own version of bed-and-breakfasts, indicated by signs reading "Zimmer frei" ("Rooms available"). Their rates may be less than €25 per person for renting a room with a shared bathroom. As a general rule, the farther from the popular and sophisticated Alpine resorts you go, the lower the rates. Note, too, that many places offer a small discount if you stay more than one night. By the same token, some places frown on staying only one night, especially during the high seasons, in summer, at Christmas, and on winter weekends. In spas and many mountain resorts a "spa tax," or *Kurtaxe*, is added to the hotel bill. It amounts to no more than €3 per person per day and allows free use of spa facilities, entry to local attractions and concerts, and use of local transportation at times.

Prices in the reviews are the lowest cost of a standard double room in high season. For expanded reviews, facilities, and current deals, visit Fodors.com.

WHAT IT COSTS IN EUROS			
	$	$$	$$$	$$$$
Restaurants	under €15	€15–€20	€21–€25	over €25
Hotels	under €100	€100–€175	€176–€225	over €225

PLANNING YOUR TIME

The Alps are spread along Germany's southern border, but are fairly compact and easy to explore. A central base like Garmisch-Partenkirchen or Berchtesgaden, the largest towns, will have the most convenient transportation connections.

Although the Alps are a popular tourist destination, the smaller communities like Mittenwald and Ettal are quieter and make for pleasant overnight stays. For an unforgettable experience, try spending the night in an Alpine hut, feasting on a simple but hearty meal and sleeping in the cool night air.

DISCOUNTS AND DEALS

One of the best deals in the area is the German Railroad's Bayern Ticket, which allows between one and five people to travel on any regional train and almost all buses in the Alps. Prices range between €23 for a single traveler to €43 for five people. Ticket holders also receive discounts on a large number of attractions in the area, including the Zugspitzbahn, a cog railroad and cable car that takes you up to the top of the Zugspitze. The city of Grainau's ZugspitzCard (three days €53) offers discounts in almost every city near the Zugspitze. Visitors to spas or spa towns receive a Kurkarte, an ID that proves payment of the spa tax, either upon check-in (the nominal fee is already included in your bill) or by

The Zugspitze is the highest mountain in Germany and is reachable from Garmisch-Partenkirchen.

dropping in at the tourist office. The document allows discounts and often free access to sights in the town or area. If you've paid the tax, be sure to show the card everywhere you go.

VISITOR INFORMATION

Tourismusverband München Oberbayern. ⊠ *Radolfzeller Str. 15, Munich* ☎ *089/829–2180* ⊕ *www.oberbayern-tourismus.de.*

WERDENFELSER LAND AND WETTERSTEIN MOUNTAINS

With Germany's highest peak and picture-perfect Bavarian villages, the Werdenfelser Land offers a splendid mix of natural beauty combined with Bavarian art and culture. The region spreads out around the base of the Zugspitze, where the views from the top reach from Garmisch-Partenkirchen to the frescoed houses of Oberammergau, and to the serene Cloister Ettal.

GARMISCH-PARTENKIRCHEN

90 km (56 miles) southwest of Munich.

More commonly known by American travelers as Garmisch, Garmisch-Partenkirchen is comprised of two separate communities that were fused together in 1936 to accommodate the Winter Olympics. Since then, it's grown into a bustling, year-round resort and spa town. Today, with a population of 28,000, the area is the center of the Werden-felser Land and large enough to offer every facility expected from a major Alpine resort. Garmisch is more urban, with a pedestrian zone, wide car-friendly streets, and hordes of tourists. The narrow streets and quaint architecture of smaller Partenkirchen look more charming and make it a slightly better choice if you're looking for a quiet, rural stay. In both parts of town pastel frescoes of biblical and bucolic scenes decorate facades.

Winter sports rank high on the agenda here. There are more than 60 km (37 miles) of downhill ski runs, 40 ski lifts and cable cars, and 180 km (112 miles) of *Loipen* (cross-country ski trails). One of the principal stops on the international winter-sports circuit, the area hosts a week of races every January. You can usually count on good skiing from December through April (and into May on the Zugspitze).

GETTING HERE AND AROUND

Garmisch-Partenkirchen is the cultural and transportation hub of the Werdenfelser Land. The autobahn A-95 links Garmisch directly to Munich. Regional German Rail trains head directly to Munich (90 minutes), Innsbruck (80 minutes), and Mittenwald (20 minutes). German Rail operates buses that connect Garmisch with Oberammergau, Ettal, and the Wieskirche. Garmisch is a walkable city; you probably won't need to use its frequent city-bus services.

Partenkirchen was founded by the Romans, and you can still follow the Via Claudia they built between Partenkirchen and neighboring Mittenwald, which was part of a major route between Rome and Germany well into the 17th century.

Bus tours can be coordinated by the local tourist office with one of the local agencies; regular trips are available to King Ludwig II's castles at Neuschwanstein and Linderhof and to the Ettal Monastery, near Oberammergau, as well as into the neighboring Austrian Tyrol.

The Garmisch mountain railway company, the Bayerische Zugspitzbahn, offers special excursions to the top of the Zugspitze, Germany's highest mountain, by cog rail and cable car.

ESSENTIALS

Bus Tours Weiss-Blau-Reisen. ✉ *Promenadestr. 5* ☎ *08821/6230* ⊕ *www. weiss-blau-reisen.de.*

Railway Tour Bayerische Zugspitzbahn. ✉ *Olympiastr. 27* ☎ *08821/7970* ⊕ *www.zugspitze.de.*

Visitor Information Garmisch-Partenkirchen. ✉ *Richard-Strauss-Pl. 1a* ☎ *08821/180–700* ⊕ *www.gapa.de.*

EXPLORING

Richard Strauss Institut. On the eastern edge of Garmisch, at the end of Zöppritzstrasse, stands the home of composer Richard Strauss, who lived there until his death in 1949. It's not open to visitors, but this institute, across town, has an exhibition about Strauss. It's also the center of activity during the *Richard-Strauss-Tage,* an annual music festival held in mid-June that features concerts and lectures on the town's most famous son. Other concerts are given year-round. ✉ *Schnitzschulstr.*

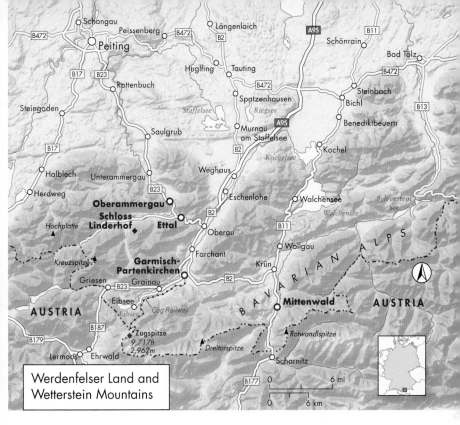

Werdenfelser Land and
Wetterstein Mountains

*19 ⊕ www.richard-strauss-institut.de ⌲ €3.50 for exhibit ⊙ Weekdays
10–4.*

St. Martin Church. Beautiful examples of Upper Bavarian houses line
Frühlingstrasse, and a pedestrian zone begins at Richard-Strauss-Platz.
Off Marienplatz, at one end of the car-free zone, is this unassuming 18th-
century parish church which contains some significant stuccowork by
the Wessobrunn artist Jospeh Schmutzer and rococo work by Matthäus
Günther that was recently restored to its original vibrancy. ⊠ *Marien-
platz* ⊕ *www.erzbistum-muenchen.de/Pfarrei/Page007033.aspx* ⌲ *Free*
⊙ *May–Sept., daily 8–7; Oct.–Apr., daily 8–6 (except during Mass).*

St. Martin Church (Die Alte Kirche). Across the Loisach River stands the
original St. Martin church (also known as "Die Alte Kirche" or the
Old Church), whose original foundation was laid in the 11th century.
Its current building dates to 1280 and showcases Gothic wall paintings from throughout the centuries, including a 7-meter-high (21-foot-
high), larger-than-life-size figure of St. Christopher from 1330 and a
Passion of the Christ fresco dating to the 1400s. ⊠ *Pfarrerhausweg
4* ⊕ *www.erzbistum-muenchen.de/Pfarrei/Page007033.aspx* ⌲ *Free*
⊙ *May–Sept., daily 8–7; Oct.–Apr., daily 8–6 (except during Mass).*

Werdenfels Museum. Objects and exhibitions on the region's history can
be found in this excellent museum, which is itself housed in a building

dating back to around 1200. The museum is spread over 19 rooms and five floors, and explores every aspect of life in the Werdenfelser region, which was an independent state for more than 700 years, until 1802. ✉ *Ludwigstr. 47* ☎ *08821/751–710* 🌐 *www.werdenfels-museum.de* 🎫 *€2.50* ⏰ *Tues.–Sun. 10–5.*

Fodor's Choice ★ **Zugspitze.** The highest mountain (9,717 feet) in Germany, this is the number one attraction in the Garmisch-Partenkirchen area. There are two ways up the mountain: a leisurely 75-minute ride on a cog railroad from Olympiastrasse 27, in the town center, combined with a cable-car ride up the last stretch; or a 10-minute hoist by cable car, which begins its giddy ascent from the Eibsee, 10 km (6 miles) outside town on the road to Austria. There are two restaurants with sunny terraces at the summit and another at the top of the cog railroad. A round-trip combination ticket allows you to mix your modes of travel up and down the mountain. Prices are lower in winter than in summer, even though winter rates include use of all the ski lifts on the mountain. You can rent skis at the top. Ascending the Zugspitze from the Austrian side is cheaper and more scenic. The *Tiroler Zugspitzbahn* departs three times per hour from near the village of Ehrwald. The round-trip ticket costs €37.50 and buses connect the gondolas to the Ehrwald train station. There are also a number of other peaks in the area with gondolas, but the views from the Zugspitze are the best. A four-seat cable car goes to the top of one of the lesser peaks: the 5,840-foot **Wank**. From there, you can tackle both mountains on foot, provided you're properly shod and physically fit. Or stop over at the **Alpspitze,** from where you can hike as well. ✉ *Garmisch-Partenkirchen* ☎ *08821/7970* 🌐 *www.zugspitze.de* 🎫 *Funicular or cable car €50 round-trip; €43.50 round-trip in winter* ⏰ *Daily 8:15–4:30 (subject to weather conditions and seasonal variation).*

WHERE TO EAT

$ GERMAN 🍴 **Bräustüberl.** Though its name refers to a brewery, and drinking does take place, this small restaurant has a more intimate atmosphere than a traditional beer hall. Its exterior is adorned in frescoes and inside, the fare is standard Bavarian pub food, with a few offerings like potato pancakes for kids. [$] *Average main: €11* ✉ *Fürstenstr. 23* ☎ *08821/2312* 🌐 *www.braeustueberl-garmisch.de* 💳 *No credit cards.*

$$ GERMAN 🍴 **Gasthaus zur Schranne.** In picturesque Partenkirchen, this small guesthouse in a historical building dating back to 1610 has an interior typical of southern Bavaria with exposed timber beams and a menu standard for the area. Fish and a variety of schnitzel are on the menu alongside vegetarian options like the eggy fried-dough specialty, *Spätzle*; most of the dishes contain regionally sourced seasonal ingredients. In summer, you can sit on a terrace with tables overlooking the Zuspitze. [$] *Average main: €16* ✉ *Griessstr. 4* ☎ *08821/909–8030* 🌐 *www.zurschranne.de* 💳 *No credit cards.*

$$ GERMAN 🍴 **Zum Wildschütz.** A hidden gem in a tourist-heavy district, this restaurant does standard Bavarian fare like pork knuckle in a gourmet version that keeps locals coming back repeatedly. Reservations are highly recommended. [$] *Average main: €16* ✉ *Bankg. 9* ☎ *08821/3290* 💳 *No credit cards.*

EATING WELL IN THE BAVARIAN ALPS

Bavarian cooking originally fed a farming people, who spent their days out of doors doing heavy manual labor. *Semmelknödel* (dumplings of old bread), pork dishes, sauerkraut, bread, and hearty soups were felt necessary to sustain a person facing the elements. The natural surroundings provided further sustenance, in the form of fresh trout from brooks, *Renke* (pike-perch) from the lakes, venison, and mushrooms. This substantial fare was often washed down with beer, which was nourishment in itself, especially during the Lenten season, when the dark and powerful "Doppelbock" was on the market. Today this regimen will suit sporty types who have spent a day hiking in the mountains, skiing in the bracing air, or swimming or windsurfing in chilly lakes.

Bavaria is not immune to eclectic culinary trends, but the most recent trend is a return to the basics. Regional cuisine comprised of locally grown ingredients seems to be on every menu nowadays, although you may find minimalist Asian daubs here, a touch of French sophistication and Italian elegance there. Menus often include large sections devoted to salads, and there are tasty vegetarian dishes even in the most traditional regions. Yes, Bavarian cooking—hearty, homey, and down-to-earth—is actually becoming lighter.

One area remains an exception: desserts. The selection of sinfully creamy cakes in the *Konditorei* (cake shop), often enjoyed with whipped-cream-topped hot chocolate, continues to grow. These are irresistible, of course, especially when homemade. A heavenly experience might be a large portion of warm *Apfelstrudel* (apple-and-nut-filled pastry) fresh from the oven in some remote mountain refuge.

Schnapps, which customarily ends a meal, has gone from being a step above moonshine to a true delicacy extracted from local fruit by virtuoso distillers.

3

WHERE TO STAY

For information about accommodation packages with ski passes, call the Zugspitze or get in touch with the tourist office in Garmisch (☎ *08821/180–700* 🌐 *www.zugspitze.de*).

$$ B&B/INN 🏨 **Edelweiss Hotel.** Like its namesake, the "nobly white" Alpine flower of *The Sound of Music* fame, this small downtown hotel has plenty of mountain charm. **Pros:** comfortable; homey. **Cons:** small hotel. [$] *Rooms from: €112* ✉ *Martinswinkelstr. 15–17* ☎ *08821/2454* 🌐 *www.hoteledelweiss.de* 🛏 *31 rooms* 🍴 *Breakfast.*

$ B&B/INN 🏨 **Gasthof Fraundorfer.** You can ride to dreamland in this beautiful old Bavarian Gasthof in the center of Partenkirchen—some of the bed frames are carved like antique automobiles and sleighs. **Pros:** free Wi-Fi; great location and dining experience. **Cons:** noise a problem for the rooms in the back of hotel. [$] *Rooms from: €86* ✉ *Ludwigstr. 24* ☎ *08821/9270* 🌐 *www.gasthof-fraundorfer.de* 🛏 *20 rooms, 7 suites* 🍴 *Breakfast.*

DER GASTHOF

The *Gasthof*, or guesthouse, is a typically Bavarian institution that originated as a place where stagecoach travelers could stop, eat, and rest for the night. Today these establishments are a combination of pub, restaurant, and small hotel. Typically, a Gasthof is a dark, half-timber house with a simple wood-paneled dining area. As a hotel, the Gasthof offers an incredible value. The mood at these spots is casual, friendly, and *gemütlich* (cozy). Expect to share a table with strangers: it's a great way to meet the locals.

$ HOTEL Fodor's Choice ★ **Hotel-Gasthof Drei Mohren.** All the simple, homey comforts you'd expect can be found in this 150-year-old Bavarian inn tucked into Partenkirchen village. **Pros:** perfect setting in a quaint corner of the town center. **Cons:** restaurant noise on the first floor; some double rooms are too small. [$] *Rooms from: €90* ✉ *Ludwigstr. 65* ☎ *08821/9130* 🌐 *www.dreimohren.de* 🛏 *29 rooms; 1 apartment* 🍴 *Breakfast.*

$$ RESORT **Hotel Waxenstein.** It's worth the 7-km (4½-mile) drive eastward to Grainau just to spend a night or a few at the delightful Waxenstein, where most rooms are a generous size and bathrooms are luxurious. **Pros:** great service; beautiful views of the Zugspitze from the north-facing rooms. **Cons:** only accessible by car; some rooms somewhat small. [$] *Rooms from: €130* ✉ *Höhenrainweg 3* ☎ *08821/9840* 🌐 *www.waxenstein.de* 🛏 *35 rooms, 6 suites* 🍴 *Breakfast.*

$$$ HOTEL **Reindl's Partenkirchner Hof.** Karl Reindl ranked among the world's top hoteliers, and his daughter Marianne Holzinger has maintained high standards since taking over this hotel. **Pros:** ample-size rooms; great views. **Cons:** front rooms are on a busy street. [$] *Rooms from: €200* ✉ *Bahnhofstr. 15* ☎ *08821/943–870* 🌐 *www.reindls.de* 🕒 *Closed Nov.* 🛏 *35 rooms, 17 suites* 🍴 *Breakfast.*

$$$$ HOTEL Fodor's Choice ★ **Staudacherhof Hotel.** A luxury spa hotel designed in Bavarian style, the Staudacherhof has wellness packages for those in search of relaxation. **Pros:** renovated, comfortable rooms; wooden touches reminiscent of surrounding area; extensive dining options. **Cons:** not ideal for kids. [$] *Rooms from: €270* ✉ *Höllentalstr. 48* ☎ *08821/9290* 🌐 *www.staudacherhof.de* 🛏 *41 rooms* 🍴 *Some meals.*

NIGHTLIFE AND PERFORMING ARTS

In season there's a busy après-ski scene. Many hotels have dance floors, and some have basement discos that pound away until the early hours. Bavarian folk dancing and zither music are regular nightlife features.

Bayernhalle. In summer there's entertainment, such as traditional Bavarian singing and dancing, every Saturday evening at the Bayernhalle. ✉ *Brauhausstr. 19* ☎ *08821/4877* 🌐 *www.vtv-garmisch.de/bayernhalle.*

Gasthof Fraundorfer. Wednesday through Monday the cozy tavern-restaurant Gasthof Fraundorfer hosts yodeling and folk dancing. ✉ *Ludwigstr. 24* ☎ *08821/9270* 🌐 *www.gasthof-fraundorfer.de.*

Spielbank Garmisch. The casino is open Sunday through Thursday 3 pm–2 am and Friday and Saturday 3 pm–3 am, with more than 150 slot machines and roulette, blackjack, and poker tables. ⊠ *Am Kurpark 10* ☎ *08821/95990* ⊕ *www.spielbanken-bayern.de.*

SPORTS AND THE OUTDOORS

HIKING AND CLIMBING

There are innumerable spectacular walks on 300 km (186 miles) of marked trails through the lower slopes' pinewoods and upland meadows. If you have the time and good walking shoes, try one of the two trails that lead to striking gorges (called *Klammen*). More expert hikers and climbers will find plenty of opportunities to explore, from the Herrgottschrofen and Gelbe Wände for all levels to the Jubiläumsgrat, which will test even the best climbers' limits. Before heading out, it's best to check with the Alpine Association for passable routes and avalanche conditions; they can also assist with finding free mountain huts for multiple-day hikes and climbs.

Deutscher Alpenverein (*German Alpine Association*). The country's leading climbing and mountaineering organization, based in Munich, has all the details on hiking and on staying in the mountain huts and keeps updates on mountain conditions for climbers as well. ⊠ *Von-Kahr-Str. 2–4, Munich* ☎ *089/140–030* ⊕ *www.alpenverein.de.*

Höllentalklamm. This route starts in the town and ends at the Zugspitze mountaintop (you'll want to turn back before reaching the summit unless you have mountaineering experience). You can park in the villages of Hammersbach or Grainau to start your tour. ⊠ *Olympia Str. 27* ⊹ *Zugspitze Mountain railroad terminal* ☎ *08821/8895* ⊕ *www. hoellentalklamm-info.de* ⊗ *May–Oct. (depending on weather).*

Partnachklamm. The Partnachklamm route is quite challenging, and takes you through a spectacular, tunneled water gorge (entrance fee), past a pretty little mountain lake, and far up the Zugspitze; to do all of it, you'll have to stay overnight in one of the huts along the way. Ride part of the way up in the **Eckbauer cable car**, which sets out from the Skistadion off Mittenwalderstrasse. The older, more scenic **Graseckbahn** takes you right over the dramatic gorges. Tickets for the country's oldest cable car cost €6.50 one way (or less, depending on how far you want to ride and time of year). There's a handy inn at the top, where you can gather strength for the hour-long walk back down to the Graseckbahn station.

Horse-drawn carriages (€16 for up to four passengers, €4 per additional person) also cover the first section of the route in summer; in winter you can skim along it in a sleigh. The carriages wait near the Skistadion. Or you can call the local coaching society, the **Lohnkutschevereinigung** (0172/860–4105; www.kutschenfahrten-garmisch.de), for information ⊠ *Garmisch-Partenkirchen* ⊕ *www.eckbauerbahn.de.*

Zugspitze Mountain railroad terminal. From the Zugspitze terminal, you can access a number of hiking trails or take one of the gondolas up the mountain and hike or ski your way down. Besides the Zuspitze itself, one of the most popular routes includes Wank, which at a height of 5,740 feet is a day-long challenge. ⊠ *Olympiastr. 27* ⊕ *www.zugspitze.de.*

SKIING AND SNOWBOARDING

Garmisch-Partenkirchen was the site of the 1936 Winter Olympics, and remains Germany's premier winter-sports resort. The upper slopes of the Zugspitze and surrounding mountains challenge the best ski buffs and snowboarders, and there are also plenty of runs for intermediate skiers and families. The area is divided into two basic regions. The **Riffelriss** with the **Zugspitzplatt** is Germany's highest skiing area, with snow pretty much guaranteed from December to May. Access is via the **Zugspitzbahn** funicular. Cost for a day pass is €52; a two-peak pass combining it with the Garmisch-Classic is €62. A three-day pass costs €88. The **Garmisch-Classic** has numerous lifts in the **Alpspitz, Kreuzeck,** and **Hausberg** regions. Day passes cost €26. The town has a number of ski schools and tour organizers, and information about all of them is available from the local tourist office. The Deutsche Alpenverein is another good contact for mountain conditions.

Alpine Auskunftstelle. The best local resource for information for all your snow sports needs is the Alpine office at the Garmisch tourist information office. ⊠ *Richard-Strauss-Pl. 2, Garmisch* ☎ *08821/180–700* ⊕ *www.gapa.de* ⊙ *Mid-Oct.–mid-Dec. and mid-Mar.–mid-May, weekdays 9–5, Sat. 9–3; mid-Dec.–mid-Mar. and mid-May–mid Oct., Mon.– Sat. 9–6, Sun. 10–noon.*

Erste Skilanglaufschule Garmisch-Partenkirchen. Cross-country skiers should check on conditions or book a course here. ⊠ *Olympia-Skistadion, Osteingang, Erster Stock* ☎ *08821/1516* ⊕ *www.ski-langlauf-schule.de.*

ETTAL

16 km (10 miles) north of Garmisch-Partenkirchen, 85 km (53 miles) south of Munich.

The village of Ettal is presided over by the massive bulk of Kloster Ettal, a great monastery and centuries-old distillery.

GETTING HERE AND AROUND

Ettal is easily reached by bus and car from Garmisch and Oberammergau. Consider staying in Oberammergau and renting a bike. The 4-km (2½-mile) ride along the river is clearly marked, relatively easy, and a great way to meet locals.

ESSENTIALS

Visitor Information Tourist Information Ettal. ⊠ *Ammergauer Str. 8* ☎ *08822/923–634* ⊕ *www.ammergauer-alpen.de/ettal.*

EXPLORING

Fodor's Choice **Kloster Ettal.** The great monastery was founded in 1330 by Holy Roman
★ Emperor Ludwig the Bavarian for a group of knights and a community of Benedictine monks. This is the largest Benedictine monastery in Germany; approximately 55 monks live here. The abbey was replaced with new buildings in the 18th century and now serves as a school. The original 10-sided church was brilliantly redecorated in 1744–53, becoming one of the foremost examples of Bavarian rococo. The church's chief treasure is its enormous dome fresco (83 feet wide), painted by Jacob Zeiller circa 1751–52. The mass of swirling clouds

The dome fresco at Kloster Ettal (Ettal Monastery) was painted by Jacob Zeiller and is an excellent example of Bavarian rococo.

and the pink-and-blue vision of heaven are typical of the rococo fondness for elaborate ceiling painting.

Today, the Kloster owns most of the surrounding land and directly operates the Hotel Ludwig der Bayer, the Kloster-Laden, and the Klostermarkt. All of the Kloster's activities, from beer production to running the hotel serve one singular purpose: to fund the famous college-prep and boarding schools which are tuition-free.

Ettaler liqueurs, made from a centuries-old recipe, are still distilled at the monastery. The monks make seven different liqueurs, some with more than 70 mountain herbs. Originally the liqueurs were made as medicines, and they have legendary health-giving properties. The ad tells it best: "Two monks know how it's made, 2 million Germans know how it tastes." You can visit the distillery right next to the church and buy bottles of the libation from the gift shop and bookstore. The honey-saffron schnapps is the best.

It's possible to tour the distillery and the brewery. For a distillery tour, call in advance; brewery tours are on Tuesday and Thursday at 1:30, and you need to register before 11 on the day of the tour. ⊠ *Kaiser-Ludwig-Pl. 1* ☎ *08822/746–228 distillery, 08822/746–450 brewery* ⊕ *www.abtei.kloster-ettal.de* ✉ *Free; distillery and brewery tour €6* ☉ *Daily 8–6 (to 7:45 in summer).*

Schaukäserei. Besides its beer and spirits, Ettal has made another local industry into an attraction, namely cheese, yogurt, butter, and other milk derivatives. You can see them in the making at this public cheese-making plant. There is even a little buffet for a cheesy break. Tours are offered daily at 11 as long as there's a minimum five people to take part.

✉ *Mandlweg 1* ☎ *08822/923–926* 🌐 *www.milch-und-kas.de* 🎟 *€1.50 for tour, or €3.50 with interpreter* ⏰ *June–Oct., daily 10–5; Nov.–May, Tues.–Sun. 10–5.*

WHERE TO EAT AND STAY

$ GERMAN 🍴 **Edelweiss.** This friendly café and restaurant next to the monastery is an ideal spot for a light lunch or coffee and homemade cakes. [$] *Average main: €9* ✉ *Kaiser-Ludwig-Pl. 3* ☎ *08822/92920* 🌐 *www.restaurant-edelweiss-ettal.de* 💳 *No credit cards.*

$$ RESORT FAMILY 🏨 **Hotel Ludwig der Bayer.** Backed by mountains, this fine old hotel is run by the Benedictine order, but there's little monastic about it, except for the exquisite religious carvings and motifs that adorn the walls. **Pros:** good value; close to Kloster; indoor pool and spa. **Cons:** can fill up quickly with tour groups. [$] *Rooms from: €104* ✉ *Kaiser-Ludwig-Pl. 10* ☎ *08822/9150* 🌐 *www.ludwig-der-bayer.de* 🛏 *70 rooms, 30 apartments* 🍽 *Breakfast.*

SCHLOSS LINDERHOF

Fodor's Choice ★ **Schloss Linderhof.** The only one of King Ludwig's three castles to have reached completion before his death, this gilded hunting lodge lies secluded in the mountains, surrounded by well-manicured gardens. Though less visited than his other castles, Schloss Linderhof tells a fantastic story about the life of a king famous for his eccentricities. ⇨ *See "The Fairy-Tale Castles of King Ludwig II" in Chapter 4.*

OBERAMMERGAU

20 km (12 miles) northwest of Garmisch-Partenkirchen, 4 km (2½ miles) northwest of Ettal, 90 km (56 miles) south of Munich.

Its location alone, in an Alpine valley beneath a sentinel-like peak, makes this small town a major attraction. Its main streets are lined with painted houses (such as the 1784 Pilatushaus on Ludwig-Thoma-Strasse), and in summer the village bursts with color. Many of these lovely houses are occupied by families whose men are highly skilled in the art of wood carving, a craft that has flourished here since the early 12th century. Oberammergau is completely overrun by tourists during the day, but at night you'll feel like you have a charming Bavarian village all to yourself.

GETTING HERE AND AROUND

The B-23 links Oberammergau to Garmsich-Partenkirchen (allow a half hour for the drive) and to the A-23 to Munich. Frequent bus services connect to Garmisch, Ettal, the Wieskirche, and Füssen. No long-distance trains serve Oberammergau, but a short ride on the Regional-Bahn to Murnau will connect you to the long-distance train network.

ESSENTIALS

Visitor Information Tourist Information Oberammergau. ✉ *Eugen-Papst-Str. 9a* ☎ *08822/922–740* 🌐 *www.oberammergau.de.*

EXPLORING

Oberammergau Museum. Here you'll find historic examples of the wood craftsman's art and an outstanding collection of Christmas crèches, which date from the mid-18th century. Numerous exhibits also document the wax and wax-embossing art, which also flourishes in Oberammergau. A notable piece is that of a German soldier carved by Georg Korntheuer on the Eastern Front in 1943: the artist was killed in 1944. ⊠ *Dorfstr. 8* ☎ *08822/94136* ⊕ *www.oberammergaumuseum.de* 🎟 *€6, includes Pilatushaus and Passionsspielhaus* ⊙ *Mar. 28–Nov. 8 and Nov. 28–Jan. 6, Tues.–Sun. 10–5.*

Oberammergau Passionsspielhaus. This immense theater is where the Passion Play is performed. Visitors are given a glimpse of the costumes, the sceneries, the stage, and even the auditorium. ⊠ *Passionswiese, Theaterstr. 16* ☎ *08822/94136* ⊕ *www.oberammergaumuseum.de; www.passionstheater.de* 🎟 *€6, includes Oberammergau Museum and Pilatushaus* ⊙ *Mar. 23–Nov. 3 and Dec. 23–Jan. 6, Tues.–Sun. 10–5; Nov. 30–Dec. 23, Tues.–Sun. 10–1.*

Pilatushaus. You'll find many wood carvers at work in town, and shop windows are crammed with their creations. Here, a workshop is open to the public, and working potters and painters can also be seen. Pilatushaus was completed in 1775, and the frescoes—considered among the most beautiful in town—were done by Franz Seraph Zwinck, one of the greatest Lüftlmalerei painters. The house is named for the fresco over the front door depicting Christ before Pilate. A collection of reverse glass paintings depicting religious and secular scenes has been moved here from the Heimatmuseum. Contact the tourist office to sign up for a weeklong course in wood carving (classes are in German), which costs from about €450 to €600, depending on whether you stay in a Gasthof or a hotel. ⊠ *Ludwig-Thoma-Str. 10* ☎ *08822/949–511 tourist office* ⊕ *www.oberammergaumuseum.de* 🎟 *€6, includes Oberammergau Museum and Passionsspielhaus* ⊙ *Mid-May–Oct., Tues.–Sat. 1–5; weekend before Easter 11–6.*

St. Peter and St. Paul Church. The 18th-century church is regarded as the finest work of rococo architect Josef Schmutzer, and it has striking frescoes by Matthäus Günther and Franz Seraph Zwinck (in the organ loft). Schmutzer's son, Franz Xaver Schmutzer, also did a lot of the stuccowork. ⊠ *Pfarrpl. 1* ⊙ *Daily 8–dusk.*

LÜFTLMALEREI

The *Lüftlmalerei* style of fresco painting is unique to Bavaria and the Tirol where the opulently painted facades were used as a display of wealth. Commonly known as trompe l'œil, the detailed frescoes give the illusion of three dimensions. They are painted directly onto fresh plaster, which preserves the painting for centuries.

The term "Lüftlmalerei" originated in Oberammergau after the famous fresco artist Franz Seraph Zwinck painted a fresco on his house, the Zum Lüftl. Zwinck became the Lüftlmaler, or the painter of the Lüftl.

WHERE TO EAT

$ ✕ **Gasthaus zum Stern.** This is a traditional place (around 500 years old),
GERMAN with coffered ceilings, thick walls, smiling waitresses in dirndls, and an
old *Kachelofen* (enclosed, tiled, wood-burning stove) that heats the dining room beyond endurance on cold winter days. The food is hearty,
traditional Bavarian. For a quieter dinner or lunch, reserve a space in
the Bäckerstube (Baker's Parlor). $ *Average main: €13* ✉ *Dorfstr. 33*
☎ *08822/867* ⊕ *www.gasthaus-stern-oberammergau.de* ☉ *Closed Wed.*

$ ✕ **Hotel Alte Post.** You can enjoy carefully prepared local cuisine, includ-
GERMAN ing several venison and boar dishes, at the original pine tables in this
350-year-old inn. There's a special children's menu, and, in summer,
meals are also served in the beer garden. The front terrace of this
delightful old building is a great place to watch traffic, both pedestrian
and automotive. $ *Average main: €12* ✉ *Dorfstr. 19* ☎ *08822/9100*
⊕ *www.altepost.com* ☉ *Closed Nov.–mid-Dec. No dinner.*

$ ✕ **Mundart.** Small and unremarkable from the outside, this is one of
GERMAN the best restaurants in Oberammergau for Bavarian dishes, like steak
or trout sourced directly from the region, served with a daily menu
reflecting the seasonal specialties. $ *Average main: €14* ✉ *Bahnhofstr.*
12 ☎ *08822/949–7565* ⊕ *www.restaurant-mundart.de* ☉ *Closed Mon.*
and Tues. ⊟ *No credit cards.*

WHERE TO STAY

$$ ⊞ **Gasthof zur Rose.** Everything is pretty rustic in this spacious remod-
B&B/INN eled barn, but the welcome and hospitality are genuine and gracious,
even by Bavarian standards. **Pros:** quiet; affordable; right off the city
center; friendly service. **Cons:** rustic and worn; few amenities. $ *Rooms*
from: €100 ✉ *Dedlerstr. 9* ☎ *08822/4706* ⊕ *www.rose-oberammergau.*
de ⊟ *No credit cards* ⇄ *19 rooms* ⏸️ *Breakfast.*

$$$$ ⊞ **Hotel Maximilian.** Modernized and luxurious, this spa retreat has won
HOTEL awards for both its hospitality and its gourmet restaurant, Ammergauer
Maxbräu. **Pros:** nice views from front rooms; great in-house restau-
rant. **Cons:** pricey for the area. $ *Rooms from: €229* ✉ *Ettalerstr. 5*
☎ *08822/948–740* ⊕ *www.maximilian-oberammergau.de* ⇄ *17 rooms,*
2 suites ⏸️ *Breakfast.*

$ ⊞ **Hotel Turmwirt.** Rich wood paneling reaches from floor to ceiling in
HOTEL this transformed 18th-century inn, set in the shadow of Oberammer-
FAMILY gau's mountain, the Kofel. **Pros:** great for families. **Cons:** service can
be brusque; nearby church bells ring every 15 minutes. $ *Rooms from:*
€99 ✉ *Ettalerstr. 2* ☎ *08822/92600* ⊕ *www.turmwirt.de* ☉ *Closed 1 wk*
in early Dec. ⇄ *22 rooms, 1 suite* ⏸️ *Breakfast.*

PERFORMING ARTS

Oberammergau Passionsspielhaus. Though the Passion Play theater was
traditionally not used for anything other than the Passion Play (next
performance: 2020), Oberammergauers decided that using it for opera
or other theatrical events during the 10-year pause between the religious
performances might be a good idea. The first performances of Verdi's
"Nabucco" and Mozart's "Magic Flute" in 2002 established a new tra-
dition. Other passion plays are also performed here. Ticket prices range

between €19 and €50. ✉ *Theaterstr. 16* ☎ *008822/045–8888* ⊕ *www. passionstheater.de.*

Passion Play. Oberammergau is best known for its Passion Play, first presented in 1634 as an offering of thanks after the Black Death stopped just short of the village. In faithful accordance with a solemn vow, it will next be performed in the year 2020, as it has every 10 years since 1680. Its 16 acts, which take 5½ hours, depict the final days of Christ, from the Last Supper through the Crucifixion and Resurrection. It's presented daily on a partly open-air stage against a mountain backdrop from late May to late September. The entire village is swept up in the production, with some 1,500 residents directly involved in its preparation and presentation. Men grow beards in the hope of capturing a key role; young women have been known to put off their weddings—the role of Mary went only to unmarried girls until 1990, when, amid much local controversy, a 31-year-old mother of two was given the part. ✉ *Passionstheater, Theaterstr. 16* ⊕ *www.passionstheater.de.*

SPORTS AND THE OUTDOORS
BICYCLING
It's easy to bike to Schloss Linderhof (14 km [9 miles]) and to Ettal (4 km [2½ miles]) on the scenic paths along the river, where there are several good places to go swimming and have a picnic. The trail to Ettal branches off in the direction of Linderhof (marked as Graswang) where it becomes part of an old forestry road. Take the branch of the Ettal path that goes via the Ettaler-Mühle (Ettal Mill); it's quieter, the river is filled with trout, and the people you meet along the way give a friendly *Grüss Gott!* (Greet God!). The path opens up at a local-heavy restaurant with fantastic views of the Kloster.

Sport-Zentrale Papistock. You can rent bikes here for €12 per day or e-bikes for €22. They are located across the street from the train station, directly at the trailhead to Ettal and Linderhof. ✉ *Bahnhofstr. 6a* ☎ *08822/4178* ⊕ *www.sportzentrale-papistock.de* ⊙ *Closed Sun.*

MITTENWALD

20 km (12 miles) southeast of Garmisch-Partenkirchen, 105 km (65 miles) south of Munich.

Many regard Mittenwald as the most beautiful town in the Bavarian Alps. It has somehow avoided the architectural sins found in other Alpine villages by maintaining a balance between conservation and the needs of tourism. Its medieval prosperity is reflected on its main street, **Obermarkt,** which has splendid houses with ornately carved gables and brilliantly painted facades. Goethe called it "a picture book come alive," and it still is. The town has even re-created the stream that once flowed through the market square. In the Middle Ages, Mittenwald was the staging point for goods shipped from the wealthy city-state of Venice by way of the Brenner Pass and Innsbruck. From Mittenwald, goods were transferred to rafts, which carried them down the Isar River to Munich. By the mid-17th century the international trade routes shifted to a different pass, and the fortunes of Mittenwald evaporated.

In 1684 Matthias Klotz, a farmer's son turned master violin maker, returned from a 20-year stay in Cremona, Italy. There, along with Antonio Stradivari, he studied under Nicolo Amati, who developed the modern violin. Klotz taught the art of violin making to his brothers and friends and before long, half the men in the village were crafting the instruments, using woods from neighboring forests. Mittenwald became known as the Village of a Thousand Violins and the locally crafted instruments are still treasured around the world. In the right weather—sunny, dry—you may even catch the odd sight of laundry lines hung with new violins out to receive their natural dark hue. The violin has made Mittenwald a small cultural oasis in the middle of the Alps. Not only is there an annual violin- (and viola-, cello-, and bow-) building contest each year in June, with concerts and lectures, but also an organ festival in the church of St. Peter and St. Paul held from the end of July to the end of September. The town also has a violin-making school.

GETTING HERE AND AROUND

The B-11 connects Mittenwald with Garmisch. Mittenwald is the last stop on the Munich–Garmisch train line.

ESSENTIALS

Visitor Information Tourist Information Mittenwald. ⊠ *Dammkarstr. 3* ☎ *08823/33981* ⊕ *www.alpenwelt-karwendel.de/en/mittenwald.*

EXPLORING

The Geigenbaumuseum. The violin-building and local museum describes in fascinating detail the history of violin making in Mittenwald. Ask the museum curator to direct you to the nearest of several violin makers—they'll be happy to demonstrate the skills handed down to them. ⊠ *Ballenhausg. 3* ☎ *08823/2511* ⊕ *www.geigenbaumuseum-mittenwald.de* 🎫 *€4.50* ☉ *Early Feb.–mid-Mar., mid-May–mid-Oct., and early Dec.–early Jan., Tues.–Sun. 10–5; early Jan.–end Jan., mid-Mar.–mid-May, and mid-Oct.–early Nov., Tues.–Sun. 11–4.*

St. Peter and St. Paul Church. On the back of the altar in this 18th-century church (as in Oberammergau, built by Josef Schmutzer and decorated by Matthäus Günther), you'll find Matthias Klotz's name, carved there by the violin maker himself. Note that on some of the ceiling frescoes, the angels are playing violins, violas da gamba, and lutes. In front of the church, Klotz is memorialized as an artist at work in vivid bronze sculpted by Ferdinand von Miller (1813–79), creator of the mighty Bavaria Monument in Munich. The church, with its elaborate and joyful stuccowork coiling and curling its way around the interior, is one of the most important rococo structures in Bavaria. The Gothic choir loft was added in the 18th century. The bold frescoes on its exterior are characteristic of Lüftlmalerei, where images, usually religious motifs, were painted on the wet stucco exteriors of houses and churches. On nearby streets you can see other fine examples on the facades of three famous houses: the Goethehaus, the Pilgerhaus, and the Pichlerhaus. Among the artists working here was the great Franz Seraph Zwinck. ⊠ *Ballenhausg.* ⊕ *www.st-peter-und-paul-mittenwald.de.*

WHERE TO EAT

$ GERMAN FAMILY 🍴 **Gasthof Stern.** This white house with brilliant blue shutters is right in the middle of Mittenwald. The painted furniture is not antique, but is reminiscent of old peasant Bavaria. Locals meet in the dining room for loud conversation and meat-heavy dinners; the beer garden with small playground is a pleasant, familial place to while away the hours with a *Bauernschmaus,* a plate of sausage with sauerkraut and homemade liver dumplings. As a Gasthof, the restaurant also has five rooms for overnight stays, with price deals for multiple nights. [$] *Average main: €12* ✉ *Fritz-Plössl-Pl. 2* ☎ *08823/8358* 🌐 *www.stern-mittenwald.de* 🕘 *Closed Mon.* 💳 *No credit cards.*

WHERE TO STAY

$ HOTEL 🏨 **Alpenrose.** Once part of a monastery and later given one of the town's most beautiful painted baroque facades, the Alpenrose is one of the area's most handsome hotels. **Pros:** great German-style interiors; friendly staff. **Cons:** some rooms are cramped; accommodations can get warm in summer. [$] *Rooms from: €76* ✉ *Obermarkt 1* ☎ *08823/92700* 🌐 *www.hotel-alpenrose-mittenwald.de* 🛏 *16 rooms, 2 apartments* 🍽 *Breakfast.*

$ HOTEL 🏨 **Bichlerhof.** Carved oak furniture gives the rooms of this Alpine-style hotel a solid German feel. **Pros:** amazing views; well-kept spa area. **Cons:** disorganized reservation system. [$] *Rooms from: €94* ✉ *Adolf-Baader-Str. 5* ☎ *08823/9190* 🌐 *www.bichlerhof-mittenwald.de* 🛏 *30 rooms* 🍽 *Breakfast.*

$$$ HOTEL 🏨 **Kranzbach.** This "English Castle," on 13 hectares (32 acres) surrounded by the Karwendel mountains, was commissioned in 1913 by an English aristocrat, Mary Portman. **Pros:** spa amenities; beautiful, quiet surroundings. **Cons:** rooms in the garden wing are more contemporary and lose the old-fashioned touch; no children under 10 allowed. [$] *Rooms from: €197* ✉ *Kranzbach 1* ✥ *Krün* ☎ *8823/928–000* 🌐 *www.daskranzbach.de* 🛏 *129 rooms* 🍽 *Some meals.*

$$ HOTEL 🏨 **Post.** The hotel retains much of its historic charm—stagecoaches carrying travelers and mail across the Alps stopped here as far back as the 17th century—though the elegant rooms come in various styles, from modern to art nouveau to Bavarian rustic. **Pros:** art nouveau rooms in the back. **Cons:** no elevator; street noise in the evening. [$] *Rooms from: €115* ✉ *Obermarkt 9* ☎ *08823/938–2333* 🌐 *www.posthotel-mittenwald.de* 🛏 *74 rooms, 7 suites* 🍽 *Breakfast.*

SPORTS AND THE OUTDOORS

Mittenwald lies literally in the shadow of the mighty **Karwendel** Alpine range, which rises to a height of nearly 8,000 feet. There are a number of small lakes in the hills surrounding Mittenwald. You can either walk to the closer ones or rent bikes and venture farther afield. The information center across the street from the train station has maps, and they can help you select a route.

The **Dammkar** run is nearly 8 km (5 miles) long and offers some of the best freeride skiing, telemarking, and snowboarding in the German Alps.

Erste Skischule Mittenwald. Skiers—cross-country and downhill—and snowboarders can find all they need, including equipment and instruction, at the Erste Skischule Mittenwald. ⊠ *Bahnhofspl. 14* ☎ *08823/3582* ⊕ *www.skischule-mittenwald.de.*

Karwendelbahn cable car. Hikers and skiers are carried to an altitude of 7,180 feet for the beginning of numerous trails down, or farther up into the Karwendel range. ⊠ *Alpenkorpsstr. 1* ☎ *08823/937-6760* ⊕ *www. karwendelbahn.de* 🎫 *€16.50 one way, €26.50 round-trip* ⊘ *May–Oct., daily 8:30–5; Nov.–Apr., daily 9–3:45.*

SHOPPING

It's not the kind of gift every visitor wants to take home, but if you'd like a violin, a cello, or even a double bass, the Alpine resort of Mittenwald can oblige. There are more than 30 craftspeople whose work is coveted by musicians throughout the world.

Anton Maller. If you're buying or even just feeling curious, call on Anton Maller. He's been making violins and other stringed instruments for more than 25 years. ⊠ *Obermarkt 2* ☎ *08823/5865* ⊕ *www.violin-maller.de.*

Gabriele Schneider's SchokoLaden. Find out where all the milk from the local cows goes with a visit to Gabriele Schneider's SchokoLaden, an artisan chocolate shop. ⊠ *Obermarkt 42* ☎ *08823/938-939* ⊕ *www. schokoladen-mittenwald.de.*

Trachten Werner. For traditional Bavarian costumes—dirndls, embroidered shirts and blouses, and lederhosen—try Trachten Werner. ⊠ *Obermarkt 39* ☎ *08823/8282* ⊕ *www.trachten-werner.de* ⊘ *Closed Sun.*

UPPER BAVARIAN LAKE DISTRICT

With its rolling hills and serene lakes in the shadow of the Alpine peaks, this region is a natural paradise and a good transition to the Alps. The main attraction is, without a doubt, the Chiemsee with the amazing palace on the Herreninsel, the biggest of the islands on the lake. The area is dotted with clear blue lakes and, although tourism is fairly well established, you may feel that you have much of the area all to yourself.

BAD TÖLZ

14 km (8 miles) north of Sylvenstein Lake, 48 km (30 miles) south of Munich.

Bad Tölz's new town, dating from the mid-19th century, sprang up with the discovery of iodine-laden springs, which allowed the locals to call their town *Bad* (bath or spa) Tölz. You can take the waters, either by drinking a cupful from the local springs or going all the way with a full course of health treatments at a specially equipped hotel. ■ TIP→ If you can, visit on a Friday morning, when a farmers' market stretches along the main street to the Isar River and on the Jungmayr-Fritzplatz.

This town clings to its ancient customs more tightly than any other Bavarian community. It is not uncommon to see people wearing traditional clothing as their daily dress. If you're in Bad Tölz on November

6, you'll witness one of the most colorful traditions of the Bavarian Alpine area: the Leonhardiritt equestrian procession, which marks the anniversary of the death in 559 of St. Leonhard of Noblac, the patron saint of animals, specifically horses. The procession ends north of town at an 18th-century chapel on the Kalvarienberg, above the Isar River.

GETTING HERE AND AROUND

Bad Tölz is on the B-472, which connects to the A-8 to Munich, and there are hourly trains from Munich. Once you're in Bad Tölz, it is easily walkable and has frequent city-bus services.

ESSENTIALS

Visitor Information **Bad Tölz Tourist-Information.** ✉ *Max-Höfler-Pl. 1* ☎ *08041/78670* 🌐 *www.bad-toelz.de.*

EXPLORING

FAMILY **The Alpamare.** Bad Tölz's very attractive spa complex pumps spa water into its pools, one of which is disguised as a South Sea beach complete with surf. Its five waterslides include a 1,082-foot-long adventure run. Another—the Alpa-Canyon—has 90-degree drops, and only the hardiest swimmers are advised to try it. A nightmarish dark tunnel is aptly named the Thriller. There is a complex price structure, depending on time spent in the spa and other wellness activities for the various individual attractions, or combo tickets for more than one. ✉ *Ludwigstr. 14* ☎ *08041/509–999* 🌐 *www.alpamare.de* 🎫 *4-hr ticket €29; €27 9:30–11 am; €23 after 5 pm* 🕒 *Daily 9:30 am–10 pm.*

The Stadtmuseum. Housed in the Altes Rathaus (Old Town Hall), the museum has a newly renovated permanent exhibition containing many fine examples of *Bauernmöbel* (farmhouse furniture), as well as fascinating information on the history of the town and its environs. ✉ *Marktstr. 48* ☎ *08041/793–5156* 🎫 *€4* 🕒 *Tues.–Sun. 10–5.*

WHERE TO STAY

$ HOTEL FAMILY 🏨 **Hotel Kolbergarten.** Near the Old Town and surrounded by a quiet garden with old trees, this hotel offers comfortable rooms, each carefully done in a particular style such as baroque or Biedermeier. **Pros:** large clean rooms; staff is great with children. **Cons:** often fully booked. [$] *Rooms from: €98* ✉ *Fröhlichg. 5* ☎ *08041/78920* 🌐 *www.hotel-kolbergarten.de* 🛏 *12 rooms, 2 suites* 🍴 *Breakfast.*

NIGHTLIFE AND PERFORMING ARTS

TanzBar KULT. With a rather wide range of themes, this bar features live music in the terrific setting of an old brewery, with barrel vaults and painted brick walls. ✉ *Wachterstr. 19* ☎ *08041/799–3699* 🌐 *www.kult-toelz.de.*

Tölzer Knabenchor Boys' Choir (*Knabenchor*). Bad Tölz is world renowned for its outstanding boys' choir. When not on tour, the choir gives regular concerts in the Kurhaus. Check with the Bad Tölz tourist information office for dates and ticket details. ✉ *Kurhaus Bad Tölz, Ludwigstr. 25* 🌐 *www.bad-toelz.de.*

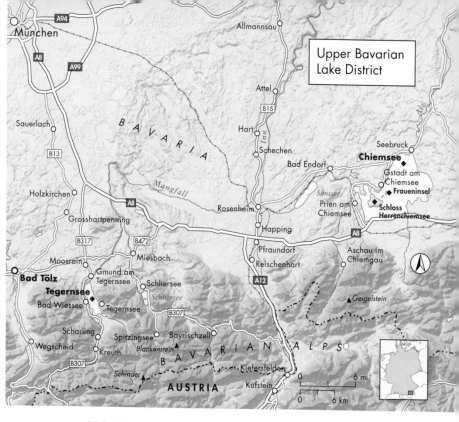

SPORTS AND THE OUTDOORS

FAMILY **Blomberg.** Bad Tölz's local mountain, the Blomberg, 3 km (2 miles) west of town, has moderately difficult ski runs and can also be tackled on a toboggan in winter and on a luge in summer. The winter run of 5 km (3 miles) is the longest in Bavaria. The concrete summer luge run snakes 3,938 feet down the mountain and is great fun; you'll want the three-ride ticket. A ski-lift ride to the start of the run and toboggan or roller luge are included in the price. ⊠ *Bad Tölz* ☎ *08041/3726* ⊕ *www. blombergbahn.de* 🎫 *€17 all-day ticket (winter); summer luge €14 for three rides* ⊙ *Check website for ski times; chairlift operates from around Nov., daily 9–4 (weather permitting). Toboggan run: summer, daily 11–6; chairlift operates 9–6.*

SHOPPING

Bad Tölz is famous for its painted farmhouse furniture (Bauernmöbel), particularly cupboards and chests, and several local shops specialize in hand-carved pine pieces. They will usually handle export formalities. Ask at your hotel or tourist-information center for a recommendation on where to shop.

Antiquitäten Schwarzwälder. For traditional Bauernmöbel furniture, try Antiquitäten Schwarzwälder. ⊠ *Badstr. 2* ☎ *08041/41222* ⊕ *www. antiquitaeten-schwarzwaelder.de* ⊙ *Weekdays 9–1 and 2–6; Sat. 10–4.*

TEGERNSEE

16 km (10 miles) east of Bad Tölz, 50 km (31 miles) south of Munich.

The beautiful shores of the Tegernsee are among the most expensive property in all of Germany. The interest in the region shown by King Maximilian I of Bavaria at the beginning of the 19th century attracted VIPs and artists, which led to a boom that has never really faded. Most accommodations and restaurants, however, still have reasonable prices, and there are plenty of activities for everyone. Tegernsee's wooded shores, rising gently to scalable mountain peaks of no more than 6,300 feet, invite hikers, walkers, and picnicking families. The lake itself draws swimmers and yachters. In fall the russet-clad trees provide a colorful contrast to the snowcapped mountains. Beer lovers are drawn to Tegernsee by one of the best breweries in Europe. There are three main towns on the lake: Tegernsee, Rottach-Egern, and Bad Wiessee. Though not directly on the lakeshore, the town of Gmund, at the lake's northern end, also has a number of attractions and is easily accessible by train.

GETTING HERE AND AROUND

The best way to reach all three towns is to take the BOB train from Munich to Tegernsee (hourly) and then take a boat ride on one of the eight boats that circle the lake year-round. The boats dock near the Tegernsee train station and make frequent stops, including the Benedictine monastery in Tegernsee, Rottach-Egern, Gmund, and Bad Wiessee. The monastery is a pleasant half-mile walk from the train station. Buses connect Tegernsee to Bad Tölz.

ESSENTIALS

Visitor Information Rottach-Egern/Tegernsee Tourist Information.
✉ *Hauptstr. 2* ☎ *08022/927–380* ⊕ *www.tegernsee.com.*

EXPLORING

Benedictine monastery. On the eastern shore of the lake, the laid-back town of Tegernsee is home to this large Benedictine monastery. Founded in the 8th century, this was one of the most productive cultural centers in southern Germany; one of the *Minnesänger* (wandering lyrical poets), Walther von der Vogelweide (1170–1230), was a welcome guest. Not so welcome were Magyar invaders, who laid waste to the monastery in the 10th century. During the Middle Ages the monastery made a lively business producing stained-glass windows, thanks to a nearby quartz quarry, and in the 16th century it became a major center of printing. The late-Gothic **church** was refurbished in Italian baroque style in the 18th century and was where heirs to the Wittelsbach dynasty were married. The frescoes inside are by Hans Georg Asam, whose work also graces the Benediktbeuren monastery in Bavaria. Secularization sealed the monastery's fate at the beginning of the 19th century: almost half the buildings were torn down. Maximilian I bought the surviving ones and had Leo von Klenze redo them for use as a summer retreat, which is still used by members of the Wittelsbach family and therefore closed to the public.

The brine pool at Alpamare spa has green water due to the mineral iodine; it is meant to stimulate circulation.

Today there is a high school on the property, and students write their exams beneath inspiring baroque frescoes in what was the monastery. The church and the **Herzogliches Bräustüberl,** a brewery and beer hall, are the only parts of the monastery open to the public. Try a *Mass* (a liter-size mug) of their legendary Tergernseer Helles or Spezial beer. ✉ *Schlosspl.*

Grosses Paraplui Hiking Path. Maximilian showed off this corner of his kingdom to Czar Alexander I of Russia and Emperor Franz I of Austria during their journey to the Congress of Verona in October 1821. You can follow their steps on a well-marked 2½-km (1½-mile) path, starting just opposite Schlossplatz in Tegernsee, through the woods to the Grosses Paraplui, one of the loveliest lookout points in Bavaria. A plaque marks the spot where they admired the open expanse of the Tegernsee and the mountains beyond. ✉ *Schlosspl.*

WHERE TO EAT

$$ GERMAN 🍴 **Boutique Hotel Relais-Chalet Wilhelmy.** Although everything is modern, this inn in Bad Wiessee takes you back to a less frantic era. Classical music accompanies unpretentious yet tasty meals. Try the fish specialties or the light guinea fowl with herb rice and enjoy tea and cake in the little garden. [$] *Average main: €16* ✉ *Freihausstr. 15, Bad Wiessee* ☎ *08022/98680* 🌐 *www.relais-chalet.com.*

$$$$ EUROPEAN 🍴 **Freihaus Brenner.** Proprietor Josef Brenner has brought a taste of nouvelle cuisine to the Tegernsee. His attractive restaurant commands fine views from high above Bad Wiessee. Try any of his suggested dishes, ranging from roast pheasant in wine sauce to fresh lake fish. There are flexible portion sizes for smaller appetites. [$] *Average main: €30*

✉ *Freihaus 4, Bad Wiessee* ☎ *08022/86560* ⊕ *www.freihaus-brenner. de* ⊘ *Closed Tues.*

$$ ✕ **Gut Kaltenbrunn.** A series of farm buildings dating back to the 19th
GERMAN century on the lake's northern shore have been renovated and expanded
FAMILY into a self-sustaining restaurant with beer garden and several dining halls. With a focus on regional delicacies created from local—preferably homegrown—ingredients, the menu here changes with the seasons but includes Tegernsee trout, greens grown in the front garden, and steaks from their own cattle. A large terrace and walls of windows provide some of the best views of the lake in town and a kid-friendly beer garden with playground keeps young visitors happy until dusk. $ *Average main: €22* ✉ *Kaltenbrunn 1, Gmund* ☎ *08022/187–0700* ⊕ *www. kaefer-gut-kaltenbrunn.de.*

$ ✕ **Herzogliches Bräustüberl.** Once part of Tegernsee's Benedictine monas-
GERMAN tery, then a royal retreat, the Bräustüberl is now an immensely popular beer hall and brewery with tasty Bavarian snacks (sausages, pretzels, all the way up to steak tartare), all for under €10. In summer, quaff your beer beneath the huge chestnut trees and admire the delightful view of the lake and mountains. $ *Average main: €10* ✉ *Schlosspl. 1* ☎ *08022/4141* ⊕ *www.braustuberl.de* ▭ *No credit cards* ⊘ *Closed Mon.*

WHERE TO STAY

$$$$ 🛏 **Althoff Seehotel Überfahrt.** Directly on the lakeshore, this trendy spa
RESORT hotel has a Michelin-recognized chef helming one of three restaurants, and draws scenesters from around the world for "wellness" weekends. **Pros:** luxurious amenities; modern, updated rooms. **Cons:** often full. $ *Rooms from: €320* ✉ *Überfahrtstr. 10, Rottach-Egern* ☎ *08022/6690* ⊕ *www.seehotel-ueberfahrt.com/de* ⏎ *122 rooms, 53 suites* ⊙| *Some meals.*

$$$ 🛏 **Bachmair Weissach.** New owners converted this old-fashioned hotel
HOTEL into a design resort with all the amenities imaginable—sushi bar, tradi-
Fodor'sChoice tional Bavarian restaurant, swimming pool, child care, and yoga classes
★ are all on offer. **Pros:** spacious rooms with balconies; friendly staff; great for families. **Cons:** no lake views; at a busy intersection. $ *Rooms from: €189* ✉ *Wiesseerstr. 1, Rottach-Egern* ☎ *08022/2780* ⊕ *www. bachmair-weissach.com* ⏎ *69 rooms, 77 suites* ⊙| *Some meals.*

$$ 🛏 **Das Tegernsee Hotel & Spa.** The elegant, turreted hotel and its two
HOTEL spacious annexes sit high above the Tegernsee, backed by the wooded slopes of Neureuth Mountain. **Pros:** historical elegance accents updated rooms; Czar Nicholas I was a frequent guest; great views. **Cons:** a little away from the hub of the town. $ *Rooms from: €159* ✉ *Neureuth-str. 23* ☎ *08022/1820* ⊕ *www.dastegernsee.de* ⏎ *63 rooms, 10 suites* ⊙| *Breakfast.*

$ 🛏 **Seehotel Zur Post.** A central location, winter garden, terrace, and a
HOTEL little beer garden make up for the lack of lake views in some rooms. **Pros:** great views from most rooms; friendly service; excellent break-fast. **Cons:** the property could do with an update. $ *Rooms from: €69* ✉ *Seestr. 3* ☎ *08022/66550* ⊕ *www.seehotel-zur-post.de* ⏎ *43 rooms* ⊙| *Breakfast.*

NIGHTLIFE AND PERFORMING ARTS

Every resort has its **spa orchestra**—in summer they play daily in the music-box-style bandstands that dot the lakeside promenades. A strong Tegernsee tradition is the summer-long program of **festivals,** some set deep in the forest. Tegernsee's lake festival in August, when sailing clubs deck their boats with garlands and lanterns, is an unforgettable experience.

Casino (*Spielbank Bad Wiessee*). Bad Wiessee's casino is near the entrance of town coming from Gmund. The main playing rooms are open daily from 3 pm, and it is the biggest and liveliest venue in town for the after-dark scene. ☒ *Winner 1, Bad Wiessee* ☎ *08022/98350* ⊕ *www.spielbanken-bayern.de/wDeutsch/wiessee/.*

> ### HIKING
>
> Well-marked and well-groomed hiking trails lead from the glorious countryside, along rivers and lakes, through woods, and high into the Bavarian Alps. If you just want an afternoon stroll, head for the lower slopes. If you're a serious hiker, make for the mountain trails of the Zugspitze, in Garmisch-Partenkirchen; the heights above Oberammergau, Berchtesgaden, or Bad Reichenhall; or the lovely Walchensee. Well-marked trails near the Schliersee or Tegernsee (lakes) lead steadily uphill and to mountaintop inns. A special treat is a hike to the Tatzelwurm Gorge near Bayrischzell.

SPORTS AND THE OUTDOORS

HIKING

Tourist Information Tegernsee. Contact the tourist office for hiking maps. ☒ *Hauptstr. 2* ☎ *08022/180–140* ⊕ *www.tegernsee.com.*

Wallberg. For the best vista in the area, climb the Wallberg, the 5,700-foot mountain at the south end of the Tegernsee. It's a hard four-hour hike or a short 15-minute cable-car ride up (€10 one way, €19 round-trip). At the summit are a restaurant and sun terrace and several trailheads; in winter the skiing is excellent. ☒ *Wallbergstr. 28, Rottach-Egern* ⊕ *www.wallbergbahn.de.*

GOLF

Tegernseer Golfclub e.V. Besides swimming, hiking, and skiing, the Tegernsee area has become a fine place for golfing. The Tegernseer Golfclub e.V. has an 18-hole course in the valley of Bad Wiessee overlooking the lake and with a view to the mountains. With three tee possibilities, the course is surrounded by old forests and has a number of hazards to challenge even the most advanced golfer. ☒ *Rohbognerhof, Bad Wiessee* ☎ *08022/271–130* ⊕ *www.tegernseer-golf-club.de* ⛳ €45 *weekdays,* €55 *weekends for 9 holes;* €80 *weekdays,* €100 *weekends for 18 holes* ⛳ *18 holes, 5500 yards, par 70.*

CHIEMSEE

80 km (50 miles) southeast of Munich, 120 km (75 miles) northeast of Garmisch-Partenkirchen.

Chiemsee is north of the Deutsche Alpenstrasse, but it demands a detour, if only to visit King Ludwig's huge palace on one of its idyllic islands. It's the largest Bavarian lake, and although it's surrounded by reedy flatlands, the nearby mountains provide a majestic backdrop. The town of **Prien** is the lake's principal resort. ■ TIP→ **The tourist offices of Prien and Aschau offer a €26 transportation package covering a boat trip, a round-trip rail ticket between the two resorts, and a round-trip ride by cable car to the top of Kampen Mountain, above Aschau.**

GETTING HERE AND AROUND

Prien is the best jumping-off point for exploring the Chiemsee. Frequent trains connect Prien with Munich and Salzburg. The regional trains are met by a narrow-gauge steam train for the short trip to Prien-Stock, the boat dock. The only way to reach the Herreninsel and the Fraueninsel is by boat.

ESSENTIALS

Visitor Information Chiemsee Infocenter. ✉ *Felden 10, Bernau am Chiemsee* ☎ *08051/965–550* 🌐 *www.chiemsee-alpenland.de.*

EXPLORING

Fraueninsel. Boats going between Stock and Herrenchiemsee Island also call at this small retreat known as Ladies' Island. The **Benedictine convent** there, founded 1,200 years ago, now serves as a school. One of its earliest abbesses, Irmengard, daughter of King Ludwig der Deutsche, died here in the 9th century. Her grave in the convent chapel was discovered in 1961, the same year that early frescoes there were brought to light. The chapel is open daily from dawn to dusk. Otherwise, the island has just a few private houses, a couple of shops, and a guesthouse where visitors wishing to take part in the nuns' quiet lives can overnight. The Benedictine Sisters make delicious fruit liqueurs and marzipan. ✉ *Fraueninsel* 🌐 *www.frauenwoerth.de.*

Fodor's Choice ★ **Schloss Herrenchiemsee.** One of three castles constructed by King Ludwig II during his reign, this palace on an island is worth the brief steamboat trip if only to see the elaborate rooms designed with French royalty in mind. *See "The Fairy-Tale Castles of King Ludwig II" in Chapter 4.*

WHERE TO STAY

$$ HOTEL 🏨 **Hotel Luitpold am See.** Boats to the Chiemsee islands tie up right outside your window at this handsome old Prien hotel, which organizes shipboard disco evenings as part of its entertainment program. **Pros:** directly on the lake (though the sister property is 328 feet away); limousine service offers pick-up from Munich airport for €100; has wheelchair-accessible rooms. **Cons:** near a busy boat dock. [$] *Rooms from: €114* ✉ *Seestr. 110, Prien am Chiemsee* ☎ *08051/609–100* 🌐 *www.luitpold-am-see.de* 🛏 *77 rooms* 🍴 *Breakfast.*

$$ B&B/INN 🏨 **Neuer am See.** Just 500 feet from the Chiemsee, this hotel benefits from its central location and some rooms have a lake view. **Pros:** great lake views from rooms with balconies; convenient location. **Cons:** strict

cancellation policy; must arrive by 8 pm; modern furnishings lend a stale feel to the interiors. $ *Rooms from: €114* ⊠ *Seestr. 104, Prien am Chiemsee* ☎ *08051/609–960* ⊕ *www.neuer-am-see.de* ⌣ *27 rooms, 4 suites* ⦿ *Some meals.*

SPORTS AND THE OUTDOORS

Chiemsee Golf-Club Prien e.V. The gentle hills of the region are ideal for golf and this parkland course makes good use of the undulating terrain, along with well-placed water hazards, to provide a moderate to difficult challenge. Fairways and greens have distant views of the mountains. ⊠ *Bauernberg 5, Prien am Chiemsee* ☎ *08051/62215* ⊕ *www.cgc-prien. de/* ⌣ *€55 weekdays, €80 weekends* ⋔ *18 holes, 6300 yards, par 72.*

SportLukas. Equipment can be provided for any kind of sport imaginable, from skiing to kayaking, climbing to curling, and it organizes tours. ⊠ *Hauptstr. 3, Schleching* ☎ *08649/243* ⊕ *www.sportlukas.de.*

Surfschule Chiemsee. For those wanting to learn windsurfing or to extend their skills, the Surfschule Chiemsee provides lessons for adults and kids and offers a package deal. You can also rent bikes or kayaks or take a lesson in stand-up paddleboarding. ⊠ *Rasthausstr. 11, Bernau am Chiemsee* ☎ *08051/970–244* ⊕ *www.surfschule-chiemsee.de.*

BERCHTESGADENER LAND

Berchtesgadener Land is the Alps at their most dramatic and most notorious. Although some points are higher, the steep cliffs, hidden mountain lakes, and protected biospheres make the area uniquely beautiful. The salt trade brought medieval Berchtesgaden and Bad Reichenhall incredible wealth, which is still apparent in the large collection of antique houses and quaint streets. Berchtesgaden's image is a bit tarnished by its most infamous historical resident, Adolf Hitler. Berchtesgaden National Park, however, is a hiker's dream, and the resounding echo of the trumpet on the Königssee shouldn't be missed.

BAD REICHENHALL

60 km (37 miles) east of Prien, 20 km (12 miles) west of Salzburg.

Bad Reichenhall is remarkably well located, near the mountains for hiking and skiing, and near Salzburg in Austria for a lively cultural scene. The town shares a remote corner of Bavaria with another prominent resort, Berchtesgaden. Although the latter is more famous, Bad Reichenhall is older, with saline springs that made the town rich. Salt is so much a part of the town that you can practically taste it in the air. Europe's largest source of brine was first tapped here in pre-Christian times; salt mining during the Middle Ages supported the economies of cities as far away as Munich and Passau. The town prospered from a spa in the early 20th century. Lately, it has successfully recycled itself from a somewhat sleepy and stodgy "cure town" to a modern, attractive center of wellness.

Schloss Herrenchiemsee, King Ludwig II's last building project, lies in the middle of Lake Chiemsee on the Herreninsel.

GETTING HERE AND AROUND

Bad Reichenhall is well connected to Berchtesgaden and Salzburg Hauptbahnhof by hourly trains; from Munich, a change in Freilassing is required. To reach the Bürgerbräu and the Predigtstuhl cable car, take Bus No. 180 and Bus No. 841 to Königssee.

ESSENTIALS

Visitor Information Tourist-Info Bad Reichenhall. ⊠ *Wittelsbacherstr. 15* ☎ *08651/6060* ⊕ *www.bad-reichenhall.de.*

EXPLORING

Alte Saline und Quellenhaus. In the early 19th century King Ludwig I built this elaborate saltworks and spa house, in vaulted, pseudomedieval style. The pump installations, which still run, are astonishing examples of 19th-century engineering. A "saline" **chapel** is part of the spa's facilities, and was built in exotic Byzantine style. An interesting museum in the same complex looks at the history of the salt trade. As the salt deposits beneath the building are no longer top quality, parts of the building have been converted to office spaces and a trendy restaurant, but you can tour the underground infrastructure. ⊠ *Alte Saline 9* ☎ *08651/700–2146* ⊕ *www.alte-saline.de* 🖾 *€8; €19 combined ticket with Berchtesgaden's salt mine* ⊘ *May–Oct., daily 10–4; Nov.–Apr., Tues.–Sat. and 1st Sun. in the month 11–3.*

Predigtstuhl. The pride and joy of the Reichenhallers is the steep, craggy mountain appropriately named the Preacher's Pulpit, which stands at 5,164 feet, southeast of town, and has been noted as one of the top 10 cable-car rides in the world for its stunning views. You can hike or just enjoy a bite to eat and drink at the **Almütte Schlegemuldel**, 15 minutes from the cable-car station. ✉ *Südtiroler Pl. 1* ☎ *08651/96850* 🌐 *www.predigtstuhl-bahn.de* 🎟 *€22 round-trip* 🕑 *Upward trips Mar.–Nov., daily 9–4 as needed; Dec.–Feb., daily 9–3 as needed. Last downward trip is when everyone is off the mountain.*

BOATING AND SAILING

All the Bavarian Alpine lakes have sailing schools that rent sailboards as well as various other types of boats. At Tegernsee you can hire motorboats at the pier in front of the Schloss Cafe, in the Tegernsee town center. Chiemsee, with its wide stretch of water whipped by Alpine winds, is a favorite for both sailing enthusiasts and windsurfers. There are boatyards all around the lake and the very good windsurfing school, Surfschule Chiemsee, at Bernau.

Rupertus Therme. Part of Bad Reichenhall's revival included building this new spa facility in 2009. Indoor and outdoor pools in the Therme section are fed by the saline deposits beneath the city; families with children will appreciate the salt-free kids' pool and slide. Saunas and steam rooms are rounded off with a host of special applications using salt, essential oils, mud packs, and massages. The Therme can be popular, especially in winter, so online reservations for any spa services are a good idea ✉ *Friedrich-Ebert-Allee 21* ☎ *08651/76220 reservation hotline* 🌐 *www.rupertustherme.de* 🎟 *Therme: full day €22, 4 hrs €18.50; family area: full day €15.50, 3 hrs €12.50* 🕑 *Daily 9 am–10 pm.*

Wandelhalle. Hotels here base spa treatments on the health-giving properties of the saline springs and the black mud from the area's waterlogged moors. The elegant, pillared pavilion of the attractive spa gardens is really a sight to behold, with its unusual misting character, said to extract salt from the water. All you need to do is walk along the 540-foot Gradierhaus, a massive wood-and-concrete construction that produces a fine salty mist by trickling brine down a 40-foot wall of dense blackthorn bundles (breathing salt-laden air is a remedy for various lung conditions). ✉ *Königlichen Kurgarten* ☎ *08651/6060 tourist office* 🎟 *Free* 🕑 *Nov.–May.*

WHERE TO EAT

$ GERMAN 🍴 **Brauereigasthof Bürgerbräu.** Each dining area in this old brewery inn reflects the social class that once met here: politicos, peasants, burghers, and salt miners. Reichenhallers from all walks of life still meet here to enjoy good conversation, hearty local beer, and excellent food prepared in traditional Bavarian style. Rooms at the inn are simple, but airy and modern, and centrally located. [$] *Average main: €11* ✉ *Waagg. 1–2* ☎ *08651/6089* 🌐 *www.brauereigasthof-buergerbraeu.de.*

$ GERMAN 🍴 **Gasthaus Obermühle.** Tucked away off the main road leading from Bad Reichenhall to the autobahn, this 16th-century mill has an intimate rural feel that draws locals in from the surrounding areas. Fish is the specialty here, though meats (the game in season is noteworthy) are also on the menu. The terrace is an inviting place for a few helpings of excellent homemade pastries. [$] *Average main: €12* ✉ *Tumpenstr. 11* ☎ *08651/2193* 💳 *No credit cards* 🕑 *Closed Mon. and Tues.*

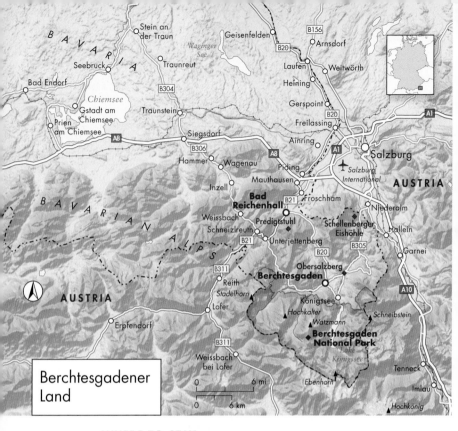

Berchtesgadener
Land

0   6 mi

0   6 km

WHERE TO STAY

$$ **Parkhotel Luisenbad.** If you fancy spoiling yourself in a typical German
HOTEL fin de siècle spa hotel, consider staying at this fine porticoed and pil-
lared building, where an imposing pastel-pink facade promises luxury
within. **Pros:** quiet; centrally located; great spa services on offer. **Cons:**
slightly old-fashioned for some tastes; some unrenovated rooms feel
stuffy. $ *Rooms from: €124* ⊠ *Ludwigstr. 33* ☎ *08651/6040* ⊕ *www.
parkhotel.de* ⇘ *70 rooms, 8 suites* ⎮◎⎮ *Breakfast.*

$ **Pension Hubertus.** This delightfully traditional family-run lodg-
B&B/INN ing stands on the shore of the tiny Thumsee, 5 km (3 miles) from
the town center. **Pros:** incredible views; private guests-only sunbath-
ing area. **Cons:** far from city center; no elevator. $ *Rooms from: €70*
⊠ *Thumsee 5* ☎ *08651/2252* ⊕ *www.hubertus-thumsee.de* ⇘ *18 rooms*
⎮◎⎮ *Breakfast.*

NIGHTLIFE AND PERFORMING ARTS

Philharmonie. Bad Reichenhall is proud of its long musical tradition
and of its orchestra, founded more than a century ago. It performs on
numerous occasions throughout the year in the chandelier-hung Kur-
gastzentrum Theater or, when weather permits, in the open-air pavil-
ion, and at a special Mozart Week in March. Call the Orchesterbüro

for program details. ⊠ *Salzburger Str. 7* ☎ *08651/762–8080 Orchesterbüro* ⊕ *www.bad-reichenhaller-philharmonie.de.*

SPORTS AND THE OUTDOORS

Though Berchtesgaden definitely has the pull for skiers, Bad Reichenhall is proud of its Predigtstuhl, which towers over the town to the south. Besides fresh air and great views, it offers snowshoeing, lots of hiking, biking, and even rock climbing. The tourist information office on Wittelsbacherstrasse, a couple of hundred yards from the train station, has all the necessary information regarding the numerous sporting activities possible in Bad Reichenhall and its surrounding area.

SHOPPING

Josef Mack Company. Using flowers and herbs grown in the Bavarian Alps, the Josef Mack Company has made medicinal herbal preparations since 1856. ⊠ *Ludwigstr. 36* ☎ *08651/78280* ⊕ *www.macknatur.de.*

FAMILY **Paul Reber.** Your sweet tooth will be fully satisfied at the confection emporium of Paul Reber, makers of the famous chocolate, nougat, and marzipan *Mozartkugel* and many other caloric depth-charges. ⊠ *Ludwigstr. 10–12* ☎ *08651/60030* ⊕ *www.reber-spezialitaeten.de/home.html* ⊙ *Closed Sun.*

BERCHTESGADEN

18 km (11 miles) south of Bad Reichenhall, 20 km (12 miles) south of Salzburg.

Berchtesgaden is a gorgeous mountain town right on the border with Austria. From its location in a 2,300-foot-high valley, you can see Germany's second-highest mountain, the Watzmann, and embark on daylong or multiday hikes through the Alps. The nature and diversity of the forests surrounding it are unparalleled in Germany, as are its snowy winters; the small town becomes a hive of activity in high winter and high summer as tourists descend in search of sporting adventure, whether it be hiking or biking, skiing or bobsledding. Perhaps historically it's best known for its brief association as the second home of Adolf Hitler, who dreamed of his "1,000-year Reich" from the mountaintop where millions of tourists before and after him drank in only the superb beauty of the Alpine panorama, but there is much more to the town than its dark past. The historic old market town and mountain

WHITE GOLD

Salt, or white gold as it was known in medieval times, has played a key role in the history of both Bad Reichenhall and Berchtesgaden. Organized salt production in the region began around 450 BC, and even included a 30-km (18-mile) wooden pipeline built in the early 1600s for salt. It wasn't until the early 19th century, however, that the town began utilizing its position and geological advantages to attract tourists. The production of salt continues to this day, as does the flow of travelers on the search for the healing saline pools.

resort has great charm. An ornate palace and working salt mine make up some of the diversions in this heavenly setting.

Salt was once the basis of Berchtesgaden's wealth. In the 12th century Emperor Barbarossa gave mining rights to a Benedictine abbey that had been founded here a century earlier. The abbey was secularized early in the 19th century, when it was taken over by the Wittelsbach rulers. Salt is still important today because of all the local wellness centers. The entire area has been declared a *Kurgebiet* ("health resort region"), and was put on the UNESCO biosphere list.

GETTING HERE AND AROUND

The easiest way to reach Berchtesgaden is with the hourly train connection, or by bus from Salzburg Hauptbahnhof. To get to Berchtesgaden from Munich requires a change in Freilassing or Salzburg. From Salzburg's renovated main train station there are regular connections to Berchtesgaden (choose the train without a Freilassing change). Once there, frequent local bus service makes it easy to explore the town and to reach Berchtesgaden National Park and the Königssee. Local bus services, except that from Documentation center to the Eagle's Nest, are included when you pay the *Kurtax*. The Schwaiger bus company runs tours of the area and across the Austrian border as far as Salzburg. An American couple runs Eagle's Nest Historical Tours out of the local tourist office, opposite the train station.

Schwaiger. ⊠ *Berchtesgaden* ☎ *08652/2525* ⊕ *www.bus-schwaiger.de/en.*

ESSENTIALS

Visitor and Tour Information Berchtesgaden Land Tourismus. ⊠ *Bahnhofpl. 4* ☎ *08652/656–5050* ⊕ *www.berchtesgadener-land.com.* **Eagle's Nest Historical Tours.** ⊠ *Königsseer Str. 2* ☎ *08652/64971* ⊕ *www.eagles-nest-tours.com.*

EXPLORING

Dokumentation Obersalzberg. This center documents the notorious history of the Third Reich, with a special focus on Obersalzberg, and some surprisingly rare archive material presented in a very well-considered manner. ⊠ *Salzbergstr. 41* ☎ *08652/947–960* ⊕ *www.obersalzberg.de* 💶 *€3* ⏱ *Apr.–Oct., daily 9–5; Nov.–Mar., Tues.–Sun. 10–3.*

FAMILY **Haus der Berge.** Opened in 2015, this interactive museum brings the surrounding national park to life for children and adults alike with a rotating exhibition focusing on the wildlife and diverse nature to be found in the area. ⊠ *Hanielstr. 7* ☎ *08652/979–0600* ⊕ *www.haus-der-berge.bayern.de* 💶 *€4* ⏱ *Daily 9–5.*

Heimatmuseum. This museum in the Schloss Adelsheim displays examples of wood carving and other local crafts. Wood carving in Berchtesgaden dates to long before Oberammergau established itself as the premier wood-carving center of the Alps. ⊠ *Schroffenbergallee 6* ☎ *08652/4410* ⊕ *www.heimatmuseum-berchtesgaden.de* 💶 *€2.50* ⏱ *Dec.–Oct., Tues.–Sun. 10–5.*

Obersalzberg. The site of Hitler's luxurious mountain retreat is part of the north slope of the Hoher Goll, high above the timber line overlooking Berchtesgaden. It was a remote mountain community of farmers and foresters before Hitler's deputy, Martin Bormann, selected the site for a complex of Alpine homes for top Nazi leaders. Hitler's chalet, the Berghof, and all the others were destroyed in 1945, with the exception of a hotel that had been taken over by the Nazis, the Hotel zum Türken.

To get there, you need to take a round-trip from Berchtesgaden's post office by bus and elevator (€16.10 per person). The bus runs mid-May through September, daily from 9 to 4:50. By car you can travel only as far as the Obersalzberg bus station. The full round-trip takes one hour. To get the most out of your visit to the Kehlsteinhaus, consider taking a tour.

Beyond Obersalzberg, the hairpin bends of Germany's highest road come to the base of the 6,000-foot peak on which sits the Kehlsteinhaus, also known as the Adlerhorst (Eagle's Nest), Hitler's personal retreat and his official guesthouse. It was Martin Bormann's gift to the führer on Hitler's 50th birthday. The road leading to it, built in 1937–39, climbs more than 2,000 dizzying feet in less than 6 km (4 miles). A tunnel in the mountain will bring you to an elevator that whisks you up to what appears to be the top of the world (you can walk up in about half an hour), and refreshments are available. ✉ *Königsseer Str. 2* ⊕ *www.kehlsteinhaus.de.*

Salzbergwerk. This salt mine is one of the chief attractions of the region. In the days when the mine was owned by Berchtesgaden's princely rulers, only select guests were allowed to see how the source of the city's wealth was extracted from the earth. Today, during a 90-minute tour, you can sit astride a miniature train that transports you nearly 1 km (½ mile) into the mountain to an enormous chamber where the salt is mined. Included in the tour are rides down the wooden chutes used by miners to get from one level to another and a boat ride on an underground saline lake the size of a football field. Although the tours take about an hour, plan an extra 45–60 minutes for purchasing the tickets and changing into and out of miners' clothing. You may wish to partake in the special four-hour **brine dinners** down in the mines (€90). These are very popular, so be sure to book early. ✉ *Bergwerkstr. 83* ☎ *08652/600–220* ⊕ *www.salzzeitreise.de* 🎫 *€15.50; €18.50 combined ticket with Bad Reichenhall's saline museum* ☉ *May–Oct., daily 9–5; Nov.–Apr., Mon.–Sat. 11–3.*

OFF THE BEATEN PATH

Schellenberger Eishöhle. Germany's largest ice caves lie 10 km (6 miles) north of Berchtesgaden. By car take B-305 to the village of Marktschellenberg, or take Bus No. 2940 (to the Eishöhle stop; €4) from the Berchtesgaden train station or Salzburg Hbf. From there you can reach the caves on foot by walking 2½ hours along the clearly marked route. A guided tour of the caves takes one hour. On the way to Marktschellenberg watch for the **Almbachklamm,** a narrow valley that is good for hikes. At its entrance is an old (1683) mill for making and polishing marbles. ✉ *Berchtesgaden* ☎ *08652/944–5300* ⊕ *www.eishoehle.net* 🎫 *€5* ☉ *June–Oct., daily 10–4.*

Schloss Berchtesgaden. The last royal resident of the Berchtesgaden abbey, Crown Prince Rupprecht (who died here in 1955), furnished it with rare family treasures that now form the basis of this permanent collection.

Fine Renaissance rooms exhibit the prince's sacred art, which is particularly rich in wood sculptures by such great late-Gothic artists as Tilman Riemenschneider and Veit Stoss. There are two weaponry rooms exhibiting hunting tools, including rifles from the 19th century, and a beautiful rose garden out back. You can also visit the abbey's original, cavernous 13th-century dormitory and cool cloisters. Just be sure to check in advance as the Wittelsbach heir still occasionally stops by for a visit, at which times the castle is closed to visitors. ✉ *Schlosspl. 2* ☎ *08652/947–980* 🌐 *www.schloss-berchtesgaden.de* 🎫 *€9.50, including tour* 🕒 *Mid-May–mid-Oct., Sun.–Fri. 10–noon and 2–4; mid-Oct.–mid-May, Sun.–Fri. 11–2.*

Watzmann Therme. Here you'll find fragrant steam rooms, saunas with infrared cabins for sore muscles, an elegant pool, whirlpools, and a special pool for children. ✉ *Bergwerkstr. 54* ☎ *08652/94640* 🌐 *www.watzmann-therme.de* 🎫 *2 hrs €10.90; 4 hrs €14.30; day pass, including sauna €16.50* 🕒 *Sun.–Wed. 10–10; Fri. and Sat. 10 am–11 pm.*

WHERE TO STAY

$$ HOTEL Fodor's Choice ★ 🏨 **Berghotel Rehlegg.** In the heart of Ramsau, just outside of Berchtesgaden, this family-run Best Western hotel has a spa and pool and a special focus on sustainability. **Pros:** quiet location; evening buffet offers something for everyone; friendly staff. **Cons:** perhaps too quiet for children. $ *Rooms from: €172* ✉ *Holzeng. 16* ✣ *Ramsau* ☎ *08657/98840* 🌐 *www.rehlegg.de* 🛏 *79 rooms, 8 suites* 🍴 *Some meals.*

$$$$ RESORT FAMILY 🏨 **Kempinski Bavarian Alps.** Nestled in the hills outside of Berchtesgaden and surrounded by quiet woods, this five-star spa hotel, dripping with luxury, has a quiet, relaxed feel. **Pros:** stunning views; well-appointed modern furnishings; quiet location. **Cons:** can get busy with conferences. $ *Rooms from: €260* ✉ *Hintereck 1* ☎ *08652/97550* 🌐 *www.kempinski.com* 🛏 *126 rooms, 12 suites* 🍴 *Breakfast.*

SPORTS AND THE OUTDOORS

Buried as it is in the Alps, Berchtesgaden is a place for the active. The Rossfeld ski area is one of the favorites, thanks to almost guaranteed natural snow. The piste down to Oberau is nearly 6 km (4 miles) long (with bus service at the end to take you back to Berchtesgaden). There is a separate snowboarding piste as well. Berchtesgaden also has many cross-country trails and telemark opportunities. The other popular area is on the slopes of the Götschenkopf, which is used for World Cup races. Snow is usually artificial, but the floodlit slopes at night and a lively après-ski scene make up for the lesser quality.

In summer, hikers, power-walkers, and paragliders take over the region. The Obersalzberg even has a summer luge track. Avid hikers should ask for a map featuring the refuges (*Berghütten*) in the mountains, where one can spend the night either in a separate room or a bunk. Simple, solid meals are offered. In some of the smaller refuges you will have to bring your own food. For more information, check out 🌐 *www.berchtesgaden.de*. And though the Königsee is beautiful to look at, only cold-water swimmers will appreciate its frigid waters.

Consider walking along the pleasant mountain path from the Eagle's Nest back to Berchtesgaden.

The gemlike Königsee Lake is the most photographed panorama in Germany.

Berchtesgadener Bergfuehrer. Professional mountaineers and rock climbers in this organization can help you find the right way up any of the surrounding mountains, including the Watzmann. ⊠ *Berchtesgadener-str. 21, Bischofswiesen* ☏ *08652/978–9690* ⊕ *www.berchtesgadener-bergfuehrer.de.*

Berchtesgaden Golf Club. Germany's highest course, the Berchtesgaden Golf Club, is on a 3,300-foot plateau of the Obersalzberg. Ten Berchtesgaden hotels offer their guests a 30% reduction on the green fee—contact the tourist office or the club for details. ⊠ *Salzbergstr. 33* ☏ *08652/2100* ⊕ *www.golfclub-berchtesgaden.de/* ▱ *€40 weekdays, €50 weekends* ⚑ *18 holes, 5680 yards, par 70.*

SHOPPING

Berchtesgadener Handwerkskunst. Handicrafts here—such as wooden boxes, woven tablecloths, wood carvings, and Christmas-tree decorations—come from Berchtesgaden, the surrounding region, and other parts of Bavaria. ⊠ *Schlosspl. 1½* ☏ *08652/979–790* ⊕ *www.berchtesgadener-handwerkskunst.de.*

BERCHTESGADEN NATIONAL PARK

5 km (3 miles) south of Berchtesgaden.

The park covers 210 square km (81 square miles) and around two-thirds of its border is shared with Austria. Characterized by mountain vistas and the beautiful Königsee, the park has over 1.2 million visitors each year, which is a true testament to the area's popularity.

GETTING HERE AND AROUND

Berchtesgaden National Park is around 150 kilometers (93 miles) southeast of Munich by car. Many people find the train connection, with a change at Freilassing, and a 30-minute bus journey (total time is around two hours 50 minutes), a more rewarding, if adventurous journey.

EXPLORING

Berchtesgaden National Park. The deep, mysterious, and fabled Königssee is the most photographed panorama in Germany. Together with its much smaller sister, the Obersee, it's nestled within the Berchtesgaden National Park, 210 square km (81 square miles) of wild mountain country where flora and fauna have been left to develop as nature intended. No roads penetrate the area, and even the mountain paths are difficult to follow. The park administration organizes guided tours of the area from June through September. ⊠ *Nationalparkhaus, Franziskanerpl. 7, Berchtesgaden* ☎ *08652/64343* ⊕ *www.nationalpark-berchtesgaden.de.*

Königssee. One less strenuous way into the Berchtesgaden National Park is by boat. A fleet of 21 excursion boats, electrically driven to avoid pollution and so that no noise disturbs the peace, operates on the Königssee (King's Lake). Only the skipper of the boat is allowed to shatter the silence—his trumpet fanfare demonstrates a remarkable echo as notes reverberate between the almost vertical cliffs that plunge into the dark green water. A cross on a rocky promontory marks the spot where a boatload of pilgrims hit the cliffs and sank more than 100 years ago. The voyagers were on their way to the tiny, twin-tower baroque chapel of St. Bartholomä, built in the 17th century on a peninsula where an early-Gothic church once stood. The princely rulers of Berchtesgaden built a hunting lodge at the side of the chapel; a tavern and restaurant now occupy its rooms.

Smaller than the Königssee but equally beautiful, the **Obersee** can be reached by a 15-minute walk from the second stop (Salet) on the boat tour. The lake's backdrop of jagged mountains and precipitous cliffs is broken by a waterfall, the Rothbachfall, which plunges more than 1,000 feet to the valley floor.

Boat service on the Königssee runs year-round, except when the lake freezes. A round-trip to St. Bartholomä and Salet, the landing stage for the Obersee, lasts almost two hours, without stops, and costs €16.90. A round-trip to St. Bartholomä lasts a little over an hour and costs €13.90. In summer the Berchtesgaden tourist office organizes evening cruises on the Königssee, which include a concert in St. Bartholomä Church and a four-course dinner in the neighboring hunting lodge. ⊠ *Boat service, Seestr. 29, Schönau* ☎ *08652/96360* ⊕ *www.bayerische-seenschifffahrt.de.*

THE ROMANTIC ROAD

WELCOME TO
THE ROMANTIC ROAD

TOP REASONS
TO GO

★ **Neuschwanstein:**
Emerald lakes and the
rugged peaks of the Alps
surround what's become
the world's most famous
storybook castle.

★ **Rothenburg-ob-
der-Tauber:** Stunning
architecture and timber-
frame houses give this
quaint walled village an
authentic Middle Ages feel,
which only increases as you
patrol the city walls with the
night watchman after the
tour buses have left town.

★ **Wieskirche:** Rising up
out of the pastoral countryside, this local pilgrimage
church is a rococo gem.

★ **Ulm's Münster:** Climb the
768 steps of this church's
tower to get a view over
the city and take in the most
elaborately designed evangelical church in Germany.

★ **Würzburg's Residenz:**
Explore the gilt and
crystal splendor of this
lavish palace, once the
home of prince-bishops.

1 Toward the Alps. Alpine meadows provide a spectacular landscape for the fairy-tale castles of Neuschwanstein and Hohenschwangau near the Austrian border. The marvelous Wieskirche (Church of the Meadow) is just up the Romantic Road, where the mountains give way to rolling fields and beer beats out wine in the small inns of towns like Landsberg and Schongau.

2 Central Romantic Road. After crossing the Danube from the south, the route takes you through the influential city of Augsburg before continuing on through the lovely Tauber valley. Vineyards slope down the hills to the small valleys, broken up only by the walled fortifications encircling charming old towns such as Nördlingen, a medieval town built in a meteoric crater; Dinkelsbühl; and Rothenburg-ob-der-Tauber.

3 Northern Romantic Road. Wine lovers should plan an extra day for the Frankish capital of Würzburg, where they can sample delicious local wines and view the Residenz Palace. A short distance down the Tauber River is the spa town of Bad Mergentheim, well known for its healing waters and 900-year association with the German Teutonic Order.

GETTING ORIENTED

The Romantic Road captures classic Germany in the 28 towns that make up its route. Beginning in Füssen on the mountainous Austrian border and just a stone's throw to Neuschwanstein, the fantastic castle built by Bavaria's "Fairy-Tale King," Ludwig II, the road follows an old trading route along the Lech River up through the handsome Renaissance city of Augsburg. From there, it winds northwest through pastoral countryside to the best-preserved medieval town on the continent, Rothenburg-ob-der-Tauber, before ending in Würzburg in central Germany, an hour from Frankfurt.

4

Updated by
Courtney Tenz

Nowhere cries "quintessential German" quite as loudly as the Romantische Strasse, or Romantic Road, a 355-km (220-mile) drive through the south-central countryside. With 28 traditional red-roofed villages, some still brimming with medieval architecture, rising out of the pastoral scenery, the route is also memorable for the castles, abbeys, and churches tucked away beyond low hills, their spires and towers just visible through the greenery.

The Romantic Road began in 1950 as a bus tour through this corner of West Germany, then occupied by the American forces, as a way to promote this historic route through Bavaria and Baden-Württemberg. Don't let the name fool you—this isn't a road for lovebirds; rather the word *romantic* is used to mean an adventurous look at the past, especially the Middle Ages.

Rich in history, the Romantic Road was traveled by the Romans 2,000 years ago. Its path criss-crosses centuries-old battlefields, most especially those of the Thirty Years' War, which destroyed the region's economic base in the 17th century. The depletion of resources prevented improvements that would have modernized the area—thereby assuring that these towns would become the quaint tourist destinations they are today.

PLANNING

WHEN TO GO

Late summer and early autumn are the best times to travel the Romantic Road, as the grapes ripen on the vines around Würzburg and the geraniums run riot on the medieval walls of towns such as Rothenburg and Dinkelsbühl. You'll also miss the high-season summer crush of tourists. Otherwise, consider visiting the region in December, when Christmas markets fill the ancient town squares and snow gives the turreted Schloss Neuschwanstein a magical touch.

PLANNING YOUR TIME

While the two bigger cities of Augsburg and Würzburg can handle large influxes of visitors, it pays to visit any of the quaint villages lining the Romantic Road to get a feel for the laid-back local lifestyle. In the two most popular places, Rothenburg-ob-der-Tauber and Neuschwanstein, an overnight stay will help beat the crowds. On summer nights, you can follow the night watchman in Rothenburg as he makes his rounds, and stroll through the town in the early morning before the bus-tour groups push through the streets. At Neuschwanstein, it's even more important to get an early start, as tickets are often booked out; even after reserving online ahead of time, expect a long wait during high season.

GETTING HERE AND AROUND

AIR TRAVEL

The major international airports serving the Romantic Road are Frankfurt and Munich.

BUS TRAVEL

Daily bus service from Frankfurt and Munich is provided by Eurolines Touring and Romantic Road Coach (the latter operated by the tourist office), and covers the entire stretch of the Romantic Road from Würzburg to Füssen. Both companies provide a hop-on, hop-off service, and tickets bought online are valid for up to six months (€84 one way, €120 round-trip). The buses run from April through October, come complete with audio guide, and stop at all the major sights along the road. Romantic Road Coach also has guides on board their weekend buses. Packages including bicycle transportation and hotel reservations can be booked directly online or through the Romantic Road official tourist office.

Bus Contacts Eurolines Touring. ✉ *Am Römerhof 17, Frankfurt* ☎ *069/7191–26261* ⊕ *www.eurolines.de.* **Romantic Road Coach.** ✉ *Segringer Str. 19, Dinkelsbühl* ☎ *09851/551–387* ⊕ *www.romantic-road.com.*

CAR TRAVEL

Most easily traveled by car, the Romantic Road offers a number of opportunities to pause at scenic overlooks to get a feel for the area. Just be sure to follow brown landmark signs marking the Road instead of following a navigation system, as it was rerouted in recent years and a GPS will likely keep you on the faster, less scenic freeways, bypassing the many quaint villages lining the route. The roads are busy, and most have only two lanes, so figure on covering no more than 70 km (43 miles) each hour, particularly in summer. If you're coming up from the south and using Munich as a gateway, Augsburg is 70 km (43 miles) from Munich via A-8. From there, you will continue north and end in Würzburg, the northernmost city on the route, which is 124 km (77 miles) from Frankfurt. If you're traveling from the north, begin in Würzburg and follow country highway B-27 south to meet roads B-290, B-19, B-292, and B-25 along the Wörnitz River. It's on the Frankfurt–Nürnberg autobahn, A-3, and is 115 km (71 miles) from Frankfurt. For route maps, with roads and sights highlighted, contact the Romantische Strasse Touristik-Arbeitsgemeinschaft (Romantic Road Central Tourist-Information) based in Dinkelsbühl.

TRAIN TRAVEL

Infrequent trains link the major towns of the Romantic Road, but both Würzburg and Augsburg are on the InterCity and high-speed Inter-City Express (ICE) routes and have fast, frequent service to and from Munich, Stuttgart, and Frankfurt.

BIKE TOURS

Alpenlandtouristik. Specializing in hiking and biking tours, this company offers a number of multiday tours, including a "luggage free" five-day castle tour from Landsberg am Lech to Neuschwanstein and Füssen. ☎ *08191/308–620* ⊕ *www.alpenlandtouristik.de* ✉ *From €298.*

Velotours. Offers a number of scenic bike tours, including four along the Romantic Road (Würzburg to Rothenburg, Rothenburg to Donau-wörth, or Donauwörth to Füssen). The first two trips can be combined for an eight-day tour. ✉ *Bücklestr. 13, Konstanz* ☎ *07531/98280* ⊕ *www.velotours.de* ✉ *from €365.*

RESTAURANTS

Restaurants in the heavily trafficked towns along the Romantic Road tend to be crowded during peak season, but if you plan your mealtimes around visits to smaller villages, you will be rewarded with Franconian or Swabian cuisine that is less expensive and may also be locally sourced. Some of the small, family-run restaurants close around 2 pm, or whenever the last lunch guests have left, and then open again at 5 or 5:30 pm. Some serve cold cuts or coffee and cake during that time, but no hot food.

Prices in the reviews are the average cost of a main course at dinner, or if dinner is not served, at lunch.

HOTELS

With a few exceptions, Romantic Road hotels are quiet and rustic, and you'll find high standards of comfort and cleanliness. If you plan to stay in one of the bigger hotels in the off-season, ask about discounted weekend rates. Make reservations as far in advance as possible if you plan to visit in summer. Hotels in Würzburg, Augsburg, Rothenburg, and Füssen are often full year-round. Tourist information offices can usually help with accommodations, especially if you arrive early in the day.

Prices in the reviews are the lowest cost of a standard double room in high season. For expanded reviews, facilities, and current deals, visit Fodors.com.

WHAT IT COSTS IN EUROS			
$	**$$**	**$$$**	**$$$$**
Restaurants	under €15	€15–€20	€21–€25	over €25
Hotels	under €100	€100–€175	€176–€225	over €225

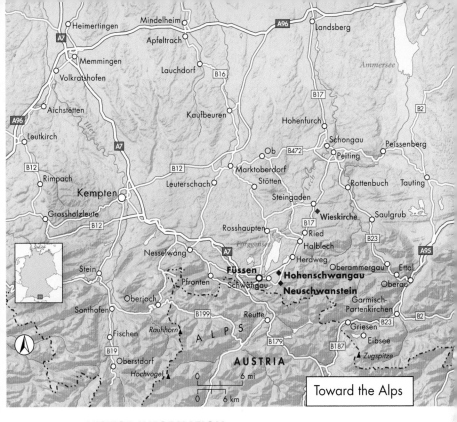

Toward the Alps

TOWARD THE ALPS

An hour west of Munich, the Romantic Road climbs gradually into the foothills of the Bavarian Alps, which burst into view between Landsberg and Schongau and grow magnificent as you continue to the route's most southern tip—the town of Füssen, on the Austrian border. Landsberg was founded by the Bavarian ruler Heinrich der Löwe (Henry the Lion) in the 12th century, and the town grew wealthy from the salt trade. Solid old houses are packed within its turreted walls; the early-18th-century Rathaus is one of the finest in the region.

Schongau has virtually intact wall fortifications, complete with towers and gates. In medieval and Renaissance times the town was an important trading post on the route from Italy to Augsburg. The steeply gabled 16th-century Ballenhaus was a warehouse before it was elevated to the rank of Rathaus. A popular Märchenwald (fairy-tale forest) lies 1½ km (1 mile) outside Schongau, suitably set in a clearing in the woods. It comes complete with mechanical models of fairy-tale scenes, deer enclosures, and an old-time miniature railway that delights both kids and adults.

HOHENSCHWANGAU AND NEUSCHWANSTEIN

103 km (64 miles) south of Augsburg, 121 km (75 miles) southwest of Munich.

These two famous castles belonging to the Wittelbachs are 1 km (½ mile) across a valley from each other, near the town of Schwangau. Bavaria's King Ludwig II (1845–86) spent many summers during his youth at Schloss Hohenschwangau (Hohenschwangau Castle). It's said that its neo-Gothic atmosphere provided the primary influences that shaped his wildly romantic Schloss Neuschwanstein (Neuschwanstein Castle), the fairy-tale castle he built after he became king. It has long been one of Germany's most recognized sights.

GETTING HERE AND AROUND

From Schwangau, 5 km (3 miles) north of Füssen, follow the road signs marked "Königschlösser" (King's Castles). After 3 km (2 miles) you come to Hohenschwangau, a small village consisting of a few houses, some good hotels, and five big parking lots (parking €6). You'll have to park and then walk to the ticket center serving both castles. If you are staying in Füssen, it is easiest to take the No. 73 or 78 bus to Hohenschwangau, which leaves from the train station in Füssen every hour from morning to night, and costs €1.60 per person one way. Tickets to the castles are for timed entry, so be sure to leave at least an hour, if not more, to get your tickets and take on the 1½-km (1-mile) uphill hike to Neuschwanstein from the ticket center. For a fee of €1.80, you can book your tickets up to two days in advance for either castle through the ticket center with a deposit or credit-card number, though in high season be sure to book several weeks in advance. You can change entrance times or cancel up to two hours before the confirmed entrance time. The main street of the small village of Hohenschwangau is lined with many souvenir shops and restaurants.

TIMING

The best time to see either castle without waiting a long time is a weekday between January and April. The prettiest time, however, is in fall. ■TIP➜ **Bear in mind that more than 1.5 million people pass through one or both castles every year. If you visit in summer, get there early and reserve ahead.**

ESSENTIALS

Ticket Center. ✉ *Alpseestr. 12, Hohenschwangau* ☎ *08362/930–830* ⊕ *www.hohenschwangau.de.*

EXPLORING

Castle concerts. Concerts by world-famous orchestras and classical singers are held throughout September in the Neuschwanstein Castle's lavishly decorated minstrels' hall. Tickets go on sale in February or March for the coming September and often sell out, so plan ahead if you want to go. ✉ *Neuschwanstein, Neuschwansteinstr. 20, Hohenschwangau* ☎ *01805/819–831* ⊕ *www.schlosskonzerte-neuschwanstein.de.*

Museum of the Bavarian Kings. Once the Alpenrose hotel, this grand building directly on the Alpensee opened in 2012 as a museum chronicling the history of the Wittelsbach kings and queens from the 11th century to the present day. Focusing primarily on King Maximilian II and his son Ludwig, it details the family's story and the influence of the Wittelsbach family in the region, from the development of Munich, their founding of the first Oktoberfest, and the family's role as resisters against the Nazi regime and their eventual imprisonment during World War II. The interactive exhibits couple state-of-the-art technology with the gold and gilt belongings of the royal family, including an elegant fur robe worn by King Ludwig II. The adjacent Alpenrose-am-See café overlooking the lake is a good spot to relax. ✉ *Alpseestr. 27, Hohenschwangau* ☎ *08362/926–4640* ⊕ *www.museumderbayerischenkoenige.de* 💶 *€9.50; combination ticket for both castles and museum €29.50* ⏰ *Apr.–Sept., daily 9–7; Oct.–Mar., daily 10–6.*

Schloss Hohenschwangau. Built by the knights of Schwangau in the 12th century, this castle was later updated by King Ludwig II's father, the Bavarian crown prince Maximilian, between 1832 and 1836. Unlike Ludwig's more famous castle across the valley, Neuschwanstein, the mustard-yellow Schloss Hohenschwangau actually feels like a noble home, where comforts would be valued as much as outward splendor. Ludwig spent his childhood summers surrounded by the castle's murals, depicting ancient Germanic legends, including those that inspired the composer Richard Wagner in his *Ring* cycle of operas. The paintings remain untouched in the dining room, as does the "Women's floor," which looks just as it did at the death of Ludwig's mother, Marie, in 1889.

After obtaining your ticket at the ticket center in the village, you can take a 20-minute walk up either of two clearly marked paths to the castle, or board one of the horse-drawn carriages that leave from in front of the Hotel Müller (uphill €6, downhill €3). ✉ *Alpseestr. 12, Hohenschwangau* ☎ *08362/930–830* ⊕ *www.hohenschwangau.de* 💶 *€12, includes guided tour; combined ticket for Hohenschwangau and Neuschwanstein €23; combined ticket for both castles and museum €29.50* ⏰ *Late Mar.–mid-Oct., daily 8–5; mid-Oct.–mid-Mar., daily 9–3:30.*

Fodor's Choice ★

Schloss Neuschwanstein. The most famous of German castles, and one of the best-known sights in all of Germany, this castle inspired Walt Disney's *Sleeping Beauty* and Disneyland castles.

See "The Fairy-Tale Palaces of King Ludwig II" in this chapter.

WHERE TO EAT AND STAY

$$$

EUROPEAN

✕ **Alpenrose am See.** There is no spot more idyllic in Hohenschwangau to enjoy excellent food and stunning views over the Alpsee and mountains beyond. The café, which is next to the Museum of Bavarian Kings, is a good choice to escape the tourist masses for lunch or afternoon coffee and cake on the terrace. The continental European cuisine includes several game and pork dishes, as well as a selection of vegetarian dishes.

The romantic five-course "Rosendinner" is served in a private room off the terrace that's filled with roses. [$] *Average main: €22* ✉ *Alpseestr. 27, Hohenschwangau* ☎ *08362/926–4660* 🌐 *www.alpenrose-am-see.de* 💳 *No credit cards.*

$$ HOTEL 🏨 **Hotel Müller.** With a convenient location between the two Schwangau castles, the Müller fits beautifully into the stunning landscape, its creamy Bavarian baroque facade a contrast to the forested mountain slopes. **Pros:** personalized service; variety of rooms; right next to castles. **Cons:** crowds during the day; expensive in season. [$] *Rooms from: €150* ✉ *Alpseestr. 16, Hohenschwangau* ☎ *08362/81990* 🌐 *www.hotel-mueller.de* 🕓 *Closed Nov. and early Jan.–late Mar.* 🛏 *39 rooms, 4 suites* 🍴 *Breakfast.*

FÜSSEN

5 km (3 miles) southwest of Schwangau, 129 km (80 miles) south of Munich.

A walled town left untouched by World War II bombs, Füssen's red roofs and turrets stand in picturesque contrast to the turquoise waters of the Lech River that rushes alongside the town, separating it from the Romantic Road. The only town with the infrastructure to accommodate the crush of tourists from the famous castles nearby, Füssen has a lot of charm of its own, with tidy, meandering streets lined with original architecture that offers an authentic slice of the past. The small town square is filled with cafés, restaurants, and shops, and a centuries-old abbey and castle round out the sights. Home to violin makers for centuries, Füssen takes pride in its musical heritage, which it showcases during an annual summer jazz festival. At the foot of the mountains that separate Bavaria from the Austrian Tyrol, it is also a great starting point for hiking and bicycle tours in the area, and on the nearby Forggensee, a reservoir created to hold glacial runoff, you can take a boat ride with stunning views of Neuschwanstein.

On the border with Austria, Füssen is the last stop on the regional express train leaving every two hours from Munich, and using the train is a highly recommended way to get to this town in the Alpine foothills. From the tourist information center next to the main train station, you can get information about bus travel in and around the region; frequency varies based on the season, but buses run at least hourly to all of the nearby castles of King Ludwig. The pedestrian-only city center is just a few hundred yards' walk from the train station.

ESSENTIALS

Visitor Information Füssen Tourismus und Marketing. ✉ *Kaiser-Maximilian-Pl. 1* ☎ *08362/93850* 🌐 *www.tourismus-fuessen.de.*

EXPLORING

Hohes Schloss (*High Castle*). One of the best-preserved late-Gothic castles in Germany, Hohes Schloss was built on the site of the Roman fortress that once guarded this Alpine section of the Via Claudia, the trade route from Rome to the Danube. Evidence of Roman occupation of the area has been uncovered at the foot of the nearby Tegelberg Mountain, and the **excavations** next to the Tegelberg cable-car station are open for visits daily. The Hohes Schloss was the seat of Bavarian rulers before Emperor Heinrich VII mortgaged it and the rest of the town to the bishop of Augsburg for 400 pieces of silver. The mortgage was never redeemed, and Füssen remained the property of the Augsburg episcopate until secularization in the early 19th century. The bishops of Augsburg used the castle as their summer Alpine residence. It has a spectacular 16th-century **Rittersaal** (Knights' Hall) with a carved ceiling, and a princes' chamber with a Gothic tile stove. ⊠ *Magnuspl. 10* ☎ *08362/903–146* 🎫 *€6* ⊙ *Apr.–Oct., Tues.–Sun. 11–5; Nov.–Mar., Fri.–Sun. 1–4.*

Kloster St. Mang. The summer presence of the bishops of Augsburg ensured that Füssen would gain an impressive number of baroque and rococo churches, and after his death, the Benedictine abbey was built at the site of his grave.

A Romanesque crypt beneath the baroque abbey church has a partially preserved 10th-century fresco, the oldest in Bavaria. In summer, chamber concerts are held in the baroque splendor of the former abbey's soaring **Fürstensaal** (Princes' Hall). Program details are available from the tourist office. ⊠ *Lechhalde 3* ⊕ *www.fuessen.de/kultur-und-kulinarik/kloster-st-mang.html* 🎫 *Free* ⊙ *Apr.–Oct., Tues.–Sun. 10–5; Nov.–Mar., Tues.–Sun. 1–4.*

OFF THE
BEATEN
PATH
Wieskirche. This church—a glorious example of German rococo architecture—stands in an Alpine meadow just off the Romantic Road. Its yellow-and-white walls and steep red roof are set off by the dark backdrop of the Trauchgauer Mountains. The architect Dominicus Zimmermann, former mayor of Landsberg and creator of much of that town's rococo architecture, built the church in 1745 on the spot where six years earlier a local woman saw tears running down the face of a picture of Christ. Although the church was dedicated as the Pilgrimage Church of the Scourged Savior, it's now known simply as the Wieskirche (Church of the Meadow). Visit it on a bright day if you can, when light streaming through its high windows displays the full glory of the glittering interior. A complex oval plan is animated by brilliantly colored stuccowork, statues, and gilt. A luminous ceiling fresco completes the decoration. Concerts are presented in the church from the end of June through the beginning of August. To get here from the village of Steingaden (22 km [14 miles] north of Füssen on the B-17), turn east and follow the signs to Wieskirche. ⊠ *Wies 12, Steingaden* ☎ *8862/932–930* ⊕ *www.wieskirche.de* 🎫 *Free (donations accepted)* ⊙ *Late Mar.–late Oct., daily 8–8; late Oct.–late Mar., daily 8–5. Closed for visits during hours of worship; check chart on website.*

WHERE TO EAT AND STAY

$ ✕ **Markthalle.** In a building that opened in 1483 as the *Kornhaus* (grain
GERMAN storage) and then became the *Feuerhaus* (fire station), at this farmers' market you can grab a quick lunch (or picnic supplies) and drink at reasonable prices. It's open weekdays 10–6 and Saturday 10–2. Try the fish soup. 💲 *Average main: €8* ⊠ *Schranneg. 12* 🚫 *No credit cards* ⊙ *Closed Sun. No dinner.*

Continued on page 192

FAIRY-TALE CASTLES OF KING LUDWIG II

By Catherine Moser

King Ludwig II's image permeates Bavarian culture—the picture of the raven-haired king with soulful eyes adorns everything from beer steins to the local autobahn. The fairy-tale palaces he built have drawn millions of visitors, but who was Ludwig II? Adopting the words of his favorite poet, Friedrich Schiller, he wrote: "I wish to remain an eternal enigma to myself and to others." A tour of his castles reveals a glimpse of the man behind the story of the "Dreamer King."

Born on August 25, 1845, in Nymphenburg Palace, Ludwig II became king at 18 after his father's, King Maximilian II's, sudden death in 1864. He would become the most famous king in the 900-year Wittelsbach dynasty, known not for his rule—he had little power, as Bavaria was governed by a constitutional monarchy—but for his eccentricities.

Ludwig attended Richard Wagner's *Lohengrin* at age 15. Identifying with the Swan Knight, he yearned for the heroic medieval world Wagner portrayed. As king, Ludwig became Wagner's greatest patron and funded the creation of his opera festival in Bayreuth. Wagner was so influential, and Ludwig's love for him so unabashed, that concerned Munich officials sent the composer away in 1865.

Seeking solace in the isolated, idealized world of his own creation, Ludwig embarked on three palace-building projects beginning in 1868. By 1885, he had amassed a personal debt of 14 million marks, putting a massive strain on the Wittelsbach fortune. A commission of doctors, enthralled with the emerging studies of psychology, was assembled to analyze the behavior of the recluse king. Led by Dr. von Gudden, the commission diagnosed the king with paranoia and declared him insane without ever examining Ludwig himself. Ludwig was arrested in the early-morning hours of June 12, 1886, and taken from Schloss Neuschwanstein to Castle Berg on the shores of Lake Starnberg. Just before midnight the following day, the bodies of Ludwig and Dr. von Gudden were found floating in the lake. Theories abound to this day about their deaths, but the truth of Ludwig's demise is unknown.

Opposite, Schloss Neuschwanstein. Above left, King Ludwig II. Above right, Golden angel fountain, Schloss Linderhof.

SCHLOSS LINDERHOF

Set in sylvan seclusion in Graswang Valley, high in the Alps, lies the royal palace of Linderhof. Built on the site of his father's hunting lodge, this was the first of Ludwig's building projects and the only one completed during his lifetime. Begun in 1868, the small villa based on the Petit Trianon of Versailles took six years to complete.

ENTRANCE HALL

Two lifesize Sèvres **peacocks** were placed outside the entry doors to signify when Ludwig was in residence. Upon entering the castle, there is a large bronze **statue of King Louis XIV**, Ludwig's idol. On the ceiling above the statue is a gold sun, symbolizing the "Sun King" of France, inscribed with his motto: *Nec Pluribus Impar* ("I stand above others").

THRONE ROOM AND BEDCHAMBER

With paintings of Louis XIV and XV watching over him, Ludwig spent hours meticulously overseeing the architectural plans of his other projects from the green and gold **throne room**. The **bedchamber**, with its three-dimensional golden tapestries set against his favorite color, royal blue, look out to a waterfall cascading down the hill to the **Neptune fountain**, with its 100-foot water jet.

DINING ROOM

Ludwig would eat alone in the adjoining **dining room**. His extreme sweet tooth had wreaked havoc on his mouth so that by the time he was 30, most of his teeth were missing and dining was a messy affair. For his privacy, the dining table could be lowered down through the floor by cables and pulleys to the kitchen below. It would then reappear

Above, Schloss Linderhof. Opposite (top) Venus grotto, (bottom) Hall of Mirrors.

with Ludwig's meal so that he never had to dine with servants in the room.

HALL OF MIRRORS
The reclusive king spent his time reading and literally reflecting in the **hall of mirrors,** with its optical illusion infinitely reflecting his image and vast collection of vases lining the walls.

LINDERHOF'S GROUNDS
In the **Venus grotto,** Ludwig spent many evenings being paddled around in a scallop-shaped boat imagining he was in the world of Wagner's *Tannhäuser.* Ludwig would gather his equerries for decadent evenings spent in the **Moorish kiosk,** which was purchased wholesale from the 1867 Paris Universal Exposition, imagining himself as an Arabian knight lounging on his magnificent **peacock throne.** Deeper into the park is the **Hunding's hut,** a medieval-style lodge based on the set designs for the opening act of Wagner's *Die Walküre.* Ludwig took moonlit rides in winter to the original Hut, set deeply in the Alpine forest, in his gilt **gala sleigh.**

GETTING HERE AND AROUND

✉ Linderhof 12, Ettal-Linderhof
☎ 08822/92030 or -21
⊕ www.schlosslinderhof.de
🎫 €8.50, €7.50 winter
🕑 Open April–Oct. 15, daily 9-6; Oct. 16–March, daily 10-4; park buildings (grotto, Moorish kiosk, etc.) closed in winter

Car Travel: Take the A–95 motorway and the B–2 to Oberau. Follow the signs in Oberau to the B–23 (Ettaler Strasse). Outside Ettal turn left onto ST–2060. In Linderhof turn right to reach the palace.

Train Travel: Take the regional Deutsche Bahn train from Munich Hauptbahnhof to Oberammergau. Buy the Bayern Ticket, which allows for a full day of travel, including bus fare, for €25 for up to five people. From there, take bus 9622 to Linderhof.

Bus Tours: There are several tours combining both Linderhof and Neuschwanstein castles, but none that go just to Linderhof. **Gray Line Tours** (☎ 8954/907–560 ⊕ *www.grayline.com*) offers a day trip, including Linderhof, Neuschwanstein, and a short stop to shop in Oberammergau. It leaves daily at 8:30 am from the Karstadt Department store in front of the Munich Hauptbahnhof. Tickets are €72 for adults and €35 for children, not including admission.

SCHLOSS NEUSCHWANSTEIN

Neuschwanstein, the most famous of the three castles, was King Ludwig's crowning achievement. The castle soars from its mountainside like a stage creation—it should hardly come as a surprise that Walt Disney took it as the model for his castle in the movie *Sleeping Beauty* and later for the Disneyland castle itself.

Prince Ludwig spent idyllic childhood summers at **Hohenschwangau,** the neighboring medieval-style palace. The young prince was undoubtedly influenced by the vast murals of the legends of *Lohengrin* and romantic vision of these ancient times. Perhaps he envisioned his own, mightier palace when looking north to the mountains and the old ruins of a fortress of the Knights of Schwangau. Upon commencing construction in 1868, Ludwig wrote to Wagner, "The Gods will come to live with us on the lofty heights, breathing the air of heaven."

THRONE ROOM

Wagner's *Tannhäuser* inspired the Byzantine-style **throne room,** drawn from plans for the original stage set for the opera; however, the actual throne was never constructed. The massive chandelier is styled after a Byzantine crown and surrounded by images of angels, apostles, and six kings of history who were canonized as saints. Look closely at the image of St. George, the patron saint of the Wittelsbachs, slaying a dragon in front of another medieval castle. That castle, Falkenstein, was set to be the next, even grander castle of Ludwig II. The elaborate mosaic floor contains two million stones.

Above, Schloss Neuschwanstein. Opposite (top) Singers' Hall, (bottom) Ludwig II's bedchamber.

BEDCHAMBER

The king spent his last days as ruler huddled in his late-Gothic-style **bedchamber** modeled after the nuptial chamber of *Lohengrin*. It took fourteen craftsman more than four years to carve this room alone. The symbol of the swan occurs throughout Neuschwanstein, appearing here in the fixtures of the sink.

GROTTO

Reminiscent of the larger one at Linderhof, but stranger for its placement inside the palace, the **grotto** overlooking the Schwangau Valley once had a running waterfall lit by tinted lights.

SINGERS' HALL

Ludwig's favorite room, the **Singers' Hall**, was modeled after the stage design for the Forest of the Holy Grail from *Parsifal* and designed for the best acoustics. On moonless nights, the king would hike out to the Marienbrücke, over the rocky gorge, to watch the candlelit splendor of this hall. Ludwig never saw a performance here, but concerts are now held every September.

GETTING HERE AND AROUND

✉ Alpseestrasse 12, Hohenschwangau

☎ 8362/930–830

🌐 www.neuschwanstein.de

💳 €12 tickets are for a set tour time, reserve ahead online. English tours every 15 minutes.

🕙 Open mid-March–mid-Oct. daily 9–6; mid-Oct.–mid-March daily 10–4

Car Travel: Take the A–7 (direction Ulm-Kempten-Füssen) to the end. From Füssen, take B–17 to Schwangau, then follow signs to Hohenschwangau.

Train Travel: Take the regional Deutsche Bahn train from Munich Hauptbahnhof to Füssen (buy the Bayern Ticket). From Füssen, take either bus 73 toward Steingaden/Garmisch-Partenkirchen or bus 78 toward Schwangau until the Hohenschwangau/Alpseestrasse stop.

Getting to the Castle: Allow 30–40 minutes for the uphill walk from the ticket center to the castle. In summer, you can take a a bus (€1.80 uphill, €1 downhill) or horse-drawn carriage (€6 uphill, €3 downhill) up to the castle.

Bus Tours: Bus Bavaria (☎ 89255/43987 or -988 🌐 mikesbiketours.com) leaves from central Munich daily from mid-April through mid-October. Tours cost €39–€49, not including admission.

SCHLOSS HERRENCHIEMSEE

The third and what would be the last of King Ludwig II's building projects, Herrenchiemsee, modeled after Louis XIV's Versailles, stands as a monument to the institution of the monarchy and the Bourbon kings he idolized. Ludwig never intended to use this palace as a place to live but rather a place to visit to transport himself to the days when the Sun King ruled the glorious court of Versailles. Ludwig stayed at this palace only once, for a brief ten-day visit in September 1885.

CONSTRUCTION OF HERRENCHIEMSEE

Ludwig purchased the Herreninsel, the biggest of the three islands on Lake Chiemsee in 1873. Work soon began on gardens to rival the ones at Versailles.

By the time the foundation stone of the palace was laid in 1878, the soaring fountains were already in use. Although 300 local craftsmen worked day and night to replicate the Sun King's palace, only 20 of the planned 70 rooms saw completion during the following eight years of construction. They abound with marble, gilt, and paintings of the Bourbon court, the French style replicated by skilled Bavarian artists.

PARADE BEDCHAMBER

The sumptuous red brocade bedspread and wall hangings in the **parade bedchamber**, which is twice the size of the original in Versailles, took 30 women seven years to embroider. Red silk curtains can be pulled over the bay windows to give the room a glow of regal red, the symbolic color of the Bourbon court. Ludwig never slept in this room; it was created in memory of Louis XIV. Instead, Ludwig slept in the **king's bed-**

chamber, softly lit by blue candlelight from the large blue orb over his bed.

HALL OF MIRRORS

In the **hall of mirrors,** longer than the original in Versailles, Ludwig held private concerts during his short stay here. A team of 35 servants took a half-hour to light the 2,000 candles of the chandeliers and candelabra lining the golden room.

LUDWIG II MUSEUM

Ludwig gave strict orders that no image of the Wittelsbach rulers or of himself should be found in his French palace. Today, however, this is the only one of his three palaces to have a museum devoted to the king. You can see his christening gown, uniforms, architectural plans for future building projects, and even sample his favorite cologne in the castle's **Ludwig II Museum.**

GETTING HERE AND AROUND

✉ Herrenchiemsee

☎ 8051/68870

⊕ www.herrenchiemsee.de

🎫 €8

🕐 Open April–Oct. 15, daily 9–6; Oct. 16–March, daily 9:40-4:15

Boat Travel: Herrenchiemsee lies on the island of Herreninsel in Lake Chiemsee. **Chiemsee Schifffahrt's** (✉ *Seestrasse 108, Prien am Chiemsee* ☎ *8051/6090* ⊕ *www.chiemsee-schifffahrt.de*) ferries leave regularly from Prien/Stock daily from 7 am–6:30 pm. Tickets cost €6.90.

Car Travel: Take the A-8 motorway (Salzburg-Munich), leaving at the Bernau exit to continue to Prien am Chiemsee. At the roundabout outside Prien follow the signs to Chiemsee or Königsschloss.

Train Travel: Take the regional Deutsche Bahn train to Prien am Chiemsee, about an hour's ride from Munich (buy the Bayern Ticket). From the station, take the quaint **Chiemsee Bahn,** which winds through the town to the boats. It runs from April–October. Train and boat combination tickets cost €9.

Bus Tours: Gray Line Tours (☎ 8954/907-560 ⊕ www.grayline.com) offers a day trip, including the boat trip out to the castle (but not admission) and a visit to the Fraueninsel on Chiemsee for €47.

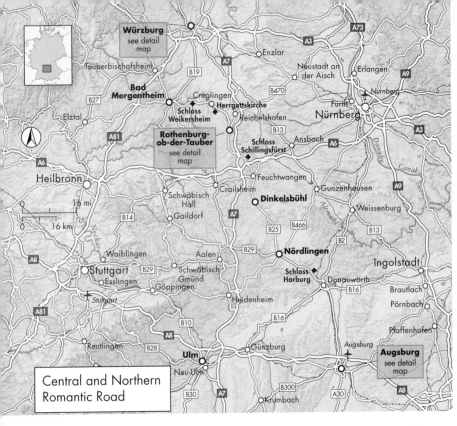

Central and Northern Romantic Road

$ **HOTEL** 🏨 **Altstadthotel Zum Hechten.** Directly below the castle, this is one of the town's oldest inns, family-run and with updated, airy rooms that are tidy and comfortable. **Pros:** in the center of town; parking available; good restaurants. **Cons:** difficult stairs to climb. $ *Rooms from: €97* ✉ *Ritterstr. 6* ☎ *08362/91600* ⊕ *www.hotel-hechten.com* 🛏 *35 rooms* ❍ *Breakfast.*

$$ **HOTEL** 🏨 **Hotel Hirsch.** Right on the main street, this family-owned hotel pays homage to traditional Bavarian style and its roof terrace has gorgeous views. **Pros:** in the center of town; good restaurant; rooms available for guests in wheelchairs. **Cons:** front rooms are noisy. $ *Rooms from: €125* ✉ *Kaiser-Maximilian-Pl. 7* ☎ *08362/93980* ⊕ *www.hotelhirsch. de* 🛏 *67 rooms* ❍ *Breakfast.*

$$$ **B&B/INN** **FAMILY** **Fodor's Choice** ★ 🏨 **Schlossanger Alp.** A century of family tradition embraces guests at this superb hotel combining the surroundings of a grand alpine hotel with the intimacy of a bed-and-breakfast. **Pros:** great food; attentive service; great for families. **Cons:** you'll need GPS to find it; a half-hour drive from Neuschwanstein; expensive. $ *Rooms from: €210* ✉ *Am Schlossanger 1, Pfronten* ☎ *08363/914–550* ⊕ *www.schlossanger.de* 🛏 *35 rooms* ❍ *Breakfast.*

EATING WELL ON THE ROMANTIC ROAD

To sample the authentic food of this area, venture off the beaten track of the official Romantic Road into any small town with a nice-looking *Gasthof* or *Wirtshaus*. Order *Sauerbraten* (roast beef marinated in a tangy sauce) with *Spätzle* (small boiled ribbons of rolled dough), or try *Maultaschen* (oversize Swabian ravioli stuffed with meat and herbs), another typical regional dish.

Franconia (the *Franken* region, which has its "capital" in Würzburg) is the sixth-largest wine-producing area of Germany. Franconian wines—half of which are made from the Müller-Thurgau grape hybrid, made from crossing Riesling with another white-wine grape—are served in distinctive green, flagon-shape wine bottles. Riesling and red wines account for only about 5% of the total production of Franconian wine.

Before you travel north on the Romantic Road, be sure to enjoy the beer country in the south. There is a wide range of Franconian and Bavarian brews available, from *Rauchbier* (literally, "smoked beer") to the lighter Pilsners of Augsburg. If this is your first time in Germany, beware of the potency of German beer—some can be quite strong. (In the past few years more and more breweries offer excellent alcohol-free versions of their products.) The smallest beers are served at 0.3 liters (slightly under 12 ounces). Restaurants typically serve 0.5 liters at a time; in most beer tents and beer gardens the typical service is a full 1-liter stein.

CENTRAL ROMANTIC ROAD

Picturesque Rothenburg-ob-der-Tauber is the highlight of this region, though certainly not the road less traveled. For a more intimate experience check out the medieval towns of Dinkelsbühl or Nördlingen, or take a side trip off the Romantic Road to see the tower at Ulm's famous protestant *Münster* (church).

AUGSBURG

70 km (43 miles) west of Munich.

Bavaria's third-largest city, Augsburg has long played a central role due to both its location and its religious history. It dates back to the Roman Empire, when in 15 BC a son of Augustus set up a military camp here on the banks of the Lech River. An important trading route, the Via Claudia Augusta, arose along the river connecting Italy to this silver-rich spot, and the settlement that grew up around it became known as Augusta, which is what Italians call the city to this day. The fashionable **Maximilianstrasse** lies on the Via Claudia Augusta, where the town's former wealth is still visible in its ornate architecture. City rights were granted Augsburg in 1156, and 200 years later, the Fugger family of bankers would become to Augsburg what the Medici were to Florence. Their wealth surpassed that of their Italian counterparts, though, such that they loaned funds to them from time to time. Their influence is felt throughout the city and several present-day members of the family run local charitable foundations.

GETTING HERE AND AROUND

Augsburg is on a main line of the high-speed ICE trains, which run hourly and take 45 minutes to get here from Munich. The center of town and its main attractions can be visited on foot. To continue on the Romantic Road, take a regional train from the main train station to Ulm, Donauwörth, or Nördlingen.

Walking tours (€8) set out from the tourist office on the Rathaus square daily at 2 and Saturday at 11. The tours, which are available in German and English, include entrance to the Fuggerei and the Goldener Saal in the Rathaus.

TIMING

It's easy to see the sights here, because signs on almost every street corner point the way to the main ones. See the tourist board's website for some additional walking-tour maps. You'll need a complete day to see Augsburg if you linger in any of the museums.

ESSENTIALS

Visitor Information Augsburg Tourist-Information. ⊠ *Rathauspl. 1* ☎ *0821/324–9410* ⊕ *www.augsburg-tourismus.de.*

EXPLORING

TOP ATTRACTIONS

Dom St. Maria (*Cathedral of St. Mary*). Augsburg's cathedral contains the oldest cycle of stained glass in central Europe and five important paintings by Hans Holbein the Elder, which adorn the altar. Originally built in the 9th century, the cathedral stands out because of its square Gothic towers, the product of a 14th-century update. A 10th-century Romanesque crypt also remains from the cathedral's early years. Those celebrated stained-glass windows, from the 11th century, are on the south side of the nave, and depict the prophets Jonah, Daniel, Hosea, Moses, and David.

A short walk from the cathedral will take you to the quiet courtyards and small raised garden of the former episcopal residence, a series of 18th-century baroque and rococo buildings that now serve as the Swabian regional government offices.

⊠ *Dompl., Johannisg. 8* ⊕ *www.bistum-augsburg.de* ▦ *Free* ☉ *Daily 9–dusk, except during hours of worship.*

Diözesanmuseum St. Afra. The cathedral's treasures are on display at this museum, which is directly behind the Dom. ⊠ *Kornhausg. 3–5* ⊕ *www.museum-st-afra.de* ▦ *€4* ☉ *Tues.–Sat. 10–5, Sun. noon–6.*

Fuggerei. The world's oldest social housing project, this settlement was established by the wealthy Fugger family in 1516 to accommodate Augsburg's deserving poor. The 67 homes with 140 apartments still serve the same purpose and house about 150 people today. It's financed almost exclusively from the assets of the foundation, because the annual rent of "one Rhenish guilder" (€1) hasn't changed, either. Residents must be Augsburg citizens, Catholic, and destitute through no fault of their own—and they must pray three times daily for their original

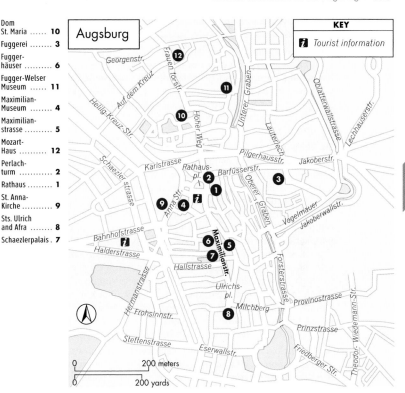

benefactors, the Fugger family. The most famous resident was Mozart's great-grandfather. ⊠ *Jakoberstr.* ☎ *0821/3198–8114* ⊕ *www.fugger.de* 🎫 *€4* ⊙ *Apr.–Oct., daily 8–8; Nov.–Mar., daily 9–6.*

Fugger-Welser Museum. This museum, housed in a fine restored Renaissance building, is dedicated to two of the city's most influential benefactors, the Fugger and Welser families, whose banking and merchant empire brought Italian art and world artifacts along with wealth to Augsburg in the 15th and 16th centuries. Providing insight into how the families contributed to the city, the museum offers both a glimpse into life in the 15th century and a hands-on lesson in Augsburg history. ⊠ *Ausser Pfaffengässchen 23* ☎ *0821/502070* ⊕ *www.fugger-und-welser-museum.de* 🎫 *€5* ⊙ *Tues.–Sun. 10–5.*

Maximilian-Museum. Augsburg's main museum houses a permanent exhibition of Augsburg arts and crafts in a 16th-century merchant's mansion. ⊠ *Fuggerpl. 1 (Philippine-Welser-Str. 24)* ☎ *0821/324–4102* ⊕ *www.kunstsammlungen-museen.augsburg.de* 🎫 *€7* ⊙ *Tues.–Sun. 10–5.*

Perlachturm (*Perlach Tower*). This plastered brick bell tower has foundations dating to the year 989 when it was constructed as a watchtower. Climbing the 258 stairs to the top of the 230-foot tower will provide you with gorgeous views of Augsburg and the countryside. Just be sure to time it to avoid being beneath the bells when they begin to chime. ⊠ *Rathauspl.* 🖳 *€2* ☉ *May–Nov., daily 10–6; Dec., Fri.–Sun. 2–6.*

Rathaus. Augsburg's town hall was Germany's largest when it was built in the early 17th century; it's now regarded as the finest secular Renaissance structure north of the Alps. Its **Goldener Saal** (Golden Hall) was given its name because of its rich decoration—8 pounds of gold are spread over its wall frescoes, carved pillars, and coffered ceiling. ⊠ *Rathauspl. 2* ⊕ *www.augsburg.de* 🖳 *€2.50* ☉ *Daily 10–6 (closed during official functions).*

Sts. Ulrich and Afra. Standing at the highest point of the city, this Catholic basilica with an attached Protestant chapel symbolizes the Peace of Augsburg, the treaty that ended the religious struggle between the two groups. On the site of a Roman cemetery where St. Afra was martyred in AD 304, the original structure was built in the late-Gothic style in 1467. St. Afra is buried in the crypt, near the tomb of St. Ulrich, a 10th-century bishop who helped stop a Hungarian army at the gates of Augsburg in the Battle of the Lech River. The remains of a third patron of the church, St. Simpert, are preserved in one of the church's most elaborate side chapels. From the steps of the magnificent altar, look back along the high nave to the finely carved baroque wrought-iron-and-wood railing that borders the entrance. As you leave, look into the separate but adjacent church of St. Ulrich, the baroque preaching hall that was added for the Protestant community in 1710, after the Reformation. ⊠ *Ulrichspl. 19* ⊕ *www.ulrichsbasilika.de* 🖳 *Free* ☉ *Daily 9–dusk.*

Schaezlerpalais. This elegant 18th-century city palace was built by the von Liebenhofens, a family of wealthy bankers. Schaezler was the name of a baron who married into the family. Today the palace rooms contain the **Deutsche Barockgalerie** (German Baroque Gallery), a major art collection that features works of the 17th and 18th centuries. The palace adjoins the former church of a Dominican monastery. A steel door behind the banquet hall leads into another world of high-vaulted ceilings, where the **Staatsgalerie Altdeutsche Meister,** a Bavarian state collection, highlights old-master paintings, among them a Dürer portrait of one of the Fuggers. ⊠ *Maximilianstr. 46* ☎ *0821/324–4102* ⊕ *www. kunstsammlungen-museen.augsburg.de* 🖳 *€7* ☉ *Tues.–Sun. 10–5.*

WORTH NOTING

Fuggerhäuser. The 16th-century house and business quarters of the Fugger family now has a restaurant in its cellar and offices on the upper floors. Only the three courtyards here are open to the public, but you can peek into the ground-floor entrance to see busts of two of Augsburg's most industrious Fuggers, Raymund and Anton. Beyond a modern glass door is the *Damenhof* (Ladies' Courtyard), originally reserved for the Fugger women. ⊠ *Maximilianstr. 36–38* 🖳 *Free* ☉ *Courtyards 11–3 and 6–midnight (summer only).*

Maximilianstrasse. Most of the city's sights are on Augsburg's main shopping street or a short walk away. It was once a medieval wine market along the Roman road, and the history still shows in the architecture. Punctuating the street are two monumental and elaborate fountains: at the north end is the **Merkur,** designed in 1599 by the Dutch master

Climb the 258 steps of the Perlachturm (Perlach Tower) beside the Rathaus for a spectacular vantage point over Augsburg.

Adrian de Vries (after a Florentine sculpture by Giovanni da Bologna) and showing winged Mercury in his classic pose; farther along is a de Vries–designed bronze **Hercules** struggling to subdue the many-headed Hydra. ⊠ *Augsburg.*

Mozart-Haus (*Mozart House*). Leopold Mozart, the father of Wolfgang Amadeus Mozart, and an accomplished composer and musician in his own right, was born in this bourgeois 17th-century residence. The house now serves as a Mozart memorial and museum, with some fascinating contemporary documents on the Mozart family, some of whom still live in the area today. ⊠ *Frauentorstr. 30* ☎ *0821/518–588* ⊕ *www. mozartgesellschaft.de* ⊠ *€3.50* ⊗ *Tues.–Sun. 10–5.*

St. Anna-Kirche (*St. Anna's Church*). This site was formerly part of a Carmelite monastery, where Martin Luther stayed in 1518 during his meetings with Cardinal Cajetanus, the papal legate sent from Rome to persuade the reformer to renounce his heretical views. Luther refused, and the place where he publicly declared his rejection of papal pressure is marked with a plaque on Maximilianstrasse. You can wander through the quiet cloisters, dating from the 14th century, and view the chapel used by the Fugger family until the Reformation. ⊠ *Anna-Str., west of Rathauspl.* ⊠ *Free* ⊗ *May–Oct., Mon. noon–5, Tues.–Sat. 10–6, Sun. 3–5; Nov.–Apr., Tues.–Sat. 10–5, Sun. 3–4.*

WHERE TO EAT

$$$
EUROPEAN
Fodor'sChoice
★

✕**Die Ecke.** In season, the venison dishes are among Bavaria's best at this imaginative restaurant, on an *Ecke* (corner) of the small square right behind Augsburg's town hall. The fish, in particular the *zander* (green pike) or the trout (sautéed in butter with herbs and lemon), is magnificent, and complemented nicely by the Riesling Gimmeldinger Meersspinne, the house wine for 40 years. In summer ask for a table on the patio. $ *Average main: €21* ✉ *Elias-Holl-Pl. 2* ☎ *0821/510–600* ⊕ *www.restaurant-die-ecke.de* ⌖ *Reservations essential.*

$

GERMAN

✕ **Ratskeller Augsburg.** Underneath the impressive Rathaus lies this vaulted redbrick destination for Bavarian food and drink, especially at the end of a long day. It's surprisingly airy, and busy with business lunches during the day. The friendly staff serves up traditional fare with plenty of choices, and it stays open late (until 1 am most nights, 2 am Friday and Saturday), after most other local restaurants have closed. There's an expansive cocktail menu that you can make the most of during the daily happy hour. $ *Average main: €13* ✉ *Ratshauspl. 2* ☎ *0821/3198–8238* ⊕ *www.ratskeller-augsburg.de* ▭ *No credit cards.*

WHERE TO STAY

$

HOTEL

🏨 **Dom Hotel.** Just around the corner from Augsburg's cathedral, this snug establishment has personality to spare, with a long history of hosting official church visitors, and an up-to-the-minute renovation that's provided good modern amenities. **Pros:** family-run, with good attention to detail; parking; nice view from upper rooms; central but quiet. **Cons:** stairs not wheelchair-friendly; no restaurant or bar. $ *Rooms from: €85* ✉ *Frauentorstr. 8* ☎ *0821/343–930* ⊕ *www.domhotel-augsburg.de* ⊗ *Closed late Dec.–1st wk of Jan.* ⟳ *44 rooms, 8 suites* ⦿ *Breakfast.*

$$

HOTEL

🏨 **Steigenberger Drei Mohren Hotel.** Kings and princes, Napoléon, and the Duke of Wellington have all slept here, and these days all the rooms have been modernized and a spa area added without detracting from the 500-year-old building's traditional luxury. **Pros:** spacious lobby with inviting bar; very good restaurants; cheaper weekend rates; spa amenities. **Cons:** can be booked out weekdays due to conventions. $ *Rooms from: €130* ✉ *Maximilianstr. 40* ☎ *0821/50360* ⊕ *www.augsburg. steigenberger.de* ⟳ *131 rooms* ⦿ *Breakfast.*

PERFORMING ARTS

Augsburg has chamber and symphony orchestras, as well as ballet and opera companies. The city stages a Mozart Festival of international stature in September.

FAMILY **Augsburger Puppenkiste** (*Puppet theater*). This children's puppet theater next to Rotes Tor has been an institution in Germany since its inception in 1948. It's still loved by kids and parents alike. Check the website for showtimes (only in German). The museum, featuring puppets in historic or fairy-tale settings, is open Tuesday–Sunday 10–7 and admission is €4.50 (€2.90 for children). ✉ *Spitalg. 15* ☎ *0821/450–3450* ⊕ *www. augsburger-puppenkiste.de* ⊗ *Closed during school summer holidays, usually July and August.*

Freilichtbühne. One of Germany's most beautiful open-air theaters, Augsburg's Freilichtbühne located directly at the Red Gate is the setting for a number of operas, operettas and musicals (all in German) from mid-June through July. ✉ *Am Roten Tor* ☎ *0821/324–4900 tourist office* ⊕ *www.theater.augsburg.de.*

ULM

85 km (53 miles) west of Augsburg.

Just off the Romantic Road, Ulm is worth a visit, if only briefly, to see its mighty Münster. The evangelical church is unusually ornate and has the world's tallest church tower (536 feet). Grown out of a medieval trading city thanks to its location on the Danube River, Ulm's Old Town is located directly on the river, which only adds to its charm. Each year, on the penultimate Monday in July—Schwörmontag—the townsfolk celebrate the mayor's "State of the Union" speech by parading down the Danube in homemade floating devices that make for a riotous sight. In the Fishermen's and Tanners' quarters the cobblestone alleys and stone-and-wood bridges over the Blau (a small Danube tributary) are especially picturesque. And down by the banks of the Danube, you'll find long sections of the old city wall and fortifications intact.

GETTING HERE AND AROUND

To get to Ulm from Augsburg, take Highway A-8 west or take a 40-minute ride on one of the ICE (InterCity Express) trains that run to Ulm every hour.

TOURS

Ulm Tourist-Information Tours. The tourist office's 90-minute tours include a visit to the Münster, the Old Town Hall, the Fischerviertel (Fishermen's Quarter), and the Danube riverbank. The departure point is the tourist office (Stadthaus) on Münsterplatz, and tours take place throughout the day. ☒ *Ulm Tourist-Information, Münsterpl. 50* ☎ *0731/161–2830* ⊕ *www.tourismus.ulm.de* ☒ *€8.*

EXPLORING

Marktplatz. The central Marktplatz is bordered by medieval houses with stepped gables. Every Wednesday and Saturday farmers from the surrounding area arrive by 6 am to erect their stands and unload their produce. Potatoes, vegetables, apples, pears, berries, honey, fresh eggs, poultry, homemade bread, and many other edible things are carefully displayed. Get here early; the market packs up around noon. ☒ *Ulm.*

Münster. Ulm's Münster, built by the citizens of their own initiative, is the largest evangelical church in Germany and one of the most elaborately decorated. Its church tower, just 13 feet higher than that of the Cologne Cathedral, is the world's highest, at 536 feet. It stands over the huddled medieval gables of Old Ulm with a single, filigree tower that challenges the physically fit to plod up the 768 steps of a giddily twisting spiral stone staircase to a spectacular observation point below the spire. On clear days, the steeple will reward you with views of the Swiss and Bavarian Alps, 160 km (100 miles) to the south. Construction on the Münster began in the late-Gothic age (1377) and took five centuries; it gave rise to the legend of the sparrow, which was said to have helped the townspeople in their building by inspiring them to pile the wood used in construction lengthwise instead of width-wise on wagons in order to pass through the city gates. Completed in the neo-Gothic years of the late 19th century, the church contains some notable treasures, including late-Gothic choir stalls and a Renaissance altar

as well as images of the inspirational sparrow. Ulm itself was heavily bombed during World War II, but the church was spared. Its mighty organ can be heard in special recitals every Sunday at noon from Easter until November. ☒ *Münsterpl. 21* ⊕ *www.ulmer-muenster.de* ☜ *Free; tower €4* ⊙ *Münster: July and Aug., daily 9–7:45; Apr.–June and Sept., daily 9–6:45; Mar. and Oct., daily 9–5:45; Jan., Feb., Nov., and Dec., daily 9–4:45. Tower: July and Aug., daily 9–6:45; Apr.–June and Sept., daily 9–5:45; Mar. and Oct., daily 9–4:45; Nov.–Feb., daily 9–3:45.*

Museum der Brotkultur (*German Bread Museum*). German bread is world renowned, so it's no surprise that a national museum is devoted to it. It's by no means as crusty or dry as you might fear, with some amusing exhibits showing how bread has been baked over the centuries. The museum is in a former salt warehouse, just north of the Münster. ☒ *Salzstadelg. 10* ☎ *0731/69955* ⊕ *www.museum-brotkultur.de* ☜ *€4* ⊙ *Daily 10–5.*

Ulmer Museum (*Ulm Museum*). The recently discovered Löwenmensch, a 40,000-year-old figure of a half-man, half-lion found in a nearby cave, is the main attraction at this natural history and art museum, which also illustrates centuries of development in this part of the Danube Valley. Art lovers will appreciate its collection of works by such modern artists as Kandinsky, Klee, Léger, and Lichtenstein. ☒ *Marktpl. 9* ☎ *0731/161–4330* ⊕ *www.museum.ulm.de* ☜ *€5* ⊙ *Tues.–Sun. 11–5.*

WHERE TO EAT AND STAY

$$
GERMAN
✕ **Zunfthaus der Schiffleute.** The sturdy half-timber Zunfthaus (Guildhall) has stood here for more than 500 years, first as a fishermen's pub and now as a charming tavern-restaurant. Ulm's fishermen had their guild headquarters here, and when the nearby Danube flooded, the fish swam right up to the door. Today they land on the menu, which also includes dry-aged steak as well as "Swabian oysters" (actually snails, drenched in garlic butter). The local beer makes an excellent accompaniment. Ⓢ *Average main: €15* ☒ *Fischerg. 31* ☎ *0731/64411* ⊕ *www. zunfthaus-ulm.de.*

$$
GERMAN
Fodor's Choice
★
✕ **Zur Forelle.** For more than 350 years Forelle ("Trout") has stood over the small, clear River Blau, which flows through a large trout basin right under the restaurant. In addition to the trout, there are five other fish dishes available, as well as excellent venison in season. On a nice summer evening, try to get a table on the small terrace. You sit over the river, with a weeping willow on one side, half-timber houses around you, and the towering cathedral in the background. Ⓢ *Average main: €19* ☒ *Fischerg. 25* ☎ *0731/63924* ⊕ *www.zurforelle.com.*

$
HOTEL
⌂ **Hotel am Rathaus/Reblaus.** Some of the rooms have vintage furniture at this family-owned hotel, which is also adorned with antique paintings and dolls. **Pros:** in the center of the city; artistic touches; good value; family-run. **Cons:** no elevator; not enough parking. Ⓢ *Rooms from: €98* ☒ *Kroneng. 8–10* ☎ *0731/968–490* ⊕ *www.rathausulm.de* ⊙ *Closed Christmas–early Jan.* ➥ *34 rooms* ⏐◯⏐ *Breakfast.*

NÖRDLINGEN

90 km (56 miles) northeast of Ulm, 72 km (45 miles) northwest of Augsburg.

In Nördlingen a medieval watchman's cry still rings out every night across the ancient walls and turrets. As in Rothenburg, its sister city, the medieval walls are completely intact, but here you can actually walk the entire circuit (about 4 km [2½ miles]) beginning at any of six original gates. Enjoy the peaceful atmosphere while taking in the riot of architecture, from the medieval to the Renaissance and the baroque, without the masses of tourists of its sister city. Or ask at the tourist office for accommodations in one of the small houses built into the city's wall for a unique overnight experience. The ground plan of the town is two concentric circles. The inner circle of streets, whose central point is St. Georg, marks the earliest medieval boundary. A few hundred yards beyond it is the outer boundary, a wall built to accommodate expansion. Fortified with 11 towers and punctuated by five massive gates, it's one of the best-preserved town walls in Germany. And if the Old Town looks a little familiar, it might be because the closing aerial shots in the 1971 film *Willy Wonka and the Chocolate Factory* were filmed over its red roofs.

Nördlingen was established along the same Roman road that goes through Augsburg, but its "foundation" goes much further back—the town is built in the center of a huge, basinlike depression, the Ries, which was at first believed to be the remains of an extinct volcano. In 1960 it was proven by two Americans that the crater, 24 km (15 miles) across, was caused by an asteroid at least 1 km (½ mile) in diameter that hit the spot some 15 million years ago. The compressed rock, or *Suevit,* formed by the explosive impact of the meteorite was used to construct many of the town's buildings, including St. Georg's tower.

GETTING HERE AND AROUND

About an hour's drive northwest from Ulm up the A-7, Nördlingen is also easily accessible from Donauworth via the B-25 by following the brown route signs directing you along the Romantic Road. During the week, a regional train can bring you from Donauworth into the city center twice hourly; weekends, the train runs every two hours.

ESSENTIALS

Visitor Information Nördlingen Tourist-Information. ✉ *Marktpl. 2* ☎ *09081/84116* ⊕ *www.noerdlingen.de.*

EXPLORING

St. Georg's Church. Watchmen still sound out the traditional "So G'sell so" ("All's well") message from the 300-foot tower of the central parish church of St. Georg at half-hour intervals between 10 pm and midnight. The tradition goes back to an incident during the Thirty Years' War, when an enemy attempted to slip into the town and was detected by a resident. You can climb the 365 steps up the tower—known locally as the Daniel—for an unsurpassed view of the town and countryside, including, on clear days, 99 villages. ✉ *Marktpl.* 🎟 *Tower €3* ⊙ *Church: Apr.–Oct., weekdays 9:30–12:30 and 2–5, weekends*

9:30–5; Nov.–Mar., Tues.–Sat. 10:30–12:30. Tower daily: July and Aug., 9–7; May, June, and Sept., 9–6; Mar., Apr., and Oct., 10–5; Dec., 9–5; Jan. and Feb., 10–4.

WHERE TO STAY

$ 🏨 **Hotel Goldene Rose.** This small, modern hotel just inside the town
HOTEL   wall is ideal for those wishing to explore Nördlingen on foot. **Pros:**
FAMILY family-friendly; parking in courtyard. **Cons:** front rooms noisy; restaurant closed Sunday. ⓈRooms from: €65 ⊠Baldingerstr. 42
☎09081/86019 ⊕www.goldene-rose-noerdlingen.de ↳17 rooms, 1
apartment ⎹⊙⎸Breakfast.

SPORTS AND THE OUTDOORS

Nördlingen Ries. Ever cycled around a huge meteor crater? You can do
just that in the Nördlingen Ries, the depression left by an asteroid that
hit the area 14.5 million years ago. This impact crater is a designated
national geopark and the best-preserved impact crater in all of Europe.
⊠Dorfstr. ✛9 km northeast of Nördlingen via B-466.

DINKELSBÜHL

32 km (20 miles) north of Nördlingen.

Within the walls of Dinkelsbühl, a beautifully preserved medieval town,
the rush of traffic seems a lifetime away. Although there is less to see
here than in Rothenburg, the town is a pleasant break from the crowds,
and you can relax among the locals at one of the Gasthauses in the
town's central Marktplatz. You can patrol the illuminated Old Town
with the night watchman at 9 pm free of charge, starting from the
Münster St. Georg.

GETTING HERE AND AROUND

About 30 minutes' drive south of Würzburg on the Romantic Road,
Dinkelsbühl is best accessed by car as it's right on the B-25. Once you
reach the city gates, however, the cobblestone streets are narrow, and
a maze of one-ways will have you lost in no time, so park outside one
of the city gates and walk.

ESSENTIALS

Visitor Information Dinkelsbühl Tourist-Information. ⊠ Marktpl.,
Altrathauspl. 14 ☎ 09851/902–440 ⊕ www.dinkelsbuehl.de. **Romantische
Strasse Touristik-Arbeitsgemeinschaft** (Romantic Road Central Tourist-Infor-
mation). ⊠ Segringerstr. 19 ☎ 09851/551–387 ⊕ www.romantischestrasse.de.

EXPLORING

Münster St. Georg (*Cathedral St. George*). Dinkelsbühl's main church
is the standout sight in town. At 235 feet long it's large enough to be
a cathedral, and is among the best examples in Bavaria of the late-
Gothic style. Note the complex fan vaulting that spreads sinuously
across the ceiling. If you can face the climb, head up the 200-foot tower
for amazing views over the jumble of rooftops. ⊠ Marktpl., Kirchhö-
flein 6 ☎ 09851/2245 ⊕ www.st-georg-dinkelsbuehl.de 🗷 Free; tower
€1.50 ⊙ Church: summer, daily 9–noon and 2–7; winter, daily 9–noon
and 2–5; tower: May–Sept., Fri.–Sun. 2–5.

WHERE TO STAY

$
B&B/INN

Goldene Rose. Since 1450 the inhabitants of Dinkelsbühl and their guests—among them Queen Victoria in 1891—have enjoyed a good night's sleep, great food, and refreshing drinks in this half-timber house, and its owners take great pride in its history. **Pros:** family-friendly; good food; parking lot. **Cons:** some rooms need renovating; front rooms are noisy. $ *Rooms from: €78* ⊠ *Marktpl. 4* ☎ *09851/57750* ⊕ *www.hotel-goldene-rose.com* 🔄 *34 rooms* ⦿| *Breakfast.*

$$
HOTEL

Hezelhof Hotel. A new addition to the Dinkelsbühl accommodations scene, the Hezelhof combines three charming timber-frame buildings from the 16th century, renovated inside to provide comfortable modern rooms with the latest designer furnishings. **Pros:** newly renovated; quiet courtyard with views; central location; old Patrician House adds charm. **Cons:** some rooms may be noisy with windows open. $ *Rooms from: €120* ⊠ *Segringer Str. 7* ☎ *09851/555–420* ⊕ *www.hezelhof.com* 🔄 *53 rooms* ⦿| *Breakfast.*

$$
HOTEL

Hotel Deutsches Haus. As you step into this medieval inn with a facade of half-timber gables and flower boxes, an old sturdy bar gives you a chance to register while sitting down and enjoying a drink. **Pros:** modern touches like free Wi-Fi. **Cons:** some rooms noisy; pricey; steps to climb. $ *Rooms from: €129* ⊠ *Weinmarkt 3* ☎ *09851/6058* ⊕ *www.deutsches-haus-dkb.de* 🔄 *16 rooms, 2 suites* ⦿| *Breakfast.*

ROTHENBURG-OB-DER-TAUBER

50 km (31 miles) north of Dinkelsbühl, 90 km (56 miles) west of Nürnberg.

Fodor'sChoice
★

Rothenburg-ob-der-Tauber (literally, the "red castle on the Tauber") is the kind of medieval town that even Walt Disney might have thought too picturesque to be true, with half-timber architecture galore and a wealth of fountains and flowers against a backdrop of towers and turrets. As late as the 17th century, it was a small but thriving market town that had grown up around the ruins of two 12th-century churches destroyed by an earthquake. Then it was laid low economically by the havoc of the Thirty Years' War, and with its economic base devastated, the town remained a backwater until modern tourism rediscovered it.

GETTING HERE AND AROUND

The easiest way to get here is via the Romantic Road bus from Augsburg via Donauwörth, Nördlingen, and Dinkelsbühl, with an optional layover on the way. If you arrive by car, there are large metered parking lots just outside the town wall. By local train it takes about 2½ hours from Augsburg, with two train changes.

All attractions within the walled town can easily be reached on foot.

TOURS

Night Watchman Tour. A local legend, the costumed night watchman conducts a one-hour tour of the town nearly every night year-round, leading the way with a lantern. The tour begins at 8 pm at the Marktplatz, and private group tours can be arranged. A 90-minute daytime tour begins at 2 pm. ⊠ *Marktpl., Rothenburg ob der Tauber* ☎ *09861/404–800 tourist office* ⊕ *www.nightwatchman.de* 🔄 *€8.*

FESTIVALS

Der Meistertrunk Festspiel (*The Master Draught Historical Fest*). From Friday through Monday over Whitsun (Pentecost) weekend every year, the town celebrates the famous wager said to have saved it from destruction in 1631, at the height of the Thirty Years' War. A play of the events takes place every day, and handicraft and artisan markets, along with food stands, fill the town squares. ⊠ *Rothenburg ob der Tauber* ⊕ *www.meistertrunk.de.*

Schäfertanz (*Shepherd's Dance*). A **Schäfertanz** (Shepherds' Dance) was once performed around the **Herterichbrunnen,** the ornate Renaissance fountain on the central Marktplatz, whenever Rothenburg celebrated a major event. Although its origins go back to local shepherds' annual gatherings, the dance is now celebrated with locals from the area costumed as maids, shepherds, soldiers, and nobility. It takes place in front of the Rathaus several times a year, chiefly at Easter, Pentecost, and in September as part of the Imperial City Festival. ⊠ *Am Marktpl., Rothenburg ob der Tauber* ⊕ *www.schaefertanzrothenburg.de.*

TIMING

Always busy with tourists, the town is best visited in early fall or late spring, when the crowds are thinner and the streets more easily explored in peace. Christmas markets in December also add a special atmosphere to brighten the short days. The best time to see the mechanical figures on the Rathaus wall is in the evening.

ESSENTIALS

Visitor Information Rothenburg-ob-der-Tauber Tourist-Information.
⊠ *Rathaus, Am Marktpl. 2, Rothenburg ob der Tauber* ☎ *09861/404–800*
⊕ *www.tourismus.rothenburg.de.*

EXPLORING

TOP ATTRACTIONS

Meistertrunkuhr. The tale of the Meistertrunk (Master Draught) and a prodigious civil servant dates to 1631, when the Protestant town was captured by Catholic forces during the Thirty Years' War. At the victory celebrations, the conquering general was embarrassed to find himself unable to drink a great tankard of wine in one go, as his manhood demanded. He volunteered to spare the town further destruction if any of the city councilors could drain the mighty six-pint draft. The mayor took up the challenge and succeeded, and Rothenburg was preserved. The tankard itself is on display at the Reichsstadtmuseum. On the north side of the main square is a fine clock, placed there 50 years after the mayor's feat. A mechanical figure acts out the epic Master Drink daily on the hour from 10 to 10. The feat is reenacted in the historical play

"The Master Draught," and celebrated at two annual pageants, when townsfolk parade through the streets in 17th-century garb. ⊠ *Am Marktpl., Rothenburg ob der Tauber.*

Stadtmauer (*City Wall*). Rothenburg's city walls are more than 4 km (2½ miles) long and dotted with 42 red-roofed watchtowers. Due to its age, only about half of the wall can be accessed on foot, but it provides an excellent way of circumnavigating the town from above. Let your imagination take you back 500 years as you explore the low, covered sentries' walkways, which are punctuated by cannons, turrets, and areas where the town guards met. Stairs every 200 or 300 yards provide ready access. There are superb views of the tangle of pointed and tiled red roofs and of the rolling country beyond. ⊠ *Rothenburg ob der Tauber.*

WORTH NOTING

Historiengewölbe (*Historic Vaults*). Below the Rathaus building are the historic vaults and dungeons, housing a museum that brings the Thirty Years' War to life with eight themed exhibition rooms, including one dedicated to the battle armor used in the 16th and 17th centuries. ⊠ *Rathaus Am Marktpl., Rothenburg ob der Tauber* ⊠ €2 ☉ *Mid-Mar.–Mar. 31, daily noon–4; Apr., daily 10–4; May–Oct., daily 9:30–5:30; Nov., weekdays 1–4, weekends 10–4; Dec., weekdays 1–4, weekends 10–7.*

Rathaus. The Rathaus's tower, in the center of town, gives you a good view. Half of the town hall is Gothic, begun in 1240; the other half is neoclassical, started in 1572, and renovated after its original facade was destroyed by a fire 500 years ago. ⊠ *Rathauspl., Am Marktpl., Rothenburg ob der Tauber* ⊕ *www.rothenburg.de* ⊠ *Tower €3* ☉ *Tower: Apr.–Oct., daily 9:30–12:30 and 1–5; Jan.–Mar. and Nov., weekends noon–3; Dec., daily 10:30–2 and 2:30–6.*

Reichsstadtmuseum (*Imperial Town Museum*). This city museum, in a former Dominican convent dating back to the 13th century, includes a cloister where one of the artifacts is the great tankard, or *Pokal*, of the Meistertrunk (Master Drink). A recent addition, the Baumann Foundation, displays valuable weapons such as hunting weapons used by Marie Antoinette and a hunting rifle belonging to Frederick the Great of Prussia. Through September 2017, a special exhibition takes a closer look at the role of propaganda during the Reformation. ⊠ *Klosterhof 5, Rothenburg ob der Tauber* ☎ *09861/939–043* ⊕ *www.reichsstadtmuseum.rothenburg.de* ⊠ *€5.50* ☉ *Apr.–Oct., daily 9:30–5:30; Nov.–Mar., daily 1–4.*

St. Jakob Church. This Lutheran parish church, constructed from 1311 to 1485, showcases 600 years of stained-glass windows and has notable Riemenschneider sculptures, including the famous *Heiliges Blut* (Holy Blood of Christ) altar. Above the altar is a crystal capsule said to contain drops of Christ's blood. The Twelve Apostles Altar, by Friedrich Herlin, has the oldest depiction of the town of Rothenburg. ⊠ *Klosterg. 15, Rothenburg ob der Tauber* ☎ *09861/700–620* ⊕ *www.rothenburgtauber-evangelisch.de* ⊠ *€2* ☉ *Jan.–Mar. and Nov., daily 10–noon and 2–4; Apr.–Oct., daily 9–5; Dec., daily 10–4:45. Tours in English Sat. at 3:30.*

Historiengewölbe **2**
Meistertrunkuhr **3**
Rathaus **1**
Reichsstadtmuseum **5**
St. Jakob Church **4**
Stadtmauer **6**

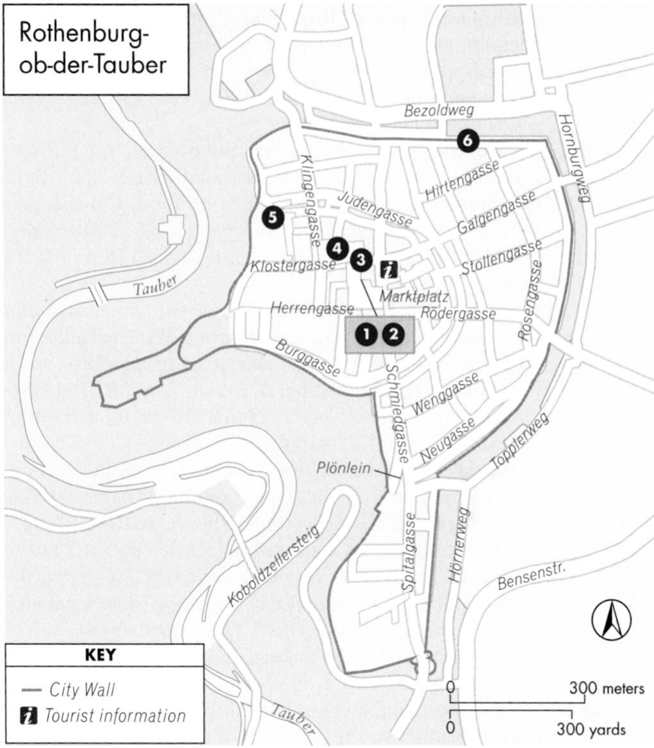
Rothenburg-ob-der-Tauber
Bezoldweg
Hornburgweg
Klingengasse
Judengasse
Hirtengasse
Galgengasse
Stollengasse
Klostergasse
Marktplatz
Rödergasse
Rosengasse
Herrengasse
Burggasse
Schmiedgasse
Wenggasse
Neugasse
Topplerweg
Plönlein
Tauber
Koboldzellersteig
Spitalgasse
Hörnerweg
Bensenstr.
KEY
City Wall
Tourist information
0
300 meters
0
300 yards

WHERE TO EAT

$ GERMAN 🍴 **Restaurant-Zur Höll.** In a building dating back to 900, the "To Hell" restaurant is a great place to head for a snack after a night watchman's tour. The basic but tasty main menu is complemented throughout the year by seasonal and local dishes and ingredients, such as *Pfefferlinge* (chanterelles, served in soups, salads, and sauces). With an extensive selection of Franconian wine and a delicious house beer, you'll have a nice late evening experience. In the busier months, reserve a table ahead of time to guarantee a spot for later in the evenings. [$] *Average main: €12* ✉ *Burgg. 8, Rothenburg ob der Tauber* ☎ *098/614–229* 🌐 *www.hoell.rothenburg.de* 💳 *No credit cards* 🕒 *Closed Mon.*

WHERE TO STAY

$$ B&B/INN Fodor's Choice ★ 🏨 **Burg-Hotel.** At this exquisite little hotel most rooms have a view of the romantic Tauber Valley, and they also have plush furnishings, with antiques or fine reproductions. **Pros:** no crowds; terrific view from most rooms; parking; bike rentals available for small fee. **Cons:** no restaurant; too quiet for kids. [$] *Rooms from: €165* ✉ *Klosterg. 1–3, Rothenburg ob der Tauber* ☎ *09861/94890* 🌐 *www.burghotel.eu* 🛏 *30 rooms, 3 apartments* 🍽 *Breakfast.*

$ B&B/INN 🏨 **Gasthof Klingentor.** This sturdy former staging post, run by the welcoming Wagenländer Family, is outside the city walls but still within a 10-minute walk of Rothenburg's historic center. **Pros:** good value; friendly restaurant popular with locals and guests. **Cons:** front rooms are noisy; no elevator. $ *Rooms from: €80* ✉ *Mergentheimerstr. 14, Rothenburg ob der Tauber* ☎ *09861/3468* ⊕ *www.hotel-klingentor.de* ⇨ *20 rooms* ⚲ *Breakfast.*

$$ ⛫ **Hotel Eisenhut.** It's fitting that the prettiest small town in Germany
HOTEL should have one of the prettiest small hotels in its center. **Pros:** elegant lobby; exceptional service; good food. **Cons:** expensive; not for kids. $ *Rooms from: €150* ✉ *Herrng. 3–5/7, Rothenburg ob der Tauber* ☎ *09861/7050* ⊕ *www.eisenhut.com* ⇨ *78 rooms, 2 suites* ⚲ *No meals.*

$ ⛫ **Hotel-Gasthof Post.** This small family-run hotel, two minutes on foot
B&B/INN from the eastern city gate, must be one of the friendliest in town. **Pros:**
FAMILY good value; family-friendly. **Cons:** front rooms noisy; no elevator; some bathrooms need renovating. $ *Rooms from: €70* ✉ *Ansbacherstr. 27, Rothenburg ob der Tauber* ☎ *09861/938–880* ⊕ *www.post-rothenburg. com* ⇨ *23 rooms* ⚲ *Breakfast.*

$$ ⛫ **Hotel Reichs-Küchenmeister.** Master chefs in the service of the Holy
B&B/INN Roman Emperor were the inspiration for the name of this historic hotel, occupying one of the oldest trader's houses in Rothenburg. **Pros:** central; excellent restaurant. **Cons:** central location means it can get noisy from crowds of tourists. $ *Rooms from: €100* ✉ *Kirchpl. 8, Rothenburg ob der Tauber* ☎ *09861/9700* ⊕ *www.reichskuechenmeister.com* ⇨ *45 rooms, 2 suites, 5 apartments* ⚲ *Breakfast.*

$$ ⛫ **Hotel-Restaurant Burg Colmberg.** East of Rothenburg, this 13th-century
B&B/INN castle converted into a hotel maintains a high standard of comfort
FAMILY within its original medieval walls without sacrificing the atmosphere. **Pros:** romantic; you're staying in a real castle. **Cons:** remote location; quite a few stairs to climb. $ *Rooms from: €110* ✉ *An der Burgenstr., Colmberg* ✛ *18 km (11 miles) east of Rothenburg* ☎ *09803/91920* ⊕ *www.burg-colmberg.de* ⇨ *24 rooms, 2 suites* ⚲ *Breakfast.*

$$ ⛫ **Romantik-Hotel Markusturm.** The Markusturm began as a 13th-century
B&B/INN customs house, an integral part of the city defense wall, and has since developed over the centuries into an inn and staging post and finally into a luxurious small hotel. **Pros:** tasteful interior design; near the city gate; responsive owner. **Cons:** stairs. $ *Rooms from: €145* ✉ *Röderg. 1, Rothenburg ob der Tauber* ☎ *09861/94280* ⊕ *www.markusturm.de* ⇨ *23 rooms, 2 suites* ⚲ *Breakfast.*

SHOPPING

Anneliese Friese. You'll find cuckoo clocks, beer tankards, porcelain, glassware, and much more at this old and atmospheric shop near the Rathaus, run by the delightful Anneliese herself. ✉ *Grüner Markt 7–8, Rothenburg ob der Tauber* ☎ *09861/7166.*

FAMILY **Käthe Wohlfahrt.** The Christmas Village part of this store is a wonderland of mostly German-made toys and decorations, particularly traditional ornaments. The Christmas museum, with a full history of the traditions over the centuries, is inside the store. ✉ *Herrng. 1, Rothenburg ob der Tauber* ☎ *09861/4090* ⊕ *www.wohlfahrt.com.*

With its half-timber houses, fountains, statues, and flowers, Rothenburg-ob-der-Tauber makes for great photo ops.

NORTHERN ROMANTIC ROAD

After heading through the plains of Swabia in the south, your tour of the Romantic Road skirts the wild, open countryside of the Spessart uplands. Bad Mergentheim can make a great overnight stop to relax before continuing on to Würzburg to see its UNESCO-recognized palace.

BAD MERGENTHEIM

24 km (15 miles) west of Creglingen.

Between 1525 and 1809, Bad Mergentheim was the home of the Teutonic Knights, one of the most successful medieval orders of chivalry. In 1809, Napoléon expelled them as he marched toward his ill-fated Russian campaign. The expulsion seemed to sound the death knell of the little town, but in 1826 a shepherd discovered mineral springs on the north bank of the river. They proved to be the strongest sodium sulfate and bitter spa waters in Europe, with supposedly health-giving properties that ensured the town's future prosperity as a health resort, which continues even today.

GETTING HERE AND AROUND

A Deutsche Bahn train runs at least twice an hour from Würzburg and the journey takes nearly 50 minutes. By car, you can reach Bad Mergentheim either via the A-7 or by the more scenic B-19, which takes only about 10 minutes longer, depending on traffic.

ESSENTIALS

Visitor Information Bad Mergentheim Tourist-Information. ✉ *Marktpl. 1* ☎ *07931/57135* 🌐 *www.bad-mergentheim.de.*

EXPLORING

Deutschordensschloss. The Teutonic Knights' former castle, at the eastern end of the town, has a museum that follows the history of the order. The castle also hosts classical concerts, lectures, and events for families and children. ✉ *Schloss 16* ☎ *07931/52212* 🌐 *www.deutschordensmuseum.de* 🎫 *€6, tours €2* ⏲ *Apr.–Oct., Tues.–Sun. 10:30–5; Nov.–Mar., Tues.–Sat. 2–5, Sun. 10:30–5.*

FAMILY **Wildpark Bad Mergentheim.** You can help feed the animals at this wildlife park just outside of Bad Mergentheim. It has the continent's largest selection of European species, including wolves and bears. ✉ *Wildpark 1* ✣ *Off the B-290, 4 km (2½ miles) south of town* ☎ *07931/41344* 🌐 *www.wildtierpark.de* 🎫 *€10* ⏲ *Mid-Mar.–Nov., daily 9–6, last entrance at 4:30.*

WHERE TO STAY

$$ HOTEL 🏨 **Best Western Parkhotel.** A glass facade has given this hotel both a pleasing appearance and a pleasant outlook over gardens and parkland. **Pros:** spacious rooms, many with balcony; several restaurants on-site; quiet location. **Cons:** chain atmosphere can feel sterile. [$] *Rooms from: €133* ✉ *Lothar-Daiker-Str. 6* ☎ *07931/5390* 🌐 *www.parkhotel-mergentheim.de* 🛏 *113 rooms, 3 suites* 🍴 *Breakfast.*

WÜRZBURG

200 km (124 miles) north of Ulm, 115 km (71 miles) east of Frankfurt.

Fodor's Choice ★ The baroque city of Würzburg, the pearl of the Romantic Road, shows what happens when great genius teams up with great wealth. Already a Celtic stronghold in 1000 BC, the city was founded as a bishopric in 742. Beginning in the 10th century, Würzburg was ruled by powerful (and rich) prince-bishops, who created the city with all the remarkable attributes you see today.

The city is at the junction of two age-old trade routes, in a calm valley backed by vineyard-covered hills. Festung Marienberg, a fortified castle on the steep hill across the Main River, overlooks the town. Constructed between 1200 and 1600, the fortress was the residence of the prince-bishops for 450 years.

Masterworks created by artists like Giovanni Battista Tiepolo abound in the city, including the Tilman Riemnschneider–designed tombstone of Prince-Bishop Rudolf von Scherenberg in the Romanesque St. Kilian church. The city is also home to the Residenz Palace, one of around 40 sites in Germany that has been recognized by UNESCO as a World Heritage Site.

Present-day Würzburg is by no means completely original. On March 16, 1945, seven weeks before Germany capitulated, Würzburg was all but obliterated by Allied saturation bombing. The 20-minute raid destroyed 87% of the city and killed at least 4,000 people. Reconstruction has returned most of the city's famous sights to their former

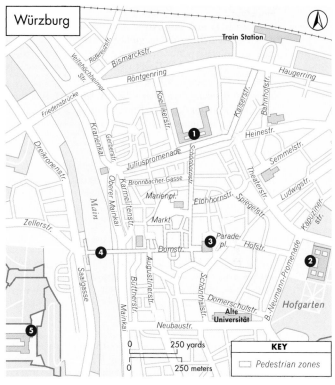

splendor. Except for some buildings with modern shops, it remains a largely authentic restoration.

GETTING HERE AND AROUND

Würzburg is on a main line of the superfast InterCity Express (ICE) trains, two hours from Munich and a bit more than an hour from Frankfurt. Most attractions in the old part of town are easily reached on foot. There's a bus to take you to Marienberg Castle, up on the hill across the river. A car is the best means of transportation if you want to continue your journey, but you can also use regional trains and buses.

The tourist office maintains a thorough app that you can download for a guided stroll through the Old Town. Or take a 40-minute City Train ride and learn about the sites as you pass by them (€8).

The Würzburger Schiffstouristik Kurth & Schiebe operates river excursions.

FESTIVALS

Würzburg is well known for its wine festivals, with celebratory tastings held nearly every weekend at sites around the city and culminating with the Wine Parade in September. But wine isn't the only cultural connector here—there's a festival honoring Mozart's contributions to classical music every May and an annual jazz festival in November.

Mozartfest. The city of Würzburg hosts its annual Mozart Festival between May and July. More than 20 venues host events, but most concerts are held in the magnificent setting of the Residenz and feature world-class performers interpreting Mozart's works. Be sure to reserve tickets early. ⊠ *Ticket Office, Rückermainstr. 2* ☎ *0931/372–336* ⊕ *www.mozartfest-wuerzburg.de.*

Weindorf Würzburg (*Würzburg Wine Village*). During this annual festival, thatched-roof "cottages" erected in the central square are stocked with wine and international foods for two weeks starting in late May. ⊠ *Marktpl.* ☎ *0931/35170* ⊕ *www.weindorf-wuerzburg.de.*

TOURS

CITY TRAIN. An English audio guide accompanies you on a 40-minute ride on this tourist train, revealing both romantic and gruesome stories from the city's history. Beginning at the Domplatz, the train takes you past all the major sites, including the Residenz Palace and Castle of the Thurn and Taxis. ⊠ *Dompl.* ☎ *09401/607–9977* ⊕ *www.city-tour. info* ⊡ *€8.*

Schiffstouristik Kurth & Schiebe. Departing from the Alte Kranen, 90-minute boat tours along the Main River show you the city from a whole new perspective. There are also day trips as far as Ochsenfurt or Gemunden, during which you can enjoy wine tastings (€8) as you glide past the vineyards. ⊠ *Alter Kranen* ☎ *0931/58573* ⊕ *www.schiffstouristik. de* ⊡ *From €13.*

TIMING

You need two days to do full justice to Würzburg. The Residenz alone demands several hours of attention. If time is short, head for the Residenz as the doors open in the morning, before the first crowds assemble, and aim to complete your tour by lunchtime. Then continue to the nearby Juliusspital Weinstuben or one of the many traditional taverns in the area for lunch. In the afternoon, explore central Würzburg. The next morning cross the Main River to visit the Festung Marienberg.

ESSENTIALS

Visitor Information Stadt Würzburg Tourist Information. ⊠ *Rückermainstr. 2* ☎ *0931/372–398* ⊕ *www.wuerzburg.de.*

EXPLORING

TOP ATTRACTIONS

Alte Mainbrücke (*Old Main Bridge*). A stone bridge—Germany's first—built in 1120 once stood on this site, over the Main River, but that ancient structure was restored beginning in 1476. Twin rows of graceful statues of saints now line the bridge, placed here in 1730, at the height of Würzburg's baroque period. They were largely destroyed in 1945, but have been lovingly restored since then. Note the *Patronna Franconiae* (commonly known as the Weeping Madonna). There's a beautiful view of the Marienberg Fortress from the bridge. ⊠ *Würzburg.*

Dom St. Kilian (*St. Kilian Basilica*). Construction on Würzburg's Romanesque cathedral, the fourth-largest of its kind in Germany, began in 1045. Centuries of design are contained under one roof; the side wings were designed in a late-Gothic style in the 16th century, followed by extensive baroque stucco work 200 years later. The majority of the building collapsed in the winter following the bombing of the city near the end of World War II. Reconstruction, completed in 1967, brought a combination of modern design influences alongside a faithful restoration of the past thousand years of the church's history. Visit the side chapel designed by the baroque architect Balthasar Neumann, and a series of tombs of the bishops of Würzburg, designed by Tilman Riemenschneider. Tours (in German) are given daily at 12:30, mid-April through October. ✉ *Domerpfarrg. 10* ☎ *0931/3866–2800* ⊕ *www. dom-wuerzburg.de* ✇ *Free. Tours €4* ⊙ *Daily 9:30–5:30 except during services.*

Festung Marienberg (*Marienberg Fortress*). This complex was the original home of the prince-bishops, beginning in the 13th century. The oldest buildings, including the **Marienkirche** (Church of the Virgin Mary) on the hilltop, date from around 700, although excavations have disclosed evidence that there was a settlement here in the Iron Age, 3,000 years ago. In addition to the rough-hewn medieval fortifications, there are a number of Renaissance and baroque apartments. Tours in English, held at 3 pm, meet at the Pferdeschwemme. To reach the Marienberg, make the fairly steep climb on foot through vineyards or take bus No. 9, starting at the Residenz, with several stops in the city. It runs about every 40 minutes from April to October. From April through October, tours around the fortress itself are offered, starting from the Scherenberg Tor. ✉ *Oberer Burgweg* ⊕ *www.schloesser.bayern.de* ✇ *Tours €4.50; tours and Fürstenbau museums €6* ⊙ *Mid-Mar.–Oct., Tues.–Sun. 9–6.*

Fürstenbaumuseum (*Princes' Quarters Museum*). The Marienberg collections are so vast that they spill over into another outstanding museum that's also part of the fortress. This one, the Fürstenbaumuseum, traces 1,200 years of Würzburg's history. The holdings include breathtaking exhibits of local goldsmiths' art. ✉ *Festung Marienberg, Oberer Burgweg* ⊕ *www.schloesser.bayern.de* ✇ *€4.50; combined ticket with Mainfränkisches museum €6* ⊙ *Mid-Mar.–Oct., Tues.–Sun. 9–6.*

Mainfränkisches Museum (*Main-Franconian Museum*). A highlight of any visit to Festung Marienberg is likely to be this remarkable collection of art treasures. Be sure to visit the gallery devoted to Würzburg-born sculptor Tilman Riemenschneider (1460–1531). Also on view are paintings by Tiepolo and Cranach the Elder, as well as porcelain, firearms, antique toys, and ancient Greek and Roman art. Other exhibits showcase enormous old winepresses and narrate the history of Franconian wine making. ✉ *Festung Marienberg, Oberer Burgweg* ☎ *0931/205–940* ⊕ *www.mainfraenkisches-museum.de* ✇ *€4; €6 combined ticket with Fürstenbaumuseum* ⊙ *Apr.–Oct., Tues.–Sun. 10–5; Nov.–Mar., Tues.–Sun. 10–4.*

Juliusspital. Founded in 1576 by Prince-Bishop Julius Echter as a foundation for the poor, the elderly, and the sick, this enormous edifice now houses a hospital and the second-largest wine estate in Germany. Wander through the hospital park and grounds, then do a wine tasting, which includes six half glasses of wine from the vineyards. All profits from the Vinothek and the neighboring restaurant go towards

The baroque Würzburg Residenz is a UNESCO World Heritage Site.

the foundation. ✉ *Juliuspromenade 19* ☎ *0931/393–1401* ⊕ *www. juliusspital.de* ✉ *Tour and six tastings €22; tour and three tastings €12* ⊙ *Vinothek: weekdays 9:30–6, Sat. 9–4.*

Fodor'sChoice ★ **Residenz** (*Residence Palace*). Würzburg's prince-bishops lived in this glorious baroque palace after moving down from the hilltop Festung Marienberg. Construction started in 1719 under the brilliant direction of Balthasar Neumann. Most of the interior decoration was entrusted to the Italian stuccoist Antonio Bossi and the Venetian painter Giovanni Battista Tiepolo. It's the spirit of the pleasure-loving Prince-Bishop Johann Philipp Franz von Schönborn, however, that infuses the Residenz. Now considered one of Europe's most sumptuous palaces, this dazzling structure is a 10-minute walk from the train station, along pedestrian-only Kaiserstrasse and then Theaterstrasse.

Tours start in the **Vestibule,** which was built to accommodate carriages drawn by six horses. The king's guests were swept directly up the **Treppenhaus,** the largest baroque staircase in the country. Halfway up, the stairway splits and peels away 180 degrees to the left and to the right. Soaring above on the vaulting is Tiepolo's giant fresco *The Four Continents,* a gorgeous exercise in blue and pink that's larger than the Sistine Chapel's ceiling. Each quarter of the massive fresco depicts the European outlook on the world in 1750—the savage Americas; Africa and its many unusual creatures; cultured Asia, where learning and knowledge originated; and finally the perfection of Europe, with Würzburg as the center of the universe. Take a careful look at the Asian elephant's trunk and find the ostrich in Africa. Tiepolo had never seen these creatures but painted on reports of them; he could only assume that the fastest and largest bird in the world would have big muscular legs. He immortalized himself and Balthasar Neumann as two of the figures—they're not too difficult to spot.

Next, make your way to the **Weissersaal** (White Room) and then beyond to the grandest of the state rooms, the **Kaisersaal** (Throne Room). Tiepolo's frescoes show the 12th-century visit of Emperor Frederick Barbarossa, when he came to Würzburg to claim his bride. If you take part in the guided tour, you'll also see private chambers of the various former residents (guided tours in English are given daily at 11 and 3). The **Spiegelkabinett** (Mirror Cabinet) was completely destroyed by Allied bombing but then reconstructed using the techniques of the original rococo artisans.

Finally, visit the formal **Hofgarten** (Court Gardens), to see its stately gushing fountains and trim ankle-high shrubs that outline geometric flowerbeds and gravel walks. **TIP→ On weekends, the Hofkeller wine cellar, below the Residenz, runs tours that include wine tasting. Ask at the ticket counter.** ✉ *Residenzpl. 2* ☎ *0931/355–170* 🌐 *www.residenz-wuerzburg.de* 🎟 *€7.50, including guided tour* 🕒 *Apr.–Oct., daily 9–6; Nov.–Mar., daily 10–4:30.*

WHERE TO EAT

$ GERMAN 🍴 **Alte Mainmühle.** Sample Frankish bratwurst cooked over a wood-fire grill and other regional dishes in this converted mill alongside the Main River. The menu also includes local fish and a variety of vegetarian options. In good weather, you can sit outside on the terrace for the best views of the Alte Mainbrücke and the Festung Marienberg. The small bar at the entrance of this easygoing restaurant serves local wine streetside, so you can get a glass of crisp Silvaner and watch the sun set over the city and surrounding vineyards. [$] *Average main: €13* ✉ *Mainkai 1* ☎ *0931/16777* 🌐 *www.alte-mainmuehle.de* 💳 *No credit cards.*

$ GERMAN 🍴 **Backöfele.** More than 400 years of tradition are embedded in this old tavern. Hidden away behind huge wooden doors on a backstreet, the Backöfele's cavelike interior is a popular meeting and eating place. The surprisingly varied menu includes local favorites such as suckling pig and marinated pot roast, as well as good fish entrées and classic desserts, all at reasonable prices. [$] *Average main: €13* ✉ *Ursulinerg. 2* ☎ *0931/59059* 🌐 *www.backoefele.de.*

$$ GERMAN 🍴 **Juliusspital Weinstuben.** Giving a gastropub's twist to traditional Franconian fare, this restaurant is also a draw for its local wines. The 400-year-old Juliusspital foundation still funds the neighboring hospital, school, and local nature preserves with profits from its vineyards and this bustling spot. While sampling local game and fish specialties, you can buy a bottle of wine to take home directly from the wait staff. In summer you can enjoy your food and drinks on a quiet terrace in the courtyard. [$] *Average main: €17* ✉ *Juliuspromenade 19, Ecke Barbarossapl.* ☎ *0931/54080* 🌐 *www.juliusspital-weinstuben.de.*

$ GERMAN 🍴 **Ratskeller.** Practically every German city has a restaurant in its city hall, but Würzburg's stands out. The daily menu offers excellent regional food, such as *Fränkischer Sauerbraten*, along with plenty of fish and vegetarian offerings. The smaller dishes offered throughout the day are a good excuse to take a break while touring. Beer is available, but local wine is what the regulars drink. As for the Gothic town hall itself, it's been the center of municipal government since 1316. [$] *Average main: €14* ✉ *Beim Grafeneckart, Langg. 1* ☎ *0931/13021* 🌐 *www.wuerzburger-ratskeller.de.*

WHERE TO STAY

$$ HOTEL **Hotel Greifensteiner Hof.** The modern Greifensteiner offers comfortable, individually furnished rooms in a quiet corner of the city, just off the market square. **Pros:** center of town; excellent restaurants; nice bar. **Cons:** no spectacular views or grand lobby. [$] *Rooms from: €130* ✉ *Dettelbacherg. 2* ☎ *0931/35170* 🌐 *www.greifensteiner-hof.de* 🛏 *49 rooms* 🍴 *Breakfast; Some meals.*

$$ HOTEL **Hotel Rebstock zu Würzburg.** This hotel's rococo facade has welcomed guests for centuries, and inside the rooms are all individually decorated and furnished in an English country-house style. **Pros:** historical building with modern amenities; quick access to the town's sights. **Cons:** sometimes fills up with conferences and other large groups. [$] *Rooms from: €140* ✉ *Neubaustr. 7* ☎ *0931/30930* 🌐 *www.rebstock.com* 🛏 *63 rooms, 9 suites* 🍴 *Breakfast.*

$$ B&B/INN **Hotel Walfisch.** Guest rooms are furnished in solid Franconian style, with farmhouse cupboards, bright fabrics, and heavy drapes. **Pros:** nice view from front rooms; good restaurant. **Cons:** difficult parking; small improvements needed. [$] *Rooms from: €130* ✉ *Am Pleidenturm 5* ☎ *0931/35200* 🌐 *www.hotel-walfisch.com* 🛏 *40 rooms* 🍴 *Breakfast.*

$$$ HOTEL **Schloss Steinburg.** Set atop vineyards and overlooking the towers of Würzburg, the Schloss Steinburg offers regal manor rooms as well as crisp and serene modern lodgings. **Pros:** beautiful views; nice variety of rooms; pool open year-round. **Cons:** outside the city center. [$] *Rooms from: €210* ✉ *Mittlerer Steinburgweg 100* ☎ *0931/97020* 🌐 *www.steinburg.com* 💳 *No credit cards* 🛏 *69 rooms* 🍴 *Breakfast.*

SPORTS AND THE OUTDOORS

Stein-Wein-Pfad. Wine lovers and hikers should visit the Stein-Wein-Pfad, a signposted trail through the vineyards that rise up from the northwest edge of Würzburg. The starting point is the Weingut am Stein (Ludwig Knoll vineyard), 10 minutes on foot from the main train station. A two-hour round-trip affords stunning views of the city as well as the chance to try the excellent local wines directly at the source. From May through mid-October, you can join a guided tour of the wineries every other Saturday for €8, which includes a glass of wine. ✉ *Mittlerer Steinbergweg 5* 🌐 *www.wuerzburger-steinweinpfad.de.*

SHOPPING

Würzburg is the true wine center of the Romantic Road. Visit any of the vineyards that rise from the Main River and choose a *Bocksbeutel*, the distinctive green, flagon-shape wine bottle of Franconia. One fanciful claim is that the shape came about because wine-guzzling monks found it the easiest to hide under their robes.

FRANCONIA AND THE GERMAN DANUBE

WELCOME TO FRANCONIA AND THE GERMAN DANUBE

TOP REASONS TO GO

★ **Bamberg's Altstadt:** This one isn't just for the tourists. Bamberg may be a UNESCO World Heritage Site, but it's also a vibrant town—the center of German brewing—living very much in the present.

★ **Vierzehnheiligen:** Just north of Bamberg, this church's swirling rococo decoration earned it the nickname "God's Ballroom."

★ **Nürnberg's Kaiserburg:** Holy Roman emperors once resided in the vast complex of this imperial castle, which has fabulous views over the entire city.

★ **Steinerne Brücke in Regensburg:** This 12th-century Stone Bridge was considered an amazing feat of engineering in its time.

★ **An organ concert in Passau:** You can listen to the mighty sound the 17,774 pipes of Dom St. Stephan's organ create at weekday concerts.

1 **Northern Franconia.** As one of the few towns not destroyed by World War II, Bamberg lives and breathes German history. Wagner fans flock to Bayreuth in July and August for the classical music festival. The beer produced in Kulmbach is famous all over the country.

2 **Nürnberg (Nuremberg).** It may not be as well known as Munich, Heidelberg, or Berlin, but when you visit Nürnberg you feel the wealth, power, and sway this city has had through the centuries. Standing on the ramparts of the Kaiserburg (Imperial Castle) and looking down on the city, you'll begin to understand why emperors made Nürnberg their home.

3 **The German Danube.** Regensburg and Passau are two relatively forgotten cities tucked away in the southeast corner of Germany in an area bordered by Austria and the Czech Republic. Passau is one of the oldest cities on German soil, built by the Celts and then ruled by the Romans 2,000 years ago. Regensburg is a bit younger; about a thousand years ago it was one of the largest and most affluent cities in Germany.

GETTING ORIENTED

Franconia's northern border is marked by the Main River, which is seen as the dividing line between northern and southern Germany. Its southern border is the Danube, where Lower Bavaria (Niederbayern) begins. Despite its size, Franconia is a homogeneous region of rolling agricultural landscapes and thick forests climbing the mountains of the Fichtelgebirge. Nürnberg is a major destination in the area and makes a good base for exploration. The towns of Bayreuth, Coburg, and Bamberg are an easy day trip from one another. The Danube River defines the region as it passes through the Bavarian Forest on its way from Germany to Austria. West of Regensburg, river cruises and cyclists follow its path.

5

CZECH REPUBLIC

B22

oding   Cham

Patersdorf

B8

Straubling   **3**   B85

Rottenmann   Deggendorf

A3

Pilsting   Preying

B8

A92   Landau an der Isar   Danube   Passau

B20

AUSTRIA

GERMANY'S CHRISTMAS MARKETS

Few places in the world do Christmas as well as Germany, and the country's Christmas markets, sparkling with white fairy lights and rich with the smells of gingerbread and mulled wine, are marvelous traditional expressions of yuletide cheer.

(above and lower right) You can purchase handmade ornaments at the atmospheric Nürnberg Christkindlesmarkt. (upper right) The Spandau Christmas market is one of 60 in Berlin.

Following a centuries-old tradition, more than 2,000 *Weihnachtsmärtke* spring up outside town halls and in village squares across the country each year, their stalls brimming with ornate tree decorations and handmade pralines. Elegant rather than kitsch, the markets last the duration of Advent—the four weeks leading up to Christmas Eve—and draw festive crowds to their bustling lanes, where charcoal grills sizzle with sausages and cinnamon and spices waft from warm ovens. Among the handcrafted angels and fairies, kids munch on candy apples and ride old-fashioned carousels while their parents shop for stocking stuffers and toast the season with steaming mugs of *Glühwein* and hot chocolate.

—Jeff Kavanagh

GLÜHWEIN

The name for mulled wine, *Glühwein*, literally means "glowing wine" and a few cups of it will definitely add some color to your cheeks. Although usually made with red wine, white mulled wine is making a comeback in Franconia and Saxony. Glühwein can be fortified with a shot of schnapps. *Feuerzangenbowle*, a supercharged version, is made by burning a rum-soaked sugar cone that drips caramelized sugar into the wine.

Dating from the late Middle Ages, Christmas markets began as a way to provide people with winter supplies; families came for the sugary treats and Christmas shopping. Now a bit more touristy, a visit to a traditional Christmas market is still a quintessential German experience. Starting on the first Sunday of Advent, the pace of life slows down when the cheerful twinkling lights are lit and the smell of hot wine lingers in the air, promising respite during the drab winter.

The most famous markets are in **Nürnberg** and **Dresden**, each drawing more than 2 million visitors every year. While these provide the essential market experience, it's well worth visiting a market in a smaller town to soak in some local flavor. **Bautzen** hosts Germany's oldest Christmas market, while **Erfurt's** market, set on the Cathedral Square, is the most picturesque. **Berlin's** immigrant communities offer themed markets on weekends, most notably the Hannumas Markt at the Jewish Museum or the Finnish Christmas Market in Templehof. No matter which you choose, keep in mind that the best time to visit is during the week when the crowds are the smallest; try to go in the early evening, when locals visit the markets with their friends and family. You'll experience a carnival-like atmosphere and won't be able to resist trying a mulled wine before heading home.

Despite the market theme, the real reason to visit is to snack on greasy, sweet, and warm market food. Each market has its own specialties—gingerbread in Nürnberg and stollen in Dresden—but the thread through all is candied almonds, warm chestnuts, and local sausages. Be sure to pair your snacks with a cup of hot spiced wine, which is served in small mugs that make great souvenirs. The wine varies from region to region and special hot white wine is a trendy alternative. Other drinks include a warm egg punch, hot chocolate, and warm berry juices for children.

TIPS FOR VISITING

Always ask for local goods. Craftspeople, especially from the Ore Mountains in Saxony, produce some of the finest smoking-man incense burners, nativity scenes, candle pyramids, glass balls, and advent stars in the world.

Think about how you're getting your purchases home. Although some larger vendors will ship your purchases for you, it's wise to plan some extra baggage space and purchase some bubble wrap.

Dress warmly and wear comfortable shoes. All markets are outside and even the smallest require walking.

Bring some small bills and coins. This will make food and wine transactions faster. Plastic dishes and cups require a deposit, which is refunded to you when you return the items.

Updated by
Lee A. Evans

All that is left of the huge, ancient kingdom of the Franks is the region known today as Franken (Franconia), stretching from the Bohemian Forest on the Czech border to the outskirts of Frankfurt. The Franks were not only tough warriors but also hard workers, sharp tradespeople, and burghers with a good political nose. The word *frank* means bold, wild, and courageous in the old Frankish tongue. It was only in the early 19th century, following Napoléon's conquest of what is now southern Germany, that the area was incorporated into northern Bavaria.

Although more closely related to Thuringia, this historic homeland of the Franks, one of the oldest Germanic peoples, is now begrudgingly part of Bavaria. Franconian towns such as Bayreuth, Coburg, and Bamberg are practically places of cultural pilgrimage. Rebuilt Nürnberg (Nuremberg in English) is the epitome of German medieval beauty, though its name recalls both the Third Reich's huge rallies at the Zeppelin Field and its henchmen's trials held in the city between 1945 and 1950.

Franconia is hardly an overrun tourist destination, yet its long and rich history, its landscapes and leisure activities (including skiing, golfing, hiking, and cycling), and its gastronomic specialties place it high on the enjoyment scale. Franconia is especially famous for its wine and for the fact that it's home to more than half of Germany's breweries.

PLANNING

WHEN TO GO

Summer is the best time to explore Franconia, though spring and fall are also fine when the weather cooperates. Avoid the cold and wet months from November to March; many hotels and restaurants close, and no matter how pretty, many towns do seem quite dreary. If you're in Nürnberg in December, you're in time for one of Germany's largest and loveliest Christmas markets. Unless you plan on attending the Wagner Festival in Bayreuth, it's best to avoid this city in July and August.

GETTING HERE AND AROUND

AIR TRAVEL

The major international airport serving Franconia and the German Danube is Munich. Nürnberg's airport is served mainly by regional carriers.

Airport Information Airport Nürnberg. ⊠ *Flughafenstr. 100, Nürnberg* ☎ *0911/93700* ⊕ *www.airport-nuernberg.de.*

CAR TRAVEL

Franconia is served by five main autobahns: A-7 from Hamburg, A-3 from Köln and Frankfurt, A-81 from Stuttgart, A-6 from Heilbronn, and A-9 from Munich. Nürnberg is 167 km (104 miles) north of Munich and 222 km (138 miles) southeast of Frankfurt. Regensburg and Passau are reached by way of the A-3 from Nürnberg.

CRUISE TRAVEL

Rising from the depths of the Black Forest and emptying into the Black Sea, the Danube is the queen of rivers; cloaked in myth and legend, it cuts through the heart and soul of Europe. The name Dānuvius, borrowed from the Celts, means swift or rapid, but along the Danube, there is no hurry. Boats go with the flow and a river journey is a relaxed affair with plenty of time to drink in the history.

Whether you choose a one-hour, one-week, or the complete Danube experience, cruising Europe's historical waterway is a never-to-be-forgotten experience. On the map, the sheer length of the Danube is daunting at best; of the river's 2,848-km (1,770-mile) length, more than 2,400 km (1,500 miles) is navigable and the river flows through some of Europe's most important cities. You can head to major boating hubs, like Passau, Vienna, and Budapest or through historical stretches from Ulm to Regensburg.

The most interesting time to cruise the Danube is during the summer when the river is abustle with passenger and commercial traffic. When the leaves start to change the river is awash in a sea of color, making autumn the most picturesque time to cruise. Several companies offer Christmas market tours from Nürnberg to Regensburg, Passau, and Vienna. Spring is the least optimal time to go as the river often floods. You can board cruises from Passau, Regensburg, and Nürnberg among others.

Amadeus Cruises. This cruise line offers half a dozen cruises through Franconia and the German Danube, including a Christmastime cruise, which stops at the fascinating Christmas markets between Nürnberg and Budapest. The reverse direction is also available. ☎ *888/829–1394* ⊕ *www.amadeuscruises.com.*

Blue Water Holidays. This British cruise line offers nine cruises starting on the Rhine, some from Basel in Switzerland, which follow the Main–Danube Canal to the Danube, and four cruises from Nürnberg or Passau to Vienna or Budapest. ☎ *01756/706–500* ⊕ *www.cruisingholidays.co.uk.*

Viking River Cruises. The Grand European Tour cruises from Amsterdam to Budapest. The two-week Eastern European Odyssey starts in

Nürnberg and ends at Bucharest. The reverse direction is also available on both cruises. ☎ *800/304–9616* ⊕ *www.vikingrivercruises.com.*

TRAIN TRAVEL

Franconia has one of southern Germany's most extensive train networks and almost every town is connected by train. Nürnberg is a stop on the high-speed InterCity Express (ICE) north–south routes, and there are hourly trains from Munich direct to Nürnberg. Regular InterCity services connect Nürnberg and Regensburg with Frankfurt and other major German cities. Trains run hourly from Frankfurt to Munich, with a stop at Nürnberg. The trip takes about three hours to Munich, two hours to Nürnberg. There are hourly trains from Munich to Regensburg.

Some InterCity Express trains stop in Bamberg, about midway between Berlin and Munich. Local trains from Nürnberg connect with Bayreuth and areas of southern Franconia. Regensburg and Passau are on the ICE line from Nürnberg to Vienna.

RESTAURANTS

Many restaurants in the rural parts of this region serve hot meals only between 11:30 am and 2 pm, and from 6 to 9 pm. ■ TIP→ "**Durchgehend warme Küche" means that hot meals are also served between lunch and dinner.**

Prices in the reviews are the average cost of a main course at dinner, or if dinner is not served, at lunch.

HOTELS

Make reservations well in advance for hotels in all the larger towns and cities if you plan to visit anytime between June and September. During the Nürnberg Toy Fair at the beginning of February, rooms are at a premium. If you're visiting Bayreuth during the annual Wagner Festival in July and August, consider making reservations up to a year in advance. Remember, too, that during the festival prices can be double the normal rates.

Prices in the reviews are the lowest cost of a standard double room in high season. For expanded reviews, facilities, and current deals, visit Fodors.com.

WHAT IT COSTS IN EUROS			
$	**$$**	**$$$**	**$$$$**
Restaurants	under €15	€15–€20	€21–€25	over €25
Hotels	under €100	€100–€175	€176–€225	over €225

PLANNING YOUR TIME

Nürnberg warrants at least a day of your time. It's best to base yourself in one city and take day trips to others. Bamberg is the most central of the northern Franconia cities and makes a good base. It is also a good idea to leave your car at your hotel and make the trip downstream to Regensburg or Passau by boat, returning by train.

VISITOR INFORMATION
Franconia Tourist Board. ⊠ *Tourismusverband Franken e.V., Wilhelminen-str. 6, Nürnberg* ☎ *0911/941–510* ⊕ *www.frankentourismus.de.*

NORTHERN FRANCONIA

Three major German cultural centers lie within easy reach of one another: Coburg, a town with blood links to royal dynasties throughout Europe; Bamberg, with its own claim to German royal history and an Old Town area designated a UNESCO World Heritage Site; and Bayreuth, where composer Richard Wagner finally settled, making it a place of musical pilgrimage for Wagner fans from all over the world.

COBURG

105 km (65 miles) north of Nürnberg.

Coburg is a surprisingly little-known treasure that was founded in the 11th century and remained in the possession of the dukes of Saxe-Coburg-Gotha until 1918; the current duke still lives here. The remarkable Saxe-Coburg dynasty established itself as something of a royal stud farm, providing a seemingly inexhaustible supply of blue-blood marriage partners to ruling houses the length and breadth of Europe. The most famous of these royal mates was Prince Albert (1819–61), who married the English Queen Victoria, after which she gained special renown in Coburg. Their numerous children, married off to other kings, queens, and emperors, helped to spread the tried-and-tested Saxe-Coburg influence even farther afield. Despite all the history that sweats from each sandstone ashlar, Coburg is a modern and bustling town.

GETTING HERE AND AROUND

It takes a little more than an hour to drive to Coburg from Nürnberg, via A-73, or about 1¾ hours on the regional train service, which runs regularly throughout the day and costs €19–€24 one way. Bus No. 29 runs twice daily from Nürnberg's central bus station and takes two hours, with prices starting at €8 one way.

ESSENTIALS

Visitor Information Tourismus Coburg. ⊠ *Herrng. 4* ☎ *09561/898–000* ⊕ *www.coburg-tourist.de.*

FESTIVALS

Brazilian Samba Festival. This weekend bacchanal, with food, drink, and dancing, is held in mid-July. ⊠ *Coburg* ☎ *09561/705–370* ⊕ *www.samba-festival.de.*

EXPLORING

TOP ATTRACTIONS

Schloss Ehrenburg. Prince Albert spent much of his childhood in this ducal palace. Built in the mid-16th century, it has been greatly altered over the years, principally following a fire in the early 19th century. Duke Ernst I invited Karl Friedrich Schinkel from Berlin to redo the palace in the then-popular neo-Gothic style. Some of the original Renaissance features were kept. The rooms of the castle are quite special, especially those upstairs, where the ceilings are heavily decorated with stucco and the floors have wonderful patterns of various woods. The Hall of Giants is named for the larger-than-life caryatids that support the ceiling; the favorite sight downstairs is Queen Victoria's flush toilet, which was the first one installed in Germany. Here, too, the ceiling is worth noting for its playful, gentle stuccowork. The baroque chapel attached to Ehrenburg is often used for weddings. ⊠ *Schlosspl. 1* ☎ *09561/80880* ⊕ *www.sgvcoburg.de* ☒ *€4.50; combined ticket with Schloss Rosenau €7* ⊙ *Tour Tues.–Sun. 10–3 on the hr.*

QUICK BITES

Burgschänke. Relax and soak up centuries of history while sampling a traditional Coburg beer at this tavern. The basic menu has traditional dishes. ⊠ *Veste Coburg* ☎ *09561/80980* ⊕ *www.burgschaenke-veste-coburg.de* ⊙ *Closed Mon. and Jan.–mid-Feb.*

Fodor'sChoice ★ **Veste Coburg.** This fortress, one of the largest and most impressive in the country, is Coburg's main attraction. The brooding bulk of the castle guards the town from a 1,484-foot hill. Construction began around 1055, but with progressive rebuilding and remodeling today's predominantly late-Gothic–early-Renaissance edifice bears little resemblance to the original crude fortress. One part of the castle harbors the **Kunstsammlungen,** a grand set of collections including art, with works by Dürer, Cranach, and Hans Holbein, among others; sculpture from the school of the great Tilman Riemenschneider (1460–1531); furniture and textiles; magnificent weapons, armor, and tournament garb spanning four centuries (in the so-called **Herzoginbau,** or Duchess's Building); carriages and ornate sleighs; and more. The room where Martin Luther lived for six months in 1530 while he observed the goings-on of the Augsburg Diet has an especially dignified atmosphere. The **Jagdintarsien-Zimmer** (Hunting Marquetry Room), an elaborately decorated room that dates back to the early 17th century, has some of the finest woodwork in southern Germany. Finally, there's the **Carl-Eduard-Bau** (Carl-Eduard Building), which contains a valuable antique glass collection, mostly from the baroque age. Inquire at the ticket office for tours. ⊠ *Festungshof* ☎ *09561/8790* ⊕ *www.kunstsammlungen-coburg.de* ☒ *€6, combination ticket with Schloss Ehrenburg and Schloss Rosenau €12* ⊙ *Museums Apr.–Oct., daily 10–5; Nov.–Mar., Tues.–Sun. 1–4; courtyards daily dawn–6:30 pm (to dusk Nov.–Mar.).*

WORTH NOTING

Marktplatz (*Market Square*). A statue of Prince Albert, Victoria's high-minded consort, is surrounded by gracious Renaissance and baroque buildings in the Marktplatz. The **Stadhaus,** former seat of the local dukes, begun in 1500, is the most imposing structure here, with a forest of ornate gables and spires projecting from its well-proportioned facade. Opposite is the **Rathaus** (Town Hall). Look on the building's tympanum for the statue of the Bratwurstmännla (it's actually St. Mauritius in armor); the staff he carries is said to be the official length against which the town's famous bratwursts are measured. These tasty sausages, roasted on pinecone fires, are available on the market square. ⊠ *Coburg.*

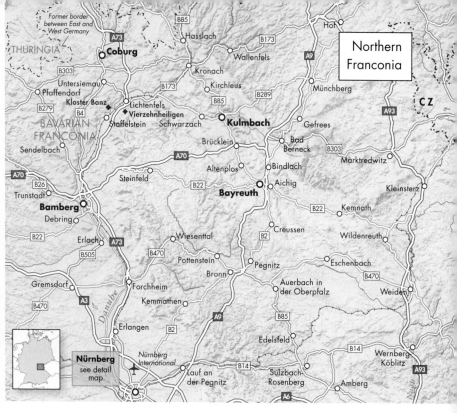

Schloss Callenberg. Perched on a hill 5 km (3 miles) west of Coburg, this was, until 1231, the main castle of the Knights of Callenberg. In the 16th century it was taken over by the Dukes of Coburg. From 1842 on it served as the summer residence of the hereditary Coburg prince and later Duke Ernst II. It holds a number of important collections, including that of the Windsor gallery; arts and crafts from Holland, Germany, and Italy from the Renaissance to the 19th century; precious baroque, Empire, and Biedermeier furniture; table and standing clocks from three centuries; a selection of weapons; and various handicrafts. The best way to reach the castle is by car via Baiersdorf. City Bus No. 5 from Coburg's Marktplatz stops at the castle only on Sunday; on other days you need to get off at the Beirsdorf stop and walk for 25 minutes. ⊠ *Callenberger Str. 1* ☎ *09561/55150* ⊕ *www.schloss-callenberg. de* ☞ *€5* ⊙ *Tues.–Sun. 11–5.*

Schloss Rosenau. Near the village of Rödental, 9 km (5½ miles) northeast of Coburg, the 550-year-old Schloss Rosenau sits in all its neo-Gothic glory in the midst of an English-style park. Prince Albert was born here in 1819, and one room is devoted entirely to Albert and his queen, Victoria. Much of the castle furniture was made especially for the Saxe-Coburg family by noted Viennese craftsmen. In the garden's Orangerie is the **Museum für Modernes Glas** (Museum of Modern Glass), which displays nearly 40 years' worth of glass sculptures (dating from 1950 to 1990) that provide an interesting juxtaposition with the venerable architecture of the castle itself. ✉ *Rosenau 1, Rödental* ☎ *09563/1606* 🌐 *www.kunstsammlungen-coburg.de* 🎫 *Castle and museum €6, museum only €3, combined ticket with Schloss Ehrenburg and Veste Coburg €12* 🕓 *Tours Apr.–Oct., daily at 10, 11, noon, 2, 3, and 4.*

WHERE TO EAT AND STAY

$ GERMAN 🍴 **Ratskeller.** The basic local specialties taste better here beneath the old vaults and within earshot of the Coburg marketplace. Try the *Tafelspitz* (boiled beef with creamed horseradish), along with a glass of crisp Franconian white wine. The prices become a little higher in the evening, when the menu adds a few more dishes. [$] *Average main: €12* ✉ *Marktpl. 1* ☎ *09561/92400* 🌐 *www.ratskeller-coburg.de* 💳 *No credit cards.*

$$ HOTEL 🏨 **Arcadia Hotel Coburg.** You can expect modern, clean, well-designed rooms that are airy and functional here. **Pros:** modern amenities; easy access; free parking and garage. **Cons:** business-oriented hotel; edge of town; surrounded by gas stations and shopping outlets; breakfast costs €15 extra. [$] *Rooms from: €120* ✉ *Ketschendorfer Str. 86* ☎ *09561/8210* 🌐 *arcadia-hotel.de* 🛏 *123 rooms* 🍽 *No meals.*

$ HOTEL 🏨 **Goldene Rose.** One of the region's oldest, this pleasant inn is about 5 km (3 miles) southeast of Coburg. **Pros:** friendly; family run; very good value; large parking lot behind the hotel. **Cons:** in a small village; front rooms overlooking the beer garden can be noisy. [$] *Rooms from: €55* ✉ *Coburgerstr. 31* ☎ *09560/92250* 🌐 *www.goldene-rose.de* 🕓 *Restaurant closed Mon.* 🛏 *14 rooms* 🍽 *Breakfast.*

$$ HOTEL 🏨 **Romantic Hotel Goldene Traube.** Rooms are individually decorated in this fine historical hotel (1756), and for dining you can choose between the elegant restaurant Esszimmer or the more casual Meer und Mehr (Sea and More), which serves fine seafood and regional specialties. **Pros:** welcoming spacious lobby; two good restaurants; center of town; nice small wineshop. **Cons:** traffic noise in front rooms; stairs up to the lobby. [$] *Rooms from: €110* ✉ *Am Viktoriabrunnen 2* ☎ *09561/8760* 🌐 *www.goldenetraube.com* 🛏 *72 rooms, 1 suite* 🍽 *Breakfast.*

SHOPPING

Coburg is full of culinary delights; its *Schmätzen* (honey gingerbread) and *Elisenlebkuchen* (almond gingerbread cake) are famous. You'll find home-baked versions in any of the many excellent patisseries or at a Grossman store (there are three in Coburg).

Hummel Museum Store. Rödental, northeast of Coburg, is the home of the world-famous M. I. Hummel figurines. There's a Hummel Museum devoted to them, with 18th- and 19th-century porcelain from other manufacturers. Besides the museum's store, there are several retail outlets in the village. ✉ *Coburgerstr. 7, Rödental* ☎ *09563/92303* 🌐 *www.mihummel.de* 🕓 *Weekdays 9–5, Sat. 9–noon.*

KULMBACH

19 km (12 miles) southeast of Kronach.

A quarter of Kulmbachers earn their living directly or indirectly from the beer that's brewed in the town. More than 22 different beers are produced here—the adventuresome try the Doppelbock Kulminator 28, which takes nine months to brew and has an alcohol content of 12%. Kulmbach celebrates its brewing traditions every year in a nine-day festival that starts on the last Saturday in July. The main festival site, a mammoth tent, is called the *Festspulhaus*—literally, "festival swill house"—a none-too-subtle dig at nearby Bayreuth and its tony Festspielhaus, where Wagner's operas are performed. If you're here in winter, be sure to try the seasonal *Eisbock*, a special dark beer that is frozen as part of the brewing process, making it stronger.

GETTING HERE AND AROUND

It's about a 45-minute drive from Coburg to Kulmbach via B-4, B-173, and B-289. Regional trains run regularly throughout the day and take the same amount of time, with one-way fares starting at €13.

ESSENTIALS

Visitor Information Kulmbach Tourismusservice. ⊠ *Stadthalle, Sutte 2* ☏ *09221/958–820* ⊕ *www.kulmbach.de.*

EXPLORING

Bayerisches Brauereimuseum Kulmbach (*Bavarian Brewery Museum*). Although a visit to the factory is almost impossible, this is the next best thing. The Kulmbacher Brewery runs this interesting museum jointly with the nearby Mönchshof-Bräu brewery and inn. The price of admission includes a "tasting" from the museum's own brewery operation. ⊠ *Hoferstr. 20* ☏ *09221/80514* ⊕ *www.kulmbacher-moenchshof.de* 🎫 *€4.50* ⊙ *Tues.–Sun. 10–5.*

FAMILY **Neuenmarkt.** In this "railway village" near Kulmbach, more than 25 beautifully preserved gleaming locomotives huff and puff in a living railroad museum. Every now and then a nostalgic train will take you to the Brewery Museum in Kulmbach, or you can enjoy a round-trip to Marktschorgast; both trips take you up the very steep "schiefe Ebene" stretch (literally, slanting level). The museum also has model trains set up in incredibly detailed replica landscapes. ⊠ *Birkenstr. 5, Neuenmarkt* ☏ *09227/5700* ⊕ *www.dampflokmuseum.de* 🎫 *€7* ⊙ *Tues.–Sun. 10–5.*

FAMILY **Plassenburg.** The most impressive Renaissance fortress in the country, the Plassenburg stands on a rise overlooking Kulmbach, a 20-minute hike from the Old Town. The first building here, begun in the mid-12th century, was torched by marauding Bavarians who were eager to put a stop to the ambitions of Duke Albrecht Alcibiades—a man who spent several years murdering, plundering, and pillaging his way through Franconia. His successors built today's castle, starting in about 1560. Externally, there's little to suggest the graceful Renaissance interior, but as you enter the main courtyard the scene changes abruptly. The tiered space of the courtyard is covered with precisely carved figures, medallions, and other intricate ornaments, the whole comprising one of the most remarkable and delicate architectural ensembles in

Europe. Inside, the **Deutsches Zinnfigurenmuseum** (Tin Figures Museum), with more than 300,000 miniature statuettes and tin soldiers, holds the largest collection of its kind in the world. The figures are arranged in scenes from all periods of history. During the day you cannot drive up to the castle. There's a shuttle bus (€2.20) that leaves from the main square every half hour from 9 to 6. ✉ *Kulmbach* ☎ *09221/947–505* 🎟 *€4.50* ⏲ *Apr.–Oct., daily 9–6; Nov.–Mar., daily 10–4.*

KULMBACH BREWS

In a country where brewing and beer drinking, despite a steady decline, still breaks all records, Kulmbach produces more beer per capita than anywhere else: 9,000 pints for each man, woman, and child. The locals claim it's the sparkling-clear spring water from the nearby Fichtelgebirge hills that makes their beer so special. The adventuresome try the Doppelbock Kulminator 28, which takes nine months to brew and has an alcohol content of 12%.

WHERE TO STAY

$ HOTEL 🏨 **Hotel Kronprinz.** This old hotel tucked away in the middle of Kulmbach's Old Town, right in the shadow of Plassenburg Castle, covers all basic needs, including an extraordinary breakfast buffet. **Pros:** center of town; excellent cakes in café; three nice rooms in annex. **Cons:** plain rooms above café; no elevator. [$] *Rooms from: €90* ✉ *Fischerg. 4–6* ☎ *09221/92180* 🌐 *www.hotel-kulmbach.eu* ⏲ *Closed Dec. 24–29* 🛏 *22 rooms* 🍴 *Breakfast.*

BAYREUTH

24 km (15 miles) south of Kulmbach, 80 km (50 miles) northeast of Nürnberg.

The small town of Bayreuth, pronounced "bye- *roit,*" owes its fame to the music giant Richard Wagner (1813–83). The 19th-century composer, musical revolutionary, ultranationalist, and Nazi poster child finally settled here after a lifetime of rootless shifting through Europe. Here he built his great theater, the Festspielhaus, as a suitable setting for his grand operas on Germanic mythological themes. The annual Wagner Festival dates to 1876, and brings droves of Wagner fans who push prices sky-high, fill hotels to bursting, and earn themselves much-sought-after social kudos in the process. The festival is held from late July until late August, so unless you plan to visit the town specifically for it, this is the time to stay away.

GETTING HERE AND AROUND

To reach Bayreuth, take the Bayreuth exit off the Nürnberg–Berlin autobahn. It's 1½ hours north of Nürnberg. The train trip is an hour from Nürnberg and costs from €33 one way. In town you can reach most points on foot.

ESSENTIALS

Visitor Information Bayreuth Kongress- und Tourismuszentrale. ✉ *Luitpoldpl. 9* ☎ *0921/88588* 🌐 *www.bayreuth.de.*

The torch-bearing figure of Apollo on his chariot adorns the Sonnentempel (Sun Temple) of Bayreuth's Neues Schloss.

EXPLORING

TOP ATTRACTIONS

Festspielhaus (*Festival Theater*). This high temple of the Wagner cult—where performances take place only during the annual Wagner Festival—is surprisingly plain. The spartan look is explained partly by Wagner's desire to achieve perfect acoustics. The wood seats have no upholstering, for example, and the walls are bare. The stage is enormous, capable of holding the huge casts required for Wagner's largest operas. The festival is still meticulously controlled by Wagner's family. ⊠ *Festspielhügel 1* ☎ *0921/78780* ⊕ *www.bayreuther-festspiele.de* ▭ *€7* ⊗ *Tours Dec.–Oct., Tues.–Sun. at 10, 11, 2, and 3. Closed during rehearsals and on performance days during festival.*

Markgräfliches Opernhaus (*Margravial Opera House*). In 1745 Margravine Wilhelmine commissioned the Italian architects Giuseppe and Carlo Bibiena to build this rococo jewel, sumptuously decorated in red, gold, and blue. Apollo and the nine Muses cavort across the baroque frescoed ceiling. It was this delicate 500-seat theater that originally drew Wagner to Bayreuth; he felt that it might prove a suitable setting for his own operas. In fact, it's a wonderful setting for the concerts and operas of Bayreuth's "other" musical festivals, which the theater hosts throughout the year. Due to restoration works, no performances are currently scheduled, but you can still visit the theater despite the ongoing work. ⊠ *Opernstr.* ☎ *0921/759–6922* ⊕ *www.bayreuth-wilhelmine.de* ▭ *€2.50* ⊗ *Apr.–Sept., daily 9–6; Oct.–Mar., daily 10–4.*

Neues Schloss (*New Palace*). This glamorous 18th-century palace was built by the Margravine Wilhelmine, a woman of enormous energy and decided tastes. Though Wagner is the man most closely associated with Bayreuth, his choice of this setting is largely due to the work of this woman, who lived 100 years before him. Wilhelmine devoured books, wrote plays and operas (which she directed and, of course, acted in), and had buildings constructed, transforming much of the town and bringing it near bankruptcy. Her distinctive touch is evident at the palace, built when a mysterious fire conveniently destroyed parts of the original one. Anyone with a taste for the wilder flights of rococo decoration will love it. Some rooms have been given over to one of Europe's finest collections of faience. ⊠ *Ludwigstr. 21* ☎ *0921/759–6921* 🖾 *Palace only €5.50, palace and "World of Wilhelmine" exhibit €12* ⊘ *Apr.–Sept., daily 9–6; Oct.–Mar., Tues.–Sun. 10–4.*

Richard-Wagner-Museum. "Wahnfried," built by Wagner in 1874 and the only house he ever owned, is now the Richard-Wagner-Museum. It's a simple, austere neoclassical building whose name, "peace from madness," was well earned. Wagner lived here with his wife Cosima, daughter of pianist Franz Liszt, and they were both laid to rest here. King Ludwig II of Bavaria, the young and impressionable "Fairy-Tale King" who gave Wagner so much financial support, is remembered in a bust before the entrance. The exhibits, arranged along a well-marked tour through the house, require a great deal of German-language reading, but it's a must for Wagner fans. The original scores of such masterpieces as *Parsifal, Tristan und Isolde, Lohengrin, Der Fliegende Holländer,* and *Götterdämmerung* are on display. You can also see designs for productions of his operas, as well as his piano and huge library. A multimedia display lets you watch and listen to various productions of his operas. The little house where Franz Liszt lived and died is right next door and can be visited with your Richard-Wagner-Museum ticket, but be sure to express your interest in advance. It, too, is heavy on the paper, but the last rooms—with pictures, photos, and silhouettes of the master, his students, acolytes, and friends—are well worth the detour. ⊠ *Richard-Wagner-Str. 48* ☎ *0921/757–2816* ⊕ *www.wagnermuseum. de* 🖾 *€8* ⊘ *Tues.–Sun. 10–6.*

WORTH NOTING

Altes Schloss Eremitage. This palace, 5 km (3 miles) north of Bayreuth on B-85, makes an appealing departure from the sonorous and austere Wagnerian mood of much of the town. It's an early-18th-century palace, built as a summer retreat and remodeled in 1740 by the Margravine Wilhelmine, sister of Frederick the Great of Prussia. Although her taste is not much in evidence in the drab exterior, the interior, alive with light and color, displays her guiding hand in every elegant line. The extraordinary **Japanischer Saal** (Japanese Room), filled with Asian treasures and chinoiserie furniture, is the finest room. The park and gardens, partly formal, partly natural, are enjoyable for idle strolling. Fountain displays take place at the two fake grottoes at the top of the hour 10–5 daily. ⊠ *Eremitagestr. 4* ☎ *0921/759–6937* 🖾 *Schloss €4.50, park free* ⊘ *Schloss Apr.–Sept., daily 9–6.*

Brauerei und Büttnerei-Museum (*Brewery and Coopers Museum*). Near the center of town, in the 1887 Maisel Brewery building, this museum reveals the tradition of brewing over the past two centuries with a

WAGNER: GERMANY'S TOP ROMANTIC

UNDERSTANDING WAGNER

Born in 1813, Richard Wagner has become modern Germany's most iconic composer. His music, which is best understood in its simple message of national glory and destiny, contributed greatly to the feeling of pan-Germanism that united Germany under the Prussian crown in 1871. However, his overtly nationalistic themes and blatant anti-Semitism also makes his music a bit controversial as it's also connected to the Nazi movement and Adolf Hitler; Hitler adored Wagner and saw him as the embodiment of his own vision for the German people. Wagner's focus on the cult of the leader and the glories of victory are prevalent in his works *Lohengrin* and *Parsifal.* Some of his most famous compositions are the four-opera cycle *The Ring of the Nibelung* (aka *Ring Cycle*) , *Parsifal*,and *Lohengrin.*

WAGNER TODAY

In 1871 Wagner moved to the city of Bayreuth and began construction of the Festspielhaus, an opera house that would only perform Wagner's operas. The performance space opened its doors in 1876 with a production of *Das Rheingold* and the first full performance of the four-part *Ring Cycle.* The Festspielhaus continues to showcase Wagner's works during the annual Bayreuther Festspiel, a pilgrimage site for die-hard Wagner fans. The waiting list for tickets is years long; it's almost impossible for mere mortals to gain entrance to the holy temple. However, almost all German opera and symphony companies perform Wagner's works throughout the year. The best places to see Wagner's longer works are at Berlin's State Opera; the National Theater in Weimar; the Gewandhaus Orchestra and Opera in Leipzig; and Munich's Bavarian State Opera.

5

focus on the Maisel's trade. The brewery operated here until 1981, when its much bigger current home was completed next door. After the 90-minute tour you can quaff a cool, freshly tapped traditional Bavarian *Weissbier* (wheat beer) in the museum's pub. The pub is also one of a handful of places to try Maisel & Friends Craft Beer, including the Citrilla Wheat, an experimental wheat-based IPA. ✉ *Kulmbacherstr. 40* ☎ *0921/401–234* 🌐 *www.maisel.com* 🎫 *€5* 🕒 *Tour daily at 2 pm; individual tours by prior arrangement.*

WHERE TO EAT

$$ GERMAN 🍴 **Oskar.** A huge glass ceiling gives the large dining room a light atmosphere even in winter. In summer, try for a table in the beer garden to enjoy fine Franconian specialties and Continental dishes. The kitchen uses the freshest produce. The room fills up at night and during Sunday brunch, especially if a jazz band is playing in one of the alcoves. [$] *Average main: €15* ✉ *Maximilianstr. 33* ☎ *0921/516–0553* 🌐 *www.oskar-bayreuth.de* 💳 *No credit cards.*

$ GERMAN 🍴 **Wolffenzacher.** This self-described "Franconian nostalgic inn" harks back to the days when the local *Wirtshaus* (inn-pub) was the meeting place for everyone from the mayor's scribes to the local carpenters. Beer and hearty traditional food are shared at wooden tables either in the rustic interior or out in the shady beer garden. The substantial Franconian specialties are counterbalanced by a few lighter Mediterranean dishes. [$] *Average main: €12* ✉ *Sternenpl. 5* ☎ *0921/64552* 🌐 *www.wolffenzacher.de* ⏲ *No lunch.*

WHERE TO STAY

$$ HOTEL Fodor's Choice ★ 🏨 **Goldener Anker.** No question about it, Bayreuth's grande dame is *the* place to stay; the hotel is right next to the Markgräfliches Opernhaus and has been entertaining composers, singers, conductors, and instrumentalists for hundreds of years. **Pros:** authentic historic setting with all modern amenities; exemplary service; excellent restaurant. **Cons:** no elevator; some rooms are on the small side; restaurant closed Monday and Tuesday, except during festival. [$] *Rooms from: €168* ✉ *Opernstr. 6* ☎ *0921/65051* 🌐 *www.anker-bayreuth.de* 🛏 *38 rooms, 2 suites* 🍴 *Breakfast.*

$$ HOTEL 🏨 **Hotel Lohmühle.** The old part of this hotel is in Bayreuth's only half-timber house, a former sawmill by a stream, just a two-minute walk from the town center. **Pros:** nice setting with reasonable prices; good food. **Cons:** stairs between hotel and restaurant; front rooms let in traffic noise. [$] *Rooms from: €175* ✉ *Badstr. 37* ☎ *0921/53060* 🌐 *www.hotel-lohmuehle.de* ⏲ *Restaurant closed for dinner Sun.* 🛏 *42 rooms* 🍴 *Breakfast.*

NIGHTLIFE AND PERFORMING ARTS

Markgräfliches Opernhaus. If you don't get Wagner Festival tickets, console yourself with visits to the exquisite 18th-century opera house. In May the *Fränkische Festwochen* (Franconian Festival Weeks) take the stage with works of Wagner, of course, but also Paganini and Mozart. ✉ *Opernstr.* ☎ *0921/759–6922.*

Wagner Festival. Opera lovers swear that there are few more intense operatic experiences than the annual Wagner Festival in Bayreuth, held July and August. You'll do best if you plan your visit several years in advance. It is nearly impossible to find a hotel room during the festival: try finding a room in Kronach instead of Bayreuth.

For tickets, obtain an order form from the Bayreuther Festspiele Kartenbüro and submit the completed form by the middle of September the year before, at the latest. Be warned: the waiting list is years long, and they only offer tickets by mail or online and will ignore any other inquiries. ✉ *Festspielhügel 1–2* ☎ *0921/78780* 🌐 *www.bayreuther-festspiele.de.*

SHOPPING

Hofgarten Passage. Off Richard-Wagner-Strasse, you'll find one of the fanciest shopping arcades in the region; it's full of smart boutiques selling everything from German high fashion to simple local craftwork. ✉ *Richard-Wagner-Str. 22.*

BAMBERG

65 km (40 miles) west of Bayreuth, 80 km (50 miles) north of Nürnberg.

Fodor's Choice ★ Sitting majestically on seven hills above the Regnitz River, the entire Alstadt of this beautiful, historic town is a UNESCO World Heritage Site. It's a must-see—few towns in Germany survived the war with as little damage as Bamberg, and its canals and bridges make it a joy to stroll. Although it exploded onto the European political scene as the capital of the Holy Roman Empire under Emperor Heinrich II, its idyllic Old Town, with winding cobblestone streets, contains one of the best-preserved collections of early-medieval half-timber structures in Europe, dominated by the cathedral, consecrated in 1237.

GETTING HERE AND AROUND

Traveling to Bamberg by train will take about 45 minutes from Nürnberg; from Munich it takes about two hours, and it's a worthwhile five-hour train trip from Berlin. Bamberg's train station is a 30-minute walk from the Altstadt (Old Town). On the A-73 autobahn, Bamberg is two hours from Munich. Everything in town can be reached on foot.

TOURS

The Bamberg Tourist Information center offers an audio tour in English for €8.50 for four hours. It also offers brewery and beer-tasting tours of the nine Bamberg breweries.

Personenschiffahrt Kropf. Boats leave daily at 11 am, March through October, for short cruises on the Regnitz River and the Main–Donau Canal. ⊠ *Kapuzinerstr. 5* ☎ *0951/26679* ⊕ *www.personenschiffahrt-bamberg.de* €7.

ESSENTIALS

Visitor Information Bamberg Tourismus und Congresservice. ⊠ *Geyerswörthstr. 5* ☎ *0951/297–6200* ⊕ *www.bamberg.info.*

EXPLORING

QUICK BITES

Rathaus-Schänke. Before heading up the hill to the main sights in the Bishops' Town, take a break with coffee, cake, small meals, or cocktails in the half-timber Rathaus-Schänke. It overlooks the river on the Burghers' Town side of the Town Hall. ⊠ *Obere Brücke 3* ☎ *0951/208–0890* ⊕ *www.rathausschaenke-bamberg.com.*

TOP ATTRACTIONS

Altes Rathaus (*Old Town Hall*). At Bamberg's historic core, the Altes Rathaus is tucked snugly on a small island in the Regnitz. To the west of the river is the so-called Bishops' Town; to the east, Burghers' Town. The citizens of Bamberg built this rickety, extravagantly decorated building on an artificial island when the bishop of Bamberg refused to give the city the land for a town hall. Its excellent collection of porcelain is a sampling of 18th-century styles, from almost sober Meissens with bucolic Watteau scenes to simple but rare Haguenau pieces from Alsace and faience from Strasbourg. ⊠ *Obere Brücke 1* ☎ *0951/871–871* €4.50 ⊘ *Tues.–Sun. 9:30–4:30.*

Dom (*Cathedral*). Bamberg's great cathedral is a unique building that tells not only the town's story but that of Germany as well. The first building here was begun by Heinrich II in 1003, and it was in this partially completed cathedral that he was crowned Holy Roman Emperor in 1012. In 1237 it was destroyed by fire, and replaced by the present late-Romanesque–early-Gothic building. The dominant features are the massive towers at each corner. Heading into the dark interior,

EATING WELL IN FRANCONIA

Franconia is known for its good and filling food and for its simple and atmospheric *Gasthäuser*. Pork is a staple, served either as *Schweinsbraten* (a plain roast) or with *Knödel* (dumplings made from either bread or potatoes). The specialties in Nürnberg, Coburg, and Regensburg are the *Bratwürste*—short, spiced sausages. The Nürnberg variety is known all over Germany; they are even on the menu on the ICE trains. You can have them grilled or heated in a stock of onions and wine (*Blaue Zipfel*). Bratwürste are traditionally served in denominations of 3, 6, or 8 with sauerkraut and potato salad or dark bread.

On the sweet side, try the *Dampfnudel*, a sweet yeast-dough dumpling that is tasty and filling. *Nürnberger Lebkuchen*, a sort of gingerbread eaten at Christmastime, is loved all over Germany. A true purist swears by *Elisenlebkuchen*,

which are made with no flour. Both Lebkuchen and the small Bratwürste are protected under German law and are only "legal" when made in or around Nürnberg.

Not to be missed are Franconia's liquid refreshments from both the grape and the grain. Franconian wines, usually white and sold in distinctive flat bottles called *Bocksbeutel*, are renowned for their special bouquet. (Silvaner is the traditional grape.) The region has the largest concentration of local breweries in the world (Bamberg alone has nine, Bayreuth seven), producing a wide range of brews, the most distinctive of which is the dark, smoky *Rauchbier* and the even darker and stronger *Schwärzla*. Then, of course, there is Kulmbach, with the Doppelbock Kulminator 28, which takes nine months to brew and has an alcohol content of 12%.

you'll find a striking collection of monuments and art treasures. The most famous piece is the **Bamberger Reiter** (Bamberg Horseman), an equestrian statue carved—no one knows by whom—around 1230 and thought to be an allegory of chivalrous virtue or a representation of King Stephen of Hungary. Compare it with the mass of carved figures huddled in the tympana above the church portals. In the center of the nave you'll find another masterpiece, the massive tomb of Heinrich and his wife, Kunigunde. It's the work of Tilman Riemenschneider. Pope Clement II is also buried in the cathedral, in an imposing tomb beneath the high altar; he's the only pope buried north of the Alps. ⊠ *Dompl.* ☎ *0951/502–330* ☐ *Free* ☉ *Apr.–Oct., daily 10–6; Nov.–Mar., daily 10–5. No visits during services.*

Kloster St. Michael (*Monastery of St. Michael*). Once a Benedictine monastery, this structure has been gazing over Bamberg since 1015. After being overwhelmed by so much baroque elsewhere, entering this haven of Romanesque simplicity is a relief. The entire choir is intricately carved, but the ceiling is gently decorated with very exact depictions of 578 flowers and healing herbs. The tomb of St. Otto is in a little chapel off the transept, and the stained-glass windows hold symbols of death and transfiguration. The monastery is now used as a home for the aged. One tract, however, was taken over by the **Franconian Brewery Museum,**

which exhibits everything that has to do with beer, from the making of malt to recipes. Due to renovation work, the church of St. Michael is closed to the public. ⊠ *Michelsberg 10f* ☎ *0951/53016* ⌦ *Museum €3.50* ⊘ *Apr.–Oct., Wed.–Sun. 1–5.*

WORTH NOTING

Diözesanmuseum (*Cathedral Museum*). Directly adjacent to the Bamberg Dom, this museum contains one of many nails and splinters of wood reputed to be from the cross of Jesus. The "star-spangled" cloak stitched with gold that was given to Emperor Heinrich II by an Italian prince is among the finest items displayed. More macabre exhibits in this rich ecclesiastical collection are the elaborately mounted skulls of Heinrich and Kunigunde. The building itself was designed by Balthasar Neumann (1687–1753), the architect of Vierzehnheiligen, and constructed between 1730 and 1733. ⊠ *Dompl. 5* ☎ *0951/502–325* ⊕ *www.dioezesanmuseum-bamberg.de* ⌦ *€5* ⊘ *Tues.–Sun. 10–5; tour in English by prior arrangement.*

Neue Residenz (*New Residence*). This glittering baroque palace was once the home of the prince-electors. Their plan to extend the immense palace even further is evident at the corner on Obere Karolinenstrasse, where the ashlar bonding was left open to accept another wing. The most memorable room in the palace is the **Kaisersaal** (Throne Room), complete with impressive ceiling frescoes and elaborate stucco. The rose garden behind the Neue Residenz provides an aromatic and romantic spot for a stroll with a view of Bamberg's roofscape. You have to take a tour to see the Residenz itself, but you can visit the Staatsbibliothek (library) at any time during its open hours.

⊠ *Dompl. 8* ☎ *0951/519–390* ⌦ *€4.50* ⊘ *By tour only: Apr.–Sept., daily 9–6; Oct.–Mar., daily 10–4.*

Obere Pfarre. Bamberg's wealthy burghers built no fewer than 50 churches. The Church of Our Lady, known simply as the Obere Pfarre (Upper Parish), dates back to around 1325, and is unusual because the exterior is entirely Gothic, while the interior is heavily baroque. The grand choir, which lacks any windows, was added much later. An odd squarish box tops the church tower; this watchman's post was placed there to keep the tower smaller than the neighboring cathedral, thus avoiding a medieval scandal. Note the slanted floor, which allowed crowds of pilgrims to see the object of their veneration, a 14th-century Madonna. Don't miss the *Ascension of Mary* by Tintoretto at the rear of the church. Around Christmas, the Obere Pfarre is the site of the city's greatest Nativity scene. Avoid the church during services, unless you've come to worship. ⊠ *Untere Seelg.* ⊘ *Daily 7–7.*

NEAR BAMBERG

Kloster Banz (*Banz Abbey*). This abbey, which some call the "holy mountain of Bavaria," proudly crowns the west bank of the Main north of Bamberg. There had been a monastery here since 1069, but the present buildings—now a political-seminar center and think tank—date from the end of the 17th century. The highlight of the complex is the **Klosterkirche** (Abbey Church), the work of architect Leonard Dientzenhofer and his brother, the stuccoist Johann Dientzenhofer (1663–1726).

Bamberg's Altes Rathaus is perched precariously on an artificial island in the middle of the Regnitz River.

Balthasar Neumann later contributed a good deal of work. Concerts are occasionally held in the church, including some by members of the renowned Bamberger Symphoniker. To get to Banz from Vierzehnheiligen, drive south to Unnersdorf, where you can cross the river. ⊠ *Kloster-Banz-Str. 1, Bad Staffelstein* ☎ *09573/7311* ⊗ *May–Oct., daily 9–5; Nov.–Apr., daily 9–noon; call to request a tour.*

Fodor's Choice ★ **Vierzehnheiligen.** In Bad Staffelstein, on the east side of the Main north of Bamberg, is a tall, elegant, yellow-sandstone edifice whose interior represents one of the great examples of rococo decoration. The church was built by Balthasar Neumann (architect of the Residenz at Würzburg) between 1743 and 1772 to commemorate a vision of Christ and 14 saints—*vierzehn Heiligen*—that appeared to a shepherd in 1445. The interior, known as "God's Ballroom," is supported by 14 columns. In the middle of the church is the *Gnadenaltar* (Mercy Altar) featuring the 14 saints. Thanks to clever play with light, light colors, and fanciful gold-and-blue trimmings, the interior seems to be in perpetual motion. Guided tours of the church are given on request; a donation is expected. On Saturday afternoon and all day Sunday the road leading to the church is closed and you have to walk the last half mile. ⊠ *Vierzehnheiligen 2, Bad Staffelstein* ✛ *36 km (22 miles) north of Bamberg via A-73* ☎ *09571/95080* ⊕ *www.vierzehnheiligen.de* ⊗ *Mar.–Oct., daily 7–8; Nov.–Feb., daily 8–5.*

WHERE TO EAT

$ ╳ **Bischofsmühle.** It doesn't always have to be beer in Bamberg. The old
GERMAN mill, its grinding wheel providing a sonorous backdrop for patrons, specializes in wines from Franconia and elsewhere. The menu offers

Franconian specialties such as the French-derived *Böfflamott,* or "beef à la mode" (beef roast, larded with bacon, marinated in red wine, and simmered in the marinade). $ *Average main: €8* ⊠ *Geyerswörthstr. 4* ☎ *0951/27570* ⊕ *www.bischofsmuehle.com* ▭ *No credit cards.*

$ ✕ **Klosterbräu.** This massive old stone-and-half-timber house has been
GERMAN standing since 1533, making it Bamberg's oldest brewpub. Regulars nurse a dark, smoky beer called Schwärzla near the big stove—though the best beer is the Klosterbraun. If you like the brew, you can buy a 5-liter bottle (called a *Siphon*) as well as other bottled beers and the requisite beer steins at the counter. The cuisine is basic, robust, filling, and tasty, with such items as a bowl of beans with a slab of smoked pork, or marinated pork kidneys with boiled potatoes. $ *Average main: €10* ⊠ *Obere Mühlbrücke* ☎ *0951/52265* ⊕ *www.klosterbraeu. de* ▭ *No credit cards.*

$ ✕ **Schlenkerla.** Set in the middle of the Old Town, this tavern has been
GERMAN serving beer inside an ancient half-timber house since 1405. The fare, atmosphere, and patrons are the definition of traditional Bamberg. Be sure to try the *Bamberger Zwiebel,* a local onion stuffed with pork, or come on Sunday for a roast dinner. But the real reason to come here is to try the *Aecht Schenkerla Rauchbier,* a beer brewed with smoked malt. This Rauchbier (smoked beer) is served from huge wooden barrels and tastes like liquid ham—it's an acquired taste, but worth sampling; locals agree that if you can choke down the first one, you'll be a fan for life. $ *Average main: €10* ⊠ *Dominikanerstr. 6* ☎ *951/56050* ⊕ *www. schlenkerla.de* ▭ *No credit cards.*

WHERE TO STAY

$$ ⌂ **Hotel-Restaurant St. Nepomuk.** This half-timber house seems to float
B&B/INN over the river Regnitz; many of the comfortable rooms have quite a
Fodor's Choice view of the water and the Old Town Hall on its island. **Pros:** great
★ views; an elegant dining room with excellent food. **Cons:** hotel on a pedestrian-only street; public garage 700 feet away. $ *Rooms from: €130* ⊠ *Obere Mühlbrücke 9* ☎ *0951/98420* ⊕ *www.hotel-nepomuk. de* ⇆ *47 rooms* ⦿ *Breakfast.*

$$ ⌂ **Romantik Hotel Weinhaus Messerschmitt.** This comfortable hotel has
HOTEL spacious and luxurious rooms, some with exposed beams and many of them lighted by chandeliers. **Pros:** elegant dining room with good food; variety of rooms to choose from. **Cons:** older property; front rooms are noisy; expensive. $ *Rooms from: €155* ⊠ *Langestr. 41* ☎ *0951/297–800* ⊕ *www.hotel-messerschmitt.de* ⇆ *67 rooms* ⦿ *Breakfast.*

PERFORMING ARTS

Capella Antiqua Bambergensis. The city's first-class ensemble, Capella Antiqua Bambergensis, specializes in ancient music featuring lute, harp, hurdy gurdy, and other early instruments. They perform (in medieval costume) at several venues in town. ⊠ *Bamberg* ⊕ *www.capella-antiqua.de.*

Dom. Throughout summer organ concerts are given Saturday at noon in the Dom. Call for program details and tickets to all cultural events. ⊠ *Dompl.* ☎ *0951/297–6200* ⊕ *bamberger-dom.de.*

E.T.A. Hoffmann Theater. Opera and operettas are performed here from September through July. ⊠ *E.T.A.-Hoffmann-Pl. 1* ☎ *0951/873–030* ⊕ *www.theater-bamberg.de.*

Kongresshalle Bamberg (*Sinfonie an der Regnitz*). This fine riverside concert hall is home to Bamberg's own world-class resident symphony orchestra, the Bamberger Symphoniker. ⊠ *Muss-Str. 1* ☎ *0951/964–7200* ⊕ *www.bamberg-ce.de, www.bamberger-symphoniker.de.*

SHOPPING

If you happen to be traveling around Christmastime, make sure you keep an eye out for crèches, a Bamberg specialty. Check the tourism website (⊕ *www.bamberg.info*) for the locations of nativity scenes and descriptions.

APFELWEIBLA

As you peruse the shops in Bamberg's Altstadt, you may notice an applelike face that adorns jewelry and housewares, the *Apfelweibla.* A replica of the Apfelweibla, a whimsical doorknob depicting an elderly woman's face, can be found at Eisgrube 14. The original doorknob is on display at the Museum of History at Domplatz. The doorknob inspired E. T. A. Hoffmann's novella *The Golden Pot.* It's said that rubbing the Apfelweibla will bring you good luck.

Café am Dom. For an edible souvenir, take home handmade chocolates like the only-in-Bamberg Rauchbier truffles made with Schlenkerla smoked beer. This café also has a roomy seating area to take a load off while you nibble a delicious pastry. ⊠ *Ringleinsg. 2* ☎ *0951/519–290* ⊕ *www.cafeamdom.de.*

Magnus Klee. This shop sells nativity scenes, called *Krippen* in German, of all different shapes and sizes, including wood carved and with fabric clothes. ⊠ *Obstmarkt 2* ☎ *0951/26037.*

Vinothek im Sand. Head to this wine store for Franconian wine as well as a sampling of Bamberg's specialty beers. ⊠ *Obere Sandstr. 8* ☎ *0151/5473–8779.*

NÜRNBERG (NUREMBERG)

With a recorded history stretching back to 1050, Franconia's main city is among the most historic in all of Germany; the core of the Old Town, through which the Pegnitz River flows, is still surrounded by its original medieval walls. Year-round floodlighting adds to the brooding romance of the moats, sturdy gateways, and watchtowers. Nürnberg has always taken a leading role in German affairs. It was here, for example, that the Holy Roman emperors traditionally held the first Diet, or convention of the estates, of their incumbency. And it was here, too, that Hitler staged the most grandiose Nazi rallies. With a sense of historical justice, Nürnberg in rubble was the site of the Allies' war trials, where top-ranking Nazis were charged with—and almost without exception convicted of—crimes against humanity. The rebuilding of Nürnberg after the war was virtually a miracle, considering the 90% destruction of the Old Town. As a major intersection on the medieval trade routes, Nürnberg became a wealthy town where the arts and sciences

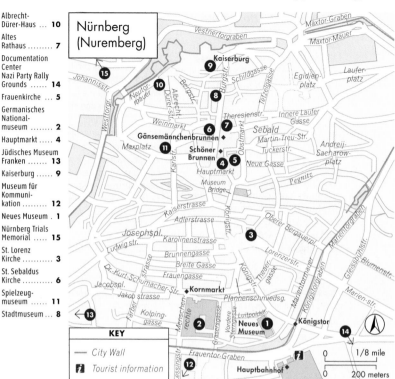

5

flowered. Albrecht Dürer (1471–1528), the first indisputable genius of the Renaissance in Germany, was born here. He married in 1509 and bought a house in the city where he lived and worked for the rest of his life. Other leading Nürnberg artists of the Renaissance include painter Michael Wolgemut (a teacher of Dürer), stonecutter Adam Kraft, and the brass founder Peter Vischer. The tradition of the Meistersinger also flourished here in the 16th century, thanks to the high standard set by the local cobbler Hans Sachs (1494–1576). The Meistersinger were poets and musicians who turned songwriting into a special craft, with a wealth of rules and regulations. They were celebrated three centuries later by Wagner in his *Meistersinger von Nürnberg*.

The Thirty Years' War (1618–48) and the shift to sea routes for transportation led to a period of decline, which ended only in the early 19th century when the first railroad opened in Nürnberg. Among a great host of inventions associated with the city, the most significant are the pocket watch, gun casting, the clarinet, and the geographic globe. Among Nürnberg's famous products are *Lebkuchen* (gingerbread of sorts) and Faber-Castell pencils.

GETTING HERE AND AROUND

Nürnberg is centrally located and well connected, an hour north of Munich and two hours east of Frankfurt by train. Five autobahns meet here: A-3 Düsseldorf–Passau, A-6 Mannheim–Nürnberg, A-9 Potzdam–München, A-73 Coburg–Feucht, and B-8 (four-lane near Nürnberg) Würzburg–Regensburg. Most places in the Old Town can be reached on foot.

Nürnberg consists of a surprisingly compact city center that is easily explored on foot. All of the downtown historical sites, restaurants, and hotels are within easy walking distance from each other. Nürnberg's fantastic bus, trolley, or subway system will help you venture out to the Nazi sites farther afield. Information about city transportation is available at the VAG-KundenCenter at the main train station.

Essentials VAG-KundenCenter. ☒ U-Bahn Verteilergeschoss, Königstorpassage, Haltestelle Hauptbahnhof, Nürnberg ⊕ www.vgn.de.

> ### UNDERGROUND NUREMBERG
>
> Beer aficionados can get a deeper look at Nürnberg's brewing history with a tour into the cellars where beer was made and stored since the 1300s. The tour, offered by Underground Nuremberg, costs €7, which includes a beer tasting, but is only offered in German. English-language group tours are available by appointment; see ⊕ www.felsengaenge-nuernberg.de.

TOURS

Neukam-Reba. This company takes visitors on a combined bus tour with a short walking tour through the Nazi Party Grounds. Tours leave daily at 10 am, May through November and during the Christmas Market. ☒ Hallpl. 36, Nürnberg ☎ 0911/200–1310 ⊕ www.neukam-reba.de ☒€17.

Nüremberg Guide Association. An English-language walking tour through the Old Town departs from the Tourist Information Office on the Hauptmarkt daily at 1 pm, April through December. The tour lasts approximately two hours and covers all the essential Nürnberg sites, with some interesting, if not canned, commentary. ☒ Hauptmarkt, Nürnberg ☎ 0911/3506–4631 ⊕ www.nuernberg-tours.de ☒€10.

TIMING

You'll need a full day to walk around Nürnberg's Old Town, two if you wish to take more time at its fascinating museums and churches. Most of the major sights are within a few minutes' walk of each other. The Kaiserburg is a must-visit on any trip to Nürnberg. Plan at least half a day for the Germanisches Nationalmuseum, which is just inside the city walls near the main station. Add another half a day to visit the Nazi Party Rally Grounds.

FESTIVALS

By far the most famous local festival is the **Christkindlesmarkt** (Christmas Market), an enormous pre-Christmas fair that runs from the Friday before Advent to Christmas Eve. One of the highlights is the candle procession, held every second Thursday of the market season, during which thousands of children parade through the city streets.

Christkindlesmarkt. Perhaps the most famous Christmas Market in Germany, the Nürnberg Christkindlesmarkt sits on the town's cobblestone main square beneath the wonderful Frauenkirche. Renowned for its food, particularly *Nürnberger Bratwurstchen,* tasty little pork and marjoram sausages, and *Lebkuchen,* gingerbread made with cinnamon and honey, the market is also famed for its little figures made out of prunes called *Nürnberger Zwetschgenmännla* (Nuremberg Prune People). ⊠ *Hauptmarkt, Nürnberg* ⊕ *www.christkindlesmarkt.de* ☉ *Nov. 25– Dec. 23, Mon.–Thurs. 9:30–8, Fri. and Sat. 9:30–10, Sun. 10:30–8; Dec. 24 9:30–2.*

Kaiserburg. From May through July classical-music concerts are given in the Rittersaal of the Kaiserburg. ⊠ *Burg 13, Nürnberg* ☎ *0911/244– 6590* ⊕ *www.kaiserburg-nuernberg.de.*

Sommer in Nürnberg. Nürnberg holds this annual summer festival from May through July, with more than 200 events. Its international organ festival in June and July is regarded as Europe's finest. ⊠ *Nürnberg.*

ESSENTIALS

Visitor Information Nürnberg Congress- und Tourismus-Zentrale. ⊠ *Frauentorgraben 3, Nürnberg* ☎ 0911/23360 ⊕ www.nuernberg.de.

EXPLORING

TOP ATTRACTIONS

Albrecht-Dürer-Haus (*Albrecht Dürer House*). The great painter Albrecht Dürer lived here from 1509 until his death in 1528. This beautifully preserved late-medieval house is typical of the prosperous merchants' homes that once filled Nürnberg. Dürer, who enriched German art with Italianate elements, was more than a painter. He raised the woodcut, a notoriously difficult medium, to new heights of technical sophistication, combining great skill with a haunting, immensely detailed drawing style and complex, allegorical subject matter, while earning a good living at the same time. A number of original prints adorn the walls, and printing techniques using the old press are demonstrated in the studio. An excellent opportunity to find out about life in the house of Dürer is the tour with a guide role-playing Agnes Dürer, the artist's wife. ⊠ *Albrecht-Dürer-Str. 39, Nürnberg* ☎ *0911/231–2568* 🔖*€5, tours with "Agnes Dürer" in English €2.50* ☉ *Tues., Wed., and Fri.–Sun. 10–5; Thurs. 10–8; guided tour in English Sat. at 2.*

Documentation Center Nazi Party Rally Grounds. On the eastern outskirts of the city, the **Ausstellung Faszination und Gewalt** (Fascination and Terror Exhibition) documents the political, social, and architectural history of the Nazi Party. The sobering museum helps illuminate the whys and hows of Hitler's rise to power during the unstable period after World War I and the end of the democratic Weimar Republic. This is one of the few museums that documents how the Third Reich's propaganda machine influenced the masses. The 19-room exhibition is inside a horseshoe-shape Congress Hall, designed for a crowd of 50,000, that the Nazis never completed. The Nazis did make infamous use of the nearby Zeppelin Field, the enormous parade ground where Hitler addressed his largest Nazi Party rallies. Today it sometimes shakes to the amplified beat of pop concerts. To get to the Documentation Center, take Tram 9 from the city center to the Doku-Zentrum stop. ⊠ *Bayernstr. 110, Nürnberg* ☎ *0911/231–5666* ⊕ *www.museen.nuernberg.de* ⤳ *€5* ⊙ *Weekdays 9–6, weekends 10–6.*

Fodor's Choice **Germanisches Nationalmuseum** (*German National Museum*). You could
★ spend a lifetime exploring the largest museum of its kind in Germany. This vast museum showcases the country's cultural and scientific achievements, ethnic background, and history. Housed in a former Carthusian monastery, complete with cloisters and monastic outbuilding, the complex effectively melds the ancient with modern extensions, giving the impression that Germany is moving forward by examining its past. The exhibition begins outside, with the tall, sleek pillars of the Strasse der Menschenrechte (Street of Human Rights), designed by Israeli artist Dani Karavan. Thirty columns are inscribed with the articles from the Universal Declaration of Human Rights. There are few aspects of German culture, from the Stone Age to the 19th century, that are not covered by the museum, and quantity and quality are evenly matched. One highlight is the superb collection of Renaissance German paintings (with Dürer, Cranach, and Altdorfer well represented). Others may prefer the exquisite medieval ecclesiastical exhibits—manuscripts, altarpieces, statuary, stained glass, jewel-encrusted reliquaries—the collections of arms and armor, the scientific instruments, or the toys. ⊠ *Kartäuserg. 1, Nürnberg* ☎ *0911/13310* ⊕ *www.gnm.de* ⤳ *€8* ⊙ *Tues. and Thurs.–Sun. 10–6, Wed. 10–9.*

QUICK BITES

Bistro Arte. Opposite the Germanisches Nationalmuseum is Bistro Arte. Al dente pasta or meat and fish dishes with excellent wines will revive you after the long hours spent in the museum. ⊠ *Kartäuserg. 12, Nürnberg* ☎ *0911/244–9774* ⊕ *www.arte-cafe.de* ⊙ *Closed Mon.*

Fodor's Choice **Kaiserburg** (*Imperial Castle*). The city's main attraction is a grand yet
★ playful collection of buildings standing just inside the city walls; it was once the residence of the Holy Roman Emperor. The complex comprises three separate groups. The oldest, dating from around 1050, is the **Burggrafenburg** (Castellan's Castle), with a craggy old pentagonal tower and the bailiff's house. It stands in the center of the complex. To the east is the **Kaiserstallung** (Imperial Stables), built in the 15th century as a granary and now serving as a youth hostel. The real interest of this vast complex of ancient buildings, however, centers on the westernmost part of the fortress, which begins at the **Sinwell Turm** (Sinwell Tower). The **Kaiserburg Museum** is here, a subsidiary of the Germanisches Nationalmuseum that displays ancient armors and has exhibits relating to horsemanship in the imperial era and to the history of the fortress. This section of the castle also has a wonderful Romanesque **Doppelkappelle** (Double Chapel). The upper part—richer, larger, and more ornate than the lower chapel—was where the emperor and his family worshipped. Also visit the **Rittersaal** (Knights' Hall) and the **Kaisersaal** (Throne Room). Their heavy oak beams, painted ceilings, and sparse interiors have changed little since they were built in the 15th

Outside the Germanisches Nationalmuseum is the "Way of Human Rights," an outdoor sculpture consisting of 30 columns inscribed with the articles from the Universal Declaration of Human Rights.

century. ⊠ *Burgstr., Nürnberg* ☎ *0911/2446–59115* ⊕ *www.kaiserburg-nuernberg.de* ✉ *€7* ⊙ *Apr.–Sept., daily 9–6; Oct.–Mar., daily 10–4.*

Neues Museum (*New Museum*). Anything but medieval, this museum is devoted to international design since 1945. The collection, supplemented by changing exhibitions, is in a slick, modern edifice that achieves the perfect synthesis between old and new. It's mostly built of traditional pink-sandstone ashlars, while the facade is a flowing, transparent composition of glass. The interior is a work of art in itself—cool stone, with a ramp that slowly spirals up to the gallery. Extraordinary things await, including a Joseph Beuys installation (*Ausfegen,* or *Sweep-out*) and *Avalanche* by François Morellet, a striking collection of violet, argon-gas-filled fluorescent tubes. The café-restaurant adjoining the museum contains modern art, silver-wrapped candies, and video projections. ⊠ *Luitpoldstr. 5, Nürnberg* ☎ *0911/240–200* ⊕ *www.nmn.de* ✉ *€4, special exhibitions €6* ⊙ *Tues.–Fri. 10–8, weekends 10–6.*

Nürnberg Trials Memorial. Nazi leaders and German organizations were put on trial here in 1945 and 1946 during the first international war-crimes trials, conducted by the victorious Allied forces of World War II. The trials were held in the Landgericht (Regional Court) in court-room No. 600 and resulted in 11 death sentences, among other convictions. The guided tours in English take place on Saturday at 2 and an English-language audio guide is available. ⊠ *Bärenschanzstr. 72, Nürnberg* ☎ *0911/231–8411* ⊕ *www.memorium-nuremberg.de* ✉ *€5, tour €3* ⊙ *Wed.–Mon. 10–6* Ⓜ *Bärenschanze.*

Climb to the top of Nürnberg's Kaiserburg (Imperial Castle) for wonderful views of the city.

WORTH NOTING

Altes Rathaus (*Old Town Hall*). This ancient building on Rathausplatz abuts the rear of St. Sebaldus Kirche; it was erected in 1332, destroyed in World War II, and subsequently reconstructed. Its intact medieval dungeons, consisting of 12 small rooms and one large torture chamber called the **Lochgefängnis** (or the Hole), provide insight into the grue-some applications of medieval law. **Gänsemännchenbrunnen** (Gooseman's Fountain) faces the Altes Rathaus. This lovely Renaissance bronze fountain, cast in 1550, is a work of rare elegance and great technical sophistication. ⊠ *Rathauspl. 2, Nürnberg* ☎ *0911/231–2690* 🖾 *€3.50, minimum of 5 people for tours* ⊙ *Tues.–Sun. 10–4.*

Frauenkirche (*Church of Our Lady*). The fine late-Gothic Frauenkirche was built in 1350, with the approval of Holy Roman Emperor Charles IV, on the site of a synagogue that was burned down during the 1349 pogrom. The modern tabernacle beneath the main altar was designed to look like a Torah scroll as a memorial to that despicable act. The church's main attraction is the **Männleinlaufen,** a clock dating from 1509, which is set into its facade. It's one of those colorful mechani-cal marvels at which Germans have long excelled. Every day at noon the seven electors of the Holy Roman Empire glide out of the clock to bow to Emperor Charles IV before sliding back under cover. It's worth scheduling your morning to catch the display. ⊠ *Hauptmarkt, Nürnberg* ⊙ *Mon.–Sat. 9–6, Sun. 12:30–6.*

Hauptmarkt (*Main Market*). Nürnberg's central market square was once the city's Jewish Quarter. When the people of Nürnberg petitioned their emperor, Charles IV, for a big central market, the emperor was in desperate need of money and, above all, political support. The Jewish Quarter was the preferred site, but as the official protector of the Jewish people, the emperor could not just openly take away their property. Instead, in 1349 he instigated a pogrom that left the Jewish Quarter in flames and more than 500 dead. He then razed the ruins and resettled the remaining Jews.

Towering over the northwestern corner of the Hauptmarkt, **Schöner Brunnen** (Beautiful Fountain) looks as though it should be on the summit of some lofty cathedral. Carved around the year 1400, the elegant 60-foot-high Gothic fountain is adorned with 40 figures arranged in tiers—prophets, saints, local noblemen, sundry electors of the Holy Roman Empire, and one or two strays such as Julius Caesar and Alexander the Great. A gold ring is set into the railing surrounding the fountain, reportedly placed there by an apprentice carver. Touching it is said to bring good luck. A market still operates in the Hauptmarkt on weekdays. Its colorful stands are piled high with produce, fruit, bread, homemade cheeses and sausages, sweets, and anything else you might need for a snack or picnic. It's here that the Christkindlmarkt is held. ✉ *Hauptmarkt, Nürnberg.*

Jüdisches Museum Franken. The everyday life of the Jewish community in Franconia and Fürth is examined in this Jewish museum: books, seder plates, old statutes, and children's toys are among the exhibits. One of the most famous members of the Fürth community was Henry Kissinger, born here in 1923. Changing exhibitions relate to contemporary Jewish life in Germany, and in the basement is the *Mikveh*, the ritual bath, which was used by the family who lived here centuries ago. In the museum you will also find a good Jewish bookshop as well as a nice small café. A subsidiary to the museum, which houses special exhibitions, is in the former synagogue in nearby Schnaittach. ✉ *Königstr. 89, 10 km (6 miles) west of Nürnberg, Fürth* ☎ *0911/770–577* ⊕ *www.juedisches-museum. org/* ⊡ *€5* ⊙ *Wed.–Sun. 10–5, Tues. 10–8* Ⓜ *Rathaus.*

Museum für Kommunikation (*Communication Museum*). Two museums about how people stay connected have been amalgamated under a single roof here: the German Railway Museum and the Museum of Communication. Germany's first train began its inaugural journey on December 7, 1835 and ran from Nürnberg to nearby Fürth. A model of the epochal train is here, along with a series of original 19th- and early-20th-century trains and stagecoaches. Philatelists will want to check out some of the 40,000-odd stamps in the extensive exhibits on the German postal system. You can also find out about the history of sending messages— from old coaches to fiber-optic networks. ✉ *Lessingstr. 6, Nürnberg* ☎ *0911/219–2428* ⊕ *www.mfk-nuernberg.de* ⊡ *€5* ⊙ *Tues.–Sun. 10–5.*

St. Lorenz Kirche (*St. Laurence Church*). In a city with several striking churches, St. Lorenz is considered by many to be the most beautiful. Construction began around 1250 and was completed in about 1477; it later became a Lutheran church. Two towers flank the main entrance, which is covered with a forest of carvings. In the lofty interior, note the works by sculptors Adam Kraft and Veit Stoss: Kraft's great stone tabernacle, to the left of the altar, and Stoss's *Annunciation*, at the east end of the nave, are their finest works. There are many other carvings throughout the building, testimony to the artistic wealth of late-medieval Nürnberg. ✉ *Lorenzer Pl., Nürnberg* ⏲ *Mon.–Sat. 9–5, Sun. noon–4.*

St. Sebaldus Kirche (*St. Sebaldus Church*). Although St. Sebaldus lacks the quantity of art treasures found in its rival St. Lorenz, its nave and choir are among the purest examples of Gothic ecclesiastical architecture in Germany: elegant, tall, and airy. Veit Stoss carved the Crucifixion group at the east end of the nave, while the elaborate bronze shrine containing the remains of St. Sebaldus himself was cast by Peter Vischer and his five sons around 1520. Not to be missed is the **Sebaldus Chörlein,** an ornate Gothic oriel that was added to the Sebaldus parish house in 1361 (the original is in the Germanisches Nationalmuseum). ✉ *Albrecht-Dürer-Pl. 1, Nürnberg* ☎ *0911/214–2500* 🎟 *Free* ⏲ *Daily 10–5.*

FAMILY **Spielzeugmuseum** (*Toy Museum*). Young and old are captivated by this playful museum, which has a few exhibits dating from the Renaissance; most, however, are from the 19th century. Simple dolls vie with mechanical toys of extraordinary complexity, such as a wooden Ferris wheel from the Ore Mountains adorned with little colored lights. The top floor displays Barbies and intricate Lego constructions. ✉ *Karlstr. 13–15, Nürnberg* ☎ *0911/231–3164* 🎟 *€5* ⏲ *Tues.–Sun. 10–5.*

Stadtmuseum (*City Museum*). This city history museum is in the Fembohaus, a dignified patrician dwelling completed in 1598. It's one of the finest Renaissance mansions in Nürnberg. Each room explores another aspect of Nürnberg history, from crafts to gastronomy. The 50-minute multivision show provides a comprehensive look at the city's long history. ✉ *Burgstr. 15, Nürnberg* ☎ *0911/231–2595* 🎟 *€5* ⏲ *Tues.–Sun. 10–5.*

WHERE TO EAT

$$$$ GERMAN Fodor's Choice ★ 🍴 **Essigbrätlein.** The oldest restaurant in Nürnberg is also the top restaurant in the city and among the best in Germany. Built in 1550, it was originally used as a meeting place for wine merchants. Today its tiny but elegant period interior caters to the distinguishing gourmet with a taste for special spice mixes (owner Andrée Köthe's hobby). The dinner menu changes daily, but the four-course menu can't be beat. There's a limited lunch menu, but this is really a place to come for dinner. Don't be put off if the restaurant looks closed—just ring the bell and a friendly receptionist will help you. [$] *Average main: €30* ✉ *Weinmarkt 3, Nürnberg* ☎ *0911/225–131* 🌐 *www.essigbraetlein.de* ⏲ *Closed Sun., Mon. (but open Mon. in Dec.), and late Aug.* ✍ *Reservations essential.*

$ GERMAN 🍴 **Hausbrauerei Altstadthof.** For traditional regional food, such as Nürnberg bratwurst, head to this atmospheric brewery. You can see the copper kettles where the brewery's organic *Rotbier* (red beer) is made. For a bit of shopping after lunch, the brewery store sells a multitude of beer-related products such as beer vinegar, brandy, and soap. Located above a network of deep, dark cellars where beer was once brewed and stored, this brewery is the meeting point for cellar tours (in English on Sunday at 11:30 am; €5.50; historische-felsengaenge.de). [$] *Average main: €10* ✉ *Bergstr. 19–21, Nürnberg* ☎ *911/244–9859* 🌐 *www.hausbrauerei-altstadthof.de* 💳 *No credit cards.*

$ ✕ **Heilig-Geist-Spital.** Heavy wood furnishings and a choice of more than
GERMAN 100 wines make this huge, 650-year-old wine tavern—built as the refectory of the city hospital—a popular spot. Try for a table in one of the alcoves, where you can see the river below as you eat your seasonal fresh fish. The menu also includes grilled pork chops, panfried potatoes, and other Franconian dishes. **$** *Average main: €14* ⊠ *Spitalg. 16, Nürnberg* ☎ *0911/221–761* ⊕ *www.heilig-geist-spital.de.*

$ ✕ **Historische Bratwurst-Küche Zum Gulden Stern.** The city council meets
GERMAN here to decide the official size and weight of the Nürnberg bratwursts,
FAMILY so this should be your first stop to try the ubiquitous Nürnberg delicacy. The sausages have to be small enough to fit through a medieval keyhole, which in earlier days enabled pub owners to sell them after hours. It's a fitting venue for such a decision, given that this house, built in 1375, holds the oldest bratwurst restaurant in the world. The famous Nürnberg bratwursts are always freshly roasted on a beech-wood fire. *Saure Zipfel,* the boiled variation, is prepared in a tasty stock of Franconian wine and onions. **$** *Average main: €9* ⊠ *Zirkelschmiedg. 26, Nürnberg* ☎ *0911/205–9288* ⊕ *www.bratwurstkueche.de.*

WHERE TO STAY

$ ⌂ **Agneshof.** This comfortable hotel is north of the Old Town, between
HOTEL the fortress and St. Sebaldus Church, and its interiors are very modern and tastefully done. **Pros:** many rooms have great views of the castle; warm yet professional welcome. **Cons:** deluxe rooms overpriced; parking and hotel access difficult; no restaurant. **$** *Rooms from: €85* ⊠ *Agnesg. 10, Nürnberg* ☎ *0911/214–440* ⊕ *www.agneshof-nuernberg.de* ⇲ *72 rooms* ⦿❘ *Breakfast.*

$ ⌂ **Burghotel Stammhaus.** At this quaint hotel the accommodations are
HOTEL small but cozy and the service is familial and friendly. **Pros:** great location in the city center; comfortable; pool; good value. **Cons:** small rooms; tiny lobby; parking not easy; service sometimes too casual. **$** *Rooms from: €67* ⊠ *Schildg. 14, Nürnberg* ☎ *0911/203–040* ⊕ *www.invite-hotels.de* ⇲ *21 rooms, 1 suite* ⦿❘ *Breakfast.*

$$ ⌂ **Hotel Drei Raben.** Legends and tales of Nürnberg form the leitmotif
HOTEL running through the designer rooms at this hotel. **Pros:** free drink at the reception desk; designer rooms; valet parking; Wi-Fi. **Cons:** neon-lighted bar isn't relaxing; no restaurant. **$** *Rooms from: €150* ⊠ *Königstr. 63, Nürnberg* ☎ *0911/274–380* ⊕ *www.hotel-drei-raben.de* ⇲ *25 rooms* ⦿❘ *Breakfast.*

$$ ⌂ **Hotel-Weinhaus Steichele.** An 18th-century bakery has been skillfully
HOTEL converted into this hotel, which has been managed by the same family for four generations. **Pros:** comfortable; good location; good restaurants. **Cons:** small rooms and lobby; some rooms show their age. **$** *Rooms from: €109* ⊠ *Knorrstr. 2–8, Nürnberg* ☎ *0911/202–280* ⊕ *www.steichele.de* ⇲ *56 rooms* ⦿❘ *Breakfast.*

$$$ ⌂ **Le Meridien Grand Hotel.** Across the square from the central train station, this stately building with the calling card "Grand Hotel" arching
HOTEL over its entranceway has a spacious and imposing lobby with marble pillars, which feels grand and welcoming. **Pros:** luxury property; impressive lobby; excellent food; valet parking. **Cons:** expensive, with

additional fees for every possible contingency; Germanic efficiency at reception desk; access from the station can be difficult with luggage, via an underpass with stairs. $ *Rooms from: €189* ⊠ *Bahnhofstr. 1, Nürnberg* ☎ *0911/23220* ⊕ *www.nuremberg.lemeridien.com* ⤳ *186 rooms, 5 suites* ⏸⏺ *Breakfast; Some meals.*

SHOPPING

Handwerkerhof. Step into this "medieval mall," in the tower at the Old Town gate (Am Königstor) opposite the main train station, and you'll think you're back in the Middle Ages. Craftspeople are busy at work turning out the kind of handiwork that has been produced in Nürnberg for centuries: pewter, glassware, basketwork, wood carvings, and, of course, toys. The Lebkuchen specialist **Lebkuchen-Schmidt** has a shop here as well. ⊠ *Am Königstor, Nürnberg* ⊕ *www.handwerkerhof.de* ⊙ *Closed Sun. and holidays late Mar.–Dec. 30.*

THE GERMAN DANUBE

For many people, the sound of the Danube River (Donau in German) is the melody of *The Blue Danube*, the waltz written by Austrian Johann Strauss. The famous 2,988-km-long (1,857-mile-long) river, which is actually a pale green, originates in Germany's Black Forest and flows through 10 countries. In Germany it's mostly a rather unremarkable stream as it passes through cities such as Ulm on its southeasterly route. However, that changes at Kelheim, just west of Regensburg, where the Main–Donau Canal (completed in 1992) brings big river barges all the way from the North Sea. The river becomes sizable in Regensburg, where the ancient Steinerne Brücke (Stone Bridge) needs 15 spans of 30 to 48 feet each to bridge the water. Here everything from small pleasure boats to cruise liners joins the commercial traffic. In the university town of Passau, two more rivers join the waters of the Danube before Europe's longest river continues into Austria.

REGENSBURG

85 km (53 miles) southeast of Nürnberg, 120 km (75 miles) northwest of Munich.

Few visitors to Bavaria venture this far off the well-trodden tourist trails, and even Germans are surprised when they discover medieval Regensburg. ■ TIP➔ **The town escaped World War II with no major damage, and it is one of the best-preserved medieval cities in Germany.**

Regensburg's story begins with the Celts around 500 BC. In AD 179, as an original marble inscription in the Historisches Museum proclaims, it became a Roman military post called Castra Regina. The Porta Praetoria, or gateway, built by the Romans, remains in the Old Town, and whenever you see huge ashlars incorporated into buildings, you are looking at bits of the old Roman settlement. When Bavarian tribes migrated to the area in the 6th century, they occupied what remained of the Roman town and, apparently on the basis of its Latin name,

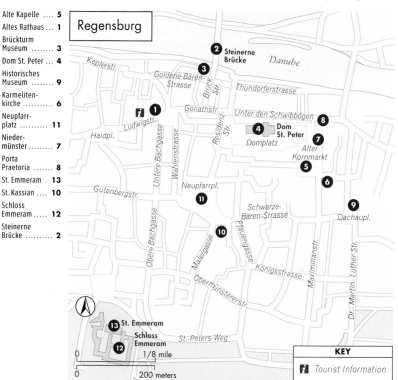

Regensburg

called it Regensburg. Anglo-Saxon missionaries led by St. Boniface in 739 made the town a bishopric before heading down the Danube to convert the heathen in even more far-flung lands. Charlemagne, first of the Holy Roman emperors, arrived at the end of the 8th century and incorporated Regensburg into his burgeoning domain. Regensburg benefited from the fact that the Danube wasn't navigable to the west, and thus it was able to control trade as goods traveled between Germany and Central Europe.

By the Middle Ages Regensburg had become a political, economic, and intellectual center. For many centuries it was the most important city in southeast Germany, serving as the seat of the Perpetual Imperial Diet from 1663 until 1806, when Napoléon ordered the dismantling of the Holy Roman Empire.

Today the ancient and hallowed walls of Regensburg continue to buzz with life. Students from the university fill the restaurants and pubs, and locals tend to their daily shopping and run errands in the inner city, where small shops and stores have managed to keep international consumer chains out.

GETTING HERE AND AROUND

Regensburg is at the intersection of the autobahns 3 and 93. It is an hour away from Nürnberg and two hours from Munich by train. Regensburg is compact; its Old Town center is about 1 square mile. All of its attractions lie on the south side of the Danube, so you won't have to cross it more than once—and then only to admire the city from the north bank.

English-language guided walking tours are conducted May through September and during the Christmas markets, Wednesday and Saturday at 1:30. They cost €6 and begin at the tourist office.

TIMING

Although the Old Town is quite small, you can easily spend half a day strolling through its narrow streets. Any serious tour of Regensburg includes an unusually large number of places of worship. If your spirits wilt at the thought of inspecting them all, you should at least see the Dom, famous for its Domspatzen (boys' choir—the literal translation is "cathedral sparrows"). You'll need about another two hours or more to explore Schloss Emmeram and St. Emmeram church.

ESSENTIALS

Personenschifffahrt Klinger. All boats depart from the Steinerne Brücke, and the most popular excursions are boat trips to Ludwig I's imposing Greek-style Doric temple of Walhalla. There are daily sailings at 10:30 and 2 to Walhalla from Easter through October. The round-trip takes three hours, including about an hour to explore the temple. Don't bother with the trip upriver from Regensburg to Kelheim. ⊠ *Thundorfstr. 1* ☎ *0941/55359* ⊕ *www.schifffahrtklinger.de* ⊠ *€10.50.*

Visitor Information Regensburg Tourismus. ⊠ *Altes Rathaus, Rathauspl. 4* ☎ *0941/507–4410* ⊕ *www.regensburg.de.*

EXPLORING

TOP ATTRACTIONS

Altes Rathaus (*Old Town Hall*). The picture-book complex of medieval half-timber buildings, with windows large and small and flowers in tubs, is one of the best-preserved town halls in the country, as well as one of the most historically important. It was here, in the imposing Gothic **Reichssaal** (Imperial Hall), that the Perpetual Imperial Diet met from 1663 to 1806. This parliament of sorts consisted of the emperor, the electors (seven or eight), the princes (about 50), and the burghers, who assembled to discuss and determine the affairs of the far-reaching German lands of the Holy Roman Empire. The hall is sumptuously appointed with tapestries, flags, and heraldic designs. Note the wood ceiling, built in 1408, and the different elevations for the various estates. The Reichssaal is occasionally used for concerts. The neighboring **Ratssaal** (Council Room) is where the electors met for their consultations. The cellar holds the city's torture chamber; the **Fragstatt** (Questioning Room); and the execution room, called the **Armesünderstübchen** (Poor Sinners' Room). Any prisoner who withstood three degrees of questioning without confessing was considered innocent and released—which tells you something about medieval notions of justice. ⊠ *Rathauspl.* ☎ *0941/507–4411* ⊠ *€8* ⊗ *Guided tours in English Apr.–Oct., daily at 3.*

Regensburg's Dom St. Peter is an excellent example of the French Gothic style.

QUICK BITES

Prinzess Confiserie Café. Just across the square from the Altes Rathaus is the Prinzess Confiserie Café, Germany's oldest coffeehouse, which first opened its doors in 1686. The homemade chocolates are highly recommended, as are the rich cakes. ⊠ *Rathauspl. 2* ☎ *0941/595–310.*

Brückturm Museum (*Bridge Tower Museum*). With its tiny windows, weathered tiles, and pink plaster, this 17th-century tower stands at the south end of the Steinerne Brücke. The tower displays a host of items relating to the construction and history of the old bridge. It also offers a gorgeous view of the Regensburg roof landscape. The brooding building with a massive roof to the left of the Brückturm is an old salt warehouse. ⊠ *Steinerne Brücke, Weisse-Lamm-G. 1* ☎ *0941/507–5888* ☜ *€2* ☺ *Apr.–Oct., daily 10–5; call ahead to ask about tours in English.*

Dom St. Peter (*St. Peter's Cathedral*). Regensburg's transcendent cathedral, modeled on the airy, powerful lines of French Gothic architecture, is something of a rarity this far south in Germany. Begun in the 13th century, it stands on the site of a much earlier Carolingian church. Remarkably, the cathedral can hold 6,000 people, three times the population of Regensburg when building began. Construction dragged on for almost 600 years, until Ludwig I of Bavaria, then ruler of Regensburg, finally had the towers built. These had to be replaced in the mid-1950s. Behind the Dom is a little workshop where a team of 15 stonecutters is busy full-time in summer recutting and restoring parts of the cathedral.

Before heading into the Dom, take time to admire the intricate and frothy carvings of its facade. Inside, the glowing 14th-century stained glass in the choir and the exquisitely detailed statues of the archangel

Gabriel and the Virgin in the crossing (the intersection of the nave and the transepts) are among the church's outstanding features.

Due to renovation work the **Kreuzgang** (Cloisters), reached via the garden, the **Allerheiligenkapelle** (All Saints' Chapel), and the ancient shell of **St. Stephan's Church** are inaccessible until 2020.

⊠ *Dompl. 50* ☎ *0941/586–5500* 🖾 *Free; €3 for tour* ☉ *Daily 6:30 am–7 pm. Tour daily at 2 (only in German; for tours in English call ahead).*

Domschatzmuseum (*Cathedral Museum*). This museum contains valuable treasures going back to the 11th century. Some of the vestments and the monstrances, which are fine examples of eight centuries' worth of the goldsmith's trade, are still used during special services. The entrance is in the nave. ⊠ *Dompl.* ☎ *0941/597–2530* 🖾 *€3* ☉ *Apr.–Oct., Tues.– Sat. 10–5, Sun. noon–5; Dec.–Mar., Fri. and Sat. 10–4, Sun. noon–4.*

NEED A BREAK?

Haus Heuport. The restaurant Haus Heuport, opposite the entrance to the Dom, was once one of the old and grand private ballrooms of the city. The service is excellent, and the tables at the windows have a wonderful view of the Dom. In summer, head for the bistro area in the courtyard for sandwiches and salads. ⊠ *Dompl. 7* ☎ *0941/599-9297* ⊕ *www.heuport.de.*

Historisches Museum. The municipal museum vividly relates the cultural history of Regensburg. It's one of the highlights of the city, both for its unusual and beautiful setting—a former Gothic monastery—and for its wide-ranging collections, from Roman artifacts to Renaissance tapestries and remains from Regensburg's 16th-century Jewish ghetto. The most significant exhibits are the paintings by Albrecht Altdorfer (1480–1538), a native of Regensburg and, along with Cranach, Grünewald, and Dürer, one of the leading painters of the German Renaissance. Altdorfer's work has the same sense of heightened reality found in that of his contemporaries, in which the lessons of Italian painting are used to produce an emotional rather than a rational effect. His paintings would not have seemed out of place among those of 19th-century Romantics. Far from seeing the world around him as essentially hostile, or at least alien, he saw it as something intrinsically beautiful, whether wild or domesticated. Altdorfer made two drawings of the old synagogue of Regensburg, priceless documents that are on exhibit here. ⊠ *Dachaupl. 2–4* ☎ *0941/507–2448* 🖾 *€5* ☉ *Tues.–Sun. noon–4.*

Schloss Emmeram (*Emmeram Palace*). Formerly a Benedictine monastery, this is the ancestral home of the princely Thurn und Taxis family, which made its fame and fortune after being granted the right to carry official and private mail throughout the empire and Spain by Emperor Maximilian I (1493–1519) and by Philip I, king of Spain, who ruled during the same period. Their business extended over the centuries into the Low Countries (Holland, Belgium, and Luxembourg), Hungary, and Italy. The horn that still symbolizes the post office in several European countries comes from the Thurn und Taxis coat of arms. In its heyday Schloss Emmeram was heavily featured in the gossip columns thanks to the wild parties and somewhat extravagant lifestyle of the young dowager Princess Gloria von Thurn und Taxis. After the death of her

The Golden Gate Bridge may be better known today, but the 12th-century Steinerne Brücke (Stone Bridge) was its match in terms of engineering ingenuity and importance in its day.

husband, Prince Johannes, in 1990, she had to auction off belongings in order to pay inheritance taxes. Ultimately a deal was cut, allowing her to keep many of the palace's treasures as long as they were put on display.

The **Thurn und Taxis Palace,** with its splendid ballroom and throne room, allows you to witness the setting of courtly life in the 19th century. A visit usually includes the fine **Kreuzgang** (cloister) of the former Benedictine abbey of St. Emmeram. The palace can only be visited by taking the guided tour. The items in the **Thurn und Taxis Museum,** which is part of the Bavarian National Museum in Munich, have been carefully selected for their fine craftsmanship—be it dueling pistols, a plain marshal's staff, a boudoir, or a snuffbox. The palace's **Marstallmuseum** (former royal stables) holds the family's coaches and carriages as well as related items. ⊠ *Emmeramspl. 5* ☎ *0941/504–8133* ⊕ *www.thurnundtaxis.de* 🖼 *Museum €4.50, palace and cloisters with mandatory tour €13.50* 🕐 *Museum Apr.–Oct., daily 1–5. Tours of palace and cloisters: premium tour (approx. 90 mins) daily 10:30, 12:30, 2:30, 4:30; compact tour (approx. 60 mins) daily 11:30 and 2:30.*

Fodor's Choice
★

Steinerne Brücke (*Stone Bridge*). This impressive old bridge resting on massive pontoons is Regensburg's most celebrated sight. It was completed in 1146 and was rightfully considered a miraculous piece of engineering at the time. As the only crossing point over the Danube for miles, it effectively cemented Regensburg's control over trade. The significance of the little statue on the bridge is a mystery, but the figure seems to be a witness to the legendary rivalry between the master builders of the bridge and those of the Dom. ⊠ *Regensburg.*

WORTH NOTING

Alte Kapelle (*Old Chapel*). Erected by the Carolingian order in the 9th century, the Old Chapel's dowdy exterior hides joyous rococo treasures within—extravagant concoctions of sinuous gilt stucco, rich marble, and giddy frescoes, the whole illuminated by light pouring in from the upper windows. ⊠ *Alter Kornmarkt 8* 🔳 *Free* 🕙 *Daily 9–dusk.*

Karmelitenkirche (*Church of the Carmelites*). This lovely church, in the baroque style from crypt to cupola, stands next to the Alte Kapelle. It has a finely decorated facade designed by the 17th-century Italian master Carlo Lurago. ⊠ *Alter Kornmarkt* 🔳 *Free* 🕙 *Mon., Tues., Thurs., and Fri. 9–11 and 3–5, Wed. 9–11, Sun. 8:25 am–9:45 pm.*

Neupfarrplatz. This oversize square was once the heart of the Jewish ghetto. Hard economic times and superstition led to their eviction by decree in 1519. While the synagogue was being torn down, one worker survived a very bad fall. A church was promptly built to celebrate the miracle, and before long a pilgrimage began. The **Neupfarrkirche** (New Parish Church) was built as well to accommodate the flow of pilgrims. During the Reformation, the Parish Church was given to the Protestants, hence its bare-bones interior. In the late 1990s, excavation work (for the power company) on the square uncovered well-kept cellars and, to the west of the church, the old synagogue, including the foundations of its Romanesque predecessor. Archaeologists salvaged the few items they could from the old stones (including a stash of 684 gold coins) and, not knowing what to do with the sea of foundations, ultimately carefully reburied them. Recovered items were carefully restored and are on exhibit in the Historisches Museum. Only one small underground area to the south of the church, the **Document,** accommodates viewing of the foundations. In a former cellar, surrounded by the original walls, visitors can watch a short video reconstructing life in the old Jewish ghetto. Over the old synagogue, the Israeli artist Dani Karavan designed a stylized plaza where people can sit and meet. Call the educational institution VHS for a tour of the Document (reservations are requested). For spontaneous visits, tickets are available at Tabak Götz on the western side of the square, at Neupfarrplatz 3. ⊠ *Neupfarrpl.* 📞 *0941/507–2433 for tours led by VHS* ⊕ *www.vhs-regensburg.de* 🔳 *Document €5* 🕙 *Church daily 9–dusk, Document tour Thurs.–Sat. at 2:30.*

NEED A BREAK?	**Dampfnudel Uli.** A *dampfnudel* is a steamed, often sweet but sometimes savory, yeast-dough dumpling that is tasty and filling. The best in Bavaria can be had at this small establishment in a former chapel. The decoration is incredibly eclectic, from Bavarian crafts to an autographed portrait of Ronald Reagan. ⊠ *Watmarkt 4* 📞 *0941/53297* ⊕ *www.dampfnudel-uli.de* 🕙 *Tues.–Fri. 10–6, Sat. 10–4.*

Niedermünster. This 12th-century building with a baroque interior was originally the church of a community of nuns, all of them from noble families. ⊠ *Alter Kornmarkt 5* 🔳 *Free* 🕙 *Irregular hours, usually late afternoon for services.*

Porta Praetoria. The rough-hewn former gate to the old Roman camp, built in AD 179, is one of the most interesting relics of Roman

Regensburg. Look through the grille on its east side to see a section of the original Roman road, about 10 feet below today's street level. ✉ *Unter den Schwibbögen* ✛ *North side of Alter Kornmarkt.*

St. Emmeram. The family church of the Thurn und Taxis family stands across from their ancestral palace, the Schloss Emmeram. The foundations of the church date to the 7th and 8th centuries. A richly decorated baroque interior was added in 1730 by the Asam brothers. St. Emmeram contains the graves of the 7th-century martyred Regensburg bishop Emmeram and the 10th-century saint Wolfgang. ✉ *Emmeramspl. 3* ☎ *0941/51030* 🖾 *Free* ✪ *Mon.–Thurs. and Sat. 10–4:30, Fri. 1–4:30, Sun. noon–4:30.*

St. Kassian. Regensburg's oldest church was founded in the 8th century. Don't be fooled by its plain exterior; inside, it's filled with ornate rococo decoration. ✉ *St. Kassianpl. 1* 🖾 *Free* ✪ *Daily 9–5:30.*

NEAR REGENSBURG

Walhalla. Walhalla (11 km [7 miles] east of Regensburg) is an excursion you won't want to miss, especially if you have an interest in the wilder expressions of newfound 19th-century pan-Germanic nationalism. Walhalla—a name resonant with Nordic mythology—was where the god Odin received the souls of dead heroes. Ludwig I erected this monumental pantheon temple in 1840 to honor important Germans from ages past, kept current with busts of Albert Einstein and Sophie Scholl. In keeping with the neoclassic style of the time, the Greek-style Doric temple is actually a copy of the Parthenon in Athens. The expanses of costly marble are evidence of both the financial resources and the craftsmanship at Ludwig's command. Walhalla may be kitschy, but the fantastic view it affords over the Danube and the wide countryside is definitely worth a look.

A boat ride from the Steinerne Brücke in Regensburg is the best way to go. On the return trip, you can steer the huge boat for about half a mile, and, for €5 extra, you can earn an "Honorary Danube Boat Captain" certificate. Kids and adults love it. To get to the temple from the river, you'll have to climb 358 marble steps.

✉ *Walhalla-Str. 48, Donaustauf* ✛ *Take the Danube Valley country road (unnumbered) east from Regensburg 8 km (5 miles) to Donaustauf. The Walhalla temple is 1 km (½ mile) outside the village and well signposted* ⊕ *www.walhalla-regensburg.de.*

Weltenburg Abbey (*Abbey Church of Sts. George and Martin*). Roughly 25 km (15 miles) southwest of Regensburg you'll find the great Weltenburg Benedictine Abbey perched on the bank of the Danube River. The most dramatic approach to the abbey is by boat (€10.50 round-trip) from Kelheim, 10 km (6 miles) downstream. On the stunning ride the boat winds between towering limestone cliffs that rise straight up from the tree-lined riverbanks. The abbey, constructed between 1716 and 1718, is commonly regarded as the masterpiece of the brothers Cosmas Damian and Egid Quirin Asam, two leading baroque architects and decorators of Bavaria. Their extraordinary composition of painted figures whirling on the ceiling, lavish and brilliantly polished marble, highly wrought statuary, and stucco figures dancing in rhythmic arabesques across the curving walls is the epitome of Bavarian baroque. Note especially the bronze equestrian statue of St. George above the high altar, reaching down imperiously with his flamelike, twisted gilt sword to dispatch the winged dragon at his feet. In Kelheim there are two boat companies that offer trips to Kloster Weltenburg every 30 minutes in summer. You cannot miss the landing stages and the huge parking lot. No Bavarian monastery is complete without a brewery and Kloster Weltenburg's is well worth visiting. ⊠ *Asamstr. 32, Kelheim* ✆ *Free* ⊙ *Daily 9–dusk.*

WHERE TO EAT

$ × **Café Felix.** A modern two-level café and bar, Felix offers everything
CAFÉ   from sandwiches to steaks, and buzzes with activity from breakfast until the early hours. Light from an artsy chandelier and torchlike fixtures bounces off the many large framed mirrors. The crowd tends to be young. $ *Average main: €10* ⊠ *Fröhliche-Türkenstr. 6* ✆ *0941/59059* ⊕ *www.cafefelix.de* ⊟ *No credit cards.*

$ × **Historische Wurstküche.** At the world's oldest, and possibly smallest,
GERMAN   bratwurst grill, just by the Stone Bridge, succulent Regensburger sausages—the best in town—are prepared right before your eyes on an open beech-wood charcoal grill. If you want to eat them inside in the tiny dining room, you'll have to squeeze past the cook to get there. On the walls—outside and in—are plaques recording the levels the river reached over a century of floods that temporarily interrupted service. $ *Average main: €9* ⊠ *Thundorferstr. 3* ✆ *0941/466–210* ⊕ *www. wurstkuchl.de* ⊟ *No credit cards.*

$ × **Leerer Beutel.** The "Empty Sack" prepares excellent international cui-
ECLECTIC   sine—from antipasti to solid pork roast—served in a pleasant vaulted room supported by massive rough-hewn beams. The restaurant is in a huge warehouse that's also a venue for concerts, exhibitions, and film screenings, making it a good place to start or end an evening. $ *Average main: €14* ⊠ *Bertoldstr. 9* ✆ *0941/58997* ⊕ *www.leerer-beutel.de.*

WHERE TO STAY

$ ⊤ **Am Peterstor.** The clean and basic rooms of this popular hotel in the
HOTEL   heart of the Old Town are a solid value. **Pros:** low prices; good location. **Cons:** spartan rooms; no restaurant or bar; no phones in rooms; breakfast not included (€5). $ *Rooms from: €50* ⊠ *Fröhliche-Türken-Str. 12* ✆ *0941/54545* ⊕ *www.hotel-am-peterstor.de* ⤵ *36 rooms* ⫽Ο⫽ *No meals.*

$$ ⊤ **Grand Hôtel Orphée.** It's difficult to choose between the very spacious
HOTEL   rooms at the three properties that comprise the Hôtel Orphée—the
Fodor'sChoice   Grand Hotel Orphée; the Petit Hotel Orphée on the next street; and
★   the Country Manor Orphée on the other side of the river about 2 km (1 mile) away. **Pros:** tastefully apportioned rooms; excellent restaurant; center of town. **Cons:** difficult parking; front rooms are noisy. $ *Rooms from: €100* ⊠ *Untere Bachg. 8* ✆ *0941/596–020* ⊕ *www.hotel-orphee. de* ⤵ *34 rooms* ⫽Ο⫽ *Breakfast; Some meals.*

$$ ⊤ **Hotel Münchner Hof.** This little hotel provides top service at a good
HOTEL   price, with Regensburg at your feet and the Neupfarrkirche nearby. **Pros:** some rooms with historic features; center of town; nice little lobby. **Cons:** entrance on narrow street; difficult parking. $ *Rooms from: €102*

✉ *Tändlerg. 9* ☎ *0941/58440* 🌐 *www.muenchner-hof.de* 🛏 *53 rooms* 🍴 *Breakfast; Some meals.*

$$ HOTEL 🏨 **Hotel-Restaurant Bischofshof am Dom.** This is one of Germany's most historic hostelries, a former bishop's palace where you can sleep in an apartment that includes part of a Roman gateway. **Pros:** historic building; no-smoking rooms only; nice courtyard beer garden. **Cons:** restaurant not up to hotel's standards; no air-conditioning. [$] *Rooms from: €150* ✉ *Krauterermarkt 3* ☎ *0941/58460* 🌐 *www.hotel-bischofshof.de* 🛏 *55 rooms, 4 suites* 🍴 *Breakfast; Some meals.*

$ HOTEL 🏨 **Kaiserhof am Dom.** Renaissance windows punctuate the green facade of this historic city mansion, but the rooms are 20th-century modern. **Pros:** front rooms have a terrific view; historic breakfast room. **Cons:** front rooms are noisy; no restaurant or bar. [$] *Rooms from: €95* ✉ *Kramg. 10–12* ☎ *0941/585–350* 🌐 *www.kaiserhof-am-dom.de* 🕓 *Closed Dec. 21–Jan. 8* 🛏 *30 rooms* 🍴 *Breakfast.*

SHOPPING

The winding alleyways of the Altstadt are packed with boutiques, ateliers, jewelers, and other small shops offering a vast array of arts and crafts. You may also want to visit the Neupfarrplatz market (Monday through Saturday 9–4), where you can buy regional specialties such as *Radi* (juicy radish roots), which locals wash down with a glass of wheat beer.

NIGHTLIFE AND PERFORMING ARTS

Regensburg offers a range of musical experiences, though none so moving as a choral performance at the cathedral. **TIP→ Listening to the Regensburger Domspatzen, the boys' choir at the cathedral, can be a remarkable experience, and it's worth scheduling your visit to the city to hear them (0941/796–2260; www.domspatzen.de). The best sung Mass is held on Sunday at 9 am.** If you're around in summer, look out for the Citizens Festival (Bürgerfest) and the Bavarian Jazz Festival (Bayerisches Jazzfest 🌐 *www.bayernjazz.de*) in July, both in the Old Town.

The kind of friendly, mixed nightlife that has become hard to find in some cities is alive and well in this small university city in the many *Kneipen,* combination bars and restaurants, such as the Leerer Beutel.

PASSAU

137 km (85 miles) southeast of Regensburg, 179 km (111 miles) northeast of Munich.

Flanking the borders of Austria and the Czech Republic, Passau dates back more than 2,500 years. Originally settled by the Celts, then by the Romans, it later passed into the possession of prince-bishops whose domains stretched into present-day Hungary. In 752 a monk named Boniface founded the diocese of Passau, which at its height would be the largest church subdivision in the entire Holy Roman Empire.

Passau's location is truly unique. Nowhere else in the world do three rivers—the Ilz from the north, the Danube from the west, and the Inn from the south—meet. Wedged between the Inn and the Danube, the Old Town is a maze of narrow cobblestone streets lined with beautifully preserved burgher and patrician houses and riddled with churches. Many streets have been closed to traffic, making the Old Town a fun and mysterious place to explore.

GETTING HERE AND AROUND

Passau is on the A-3 autobahn from Regensburg to Vienna. It's an hour from Regensburg and about four hours from Vienna by train.

TOURS

The Passau tourist office leads tours May through October at 10:30 and 2:30 on weekdays and at 2:30 on Sunday; November through April the tours are held weekdays at noon. Tours start at the entrance to the cathedral. A one-hour tour costs €4.

Donauschiffahrt Wurm + Köck. In Passau cruises on the three rivers begin and end at the Danube jetties on Fritz-Schäffer Promenade. Donauschiffahrt Wurm + Köck runs 12 ships with capacity varying from 250 to 1,100 passengers. Options for tours include city sightseeing from the water, excursions with time ashore, an evening cruise with dinner, and a popular full-day excursion to the Austrian city of Linz, which departs at 9 am. ⊠ *Passau* ☎ *0851/929–292* ⊕ *www.donauschiffahrt. de* ⛴ *From €8.70; dinner cruises from €28.50.*

TIMING

Passau can be toured in the course of one leisurely day. Try to visit the Dom at noon to hear a recital on the world's largest organ. Early morning is the best time to catch the light falling from the east on the Old Town walls and the confluence of the three rivers.

FESTIVALS

Christkindlmarkt. Passau's Christmas market is the biggest and most spectacular of the Bavarian Forest. It's held in the heart of the city's Altstadt, at the steps of Dom St. Stephan, from late November until just before Christmas. ⊠ *Dompl.* ⊕ *www.passauer-christkindlmarkt.de.*

Europäische Wochen (*European Weeks*). Passau is the cultural center of Lower Bavaria. Its *Europäische Wochen* festival—featuring everything from opera to pantomime—is a major event on the European music calendar. The festival runs from mid-June to July or early August and is held in venues all over the city. ⊠ *Dr.-Hans-Kapfinger-Str. 22* ⊕ *www. ew-passau.de.*

ESSENTIALS

Visitor Information Tourist-Information Passau. ⊠ *Rathauspl. 3* ☎ *0851/955–980* ⊕ *www.passau.de.*

EXPLORING

TOP ATTRACTIONS

Fodor's Choice ★ **Dom St. Stephan** (*St. Stephan's Cathedral*). The cathedral rises majestically on the highest point of the earliest-settled part of the city. A baptismal church stood here in the 6th century, and 200 years later, when Passau became a bishop's seat, the first basilica was built. It was dedicated to St. Stephan and became the original mother church of St. Stephan's Cathedral in Vienna. A fire reduced the medieval basilica to ruins in 1662; it was then rebuilt by Italian master architect Carlo Lurago. What you see today is the largest baroque basilica north of

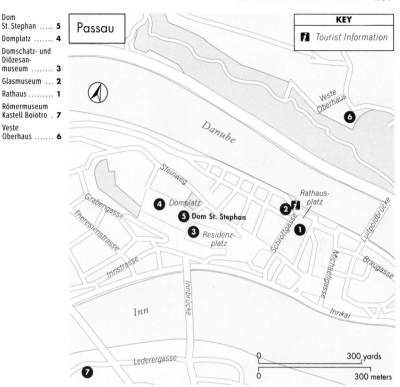

Passau

KEY

🛈 *Tourist Information*

the Alps, complete with an octagonal dome and flanking towers. Little in its marble- and stucco-encrusted interior reminds you of Germany, and much proclaims the exuberance of Rome. Beneath the dome is the largest church organ assembly in the world. Built between 1924 and 1928 and enlarged in 1979–80, it claims no fewer than 17,774 pipes and 233 stops. The church also houses the most powerful bell chimes in southern Germany. ✉ *Dompl.* ☎ *0851/3930* 🖃 *Free; concerts midday €4, evening €8* ⊙ *Daily 6:30–10:45 and 11:30–6. Tours May–Oct., weekdays at 12:30; Nov.–Apr., weekdays at noon.*

Domplatz (*Cathedral Square*). This large square in front of the Dom is bordered by sturdy 17th- and 18th-century buildings, including the **Alte Residenz,** the former bishop's palace and now a courthouse. The neoclassical statue at the center is Bavarian King Maximilian I, who watches over the Christmas market in December. ✉ *Passau.*

Domschatz- und Diözesanmuseum (*Cathedral Treasury and Diocesan Museum*). The cathedral museum houses one of Bavaria's largest collections of religious treasures, the legacy of Passau's rich episcopal history. The museum is part of the **Neue Residenz,** which has a stately baroque entrance opening onto a magnificent staircase—a scintillating study in marble, fresco, and stucco. ✉ *Residenzpl.* 🖃 *€1.50* ⊙ *May–Oct., Mon.–Sat. 10–4.*

Veste Oberhaus (*Upper House Stronghold*). The powerful fortress and summer castle commissioned by Bishop Ulrich II in 1219 looks over Passau from an impregnable site on the other side of the river, opposite the Rathaus. Today the Veste Oberhaus is Passau's most important museum, containing exhibits that illustrate the city's 2,000-year history. From the terrace of its café-restaurant (open Easter–October), there's a magnificent view of Passau and the convergence of the three rivers. ⊠ *Oberhaus 125* ☎ *0851/493–3512* ⊕ *www.oberhausmuseum. de* 🖃 *€5* ☉ *May–Oct., weekdays 9–5, weekends 10–6* 🚌 *Bus (€5) from Rathauspl. Apr.–Nov., daily every ½ hr 10:30–5.*

WORTH NOTING

Glasmuseum (*Glass Museum*). The world's most comprehensive collection of European glass is housed in the lovely Hotel Wilder Mann. The history of Central Europe's glassmaking is captured in 30,000 items, from baroque to art deco, spread over 35 rooms. The museum also houses the world's largest collection of cookbooks. ⊠ *Höllg. 1* ☎ *0851/35071* ⊕ *www.glasmuseum.de* 🖃 *€7* ☉ *Daily 1–6.*

Rathaus. Passau's 14th-century Town Hall sits like a Venetian merchant's house on a small square fronting the Danube. It was the home of a wealthy German merchant before being declared the seat of city government after a 1298 uprising. Two assembly rooms have wall paintings depicting scenes from local history and legend, including the (fictional) arrival in the city of Siegfried's fair Kriemhild, from the Nibelungen fable. The Rathaus tower has Bavaria's largest glockenspiel, which plays daily at 10:30, 2, and 7:25, with an additional performance at 3:30 on Saturday. ⊠ *Rathauspl.* ☎ *0851/3960* 🖃 *€1.50* ☉ *Apr.–Oct. and late Dec.–early Jan., daily 10–4.*

Römermuseum Kastell Boiotro (*Roman Museum*). While excavating a 17th-century pilgrimage church, archaeologists uncovered a stout Roman fortress with five defense towers and walls more than 12 feet thick. The Roman citadel Boiotro was discovered on a hill known as the Mariahilfberg on the south bank of the river Inn, with its Roman well still plentiful and fresh. Pottery, lead figures, and other artifacts from the area are housed in this museum at the edge of the site. ⊠ *Ledererg. 43* ☎ *0851/34769* 🖃 *€4* ☉ *Mar.–Nov., Tues.–Sun. 10–4.*

WHERE TO EAT

$ ✕**Hacklberger Bräustüberl.** Shaded by magnificent old trees, locals sit
GERMAN in this famous brewery's enormous beer garden (seating more than 1,000), sipping a Hacklberger and tucking into a plate of sausages. In winter they simply move to the wood-panel interior, where beer has been on tap from the brewery next door since 1618. 🖫 *Average main: €11* ⊠ *Bräuhauspl. 7* ☎ *0851/58382* ⊕ *www.hacklbergers.de.*

$$ ✕**Heilig-Geist-Stiftsschenke.** For atmospheric dining this 14th-century
GERMAN monastery-turned-wine cellar is a must. In summer eat beneath chestnut trees; in winter seek out the warmth of the vaulted, dark-paneled dining rooms. The wines—made in Austria from grapes from the Spitalkirche Heiliger Geist vineyards—are excellent and suit all seasons. The fish comes from the Stift's own ponds. 🖫 *Average main:*

€16 ✉ Heilig-Geist-G. 4 ☎ 0851/2607 🌐 www.stiftskeller-passau.de ⏲ Closed Wed. and last 3 wks in Jan.

$ GERMAN 🍴 **Peschel Terrasse.** The beer you sip on the high, sunny terrace overlooking the Danube is brought fresh from Peschl's own brewery below, which, along with this traditional Bavarian restaurant, has been in the same family since 1855. [$] *Average main: €11 ✉ Rosstränke 4 ☎ 0851/2489 🌐 www.peschl-terrasse.de.*

$ GERMAN 🍴 **Zum Suppentopf.** Serving rustically home-style soups, just like your German grandmother makes, Zum Suppentopf is loved by locals and visitors alike, but keep a lookout—it's easy to walk by this small restaurant without noticing. The owner, Jacques, pours his soul into every bowl, and the large selection of daily offerings—rare in a venue this size—are all freshly prepared using local ingredients. The bracing *Erbseneintopf* (pea stew) is a must on Passau's misty fall afternoons. [$] *Average main: €7 ✉ Grabeng. 13/L ☎ 0851/490–8560 💳 No credit cards.*

WHERE TO STAY

$$ HOTEL 🏨 **Hotel König.** Though built in 1984, the König blends successfully with the graceful Italian-style buildings alongside the elegant Danube waterfront. **Pros:** some rooms have an impressive view of the Danube; most rooms are spacious. **Cons:** no restaurant; uninspired bathrooms; some small rooms. [$] *Rooms from: €120 ✉ Untere Donaulände 1 ☎ 0851/3850 🌐 www.hotel-koenig.de 🛏 61 rooms 🍽 Breakfast.*

$ HOTEL 🏨 **Hotel Weisser Hase.** The "White Rabbit" began accommodating travelers in the early 16th century but is thoroughly modernized. **Pros:** good location in the heart of Passau; friendly staff; great breakfast. **Cons:** street noise in the early morning; no air-conditioning. [$] *Rooms from: €85 ✉ Heiliggeistg. 1 ☎ 0851/92110 🌐 www.weisser-hase.de ⏲ Closed Jan.–mid-Feb. 🛏 108 rooms, 1 suite 🍽 Breakfast; Some meals.*

$ HOTEL 🏨 **Hotel Wilder Mann.** Passau's most historic hotel dates from the 11th century and is near the ancient Town Hall on the waterfront market square. **Pros:** historic hotel with some luxurious suites; center of town; some rooms with nice view of the river; others are a good value. **Cons:** some rooms showing their age; no restaurant or bar. [$] *Rooms from: €88 ✉ Am Rathauspl. 1 ☎ 0851/35071 🌐 www.wilder-mann.com 🛏 49 rooms, 5 suites 🍽 Breakfast.*

$ HOTEL 🏨 **Schloss Ort.** This 13th-century castle's large rooms have views of the Inn River, which flows beneath the hotel's stout walls. **Pros:** nice garden; good restaurant. **Cons:** old linens; thin walls; not in the center of town. [$] *Rooms from: €97 ✉ Ort 11 ☎ 0851/34072 🌐 www.schlosshotel-passau.de 🛏 18 rooms 🍽 Breakfast.*

THE BODENSEE

WELCOME TO THE BODENSEE

TOP REASONS TO GO

★ **The Bodensee:** Whether you're circling the lake on foot, or by bike, car, or train, crossing the water by boat, or dipping into it on a hot summer's day, the beautiful Bodensee affords myriad pleasures.

★ **Zeppelin Museum, Friedrichshafen:** Step inside the gracious passenger rooms of the airship, and you may question whether the air transport of today, though undeniably bigger and faster, is a real improvement.

★ **Altes Schloss in Meersburg:** Explore the oldest continuously inhabited castle in Germany, from the sinister dungeons to the imposing knights' hall.

★ **Schloss Salem, near Überlingen:** The castle itself offers plenty to see, with furnished rooms, stables, gardens, and museums.

★ **Mainau Island:** More than a million tulips and narcissi grace the flower island in spring—later they're followed by rhododendrons and azaleas, roses and dahlias.

1 The Northern Shore. A dozen charming little villages and towns line the northern shore of the lake. In good weather there's a wonderful view across the water to the Swiss mountains.

2 The Upper Swabian Baroque Road. Nearly every village has its own baroque treasure, from the small village church to the mighty Basilica Weingarten. The more miles between you and the Bodensee, the easier it is on your wallet, which may be reason enough to venture to this region.

GETTING ORIENTED

The Bodensee (Lake Constance) is off the beaten path for visitors from overseas and from other parts of Europe. If you venture here, you can be pretty sure you won't meet anyone else from back home. Even the Swiss and the Austrians, who own part of the shore of the Bodensee, tend to vacation elsewhere. For Germans, however, it's a favorite summer vacation spot, so it's wise to reserve rooms in advance.

6

3 Around the Bodanrück Peninsula. Konstanz is the biggest city on the international lakeshore, situated on the Bodanrück Peninsula and separated from the northern shore by a few miles of water. Konstanz survived World War II unscathed by leaving its lights burning every night, so the Allied bomber pilots could not distinguish it from the neighboring Swiss city of Kreuzlingen. The small towns of the "Unter-see" (Lower Lake), as this part of the Bodensee is called, have a more rural atmosphere than those of the northern shore.

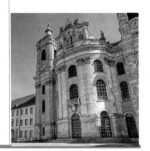

BIKING THE BODENSEE

The best way to experience the Bodensee area is by bike. In as little as three days, you can cross the borders of three nations. The largely flat landscape makes this cycle tour suitable for all ages and fitness levels.

(above and upper right) Cyclists on the banks of the Bodensee.

You could start and finish anywhere, but this three-day tour circumnavigates the entire lake. Book a room in Meersburg or Konstanz for the first night; in Arbon, Switzerland, for the second; and in Lindau for the third. Store your baggage, bringing with you only what you can comfortably carry on your back or in panniers (don't forget your bathing suit). A sign displaying a bicyclist with a blue back wheel will be your guide through all three countries. Much of the route follows dedicated bike paths—some lakeside, some farther away. However, you'll occasionally find yourself riding along the road, so a helmet is recommended, although it's not required by law. At some points, you might like to disregard this official route in favor of a more scenic path. Follow your instincts—even without the signs or a map, the water is an easy point of reference.

—Leonie Schaumann

BIKING ESSENTIALS

You can rent a bike as a guest at many hotels, at some tourist offices, from bike shops, and from bicycle-tour operators. Biking maps are available from newspaper stands, bookshops, and tourist offices, and you can leave your baggage in the long-term storage available at the train stations in Konstanz, Überlingen, Friedrichshafen, and Lindau. You can cut across the lake on a ferry at numerous points.

ITINERARY

Departing **Lindau,** head west along the lake toward Wasserburg, 5 km (3 miles) away. Continue on through meadows, marshland, and orchards, passing charming villages like **Nonnenhorn** and **Langenargen**—9 km (5½ miles) from Wasserburg. **Friedrichshafen** is another 10 km (6 miles) from Langenargen. Pay a visit to the **Zeppelin Museum.** After **Friedrichshafen** the path runs along the main road; follow the sign to **Immenstaad** (10 km [6 miles]) to get away from the traffic. Pass through the village and continue to **Hagnau.** After another 5 km (3 miles), stay overnight in lovely **Meersburg,** rising early to catch the ferry to **Konstanz.**

When you come off the ferry, head to the flower island of **Mainau** to enjoy the blooms. Continue onward to **Konstanz,** pass the ferry dock again, and keep as close as you can to the water, which will bring you into **Konstanz** through the scenic "back entrance." Cross the bridge over the **Rhine.** Take in the old town, and the buzzing small harbor. When you set off again, you'll be in the Swiss city of **Kreuzlingen** in a few minutes. Head east out of the city. After 32 km (20 miles) of rolling Swiss countryside, you'll arrive in **Arbon** for your second overnight.

Leave **Arbon** early in the morning, passing **Rorschach** (after 7 km [4½ miles]) and Rheineck on the Austrian border (another 9 km [5½ miles]). After the border, keep as close to the lake as possible, and you'll pass through protected marshlands and lush meadows. Twenty kilometers (12 miles) beyond the border is **Bregenz,** Austria. Ascend the **Pfänder cable car** 3,870 feet for a marvelous view. Bike the 9 km (5½ miles) back to **Lindau,** or take a train or ferry ride.

REFUELING

Copious amounts of fresh lake air and pedaling are bound to trigger your appetite. If the weather is ripe for a picnic, be on the lookout for supermarket chains such as Rewe, Edeka, and Lidl, where you can fill your picnic basket. For *Brot* (bread), a fresh *Brezel* (pretzel) or *Kaffee und Kuchen* (coffee and cake), seek out a local *Bäckerei* (bakery) or *Stehcafé* (standing café). Don't be shy about venturing into the village *Metzgerei* (butcher), either. Most of them offer delicious *Leberkässemmel* or *Fleischkäsweckle* (its respective names in Bavaria and Baden Württemburg)—a slice of warm sausage-meat loaf in a bread roll. Or, try some sliced *Fleischwurst* (bologna sausage) in various flavors, or tangy *Fleischsalat* (sliced sausage-meat salad and pickles with salad dressing)—both best eaten on bread fresh from the bakery.

6

Updated by Leonie Schaumann

A natural summer playground, the Bodensee (Lake Constance) is ringed with little towns and busy resorts. Lapping the shores of Germany, Switzerland, and Austria, the Bodensee, at 65 km (40 miles) long and 15 km (9 miles) wide, is the largest lake in the German-speaking world.

Though called a lake, it's actually a vast swelling of the Rhine, gouged out by a massive glacier in the Ice Age and flooded by the river as the ice receded. The Rhine flows into its southeast corner, where Switzerland and Austria meet, and flows out at its west end. On the German side, the Bodensee is bordered almost entirely by the state of Baden-Württemberg (a small portion of the eastern tip, from Lindau to Nonnenhorn, belongs to Bavaria).

It's one of the warmest areas of the country, not just because of its southern latitude but also owing to the warming influence of the water, which gathers heat in summer and releases it in winter. The lake itself practically never freezes over—it has done so only once in the past two centuries. The climate is excellent for growing fruit, and along the roads you'll find stands and shops selling apples, peaches, strawberries, jams, juices, wines, and schnapps, much of it homemade.

PLANNING

WHEN TO GO

The Bodensee's temperate climate makes for pleasant weather from April to October. In spring, orchard blossoms explode everywhere, and on Mainau, the "island of flowers," more than a million tulips, hyacinths, and narcissi burst into bloom. Holiday crowds come in summer, and autumn can be warm and mellow. Some hotels and restaurants as well as many tourist attractions close for winter.

GETTING HERE AND AROUND

AIR TRAVEL

The closest major international airport is in Zürich, Switzerland, 60 km (37 miles) from Konstanz, connected by the autobahn. There are also direct trains from the Zürich airport to Konstanz. There are several domestic and international (primarily of United Kingdom and European origin) flights to the regional airport at Friedrichshafen—these are mostly operated by budget airlines.

Airport Contacts Flughafen Friedrichshafen (FDH). ⊠ *Am Flugpl. 64, Friedrichshafen* ☎ *07541/28401* ⊕ *www.fly-away.de.* **Zürich Airport (ZRH).** ⊠ *Flughafenstr., Kloten* ☎ *410/4381–62211 for general enquiries, 0900/300–313 for flight-related enquiries (1.99 CHF/min)* ⊕ *www.zurich-airport.com.*

BOAT AND FERRY TRAVEL

■ **TIP→ Note that the English pronunciation of "ferry" sounds a lot like the German word "fähre," which means car ferry. "Schiffe" is the term used for passenger ferries.** Car and passenger ferries have different docking points in the various towns. The car ferries run all year; in summer you may have to wait in line. The passenger routes, especially the small ones, often do not run from November to March. Sailing on a car ferry as a passenger can be cheaper than taking a passenger ferry—and most car ferries are reasonably comfortable. Bicycles can be taken on both types of ferry.

The Weisse Flotte line of boats, which is run by the BSB, or Bodensee-Schiffsbetriebe, links most of the larger towns and resorts. One of the nicest trips is from Konstanz to Meersburg and then on to the island of Mainau. Excursions around the lake last from one hour to a full day. Many cross to Austria and Switzerland; some head west along the Rhine to Schaffhausen and the Rheinfall, the largest waterfall in Europe. Information on lake excursions is available from all local tourist offices and travel agencies.

Bodensee-Schiffsbetriebe. Ticket offices for this ferry line are in Konstanz, Überlingen, Meersburg, Friedrichshafen, and Lindau. ⊠ *Hafenstr. 6, Konstanz* ☎ *07531/36400* ⊕ *www.bsb.de.*

BUS TRAVEL

Buses serve most smaller communities that have no train links, but service is infrequent. Along the shore there are buses that run regularly throughout the day from Überlingen to Friedrichshafen, stopping in towns such as Meersburg, Hagnau, and Immenstaad.

CAR TRAVEL

The A-96 autobahn provides the most direct route between Munich and Lindau. For a more scenic, slower route, take B-12 via Landsberg and Kempten. For another scenic and slower route from Frankfurt, take B-311 at Ulm and follow the Oberschwäbische Barockstrasse (Upper Swabian Baroque Road) to Friedrichshafen. From Stuttgart, follow the A-81 autobahn south. At Exit 40 take B-33 to Konstanz, or the A-98 autobahn and B-31 for the northern shore. Lindau is also a terminus of the picturesque Deutsche Alpenstrasse (German Alpine Road), running east–west from Salzburg to Lindau.

Lakeside roads, particularly those on the northern shore, boast wonderful vistas but experience occasional heavy traffic in summer, and on weekends and holidays year-round. Stick to the speed limits in spite of tailgaters—speed traps are frequent, especially in built-up areas. Formalities at border-crossing points are few. However, in addition to your passport you'll need insurance and registration papers for your car. For rental cars, check with the rental company to make sure you are allowed to take the car into other countries. Crossing into Switzerland, you're required to have an autobahn tax sticker (CHF40/€40, purchasable in euros or Swiss francs) if you plan to drive on the Swiss autobahn. These are available from border customs offices, and from petrol stations and post offices in Switzerland. This sticker is not necessary if you plan to stick to nonautobahn roads. Car ferries link Romanshorn, in Switzerland, with Friedrichshafen, as well as Konstanz with Meersburg. Taking either ferry saves substantial mileage. The fare depends on the size of the car.

TRAIN TRAVEL

From Frankfurt to Friedrichshafen and Lindau, take the ICE (InterCity Express) to Ulm and then transfer (total time 4 hours). A combination of ICE and regional train gets you to Konstanz from Frankfurt in 4½ hours, passing through the beautiful scenery of the Black Forest. From Stuttgart to Konstanz, take the IC (InterCity) to Singen, and transfer to an RE or IRE (Regional/InterRegio Express) for the brief last leg to Konstanz (total time 2½ hours). From Munich to Lindau, the EC (Europe Express) train or the ALX (Alex) train take 2½ hours. From Zürich to Konstanz, the trip lasts 1½ hours. Local trains encircle the Bodensee, stopping at most towns and villages.

TOURS

Most of the larger tourist centers have city tours with English-speaking guides. The Bodensee is a great destination for bike travelers, with hundreds of miles of well-signposted paths that keep riders safe from cars. You can go on your own or enjoy the comfort of a customized tour with accommodations and baggage transport (and a rental bike, if need be). Wine-tasting tours are available in Überlingen, Konstanz, and Meersburg. Call the local tourist offices for information. Zeppelin tours operated by the DZR (Deutsche Zeppelin Reederei) are not cheap (sightseeing trips cost €210–€785), but they do offer a special experience and a reminder of the grand old days of flight. The zeppelins depart from the airport in Friedrichshafen.

Deutsche Zeppelin Reederei. Perfect for aviation enthusiasts, and those looking for a unique way to experience the Bodensee: glide silently above it in a Zeppelin. ⊠ *Messestr. 132, Friedrichshafen* ☎ *07541/59000* ⊕ *www.zeppelinflug.de* ✉ *From €210.*

Radweg-Reisen GmbH. This cycle-hire company's most popular tour circumnavigates the Bodensee in a relaxed eight days, with hotel accommodation and breakfast included. ⊠ *Fritz-Arnold-Str. 16a, Konstanz* ☎ *07531/819–930* ⊕ *www.radweg-reisen.com* ✉ *From €479.*

Velotours Touristik GmbH. Velotours offers a variety of cycle-tour options around the Bodensee. Their Eastern Bodensee route begins and ends in

Konstanz, taking in highlights in Germany, Austria, and Switzerland, including a ferry "shortcut" from Konstanz to Meersburg. ⊠ *Bücklestr. 13, Konstanz* ☎ *07531/98280* ⊕ *www.velotours.de* ☒ *From €475.*

RESTAURANTS

In this area, international dishes are not only on the menu but also on the map—you have to drive only a few miles to try the Swiss or Austrian dish you're craving in its own land. *Seeweine* (lake wines) from vineyards in the area include Müller-Thurgau, Spätburgunder, Ruländer, and Kerner.

Prices in the reviews are the average cost of a main course at dinner, or if dinner is not served, at lunch.

HOTELS

Accommodations in the towns and resorts around the lake include venerable wedding-cake-style, fin de siècle palaces as well as more modest *Gasthöfe*. If you're visiting in July and August, make reservations in advance. For lower rates in a more rural atmosphere, consider staying a few miles away from the lake.

Prices in the reviews are the lowest cost of a standard double room in high season. For expanded reviews, facilities, and current deals, visit Fodors.com.

6

WHAT IT COSTS IN EUROS			
$	**$$**	**$$$**	**$$$$**
Restaurants	under €15	€15–€20	€21–€25	over €25
Hotels	under €100	€100–€175	€176–€225	over €225

PLANNING YOUR TIME

Choosing a place to stay is a question of finance and interest. The closer you stay to the water, the more expensive and lively it becomes. Many visitors pass by on their way from one country to another, so during the middle of the day, key hubs like Konstanz, Mainau, Meersburg, and Lindau tend to be crowded. Try to visit these places either in the morning or in the late afternoon, and make your day trips to the lesser-known destinations: the baroque churches in upper Swabia, the Swiss towns along the southern shore, or the nearby mountains.

VISITOR INFORMATION

Visitor Information Internationale Bodensee Tourismus. ⊠ *Hafenstr. 6, Konstanz* ☎ *07531/909–490* ⊕ *www.bodensee.eu.*

THE NORTHERN SHORE

There's a feeling here, in the midst of a peaceful Alpine landscape, that the Bodensee is part of Germany and yet separated from it—which is literally the case for Lindau, which sits in the lake tethered to land by a causeway. Überlingen, a beautiful resort at the northwestern finger of the lake, attracts many vacationers and spa goers. Clear days reveal the snowcapped mountains of Switzerland to the south and the peaks of the Austrian Vorarlberg to the east.

LINDAU

180 km (112 miles) southwest of Munich.

By far the best way to get to know this charming old island town is on foot. Lose yourself in the maze of small streets and passageways flanked by centuries-old houses. Wander down to the harbor for magnificent views, with the Austrian shoreline and mountains close by to the east. Just 13 km (8 miles) away, they are nearer than the Swiss mountains visible to the southwest.

Lindau was made a Free Imperial City within the Holy Roman Empire in 1275. It had developed as a fishing settlement and then spent hundreds of years as a trading center along the route between the rich lands of Swabia and Italy. The Lindauer Bote, an important stagecoach service between Germany and Italy in the 18th and 19th centuries, was based here; Goethe traveled via this service on his first visit to Italy in 1788. The stagecoach was revived a few years ago, carrying passengers on a 13-day journey to Italy. This service only runs occasionally—ask at the Lindau tourist office.

As the German empire crumbled toward the end of the 18th century, battered by Napoléon's revolutionary armies, Lindau fell victim to competing political groups. It was ruled by the Austrian Empire before passing into Bavarian control in 1805. Lindau's harbor was rebuilt in 1856.

GETTING HERE AND AROUND

Lindau is halfway between Munich and Zürich, and about two hours from both on the EC (European Express) train. From Frankfurt it takes about four hours—change from the ICE (InterCity Express) train in Ulm to the IRE (InterRegio Express) train. You can also reach Lindau by boat: it takes about 20 minutes from Bregenz across the bay. Once in Lindau, you can reach everything on foot. Its *Altstadt* (Old Town) is a maze of ancient streets with half-timber and gable houses making up most of the island. The center and main street is the pedestrian-only Maximilianstrasse.

ESSENTIALS

Visitor Information Lindau Tourist-Information. ✉ *Alfred-Nobel-Pl. 1* ☎ *08382/260–030* ⊕ *www.lindau-tourismus.de.*

EXPLORING

TOP ATTRACTIONS

Altes Rathaus (*Old Town Hall*). The Old Town Hall is the finest of Lindau's handsome historic buildings. It was constructed between 1422 and 1436 in the midst of a vineyard and given a Renaissance face-lift 150 years later, though the original stepped gables remain. Emperor Maximilian I held an imperial diet (deliberation) here in 1496; a fresco on the south facade depicts the scene. The building retains city government functions, thus its interior is closed to the public. ✉ *Bismarckpl. 4* ⊕ *www.lindau-tourismus.de.*

Der Bayerische Löwe (*Bavarian Lion*). A proud symbol of Bavaria, the lion is Lindau's most striking landmark. Carved from Bavarian marble and standing 20 feet high, the lion stares out across the lake from a massive plinth. ⊠ *Lindau Harbor entrance, Römerschanze* ⊕ *www.lindau-tourismus.de.*

FAMILY **Mangenturm** (*Mangturm*). At the harbor's inner edge, across the water from the Neuer Leuchtturm, stands this 13th-century former lighthouse, one of the lake's oldest. After a lightning strike in the 1970s, the roof tiles were replaced, giving the tower the bright top it now bears. The interior of the tower can be visited as part of the kid-oriented Märchenstunden (Story Time) tours run in August—contact the Lindau Tourism organization. ⊠ *Hafenpl. 4.*

> ## BREGENZ, AUSTRIA
>
> Bregenz is a mere 13 km (8 miles) from Lindau, on the other side of the bay. It's a 20-minute boat ride to get there, which makes for a great side trip. Wander around the lakeshore and the lovely, romantic remains of the once-fortified medieval town. An enormous floating stage is the site for performances of grand opera and orchestral works under the stars. Ascend Pfänder Mountain, in Bregenz's backyard, via the *Pfänderbahn* cable tramway for views that stretch as far as the Black Forest and the Swiss Alps.

Neuer Leuchtturm (*New Lighthouse; Neuer Lindauer Leuchtturm*). Germany's southernmost lighthouse stands sentinel with the Bavarian Lion across the inner harbor's passageway. A viewing platform at the top is intermittently open (generally during summer, in good weather). Climb the 139 steps for views over the harbor. ⊠ *Schützingerweg* ⚎ *€1.80.*

WORTH NOTING

Barfüsserkirche — Stadttheatre Lindau and Lindauer Marionettenoper (*Church of the Barefoot Pilgrims*). This church, built from 1241 to 1270, is now Lindau's principal theater, and it also hosts the Lindauer Marionettenoper (Puppet Theater). Tickets for shows—starring humans or puppets—are available at the adjacent box office. ⊠ *Fischergasse 37* ☎ *08382/944–650* ⊕ *www.kultur-lindau.de* ⊙ *Ticket office Mon.– Thurs. 10–1:30 and 3–5:15.*

Haus zum Cavazzen (*Stadtmuseum Lindau*). Dating to 1729, this house belonged to a wealthy merchant and is now considered one of the most beautiful in the Bodensee region, owing to its rich decor of frescoes. Today it serves as a local history museum, with collections of glass and pewter items, paintings, and furniture from the past five centuries, alongside touring exhibitions. ⊠ *Marktpl. 6* ☎ *08382/944–073* ⊕ *www. kultur-lindau.de/museum* ⚎ *€3* ⊙ *Apr.–Aug., daily 10–6.*

Marktplatz. Lindau's market square is lined by a series of sturdy and attractive old buildings. The Gothic **Stephanskirche** (St. Stephen's Church) is simple and sparsely decorated, as befits a Lutheran place of worship. It dates to the late 12th century but went through numerous transformations. One of its special features is the green-hue stucco ornamentation on the ceiling, which immediately attracts the eye toward the heavens. In contrast, the Catholic **Münster Unserer Lieben Frau** (St. Mary's

6

EATING WELL BY THE BODENSEE

On a nice day you could sit on the terrace of a Bodensee restaurant forever, looking across the sparkling waters to the imposing heights of the Alps in the distance. The fish on your plate, possibly caught that very morning in the lake, is another reason to linger. Fish predominates on the menus of the region; 35 varieties swim in the lake, with *Felchen* (whitefish) the most highly prized. Felchen belongs to the salmon family and is best eaten *blau* ("blue"—poached in a mixture of water and vinegar with spices, called *Essigsud*) or *Müllerin* (baked in almonds). A white *Seewein* (lake wine) from one of the vineyards around the lake provides the perfect pairing. Sample a German and a Swiss version. Both use the same kind of grape, from vineyards only a few miles apart, but they produce wines with very different tastes. The Swiss like their wines very dry, whereas the Germans prefer them slightly sweeter.

One of the best-known Swabian dishes is *Maultaschen*, a kind of ravioli, usually served floating in a broth strewn with chives. Another specialty is *Pfannkuchen* (pancakes), generally filled with meat, or chopped into fine strips and scattered in a clear consommé known as *Flädlesuppe*. Hearty *Zwiebelrostbraten* (beef steak with lots of fried onions) is often served with a side of *Spätzle* (hand-cut or pressed, golden soft-textured egg noodles) and accompanied by a good strong Swabian beer.

Church), which stands right next to the Stephanskirche, is exuberantly baroque. ⊠ *Marktpl.*

Peterskirche (*St. Peter's Church, Krieger Gedächtnis Kapelle*). This solid 10th-century Romanesque building may be the oldest church in the Bodensee region. On the inside of the northern wall, frescoes by Hans Holbein the Elder (1465–1524) depict scenes from the life of St. Peter, the patron saint of fishermen. Peterskirche houses a memorial to fallen German soldiers from World Wars I and II, and a memorial plaque for victims of Auschwitz. Attached to the church is the 16th-century bell foundry, now a pottery works. Also of note is the adjacent fairy-tale-like **Diebsturm.** Look closely and you might see Rapunzel's golden hair hanging from this 13th-century tower, awaiting a princely rescuer. Follow the old city wall behind the tower and church to the adjoining Unterer Schrannenplatz, where the bell-makers used to live. A 1989 fountain depicts five of the *Narren* (Fools) that make up the VIPs of *Fastnacht*, the annual Alemannic Carnival celebrations. ⊠ *Oberer Schrannenpl.*

WHERE TO EAT

$$
GERMAN   ✕ **Gasthaus zum Sünfzen.** This ancient inn was serving warm meals to the patricians, officials, merchants, and other good burghers of Lindau back in the 14th century. The current chef insists on using fresh ingredients preferably from the region, such as fish from the lake in season, venison from the mountains, and apples—pressed to juice or distilled to schnapps—from his own orchard. Try the herb-flavored *Maultaschen* (large ravioli), the excellent *Felchen* (whitefish) fillet, or the

peppery Schübling sausage. $ *Average main: €15* ✉ *Maximilianstr. 1* ☎ *08382/5865* ⊕ *www.suenfzen.de* ⊘ *Closed Thurs. mid-Jan.–mid-Mar.*

WHERE TO STAY

$$
HOTEL
🛏 **Gasthof Engel.** Tucked into one of the Old Town's ancient, narrow streets, this ancient property with a pedigree dating back to 1390 positively exudes history. **Pros:** historic building; in the center of town; freshly redecorated rooms. **Cons:** no elevator; steep, narrow stairs. $ *Rooms from: €128* ✉ *Schafg. 4* ☎ *08382/5240* ⊕ *www.engel-lindau.de* 🛏 *10 rooms* ⦿⦿ *Breakfast.*

$$$
HOTEL
🛏 **Hotel Bayerischer Hof.** This is *the* address in town, a stately hotel directly on the edge of the lake, its terrace lush with semitropical, long-flowering plants, trees, and shrubs. **Pros:** pretty lake view from many rooms; elegant dining room with good food; majority of rooms air-conditioned. **Cons:** not all rooms have a lake view; no free parking; on weekends in summer parking is difficult; expensive. $ *Rooms from: €210* ✉ *Hafenpl.* ☎ *08382/9150* ⊕ *www.bayerischerhof-lindau.de* 🛏 *95 rooms, 6 junior suites, 4 suites* ⦿⦿ *Breakfast.*

$$
HOTEL
🛏 **Insel-Hotel.** In fine weather, you can enjoy breakfast alfresco as you watch the town come alive at this friendly central hotel on the pedestrian-only Maximilianstrasse. **Pros:** center of town; family run; recently renovated. **Cons:** no free parking. $ *Rooms from: €128* ✉ *Maximilianstr. 42* ☎ *08382/5017* ⊕ *www.insel-hotel-lindau.de* 🛏 *26 rooms* ⦿⦿ *Breakfast.*

NIGHTLIFE AND PERFORMING ARTS

Fodor's Choice
★
Bregenzer Festspiele (*Bregenz Music Festival*). A dramatic floating stage supports orchestras and opera stars during the famous Bregenzer Festspiele from mid-July to the end of August. Make reservations well in advance. The Austrian town of Bregenz is 13 km (8 miles) from Lindau, on the other side of the bay. ✉ *Pl. Der Wiener Symphoniker 1, Bregenz* ☎ *0043/5574–4076* ⊕ *www.bregenzerfestspiele.com.*

Spielbank Lindau Casino. You can play roulette, blackjack, poker, and slot machines at the town's modern and elegant casino. The dress code requires that men wear a sports jacket and shirt. Sports jackets can be rented at the coat-check area. ✉ *Chelles-Allee 1* ☎ *08382/27740* ⊕ *www.spielbanken-bayern.de* ⊘ *Sun.–Thurs. noon–2 am, Fri. and Sat. noon–3 am.*

SPORTS AND THE OUTDOORS

Bodensee-Schiffsbetriebe. The best way to see Lindau is from the lake. Take one of the pleasure boats of the Bodensee-Schiffsbetriebe (sometimes referred to locally as the *Weisse Flotte*—white fleet), which leave Lindau's harbor several times a day for the 20-minute ride to Bregenz in Austria. These large boats carry up to 800 people on three decks. Round-trip costs €11. ✉ *Schützingerweg 2* ☎ *08382/275–840* ⊕ *www.bsb.de.*

Bodensee Yachtschule. This sailing school in Lindau charters yachts and offers sailing courses for all ages, from beginner to advanced levels. ✉ *Schiffswerfte 2* ☎ *08382/944–588* ⊕ *www.bodensee-yachtschule.de.*

6

Surfschule Kreitmeir. You can rent boards and take windsurfing and stand-up paddleboarding lessons at Surfschule Kreitmeir. ✉ *Strandbad Eichwald, Eichwaldstr. 20* ☎ *08382/279–9459* ⊕ *www.surfschule-lindau.de.*

SHOPPING

Biedermann en Vogue. This high-end boutique carries various luxury fashion brands, as well as custom-made clothing, cashmere sweaters, and Italian shoes. ✉ *Maximilianstr. 2* ☎ *08382/944–913.*

Böhm. A destination for interior decorators, Böhm consists of three old houses full of lamps, mirrors, precious porcelain, and elegant furniture. ✉ *Maximilianstr. 21* ☎ *08382/94880* ⊕ *www.boehm-dieeinrichtungen.de.*

Internationale Bodensee-Kunstauktion. Michael Zeller organizes the celebrated International Bodensee Art Auction, held four times yearly. Visit the website for the catalog and dates of upcoming auctions. ✉ *Binderg. 7* ☎ *08382/93020* ⊕ *www.zeller.de.*

EN ROUTE

Wasserburg. Six kilometers (4 miles) west of Lindau lies Wasserburg, whose name means "water castle," a description of what this enchanting island town once was—a fortress. It was built by the St. Gallen monastery in 924, and the owners, the counts of Montfort zu Tettnang, sold it to the Fugger family of Augsburg. The Fuggers couldn't afford to maintain the drawbridge that connected the castle with the shore and instead built a causeway. In the 18th century the castle passed into the hands of the Habsburgs, and in 1805 the Bavarian government took it over. Wasserburg has some of the most photographed sights of the Bodensee: the yellow, stair-gabled presbytery; the fishermen's St. Georg Kirche, with its onion dome; and the little Malhaus museum, with the castle, Schloss Wasserburg (now a luxury hotel), in the background. ✉ *Lindau* ⊕ *www.wasserburg-bodensee.de.*

Schloss Montfort (*Montfort Castle*). Another 8 km (5 miles) west of Wasserburg is the small, pretty town of Langenargen, famous for the region's most unusual castle, Schloss Montfort. Named for the original owners, the counts of Montfort-Werdenberg, this structure was a conventional medieval fortification until the 19th century, when it was rebuilt in pseudo-Moorish style by its new owner, King Wilhelm I of Württemberg. If you can, see it from a passenger ship on the lake; the castle is especially memorable in the early morning or late afternoon. The castle houses a restaurant, open for dinner from Tuesday to Sunday, March through October, and on weekends during the colder months. The restaurant is also open for Sunday brunch year-round (10–2, €25 per person, all-you-can-eat German buffet-brunch style). A new wine bar features in the atmospheric cellar, open Friday nights. You can also climb the wooden spiral staircase to the top of the tower for views across the lake to Switzerland, Austria, and over the rolling German countryside. ✉ *Untere Seestr. 3, Langenargen* ☎ *07543/912–712* ⊕ *www.vemax-gastro.de* ✉ *Tower €2* ☉ *Tower Apr.–Oct., daily 10–noon and 1–5.*

FRIEDRICHSHAFEN

24 km (15 miles) west of Lindau.

Named for its founder, King Friedrich I of Württemberg, Friedrich-shafen is a relatively young town (dating to 1811). In an area otherwise given over to resort towns and agriculture, Friedrichshafen played a central role in Germany's aeronautics tradition, which saw the development of the zeppelin airship before World War I and the Dornier seaplanes in the 1920s and '30s. The zeppelins were once launched from a floating hangar on the lake, and the Dornier water planes were tested here. The World War II raids on its factories virtually wiped the city off the map. The current layout of the streets is the same, but the buildings are all new and not necessarily pretty. The atmosphere, however, is good and lively, and occasionally you'll find a plaque with a picture of the old building that stood at the respective spot. The factories are back, too. Friedrichshafen is home to such international firms as EADS (airplanes, rockets, and helicopters) and ZF (gear wheels).

GETTING HERE AND AROUND

It takes about two hours from Ulm on the IRE (InterRegio Express) train, then a bus or BOB (Bodensee Oberschwaben Bahn). Most trains stop at Friedrichshafen airport. The car ferry takes you on a 40-minute run across the lake to Romanshorn in Switzerland, where you have direct express trains to the airport and Zürich. In town you can reach most places on foot.

ESSENTIALS

Airplane Tours Konair. ⊠ *Riedstr. 82, Konstanz* ☎ *07531/361–6905* ⊕ *www.konair.aero.*

Visitor Information Friedrichshafen. ⊠ *Tourist-Information, Bahnhofpl. 2* ☎ *07541/30010* ⊕ *www.friedrichshafen.info.*

EXPLORING

Fodor'sChoice ★ **Deutsche Zeppelin Reederei GmbH.** For an unforgettable experience, take a scenic zeppelin flight out of Friedrichshafen airport. The flying season runs from March to November, and prices start at €210 for half an hour. For those who prefer to stay grounded, you can also tour the *Zeppelin NT* (New Technology) in its hangar. ⊠ *Messestr. 132* ☎ *07541/59000* ⊕ *www.zeppelinflug.de.*

Dornier Museum. Explore a century of pioneering aviation history. Alongside the main focuses on Claude Dornier and his company, restored classic Dornier aircraft and Dornier's explorations into aerospace technology, temporary exhibitions on various aviation themes are shown. A special Dornier Museum/Zeppelin Museum combination ticket (€15) provides a discount for those exploring the major aviation attractions of Friedrichshafen. ⊠ *Claude-Dornier-Pl. 1* ✛ *at Friedrichshafen Airport* ☎ *07541/487–3600* ⊕ *www.dorniermuseum.de* ⌨ *€9* ⊗ *May–Oct., daily 9–5; Nov.–Apr., Tues.–Sun. 10–5.*

Schloss Hofen (*Hofen Castle*). A short walk from town along the lakeside promenade is a small palace that served as the summer residence of Württemberg kings until 1918. The palace was formerly a priory—its foundations date from the 11th century. Today it is the private home of Duke Friedrich von Württemberg and isn't open to the public. You can visit the adjoining priory **church,** a splendid example of regional baroque architecture. The swirling white stucco of the interior was executed by the Schmuzer family from Wessobrunn whose master craftsman, Franz Schmuzer, also created the priory church's magnificent marble altar. ✉ *Klosterstr. 3* ⏲ *Easter–Oct., Sat.–Thurs. 9–6, Fri. 11–6; Nov.–Easter, Sun. 9–6.*

> **SWISS STOPS**
>
> There are two towns on the Swiss shores of the Bodensee that are convenient for quick trips from Germany. Ferries travel between Friedrichshafen in Germany and **Romanshorn,** a yachting and sportfishing center, in Switzerland. You can catch trains in Romanshorn to eastern Switzerland and to Zürich. **Kreuzlingen** is the small Swiss city across the border from Konstanz. There's little to see here, but you can catch a train to Zürich.

Zeppelin Museum. Graf Zeppelin (Ferdinand Graf von Zeppelin) was born across the lake in Konstanz, but Friedrichshafen was where, on July 2, 1900, his first "airship"—the LZ 1—was launched. The story is told in the Zeppelin Museum, which holds the world's most significant collection of artifacts pertaining to airship history. In a wing of the restored Bauhaus **Friedrichshafen Hafenbahnhof** (harbor railway station), the main attraction is the reconstruction of a 108-foot-long section of the legendary *Hindenburg,* the LZ 129 that exploded at its berth in Lakehurst, New Jersey, on May 6, 1937. (The airships were filled with hydrogen, because in 1933 the United States had passed an act banning helium sales to foreign governments due to its military usefulness and scarcity at that time.) Climb aboard the airship via a retractable stairway and stroll past the authentically furnished passenger room, the original lounges, and the dining room. The illusion of traveling in a zeppelin is followed by exhibits on the history and technology of airship aviation: propellers, engines, dining-room menus, and films of the airships traveling or at war. Car fans will appreciate the great Maybach standing on the ground floor; passengers once enjoyed being transported to the zeppelins in it. The museum's restaurant, a good place to take a break, is open for lunch and dinner. ✉ *Seestr. 22* ☎ *07541/38010* 🌐 *www.zeppelin-museum.de* 🎫 *€8* ⏲ *May–Oct., daily 9–5 (last entry at 4:30); Nov.–Apr., Tues.–Sun. 10–5.*

WHERE TO EAT

$$ ECLECTIC 🍴 **Lukullum.** This lively, novel restaurant is divided into seven *Stuben* (rooms), all themed: sit in a wine barrel, dine in Tirol, relax under the image of an airship in the Zeppelin Bräustüble—or enjoy the beer garden in summer. Dishes are good and basic, with some international touches. Friendly service keeps up with the pace of the socializing at this friendly dining spot. Great for late diners; the kitchen is open until 11 at night (9:30 on Sundays). [$] *Average main: €16* ✉ *Friedrichstr. 21* ☎ *07541/6818* 🌐 *www.lukullum.de* ⏲ *Closed Mon. No lunch Tues.–Fri.*

$$ ECLECTIC 🍴 **Zeppelin-Museumrestaurant.** A grand view of the harbor and the lake is only one of the attractions of this art deco–styled restaurant in the Zeppelin Museum. Soak up the retro airship travel theme as you enjoy

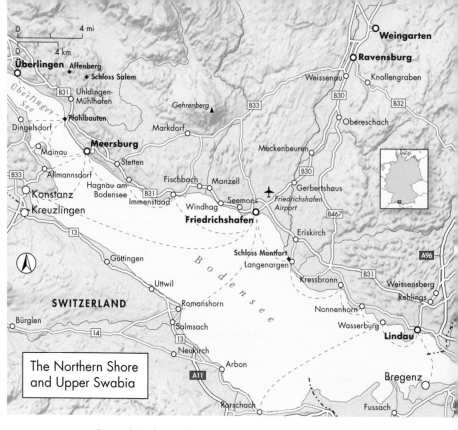

The Northern Shore and Upper Swabia

cakes and drinks, and a range of Swabian, Italian, and Asian-influenced meals. $ *Average main: €15* ✉ *Seestr. 22* ☎ *07541/953–0088* ⊕ *www.zeppelinmuseum-restaurant.de* ⊗ *Closed Mon. Nov.–Apr. No dinner Sun. and Mon.*

WHERE TO STAY

$$ 🏨 **Buchhorner Hof.** This traditional family-run hotel near the train station
HOTEL is decorated with hunting trophies, leather armchairs, and Turkish rugs; bedrooms are large and comfortable. **Pros:** business floor; cozy and big lobby; excellent restaurant; many rooms have nice views. **Cons:** many rooms look onto a busy main street; parking is difficult. $ *Rooms from: €100* ✉ *Friedrichstr. 33* ☎ *07541/2050* ⊕ *www.buchhorn.de* ➷ *92 rooms, 4 suites, 2 apartments* ⊙ *Breakfast.*

$$ 🏨 **Flair Hotel Gerbe.** A former farm and tannery that's about 5 km (3
HOTEL miles) from the city center, is now a pleasant, spacious hotel; its rooms (many with balconies) overlook the gardens, the countryside, and—on a clear day—the Swiss mountains. **Pros:** spacious rooms with good views; ample parking; indoor swimming pool. **Cons:** 5 km (3 miles) from center of town; some rooms have street noise. $ *Rooms from: €128* ✉ *Hirschlatterstr. 14, Ailingen* ☎ *07541/5090* ⊕ *www.hotel-gerbe.de* ➷ *59 rooms* ⊙ *Breakfast.*

$$ **Ringhotel Krone.** This large Bavarian-themed hotel in the Schnetzen-
HOTEL hausen district's semirural surroundings, 6 km (4 miles) from the cen-
ter of town, has a lot to offer active guests, including tennis, minigolf,
bicycles to rent, a gym, saunas, and indoor and outdoor pools. **Pros:**
great variety of rooms; good food; lots of parking. **Cons:** not near the
center of town; a few rooms have street noise. $ *Rooms from: €164*
✉ *Untere Mühlbachstr. 1, Schnetzenhausen* ☎ *07541/4080* ⊕ *www.
ringhotel-krone.de* ⤴ *140 rooms* ⎟◯⎟ *Breakfast.*

NIGHTLIFE AND PERFORMING ARTS

Café Bar Belushi. College students and a mostly young crowd raise their
glasses and voices above the din at Café Bar Belushi. ✉ *Montfortstr. 3*
☎ *07541/32531* ⊕ *www.cafe-bar-belushi.de* ☽ *Closed Sun.*

Graf-Zeppelin-Haus. This modern convention center on the lakeside
promenade also functions as a cultural center, where musicals, light
opera, and classical as well as pop-rock concerts take place several
times a week. The Graf-Zeppelin-Haus has a good modern restaurant
with a big terrace overlooking the harbor. ✉ *Olgastr. 20* ☎ *07541/2880*
⊕ *www.gzh.de.*

SHOPPING

Marktkörble Ebe. This century-old gift shop sells tableware and kitch-
enware, handmade candles, toys, stationery, and postcards, alongside
some clothing and accessories. ✉ *Buchhornpl. 5* ☎ *07541/388–430*
⊕ *www.marktkoerble.de.*

Weber & Weiss. Excellent chocolates are sold at Weber & Weiss. Look
for the special zeppelin airship–shape chocolates and candies. ✉ *Char-
lottenstr. 11* ☎ *07541/21771* ⊕ *www.weber-weiss.de.*

MEERSBURG

18 km (11 miles) west of Friedrichshafen.

Meersburg is one of the most romantic old towns on the German shore
of the lake. Seen from the water on a summer afternoon with the sun
slanting low, the steeply terraced town looks like a stage set, with its
bold castles, severe patrician dwellings, and a gaggle of half-timber
houses arranged around narrow streets. It's no wonder that cars have
been banned from the center: the crowds of people who come to visit
the sights on weekends fill up the streets. The town is divided into the
Unterstadt (Lower Town) and Oberstadt (Upper Town), connected by
several steep streets and stairs.

ESSENTIALS

Visitor Information Tourism Meersburg. ✉ *Tourism Meersburg, Kirchstr. 4*
☎ *07532/440–400* ⊕ *www.meersburg.de.*

EXPLORING

Altes Schloss (*Old Castle; Burg Meersburg*). Majestically guarding the
town is the Altes Schloss, the original Meersburg ("sea castle"). It's
Germany's oldest inhabited castle, founded in 628 by Dagobert, king
of the Franks. The massive central tower, with walls 10 feet thick, is
named after him. The bishops of Konstanz used it as a summer residence

until 1526, at which point they moved in permanently. They remained until the mid-18th century, when they built themselves what they felt to be a more suitable residence—the baroque Neues Schloss. Plans to tear down the Altes Schloss in the early 19th century were shelved when it was taken over by Baron Joseph von Lassberg, a man much intrigued by the castle's medieval romance. He turned it into a home for like-minded poets and artists, among them the Grimm brothers and his sister-in-law, the poet Annette von Droste-Hülshoff (1797–1848). The Altes Schloss is still private property, but much of it can be visited, including the richly furnished rooms where Droste-Hülshoff lived and the chamber where she died, as well as the imposing knights' hall, the minstrels' gallery, and the sinister dungeons. The **Altes Schloss Museum** (Old Castle Museum) contains a fascinating collection of weapons and armor, including a rare set of medieval jousting equipment. ✉ *Schlosspl. 10* ☎ *07532/80000* 🌐 *www.burg-meersburg.de* 🎟 *€9.50* 🕒 *Mar.–Oct., daily 9–6:30; Nov.–Feb., daily 10–6.*

Fürstenhäusle (*Prince's Little House, Droste Museum*). An idyllic retreat almost hidden among the vineyards, the Fürstenhäusle was built in 1640 by a local vintner and later used as a holiday house by the poet Annette von Droste-Hülshoff. It's now the Droste Museum, containing many of her personal possessions and giving a vivid sense of Meersburg in her time. You'll need to join a guided tour to enter the museum. ✉ *Stettenerstr. 11, east of Obertor, the town's north gate* ☎ *07532/6088* 🌐 *www.fuerstenhaeusle.de* 🎟 *€5* 🕒 *Apr.–Oct., Tues.–Sat. 10–12:30 and 2–6, Sun. 2–6.*

Heilig Geist Spital (*Haus für Wein, Kultur, Geschichte; Museum of Wine, Culture and History*). Take a fascinating look into Meersburg's cultural—and vinicultural—history at this museum space housed in the city's historic hospital building, the Heilig Geist Spital (Hospital of the Holy Spirit). Temporary exhibitions have been showing in the under-renovation building since 2015, with the new museum set to open in full by mid-2016. ✉ *Vorburgg. 11* ☎ *07532/440–400* 🌐 *www.meersburg.de* 🎟 *€6* 🕒 *Tues.–Sun. 11–6.*

Neues Schloss. The spacious and elegant "New Castle" is directly across from its predecessor. Designed by Christoph Gessinger at the beginning of the 18th century, it took nearly 50 years to complete. The grand double staircase, with its intricate grillwork and heroic statues, was the work of Balthasar Neumann. The interior's other standout is the glittering **Spiegelsaal** (Hall of Mirrors). ✉ *Schlosspl. 12* ☎ *07532/807–9410* 🌐 *www.neues-schloss-meersburg.de* 🎟 *€5* 🕒 *Apr.–Oct., daily 9–6.30; Nov.–Mar., weekends and holidays noon–5.*

WHERE TO EAT

$$$ GERMAN 🍴 **Winzerstube zum Becher.** Fresh fish from the lake is a specialty at this traditional restaurant, which has been in the Benz family for three generations. You can pair the day's catch with white wine from their own vineyard. A popular entrée is *badische Ente* (duck with bacon and apples in a wine-kirsch sauce). The restaurant is near the New Castle, and reservations are recommended. [$] *Average main: €22* ✉ *Höllg. 4* ☎ *07532/9009* 🌐 *www.winzerstube-zum-becher.de* 🕒 *Closed Mon. and 1 wk in Jan.*

6

The Altes Schloss in Meersburg, a true medieval castle, has a museum with armor and jousting equipment.

WHERE TO STAY

$
HOTEL
🏨 **Gästehaus am Hafen.** This family-run, half-timber pension is in the middle of the Old Town, near the harbor. **Pros:** close to the harbor; in the center of the Lower Town; good value. **Cons:** small rooms; no credit cards; parking is five minutes away on foot. ⓢ *Rooms from: €58* ✉ *Spitalg. 3–4* ☎ *07532/7069* ⊕ *www.amhafen.eu* ⊟ *No credit cards* 🕑 *Closed Nov.–Mar.* 🛏 *7 rooms* ⑪ *Breakfast.*

$
HOTEL
🏨 **Hotel Weinstube Löwen.** Rooms at this local landmark—a centuries-old, ivy-clad tavern on Meersburg's market square—have their own corner sitting areas, some with genuine Biedermeier furniture. **Pros:** center of town; pleasant rooms; good food in a cozy restaurant. **Cons:** lots of daytime noise from tourists; no elevator. ⓢ *Rooms from: €90* ✉ *Marktpl. 2* ☎ *07532/43040* ⊕ *www.hotel-loewen-meersburg.de* 🛏 *20 rooms* ⑪ *Breakfast.*

$$$
HOTEL
🏨 **Romantik Hotel Residenz am See.** This tastefully modern hotel overlooking the lake features two restaurants, including the Michelin-starred Casala, and Residenz Restaurant, which specializes in regional fare. **Pros:** good food; pleasant rooms with lake view; quiet rooms toward the vineyards. **Cons:** not in center of town. ⓢ *Rooms from: €198* ✉ *Uferpromenade 11* ☎ *07532/80040* ⊕ *www.hotel-residenz-meersburg.com* 🛏 *23 rooms, 2 suites* ⑪ *Breakfast; Some meals* ☞ *Casala restaurant closed Mon.–Wed. and Nov. Residenz restaurant closed Tues., in winter also Mon.*

$$
HOTEL
🏨 **See Hotel Off.** Nearly all rooms at this bright, airy and crisply renovated hotel just a few steps from the shore offer balconies with views across the lake or vineyards. **Pros:** close to the lake; individually decorated rooms; away from center of town. **Cons:** not in center of town.

$ *Rooms from: €107* ⊠ *Uferpromenade 51* ☎ *07532/44740* ⊕ *www. seehotel-off.de* ⊘ *Closed Jan.* ⇱ *13 rooms, 7 junior suites* ❑ *Breakfast.*

$
HOTEL

⊡ **Zum Bären.** Individually furnished rooms lend character to this historic hotel, whose ivy-covered facade, with its characteristic steeple, hasn't changed much over the centuries. **Pros:** center of town; historic building; good value; own parking garage. **Cons:** no elevator; some rooms are small; no credit cards. $ *Rooms from: €88* ⊠ *Marktpl. 11* ☎ *07532/43220* ⊕ *www.baeren-meersburg.de* ⊟ *No credit cards* ⊘ *Closed mid-Nov.–mid-Mar.* ⇱ *20 rooms* ❑ *Breakfast.*

SPORTS AND THE OUTDOORS

FAMILY **Meersburg Therme** (*Meersburg Spa*). This lakeside pool complex east of the harbor has three outdoor pools, an indoor "adventure" pool, an indoor-outdoor thermal bath (34°C [93.2°F]), and an indoor-outdoor "sauna world" with a wide variety of saunas, including two "Pfahlbau saunas" built to look like traditional *Pfahlbauten* (lake dwellings). ⊠ *Uferpromenade 12* ☎ *07532/440-2850* ⊕ *www.meersburg-therme.de* ⊡ *Bathing and sauna (3 hrs) €18, full day €22* ⊘ *Mon.–Thurs. 10–10, Fri. and Sat. 10 am–11 pm, Sun. 9 am–10 pm.*

SHOPPING

FAMILY **Omas Kaufhaus.** If you can't find something at this incredible gift shop (with nostalgic retro toys, enamelware, books, dolls, model cars, and much more), then you should at least see the exhibition of toy trains and tin boats on the first floor. The boats are displayed in a long canal filled with real water. ⊠ *Cnr. Kirchstr. and Steigstr.* ☎ *07532/433–9611* ⊡ *Entry to the exhibition €2* ⊘ *Daily 10–6:30* ⊘ *Exhibition closed in the winter months, except around Christmas.*

EN
ROUTE

Pfahlbauten. As you proceed northwest along the lake's shore, a settlement of "pile dwellings"—a reconstructed village of Stone Age and Bronze Age houses built on stilts—sticks out of the lake. This is how the original lake dwellers lived, surviving off the fish that swam outside their humble huts. Real dwellers in authentic garb give you an accurate picture of prehistoric lifestyles. The on-site **Pfahlbaumuseum** (Lake Dwelling Open-Air Museum and Research Institute) contains actual finds excavated in the area. Admission includes a 45–60-minute tour. ⊠ *Strandpromenade 6, Unteruhldingen* ☎ *07556/928–900* ⊕ *www. pfahlbauten.com* ⊡ *€9* ⊘ *Apr.–Sept., daily 9–6:30; Oct., daily 9–5; Nov.–Mar., hrs vary.*

ÜBERLINGEN

13 km (8 miles) west of Meersburg, 24 km (15 miles) west of Friedrichshafen.

This Bodensee resort has an attractive waterfront and an almost Mediterranean feel. It's midway along the north shore of the Überlingersee, a narrow finger of the Bodensee that points to the northwest. Überlingen is ancient—it's first mentioned in records dating back to 770. In the 14th century it earned the title of Free Imperial City and was known for its wines. No fewer than seven of its original city gates and towers remain from those grand days, as well as substantial portions of the old city walls. What was once the moat is now a grassy walkway, with the walls of the Old Town towering on one side and the Stadtpark stretching away on the other. The **Stadtgarten** (city garden), which opened in 1875, cultivates exotic plants and has a famous collection of cacti, a fuchsia garden, and a small deer corral. The heart of the city is the Münsterplatz.

ESSENTIALS

Visitor Information **Überlingen.** ⊠ *Tourist-Information, Landungspl. 5* ☎ *07551/947–1522* ⊕ *www.ueberlingen-bodensee.de.*

EXPLORING

Altes Rathaus (*Old Town Hall*). Inside the late-Gothic Altes Rathaus is a high point of Gothic decoration, the **Rathaussaal,** or council chamber, which is still in use today. Its most striking feature amid the riot of carving is the series of figures, created between 1492 and 1494, representing the states of the Holy Roman Empire. To visit the interior, you'll need to take the short guided tour. Tours are free; simply show up shortly before the set start time. ⊠ *Münsterstr. 15* ☎ *07551/991–011* ⊕ *www. ueberlingen-bodensee.de* ☉ *Tours: Wed. and Thurs. at 11.*

Münster St. Nikolaus (*Church of St. Nicholas*). The huge Münster St. Nikolaus was built between 1512 and 1563 on the site of at least two previous churches. The interior is all Gothic solemnity and massiveness, with a lofty stone-vaulted ceiling and high, pointed arches lining the nave. The single most remarkable feature is not Gothic at all but opulently Renaissance—the massive high altar, carved by Jörg Zürn from lime wood that almost looks like ivory. The subject of the altar carvings is the Nativity. ⊠ *Münsterpl.* ☎ *07551/92720* ⊕ *Daily 8–6.*

FAMILY

Fodor's Choice

★

Schloss Salem (*Salem Castle*). This huge castle in the tiny inland village of Salem, 10 km (6 miles) north of Überlingen, began its existence as a convent and large church. After many architectural permutations, it was transformed into a palace for the Baden princes, though traces of its religious past can still be seen. You can view the royally furnished rooms of the abbots and princes, a library, stables, and the church. The castle also houses an interesting array of museums, workshops, and activities, including a museum of firefighting, a potter, a musical instrument builder, a goldsmith shop, a glassblowing shop, pony farms, a golf driving range, and a fantasy garden for children. There is a great path that leads from the southwestern part of the grounds through woods and meadows to the pilgrimage church of Birnau. The route was created by the monks centuries ago and is still called the Prälatenweg (path of the prelates) today. It's an 8-km (5-mile) walk (no cars permitted). ⊠ *Salem* ☎ *07553/916–5336* ⊕ *www.salem.de* ☐ *€9* ☉ *Apr.–Oct., Mon.–Sat. 9:30–6, Sun. 10:30–6; Nov.–Mar., Sun. 3 pm guided tour only.*

Städtisches Museum (*City Museum*). This museum is housed in the Reichlin-von-Meldegg house, built in 1462, one of the earliest Renaissance dwellings in Germany. It displays exhibits tracing Bodensee history and Germany's largest collection of antique dollhouses. ⊠ *Krummebergstr. 30* ☎ *07551/991–079* ⊕ *www.museum-ueberlingen.de* ☐ *€5* ☉ *Apr.–Oct., Tues.–Sat. 9–12:30 and 2–5, Sun. 10–3.*

Near Überlingen, Schloss Salem was constructed as a convent and then transformed into a palace. Leading from the palace grounds is a 5-mile path to Wallfahrtskirche Birnau (Pilgrimage Church).

Wallfahrtskirche Birnau (*Pilgrimage Church; Basilika Birnau*). Just northwest of Unteruhldingen, the Wallfahrtskirche Birnau stands among vineyards overlooking the lake. The church was built by the master architect Peter Thumb between 1746 and 1750. Its exterior consists of pink-and-white plaster and a tapering clock-tower spire above the main entrance. The interior is overwhelmingly rich, full of movement, light, and color. It's hard to single out highlights from such a profusion of ornament, but look for the *Honigschlecker* ("honey sucker"), a gold-and-white cherub beside the altar, dedicated to St. Bernard of Clairvaux, "whose words are sweet as honey" (it's the last altar on the right as you face the high altar). The cherub is sucking honey from his finger, which he's just pulled out of a beehive. The fanciful spirit of this play on words is continued in the small squares of glass set into the pink screen that rises high above the main altar; the gilt dripping from the walls; the swaying, swooning statues; and the swooping figures on the ceiling. ⊠ *Birnau-Maurach 5, Uhldingen-Mühlhofen* ☎ *07556/92030* ⊕ *www.birnau.de* ⊗ *May–Sept., daily 7:30–7; Oct.–Apr., daily 7:30–5.*

OFF THE BEATEN PATH

Affenberg (*Monkey Mountain*). On the road between Überlingen and Salem, the Affenberg (Monkey Mountain) is a 50-plus-acre park that serves as home to more than 200 free-roaming Barbary apes, as well as deer, aquatic birds, gray herons, ducks, coots, and—during nesting time—a colony of white storks. ⊠ *Mendlishauser Hof* ✢ *On road between Überlingen and Salem* ☎ *07553/381* ⊕ *www.affenberg-salem. de* ⊠ *€8.50* ⊗ *Mid-Mar.–Oct., daily 9–6; last entry at 5:30.*

WHERE TO STAY

$ Ⓣ **Landgasthof zum Adler.** This unpretentious, rustic country inn in a vil-
HOTEL   lage a few miles north of Überlingen has a blue-and-white half-timber
FAMILY facade, scrubbed wooden floors, maple-wood tables, and thick down
comforters on the beds. **Pros:** good food in old wooden restaurant;
modern rooms in annex; family-friendly. **Cons:** rooms on the street
side can be noisy; a bit far from Überlingen; family-oriented. $ *Rooms
from: €78* ✉ *Hauptstr. 44, Lippertsreute* ☎ *07553/82550* ⊕ *www.adler-
lippertsreute.de* ↪ *16 rooms* ⦿ *Breakfast.*

$$ Ⓣ **Romantik Hotel Johanniter Kreuz.** Parts of this half-timber hotel in a
HOTEL   small village north of Überlingen date from the 17th century, setting a
romantic tone that's further enhanced by the huge fireplace in the center
of the restaurant. **Pros:** choice of very different rooms; spacious; mod-
ern, and yet welcoming lobby; family run; cozy restaurant; golf course
close by. **Cons:** 3 km (2 miles) from center of town; long corridors from
historic part of hotel to reach elevator in new part. $ *Rooms from:*
€136 ✉ *Johanniterweg 11, Andelshofen* ☎ *07551/937–060* ⊕ *www.*
johanniter-kreuz.de ↪ *29 rooms* ⦿ *Breakfast.*

$$ Ⓣ **Schäpfle.** The charm of this vine-covered hotel in the center of town
HOTEL   has been preserved and supplemented through time—in the hallways
you'll find quaint furniture and even an old Singer sewing machine
painted with flowers. **Pros:** center of town; local atmosphere in restaurant; annex with lake view. **Cons:** parking nearby, but for a fee; no
credit cards. $ *Rooms from: €109* ✉ *Jakob-Kessenringstr. 12 and 14*
☎ *07551/83070* ⊕ *www.schaepfle.de* ▭ *No credit cards* ↪ *32 rooms*
in 2 houses ⦿ *Breakfast.*

SHOPPING

The beauty and charm of Überlingen is one reason so many artists work
and live here; there are more than 20 workshops and artists' shops
where you can browse and buy at reasonable prices. ■**TIP➜ Ask at the
tourist office for the brochure listing all the galleries.**

Holzer Goldschmiede. You'll find this master goldsmith's studio near the
city's Franziskanertor. ✉ *Turmg. 8, Am Franziskanertor* ☎ *07551/61525*
⊕ *www.goldschmiede-holzer.de.*

THE UPPER SWABIAN BAROQUE ROAD

From Friedrichshafen, B-30 leads north along the valley of the little
River Schussen and links up with one of Germany's lesser-known but
most attractive scenic routes. The Oberschwäbische Barockstrasse
(Upper Swabian Baroque Road) follows a rich series of baroque
churches and abbeys, including Germany's largest baroque church, the
basilica in Weingarten.

RAVENSBURG

20 km (12 miles) north of Friedrichshafen.

The Free Imperial City of Ravensburg once competed with Augsburg
and Nürnberg for economic supremacy in southern Germany. The

Thirty Years' War put an end to the city's hopes by reducing it to little more than a medieval backwater. The city's loss proved fortuitous only in that many of its original features have remained much as they were built (in the 19th century, medieval towns usually tore down their medieval walls and towers, which were considered ungainly and constraining). Fourteen of Ravensburg's town gates and towers survive, and the Altstadt is among the best preserved in Germany.

GETTING HERE AND AROUND
Consider taking an official tour of the city, which grants you access to some of the towers for a splendid view of Ravensburg and the surrounding countryside. Tours are available at the tourist office.

ESSENTIALS
Visitor Information Ravensburg Tourist-Information. ⊠ *Tourist-Information, Kirchstr. 16* ☎ *0751/82800* ⊕ *www.ravensburg.de.*

EXPLORING
TOP ATTRACTIONS
Defensive Towers. Ravensburg is home to a remarkable collection of well-preserved medieval towers and city gates. Highlights include the **Grüner Turm** (Green Tower), so called for its green tiles, many of which are 14th-century originals. Another stout defense tower is the massive **Obertor** (Upper Tower), the oldest gate in the city walls. The curiously named **Mehlsack** (Flour Sack) tower—so called because of its rounded shape and whitewash exterior—stands 170 feet high and sits upon the highest point of the city. From April to October, visitors can climb to the top of the **Blaserturm** (Trumpeter's Tower) for rooftop views over the city. ⊠ *Ravensburg* ☎ *0751/82800* ⊕ *www.ravensburg.de* 🔖 *Towers €1.50* 🕙 *Apr.–Oct., daily 11–5.*

Marienplatz. Many of Ravensburg's monuments that most recall the town's wealthy past are concentrated on this central square. To the west is the 14th-century **Kornhaus** (Granary); once the corn exchange for all of Upper Swabia, it now houses the public library. The late-Gothic **Rathaus** is a staid, red building with a Renaissance bay window and imposing late-Gothic rooms inside. Next to it stands the 15th-century **Waaghaus** (Weighing House), the town's weigh station and central warehouse. Its tower, the **Blaserturm** (Trumpeter's Tower), which served as the watchman's abode, was rebuilt in 1556 after a fire and now bears a pretty Renaissance helmet. Finally there's the colorfully frescoed **Lederhaus,** once the headquarters of the city's leather workers, and now home to a café. On Saturday morning the square comes alive with a large market. ⊠ *Ravensburg.*

WORTH NOTING
Evangelische Stadtkirche (*Protestant Church*). That ecclesiastical and commercial life were never entirely separate in medieval towns is evident in this church, once part of a 14th-century monastery. The stairs on the west side of the church's chancel lead to the meeting room of the Ravensburger Gesellschaft (Ravensburg Society), an organization of linen merchants established in 1400. After the Reformation, Catholics and Protestants shared the church, but in 1810 the Protestants were given the entire building. The neo-Gothic stained-glass windows on the

DID YOU KNOW?

The Weingarten Basilica's altar is said to hold a vial of Christ's blood. On the day after Ascension Thursday, a huge procession of pilgrims makes its way to the basilica.

west side, depicting important figures of the Reformation such as Martin Luther and Ulrich Zwingli, were sponsored by wealthy burghers. ✉ *Marienpl. 5* 🌐 *www.ravensburg-evangelisch.de.*

Humpis-Quartier Museum. Glass walkways, stairways, and a central courtyard connect the well-preserved medieval residences at this museum, where visitors can take a close look into the lives of Ravensburgers in the Middle Ages. The residences once belonged to the Humpis family, who were traders in the 15th century. ✉ *Marktstr. 45* ☎ *0751/82820* 🌐 *www.museum-humpis-quartier.de* 🎫 *€4* 🕒 *Tues., Wed., and Fri.–Sun. 11–6, Thurs. 11–8.*

Kirche St. Peter und Paul (*St. Petrus und Paulus*). Just to the southwest of Ravensburg in the village of Weissenau stands this old church, which was part of a 12th-century Premonstratensian monastery and now has a high baroque facade. The interior is a stupendous baroque masterpiece, with ceiling paintings by Joseph Hafner that create the illusion of cupolas, and vivacious stuccowork by Johannes Schmuzer, one of the famous stucco artists from Wessobrunn. ✉ *Abteistr. 2–3* ☎ *0751/61590* 🌐 *www.kath-rv.de* 🕒 *Daily 9–6.*

Liebfrauenkirche (*Church of Our Lady*). Ravensburg's true parish church, the Gothic 14th-century Liebfrauenkirche, is elegantly simple on the outside but almost entirely rebuilt inside, having reopened in early 2011 following major renovations. Among the finest treasures within are the 15th-century stained-glass windows in the choir and the heavily gilt altar. In a side altar is a copy of a carved Madonna, the *Schutzmantelfrau*; the late-14th-century original is in Berlin's Dahlem Museum. ✉ *Kirchstr. 18* ☎ *0751/361–960* 🌐 *www.kath-rv.de* 🕒 *Daily 7–7.*

FAMILY **Museum Ravensburger.** Ravensburg is a familiar name to all jigsaw-puzzle fans, because the Ravensburg publishing house produces the world's largest selection of puzzles, in addition to many other children's games. Here you can explore the history of the company, founded in 1883 by Otto Robert Maier. Be sure to try out new and classic games via the interactive game stations throughout the museum. ✉ *Marktstr. 26* ☎ *0751/861–377* 🌐 *www.museum-ravensburger.de* 🎫 *€7.50* 🕒 *Apr.–Sept., Tues.–Sun. 10–6; Oct.–Mar., Tues.–Sun. 11–6.*

WHERE TO EAT AND STAY

$ ITALIAN 🍴 **Firenze Caffé e Gelateria.** This bustling multilevel café opens early and closes late and offers a mind-boggling array of ice-cream dishes and other sweet and savory fare. For a quick and inexpensive meal, consider the tasty breakfasts, sandwiches, and German- and Italian-influenced items on offer. [$] *Average main: €10* ✉ *Marienpl. 47* ☎ *0751/24665* 💳 *No credit cards.*

$ HOTEL 🏨 **Gasthof Ochsen and Ochsen Hotel am Mehlsack.** A typical, family-owned Swabian inn, the Ochsen consists of a traditional Gasthof, and the adjoining, newly renovated Ochsen Hotel am Mehlsack featuring more modern (and pricier) rooms. **Pros:** warm atmosphere and good Swabian food in two cozy restaurants; many rooms newly refurbished. **Cons:** parking not on-site. [$] *Rooms from: €99* ✉ *Burgstr. 1* ☎ *0751/25480* 🌐 *www.ochsen-rv.de* 🛏 *23 rooms, 2 suites, 1 penthouse room* 🍽 *Breakfast.*

$$ ⚏ **Romantikhotel Waldhorn.** This historic hostelry in the heart of Ravens-
HOTEL   burg has been in the Dressel-Bouley family for more than 150 years. **Pros:**
family-run historic institution; recently renovated. **Cons:** very limited
on-site parking. $ *Rooms from: €109* ⌧ *Marienpl. 15* ☏ *0751/36120*
⊕ *www.waldhorn.de* ⇱ *11 rooms, 1 suite, 9 apartments* ⦿| *Breakfast.*

WEINGARTEN

5 km (3 miles) north of Ravensburg.

Weingarten is famous throughout Germany for its huge and hugely
impressive basilica, which you can see up on a hill from miles away,
long before you get to the town. The city has grown during the last
century as several small and midsize industries settled here. It's now
an interesting mixture, its historic Old Town surrounded by a small,
prosperous industrial city.

ESSENTIALS

Visitor Information Weingarten Amt für Kultur- und Tourismus.
⌧ *Münsterpl. 1* ☏ *0751/405–232* ⊕ *www.weingarten-online.de.*

EXPLORING

Alemannenmuseum. If you want to learn about early Germans—resi-
dents from the 6th, 7th, and 8th centuries whose graves are just outside
town—visit the Alemannenmuseum in the Kornhaus, which was once a
granary. Archaeologists discovered the hundreds of Alemannic graves
in the 1950s. ⌧ *Karlstr. 28* ☏ *0751/49343* ⊕ *www.weingarten-online.
de* ⌧ *€2* ⊘ *Wed.–Sun. 2–5.*

Weingarten Basilica (*St. Martin Basilica*). At 220 feet high and more
than 300 feet long, Weingarten Basilica is the largest baroque church
in Germany. It was built as the church of one of the oldest and most
venerable convents in the country, founded in 1056 by the wife of
Guelph IV. The Guelph dynasty ruled large areas of Upper Swabia, and
generations of family members lie buried in the church. The majestic
edifice was renowned because of its little vial said to contain drops
of Christ's blood. First mentioned by Charlemagne, the vial passed
to the convent in 1094, entrusted to its safekeeping by the Guelph
queen Juditha, sister-in-law of William the Conqueror. Weingarten then
became one of Germany's foremost pilgrimage sites. To this day, on the
day after Ascension Thursday, the anniversary of the day the vial of
Christ's blood was entrusted to the convent, a huge procession of pil-
grims wends its way to the basilica. It's well worth seeing the procession,
which is headed by nearly 3,000 horsemen (many local farmers breed
horses just for this occasion). The basilica was decorated by leading
early-18th-century German and Austrian artists: stuccowork by Franz
Schmuzer, ceiling frescoes by Cosmas Damian Asam, and a Donato
Frisoni altar—one of the most breathtakingly ornate in Europe, with
nearly 80-foot-high towers on either side. The organ, installed by Josef
Gabler between 1737 and 1750, is among the largest in the country.
⌧ *Kirchpl. 6* ⊕ *www.st-martin-weingarten.de* ⊘ *Nov.–Mar., daily 8–5;
Apr.–Oct., daily 8–7.*

Around the Bodanrück Peninsula

AROUND THE BODANRÜCK PENINSULA

The immense Bodensee owes its name to a small, insignificant town, Bodman, on the Bodanrück Peninsula, at the northwestern edge of the lake. ■TIP→ **The peninsula's most popular destinations, Konstanz and Mainau, are reachable by ferry from Meersburg—by far the most romantic way to get to the area.** The other option is to take the road (B-31, then B-34, and finally B-33) that skirts the western arm of the Bodensee and ends its German journey at Konstanz.

KONSTANZ

A ½-hr ferry ride from Meersburg.

The university town of Konstanz is the largest on the Bodensee; it straddles the Rhine as it flows out of the lake, placing it both on the Bodanrück Peninsula and the Switzerland side of the lake, where it adjoins the Swiss town of Kreuzlingen. Konstanz is among the best-preserved medieval towns in Germany; during the war the Allies were unwilling to risk inadvertently bombing neutral Switzerland. On the peninsula side of the town, east of the main bridge connecting Konstanz's two halves, runs **Seestrasse,** a stately promenade of neoclassical mansions with views of the Bodensee. The Old Town center is a labyrinth of narrow streets lined with restored half-timber houses and dignified merchant dwellings. This is where you'll find restaurants, hotels, pubs, and much of the nightlife.

It's claimed that Konstanz was founded in the 3rd century by Emperor Constantine Chlorus, father of Constantine the Great. The story is probably untrue, though it's certain there was a Roman garrison here. In the late 6th century Konstanz was made a bishopric; in 1192 it became a Free Imperial City. What put it on the map was the Council of Constance, held between 1414 and 1418 to settle the Great Schism (1378–1417), the rift in the church caused by two separate lines of popes, one ruling from Rome, the other from Avignon. The Council resolved the problem in 1417 by electing Martin V as the true, and only, pope. The church had also agreed to restore the Holy Roman emperor's (Sigismund's) role in electing the pope, but only if Sigismund silenced the rebel theologian Jan Hus, of Bohemia. Even though Sigismund had allowed Hus safe passage to Konstanz for the Council, he won the church's favor by having Hus burned at the stake in July 1415. In a satiric short story, the French author Honoré de Balzac created the character of Imperia, a courtesan of great beauty and cleverness, who raised the blood pressure of both religious and secular VIPs during the council. No one visiting the harbor today can miss the 28-foot statue of **Imperia** standing out on the breakwater. Dressed in a revealing and alluring style, in her hands she holds two dejected figures: the emperor and the pope. This hallmark of Konstanz, created by Peter Lenk, caused controversy when it was unveiled in April 1993.

Most people enjoy Konstanz for its worldly pleasures—the elegant Altstadt, trips on the lake, walks along the promenade, elegant shops, the restaurants, the views. The heart of the city is the **Marktstätte** (Marketplace), near the harbor, with the simple bulk of the Konzilgebäude looming behind it. Erected in 1388 as a warehouse, the **Konzilgebäude** (Council Hall) is now a concert hall. Beside the Konzilgebäude are statues of Jan Hus and native son Count Ferdinand von Zeppelin (1838–1917). The Dominican monastery where Hus was held before his execution is still here, doing duty as a luxurious hotel, the Steigenberger Insel-Hotel.

GETTING HERE AND AROUND

Konstanz is in many ways the center of the lake area. You can reach Zürich airport by direct train in about an hour, and Frankfurt in 4½ hours. Swiss autobahn access to Zürich is about 10 minutes away, and you can reach the autobahn access to Stuttgart in about the same time. To reach the island of Mainau, you can take a bus, but a much more pleasant way to get there is by boat, via Meersburg. You can take another boat downriver to Schaffhausen in Switzerland, or east to the northern shore towns as well as Bregenz in Austria. The Old Town is manageable on foot.

ESSENTIALS

Visitor Information Tourist-Information Konstanz. ⊠ *Bahnhofpl. 43* ☎ *07531/133–030* ⊕ *www.konstanz-tourismus.de.*

EXPLORING

Altes Rathaus (*Old Town Hall*). This old town hall was built during the Renaissance and painted with vivid frescoes—swags of flowers and fruits, shields, and sturdy knights wielding immense swords. Walk into the courtyard to admire its Renaissance restraint. ⊠ *Kanzleistr. 13.*

Münster. Konstanz's cathedral, the **Münster**, was the center of one of Germany's largest bishoprics until 1827, when the seat was moved to Freiburg. Construction on the cathedral continued from the 10th through the 19th century, resulting in an interesting coexistence of architectural styles: the twin-tower facade is sturdily Romanesque; the elegant and airy chapels along the aisles are full-blown 15th-century Gothic; the complex nave vaulting is Renaissance; and the choir is severely neoclassical. The Mauritius Chapel behind the altar is a

For views of the Bodensee from Konstanz, head to the Seestrasse promenade.

13th-century Gothic structure, 12 feet high, with some of its original vivid coloring and gilding. It's studded with statues of the Apostles and figures depicting the childhood of Jesus. Climb the **Münsterturm** (Münster Tower) for views over the city and lake. ⊠ *Münsterpl. 4* ✉ *€2* ⊙ *Daily 8–6. Tower: Mon.–Sat. 10–5 and Sun. 12:30–5.*

Niederburg. The Niederburg, the oldest part of Konstanz, is a tangle of twisting streets leading to the Rhine. From the river take a look at two of the city's old towers: the **Rheintorturm** (Rhine Tower), the one nearer the lake, and the aptly named **Pulverturm** (Powder Tower), the former city arsenal. ⊠ *Konstanz.*

Rosgartenmuseum (*Rose Garden Museum*). Within the medieval guild-hall of the city's butchers, this museum has a rich collection of art and artifacts from the Bodensee region. Highlights include exhibits of the life and work of the people around the Bodensee, from the Bronze Age through the Middle Ages and beyond. There's also a collection of sculpture and altar paintings from the Middle Ages. ⊠ *Rosgartenstr. 3–5* ☎ *07531/900–246* ⊕ *www.rosgartenmuseum-konstanz.de* ✉ *€3* ⊙ *Tue.–Fri. 10–6, weekends 10–5.*

FAMILY **Sealife.** This huge aquarium has gathered all the fish species that inhabit the Rhine and the Bodensee, from the river's beginnings in the Swiss Alps to its end in Rotterdam and the North Sea. Also check out the **Bodensee Naturmuseum** at the side entrance, which gives a comprehensive overview of the geological history of the Bodensee and its fauna and flora right down to the microscopic creatures of the region. You can buy tickets in advance online for a significantly cheaper price. ⊠ *Hafenstr.*

9 ☎ 07531/128–270 🌐 www.sealife.de 🎫 €19.50 🕒 Sept.–June, daily 10–5, July and Aug., daily 10–6.

WHERE TO EAT

$ GERMAN 🍴 **Brauhaus Joh. Albrecht.** This small brewery with shiny copper cauldrons, part of a chain of five throughout Germany, serves simple dishes as well as regional specialties and vegetarian food on large wooden tables. [$] *Average main: €14* ✉ *Konradig. 2* ☎ *07531/25045* 🌐 *konstanz.brauhaus-joh-albrecht.de.*

$$ GERMAN 🍴 **Hafenhalle.** Enjoy eclectic cooking—including Italian, Bavarian, and Swabian fare—at this warm-weather spot on the harbor. Sit outside on the terrace and watch the busy harbor traffic, or enjoy the beer garden with sandbox for children and big TV screen for watching sports. The restaurant frequently presents sporting, culinary, and live-music events. If you're in town on Ash Wednesday at the end of the Swabian-Alemannic Fastnacht (carnival) celebrations, try to get a spot at Hafenhalle's annual fish-and-snails dining event, which marks the reopening of the restaurant after their period of winter closure. [$] *Average main: €15* ✉ *Hafenstr. 10* ☎ *07531/21126* 🌐 *www.hafenhalle.com* 🕒 *Closed Jan. and Feb.*

WHERE TO STAY

$$ HOTEL 🏨 **ABC Hotel.** This hotel offers large, comfortable, individually furnished rooms, all with kitchen facilities; book the unusual Turmsuite (Tower Suite) for an especially memorable stay among exposed beams and steeply sloping walls, and with private access to the top of the tower. **Pros:** warm welcome; large airy rooms; quiet location; free on-site parking; free Wi-Fi. **Cons:** not in the center of town; no elevator. [$] *Rooms from: €119* ✉ *Steinstr. 19* ☎ *07531/8900* 🌐 *www.abc-hotel.de* 🛏 *36 rooms, 1 suite* 🍽 *Breakfast.*

$ HOTEL 🏨 **Barbarossa.** This historic hotel in the heart of Old Town has been modernized inside, but such original elements as wooden support beams lend a romantic, authentic feel. **Pros:** historic building; cozy restaurant with good food; free hotel-wide Wi-Fi. **Cons:** some rooms simply furnished; parking available but a third of a mile walk away. [$] *Rooms from: €99* ✉ *Obermarkt 8–12* ☎ *07531/128–990* 🌐 *www.hotelbarbarossa.de* 🛏 *50 rooms* 🍽 *Breakfast.*

$$ HOTEL 🏨 **Stadthotel.** It's a five-minute walk to the lake from this friendly hotel, where rooms are modern, airy, and decorated in bright colors. **Pros:** center of town; quiet location with little traffic. **Cons:** no restaurant; parking garage five minutes away on foot. [$] *Rooms from: €115* ✉ *Bruderturmg. 2* ☎ *07531/90460* 🌐 *www.stadthotel-konstanz.com* 🛏 *24 rooms* 🍽 *Breakfast.*

$$$ HOTEL Fodor's Choice ★ 🏨 **Steigenberger Insel-Hotel.** With its original cloisters intact, this former 16th-century monastery is now the most luxurious lodging in town. **Pros:** wonderful lake views; luxurious; good restaurants; several rooms newly refurbished. **Cons:** a few rooms look out on railroad tracks; some rooms need refurbishing; expensive. [$] *Rooms from: €210* ✉ *Auf der Insel 1* ☎ *07531/1250* 🌐 *www.konstanz.steigenberger.com* 🛏 *100 rooms, 2 suites* 🍽 *Breakfast.*

NIGHTLIFE AND PERFORMING ARTS

K9 (*Kommunales Kunst-und Kulturzentrum K9*). This cultural center draws all ages with its music and dance club, theater, comedy, and cabaret. It's in the former Church of St. Paul. ⊠ *Hieronymusg. 3* ☎ *07531/16713* ⊕ *www.k9-kulturzentrum.de.*

Kulturladen (*Kula*). Concerts and variously themed DJ nights are held at Kulturladen. ⊠ *Joseph Belli Weg 5* ☎ *07531/52954* ⊕ *www. kulturladen.de.*

Rock am See. This annual late-summer rock music festival has been drawing rock fans to the Bodensee since 1985. Held at Bodensee-Stadion in Konstanz, the festival features both German and international acts. ⊠ *Bodensee-Stadion, Eichhornstr. 89* ☎ *07531/90880 ticket service* ⊕ *www.rock-am-see.de* ⊡ *Approx. €90.*

Seekuh. This cozy and crowded Italian restaurant ($) and bar features the occasional live jazz night and also screens live football games from time to time. ⊠ *Konzilstr. 1* ☎ *07531/27232* ⊕ *www.seekuh.de* ⟳ *Open daily from 5.*

Seenachtfest (*Lake Night Festival*). In August, Konstanz shares this one-day city festival with neighboring Kreuzlingen in Switzerland, with street events, music, clowns, and magicians, and ending with fireworks over the lake. ⊠ *Lakefront* ⊕ *www.seenachtfest.de* ⊡ *€19.*

Stadttheater (*Theater Konstanz*). The Stadttheater, Germany's oldest active theater, has staged plays since 1609 and has its own repertory company. ⊠ *Konzilstr. 11* ☎ *07531/900–150 (tickets)* ⊕ *www. theaterkonstanz.de* ⟳ *Ticket office open weekdays 10–7, Sat. 10–1.*

SPORTS AND THE OUTDOORS

BICYCLING

Bike rentals generally cost €12 per day.

Kultur-Rädle. This friendly store rents bikes at the main train station. A two-day rental costs €25. ⊠ *Bahnhofpl. 29* ☎ *07531/27310* ⊕ *www. kultur-raedle.de.*

Velotours Touristik GmbH. You can book bicycle tours and rent bikes at Velotours Touristik GmbH. ⊠ *Bücklestr. 13* ☎ *07531/98280* ⊕ *www. velotours.de.*

BOATING

Wilde Flotte—Segel & Wassersportschule Konstanz Wallhausen (*Wild Fleet*). This sailing school offers boat charters—both skippered and solo—as well as lessons in sailing, wakeboarding, and waterskiing. ⊠ *Uferstr. 16, Wallhausen* ☎ *07533/997–8802* ⊕ *www.wilde-flotte.de.*

Yachtcharter Konstanz. Sail and motor yachts are available at Yachtcharter Konstanz. ⊠ *Hafenstr. 7b* ☎ *07531/363–3970* ⊕ *www.yachtcharter-konstanz.de.*

SHOPPING

It's worthwhile to roam the streets of the old part of town, where there are several gold- and silversmiths and jewelers.

Modehaus Fischer. This elegant fashion store has enough style for a city 10 times the size of Konstanz. Much of its business comes from wealthy

Mainau Island, on the Bodensee, is covered with flowering gardens.

Swiss who visit Konstanz for what they consider bargain prices. Mode-haus Fischer deals in well-known international fashion stock, including handbags and exquisite shoes. The store is actually spread over three branches a few blocks apart—two for women, and one for men at Obermarkt. ⊠ *Rosgartenstr. 36, Hussenstr. 29, and Obermarkt.* ☎ *07531/363–250* ⊕ *www.modefischer.de.*

MAINAU

7 km (4½ miles) north of Konstanz by road; by ferry, ½–1 hr from Konstanz (depending on route), or 20 mins from Meersburg.

Fodor'sChoice ★ One of the most unusual sights in Germany, Mainau is a tiny island given over to the cultivation of rare plants and splashy displays of more than a million tulips, hyacinths, and narcissi. Rhododendrons and roses bloom from May to July; dahlias dominate the late summer. A greenhouse nurtures palms and tropical plants.

The island was originally the property of the Teutonic Knights, who settled here during the 13th century. In the 19th century Mainau passed to Grand Duke Friedrich I of Baden, a man with a passion for botany. He laid out most of the gardens and introduced many of the island's more exotic specimens. His daughter Victoria, later queen of Sweden, gave the island to her son, Prince Wilhelm, and it has remained Swedish ever since. Today it's owned by the family of Prince Wilhelm's son, Count Lennart Bernadotte. In the former main reception hall in the castle are changing art exhibitions.

GETTING HERE AND AROUND

Ferries to the island from Meersburg and Konstanz depart from April to October approximately every 1½ hours between 9 and 5. You must purchase a ticket to enter the island, which is open year-round from dawn until dusk. There's a small bridge to the island. At night you can drive across it to the restaurants.

ESSENTIALS

Visitor Information Insel Mainau. ✉ *Mainaustr. 1, Konstanz* ☎ *07531/3030* 🌐 *www.mainau.de.*

EXPLORING

Das Schmetterlinghaus. Beyond the flora, the island of Mainau's other colorful extravagance is Das Schmetterlinghaus, Germany's largest butterfly conservatory. On a circular walk through a semitropical landscape with water cascading through rare vegetation, you'll see hundreds of butterflies flying, feeding, and mating. The exhibition in the foyer explains the butterflies' life cycle, habitats, and ecological connections. Like the park, this oasis is open year-round. ✉ *Insel Mainau, Mainaustr. 1, Konstanz* 🌐 *www.mainau.de/schmetterlingshaus.html* 🕒 *Spring and summer 10–7, fall and winter 10–5.*

6

Gärtnerturm. At the middle of the island, the Gärtnerturm (Gardener's Tower) contains an information center, a shop, and an exhibition space. Several films on Mainau and the Bodensee are also shown. ✉ *Gärtnerturm.*

WHERE TO EAT

There are nine restaurants and cafés on the island, but nowhere to stay overnight.

$$ SCANDINAVIAN

🍴 **Schwedenschenke.** The lunchtime crowd gets what it needs here—fast and good service. At dinnertime candlelight adds some extra style. The resident Bernadotte family is Swedish, and so are the specialties of the chef. Have your hotel reserve a table for you. After 6 pm your reservation will be checked at the gate, and you can drive onto the island without having to pay admission. [$] *Average main: €18* ✉ *Insel Mainau* ☎ *07531/303–156* 🌐 *www.mainau.de/schwedenschenke.html* 🕒 *Closed mid-Nov.–mid-Mar.*

REICHENAU

10 km (6 miles) northwest of Konstanz, 50 mins by ferry from Konstanz.

Reichenau is an island rich in vegetation, but unlike Mainau, it features vegetables, not flowers. In fact, 15% of its area (the island is 5 km [3 miles] long and 1½ km [1 mile] wide) is covered by greenhouses and crops of one kind or another. It also has three of Europe's most beautiful Romanesque churches, a legacy of Reichenau's past as a monastic center in the early Middle Ages. The churches are in each of the island's villages—**Oberzell, Mittelzell,** and **Niederzell,** which are separated by only 1 km (½ mile). Along the shore are pleasant pathways for walking or biking.

ESSENTIALS

Visitor Information Reichenau. ✉ *Tourist-Information, Pirminstr. 145* ☎ *07534/92070* ⊕ *www.reichenau-tourismus.de.*

EXPLORING

Münster of St. Maria and St. Markus. Begun in 816, the Münster of St. Maria and St. Markus, the monastery's church, is the largest and most important of Reichenau's Romanesque churches. Perhaps its most striking architectural feature is the roof, whose beams and ties are open for all to see. The monastery was founded in 725 by St. Pirmin and became one of the most important cultural centers of the Carolingian Empire. It reached its zenith around 1000, when 700 monks lived here. It was then probably the most important center of book illumination in Germany. The building is simple but by no means crude. Visit the **Schatzkammer** (Treasury) to see some of its more important holdings. They include a 5th-century ivory goblet with two carefully incised scenes of Christ's miracles, and some priceless stained glass that is almost 1,000 years old. ✉ *Münsterpl. 3, Mittelzell* ☎ *07534/92070* ⊕ *www.reichenau-tourismus.de/kultur3/kirchen* ⊙ *Daily 9–5.*

Stiftskirche St. Georg (*Collegiate Church of St. George*). The Stiftskirche St. Georg, in Oberzell, was built around 900; now cabbages grow in ranks up to its rough plaster walls. Small round-head windows, a simple square tower, and massive buttresses signal the church's Romanesque origin from the outside. The interior is covered with frescoes painted by the monks in around 1000. They depict the eight miracles of Christ. Above the entrance is a depiction of the Resurrection. ✉ *Seestr. 4, Oberzell* ⊕ *www.reichenau-tourismus.de/kultur3/kirchen* ☑ *Free. Tours €2* ⊙ *Daily 9–5; tours May–Sept., daily at noon and 4.*

Stiftskirche St. Peter und Paul (*St. Peter and Paul Parish Church*). The Stiftskirche St. Peter und Paul, at Niederzell, was revamped around 1750. The faded Romanesque frescoes in the apse contrast with bold rococo paintings on the ceiling and flowery stucco. ✉ *Cnr. Eginostr. and Fischerg., Niederzell* ⊕ *www.reichenau-tourismus.de/kultur3/kirchen* ⊙ *Daily 9–5.*

WHERE TO EAT AND STAY

$ ✕ **Kiosk am Yachthafen.** This kiosk-style restaurant at Reichenau's yacht
GERMAN   harbor provides an ideal lunch, drink, or snack stop when wandering the island. In good weather, you can sit outside and watch the boats come and go. It's also a perfect place to try the Bodensee specialty *Zanderknusperle* (crispy battered pike-perch bites)—fresh out of the lake. $ *Average main: €10* ✉ *Yacht Harbor, Hermannus-Contractus-Str. 30* ☎ *07534/999–655* ⊕ *www.sbrestaurant-reichenau.de* ▭ *No credit cards* ⊙ *Closed Nov.–Mar.*

$$ ☷ **Strandhotel Löchnerhaus.** Standing commandingly on the water's edge
HOTEL   fronted by its own boat pier, the Strandhotel (Beach Hotel) Löchnerhaus exudes a retro Riviera feel. **Pros:** nice location; views over the lake into Switzerland; quiet; free bicycle rental. **Cons:** closed in winter; some rooms expensive. $ *Rooms from: €155* ✉ *An der Schiffslände 12* ☎ *07534/8030* ⊕ *www.loechnerhaus.de* ⊙ *Closed Nov.–mid-Mar.* ↰ *41 rooms* ⊖| *Breakfast.*

THE BLACK FOREST

WELCOME TO THE BLACK FOREST

TOP REASONS TO GO

★ **Excellent eats:** Enjoy extraordinary regional specialties like Black Forest cake, Schwarzwald ham, and incredible brews from the Alpirsbach Brewery before feasting on Baiersbronn's gourmet offerings.

★ **Freiburg Münster:** One of the most beautiful Gothic churches in Germany, the Cathedral of Freiburg survived the war unscathed. The view from the bell tower is stunning.

★ **Stunning scenery:** From the country's largest waterfall in Triberg to the glacially carved Titisee Lake, the landscape in the Black Forest National Park is unparalleled.

★ **Healing waters:** The region is home to more than 30 spas with a wide range of treatments, including a 3½-hour session at the Friedrichsbad in Baden-Baden, the ultimate place for relaxation.

★ **Libations at Kaiserstuhl:** With a diversity of wine like nowhere else in Germany, the sunny border region is especially pretty when the grapes are being harvested.

 **The Northern Black Forest.** The elegance of the region also known as the High Black Forest is unmatched in Germany. Whether in the genteel spa town of Baden-Baden or the quiet resort village of Baiersbronn, the beauty of the lush forest landscape abutting the rolling vineyards along the Badische Wine Route is unparalleled.

2 The Central Black Forest. The stereotypes representing the Black Forest, from Alpirsbach's half-timber houses to Triberg's cuckoo clocks, and the nation's highest waterfalls all abound in the central Black Forest, a national park with thick pine forests and a series of steep-sided valleys.

3 The Southern Black Forest. Freiburg is one of the country's most historic cities; just to the west is the sunny and temperate wine-growing region of Kaiserstuhl; to the east, one of the country's most beautiful lakes, Titisee

Rastatt
Oberndorf
Pforzheim
A8
B463

1

Calmbach
Bad Liebenzell

Mt Merkur
Baden-Baden
B462
Calw

B3
Bühl
B500
Gernsbach
A5
Sand
B294
B463
Achern
Wildberg

Altensteig

Baiersbronn
B28
Nagold
B28
Durbach
Löcherberg
Freudenstadt
Horb

B294

Alpirsbach

Haslach
Wolfach
Schiltach
Gutach
B462
Katzenmoos
B33
Schramberg

Triberg
Peterzell
Rohrhardsberg

Furtwangen
B500

Hinterzarten
Titisee
B31
B500
B315

B L A C K   F O R E S T

0   10 mi
0   10 km

GETTING ORIENTED

Germany's southwest corner shifts from the wide flat plains of the Rhine River Valley, which stretches to the French border in the west, into a hilly region dotted with glacier-carved lakes. Along the way, the Black Forest grows thick as you leave the bigger cities of Karlsruhe and Baden-Baden behind and escape up winding mountain roads dotted with picturesque villages.

7

SPAS

The restorative power of relaxation is something Germans take quite seriously, and nowhere is this better exemplified than in the country's sauna culture. Whether soaking in a hot pool or sweating it out in a 190-degree sauna, after just a short time, you'll find there really is something to this method of regeneration.

(above) Relax in the warm thermal pools of the Black Forest's spas. (upper right) Waterfall at the Caracalla Therme in Baden-Baden.

Seeking relief from the pains of battle, the Romans erected baths here almost 2,000 years ago, a pastime resurrected in the 19th century as spa towns across the country flourished and Europe's upper classes began to appreciate the soothing effects of fresh air and mineral waters. These days there are hundreds of facilities throughout the country ranging from sophisticated resorts offering precious-stone massages and chocolate baths to smaller "wellness" hotels with not much more than a sauna and a relaxation room.

—Courtney Tenz

DRINKING IT IN

Bad Mergentheim and Baden-Baden are renowned for their drinking-water springs and the healing properties of the mineral waters that spill from them. Used for everything from the stimulation of the pancreas to curing a sore throat, they are drunk by thousands of visitors every year.

SPA ETIQUETTE

NUDITY

Every European culture has its own rules about how best to enjoy the sauna experience and in Germany, that includes embracing nudity. Though sitting naked in a dimly lit, scorching-hot room or floating au naturel in a thermal pool among a group of strangers may not be everyone's idea of relaxation, the saunas, steam rooms, and hot pools in a spa are "textile-free" areas. They're also mainly mixed sex, except on marked days, and the prevailing attitude is that one's body is nothing to be ashamed of. The theory is that the body needs to be unencumbered to enjoy the full curative effects of the heat and water, and this becomes particularly understandable when the treatments include rubbing hot chocolate, honey, or salt on your skin while sweating it out. Bring a robe and a large towel to preserve your modesty in common areas, and if you're unsure what to take off and what to leave on, don't be afraid to ask.

BATHROBES, TOWELS, AND SANDALS

While the more upscale wellness locations will provide you with all three, most public spas will expect you to at least bring your own towel. Bathrobes and sandals should be worn in relaxation areas but left outside saunas and steam baths. Towels must be laid beneath you in the sauna to absorb excess sweat. Most facilities provide these items for purchase or will loan them to you for a small fee.

COLD SHOWERS

A quick shower before entering the sauna area is expected. A refreshing rinse between each sauna session is also part of the procedure, not just for hygiene but also for its therapeutic effects. Taking a cold shower directly upon leaving the sweaty sauna is said to invigorate your circulation while also closing all your pores before you hit the icy waters of the plunge pool.

QUIET TIME

Given that spas are designed to be oases of wellness and relaxation, loud conversation is forbidden and even whispers—particularly in saunas, steam rooms, and relaxation lounges or reading rooms—may be met with sighs of disapproval or even a telling-off.

SPA GLOSSARY

Algae and mud therapy: Applied as packs or full-body bath treatments to nourish the skin and draw out toxins.

Aromatherapy baths: Oils such as bergamot, cypress, and sandalwood are added to hot baths in order to lift the spirits and reduce anxiety.

Ayurveda: Refers to Indian techniques including massage, oils, herbs, and diet to encourage perfect body balance.

Jet massage: Involves standing upright and being sprayed with high-pressure water jets that follow the direction of your blood flow, thereby stimulating circulation.

Liquid sound therapy: A relaxation technique that entails lying in body-temperature saltwater and listening to classical or electronic music being played through the water while a kaleidoscope of colors illuminates your surroundings.

Reflexology: Massage on the pressure points of feet, hands, and ears.

Thalassotherapy: A spa treatment employing sea air, water, and mud to heal the body.

7

Updated by
Courtney Tenz

A wood so dense that the sun couldn't penetrate the thick pine trees—that's how the Black Forest—*Schwarzwald* in German—got its name. Stretching west to the Rhine River and south into the Alpine foothills in Switzerland, this southwest corner of Baden-Württemberg (in the larger region known as Swabia) has one of Germany's most beautiful natural landscapes.

The Romans arrived in southern Germany nearly 2,000 years ago, bringing with them a spa culture that has remained since the Roman emperor Caracalla and his army rested and soothed their battle wounds in the natural-spring waters at what later became Baden-Baden. Though the area changed hands several times over the course of history, the Black Forest really came into its own in the 19th century, as the dark woods opened up to the outside world.

Europe's upper-crust society discovered Baden-Baden when it convened nearby for the Congress of Rastatt from 1797 to 1799, which attempted to end the wars of the French Revolution. In the 19th century kings, queens, emperors, princes, princesses, members of Napoléon's family, and the Russian nobility, along with actors, writers, and composers, flocked to the little spa town. Turgenev, Dostoyevsky, and Tolstoy were among the Russian contingent. Victor Hugo was a frequent visitor. Brahms composed lilting melodies in this calm setting. Queen Victoria spent her vacations here. Mark Twain put the Black Forest on the map for Americans by stating, "Here . . . you lose track of time in ten minutes and the world in twenty," in his 1880 book *A Tramp Abroad*.

While today the city has become a favorite getaway for movie stars and millionaires, it's the national park surrounding Baden-Baden that is the area's biggest draw for the everyday traveler. Within its protected areas, an adventurous sporting scene has sprouted, with possibilities for kayaking, biking, and hiking. The Schwarzwald-Verein, an outdoors association in the region, maintains no fewer than 30,000 km (18,000 miles) of hiking trails. In winter the terrain is ideally suited for cross-country skiing. A river cruise along the Rhine is worthwhile at any time of year, with its unique perspective on the landscape.

PLANNING

WHEN TO GO

The Black Forest is one of the most visited mountain regions in Europe and despite its name, one of the sunniest places in Germany. Be sure to make reservations well in advance for spas and hotels, especially from June to August. The area around Titisee is particularly crowded then. In early fall and late spring, when the weather turns more temperate, the Black Forest is less crowded, but just as beautiful. Some hotels in small towns close for a month or so in winter so be sure to check ahead.

GETTING HERE AND AROUND

AIR TRAVEL

The closest international airport in Germany is Frankfurt. Strasbourg, in neighboring French Alsace, and the Swiss border city of Basel, the latter just 70 km (43 miles) from Freiburg, are also reasonably close. An up-and-coming airport is the Baden-Airpark, now known more commonly as Karlsruhe-Baden, near Baden-Baden. It is used by European budget carriers including Ryanair (⊕ *www.ryanair.com*) and Air Berlin (⊕ *www.airberlin.com*), serving short-haul international destinations such as London, Dublin, and Barcelona.

Airport Information Aeroport International de Strasbourg. ✉ *Strasbourg* ☎ 00333/8864–6767 ⊕ www.strasbourg.aeroport.fr. **EuroAirport Basel-Mulhouse-Freiburg.** ✉ *Saint Louis Cedex* ☎ 0389/903–111 ⊕ www.euroairport.com. **Flughafen Frankfurt Main.** ✉ *Frankfurt* ☎ 01805/372–4636 ⊕ www.frankfurt-airport.de. **Karlsruhe-Baden.** ✉ *Halifax Ave.* ☎ 07229/662–000 ⊕ www.badenairpark.de.

BUS TRAVEL

A number of long-distance bus lines have opened up in recent years, including the Post Bus, Eurolines, and Flix Bus. Regionally, the bus system is partially owned by and coordinated with the German Railways, so it's easy to reach every corner of the Black Forest by bus and train. Regional bus stations are usually at or near the train station. For more information, contact the Regionalbusverkehr Südwest (Regional Bus Lines) in Karlsruhe.

Bus Information Regionalbusverkehr Südwest (*Regional Bus Lines*). ✉ *Karlsruhe* ☎ 0721/84060 ⊕ www.suedwestbus.de.

CAR TRAVEL

The main autobahns are the A-5 (Frankfurt–Karlsruhe–Basel), which runs through the Rhine Valley along the western length of the Black Forest; A-81 (Stuttgart–Bodensee) in the east; and A-8 (Karlsruhe–Stuttgart) in the north. Good two-lane highways crisscross the entire region. B-3 runs parallel to A-5 and follows the Baden Wine Road. Traffic jams on weekends and holidays are not uncommon. Taking the side roads might not save time, but they are a lot prettier. The Schwarzwald-Hochstrasse is one of the area's most scenic routes, running from

Freudenstadt to Baden-Baden. The region's tourist office has mapped out thematic driving routes: the Valley Road, the Spa Road, the Baden Wine Road, the Asparagus Road, and the Clock Road. Most points along these routes can also be reached by train or bus.

Freiburg, the region's major city, is 275 km (170 miles) south of Frankfurt and 410 km (254 miles) west of Munich.

TRAIN TRAVEL

Karlsruhe, Baden-Baden, and Freiburg are served by fast ICE trains zipping between Frankfurt-am-Main and Basel in Switzerland. Regional express trains also link these hubs with many other places locally, including Freudenstadt, Titisee, and, in particular, the spectacular climb from Baden-Baden to Triberg, one of the highest railroads in Germany.

Local lines connect most of the smaller towns. Two east–west routes—the Schwarzwaldbahn (Black Forest Railway) and the Höllental Railway—are among the most spectacular in the country. Many small towns participate in the KONUS program that allows you to travel for free on many Black Forest train lines while staying in the region. Details are available from Deutsche Bahn.

Train Information Deutsche Bahn. ☎ 11861 ⊕ www.bahn.de.

RESTAURANTS

Restaurants in the Black Forest range from award-winning dining rooms to simple country inns. Old *Kachelöfen* (tile stoves) are still in use in many area restaurants; try to sit near one if it's cold outside.

Prices in the reviews are the average cost of a main course at dinner, or if dinner is not served, at lunch.

HOTELS

Accommodations in the Black Forest are varied and plentiful, from simple rooms in farmhouses to five-star luxury. Some properties have been passed down in the same family for generations. *Gasthöfe* offer low prices and local color. Keep in mind that many hotels in the region do not offer air-conditioning.

Prices in the reviews are the lowest cost of a standard double room in high season. For expanded reviews, facilities, and current deals, visit Fodors.com.

WHAT IT COSTS IN EUROS			
	$	$$	$$$	$$$$
Restaurants	under €15	€15–€20	€21–€25	over €25
Hotels	under €100	€100–€175	€176–€225	over €225

PLANNING YOUR TIME

The lively, student-driven city of Freiburg, Germany's "greenest" town, is the largest, most obvious base from which to explore the Black Forest, but you may do well to stay in one of the smaller nearby villages in Kaiserstuhl or Titisee, where the accommodations are nicer and the scenery more breathtaking. Don't miss "taking the waters" at a spa in Baden-Baden, a charming place with loads of cultural offerings and luxury to spare. Bear in mind that the winding, often steep Black Forest highways can make for slow driving, so you may want to consider adding overnight stays at other locations. Freudenstadt's vast market square lends it a uniquely pleasant atmosphere, and Triberg's mountain location is picturesque. Baiersbronn has gained a reputation as one of the country's leading high-end resort towns, with good reason. If there is one place in the region to go out of your way to get a beer, head to Alpirsbach.

TOURS

Bicycles can be rented in nearly all towns and many villages, as well as at the Deutsche Bahn train stations. Several regional tourist offices sponsor tours on which the biker's luggage is transported separately from one overnight stop to the next and you may be able to secure an e-bike for a bit of help in getting up the hills. Six- to 10-day tours are available at reasonable rates, including bed-and-breakfast and bike rental. This region is also ideal for hikers. Similar to the bike tours, *Wandern ohne Gepäck* (hike without luggage) tours are available; get details from tourist offices.

VISITOR INFORMATION

Schwarzwald Tourismus GmbH. ⊠ *Hapsburger Str. 132, Freiburg* ☎ *0761/896–460* ⊕ *www.schwarzwald-tourismus.info.*

THE NORTHERN BLACK FOREST

This region is densely wooded, and dotted with little lakes such as the Mummelsee and the Wildsee. The Black Forest Spa Route (270 km [168 miles]) links many of the spas in the region, from Baden-Baden (the best known) to Bad Wildbad. Other regional treasures are the lovely Nagold River; ancient towns such as Hirsau; and the magnificent abbey at Maulbronn, near Pforzheim.

PFORZHEIM

35 km (22 miles) southeast of Karlsruhe, just off the A-8 autobahn, the main Munich–Karlsruhe route.

Although Pforzheim is not exactly the attractive place the Romans found at the junction of three rivers—the Nagold, the Enz, and the Würm—it is the "gateway to the Black Forest." Pforzheim still owes its prosperity to its role in Europe's jewelry trade and its wristwatch industry. To get a sense of the "Gold City," explore the jewelry shops on streets around Leopoldplatz and the pedestrian area.

GETTING HERE AND AROUND

Connected with a twice-hourly InterCity train as well as to the Karlsruhe Stadtbahn network, Pforzheim is easily accessible for those coming south from nearby Karlsruhe or north from Stuttgart. Once there, buses that stop at the ZOB southeast of the main train station can take you to major stops across the city.

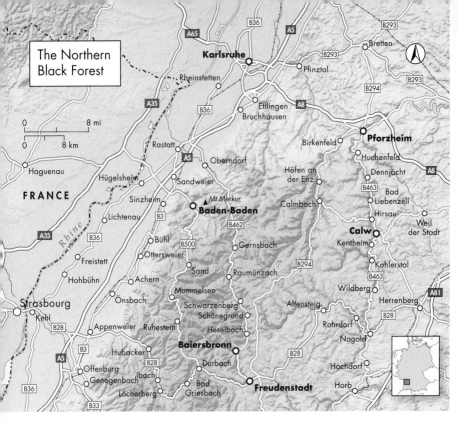

The Northern
Black Forest

ESSENTIALS

Visitor Information Tourist-Information Pforzheim. ✉ *Schlossberg 15–17*
☎ *07231/393–700* ⊕ *www.pforzheim.de.*

EXPLORING

Gasometer Pforzheim. A former gas storage tank has been converted into
a work of art, inside which artist Yadegar Asisi has created a 360-degree
panoramic view of Rome in the year 312 spanning 3,500 square meters.
You can ascend a platform to view the artwork from above while a special sound-and-light show immerses you in the ancient times represented
below. ✉ *Hohwiesenweg 6* ☎ *07231/776–0997* ⊕ *www.gasometer-
pforzheim.de* 🎟 *€11.*

Kloster Maulbronn (*Maulbronn Monastery*). The little town of Maulbronn, 18 km (11 miles) northeast of Pforzheim, is home to the best-
preserved medieval monastery north of the Alps, with an entire complex
of 30 buildings on UNESCO's World Heritage list. The name Maulbronn (Mule Fountain) derives from a legend. Monks seeking a suitably
watered site for their monastery considered it a sign from God when
one of their mules discovered and drank at a spring. The Kloster is
also known for inventing the *Maultasche*, a kind of large ravioli. The
monks thought that by coloring the meat filling green by adding parsley and wrapping it inside a pasta pocket, they could hide it from God

on fasting days. Today the maultasche is the cornerstone of Swabian cuisine. An audio guide in English is available. ✉ *Off B-35, Klosterhof 5, Maulbronn* ☎ *07043/926–610* 🌐 *www.kloster-maulbronn.de* 🎫 *€7* 🕒 *Mar.–Oct., daily 9–5:30; Nov.–Feb., Tues.–Sun. 9:30–5; guided tours daily at 11:15 and 3.*

St. Michael's Church. The restored church of St. Michael, near the train station, is the final resting place of Baden royalty. The original mixture of 13th- and 15th-century styles has been faithfully reproduced; compare the airy Gothic choir with the church's sturdy Romanesque entrance. A museum dedicated to the life of Johannes Reuchlin, one of Europe's greatest humanists, is attached. ✉ *Schlossberg 10* 🕒 *May–Sept., weekdays 9–6; Oct.–Apr., weekdays 3–6.*

Schmuckmuseum (*Jewelry Museum*). The Reuchlinhaus, the city's cultural center, houses this collection of jewelry, which, with pieces from five millennia, is one of the finest in the world. The museum nearly doubled in size in 2006, adding pocket watches and ethnographic jewelry to its collection, plus a shop, a café, and a gem gallery where young designers exhibit and sell their work. Guided tours in English are available on request. ✉ *Jahnstr. 42* ☎ *07231/392–126* 🌐 *www.schmuckmuseum-pforzheim.de* 🎫 *€3* 🕒 *Tues.–Sun. 10–5.*

Technisches Museum (*Technical Museum*). Pforzheim has long been known as a center of the German clock-making industry. In the Technisches Museum, one of the country's leading museums devoted to the craft, you can see makers of watches and clocks at work; there's also a reconstructed 18th-century clock factory. ✉ *Bleichstr. 81* ☎ *07231/392–869* 🌐 *www.technisches-museum.de* 🎫 *Free* 🕒 *Wed. 2–5, Sun. 10–5.*

WHERE TO EAT

$$$$
MODERN FRENCH

🍴 **Chez Gilbert.** The Alsatian owners of this cozy restaurant serve classic French-inspired cuisine, using the freshest local seasonal ingredients. The menu and wine lists are relatively small, but from the moment you're greeted by Frau Nosser until the time you leave, you'll be convinced that everything was planned just for you. The best bet is one of the seasonal four-course menus for €57. If you must dine à la carte, try the duck with raspberries or the foie gras with peaches. [$] *Average main: €28* ✉ *Altstädter Kirchenweg 3* ☎ *07231/441–159* 🌐 *www.chez-gilbert.de* 🕒 *Closed Mon. and 2 wks in Aug. No dinner Sun.*

CALW

28 km (17 miles) south of Pforzheim on B-463.

Calw, one of the Black Forest's prettiest towns, is the birthplace of Nobel Prize–winning novelist Hermann Hesse (1877–1962). The town's market square, with its two sparkling fountains, is surrounded by 18th-century half-timber houses whose sharp gables pierce the sky. It's an ideal spot for relaxing, picnicking, or people-watching, especially during market time.

GETTING HERE AND AROUND

Calw is best reached by car as it's no longer serviced by trains. Bus connections to nearby destinations, including Weil and Boebelingen, are available daily by several companies, including the Deutsche Bahn's Südwest Bus.

ESSENTIALS

Visitor Information **Stadtinformation Calw.** ⊠ *Sparkassenpl. 2* ☏ *07051/167–399* ⊕ *www.calw.de.*

EXPLORING

Hermann Hesse Museum. The museum recounts the life of the Nobel Prize–winning writer Hermann Hesse, author of *Steppenwolf* and *Siddharta*, who rebelled against his middle-class German upbringing to become a pacifist and the darling of the Beat Generation. The museum tells the story of his life in personal belongings, photographs, manuscripts, and other documents. ⊠ *Marktpl. 30* ☏ *07051/7522* ⊕ *www.calw.de/museum-hermann-hesse* ⊡ *€5* ⊗ *Apr.–Oct., Tues.–Sun. 11–5; Nov.–Mar., Tues.–Thurs. and weekends 11–4. Guided tours Fri. by appointment.*

Hirsau. 3 km (2 miles) north of Calw, Hirsau has ruins of a 9th-century monastery, now the setting for the Klostersummer (open-air concerts) in July and August. Buy advance tickets at the Calw tourist office. ⊠ *Calw* ⊕ *www.klostersommer.de.*

WHERE TO STAY

$$
HOTEL
Hotel Kloster Hirsau. A model of comfort and gracious hospitality, this hotel is in Hirsau, 3 km (2 miles) from Calw. **Pros:** quiet location; homey atmosphere. **Cons:** a bit out of town. ⓢ *Rooms from: €124* ⊠ *Hirsau, Wildbaderstr. 2* ☏ *07051/96740* ⊕ *www.hotel-kloster-hirsau.de* ⌑ *42 rooms* ⦿ *Breakfast.*

$
HOTEL
Ratsstube. Most of the original features, including 16th-century beams and brickwork, are preserved at this historic house in the center of Calw, next to Hesse's birthplace. **Pros:** great location overlooking historic market square; beautiful old half-timber building. **Cons:** parking around the corner; some rooms quite small; historic building means no elevator. ⓢ *Rooms from: €70* ⊠ *Marktpl. 12* ☏ *07051/92050* ⊕ *www.hotel-ratsstube-calw.de* ⌑ *13 rooms* ⦿ *Breakfast.*

FREUDENSTADT

65 km (40 miles) south of Calw, 22 km (14 miles) southwest of Altensteig.

At an altitude of 2,400 feet, Freudenstadt claims to be the "better climate" in Germany and it has the sunny days to prove it. Founded in 1599 by Duke Frederick I of Württemberg, the "city of joy" has the country's largest market square, more than 650 feet long and edged with arcaded shops. The square still awaits the palace that was supposed to be built here for the city's founder, who died before its construction began, though it is difficult to admire its vastness, since a busy, four-lane street cuts it nearly in half. The city's location along three scenic driving routes (the Valley Route, the Spa Route, and the Black Forest Mountain

Route) makes it an ideal place for an overnight stay. ■ TIP→ **When the fountains all spout on this square, it can be quite a sight, and a refreshing one as well.**

GETTING HERE AND AROUND

Freudenstadt is served by regular trains from both Karlsruhe and Stuttgart. The huge main square makes the city feel larger than it actually is. The central zone can easily be covered on foot.

ESSENTIALS

Visitor Information Freudenstadt. ✉ *Marktpl. 64* ☎ *07441/8640* 🌐 *www.freudenstadt.de.*

EATING WELL IN THE BLACK FOREST

Don't pass up the chance to try *Schwarzwälder Schinken* (pinecone-smoked ham) and *Schwarzwälder Kirschtorte* (a dense layered cake with chocolate sponge soaked in cherry liqueur and covered in a fluffy whipped-cream frosting). *Kirschwasser,* locally called *Chriesewässerle* (from the French *cerise,* meaning "cherry"), is cherry brandy, the most famous of the region's excellent schnapps varieties. If traveling from May to June, keep an eye out for the "king of vegetables," white asparagus. Most restaurants create special menus that feature this locally grown delicacy.

EXPLORING

Stadtkirche. Don't miss Freudenstadt's Protestant Stadtkirche, a Gothic-influenced Renaissance church just off the Market Square. Its lofty L-shaped nave is a rare architectural feature built in 1608, constructed this way so that male and female worshippers would be separated and unable to see each other during services. ✉ *Marktpl. 36* 🎟 *Free* 🕑 *Daily 9–7.*

WHERE TO EAT

$ GERMAN 🍴 **Berghütte Lauterbad.** A traditional mountain hut, set in the woods and run by the nearby Hotel Lauterbad, this restaurant has an outdoor seating area and a beautiful panoramic view that you can enjoy while munching regional delicacies after a hike. [$] *Average main: €10* ✉ *Am Zollernblick 1* ☎ *07441/950–990* 💳 *No credit cards.*

$ GERMAN 🍴 **Turmbräu Freudenstädter.** Lots of wood paneling, exposed beams, and a sprinkling of old sleds and hay wagons give this place, right on the main square, its rustic atmosphere. So do the large brass kettle and the symphony of pipes that produce the establishment's own beer. The restaurant serves hearty solid local fare, including the Alsatian flatbread *Flammkuchen,* and a kebab of various types of meat marinated in wheat beer. Fondue is offered on Wednesday. Part of the restaurant turns into a disco on weekends. [$] *Average main: €11* ✉ *Brauhaus am Markt, Marktpl. 64* ☎ *07441/905–121* 🌐 *www.turmbraeu.de.*

$$$ GERMAN 🍴 **Warteck.** The leaded windows with stained glass, vases of flowers, and beautifully upholstered banquettes create a bright setting in the two dining rooms of this hotel. The chef uses only organic products and spotlights individual ingredients. The various seasonal menus (€40) are always a good choice. Top off the meal with one of the many types of schnapps on offer. [$] *Average main: €25* ✉ *Stuttgarterstr. 14* ☎ *07441/91920* 🌐 *www.warteck-freudenstadt.de/* 🕑 *Closed Tues. No lunch.*

WHERE TO STAY

$ **Bären.** The Montigels have owned this sturdy old hotel and restau-
HOTEL rant, just two minutes from the marketplace, since 1878, and the family
strives to maintain tradition with personal service. **Pros:** great central
location; friendly atmosphere. **Cons:** some rooms on the small side;
restaurant doesn't serve lunch and is closed Sunday. *$ Rooms from:
€80 ⊠ Langestr. 33 ☏ 07441/2729 ⊕ www.hotel-baeren-freudenstadt.
de ⤳ 33 rooms ❍❙ Breakfast.*

$ **Hotel Adler.** This simple hotel sits between the main square and the
HOTEL train station, and some of the very affordable rooms even have bal-
conies, so you can enjoy a view of behind-the-scenes Freudenstadt.
Pros: friendly; informal; centrally located. **Cons:** some rooms are small;
furnishings are from 1970s and quite modest. *$ Rooms from: €82
⊠ Forststr. 15–17 ☏ 07441/91520 ⊕ www.adler-fds.de ⤳ 16 rooms
❍❙ Breakfast.*

$ **Hotel Schwanen.** This bright, white building just a few steps from the
HOTEL main square has one guest room with a waterbed for those with allergies
and an extra-large suite for those traveling with kids. **Pros:** great location; excellent-value restaurant. **Cons:** no elevator in historic building.
*$ Rooms from: €99 ⊠ Forststr. 6 ☏ 07441/91550 ⊕ www.schwanen-
freudenstadt.de ⤳ 17 rooms, 1 family suite ❍❙ Breakfast.*

SHOPPING

Germans prize Black Forest ham (*Schwarzwaldschinken*) as an aromatic
souvenir, although visitors from North America will not be permitted
to bring one back home. Be content, instead, with the vacation experience, especially when planning a picnic. You can buy the ham at any
butcher shop in the region, but it's more fun to visit a *Schinkenräucherei*
(smokehouse), where it is actually cured in a stone chamber. By law, the
ham must be smoked over pinecones.

Hermann Wein. In the village of Musbach, near Freudenstadt, this is
one of the leading smokehouses in the area. If you have a group of
people, call ahead to find out if the staff can show you around. If you
are looking for Black Forest ham, this is the place to go. ⊠ Dornstet-
terstr. 29 ☏ 07443/2450 ⊕ www.schinken-wein.de ☾ Weekdays 7:30–6,
Sat. 7:30–1.

BAIERSBRONN

6 km (4 miles) northwest of Freudenstadt.

The mountain resort of Baiersbronn—actually comprised of nine separate villages, all named after the valleys they inhabit—has become a
high-end destination thanks to an incredible collection of hotels and
bed-and-breakfasts providing not only rest and relaxation in beautiful
surroundings, but also a gourmet experience. With eight Michelin stars
among three of the restaurants and spa resorts, the village has become
a favorite location to unwind and indulge in culinary delights—head
to the Bareiss Restaurant, the Restaurant Schlossberg, or the Schwar-
zwaldstube, all in area hotels. The natural surroundings in the midst
of the national park make this an ideal place to walk, ski, golf, and
ride horseback.

GETTING HERE AND AROUND

On one of the most scenic roads in all of Germany, the Hochschwarzwaldstrasse (High Black Forest Highway), Baiersbronn is best accessed by car. There is also regular weekday regional train service every two hours from nearby Karlsruhe.

ESSENTIALS

Visitor Information Baiersbronn Touristik. ✉ *Rosenpl. 3* ☎ *07442/84140* 🌐 *www.baiersbronn.de.*

EXPLORING

FAMILY **Hauffs Märchenmuseum** (*Fairy-Tale Museum*). Near the town hall and church in the upper part of town is the little Hauffs Märchenmuseum, devoted to the crafts and life around Baiersbronn and the fairy-tale author Wilhelm Hauff (1802–27). ✉ *Alte Reichenbacherstr. 1* ☎ *07442/84140* 🎟 *€1.50* 🕒 *Mid-Dec.–mid-Nov., Wed. and weekends 2–5.*

WHERE TO STAY

$$$$ RESORT Fodor's Choice ★ 🏨 **Bareiss.** This luxury hotel has won numerous awards since its founding by Hermione Bareiss in 1951 and continues to impress, recently being noted as one of the top 10 hotels in Europe and number two in Germany. **Pros:** beautiful, secluded location; relaxing facilities; friendly, competent staff; excellent restaurants. **Cons:** expensive; credit cards only accepted in the restaurants and shops; hotel must be paid by check, debit card, or cash. [$] *Rooms from: €470* ✉ *Gärtenbühlweg 14, Mitteltal* ☎ *07442/470* 🌐 *www.bareiss.com* 💳 *No credit cards* 🛏 *99 rooms* 🍴 *Some meals.*

$$ HOTEL FAMILY 🏨 **Hotel-Café Sackmann.** This imposing cluster of white houses, set in the narrow Murg Valley north of Baiersbronn, has broad appeal—families can nest here thanks to children's programs, wellness-seekers can take advantage of the spa facilities on the roof, and sightseers can use this as a base for exploring much of the Black Forest. **Pros:** good for families; beautiful location; gourmet restaurant on-site. **Cons:** payment for accommodations only by cash or certain debit cards (credit cards are accepted in the restaurant only). [$] *Rooms from: €170* ✉ *Murgtalstr. 602, Schwarzenberg* ☎ *07447/2980* 🌐 *www.hotel-sackmann.de* 🛏 *65 rooms* 🍴 *Breakfast.*

$$ HOTEL 🏨 **Hotel Lamm.** The steep-roof exterior of this 200-year-old typical Black Forest building offers an unmistakable clue to the heavy oak fittings and fine antiques inside. **Pros:** beautiful traditional building; friendly staff. **Cons:** can feel remote in winter. [$] *Rooms from: €120* ✉ *Ellbacherstr. 4, Mitteltal* ☎ *07442/4980* 🌐 *www.lamm-mitteltal.de* 🛏 *33 rooms, 13 apartments* 🍴 *Breakfast.*

$$$$ HOTEL FAMILY Fodor's Choice ★ 🏨 **Traube Tonbach.** Dating from 1778, this luxurious hotel is true to the original, yet the rooms, each of which presents a sweeping view of the Black Forest, meet contemporary standards, and the spa and swimming pool area, along with on-site child care, creates an air of relaxation. **Pros:** beautiful countryside setting; friendly and efficient staff; good choice of dining. **Cons:** expensive; credit cards only accepted in the restaurants, not in the hotel. [$] *Rooms from: €249* ✉ *Tonbachstr. 237* ☎ *07442/4920* 🌐 *www.traube-tonbach.de* 💳 *No credit cards* 🛏 *135 rooms, 12 suites, 23 apartments* 🍴 *Breakfast.*

BADEN-BADEN

51 km (32 miles) north of Freudenstadt, 24 km (15 miles) north of Mummelsee.

Fodor'sChoice
★

Perhaps best known as Europe's most fashionable spa town, Baden-Baden is more than its name implies. With a storied history, original 19th-century French-influenced architecture, world-class cultural offerings, and a sunny location in a valley at the edge of the Black Forest, the city has more to offer than just a relaxing soak. It sits atop extensive underground hot springs and can trace its spa heritage back to the time of the Roman emperor Caracalla, whose legions discovered the springs and named the area Aquae Aureliae. The ruins of these Roman baths can still be seen in the city center, next to the more modern Friedrichsbad and Caracalla Therme, two spas that continue to attract visitors to the area.

In the 19th century, Baden-Baden began to attract the upper classes from around Europe, thanks to its comfortable climate. Seeking leisurely pursuits, cultural heavyweights, including Richard Wagner and Fyodor Dostoyevsky, joined many European royal families in their unofficial summer residence. Palatial homes and stately villas from that time survived unscathed by the war, gracing the tree-lined avenues; the spa tradition continues at many of the city's resorts, making it a nice last stop on the way home, as Baden-Baden is just 1½ hours from Frankfurt Airport by train.

Though some may come here for the spas, the city has also made a name for itself as a cultural power player. As home to Europe's second-largest festival hall, the Festspielhaus—a concert hall originally planned by Richard Wagner before King Ludwig convinced him to construct in Bayreuth—Baden-Baden hosts some of the world's best symphonies, opera singers, and ballet troupes each year, from St. Petersburg's Mariinsky Ballet to the Berlin Philharmonie to violin soloist Anne-Sophie Mutter. Four museums add to the city's unique cultural repertoire.

GETTING HERE AND AROUND

High-speed ICE trains stop at Baden-Baden en route between Frankfurt and Basel. The station is some 4 km (2½ miles) northwest of the center. To get downtown, take one of the many buses that leave from outside the station. Once in the center, Baden-Baden is manageable on foot, but there is a range of alternatives available if you get tired, including a hop-on, hop-off tourist train and horse-drawn carriages.

ESSENTIALS

Visitor Information Baden-Baden Tourism. ⊠ *Schwarzwaldstr. 52*
✚ *Trinkhalle* ☎ *07221/275–200* ⊕ *www.baden-baden.de.*

EXPLORING

TOP ATTRACTIONS

Casino. Germany's oldest casino, this testament to 19th-century decadence was the brainchild of Parisian Jacques Bénazet, who persuaded the sleepy little Black Forest spa town to build gambling rooms to enliven its evenings after gambling was banned in France (just 10 km [6 miles] away). Opened in 1855, the sumptuous interior was modeled on

Baden-Baden's Festspielhaus (Festival Hall) hosts concerts, operas, and ballets throughout the year; outside is a sculpture by Henry Moore.

Versailles, right down to the Pompadour Room, home to a "practice" roulette table, and the luminous Winter Garden, with white marble and antique Chinese vases. The richly decorated gaming rooms could make even an emperor feel at home—Kaiser Wilhelm I was a regular patron, as was his chancellor, Bismarck. Russian novelist Dostoyevsky related his experiences here in his novella, *The Gambler*, and Marlene Dietrich reputedly called it the best casino in the world. Passports are necessary as proof of identity. Come in the morning before the doors open to players for a guided tour (40 minutes), available in English on request. To play, see Nightlife for further information. ⊠ *Kaiserallee 1* ☎ *07221/30240* ⊕ *www.casino-baden-baden.de* ⊠ *Tour €6* ⊗ *Sun.– Thurs. 2 pm–2 am, Fri. and Sat. 2 pm–3:30 am. Tours Apr.–Oct., daily 9:30, 10:15, 11, 11:45 am; Nov.–Mar., daily 10, 10:45, 11:30 am.*

Russian church. The sandstone church is on the corner of Robert Koch-strasse and Lichtentalerstrasse. The Russian diaspora community in Baden-Baden consecrated it in 1882; it's identifiable by its golden onion dome. ⊠ *Lichtentaler Str. 76* ⊠ *€1* ⊗ *Feb.–Nov., daily 10–6.*

WORTH NOTING

Fabergé Museum. The first museum dedicated to the work of Russian jeweler Carl Peter Fabergé holds up to 700 masterpieces from the private collection of Muscovite businessman A. Ivanov. Priceless pieces from the late 19th century include several of the 52 unique eggs gifted to members of Russian royalty, including the first of its kind, a modest egg made of white enamel inside of which a gold yolk, tiny chick, and diamond-emblazoned crown are nested. A Buddha made of nephrite—a green stone unique to Russia—with ruby eyes was originally a gift to the

King of Siam. Multilingual staff are on hand to explain the collection in detail. ⊠ *Sophienstr 30* ☎ *07221/970–890* ⊕ *www.faberge-museum. de* 🎟 *€18* ⊙ *Daily 10–6.*

Lichtentaler Allee. A well-groomed park bordering the slender Oos River, this green, tree-lined pedestrian boulevard is a perfect place to stroll, take in the atmosphere, and forget you're in a city. Lined with 19th-century villas, it's home to four museums and an extensive rose garden, the **Gönneranlage,** which contains more than 400 types of roses. ⊠ *Baden-Baden.*

Museum Frieder Burda. Built as an exhibition hall for the private collection of businessman Frieder Burda, this modern structure was created by acclaimed New York architect Richard Meier. Continually rotating, the private collection focuses on classic modern and contemporary art. Highlights include a number of pieces by Gerhard Richter as well as works by Picasso, German expressionists, the New York School, and American abstract expressionists. ⊠ *Lichtentaler Allee 8b* ☎ *07221/398–980* ⊕ *www.museum-frieder-burda.de* 🎟 *€12* ⊙ *Tues.– Sun. 11–6.*

Rebland Vineyard Region. The soft slopes between the Rhine plains and the Black Forest on the outskirts of Baden-Baden enjoy a mild climate that's perfect for the vineyards growing Riesling here. A part of the Baden Wine Route, the Rebland area is home to a number of small, family-run vineyards that offer tours and tastings. ⊠ *Mauerburgstr. 32* ☎ *07223/96870 to arrange group tours at any member of the wine growers association* ⊕ *www.baden-badener-wg.de.*

Römische Badruinen. The remains of the original Roman settlement and a brief history of spa culture from the 1st century AD can be seen at the Römische Badruinen, next to the present-day thermal baths. ⊠ *Römerpl. 1, 76530* 🎟 *€2.50* ⊙ *Mar.–Nov., daily 11–1 and 2–5.*

WHERE TO EAT

$$$$ ✕ **Le Jardin de France.** This clean, crisp little French restaurant, whose
FRENCH owners are actually French, emphasizes elegant, imaginative dining in a modern setting. The restaurant sits in a quiet courtyard away from the main street, offering the possibility of alfresco dining in summer. The milk-fed suckling pig and Russian dishes are well worth the visit. It also runs a school for budding chefs. $ *Average main: €40* ⊠ *Lichtentalerstr. 13* ☎ *07221/300–7860* ⊕ *www.lejardindefrance.de* ⊙ *Closed Sun. and Mon. Mar.–Dec.; closed Sun.–Tues. Jan. and Feb. (except public holidays).*

$$ ✕ **Rizzi.** This trendy lounge with an eclectic menu featuring everything
FUSION from Italian ravioli dishes to tuna steak has quickly become a beloved institution. The food is noteworthy, the modern interior complements the 19th-century palace housing it, and an enclosed patio gets crowded quickly on sunny days. Although the service could use a course in proper table etiquette, this is a see-and-be-seen kind of place. $ *Average main: €17* ⊠ *Augustapl. 1* ☎ *07221/25838* ⊕ *www.rizzi-baden-baden. de* ⊟ *No credit cards.*

$ ✕ **Weinstube im Baldreit.** This lively little wine bar enchants you with
WINE BAR its lovely terraces and courtyard. It's nestled in the middle of the Old

Town, making the garden and terrace the perfect place to meet friends over a dry Riesling. Enjoy some of the best *Maultaschen* (ravioli) and solid Black Forest cuisine near the fireplace in the huge barrel-vaulted cellar. [$] *Average main: €11* ✉ *Küferstr. 3* ☎ *07221/23136* ⏲ *Closed Sun. and Mon. No lunch.*

WHERE TO STAY

$$$$ HOTEL 🏨 **Brenner's Park Hotel & Spa.** This stately and exclusive hotel on the Lichtentaller Allee is one of Germany's most celebrated and storied retreats—a favorite of royalty, from Queen Victoria to Czar Alexander II, and their contemporaries. **Pros:** elegant rooms; good location; quiet. **Cons:** fellow guests can be aloof. [$] *Rooms from: €375* ✉ *Schillerstr. 6* ☎ *07221/9000* 🌐 *www.brenners.com* 🛏 *68 rooms, 32 suites* 🍴 *No meals.*

$$$ HOTEL Fodor's Choice ★ 🏨 **Der Kleine Prinz.** Owner Norbert Rademacher, a veteran of New York's Waldorf-Astoria, and his interior-designer wife, Edeltraud, have skillfully combined two elegant city mansions into a unique, antiques-filled lodging. **Pros:** friendly and welcoming staff; some rooms have wood-burning fireplaces; most bathrooms have whirlpool tubs. **Cons:** stairs; some rooms may get noisy. [$] *Rooms from: €199* ✉ *Lichtentalerstr. 36* ☎ *07221/346–600* 🌐 *www.derkleineprinz.de* 🛏 *24 rooms, 16 suites* 🍴 *Breakfast.*

$$$$ HOTEL Fodor's Choice ★ 🏨 **Hotel Belle Epoque.** Started by Norbert Rademacher after his lengthy stint in New York at hotels like the Waldorf-Astoria, this hotel reflects the beautiful era of its name, with large rooms, soaring ceilings, spacious beds, genuine antiques from Louis XV to art deco, luxurious baths, and a beautiful enclosed garden. **Pros:** beautiful gardens; room price includes breakfast and afternoon tea; personal and friendly service. **Cons:** only the newer wing has an elevator. [$] *Rooms from: €230* ✉ *Maria-Viktoriastr. 2c* ☎ *07221/300–660* 🌐 *www.hotel-belle-epoque.de* 🛏 *20 rooms* 🍴 *Breakfast.*

$ HOTEL 🏨 **Merkur.** The large, comfortable rooms here typify the high standards of German lodgings, and though it's in the middle of Baden-Baden, the setting is quiet. **Pros:** good deals for stays of three days or more; central location; quiet street. **Cons:** views not great. [$] *Rooms from: €98* ✉ *Merkurstr. 8* ☎ *07221/3030* 🌐 *www.hotel-merkur.com* 🛏 *34 rooms, 2 suites* 🍴 *Breakfast.*

NIGHTLIFE AND PERFORMING ARTS

Nightlife revolves around Baden-Baden's elegant **casino.**

NIGHTLIFE

Casino. The opulent rooms of the casino's lower floors overflow with the decadent atmosphere where many of the European elite have come to play. Try your hand at either French or American roulette, blackjack or Texas hold'em or plan your visit to coincide with one of the regular club nights appealing to younger crowds (21 and over only). Passports are required for entry and the dress code (jacket for men, no sneakers) must be strictly observed. ✉ *Kaiserallee 1* ☎ *07221/30240* 🌐 *www.casino-baden-baden.de* 🎟 *€5.*

Trinkhalle. Baden-Baden attracts a rather mature crowd, but the deep leather seats of the Trinkhalle make a hip lounge for those under age 40. At night this daytime bistro also takes over the portion of the hall

7

where the tourist office has a counter, transforming it into a dance floor. ⊠ *Kaiserallee 3*.

PERFORMING ARTS

Fodor's Choice ★ **Festspielhaus.** The entryway to Europe's second-largest performing arts center is the renovated former train station, whose grand foyer down to the ticketing window was retained. A modern, state-of-the-art theater with 2,500 seats and a 900-square-meter stage was attached where the former train tracks had once lain. More than 120 events annually draw culture lovers and performers from the world over, including violinist Anne-Sophie Mutter, John Neumeier's Hamburg Ballet, and the Berliner Philharmonie. ⊠ *Beim Alten Bahnhof 2* ☎ *07221/301–3101* ⊕ *www. festspielhaus.de*.

Kurhaus. The Kurhaus adjoining the casino is an intimate concert hall in an inspired venue that hosts classical music concerts year-round. ⊠ *Kaiserallee 1* ☎ *07221/353–202* ⊕ *www.kurhaus-baden-baden.de*.

Theater Baden-Baden. Baden-Baden has one of Germany's most beautiful performance halls in the Theater Baden-Baden, a late-baroque jewel built in 1860–62 in the style of the Paris Opéra. It opened with the world premiere of Berlioz's opera *Beatrice et Benedict*. Today the theater presents a regular series of dramas. ⊠ *Goethepl. 1* ☎ *07221/932– 700* ⊕ *www.theater.baden-baden.de*.

SPORTS AND THE OUTDOORS

HORSE RACING

Iffezheim. The racetrack at nearby Iffezheim harks back to the days when Baden-Baden was a magnet for royalty and aristocrats. Its tradition originated in 1858; now annual international meets take place in late May, late August/early September, and October, and the occasions call for attire similar to that worn at the Kentucky Derby, with a special hat shop on-site for those who arrive bare-headed. ⊠ *Rennbahnstr. 16, Iffezheim* ☎ *07229/1870*.

HORSEBACK RIDING

Reitzentrum Balg. Those wishing to ride can rent horses and get instruction at the Reitzentrum Balg. ⊠ *Buchenweg 42* ☎ *07221/55920*.

SHOPPING

SPAS

The history of "taking the waters" in Baden-Baden dates back to AD 75, when the Roman army established the city of Aquæ Aureliæ. The legions under Emperor Caracalla soon discovered that the region's salty underground hot springs were just the thing for aching joints.

In a modern sense, bathing became popular within the upper-class elite when Friedrich I banned gambling in 1872. Everyone from Queen Victoria to Karl Marx dangled their feet in the pool and sang the curative praises of the salty warm water bubbling from the ground.

FAMILY **Caracalla Therme.** Less of a relaxing "forget-the-outside-world" experience than the neighboring Friedrichsbad, the Caracalla Therme maintains a series of indoor–outdoor swimming pools with temperatures between 18°C and 38°C (64°F–100°F) that are ideal for the more modest traveler and those with families, since bathing suits are required here. Though children under seven are not allowed in the spa upstairs and those under 14 must be accompanied by an adult, the swimming area offers whirlpools, Jacuzzis, and waterfalls to complement the warm waters. A series of saunas on the upper level are clothing-free and provide an escape from the hustle and bustle of the pool area below. Be sure to bring your own robe and bath towel, as they are not a part of the package here. ⊠ *Römerpl. 1* ☎ *07221/275–940* ⊕ *www.carasana.de* 🖭 *€18 for 3 hrs* ☉ *Daily 8 am–10 pm* ☞ *Childcare also available on-site.*

Fodor's Choice **Friedrichsbad.** Also known as the Roman-Irish Baths, Friedrichsbad
★ offers a one-of-a-kind spa experience. With 17 stations that take you through warm and hot dry saunas, ice baths, and thermal pools, there is a method to the ultimate relaxation on offer. Housed in a building dating back to 1877, this "temple of well-being" was considered the most modern bathing establishment in Europe and its ornate copper and terra-cotta temple only adds to the unique ambience. As with all spas in Germany, this one is textile-free; the 3½-hour spa treatment package includes a honey peeling or soap-and-brush massage. Note that no cameras or children under 14 are allowed. ⊠ *Römerpl. 1* ☎ *07221/275–920* ⊕ *www.carasana.de* 🖭 *€59 for 4 hrs all-inclusive, €25 with no massage.* ☉ *Daily 9 am–10 pm* ☞ *Mixed bathing: Tues., Wed., Fri., and Sun; gender-separate bathing: Mon., Thurs., and Sat.*

KARLSRUHE

10 km (6 miles) north of Ettlingen.

Karlsruhe, founded at the beginning of the 18th century, is a young upstart, but what it lacks in years it makes up for in industrial and administrative importance, sitting as it does astride a vital autobahn and rail crossroads. It's best known as the seat of Germany's Supreme Court, and has a high concentration of legal practitioners.

GETTING HERE AND AROUND

The autobahn A-5 connects Freiburg, Baden-Baden, and Karlsruhe. Karlsruhe's train station is an easy 15-minute walk from the city center and trains run frequently throughout the region; south to Baden-Baden (15 minutes) and Freiburg (1 hour), and east to Pforzheim (25 minutes) and Frankfurt (1 hour).

ESSENTIALS

Visitor Information Tourist-Information Karlsruhe. ⊠ *Bahnhofpl. 6* ☎ *0721/3720–5383* ⊕ *www.karlsruhe-tourismus.de.*

EXPLORING

Badisches Landesmuseum (*Baden State Museum*). Housed in the Schloss Karlsruhe, this museum has a large number of Greek and Roman antiquities and trophies that Ludwig the Turk brought back from campaigns in Turkey in the 17th century. Most of the other exhibits are devoted to local history. ⊠ *Schloss, Schlossbezirk 10* ☎ *0721/926–6514* ⊕ *www.landesmuseum.de* 🖭 *€4; free after 2 pm Fri.* ☉ *Tues.–Thurs. 10–5, Fri.–Sun. 10–6.*

Schloss Karlsruhe. The town quite literally grew up around the former Schloss of the Margrave Karl Wilhelm, which was begun in 1715 and was in use for more than 200 years. Thirty-two avenues radiate from the palace, 23 leading into the extensive grounds, and the remaining nine forming the grid of the Old Town. Today, the palace is home to the Badisches Landmuseum. ✉ *Schlossbezirk 10.*

Staatliche Kunsthalle (*State Art Gallery*). One of the most important collections of paintings in the Black Forest region hangs in this gallery. Look for masterpieces by Grünewald, Holbein, Rembrandt, and Monet, and also for work by the Black Forest painter Hans Thoma. The **Kunsthalle Orangerie** next door houses work by such modern artists as Braque and Beckmann. ✉ *Hans-Thoma-Str. 2–6* ☎ *0721/926–3359* 🌐 *www.kunsthalle-karlsruhe.de* 🎟 *€12, includes both galleries* 🕓 *Tues.–Sun. 10–6.*

FAMILY **Zentrum für Kunst und Medientechnologie** (*Center for Art and Media Technology*). In a former munitions factory, the vast Zentrum für Kunst und Medientechnologie, or simply ZKM, is an all-day adventure consisting of two separate museums. At the **Medienmuseum** (Media Museum) you can watch movies, listen to music, try out video games, flirt with a virtual partner, or sit on a real bicycle and pedal through a virtual New York City. The **Museum für Neue Kunst** houses a top-notch collection of media art, in all genres, from the end of the 20th century.

✉ *Lorenzstr. 19* ☎ *0721/81000* 🌐 *www.zkm.de* 🎟 *€6 for one museum or €10 for both* 🕓 *Wed.–Fri. 10–6, weekends 11–6.*

WHERE TO STAY

$$ HOTEL 🏨 **Schlosshotel.** A few steps from the main station, the hotel exterior looks like a palace, and inside you'll find marble bathrooms and a mirrored elevator dating from 1914, but the guest rooms are pretty much in standard modern hotel style. **Pros:** friendly service; advance online booking can save up to €50. **Cons:** on a noisy street; modern rooms don't live up to the historic feel. [$] *Rooms from: €140* ✉ *Bahnhofpl. 2* ☎ *0721/38320* 🌐 *www.schlosshotel-karlsruhe.de* 🛏 *93 rooms, 3 suites* 🍴 *Breakfast; Some meals.*

PERFORMING ARTS

Badisches Staatstheater. One of the best opera houses in the region is Karlsruhe's Badisches Staatstheater, which also serves as a venue for the local theater troupe and ballet. ✉ *Baumeisterstr. 11* ☎ *0721/35570* 🌐 *www.staatstheater.karlsruhe.de.*

THE CENTRAL BLACK FOREST

The Central Black Forest is hilly, a rural forest that includes the Simonswald, Elz, and Glotter valleys as well as Triberg and Furtwangen. It's where the clichés all come together—pom-pom hats, thatch-roof farmhouses, and cuckoo clocks abound. The area around the Triberg Falls—the highest falls in Germany—is especially scenic. The Schwarzwaldbahn (Black Forest Railway; Offenburg–Villingen line), which passes through Triberg, is one of the most scenic in all of Europe.

ALPIRSBACH

16 km (10 miles) south of Freudenstadt.

The hamlet of Alpirsbach was founded in 1035 and developed around the Benedictine monastery Kloster Alpirsbach. Although the Reformation forced the abbey to close its doors in 1535, the tradition of brewing is still going strong. Locals claim that it's the pristine artesian water that makes the beer from the Alpirsbacher Klosterbräu (brewery) so incredible. The village maintains a preserved historic core with a fine collection of half-timber houses that only add to the charm.

GETTING HERE AND AROUND

Alpirsbach is on the direct train line between Freudenstadt and Offenburg, and is a great day trip by train from Freiburg (two hours with a change in Offenburg).

ESSENTIALS

Visitor Information Alpirsbach Tourist-Information. ✉ *Hauptstr. 20* ☎ *07444/951–6281* 🌐 *www.alpirsbach.de.*

EXPLORING

Brauerei Museum (*brewery*). The Brauerei was once part of the monastery, and has brewed beer since the Middle Ages. The unusually soft water gives the beer a flavor that is widely acclaimed. There are guided tours of the brewery museum daily at 2:30. If there is one place in Germany to go out of your way for a beer, Alpirsbach is it! ✉ *Marktpl. 1* ☎ *07444/67149* 🌐 *www.alpirsbacher.de* 🎟 *Tour €7* 🕓 *Mar.–Oct., weekdays 9:30–4:30, weekends 11–3; Nov.–Feb., daily 11–3.*

WHERE TO EAT

$ GERMAN 🍴 **Zwickel & Kaps.** The name is a highly sophisticated brewing term, describing the means by which the brewmaster samples the fermenting product. Sit down at one of the simple beech-wood tables and order a satisfying Swabian lentil stew with dumplings and sausages, or something more Mediterranean, such as salmon with pesto. All the pasta, bread, and sauces are house-made. [$] *Average main: €11* ✉ *Marktstr. 3* ☎ *07444/51727* 🕓 *No lunch. Closed Mon. and end Dec.–mid-Jan.*

GUTACH

17 km (11 miles) north of Triberg.

Gutach lies in Gutachtal, a valley famous for the traditional costumes, complete with pom-pom hats, worn by women on feast days and holidays. Married women wear black pom-poms, unmarried women red ones. The village is one of the few places in the Black Forest where you can still see thatch roofs. However, escalating costs caused by a decline in skilled thatchers, and soaring fire-insurance premiums, have made them rare.

GETTING HERE AND AROUND

Gutach is a 20-minute train ride from Freiburg. Trains leave once per hour.

7

EXPLORING

Schwarzwälder Freilichtmuseum Vogtsbauernhof (*Black Forest Open-Air Museum*). Near Gutach, this is one of the most appealing museums in the Black Forest. Farmhouses and other rural buildings from all parts of the region have been transported here and reassembled, complete with traditional furniture, to create a living-history museum of Black Forest architecture through the centuries. Demonstrations ranging from traditional dances to woodworking capture life as it was in centuries past; be sure to check the website for daily shows. ⊠ *B–33 Vogtsbauernhof* ☎ *07831/93560* ⊕ *www.vogtsbauernhof.org* ✉ *€8* ⊗ *Apr.–July, Sept., and Oct., daily 9–5; Aug., daily 9–6.*

TRIBERG

16 km (10 miles) south of Gutach.

The cuckoo clock, that symbol of the Black Forest, is at home in the Triberg area. It was invented here, it's made and sold here, it's featured in two museums, and the world's largest cuckoo clock is here.

GETTING HERE AND AROUND

Triberg is accessible via one of the prettiest train rides in Germany, with direct services to Lake Constance and Karlsruhe. The train station is at the lower end of the long main street, and the waterfalls are a stiff uphill walk away. You can take a bus up the hill from the train station to the entrance to the waterfalls, relieving most of the uphill struggle.

ESSENTIALS

Visitor Information Triberg Tourist-Information. ⊠ *Wahlfahrtstr. 4* ☎ *07722/866–490* ⊕ *www.triberg.de.*

EXPLORING

TOP ATTRACTIONS

Schwarzwaldbahn (*Black Forest Railway*). The Hornberg–Triberg–St. Georgen segment of the Schwarzwaldbahn is one of Germany's most scenic train rides. The 149-km (93-mile) Schwarzwaldbahn, built from 1866 to 1873, runs from Offenburg to Lake Constance via Triberg. It has no fewer than 39 tunnels, and at one point climbs almost 2,000 feet in just 11 km (6½ miles). It's now part of the German Railway, and you can make inquiries at any station. ⊠ *Triberg* ☎ *11861* ⊕ *www.bahn.de.*

Triberg Waterfalls. At the head of the Gutach Valley, the Gutach River plunges more than 500 feet over seven huge granite cascades at Triberg's waterfall, Germany's highest. The pleasant 45-minute walk from the center of town is well signposted. A longer walk goes by a small pilgrimage church and the old Mesnerhäuschen, the sacristan's house. You can do much of the hike free of charge but to climb to the top, you'll need to pay a fee. ⊠ *Friedrichstr.* ✉ *€4; €9 combined ticket with Schwarzwaldmuseum* ⊗ *Dawn–10 pm.*

WORTH NOTING

Eble Uhren-Park. Stop by on the hour to see the world's largest cuckoo clock, the size of a house, in action. It is also possible, for a small fee, to step inside and examine the works. In the gift shop at this huge store, you can buy a cuckoo clock, or just about any other timepiece

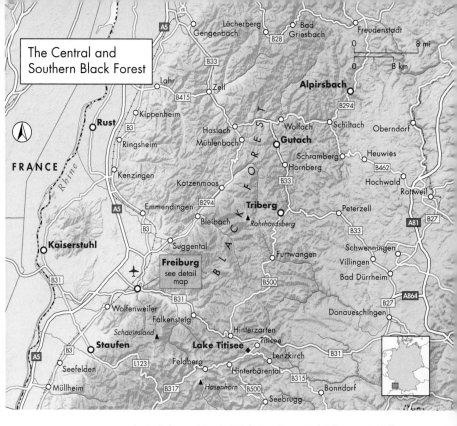

The Central and Southern Black Forest

or souvenir. ⊠ *Schonachbach 27* ⊕ *On Hwy. B-33 between Triberg and Hornberg, about 3 km (2 miles) from Triburg in the district of Shonachbach* ☎ *07722/96220* ⊕ *www.eble-uhren-park.de* ⊠ *€2 to go inside the clock* ☉ *Apr.–Oct., Mon.–Sat. 9–6, Sun. 10–6; Nov.–Mar., Mon.–Sat. 9–5:30, Sun. 10:30–5.*

Hubert Herr. This is the only factory that continues to make nearly all of its own components for its cuckoo clocks. The present proprietors are the fifth generation from Andreas and Christian Herr, who began making the clocks more than 150 years ago. The company produces a great variety of clocks, including one that, at 5¼ inches high, is claimed to be "the world's smallest." ⊠ *Hauptstr. 8* ☎ *07722/4268* ⊕ *www.hubertherr. de* ☉ *Weekdays 9–noon and 1:30–4.*

Schwarzwaldmuseum (*Black Forest Museum*). Triberg's famous Schwarzwaldmuseum is a treasure trove of the region's traditional arts: wood carving, costumes, and handicrafts. The Schwarzwaldbahn is described, with historical displays and a working model. The Black Forest was also a center of mechanical music, and, among many other things, the museum has an "Orchestrion"—a cabinet full of mechanical instruments playing like an orchestra. ⊠ *Wallfahrtstr. 4* ☎ *07722/4434* ⊕ *www.schwarzwaldmuseum.de* ⊠ *€6* ☉ *Apr.–Sept., daily 10–6; Oct.–Mar., Tues.–Sun. 10–5.*

**OFF THE
BEATEN
PATH** **Stadtmuseum.** Rottweil, 26 km (16 miles) east of Triberg, has the best of the Black Forest's Fasnet celebrations, which here are pagan, fierce, and steeped in tradition. In the days just before Ash Wednesday, usually in February, "witches" and "devils" roam the streets wearing ugly wooden masks and making fantastic gyrations as they crack whips and ring bells. If you can't make it to Rottweil during the Carnival season, you can still catch the spirit of Fasnet. There's an exhibit on it at the Stadtmuseum, and tours are organized to the shops where they carve the masks and make the costumes and bells. The name *Rottweil* may be more familiar as the name for a breed of dog. The area used to be a center of meat production, and locals bred the Rottweiler to herd the cattle. ⊠ *Hauptstr. 20, Rottweil* ☎ *0741/494–330* 🎫 *€2* ⊙ *Tues.–Sun. noon–4.*

**EN
ROUTE** **Uhren Museum** (*Clock Museum*). In the center of Furtwangen, 16 km (10 miles) south of Triberg, drop in on the Uhren Museum, the largest such museum in Germany. It charts the development of Black Forest clocks and exhibits all types of timepieces, from cuckoo clocks, church clock mechanisms, kinetic wristwatches, and old decorative desktop clocks to punch clocks and digital blinking objects. ⊠ *Robert-Gerwig-Pl. 1* ☎ *07723/920–2800* ⊕ *www.deutsches-uhrenmuseum.de* 🎫 *€6* ⊙ *Apr.–Oct., daily 9–6 (guided tours at 11); Nov.–Mar., daily 10–5 (guided tours at 2).*

WHERE TO STAY

$
HOTEL
🏨 **Hotel-Restaurant-Pfaff.** Rooms at this hotel-restaurant are very comfortable, and some have balconies overlooking the famous waterfall. **Pros:** friendly service; close to waterfall. **Cons:** some rooms quite small; no elevator. 💲 *Rooms from: €80* ⊠ *Hauptstr. 85* ☎ *07722/4479* ⊕ *www.hotel-pfaff.com* 🛏 *10 rooms* ⊙ *Breakfast.*

$$
HOTEL
🏨 **Parkhotel Wehrle.** This large mansion, which dominates the town center, has a wisteria-covered facade, steep eaves, and individually furnished, wood-accented rooms. **Pros:** elegant rooms; friendly service; small swimming pool and spa area. **Cons:** main street outside can be noisy. 💲 *Rooms from: €155* ⊠ *Gartenstr. 24* ☎ *07722/86020* ⊕ *www.parkhotel-wehrle.de* 🛏 *50 rooms, 1 suite* ⊙ *Breakfast.*

THE SOUTHERN BLACK FOREST

In the south you'll find the most spectacular mountain scenery in the area, culminating in the Feldberg—at 4,899 feet the highest mountain in the Black Forest. The region also has two large lakes, the Titisee and the Schluchsee. Freiburg is a romantic university city with a superb Gothic cathedral.

TITISEE

37 km (23 miles) south of Furtwangen; 40 km (25 miles) south of Triburg.

Beautiful Titisee, carved by a glacier in the last Ice Age, is the most scenic lake in the Black Forest. The heavily wooded landscape is ideal for long bike tours, which can be organized through the Titisee tourist office. The lake measures 2½ km (1½ miles) long and is invariably crowded in summer, but it's a refreshing place to swim as it is closed

Cuckoo for Cuckoo Clocks

"In Switzerland they had brotherly love—they had 500 years of democracy and peace, and what did that produce? The cuckoo clock."

So says Harry Lime, played by Orson Welles in the classic 1949 film *The Third Man*. He misspoke in two ways. First, the Swiss are an industrious, technologically advanced people. And second, they didn't invent the cuckoo clock. That was the work of the Germans living in the adjacent Black Forest.

CUCKOO HISTORY
The first *Kuckucksuhr* was designed and built in 1750 by Franz Anton Ketterer in Schönwald near Triberg. He cleverly produced the cuckoo sound with a pair of wooden whistles, each attached to a bellows activated by the clock's mechanism.

The making of carved wooden clocks developed rapidly in the Black Forest. The people on the farms needed ways to profitably occupy their time during the long snowbound winters, and the carving of clocks was the answer. Wood was abundant, and the early clocks were entirely of wood, even the works.

Come spring one of the sons would don a traditional smock and hat, mount the family's winter output on a big rack, hoist it onto his back, and set off into the world to sell the clocks. In 1808 there were 688 clock makers and 582 clock peddlers in the districts of Triberg and Neustadt. The *Uhrenträger* (clock carrier) is an important part of the Black Forest tradition. Guides often wear the traditional costume.

CLOCK STYLES
The traditional cuckoo clock is made with brown stained wood with a gabled roof and some sort of woodland motif carved into it, such as a deer's head or a cluster of leaves. The works are usually activated by cast-iron weights, in the form of pinecones, on chains.

Today's clocks can be much more elaborate. Dancing couples in traditional dress automatically move to the sound of a music box, a mill wheel turns on the hour, a farmer chops wood on the hour, the Uhrenträger even makes his rounds. The cuckoo itself moves its wings and beak and rocks back and forth when calling.

The day is long past when the clocks were made entirely of wood. The works are of metal and therefore more reliable and accurate. Other parts of the clock, such as the whistles, the face, and the hands, are usually of plastic now, but hand-carved wood is still the rule for the case. The industry is still centered in Triberg. There are two museums in the area with sections dedicated to it, and clocks are sold everywhere, even in kiosks.

to motorboats. A public beach with outdoor pool ensures everyone has lake access. On rainy days, head to the indoor water park on the outskirts of town to stay refreshed. Stop by one of the many lakeside cafés to enjoy some of the region's best Black Forest cherry cake with an unparalleled waterside view. ■ TIP➡ **Paddleboats and stand-up paddleboards can be rented at several points along the shore.**

East of Freiburg, just beyond the Höllental (Hell Valley), Titisee is best reached via the picturesque twice-hourly regional train, which stops in the center of the resort area, just a short walking distance from the lake. By car it's a winding 30-km (19-mile) drive along the B-31, which can be treacherous in fresh snowfall.

ESSENTIALS

Visitor Information Titisee-Neustadt Tourist-Information. ⊠ *Strandbadstr. 4, Titisee-Neustadt* ☎ *07652/1206-8100* ⊕ *www.hochschwarzwald.de.*

WHERE TO STAY

$

B&B/INN

FAMILY

☆ **Neubierhäusle.** This small guesthouse on the road between Titisee and Neustadt offers a unique charm just a few kilometers away from the crowded lakeshore. **Pros:** large rooms, some of which can be adjoined; friendly service; views of the Black Forest. **Cons:** a short bus ride or drive to the lake. $ *Rooms from: €74* ⊠ *Neustadter Str. 79, Titisee-Neustadt* ☎ *07651/8230* ⊕ *www.neubierhaeusle.com* 🖙 *24 rooms* ⦿ *Breakfast* ▭ *No credit cards.*

$$

RESORT

FAMILY

Fodor'sChoice

★

☆ **Treschers Schwarzwald Romantikhotel.** Right on the lake, this hotel has the best location in town, and most rooms have a balcony with an astounding view. **Pros:** large rooms, many with lake view; all-in-one hotel so you don't need to leave. **Cons:** several rooms face the pedestrian zone, which can get loud in summer. $ *Rooms from: €117* ⊠ *Seestr. 10, Titisee-Neustadt* ☎ *07651/8116* ⊕ *www.schwarzwaldhotel-trescher.de* 🖙 *74 rooms, 7 suites, 2 apartments* ⦿ *Breakfast.*

▌EN
ROUTE

To get to Freiburg, the largest city in the southern Black Forest, you have to brave the curves of the winding road through the **Höllental** (Hell Valley). In 1770 Empress Maria Theresa's 15-year-old daughter—the future queen Marie Antoinette—made her way along what was then a coach road on her way from Vienna to Paris. She traveled with an entourage of 250 officials and servants in some 50 horse-drawn carriages. The first stop at the end of the valley is a little village called **Himmelreich,** or Kingdom of Heaven. Railroad engineers are said to have given the village its name in the 19th century, grateful as they were to finally have laid a line through Hell Valley. At the entrance to Höllental is a deep gorge, the **Ravennaschlucht.** It's worth scrambling through to reach the tiny 12th-century chapel of **St. Oswald,** the oldest parish church in the Black Forest (there are parking spots off the road). Look for a bronze statue of a deer high on a roadside cliff, 5 km (3 miles) farther on. It commemorates the legend of a deer that amazed hunters by leaping the deep gorge at this point. Another 16 km (10 miles) will bring you to Freiburg.

FREIBURG

34 km (21 miles) west of Titisee.

Duke Berthold III founded Freiburg im Breisgau in the 12th century as a free trading city. World War II left extensive damage, but skillful restoration helped re-create the original and compelling medieval atmosphere of one of the loveliest historic towns in Germany. The 16th-century geographer Martin Waldseemüller was born here; in 1507 he was the first to put the name "America" on a map.

For an intimate view of Freiburg, wander through the car-free streets around the Münster or follow the main shopping artery of Kaiser-Joseph-Strasse. After you pass the city gate (Martinstor), follow Gerberau off to the left. You'll come to quaint shops along the banks of one of the city's larger canals, which continues past the former Augustinian cloister to the equally picturesque area around the *Insel* (island). This canal is a larger version of the *Bächle* (brooklets) running through many streets in Freiburg's Old Town. The Bächle, so narrow you can step across them, were created in the 13th century to bring fresh water into the town. Legend has it that if you accidentally step into one of them—and it does happen to travelers looking at the sights—you will marry a person from Freiburg. The tourist office sponsors English walking tours daily at 10:30, with additional tours on Friday and Saturday at 10. The two-hour tour costs €8.

GETTING HERE AND AROUND

Freiburg is on the main railroad line between Frankfurt and Basel, and regular ICE (InterCity Express) trains stop here. The train station is a short walk from the city center. Although Freiburg is a bustling metropolis, the city center is compact. In fact, the bulk of the Old Town is closed to traffic, so walking is by far the most practical and pleasurable option. The Old Town is ringed with parking garages for those who arrive by car.

ESSENTIALS

Visitor Information Kaiserstuhl Tourist-Information. ⊠ *Rhine Tourist Information Office, Marktpl. 16, Breisach* ☎ *07667/940–155* ⊕ *www.naturgarten-kaiserstuhl.de.*

EXPLORING

Augustinermuseum. A visit to Freiburg's cathedral is not really complete without also exploring the Augustinermuseum, in the former Augustinian cloister. Original sculpture from the cathedral is on display, as well as gold and silver reliquaries. The collection of stained-glass windows, dating from the Middle Ages to today, is one of the most important in Germany. ⊠ *Augustinerpl.* ☎ *0761/201–2531* ⊕ *www.museen.freiburg.de* ⊠ *€7* ⊗ *Tues.–Sun. 10–5.*

Fodor's Choice ★ **Münster Unserer Lieben Frau** (*Cathedral of Our Dear Lady*). The Münster Unserer Lieben Frau, Freiburg's most famous landmark, towers over the medieval streets. The cathedral took three centuries to build, from around 1200 to 1515. You can easily trace the progress of generations of builders through the changing architectural styles, from the fat columns and solid, rounded arches of the Romanesque period to the lofty Gothic windows and airy interior of the choir. A daily hour-long tour at 2 pm points out the architectural details. The delicately perforated 380-foot spire, the finest in Europe, can be climbed. In addition to a magnificent view, you'll get a closer look at the 16 bells, including the 1258 "Hosanna," one of Germany's oldest functioning bells. ⊠ *Münsterpl. 1* ☎ *0761/388–101* ⊠ *Bell tower €2; tour €4 donation suggested* ⊗ *Mon.–Sat. 9:30–5, Sun. 1–7:30; Tower: Mon.–Sat. 9:30–4:45, Sun. 1–5.*

Museum für Stadtgeschichte (*Museum of City History*). The former home of painter, sculptor, and architect Johann Christian Wentzinger (1710–97)

Visitors light candles at the Münster unserer Lieben Frau (Cathedral of Our Dear Lady) in Freiburg.

houses the City History Museum, which contains fascinating exhibits, including the poignant remains of a typewriter recovered from a bombed-out bank. The ceiling fresco in the stairway, painted by Wentzinger himself, is the museum's pride and joy. ✉ *Münsterpl. 30* ☎ *0761/201–2515* 🌐 *www.museen.freiburg.de* 🎟 *€3* 🕐 *Tues.–Sun. 10–5.*

Rathaus. Freiburg's famous Rathaus (Town Hall) is actually two 16th-century patrician houses joined together. Destroyed in the war, it was faithfully reconstructed in the 1950s. Among its attractive Renaissance features is an oriel, or bay window, clinging to a corner and bearing a bas-relief of the romantic medieval legend of the Maiden and the Unicorn. ✉ *Rathauspl. 2–4* 🕐 *Mon.–Thurs. 8–5:30, Fri. 8–4.*

WHERE TO EAT

$ GERMAN 🍴 **Der Goldene Engel.** Oak beams festooned with plaster casts of cherubs, and angelic paintings on the walls, combine to create a charmingly kitschy atmosphere in "the golden angel." Local dishes are the specialty here, and the Flammkuchen in particular are a good choice. Try the Schwarzwälder Kirschsteak, a wonderful pork chop with cherries. [$] *Average main: €14* ✉ *Münsterpl. 14* ☎ *0761/37933* 🌐 *www.goldenerengel-freiburg.de.*

WHERE TO STAY

$$$$ HOTEL Fodor's Choice ★ 🏨 **Colombi.** Freiburg's most luxurious hotel is one of the few where the owners are there to make sure your stay is perfect. **Pros:** friendly service; quiet location; comfortable rooms. **Cons:** business hotel; often fully booked by conference delegates. [$] *Rooms from: €264* ✉ *Rotteckring 16* ☎ *0761/21060* 🌐 *www.colombi.de* 🛏 *111 rooms, 5 suites* 🍽 *Breakfast; Some meals.*

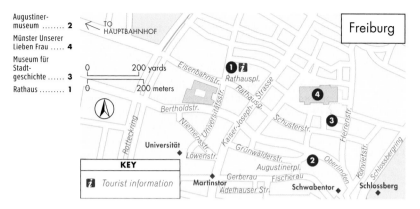

Freiburg

KEY

🛈 *Tourist information*

$ 🏨 **Hotel Schwarzwälder Hof.** In a downtown pedestrian zone, part of this
HOTEL family-run hotel occupies a former mint, complete with graceful cast-
iron railings on the spiral staircase. **Pros:** central location; clean rooms.
Cons: can be noisy. $ *Rooms from: €99* ✉ *Herrenstr. 43* ☎ *0761/38030*
⊕ *www.shof.de* ⤳ *42 rooms, 3 suites* ❖*Breakfast.*

$$ 🏨 **Oberkirchs Weinstube.** Across from the cathedral, this hotel, restau-
HOTEL rant, and wine cellar is a bastion of tradition and *Gemütlichkeit* (com-
fort and conviviality). **Pros:** great central location; personal charm.
Cons: no a/c; there are two buildings but only one overlooks the square.
$ *Rooms from: €139* ✉ *Münsterpl. 22* ☎ *0761/202–6868* ⊕ *www.
hotel-oberkirch.de* ⤳ *26 rooms* ❖*Breakfast.*

$$ 🏨 **Park Hotel Post.** This century-old building near the train station has
HOTEL seen a lot of writers come through its historic doors, and editions signed
by visiting authors—including Teju Cole, children's illustrator Janusch,
and Alice Schwarzer—line the halls. **Pros:** friendly; some rooms have
park views; within walking distance of main train station yet quiet.
Cons: outside the medieval center. $ *Rooms from: €149* ✉ *Eisenbahn-
str. 35–37* ☎ *0761/385–480* ⊕ *www.park-hotel-post.de* ⤳*43 rooms, 2
apartments* ❖*Breakfast.*

$$ 🏨 **Rappen.** This hotel's brightly painted rooms are on the sunny side
HOTEL of the cobblestone cathedral square and marketplace and some rooms
have beautiful views of the cathedral's flying buttresses. **Pros:** ideal
central location; friendly service; clean rooms. **Cons:** hard to find your
way in—go through restaurant to find lobby. $ *Rooms from: €129*
✉ *Münsterpl. 13* ☎ *0761/31353* ⊕ *www.rappen-freiburg.de* ⤳*24
rooms* ❖*Breakfast.*

$$ 🏨 **Zum Roten Bären.** The "Red Bear" claims to be the "oldest in Ger-
HOTEL many," with its history traced back 50 generations and documented in a
book. **Pros:** dripping with history; great location. **Cons:** some rooms are
quite small. $ *Rooms from: €158* ✉ *Oberlinden 12* ☎ *0761/387–870*
⊕ *www.roter-baeren.de* ⤳*22 rooms, 3 suites* ❖*Breakfast.*

NIGHTLIFE

Nightlife in Freiburg takes place in the city's *Kneipen* (pubs), wine bars, and wine cellars, which are plentiful on the streets around the cathedral. For student pubs, wander around Stühlinger, the neighborhood immediately south of the train station.

Cocktailbar Hemingway. Plenty of people take their nightcap in the Victoria Hotel's Cocktailbar Hemingway, which stays open until 2 am on weekends. ⊠ *Best Western Premier Hotel Victoria, Eisenbahnstr. 54* ☎ *0761/207–340.*

STAUFEN

20 km (12 miles) south of Freiburg via B-31.

Once you've braved Hell Valley to get to Freiburg, visit the nearby town of Staufen, where Dr. Faustus is reputed to have made his pact with the devil. The Faustus legend is remembered today chiefly because of Goethe's *Faust* (published in two parts, 1808–32). In this account, Faust sells his soul to the devil in return for eternal youth and knowledge. The historical Faustus was actually an alchemist whose pact was not with the devil but with a local baron who convinced him that he could make his fortune by converting base metal into gold. The explosion leading to his death at Gasthaus zum Löwen produced so much noise and sulfurous stink that the townspeople were convinced the devil had carried him off.

GETTING HERE AND AROUND

To reach Staufen, take the twice-hourly train from Freiburg and change at Bad Krozingen. The train station is a 15-minute walk northwest of the town center. The B-31 highway connects Staufen with Freiburg and the A-5 motorway.

EXPLORING

Gasthaus zum Löwen. You can visit the ancient Gasthaus zum Löwen, where Faust lived—allegedly in room No. 5—and died. Guests can stay overnight in the room, which has been decked out in period furniture with all modern conveniences removed (including the telephone) to enhance the effect. The inn is right on the central square of Staufen, a town with a visible inclination toward modern art in ancient settings. ⊠ *Rathausg. 8* ☎ *07633/908–9390* ⊕ *www.fauststube-im-loewen.de.*

WHERE TO STAY

$ 🍴 **Landgasthaus zur Linde.** Guests have been welcomed here for more
HOTEL   than 350 years, but the comforts inside the inn's old walls are contemporary. **Pros:** friendly; quiet; good restaurant. **Cons:** remote; no elevator. $ *Rooms from: €95* ⊠ *Krumlinden 13, 14 km (9 miles) southeast of Staufen, Münstertal* ☎ *07636/447* ⊕ *www.landgasthaus.de* ⇦ *11 rooms, 3 suites* ❙❙❙ *Breakfast.*

For a break from cathedrals and historic sites, take the kids to Europa Park in Rust.

KAISERSTUHL

20 km (12 miles) northwest of Freiburg on B-31.

The southwesternmost corner of Germany, nestled on the borders of France and Switzerland is the Kaiserstuhl (Emperor's Chair) region, a volcanic outcrop clothed in vineyards that produce some of Baden's best wines—reds from the Spätburgunder grape and whites that have an uncanny depth. A third of Baden's wines are produced in this single area, which has the warmest climate in Germany and some of the country's most beautiful countryside. The especially dry and warm microclimate has given rise to a diversity of wildlife and vegetation, including sequoias and a wide variety of orchids, and dragonflies found nowhere else in the world.

Visitor Information Kaiserstuhl Tourist-Information. ⊠ *Rhine Tourist Information Office, Marktpl. 16, Breisach* ☎ *07667/940–155* ⊕ *www.naturgarten-kaiserstuhl.de.*

EXPLORING

Geldermann Sektkellerei. A wine cellar specializing in turning white wine into the sparkling white wine known as Sekt in German, this 600-year-old building with an arched eave basement was used as a bomb shelter during the war and adapted for the years-long in-bottle fermentation process. Tours are held every day at 2 pm. Arrive 30 minutes early to watch the DVD introduction in English. ⊠ *Breisach* ☎ *07667/834–258* ⊕ *www.geldermann.de* 🎫 *€4* ⊗ *Nov.–Feb., weekdays 8–5:30, Sat. 9–1; Mar.–Oct., weekdays 8–5:30, also Sun. 1–5.*

Weinbaumuseum (*Wine Museum*). The fine little Weinbaumuseum is in a renovated barn in the center of the village of Vogtsburg. A small vineyard out front displays the various types of grapes used to make wine in the Kaiserstuhl region. ✉ *Schlossbergstr., Achkarren, Vogtsburg* ☎ *07662/81263* 🎫 *€2* 🕒 *Apr.–Oct., Wed.–Sat. 11–6.*

WHERE TO STAY

$$ B&B/INN 🏨 **Hotel Zur Krone.** The building dates to 1561, and the Höfflin-Schüssler family, now in its fourth generation as hoteliers, knows how to make visitors feel welcome. **Pros:** friendly; quiet. **Cons:** can feel remote. [$] *Rooms from: €120* ✉ *Schlossbergstr. 15, Achkarren, Vogtsburg* ☎ *07662/93130* 🌐 *www.Hotel-Krone-Achkarren.de* 🛏 *23 rooms* 🍴 *Breakfast.*

$$ HOTEL Fodor's Choice ★ 🏨 **Zollhaus.** A converted customs house, this design hotel only has four rooms but luxury to spare, and the interaction of modernity with old beams and exposed brickwork is very striking. **Pros:** quiet despite central location; friendly service; designer feel. **Cons:** only four rooms. [$] *Rooms from: €109* ✉ *Hauptstr. 3* ☎ *07642/920–2343* 🌐 *www.zollhaus-endingen.de* 🕒 *Closed 2 wks early Aug.* 🛏 *4 rooms* 🍴 *Breakfast.*

RUST

35 km (22 miles) north of Freiburg.

The town of Rust, on the Rhine almost halfway from Freiburg to Strasbourg, has a castle dating from 1577 and painstakingly restored half-timber houses. But its big claim to fame is Germany's biggest amusement park, with its own autobahn exit.

EXPLORING

FAMILY Fodor's Choice ★ **Europa Park.** Covering 160 acres, Europa Park is the continent's largest and busiest amusement park and one of Germany's best-loved attractions. It has a wide array of shows and rides, among them the "Eurosat" to take you on a virtual journey past clusters of meteors and falling stars; the "Silver Star," Europe's highest roller coaster; a Spanish jousting tournament; and even a "4-D" movie in which you might get damp in the rain or be rocked by an earthquake. ✉ *Europa-Park-Str. 2* ☎ *01805/776–688* 🌐 *www.europapark.de* 🎫 *€42.50* 🕒 *Mid-July–mid. Sept., daily 9–8; Apr.–mid-July and mid-Sept.–Oct., daily 9–6; Dec.–mid-Jan., daily 11–7.*

WHERE TO STAY

$$ HOTEL FAMILY 🏨 **Hotel am Park.** This handy hotel, with a waterfall and a statue of a "friendly dragon" in the lobby, is just across the road from the entrance to Europa Park. **Pros:** child-friendly; convenient for Europa Park. **Cons:** it can get noisy. [$] *Rooms from: €110* ✉ *Austr. 1* ☎ *07822/444–900* 🌐 *www.hotel-am-freizeitpark-rust.de* 🛏 *47 rooms* 🍴 *Breakfast.*

HEIDELBERG AND THE NECKAR VALLEY

WELCOME TO HEIDELBERG AND THE NECKAR VALLEY

TOP REASONS TO GO

★ **Heidelberg Castle:** The architectural highlight of the region's most beautiful castle is the Renaissance courtyard—harmonious, graceful, and ornate.

★ **Heidelberg's Alte Brücke:** Walk under the twin towers that were part of medieval Heidelberg's fortifications, and look back for a picture-postcard view of the city and the castle.

★ **Burg Hornberg:** With its oldest parts dating from the 12th century, this is one of the best of more than a dozen castles between Heidelberg and Stuttgart.

★ **Stuttgart's museums:** Top art collections in the Staatsgalerie and the Kunstmuseum contrast with the Mercedes and Porsche museums, where the history of the automobile is illustrated by historic classic cars and sleek racing cars.

★ **Tübingen Altstadt:** With its half-timber houses, winding alleyways, and hilltop setting overlooking the Neckar, Tübingen is the quintessential small-town German experience.

1 **Heidelberg.** The natural beauty of Heidelberg is created by the embrace of mountains, forests, vineyards, and the Neckar River, all crowned by the famous ruined castle. The Neckar and the Rhine meet at nearby Mannheim, the biggest train hub for the superfast ICE (InterCity Express) trains of Germany, a major industrial center, and the second-largest river port in Europe.

2 **The Burgenstrasse (Castle Road).** If you or your kids like castles, this is the place to go. The crowded Heidelberg Castle is a must-see, but the real fun starts when you venture up the Neckar River. There seems to be a castle on every hilltop in the valley, including Burg Hohenzollern, home to the most powerful family in German history.

3 **Swabian Cities.** Stuttgart, the state capital, has elegant streets, shops, hotels, and museums, as well as some of Germany's top industries, among them Mercedes, Porsche, and Bosch. Ludwigsburg, with its huge baroque castles and baroque flower gardens, is worth a visit. The most charmingly "Swabian" of all these cities is the old half-timber university town of Tübingen.

GETTING ORIENTED

Although not as well known as the Rhine, the Neckar River has a wonderful charm of its own. After Heidelberg, it winds through a small valley guarded by castles. It then flows on, bordered by vineyards on its northern slopes, passing the interesting and industrious city of Stuttgart, before it climbs toward the Swabian Hills. You follow the Neckar until the old half-timber university town of Tübingen. The river continues toward the eastern slopes of the Black Forest, where it originates less than 80 km (50 miles) from the source of the Danube.

8

Updated by
Evelyn Kanter

Heidelberg remains one of the best-known and most visited cities in Germany, identifiable by its graceful baroque towers and the majestic ruins of its red-sandstone castle. From this grand city, the narrow and quiet Neckar Valley makes its way east, then turns to the south, taking you past villages filled with half-timber houses and often guarded by their own castle—sometimes in ruins but often revived as a museum or hotel. This part of Germany is aptly named the *Burgenstrasse* (Castle Road).

The valley widens into one of the most industrious areas of Germany, with Stuttgart at its center. In this wealthy city, world-class art museums like the Staatsgalerie or the Kunstmuseum in the center of town contrast with the new and striking Mercedes and Porsche museums in the suburbs, adjoining their sprawling manufacturing facilities.

A bit farther south, the rolling Swabian Hills cradle the university town of Tübingen, a center of learning in a beautiful historic setting on the banks of the Neckar River. Overlooking the town is—of course—a mighty castle.

PLANNING

WHEN TO GO

If you plan to visit Heidelberg in summer, make reservations well in advance and expect to pay top rates. To get away from the crowds, consider staying out of town and driving or taking the bus or train into the city. Hotels and restaurants are much cheaper just a little upriver. A visit in late fall, when the vines turn a faded gold, or early spring, with the first green shoots of the year, can be captivating. In the depths of winter, river mists creep through the narrow streets of Heidelberg's Old Town and awaken the ghosts of a romantic past.

GETTING HERE AND AROUND

AIR TRAVEL

From the Frankfurt and Stuttgart airports, there's fast and easy access, by car and train, to all major centers along the Neckar.

BUS AND SHUTTLE TRAVEL

From Frankfurt Airport to Heidelberg, hop aboard the Lufthansa Airport Bus, which takes about an hour and is not restricted to Lufthansa passengers. Buses depart every 90 minutes from the charter bus lane at Arrivals Hall B of Terminal 1. Airport-bound buses leave the Crowne Plaza Heidelberg between 5:30 am and 8 pm. One-way tickets are €25 per person. With advance reservations you can also get to downtown Heidelberg via the shuttle service TLS. The trip costs €35 per person. Vans leave hourly, 8 am to 6 pm weekdays and 8 am to 1 pm on Saturdays.

Bus Information Lufthansa Airport Bus. ☎ *06152/976–9099* ⊕ *www. transcontinental-group.com/en/frankfurt-airport-shuttles.* **TLS.** ☎ *06221/770– 077* ⊕ *www.tls-heidelberg.de.*

CAR TRAVEL

Heidelberg is a 15-minute drive (10 km [6 miles]) on A-656 from Mannheim, a major junction of the autobahn system. The Burgenstrasse (Route B-37) follows the north bank of the Neckar River from Heidelberg to Mosbach, from which it continues south to Heilbronn as B-27, the road parallel to and predating the autobahn (A-81). B-27 still leads to Stuttgart and Tübingen.

TRAIN TRAVEL

Heidelberg is 17 minutes from Mannheim, by S-bahn regional train, or 11 minutes on hourly InterCity Express (ICE) trains. These sleek, super-high-speed trains reach 280 kph (174 mph), so travel time between Frankfurt Airport and Mannheim is a half hour. From Heidelberg to Stuttgart, direct InterCity (IC) trains take 40 minutes. Local services link many of the smaller towns.

RESTAURANTS

Mittagessen (lunch) in this region is generally served from noon until 2 or 2:30, *Abendessen* (dinner) from 6 until 9:30 or 10. *Durchgehend warme Küche* means that hot meals are also served between lunch and dinner. While credit cards are widely accepted, many small family-owned restaurants, cafés, and pubs will accept only cash or debit cards issued by a German bank. Casual attire is typically acceptable at restaurants here, and reservations are generally not needed.

Prices in the reviews are the average cost of a main course at dinner, or if dinner is not served, at lunch.

HOTELS

This area is full of castle-hotels and charming country inns that range in comfort from upscale rustic to luxurious. For a riverside view, ask for a *Zimmer* (room) or *Tisch* (table) *mit Neckarblick* (with a view of the Neckar). The Neckar Valley offers idyllic alternatives to the cost and crowds of Heidelberg. Driving or riding the train from Neckargemünd, for example, takes 20 minutes.

Prices in the reviews are the lowest cost of a standard double room in high season. For expanded reviews, facilities, and current deals, visit Fodors.com.

WHAT IT COSTS IN EUROS			
$	**$$**	**$$$**	**$$$$**
Restaurants	under €15	€15–€20	€21–€25	over €25
Hotels	under €100	€100–€175	€176–€225	over €225

PLANNING YOUR TIME

To fully appreciate Heidelberg, try to be up and about before the tour buses arrive. After the day-trippers have gone and many shops have closed, the good restaurants and the nightspots open up. Visit the castles on the Burgenstrasse at your leisure, perhaps even staying overnight. Leaving the valley toward the south, you'll drive into wine country. Even if you are not a car enthusiast, the museums of Mercedes and Porsche in Stuttgart are well worth a visit. Try to get to Tübingen during the week to avoid the crowds of Swabians coming in for their *Kaffee und Kuchen* (coffee and cake). During the week, try to get a room and spend a leisurely evening in this charming half-timber university town.

VISITOR INFORMATION

Visitor Information Die Burgenstrasse. ✉ Allee 28, Heilbronn ☎ 07131/564–028 ⊕ www.burgenstrasse.de. **State Tourist Board Baden-Württemberg.** ✉ Esslingerstr. 8, Stuttgart ☎ 0711/238–580 ⊕ www.tourismus-bw.de.

HEIDELBERG

57 km (35 miles) northeast of Karlsruhe.

If any city in Germany encapsulates the spirit of the country, it is Heidelberg. Scores of poets and composers—virtually the entire 19th-century German Romantic movement—have sung its praises. Goethe and Mark Twain both fell in love here: the German writer with a beautiful young woman, the American author with the city itself. Sigmund Romberg set his operetta *The Student Prince* in the city; Carl Maria von Weber wrote his lushly Romantic opera *Der Freischütz* here. Composer Robert Schumann was a student at the university. The campaign these artists waged on behalf of the town has been astoundingly successful. Heidelberg's fame is out of all proportion to its size (population 140,000); more than 3½ million visitors crowd its streets every year.

Heidelberg was the political center of the Lower Palatinate. At the end of the Thirty Years' War (1618–48), the elector Carl Ludwig married his daughter to the brother of Louis XIV in the hope of bringing peace to the Rhineland. But when the elector's son died without an heir, Louis XIV used the marriage alliance as an excuse to claim Heidelberg, and in 1689 the town was sacked and laid to waste. Four years later he sacked the town again. From its ashes arose what you see today: a baroque town built on Gothic foundations, with narrow, twisting streets and alleyways.

Above all, Heidelberg is a university town, with students making up some 20% of its population. And a youthful spirit is felt in the lively restaurants and pubs of the Altstadt (Old Town). In 1930 the university was expanded, and its buildings now dot the entire landscape of Heidelberg and neighboring suburbs. Modern Heidelberg changed as U.S. Army barracks and industrial development stretched into the suburbs, but the old heart of the city remains intact, exuding the spirit of romantic Germany.

GETTING HERE AND AROUND

Heidelberg is 15 minutes from Mannheim, where four ICE trains and five autobahn routes meet. Everything in town may be reached on foot, but wear sturdy, comfortable shoes, since much of the Old City is uneven cobblestones. A funicular takes you up to the castle and Heidelberg's Königstuhl Mountain, and a streetcar runs from the city center to the main train station. From April through October there are daily walking tours of Heidelberg in German (Friday and Saturday also in English) at 10:30 am; from November through March, tours are in German only, Friday at 2:30 and Saturday at 10:30; the cost is €7. They depart from the main entrance to the Rathaus (Town Hall). Bilingual bus tours run April through October on Thursday and Friday at 1:30 and on Saturday at 1:30 and 3. From November through March, bus tours are on Saturday at 1:30. They cost €17 and depart from Universitätsplatz.

DISCOUNTS AND DEALS

The two-day HeidelbergCARD, which costs €14.50 per person or €31.50 for a family of up to five people, includes free or reduced admission to most tourist attractions as well as free use of all public transportation—including the Bergbahn (funicular) to the castle—and other extras such as free entrance to the castle courtyard, free guided walking tours, discounts on bus tours, and a city guidebook. It can be purchased at the tourist-information office at the main train station or the Rathaus, and at many local hotels.

TIMING

Walking the length of Heidelberg's Hauptstrasse (main street) will take an hour—longer if you are easily sidetracked by the shopping opportunities. Strolling through the Old Town and across the bridge to look at the castle will add at least another half hour, not counting the time you spend visiting the sites.

TOURING TIPS

Information: Tourist offices in front of the main train station and in the Rathaus have maps and brochures, as well as discount cards.

Scenic spot: From the Old Bridge over the Neckar you'll have an excellent view toward Heidelberg's Altstadt (Old Town) and its famous castle.

Scenic spot: Looking down from the ramparts of Heidelberg's Castle you can see the Neckar flowing toward the Rhine.

8

ESSENTIALS

Visitor Information Heidelberg Tourist Information. ✉ *Tourist-Information im Rathaus, Marktpl.* ☎ *06221/58444* ⊕ *www.heidelberg-marketing.de.* **Heidelberg Tourist Information.** ✉ *Willy-Brandt-Pl. 1* ☎ *06221/19433* ⊕ *www. heidelberg-marketing.de.*

EXPLORING

TOP ATTRACTIONS

Alte Brücke (*Old Bridge*). Framed by two *Spitzhelm* towers (so called for their resemblance to old German helmets), this bridge was part of Heidelberg's medieval fortifications. In the west tower are three dank dungeons that once held common criminals. Above the portcullis you'll see a memorial plaque that pays warm tribute to the Austrian forces that helped Heidelberg beat back a French attempt to capture the bridge in 1799. The bridge itself is one of many to be built on this spot; ice floes and floods destroyed its predecessors. The elector Carl Theodor, who built it in 1786–88, must have been confident this one would last: he had a statue of himself erected on it, upon a plinth decorated with river gods and goddesses (symbolic of the Neckar, Rhine, Danube, and Mosel rivers). As you enter the bridge from the Old Town, you'll also notice a statue of an animal that appears somewhat catlike. It's actually a monkey holding a mirror. Legend has it the statue was erected to symbolize the need for both city-dwellers and those who lived on the other side of the bridge to take a look over their shoulders as they crossed—reminding them that neither group was more elite than the other. The pedestrian-only bridge is at the end of Steingasse, not far from the Marktplatz. ✉ *End of Steing.*

Alte Universität (*Old University*). The three-story baroque structure was built between 1712 and 1735 at the behest of the elector Johann Wilhelm, although Heidelberg's Ruprecht Karl University was originally founded in 1386. Today it houses the **University Museum**, with exhibits that chronicle the history of Germany's oldest university. The present-day Universitätsplatz (University Square) was built over the remains of an Augustinian monastery that was destroyed by the French in 1693. ✉ *Grabeng. 1–3* ☎ *06221/542–152* ⌑ *€3* ☉ *Apr.–Sept., Tues.–Sun. 10–6; Oct., Tues.–Sun. 10–4, Nov.–Mar., Tues.–Sat. 10–4.*

Friedrich-Ebert-Gedenkstätte (*Friedrich Ebert Memorial*). The humble rooms of a tiny backstreet apartment were the birthplace of Friedrich Ebert, Germany's first democratically elected president (in 1919) and leader of the ill-fated Weimar Republic. The display tells the story of the tailor's son who took charge of a nation accustomed to being ruled by a kaiser. ✉ *Pfaffeng. 18* ☎ *06221/91070* ⊕ *www.ebert-gedenkstaette. de* ⌑ *Free* ☉ *Tues.–Sun. 10–6 (to 8 Thurs.).*

Heiliggeistkirche (*Church of the Holy Ghost*). The foundation stone of this Gothic church was laid in 1398, but it was not actually finished until 1544. The gargoyles looking down on the south side (where Hauptstrasse crosses Marktplatz) are remarkable for their sheer ugliness. The church fell victim to plundering by the Catholic League during the Thirty Years' War, when the church's greatest treasure—the

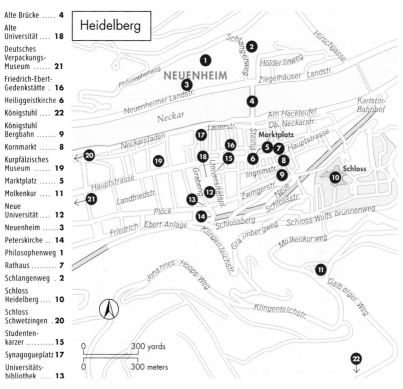

Bibliotheca Palatina, at the time the largest library in Germany—was loaded onto 500 carts and trundled off to the Vatican. Few volumes found their way back. At the end of the 17th century, French troops plundered the church again, destroying the tombs; only the 15th-century tomb of Elector Ruprecht III and his wife, Elisabeth von Hohenzollern, remain. Today, the huge church is shared by Heidelberg's Protestant and Catholic populations. ⊠ *Marktpl.* ☎ *06221/21117* ⊘ *Late Mar.–Oct., Mon.–Sat. 11–5, Sun. 12:30–5; Nov.–mid-Mar., Fri. and Sat. 11–3, Sun. 12:30–3.*

Königstuhl (*King's Throne*). The second-highest hill in the Odenwald range—1,800 feet above Heidelberg—is only a hop, skip, and funicular ride from Heidelberg. On a clear day you can see as far as the Black Forest to the south and west to the Vosges Mountains of France. The hill is at the center of a close-knit network of hiking trails. Well-marked trail signs from the top lead hikers through the woods of the Odenwald. ⊠ *Heidelberg.*

Fodor's Choice **Königstuhl Bergbahn** (*funicular*). Hoisting visitors to the summit of the
★ Königstuhl in 17 minutes, the funicular stops on the way at the ruined Heidelberg Schloss and Molkenkur. A modern funicular usually leaves every 10 minutes, and a historical train comes every 20 minutes. ⊠ *Kornmarkt* ⊕ *www.bergbahn-heidelberg.de* ⊠ *Königstuhl €12 (round-trip),*

Schloss €6.50 (round-trip; additional charge to visit Schloss) ⊙ *Mid-Apr.–mid-Oct., daily 9–8:25; mid-Oct.–mid-Apr., daily 9–5:45.*

Kurpfälzisches Museum (*Palatine Museum*). This baroque palace was built as a residence for a university professor in 1712, and since turned into an art and archeology museum with two standout exhibits worth the visit. One is a replica of the jaw of Heidelberg Man, a key link in the evolutionary chain thought to date from a half-million years ago (the original was unearthed near the city in 1907). The larger attraction is the *Windsheimer Zwölfbotenaltar (Twelve Apostles Altarpiece)*, one of the largest and finest works of early Renaissance sculptor Tilman Riemenschneider. Its exquisite detailing and technical sophistication are evident in the simple faith that radiates from the faces of the Apostles. The top floor of the museum showcases 19th-century German paintings and drawings, many depicting Heidelberg. The restaurant in the museum's quiet courtyard is a good place for a break. ⊠ *Hauptstr. 97* ☎ *06221/583–4020* ⊕ *www.museum-heidelberg.de* 🖼 *€3* ⊙ *Tues.–Sun. 10–6.*

Marktplatz (*Market Square*). Heidelberg's main square, with the Rathaus (Town Hall) on one side and the Heiliggeistkirche on the other, has been its focal point since the Middle Ages. Public courts of justice were held here in earlier centuries, and people accused of witchcraft and heresy were burned at the stake. The baroque fountain in the middle, the *Herkulesbrunnen* (Hercules Fountain), is the work of 18th-century artist H. Charrasky. Until 1740 a rotating, hanging cage stood next to it. For minor crimes, people were imprisoned in it and exposed to the abuse of their fellow citizens. Today the Marktplatz hosts outdoor markets every Wednesday and Saturday. ⊠ *Heidelberg.*

Molkenkur. The next stop after the castle on the Königstuhl funicular, Molkenkur was the site of Heidelberg's second castle. Lightning struck it in 1537, and it was never rebuilt. Today it's occupied by a small restaurant—which bears the creative name Molkenkur Restaurant—with magnificent views of the Odenwald and the Rhine plain. ⊠ *Off Klingenteichstr., Molkenkurweg.*

Philosophenweg (*Philosophers' Path*). You can reach this trail high above the river in one of two ways—either from Neuenheim or by taking the **Schlangenweg** (Snake Path). Both are steep climbs, but you'll be rewarded with spectacular views of the Old Town and castle. From Neuenheim, turn right after crossing the bridge and follow signs to the walking path. ⊠ *Heidelberg.*

Rathaus (*Town Hall*). Work began on the town hall in 1701, a few years after the French destroyed the city. The massive coat of arms above the balcony is the work of Heinrich Charrasky, who also created the statue of Hercules atop the fountain in the middle of the square. ⊠ *Marktpl.*

Schlangenweg (*Snake Path*). This walkway starts just above the Alte Brücke opposite the Old Town and cuts steeply through terraced vineyards until it reaches the woods, where it crosses the Philosophenweg (Philosophers' Path). ⊠ *Off Ziegelhäuser Landstr.*

Fodor's Choice ★   **Schloss Heidelberg** (*Castle*). What's most striking is the architectural variety of this great complex. The oldest parts still standing date from the 15th century, though most of the castle was built during the Renaissance in the baroque styles of the 16th and 17th centuries, when the castle was the seat of the Palatinate electors. There's an "English wing," built in 1612 by the elector Friedrich V for his teenage Scottish bride, Elizabeth Stuart; its plain, square-window facade is positively foreign compared to the castle's more opulent styles. (The enamored Friedrich also had a charming garden laid out for his young bride; its imposing arched entryway, the Elisabethentor, was put up overnight as a surprise for her 19th birthday.) The architectural highlight remains the Renaissance courtyard—harmonious, graceful, and ornate.

> ## LOCAL LEGEND
>
> During the rule of the elector Carl Philip, the Great Cask in the Schloss was guarded by the court jester, a Tyrolean dwarf called Perkeo. When offered wine, he always answered, *"Perche no?"* ("Why not?"), hence his nickname. Legend has it that he could consume frighteningly large quantities of wine and that he died when he drank a glass of water by mistake. A statue of Perkeo stands next to the two-story-high barrel.

Even if you have to wait, make a point of seeing the *Grosses Fass* (Great Cask) in the cellar, possibly the world's largest wine barrel, made from 130 oak trees and capable of holding 58,500 gallons. It was used to hold wines paid as taxes by wine growers in the Palatinate. In summer there are fireworks displays, on the first Saturday in June and September and the second Saturday in July, to commemorate when the castle went up in flames in 1689, 1693, and 1764. In July and August the castle hosts a theater festival. Performances of *The Student Prince* often figure prominently. Take the Königstuhl Bergbahn, or funicular (€6.50 round-trip), faster and less tiring than hiking to the castle on the Burgweg. Audio guides are available in seven languages. ⊠ *Schlosshof* ☎ *06221/538–431* ⊕ *www.heidelberg-schloss.de* ▨ *€6 (funicular round-trip an additional €6.50); audio guide €4* ⊗ *Daily 8–6; tours in English daily 11:15–3:15, when demand is sufficient.*

Deutsches Apotheken–Museum. This museum, on the lower floor of the Ottheinrichsbau (Otto Heinrich Building), is filled with ancient flagons and receptacles (each with a carefully painted enamel label), beautifully made scales, little drawers, shelves, dried beetles and toads, and marvelous reconstructions of six apothecary shops from the 17th through the 20th century. The museum also offers young visitors the chance to smell various herbs and mix their own teas. ⊠ *Heidelberg* ☎ *06221/25880* ⊕ *www.deutsches-apotheken-museum.de* ⊗ *Apr.–Oct., daily 10–6; Nov.–Mar., daily 10–5:30.*

WORTH NOTING

Deutsches Verpackungs-Museum (*German Packaging Museum*). A former church was innovatively converted to house this fascinating documentation of packaging and package design of brand-name products. Representing the years 1800 to the present, historic logos and slogans are a trip down memory lane. The entrance is in a courtyard reached via an alley. ⊠ *Hauptstr. 22* ☎ *06221/21361* ⊕ *www.verpackungsmuseum.de* ▨ *€5* ⊗ *Weekdays 1–6, weekends and public holidays 11–6.*

Heidelberg's Alte Brücke (Old Bridge), now a pedestrian walkway with picture-postcard views, was part of the city's medieval fortifications and is a top site.

Kornmarkt (*Grain Market*). A baroque statue of the Virgin Mary is in the center of this old Heidelberg square, which has a view of the castle ruins. ⊠ *Heidelberg.*

Neue Universität (*New University*). The plain building on the south side of Universitätsplatz was erected between 1930 and 1932 through funds raised by the U.S. ambassador to Germany, J. G. Schurman, who had been a student at the university. The only decoration on the building's three wings is a statue of Athena, the Greek goddess of wisdom, above the entrance. The inner courtyard contains a medieval tower from 1380, the **Hexenturm** (Witches' Tower). Suspected witches were locked up there in the Middle Ages. It later became a memorial to former students killed in World War I. ⊠ *Graben.*

OFF THE BEATEN PATH

Neuenheim. To escape the crowds of central Heidelberg, walk across the Theodor Heuss Bridge to the suburb of Neuenheim. At the turn of the 20th century this old fishing village developed into a residential area full of posh art nouveau villas. North of the Brückenkopf (bridge-head) you'll find antiques and designer shops and boutiques, and cafés on Brückenstrasse, Bergstrasse (one block east), and on Ladenburger Strasse (parallel to the river). To savor the neighborhood spirit, visit the charming farmers' market on Wednesday or Saturday morning at the corner of Ladenburger and Luther streets. ⊠ *Heidelberg.*

Peterskirche (*St. Peter's Church*). Many famous Heidelberg citizens' tombstones, some more than 500 years old, line the outer walls of the city's oldest parish church, dating from the 1300s. While still used for ecumenical services, it is now primarily an event space for concerts and exhibitions. ✉ *Plöck 70* 🌐 *www.peterskirche-heidelberg.de* ⏲ *Weekdays 11–5, weekends 11–4.*

Studentenkarzer (*Student Prison*). Between 1778 and 1914, university officials used this as a lock-up for students, mostly incarcerated for minor offenses. They could be held for up to 14 days and were left to subsist on bread and water for the first three days; thereafter, they were allowed to attend lectures, receive guests, and have food brought in from the outside. There's bravado, even poetic flair, to be deciphered from two centuries of graffiti that cover the walls and ceilings of the narrow cells. ✉ *Augustinerg. 2* ☎ *06221/543–554* 🎟 *€2.50; discounted with HeidelbergCARD* ⏲ *Apr.–Oct., Tues.–Sun. 10–6; Nov.–Mar., Tues.–Sat. 10–4.*

Synagogueplatz. The site of the former Heidelberg Synagogue, built in 1877 and burned down in 1938, is now a memorial to the local Jewish population lost in World War II, their names listed on a bronze plaque on an adjoining building. On this residential corner, 12 stone blocks represent the synagogue's pews and the 12 tribes of Israel. ✉ *Corner of Lauerstr. and Grosse Mantelg.* 🌐 *www.tourism-heidelberg.com.*

Universitätsbibliothek (*University Library*). The 3½ million volumes in this Gothic redbrick building include the 14th-century *Manesse Codex,* a unique collection of medieval songs and poetry once performed in the courts of Germany by the *Minnesänger* (troubadors). The original is too fragile to be exhibited, so a copy is on display. ✉ *Plöck 107–109* ☎ *06221/542–380* 🌐 *www.ub.uni-heidelberg.de* 🎟 *Free* ⏲ *Daily 10–6.*

WHERE TO EAT

$ CAFÉ 🍴 **Café Knösel.** Heidelberg's oldest (1863) coffeehouse has always been a popular meeting place for students and professors, and offers traditional Swabian food, pastries, and ambience. A historic change is that the café no longer produces café founder Fridolin Knösel's *Heidelberger Studentenkuss.* This iconic "student kiss" is a chocolate wrapped in paper showing two sets of touching lips—an acceptable way for 19th-century students to "exchange kisses" in public. They are now being sold exclusively in Knösel Chocolatier, a small, charming shop, owned by the Knösel family, just down the street. [$] *Average main: €10* ✉ *Haspelg. 20* ☎ *06221/727–2754* 🌐 *www.cafek-hd.de.*

$$$$ GERMAN 🍴 **Scharff's Schlossweinstube.** Elegant, romantic, and expensive, this baroque dining room inside the famous Heidelberg castle specializes in *Ente von Heidelberg* (roast duck), but there's always something new on the seasonal menu. Whatever you order, pair it with a bottle from the extensive selection of international wines. Less pricey is the adjacent Bistro Backhaus, which has rustic furnishings and a nearly 50-foot-high *Backkamin* (baking oven). Light fare as well as coffee and cake are served indoors and on the shaded terrace. You can sample rare wines (Eiswein, Beerenauslese) by the glass in the shared wine cellar, or pick up a bottle with a designer label depicting Heidelberg. Reservations are essential for terrace seating in summer. [$] *Average main: €75* ✉ *Schlosshof, on castle grounds* ☎ *06221/872–7010* 🌐 *www.*

EATING WELL IN THE NECKAR VALLEY

Fish and *Wild* (game) from the streams and woods lining the Neckar Valley, as well as seasonal favorites—*Spargel* (asparagus), *Pilze* (mushrooms), *Morcheln* (morels), *Pfifferlinge* (chanterelles), and *Steinpilze* (porcini)—are regulars on menus. Pfälzer specialties are also common, but the penchant for potatoes yields to *Knödel* (dumplings) and pasta farther south. The latter includes the Swabian and Baden staples *Maultaschen* ("pockets" of pasta stuffed with meat or spinach) and *Spätzle* (roundish egg noodles), as well as *Schupfnudeln* (finger-size noodles of potato dough), also called *Buwespitzle*. Look for *Linsen* (lentils) and sauerkraut in soups or as sides. *Schwäbischer Rostbraten* (beefsteak topped with fried onions) and *Schäufele* (pickled and slightly smoked pork shoulder) are popular meat dishes, along with a variety of *Würste*.

Considerable quantities of red wine are produced along the Neckar Valley. Crisp, light Trollinger is often served in the traditional *Viertele*, a round, quarter-liter (8-ounce) glass with a handle. Deeper-color, more substantial reds include Spätburgunder (Pinot Noir) and its mutation Schwarzriesling (Pinot Meunier), Lemberger, and Dornfelder. Riesling, Kerner, and Müller-Thurgau (synonymous with Rivaner), as well as Grauburgunder (Pinot Gris) and Weissburgunder (Pinot Blanc), are the typical white wines. A birch broom or wreath over the doorway of a vintner's home signifies a *Besenwirtschaft* ("broomstick inn"), a rustic pub where you can enjoy wines with snacks and simple fare. Many vintners offer economical B&Bs. These places are ideal spots to try out your newly learned German phrases; you'll be surprised how well you speak German after the third glass of German wine.

heidelberger-schloss-gastronomie.de ☉ *Closed late Dec.–Jan. and Wed. No lunch* ⌧ *Reservations essential* 🗎 *Jacket required.*

$

GERMAN

Fodor'sChoice

★

✕ **Schnitzelbank.** Little more than a hole in the wall, this former cooper's (barrel maker's) workshop has been transformed into a candlelighted pub. No matter when you go, it seems to be filled with people seated around the wooden tables. The menu features specialties from Baden and the Pfalz, such as *Schäufele* (pickled and slightly smoked pork shoulder); or a hearty platter of bratwurst, *Leberknödel* (liver dumplings), and slices of *Saumagen* (a spicy meat-and-potato mixture encased in a sow's stomach). $ *Average main: €12* ⌧ *Bauamtsg. 7* ☎ *06221/21189* ⊕ *www.schnitzelbank-heidelberg.de* ☉ *No lunch weekdays.*

$

GERMAN

✕ **Schnookeloch.** This lively old tavern dates from 1703 and is inextricably linked with Heidelberg's history and university. Young and old alike crowd around the wooden tables in the wood-panel room, decorated with historic photos and maps, and piano music adds to the din Wednesday through Saturday nights. From salads and pasta to hearty roasts and steaks, there's a broad selection of food, and beer is served from 7:30 am until closing. Upstairs are modern, pleasantly furnished guest rooms. $ *Average main: €14* ⌧ *Haspelg. 8* ☎ *06221/138–080.*

$$$

MEDITERRANEAN

✕ **Simplicissimus.** Saddle of lamb and sautéed liver in honey-pepper sauce are specialties here, as are seasonal preparations with asparagus and mushrooms. The menu changes every six weeks. The *Dessertteller,* a sweet sampler, is a crowning finish to any meal. The wine list focuses on old-world estates, particularly clarets. The elegant art nouveau interior is done in shades of red with dark-wood accents, and a quiet courtyard offers alfresco dining in summer. $ *Average main: €25* ✉ *Ingrimstr. 16* ☎ *06221/673–2588* ⊕ *www.restaurant-simplicissimus.de* ✆ *Closed Sun. No lunch.*

$ ✕ **Trattoria Toscana.** Traditional Italian fare is on offer here, including
ITALIAN antipasti platters, pasta dishes, pizzas, and special daily offerings, all served in generous portions. The restaurant is in a central location in the main square, and in warm weather you can opt for a table outside on the cobblestones—perfect for people-watching with your meal. $ *Average main: €12* ✉ *Marktpl. 1* ☎ *06221/28619.*

$$ ✕ **Zum Roten Ochsen.** Many of the rough-hewn oak tables here have ini-
GERMAN tials carved into them, a legacy of the thousands who have visited Hei-
Fodor's Choice delberg's most famous old tavern. Mark Twain, Marilyn Monroe, and
★ John Wayne may have left their mark—they all ate here, and Twain's photo is on one of the memorabilia-covered walls. Wash down simple fare, such as goulash soup and bratwurst, or heartier dishes like *Tellerfleisch* (boiled beef) or Swabian *Maultaschen* (meat-filled ravioli) with regional German wines or local Heidelberg beer. The "Red Ox" has been run by the same family for more than 170 years. Come early to get a good seat, and stay late for the piano player and *Gemütlichkeit* (easygoing friendliness). $ *Average main: €15* ✉ *Hauptstr. 217* ☎ *06221/20977* ⊕ *www.roterochsen.de* ✆ *Closed Sun. and mid-Dec.– mid-Jan. No lunch Nov.–Mar.*

$$ ✕ **Zum Weissen Schwanen.** Founded in 1398 and in this location on Hei-
GERMAN delberg's Hauptstrasse (main street) since 1778—so you know they are doing something right—the White Swan specializes in regional fare. The menu includes several versions of Maultaschen (traditional Swabian ravioli) and local mushrooms and asparagus are featured in season. Unlike most German restaurants and pubs, which serve one local brew, there are a dozen on tap here; the most popular are Klosterhof and Heidelberger. $ *Average main: €15* ✉ *Hauptstr. 143* ☎ *06221/659–692* ⊕ *zumweissenschwanen.de* 🚫 *No credit cards.*

$$$ ✕ **Zur Herrenmühle.** A 17th-century grain mill has been transformed into
EUROPEAN this romantic restaurant in the heart of Altstadt (Old Town). The old beams add to the warm atmosphere. In summer, try to arrive early to get a table in the idyllic courtyard. Fish, lamb, and homemade pasta are specialties. Or, opt for the three-course or four-course prix-fixe menu. $ *Average main: €21* ✉ *Near Karlstor, Hauptstr. 239* ☎ *06221/602– 909* ⊕ *www.herrenmuehle-heidelberg.de* ✆ *Closed Mon. No lunch.*

WHERE TO STAY

$$ 🛏 **Bergheim 41.** This sleek and trendy hotel in the "new" part of Heidel-
HOTEL berg is built into one side of the Alten Hallenbad, the covered former city pool that is now a popular upscale international food court. **Pros:** roof garden; some rooms have views of the Schloss. **Cons:** no parking; 15 minutes from Old City; on a busy street (although windows are soundproofed); no restaurant. $ *Rooms from: €110* ✉ *Bergheim*

41 ☎ 06221/750–040 🌐 www.bergheim41.de 💳 No credit cards 🛏 32 rooms, 4 suites 🍴 Breakfast.

$$ HOTEL
🏨 **Crowne Plaza Heidelberg.** This grand hotel has a spacious lobby, stylish furnishings, soaring ceilings, and an enviable location—it's a five-minute walk from Old Town. **Pros:** parking garage; pool and fitness center; direct shuttle from Frankfurt airport (80 km [50 miles] away). **Cons:** chain-hotel feel. [$] *Rooms from: €140 ✉ Kurfürsten-Anlage 1 ☎ 06221/9170 🌐 www.crowneplaza.com 🛏 232 rooms, 4 suites 🍴 No meals.*

$$$ HOTEL Fodor's Choice ★
🏨 **Der Europäische Hof–Hotel Europa.** On secluded grounds next to the Old Town, this most luxurious of Heidelberg hotels has been welcoming guests since 1865. **Pros:** indoor pool; castle views from the two-story fitness and spa center. **Cons:** restaurant closed in July and August; limited parking. [$] *Rooms from: €209 ✉ Friedrich-Ebert-Anlage 1 ☎ 06221/515–512 🌐 www.europaeischerhof.com 🛏 100 rooms, 14 suites, 3 apartments, 1 penthouse 🍴 Breakfast.*

$$ B&B/INN
🏨 **Gasthaus Backmulde.** This traditional family-owned Gasthaus on a residential street in the heart of Heidelberg has very nice modern rooms at affordable prices. **Pros:** quiet rooms; nice restaurant, dinner only; cooking classes with chef in restaurant kitchen. **Cons:** difficult parking; some rooms have shared baths; restaurant closed Sunday. [$] *Rooms from: €135 ✉ Schiffg. 11 ☎ 06221/53660 🌐 www.gasthaus-backmulde.de 🛏 26 rooms 🍴 Breakfast.*

$$ HOTEL
🏨 **Holländer Hof.** Opposite the Alte Brücke, and with views across the busy Neckar River to the forested hillside beyond, this ornate 19th-century building is in a prime Old Town location. **Pros:** nice view of river and beyond; comfortable accommodations; some rooms are wheelchair accessible. **Cons:** noisy at times; no restaurant or bar (although both are in adjoining building). [$] *Rooms from: €112 ✉ Neckarstaden 66 ☎ 06221/60500 🌐 www.hollaender-hof.de 🛏 38 rooms, 1 suite 🍴 Breakfast.*

$$$ HOTEL Fodor's Choice ★
🏨 **Hotel Die Hirschgasse.** A stunning castle view, fine restaurants, a literary connection, and a touch of romance distinguish this historic inn (1472) across the river from the Old Town, opposite Karlstor. **Pros:** terrific view; very good food in both restaurants; close to "museum row". **Cons:** limited parking; 15-minute walk to Old Town. [$] *Rooms from: €205 ✉ Hirschg. 3 ☎ 06221/4540 🌐 www.hirschgasse.de 🕓 Le Gourmet closed Sun. and Mon., 2 wks in early Jan., and 2 wks in early Aug.; Mensurstube closed Sun. No lunch at either restaurant 🛏 20 suites 🍴 Breakfast; Some meals.*

$$ HOTEL Fodor's Choice ★
🏨 **Hotel zum Ritter.** If this is your first visit to Germany, or to Heidelberg, try to stay here. **Pros:** charm and elegance; nice views; spacious rooms. **Cons:** off-site parking; rooms facing the square can be noisy. [$] *Rooms from: €115 ✉ Hauptstr. 178 ☎ 06221/1350 🌐 www.hotel-ritter-heidelberg.com 🛏 36 rooms, 1 suite 🍴 Breakfast.*

$$ HOTEL
🏨 **KulturBrauerei Heidelberg.** Rooms with warm, sunny colors and modern style are brilliantly incorporated into this old brewery in the heart of Old Town. **Pros:** stylish rooms; lively restaurant; Wi-Fi in most rooms; beer garden. **Cons:** noisy in summer; difficult parking; rooms above Zum Seppl restaurant are accessed by steep, narrow stairs and dark hallways, and you have to walk a block to get breakfast. [$] *Rooms*

from: €110 ✉ *Leyerg. 6* ☎ *06221/502–980* 🌐 *www.heidelberger-kulturbrauerei.de* 🛏 *41 rooms, 2 suites* 🍴 *Breakfast.*

$$ HOTEL 🏨 **NH Heidelberg.** The glass-covered entrance hall of this primarily business hotel is spacious—not surprising, as it was the courtyard of a former brewery. **Pros:** gym and spa; underground garage; wheelchair-accessible rooms. **Cons:** lacks charm; 15-minute walk to Old Town; breakfast expensive. [$] *Rooms from: €125* ✉ *Bergheimerstr. 91* ☎ *06221/13270* 🌐 *www.nh-hotels.com* 🛏 *156 rooms, 18 suites* 🍴 *No meals.*

$$ HOTEL 🏨 **Weisser Bock.** Exposed beams, stucco ceilings, warm wood furnishings, and individually decorated, comfortable rooms are all part of this hotel's charm. **Pros:** nicely decorated rooms; exceptional food; this is a smoke-free facility. **Cons:** parking difficult to find; not all rooms accessible by elevator; breakfast not included in room rate. [$] *Rooms from: €115* ✉ *Grosse Mantelg. 24* ☎ *06221/90000* 🌐 *www.weisserbock.de* 🛏 *21 rooms, 2 suites* 🍴 *No meals.*

NIGHTLIFE AND PERFORMING ARTS

Information on all upcoming events can be found in the monthly *Heidelberg aktuell,* free and available from the tourist office or on the Internet (🌐 *www.heidelberg-aktuell.de*).

NIGHTLIFE

Heidelberg nightlife is concentrated in the area around the Heiliggeistkirche (Church of the Holy Ghost), in the Old Town. Don't miss a visit to one of the old student taverns that have been in business for generations.

Today's students, however, are more likely to hang out in one of the dozen or more cafés and bars on **Untere Strasse,** which runs parallel to and between Hauptstrasse and the Neckar River, starting from the market square.

Billy Blues (im Ziegler). This restaurant, bar, and disco, popular with university students, has live music on Thursday and a salsa party on Wednesday. There also are a few small, efficiently decorated, budget-priced rooms upstairs. ✉ *Bergheimer Str. 1b* ☎ *06221/25333* 🌐 *www.billyblues.de* ⏲ *Closed Sun.–Tues.*

Destille. The club plays rock music until 2 am on weekdays and 3 am on weekends, and the young crowd that packs the place is always having a good time. A tree in the middle of this club is decorated according to season. This is also an art gallery; paintings by local artists decorate the walls and are for sale. ✉ *Untere Str. 16* ☎ *06221/22808* 🌐 *www.destilleonline.de.*

Nachtschicht. In the Landfried complex near the main train station, this is Heidelberg's biggest disco, pulsing with 15,000 LEDs that change colors and pattern with the music. Nachtschicht (night story) is open until 4 am Thursday through Saturday. ✉ *Bergheimer Str. 147* ☎ *06221/438–550* 🌐 *www.nachtschicht.com.*

Print Media Lounge. Facing the main train station, this is a chic, modern place where you can dine all day, including weekday lunch specials popular with the business crowd, or dance till the wee hours.

It's open Monday–Saturday, with DJs Friday and Saturday and live bands and free admission on Mondays. ⊠ *Kurfürsten–Anlage 52-60* ☎ *06221/653–949* ⊕ *www.printmedialounge.de* ⊘ *Closed Sun. and 2 wks mid-August. No lunch Sat.*

Schnookeloch. In the same location since 1703, it was a favorite of the *Burschenschaften*, or dueling fraternities for two centuries. These days, it's popular with Heidelberg's university students, locals, and visitors for its traditional ambience and well-priced food and beer that starts flowing at 7:30 am daily. The wood-paneled walls are filled with historic photos and maps. There also are budget-priced rooms upstairs. ⊠ *Haspelg. 8* ☎ *06221/138–080.*

Schwimmbad Musikclub. Near the zoo, this is a fixture of Heidelberg's club scene. It occupies what was once a swimming pool, hence the name. It's open Thursday to Saturday with two floors plus an open-air disco when weather permits, and a rotating schedule of live and DJ music. ⊠ *Tiergartenstr. 13* ☎ *06221/470–201* ⊕ *www.schwimmbad-club.de.*

SKYlounge Der Turm. For a nice view of the town, a menu of 120 cocktails, and relaxing music, head for the glass-walled SKYlounge. Choose between the dark-red walls on the seventh floor or the deep-blue shades on the eighth floor. ⊠ *Alte Glockengiesserei 9* ☎ *06221/434–968* ⊕ *www.skylounge-heidelberg.de* ⊘ *Restaurant closed Mon.–Thurs.*

Vetters Alt-Heidelberger Brauhaus. It's worth elbowing your way into this bar for the brewed-on-the-premises beer. Try the Dunkles Hefeweizen, or dark wheat beer, which is not produced as widely as the lighter version. As with most German brewpubs, there's a full menu, too, including a long list of wurst dishes. ⊠ *Steing. 9* ☎ *06221/165–850* ⊕ *www.brauhaus-vetter.de.*

Fodor's Choice ★ **Zum Roten Ochsen.** Mark Twain rubbed elbows with students here during his 1878 stay in Heidelberg—look for his photo on one of the memorabilia-covered walls. Zum Roten Oschen is popular with students and local residents for its friendly atmosphere and hearty meals at reasonable prices The Red Ox has been operated by the Spengel family for more than 170 years. A pianist plays German and international favorites, starting at 7:30 pm, likely to turn into a singalong after several refills of regional German wines and local Heidelberg beer. ⊠ *Hauptstr. 217* ☎ *06221/20977* ⊕ *www.roterochsen.de.*

Zum Seppl. When this traditional restaurant and bar opened at the end of the 17th century, it had its own brewery on the premises; now the brewery is a block away and called Kulturbrauerei Heidelberg. The Seppl crowd is a mix of Heidelberg students, local residents, and visitors, all attracted by the traditional old-world charm and ample servings of traditional German specialties. Every inch of wall space is covered with historic photos, menus, and other memorabilia. ⊠ *Hauptstr. 213* ☎ *06221/502–980* ⊕ *www.heidelberger-kulturbrauerei.de/en/ scheffels-wirtshaus-zum-seppl.*

PERFORMING ARTS

Heidelberg has a thriving theater and concert scene.

heidelbergTicket. Theater tickets may be purchased here. ⊠ *Theaterstr. 4* ☎ *06221/582–0000* ⊕ *www.theaterheidelberg.de.*

Kulturhaus Karlstorbahnhof. This 19th-century train station has been repurposed as a theater and concert venue. ⊠ *Am Karlstor 1* ☎ *06221/978– 911* ⊕ *www.karlstorbahnhof.de.*

Schlossfestspiele. Theatrical and musical performances are held at the Heidelberg castle during this annual festival from late June through July. ⊠ *Heidelberg* ☎ *06221/582–0000 (ticket agency)* ⊕ *www. schlossfestspiele-heidelberg.de.*

Theater & Orchester Heidelberg. This is the best-known theater company in town, with a variety of theater, opera, and concert performances. The historic theater reopened in 2013 after a renovation and the addition of a modern second stage in the new adjoining building. ⊠ *Theaterstr. 10* ☎ *06221/582–0000* ⊕ *www.theaterheidelberg.de.*

Zimmertheater. Avant-garde theater productions are staged here. ⊠ *Hauptstr. 118* ☎ *06221/21069* ⊕ *www.zimmertheaterhd.de.*

SPORTS AND THE OUTDOORS

The riverside path is an ideal route for walking, jogging, and bicycling, since it's traffic-free and offers excellent views of the area. If you access the paved pathway in the center of town, you can follow it for many kilometers in either direction.

SHOPPING

Heidelberg's **Hauptstrasse,** or Main Street, is a pedestrian zone lined with shops, sights, and restaurants that stretches more than 1 km (½ mile) through the heart of town. But don't spend your money before exploring the shops on such side streets as **Plöck, Ingrimstrasse,** and **Untere Strasse,** where there are candy stores, bookstores, and antiques shops on the ground floors of baroque buildings. If your budget allows, the city can be a good place to find reasonably priced German antiques, and the Neckar Valley region produces fine glass and crystal.

Aurum & Argentum. The finely executed, modern gold and silver pieces here are impeccably crafted, in a sleek store design unusual for this historic city. ⊠ *Brückenstr. 22* ☎ *06221/473–453* ☉ *Tues.–Fri. 2:30–6:30, Sat. 10–2.*

Farmers' markets. Heidelberg has open-air farmers' markets on Wednesday and Saturday mornings on Marktplatz and Tuesday and Friday mornings, as well as Thursday afternoons, on Friedrich-Ebert-Platz. ⊠ *Heidelberg.*

Fodor's Choice
★
Heidelberger Zuckerladen. The old glass display cases and shelves here are full of lollipops and "penny" candy. If you're looking for an unusual gift or special sweet treat, the shop fashions colorful, unique items out of sugary ingredients such as marshmallow and sweetened gum. Avoid early afternoon, when the tiny shop is crowded with schoolchildren. ⊠ *Plöck 52* ☎ *06221/24365* ⊕ *www.zuckerladen.de* ☉ *Tues.–Fri. noon–7, Sat. 11–3.*

OFF THE
BEATEN
PATH
Schloss Schwetzingen. This formal 18th-century palace was constructed as a summer residence by the Palatinate electors. It is a noble rose-color building, imposing and harmonious; a highlight is the rococo theater in one wing. The extensive park blends formal French and informal English styles, with neatly bordered gravel walks trailing off into the dark woodland. Fun touches include an exotic mosque, complete with minarets and a shimmering pool (although they got a little confused and gave the building a very baroque portal), and the "classical ruin" that was de rigueur in this period. The palace interior can only be visited by tour. At this writing, the castle is closed for renovations, but it is due to reopen in 2016—call before you visit. ⊠ *Schloss Mittelbau, Schwetzingen* ☎ *06202/742–770* ⊕ *www.schloss-schwetzingen.de* ☎ *€9 Apr.–Oct., €7 Nov.–Mar. (includes palace tour and gardens); gardens only: €5 Apr.–Oct., €3 Nov.–Mar.* ☉ *Apr.–Oct., daily 9–8; Nov.–Mar., daily 9–5, last admission 30 mins before closing. Palace tours (in German): Apr.–Oct., weekdays hourly 11–4, weekends and holidays 11–5; Nov.–Mar., Fri. at 2, weekends and holidays 11, 1:30, and 3; tours in English weekends at 2, or by arrangement.*

THE BURGENSTRASSE (CASTLE ROAD)

The Neckar Valley narrows upstream from Heidelberg, presenting a landscape of orchards, vineyards, and wooded hills crowned with castles rising above the gently flowing stream. It's one of the most impressive stretches of the Burgenstrasse. Along the B-37 are small valleys—locals call them *Klingen*—that cut north into the Odenwald and are off-the-beaten-track territory. One of the most atmospheric is the Wolfsschlucht, which starts below the castle at Zwingenberg. The dank, shadowy little gorge inspired Carl Maria von Weber's opera *Der Freischütz* (*The Marksman*).

NECKARGEMÜND

11 km (7 miles) from Heidelberg.

Coming from the hustle and bustle of Heidelberg, you'll find the hamlet of Neckargemünd is a quiet place where you can relax by the Neckar River and watch the ships go by. The town also makes a good base from which to visit Heidelberg. Leave the car here and enjoy the 10-minute ride by bus or train.

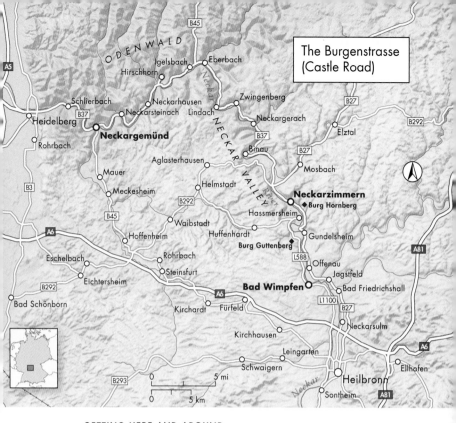

The Burgenstrasse (Castle Road)

GETTING HERE AND AROUND

The S1, S2, S5, and S51 commuter trains from Heidelberg run every few minutes and will get you here in less than 10 minutes. By car, it will take 25 minutes via the B-37. Once here, the Altstadt (Old Town) and Neckar River views are walkable, but you'll need a car or take a taxi to visit the Schloss Zwingennberg, about a half hour distant via the S1 (toward Osterburken) or the B-37 and B-45.

WHERE TO STAY

$
B&B/INN
FAMILY
Art Hotel. In a historic building in the heart of the Altstadt (Old City), this stylish hotel has spacious rooms and suites, including three- and four-bed junior suites that are perfect for families. **Pros:** good for families; reasonable rates. **Cons:** on a busy street; no elevator; no restaurant. $ *Rooms from: €95 ⊠ Hauptstr. 40 ☎ 06223/862–768 ⊕ www. art-hotel-neckar.de ⟿ 7 rooms, 6 suites ⊙| Breakfast.*

$
B&B/INN
Gasthaus Reber. If you're looking for a clean, simple, and inexpensive room, this small inn is an ideal candidate, and it's conveniently located opposite the railway station for trips to or from Heidelberg. **Pros:** unbeatable rates; close to public transportation. **Cons:** on busy street; not all rooms have an en suite bathroom. $ *Rooms from: €70 ⊠ Bahnhofstr. 52 ☎ 06223/8779 ⊕ www.gasthaus-reber.de ▬ No credit cards ⊙ Restaurant closed Wed. No lunch weekdays ⟿ 10 rooms ⊙| Breakfast.*

**EN
ROUTE**

Mosbach. The little town of Mosbach, 78 km (48 miles) southeast of Heidelberg, is one of the most charming towns on the Neckar. Its main street is pure half-timber, and its ancient market square contains one of Germany's most exquisite half-timber buildings—the early-17th-century Palm'sches Haus (Palm House), its upper stories laced with intricate timbering. The Rathaus, built 50 years earlier, is a modest affair by comparison. ⊠ *Mosbach.*

NECKARZIMMERN

83 km (52 miles) from Heidelberg.

The main attraction here is the Burg Hornberg castle high above the town, but visitors will find the village itself to be a charming respite, with a traditional town square surrounded by historic buildings, and pleasant riverfront walks.

GETTING HERE AND AROUND

By road from Heidelberg, take the E-5 autobahn south (toward Bruschal) then the E-6 east to Sinsheim, where you connect with local road 292 northeast past Mossbach to Neckarzimmern, then follow signs. If you have time en route, stop off at the Sinsheim Auto & Technik Museum for displays including Formula 1 racecars and a Concorde supersonic jet.

EXPLORING

Fodor'sChoice
★

Burg Hornberg. The largest and oldest castle in the Neckar Valley, the circular bulk of Burg Hornberg rises above the town of Neckarzimmern. The road to the castle leads through vineyards that have been providing dry white wines for centuries. These days, the castle is part hotel (23 rooms, 1 suite) and part museum. In the 16th century it was home to the larger-than-life Götz von Berlichingen (1480–1562). When the knight lost his right arm in battle, he had a blacksmith fashion an iron replacement. Original designs for this fearsome artificial limb are on view in the castle, as is his suit of armor. For most Germans, this larger-than-life knight is best remembered for a remark that was faithfully reproduced in Goethe's play *Götz von Berlichingen.* Responding to an official reprimand, von Berlichingen told his critic, more or less, to "kiss my ass" (the original German is a bit more earthy: Er kann mich am Arsche lecken). To this day the polite version of this insult is known as a *Götz von Berlichingen.* Inquire at the hotel reception about visiting the castle, or just enjoy the walking trails and views from the top of the hill. ⊠ *Hornbergerweg* ☎ *06221/5001* ⊕ *www.burg-hornberg.de* 🎫 *€5* ⊙ *Daily 9–6.*

WHERE TO STAY

$$
HOTEL
Fodor'sChoice
★

Burg Hornberg Hotel. Your host at this antiques-filled hotel with comfortable, modern rooms is the present baron of the Burg Hornberg castle. **Pros:** historic setting; nice restaurant; on-site wineshop. **Cons:** no elevator; restaurant can be crowded in season on weekends; not enough parking. Ⓢ *Rooms from: €110* ⊠ *Marcus Freiherr von Gemmingen* ☎ *06261/92460* ⊕ *www.castle-hotel-hornberg.com* ⊙ *Closed late Dec.–late Jan.* 🛏 *23 rooms, 1 suite* ❚⊙❚ *Breakfast.*

You can tour Burg Hornberg or spend the night at this spectacular castle.

EN
ROUTE

Burg Guttenberg. One of the best-preserved Neckar castles is the 15th-century Burg Guttenberg. Within its stone walls are a museum and a restaurant (closed January, February, and Monday) with views of the river valley. The castle also is home to Europe's leading center for the study and protection of birds of prey, the German Raptor Research Center, with 100 falcons and other birds of prey. There are demonstration flights from the castle walls from April through October, daily at 11 and 3. ⊠ *6 km (4 miles) west of Gundelsheim, Burgstr., Neckarmühlbach* ☎ *06266/388* ⊕ *www.burg-guttenberg.de* ⊠ *Castle €5, castle and flight demonstration €11* ⊙ *Apr.–Oct., daily 10–6; Mar., weekends 10–5.*

BAD WIMPFEN

8 km (5 miles) south of Neckarzimmern.

Fodor'sChoice
★

At the confluence of the Neckar and Jagst rivers, Bad Wimpfen is one of the most stunning towns of the Neckar Valley. The Romans built a fortress and a bridge here, on the riverbank site of an ancient Celtic settlement, in the 1st century AD. A millennium later, the Staufen emperor Barbarossa chose this town as the site of his largest *Pfalz* (residence). The ruins of this palace still overshadow the town and are well worth a stroll.

GETTING HERE AND AROUND

There's a direct regional commuter train from Heidelberg that will get you to Bad Wimpfen in 45 minutes, and from Neckarzimmern there's an hourly service that takes 30 minutes. By road, take the B-27 east from Neckarzimmern to the L-1100. The old city is good for walking, but wear comfortable shoes for the uneven cobblestones.

TOURS

Medieval Bad Wimpfen offers a town walk year-round, Sunday at 2 (€2), departing from the visitor center inside the old train station. Private group tours may also be arranged for other days by calling the visitor center in advance.

DISCOUNTS AND DEALS

On arrival, ask your hotel for a free *Bad Wimpfen à la card* for reduced or free admission to historic sights and museums.

FESTIVALS

Zunftmarkt. On the last weekend in August, the Old Town's medieval past comes alive during the Zunftmarkt, a historical market dedicated to the *Zünfte* (guilds). "Artisans" in period costumes demonstrate the old trades and open the festivities with a colorful parade on horseback. ⊠ *Bad Wimpfen* ⊕ *www.zunftmarkt.de.*

ESSENTIALS

Visitor Information Bad Wimpfen–Gundelsheim Tourist-Information. ⊠ *Carl-Ulrich-Str. 1* ☎ *07063/97200* ⊕ *www.badwimpfen.de.*

EXPLORING

Ritterstiftskirche St. Peter. Wimpfen im Tal (Wimpfen in the Valley), the oldest part of town, is home to the Benedictine monastery of Gruessau and its church, Ritterstiftskirche St. Peter, which dates from the 10th and 13th centuries. The cloisters are an example of German Gothic at its most uncluttered. ⊠ *Lindenpl.* ⊕ *www.badwimpfen.de.*

Stadtkirche (*City Church*). The 13th-century stained glass, wall paintings, medieval altars, and the stone pietà in the Gothic Stadtkirche are worth seeing, as are the Crucifixion sculptures (1515) by the Rhenish master Hans Backoffen on Kirchplatz, behind the church. ⊠ *Kirchsteige 8* ⊕ *www.kirche-badwimpfen.de.*

Steinhaus. Germany's largest Romanesque living quarters and once the imperial women's apartments, this is now a history museum with relics from the Neolithic and Roman ages along with the history of the Palatinate, including medieval art, armor and weapons, and ceramics. Next to the Steinhaus are the remains of the northern facade of the palace, an arcade of superbly carved Romanesque pillars that flanked the imperial hall in its heyday. The imperial chapel, next to the Red Tower, holds a collection of religious art. ⊠ *Burgviertel 25* ☎ *07063/97200* 💳 *€2.50* ⊙ *Mid-Apr.–mid.-Oct., Tues.–Sun. 10–noon and 2–4:30.*

WHERE TO EAT AND STAY

$ × **Weinstube Feyerabend.** There are three adjoining eateries here: the Weinstube for a glass of good Swabian wine with a snack, the Restaurant for a full meal at lunch or dinner, or let yourself be tempted by the good-looking cakes from their own bakery in the Konditerei/Cafe. Ⓢ *Average main: €12* ⊠ *Hauptstr. 74* ☎ *07063/950–566* ⊕ *www.friedrich-feyerabend.de* ☐ *No credit cards* ⊙ *Closed Mon.*

GERMAN

$ 🛏 **Hotel Neckarblick.** You get a good *Neckarblick* (Neckar view) from the terrace, the dining room, and most guest rooms of this pleasant lodging. **Pros:** terrific view; personal touch. **Cons:** no restaurant or

HOTEL

bar; not enough parking. $ *Rooms from: €59* ✉ *Erich-Sailer-Str. 48* ☎ *07063/961–620* ⊕ *www.neckarblick.de* 🛏 *14 rooms* ⏐◯⏐ *Breakfast.*

OFF THE
BEATEN
PATH

Deutsches Zweirad–Museum (*German Motorcycle Museum*). Although its name is the German Motorcycle Museum, there are historic cars here, too. Displays include the 1885 Daimler machine that started us on the road to motorized mobility, the world's first mass-produced motorcycles (Hildebrand and Wolfmüller), and exhibits on racing. Also here is the NSU Museum, an early motorbike manufacturer acquired by the precedessor of the company now called Audi, which has an auto production facility in Neckarsulm. The collections are arranged over five floors in a handsome 400-year-old castle that belonged to the Teutonic Knights until 1806. The Audi factory offers tours. ✉ *Urbanstr. 11, Neckarsulm* ☎ *07132/35271* ⊕ *www.zweirad-museum.de* 🎫 *€4.50* ☉ *Tues.–Sun. 9–5, Thurs. to 7.*

SWABIAN CITIES

Ludwigsburg, Stuttgart, and Tübingen are all part of the ancient province of Swabia, a region strongly influenced by Protestantism and Calvinism. The inhabitants speak the Swabian dialect of German. Ludwigsburg is known for its two splendid castles. Stuttgart, the capital of the state of Baden-Württemberg, is one of Germany's leading industrial cities, home to both Mercedes and Porsche, and is cradled by hills on three sides, with the fourth side opening up toward its river harbor. The medieval town of Tübingen clings to steep slopes and hilltops above the Neckar.

8

LUDWIGSBURG

15 km (9 miles) north of Stuttgart.

Although its residents would never call it a suburb of Stuttgart, its proximity to the modern industrial and commercial center of Baden-Wurttenberg has made it one. Ludwigsburg's attraction is its fabulous baroque castle, with more than 450 rooms spread over 18 buildings, surrounded by the beautiful Schlosspark (gardens). A music festival, held each summer since 1932, features performances both outdoors and in the original palace theater.

GETTING HERE AND AROUND

There is regular commuter rail service from Stuttgart's Hauptbahnhof (main train station). Take the S4 or S5 for the journey of around 45 minutes. The castle is close enough to the station to walk, or you can take a taxi.

EXPLORING

Fodor's Choice ★ **Residenzschloss Ludwigsburg.** One of Europe's largest palaces to survive in its original condition, Residenzschloss Ludwigsburg certainly merits a visit for its sumptuous interiors and exquisite gardens. The main palace is also home to the **Keramikmuseum,** a collection of historical treasures from the porcelain factories in Meissen, Nymphenburg, Berlin, Vienna, and Ludwigsburg, as well as an exhibit of contemporary ceramics. The

Barockgalerie is a collection of German and Italian baroque paintings from the 17th and 18th centuries. The **Modemuseum** showcases three centuries of fashion, particularly royal clothing of the 18th century. In another part of the palace you'll find the **Porzellan-Manufaktur Ludwigsburg** (*www.ludwigsburger-porzellan.de*); you can tour the porcelain factory where each piece is handmade and hand-painted. The castle is surrounded by the fragrant, colorful 74-acre park **Blühendes Barock** (Blooming Baroque), filled with thousands and thousands of tulips, huge masses of rhododendrons, and fragrant roses. A Märchengarten (fairy-tale garden) delights children of all ages. In the midst of it all, you can take a break in the cafeteria in the Rose Garden. Guided tours in English are at 1:30 on weekdays, and at 11, 1:30, and 3:15 on weekends. There also are performances in the ornate theater, dating from 1758, during the Ludwigsburg Theater Festival each summer. ⊠ *Schloss Str. 30* ☎ *07141/182–004* ⊕ *www.schloesser-und-gaerten.de* ⌦ *Palace €7, park €8, museums with audio guide €3.50, museum tour with audio guide €6.50, combination ticket €17* ⊙ *Park daily 7:30 am–8:30 pm, palace and museums daily 10–5.*

STUTTGART

50 km (31 miles) south of Heilbronn.

Stuttgart is a city of contradictions. It has been called, among other things, "Germany's biggest small town" and "the city where work is a pleasure." For centuries Stuttgart, whose name derives from *Stutengarten,* or "stud farm," remained a pastoral backwater along the Neckar. Then the Industrial Revolution propelled the city into the machine age. Leveled in World War II, Stuttgart has regained its position as one of Germany's top industrial centers.

This is Germany's can-do city, whose natives have turned out Mercedes-Benz and Porsche cars, Bosch electrical equipment, and a host of other products exported worldwide. Yet Stuttgart is also a city of culture and the arts, with world-class museums, opera, and ballet. Moreover, it's the domain of fine local wines; the vineyards actually approach the city center in a rim of green hills. Forests, vineyards, meadows, and orchards compose more than half the city, which is enclosed on three sides by woods. Each year in October, Stuttgart is home to Germany's second-largest Oktoberfest (after Munich), called the Canstatter Volksfest.

An ideal introduction to the contrasts of Stuttgart is a guided city bus tour. Included is a visit to the needle-nose TV tower, high on a mountaintop above the city, affording stupendous views. Built in 1956, it was the first of its kind in the world. The tourist office also offers superb walking tours. On your own, the best place to begin exploring Stuttgart is the Hauptbahnhof (main train station); from there walk down the pedestrian street Königstrasse to Schillerplatz, a small, charming square named after the 18th-century poet and playwright Friedrich Schiller, who was born in nearby Marbach. The square is surrounded by historic buildings, many of which were rebuilt after the war.

GETTING HERE AND AROUND

Stuttgart is the major hub for the rail system in southwestern Germany, and two autobahns cross here. It's about 2½ hours away from Munich and a bit more than an hour from Frankfurt. The downtown museums and the main shopping streets are doable on foot. For the outlying attractions and to get to the airport, there is a very efficient S-bahn and subway system.

TOURS

The tourist office is the meeting point for city walking tours in German (year-round, Saturday at 10) for €8. There are daily bilingual walks April–October at 11 am for €18. Bilingual bus tours costing €8 depart from the bus stop around the corner from the tourist office, in front of Hotel am Schlossgarten (April–October, daily at 1:30; November–March, Friday–Sunday at 1:30). All tours last from 1½ to 2½ hours. Stuttgart Tourist-Information offers 12 different special-interest tours altogether. Call for details.

DISCOUNTS AND DEALS

The three-day **StuttCard** (€9.70) offers discounts to museums and attractions, with or without a free public-transit pass (€22 includes a transit card valid in the whole city; €18 for the city center only). All the cards are available from the Stuttgart tourist office opposite the main train station.

ESSENTIALS

Visitor Information Stuttgart Touristik-Information i-Punkt. ☒ *Königstr. 1A* ☏ *0711/222–8246* ⊕ *www.stuttgart-tourist.de.*

EXPLORING

TOP ATTRACTIONS

Kunstmuseum Stuttgart (*Stuttgart Art Museum*). This sleek structure encased in a glass facade is a work of art in its own right. The museum contains artwork of the 19th and 20th centuries and the world's largest Otto Dix collection, including the *Grossstadt* (*Metropolis*) triptych, which captures the essence of 1920s Germany. The bistro-café on the rooftop terrace affords great views; the lobby houses another café and the museum shop. ☒ *Kleiner Schlosspl. 1, Mitte* ☏ *0711/216–19600* ⊕ *www.kunstmuseum-stuttgart.de* ☒ *€6; special exhibitions €10; guided tours €2.50* ⊙ *Tues.–Th. and weekends 10–6; Fri. 10–9.*

FAMILY
Fodor'sChoice
★

Mercedes-Benz Museum. The stunning futuristic architecture of this museum is an enticement to enter, but the stunning historic and futuristic vehicles inside are the main attraction. Visitors are whisked to the top floor to start this historical timeline tour of motorized mobility in the 1880s, with the first vehicles by Gottlieb Daimler and Carl Benz. Other museum levels focus on a particular decade or category of vehicle, such as trucks and buses, race cars, concept cars, and future technology, including fuel cells. Historic photos and other artifacts line the walls of the circular walkway that links the levels. A restaurant on the lower level serves mostly German cuisine with a modern twist, and stays open after the museum has closed, and there's a huge gift shop with all kinds of Mercedes-Benz–branded items. In the adjoining new-car showroom you can muse over appealing models that are sold in Europe but not in North America. Guided tours of the factory are also available. ☒ *Mercedesstr. 100, Untertürkheim* ☏ *0711/173–0000* ⊕ *www.mercedes-benz-classic.com* ☒ *€8 (€4 after 4:30); guided tour €4; factory tour €4* ⊙ *Tues.–Sun. 9–6 (last admission 5).*

FAMILY
Fodor'sChoice
★

Porsche Museum. In the center of the Porsche factory complex in the northern suburb of Zuffenhausen, the architecturally dramatic building expands outward and upward from its base. Inside is a vast collection of around 100 legendary and historic Porsche cars including racing cars, nearly 1,000 racing trophies and design and engineering awards, and several vehicles designed by Ferdinand Porsche that eventually became the VW Beetle. It is astounding how some 1930s models still look contemporary today. The museum includes a coffee shop, snack bar, and the sophisticated Christophorus restaurant, regarded as the best American-style steak house in Stuttgart, open for lunch and dinner beyond museum hours. The gift shop sells some Porsche logo clothing, but mostly miniature collectibles. Stand under the special "cones" on the upper level to hear the different engine sounds of various Porsche models, and try out the interactive "touch wall" timeline to explore nine decades of automotive history. Factory tours also are available with advance arrangement. ☒ *Porschepl. 1, Zuffenhausen* ☏ *0711/911–20911* ⊕ *www.porsche.com/museum* ☒ *€8* ⊙ *Tues.–Sun. 9–6.*

The postmodern Neue Staatsgalerie (New State Gallery) is where you'll find 20th-century masterpieces by artists including Picasso and Chagall.

Schlossplatz (*Palace Square*). A huge area enclosed by royal palaces and planted gardens, the square has elegant arcades branching off to other stately plazas. The magnificent baroque **Neues Schloss** (New Palace), now occupied by Baden-Württemberg state government offices, dominates the square. Schlossplatz is the extension of the Koenigstrasse pedestrian shopping street, dotted with outdoor cafés in season. ⊠ *Corner of Koenigstr. and Planie, Mitte.*

Fodor'sChoice
★
Staatsgalerie (*State Gallery*). This not-to-be-missed museum displays one of the finest art collections in Germany. The old part of the complex, dating from 1843, has paintings from the Middle Ages through the 19th century, including works by Cranach, Holbein, Hals, Memling, Rubens, Rembrandt, Cézanne, Courbet, and Manet. Connected to the original building is the **Neue Staatsgalerie** (New State Gallery), designed by British architect James Stirling in 1984 as a melding of classical and modern, sometimes jarring, elements (such as chartreuse window mullions). Considered one of the most successful postmodern buildings, it houses works by such 20th-century artists as Braque, Chagall, de Chirico, Dalí, Kandinsky, Klee, Mondrian, and Picasso. ⊠ *Konrad-Adenauer-Str. 30–32, Mitte* ☎ *0711/470–400, 0711/4704–0249 infoline* ⊕ *www.staatsgalerie.de* ✉ *Permanent collection €7 (free Wed.); special exhibitions €8–€12; guided tours €5* ☉ *Tues.–Wed. and Fri.– Sun. 10–6; Thurs. 10–8.*

WORTH NOTING

FAMILY
Fodor'sChoice
★
Altes Schloss (*Old Castle*). Across the street from the Neues Schloss stands this former residence of the counts and dukes of Württemberg, which was originally built as a moated castle around 1320. Wings

were added in the mid-15th century, creating a Renaissance palace. The palace now houses the **Landesmuseum Württemberg** (Württemberg State Museum), with imaginative exhibits tracing the area's development from the Stone Age to modern times. There's also a separate floor dedicated to a children's museum. The second floor includes jaw-dropping family jewels of the fabulously rich and powerful Württemberg royals. ⊠ *Schillerpl. 6, Mitte* ☎ *0711/8953–5111* ⊕ *www.landesmuseum-stuttgart.de* ⊠ *€12* ⊗ *Mon.–Thurs. 9–4, Fri. 9–2.*

Haus der Geschichte Baden-Württemberg (*Museum of the History of Baden-Württemberg*). Adjoining the Staatsgalerie (State Gallery), this museum chronicles the history of Baden-Württemberg state during the 19th and 20th centuries. Multimedia presentations enable you to interact with the thousands of objects on display. ⊠ *Konrad-Adenauer-Str. 16, Mitte* ☎ *0711/212–3989* ⊕ *www.hdgbw.de* ⊠ *€4* ⊗ *Tues.–Wed. and Fri–Sun. 10–6; Thurs. 10–9.*

FAMILY **Schweine Museum.** Billed as the world's only pig museum, it is housed in a former slaughterhouse, with displays on more than you ever wanted to know about breeding and porcine anatomy. Exhibits of piggy banks and other pig-themed memorabilia are fun to peruse. There's also a restaurant and an outdoor beer garden, and a play area for the kids where everything is pig themed, from the seesaws to the garbage containers. ⊠ *Schlachthofstr. 2* ⊕ *www.schweinemuseum.de* ⊠ *€5.90; playground free* ⊗ *Daily 11–7:30 (last admission 6:45).*

Schlossgarten (*Palace Garden*). This huge city park borders the Schlossplatz and extends northeast across Schillerstrasse all the way to Bad Cannstatt on the Neckar River. The park is graced by an exhibition hall, planetarium, lakes, sculptures, and the hot-spring mineral baths Leuze and Berg. ⊠ *Off Cannstatterstr.*

Stiftskirche (*Collegiate Church of the Holy Cross*). Just off Schillerplatz, this is Stuttgart's most familiar sight, with its two oddly matched towers. Built in the 12th century, it was later rebuilt in a late-Gothic style. The choir has a famous series of Renaissance figures of the counts of Württemberg sculpted by Simon Schlör (1576–1608). ⊠ *Stiftstr. 12, Mitte.*

FAMILY **Wilhelma Zoologische-Botanische Garten** (*Wilhelma Zoological and Botanical Garden*). Adjacent to Rosenstein Park, this wildlife park and zoological garden, with more than 9,000 animals in more than 1,000 species and around 7,000 species of plants and flowers, was originally intended as a garden for King Wilhelm I. The Moorish-style buildings are why it's referred to as the "Alhambra on the Neckar." There are two restaurants on-site and a less formal bistro-café with outdoor seating in warm weather. A modern Ape House opened in 2013, with gorillas and bonobos. ⊠ *Wilhemapl. 13, Wilhelma* ☎ *0711/54020* ⊕ *www.wilhelma. de* ⊠ *€16; €10 Nov.–Feb. and after 4 pm Mar.–Oct.* ⊗ *May–Aug., daily 8:15–6; Sept.–Apr., daily 8:15–4.*

WHERE TO EAT

$$ ✕ **Alte Kanzlei.** Steps from the Altes Schloss, the building dates from
GERMAN 1565, but the menu is modern, albeit with traditional Swabian special-
Fodor's Choice ties including Maultaschen, or meat-filled ravioli. The *Käsespätzle*, or
★ noodles with cheese, is served with a salad, and it's enough for lunch

The fountain in Schlossplatz (Palace Square) is a great place for people-watching, or to contemplate the surrounding architecture.

or a light dinner, especially when combined with *Opfenschulpfer,* an airy bread pudding topped with vanilla sauce. There are daily beer and wine specials featuring local and regional producers. It's popular with local office workers for its location, service, and good prices. $ *Average main: €15* ✉ *Schillerpl. 5A, Mitte* ☎ *0711/294–457* ⊕ *www.alte-kanzlei-stuttgart.de* ✍ *Reservations essential.*

$$
GERMAN
✕ **Paulaner am Alten Postplatz** (*Paulaner Brewpub*). The motto here is "wurst and bier are friends," and there's plenty of both consumed in this popular brewpub. Paulaner is a Munich beer, so you'll find traditional Bavarian fare, including *Weisswurst,* or veal sausages, on the menu along with Swabian favorites such as house-made Maultaschen. There's even an Austrian dessert, *Kaisershmarrn,* named for the ruler who loved pancakes cut in small pieces and mixed with fresh fruits and whipped cream. Tables upstairs are quieter, and there's an outdoor beer garden in season. $ *Average main: €15* ✉ *Calwerstr. 45, Mitte* ☎ *711/214450* ⊕ *www.paulaner-stuttgart.de/.*

$
GERMAN
✕ **Tobi's.** Take out or eat in at this regional minichain. You won't find burgers or chicken nuggets, but, rather, schnitzel, currywurst, spaetzle, several types of Maultaschen, and German-style fries. Service is fast and friendly, it's bright and clean, and there's a daily happy hour from 4 pm to 7 pm with €1.20 draft beers, and a small sidewalk café in season. $ *Average main: €5* ✉ *Bolzstr. 7, Mitte* ☎ *7111/229–3307* ⊕ *www.todis.de/stuttgart* ✍ *Reservations not accepted* ▭ *No credit cards.*

$$$$
EUROPEAN
✕ **Wielandshöhe.** One of Germany's top chefs, Vincent Klink, and his wife, Elisabeth, are very down-to-earth, cordial hosts. Her floral arrangements add a baroque touch to the otherwise quiet interior,

designed to focus on the artfully presented cuisine. To the extent possible, all ingredients are grown locally and identified on the menu. House specialties, such as saddle of lamb with a potato gratin and green beans or the Breton lobster with basil potato salad, are recommended. The wine list is exemplary. $ *Average main: €45 ⊠ Alte Weinsteige 71, Degerloch ☎ 0711/640–8848 ⊕ www.wielandshoehe.de ⊗ Closed Sun. and Mon. ⌕ Reservations essential ⌂ Jacket required.*

WHERE TO STAY

$$$ ⊡ **Am Schlossgarten.** Stuttgart's top accommodations are in a modern
HOTEL structure set in spacious gardens, a stone's throw from many of the top sights and opposite the main station. **Pros:** views of the park; welcoming lobby; close to museums, ballet, opera. **Cons:** not all rooms face the park; rates are on the high end; parking is limited and expensive. $ *Rooms from: €200 ⊠ Schillerstr. 23, Mitte ☎ 0711/20260 ⊕ www. hotelschlossgarten.com ⊗ Zirbelstube closed 1st 2 wks Jan., 3 wks Aug., Sun., and Mon. ⌐ 106 rooms, 10 suites ⊠ Breakfast.*

$$$ ⊡ **Der Zauberlehrling.** The "Sorcerer's Apprentice" is aptly named, as
B&B/INN Karen and Axel Heldmann have conjured up an unusual luxury hotel with each room's style based on a theme. **Pros:** fabulous rooms with lots of surprises; enjoyable restaurant. **Cons:** minuscule lobby; no elevator. $ *Rooms from: €190 ⊠ Rosenstr. 38, Bohnenviertel ☎ 0711/237–7770 ⊕ www.zauberlehrling.de ⌐ 13 rooms, 4 suites ⊠ Breakfast.*

$$ ⊡ **Hotel Wartburg.** This comfortable hotel is on a quiet side street a five-
HOTEL minute walk from the Konigstrasse pedestrian mile and the museums around Schlossplatz. **Pros:** free parking; close to shopping and theaters. **Cons:** rooms facing street can be noisy. $ *Rooms from: €125 ⊠ Langestr. 49, Mitte ☎ 0711/20450 ⊕ www.hotel-wartburg-stuttgart.de ⌐ 74 rooms ⊠ Breakfast.*

$$ ⊡ **Mövenpick Hotel Stuttgart Airport.** Across the street from Stuttgart Air-
HOTEL port, the doors of this hotel open into a completely soundproof glass palace. **Pros:** discount for booking online; modern yet welcoming; fitness equipment, sauna, steam room. **Cons:** swells with business travelers; 15 minutes from downtown museums, theater, or shopping. $ *Rooms from: €150 ⊠ Flughafenstr. 50, Flughafen ☎ 0711/553–440 ⊕ www. movenpick.com/Stuttgart ⌐ 326 rooms, 12 junior suites ⊠ No meals.*

$$ ⊡ **Wald Hotel.** On the edge of a forest (wald) with miles of hiking and
RESORT biking trails, yet just a 10-minute streetcar ride from downtown, this
Fodor's Choice modern resort hotel offers lots of amenities and peaceful nights. **Pros:**
★ free Wi-Fi; ample free parking; spacious modern bathrooms. **Cons:** walk from streetcar station after dark is not well lit. $ *Rooms from: €150 ⊠ Guts-Muths-Weg 18, Degerloch ☎ 0711/185–720, 0711/185–72120 ⊕ www.waldhotel-stuttgart.de ⌐ 94 rooms, 2 suites ⊠ Breakfast.*

NIGHTLIFE AND PERFORMING ARTS
NIGHTLIFE
There's no shortage of rustic beer gardens, wine pubs, or sophisticated cocktail bars in and around Stuttgart. Night owls should head for the **Schwabenzentrum** on Eberhardstrasse; the **Bohnenviertel**, or "Bean Quarter" (Charlotten-, Olga-, and Pfarrstrasse); the "party mile" along **Theodor-Heuss-Strasse; Calwer Strasse**; and **Wilhelmsplatz**.

Café Stella. If you enjoy live music, visit this trendy restaurant and bar, perfect for an evening of dinner and drinks. The entertainment focus is on singer-songwriters, but includes jazz, comedy, and literary events, with swing dancing to a DJ every Sunday. ⊠ *Hauptstätterstr. 57, Mitte* ☎ *0711/640–2583* ⊕ *www.cafe-stella.de.*

PERFORMING ARTS

i-Punkt tourist office. Across the street from the main train station, this is the place to check out a current calendar of events and buy discount tickets. There is also an i-Punkt kiosk at the Stuttgart Airport, Terminal 3, Level 2. ⊠ *Königstr. 1A, Mitte* ☎ *0711/22280 ticket hotline (weekdays 8:30–6)* ⊕ *www.stuttgart-tourist.de* ☽ *Weekdays 9–8, Sat. 9–6, Sun. and public holidays 10–6.*

SI-Centrum. Built to showcase big-budget musicals, including American imports such as *42nd Street,* this entertainment complex contains theaters, hotels, bars, restaurants, a casino, a wellness center, movie theaters, and shops. A calendar of events can be found on its website. ⊠ *Plieninger Str. 100, Möhringen* ☎ *0711/721–1111* ⊕ *www. si-centrum.de.*

Staatstheater. Stuttgart's internationally renowned ballet company performs at this elegant historic theater. The ballet season—including works choreographed by Stuttgart Ballet's John Cranko—is September through July and alternates with the highly respected State Opera. The box office is open weekdays 10–8, Saturday 10–2. ⊠ *Oberer Schlossgarten 6, Mitte* ☎ *0711/20320* ⊕ *www.staatstheater.stuttgart.de.*

SPORTS AND THE OUTDOORS

BOAT TRIPS

Neckar-Käpt'n. From the pier opposite the entrance to the zoo, Neckar-Käpt'n offers a wide range of boat trips, as far north as scenic Besigheim. ⊠ *Off Neckartalstr., Am Leuzebad* ☎ *0711/5499–7060* ⊕ *www.neckar-kaeptn.de* 🎫 *€7–€32, depending on distance.*

HIKING

Stuttgart has a 53-km (33-mile) network of marked hiking trails in the nearby hills; follow the signs with the city's emblem: a horse set in a yellow ring.

SWIMMING AND SPAS

Mineralbad Cannstatt. Bad Cannstatt's mineral springs are more than 2,000 years old and, with a daily output of about 5.8 million gallons, the second most productive in Europe (after Budapest). There are indoor and outdoor mineral pools, hot tubs, a sauna, a steam room, and spa facilities. ⊠ *Sulzerrainstr. 2, Bad Cannstatt* ☎ *0711/2166–6270.*

Mineralbad Leuze. On the banks of the Neckar near the König-Karl Bridge is the Mineralbad Leuze, with eight pools indoors and out and an open-air mineral-water sauna. ⊠ *Am Leuzebad 2–6, Bad Cannstatt* ☎ *0711/2169–9701.*

SHOPPING

Stuttgart is a shopper's paradise, from the department stores on the Königstrasse to the boutiques in the Old Town's elegant passages and the factory outlet stores.

8

Bohnenviertel (*Bean Quarter*). Some of Stuttgart's more unique shops are found in this older quarter. A stroll through the neighborhood's smaller streets reveals many tucked-away shops specializing in fashion, jewelry, artwork, and gifts. ⊠ *Stuttgart.*

Breuninger. The flagship store of this upscale regional department-store chain has glass elevators that rise and fall under the dome of the central arcade, whisking you to multiple floors of designer boutiques. There is also a clearance Breuninger Outlet at Rotebühlplatz 25. ⊠ *Marktstr. 1–3, Mitte* ☎ *0711/2110* ⊕ *www.breuninger.de* ⊗ *Main store and Outlet: weekdays 10–8, Sat. 9:30–8.*

Calwerstrasse. You'll find several blocks of boutiques, cafés, and restaurants between the main shopping streets of Koenigstrasse and Theodore-Heuss-Strasse, but far less busy. The restaurants spill into the pedestrian-only street in warm weather. ⊠ *Calwerstr., Mitte.*

Fodor'sChoice ★ **Markthalle.** The beautiful art nouveau Markthalle on Dorotheenstrasse is one of Germany's finest market halls, with a curved glass ceiling for natural light to show off a mouthwatering selection of exotic fresh fruits, spices, meats, cheeses, chocolates, honeys, flowers, and handmade jewelry and crafts, including holiday decorations in season. Check out the huge ceramic fountain, which spouts water from the original well. The restaurant balcony overlooks the action, which starts at 7 am. ⊠ *Dorotheenstr. 4* ⊕ *www.markthalle-stuttgart.de* ⊗ *Weekdays 7–6:30, Sat. 7–5.*

BEBENHAUSEN

6 km (4 miles) north of Tübingen.

Between Stuttgart and Tübingen lies this small hamlet consisting of a few houses, a monastery, and the Waldhorn, an excellent and well-known restaurant. The monastery was founded in the 12th century by the count of Tübingen. Today it belongs to the state.

GETTING HERE AND AROUND

To get here by public transportation, take the train from Stuttgart to Tübingen (45 minutes) then a bus to Bebenhausen (15 minutes). Trains and bus connections are several times an hour on weekdays, less on weekends. If you're driving, take the B-27 and B-464 south from Stuttgart.

EXPLORING

Fodor'sChoice ★ **Zisterzienzerkloster** (*Cistercian Monastery*). This is a rare example of a well-preserved medieval monastery from the late 12th century. Following the secularization of 1806, the abbot's abode was rebuilt as a hunting castle for King Frederick of Württemberg. Expansion and restoration continued as long as the palace and monastery continued to be a royal residence. Visits to the palace are with guided tours only. ⊠ *Im Schloss* ☎ *07071/602–802* ⊠ *Monastery €4, palace €4.50* ⊗ *Nov.–Mar., Tues.–Sun. 10–noon and 1–5; Apr.–Oct. daily 9–5.*

WHERE TO EAT

$$$$ ✕ **Waldhorn.** Old favorites such as the *Vorspeisenvariation* (a medley of
EUROPEAN appetizers), local fish, and goose keep people coming back to this his-
Fodor's Choice toric eatery. The wine list features a well-chosen selection of top Baden
★ and Württemberg wines. Garden tables have a castle view. A meal here
is a perfect start or finale to the concerts held on the monastery-cas-
tle grounds in the summer. $ *Average main: €30* ⊠ *Schönbuchstr. 49*
☎ *07071/61270* ⊕ *www.waldhorn-bebenhausen.de* ▬ *No credit cards*
⊗ *Closed Mon. and Tues.* ⪼ *Reservations essential.*

TÜBINGEN

40 km (25 miles) south of Stuttgart.

With its half-timber houses, winding alleyways, and hilltop setting
overlooking the Neckar, Tübingen provides the quintessential German
experience. The medieval flavor is quite authentic, as the town was
untouched by wartime bombings. Dating to the 11th century, Tübingen
flourished as a trade center; its weights and measures and currency were
the standard through much of the area. The town declined in importance after the 14th century, when it was taken over by the counts of
Württemberg. Between the 14th and the 19th century, its size hardly
changed as it became a university and residential town, its castle the
only symbol of ruling power.

Yet Tübingen hasn't been sheltered from the world. It resonates with
a youthful air. Even more than Heidelberg, Tübingen is virtually synonymous with its university, a leading center of learning since it was
founded in 1477. The best way to see and appreciate Tübingen is simply
to stroll around, soaking up its age-old atmosphere of quiet erudition.

8

GETTING HERE AND AROUND

By regional train or by car on the autobahn, Tübingen is an hour south
of Stuttgart on B-27. Trains run several times an hour on weekdays,
less often on weekends. In the Old Town you reach everything on foot.

TOURS

The Tübingen tourist office runs guided city tours year-round at 2:30.
From March through October tours take place daily and cost €9. From
November through February, tours are on weekends only. Tours start
at the Rathaus on the market square.

DISCOUNTS AND DEALS

Overnight guests receive a free Tourist-Regio-Card from their hotel
(ask for it) for reduced admission fees to museums, concerts, theaters,
and sports facilities.

TIMING

A leisurely walk around the old part of town will take you about two
hours, if you include the castle on the hill and Platanenallee, where you
look at the Old Town from across the river.

ESSENTIALS

Visitor Information Verkehrsverein Tübingen. ⊠ *Tübingen* ☎ *07071/91360*
⊕ *www.tuebingen-info.de.*

EXPLORING
TOP ATTRACTIONS

FAMILY   **Boxenstop Museum.** A wealth of vintage toys, model trains, and vehicles,
Fodor'sChoice   including motorcycles, awaits children of all ages. This private collec-
★   tion, open to the public, includes Porsche, Ferrari, and Maserati racecars, an original 1957 VW Beetle, and a rare 1954 Lloyd. Ask a docent
to start up the HO trains or one of the antique musical toys. Kids can
ride one of the old pedal cars. There's also a small café. ⊠ *Brunnenstr.
18* ☎ *7071/929–090* ⊕ *www.boxenstop-tuebingen.de* ⬚ *€6.50* ⊙ *Mid-
Jan.–Oct., Wed.–Fri. 10–noon and 2–5; Nov.–Dec. 21, weekends 10–5.*

Marktplatz (*Market Square*). Houses of prominent burghers of centuries gone by surround this square. At the open-air market on Monday,
Wednesday, and Friday from 7 to 5 in the summer and 9 to 3 in winter, you can buy flowers, bread, pastries, poultry, sausage, and cheese.
⊠ *Tübingen.*

Rathaus (*Town Hall*). Begun in 1433, this building slowly expanded over
the next 150 years. Its ornate Renaissance facade is bright with colorful murals and a marvelous astronomical clock dating from 1511. The
halls and reception rooms are adorned with half-timber and paintings
from the late 19th century. ⊠ *Marktpl.*

Stiftskirche (*Collegiate Church*). The late-Gothic church has been well
preserved; its original features include the stained-glass windows, the
choir stalls, the ornate baptismal font, and the elaborate stone pulpit.
The windows are famous for their colors and were much admired by
Goethe. The dukes of Württemberg, from the 15th through the 17th
century, are interred in the choir. ⊠ *Holzmarkt* ☎ *0707/43151* ⊕ *www.
stiftskirche-tuebingen.de/* ⊙ *Daily 9–4.*

WORTH NOTING

Alte Aula (*Old Auditorium*). Erected in 1547, the half-timber university
building was significantly altered in 1777, when it acquired an Italian
roof, a symmetrical facade, and a balcony decorated with two crossed
scepters, symbolizing the town's center of learning. In earlier times grain
was stored under the roof as part of the professors' salaries. ⊠ *Münzg.*

Bursa (*Student Dormitory*). The word *bursa* meant "purse" in the Middle Ages and later came to refer to student lodgings such as this former
student dormitory. Despite its classical facade, which it acquired in the
early 19th century, the building actually dates back to 1477. Medieval
students had to master a broad curriculum that included the *septem
artes liberales* (seven liberal arts) of grammar, dialectic, rhetoric, arith-
metic, geometry, astronomy, and music. The interior of the Bursa is
not open for visits, but it's worth strolling by for a look at the outside.
⊠ *Bursag. 4.*

Hölderlinturm (*Hölderlin's Tower*). Friedrich Hölderlin, a visionary poet
who succumbed to madness in his early thirties, lived here until his
death in 1843, in the care of the master cabinetmaker Zimmer and his
daughter. There's a small literary museum and art gallery inside, and a
schedule of events includes concerts and poetry readings. ⊠ *Bursag. 6*
☎ *07071/22040* ⊕ *www.hoelderlin-gesellschaft.de* ⬚ *€2.50* ⊙ *Tues.–
Fri. 10–noon and 3–5.*

Kornhaus (*Grain House*). During the Middle Ages, townspeople stored and sold grain on the first floor of this structure built in 1453; social events took place on the second floor. It now houses the City Museum with changing exhibitions and a permanent exhibition about the history of Tübingen. ✉ *Kornhausstr. 10* ☎ *07071/204–1711* 🎟 *€2.50* 🕓 *Tues.–Sun. 11–5.*

Schloss Hohentübingen. The original castle of the counts of Tübingen (1078) was significantly enlarged and altered by Duke Ulrich during the 16th century. Particularly noteworthy is the elaborate Renaissance portal patterned after a Roman triumphal arch. The coat of arms of the duchy of Württemberg depicted in the center is framed by the emblems of various orders, including the Order of the Garter. Today the castle's main attraction is its magnificent view over the river and town. It's a 90-minute walk from Schlossbergstrasse, over the Spitzberg, or via the Kapitänsweg that ends north of the castle. ✉ *Burgsteige 11.*

TOURING TIPS

Information: The tourist office at the Neckarbrücke has maps, brochures, and information on hotels.

Scenic spot: From the ramparts of the Hohentübingen Castle you have an excellent view over the Old Town.

Scenic spot: Walking along Kirchgasse, which opens up into the Marktplatz, you find yourself surrounded by the imposing houses that belonged to the leading families of the town.

WHERE TO EAT AND STAY

$$ GERMAN Fodor's Choice ★

🍴 **Forelle.** Beautiful ceilings painted with vine motifs, exposed beams, wooden wainscotting and an old tile stove make for a *gemütlich* (cozy) atmosphere. This small restaurant fills up fast, not least because of the Swabian cooking, including the region's signature Maultaschen (filled pasta pockets). The chef makes sure the ingredients are from the region, including the inn's namesake, trout, often served as French-style *almondine*. Save room for dessert, especially the house-made *Schwäbische Apfelküchle* (Swabian apple cake) with vanilla sauce. [$] *Average main: €17* ✉ *Kronenstr. 8* ☎ *07071/24094* 🌐 *www.weinstube-forelle.de.*

$ GERMAN Fodor's Choice ★

🍴 **Wurstküche.** For more than 200 years, all sorts of people have come here: students, because many of the dishes are filling yet inexpensive; locals, because the food is the typical Swabian fare their mothers made; and out-of-town visitors, who love the old-fashioned atmosphere. In summer try to get a seat at one of the sidewalk tables. Try the Alb-Leisa ond Schbatza, or sausages with spaetzle and lentils. [$] *Average main: €13* ✉ *Am Lustnauer Tor 8* ☎ *07071/92750* 🌐 *www.wurstkueche.com.*

$$ HOTEL

🏨 **Hotel Am Schloss.** There are lovely views of the Old Town from the rooms in this charming small hotel, and it's close to the castle that towers over the town. **Pros:** lovely views of castle and valley; excellent restaurant. **Cons:** no elevator; difficult parking. [$] *Rooms from: €118* ✉ *Burgsteige 18* ☎ *07071/92940* 🌐 *www.hotelamschloss.de* 🛏 *37 rooms* 🍽 *Breakfast.*

$$ HOTEL

🏨 **Hotel Hospiz.** This family-run hotel provides friendly service, comfortable rooms, and a convenient Altstadt location near the castle. **Pros:** convenient location. **Cons:** many stairs in spite of elevator; rooms simply furnished; no bar or restaurant. $ *Rooms from: €110* ⊠ *Neckarhalde 2* ☎ *07071/9240* ⊕ *www.hotel-hospiz.de* ➴ *45 rooms* ⦿ *Breakfast.*

NIGHTLIFE AND PERFORMING ARTS

Die Kelter. You'll find jazz, light fare, and a wineshop here, and a more sophisticated crowd than at the student pubs. ⊠ *Schmiedtorstr. 17* ☎ *07071/254–690* ⊕ *www.diekelter.de* ☉ *Closed Mon.*

Jazzkeller. Like all the Old Town student pubs, Jazzkeller attracts a lively crowd after 9. ⊠ *Haagg. 15/2* ☎ *07071/550–906* ⊕ *www.jazz-keller.eu* ☉ *Closed Sun.*

Tangente-Jour. This café morphs into a bistro and cocktail lounge after dark, so you can find action from breakfast until past midnight, next to the Stiftskirche. ⊠ *Münzg. 17* ☎ *07071/24572* ⊕ *www.tangente-marktschenke.de.*

SPORTS AND THE OUTDOORS

The Tübingen tourist office has maps with hiking routes around the town, including historical and geological *Lehrpfade,* or educational walks. A classic Tübingen walk goes from the castle down to the little chapel called the **Wurmlinger Kapelle,** taking about two hours. On the way you can stop off at the restaurant Schwärzlocher Hof (closed Monday and Tuesday) for a glass of *Most* (apple wine), bread, and sausages—all are homemade.

OFF THE BEATEN PATH

Burg Hohenzollern. The majestic silhouette of this massive castle is visible from miles away. The Hohenzollern House of Prussia was the most powerful family in German history. It lost its throne when Kaiser William II abdicated after Germany's defeat in World War I. The Swabian branch of the family owns one-third of the castle, the Prussian branch two-thirds. Today's neo-Gothic structure, perched high on a conical wooded hill, is a successor of a castle dating from the 11th century. On the fascinating 45-minute castle tour you'll see the Prussian royal crown and beautiful period rooms, all opulent from floor to ceiling, with such playful details as door handles carved to resemble peacocks and dogs. The restaurant on the castle grounds, Burgschänke (closed January and Monday in February and March) serves regional food, and there's an outdoor beer garden in season. From the castle parking lot it's a 20-minute walk to the entrance, or in summer take the shuttle bus (€3.10 round-trip, €1.90 one way). ⊠ *25 km (15 miles) south of Tübingen on B–27, Hechingen* ☎ *07471/2428* ⊕ *www.burg-hohenzollern. com* ➴ *€12 including interior rooms; €7 without* ☉ *Castle and shuttle bus: mid-Mar.–Oct., daily 9–5:30; Nov.–mid-Mar., daily 10–4:30.*

FRANKFURT

WELCOME TO FRANKFURT

TOP REASONS TO GO

★ **Sachsenhausen:** Frankfurt's South Bank, with its riverbank row of world-class museums, upscale restaurants, fast-food joints, bars with live music, and traditional Apfelwein pubs, is one big outdoor party in summer.

★ **Paleontology paradise:** Beyond a huge dinosaur skeleton, the Senckenberg Natural History Museum has exhibits of many other extinct animals and plants, plus dioramas of animals in their habitats.

★ **Enjoy the outdoors:** The parks and riverbanks are popular with locals and tourists for strolls, sunbathing, and picnics.

★ **Get some wheels:** Hop on and tour the city sites from a bike; you'll be in good company alongside locals.

★ **Exotic experience:** Head to the Frankfurt Zoo's "exotarium," where coral, fish, snakes, alligators, amphibians, insects, and spiders are on display.

1 Altstadt and City Center. Frankfurt's downtown includes the Altstadt (Old City), parts of which have been carefully restored after wartime destruction; the Zeil, allegedly Germany's number one "shop 'til you drop" mile; the Fressgass ("Pig-Out Alley"); and the bank district.

2 Ostend. This area near the East Harbor is where you'll find lots of corporations and banks, although there are also some sights, including the zoo, as well as restaurants, cafés, and clubs catering to those working in the neighboring skyscrapers.

3 Messe and Westend. The Westend is a mix of the villas of the prewar rich and a skyscraper extension of the business district. It's a popular place for the city's elite to live. Messe is the area around Frankfurt's huge and busy convention center (Messe), but unless you are attending the huge book fair here or Europe's largest auto show and need a nearby beer or meal to refuel, there's not much reason to go.

4 Nordend and Bornheim. These residential areas are a great place to get away from the crowds and enjoy small neighborhood restaurants and shops.

KEY

S	S-Bahn
i	Tourist information
U	U-Bahn

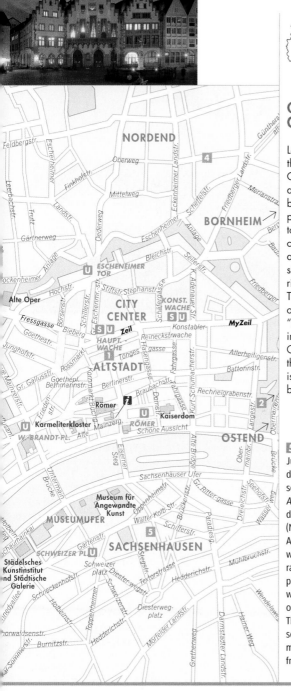

GETTING ORIENTED

Legend has it that the Frankish Emperor Charlemagne was chasing a deer on the Main's south bank when the animal plunged into the river and, to the emperor's amazement, crossed it with its head always above water. A stone ridge had made the river shallow at that point. That supposedly was the origin of Frankfurt (literally "Frankish Ford") as an important river crossing. Commerce flourished from then on: to this day Frankfurt is an important center of business and finance.

9

5 Sachsenhausen.
Just across the river from downtown, Sachsenhausen is distinguished by the *Apfelwein* (Apple Wine) district and the *Museumufer* (Museum Riverbank). The Apple Wine district, now with every sort of restaurant and tavern, is one big party, especially in summer, when the tables spill out onto traffic-free streets. The Museum Riverbank has seven museums within as many blocks along the riverfront street Schaumainkai.

GERMAN SAUSAGES

(above) Landjäger sausage. (lower right) Thüringer Rostbratwurst. (upper right) Frankfurter.

The one thing you're guaranteed to find wherever your travels in Germany take you: sausages. Encased meats are a serious business here, and you could spend a lifetime working your way through 1,500 varieties of German sausages, also known as *Wurst*.

The tradition of making sausages goes back centuries, both as a method to preserve food long before refrigeration and as the best way to use every last piece of precious meat. Sausage recipes go back for generations, and like most German cooking, sausage types vary from region to region. There's also an abundance of ways to serve a sausage—grilled sausages are served up in a small roll, essentially just a sausage "holder"; Weisswursts come to the table after a gentle bath in warm water; cured sausages often are served sliced, while other cooked sausages are dished up with sauerkraut. Germans don't mess around when it comes to their love for sausage, eating about 62 pounds of sausage per person each year.

—Tania Ralli

WEISSWURST ETIQUETTE

Weisswurst is a delicate white sausage made with veal, bacon, lemon, and parsley. It's traditional in the southern state of Bavaria, where they are sticklers about the way to eat them. The casing is never eaten; instead, you *zuzeln* (suck) out the meat. Make a slit at the top, dunk it in sweet mustard, and suck out the insides. It's all right to slit and peel it as well.

FRANKFURTER

In Germany a frankfurter isn't something that must be doused in condiments to make it palatable, like a subpar ballpark frank—instead you'll immediately notice the crisp snap of the frankfurter's skin and a delicious smoky taste. Frankfurters are long and narrow by design, to absorb as much flavor as possible during cold smoking. When served on a plate for lunch or dinner, they're normally served in a pair, and you should eat them dipped in mustard, with your fingers. Frankfurters and other *Würste* also are served inside a small roll, called a *Brotchen*. The only condiment used is mustard, never sauerkraut or other toppings.

THÜRINGER ROSTBRATWURST

This bratwurst dates back to 1613 and it's clear why it has stood the test of time: it's one of Germany's most delicious sausages. The *Rostbratwurst* is a mix of lean pork belly, veal, and beef, seasoned with herbs and spices. Most families closely guard their recipes, but often use garlic, caraway, or nutmeg. You'll smell the scent of grilled *Thüringer* wafting through the streets because they're popular at street markets and festivals.

LANDJÄGER

This small, narrow, and dense rectangular sausage is sold in pairs. It's cured by air-drying, so it resembles a dry salami in color and texture. *Landjäger* are made of beef, sometimes with pork, and red wine and spices. Historically, fieldworkers and wine-grape harvesters liked to eat these salty sausages. Landjäger keep well, so they're a great snack to tuck in your backpack when you head out for a day of hiking in the mountains.

BLUTWURST

Sometimes called *Rotwurst* (red sausage), *Blutwurst* is a combination of ground pork, spices, and—the key ingredient—blood, fresh from the slaughter. After it's been cooked and smoked, the blood congeals, and the sausage takes on a dark hue and looks almost black. Depending on the region, it can be studded with bacon, pickled ox tongue, or potatoes. For most of its history Blutwurst has been considered a luxury item.

BOCKWURST

This sausage got its name when hungry students ordered it with a round of *Bockbier*, a style of beer, in Berlin in 1889. The sausage came from a nearby Jewish butcher, who made it with veal and beef. *Bockwurst* is a thick sausage seasoned with salt, white pepper, and paprika, in a natural casing. It's usually boiled and served hot, but it can also be grilled. It's one of Germany's most popular sausages, so you'll find it on menus all over the country.

9

Updated by
Evelyn Kanter

Although many consider Frankfurt more or less a gateway to their European travels, the city's rich culture and history, dining, and amusement options might just surprise you.

Standing in the center of the Römerberg (medieval town square), you'll see the city's striking contrasts at once. Re-creations of neo-Gothic houses and government buildings enfold the square, while just beyond them modern skyscrapers pierce the sky. The city cheekily nicknamed itself "Mainhattan," using the name of the Main River that flows through it to suggest that other famous metropolis across the Atlantic. Although only fifth in size among German cities, with a population of nearly 700,000, Frankfurt is Germany's financial powerhouse. The German Central Bank (*Bundesbank*) is here, as is the European Central Bank (ECB), which manages the euro. Some 300 credit institutions (more than half of them foreign banks) have offices in Frankfurt, including the headquarters of five of Germany's largest banks. You can see how the city acquired its other nickname, "Bankfurt am Main." It's no wonder that Frankfurt is Europe's financial center. The city's stock exchange, one of the most important in the world, was established in 1585, and the Rothschild family opened their first bank here in 1798.

The long history of trade might help explain the temperament of many Frankfurters—competitive but open-minded. It's also one of the reasons Frankfurt has become Germany's most international city. Close to a quarter of its residents are foreign, with a growing number from Eastern Europe and the Middle East.

Because of its commercialism, Frankfurt has a reputation for being cold and boring, but people who know the city think this characterization is unfair. The district of Sachsenhausen is as *gemütlich* (fun, friendly, and cozy) as you will find anywhere. The city has world-class ballet, opera, theater, and art exhibitions; an important piece of Germany's publishing industry (and the world's largest annual book fair); a large university (43,000 students); and two of the three most important daily newspapers in Germany. Despite the skyscrapers, especially in the *Hauptbahnhof* (main train station) area and adjoining Westend district, there's much here to remind you of the Old World, along with much that explains the success of postwar Germany.

PLANNING

WHEN TO GO

The weather in Frankfurt is moderate throughout the year, though often damp and drizzly. Summers are mild, with the occasional hot day, and it rarely gets very cold in winter and hardly ever snows. Because Frankfurt is one of the biggest trade fair cities in all of Europe, high season at all hotels is considered to be during trade shows throughout the year. Be sure to check dates to avoid paying premium price for a room or even finding yourself without a place to stay.

GETTING HERE AND AROUND

AIR TRAVEL

There are two airports with the name "Frankfurt": Flughafen Frankfurt Main (FRA), which receives direct flights from many U.S. cities and from all major cities in Europe, Africa, Asia, and the Mideast; and Frankfurt-Hahn (HHN), a former U.S. air base a full 112 km (70 miles) west of Frankfurt that handles some bargain flights, mainly to and from secondary European airports.

Airport Contacts Flughafen Frankfurt Main (FRA). ✉ 200 Flughafen Frankfurt am Main ☎ 180/6372–4636 toll call ⊕ www.frankfurt-airport.de. **Frankfurt-Hahn** (HHN). ✉ 1 Saonestr., Hahn-Flughafen ☎ 06543/509–113, ⊕ www.hahn-airport.de.

AIRPORT TRANSFERS

Flughafen Frankfurt Main is 10 km (6 miles) southwest of downtown via the A-5 autobahn, and has its own railway station for high-speed InterCity (IC) and InterCity Express (ICE) trains. Getting into Frankfurt from the airport is easy, via S-bahn line Nos. 8 and 9 that run between the airport and downtown. Most travelers get off at the Hauptbahnhof (main train station, or HBF) or at Hauptwache, in the heart of Frankfurt. Trains run at least every 15 minutes, and the trip takes about 15 minutes. The one-way fare is €4.25. A taxi from the airport into the City Center normally takes around 25 minutes (double that during rush hours). The fare is around €35. If you are driving a rental car from the airport, take the main road out of the airport and follow the signs reading "Stadtmitte" (downtown).

Bohr Busreisen offers a regular bus service to and from Frankfurt-Hahn Airport. It leaves every hour to every 1½ hours, 3 am to 8 pm, from the south side of the Frankfurt Hauptbahnhof, with a stop 15 minutes later at the Terminal 1 bus station at Flughafen Frankfurt Main. The trip to Frankfurt-Hahn takes an hour and 45 minutes, and costs €14.

BUS AND SUBWAY TRAVEL

Frankfurt's smooth-running, well-integrated public transportation system (called RMV) consists of the U-bahn (subway), S-bahn (suburban railway), Strassenbahn (streetcars), and buses. Buses are the public-transit option between 1 am and 4 am.

Fares for the entire system, which includes an extensive surrounding area, are uniform, though they are based on a complex zone system. Within the time that your ticket is valid (one hour for most inner-city destinations), you can transfer from one part of the system to another.

9

Tickets may be purchased from automatic vending machines, which are at all U-bahn and S-bahn stations. Weekly and monthly tickets are sold at central ticket offices and newsstands. A basic one-way ticket for a ride in the inner zone costs €2.60 during the peak hours of 6 am–9 am and 4 pm–6:30 pm weekdays (€2.30 the rest of the time). There's also a reduced *Kurzstrecke* ("short stretch") fare of €1.60 the whole day. A day ticket for unlimited travel in the inner zones costs €6.60. If you're caught without a ticket, there's a fine of €40.

Some 200 European cities have bus links with Frankfurt, largely through Deutsche Touring. Buses arrive at and depart from the south side of the Hauptbahnhof and Terminal 1 at the Frankfurt Main airport. Eurolines provides tours to nearby cities, including Mannheim, Hamburg, and Hanover.

Bus Contacts Bohr Busreisen. ⊠ *Frankfurt* ☎ *0654/350–190* ⊕ *www. omnibusse.bohr.de.* **Eurolines.** ⊠ *Mannheimerstr. 15, City Center* ☎ *069/4609– 2780* ⊕ *www.eurolines.de/en.* **Verkehrsgesellschaft Frankfurt am Main** (*Municipal Transit Authority*). ⊠ *Frankfurt* ☎ *069/19449* ⊕ *www.vgf-ffm.de.*

CAR TRAVEL

Frankfurt is the meeting point of a number of major autobahns. The most important are A-3, running south from Köln and then on east to Würzburg and Nürnberg, and A-5, running south from Giessen and then on toward Heidelberg and Basel.

In Frankfurt, hidden cameras are used to catch speeders, so be sure to stick to the speed limit. Tow trucks cruise the streets in search of illegal parkers. There are many reasonably priced parking garages around the downtown area and a well-developed "park-and-ride" system with the suburban train lines. The transit map shows nearly a hundred outlying stations with a blue "P" symbol beside them, meaning there is convenient parking there.

TAXI TRAVEL

Cabs are not always easy to hail from the sidewalk; some stop, but others will pick up only from the city's numerous taxi stands or outside hotels or the train station. You can always order a cab. Fares start at €2.80 (€3.30 in the evening) and increase by a per-kilometer (½ mile) charge of €1.75 (€1.60 after 10 km). Frankfurt also has Velotaxis, covered tricycles seating two passengers and a driver that are useful for sightseeing or getting to places on the traffic-free downtown streets. They charge €2.50 per km.

Taxi Contacts Taxis. ⊠ *Frankfurt* ☎ *069/230–001.* **Velotaxi.** ⊠ *Frankfurt* ☎ *0700/8356–8294* ⊕ *www.velotaxi.de.*

TRAIN TRAVEL

EuroCity, InterCity (IC), and InterCity Express (ICE) trains connect Frankfurt with all German cities and many major European ones. The InterCity Express line links Frankfurt with Berlin, Hamburg, Munich, and a number of other major hubs. All long-distance trains arrive at and depart from the Hauptbahnhof, and many also stop at the long-distance train station at the main airport. The red-light district southwest of the main station should be avoided.

Train Contact Deutsche Bahn (*German Railways*). ✉ *Bahnhof* ☎ *01805/996–633* ⊕ *www.bahn.de.*

VISITOR INFORMATION

Tourismus und Congress GmbH Frankfurt–Main has its main office at Römerberg 27, in Old Town. It's open weekdays 9:30–5:30 and weekends 9–6.

The airport's information office is on the first floor of Arrivals Hall B and open daily 7 am–10:30 pm. Another information office in the main hall of the railroad station is open weekdays 8 am–9 pm, weekends 9–6. Both can help you find accommodations.

Visitor Information Tourismus und Congress GmbH Frankfurt/Main.
✉ *Römerberg 27, City Center* ☎ *069/2123–8800* ⊕ *www.frankfurt-tourismus.de.*

DISCOUNTS AND DEALS

The Frankfurt tourist office offers a one- or two-day ticket—the Frankfurt Card (€9.20 for one day, €13.50 for two days)—allowing unlimited travel on public transportation in the inner zone, and to the airport. It also includes a 50% reduction on admission to 24 museums, the zoo, and the Palmengarten, and price reductions at some restaurants and stores.

TOURS

Two-hour city bus tours with English-speaking guides are available from the Frankfurt Tourist Office throughout the year.

Ebbelwei Express. The one-hour Apple Wine Express tour in a vintage streetcar is offered hourly weekends and some holidays. It gives you a quick look at the city's neighborhoods, a bit of Frankfurt history, and a chance to sample Apfelwein (a bottle, along with pretzels, is included in the fare). ☎ *069/2132–2425* ⊕ *www.ebbelwei-express.com* 🎫 *From €8.*

Frankfurt Personenschiffahrt Primus-Linie. Day trips on the Main River and Rhine excursions run from April through October and leave from the Frankfurt Mainkai am Eiserner Steg, just south of the Römer complex. ■TIP→ **The boats are available for private parties, too.** ✉ *Mainkai 36, Altstadt* ☎ *069/133–8370* ⊕ *www.primus-linie.de* 🎫 *From €8.95.*

EXPLORING FRANKFURT

ALTSTADT

Altstadt (Old City) is the historic, cultural, and culinary heart of Frankfurt, with restored medieval buildings around a huge town square, notable churches and museums, and historic restaurants serving traditional local fare. Be sure to walk to Fressgasse (eating street), a pedestrian-only street of cafés, gourmet food shops, and jazz clubs.

TOP ATTRACTIONS

Alte Oper (*Old Opera House*). Kaiser Wilhelm I traveled from Berlin for the gala opening of this opera house in 1880. Gutted in World War II, it remained a hollow shell for 40 years while controversy raged over its reconstruction. The exterior and lobby are faithful to the original,

Goethe's House and Museum is filled with the manuscripts and paintings of Germany's best-loved poet.

though the remainder of the building is more like a modern multipurpose hall. Although classical music and ballet performanaces are held here, most operas these days are staged at the Frankfurt Opera. ⊠ *Opernpl. 1, Altstadt* ☎ *069/13400* ⊕ *www.alteoper.de* Ⓜ *Alte Oper (U-bahn).*

Fodor's Choice
★

Fressgass. Grosse Bockenheimer Strasse is the proper name of this pedestrian street, but it's nicknamed "Pig-Out Alley" because of its amazing choice of delicatessens, wine merchants, cafés, and restaurants, offering everything from crumbly cheeses and smoked fish to vintage wines and chocolate creams. Check the side streets for additional cafés and restaurants. ⊠ *Grosse Bockenheimerstr., Altstadt* ⊕ *www.frankfurt-fressgass. de* Ⓜ *Hauptwache (U-bahn and S-bahn), Alte Oper (U-bahn).*

Goethehaus und Goethemuseum (*Goethe's Residence and Museum*). The house where Germany's most famous poet was born is furnished with many original pieces that belonged to his family, including manuscripts in his own hand. The original house, which was destroyed by Allied bombing, has been carefully rebuilt and restored. Johann Wolfgang von Goethe (1749–1832) studied law and became a member of the bar in Frankfurt, but he was quickly drawn to writing, and in this house he eventually wrote the first version of his masterpiece, *Faust*. The adjoining museum contains works of art that inspired Goethe (he was an amateur painter) and works associated with his literary contemporaries. ⊠ *Grosser Hirschgraben 23–25, Altstadt* ☎ *069/138–800* ⊕ *www.goethehaus-frankfurt.de* ☜ *€7* ⊗ *Mon.–Sat. 10–6, Sun. 10–5:30* Ⓜ *Hauptwache or Willy-Brandt-Platz (U-bahn and S-bahn).*

FAMILY

Historisches Museum (*Historical Museum*). This fascinating museum in a building in Römer Square that dates from the 1300s has doubled in size with the addition of an adjoining wing, which opened in summer 2015. The city's oldest museum encompasses 630,000 objects and 2,000 years of all aspects of Frankfurt's history, including what the city of the future might look like. Standout exhibits include scale models of historic Frankfurt at various periods, with every street, house, and church, plus photos of the devastation of World War II. The new wing blends in with the surrounding historic architecture with its gabled roof and carved sandstone sides, and offers both a café and city views from the top floor. ⊠ *Fahrtor 2 (Römerberg), Altstadt* ☏ *069/2123–5599* ⊕ *www. historisches-museum.frankfurt.de* ▧ *€6, scale models €1* ☉ *Tues.–Sun. 10–6 (Wed. until 8)* Ⓜ *Römer (U-bahn).*

Kaiserdom. Because the Holy Roman emperors were chosen and crowned here from the 16th to the 18th century, the church is known as the Kaiserdom (Imperial Cathedral), even though it isn't the seat of a bishop. Officially the Church of St. Bartholomew, but called simply "The Dom" by locals, it was built largely between the 13th and 15th centuries and survived World War II with the majority of its treasures intact. The most impressive exterior feature is the tall, red-sandstone tower (almost 300 feet high), which was added between 1415 and 1514. Climb it for a good view. The **Dommuseum** (Cathedral Museum) occupies the former Gothic cloister. ⊠ *Dompl. 1, Altstadt* ☏ *069/297–0320* ⊕ *www.dom-frankfurt.de* ▧ *Dommuseum €2* ☉ *Daily 10–1 and 2–5* Ⓜ *Römer (U-bahn).*

Museum für Moderne Kunst (*Museum of Modern Art*). Austrian architect Hans Hollein (born in 1934) designed this distinctive triangular building, shaped like a wedge of cake. The collection features works by artists such as Andy Warhol and Joseph Beuys. There are free guided tours in English on Saturdays at 4 pm, and the museum is wheelchair accessible. ⊠ *Domstr. 10, Altstadt* ☏ *069/2123–0447* ⊕ *www.mmk-frankfurt.de* ▧ *€16* ☉ *Tues.–Sun. 10–6 (Wed. until 8)* Ⓜ *Willy-Brandt Platz (U-bahn).*

Paulskirche (*St. Paul's Church*). The first all-German parliament was held here in 1848. The parliament lasted only a year, having achieved little more than offering the Prussian king the crown of Germany. Today the church, which has been extensively restored, remains a symbol of German democracy and is used mainly for ceremonies. The most striking feature of the interior is a giant, completely circular mural showing an "endless" procession of the people's representatives into the Paulskirche. The plenary chamber upstairs is flanked by the flags of Germany, the 16 states, and the city of Frankfurt. ⊠ *Paulspl. 11, Altstadt* ☏ *069/2123–4920* ▧ *Free* ☉ *Daily 10–5* Ⓜ *Römer (U-bahn).*

Fodor's Choice ★ **Römer** (*City Hall*). Three individual patrician buildings make up the Römer, Frankfurt's town hall. The mercantile-minded Frankfurt burghers used the complex for political and ceremonial purposes as well as for trade fairs and other commercial ventures. Its gabled facade with an ornate balcony is widely known as the city's official emblem.

The most important events to take place here were the festivities celebrating the coronations of the Holy Roman emperors. The first was in 1562 in the glittering **Kaisersaal** (Imperial Hall), which was last used in 1792 to celebrate the election of the emperor Francis II, who would later be forced by Napoléon to abdicate. Unless official business is being conducted you can see the impressive, full-length 19th-century portraits of the 52 emperors of the Holy Roman Empire, which line the walls of the reconstructed banquet hall. ⊠ *West side of Römerberg, Römerberg 27, Altstadt* ☎ *069/2123–4814* ⊠ *€3* ⊘ *Weekdays 9–noon and 2–5; often closed for events, check hrs before going* Ⓜ *Römer (U-bahn).*

Römerberg. This square a few blocks north of the Main River, restored after wartime bomb damage, is the historical focal point of the city. The Römer, the Nikolaikirche, and the half-timber Ostzeile houses are all clustered around this huge plaza. The 16th-century Fountain of Justitia (Justice), which flows with wine on special occasions, stands in the center of the Römerberg. The square is also the site of many public festivals throughout the year, including the Christmas market in December. Kleine Krame is a pedestrian street just north of the square that's lined with snack shops and cafés. ⊠ *Between Braubachstr. and Main River, Altstadt* Ⓜ *Römer (U-bahn).*

Zeil. The heart of Frankfurt's shopping district is this bustling pedestrian street running east from Hauptwache Square. It's lined with a mix of department stores, boutiques, drugstores, cell-phone franchises, electronics shops, restaurants, and more. Stop in at the outdoor farmers' market every Thursday and Saturday for a freshly grilled bratwurst and a beer. ⊠ *Hauptwache Square, Altstadt* Ⓜ *Hauptwache, Konstablerwache (U-bahn and S-bahn).*

WORTH NOTING

Alte Nikolaikirche (*Old St. Nicholas Church*). This small red-sandstone church was built in the late 13th century as the court chapel for emperors of the Holy Roman Empire. Try to time your visit to coincide with the chimes of the carillon, which rings three times a day, at 9:05 in the morning, and at 12:05 and 5:05 in the afternoon. ⊠ *South side of Römerberg, Altstadt* ☎ *069/284–235* ⊕ *www.paulsgemeinde.de/alte_nikolaikirche* ⊘ *Oct.–Mar., daily 10–6; Apr.–Sept., daily 10–8* Ⓜ *Römer (U-bahn).*

Archäologisches Museum (*Archeology Museum*). The soaring vaulted ceilings make the Gothic Karmeliterkirche (Carmelite Church) an ideal setting for huge Roman columns and other local and regional artifacts, including Stone Age and Neolithic tools and ancient papyrus documents. Modern wings display Greek, Roman, and Persian pottery, carvings, and more. Adjacent buildings house the city's Institut für Stadtgeschichte (Institute of History). The basement, titled "Die Schmiere" (The Grease), is a satirical theater.

The main cloister displays the largest religious fresco north of the Alps, a 16th-century representation of Christ's birth and death by Jörg Ratgeb. ⊠ *Karmeliterg. 1, Altstadt* ☎ *069/2123–5896* ⊕ *www.archaeologisches-museum.frankfurt.de* ⊠ *Museum €7, free last Sat. of month* ⊘ *Tues.–Sun. 10–5 (Wed. until 8)* Ⓜ *Willy-Brandt-Platz (U-bahn).*

Eiserner Steg (*Iron Bridge*). A pedestrian walkway and the first suspension bridge in Europe, the Eiserner Steg connects the city center with

Sachsenhausen and offers great views of the Frankfurt skyline. Excursions by boat leave from here. ✉ *Mainkai, Altstadt.*

Hauptwache. The attractive baroque building with a steeply sloping roof is the actual Hauptwache (Main Guardhouse), from which the square takes its name. The 1729 building was partly demolished to permit excavation for a vast underground shopping mall. It was then restored to its original appearance and is now considered the heart of the Frankfurt pedestrian shopping area. The outdoor patio of the building's restaurant-café is a popular people-watching spot on the Zeil. ✉ *An der Hauptwache 15, Altstadt* Ⓜ *Hauptwache (U-bahn and S-bahn).*

Schirn Kunsthalle (*Schirn Art Gallery*). One of Frankfurt's most modern museums is devoted exclusively to changing exhibits of modern art and photography. The gallery, right beside the Kaiserdom, has a restaurant. ✉ *Römerberg, Altstadt* ☎ *069/299–8820* ⊕ *www.schirn.de* 💶 *€7–€10, varies by exhibit* ⊙ *Tues. and Fri.–Sun. 10–7, Wed. and Thurs. 10–10* Ⓜ *Römer (U-bahn).*

CITY CENTER

Frankfurt was rebuilt after World War II with little attention paid to the past. Nevertheless, important historical monuments can still be found among the modern architecture. The city is very walkable; its growth hasn't encroached on its parks, gardens, pedestrian arcades, or outdoor cafés. The riverbank paths make for great strolls or bike rides.

TOP ATTRACTIONS

OFF THE
BEATEN
PATH

Alter Jüdischer Friedhof (*Old Jewish Cemetery*). Containing hundreds of moss-covered gravestones, this cemetery was in use between the 13th and mid-19th centuries, and is one of the few reminders of prewar Jewish life in Frankfurt. It suffered minimal vandalization in the Nazi era, even though its adjoining grand Börneplatz Synagogue was destroyed on Kristallnacht, in 1938. That space is now part of Museum Judengasse; ask the admissions desk for the key to open the vandal-proof steel gates to the cemetery. Mayer Amschel Rothschild, founder of the banking family, who died in 1812, is buried here, along with some family members (the Rothschild mansion is now the main Jewish Museum). The wall around the cemetery is dotted with more than 1,000 small memorial plaques, each with the name of a Jewish Frankfurter and the concentration camp where they died. There is a newer Jewish cemetery at Eckenheimer Landstrasse 238 (about 2½ km [1½ miles] north). ✉ *Battonnstr. 2, City Center* ☎ *069/2127–0790* ⊕ *juedischesmuseum.de/museumjudengasse* 💶 *Free* ⊙ *Sun.–Fri. 8:30–4:30* Ⓜ *Bornerplatz (S-bahn).*

Museum Judengasse. This branch of the Jewish Museum (the main museum is closed for renovation through early 2018) is built on the site of the Bornerplatz Synagogue, destroyed in 1938, and the foundations of mostly 18th-century buildings that were once part of the Jewish quarter, or Judengasse. ✉ *Kurt-Schumacher-Str. 10, City Center* ☎ *069/297–7419* ⊕ *www.juedischesmuseum.de/* 💶 *€3* ⊙ *Tues.–Sun. 10–5 (Wed. until 8)* Ⓜ *Bornerplatz (U-bahn).*

9

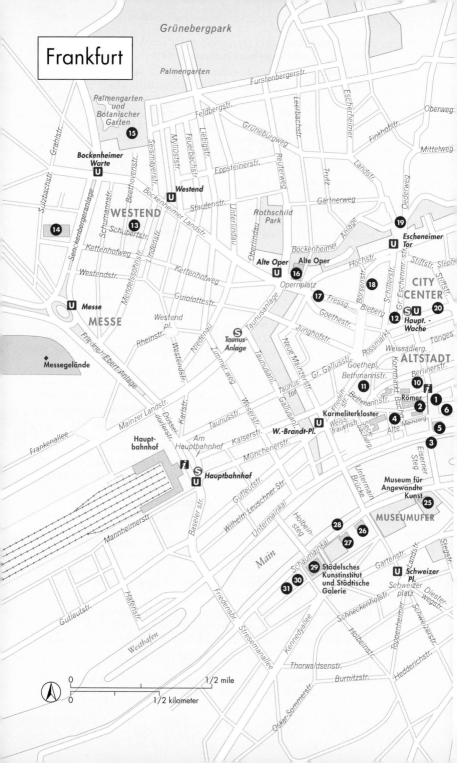

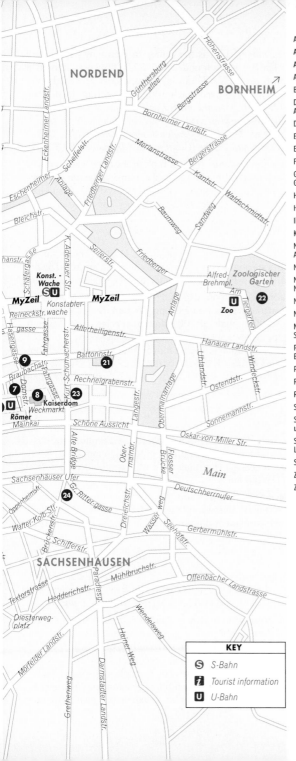

KEY

S *S-Bahn*
i *Tourist information*
U *U-Bahn*

WORTH NOTING

Börse (*Stock Exchange*). This is the center of Germany's stock and money market. The Börse was founded in 1585, but the present domed building dates from the 1870s. These days computerized networks and telephone systems have removed much of the drama from the dealers' floor, but it's still fun to visit the visitor gallery and watch the hectic activity. You must reserve your visit 24 hours in advance. ⊠ *Börsenpl. 4, City Center* ☎ *069/211–1515* ⊕ *www.boerse-frankfurt.de* ⊠ *Free* ⊗ *Weekdays 9–5* Ⓜ *Hauptwache (U-bahn and S-bahn)*.

Eschenheimer Turm (*Eschenheim Tower*). Built in the early 15th century, this tower, a block north of the Hauptwache, remains the finest example of the city's original 42 towers. It now contains a restaurant–bar. ⊠ *Eschenheimer Tor, City Center* Ⓜ *Eschenheimer Tor (U-bahn)*.

OSTEND

Named for its location around the city's East Harbor, the business-oriented Ostend is sprouting new restaurants and cafés, attracted by the 2014 opening of the new European Central Bank headquarters building.

FAMILY **Zoologischer Garten** (*Zoo*). Founded in 1858, this is one of the most important and attractive zoos in Europe. Its remarkable collection includes some 4,500 animals of 500 different species, an exotarium (an aquarium plus reptiles), a large ape house, and an aviary, one of the largest in Europe. Nocturnal creatures move about in a special section. ⊠ *Bernhard-Grzimek-Allee 1, Ostend* ☎ *069/2123–3735* ⊕ *www.zoo-frankfurt.de* ⊠ *€10, family ticket €25* ⊗ *Nov.–Mar., daily 9–5; Apr.–Oct., daily 9–7* Ⓜ *Zoo (U-bahn)*.

MESSE AND WESTEND

The city's huge, sprawling convention center (Messe) is one of the busiest in Europe, and the area around it isn't especially interesting. Westend, on the other hand, is a charming residential neighborhood dotted with some good restaurants.

FAMILY **Naturkundemuseum Senckenberg** (*Natural History Museum*). The important collection of fossils, animals, plants, and geological exhibits here is upstaged by the permanent dinosaur exhibit: it's the most extensive of its kind in all of Germany. The diplodocus dinosaur, imported from New York, is the only complete specimen of its kind in Europe. Many of the exhibits of prehistoric animals, including a series of dioramas, have been designed with children in mind. ⊠ *Senckenberganlage 25, Westend* ☎ *069/75420* ⊕ *www.senckenberg.de* ⊠ *€9* ⊗ *Weekdays 9–5 (Wed. until 8), weekends 9–6* Ⓜ *Bockenheimer Warte (U-bahn)*.

Fodor's Choice ★

FAMILY **Palmengarten und Botanischer Garten** (*Botanical Gardens*). The splendid cluster of tropical and semitropical greenhouses here contains cacti, orchids, palms, and other plants. The surrounding park, which can be surveyed from a miniature train, has many recreational facilities, including a small lake where you can rent rowboats, a play area for children, and a wading pool. The Palmengarten offers free tours on a variety of topics on Sunday. In summer there's also an extensive concert program

Climb to the top of Kaiserdom, officially called the Church St. Bartholomew, for a fantastic view of the city.

that takes place in an outdoor pavilion. ⊠ *Siesmayerstr. 63, Westend* ☎ *069/2123–3939* ⊕ *palmengarten.frankfurt.de* ⌛€7 ⊗ *Feb.–Oct., daily 9–6; Nov.–Jan., daily 9–4* Ⓜ *Westend (U-bahn)*.

FAMILY **Struwwelpeter Museum** (*Slovenly Peter Museum*). This charming little museum honors the Frankfurt physician who created the sardonic children's classic *Struwwelpeter*, or Slovenly Peter. Heinrich Hoffmann wrote the poems and drew the rather amateurish pictures in 1844, to warn children of the dire consequences of being naughty. The book has seen several English translations, including one by Mark Twain, which can be purchased at the museum. The kid-friendly museum has a puppet theater and game room, and is popular for birthday parties. ⊠ *Schubertstr. 20, Westend* ☎ *069/747–969* ⊕ *www.struwwelpeter-museum.de* ⌛€5 ⊗ *Tues.–Sun. 10–5* Ⓜ *Westend (U-bahn)*.

NORDEND AND BORNHEIM

Nordend was the center of antigovernment student demonstrations in the 1960s and 1970s—it still retains a little shabby, bohemian flavor. For its part, Bornheim holds on to some of the liveliness it had as the city's red-light district a century ago. Both have some pleasant, small shops and restaurants.

SACHSENHAUSEN

The old quarter of Sachsenhausen, on the south bank of the Main River, has been sensitively preserved, and its cobblestone streets, half-timber houses, and beer gardens make it a popular area to stroll.

Sachsenhausen's two big attractions are the **Museumufer** (Museum Riverbank), which has nine museums almost next door to one another and offers beautiful views of the Frankfurt skyline, as well as the famous Apfelwein taverns around the Rittergasse pedestrian area. You can eat well—and quite reasonably—in these small traditional establishments.

TOP ATTRACTIONS

FAMILY
Fodor'sChoice
★
Deutsches Filmmuseum (*German Film Museum*). Germany's first museum of cinematography, set in a historic villa on "museum row," offers visitors a glimpse at the history of film, with artifacts that include "magic lanterns" from the 1880s, costume drawings from Hollywood and German films, and multiple screens playing film clips. Interactive exhibits show how films are photographed, given sound, and edited, and let visitors play with lighting and animation. A theater in the basement screens every imaginable type of film, from historical to avant-garde to *Star Wars*. ⊠ *Schaumainkai 41, Sachsenhausen* ☎ *069/9612–20220* ⊕ *www.deutschesfilmmuseum.de* ⊡ *€5* ⊘ *Tues.–Sun. 10–6 (Wed. until 8)* Ⓜ *Schweizer Platz (U-bahn)*.

Ikonen-Museum (*Icon Museum*). This is one of very few museums in the world to exhibit a wide spectrum of the Christian Orthodox world of images. The art and ritual of icons from the 15th to the 20th century are on display here in a collection that totals more than 1,000 artifacts. Admission is free on the last Saturday of the month. ⊠ *Brückenstr. 3–7, Sachsenhausen* ☎ *069/2123–6262* ⊕ *www.ikonenmuseumfrankfurt.de* ⊡ *€4* ⊘ *Tues.–Sun. 11–5 (Wed. until 7)*.

Museum für Kommunikation (*Museum for Communication*). This is the place for visiting the past and the future of communication technology, in an airy, modern glass building. Exhibitions on historic methods include mail coaches, a vast collection of stamps from many countries and eras, and ancient dial telephones, with their clunky switching equipment. ⊠ *Schaumainkai 53, Sachsenhausen* ☎ *069/60600* ⊕ *www.museumsstiftung.de* ⊡ *€3* ⊘ *Tues.–Fri. 9–6, weekends 11–7* Ⓜ *Schweizer Platz (U-bahn)*.

Museum Giersch. This museum, part of Goethe University, is set in a beautiful neoclassical villa along the strip of museums in Sachsenhausen and focuses on paintings from the 19th century and early 20th century. The artists are drawn mainly from the Rhine-Main region. ⊠ *Schaumainkai 83, Sachsenhausen* ☎ *069/6330–4128* ⊕ *www.museum-giersch.de* ⊡ *€5* ⊘ *Mon., Wed., and Thurs. 10–7, weekends 10–6*.

Fodor'sChoice
★
Städelsches Kunstinstitut und Städtische Galerie (*Städel Art Institute and Municipal Gallery*). This is one of Germany's most important art collections, covering 700 years of paintings and sculpture, with a vast collection of paintings by Dürer, Vermeer, Rembrandt, Rubens, Monet, Renoir, and other masters. The downstairs annex features a large collection of works from contemporary artists, including a huge portrait of Goethe by Andy Warhol. The section on German expressionism is particularly strong, with representative works by the Frankfurt artist Max Beckmann and Ernst Ludwig Kirchner. A free smartphone app with a built-in audio guide enhances the experience. There is also a café-restaurant, Holbein's. ⊠ *Schaumainkai 63, Sachsenhausen* ☎ *069/605–0980*

Sachsenhausen comes alive at night with a lively restaurant and bar scene.

⊕ *www.staedelmuseum.de* ⊠ *€14* ⊙ *Tues., Wed., and weekends 10–6, Thurs. and Fri. 10–9* Ⓜ *Schweizer Platz (U-bahn).*

WORTH NOTING

Deutsches Architekturmuseum. The German Architecture Museum is housed in a late-19th-century villa, which was converted in the early 1980s by the Köln-based architect Oswald Mathias Ungers. He created five levels, including a simple basement space with a visible load-bearing structure, a walled complex on the ground floor, and a house-within-a-house on the third floor. With more than 180,000 drawings and plans, and 600 scale models, the museum features a wealth of documents on the history of architecture and hosts debates and exhibitions on its future, including sustainable urban design. A permanent exhibit features the most comprehensive collection of model panoramas in the history of German architecture. ⊠ *Schaumainkai 43, Sachsenhausen* ☎ *069/2123–8844* ⊕ *www.dam-online.de* ⊠ *€9* ⊙ *Tues. and Thurs.–Sat. 11–6, Sun. 11–7, Wed. 11–8* Ⓜ *Schweizer Platz (U-bahn).*

Museum für Angewandte Kunst (*Museum of Applied Arts*). More than 30,000 decorative objects are exhibited in this modern white building designed by American star architect Richard Meier. Chairs and furnishings and medieval craftwork are some of the thematic sections you'll find on the same floor. The exhibits are mainly from Europe and Asia, including nine rooms from the historic Villa Metzler, spanning baroque to art deco. ⊠ *Schaumainkai 17, Sachsenhausen* ☎ *069/2123–4037* ⊕ *www.museumfuerangewandtekunst.frankfurt.de* ⊠ *€9, free last Sat. of month* ⊙ *Tues.–Sun. 10–5 (Wed. until 9)* Ⓜ *Schweizer Platz (U-bahn).*

Städtische Galerie Liebieghaus (*Liebieg Municipal Museum of Sculpture*). The sculpture collection here represents 5,000 years of civilization and is considered one of the most important in Europe. Ancient Greece and Rome, the Middle Ages, the Renaissance, classicism, and the baroque are all represented. Some pieces are exhibited in the lovely gardens surrounding the historic brick villa with its signature turret tower. Don't miss out on the freshly baked German cakes in the museum café. ⊠ *Schaumainkai 71, Sachsenhausen* ☎ *069/650–0490* ⊕ *www. liebieghaus.de* 🖅 *€9* ⊗ *Tues.–Sun. 10–6 (Thurs. until 9)* Ⓜ *Schweizer Platz (U-bahn).*

WHERE TO EAT

Many international cuisines are represented in the financial hub of Europe. For vegetarians there's usually at least one meatless dish on a German menu, and substantial salads are popular, too (though often served with speck, or bacon). The city's most famous contribution to the world's diet is the *Frankfurter Würstchen*—a thin smoked pork sausage—served with bread and mustard, but not with sauerkraut like the American hot dog also called a frankfurter. *Grüne Sosse* is a thin cream sauce of herbs served with potatoes and hard-boiled eggs. The oddly named *Handkäs mit Musik* (literally, "hand cheese with music") consists of slices of cheese covered with raw onions, oil, and vinegar, served with dark bread and butter (an acquired taste for many). There is the *Rippchen,* or cured pork chop, served on a mound of sauerkraut, and the *Schlachtplatte,* an assortment of sausages and smoked meats. All are served with Frankfurt's distinctive hard cider drink, Apfelwein, by the glass or ceramic pitcher.

Smoking is prohibited inside Frankfurt's bars and restaurants, but allowed in most beer gardens.

Prices in the reviews are the average cost of a main course at dinner, or if dinner is not served, at lunch. Use the coordinates (⊕ C3) at the end of each listing to locate a site on the corresponding map.

WHAT IT COSTS IN EUROS				
	$	**$$**	**$$$**	**$$$$**
AT DINNER	under €15	€15–€20	€21–€25	over €25

ALTSTADT

$

VEGETARIAN

✕ **Langosch am Main.** This eclectic vegetarian and vegan spot, a rarity in Frankfurt, serves breakfast, lunch, dinner, and late-night snacks made only with organic ingredients. There's also organic wine and beer and homemade drinks such as lemonade garnished with sprigs of fresh mint and rosemary. Homemade desserts are made with honey instead of refined sugar. Centrally located a few blocks from the Dom, the café has low lighting and rough-hewn wood tables; the rock 'n' roll and Motown tunes are played here at a volume low enough not to discourage quiet conversation. $ *Average main: €10* ✉ *Fahrg. 3, Altstadt* ☎ *069/9203–9510* ⊕ *www.langosch-frankfurt.com* ✛ *F4.*

$$
INTERNATIONAL

✕ **Margarete.** This modern restaurant with an open-kitchen design is named for the Viennese architect Margarete Scütte-Lihotzky, who created the style in the 1920s. There are three-course prix-fixe menus both for lunch (€25) and dinner (€38), or order à la carte from an eclectic and creative menu including homemade soups, risotto, and meats with the ubiquitous Frankfurter herb sauce. The chocolate tart with bitter orange marmalade and berry sorbet is a standout. $ *Average main: €20* ✉ *Braubachstr. 18–22, Altstadt* ☎ *069/1306–6500* ⊕ *www.margarete-restaurant.de* Ⓜ *Willy-Brandt-Platz (U-bahn), Dom (U-bahn)* ✛ *E4.*

$
CAFÉ

✕ **Metropol.** Breakfast is the main attraction at this café near the Römerberg and Dom. The dining room is large, and in the warmer months there are also tables on a garden patio. In addition to the daily selection of tantalizing cakes and pastries, the menu features salads, pastas, and traditional German dishes. The kitchen serves until 11 pm. Reservations are accepted for dinner only, and not for the terrace. $ *Average main: €12* ✉ *Weckmarkt 13–15, Altstadt* ☎ *069/288–287* ⊕ *www.metropolcafe.de* ⊘ *Closed Mon.* Ⓜ *Römer (U-bahn)* ✛ *E4.*

$
FAST FOOD

✕ **Souper.** Hearty soups seem to be the favorite light lunch in Frankfurt these days. The best selection can be found in this place near the Hauptwache, although the bowls seem a little small for the price. The daily selection may include such creations as Thai-style coconut chicken or lentil with sausage in cold weather and gazpacho in warm. Eat at the counter or take your soup to go. $ *Average main: €5* ✉ *Weissadlerg. 3, Altstadt* ☎ *069/2972–4545* ⊕ *www.souper.de* ⊘ *No dinner. Closed Sun.* ✍ *Reservations not accepted* Ⓜ *Hauptwache (U-bahn and S-bahn)* ✛ *E4.*

$$
GERMAN

✕ **Zum Schwarzen Stern.** Housed in a historic half-timber house that dates from 1453, the menu focuses on traditional Hessian food, but presented in a modern way, with carefully arranged plating. The Frankfurter Teller, a sampler of sausages, pork loin, and crispy pork knuckle, is for one hearty appetite or for two to share. Lighter chicken and fish dishes also are available, and mushroom and asparagus dishes in season. Try to get a table by the windows for people-watching across the busy square. The restaurant is named for the historic six-pointed black metal star which marks the entrance. $ *Average main: €20* ✉ *Römerberg 6, Altstadt* ☎ *069/291–979* ⊕ *www.schwarzerstern.de/en/* Ⓜ *Römer (U-bahn)* ✛ *E4.*

9

CITY CENTER

$$
ECLECTIC

✕ **Embassy.** This modern restaurant, bar, and lounge near many of the city's largest banks makes it a natural for business lunches, but it also attracts many young professionals for after-work socializing and dinner. The moderately priced menu of contemporary dishes includes nearly two dozen varieties of pizzas, plus pastas, salads, and meat and fish dishes. $ *Average main: €15* ✉ *Zimmerweg 1, corner of Mainzer Landstr., City Center* ☎ *069/7409–0844* ⊕ *www.embassy-frankfurt.de* ⊘ *Closed weekends* Ⓜ *Taunusanlage (S-bahn)* ✛ *C4.*

$$$
ECLECTIC

✕ **Frankfurter Botschaft.** Frankfurt's Westhafen (West Harbor), once busy and commercial, has been transformed into an upscale neighborhood

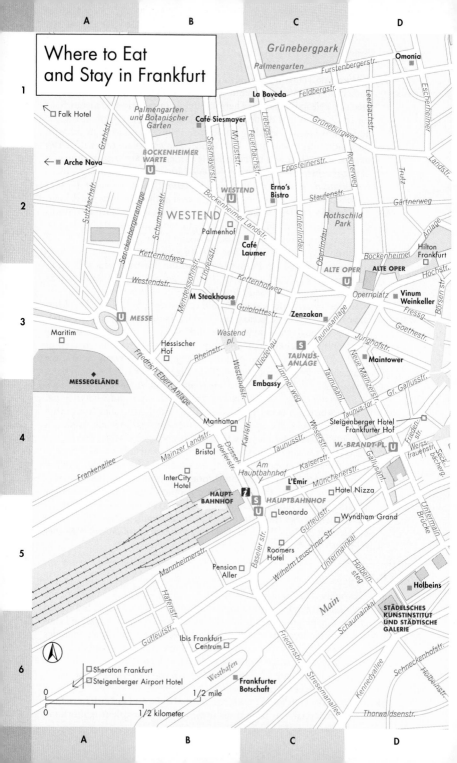

Where to Eat and Stay in Frankfurt

Grünebergpark

Palmengarten

Omonia

La Boveda

Palmengarten und Botanischer Garten

Café Siesmayer

Falk Hotel

BOCKENHEIMER WARTE Ⓤ

← ■ Arche Nova

WESTEND

Erno's Bistro

WESTEND

Palmenhof

Café Laumer

Rothschild Park

Hilton Frankfurt

ALTE OPER Ⓤ

ALTE OPER

Kettenhofweg

M Steakhouse

Opernplatz

Vinum Weinkeller

MESSE Ⓤ

Maritim

Westend pl.

Zenzakan

Hessischer Hof

TAUNUS-ANLAGE Ⓢ

Maintower

MESSEGELÄNDE

Embassy

Steigenberger Hotel Frankfurter Hof

Manhattan

W.-BRANDT-PL. Ⓤ

Bristol

Am Hauptbahnhof

InterCity Hotel

L'Emir

Hotel Nizza

HAUPT-BAHNHOF

🛈

Ⓢ Ⓤ HAUPTBAHNHOF

Leonardo

Wyndham Grand

Roomers Hotel

Pension Aller

Holbeins

Main

STÄDELSCHES KUNSTINSTITUT UND STÄDTISCHE GALERIE

Ibis Frankfurt Centrum

Sheraton Frankfurt

Steigenberger Airport Hotel

Frankfurter Botschaft

0   1/2 mile

0   1/2 kilometer

A   B   C   D

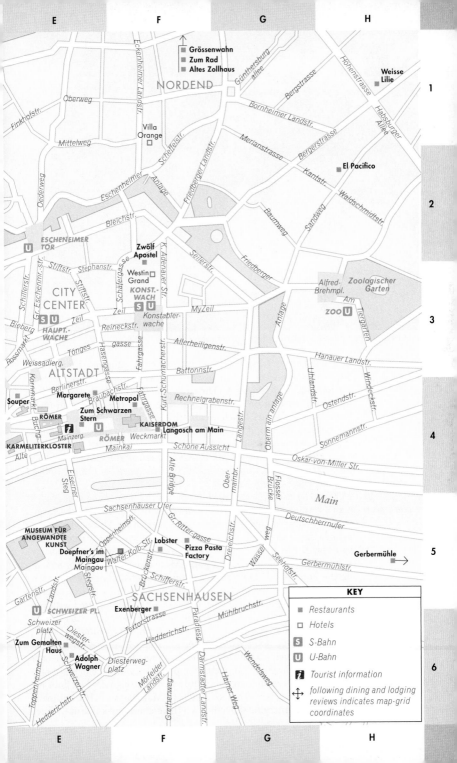

Don't leave Frankfurt without sampling a tall glass of Apfelwein.

of apartments, a yacht club, and waterfront restaurants. One of the chicest is Frankfurter Botschaft, with a glass facade and a big terrace overlooking the Main River. The city's elite descend here for business lunches, a cocktail on the terrace at sunset, or the Sunday brunch. There is also a sandy beach area with folding chairs and umbrellas. The international food is mainly organic, and even the dinnerware is of a prize-winning design. $ *Average main: €24* ⊠ *Westhafenpl. 6–8, City Center* ☎ *069/2400–4899* ⊕ *www.frankfurter-botschaft.de* ⊘ *No lunch Sat.* ⌖ *Reservations essential* 🏛 *Jacket required* Ⓜ *Hauptbahnhof (U-bahn and S-bahn)* ✛ *B6.*

$$ ✕ **L'Emir.** The atmosphere is right out of *One Thousand and One Nights*

MIDDLE EASTERN at this restaurant near the train station, with belly dancers performing every Saturday night urging patrons to join in. Those who are so inclined can retire to the lounge and smoke flavored tobacco from a water pipe. The Middle Eastern menu is largely vegetarian and heavy on garlic, olive oil, and lemon juice. Meat dishes favor lamb, including the house-made lamb sausage and marinated chops grilled over charcoal. Save room for dessert, either baklava, flaky pastry layered with honey and nuts, or *amar eilden*, apricot pudding dotted with raisins. $ *Average main: €18* ⊠ *Ramada Hotel, Weserstr. 17, City Center* ☎ *069/2400–8686* ⊕ *www.lemir.de* ⌖ *Reservations essential* Ⓜ *Hauptbahnhof (U-bahn and S-bahn)* ✛ *C4.*

$$$$ ✕ **Maintower.** On the 53rd floor of the skyscraper that houses the Helaba

GERMAN Landesbank Hessen-Thüringen, this popular cocktail bar and high-end restaurant captures an unbeatable view. Through 25-foot floor-to-ceiling windows, you can take in all of "Mainhattan." The cuisine is part global, part regional. Dinner is a three-course prix fixe at €79 per

CLOSE UP

Apfelwein

Apfelwein, the local hard cider and the quintessential Frankfurt drink, is more sour than the sweet versions you may be used to. To produce Apfelwein, the juice of pressed apples is fermented for approximately eight weeks. Its alcohol content of 5%–7% makes it comparable to beer. Straight up, it is light and slightly fizzy. You can also try it carbonated with seltzer (*Sauergespritzer*), or sweetened with lemonade (*Süssgespritzer*).

Apfelwein is drunk from a lattice-patterned glass called a *Gerippte*.

When among friends, it is poured from blue stoneware pitchers called *Bembels*, which range in size from big (a liter) to enormous (4 liters and up).

Popular throughout the state of Hesse, locals drink Apfelwein with pride. The largest concentration of Frankfurt's Apfelwein establishments is in the old neighborhood of Sachsenhausen. Look for establishments with a pine wreath hanging over the door; this signifies that Apfelwein is sold. There is also an annual weeklong Apfelwein Festival in Rossmarkt square in mid-August.

person, not counting drinks or the €4.50 fee for the elevator. Lunch is an open menu with no minimum, as is the lounge for drinks and bar snacks, which opens at 6 pm. Both the restaurant and the Tower Lounge are open until midnight. $ *Average main: €40* ⊠ *Neue Mainzerstr. 52–58, City Center* ☎ *069/3650–4770* ⊕ *www.maintower-restaurant. de* ☯ *Closed Sun. and Mon. No lunch Tues. or Sat.* ⚏ *Reservations essential* 🎩 *Jacket required* Ⓜ *Alte Oper (U-Bahn), or Taunusanlage (S-Bahn)* ✛ *D3.*

$$
GERMAN
Fodor's Choice
★

✕ **Vinum Weinkeller.** Housed in a former wine cellar that dates from 1893 in one of the alleys off Fressgasse, Vinum specializes in regional wines, by the glass or bottle, and the burnished brickwork and low lighting adds to the charm. The wine-themed decor includes such items as glass bowls filled with wine corks. Menu choices focus on wine-friendly dishes, including cheese platters, as well as German specialties more often associated with beer, such as wursts and sauerbraten with dumplings and red cabbage. $ *Average main: €15* ⊠ *Kleine Hochstr. 9, City Center* ☎ *069/293–037* ⊕ *www.vinum-frankfurt.de* ☯ *No lunch. Closed Sun., Oct.–Apr.* ✛ *D3.*

$
GERMAN

✕ **Zwölf Apostel.** There are few inner-city restaurants that brew their own beer, and the Twelve Apostles is one of the pleasant exceptions. Enjoy homemade pilsners in the dimly lighted, cavernous cellar, and sample traditional international and Croatian dishes. Servings are large, prices are reasonable, and you can have a small portion at half price. $ *Average main: €11* ⊠ *Rosenbergerstr. 1, City Center* ☎ *069/288–668* ⊕ *www.12aposteln-frankfurt.de* ▭ *No credit cards* Ⓜ *Konstablerwache (U-bahn and S-bahn)* ✛ *F2.*

MESSE AND WESTEND

$ ✕**Café Laumer.** The ambience of an old-time Viennese café pervades
CAFÉ this popular spot, where there's a lovely garden in summer—as well
as some of the city's best freshly baked pastries and cakes year-round,
best teamed with a *cafe mit schlag* (coffee with whipped cream). Homemade soups, quiches, and wurst plates also are on the menu. The café
closes at 7 pm. $ *Average main: €8 ⊠ Bockenheimer Landstr. 67, Wes-
tend* ☎ *069/727–912* ⊕ *www.cafe-laumer.de* ⊙ *No dinner* Ⓜ *Westend
(U-bahn)* ⊹ *C2.*

$ ✕**Café Siesmayer.** This sleek establishment is at the Palmengarten, acces-
GERMAN sible either from the botanical garden or from the street, for fresh-baked
pastries throughout the day and a limited prix-fixe lunch menu that
changes daily, with a splendid garden view. There's also the Linden
Terrace for snacks in season, and the elegant and pricey Restaurant
Lafleur for dinner. Note that the café closes at 7. $ *Average main: €14
⊠ Siesmayerstr. 59, Westend* ☎ *069/9002–9200* ⊕ *www.palmengarten-
gastronomie.de* ⊙ *No dinner* Ⓜ *Westend (U-bahn)* ⊹ *B1.*

$$$$ ✕**Erno's Bistro.** This tiny, unpretentious place in a quiet Westend neighbor-
FRENCH hood seems an unlikely candidate for the best restaurant in Germany. Yet
Fodor'sChoice that's what one French critic called it. The bistro's specialty, fish, is often
★   flown in from France, as are the wines (the wine list is 600 choices). It's
closed weekends, during the Christmas and Easter seasons, and during
much of summer—in other words, when its patrons, well-heeled business
executives, are unlikely to be in town. $ *Average main: €45 ⊠ Liebigstr.
15, Westend* ☎ *069/721–997* ⊕ *www.ernosbistro.de* ⊙ *Closed weekends
and for 6 wks during Hesse's summer school vacation* ⌕ *Reservations
essential* 🎩 *Jacket required* Ⓜ *Westend (U-bahn)* ⊹ *C2.*

$$ ✕**La Boveda.** This quaint Spanish restaurant is inside the dimly lit base-
SPANISH ment of a Westend residential building. (Appropriate, as the name
means "wine cellar.") Instead of the somewhat pricey entrées, make
a meal of several smaller plates of tapas and one of the mussel or
clam dishes, or the three-course prix-fixe lunch for €10.50. True to
its name, La Boveda offers an extensive wine menu. Reservations are
recommended on weekends. $ *Average main: €20 ⊠ Feldbergstr. 10,
Westend* ☎ *069/723–220* ⊕ *www.la-boveda.de* ⊙ *No lunch weekends*
Ⓜ *Westend (U-bahn)* ⊹ *C1.*

$$$$ ✕**M Steakhouse.** Many say the M Steakhouse serves the best steak in
STEAKHOUSE Germany, all of it imported Nebraska beef, most often ordered as Amer-
Fodor'sChoice ican-style porterhouse, sirloin, and rib eye. A set of steps leads down
★   into the restaurant's beautifully lit outdoor patio, a perfect setting for a
private romantic dinner. The main dining room inside is warm, welcom-
ing, and intimate. Prices are in line with the quality of meat, and the
sides complement the dishes perfectly. The restaurant doesn't serve any
seafood main courses, but the same restaurant group operates Surf 'n
Turf a few blocks away, with similar prices and ambience, and seafood
dishes in addition to the steaks. $ *Average main: €30 ⊠ Feuerbachstr.
11a, Westend* ☎ *069/7103–4050* ⊕ *www.mook-group.de* ▭ *No credit
cards* ⊙ *Closed Sun. No lunch Sat.* ⌕ *Reservations essential* 🎩 *Jacket
required* ⊹ *B3.*

$$ **Omonia.** This cozy cellar serves the city's best Greek cuisine. If you

GREEK have a big appetite, try the Omonia platter, with lamb cooked several ways and accompanied by Greek-style pasta. Vegetarians go for the *mestos sestos,* a plate of lightly breaded grilled vegetables served in a rich tomato-and-feta sauce. This family-owned place is popular, so make a reservation for one of the few tables. $ *Average main: €15* ⊠ *Vogtstr. 43, Westend* ☎ *069/593–314* ⊕ *www.omonia.de* ⊘ *No lunch* ⚷ *Reservations essential* Ⓜ *Holzhausenstrasse (U-bahn)* ✛ *D1.*

$$$$ **Zenzakan.** Hailed as a sort of pan-Asian supper club, this large res-

JAPANESE taurant with Buddha heads and other Asian decor has a bar scene that's just as good a reason to visit as its exceptional food, especially its sushi. Beef lovers also will find plenty to choose from, including sliced hangar steak with Japanese barbecue sauce. The equally innovative cocktails at the bar include a lemograss martini and the Balsamic Touch, and there's a smokers' lounge, rare in smoke-free Frankfurt, featuring Japanese vodka. $ *Average main: €30* ⊠ *Taunusanlage 15, Westend* ☎ *069/9708–6908* ⊕ *www.mook-group.de/zenzakan* ⊟ *No credit cards* ⊘ *No lunch. Closed Sun.* ⚷ *Reservations essential* ✛ *C3.*

NORDEND AND BORNHEIM

$ **El Pacifico.** Some of Frankfurt's best Mexican cuisine is found in this

MEXICAN festive little place. Warm and colorful, this restaurant serves a variety of fruity margaritas and is well known for its hearty chicken-wings appetizer, fajitas, and extensive selection of tequilas. The dimly lighted dining room is fairly small; reservations are recommended on weekends. $ *Average main: €14* ⊠ *Sandweg 79, Bornheim* ☎ *069/446–988* ⊕ *www.el-pacifico-ffm.de* ⊘ *No lunch Mon.–Sat.* Ⓜ *Merianplatz (U-bahn)* ✛ *H2.*

$$ **Grössenwahn.** The Nordend is noted for its trendy establishments, and

ECLECTIC this corner restaurant, which is often crowded, is one of the best. The name translates as "megalomania," which says it all. The menu is creative, with German, Greek, Italian, and French elements. Reservations essential on weekends. $ *Average main: €15* ⊠ *Lenaustr. 97, Nordend* ☎ *069/599–356* ⊕ *www.cafe-groessenwahn.de* ⊘ *No lunch* ⚷ *Reservations essential* Ⓜ *Glauburgstrasse (U-bahn)* ✛ *F1.*

$ **Weisse Lilie.** Come to this Bornheim favorite for the delicious selection

SPANISH of tapas, paella, and other Spanish specialties and reasonably priced

Fodor's Choice red wines. The dark interior has wooden tables brightened by fresh-

★ cut flowers and candles, making it a good spot for an intimate dinner. In summer you can dine outside, German style, at long tables. $ *Average main: €10* ⊠ *Bergerstr. 275, Bornheim* ☎ *069/453–860* ⊕ *www. weisse-lilie.com* ⊘ *No lunch* ⚷ *Reservations essential* Ⓜ *Bornheim Mitte (U-bahn)* ✛ *H1.*

SACHSENHAUSEN

$ **Adolf Wagner.** With sepia-tone murals of merrymaking above the

GERMAN dark-wood wainscotting, this Apfelwein classic succeeds in being tour-

Fodor's Choice isty and traditional all at once, and it's a genuine favorite of local resi-

★ dents. The kitchen produces the same hearty German dishes as other

CLOSE UP

Riesling: Try It Dry

Germany's mild, wet climate and a wine-making tradition that dates back 2,000 years combine to produce some of the world's finest white wines.

The king of German varietals is Riesling. Grown on the banks of Germany's many rivers, most notably the Rhine, the grape produces wines of stunning variety and quality. Rieslings are noted for their strong acidity, sometimes-flowery aroma, and often mineral-tasting notes—stemming from the grape's susceptibility to influences from the soil. Riesling made its name throughout the world through sweet (*lieblich*) wines, but many Germans prefer them dry (*trocken*). Importers, especially in the United States, don't bring over many dry German Rieslings, so take the opportunity to sample some while in Frankfurt.

SIP IT HERE

The **Bockenheimer Weinkontor** (✉ Schlossstr. 92 ☎ 069/702–031 ⊕ www.bockenheimer-weinkontor.de Ⓜ *Bockenheimer Warte [U-bahn]*) is nearby the Messegelände (Exhibition Center), in the Bockenheim area. Through a courtyard and down a set of stairs, the cozy bar offers 15–20 reasonably priced local wines by the glass. The trellis-covered back garden is a treat.

For prestige wines, head to **Piccolo** (✉ Bornheimer Landstr. 56 ☎ 069/9441–1277 ⊕ www.weinbar-piccolo.de Ⓜ *Merianplatz [U-bahn]*), where the bilingual staff make solid recommendations. Try a glass from the Markus Molitor or Alexander Freimuth wineries. Along with wine, they serve a range of snacks and main courses. The space is small, so make reservations if you plan to dine here.

---

nearby taverns, only better. Try the schnitzel or the *Tafelspitz mit Frankfurter Grüner Sosse* (stewed beef with a sauce of green herbs), or come on Friday for fresh fish. Cider is served in large quantities in the noisy, crowded dining room. Reservations recommended on weekends. Warning: it serves no beer! The family also operates a hotel upstairs. $ *Average main: €12* ✉ *Schweizerstr. 71, Sachsenhausen* ☎ 069/612–565 ⊕ *www.apfelwein-wagner.com* Ⓜ *Schweizer Platz (U-bahn)* ✚ F6.

$$$
GERMAN
Fodor'sChoice
★

✕ **Doepfner's im Maingau.** Chef Jörg Döpfner greets you himself and lights your candle at this excellent restaurant. A polished clientele is drawn by the linen tablecloths, subdued lighting, and such nearly forgotten practices as carving the meat at your table. The menu includes asparagus salad with homemade wild-boar ham, braised veal cheek with wild-garlic risotto, and some vegetarian dishes. The place also has a cellar full of rare German wines, and a small outdoor area in season. $ *Average main: €22* ✉ *Schifferstr. 38–40, Sachsenhausen* ☎ 069/610–752 ⊕ *maingau.de/de/restaurant* ☉ *Closed Mon. and Tues.* ⌂ *Reservations essential* ⌂ *Jacket required* Ⓜ *Schweizer Platz (U-bahn)* ✚ F5.

$
GERMAN

✕ **Exenberger.** The menu is typical of Old Sachsenhausen: apple wine and sauerkraut are served, but the interior is bright and modern and the Frankfurt specialties are a cut above the rest. As proprietor Kay Exenberger puts it: "We're nearly as fast as a fast-food restaurant, but as gemütlich (quaint) as an apple wine locale must be." It's so popular that reservations are a good idea even at lunch, and everything can be wrapped up to go. Many rave about the chocolate pudding with vanilla sauce. $ *Average main: €8* ⊠ *Bruchstr. 14, Sachsenhausen* ☎ *069/6339–0790* ⊕ *www.exenberger-frankfurt.de* ⊟ *No credit cards* ⊘ *Closed Sun.* ⊱ *Reservations essential* Ⓜ *Südbahnhof (U-bahn and S-bahn)* ✛ *F6.*

$$$
ECLECTIC
✕**Holbeins.** On the ground floor of the Städel art museum, Holbein's changes from a casual bistro at lunch to an elegant restaurant open until midnight. Lunch features pastas and paninis, or a prix-fixe three-course business lunch. The dinner menu changes every two months to take advantage of seasonal items such as chanterelles, but always includes German favorites such as schnitzel and international favorites including sushi. The café is open between lunch and dinner for coffee and pastries. $ *Average main: €22* ⊠ *Holbeinstr. 1, Sachsenhausen* ☎ *069/6605–6666* ⊕ *www.meyer-frankfurt.de* ⊘ *Closed Mon. in July* ⊱ *Reservations essential* Ⓜ *Schweizer Platz (U-bahn)* ✛ *D5.*

$$
SEAFOOD
✕**Lobster.** This small restaurant is a favorite of locals and visitors alike. The menu, dramatically different from those of its neighbors, includes mostly seafood. Oddly, lobster's not on the menu, but it does occasionally come up as a special or sauce on other dishes. The fish and shellfish are prepared in a variety of styles, but the strongest influence is French, including lamb Provençale. For dessert, try the vanilla ice cream with warm raspberry sauce. There's an extensive choice of regional wines by the glass. Reservations are strongly recommended on weekends. $ *Average main: €17* ⊠ *Wallstr. 21, Sachsenhausen* ☎ *069/612–920* ⊕ *www.lobster-weinbistrot.de* ⊘ *Closed Sun. No lunch* Ⓜ *Schweizer Platz (U-bahn)* ✛ *F5.*

$
ITALIAN
FAMILY
✕**Pizza Pasta Factory.** This restaurant started off with a proven theory: if you offer your food cheaply enough, you can make up the difference by selling a lot of it. So between 11:30 am and 4 pm and after 10 pm, this place sells its pizzas with three toppings, and pastas (except lasagna), for only €4.80. There are 37 possible toppings, including some unlikely ones like pineapple, corn, and eggs. Prosecco and espresso are a bargain €1.80 all day, and there's a play area for the stroller crowd. $ *Average main: €5* ⊠ *Martin Luther Str. 33, Sachsenhausen* ☎ *069/6199–5004* ⊕ *www.pizzapastafactoria.de* ⊟ *No credit cards* Ⓜ *Lokalbahnhof (S-bahn)* ✛ *F5.*

$
GERMAN
Fodor's Choice
★
✕**Zum Gemalten Haus.** There aren't many classic Apfelwein locales left, but this is one of them. It's just as it has been since the end of the 19th century: walls covered with giant paintings darkened with age, giant stoneware pitchers called *Bembels,* glasses that are ribbed to give greasy hands traction, long tables that can seat 12 people, schmaltzy music, hearty food with daily specials, and, as is traditional, no beer. Try this one if you want to truly capture the spirit of Old Sachsenhausen. $ *Average main: €8* ⊠ *Schweizerstr. 67, Sachsenhausen* ☎ *069/614–559* ⊕ *www.zumgemaltenhaus.de* ⊘ *Closed Mon. and 1st 2 wks Aug.* Ⓜ *Schweizer Platz (U-bahn)* ✛ *E6.*

9

OUTER FRANKFURT

$$ ✕**Altes Zollhaus.** The Old Customs House was built in 1775, and
GERMAN remains an excellent example of a half-timber house. Excellent versions of traditional German and international specialties are served. If
you're here in season, try a game or mushroom dish. In summer you
can eat in the beautiful garden. Menu specials change monthly. To get
here, take Bus 30 from Konstablerwache to Heiligenstock, or drive
out on Bundesstrasse 521 in the direction of Bad Vilbel. Reservations
recommended, especially for the outdoor garden. $ Average main: €18
✉ Friedberger Landstr. 531, Seckbach ☎ 069/472–707 ⊕ www.altes-
zollhaus-frankfurt.de ⊙ Closed Mon. No lunch Tues.–Sat. ✦ F1.

$$ ✕**Arche Nova.** This sunny establishment is a feature of Frankfurt's Öko-
VEGETARIAN haus, which was built according to environmental principles (solar panels, catching rainwater, etc.). It's mainly vegetarian, with such dishes as
a vegetable platter with feta cheese or curry soup with grated coconut
and banana. Meat, fish, and poultry dishes include goose, not often
found on German menus these days. Much of what's served, including
some of the beer, is organic. $ Average main: €15 ✉ Kasselerstr. 1a,
Bockenheim ☎ 069/707–5859 ⊕ www.arche-nova.de ⊙ No dinner Sun.
Ⓜ Westbahnhof (S-bahn) ✦ A2.

$$ ✕**Gerbermühle.** So beautiful that it inspired works by Goethe, a frequent
GERMAN visitor, this 14th-century building is now a restaurant once again, and
the century-long-plus tradition of hiking or biking to the chestnut-
tree-shaded, riverside beer garden has returned. The garden is as nice
as ever, and there's an indoor restaurant, guest rooms, an attractive
bar with the original stone walls, burnished leather chairs, and even a
bust of Goethe. The specialty of the house is frankfurters with Grüne
Sosse. Reservations recommended on the weekend. $ Average main:
€20 ✉ Gerbermühlestr. 105, Oberrad ☎ 069/6897–7790 ⊕ www.
gerbermuehle.de Ⓜ S16 to Oberad (S-bahn) ✦ H5.

$ ✕**Zum Rad.** Named for the huge *Rad* (wagon wheel) that serves as a
GERMAN centerpiece, this is one of the few Apfelwein taverns in Frankfurt that
makes its own apple wine, which it's been doing since 1806. It's located
in the villagelike district of Seckbach, on the northeastern edge of the
city. Outside tables are shaded by chestnut trees in an extensive courtyard. The typically Hessian cuisine, with giant portions, includes such
dishes as *Ochsenbrust* (brisket of beef) with the ubiquitous herb sauce,
and several kinds of schnitzel. Reservations recommended on weekends.
$ Average main: €10 ✉ Leonhardsg. 2, Seckbach ✦ U-4 to Seckbacher
Landstr. then Bus 43 to Draisbornstr. ☎ 069/479–128 ⊕ www.zum-rad.
de ▭ No credit cards ⊙ Closed Tues. No lunch Mon.–Sat. ✦ F1.

WHERE TO STAY

Businesspeople descend on Frankfurt year-round, so most hotels in the
city are frequently booked up well in advance and are expensive (though
many offer significant reductions on weekends). Many hotels add as
much as a 50% surcharge during trade fairs (*Messen*), of which there
are about 30 a year. The majority of the larger hotels are close to the

In summer, riverside bars and DJs spinning music are all part of the local scene.

main train station, fairgrounds, and business district (Bankenviertel). The area around the station has a reputation as a red-light district, but is well policed. More atmosphere is found at smaller hotels and pensions in the suburbs; the efficient public transportation network makes them easy to reach.

Prices in the reviews are the lowest cost of a standard double room in high season. For expanded reviews, facilities, and current deals, visit Fodors.com. Use the coordinates (✥ C3) at the end of each listing to locate a site on the corresponding map.

	WHAT IT COSTS IN EUROS			
	$	**$$**	**$$$**	**$$$$**
FOR TWO PEOPLE	under €100	€100–€175	€176–€225	over €225

CITY CENTER

$$ HOTEL **Bristol.** One of the nicest hotels in the neighborhood around the main train station, this stylish choice features modern, minimalist decor in soothing earth tones, and air-conditioning adds to the appeal. **Pros:** lobby bar is open 24 hours; beautiful garden patio; recently installed air-conditioning. **Cons:** unappealing neighborhood; small rooms. [$] *Rooms from: €150* ✉ *Ludwigstr. 15, City Center* ☎ *069/242–390* 🌐 *www.bristol-hotel.de* 🛏 *145 rooms* 🍴 *Breakfast* [M] *Hauptbahnhof (U-bahn and S-bahn)* ✥ *B4.*

$$$$
HOTEL
FAMILY
Fodor's Choice
★

Hilton Frankfurt. This international chain's downtown Frankfurt outpost has all the perks the business traveler wants, from secretarial services to video conferencing facilities and a hip lobby bar, Gekkos, which is definitely worth a visit. **Pros:** child-friendly and pet-friendly facilities; indoor pool; large terrace overlooking a park. **Cons:** expensive; small bathrooms. $ *Rooms from: €260* ⊠ *Hochstr. 4, City Center* ☎ *069/133–8000* ⊕ *www.frankfurt.hilton.com* ⇌ *342 rooms* ⊚ *No meals* Ⓜ *Eschenheimer Tor (U-bahn)* ♦ *D2.*

$$
HOTEL

Hotel Nizza. This beautiful Victorian building close to the main train station is filled with antiques and hand-painted murals by the owner, and features a lovely roof garden with a view of the skyline. **Pros:** antique furnishings; roof garden with shrubbery and a view of the skyline; very comfortable. **Cons:** the hotel is in the Bahnhof district, which can be a bit seedy at night; not all rooms have a private bathroom. $ *Rooms from: €110* ⊠ *Elbestr. 10, City Center* ☎ *069/242–5380* ⊕ *www.hotelnizza.de* ⇌ *26 rooms* ⊚ *Breakfast* Ⓜ *Willy-Brandt-Platz (U-bahn and S-bahn) or Hauptbahnhof (U-bahn and S-bahn)* ♦ *C4.*

$$
HOTEL
Fodor's Choice
★

Ibis Frankfurt Centrum. The Ibis is a reliable budget hotel chain, and this location offers simple, straightforward rooms on a quiet street near the river. **Pros:** short walk from the station and museums; 24-hour bar; family rooms and wheelchair-accessible rooms. **Cons:** far from stores and theaters; small rooms. $ *Rooms from: €105* ⊠ *Speicherstr. 4, City Center* ☎ *069/273–030* ⊕ *www.ibishotel.com* ⇌ *233 rooms* ⊚ *No meals* Ⓜ *Hauptbahnhof (U-bahn and S-bahn)* ♦ *B6.*

$
HOTEL
Fodor's Choice
★

InterCity Hotel. If there ever was a hotel at the vortex of arrivals and departures, it's this centrally located one in an elegant old-world building across the street from the main train station. **Pros:** free passes for local transportation; discount rates for seniors. **Cons:** on a busy street so can be noisy; no restaurant. $ *Rooms from: €70* ⊠ *Poststr. 8, City Center* ☎ *069/273–910* ⊕ *www.intercityhotel.com* ⇌ *384 rooms, 2 suites* ⊚ *Breakfast* Ⓜ *Hauptbahnhof (U-bahn and S-bahn)* ♦ *B4.*

$
HOTEL

Leonardo. Across the street from the main train station, this modern, sparkling hotel has its own underground garage. **Pros:** underground garage; quiet summer garden. **Cons:** on a busy street; parking expensive. $ *Rooms from: €68* ⊠ *Münchenerstr. 59, City Center* ☎ *069/242–320* ⊕ *www.leonardo-hotels.com* ⇌ *106 rooms* ⊚ *Breakfast* Ⓜ *Hauptbahnhof (U-bahn and S-bahn)* ♦ *C5.*

$$
HOTEL

Manhattan. Get to all parts of town quickly from this centrally located hotel. **Pros:** close the main train station; all rooms non-smoking and air-conditioned. **Cons:** no restaurant; neighborhood can be somewhat seedy at night. $ *Rooms from: €100* ⊠ *Düsseldorferstr. 10, City Center* ☎ *069/269–5970* ⊕ *www.manhattan-hotel.com* ⇌ *60 rooms* ⊚ *Breakfast* Ⓜ *Hauptbahnhof (U-bahn and S-bahn)* ♦ *B4.*

$
B&B/INN

Pension Aller. Quiet, solid comforts come with a modest price and a friendly welcome at this pension near the river. **Pros:** economical; near the station. **Cons:** need to reserve well in advance. $ *Rooms from: €62* ⊠ *Gutleutstr. 94, City Center* ☎ *069/252–596* ⊕ *www.pension-aller.de* ⇌ *10 rooms* ⊚ *Breakfast* Ⓜ *Hauptbahnhof (U-bahn and S-bahn)* ♦ *B5.*

$$$ | ⌂ **Roomers Hotel.** This lively boutique hotel features modern and sleek
HOTEL | designs everywhere you look, including rooms heavy on black lacquer
Fodor'sChoice | furniture offset by white bedspreads and chairs and large, airy win-
★ | dows. **Pros:** trendy design; convenient location close to train station and museums. **Cons:** expensive; probably not the best choice for families. $ *Rooms from: €220* ⌂ *Gutleutstr. 85, City Center* ☎ *069/271–3420* ⊕ *www.roomers.eu* ⬳ *116 rooms* ❍| *No meals* ⊹ *C5.*

$$$$ | ⌂ **Steigenberger Hotel Frankfurter Hof.** The neo-Gothic Frankfurter Hof
HOTEL | is the first choice of visiting heads of state and business moguls, who
Fodor'sChoice | keep coming back because of its impeccable service and luxurious
★ | rooms. **Pros:** old-fashioned elegance; central location close to Alt-stadt and museums; fresh flowers; thick carpeting. **Cons:** expensive rates. $ *Rooms from: €249* ⌂ *Am Kaiserpl., City Center* ☎ *069/21502* ⊕ *www.frankfurter-hof.steigenberger.de* ⬳ *280 rooms, 41 suites* ❍| *No meals* Ⓜ *Willy-Brandt-Platz (U-bahn)* ⊹ *D4.*

$$ | ⌂ **Westin Grand.** Those who like downtown Frankfurt will appreciate
HOTEL | the Westin's location, just steps from the famous Zeil shopping street,
FAMILY | plus all the features of a high-end chain hotel, including a fitness room, spa, pool, and sauna. **Pros:** kids stay free; handy to downtown; loaner work-out gear for the gym. **Cons:** on a noisy street; chain hotel feel; free in-room Wi-Fi only for members of Starwood frequent-stay rewards program. $ *Rooms from: €165* ⌂ *Konrad Adenauer Str. 7, City Center* ☎ *069/29810* ⊕ *www.westingrandfrankfurt.com* ⬳ *371 rooms* ❍| *No meals* Ⓜ *Konstablerwache (U-bahn and S-bahn)* ⊹ *F3.*

$$ | ⌂ **Wyndham Grand.** This recent addition to the "Mainhattan" skyline
HOTEL | caters to business guests with free Wi-Fi, air-conditioning (unusual in German hotels), and great city views from floor-to-ceiling windows. **Pros:** central location; modern decor. **Cons:** expensive; busy lobby. $ *Rooms from: €139* ⌂ *Wilhelm-Leuschner-Str. 32/34, City Center* ☎ *69/9074–5335* ⊕ *www.wyndhamgrandfrankfurt.com* ⬳ *285 rooms, 8 suites* ❍| *No meals* ⊹ *C5.*

MESSE AND WESTEND

$$$$ | ⌂ **Hessischer Hof.** This is the choice of many businesspeople, not just for
HOTEL | its location across from the convention center but also for the air of class that pervades its handsome interior. **Pros:** close to the convention center and public transportation; site of Jimmy's, one of the town's cult bars. **Cons:** lobby can be crowded; expensive. $ *Rooms from: €250* ⌂ *Friedrich-Ebert-Anlage 40, Messe* ☎ *069/75400* ⊕ *www.hessischer-hof.de* ⬳ *110 rooms, 7 suites* ❍| *No meals* Ⓜ *Messe (S-bahn)* ⊹ *B3.*

$$ | ⌂ **Maritim.** It's so close to the Messegelände (Exhibition Center) that
HOTEL | you can reach the exhibition halls, as this top-notch business hotel puts it, "with dry feet." It has its own underground garage, a sauna, steam bath, and indoor pool, and a sushi bar that draws many non–hotel guests. **Pros:** direct access to the convention center; indoor pool. **Cons:** online booking site is German only; hectic during fairs. $ *Rooms from: €110* ⌂ *Theodor-Heuss-Allee 3, Messe* ☎ *069/75780* ⊕ *www.maritim.de* ⬳ *519 rooms, 24 suites* ❍| *No meals* Ⓜ *Messe (S-bahn)* ⊹ *A3.*

$$ | ⌂ **Palmenhof.** This luxuriously modern hotel, held in the same family
HOTEL | for three generations, occupies a renovated art nouveau building dating

9

from 1890. **Pros:** near the Palmengarten; less expensive than similar hotels. **Cons:** no restaurant; top floor can get very hot. $ *Rooms from: €165* ✉ *Bockenheimer Landstr. 89–91, Westend* ☎ *069/753–0060* ⊕ *www.palmenhof.com* ⇆ *45 rooms, 37 apartments, 1 suite* ⦿ *Breakfast* Ⓜ *Westend (U-bahn)* ✛ *B2.*

NORDEND AND BORNHEIM

$$

HOTEL

🏨 **Villa Orange.** Frankfurt's first eco-hotel features modern, natural-wood furniture, including canopy beds, and organic cotton sheets and towels. **Pros:** certified BIO hotel with organic furnishings and food; on a quiet residential street; all rooms are smoke-free. **Cons:** hard beds; not close to museums and shopping. $ *Rooms from: €158* ✉ *Hebelstr. 1, Nordend* ☎ *069/405–840* ⊕ *www.villa-orange.de* ⇆ *38 rooms* ⦿ *Breakfast* Ⓜ *Musterschule (U-bahn)* ✛ *F1.*

SACHSENHAUSEN

$$

HOTEL

🏨 **Maingau.** This pleasant hotel in the middle of the lively Sachsenhausen quarter has recently renovated rooms that are modest but comfortable; the nightly rate includes a substantial breakfast buffet. **Pros:** close to nightlife; fantastic restaurant; smoke-free hotel. **Cons:** on a busy street. $ *Rooms from: €100* ✉ *Schifferstr. 38–40, Sachsenhausen* ☎ *069/609–140* ⊕ *www.maingau.de* ⇆ *78 rooms* ⦿ *Breakfast* Ⓜ *Schweizer Platz (U-bahn)* ✛ *F5.*

OUTER FRANKFURT

$$

HOTEL

🏨 **Falk Hotel.** In the heart of Bockenheim and near numerous cafés, bars, shops, and the Messe (trade center) this hotel is a good deal, especially on weekends. **Pros:** fairly low rates, especially weekends. **Cons:** outside the city center; small rooms; no restaurant. $ *Rooms from: €134* ✉ *Falkstr. 38A, Bockenheim* ☎ *069/7191–8870* ⊕ *www.hotel-falk.de* ⇆ *29 rooms* ⦿ *Breakfast* Ⓜ *Leipzigerstrasse (U-bahn)* ✛ *A1.*

$$$$

HOTEL

🏨 **Sheraton Frankfurt.** This huge hotel is connected to one of Frankfurt Airport's terminals. **Pros:** close to the airport and the autobahn; 24-hour amenities including business center. **Cons:** smoke-free rooms not always available; long walk to the elevator; expensive; free Internet in lobby only. $ *Rooms from: €559* ✉ *Hugo-Eckener-Ring 15, Flughafen Terminal 1, Airport* ☎ *069/69770* ⊕ *www.sheraton.com/frankfurt* ⇆ *1,008 rooms, 28 suites* ⦿ *Breakfast* Ⓜ *Flughafen (S-bahn)* ✛ *A6.*

$$$

HOTEL

FAMILY

🏨 **Steigenberger Airport Hotel.** The sylvan beauty of this skyscraper hotel is surprising, considering that it's just a half mile from the airport and connected to it by a steady stream of shuttle buses that operate 24 hours. **Pros:** conveniently located near the airport; indoor pool and gym; four restaurants, including a 24-hour bistro. **Cons:** restaurants are expensive; far from downtown. $ *Rooms from: €200* ✉ *Unterschweinstiege 16, Airport* ☎ *069/69750* ⊕ *www.steigenberger.com/en/Frankfurt_Airport* ⇆ *550 rooms, 20 suites* ⦿ *No meals* Ⓜ *Flughafen (S-bahn)* ✛ *A6.*

NIGHTLIFE AND PERFORMING ARTS

NIGHTLIFE

Most bars close between 2 am and 4 am. Nightclubs typically charge entrance fees ranging from €5 to €20. In addition, some trendy places, such as King Kamehameha, enforce dress codes—usually no jeans, sneakers, shorts, or khaki pants admitted.

Sachsenhausen (Frankfurt's "Left Bank") is a good place for bars, clubs, and traditional Apfelwein taverns. The fashionable Nordend has an almost equal number of bars and clubs but fewer tourists. Frankfurt was a real pioneer in the German jazz scene, and also has done much for the development of techno music. Jazz musicians make the rounds from smoky backstreet cafés all the way to the Old Opera House, and the local broadcaster Hessischer Rundfunk sponsors the German Jazz Festival in fall. The Frankfurter Jazzkeller has been the most noted venue for German jazz fans for decades.

CITY CENTER

DANCE AND NIGHTCLUBS

Gibson Club. This nightclub in the heart of the Zeil attracts a mostly young crowd with its live music performances by international musicians. It's open Thursday from 8 pm and Friday and Saturday from 11 pm. Concert tickets from €21. ⊠ *Zeil 85–93, City Center* ☎ *069/9494–7770* ⊕ *www.gibson-club.de.*

Odeon. The type of crowd depends on the night. The large club hosts student nights on Thursday, a "27 Up Club" on Friday (exclusively for guests 27 or older), disco nights on Saturday, as well as "Black Mondays"—a night of soul, hip-hop, and R&B. It's housed in a beautiful white building that looks like a museum. There's lots of neon and pulsing lights, including under the see-through dance floor. ⊠ *Seilerstr. 34, City Center* ☎ *069/285–055* ⊕ *www.theodeon.de.*

JAZZ

Der Frankfurter Jazzkeller. The oldest jazz cellar in Germany, Der Frankfurter Jazzkeller was founded by legendary trumpeter Carlo Bohländer. The club, which once hosted such luminaries as Louis Armstrong and Ella Fitzgerald, now offers hot, modern jazz, at a cover of €5 to €25. There are jam sessions on Wednesday and "Latin-funky" dances on Friday. Jazzkeller is located on a difficult-to-find alleyway off "Fressgasse," which just adds to its charm and legend. ⊠ *Kleine Bockenheimerstr. 18, City Center* ☎ *069/284–927* ⊕ *www.jazzkeller.com* ⊙ *Closed Sun.– Tues. and last wk Aug.*

Zoom. Sinkkasten, a Frankfurt musical institution, was renamed Zoom in 2013. By any name it is a great place for blues, jazz, pop, and rock. Saturday nights are Hit Happens, with hip-hop and techno-electro music. There are live performances nightly. Zoom is open from 9 pm to 1 am every day but Monday. ⊠ *Brönnerstr. 5, City Center* ☎ *069/280–385* ⊕ *www.zoomfrankfurt.de.*

9

Beer Bitte

The lager style that most of the world has come to know as "beer" originated in Germany. However, Germans don't just produce one beverage called beer; they brew more than 5,000 varieties in about 1,300 breweries. The hallmark of the country's dedication to beer is the Purity Law, *das Reinheitsgebot,* unchanged since Duke Wilhelm IV introduced it in Bavaria in 1516. The law decrees that only malted barley, hops, yeast, and water may be used to make beer, except for the specialty *Weiss* or *Weizenbier* (wheat beers). Although the law has been repealed, nearly all breweries continue to follow its precepts, even if some modern brewers are tinkering with flavorings including spices.

The beer preferred in most of Germany is *Pils* (Pilsner), which has a rich yellow hue, hoppy flavor, and an alcohol content of about 5%. Frankfurt's local Pils brands are Binding and Henninger, but Licher, from the village of Lich nearby, is especially well balanced and crisp. The area is also home to Schöfferhofer, which brews Germany's number two style, *Hefeweizen* (wheat beer), which is cloudy, since it is

unfiltered, and yeasty. Light, or *helles,* is sweeter than *dunkel,* or dark.

Few German bars offer more than one type of Pils or Weizen on tap, so you'll need to hit a few bars to sample a good variety. Not a bad proposition.

QUAFF IT HERE

Begin a night at **Klosterhof** (⊠ Weissfrauenstr. 3 ☎ 069/9139–9000 ⊕ www.klosterhof-frankfurt. de Ⓜ Willy-Brandt-Platz [U-bahn]), a traditional restaurant and beer garden in the City Center, where you can try Hessian favorites like *Handkäs mit Musik* (literally, hand cheese with music, a strong soft cheese served with chopped onions, oil, and vinegar), as well as their custom-brewed *Naturtrüb,* an unfiltered (and thus naturally cloudy) lager.

Eckhaus (⊠ Bornheimer Landstr. 45 ☎ 069/491–197 Ⓜ Merianplatz [U-bahn]) is the perfect neighborhood bar to down a cold Binding or two. The restaurant, in a great location just off the Berger Strasse strip in leafy Nordend, offers a solidly executed menu of standards like schnitzel and roast chicken, along with a few creative specials.

OSTEND

JAZZ

Jazzlokal Mampf. With posters of Chairman Mao on the walls, time seems to have stood still at the Jazzlokal Mampf. It looks straight out of the 1970s, but with live music to match, many don't think that's so bad. Since it opens at 6 pm for dinner and drinks, there's a lively after-work crowd on weekdays. Live jazz performances begin at 8:30 pm. Closed Wednesday and Thursday. ⊠ *Sandweg 64, Ostend* ☎ *069/448–674* ⊕ *www.mampf-jazz.de* ☉ *Sun.–Tues. 6–1, Fri. and Sat. 6–2* Ⓜ *Merianplatz (U-bahn).*

HAUSEN

LIVE MUSIC

Brotfabrik. An important address for jazz, rock, salsa, and disco, the "Bread Factory" really is set in a former bakery in an area of town that's still primarily industrial. The building houses two stages, a concert hall, two restaurants, three not-for-profit projects, an ad agency, and a gallery. ✉ *Bachmannstr. 2–4, Hausen* ☎ *069/2479–0800* ⊕ *www.brotfabrik.info* Ⓜ *Fischstein (U-bahn)*.

MESSE AND WESTEND

BARS

Champion's - The American Sports Bar and Restaurant. Like the rest of the Marriott Hotel, this sports bar is designed to make Americans feel at home. The walls are lined with team jerseys, autographed helmets, and photographs of professional athletes. The 23 TVs can be tuned to the American Forces Network, which carries the full range of American sports. Food leans toward buffalo wings, hamburgers, and brownies. ✉ *Hamburger Allee 2, Messe* ☎ *069/7955–8305* ⊕ *www.champions-frankfurt.de* ☞ *Festhalle/Messe (U-bahn)*.

Fox and Hound. Frankfurt is teeming with Irish pubs, but there is an occasional English pub, too. A good example is the Fox and Hound. Its patrons, mainly British, come to watch the latest football (soccer to Americans), rugby, and cricket matches. Enjoy the authentic British pub food; 35 whiskies, bitters, and stout; and the basket of chips. Monday is steak night, with American-style sirloins and rib eyes. ✉ *Niedenau 2, Westend* ☎ *069/9720–2009* ⊕ *www.foxandhound.de* Ⓜ *Festhalle/Messe (U-bahn)*.

Jimmy's Bar. Jimmy's Bar, the meeting place of business executives since 1951, is classy and expensive—just like the hotel it's in. There is live piano music, mostly jazz, every evening from 10 pm to 3 am, and the kitchen is open just as late. You must ring the doorbell to get in, although regulars have their own keys. ✉ *Hessischer Hof, Friedrich-Ebert-Anlage 40, Messe* ☎ *069/7540–2461* ⊕ *www.hessischer-hof.de/en/hotel-bar-frankfurt*.

SACHSENHAUSEN

BARS

Stereobar. University students and young professionals frequent this bar in a cellar beneath a narrow Sachsenhausen alleyway. DJs usually spin the music, although there are occasional live acts on weekends. There's a tiny dance floor if you feel like showing off your moves. ✉ *Abstgässchen 7, Sachsenhausen* ☎ *069/617–116* ⊕ *www.stereobar.de* Ⓜ *Offenbach (S-bahn)*.

LIVE MUSIC

Balalaika. The spacious club has an intimate feel, as candles are just about the only source of light. The proprietor is Anita Honis, an American singer from Harlem, who likes to get out her acoustic guitar and perform on occasion. Everyone is invited to sing or play on the piano, which is set up for impromptu and scheduled performances. ✉ *Schifferstr. 3, Sachsenhausen* ☎ *069/612–226* Ⓜ *Bus 36 to Affentorplatz*.

9

PERFORMING ARTS

The Städtische Bühnen—municipal theaters, including the city's opera company—are the prime venues for Frankfurt's cultural events. The city has what is probably the most lavish theater in the country, the Alte Oper, a magnificently ornate 19th-century opera house that's now a multipurpose hall for pop and classical concerts, and dances. (These days operas are presented at the Städtische Bühnen.)

Best Tickets. Tickets for theater, concerts, and sports events can be purchased from Best Tickets downtown in the Zeilgalerie. ⊠ *Zeil 112–114, City Center* ☎ *069/20228, 069/296–929* ⊕ *www.journal-ticketshop.de.*

BALLET, CONCERTS, AND OPERA

Alte Oper. The most glamorous venue for classical-music concerts and ballet is the Alte Oper, one of the most beautful buildings in Frankfurt. Tickets to performances can range from €20 to nearly €150. There is a bar or bistro on each level for drinks, coffee, and pastries during intermission, and the elegant Restaurant Opera for dining before or after performances. ⊠ *Opernpl., City Center* ⊕ *www.alteoper.de.*

Bockenheimer Depot. Frankfurt's ballet company performs in the Bockenheimer Depot, a former trolley barn also used for other theatrical performances and music events. ⊠ *Carlo-Schmidt-Pl. 1, Bockenheim* ⊕ *www.bockenheimer-depot.de/.*

Festhalle. The huge glass-domed Festival Hall, commissioned by Kaiser Wilhelm II in 1905, Festhalle is the scene of many rock concerts, horse shows, ice shows, sporting events, circus and other large-scale spectaculars including trade fairs. It is on the city's fairgrounds, just 10 minutes from downtown by subway. Tickets are available through Frankfurt Ticket. ⊠ *Ludwig-Erhard-Anlage 1, Messe* ☎ *069/9200–9213* ⊕ *festhalle.messefrankfurt.com/frankfurt/en/besucher/willkommen. html* Ⓜ *Festhalle/Messe (U-bahn).*

Frankfurt Opera. Widely regarded as one of the best in Europe, the Frankfurt Opera is known for its dramatic artistry. Richard Wagner and Richard Strauss both oversaw their own productions for the company, now housed in a modern glass-walled building in the city center. In an effort to introduce a new generation to opera, there are special family programs with free tickets for children and teens to 19. ⊠ *Städtische Bühnen, Untermainanlage 11, City Center* ☎ *069/2124–9494* ⊕ *www. oper-frankfurt.de* Ⓜ *Willy-Brandt-Platz (U-bahn).*

Kammermusiksaal. The city is the home of the Radio-Sinfonie-Orchester Frankfurt, part of Hessischer Rundfunk. Considered one of Europe's best orchestras, it performs regularly in the 850-seat Kammermusiksaal, part of that broadcasting operation's campuslike facilities. ⊠ *Bertramstr. 8, Dornbusch* ☎ *069/155–2000* ⊕ *termine.koeln.de/frankfurt-am-main/124341_frankfurter-sparkasse-von-1822-kammermusiksaal-frankfurt-am-main.*

THEATER

Theatrical productions in Frankfurt are usually in German, except for those at the English Theater.

The Eiserner Steg (Iron Bridge) was Europe's very first suspension bridge, and a walk across promises great photo ops of Frankfurt's skyline.

Die Schmiere. For a zany theatrical experience, try Die Schmiere, which offers trenchant cabaret-style satire and also disarmingly calls itself "the worst theater in the world." The theater is closed in summer for a "creative break." ⊠ *Seckbächerg. 4, City Center* ☏ *069/281–066* ⊕ *www. die-schmiere.de.*

English Theatre. For English-language productions, try the English Theatre, continental Europe's largest English-speaking theater, which offers an array of musicals, thrillers, dramas, comedies, and poetry readings with British or American casts. The bar, James, is open before and after performances. ⊠ *Gallusanlage 7, City Center* ☏ *069/2423–1620* ⊕ *www.English-theatre.org* ☉ *Closed July.*

Internationales Theater Frankfurt. The Internationales Theater Frankfurt bills itself as presenting "the art of the world on the Main." It has regular performances in English, as well as in German, French, Spanish, Italian, Romanian, and Russian, and concerts by international jazz, folk, and pop rock musicians. ⊠ *Hanauer Landstr. 7, Ostend* ☏ *069/499–0980* ⊕ *www.internationales-theater.de* Ⓜ *Ostendstrasse (S-bahn).*

Künstlerhaus Mousonturm. This cultural center hosts an eclectic mix of concerts of all kinds, as well as plays, dance performances, and exhibits. ⊠ *Waldschmidtstr. 4, Nordend* ☏ *069/4058–9520* ⊕ *www. mousonturm.de* Ⓜ *Zoo station (U-bahn).*

Schauspielhaus (*Playhouse*). The municipally owned Schauspielhaus has a repertoire that includes works by Sophocles, Goethe, Shakespeare, Brecht, and Beckett, along with more contemporary plays. All are performed with modern, even avant-garde staging. ⊠ *Willy-Brandt-Pl.,*

The elegant illumination of the Alte Oper (Old Opera House) and fountain make for magical nighttime viewing.

Neue Mainzer Str. 17, City Center ☎ *069/2124–9494* ⊕ *www.schauspielfrankfurt.de* Ⓜ *Willy-Brandt-Platz (U-bahn).*

Tigerpalast. There's not much that doesn't take place at this international variety theater. Guests are entertained by international cabaret performers and the Palast's own variety orchestra. There's an excellent French restaurant that has been awarded a Michelin star, and the cozy Palastbar, under the basement arches, looks like an American bar from the 1920s. Despite pricey show tickets, shows often sell out, so book tickets as far in advance as possible. Dinner and show packages start at €70. It's located one block from the Zeil pedestrian shopping area. ⊠ *Heiligkreuzg. 16–20, City Center* ☎ *069/920–0220* ⊕ *www.tigerpalast.de* ⊗ *Closed Mon.*

SPORTS AND THE OUTDOORS

Despite an ever-growing number of skyscrapers, Frankfurt is full of parks and other green oases where you can enjoy wide-open spaces.

Lohrberg Hill. In the Seckbach district, northeast of the city, Frankfurters hike the 590-foot Lohrberg Hill for a fabulous view of the town and the Taunus, Spessart, and Odenwald hills. Along the way you'll also see the last remaining vineyard within the Frankfurt city limits, the Seckbach Vineyard. Take the U-4 subway to Seckbacher Landstrasse, then Bus 43 to Draisbornstrasse. ⊠ *Frankfurt.*

Stadtwald. South of the city lies Sachsenhausen, the huge, 4,000-acre Stadtwald (city forest), which makes Frankfurt one of Germany's greenest metropoles. The forest has innumerable paths and trails, bird sanctuaries, impressive sports stadiums, and a good restaurant. The Oberschweinstiege stop on streetcar Line 14 is right in the middle of the park. ⊠ *Sachsenhausen.*

Taunus Hills. The Taunus Hills are a great getaway for Frankfurters. Take U-bahn 3 to Hohemark.

BICYCLING

There are numerous biking paths within the city limits. The Stadtwald in the southern part of the city is crisscrossed with well-tended paths that are nice and flat. The city's riverbanks are, for the most part, lined with paths open to bikers. These are not only on both sides of the Main but also on the banks of the little Nidda River, which flows through Heddernheim, Eschersheim, Hausen, and Rödelheim before joining the Main at Höchst. Some bikers also like the Taunus Hills, but note that word, "Hills."

JOGGING

Anlagenring. The Anlagenring ("Cityring") consists of two parallel roads that were formerly the city walls. Both are one-way streets, with the inner ring running clockwise and the outer counterclockwise to form the city center. Today it is a popular running route along many of Frankfurt's sights. ⊠ *Frankfurt.*

SHOPPING

Frankfurt, and the rest of Germany, no longer has the restrictive laws that once kept stores closed evenings and Saturday afternoons, the very times working people might want to shop. Stores now can stay open until 10 pm, but pretty much everything is still closed on Sunday except for restaurants and bakeries.

The tree-shaded pedestrian zone of the **Zeil** is said to be one of the richest shopping strips in Germany. The section between Hauptwache and Konstablerwache is famous for its incredible variety of department and specialty stores. But there's much more to downtown shopping. The subway station below the Hauptwache also doubles as a vast underground mall. West of the Hauptwache are two parallel streets highly regarded by shoppers. One is the luxurious **Goethestrasse,** lined with trendy boutiques, art galleries, jewelry stores, and antiques shops. The other is **Grosse Bockenheimer Strasse,** better known as the Fressgass ("Pig-Out Alley"), an extension of the Zeil that's lined with cafés, restaurants, and pricey food shops.

One gift that's typical of the city is the Apfelwein. You can get a bottle of it at any grocery store, but more enduring souvenirs would be the Bembel pottery pitchers and ribbed glasses that are an equal part of the Apfelwein tradition. Then there is the sausage. You can get the "original hot dog" in cans or vacuum-packed at any grocery store.

For a total shopping blitz, head to the Zeil, where you'll find some of Germany's most upscale shops.

CITY CENTER

CLOTHING

Peek & Cloppenburg. At this huge branch of the clothing chain, men and women can find what they need for the office, gym, and nightclub. Prices range from easily affordable to sky-high for top designer labels. There's also a branch at the new Skyline Plaza shopping mall near the Messe. ⊠ *Zeil 71–75, City Center* ☎ *069/298–950* ⊕ *www.peek-cloppenburg.de/* ⊘ *Closed Sun.*

Pfüller Modehaus. Find upscale designer day wear, evening wear, jeans, handbags, and other accessories for women, ranging from classic to trendy. While there's mostly well-known brands such as Valentino and Diane von Furstenburg, new, innovative names on the fashion scene are also well represented. Everything is displayed elegantly, and personal service is impeccable in this three-story shopping destination. Pfüller has separated its equally upscale children's collection to a separate multifloor store directly across the street, called Pfüller Kids. Both stores have the same opening hours. ⊠ *Goethestr. 15–17, City Center* ☎ *069/1337–8060* ⊕ *www.august-pfueller.de/en/women* ⊘ *Closed Sun.*

Schillerpassage. The Schillerpassage shopping area is lined with men's and women's fashion boutiques. ⊠ *Rahmhofstr. 2, City Center.*

FOOD AND WINE

Café Mozart. Reminiscent of a traditional coffeehouse, this café offers all types of sweets and pastries, along with breakfast, lunch, and dinner. Open daily, it's on a quiet, tucked-away street that's steps from the main shopping area, Zeil. ⊠ *Töngesg. 23, City Center* ☎ *069/291–954* ⊕ *www.cafemozart-frankfurt.de/english.*

Kleinmarkthalle. The large and airy Kleinmarkthalle is a treasure trove of stands selling spices, herbs, teas, exotic fruits, cut flowers, meats, live fish flown in from the Atlantic, and more varieties of wursts and cheeses than you can count. Plus, it offers all kinds of snacks in case you need a break while shopping. ⊠ *Haseng. 5–7, City Center* ☎ *069/2123–3696* ⊕ *www.kleinmarkthalle.com* ⊗ *Closed. Sun.* Ⓜ *Hauptwache (S-bahn), Dom (U-bahn).*

Weinhandlung Dr. Teufel. Weinhandlung Dr. Teufel is well known for its wide selection of regional wines, many priced under € 10, plus rare vintages costing three figures or more. There are also chocolate and cigars, a complete line of glasses, carafes, corkscrews, and other accessories, and books on all aspects of viticulture. The store also has a location in the Westend. ⊠ *Kleiner Hirschgraben 4, City Center* ☎ *069/448–989* ⊕ *www.weinteufel.de.*

SHOPPING MALLS AND DEPARTMENT STORES

Galeria Kaufhof. One of Germany's biggest and most popular department stores, the Galeria Kaufhof carries clothing, jewelry, sports equipment, cosmetics, toys, and more. The Frankfurt branch has a food hall on the bottom floor; the restaurant on the top floor has great city views. ⊠ *Zeil 116–126, City Center* ☎ *069/21910* ⊗ *Closed Sun.* Ⓜ *Hauptwache (U-bahn).*

Karstadt. One of Germany's biggest department store chains, Karstadt is known for both its upscale brand-name designer offerings, including popular German designers Betty Buckley and Gerry Weber (for women), and its splendid food and drink department, with plenty of opportunity to try the offerings. ⊠ *Zeil 90, City Center* ☎ *069/929–050* ⊕ *www. karstadt.de/jsp/filialen/frankfurt-zeil.jsp* ⊗ *Closed Sun.*

MyZiel. The moderately priced multilevel MyZeil shopping mall has dozens of clothing and electronics shops and a food court. ⊠ *Zeil 112–114, City Center* ☎ *069/2972–3970* ⊗ *Closed Sun.*

Skyline Plaza. Opened in 2015 in the Messe section of the city, this multilevel shopping mall contains more than 170 shops, including clothing, shoes, jewelry, and accessories, and the biggest food court in Frankfurt. Unfortunately, it feels like an American mall, with all its familiar food and fashion chains dominating the European and German brands. Head to the roof garden for a picture-postcard view of the skyline year-round, and outdoor dining in season. ⊠ *Europa-Allee 6, Messe* ☎ *069/2972– 8700* ⊗ *Closed Sun.* Ⓜ *Festhalle/Messe (U-bahn).*

WESTEND

FOOD

Café Laumer. The pastry shop at Café Laumer has local delicacies such as *Bethmännchen und Brenten* (marzipan cookies) and *Frankfurter Kranz* (a kind of creamy cake). It's open daily. ⊠ *Bockenheimer Landstr. 67, Westend* ☎ *069/727–912* ⊕ *www.cafelaumer.de.*

9

SACHSENHAUSEN

MARKET

Flohmarkt (*Flea Market*). Sachsenhausen's weekend flea market is on Saturday from 9 to 2 on the riverbank between Dürerstrasse and the Eiserner Steg. Purveyors of the cheap have taken over, and there's lots of discussion as to whether it is a good use for the elegant, museum-lined riverbank. ■TIP→ **Get there early for the bargains, as the better-quality stuff gets snapped up quickly.** Shopping success or no, the market can be fun for browsing. ⊠ *Southern bank of the Main River between Eiserner Steg and Holbeinsteg, Sachsenhausen* ☎ *069/212–48562.*

SIDE TRIPS FROM FRANKFURT

Destinations reachable by the local transportation system include Höchst and the Taunus Hills, which include Bad Homburg and Kronberg. Just to the northwest and west of Frankfurt, the Taunus Hills are an area of mixed pine and hardwood forest, medieval castles, and photogenic towns many Frankfurters regard as their own backyard. It's home to Frankfurt's wealthy bankers and business executives, and on weekends you can see them enjoying their playground: hiking through the hills, climbing the Grosse Feldberg, taking the waters at Bad Homburg's health-enhancing mineral springs, or just lazing in elegant stretches of parkland.

BAD HOMBURG

12 km (7 miles) north of Frankfurt.

Emperor Wilhelm II, the infamous "Kaiser" of World War I, spent a month each year at Bad Homburg, the principal city of the Taunus Hills. Another frequent visitor to Bad Homburg was Britain's Prince of Wales, later King Edward VII, who made the name *Homburg* world famous by associating it with a hat.

GETTING HERE AND AROUND

Bad Homburg is reached easily by the S-bahn from Hauptwache, the main station, and other points in downtown Frankfurt. The S5 goes to Bad Homburg. There's also a Taunusbahn (from the main station only) that stops in Bad Homburg and then continues into the far Taunus, including the Römerkastell-Saalburg and Wehrheim, with bus connections to Hessenpark. Bad Homburg is about a 30- to 45-minute drive north of Frankfurt on A-5.

ESSENTIALS

Visitor Information Kur- und Kongress GmbH Bad Homburg. ⊠ *Louisenstr. 58, Bad Homburg vor der Höhe* ☎ *06172/1000* ⊕ *www.bad-homburg.de.*

EXPLORING

FAMILY **Freilichtmuseum Hessenpark.** About an hour's walk through the woods along a well-marked path from the Römerkastell-Saalburg is an open-air museum at Hessenpark, near Neu-Anspach. The museum presents a clear picture of the world in which 18th- and 19th-century Hessians lived, using 135 acres of rebuilt villages with houses, schools, and farms typical of the time. The park, 15 km (9 miles) outside Bad Homburg in the direction of Usingen, can also be reached by public transportation. Take the Taunusbahn from the Frankfurt main station to Wehrheim; then transfer to Bus 514. ⊠ *Laubweg 5, Neu-Anspach* ☎ *06081/5880* ⊕ *www.hessenpark.de* ☜ *€6* ⊘ *Mar.–Oct., daily 9–6; Nov., daily 10–5.*

Grosser Feldberg. A short bus ride from Bad Homburg takes you to the highest mountain in the Taunus, the 2,850-foot, eminently hikable Grosser Feldberg. ⊠ *Bad Homburg vor der Höhe.*

Kurpark (*spa*). Bad Homburg's greatest attraction has long been the Kurpark, in the heart of the Old Town, with more than 31 fountains. Romans first used the springs, which were rediscovered and made famous in the 19th century. In the park you'll find the popular, highly salty Elisabethenbrunnen spring as well as a Thai temple and a Russian chapel, mementos left by royal guests—King Chulalongkorn of Siam and Czar Nicholas II. ⊠ *Bad Homburg vor der Höhe* ⊕ *www. bad-homburg-tourismus.de/en/entdecken/freizeit_kurpark.htm.*

FAMILY **Römerkastell-Saalburg** (*Saalburg Roman Fort*). The remains of a Roman fortress built in AD 120, the Römerkastell-Saalburg could accommodate a cohort (500 men) and was part of the fortifications along the Limes Wall, which ran from the Danube to the Rhine and was meant to protect the Roman Empire from barbarian invasion. The fort was restored more than a century ago. The site, which includes a museum of Roman artifacts, is 6½ km (4 miles) north of Bad Homburg on Route 456 in the direction of Usingen; there's a direct bus from Bad Homburg. ⊠ *Archäologischer Park, Saalburg 1, Bad Homburg vor der Höhe* ☎ *06175/93740* ⊕ *www.saalburgmuseum.de* ☜ *€5* ⊘ *Mar.–Oct., daily 9–6; Nov.–Feb., Tues.–Sun. 9–4.*

Schloss Homburg. The most historically noteworthy sight in Bad Homburg is the 17th-century Schloss, where the kaiser stayed when he was in town. The state apartments are exquisitely furnished, and the Spiegelkabinett (Hall of Mirrors) is especially worthy of a visit. In the surrounding park look for two cedars from Lebanon, both now about 200 years old. The museum holds artifacts from much earlier, including from archeological digs on the site. ⊠ *Schloss, Bad Homburg vor der Höhe* ☎ *06172/926–2148* ⊕ *www.schloss-homburg.de* ☜ *€5* ⊘ *Tues.– Sun. 10–5.*

Spielbank Bad Homburg. This casino boasts with some justice that it is the "Mother of Monte Carlo." The first casino in Bad Homburg, and one of the first in the world, was established in 1841, but closed in 1866 because Prussian law forbade gambling. Proprietor François Blanc then established the famous Monte Carlo casino on the French Riviera, and the Bad Homburg casino wasn't reopened until 1949. Classic table games such as roulette and blackjack have been joined by poker variations Texas Hold 'Em and Three Card Poker, plus slot machines and other electronic games including electronic roulette. A bus from the south side of Frankfurt's Hauptbahnhof leaves every 60 to 90 minutes between 2 pm and 1 am. Buses back to Frankfurt run every one–two hours from 4:30 pm to 4 am. The trip takes one hour each way. The €10 fare will be refunded after the casino's full entry fee has been deducted. A passport or other government-issued identification is required for admission. ⊠ *Kisseleffstr. 35, Bad Homburg vor der Höhe* ☏ *06172/17010* ⊕ *www.spielbank-bad-homburg.de* ⊡ *Slot-machine area free, gaming area €2.50* ⊘ *Daily 2:30 pm–3 am.*

WHERE TO EAT AND STAY

$ ✕ **Kartoffelküche.** This simple restaurant serves traditional dishes accom-
GERMAN   panied by potatoes cooked every way imaginable. The potato-and-broc-coli gratin and the potato pizza are excellent. For dessert, try potato strudel with vanilla sauce. The charming decor includes colorful art deco dishes and lamps. ⓢ *Average main: €9* ⊠ *Audenstr. 4, Bad Homburg vor der Höhe* ☏ *06172/21500* ⊕ *www.kartoffelkueche.com* ⊘ *No lunch Mon.–Thurs.*

$ ⌂ **Maritim Kurhaus Hotel.** The hotel offers large, richly furnished rooms
HOTEL   with king-size beds and deep armchairs. **Pros:** quiet location near Kurpark; indoor pool. **Cons:** expensive parking. ⓢ *Rooms from: €100* ⊠ *Ludwigstr. 3, Bad Homburg vor der Höhe* ☏ *06172/6600* ⊕ *www.maritim.de* ⇆ *148 rooms, 10 suites* |◯| *Breakfast.*

$$$ ⌂ **Steigenberger Bad Homburg.** This hotel, which opened in 1883, was
HOTEL   renowned for catering to Europe's royalty in its pre–World War I hey-day, and it's still good at pleasing a well-heeled clientele. **Pros:** old-world class; handy to the Kurpark; fitness equipment and sauna. **Cons:** expensive; parking is difficult; access to pool, sauna, and steam room is a whopping €60 daily fee. ⓢ *Rooms from: €180* ⊠ *Kaiser-Friedrich-Promenade 69–75, Bad Homburg vor der Höhe* ☏ *06172/1810* ⊕ *www.bad-homburg.steigenberger.de* ⇆ *148 rooms, 17 suites* |◯| *No meals.*

THE PFALZ AND
RHINE TERRACE

WELCOME TO THE PFALZ AND RHINE TERRACE

TOP REASONS TO GO

★ **Wine:** German Rieslings are some of the most versatile white wines in the world. If you've only tried the sweet style, the rest may be a revelation.

★ **Festivals:** Wine is a great excuse for merrymaking, and wine festivals take place in almost every town and village across the region from May through October. The largest wine festival in the world takes place in the town of Bad Dürkheim, in front of a wine barrel the size of a building.

★ **Pfälzerwald:** The Palatinate Forest is a paradise for hiking and cycling. Even a short stroll under the beautiful pine and chestnut trees is a relaxing and way to spend an afternoon.

★ **Castles:** Burg Trifels and Schloss Villa Ludwigshöhe contrast strikingly in style, inside and out. Both are wonderful settings for concerts.

★ **Cathedrals:** The cathedrals in Speyer, Worms, and Mainz are the finest examples of grand-scale Rhenish Romanesque architecture in Germany.

1 **The German Wine Road.** The picturesque *Deutsche Weinstrasse* (German Wine Road) weaves through the valleys and among the lower slopes of the Haardt Mountains. Along its length is a string of pretty half-timber wine-producing villages, each more inviting than the last.

2 **The Rhine Terrace.** Rheinhessen, or the "Rhine Terrace," is a broad, fertile river valley, where grapes are but one of many crops. Here the medieval cities of Mainz, Worms, and Speyer all bear testament to the great power and wealth brought by the important trading route created by the mighty Rhine itself.

GETTING ORIENTED

If you're arriving from the dramatic stretch of the river Rhine centered on the Loreley and Koblenz to the north, you'll notice that the landscape here is far gentler. So, too, is the climate: this region, guarded at its northern edge by the medieval city of Mainz and touching the French border at its southern extreme, is one of Germany's warmest. This helps the land give birth to plentiful fruits such as apricots and figs, and to some of Germany's greatest wines.

10

DRIVING THE GERMAN WINE ROAD

Due to its sunny skies, warm weather, and fertile fields, many Germans consider the Pfalz their version of Tuscany. In addition to vineyards, the mild climate fosters fig, lemon, and chestnut trees.

(above) Autumn is a gorgeous time of year to tour the region. (upper right) Vineyards in Pfalz.

The best time for a drive is early spring, when the route is awash with pink and white almond blossoms, or early fall, when you can sample sweet young wines. The Deutsche Weinstrasse begins in Schweigen-Rechtenbach and runs alongside the *Bundesstrassen* (highways) B-38 and B-271. Yellow signs depicting a cluster of grapes guide visitors along a picturesque path of villages and vineyards north, to the end of the route at the "House of the German Wine Road" in Bockenheim. The entire road is just a little more than 50 miles and can be driven in a few hours. However, it can easily turn into a two-day drive (or longer!) if you stop to sample the local food and wines. Get an early start and allow yourself to get lost in the charming villages along the way, leaving time for a hike (or a bike ride) among the beautiful vines.

—Updated by Christie Dietz

DRINKING AND DRIVING

Germany has strict laws against driving (and biking) under the influence, so if you're planning to take advantage of the numerous *Weinprobe* (wine samples) offered along the route, make sure you have a designated driver. Alternatively, just let the vintner know what you like, and he can help you pick a bottle to enjoy when you reach your final destination.

The entire route is scenic, but if you're short on time, the stretch between Gleiszellen and Bad Dürkheim is particularly rich with castles, vineyards, and vistas. Pick up the route in **Gleiszellen,** where you should stop to savor a glass of the hard-to-find Muskateller wine, with its distinctly sweet aroma. **Weinstube Wissing** has a homey atmosphere and offers Muskateller in red, yellow, and rosé varieties.

Depending on the time of year, your trip may coincide with a local wine or produce festival—as you drive, keep your eyes peeled for signs advertising "Weinfest." Summer is the best time for festivals, but the seasons are celebrated with roadside stands selling local produce all year round. When you arrive in **Edenkoben,** stretch your legs at the Pompeian-style palace **Schloss Villa Ludwigshöhe,** then continue uphill via the Rietburgbahn chairlift to the vantage point at the **Rietburg Castle Ruins.** During the summer months, early evening is a lovely time for the journey. If you plan to split your drive into two days, the neighboring village of **St. Martin** is approximately halfway through the journey, making it an ideal place to overnight. Spend the next morning exploring the winding streets of this charming village on foot.

Continue north, stopping for lunch in the picturesque town of **Deidesheim,** home to three of the region's most famous wineries and some of its very best restaurants. Drive leisurely through the vineyards of **Forst,** stop off at the imposing ruins of **Burgruine Hardenburg** (Hardenburg Fortress), and end your day with a visit to the world's biggest wine barrel in **Bad Dürkheim.**

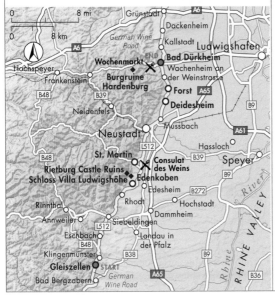

QUICK BITES

Consulat des Weines. Oenophiles won't want to miss this Vinothek in the charming village of St. Martin. It offers more than 80 varieties of wine from its vineyards in St. Martin and nearby Edenkoben (cash only). The sheer variety makes it easy to overindulge—good thing there's a hotel and restaurant on-site. There's a second location, also on Maikammerer Strasse near the St. Martiner Castell hotel (closed Sundays). ⊠ *Maikammerer Str. 44, St. Martin* ☎ *06323/8040* ⊕ *www.consulat-des-weins.de* ⊗ *Closed Sun. after noon.*

Wochenmarkt. If you're in Bad Dürkheim on a Wednesday or Saturday morning, head to the farmers' market for flowers, bread, wine, meats, cheeses, and vinegars. ⊠ *Am Obermarkt, Bad Dürkheim* ☎ *06323/8040* ⊕ *www. wochenmarkt-duerkheim. de* ⊗ *Wed. and Sat. 7 am–1 pm.*

10

Updated by
Christie Dietz

Pfalz and wine go hand in hand. This region of vineyards and picturesque villages is the home of the German Wine Road and the country's greatest wine festival at Bad Dürkheim. Six of Germany's 13 wine-growing regions are in the area.

The Pfalz has a mild, sunny climate, and that seems to affect the mood here, too. Vines carpet the foothills of the thickly forested Haardt Mountains, an extension of the Alsatian Vosges. The Pfälzerwald (Palatinate Forest) with its pine and chestnut trees is the region's other natural attraction. Hiking and cycling trails lead through the vineyards, the woods, and up to castles on the heights.

The border between the Pfalz and Rheinhessen is invisible, but you begin to get a sense of Rheinhessen's character soon after crossing it. It's a region of gentle, rolling hills and expansive farmland, where grapes are but one of many crops; vineyards are often scattered miles apart. The slopes overlooking the Rhine between Worms and Mainz—the so-called Rhine Terrace—are a notable exception, with a nearly uninterrupted ribbon of vines, including the famous vineyards of Oppenheim, Nierstein, and Nackenheim on the outskirts of Mainz.

PLANNING

WHEN TO GO
After countless celebrations of the *Mandelblüten* (blossoming of the almond trees) along the Wine Road in March, the wine festival season picks up in May and continues through October. The landscape alters dramatically in May as the vines' tender shoots and leaves begin to appear, and as the wine harvest progresses in September and October, foliage takes on reddish-golden hues.

FESTIVALS
Attending a wine festival is a fun and memorable part of any vacation in wine country. You can sample local food and wine inexpensively, and meet winegrowers at their stands without making an appointment.

Wine, *Sekt* (sparkling wine), and *Weinschorlen* (wine spritzers) flow freely at festivals all over the region, from tiny villages to the larger towns. The bigger events often involve live music, parades, fireworks, and rides. See ⊕ *www.germanwines.de* for an events calendar with an up-to-date overview of the many smaller, local wine festivals that take place in virtually every village.

Brezelfest (*Pretzel Festival*). Beer and pretzels are central to this annual six-day celebration held in Speyer over the second weekend in July. Other highlights include carnival rides and games, fireworks, and a grand parade. ⊠ *Festpl., Speyer* ⊕ *www.brezelfest-speyer.de.*

Deidesheim Weinkerwe. For 10 days in August, the wine town of Deidesheim fills up with stalls where visitors can sample local wines and hearty cuisine. Deidesheim's wineries also stay open late, offering live entertainment most nights during the festival. ⊠ *Marktpl., Deidesheim.*

Deutsches Weinlesefest (*German Wine Harvest Festival*). In Neustadt, the German Wine Queen is crowned during this 10-day wine festival in early October. The festival includes wine tastings, the largest wine festival parade in Germany, and a huge fireworks display on the final night. ⊠ *Various locations including the Saalbau, Heztelpl., and Bahnhofsvorpl., Neustadt* ⊕ *www.neustadt.eu/.*

Dürkheimer Wurstmarkt (*Sausage Market*). The Pfalz is home to the world's largest wine festival, held in Bad Dürkheim in mid-September in front of the world's largest wine barrel. Some 400,000 pounds of sausage are consumed during eight days of merrymaking. ⊠ *Sankt-Michaels-Allee 1, Bad Dürkheim* ⊕ *www.duerkheimer-wurstmarkt.de.*

Mainzer Johannisnacht (*The Mainz Midsummer St. John's Night Festival*). In addition to carnival rides, a craft market, fireworks, and plenty of food and drink, live performances from local and international bands, as well as theater and cabaret performances, take place on six stages in the city center in late June. Since the festival is at least nominally in honor of Johannes Gutenberg, printers' apprentices are dunked in water in front of the Gutenberg Museum as part of a "printers' baptism" ceremony. ⊠ *Various locations, Mainz* ⊕ *www.johannisnacht.de.*

Wormser Backfischfest (*Fried Fish Festival*). Carnival rides, traditional folk music and dance, jousting on the Rhine, and fireworks create a jovial atmosphere at this annual festival, starting in late August, which honors the city's fishermen. Don't pass up the chance to taste more than 400 wines at the festival's Wonnegauer Wine Cellar. ⊠ *Festpl., Worms* ⊕ *www.backfischfest.de* ⊗ *Late Aug.–early Sept.*

PLANNING YOUR TIME

Central hubs such as Bad Dürkheim or Neustadt make good bases for exploring the region; smaller towns such as St. Martin, Deidesheim, and Gleiszellen are worth an overnight stay because of their charm. Driving the Wine Road takes longer than you might expect, and will probably involve spur-of-the-moment stops, so you may want to consider a stopover in one of the many country inns en route.

When traveling with children, Neustadt and Worms are convenient bases from which to explore nearby Holiday Park.

GETTING HERE AND AROUND

AIR TRAVEL

Frankfurt-Main is the closest major international airport for the entire Rhineland. International airports in Stuttgart and France's Strasbourg are closer to the southern end of the German Wine Road. If you're traveling from within Europe, the frequently disparaged Ryanair hub in the remote Frankfurt suburb of Hahn is actually a convenient jumping-off point for a tour of the region, with bus services to Mainz, Koblenz, Heidelberg, and Karlsruhe.

BIKE TRAVEL

There's no charge for transporting bicycles on local trains throughout Rheinland-Pfalz; carriages suitable for traveling with them are indicated by stickers depicting bicycles. For maps, suggested routes, bike-rental locations, and details on *Pauschalangebote* (package deals) or *Gepäck-transport* (luggage-forwarding service), contact the Pfalz or Rhine Terrace tourist service centers.

CAR TRAVEL

It's 162 km (100 miles) between Schweigen-Rechtenbach and Mainz, the southern- and northernmost points of this region. The main route is the Deutsche Weinstrasse, which is a Bundesstrasse, abbreviated "B," as in B-38, B-48, and B-271. The route from Worms to Mainz is the B-9.

TRAIN TRAVEL

Mainz is on the high-speed ICE (InterCity Express) train route linking Wiesbaden, Frankfurt, and Dresden, and so forms a convenient gateway to the region. The excellent networks of public transportation called the **Rheinland-Pfalz-Takt** and **Rhein-Main Verkehrsverbund** operate throughout the region with well-coordinated **RegioLinie** (buses) and **Nahverkehrszüge** (local trains). Regional trains link Mainz with other towns along the Rhine Terrace, including Worms and Speyer, while local branch lines serve key hubs along the Wine Road such as Neustadt and Bad Dürkheim. Smaller towns and villages connect with these hubs by an excellent network of local buses.

■ TIP→ **The Rheinland-Pfalz Ticket is a great value if you plan to travel on the train.** The ticket costs €24 for the first person and €4 for each additional person, up to five people. It's valid for a whole day, beginning at 9 am on weekdays and midnight on weekends and holidays, until 3 am the following morning. It can be used on all regional trains and buses, but not the high-speed ICE trains; ensure you write your name on your ticket after purchase.

RESTAURANTS

Lunch in this region is generally served from noon until 2 or 2:30, dinner from 6 until 9:30 or 10. Credit cards have gained a foothold, but many restaurants will accept only cash or debit cards issued by a German bank. Casual attire is typically acceptable at restaurants here, and reservations are generally not needed.

Prices in the reviews are the average cost of a main course at dinner, or if dinner is not served, at lunch.

HOTELS

Book in advance if your visit coincides with a large festival. Bed-and-breakfasts abound. Look for signs reading "Fremdenzimmer" or "Zimmer frei" (rooms available). A *Ferienwohnung* (holiday apartment), abbreviated FeWo in tourist brochures, is an economical option if you plan to stay in one location for several nights.

Prices in the reviews are the lowest cost of a standard double room in high season. For expanded reviews, facilities, and current deals, visit Fodors.com.

WHAT IT COSTS IN EUROS			
	$	$$	$$$	$$$$
Restaurants	under €15	€15–€20	€21–€25	over €25
Hotels	under €100	€100–€175	€176–€225	over €225

VISITOR INFORMATION

Contacts Pfalz.Touristik. ⊠ *Martin-Luther-Str. 69, Neustadt* ☎ *06321/39160* ⊕ *www.pfalz.de.* **Rheinhessen-Touristik.** ⊠ *Friedrich-Ebert-Str. 17, Ingelheim am Rhein* ☎ *06731/9510–7440 info hotline: Mon.–Thurs. 8:30–4:30, Fri. 8:30–12:30* ⊕ *www.rheinhessen.de.* **Rheinland-Pfalz Tourismus.** ☎ *01805/915–200 info hotline, € 0.14/min, mobile max €0.42/min* ⊕ *www.gastlandschaften.de.* **Südliche Weinstrasse.** ⊠ *An der Kreuzmühle 2, Landau* ☎ *06341/940–407* ⊕ *www.suedlicheweinstrasse.de.*

THE GERMAN WINE ROAD

The Wine Road spans the length of the Pfalz wine region, north to south, and makes for a memorable road trip in either direction. Given its central location, the Pfalz is convenient to visit before or after a trip to the Black Forest, Heidelberg, or the northern Rhineland.

SCHWEIGEN-RECHTENBACH

10

21 km (13 miles) southwest of Landau on B-38.

The southernmost wine village of the Pfalz lies on the French border. During the economically depressed 1930s, local vintners established a route through the vineyards to promote tourism. The German Wine Road was inaugurated in 1935; a year later the massive stone Deutsches Weintor (German Wine Gate) was erected to add visual impact to the marketing concept. Halfway up the gateway is a platform that offers a fine view of the vineyards—to the south, French, to the north, German. Schweigen's 1-km (½-mile) Weinlehrpfad (educational wine path) wanders through the vineyards and, with signs and exhibits, explains the history of viticulture from Roman times to the present.

BAD BERGZABERN

10 km (6 miles) north of Schweigen-Rechtenbach on B-38.

The landmark of this little spa town is the baroque **Schloss** (palace) of the dukes of Zweibrücken. The Gasthaus Zum Engel (Königstrasse 45) is an impressive Renaissance house with elaborate scrolled gables and decorative oriels. **TIP→ Visit Café Herzog (Marktstrasse 48) for scrumptious, homemade chocolates, cakes, and ice creams made with unexpected ingredients, such as wine, pepper, cardamom, curry, thyme, or fig vinegar. The café is closed Mondays.**

GETTING HERE AND AROUND

From Landau, you can take the regional train to Bad Bergzabern, which takes about 30 minutes and requires a change in Winden (Pfalz). Bus No. 543 also connects Bad Bergzabern along the Wine Road to Schweigen, over the French border to Wissembourg. The Rheinland-Pfalz ticket is valid on both train and bus until the French border.

WHERE TO STAY

$$ HOTEL 🏨 **Hotel-Restaurant Krone.** Behind a simple facade is this inn, with modern facilities, upscale and tasteful furnishings, an open fireplace perfect for cold winters, and, above all, a warm welcome from the Kuntz family. **Pros:** quiet location; friendly atmosphere; great food; free Wi-Fi. **Cons:** a detour off the Wine Road (about a half-hour drive); not many activities in the surrounding area. [$] *Rooms from: €135* ✉ *Hauptstr. 62–64, Hayna* ☎ *07276/5080* 🌐 *www.hotelkrone.de* 🕒 *Restaurant Zur Krone closed Mon. and Tues., 1st 2 wks in Jan., and 3 wks in Aug. No lunch.* 🛏 *60 rooms, 6 suites* 🍴 *Breakfast.*

GLEISZELLEN

4 km (2½ miles) north of Bad Bergzabern on B-48.

Gleiszellen's **Winzergasse** (Vintners' Lane) is a little vine-canopied street lined with a beautiful ensemble of half-timber houses. Try a glass of the town's specialty: spicy, aromatic Muskateller wine, a rarity seldom found even elsewhere in Germany.

GETTING HERE AND AROUND

Gleiszellen is on the No. 543 bus line that runs from Landau to the French border town of Wissembourg. The bus runs hourly.

OFF THE BEATEN PATH

Burg Trifels. Burg Trifels is on the highest of three sandstone bluffs overlooking Annweiler, which is 15 km (9 miles) northwest of Gleiszellen. Celts, Romans, and Salians all had settlements on this site, but it was under the Hohenstaufen emperors (12th and 13th centuries) that Trifels was built on a grand scale. It housed the crown jewels from 1125 to 1274 (replicas are on display today). It was also an imperial prison, perhaps where Richard the Lion-Hearted was held captive in 1193–94.

Although it was never conquered, the fortress was severely damaged by lightning in 1602. Reconstruction began in 1938, shaped by visions of grandeur to create a national shrine to the imperial past. Accordingly, the monumental proportions of some parts of today's castle bear no

CLOSE UP

The Wines of Rheinland-Pfalz

The Romans planted the first Rhineland vineyards 2,000 years ago, finding the mild, wet climate hospitable to grape growing. By the Middle Ages viticulture was flourishing and a bustling wine trade had developed. Wine making and splendid Romanesque cathedrals are the legacies of the bishops and emperors of Speyer, Worms, and Mainz. This region, now the state of Rheinland-Pfalz (Rhineland Palatinate), remains a major wine center, with two of the largest wine districts in the country, Rheinhessen and the Pfalz.

In the Pfalz, you can follow the Deutsche Weinstrasse as it winds its way north from the French border. Idyllic wine villages beckon with flower-draped facades and courtyards full of palms, oleanders, and fig trees. "Weinverkauf" (wine for sale) and "Weinprobe" (wine-tasting) signs are posted everywhere—an invitation to stop in to sample the wines.

Most of the wines from both Pfalz and Rheinhessen are white, and the ones from Rheinhessen are often fragrant and sweeter than their counterparts from the Pfalz. Many are sold as *offene Weine* (wines by the glass). The classic white varieties are Riesling, Silvaner, Müller-Thurgau (also called Rivaner), Grauburgunder (Pinot Gris), and Weissburgunder (Pinot Blanc). Spätburgunder (Pinot Noir), Dornfelder, and Portugieser are the most popular red wines. The word *Weissherbst,* after the grape variety, indicates a rosé wine.

Riesling is the king of German grapes. It produces wines that range widely in quality and character: Rieslings are noted for their strong acidity, sometimes-flowery aroma, and often mineral-tasting notes—all reflections of the soil in which they're grown. Riesling made its name throughout the world as a sweet (*lieblich*) wine, but many Germans (and, increasingly, others) prefer dry (*trocken*) or semi-dry (*halbtrocken*) versions. Importers, especially in the United States, have tended not to bring over many dry Rieslings, so take the opportunity to sample some while in Germany.

10

resemblance to those of the original Romanesque structure. The imperial hall is a grand setting for the *Serenaden* (concerts) held in summer.

Arriving on foot: From the main train station in Annweiler, follow the local signs for Burg Trifels. The hike is about an hour. **Arriving by car:** Follow the A-65 direction Karl-Ludwigshafen, take exit Landau-Sued, then B-10 to Annweiler west. From there follow the local signs. Parking is at the foot of the fortress, a 20-minute walk from the top. ✉ *Burg Trifels, Annweiler* ☎ *06346/8470* 🌐 *www.burgen-rlp.de* 🎟 *€3* 🕒 *Apr.–Sept., daily 9–6; Oct., Nov., and Jan.–Mar., daily 9–5.*

WHERE TO EAT AND STAY

$ WINE BAR 🍴 **Weinstube Wissing.** Friendly service and a homey atmosphere await guests at this restaurant. Wines, fine spirits, and regional delicacies are offered in the former premises of the family-owned distillery. Don't miss a chance to sample their fruity Muskateller wine, and you might also want to pick up a bottle of their fresh red or white *Pfälzer Traubensaft* (grape juice) as a tasty souvenir. [$] *Average main: €13*

Some wineries offer seasonal outdoor seating areas where guests can enjoy samples.

✉ *Winzerg. 34* ☎ *06343/4711* 🌐 *www.weingut-wissing.de* 💳 *No credit cards* ⏲ *Closed Mon. and Tues. No lunch Wed.–Sat. Check website for summer holiday closure.*

$ B&B/INN Fodor's Choice ★ 🏨 **Gasthof Zum Lam.** Flowers cascade from the windowsills of this 250-year-old half-timber inn in the heart of town, where the good rates include free Wi-Fi and an enjoyable breakfast buffet. **Pros:** quiet location; charming courtyard; beautiful old building. **Cons:** no elevator; no air-conditioning. [$] *Rooms from: €90* ✉ *Winzerg. 37* ☎ *06343/939–212* 🌐 *www.zum-lam.de* ⏲ *Restaurant closed Wed. No lunch Nov.–Mar.* 🛏 *20 double rooms* 🍴 *Breakfast.*

SCHLOSS VILLA LUDWIGSHÖHE

24 km (15 miles) north of Annweiler, slightly west of Edenkoben on the Wine Road.

For a cultural break from all that wine tasting, head to this Pompeian-style palace, the former summer residence of King Ludwig I, which overlooks what he described as "the most beautiful square mile of my realm," where the Palatinate vineyards end and the forests begin. The layout and decor of the neoclassical palace—Pompeian-style murals, splendid parquet floors, and Biedermeier and Empire furnishings—are quite a contrast to those of medieval castles elsewhere in the Pfalz. Follow up your visit with a chairlift ride to the vantage point of the Rietburg Castle Ruins, or get your heart racing by following the example of the hardy German tourists who can often be seen hiking uphill between the two sights.

FAMILY **Rietburg Castle Ruins.** From Schloss Villa Ludwigshöhe you can hike (30 minutes) or ride the Rietburgbahn chairlift (10 minutes) up to the Rietburg ruins for a sweeping view of the Pfalz. During a festive *Lampionfahrt* in July and August (dates vary each year), the chairlift operates until midnight on Saturdays, and the route is lit by dozens of Chinese lanterns. A restaurant, game park, and playground are on the grounds. ✉ *Villastr. 67, Edenkoben* ☎ *06323/1800* 🌐 *www.rietburgbahn-edenkoben.de* 🎟 *Chairlift €7 round-trip, €4.50 one way* 🕒 *Mar., Sun. 9–5; Apr. and May, weekdays 9–5, weekends 9–6; June–Oct., weekdays 9–5:30, weekends 9–6; Nov. 1–8, daily 9–5.*

Fodor's Choice ★ **Schloss Villa Ludwigshöhe.** Bavaria's King Ludwig I's Italian-style villa sits on the slopes overlooking Edenkoben and Rhodt unter Rietburg. The house is now used as a space for art exhibitions and musical events: the former dining room is used for classical concerts; the cellars house exhibitions of 20th-century ceramics; and an extensive collection of paintings and prints by the leading German impressionist Max Slevogt (1868–1932) is also on display. Hourly tours are included in the admission fee.

Schloss Villa Ludwigshöhe is reachable by car, bus, or foot; the 506 Palatina bus goes directly from Edenkoben on Sundays and holidays. If you opt to walk, the *Weinlehrpfad* (educational trailpath) takes about 45 minutes. Historical winepresses and vintners' tools are displayed at intervals along the path, which starts at the corner of Landauer Strasse and Villa Strasse in Edenkoben. ✉ *Schloss Villa Ludwigshöhe, Villastr. 64, Edenkoben* ☎ *06323/93016* 🌐 *www.schloss-villa-ludwigshoehe.de* 🎟 *€6* 🕒 *Apr.–Sept., daily 9–6; Oct., Nov., and Jan.–Mar., daily 10–5.*

WHERE TO STAY

$$$ HOTEL 🏨 **Alte Rebschule.** Fireside seating in the lobby lounge and spacious rooms (all with a balcony) make for a pleasant, peaceful stay in this former *Rebschule* (vine nursery) on the edge of the forest. **Pros:** beautiful vineyard views; quiet. **Cons:** room decor a bit old-fashioned. [$] *Rooms from: €196* ✉ *3 km (2 miles) west of Schloss Villa Ludwigshöhe, Theresienstr. 200, Rhodt unter Rietburg* ☎ *06323/70440* 🌐 *www.alte-rebschule.de* 🛏 *34 rooms, 3 suites* 🍴 *Breakfast.*

ST. MARTIN

26 km (16 miles) north of Annweiler, slightly west of the Wine Road. Turn left at the northern edge of Edenkoben.

This is one of the most charming wine villages in the Pfalz. Narrow cobblestone streets are lined by historic half-timber houses that are now home to inns, restaurants, and wineshops, making the compact, historically preserved *Altstadt* (Old Town) a pleasure to stroll.

GETTING HERE AND AROUND

The easiest way to reach St. Martin is by car. There's no train station, but Bus Nos. 500 and 501 connect St. Martin with Neustadt and Edenkoben. The trip takes about 20 minutes from Neustadt, a further five to Edenkoben in the same direction, and the buses run approximately every half hour. Alight at "St. Martin, Ort."

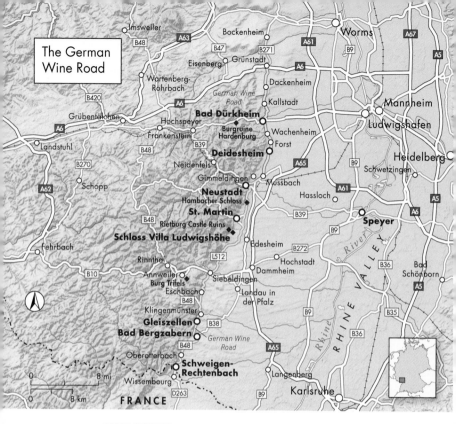

The German Wine Road

EXPLORING

Katholische Pfarrkirche St. Martin (*Catholic church of St. Martin*). Perched dramatically on the northern edge of St. Martin against a backdrop of vineyards, this late-Gothic church was thought to have been built around 1200 (the interior was renovated in the mid-1980s). Renaissance tombstones and a Madonna sculpture carved from a single piece of oak are among the intriguing artworks found inside. ⊠ *Kirchg. 6* ☎ *06323/5100*.

Schloss Kropsburg. Now romantic ruins, this castle was originally constructed in the early 13th century and used by the bishops of Speyer; during the 15th to the 19th centuries, the Knights of Dalberg resided there. You can see Schloss Kropsburg from the hills above St. Martin. It's not open to the public, but if you hike up to the castle's outskirts, you can enjoy a traditional sausage lunch at the charming inn and restaurant Burgschänke an der Kropsburg ($, closed on Tuesdays) while admiring the views. ⊠ *Kropsburg* ☉ *Restaurant closed on Tues. No dinner.*

WHERE TO STAY

$ 🏠 **Landhaus Christmann.** This bright, modern house in the midst of the
B&B/INN   vineyards outside of St. Martin has stylish rooms decorated with both antiques and modern furnishings, and is close enough to walk into town. **Pros:** excellent-value rooms; quiet location; free Wi-Fi. **Cons:**

EATING WELL IN THE PFALZ

Wine has a big influence on the cuisine here, turning up both in dishes and as an accompaniment to them. *Weinkraut* is sauerkraut braised in white wine; *Dippe-Has'* is hare and pork belly baked in red wine; and *Backes Grumbeere* is scalloped potatoes cooked with bacon, sour cream, white wine, and a layer of pork. Among the regional dishes well suited to wine is the *Pfälzer Teller,* a platter of bratwurst, *Leberknödel* (liver dumplings), and slices of *Saumagen* (a spicy meat-and-potato mixture cooked in a sow's stomach) with *Kartoffelpüree* (mashed potatoes) on the side. Seasonal favorites include *Spargel* (white asparagus), *Wild* (game), *Maronen* (chestnuts), and mushrooms, particularly *Pfifferlinge* (chanterelles) and *Steinpilz* (porcini). During the grape harvest, from September through November, try a slice of *Zwiebelkuchen* (onion tart) with a glass of *Federweisser,* fermenting young grape juice—just drink it slowly as it tastes nonalcoholic but can be very potent.

rooms are very simple; extra charge for breakfast (€10) and daily room cleaning (€12) for apartments. $ *Rooms from: €94* ✉ *Riedweg 1* ☎ *06323/94270* 🌐 *www.landhaus-christmann.de* *6 rooms, 3 apartments* 🍽 *Breakfast.*

$$ HOTEL Fodor's Choice ★ **St. Martiner Castell.** The Mücke family transformed a simple vintner's house into a fine, family-friendly hotel and restaurant, retaining many of the original features, such as exposed beams and an old winepress. **Pros:** beautiful old house; free Wi-Fi in rooms; free parking; breakfast included. **Cons:** can be noisy; fee charged for cots (€9.50) and extra beds (€13–€26). $ *Rooms from: €115* ✉ *Maikammerer Str. 2* ☎ *06323/9510* 🌐 *www.martinercastell.de* ⊙ *Restaurant closed Tues.* *22 rooms, 2 suites* 🍽 *Breakfast.*

PERFORMING ARTS

Schloss Villa Ludwigshöhe, Kloster Heilsbruck (a former Cistercian convent near Edenkoben), and **Schloss Edesheim** serve as backdrops for concerts and theater in summer. For a calendar of events, contact the Südliche Weinstrasse regional tourist office in Landau (☎ *06341/940–407* 🌐 *www.suedlicheweinstrasse.de*).

SHOPPING

Weinessiggut Doktorenhof. Artist Georg Wiedemann is responsible for both the contents and the design of the containers at Germany's premier wine-vinegar estate, Doktorenhof. Vinegar tastings and cellar tours take place on Saturday mornings (90 minutes, €25); pick up a gift in the shop afterwards (cash only). The estate's in Venningen, 2 km (1 mile) east of Edenkoben. ✉ *Raiffeisenstr. 5, Venningen* ☎ *06323/5505* 🌐 *www.doktorenhof.de* ⊙ *Mon., Tues., Thurs., and Fri. 8–4, Wed. 8–6, Sat. 9–2.*

EN ROUTE **Hambacher Schloss.** On the Wine Road, it's a brief drive to the Neustadt suburb of Hambach. The sturdy block of Hambacher Schloss is considered the cradle of German democracy. It was here, on May 27, 1832, that 30,000 patriots demonstrated for German unity, raising the German colors for the first time. Inside there are exhibits about the

10

uprising and the history of the castle. The French destroyed the 11th-century imperial fortress in 1688. Reconstruction finally began after World War II, in neo-Gothic style, and the castle is now an impressive setting for theater and concerts. On a clear day, you can see the spire of Strasbourg Cathedral and the northern fringe of the Black Forest from the terrace restaurant.

Group tours can be booked in advance; audio guides are available. ⊠ *Hambacher Schloss, Neustadt* ☎ *06321/926–290* ⊕ *www.hambacher-schloss.de* ⊠ *€4.50* ⊗ *Apr.–Oct., daily 10–6; Nov. and Dec., daily 11–5.*

NEUSTADT

8 km (5 miles) north of St. Martin, 5 km (3 miles) north of Hambach on the Wine Road.

Neustadt and its nine wine suburbs are at the midpoint of the Wine Road and the edge of the district known as Deutsche Weinstrasse–Mittelhaardt. With around 5,000 acres of vines, they together make up Germany's largest winemaking community.

GETTING HERE AND AROUND

Regular trains connect Neustadt with Ludwigshafen (which connects further to Worms and Mainz). Coming from Speyer, change in Schifferstadt. Local buses connect Neustadt to other towns along the Wine Road. Once you're in Neustadt, the best way to get around is on foot.

ESSENTIALS

Visitor Information Tourist-Information. ⊠ *Tourist-Information, Hetzelpl. 1* ☎ *06321/926–892* ⊕ *www.neustadt.pfalz.com.*

EXPLORING

FAMILY **Eisenbahn Museum.** Thirty historic train engines and railway cars are on display at the Eisenbahn Museum behind the main train station. Take a ride through the Palatinate Forest on one of the museum's historic steam trains, the *Kuckucksbähnel* (€14 round-trip), which departs from Track 5 around 10:45 am some Sundays and Wednesdays between Easter and mid-October (check the website for the latest schedule). It takes a little over an hour to cover the 13-km (8-mile) stretch from Neustadt to Elmstein. ⊠ *Neustadt train station, close to the Schillerstr. entrance* ☎ *06321/30390* ⊕ *www.eisenbahnmuseum-neustadt.de* ⊠ *€2* ⊗ *Mar.–Dec. 23, Tues.–Fri. 10–1, weekends 10–4; Dec. 24–Feb., Sat. 10–4. Closed some holidays.*

FAMILY **Elwetrischen-Brunnen.** While in the Pfalz, keep your eyes peeled for the elusive *Elwetritschen*—mythical, birdlike creatures rumored to roam the forest and vineyards at night. Hunting the creatures is something of a local prank. Sculptor Gernot Rumpf has immortalized the Elwetrischen in a fountain (*Brunnen*) on Marstallplatz. Near the market square, search for the one that "escaped" from its misty home. ⊠ *Marstallpl.*

Marktplatz (*Market square*). The Marktplatz is the focal point of the Old Town and a beehive of activity when farmers come to sell their wares on Tuesdays and Saturdays, plus Thursdays from April to October. The square itself is ringed by baroque and Renaissance buildings (Nos. 1, 4, 8, and 11) and the Gothic **Stiftskirche** (Collegiate Church),

Pink and white almond blossoms line the roads of the region in spring.

built as a burial church for the Palatinate counts. In summer, concerts take place in the church (Saturday 11:30–noon). Afterward, you can ascend the southern tower (187 feet) for a bird's-eye view of the town. The world's largest cast-iron bell—weighing more than 17 tons—hangs in the northern tower. Indoors, see the elaborate tombstones near the choir and the fanciful grotesque figures carved into the baldachins and corbels. ⊠ *Marktpl.* ⊕ *www.stiftskirche-nw.de.*

QUICK BITES **Café Sixt.** For the best coffee, cake, and handcrafted truffles and pralines in town, head to Café Sixt. The *Pfälzer Kirschtorte* (cherry torte) is a favorite. They also offer breakfasts, a small daily lunch menu, and can cater for some allergies. ⊠ *Hauptstr. 3* ☎ *06321/2192* ⊕ *www.cafesixt.de.*

Otto Dill Museum. The impressionist painter Otto Dill (1884–1957), a native of Neustadt, is known for his powerful animal portraits (especially lions, tigers, and horses) and vivid landscapes. The Otto Dill Museum displays some 100 oil paintings and 50 drawings and watercolors from the Manfred Vetter collection. ⊠ *Bachgängel 8, Ecke Rathausstr. 12* ☎ *06321/398–321* ⊕ *www.otto-dill-museum.de* 🖃*€2.50* 🕗 *Tues.–Fri. 2–5, weekends 11–5.*

WHERE TO EAT

$$
GERMAN
✕ **Altstadtkeller bei Jürgen.** Tucked behind a wooden portal on a cobblestone street, this vaulted sandstone "cellar" (it's actually on the ground floor) feels very cozy. Equally inviting is the Tuscan-style terrace, with its citrus, olive, palm, and fig trees. The regular menu includes a number of salads and a good selection of fish and steaks. Owner Jürgen Reis is a wine enthusiast, and his well-chosen list shows it. $ *Average*

BIKING, HIKING, AND WALKING

Country roads and traffic-free vineyard paths make the area perfect for cyclists. There are also well-marked cycling trails, such as the **Radwanderweg Deutsche Weinstrasse,** which runs parallel to its namesake from the French border to Bockenheim, and the **Radweg** (cycling trail) along the Rhine between Worms and Mainz. The Palatinate Forest, Germany's largest single tract of woods, has more than 10,000 km (6,200 miles) of paths.

The **Wanderweg Deutsche Weinstrasse,** a walking route that traverses vineyards, woods, and wine villages, covers the length of the Pfalz. It connects with many trails in the Palatinate Forest that lead to Celtic and Roman landmarks and dozens of castles dating primarily from the 11th to 13th century. In Rheinhessen, you can hike two marked trails parallel to the Rhine: the **Rheinterrassenwanderweg** and the **Rheinhöhenweg** along the heights.

main: €18 ✉ *Kunigundenstr. 2* ☎ *06321/32320* 🌐 *www.altstadtkeller-neustadt.de* ⏲ *Closed Sun. and Mon.*

$$$ GERMAN Fodor's Choice ★ 🍴 **NETTS Restaurant-Weinbar.** Susanne and Daniel Nett operate a chic wine restaurant-bar filled with modern art within a 16th-century vaulted stone cellar at Weingut A. Christmann, a top wine estate. The short, seasonal menu has a Mediterranean influence, offering dishes such as green gazpacho with prawns, and cod wrapped in courgette with a sweet potato torte and fennel foam; and there's also a children's menu. The thoughtful wine list includes lots of Pfälzer wines by the glass, including those from the Christmann winery. Dining in the intimate courtyard overlooking the vineyards is a romantic option in summer, when they also open their garden for coffee, cake, and *Flammkuchen* (a thin-crust, rectangular pizza covered in crème fraîche and various toppings). The Netts also offer seven rooms ($) for overnight guests, each with hardwood floors and Wi-Fi. [$] *Average main: €23* ✉ *Meerspinnstr. 46, Gimmeldingen* ☎ *06321/60175* 🌐 *www.nettsrestaurant.de* 💳 *No credit cards* ⏲ *Closed Mon. and Tues. No lunch.*

$$$$ GERMAN Fodor's Choice ★ 🍴 **Urgestein.** Dine inside the cozy brick-lined former horse stables or outside on the lovely patio at this restaurant inside the historic stone houses of the Steinhauser Hof hotel. The ambitious tasting menus highlight local produce and are best paired with one of the 350 Pfalz wines on the wine list. There's no à la carte ordering: try the €85 four-course or €100 five-course menus (wine is extra) featuring dishes such as miso cod with roast fennel salad, or egg yolk with truffle, or splurge on the six-course surprise menu for €140 (including wine pairings). There's also a vegetarian menu. Leave room for the tasty desserts, which include rhubarb with nougat ganache and hazlenuts. [$] *Average main: €100* ✉ *Rathausstr. 6* ☎ *06321/489–060* 🌐 *www.restaurant-urgestein.de* ⏲ *Closed Sun. and Mon. No lunch.*

$ WINE BAR 🍴 **Weinstube Eselsburg.** The *Esel* (donkey) lends its name to his wine pub and one of its specialties, *Eselssuppe,* a hearty soup of pork, beef, and vegetables. The season dictates the menu here, and it's popular with regulars throughout the year. In summer, savor top Pfälzer wines

The Marktplatz in Neustadt is your best bet for a meal alfresco.

in the flower-filled courtyard, or in the warmth of an open hearth in winter. From October to April, try the *Schlachtfest* (meat and sausages from freshly slaughtered pigs; check with restaurant for dates). $ *Average main: €14* ⊠ *Kurpfalzstr. 62* ☎ *06321/66984* ⊕ *www.eselsburg.de* ⊗ *Closed Sun. and Mon. No lunch, except during Schlachtfest.*

WHERE TO STAY

$
B&B/INN

⛺ **Gästehaus Rebstöckel.** This 17th-century stone guesthouse has a beautiful cobblestone courtyard and magnificent fig tree; all the rooms have blond-wood furnishings, and some have kitchenettes. **Pros:** quiet; friendly; rustic location. **Cons:** light from street lamp may bother light sleepers; additional fee for baby bed/room charge for children. $ *Rooms from: €79* ⊠ *Kreuzstr. 11, Diedesfeld* ☎ *06321/484–060* ⊕ *www.rebstoeckel.eu* ⊟ *No credit cards* ⌁ *5 rooms* ⦿ *Breakfast.*

$
HOTEL

⛺ **Steinhäuser Hof.** This architectural gem dates back to 1276 and is one of the oldest preserved stone mansions in Rhineland-Palatinate. **Pros:** beautiful old building; central location; friendly staff; renowned restaurant; free Wi-Fi. **Cons:** basic rooms; some street noise; no elevator. $ *Rooms from: €82* ⊠ *Rathausstr. 6* ☎ *06321/489–060* ⊕ *www. steinhaeuserhof.de* ⊗ *Restaurant closed Sun. and Mon. No lunch.* ⌁ *6 rooms* ⦿ *No meals.*

EN
ROUTE

Holiday Park. The Holiday Park, in Hassloch, 10 km (6 miles) east of Neustadt, is one of Europe's largest amusement parks. The admission fee covers all attractions, shows, special events, and the children's world. The free-fall tower, hell barrels, and Thunder River rafting are long-standing favorites, and Expedition GeForce is one of the largest roller coasters in Europe, with a steep drop of 82 degrees. For a great panoramic view of the surroundings, whirl through the air on Lighthouse-Tower, Germany's tallest carousel (265 feet). On Friday and Saturday in summer, the "Summer Nights" spectacular features live music and an outdoor laser light show. ⊠ *Holiday Parkstr. 1–5* ☎ *06324/59930* ⊕ *www.holidaypark.de* ✑ *€28.45* ⊙ *Irregular hrs: see website.*

SPEYER

25 km (15 miles) east of Neustadt via B-39, 22 km (14 miles) south of Mannheim via B-9 and B-44.

Speyer is a picturesque and easily walkable town filled with interesting sights and a wonderful Christmas market in the winter. It's also a must-visit for those who like to eat well: there's a huge choice of traditional German restaurants and pretty beer gardens, and in summer, the main street (Maximilianstrasse) is packed with the tables and chairs of the plethora of cafés that line it. It was one of the great cities of the Holy Roman Empire, founded in pre-Celtic times, taken over by the Romans, and expanded in the 11th century by the Salian emperors. Between 1294, when it was declared a Free Imperial City, and 1570, no fewer than 50 imperial diets were convened here. The term "Protestant" derives from the Diet of 1529, referring to those who protested when the religious freedom granted to evangelicals at the Diet of 1526 was revoked and a return to Catholicism was decreed. The neo-Gothic **Gedächtniskirche** on Bartolomäus-Weltz-Platz commemorates those 16th-century Protestants.

GETTING HERE AND AROUND
Speyer is a little way off the German Wine Road. It is served by regular trains from Mannheim (takes around 30 minutes) and Mainz (approximately 1 hour). Buses go down the main street, but the center is compact enough that getting around on foot is not a problem.

ESSENTIALS
Visitor Information Speyer. ⊠ *Tourist Office, Maximilianstr. 13* ☎ *06232/142–392* ⊕ *www.speyer.de.*

EXPLORING
Altpörtel. Ascend the Altpörtel, the impressive town gate, for a grand view of Maximilianstrasse, the now busy shopping street that once led kings and emperors straight to the cathedral. ⊠ *Postpl.* ✑ *€1.50* ⊙ *Apr.–Oct., weekdays 10–noon and 2–4, weekends 10–5.*

Historisches Museum der Pfalz (*Palatinate Historical Museum*). Opposite the cathedral, the museum houses the **Domschatz** (Cathedral Treasury). Other collections chronicle the art and cultural history of Speyer and the Pfalz from the Stone Age to modern times. Don't miss the "Golden Hat of Schifferstadt," a Bronze Age headdress used in religious ceremonies dating back to approximately 1300 BC. The **Wine Museum** houses the world's oldest bottle of wine, which is still liquid and dates to circa AD 300. The giant 35-foot-long wooden winepress from 1727 is also worth a look. ⊠ *Dompl. 4* ☎ *06232/620–222 service point, 06232/13250* *general office* ⊕ *www.museum.speyer.de* ✉ *€7; additional fee for special exhibitions* ⊙ *Tues.–Sun. 10–6.*

Fodor's Choice **Jewish Quarter.** Speyer was an important medieval Jewish cultural center.
★ Behind the Palatinate Historical Museum is the Jewish quarter, where you'll find synagogue remains from 1104; Germany's oldest (circa 1126) ritual baths, the 33-foot-deep *Mikwe;* and the Museum SchPIRA, which displays objects such as gravestones and coins from the Middle Ages . ✉ *Kleine Pfaffeng. 21, near Judeng.* ☎ *06232/291–971* ✉ *€3* ⊙ *Apr.–Oct., daily 10–5; Nov.–Mar., Tues.–Sun. 10–4.*

Fodor's Choice **Kaiserdom** (*Imperial Cathedral*). The Kaiserdom, one of the finest
★ Romanesque cathedrals in the world and a UNESCO World Heritage site, conveys the pomp and majesty of the early Holy Roman emperors. It was built between 1030 and 1061 by the emperors Konrad II, Henry III, and Henry IV. The last replaced the flat ceiling with groin vaults in the late 11th century, an innovative feat in its day. A restoration program in the 1950s returned the building to almost exactly its original condition. There's a fine view of the east end of the structure from the park by the Rhine. Much of the architectural detail, including the dwarf galleries and ornamental capitals, was inspired and executed by stonemasons from Lombardy, which belonged to the German Empire at the time. The four towers symbolize the four seasons and the idea that the power of the empire extends in all four directions. Look up as you enter the nearly 100-foot-high portal; it's richly carved with mythical creatures. In contrast to Gothic cathedrals, whose walls are supported externally by flying buttresses, allowing for a minimum of masonry and a maximum of light, at Speyer the columns supporting the roof are massive. The **Krypta** (crypt, €3.50, audio guide available) lies beneath the chancel. It's the largest crypt in Germany and is strikingly beautiful in its simplicity. Four emperors, four kings, and three empresses are buried here. ✉ *Edith-Stein-Pl.* ☎ *06232/102–118* ✉ *Donation requested* ⊙ *Apr.–Oct., Mon.–Sat. 9–7, Sun. noon–6; Nov.–Mar., Mon.–Sat. 9–5, Sun. noon–6; closed during services.*

Fodor's Choice **Technik Museum** (*The Technical Museum of Speyer*). Built on the site of
★ a former aircraft works just outside the city center (about a 10-minute walk from the Kaiserdom), the Technik Museum houses 300 exhibits including space suits, a landing capsule, and an original Russian BURAN space shuttle as part of Europe's largest aerospace exhibition. In addition, there are walk-in exhibits including a Boeing 747 and a 46-meter-long U9 submarine; and there's also a collection of vintage cars, ships, locomotives, and motorcycles. While you're here, don't miss one of the world's biggest collections of mechanical musical instruments at the Wilhelmsbau Museum (entry included in ticket price) or a movie on the curved screen of the IMAX DOME theater. Allow at least three hours to visit this extensive museum, which covers several large buildings. ✉ *Am Technik Museum 1* ☎ *06232/67080* ⊕ *speyer.technik-museum.de/de/* ✉ *€14* ⊙ *Weekdays 9–6, weekends and holidays 9–7.*

10

WHERE TO EAT

$ ✕ **Alter Hammer.** A pleasant 15-minute stroll through the gardens behind
GERMAN the cathedral will bring you to the oldest beer garden in Speyer, opened
in 1919, where the portions of rustic, regional fare are enormous. Try
the regional specialty *Maultaschen* (ground-beef ravioli) or their special (but not entirely traditional) "WuPo,", *Wurstsalat mit Pommes*,
a salad made from strips of bologna sausage, onions, and gherkins,
dressed with oil and vinegar and served with fries. Service is quick and
friendly, and, in summer, the popular, leafy riverside beer garden is a
pleasant spot to pass the afternoon. $ *Average main: €12* ⊠ *Leinpfad
1c* ☎ *06232/75539* ⊕ *www.alter-hammer.de* ⊟ *No credit cards.*

$$ ✕ **Ratskeller.** Friendly service and fresh seasonal dishes make for an
GERMAN enjoyable dining experience in the town hall's vaulted cellar (1578).
The frequently changing menu offers creative soups and other starters
(pretzel soup, Tuscan bread soup) and entrées such as *Sauerbraten nach
Grossmutters Art* (sour beef pot roast the way grandma used to make
it) or *Bachsaibling* (brook trout) in a red-wine-butter sauce. Wines
from the Pfalz predominate, with many available by the glass. Small
plates and drinks are served in the courtyard May through September.
$ *Average main: €15* ⊠ *Maximilianstr. 12* ☎ *06232/78612* ⊕ *www.
ratskeller-speyer.de* ⊗ *Closed Mon. No dinner Sun.*

$ ✕ **Weinstube Rabennest.** It's small and often packed with local families,
GERMAN but the rustic cooking in this cozy restaurant is worth the wait. Hearty
portions of regional specialties will delight both your mouth and your
wallet. The *Leberknoedel* (liver dumplings) and *Rumpsteak* (rump
steak) are both excellent, and there's also a nice selection of fresh sal-
ads. In the summer months, the patio seating is great for people-watch-
ing. $ *Average main: €10.50* ⊠ *Korng. 5* ☎ *06232/623–857* ⊕ *www.
weinstube-rabennest.de* ⊟ *No credit cards* ⊗ *Closed Sun.*

$$ ✕ **Wirtschaft Zum Alten Engel.** This 200-year-old vaulted brick cellar has
GERMAN rustic wood furnishings and cozy niches. Seasonal dishes made from
local ingredients supplement the large selection of Pfälzer and Alsatian
specialties, such as Maultaschen (large ravioli), *Blutwurst* (blood sausage), and the *Winzerteller* ("vintner's dish," a platter of bratwurst,
Saumagen, and Leberknödel with sauerkraut and home-fried potatoes).
The drinks menu features a large collection of Pfälzer, European, and
New World wines plus a selection of fruit brandies and German liqueurs
$ *Average main: €18* ⊠ *Mühlturmstr. 7* ☎ *06232/70914* ⊕ *www.
zumaltenengel.de* ⊗ *No lunch.*

WHERE TO STAY

$$ ▦ **Hotel Domhof.** Positioned a very short walk from the cathedral end
HOTEL of Maximilianstrasse, the Domhof makes for an ideal base for explor-
ing the town. **Pros:** very central; breakfast can be eaten on the ter-
race in summer. **Cons:** the cathedral bells may disturb light sleepers.
$ *Rooms from: €125* ⊠ *Bauhof 3* ☎ *06232/13290* ⊕ *www.domhof.de*
⤳ *49 rooms* ⦿ *Breakfast.*

$ ▦ **Hotel Goldener Engel.** A scant two blocks west of the Altpörtel is the
HOTEL "Golden Angel," a friendly, family-run hotel that has recently reno-
vated rooms all individually furnished with antiques and innovative
metal-and-wood designer furniture. **Pros:** friendly; good location;

THE ALTRHEIN

From April to October, you can take a short river cruise through the network of branching arms of the river to the north or south of Speyer to discover the idyllic landscape of the ancient, forested islands along the *Altrhein,* the original course of the Rhine. The islands are home to rare flora, fauna, and many birds; and there are grand views of the cathedral from the boat.

Fahrgastschifffahrt Speyer. From March to November, boat tours depart from just outside the Sea Life Aquarium at noon, 2, and 4. The trip lasts about 1½ hours and offers a unique look at Speyer's old harbor and its fascinating network of rivers. ✉ *Hafenstr. 22* ☎ *06232/291–150* 🌐 *www.ms-sealife.de* 🎫 *€10.*

Pfälzerland Fahrgastschiff. Enjoy a peaceful tour of the Speyer harbor and its surrounding river network on a ship built for 200 passengers. Homemade cakes and drinks are available on board. Tuesday through Friday, 1½-hour tours depart at 1 and 3, on Saturday at 1:30, 3, and 5 and on Sunday at 1, 3, and 5. The pickup and drop-off point is on the Leinpfad. ✉ *Dock: Leinpfad [via Rheinallee], on the Rhine riverbank, Rheinalle 2* ☎ *06232/71366* 🌐 *www. personenschifffahrt-streib.de* 🎫 *€10.*

free Wi-Fi. **Cons:** some rooms are a little small; no air-conditioning; a small amount of noise from the main street may disturb light sleepers. [$] *Rooms from: €92* ✉ *Mühlturmstr. 5–7* ☎ *06232/13260* 🌐 *www. goldener-engel-speyer.de* 🛏 *44 rooms, 2 apartments* 🍴 *Breakfast.*

NIGHTLIFE AND PERFORMING ARTS

City highlights for music lovers are **Orgelfrühling,** the organ concerts in the Gedächtniskirche (Memorial Church) in spring, the jazz festival in mid-August, and the concerts in the cathedral during September's **Internationale Musiktage.** Contact the Speyer tourist office for program details and tickets.

Kulturhof Flachsgasse. Walk into the town-hall courtyard to enter the Kulturhof Flachsgasse, home of the city's art collection and special exhibitions. ✉ *Flachsg. 3* ☎ *06232/142–399* 🎫 *Free* ⏲ *Thurs.–Sun. 11–6.*

DEIDESHEIM

8 km (5 miles) north of Neustadt via the Wine Road, B-271.

The immaculately preserved half-timber houses and historical facades lining its narrow streets fit perfectly with Deidesheim's reputation as one of the most renowned wine towns in the Pfalz. The grapes have made winemakers here a great deal of money over the centuries, and it shows: despite its size, it's a town that boasts Michelin-starred restaurants and world-class hotels owned by each of its biggest wine producers, Bassermann, Buhl, and Bürklin-Wolf. Sites of interest include the Gothic Church of St. Ulrich, the Rathaus, and the elegant Hotel Deidesheimer Hof. In August, the Deidesheim Weinkerwe (wine festival) begins at the Marktplatz, and in December, it's the site of a lively Christmas market. The main reason to visit, however, remains the opportunity to taste some of the best wines the Pfalz has to offer. Most of the local *Weingüter* (wineries) lining the streets are open to visitors year-round.

ESSENTIALS

Visitor Information Deidesheim. ⊠ *Tourist Service Center, Bahnhofstr. 5* ☎ *06326/96770* ⊕ *www.deidesheim.de.*

EXPLORING

Church of St. Ulrich. A Gothic gem inside and out, this is the only 15th-century church in the Palatinate region whose walls have been entirely preserved, though the interior has changed according to the style of the times. Despite having been looted during the French Revolution and turned first into a wine warehouse and later a military prison, the basic exterior structure of the church hasn't been altered. The interior includes stained glass that dates from the Middle Ages and wooden figures from around 1500. ⊠ *Marktpl.* ☎ *06326/345* ⊕ *www.st-ulrich-deidesheim.de* ⊘ *Closed during services.*

Rathaus und Museum für Weinkultur (*Town Hall and Museum of Viniculture*). The old Rathaus, whose doorway is crowned by a baldachin and baroque dome, is at the Marktplatz. The attractive open staircase leading up to the entrance is the site of the festive *Geissbock-Versteigerung* (billy-goat auction) every Pentecost Tuesday, followed by a parade and folk dancing. The goat is the tribute neighboring Lambrecht has paid Deidesheim since 1404 for grazing rights. Inside, in addition to a richly appointed Ratssaal (council chamber), is a museum of wine culture, which examines the importance of wine throughout history. There's also a wine bar where you can taste and buy wines from the area. ⊠ *Historisches Rathaus, Marktpl. 9* ☎ *06326/981–561* ⊕ *www.weinkultur-deidesheim. de* ⊠ *Donation requested* ⊘ *Mar.–Dec., Wed.–Sun. and holidays 4–6.*

Schloss Deidesheim. Vines, flowers, and fig trees cloak the houses behind St. Ulrich on Heumarktstrasse and its extension, Deichelgasse (nicknamed Feigengasse because of its *Feigenbäume*—fig trees). To see the workshops and ateliers of about a dozen local artists, sculptors, and goldsmiths, follow the *Künstler-Rundweg,* a signposted trail (black on yellow signs). The tourist office has a brochure with a map and opening hours. Cross the Wine Road to reach the grounds of Schloss Deidesheim, now a pub. The bishops of Speyer built a moated castle on the site in the 13th century. Twice destroyed and rebuilt, the present castle dates from 1817, and the moats have been converted into gardens. ⊠ *Schlossstr. 4* ☎ *06326/96690* ⊕ *www.schloss-deidesheim.de* ⊘ *Pub: Apr.–Oct., closed Tues. and Wed. and no lunch Mon. or Thurs.; Nov. and Dec., no lunch Fri.–Sun.*

WHERE TO EAT AND STAY

$$$ ✕ **Gasthaus Zur Kanne.** This friendly family-run restaurant, with its out-
GERMAN door stone-walled patio hidden inside a lovely courtyard, has been a guesthouse of some sort since 1160. The short but smart menu changes daily, focusing on local, seasonal ingredients and listing the origin of every product; the Pfalz-focused wine list is organized by the towns where the bottles were produced. The set menu of three courses for €30 is a good deal and if they're available, the venison meatballs and chanterelles with dumplings are both delicious regional options.

$ *Average main: €21* ⊠ *Weinstr. 31* ☎ *06326/96600* ⊕ *www.gasthauszurkanne.de* ▭ *No credit cards* ⊘ *Closed Mon. and Tues.*

$$$$ ✕**L.A. Jordan im Ketschauer Hof.**
FUSION An 18th-century complex is the
Fodor's Choice home to the Bassermann-Jordan
★ wine estate and an elegant restaurant, which has one Michelin star. Choose to sit in the sleek new conservatory or the more formal restaurant, where elements of the original structures harmonize with modern, minimalist decor. Pick your own five- or seven-course menu from the selection of Mediterranean-influenced Asian dishes or order à la carte; and select a wine from over 500 bottles from all over the world. The restaurant is also open for lunch Thursday–Saturday from May to September. $ *Average main: €33* ⊠ *Ketschauerhofstr. 1* ☎ *06326/70000* ⊕ *www.ketschauer-hof.com* ⊘ *Restaurant closed Sun. and Mon. Check website for annual holiday.*

$$$ ✕**Restaurant St. Urban.** Named after the patron saint of the wine industry,
GERMAN this upscale restaurant offers traditional Palatinate cuisine and what is probably the best wine list in the region, featuring the wines of more than 50 local wineries. If the weather is good, sit at a table on the market square with a glass of Riesling and pick from the affordable lunch menu, which features dishes such as a taster board of local meats and cheeses known as a *Vesperbrett*. Downstairs, the Michelin-starred Schwarzer Hahn ($$$$, dinner only, Wednesday–Saturday) has served its elaborate regional haute cuisine to royal and political figures from around the globe. $ *Average main: €21* ⊠ *Hotel Deidesheimer Hof, Marktpl. 1* ☎ *06326/96870* ⊕ *www.deidesheimerhof.de* ⊘ *Check website for annual holidays.*

$$ ⊞**Hotel Deidesheimer Hof.** Despite the glamour of some of its clientele—
HOTEL heads of state, entertainers, and sports stars line the guest book—this
Fodor's Choice hotel retains its country charm and friendly service. **Pros:** some rooms
★ have whirlpool baths; friendly staff; central location on the Marktplatz. **Cons:** breakfast costs an impressive €21. $ *Rooms from: €125* ⊠ *Marktpl. 1* ☎ *06326/96870* ⊕ *www.deidesheimerhof.de* ⊘ *Check website for annual holiday closing* ⟿ *24 rooms, 4 suites* ⟦◉⟧*No meals.*

$$$$ ⊞**Hotel Ketschauer Hof.** This sleek, sophisticated former manor house,
HOTEL one of the few modern design hotels in the region, attracts a discerning crowd. **Pros:** high-speed Wi-Fi included; close to the center of town; friendly service. **Cons:** expensive, and breakfast costs €25 extra; few public spaces in the hotel. $ *Rooms from: €200* ⊠ *Ketschauerhofstr. 1* ☎ *06326/70000* ⊕ *www.ketschauer-hof.com* ⟿ *5 rooms, 13 suites* ⟦◉⟧*No meals.*

$$ ⊞**Kaisergarten.** At the younger, trendier sister of the nearby Ketschauer
HOTEL Hof, the ambience is relaxed but classy. **Pros:** free high-speed Wi-Fi; use
Fodor's Choice of gym, spa, and pool included; all rooms are air-conditioned; elevator.
★ **Cons:** breakfast costs €19; parking costs extra. $ *Rooms from: €140*

SWEET SOUVENIRS

Josef Biffar & Co. The Biffar family not only runs a first-class wine estate but also manufactures candied fruits and ginger that make for delicious souvenirs. ⊠ *Confisserieshop, Weinstr. 27, Deidesheim* ☎ *06326/982-827* ⊕ *www.biffar.com* ⊘ *Weekdays 9:30–1 and 2–6, Sat. 9:30–4, Sun. 11:30–4.*

10

✉ *Weinstr. 12* ☎ *06326/700–077* 🌐 *www.kaisergarten-deidesheim.com* 🛏 *77 rooms, 8 suites* 🍴 *No meals.*

$ HOTEL 🏨 **Landhotel Lucashof.** The beautifully decorated, modern guest rooms are named after famous vineyards in Forst, and six have balconies—the Pechstein room is particularly nice. **Pros:** quiet location; friendly; good value. **Cons:** far from the sights; difficult to reach without a car; no Wi-Fi. [$] *Rooms from: €92* ✉ *Wiesenweg 1a, Forst* ☎ *06326/336* 🌐 *www.lucashof.de* 💳 *No credit cards* 🕒 *Closed Christmas.–Feb.* 🛏 *7 rooms* 🍴 *Breakfast.*

EN ROUTE **Forst** and **Wachenheim,** both a few minutes' drive north of Deidesheim, complete the trio of famous wine villages. As you approach Forst, depart briefly from B-271 (take the left fork in the road) to see the Old Town and its vine- and ivy-clad sandstone and half-timber vintners' mansions. Peek through the large portals to see the lush courtyards. Many estates on this lane have pubs, as does the town's *Winzerverein* (cooperative winery). Wachenheim is another 2 km (1 mile) down the road. Its cooperative, Wachtenburg Winzer (with a good restaurant), is on the left at the entrance to town; walk towards the town center from there and you'll pass Sektkellerei Schloss Wachenheim on the left, which produces some of Germany's best Sekt. Head for the Wachtenburg (castle) ruins up on the hill for a glass of wine overlooking the vineyards. The *Burgschänke* (castle pub) is open if the flag is flying.

BAD DÜRKHEIM

6 km (4 miles) north of Deidesheim on B-271.

This pretty spa town is nestled into the hills at the edge of the Palatinate Forest and ringed by vineyards. The saline springs discovered here in 1338 are the source of today's drinking and bathing cures, and at harvest time there's a detoxifying *Traubenkur* (grape-juice cure). The town is the site of the Dürkheimer Wurstmarkt, the world's largest wine festival, held in mid-September. Legendary quantities of *Weck, Worscht, und Woi* (dialect for bread rolls, sausage, and wine) are consumed at the fair, including enough wine to fill half a million *Schoppen,* the region's traditional glasses, which hold a half liter (about a pint). The festival grounds are also the site of the world's largest wine cask, the **Dürkheimer Riesenfass,** with a capacity of 450,000 gallons. Built in 1934 by an ambitious cooper, the cask is now a restaurant that can seat more than 450 people.

GETTING HERE AND AROUND

Regional trains link Bad Dürkheim with Freinsheim and Neustadt. Once in town, all the hotels and restaurants are within easy walking distance.

ESSENTIALS

Visitor Information Bad Dürkheim Tourist Information. ✉ *Tourist Information, Kurbrunnenstr. 14* ☎ *06322/935–140* 🌐 *www.bad-duerkheim.com.*

EXPLORING

Burgruine Hardenburg (*Hardenburg Castle Ruins*). The massive ruins of 13th-century Hardenburg Castle lie 3 km (2 miles) west of Kloster Limburg (via B-37). In its heyday, it was inhabited by more than 200 people, but it burned down in 1794. In the visitor center there's an exhibit about the fascinating history of the castle, and various events are held here throughout the year, including a medieval market in September. ⊠ *Kaiserslauterer Str.* ☎ *06322/7530* ⊕ *www.schloss-hardenburg. de* ⊡ *€3* ⊙ *Jan.–Mar., Oct., and Nov., Tues.–Sun. 9–4:30; Apr.–Sept., Tues.–Sun. 9–6.*

Heidenmauer (*Heathen Wall*). One kilometer (½ mile) northwest of town lies the Heidenmauer, the remains of an ancient Celtic ring wall more than 2 km (1 mile) in circumference and up to 20 feet thick in parts. The remnants are on the Kastanienberg, above the quarry. Nearby are the rock drawings at **Kriemhildenstuhl,** an old Roman quarry where the legionnaires of Mainz excavated sandstone. ⊠ *Bad Dürkheim.*

Kloster Limburg (*Limburg Abbey*). Overlooking the suburb of Grethen are the ruins of Kloster Limburg. Emperor Konrad II laid the cornerstone in 1030, supposedly on the same day that he laid the cornerstone of the Kaiserdom in Speyer. The monastery was never completely rebuilt after a fire in 1504, but it's a majestic backdrop for open-air performances in summer. On the tree-shaded terrace of the adjacent restaurant Spötzl's Klosterschänke Limburg ($–$$, closed Monday and Tuesday, no lunch Wednesday–Saturday), you can combine good food and wine with a great view. ⊠ *Luitpoldweg 1* ☎ *06322/935–140* ⊕ *www.klosterschaenkelimburg.de* ⊡ *€1 for tower visit* ⊙ *Nov.–Easter, Fri.–Sun. and holidays from 11:30; Easter–Oct., Tues.–Thurs. 11:30–6, Fri and Sat. 11:30–9, Sun. and holidays 11:30–7.*

WHERE TO EAT

$

GERMAN

✕ **Dürkheimer Riesenfass.** Sure, it's a bit of a tourist trap, but then again, how often do you get the chance to eat in the world's biggest wine barrel? The two-story "giant cask" is divided into various rooms and niches with rustic wood furnishings. Venture upstairs to see the impressive *Festsaal mit Empore* (banquet hall with gallery). There's also extensive outdoor seating if the weather's nice. Regional wines, Pfälzer specialties, and international dishes are served year-round. Ⓢ *Average main: €14* ⊠ *St. Michael Allee 1* ☎ *06322/2143* ⊕ *www.duerkheimer-fass.de.*

$$

GERMAN

✕ **Weinstube Petersilie.** Behind a group of lush, potted plants and a sign on a pink-and-white house reading "Bier- und Weinstube Tenne" is Petersilie, a traditional wine tavern that stands out from the many other cafés and eateries on Römerplatz. Patio seating is great for people-watching; indoors is warm and cozy, with rustic wooden tables, beamed ceilings, and pillow-lined benches. The menu offers both homey Pfälzer fare and international cuisine. Ⓢ *Average main: €15* ⊠ *Römerpl. 12* ☎ *06322/4394* ⊕ *www.weinstube-petersilie.de* ▭ *No credit cards.*

WHERE TO STAY

$$

HOTEL

🛏 **Mercure Hotel Bad Dürkheim an den Salinen.** Within walking distance to the center of town, this well-maintained chain hotel offers free admission to the Salinarium water park and spa next door, where there are indoor and outdoor pools and wellness treatments. **Pros:** free Wi-Fi; plenty of free parking; three restaurants and two bars in the hotel. **Cons:** not a lot of character. Ⓢ *Rooms from: €130* ⊠ *Kurbrunnenstr. 30–32* ☎ *06322/6010* ⊕ *www.mercure.com* ⇱ *100 rooms* ⦿ *Breakfast.*

10

$$ 🍷**Weingut Fitz-Ritter.** At the Fitz-Ritter wine estate there are two dif-
B&B/INN ferent places to stay: a centuries-old stone cottage that sleeps up to
four people and has its own pool on the parklike grounds, and a suite
that sleeps four, plus four further rooms with shared bathroom and
kitchen facilities in a courtyard full of oleanders, palms, fig trees, and
nesting swallows. **Pros:** quiet location amid the vines; friendly staff;
short walk to the town center; free Wi-Fi. **Cons:** minimum stay in the
cottage is seven nights; on weekends Apr.–Oct., all four rooms need
to be rented together; no breakfast. $ *Rooms from: €100* ⊠ *Weinstr.
Nord 51* ☎ *06322/5389* ⊕ *www.fitz-ritter.de* ⇌ *1 cottage, 4 rooms, 1
suite* ⎮⚪⎮ *No meals.*

$ 🍷**Weingut und Gästehaus Ernst Karst und Sohn.** Rooms at this cheerful
B&B/INN guesthouse in the middle of the vineyards are airy and furnished mostly
in pine; all of them have splendid views of the countryside, which you
are invited to explore on bikes that you can borrow. **Pros:** quiet vineyard
location; friendly staff. **Cons:** rooms include breakfast, but apartments
don't; far from the sights. $ *Rooms from: €80* ⊠ *In den Almen 15*
☎ *06322/2862* ⊕ *www.weingut-karst.de* ⊟ *No credit cards* ⊘ *Closed
Nov.–Feb.* ⇌ *4 rooms, 2 apartments* ⎮⚪⎮ *Breakfast.*

NIGHTLIFE

Spielbank (*Casino*). This casino is open daily at 11 am for the slot
machines, 2 pm for roulette and poker, and 6 pm for blackjack; jacket
and tie are no longer required, but tennis shoes, T-shirts, and shorts are
not allowed. Be certain to bring your passport for identification; the
minimum age is 18. ⊠ *Kurparkhotel, Schlosspl. 6* ⊕ *www.casino-bad-
duerkheim.de* ⊘ *Check website for holiday closing times.*

SHOPPING

Weindom. Several hundred wines from Bad Dürkheim and the vicinity
can be sampled and purchased at this shop next to the Dürkheimer
Riesenfass. The shop also sells other grape products and accesso-
ries. ⊠ *St.-Michaels-Allee 10* ☎ *06322/949–222* ⊕ *www.weindom.de*
⊘ *Daily 10–6.*

SPORTS AND THE OUTDOORS

Kurhaus Staatsbad. The Kurhaus Staatsbad houses all kinds of bathing
facilities, including thermal baths, herbal steam baths, a sauna, and a
hammam (Turkish bath). ⊠ *Kurbrunnenstr. 14* ☎ *06322/9640* ⊕ *www.
kurzentrum-bad-duerkheim.de* ⊘ *Mon., Tues., Thurs., Fri. 9–8, Wed.
8–8, Sat. 9–5, Sun. 9–2:30.*

THE RHINE TERRACE

Like Speyer, the cities of Worms and Mainz were Free Imperial Cities
and major centers of Christian and Jewish culture in the Middle Ages.
Germany's first synagogue and Europe's oldest surviving Jewish cem-
etery, both from the 11th century, are in Worms. The imperial diets of
Worms and Speyer in 1521 and 1529 stormed around Martin Luther
(1483–1546) and the rise of Protestantism. In 1455 Johannes Gutenberg
(1400–68), the inventor of the printing press and of movable type in
Europe, printed the first Gutenberg Bible in Mainz.

WORMS

15 km (9 miles) east of Bockenheim via B-47 from Monsheim, 45 km (28 miles) south of Mainz on B-9.

In addition to having a great Romanesque cathedral, Worms is a center of the wine trade, as well as one of the most storied cities in Germany, with a history going back some 6,000 years. Settled by the Romans, Worms (pronounced *vawrms*) later became one of the imperial cities of the Holy Roman Empire. More than 100 Imperial diets (assemblies) were held here, including the 1521 meeting where Martin Luther pleaded his cause.

Worms developed into an important garrison town under the Romans, but it's better known for its greatest legend, the *Nibelungenlied*, derived from the short-lived kingdom established by Gunther and his Burgundian tribe in the early 5th century. The complex and sprawling story was given its final shape in the 12th century and tells of love, betrayal, greed, war, and death. It ends when Attila the Hun defeats the Nibelungen (Burgundians), who find their court destroyed, their treasure lost, and their heroes dead. One of the most famous incidents tells how Hagen, treacherous and scheming, hurls the court riches into the Rhine. Near the Nibelungen Bridge there's a bronze statue of him caught in the act. The Nibelungenlied may be legend, but the story is based on fact. A Queen Brunhilda, for example, is said to have lived here. It's also known that a Burgundian tribe was defeated in 436 by Attila the Hun in what is present-day Hungary.

Not until Charlemagne resettled Worms almost 400 years later, making it one of the major cities of his empire, did the city prosper again. Worms was more than an administrative and commercial center—it was a great ecclesiastical city as well. The first expression of this religious importance was the original cathedral, consecrated in 1018. Between 1130 and 1181 it was rebuilt in three phases into the church you see today.

GETTING HERE AND AROUND

Worms can be reached by direct trains from both Mannheim and Mainz (approximately 30 minutes from each). The city center is quite compact and negotiable on foot.

ESSENTIALS

Visitor Information **Tourist Information.** ⊠ *Neumarkt 14* ☎ *06241/853–7306* ⊕ *www.worms.de.*

EXPLORING

TOP ATTRACTIONS

Heylshofgarten. An imperial palace once stood in this park just north of the cathedral. It was the site of the fateful 1521 meeting between Luther and Emperor Charles V that ultimately led to the Reformation. Luther refused to recant his theses demanding Church reforms and went into exile in Eisenach, where he translated the New Testament in 1521 and 1522. ⊠ *Stephansg. 9.*

Judenfriedhof Heiliger Sand (*Holy Sand Jewish Cemetery*). This is the oldest Jewish cemetery in Europe and also one of the most atmospheric

10

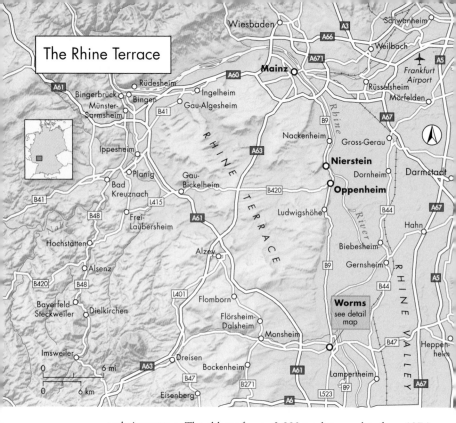

The Rhine Terrace

and picturesque. The oldest of some 2,000 tombstones date from 1076. Entry is via the gate on Willy-Brandt-Ring. ⊠ *Andreasstr. and Willy-Brandt-Ring* ☉ *Summer, daily 8–8; winter, daily 8–sunset (except Jewish holidays).*

Kunsthaus Heylshof (*Heylshof Art Gallery*). Located in the Heylshof-garten, this is one of the leading art museums of the region. It has an exquisite collection of German, Dutch, and French paintings as well as stained glass, glassware, porcelain, and ceramics dating from the 15th to the 19th century. ⊠ *Stephansg. 9* ☎ *06241/22000* ⊕ *www.heylshof. de* ⊠ *€3.50* ☉ *Mar.–Dec., Tues.–Sat. 2–5, Sun. and holidays 11–5.*

Fodor's Choice ★

Liebfrauenkirche (*Church of Our Lady*). This twin-towered Gothic church is set amid vineyards on the northern outskirts of Worms. It's the namesake of the popular, sweet white wine Liebfraumilch, literally, the "Milk of Our Lady." The wine (Blue Nun is the most well known brand) was originally made from the grapes of the small vineyard surrounding the church, but today it's produced throughout Rheinhessen, the Pfalz, the Nahe, and the Rheingau wine regions. ⊠ *Liebfrauenring 21* ⊕ *www.liebfrauen-worms.de* ☉ *Closed during services.*

Lutherdenkmal. This monument commemorates Luther's appearance at the Diet of Worms. He ended his speech with the words: "Here I stand. I have no choice. God help me. Amen." The 19th-century monument includes a large statue of Luther ringed by other figures from the Reformation. It's set in a small park on the street named Lutherring. ⊠ *Lutherpl./Lutherring.*

Nibelungen Museum. This stunning sight-and-sound exhibition is dedicated to *Das Nibelungenlied* (*Song of the Nibelungs*), the epic German poem dating to around 1200. Cleverly installed in two medieval towers and the portion of the Old Town wall between them, the exhibition brings to life the saga of the dragon slayer Siegfried. The architecture of the structure itself is also fascinating, and the rampart provides a wonderful view of the town. The tour script (via headphones and printed matter) is offered in English. Allow 1½ hours for a thorough visit. ⊠ *Fischerpförtchen 10* 🕾 *06241/202–120* ⊕ *www.nibelungen-museum.de* 🖸 *€5.50* ☉ *Tues.– Fri. 10–5, weekends and holidays 10–6. Check website for summer holiday closing time.*

Synagogue. This first synagogue in Worms was built in 1034, rebuilt in 1175, and expanded in 1213 with a synagogue for women. Destroyed in 1938, it was rebuilt in 1961 using as much of the original masonry as had survived. It is located in the Jewish quarter, which is along the town wall between Martinspforte and Friesenspitze and between Judengasse and Hintere Judengasse. ⊠ *Synagogenpl.* 🕾 *06241/853–4700* ☉ *Apr.– Oct., daily 10–12:30 and 1:30–5; Nov.–Mar., daily 10–noon and 2–4; closed during services.*

Fodor's Choice ★ **Wormser Dom St. Peter** (*Cathedral of St. Peter*). In contrast to Speyer's Romanesque cathedral, the Worms Cathedral of St. Peter is much more Gothic. In part this is simply a matter of chronology, since Speyer Cathedral was finished in 1061, nearly 70 years before the one in Worms was even begun—and long before the lighter, more vertical lines of the Gothic style evolved. In addition, Speyer Cathedral was left largely untouched, but the Worms Cathedral underwent frequent remodeling. The Gothic influence here can be seen both inside and out, from the elaborate tympanum with biblical scenes over the southern portal (today's entrance) to the great rose window in the west choir and the five sculptures in the north aisle recounting the life of Christ. The cathedral was gutted by fire in 1689 in the War of the Palatinate Succession. For this reason many of the furnishings are baroque, including the magnificent gilt high altar from 1742, designed by the master architect Balthasar Neumann (1687–1753). The choir stalls are no less decorative. They were built between 1755 and 1759 in rococo style. Walk around the building to see the artistic detail of

> **TOURING TIPS**
>
> **Information:** The tourist office is near the cathedral. Pick up "Two Thousand Years of History," a handy map with suggested walking tours and descriptions of the main sights.
>
> **Scenic spot:** The Old Town wall between the two towers of the Nibelungen Museum affords a great view of the town.
>
> **Scenic spot:** From the Holy Sand Jewish Cemetery there's a good view of a portion of the massive Old Town wall, and the cemetery itself is worth exploring.

10

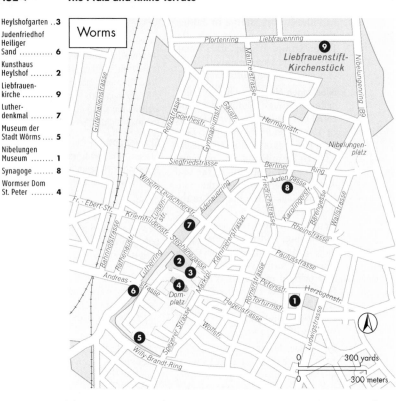

the exterior. ⊠ *Lutherring 9* ☎ *06241/6115* ⊕ *www.wormser-dom. de* ⊠ *Donation requested* ⊙ *Summer, daily 9–6; winter, daily 10–5. Closed during services.*

WORTH NOTING

Museum der Stadt Worms (*Municipal Museum*). To find out more about the history of Worms, visit this museum, housed in the cloisters of a Romanesque church in the Andreasstift. The collection includes artifacts from the Roman period (it features one of the largest collections of Roman glass in Germany), all the way up to local art from the 20th century. ⊠ *Weckerlingpl. 7* ☎ *06241/946–390* ⊠ *€3* ⊙ *Tues.–Sun. 10–6.*

WHERE TO EAT

$ ✕ **Gasthaus Hagenbräu.** Located a little to the west of the center, by the
GERMAN banks of the Rhine, this house brewery serves a good range of classic German dishes such as meatloaf with *Spätzle* (egg noodles) as well as regional specialties. Service and decor are bright and cheery, and you will be surrounded by copper vats and oak barrels as you dine. The summer terrace by the river is a chance to enjoy a brew with a view. $ *Average main: €12* ⊠ *Am Rhein 3* ☎ *06241/921–100* ⊕ *www.hagenbraeu. de* ⊙ *Closed Mon. and Tues. Nov.–Feb.*

One of the focal points of the Gothic Wormser Dom St. Peter (Worms Cathedral of St. Peter) is the rose window.

WHERE TO STAY

$$ **Dom-Hotel.** The appeal of this hotel, with comfortable if somewhat
HOTEL bland rooms, lies in its friendly staff and its terrific location in the heart
of the pedestrian zone (a parking garage is available for free). **Pros:**
central location; breakfast included; free Wi-Fi. **Cons:** building design
doesn't have much charm; hotel in need of a refresh. $ *Rooms from:*
€105 ✉ *Obermarkt 10* ☎ *06241/9070* ⊕ *www.dom-hotel.de* ⤴ *53*
rooms, 2 apartments ❒ *Breakfast.*

$ **Land- und Winzerhotel Bechtel.** The friendly Bechtel family, winegrow-
HOTEL ers and proud parents of a former German Wine Queen, offer very
pleasant accommodations on the grounds of their wine estate in the
suburb of Heppenheim, about 10 km (6 miles) west of Worms. **Pros:**
quiet location; excellent value; rooms have balconies. **Cons:** far from
the sights; extra charge for breakfast; checkout is on the early side,
at 10 am. $ *Rooms from: €65* ✉ *Pfälzer Waldstr. 100* ☎ *06241/506–*
1332 ⊕ *www.landhotel-bechtel.de* ⊙ *Restaurant closed Tues. No lunch*
Mon.–Sat. ⤴ *11 rooms* ❒ *No meals.*

$ **Landhotel Zum Schwanen.** Bärbel Berkes runs this lovingly restored
HOTEL country inn in Osthofen, 10 km (6 miles) northwest of Worms. **Pros:**
quiet location; friendly staff; free Wi-Fi in rooms. **Cons:** far from the
sights; no elevator. $ *Rooms from: €98* ✉ *Friedrich-Ebert-Str. 40, west*
of B-9, Osthofen ☎ *06242/9140* ⊕ *www.zum-schwanen-osthofen.de*
⊙ *Restaurant closed Sun. No lunch Sat.* ⤴ *30 rooms* ❒ *Breakfast.*

10

SHOPPING

Star Region. Eat, drink and shop: this store and restaurant specializes in culinary items, including gift baskets, from Rheinhessen, Odenwald, and Pfalz. They also offer wine tastings and city tours. ✉ *Kammererstr. 60* ☎ *06241/269–796* ⊕ *www.starregion.de* ☯ *Closed Sun.*

OPPENHEIM

26 km (16 miles) north of Worms, 23 km (14 miles) south of Mainz on B-9.

Oppenheim is slightly off the beaten path, making it an ideal destination if you're looking to avoid the hordes of tourists that often descend on the Wine Road in midsummer. It's a steep walk from the train station up to the picturesque old town and market square, but worth the effort to reach the Katharinenkirche, Oppenheim's obvious crown, and the town's mysterious hidden gem: the Oppenheimer Kellerlabyrinth.

GETTING HERE AND AROUND

An excellent network of regional trains connect Oppenheim with Mainz and Worms. Both journeys take about 20 minutes, and trains depart every half hour. Nierstein is just one stop away on the same regional train.

ESSENTIALS

Oppenheim Tourist Office. ✉ *Merianstr. 2* ☎ *06133/490–919, 06133/490–914* ⊕ *www.stadt-oppenheim.de/* ☯ *Nov.–Mar., daily 10–5; Oct.–Apr., weekends 10–5.*

EXPLORING

Deutsches Weinbaumuseum (*German Viticultural Museum*). Oppenheim and its neighbors to the north, Nierstein and Nackenheim, are home to some of Rheinhessen's best-known vineyards. The Deutsches Weinbaumuseum has wine-related artifacts that chronicle the region's 2,000-year-old wine-making tradition, not to mention the world's largest collection of mousetraps and more than 2,000 corkscrews. ✉ *Wormser Str. 49* ☎ *06133/2544* ⊕ *www.dwb-museum.de* 🖾 *€4* ☯ *Apr.–Oct., Tues.–Fri. 2–5, weekends and holidays 10–5.*

Katharinenkirche (*St. Catherine's Church*). On the way to Oppenheim, the vine-covered hills parallel to the Rhine gradually steepen. Then, unexpectedly, the spires of Oppenheim's Gothic St. Catherine's Church come into view. The contrast of its pink sandstone facade against a bright blue sky is striking. Built between 1225 and 1439, it's the most important Gothic church between Strasbourg and Köln. The interior affords a rare opportunity to admire magnificent original 14th-century stained-glass windows including two rose windows, the Lily Window and the Oppenheim Rose. The church houses masterfully carved tombstones, and the chapel behind it has a *Beinhaus* (charnel house) containing the bones of 20,000 citizens and soldiers from the 15th to 18th century. ✉ *Katharinenstr. 1* ☎ *06133/579–217 or 2381* ⊕ *www. katharinen-kirche.de* ☯ *Apr.–Oct., daily 8–6; Nov.–Mar., daily 9–5.*

Fodor's Choice **Oppenheimer Kellerlabyrinth** (*Oppenheim cellar labyrinth*). Beneath
★ Oppenheim's surface, there are five layers of cellars, tunnels, and stairways. Thought to have been built in the 14th century, their purpose

remains unknown. Of the 40 km (24 miles) of complex underground passageways, today ¾ km (½ mile) is open to the public; contact the Oppenheim tourist office to arrange a tour. ✉ *Merianstr. 2a* ☎ *06133/490–921* ⊕ *www.stadt-oppenheim.de/* 💲 *€7.50.*

NIGHTLIFE AND PERFORMING ARTS

FAMILY **Burgruine Landskron.** During the Oppenheim Festival, from the end of August till the end of September, concerts are held at St. Catherine's, and open-air theater takes place in the Burgruine Landskron, the 12th-century imperial fortress ruins. From here, there's a wonderful view of the town and the vineyards, extending all the way to Mannheim and Frankfurt on a clear day. The castle ruins are northwest of the church. Follow Dalbergerstrasse north; from there it's a short, steep walk up to the ruins. For tickets to the open-air theater performances contact the Oppenheim tourist office. ✉ *Oppenheim.*

NIERSTEIN

3 km (2 miles) north of Oppenheim on B-9.

Surrounded by 2,700 acres of vines, Nierstein is a small, quaint town that's home to the largest wine-growing community on the Rhine. It is also home to Glöck, Germany's **oldest documented vineyard** (AD 742), which surrounds St. Kilian's Church.

GETTING HERE AND AROUND

Regional trains leave every 30 minutes between Nierstein and both Mainz and Worms. The journey takes about 20 minutes.

EXPLORING

Winzergenossenschaft. The Winzergenossenschaft can be the starting point of an easy hike or drive to the vineyard heights and the vantage point at the *Wartturm* (watchtower). In the summer, the *Niersteiner Weinwanderung* (wine walk) takes place along the *roten Hang,* or "red slope" of the vineyards—the soil here has a lot of red clay in it—with food and wine-tasting stands set up along the way. From up there, there's a stunning view of the Rhine. ✉ *Karolingerstr. 6* ☎ *06133/971– 720* ⊕ *www.roter-hang.de.*

WHERE TO STAY

$$ 🏨 **Best Western Wein & Parkhotel.** Spacious, light rooms decorated in HOTEL warm shades of ochre, chic bathrooms, and an inviting lounge and terrace make for comfortable, relaxing quarters here. **Pros:** friendly; quiet location; free Wi-Fi throughout hotel. **Cons:** a chain hotel with few surprises; not all rooms are nonsmoking. 💲 *Rooms from: €150* ✉ *An der Kaiserlinde 1* ☎ *06133/5080* ⊕ *www.weinhotel.bestwestern. de* 🛏 *55 rooms* ⊗ *Breakfast.*

$ 🏨 **Jordan's Untermühle.** The spacious grounds of an old mill are home to B&B/INN a country inn, a restaurant, and a Vinothek (wine store). **Pros:** beautiful Fodor's Choice buildings; great value; very quiet; the suite has its own sauna. **Cons:** ★ a long way from anywhere; difficult to reach without a car. 💲 *Rooms from: €57.50* ✉ *Ausserhalb 1, Köngernheim* ✛ *West of B-9, at Nierstein turn left on B-420 (toward Wörrstadt), drive through Köngernheim and*

10

turn right toward Selzen ☎ *06737/71000* ⊕ *www.jordans-untermuehle. de* ⇆ *25 rooms, 4 studios, 1 suite* ❍❘ *Breakfast.*

MAINZ

14 km (9 miles) north of Nackenheim, 45 km (28 miles) north of Worms on B-9, and 42 km (26 miles) west of Frankfurt on A-3.

Mainz is the capital of the state of Rheinland-Pfalz. It's a lively university town with friendly locals renowned for their community spirit, whether it be in supporting the local soccer team, Mainz 05, enjoying wine tavern culture in the cobbled Old Town, or partying at *Karneval* (carnival). Today's city was built on the site of a Roman citadel dating back to 38 BC, and given its central location at the confluence of the Main and Rhine rivers, it's not surprising that Mainz has always been an important trading center, rebuilt time and again in the wake of wars.

GETTING HERE AND AROUND

As the regional hub, Mainz is well served by trains, with fast connections to Frankfurt (40 minutes) and Köln (1 hour, 40 minutes). The station is a short walk west of the center. A comprehensive network of local buses makes getting around the city a breeze (route maps and timetables are posted at bus stops), while the upper areas of town are also served by trams. Although the sights are fairly spread out, they're manageable on foot if you're in reasonably good shape.

DISCOUNTS AND DEALS

■TIP➜ Head to the Tourist Service Center to pick up a mainzcardplus for €9.95, or €25 for up to five people. The card covers 48 hours of unlimited public transportation in the specified area, free entry to museums and the casino, free walking tours, plus discounts on theater tickets and trips with the Koln-Düsseldorf Rheinschiffahrt and Gutenberg-Express sightseeing train.

ESSENTIALS

VISITOR INFORMATION **Tourist Service Center.** Mainz offers year-round tours of the city, including its Roman and medieval areas, the cathedral, and the modern city center, departing Saturday at 2 pm from outside the Tourist Service Center. Drop in to ask about arranging a personalized tour at a different time or a guided visit to the Gutenberg Museum or St. Stephen's Church. ⊠ *Tourist Service Center, Brückenturm am Rathaus, Rheinstr. 55* ☎ *06131/242–888* ⊕ *www.mainz-tourismus.com* ⊗ *Weekdays 9–5, Sat. 10–4, Sun. and holidays 11–3.*

EXPLORING

TOP ATTRACTIONS

Fodor's Choice ★ **Dom** (*St. Martin's Cathedral*). This cathedral's interior is a virtual sculpture gallery of elaborate monuments and tombstones of archbishops, bishops, and canons, many of which are significant artworks in their own right. Emperor Otto II began building the oldest of the Rhineland's trio of grand Romanesque cathedrals in 975, the year in which he named Willigis archbishop and chancellor of the empire. Henry II, the last Saxon emperor of the Holy Roman Empire, was crowned here in 1002, as was his successor, Konrad II, the first Salian emperor, in 1024.

In 1009, on the very day of its consecration, the cathedral burned to the ground. It was the first of seven fires the Dom has endured. Today's cathedral dates mostly from the 11th to 13th century. During the Gothic period, remodeling diluted the Romanesque identity of the original; an imposing baroque spire was added in the 18th century. Nevertheless, the building remains essentially Romanesque, and its floor plan demonstrates a clear link to the cathedrals in Speyer and Worms. Individual and group tours can be arranged through the Tourist Service Center. ✉ *Domstr. 3 ✚ On the Marktplatz* ☎ *06131/253–412* ⊕ *www.mainz-dom.de/* ✉ *Donations requested* ⊗ *Mar.–Oct., weekdays 9–6:30, Sat. 9–4, Sun. 12:45–3 and 4–6:30; Nov.–Feb., weekdays 9–5, Sat. 9–4, Sun. 12:45–3 and 4–5; closed during services.*

Dom und Diözesanmuseum. From the Middle Ages until secularization in the early 19th century, the archbishops of Mainz, who numbered among the imperial electors, were extremely influential politicians and property owners. The wealth of religious art treasures they left behind can be viewed in the cathedral cloisters. ✉ *Domstr. 3* ☎ *06131/253–344* ⊕ *www. dommuseum-mainz.de* ✉ *€5* ⊗ *Tues.–Fri. 10–5, weekends 11–6.*

Gutenberg Museum. Opposite the east end of the cathedral (closest to the Rhine) stands this fascinating museum, which is devoted to the history of writing, printing, and books. Exhibits include historical printing presses, incunabula (books printed in Europe before 1501), and medieval manuscripts with illuminated letters, as well as two precious 42-line Gutenberg bibles printed circa 1455. A replica workshop demonstrates how Gutenberg implemented his invention of movable type. ✉ *Liebfrauenpl. 5* ☎ *06131/122–640* ⊕ *www.gutenberg-museum.de* ✉ *€5* ⊗ *Tues.–Sat. 9–5, Sun. 11–5.*

Kupferberg Terrasse. These hillside sparkling wine cellars were built in 1850 on a site where the Romans had cultivated vines and cellared wine. The Kupferberg family expanded them to create 60 seven-story-deep vaulted cellars—the deepest in the world. The winery has a splendid collection of glassware; posters from the belle epoque period (1898–1914); richly carved casks from the 18th and 19th centuries; and the **Traubensaal** (Grape Hall), a tremendous example of the art nouveau style. Tours of the cellars and museum last one hour plus time for a sparkling wine tasting. Reservations are required, either online at the Kupferberg Terrasse website or by telephone with the Tourist Service Center. The Kupferberg Terrassen restaurant ($$$) here is a lovely place to dine before or after your tour. ✉ *Kupferbergterrasse 17–19* ☎ *06131/9230* ⊕ *www. kupferbergterrasse.com* ✉ *From €9 for tour plus 1 glass sparkling wine* ⊗ *Weekdays 11–4.*

Landesmuseum. The various collections of the Museum of the State of Rheinland-Pfalz are in the former electors' stables, easily recognized by the statue of a golden stallion over the entrance. Exhibits range from the Middle Ages to the 20th century. Among the highlights are paintings by Dutch masters, artworks from the baroque to art-nouveau period, and collections of porcelain and faience. ✉ *Grosse Bleiche 49–51* ☎ *06131/28570* ⊕ *www.landesmuseum-mainz.de* ✉ *€6* ⊗ *Tues. 10–8, Wed.–Sun. 10–5.*

In addition to Bibles printed circa 1455, the Gutenberg Museum has artifacts that tell the story of the printed word, including ancient manuscripts and presses.

Römisch-Germanisches Zentralmuseum. The wonderful collection here chronicles cultural developments in the area up to the early Middle Ages. One of the highlights is a tiny Celtic glass dog from the 1st or 2nd century BC. The entrance for the museum, which is in the Kurfürstliches Schloss (Electoral Palace), is around the back, on the river (east) side of the building. ⊠ *Ernst-Ludwig-Pl. 2* ☎ *06131/91240* ⊕ *www.rgzm. de* ⊡ *Free* ⊗ *Tues.–Sun. 10–6.*

Fodor's Choice
★

St. Stephanskirche (*St. Stephen's Church*). It's just a short walk up Gaustrasse from Schillerplatz to the church, which affords a hilltop view of the city. Nearly 200,000 people make the trip each year to see the nine magnificent blue stained-glass windows designed by the Russian-born artist Marc Chagall. ⊠ *Kleine Weissg. 12, via Gaustr.* ☎ *06131/231–640* ⊕ *www.st-stephan-mainz.de* ⊗ *Mar.–Oct., Mon.–Sat. 10–5, Sun. noon–5; Nov.–Feb., Mon.–Sat. 10–4:30, Sun. noon–4:30. Closed during services.*

WORTH NOTING

FAMILY **Marktplatz.** The area around the cathedral and the adjacent *Höfchen* (little courtyard) is the focal point of the city. The *Marktplatz* (market place) is especially colorful on Tuesdays, Fridays, and Saturdays, from 7 am to 2 pm, when farmers, butchers, cheesemongers, and florists set up stands to sell their produce. On Saturdays at 9 am from March to November join friendly Mainzers in the adjoining Liebfrauenplatz for the *Mainzer Marktfrühstuck* (Mainz Market Breakfast), where you can sample local wines alongside a traditional local breakfast of *Fleischwurst* (German bologna sausage) with mustard and a crusty bread roll. ⊠ *Marktpl.*

Museum für Antike Schiffahrt (*Museum of Ancient Navigation*). The main attractions at this bright, airy museum are the fascinating remains of five 4th-century wooden Roman warships, on display with two full-size replicas. The remains were unearthed in 1981, when the foundation for an expansion to the Hilton hotel was dug. For more than a decade, the wood was injected with a water-and-paraffin mixture to restore its stability. There's also an extensive exhibit dedicated to the history of shipbuilding and an educational area for children. To arrange a tour, contact the service office. ⊠ *Neutorstr. 2b* ☎ *06131/912–4170 service office (for tours)* ⊕ *web.rgzm.de/* ⊒ *Free* ⊙ *Tues.–Sun. 10–6.*

Schillerplatz. This square, lined by a number of beautiful baroque aristocratic houses, is the site of a memorial to the 18th-century German writer and philosopher Friedrich Schiller as well as the ebullient **Fastnachtsbrunnen** (Carnival Fountain), which features 200 figures related to Mainz's "fifth season" of the year. ⊠ *Schillerpl.*

WHERE TO EAT

$

GERMAN

✕ **Eisgrub-Bräu.** It's loud, it's busy, and the small selection of high-quality beer is brewed on-site in a labyrinth of vaulted cellars. The menu offers regional snacks such as *Handkäs' mit Musik* (hand-formed sour-milk cheese with chopped onions, caraway, and vinegar) as well as hearty Bavarian fare, from *Schweinehaxen* (pork knuckle) to sauerkraut . During the week, there's a lunch special for €6.90. Brewery tours are free, but must be arranged in advance. It's open most days from 11:30 am–midnight, and on Friday and Saturday until 1 am. $ *Average main: €12* ⊠ *Weisslilieng. 1a* ☎ *06131/221–104* ⊕ *www.eisgrub.de.*

$$$

GERMAN

✕ **Gebert's Weinstuben.** Gebert's smart yet traditional wine tavern serves refined versions of regional favorites and modern European cuisine using fresh, seasonal ingredients. The *geeister Kaffee* (coffee ice cream and a chocolate praline in a cup of coffee) uses delicious, handmade chocolate pralines. German wines, from the Rhine Terrace in particular, dominate the excellent wine list. You can also dine outside in the appealing courtyard. $ *Average main: €21* ⊠ *Frauenlobstr. 94* ☎ *06131/611–619* ⊕ *www.geberts-weinstuben.de* ⊙ *Closed Mon. and Tues. and for 3 wks during July and Aug.*

$$

MEDITERRANEAN

✕ **Heiliggeist.** This lively café-bistro-bar serves elaborate salad platters, creatively spiced fish and meat dishes, and the house specialty, *Croustarte,* an upscale version of pizza. Choose from an extensive drinks menu that includes a crowd-pleasing cocktail list: in summer, do as the locals do and sit out in the beer garden with a refreshing *Hugo* (Prosecco with mint, elderflower, soda, and lime). Heiliggeist's modern, minimal decor is a striking contrast to the historic vaulted ceilings in this former almshouse and hospital church, which was built in 1236. $ *Average main: €16* ⊠ *Mailandsg. 11* ☎ *06131/225–757* ⊕ *www.heiliggeist-mainz.de* ⊟ *No credit cards* ⊙ *No lunch weekdays* ⊴ *Reservations not accepted.*

$$

GERMAN

Fodor's Choice

★

✕ **Weinhaus Schreiner.** It's one of the more formal Mainz wine taverns, yet Schreiner still attracts a mixed, jovial clientele who come to enjoy excellent local wines and delicious, refined takes on traditional German cuisine. The compact, seasonal menu offers regional favorites such as Saumagen (sliced stuffed pig's stomach) as well as lighter dishes with a Mediterranean twist. In winter, the succulent roast goose with red

10

CLOSE UP

Gutenberg: The Father of Modern Printing

His invention—printing with movable type—transformed the art of communication, yet much about the life and work of Johannes Gutenberg is undocumented, starting with his year of birth. It's conjectured that he was born in Mainz circa 1400, into a patrician family that supplied the city mint with metal for coining. Gutenberg's later accomplishments attest to his own skill in working with metals. Details about his education are unclear, but he probably helped finance his studies by copying manuscripts in a monastic scriptorium. He moved to Strasbourg around 1434, where he was a goldsmith by day and an inventor by night. It was here that he worked—in great secrecy—to create movable type and develop a press suitable for printing by adapting the screw press conventionally used for making wine. By 1448, Gutenberg

had returned to Mainz. Loans from a wealthy businessman enabled him to set up a printer's workshop and print the famous 42-line Bible. The lines of text are in black ink, yet each of the original 180 Bibles printed from 1452 to 1455 is unique, thanks to the artistry of the hand-painted illuminated letters.

Despite its significance, Gutenberg's invention was not a financial success. His quest for perfection rather than profit led to a legal battle during which his creditor was awarded the workshop and the Bible type. Gutenberg's attempts to set up another print shop in Mainz failed, but from 1465 until his death in 1468 he received an allowance for service to the archbishop of Mainz, which spared the "father of modern printing" from dying in poverty.

cabbage and dumplings is not to be missed. During periods of warm weather, the garden is open from 5 pm weekdays and from 11:30 am Saturday. $ *Average main: €17* ✉ *Rheinstr. 38* ☎ *06131/225–720* ⊕ *www.weinhausschreiner.de* ⊘ *Closed Sun.* ☐ *No credit cards.*

$
GERMAN
✕ **Weinstube zum Bacchus.** A tiny wine tavern with a narrow, rickety staircase up to a tightly packed, wood-paneled room in addition to the cozy space downstairs, Bacchus offers traditional Mainzer appetizers such as Handkäs' mit Musik as well as mains such as salads, baked potatoes, Flammkuchen, and elegant versions of classic seasonal German dishes, from schnitzel with green sauce in the spring, to goose with dumplings at Christmastime. From the international selection, the curried dishes are always good. In addition to local wines, they also offer a small selection of German craft beers. $ *Average main: €12* ✉ *Jakobsbergstr. 7* ☎ *06131/487–5548* ⊕ *www.weinstube-zum-bacchus.de* ⊘ *No lunch.*

$
GERMAN
✕ **Zum Goldstein.** This cozy wine tavern offers simple, traditional German fare, from pickled herrings with sour cream, apple, and vinegar to schnitzel with fried potatoes and mushroom sauce, as well as a handful of international dishes. Pick a glass of Riesling from their wine list and enjoy a leisurely summer's evening in the popular walled beer garden, which sits in the shade of an enormous tree lit with fairy lights. $ *Average main: €14* ✉ *Kartäuserstr. 3* ☎ *06131/236–576* ⊕ *www.zum-goldstein.de/* ⊘ *No lunch.*

CARNIVAL IN MAINZ

Carnival season runs from November 11 at 11:11 am to Ash Wednesday. There are dozens of costume balls, parties, and political cabaret sessions during this period, but the heavy celebrating doesn't begin until *Weiberfastnacht*, the Thursday preceding Ash Wednesday. The "fifth season" ends with a huge parade of colorful floats and marching bands through downtown on the *Rosenmontag* (Rose Monday), the Monday before Lent.

A visit to Mainz during carnival week isn't for the faint-hearted: Mainzers—and the half million or so visitors who come for the Rosenmontag parade—party nonstop all week in every corner of the town, so a quiet meal out or a gentle stroll to take in the sights simply isn't an option. If you're brave enough to throw yourself into the celebrations, however, carnival in Mainz is an experience not to be missed.

WHERE TO STAY

$$
HOTEL

FAVORITE parkhotel. Mainz's city park is a lush setting for this amenity-filled hotel about a half hour away from the Old Town. **Pros:** quiet location; friendly staff; good views. **Cons:** a bit far from the sights; you can hear the train from some rooms; standard rooms do not have air-conditioning. $ *Rooms from: €145* ⌧ *Karl-Weiser-Str. 1* ☎ *06131/80150* ⊕ *www.favorite-mainz.de* �》 *Favorite restaurant closed Mon. and Tues.* ↻ *115 rooms, 7 suites* ⊙ *Breakfast.*

$$$$
HOTEL
FAMILY
Fodor's Choice
★

Hyatt Regency Mainz. From the spacious atrium lobby to the luxurious rooms and spa, everything is sleek, modern, and comfortable at this award-winning hotel. **Pros:** grand public spaces; friendly staff; riverside location; 24-hour room service. **Cons:** expensive; breakfast costs €29. $ *Rooms from: €229* ⌧ *Malakoff-Terrasse 1* ☎ *06131/731–234* ⊕ *www.mainz.regency.hyatt.com* ↻ *265 rooms, 3 suites* ⊙ *No meals.*

$
HOTEL

Ibis Mainz City. Here you'll find modern and functional rooms and a great location on the edge of the Old Town. **Pros:** central location; good rates and deals; air-conditioning in all rooms; free Wi-Fi. **Cons:** chain hotel lacking in character; €9 per night for garage parking (when space is available). $ *Rooms from: €58* ⌧ *Holzhofstr. 2* ☎ *06131/2470* ⊕ *www.ibishotel.com* ↻ *144 rooms* ⊙ *Breakfast.*

NIGHTLIFE AND PERFORMING ARTS

Mainz supports a broad spectrum of cultural events—classical as well as avant-garde music, dance, opera, and theater performances—at many venues throughout the city. Music lovers can attend concerts in venues ranging from the cathedral and the Rathaus to the market square and historic churches.

Nightlife centers on its numerous *Weinstuben* (wine taverns). Rustic and cozy, they're packed with locals who come to enjoy a meal or snack with a glass (or more) of local wine—expect to share your table when they're busy. Most are on the Old Town's main street, Augustinerstrasse, and its side streets (Grebenstrasse, Kirschgarten, Kartäuserstrasse, Jakobsbergstrasse).

10

Doctor Flotte. It offers a full menu of regional favorites, but this friendly Weinstube, with its small, leafy courtyard, is more of a pub than the other wine taverns in town, so there's no pressure to order dinner and there's a good selection of beers as well as wines. However, a dish of tasty *Spundekäs* (cream cheese with onions, paprika, and garlic) with crunchy pretzels goes down very well with a tall glass of beer. ⊠ *Kirschgarten 21* ☎ *06131/234–170.*

Weinhaus Wilhelmi. Over 120 years old, this tiny, wood-paneled pub close to the river is a favorite with postcollegiates, who come to enjoy glasses of local wine while nibbling on traditional sausage and cheeses or heartier fare such as fried pork steak with onions, or, in spring, schnitzel with white asparagus. ⊠ *Rheinstr. 53* ☎ *06131/224–949* ⊕ *www.weinhaus-wilhelmi.de* ⊗ *No lunch.*

SHOPPING

The Old Town is full of boutiques selling clothes, jewelry, and gifts, and the shopping district stretches between Schillerplatz, the Marktplatz, Höfchen, and **Am Brand,** an ancient marketplace that is now a pedestrian zone full of clothes stores.

Fodor's Choice
★
Gutenberg-Shop. The Gutenberg-Shop in the building of the local newspaper, *Allgemeine Zeitung Mainz,* offers splendid souvenirs and gifts, including pages from the Bible, books, posters, pens, and stationery. The friendly staff will also arrange to ship your purchases outside the country. There's a similar selection at the shop in the Gutenberg Museum. ⊠ *Markt 17* ☎ *06131/143–666* ⊕ *www.gutenberg-shop.de* ⊗ *Closed Sun.*

Krempelmarkt. Antiques and perhaps a few hidden treasures await the patient shopper at Krempelmarkt. The flea market is on the banks of the Rhine (Rheinufer) between the Hilton hotel and Kaiserstrasse. At the Theodor Heuss Bridge is the children's flea market, where the youngest sellers offer clothes, toys, and books. ⊠ *Rheinufer.*

Römerpassage. This city-center shopping mall offers a standard selection of German chain stores, cafés, and kiosks, but if you're a keen chef then go upstairs to kitchen store *cookmal!* to pick up excellent-quality cooking utensils or a traditional German clay cooking pot (a *Römertopf*). The Römerpassage also houses the remains of a Roman temple (AD 1) discovered in 1999 during the construction of the mall. The temple, which is dedicated to the goddess Isis and Magna Mater, is in the basement and can be visited during mall opening times (donation requested). ⊠ *Adolf-Kolping-Str. 4* ☎ *06131/600–7100* ⊕ *www.roemerpassage.com* ⊗ *Closed Sun.*

THE RHINELAND

WELCOME TO THE RHINELAND

TOP REASONS TO GO

★ **Drachenfels:** This dramatic castle in Königswinter crowns a high hill overlooking the Rhine.

★ **Fastnacht:** Germany's Carnival season culminates with huge parades, round-the-clock music, and dancing in Düsseldorf, Köln, and Mainz the week before Ash Wednesday.

★ **Rhine in Flames:** These massive displays of fireworks take place the first Saturday in May in Linz-Bonn; the first Saturday in July in Bingen-Rüdesheim; the second Saturday in August in Koblenz; the second Saturday in September in Oberwesel; and the third Saturday in September in St. Goar.

★ **The romance of the Rhine:** From cruises to Rhine-view rooms, castles to terraced vineyards, the Rhine does not disappoint.

★ **Spectacular wine:** A whole culinary tradition has grown up around the distinctive light white wines of the Rhine and Mosel.

1 The Rheingau. Though the course of the Rhine is generally south to north, it bends sharply at Wiesbaden and flows east to west for 31 km (19 miles) to Rüdesheim. This means that the steep hills on its right bank have a southern exposure, and that vineyards there produce superb wines.

2 The Mittelrhein. The romance of the Rhine is most apparent in the Middle Rhine, from Bingen to Koblenz. The 65-km (40-mile) stretch of the Upper Middle Rhine Valley was designated a UNESCO World Heritage Site in 2002 with its concentration of awesome castles, medieval towns, and the vineyards of the Rhine Gorge.

3 The Mosel Valley. Koblenz and Trier aren't very far apart as the crow flies, but the driving distance along the incredible twists and turns of the Mosel River is 201 km (125 miles). The journey is worth it, though. The region is unspoiled, the towns gemlike, the scenery a medley of vineyards and forests, and there's a wealth of Roman artifacts, medieval churches, and castle ruins to admire.

4 Bonn and the Köln (Cologne) lowlands. North of Koblenz, the Rhine is less picturesque, but it does shoulder the cosmopolitan cities Köln and Düsseldorf, as well as the former capital city of Bonn.

GETTING ORIENTED

The most spectacular stretch of the Rhineland is along the Middle Rhine, between Mainz and Koblenz, which takes in the awesome castles and vineyards of the Rhine Gorge. Highways hug the river on each bank (B-42 on the north and eastern sides, and B-9 on the south and western sides), and car ferries crisscross the Rhine at many points. Cruises depart from many cities and towns, including as far south as Frankfurt. Trains service all the towns, and the Mainz–Bonn route provides river views all the way.

Willroth
A3
Neuwied A48
Bendorf
9
Koblenz
Winningen
Braubach Pohl
A61 Boppard
B260 B54
St. Goar
2 Kemel
Oberwesel Kaub
Bacharach
A3
Wiesbaden
Eltville
B9 **Rüdesheim** A60 **Mainz**
B50
A61 Bingen
Rüdesheim A63
Laubenheim

Updated by
Dan Allen

The banks of the Rhine are crowned by magnificent castle after castle and by breathtaking, vine-terraced hills that provide the livelihood for many of the villages hugging the shores. In the words of French poet Victor Hugo, "The Rhine combines everything. The Rhine is swift as the Rhône, wide as the Loire, winding as the Seine . . . royal as the Danube and covered with fables and phantoms like a river in Asia."

The importance of the Rhine can hardly be overestimated. Although not the longest river in Europe (the Danube is more than twice as long), the Rhine has been the main river-trade artery between the heart of the continent and the North Sea (and Atlantic Ocean) throughout recorded history. The Rhine runs 1,230 km (764 miles) from the Bodensee (Lake Constance) west to Basel, then north through Germany, and, finally, west through the Netherlands to Rotterdam.

Vineyards, a legacy of the Romans, are an inherent part of the Rhine landscape from Wiesbaden to Bonn. The Rhine tempers the climate sufficiently for grapes to ripen this far north, and the world's finest Rieslings come from the Rheingau and from the Rhine's most important tributary, the Mosel. Thanks to the river, these wines were shipped far beyond the borders of Germany, giving rise to the wine trade that shaped the fortune of many riverside towns. Rüdesheim, Bingen, Koblenz, and Köln (Cologne) remain important commercial wine centers to this day.

The river is steeped in legend and myth. The Loreley, a jutting sheer slate cliff, was once believed to be the home of a beautiful and bewitching maiden who lured boatmen to a watery end in the swift currents. Heinrich Heine's poem *Song of Loreley* (1827), inspired by Clemens Brentano's *Legend of Loreley* (1812) and set to music in 1837 by Friedrich Silcher, has been the theme song of the landmark ever since. The Nibelungen, a legendary Burgundian people said to have lived on the banks of the Rhine, serve as subjects for Wagner's epic opera cycle *Der Ring des Nibelungen* (1852–72).

11

William Turner captured misty Rhine sunsets on canvas. Famous literary works, such as Goethe's *Sankt-Rochus-Fest zu Bingen* (*The Feast of St. Roch*; 1814), Lord Byron's *Childe Harold's Pilgrimage* (1816), and Mark Twain's *A Tramp Abroad* (1880), captured the spirit of Rhine Romanticism on paper, encouraging others to follow in their footsteps.

PLANNING

WHEN TO GO

The peak season for cultural, food, and wine festivals is March–mid-November, followed by colorful Christmas markets in December. The season for many hotels, restaurants, riverboats, cable cars, and sights is from Easter through October, particularly in smaller towns. Opening hours at many castles, churches, and small museums are shorter in winter. Orchards blossom in March, and the vineyards are verdant from May until late September, when the vines turn a shimmering gold.

GETTING HERE AND AROUND

AIR TRAVEL

The Rhineland is served by three international airports: Frankfurt, Düsseldorf, and Köln-Bonn. Bus and rail lines connect each airport with its respective downtown area and provide rapid access to the rest of the region. There are direct trains from the Frankfurt airport to downtown Köln and Düsseldorf.

No-frills carriers that fly within Europe are based at smaller Frankfurt-Hahn Airport in Lautzenhausen, between the Rhine and Mosel valleys (a one-hour drive from Wiesbaden or Trier; a 90-minute bus ride from Frankfurt Airport). The Luxembourg Findel International Airport (a 30-minute drive from Trier) is close to the upper Mosel River valley.

Airport Contacts Flughafen Düsseldorf. ☎ *0211/4210* ⊕ *www.dus. com.* **Flughafen Frankfurt.** ☎ *01806/372–4636* ⊕ *www.frankfurt-airport. com.* **Flughafen Frankfurt-Hahn.** ☎ *06543/509–200* ⊕ *www.hahn-airport.de.* **Flughafen Köln/Bonn.** ☎ *02203/404–001* ⊕ *www.koeln-bonn-airport.de.* **Luxembourg Findel International Airport.** ☎ *00352/24640* ⊕ *www.lux-airport.lu.*

CRUISE TRAVEL

While the fastest way to get around the region is by car or train, the Rhine and Mosel Rivers have been navigated by ship for thousands of years, and this option remains the most scenic, not to mention the safest for visitors looking to drink wine while soaking up a little history. The Rhine is the more popular of the two rivers, but many find its little sister, the Mosel, even more beautiful with its narrow, twisting landscapes.

Many Rhine trips are available from Köln and Düsseldorf, but the river doesn't truly turn scenic until south of Bonn. The most popular starting point is Koblenz, where the Rhine and Mosel converge. The area between Koblenz and Bingen, the Rhine Gorge, offers the shortest cruises with the highest concentration of castles.

Trips along the Rhine and Mosel range in length from a few hours to days or weeks. Day-trippers don't generally need advance reservations, and the tourist offices in any major Rhine or Mosel town can provide information about short round-trip cruises (*Rundfahrten*) or hop-on/hop-off waterbuses (*Linienfahrten*), which generally run on the Rhine daily from Easter to late October and on the Mosel from June through September. Some multiday cruises also make extra trips in November and December to stop at Christmas markets.

MULTIDAY CRUISES **CroisiEurope.** Europe's largest river cruise line, this French company offers numerous affordable multiday cabin cruises on both the Rhine and Mosel. ☎ *800/768–7232 in U.S.* ⊕ *www.croisieuroperivercruises.com.*

Uniworld. A variety of multiday luxury cabin cruises are offered on both the Rhine and Mosel. ☎ *800/257–2407 in U.S.* ⊕ *www.uniworld.com.*

Viking River Cruises. Multiday luxury cabin cruises sail between Amsterdam and Basel and between Basel and Paris. ☎ *800/706–1483 in U.S.,* ⊕ *www.vikingrivercruises.com.*

SHORT CRUISES **Bingen-Rüdesheimer.** Short Loreley and castle cruises along the Middle Rhine are available, plus ferry service between Bingen and Rüdesheim. ☎ *06721/14140* ⊕ *www.bingen-ruedesheimer.de.*

Köln-Düsseldorfer Deutsche Rheinschiffahrt (*KD Rhine Line*). One of the region's most popular short-journey lines, this company offers day trips and water taxi service on the Rhine and Main between Köln and Mainz, and on the Mosel between Koblenz and Cochem. There's a 20% discount for German Rail Pass holders. ☎ *0221/208–8318* ⊕ *www.k-d.com.*

Mosel-Schiffstouristic Hans Michels. Short cruises on the middle Mosel mostly begin at Bernkastel and last about two hours. ☎ *06531/8222* ⊕ *www.mosel-personenschifffahrt.de.*

Personenschifffahrt Kolb. Cruising mostly shorter stretches of the Mosel between Koblenz and Trier, Kolb also offers day trips and combination tickets that include city tours on land. ☎ *02673/1515* ⊕ *www.moselfahrplan.de.*

Personenschifffahrt Merkelbach. Castle cruises on the Rhine run from Koblenz to Schloss Stolzenfels (60 mins) or to the Marksburg (100 mins). ☎ *0261/76810* ⊕ *www.merkelbach-personenschiffe.de.*

Primus-Linie. Frankfurt-originating short cruises call at the Loreley and Rüdesheim/St. Goarshausen. ☎ *069/133–8370* ⊕ *www.primus-linie.de.*

Rheinschifffahrt Hölzenbein. This is a Koblenz-based line, with regular short Rhine cruises to Rüdesheim. ☎ *0261/37744* ⊕ *www.hoelzenbein.de.*

Rösslerlinie. Rhine castle and Loreley day cruises depart from Rüdesheim. ☎ *06722/2353* ⊕ *www.roesslerlinie.de.*

TRAIN TRAVEL

InterCity and EuroCity expresses connect all the cities and towns of the area. Hourly InterCity routes run between Düsseldorf, Köln, Bonn, and Mainz, with most services extending as far south as Munich and as far north as Hamburg. German Rail Passes are valid on these and all Deutsche Bahn trains; passes come in many configurations and include Rhineland-specific bonuses like discounts on KD Rhine Line cruises. The city transportation networks of Bonn, Köln, and Düsseldorf are linked by S-bahn, regional, and local trains (for information contact the KVB).

Train Contacts **Deutsche Bahn.** ☎ *01806/996–633* ⊕ *www.bahn.de.* **German Rail Pass.** ⊕ *www.germanrailpasses.com.* **Kölner Verkehrs-Betriebe** (*KVB*). ☎ *01806/504-030* ⊕ *www.kvb-koeln.de.*

RESTAURANTS

Although Düsseldorf, Köln, and Wiesbaden are home to many talented chefs, some of Germany's most creative classic and contemporary cooking is found in smaller towns or country inns.

Prices in the reviews are the average cost of a main course at dinner, or if dinner is not served, at lunch.

HOTELS

The most romantic places to lay your head are the old riverside inns and castle hotels. Ask for a *Rheinblick* (Rhine-view) room. Hotels are often booked well in advance, especially for festivals and when there are trade fairs in Köln, Düsseldorf, or Frankfurt, making rooms even in Wiesbaden and the Rheingau scarce and expensive. Many hotels close for winter.

Prices in the reviews are the lowest cost of a standard double room in high season. For expanded reviews, facilities, and current deals, visit Fodors.com.

WHAT IT COSTS IN EUROS			
	$	$$	$$$	$$$$
Restaurants	under €15	€15–€20	€21–€25	over €25
Hotels	under €100	€100–€175	€176–€225	over €225

PLANNING YOUR TIME

Those seeking "Rhine romance" should probably concentrate on its southern part, particularly the Rhine Gorge, with its castles, vineyards, and the Loreley. If nightlife and culture are your preferences, you'll like the cathedral city of Köln and cosmopolitan Düsseldorf; you can still take a day cruise along the Rhine from Köln.

VISITOR INFORMATION

Rheingau–Taunus Kultur & Tourismus. ⊠ *Pfortenhaus-Kloster Eberbach, Eltville* ☎ *06723/99550* ⊕ *www.kulturland-rheingau.de.*

Rheinland-Pfalz Tourismus. ⊠ *Löhrstr. 103–105, Koblenz* ☎ *01805/757–4636* ⊕ *www.romantic-germany.info.*

THE RHEINGAU

The heart of the region begins in Wiesbaden, where the Rhine makes a sharp bend and flows east to west for some 30 km (19 miles) before resuming its south to north course at Rüdesheim. Wiesbaden is a good starting point for touring any of the well-marked cycling, hiking, and driving routes through the Rheingau's villages and vineyards.

■TIP➜ **Nearly every Rheingau village has an outdoor Weinprobierstand (wine-tasting stand), usually near the riverbank. It is staffed and stocked by a different wine estate every weekend in summer.**

EATING WELL IN THE RHINELAND

The Rhineland's regional cuisine features fresh fish and *Wild* (game), as well as sauces and soups based on the local Riesling and Spätburgunder (Pinot Noir) wines. Boiled beef, once known in the region as *Tellerfleisch* ("dish meat") or *Ochsenbrust* (brisket), is nowadays called by the more familiar Austrian name *Tafelspitz*. *Rheinischer Sauerbraten* (Rhenish marinated pot roast in a sweet-and-sour raisin gravy) is another traditional favorite. The *Kartoffel* (potato) is prominent in soups, *Reibekuchen* and *Rösti* (potato pancakes), and *Dibbe*-or *Dippekuchen* (dialect: *Döppekoche*), a casserole baked in a cast-iron pot and served with apple compote. *Himmel und Erde*, literally "heaven and earth," is a mixture of mashed potatoes and chunky applesauce, topped with panfried slices of blood sausage and onions.

The region is known for its wines: Riesling is the predominant white grape, and Spätburgunder the most important red variety in the Rheingau, Mittelrhein, and Mosel wine regions , *all covered in this chapter*. Three abutting wine regions—Rheinhessen and the Nahe, near Bingen, and the Ahr, southwest of Bonn—add to the variety of wines available along the route.

Wines of Germany, aka the German Wine Institute, provides background information and brochures about all German wine-producing regions. Tips on wine-related events and package offers are available from regional wine-information offices, and any visitor-information center along the Rhine and Mosel will put you in touch with local winegrowers.

WINE INFORMATION
Wines of Germany. ☎ *212/994–7523* ⊕ *www.germanwineusa.com, www.germanwines.de.*

WIESBADEN

40 km (25 miles) west of Frankfurt.

Wiesbaden, the capital of the state of Hesse, is a small city of tree-lined avenues with elegant shops and handsome facades. Its hot mineral springs have been a drawing card since the days when it was known as Aquis Mattiacis ("the waters of the Mattiaci")—the words boldly inscribed on the portal of the Kurhaus—and Wisibada ("the bath in the meadow").

In the 1st century AD the Romans built thermal baths here, a site then inhabited by a Germanic tribe, the Mattiaci. Modern Wiesbaden dates from the 19th century, when the dukes of Nassau and, later, the Prussian aristocracy commissioned the grand public buildings and parks that shape the city's profile today. Wiesbaden developed into a fashionable spa that attracted the rich and the famous. Their ornate villas on the Neroberg and turn-of-the-20th-century town houses are part of the city's flair.

GETTING HERE AND AROUND
If you're driving, take the A-66 from Frankfurt.

THermine. For a one-hour ride through the city, board this little train. A one-day ticket enables you to get on and off as often as you like to explore the sights. From April through October, and late November to mid-December, it departs numerous times daily, 10–4:30, from Café Lumen (behind the Marktkirche), and stops at the Greek Chapel and the Neroberg train station. In March and November it operates on weekends. ☎ *0611/5893–9464* ⊕ *www.thermine.de* 🎫 *€8 for all-day ticket.*

Walking Tours. English-language guided walking tours of Wiesbaden lasting about 90 minutes depart from the tourist-information office every Saturday at 2, June through September. 🎫 *€9.*

ESSENTIALS
Visitor Information Wiesbaden Tourist-Information. ✉ *Marktpl. 1* ☎ *0611/172–9930* ⊕ *www.wiesbaden.eu.*

EXPLORING
TOP ATTRACTIONS
Altstadt. Called *Schiffchen* (Little Ship) for its boatlike shape, Wiesbaden's pretty Old Town is packed with restaurants, cafés, shops, and goldsmith workshops. It's located just behind the Stadtschloss (a former duke's palace, now the seat of state parliament, the Hessischer Landtag) on Grabenstrasse, Wagemannstrasse, and Goldgasse. ✉ *Wiesbaden.*

Fodor'sChoice ★ **Kurhaus.** Built in 1907, the neoclassical Kurhaus is the cultural center of town. It houses the casino and the Thiersch-Saal, a splendid setting for concerts. The Staatstheater (1894), opulently appointed in baroque and rococo revival styles, and two beautifully landscaped parks flank the Kurhaus. ✉ *Kurhauspl. 1* ⊕ *www.wiesbaden.de/kurhaus.*

WORTH NOTING
Kochbrunnen Fountain. Fifteen of Wiesbaden's 26 springs converge at the steaming Kochbrunnen Fountain, where the sulfurous but at least theoretically healthful waters are there for the tasting. ✉ *Kochbrunnenpl.*

Marktplatz (*Market Square*). Historic buildings ring the Schlossplatz (Palace Square) and the adjoining Marktplatz, site of the annual Rheingau Wine Festival (mid-August) and Christmas market (December). The farmers' market (Wednesday and Saturday) takes place behind the neo-Gothic brick Marktkirche (Market Church). ✉ *Marktpl.*

Museum Wiesbaden. Nature and culture come together under one roof at the Museum Wiesbaden. The natural history section exhibits a wealth of geological finds and preserved animals, and the art collection ranges from 12th-century polychromes to present-day installations. The museum is best known for its expressionist paintings, particularly the works of Russian artist Alexej Jawlensky. ✉ *Friedrich-Ebert-Allee 2* ☎ *0611/335–2250* ⊕ *www.museum-wiesbaden.de* 🎫 *€6* ☉ *Tues. and Thurs. 10–8, Wed. and Fri.–Sun. 10–5.*

WHERE TO EAT
$$$$
ECLECTIC
✕ **Käfer's Bistro.** This popular bistro with a striking art nouveau interior, a grand piano (live music nightly), and a good-size bar attracts an upscale clientele. Book a table for two in one of the window alcoves (Nos. 7, 12, 25, and 29) at least four weeks in advance for some privacy among the otherwise close-set tables. *Lachstatar* (salmon tartare) and

Bauernente (farmer's duck) are standard favorites. A few champagnes are available by the glass and bottle. Käfer's also caters the beer garden behind the Kurhaus and the Bowling Green's terrace with concerts in summer. $ *Average main: €26* ⊠ *Kurhauspl. 1* ☎ *0611/536–200* ⊕ *www.kurhaus-gastronomie.de* ⌀ *Reservations essential.*

$$
ECLECTIC

✕ **Sherry & Port.** Austrian expat Gerd Royko's friendly neighborhood bistro hosts live music on Friday and Saturday from October through March. During warm months, you can dine at outdoor tables surrounding a fountain on tree-lined Adolfsallee. In addition to the fantastic number of sherries and ports (60), there are more than 20 malt whiskies served by the glass. There is also a good selection of beers and wines to accompany the menu's tapas, salads, steaks, and well-priced daily specials. $ *Average main: €18* ⊠ *Adolfsallee 11* ☎ *0611/373–632* ⊕ *www. sherry-und-port.de* ▭ *No credit cards.*

WHERE TO STAY

$
HOTEL

Hotel de France. Behind this 1880 facade is a lovingly restored hotel and a new high-end restaurant, both with sleek, modern furnishings and lots of fresh flowers. **Pros:** centrally located. **Cons:** on a busy street; some rooms are small. $ *Rooms from: €89* ⊠ *Taunusstr. 49* ☎ *0611/959–730* ⊕ *www.hoteldefrance.de* ⤳ *34 rooms, 3 suites* ⦿ *Breakfast.*

$$$
HOTEL

Hotel Nassauer Hof. Wiesbaden's premier address for well over a century boasts luxuriously appointed rooms, top-flight service, and three restaurants—and a guest list ranging from Dostoyevsky to the Dalai Lama. **Pros:** nice location opposite the Kurhaus; warm spring-fed pool. **Cons:** expensive; breakfast is not included and costs €32. $ *Rooms from: €215* ⊠ *Kaiser-Friedrich-Pl. 3–4* ☎ *0611/1330* ⊕ *www.nassauer-hof.de* ⤳ *136 rooms, 23 suites* ⦿ *No meals.*

$
HOTEL

ibis Wiesbaden City. This modern hotel opposite the Kochbrunnen on Kranzplatz is an excellent value and has a location within walking distance of the shop-filled pedestrian zone, the Old Town, and all sights. **Pros:** bar stays open 24 hours; four wheelchair-accessible rooms. **Cons:** small rooms; breakfast not included. $ *Rooms from: €65* ⊠ *Georg-August-Zinn-Str. 2* ☎ *0611/36140* ⊕ *www.ibishotel.com* ⤳ *131 rooms* ⦿ *No meals.*

$$
HOTEL
Fodor's Choice
★

Town Hotel. Its central location (a five-minute walk from the Kurhaus, Old Town, and shopping district), particularly friendly and helpful staff, and affordability make the Gerbers' modern hotel an excellent Wiesbaden choice. **Pros:** a good deal; free telephone calls to North America and most of Europe. **Cons:** often full during the week. $ *Rooms from: €119* ⊠ *Spiegelg. 5* ☎ *0611/360–160* ⊕ *www.townhotel.de* ⤳ *24 rooms* ⦿ *No meals.*

NIGHTLIFE AND PERFORMING ARTS

In addition to the casino, restaurants, bars, and beer garden at the Kurhaus, nightlife is centered on the many bistros and pubs on Taunusstrasse and in the Old Town. The tourist office provides schedules and sells tickets for most venues listed here.

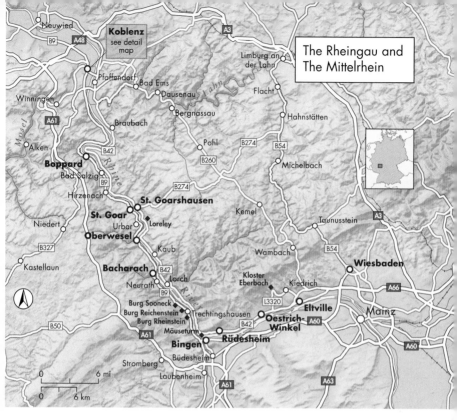

The Rheingau and The Mittelrhein

NIGHTLIFE

CASINO   **Spielbank** (*Casino*). The Klassische Spiel (roulette and blackjack) in the Kurhaus is one of Europe's grand casinos, open daily 2:45 pm to 3 am (4 am weekends, jacket required). The less formal Automatenspiel (slots and poker) in the neighboring Kolonnade is open from noon to 4 am. To enter either, you must be at least 18 (bring your passport). ⊠ *Kurhauspl. 1* ☎ *0611/536–100* ⊕ *www.spielbank-wiesbaden.de.*

PERFORMING ARTS

CONCERTS   **Kurhaus.** The Hessian State Orchestra performs several programs a year at the Kurhaus. ⊠ *Kurhauspl. 1* ☎ *0611/17290.*

Marktkirche. Many churches offer concerts, including the free organ recitals that are held Saturday at 11:30 am in the Marktkirche. ⊠ *Schlosspl. 4* ☎ *0611/900–1611* ⊕ *www.marktkirche-wiesbaden.de.*

THEATERS AND   **Hessisches Staatstheater.** Classical and contemporary opera, theater, bal-
ARTS CENTERS   let, and musicals are presented on the Hessisches Staatstheater's four stages: Grosses Haus, Kleines Haus, Studio, and Wartburg. ⊠ *Chr.-Zais-Str. 3* ☎ *0611/132–325* ⊕ *www.staatstheater-wiesbaden.de.*

Thalhaus. In addition to having an art gallery and theater, this lively multiarts venue has featured music performances, cabaret revues (sometimes performed in drag), and the occasional dance party. ⊠ *Nerotal 18* ☎ *0611/185–1267* ⊕ *www.thalhaus.de.*

SHOPPING

Broad, tree-lined Wilhelmstrasse, with designer boutiques housed in its fin de siècle buildings, is one of Germany's most elegant shopping streets. Wiesbaden is also known as one of the best places in the country to find antiques; Taunusstrasse and Nerostrasse have excellent antiques shops. The Altstadt is full of upscale boutiques; Kirchgasse and its extension, Langgasse, are the heart of the shops-filled pedestrian zone.

THERMAL SPRINGS, SPAS, AND POOLS

Kaiser-Friedrich-Therme. Pamper yourself with the thermal-spring and cold-water pools, various steam baths and saunas, two solaria, and a score of health- and wellness treatments in elegant art nouveau surroundings. Towels and robes can be rented on-site, but come prepared for bathing nude. Children under 16 are not admitted. On Tuesday the facility is for women only. ⊠ *Langg. 38–40* ☎ *0611/317–060* 🖃 *€6.50 per hr, Sept.–Apr.; €5 per hr, May–Aug.* ☉ *Sept.–Apr., Mon.–Thurs. 10–10, Fri. and Sat. 10 am–midnight; May–Aug., daily 10–10.*

Thermalbad Aukammtal. There's year-round swimming indoors and out thanks to the thermal springs (32°C [90°F]) that feed the pools here. The facility includes seven saunas, a whirlpool, massage, and various other treatments. ⊠ *Leibnizstr. 7* ⊹ *Bus No. 18 from Wilhelmstr. to Aukamm Valley* ☎ *0611/317–080* 🖃 *Pools €10, saunas €20, combined ticket €24* ☉ *Sun., Mon., Wed., and Thurs. 8 am–10 pm; Tues. 6 am–10 pm; Fri. and Sat. 8 am–midnight.*

ELTVILLE

14 km (9 miles) west of Wiesbaden.

The largest town in the Rheingau, Eltville rose to prominence in the Middle Ages as the residence of the archbishops of Mainz. Today it's cherished for its wine and roses, which are celebrated most colorfully during its *Rosentage* (Rose Days), held the first weekend of June.

Burg Crass (Crass Castle), located on the riverbank, is well worth a look, as are the half-timber houses and aristocratic manors on the lanes between the river and Rheingauer Strasse (B-42), notably the Bechtermünzer Hof (Kirchgasse 6), Stockheimer Hof (Ellenbogengasse 6), and Eltzer Hof (at the Martinstor gateway).

There are a number of prominent wineries in the area, and some offer tours and tastings. The Nussbrunnen, Wisselbrunnen, and Marcobrunn estates get their name from the *Brunnen* (wells) that are beneath the vineyards.

GETTING HERE AND AROUND

Just 9 miles from Wiesbaden, via A-66 and B-42, and 12 from Mainz via A-643, Eltville is easily accessible by road, rail, or bus service via RTV (Rheingau-Taunus-Verkehrsgesellschaft).

ESSENTIALS

Bus RTV. ☎ *06124/726–5914* ⊕ *www.r-t-v.de.*

Visitor Information Eltville Tourist Information. ⊠ *Kurfürstliche Burg, Burgstr. 1* ☎ *06123/90980* ⊕ *www.eltville.de.*

EXPLORING
TOP ATTRACTIONS

Fodor'sChoice ★ **Kloster Eberbach.** The former Cistercian monastery is idyllically set in a secluded forest clearing 3 km (2 miles) west of Kiedrich. Its Romanesque and Gothic buildings (12th–14th century) look untouched by time—one reason why the 1986 film of Umberto Eco's medieval murder mystery *The Name of the Rose* was filmed here. The monastery's impressive collection of old winepresses bears witness to a viticultural tradition that spans nearly nine centuries. The wines can be sampled year-round in the **Vinothek** or restaurant on the grounds. The church, with its excellent acoustics, and the large medieval dormitories are the settings for concerts, wine auctions, and festive wine events. ⊠ *Stiftung Kloster Eberbach* ☎ *06723/917–8115* ⊕ *www.klostereberbach.de* ⊠ *€8* ⊙ *Apr.–Oct., daily 10–6; Nov.–Mar., daily 11–5.*

Kurfürstliche Burg (*Electors' Castle*). Eltville flourished as a favorite residence of the archbishops of Mainz in the 14th and 15th centuries, and it was during this time that the castle—which now houses Eltville's tourist-information center—was built. More than 300 varieties of roses grow in the castle's courtyard garden, on the wall, and along the Rhine promenade. During "Rose Days" (the first weekend in June) the flower is celebrated in shops and restaurants (as an ingredient in recipes) throughout town. ⊠ *Burgstr. 1* ☎ *06123/909–840* ⊕ *www.eltville. de* ⊠ *Tower €3, rose garden free* ⊙ *Tower: Apr.–Oct., Mon., Tues., and Thurs. 10–1 and 2–5, Wed. 2–5, Fri. 10–1 and 2–6, weekends 10–6. Garden: Apr.–Sept., daily 9:30–7; Oct.–March, daily 10–5.*

WORTH NOTING

Kiedrich. For a good look at the central Rheingau, make a brief circular tour from Eltville. Drive 3 km (2 miles) north via the Kiedricher Strasse to the Gothic village of Kiedrich. In the distance you can see the tower of Scharfenstein Castle (built in 1215) and the spires of St. Valentine's Basilica and St. Michael's Chapel, both from the 15th century. If you attend the basilica's 9:30 am mass on Sunday, you can admire the splendid Gothic furnishings and star vaulting to the sounds of Gregorian chants and one of Germany's oldest organs, and public tours of the church begin just after every mass. The chapel next door, once a charnel house (a building near a cemetery used for storing dug-up bones), has a unique chandelier sculpted around a nearly life-size, two-sided Madonna. These Gothic gems have survived intact thanks to 19th-century restorations sponsored by the English baronet John Sutton.

Weingut Robert Weil. Built by the English aristrocrat John Sutton, this beautiful villa south of St. Valentine's Church is home to one of Germany's leading wine estates. Its famed Rieslings can be sampled in the tasting room. ⊠ *Mühlberg 5, Kiedrich* ☎ *06123/2308* ⊕ *www. weingut-robert-weil.com* ⊙ *Weekdays 8–5:30, Sat. 10–5, Sun. 11–5.*

Sts. Peter and Paul. The parish church of Saints Peter and Paul has late-Gothic frescoes, Renaissance tombstones, and a carved baptismal likely created by the Rhenish sculptor Hans Backoffen. ⊠ *Roseng.*

Steinberg. Kloster Eberbach's premier vineyard, the high-tech Steinberg, is surrounded by a 3-km (2-mile) stone wall (13th–18th century). In

Kloster Eberbach, a former Cistercian monastery, is worth a stop for its well-preserved architecture and its winery.

warmer months you can enjoy its vintages outdoors, overlooking the vines. ✉ *Domäne Steinberg* ✥ *From Eberbach, take the road toward Hattenheim, stopping at the first right-hand turnoff* 🌐 *www.kloster-eberbach.de/en/wine-estate/das-weingut-seine-domaenen/domaene-steinberg.html* 🎫 *Wine cellar tour €10, includes three tastings* ⏲ *Guided wine cellar tour Apr.–Oct., weekends at 1 and 3; Nov.–Mar., Sun. at 2.*

WHERE TO EAT

$$ GERMAN 🍴 **Gutsausschank im Baiken.** This restaurant is on a hilltop amid the Rauenthaler Baiken vineyard. The panorama from the vine-canopied terrace, the regional cooking, and local wines make for a complete "Rheingau Riesling" experience. [$] *Average main: €20* ✉ *Wiesweg 86* ☎ *06123/900–345* 🌐 *www.baiken.de* ⏲ *Closed Feb. and Mon.; also closed Tues. and Wed. Nov.–Mar. No lunch Tues.–Sat.*

$$ GERMAN 🍴 **Klosterschänke und Gästehaus Kloster Eberbach.** Beneath the vaulted ceiling of the Klosterschänke you can pair local wines with regional cuisine. Try the *Weinfleisch* (pork goulash in Riesling sauce) or *Zisterzienser Brot,* which translates to "Cistercian bread" (minced meat in a plum-and-bacon dressing with boiled potatoes). [$] *Average main: €16* ✉ *Kloster Eberbach* ✥ *Via Kiedrich or Hattenheim* ☎ *06723/993–299* 🌐 *www.klostereberbach.de* 💳 *No credit cards.*

$$$$ FRENCH Fodor's Choice ★ 🍴 **Kronenschlösschen.** The young chef here, who received a Michelin star in 2014, carries on the acclaimed culinary traditions that made this stylish and intimate art nouveau house one of the Rheingau's top restaurants. The wine list focuses on the finest local estates for whites, and Old and New World estates for reds. In warmer months, you can also enjoy sensational fish creations in the parklike garden. [$] *Average*

main: €32 ⊠ *Rheinallee* ⊹ *At Hattenheim* ☎ *06723/640* ⊕ *www.kronenschloesschen.de* ⊗ *No lunch.*

$$$$ ✕ **Schloss Reinhartshausen.** A palace in every sense of the word, this
GERMAN hotel and wine estate overlooks the Rhine and beautifully landscaped gardens. Antiques and artwork fill the house. You can enjoy breakfast, lunch, and afternoon tea with *Rieslingtorte* in the airy, glass-lined Wintergarten. Upscale dinners are served in the elegant Prinzess von Erbach. The less pricey Schloss Schänke, located in the winery courtyard, serves light fare and hearty snacks. The estate's wines are also sold daily in the Vinothek. $ *Average main: €32* ⊠ *Hauptstr. 41* ⊹ *In Erbach* ☎ *06123/6760* ⊕ *www.kempinski.com/en/eltville.*

$$$ ✕ **Zum Krug.** Winegrower Josef
GERMAN Laufer more than lives up to the hospitality promised by the wreath and *Krug* (an earthenware pitcher) hanging above the front door. The wood-paneled restaurant, with its old tiled stove, is cozy. The German fare includes wild duck, goose, game, or sauerbraten served in rich, flavorful sauces and gravies. The wine list is legendary for its scope (600 Rheingau wines) and selection of older vintages. In 2011, the former Hattenheim City Hall became part of Zum Krug's Rheingau-themed inn, nearly doubling its rooms to 15. $ *Average main: €23* ⊠ *Hauptstr. 34* ⊹ *In Hattenheim* ☎ *06723/99680* ⊕ *www.hotel-zum-krug.de* ⊗ *Closed 4 wks in Dec. and Jan. and 2 wks in July and Aug.*

WHERE TO STAY

$$ ⌑ **Weinhotel Hof Bechtermünz.** Set within a 15th-century structure on
HOTEL Eltville's Weingut Koegler complex, Weinhotel Hof Bechtermünz brings modern style to its historic setting (Johannes Gutenberg printed the world's first dictionary here in 1467). **Pros:** historic and central setting; delicious wine selection. **Cons:** no air-conditioning. $ *Rooms from: €140* ⊠ *Kirchg. 5* ☎ *06123/2437* ⊕ *www.weingut-koegler.de/weinhotel* ⊟ *No credit cards* ⊅ *16 rooms* ⦿ *Breakfast.*

OESTRICH-WINKEL

21 km (13 miles) west of Wiesbaden, 7 km (4½ miles) west of Eltville.

Oestrich's vineyard area is the largest in the Rheingau. Lenchen and Doosberg are the most important vineyards. You can sample the wines at the outdoor wine-tasting stand, opposite the 18th-century wine-loading crane on the riverbank of Oestrich (nearly opposite Hotel Schwan).

GETTING HERE AND AROUND

By road from Wiesbaden or Eltville go west on B-42.

TAKE A HIKE!

The Rheinhöhenweg (Rhine Heights Path) gives its hikers splendid views and descents into the villages en route. These marked trails run between Oppenheim on the Rhine Terrace and Bonn for 240 km (149 miles) and between Wiesbaden and Bonn-Beuel for 272 km (169 miles). The most extensive hiking trail is the Rheinsteig, from Wiesbaden to Bonn on the right side of the Rhine. It comprises 320 km (199 miles) of well-marked paths that offer everything from easy walks to challenging stretches on a par with Alpine routes.

EXPLORING

Fodor's Choice ★ **Schloss Johannisberg.** The origins of this grand wine estate date from 1100, when Benedictine monks built a monastery and planted vines on the slopes below. The striking early-18th-century palace is closed to the public, but guided tours (by appointment) explore the winery and its remarkable cellars, and there are also tastings at the estate's restaurant. ✉ *Weinbaudomäne Schloss Johannisberg, Geisenheim* ✣ *From Winkel, turn off main street at Schillerstr. and drive north all the way uphill. After the road curves to the left, watch for the left turn to the castle* ☎ *06722/70090* 🌐 *www.schloss-johannisberg.de* 🕒 *Wineshop: Mar., Apr., and Oct., weekdays 10–6, weekends 11–6; May–Sept., weekdays 10–6, weekends 11–7; Nov.–Feb., weekdays 10–6, weekends 11–5.*

HESSIAN STATE WINE DOMAINS

Sekt (sparkling wine) production in the Rheingau is concentrated in Eltville, Wiesbaden, and Rüdesheim. The tree-lined Rhine promenade in Eltville hosts the annual Sekt festival during the first weekend of July. The administrative headquarters and main cellars of the Hessian State Wine Domains, Germany's largest wine estate, are in town. The estate owns about 500 acres of vineyards throughout the Rheingau and in the Hessische Bergstrasse wine region south of Frankfurt. Its shops in the early-Gothic hospital at Kloster Eberbach stock a comprehensive regional selection.

Fodor's Choice ★ **Schloss Vollrads.** Built in 1211, Schloss Vollrads is the oldest of Germany's major wine estates. The tower, built in 1330 and surrounded by a moat, was the Greiffenclau residence for 350 years until the present palace was built in the 17th century. There is a wineshop, and the castle's period rooms can be toured during concerts, festivals, and wine tastings. It's 3 km (2 miles) north of town. ✉ *Vollradser Allee* ✣ *North on Kirchstr., continue on Vollradser Allee* ☎ *06723/6626* 🌐 *www.schlossvollrads.com* 🕒 *Apr.–Oct., weekdays 9–6, weekends 11–7; Nov.–Mar., weekdays 9–5, weekends 11–4.*

WHERE TO EAT

$$ GERMAN 🍴 **Die Wirtschaft.** Beate and Florian Kreller give you a warm welcome to their historic building on Winkel's Hauptstrasse (main street). Local dishes are the specialty, with emphasis placed on fresh, local ingredients in season. Their fixed-price lunch (€9.50 for two courses and €11 for three) is a good deal. Fresh flowers and candles top the tables set in a labyrinth of cozy niches with exposed beams and old stone walls. No less inviting is the pretty courtyard. [$] *Average main: €15* ✉ *Hauptstr. 70, Winkel* ☎ *06723/7426* 🌐 *www.die-wirtschaft.net* 💳 *No credit cards* 🕒 *Closed Mon. and 2 wks in July and Aug. No dinner Sun.*

$$ MEDITERRANEAN Fodor's Choice ★ 🍴 **Gutsrestaurant Schloss Vollrads.** The seasonal German and light Mediterranean dishes on the menu are served with the estate's wines in the cavalier house (1650) or on the flower-lined terrace facing the garden. [$] *Average main: €20* ✉ *Schloss Vollrads, Vollradser Allee, north of Winkel* ☎ *06723/660* 🌐 *www.schlossvollrads.com/restaurant.html* 🕒 *Closed late Dec.–Apr. Closed Mon. and Tues. Nov.–mid-Dec., and Wed. May–Oct.*

$$ GERMAN 🍴 **Gutsschänke Schloss Johannisberg.** The glassed-in terrace affords a spectacular view of the Rhine and the vineyards where the wine you're drinking originated. Rheingau Riesling soup and *Bauernente* (farmer's duck) are among the house specialties. [$] *Average main: €20* ✉ *Schloss Johannisberg, Geisenheim* ☎ *06722/96090* 🌐 *www.schloss-johannisberg.de* ✍ *Reservations essential.*

WHERE TO STAY

$ B&B/INN Fodor's Choice ★ 🏨 **Hotel Schwan.** Owned by the Wenckstern family since it was built in 1628, this green-and-white half-timber inn offers considerable comfort, though the rooms in the guesthouse are simpler than in the historic main building. **Pros:** nice location right at the 18th-century crane on the river; outdoor wine stands. **Cons:** rooms in the guesthouse are plain. [$] *Rooms from: €89* ✉ *Rheinallee 5* ✣ *In Oestrich* ☎ *06723/8090* 🌐 *www.hotel-schwan.de* 🛏 *52 rooms, 3 suites* 🍴 *Breakfast.*

RÜDESHEIM

30 km (19 miles) west of Wiesbaden, 9 km (5½ miles) west of Oestrich-Winkel.

Tourism and wine are the heart and soul of Rüdesheim. With south-facing slopes reaching down to the riverbanks, wine growing has thrived here for 1,000 years. Since being discovered by English and German romanticists in the early 19th century for its picturesque solitude, Rüdesheim has long lost its quiet innocence, as the narrow, medieval alleys fill with boatloads of cheerful visitors from all over the world.

GETTING HERE AND AROUND

The town is on the B-42.

ESSENTIALS

Visitor Information Rüdesheim Tourist-Information. ✉ *Rheinstr. 29a* ☎ *06722/906–150* 🌐 *www.ruedesheim.de.*

EXPLORING

Drosselgasse (*Thrush Alley*). Less than 500 feet long, Drosselgasse is a narrow, pub-lined lane between Rheinstrasse and Oberstrasse that buzzes with music and merrymaking from noon until well past midnight every day from Easter through October. ✉ *Rüdesheim.*

Luftsport-Club Rheingau. With the wings of a glider you can silently soar over the Rhine Valley. At the Luftsport-Club Rheingau you can catch a 30- to 60-minute *Segelflug* (glider flight) between Rüdesheim and the Loreley; allow 1½ hours for pre- and postflight preparations. ✉ *Flugplatz Eibinger Forstwiesen, Kammerforsterstr., 3 km (2 miles) north of Niederwald-Denkmal and Landgut Ebenthal* ☎ *06722/2979* 🌐 *www.lsc-rheingau.de* 🎫 *€15 for first 5 mins; each additional min €0.50; first 15 mins in glider with motor €30, each additional min €2* 🕓 *Apr.–Oct., weekends and public holidays 10–7.*

Niederwalddenkmal. High above Rüdesheim and visible for miles stands Germania, a colossal female statue crowning the Niederwald Monument. This tribute to German nationalism was built between 1877 and 1883 to commemorate the rebirth of the German Empire after the

Franco-Prussian War (1870–71). Germania faces across the Rhine toward its eternal enemy, France. At her base are the words to a stirring patriotic song: "Dear Fatherland rest peacefully! Fast and true stands the watch, the watch on the Rhine!" There are splendid panoramic views from the monument and from other vantage points on the edge of the forested plateau. You can reach the monument on foot, by car (via Grabenstrasse), or over the vineyards in the *Seilbahn* (cable car). There's also a *Sessellift* (chairlift) to and from Assmannshausen, a red-wine enclave, on the other side of the hill; for €14, a "Ringticket" will take you from the Old Town to Niederwald by

> ### BETTER LATE
>
> Schloss Johannisberg was once owned by the prince-abbots of Fulda, and every autumn a courier was sent from Johannisberg to Fulda to obtain permission to harvest the grapes. In 1775 the courier returned after considerable delay. The harvest was late and the grapes were far riper than usual; the resulting wines were exceptionally rich and fruity. *Spätlese* (literally, "late harvest," pronounced *shpate*-layzeh) wines have been highly esteemed ever since. A statue in the courtyard commemorates the "late rider."

Seilbahn, from Niederwald to Assmannshausen by Sessellift, and back to Rüdesheim by boat. ✉ *Oberstr. 37* ☎ *06722/2402* ⊕ *www.seilbahn-ruedesheim.de* 💶 *€5 one way, €7 round-trip, or €8 combined ticket for cable car and chairlift* ⊙ *Mar., Apr., and Oct., weekdays 9:30–5, weekends 9:30–6; May, daily 9:30–6; June and Sept., weekdays 9:30–6, weekends 9:30–7; July and Aug., daily 9:30–7; Nov., daily 9:30–4; early Dec.–mid-Dec., weekdays 11–6, weekends 11–7.*

Weinmuseum Brömserburg (*Brömserburg Wine Museum*). Housed in one of the oldest castles on the Rhine (it was built around the year 1000), the museum displays wine-related artifacts and drinking vessels dating from Roman times. There are great views from the roof and the terrace, where there are occasionally wine tastings (ask at the desk). ✉ *Rheinstr. 2* ☎ *06722/2348* ⊕ *www.rheingauer-weinmuseum.de* 💶 *€5* ⊙ *Mar.–Oct., daily 10–6.*

WHERE TO STAY

$$
HOTEL

⚜ **Breuer's Rüdesheimer Schloss.** Vineyard views grace most of the rooms at this stylish, historic hotel where guests are welcomed with a drink from the family's Rheingau wine estate. **Pros:** right off the Drosselgasse; numerous rate packages. **Cons:** noisy tourist area. 💲 *Rooms from: €135* ✉ *Steing. 10* ☎ *06722/90500* ⊕ *www.ruedesheimer-schloss. com* ⊙ *Closed late Dec.–early Jan.* ⮌ *23 rooms, 3 suites* ⦿ *Breakfast.*

$$
HOTEL
Fodor'sChoice
★

⚜ **Hotel Krone Assmannshausen.** From its humble beginnings in 1541 as an inn for sailors and ferrymen, the Krone evolved into an elegant, antiques-filled hotel with a fine restaurant. **Pros:** restaurant has a terrace overlooking the Rhine; lovely views of vineyards as well as river. **Cons:** right on a main railroad line; rooms at the back have a less than spectacular view. 💲 *Rooms from: €170* ✉ *Rheinuferstr. 10, Assmannshausen* ☎ *06722/4030* ⊕ *www.hotel-krone.com* ⮌ *53 rooms, 12 suites, 1 penthouse* ⦿ *Breakfast.*

Take the Seilbahn over picturesque vineyards to the Niederwald-Denkmal monument above Rüdesheim.

THE MITTELRHEIN

Bingen, like Rüdesheim, is a gateway to the Mittelrhein. From here to Koblenz lies the greatest concentration of Rhine castles. Most date from the 12th and 13th centuries, but were destroyed after the invention of gunpowder, mainly during invasions by the French. It's primarily thanks to the Prussian royal family and its penchant for historical preservation that numerous Rhine castles were rebuilt or restored in the 19th and early 20th centuries.

Two roads run parallel to the Rhine: B-42 (east side) and B-9 (west side). The spectacular views from the heights can best be enjoyed on the routes known as the Loreley-Burgenstrasse (east side), from Kaub to the Loreley to Kamp-Bornhofen; or the Rheingoldstrasse (west side), from Rheindiebach to Rhens.

BINGEN

35 km (22 miles) west of Wiesbaden.

Bingen overlooks the Nahe-Rhine conflux near a treacherous stretch of shallows and rapids known as the Binger Loch (Bingen Hole). Early on, Bingen developed into an important commercial center, for it was here—as in Rüdesheim on the opposite shore—that goods were moved from ship to shore to circumvent the impassable waters. Bingen was also the crossroads of Roman trade routes between Mainz, Koblenz, and Trier. Thanks to this central location, it grew into a major center of the wine trade and remains so today. Wine is celebrated during 11 days of merrymaking in late August and early September at the annual **Winzerfest.**

GETTING HERE AND AROUND

From Wiesbaden by road, take A-60 via Mainz. If you're coming from Rüdesheim, you can hop on a ferry from the wharf opposite the train station.

ESSENTIALS

Visitor Information Bingen Tourist-Information. ✉ *Rheinkai 21* ☎ *06721/184-205* ⊕ *www.bingen.de.*

EXPLORING

Basilika St. Martin. The late-Gothic Basilika St. Martin was built on the site of a Roman temple and first mentioned in 793. The 11th-century crypt and Gothic and baroque furnishings make it worth a visit. Not far away is the thousand-year-old Drususbrücke, a stone bridge that runs over the Nahe. ✉ *Basilikastr. 1* ⊗ *Mon. and Wed.–Fri. 8–5; Tues. and weekends 8–8.*

Burg Klopp. Bingen was destroyed repeatedly by wars and fires; thus there are many ancient foundations but few visible architectural remains of the past. Since Celtic times the Kloppberg (Klopp Hill), in the center of town, has been the site of a succession of citadels, all named Burg Klopp, since 1282. Here you'll find a terrace with good views of the Rhine, the Nahe, and the surrounding hills and from April to October you can climb the tower for a more lofty view. ✉ *Kloppg. 1* ⊗ *Tower Apr.–Oct., daily 8–6.*

Hildegard Forum. Near the St. Roch Chapel, the Hildegard Forum has exhibits related to St. Hildegard, a medieval herb garden, and a restaurant serving tasty, wholesome foods (many based on Hildegard's theories of nutrition) and a nice selection of local wines. The lunch buffet is a good value. ✉ *Rochusberg 1* ☎ *06721/181-000* ⊕ *www. hildegard-forum.de* ⊗ *Tues.–Sun. 11–6.*

Fodor'sChoice
★
Historisches Museum am Strom (*History Museum*). Here you can see the most intact set of Roman surgical tools ever discovered (2nd century), period rooms from the Rhine Romantic era, and displays about Abbess St. Hildegard von Bingen (1098–1179), one of the most remarkable women of the Middle Ages. An outspoken critic of papal and imperial machinations, she was a highly respected scholar, naturopath, and artist whose mystic writings and (especially) music became very popular from the 1990s onward. An excellent illustrated booklet in English on Rhine Romanticism, *The Romantic Rhine,* is sold at the museum shop. The museum is housed in a former power station (1898) on the riverbank. ✉ *Museumsstr. 3* ☎ *06721/184-353* ⊕ *www.bingen.de* 🎫*€3* ⊗ *Tues.–Sun. 10–5.*

Rochuskapelle (*St. Roch Chapel*). The forested plateau of the Rochusberg (St. Roch Hill) is the pretty setting of the Rochuskapelle. Originally built in 1666 to celebrate the end of the plague, it has been rebuilt twice. On August 16, 1814, Goethe attended the consecration festivities, the forerunner of today's Rochusfest, a weeklong folk festival in mid-August.

The chapel (open during Sunday services at 8 and 10) contains an altar dedicated to St. Hildegard and relics and furnishings from the convents she founded on the Ruppertsberg (in the suburb of Bingerbrück) and in Eibingen (east of Rüdesheim). ✉ *Rochusberg 3* ☎ *06721/14225.*

WHERE TO EAT

$$$$ EUROPEAN Fodor's Choice ★ 🍴 **Johann Lafer's Stromburg.** It's a pretty 15-minute drive through the Binger Wald (Bingen Forest) to this luxurious castle hotel and restaurant overlooking Stromberg. Johann Lafer is a prolific chef who pioneered cooking shows in Germany. In the elegant Val d'Or the *Variationen* (medley) of foie gras and the *Hirschrücken mit Rosenkohl* (venision with Brussels sprouts) are classics. The less formal Bistro d'Or serves tasty regional dishes. The wine list features some 200 top Nahe wines and several hundred Old and New World wines, with a particularly fine collection from Bordeaux and Burgundy. [$] *Average main: €46* ✉ *Am Schlossberg 1, Stromberg* ✣ *12 km (7½ miles) west of Bingerbrück via Weiler and Waldalgesheim* ☎ *06724/93100* 🌐 *www.johannlafer.de/stromburg* ⏲ *Le Val d'Or closed Mon. and Tues. No lunch weekdays* ✍ *Reservations essential.*

$$ GERMAN 🍴 **Weinstube Kruger-Rumpf.** It's well worth the 10-minute drive from Bingen (just across the Nahe River) to enjoy the refined country cooking and exquisite Nahe wines produced by the Rumpf family. Seasonal house specialties include *geschmorte Schweinebacken* (braised pork jowls) with kohlrabi, boiled beef with green herb sauce, and *Winzerschmaus* (a casserole of potatoes, sauerkraut, bacon, cheese, and herbs). The house dates from 1790; the wisteria-draped garden beckons in summer. [$] *Average main: €17* ✉ *Rheinstr. 47, Münster-Sarmsheim* ✣ *4 km (2½ miles) southwest of Bingen* ☎ *06721/43859* 🌐 *www.kruger-rumpf.com* ⏲ *Closed Mon. and 2 wks in Jan. No lunch weekdays* ✍ *Reservations essential.*

EN ROUTE **Mäuseturm** (*Mouse Tower*). On the 5-km (3-mile) drive on B-9 to Trechtingshausen you will pass by Bingen's landmark, the Mäuseturm, perched on a rocky island near the Binger Loch. The name derives from a gruesome legend. One version tells that during a famine in 969 the miserly Archbishop Hatto hoarded grain and sought refuge in the tower to escape the peasants' pleas for food. The stockpile attracted scads of mice to the tower, where they devoured everything in sight, including Hatto. In fact, the tower was built by the archbishops of Mainz in the 13th and 14th centuries as a *Mautturm* (watch tower and toll station) for their fortress, Ehrenfels, on the opposite shore (now a ruin). It was restored in neo-Gothic style by the king of Prussia in 1855, who also rebuilt Burg Sooneck, but you can't go inside. ✉ *Mäuseturminsel.*

The three castles open for visits near Trechtingshausen (turnoffs are signposted on B-9) will especially appeal to lovers of history and art. As you enter each castle's gateway, consider what a feat of engineering it was to have built such a massive Burg (fortress or castle) on the stony cliffs overlooking the Rhine. They have all lain in ruin once or more during their turbulent histories. Their outer walls and period rooms still evoke memories of Germany's medieval past as well as the 19th-century era of Rhine Romanticism.

Burg Rheinstein. This castle was the home of Rudolf von Habsburg from 1282 to 1286. To establish law and order on the Rhine, he destroyed the neighboring castles of Burg Reichenstein and Burg Sooneck and hanged their notorious robber barons from the oak trees around the Clemens Church, a late-Romanesque basilica near Trechtingshausen. The Gobelin tapestries, 15th-century stained glass, wall and ceiling frescoes, a floor of royal apartments, and antique furniture—including a rare "giraffe spinet," which Kaiser Wilhelm I is said to have played— are the highlights here. All of this is illuminated by candlelight on some summer Fridays. Rheinstein was the first of many a Rhine ruin to be rebuilt by a royal Prussian family in the 19th century. ⊠ *Trechtingshausen* ✣ *From A-61, take exit AS Bingen center. Continue on B-9 through Bingerbrück towards Trechtingshausen; parking is below the castle* ☎ *06721/6348* ⊕ *www.burg-rheinstein.de* ⊠ *€5.50* ☉ *Mid-Mar.– mid-Nov., daily 9:30–6; mid-Nov.–late Dec. and early to mid-Mar., weekends only 10–5 (weather permitting—call ahead).*

Burg Reichenstein. Under new ownership since 2014 and on the fast track to becoming a stylish castle hotel with two restaurants, Reichenstein also has an interesting museum with collections of decorative cast-iron slabs (from ovens and historical room-heating devices), hunting weapons and armor, period rooms, and paintings. It's the only one of the area's three castles directly accessible by car. ⊠ *Burgweg 7, Trechtingshausen* ☎ *06721/6117* ⊕ *www.burg-reichenstein.com* ⊠ *€5* ☉ *Museum Feb.–Dec., Tues.–Sun. 10–6.*

Burg Sooneck. Perched on the edge of the Soon (pronounced *zone*) Forest, this imposing 11th-century castle houses a valuable collection of Empire, Biedermeier, and neo-Gothic furnishings, medieval weapons, and paintings from the Rhine Romantic era. ⊠ *Sooneckstr. 1, Niederheimbach* ☎ *06743/6064* ⊕ *www.burgen-rlp.de* ⊠ *€4* ☉ *Apr.–Sept., Tues.–Sun. 9–6; Oct., Nov., and Jan.–Mar., Tues.–Sun. 9–5.*

BACHARACH

16 km (10 miles) north of Bingen, ferry 3 km (2 miles) north of town, to Kaub.

Bacharach, whose name may derive from the Latin *Bacchi ara* (altar of Bacchus), has long been associated with wine. Like Rüdesheim, Bingen, and Kaub, it was a shipping station where barrels would interrupt their Rhine journey for land transport. Riesling wine from the town's most famous vineyard, the Bacharacher Hahn, is served on the KD Rhine steamers, and Riesling is used in local cooking for marinades and sauces; you can even find Riesling ice cream. In June you can sample wines at the Weinblütenfest (Vine Blossom Festival) in the side-valley suburb of Steeg, and, in late August, at Kulinarische Sommernacht in Bacharach proper (⊕ *www.kulinarische-sommernacht.de*).

Park on the riverbank and enter the town through one of its medieval gateways. You can ascend the 14th-century town wall for a walk along the ramparts around the town, then stroll along the main street (one street but three names: Koblenzer Strasse, Oberstrasse, and Mainzer Strasse) for a look at patrician manors, typically built around a *Hof* (courtyard), and half-timber houses. Haus Sickingen, Posthof, Zollhof, Rathaus (Town Hall), and Altes Haus are fine examples.

ESSENTIALS

Visitor Information Bacharach Tourist-Information. ✉ *Oberstr. 10* ☎ *06743/919–303* 🌐 *www.rhein-nahe-touristik.de.*

EXPLORING

St. Peter. The massive tower in the center of town belongs to the parish church of St. Peter. A good example of the transition from Romanesque to Gothic styles, it has an impressive four-story nave. ✉ *Blücherstr. 1.*

Wernerkapelle. From the parish church a set of stone steps (signposted) leads to Bacharach's landmark, the sandstone ruins of the Gothic Wernerkapelle, highly admired for its filigree tracery. The chapel's roof succumbed to falling rocks in 1689, when the French blew up Burg Stahleck. Originally a Staufen fortress (11th century), the castle lay dormant until 1925, when a youth hostel was built on the foundations. The sweeping views from there are worth the 10-minute walk. ✉ *Obertstr.*

WHERE TO EAT AND STAY

$ GERMAN Fodor's Choice ★ 🍴 **Altes Haus.** This charming medieval half-timber house (1368) is a favorite setting for films and photos. The restaurant uses the freshest ingredients possible and buys meat and game from local butchers and hunters. *Rieslingrahmsuppe* (Riesling cream soup), *Reibekuchen* (potato pancakes), and a refined version of boiled beef with horseradish sauce, *Tafelspitz mit Wasabi*, are favorites, in addition to the seasonal specialties. There is also a good selection of local wines. [$] *Average main: €10* ✉ *Oberstr. 61* ☎ *06743/1209* ⏲ *Closed Wed. and Dec.–Easter; closed weekdays in Apr. and Nov.*

$ GERMAN 🍴 **Gutsausschank Zum Grünen Baum.** The Bastian family (also owners of the vineyard Insel Heyles'en Werth, on the island opposite Bacharach) runs this cozy tavern in a half-timber house dating from 1421. The "wine carousel" is a great way to sample a full range of wine flavors and styles (15 wines). Snacks are served (from noon), including delicious *Wildsülze* (game in aspic), with potato salad, sausages, and cheese. Reservations are a good idea on summer weekends. [$] *Average main: €12* ✉ *Oberstr. 63* ☎ *06743/1208* 🌐 *www.weingut-bastian-bacharach.de* ⏲ *Closed Thurs. and Jan.–mid-Mar.*

$ HOTEL 🏨 **Altkölnischer Hof.** Flowers line the windows of country-style rooms in this pretty half-timber hotel near the market square. **Pros:** half-timber romance. **Cons:** noisy tourist area; 10-minute walk from the station. [$] *Rooms from: €92* ✉ *Blücherstr. 2* ☎ *06743/1339* 🌐 *www.altkoelnischer-hof.de* ⏲ *Closed Nov.–Mar.* 🛏 *18 rooms, 2 suites, 4 apartments* 🍽 *Breakfast.*

$$ HOTEL 🏨 **Rhein-Hotel Bacharach.** The modern rooms in this friendly, family-run operation, each of them named after a vineyard, come with Rhine and castle views. **Pros:** Rhine and castle views; free bike and laptop loans for hotel guests. **Cons:** no elevator; next to railroad. [$] *Rooms from: €110* ✉ *Langstr. 50* ☎ *06743/1243* 🌐 *www.rhein-hotel-bacharach.de* ⏲ *Closed late Dec.–Feb.* 🛏 *13 rooms, 1 apartment* 🍽 *Breakfast.*

OBERWESEL

8 km (5 miles) north of Bacharach.

Oberwesel retains its medieval silhouette. Sixteen of the original 21 towers and much of the town wall still stand in the shadow of Schönburg Castle. The "town of towers" is also renowned for its Riesling wines, which are celebrated during a festival held the first half of September. Both Gothic churches, on opposite ends of town, are worth visiting.

ESSENTIALS

Visitor Information Oberwesel Tourist-Information. ✉ *Rathausstr. 3* ☎ *06744/710–624* 🌐 *www.oberwesel.de.*

EXPLORING

Liebfrauenkirche (*Church of Our Lady*). Popularly known as the "red church" because of its brightly colored exterior, Liebfrauenkirche has superb sculptures, tombstones and paintings, and one of Germany's oldest altars (1331). ✉ *Kirchstr. 1.*

St. Martin. Set on a hill and with a fortresslike tower, the so-called "white church" has beautifully painted vaulting and a magnificent baroque altar. ✉ *Martinsberg 1.*

Stadtmuseum Oberwesel. Oberwesel's city museum offers a virtual tour of the town, as well as a multimedia "journey through time" showing the area from the Stone Age to the present day. It also houses a fine collection of old etchings and drawings of the Rhine Valley, including one by John Gardnor, an English clergyman and painter, who published a book of sketches upon his return to England and kicked off a wave of Romantic tourism in the late 18th century. ✉ *Rathausstr. 23* ☎ *06744/714–726* 🌐 *www.kulturhaus-oberwesel.de* 🎟 *€3* 🕒 *Apr.–Oct., Tues.–Fri. 10–5, weekends 2–5; Nov.–Mar., Tues.–Fri. 10–2.*

WHERE TO EAT AND STAY

$ GERMAN 🍴 **Historische Weinwirtschaft.** Tables in the flower-laden garden in front of this lovingly restored half-timber house are at a premium in summer, though the seats in the nooks and crannies indoors are just as inviting. Dark beams, exposed stone walls, and antique furniture set the mood on the ground and first floors, and the vaulted cellar houses contemporary-art exhibitions. Ask Iris Marx, the ebullient proprietor, for an English menu if you're stumbling over the words in local dialect. She offers country cooking at its best. The wine list has 32 wines by the glass. [$] *Average main: €13* ✉ *Liebfrauenstr. 17* ☎ *06744/8186* 🌐 *www.historische-weinwirtschaft.de* 🕒 *Closed Tues. and Jan. No lunch Mon.–Sat.*

$$$$ B&B/INN Fodor's Choice ★ 🏨 **Burghotel "Auf Schönburg".** Antique furnishings and historic rooms—a library, chapel, and prison tower—make for an unforgettable stay at this lovingly restored hotel and restaurant in the 12th-century Schönburg Castle complex. **Pros:** castle right out of a storybook. **Cons:** lots of climbing; parking lot 100 yards downhill; train tracks nearby; very expensive. [$] *Rooms from: €290* ✉ *Oberwesel* ☎ *06744/93930* 🌐 *www.hotel-schoenburg.com* 🕒 *Closed early Jan.–mid-Mar.* 🛏 *20 rooms, 5 suites* 🍽 *Breakfast.*

ST. GOAR

7 km (4½ miles) north of Oberwesel.

St. Goar and St. Goarshausen, its counterpoint on the opposite shore, are named after a Celtic missionary who settled here in the 6th century. He became the patron saint of innkeepers—an auspicious sign for both towns, which now live off tourism and wine. September is especially busy, with Weinforum Mittelrhein (a major wine-and-food presentation in Burg Rheinfels) on the first weekend, and the annual wine festivals and the splendid fireworks display "Rhine in Flames" on the third weekend.

> ### BIKE THE MIDDLE RHINE
>
> There is a 132-km (82-mile) cycle path (Rheinradweg) through the Middle Rhine Valley running parallel to the road and the railroad tracks from Bingen to Bonn. It's an ideal way of combining sightseeing with some not-so-strenuous exercise, unless you attempt to reach the castles on the hills. Watch out for pedestrians and other bicyclists.

GETTING HERE AND AROUND

Highway B-9 and train service link St. Goar to other towns on the Mittelrhein's west side; ferries to St. Goarshausen connect it to the east.

ESSENTIALS

St. Goar Tourist-Information. ⊠ *Heerstr. 86* ☎ *06741/383* ⊕ *www.st-goar.de.*

EXPLORING

FAMILY **Burg Rheinfels.** The castle ruins overlooking the town bear witness to the fact that St. Goar was once the best-fortified town in the Mittelrhein. From its beginnings in 1245, it was repeatedly enlarged by the counts of Katzenelnbogen, a powerful local dynasty, and their successors, the Landgraviate of Hesse. Rheinfels was finally blasted by the French in 1797. Take time for a walk through the impressive ruins and the museum, which has a detailed model of how the fortress looked in its heyday. To avoid the steep ascent on foot, buy a round-trip ticket (€4) for the Burgexpress, which departs from the bus stop on Heerstrasse, opposite the riverside parking lot for tour buses. ⊠ *Off Schlossberg Str.* ☎ *06741/7753* ⊕ *www.burg-rheinfels.com* ☒ *€5* ⊗ *Mid-Mar.–late Oct., daily 9–6; late Oct.–early Nov., daily 9–5.*

Stiftskirche. This 15th-century collegiate church was built atop the tomb of St. Goar, despite the fact that the tomb itself (an ancient pilgrimage site) was discovered to be empty during the church's construction. The 11th-century crypt has been called the most beautiful to be found on the Rhine, between Köln and Speyer. ⊠ *Marktpl.* ☒ *Free* ⊗ *Apr.–Oct., daily 10–6; Nov.–Mar., daily 11–6.*

WHERE TO EAT AND STAY

$$
GERMAN ✕ **Weinhotel Landsknecht.** Members of the Lorenz and Nickenig-Kehring families make everyone feel at home in their riverside restaurant and hotel north of St. Goar. Martina Lorenz and her winemaker husband Joachim operate the Vinothek, where you can sample his delicious Bopparder Hamm wines. These go well with the hearty local dishes, such as Rhine-style sauerbraten or seasonal specialties (asparagus, game), at

the Ausblick restaurant. The hotel is an official Rheinsteig and Rhein-Burgen trail partner—perfect for hikers. $ *Average main: €16* ⊠ *Rheinuferstr. B–9* ☎ *06741/2011* ⊕ *www.hotel-landsknecht.de.*

$$

HOTEL

Fodor'sChoice

★

🏨 **Romantik Hotel Schloss Rheinfels.** Directly opposite Burg Rheinfels, this hotel offers modern comfort and expansive views from rooms furnished in country-manor style. **Pros:** marvelous views of the Rhine and the town. **Cons:** villa section some distance from main hotel and lacks charm. $ *Rooms from: €175* ⊠ *Schlossberg 47* ☎ *06741/8020* ⊕ *www.schloss-rheinfels.de* ⇄ *55 rooms, 4 apartments, 4 suites* ⦿ *Breakfast.*

ST. GOARSHAUSEN

29 km (18 miles) north of Rüdesheim.

The town closest to the famous Loreley rock, pretty St. Goarshausen even calls itself *Die Loreleystadt* (Loreley City), and it's a popular destination for Rhineland travelers, especially during the Weinwoche (Wine Week festival), which leads up to the third weekend in September.

Overlooking the town are two 14th-century castles whose names, Katz (Cat) and Maus (Mouse), reflect but one of the many power plays on the Rhine in the Middle Ages. Territorial supremacy and the privilege of collecting tolls fueled the fires of rivalry. In response to the construction of Burg Rheinfels, the archbishop of Trier erected a small castle north of St. Goarshausen to protect his interests. In turn, the masters of Rheinfels, the counts of Katzenelnbogen, built a bigger castle directly above the town. Its name was shortened to Katz, and its smaller neighbor was scornfully referred to as Maus. Neither castle is open to the public.

GETTING HERE AND AROUND

Roads (B-42 and B-274) and rail service connect St. Goarshausen to neighboring towns on the east side of the Mittelrhein. Ferries to St. Goar link it to the west.

EXPLORING

Liebenstein and Sterrenberg. Some 10 km (6 miles) north of the Maus castle, near Kamp-Bornhofen, is a castle duo separated by a "quarrel wall": Liebenstein and Sterrenberg, known as the *Feindliche Brüder* (rival brothers). Liebenstein is now home to a charming hotel, and both restored palaces have terrace cafés with good views. ⊠ *Zu den Burgen 1, Kamp-Bornhofen* ⊕ *www.castle-liebenstein.com.*

Loreley. One of the Rhineland's main attractions lies 4 km (2½ miles) south of St. Goarshausen: the steep (430-foot-high) slate cliff named after the beautiful blonde nymph Loreley. Here she supposedly sat, singing songs so lovely that sailors and fishermen were lured to the treacherous rapids—and their demise. The rapids really were treacherous: the Rhine is at its narrowest here and the current the swiftest. The Loreley nymph was invented in 1801 by author Clemens Brentano, who drew his inspiration from the sirens of Greek legend. Her tale was retold as a ballad by Heinrich Heine and set to music by Friedrich Silcher at the height of Rhine Romanticism in the 19th century. The haunting melody is played on the PA systems of the Rhine boats whenever the Loreley is approached. ⊠ *St. Goarshausen.*

Loreley Besucherzentrum. The 3-D, 20-minute film and hands-on exhibits at this visitor center are entertaining ways to learn about the region's flora and fauna, geology, wine, shipping, and, above all, the myth of the Loreley. You can stock up on souvenirs in the shop and have a snack at the bistro before heading for the nearby vantage point at the cliff's summit. The center is on the Rheinsteig trail, and other hiking trails are signposted in the landscaped park. From Easter to October there's hourly bus service to and from the KD steamer landing in St. Goarshausen. ⊠ *Auf der Loreley 7* ☎ *06771/599–093* ⊕ *www.loreley-besucherzentrum.de* 🎫 *€2.50* ⊘ *Apr.–Oct., daily 11–5.*

BOPPARD

17 km (11 miles) north of St. Goar, ferry to Filsen.

Boppard is a pleasant little resort that evolved from a Celtic settlement into a Roman fortress, Frankish royal court, and Free Imperial City. Boppard's tourism board conducts walking tours (in German, €3) mid-April to mid-October, Saturday at 11, starting at its office on the market square. Special tours in English are also bookable for groups.

ESSENTIALS

Visitor Information Boppard Tourist-Information. ⊠ *Altes Rathaus, Am Marktpl.* ☎ *06742/3888* ⊕ *www.boppard-tourismus.de.*

EXPLORING

Bodobrica. The Roman garrison Bodobrica, established here in the 4th century, was enclosed by a 26-foot-high rectangular wall (1,010 by 505 feet) with 28 defense towers. You can see portions of these in a fascinating open-air archaeological park. ⊠ *Angertstr.* ✛ *Near B-9 and the railroad tracks* 🎫 *Free* ⊘ *Always accessible.*

Karmeliterkirche (*Carmelite Church*). Two baroque altars dominate the interior of the Gothic Karmeliterkirche on Karmeliterstrasse, near the Rhine. It houses intricately carved choir stalls and tombstones and several beautiful Madonnas. Winegrowers still observe the old custom of laying the first-picked *Trauben* (grapes) at the foot of the Traubenmadonna (1330) to ensure a good harvest. The annual wine festival takes place in late September or early October, just before the Riesling harvest. ⊠ *Karmeliterstr.*

Severuskirche (*Church of St. Severus*). Excavations in the 1960s revealed ancient Roman baths beneath the twin-tower, Romanesque Severuskirche on the market square. The large triumphal crucifix over the main altar and a lovely statue of a smiling Madonna date from the 13th century. ⊠ *Marktpl.*

Vierseenblick. From the Mühltal station, let the Sesselbahn (chairlift) whisk you a half-mile uphill to the Vierseenblick, from where the Rhine looks like a chain of lakes. ⊠ *Mühltal 12* ☎ *06742/2510* ⊕ *www.sesselbahn-boppard.de* 🎫 *€7.50 round-trip* ⊘ *Mid-Apr.–Sept., daily 10–6; Oct. 1–15, daily 10–5:30; Apr. 1–15 and Oct. 15–31, daily 10–5.*

WHERE TO EAT AND STAY

$ GERMAN 🍴 **Weinhaus Heilig Grab.** This wine estate's tavern, Boppard's oldest, is full of smiling faces: the wines are excellent, the food is simple and hearty, and the welcome is warm. Old chestnut trees shade tables in the courtyard. If you'd like to visit the cellars or vineyards, ask the friendly hosts. [$] *Average main: €8* ✉ *Zelkesg. 12* ☎ *06742/2371* 🌐 *www.heiliggrab.de* 🕒 *Closed Tues. and late Dec.–Jan. No lunch.*

$$ HOTEL 🏨 **Best Western Bellevue Rheinhotel.** In this traditional hotel now run by the fourth and fifth generations of the same family, you can enjoy a Rhine view from many of the rooms, or from the terrace next to the waterfront promenade. **Pros:** marvelous views. **Cons:** parking is a problem; breakfast costs €11 extra. [$] *Rooms from: €128* ✉ *Rheinallee 41* ☎ *06742/1020* 🌐 *www.bellevue-boppard.de* 🛏 *93 rooms, 1 suite* 🍽 *No meals.*

SPORTS AND THE OUTDOORS

Mittelrhein Klettersteig. If you have Alpine hiking ambitions, try this climbing path—a "via ferrata" complete with cables, steps, and ladders to help reach heights more quickly. It's an alternate route of the Rhein-Burgen-Wanderweg (hiking trail from Koblenz to Bingen). The trail starts at St.-Remigius-Platz, about 1 km (½ mile) from Boppard Hauptbahnhof. Allow two to three hours for the climb, though there are several possibilities to return to the "normal" path in-between climbs. Rent the necessary gear at the Aral gas station on Koblenzer Strasse in Boppard. ✉ *St.-Remigius-Pl.* ☎ *06742/2447 Aral gas station.*

Weinwanderweg (*Wine Hiking Trail*). The 10-km (6-mile) hiking trail from Boppard to Spay begins north of town on Peternacher Weg. Many other marked trails in the vicinity are outlined on maps and in brochures available from the tourist office.

KOBLENZ

20 km (12 miles) north of Boppard.

The ancient city of Koblenz is at a geographic nexus known as the **Deutsches Eck** (German Corner) in the heart of the Mittelrhein region. Rivers and mountains converge here: the Mosel flows into the Rhine on one side; the Lahn flows in on the other a few miles south; and three mountain ridges intersect.

Founded by the Romans in AD 9, the city was first called Castrum ad Confluentes (Fort at the Confluence). It became a powerful center in the Middle Ages, when it controlled trade on both the Rhine and the Mosel. Air raids during World War II destroyed 85% of the city, but extensive restoration has done much to re-create its former atmosphere. As the host of Germany's Federal Horticultural Show in 2011, the city saw widespread urban development, including the new Seilbahn that transports visitors across the river and up to the Ehrenbreitstein fortress.

GETTING HERE AND AROUND

You can get here speedily by autobahn or train, or via a leisurely scenic drive along the Rhine (or even more mellow, by cruise boat). The Koblenz tourist office has guided English-language tours on Saturday at 3 from April to October. Tours are €7 and depart from the Tourist-Information office.

ESSENTIALS

Visitor Information Koblenz Tourist-Information. ⊠ *Forum Confluentes, Zentralpl. 1* ☎ *0261/19433* ⊕ *www.koblenz-touristik.de.*

EXPLORING

TOP ATTRACTIONS

Deutsches Eck (*German Corner*). This pointed bit of land, jutting into the river like the prow of an early ironclad warship, is at the sharp intersection of the Rhine and Mosel rivers. One of the more effusive manifestations of German nationalism—an 1897 equestrian statue of Kaiser Wilhelm I, first emperor of the newly united Germany—was erected here. It was destroyed at the end of World War II and replaced in 1953 with a ponderous monument to Germany's unity. After German reunification a new statue of Wilhelm was placed atop this monument in 1993. Pieces of the Berlin Wall stand on the Mosel side—a memorial to those who died as a result of the partitioning of the country.

Fodor'sChoice ★ **Festung Ehrenbreitstein.** Europe's largest fortress, towering 400 feet above the left bank of the Rhine, offers a magnificent view over Koblenz and where the Mosel and the Rhine rivers meet. The earliest buildings date from about 1100, but the bulk of the fortress was constructed in the 16th century. In 1801 it was partially destroyed by Napoléon, and the French occupied Koblenz for the next 18 years. For an introduction to the fortress and its history, head for the *Besucherdienst* (visitor center). English-language tours are for groups only, but you can often join a group that is registered for a tour.

A Seilbahn (cable car) carries you a half mile from Konrad-Adenauer-Ufer over the river to Ehrenbreitstein, with spectacular views of the Deutsches Eck below. Lifts can accommodate 7,000 passengers in an hour, and operate continually throughout the day from a half-hour before the site opens until a half-hour after it closes.

⊠ *Felsenweg* ☎ *0261/6675–4000* ⊕ *www.diefestungehrenbreitstein.de* 🎫 *Fortress €6, Seilbahn ride round-trip €9, combined ticket €11.80* ⊙ *Mid-Apr.–Oct., daily 10–6; Nov.–mid-Apr., daily 10–5; year-round free access to grounds.*

Landesmuseum Koblenz (*State Museum*). The Festung Ehrenbreitstein's museum has exhibits on the history of local industries, from wine growing to technology. Pride of place is given to the fortress's 16th-century Vogel Greif cannon, which has done a lot of traveling over the years. The French absconded with it in 1794, the Germans took it back in 1940, and the French commandeered it again in 1945. The 15-ton cannon was peaceably returned by French president François Mitterrand in 1984. ⊠ *Festung Ehrenbreitstein, Felsenweg* ☎ *0261/66750* ⊕ *www.landesmuseum-koblenz.de* 🎫 *Included in €6 fortress admission* ⊙ *Apr.–Oct., daily 10–6; Nov.–mid-Mar., weekends 10–5.*

Ludwig Museum. Just behind the Deutsches Eck, this museum is housed in the spic-and-span Deutschherrenhaus, a restored 13th-century building. Industrialist Peter Ludwig, one of Germany's leading contemporary-art

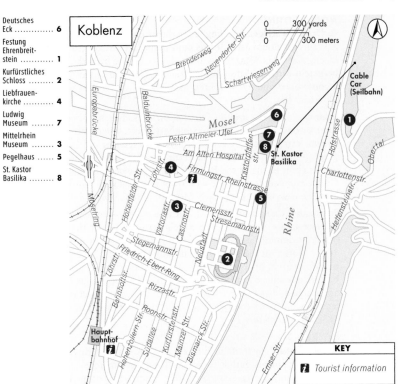

11

collectors, has filled this museum with part of his huge collection. ✉ *Danziger Freiheit 1* ☎ *0261/304–040* ⊕ *www.ludwigmuseum.org* 🎫 *€5* 🕙 *Tues.–Sat. 10:30–5, Sun. 11–6.*

Mittelrhein Museum. Relocated in 2013 to the new Forum Confluentes, this museum houses the city's art collection, including extensive holdings of landscapes focusing on the Rhine. It also has a notable collection of secular medieval art and works by regional artists. ✉ *Zentralpl. 1* ☎ *0261/129–2520* ⊕ *www.mittelrhein-museum.de* 🎫 *€6, special exhibitions €6, €10 for both* 🕙 *Tues.–Sun. 10–6.*

St. Kastor Basilika (*St. Castor Basilica*). It was in this sturdy Romanesque basilica, consecrated in 836, that plans were drawn for the Treaty of Verdun a few years later, formalizing the division of Charlemagne's great empire and leading to the creation of Germany and France as separate states. Inside, compare the squat Romanesque columns in the nave with the intricate fan vaulting of the Gothic sections. The **St. Kastor Fountain** outside the church is an intriguing piece of historical one-upmanship. It was built by the occupying French to mark the beginning of Napoléon's ultimately disastrous Russian campaign of 1812. ✉ *Kastorhof* ⊕ *www.sankt-kastor-koblenz.de* 🎫 *Free* 🕙 *Daily 9–6.*

WORTH NOTING

Kurfürstliches Schloss. Strolling along the promenade toward town, you'll pass this gracious castle. It was built in the late 18th century by Prince-Elector Clemens Wenzeslaus as an elegant escape from the grim Ehrenbreitstein fortress. Though the palace is primarily used these days as a conference and event center, its Grand Café is open to the public ✉ *Neustadt.*

Liebfrauenkirche (*Church of Our Lady*). This church stands on Roman foundations at the Old Town's highest point, where, on surrounding streets, war damage is evidenced by the blend of old buildings and modern store blocks. The bulk of the church is of Romanesque design, but its choir is one of the Rhineland's finest examples of 15th-century Gothic architecture, and the west front is graced with two 17th-century baroque towers. ✉ *Am Plan* 🕒 *Mon.–Sat. 8–6, Sun. 9–8.*

Pegelhaus (*Rheinkran*). Part of a Rhine-wide system that keeps track of river levels, Koblenz's squat Pegelhaus is one of the city's landmarks, originally a Rheinkran (Rhine crane) when it was built in 1611. Marks on the side of the building indicate the heights reached by floodwaters of bygone years. In the mid-19th century a pontoon bridge consisting of a row of barges spanned the Rhine here; when ships approached, two or three barges were simply towed out of the way to let them through. Today a restaurant operates within the Pegelhaus. ✉ *Konrad-Adenauer-Ufer.*

WHERE TO EAT

$$ ECLECTIC 🍴 **Café Einstein.** Portraits of Einstein line the walls of this busy restaurant, where locals gather to watch live soccer matches. The friendly Tayhus family serves tasty fare daily, from a hearty breakfast buffet (there's brunch on Sunday—reservations recommended) to late-night finger food. Fish specials are served year-round. [$] *Average main: €15* ✉ *Firmungstr. 30* ☎ *0261/914–4999* 🌐 *www.einstein-koblenz.de.*

$$$ GERMAN 🍴 **Da Vinci.** At this smart restaurant in the heart of the Old Town, da Vinci reproductions, including an original-size rendition of *The Last Supper,* adorn the walls. Leather upholstery, an elegant bar, and soft lighting round out the stylish interior. The chef presents a modernized Mediterranean menu with innovative dishes like crab with grapefuit, curry, shellfish jelly, and pink ginger. The wine list includes more than 200 bottles, with a focus on German, Italian, and French wines. [$] *Average main: €23* ✉ *Firmungstr. 32b* ☎ *0261/921–5444* 🌐 *www.davinci-koblenz.de.*

$ GERMAN 🍴 **Weindorf-Koblenz.** This reconstructed "wine village" of half-timber houses is grouped around a tree-shaded courtyard with an adjacent vineyard. The fresh renditions of traditional Rhine and Mosel specialties, a good selection of local wines, and a fabulous Sunday brunch (reservation recommended) where wine, beer, and nonalcoholic beverages are included in the price (€31.90) all make this a popular spot. [$] *Average main: €12* ✉ *Julius-Wegeler-Str. 2* ☎ *0261/133–7190* 🌐 *www.weindorf-koblenz.de* 🕒 *Closed Tues. No lunch Nov.–Mar.*

$ GERMAN 🍴 **Weinhaus Hubertus.** Hunting scenes and trophies line the wood-panel walls of this cozy wine restaurant, named after the patron saint of hunters, and the decorations also include 100-year-old murals. Hearty

Stroll through Koblenz's Old Town, stopping for a bite at a sidewalk café along one of the squares, such as Jesuitenplatz.

portions of fresh, traditional fare (à la *Wildschwein Würstchen,* or wild boar sausages) are what you'll find on offer. [$] *Average main: €14* ✉ *Florinsmarkt 6* ☎ *0261/31177* 🌐 *weinhaus-hubertus.de* 🕒 *No lunch weekdays.*

$$ GERMAN 🍴 **Zum Weissen Schwanen.** Guests have found a warm welcome in this half-timber inn and mill since 1693, a tradition carried on by the Kunz family. This is a charming place to enjoy a dinner of well-prepared, contemporary German cuisine with regional specialties. Brasserie Brentano serves lighter dishes as well as lunch and Sunday brunch. It's next to the 13th-century town gateway of Braubach, just below the Marksburg. The hotel is an official Rheinsteig trail partner. [$] *Average main: €20* ✉ *Brunnenstr. 4, Braubach* ✥ *12 km (7½ miles) south of Koblenz via B-42* ☎ *02627/9820* 🌐 *www.zum-weissen-schwanen.de.*

WHERE TO STAY

$$ HOTEL 🏨 **Hotel Kleiner Riesen.** You can literally watch the Rhine flowing by from the four front rooms of this friendly, family-operated hotel, about a 10-minute walk from the station. **Pros:** quiet; on the river; close to piers. **Cons:** 20-minute walk from city center. [$] *Rooms from: €100* ✉ *Januarius-Zick Str. 11* ☎ *0261/303–460* 🌐 *www.hotel-kleinerriesen.de* 🛏 *19 rooms, 3 suites* 🍽 *Breakfast.*

NIGHTLIFE AND PERFORMING ARTS

Café Hahn. In the suburb of Güls, this place features cabaret, stand-up comedians, popular musicians and bands, and other shows. ✉ *Neustr. 15* ☎ *0261/42302* 🌐 *www.cafehahn.de.*

Circus Maximus. You'll find dancing, live music, and theme parties practically every evening here. On a balmy night, visit Circus Maximus's Statt Strand beach bar, on Universitätsstrasse on the banks of the Mosel near the university. ⊠ *Stegemannstr. 30 at Viktoriastr.* ☎ *0261/300–2357* ⊕ *www.circus-maximus.org, www.strand-koblenz.de.*

Staatsorchester Rheinische Philharmonie (*Rhenish Philharmonic Orchestra*). The Philharmonic plays regularly at various concert venues around town. ⊠ *Eltzerhofstr. 6a* ☎ *0261/301–2272* ⊕ *www.rheinische-philharmonie.de.*

Theater Koblenz. Built in 1787, this gracious neoclassic theater is still in regular use and has resident drama, ballet, and musical theater ensembles. ⊠ *Clemensstr. 1–5* ☎ *0261/129–2870* ⊕ *www.theater-koblenz.de.*

SHOPPING

Koblenz's most pleasant shopping is in the Old Town streets around the market square, Am Plan.

Löhr Center. This modern mall has some 130 shops and restaurants. ⊠ *Hohenfelder Str. 22* ☎ *0261/133–906* ⊕ *www.loehr-center.de.*

THE MOSEL VALLEY

The Mosel is one of the most hauntingly beautiful river valleys on Earth—with the added draw of countless ancient vineyards on the banks, creating abundant opportunities for sampling some of Germany's best wines. Here, as in the Rhine Valley, forests and vines carpet steep hillsides; castles and church spires dot the landscape; and medieval wine hamlets line the riverbanks. The Mosel landscape is no less majestic, but is narrower and more peaceful than that of the Rhine Gorge; the river's countless bends and loops slow its pace and lend the region a leisurely charm.

WINNINGEN

11 km (7 miles) southwest of Koblenz.

Winningen is a gateway to the Terrassenmosel (Terraced Mosel), the portion of the river characterized by steep, terraced vineyards. Winches help haul miniature monorails, with the winegrowers and their tools aboard, up the steep incline, but tending and harvesting the vines are all done by hand. ■TIP→ **For a bird's-eye view of the valley, drive up Fährstrasse to Am Rosenhang, the start of a pleasant walk along the Weinlehrpfad (Educational Wine Path).**

As you head upstream toward Kobern-Gondorf, you'll pass the renowned vineyard site, Uhlen. In Kobern, the Oberburg (upper castle) and the St. Matthias Kapelle, a 12th-century chapel, are good vantage points. Half-timber houses reflecting the architectural styles of three centuries ring the town's pretty market square.

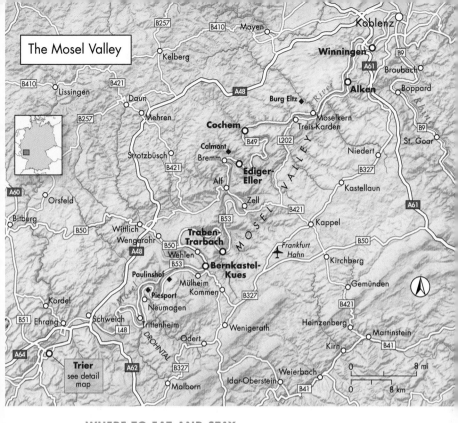

The Mosel Valley

WHERE TO EAT AND STAY

$$$ ✕ **Alte Mühle Thomas Höreth.** Thomas and Gudrun Höreth's enchanting
GERMAN country inn is a labyrinth of little rooms and cellars grouped around ole-
ander-lined courtyards. They have restored this former mill, originally
dating to 1026, and furnished it with thoughtful details and authentic
materials. Highlights of the menu include homemade cheeses, terrines,
pâtés, and *Entensülze* (goose in aspic), served with the Höreths' own
wines. For those who want to get away from the river, the Höreths have
a pleasing hotel in the forest, Höreth im Wald. $ *Average main: €23*
✉ *Mühlental 17, Kobern-Gondorf* ⊹ *Via B-416* ☎ *02607/6474* ⊕ *www.
thomas-hoereth.de* ⊘ *No lunch weekdays.*

$ ⌂ **Hotel Simonis.** Two of the suites in this traditional hotel on Kobern-
B&B/INN Gondorf's market square, 6 km (4 miles) from Winningen, are across
the courtyard, in what might be Germany's oldest half-timber house
(1321). **Pros:** half-timber setting. **Cons:** no elevator. $ *Rooms from:*
€89 ✉ *Marktpl. 4, Kobern-Gondorf* ☎ *02607/974–8537* ⊕ *www.
hotelsimonis.com* ⊘ *Closed Jan. and Feb.* ⇋ *13 rooms, 2 suites*
⦿ *Breakfast.*

ALKEN

22 km (14 miles) southwest of Koblenz.

One of the Mosel's oldest towns (the Celts were here by 450 BC), today Alken is best known for its 12th-century castle, Burg Thurant. With a pretty waterside setting backdropped by rolling vineyards and the castle above, Alken's among the lovelier wine village stops along the Untermosel (Lower Mosel) between Koblenz and Pünderich.

GETTING HERE AND AROUND

The B-49 connects Alken to Koblenz. The nearest train stop, on the Regionalbahn from Koblenz, is at Löf, across the river and linked to Alken by a bridge and a 2½-km (1½-mile) walk.

EXPLORING

Burg Thurant. This 12th-century castle towers over the village and the Burgberg (castle hill) vineyard. Castle tours include the chapel, cellar, tower, and a weapons display, and wine and snacks are served in the courtyard. Allow a good half hour for the climb from the riverbank. ⊠ *Alken* ☎ *02605/2004* ⊕ *www.thurant.de* ☞ *€3.50* ☼ *Mar. and Apr., daily 10–5; May–mid-Nov., daily 10–6.*

EN ROUTE

Burg Eltz (*Eltz Castle*). Genuinely medieval (12th–16th century) and genuinely stunning, Burg Eltz deserves as much attention as King Ludwig's trio of castles in Bavaria. For the 40-minute English-language tour, given when enough English speakers gather, ask at the souvenir shop. It guides you through the period rooms and massive kitchen. There's also a popular treasure vault filled with gold and silver. To get here, exit B-416 at Hatzenport (opposite and southwest of Alken), proceed to Münstermaifeld, and follow signs to the parking lot near the Antoniuskapelle. From here it's a 15-minute walk, or take the shuttle bus (€2). Hikers can reach the castle from Moselkern in about an hour. ⊠ *Burg Eltz, Münstermaifeld* ☎ *02672/950–500* ⊕ *www.burg-eltz.de* ☞ *Tour and treasure vault €10* ☼ *Late Mar.–Oct., daily 9:30–5:30.*

COCHEM

51 km (32 miles) southwest of Koblenz, approximately 93 km (58 miles) from Trier.

Cochem is one of the most attractive towns of the Mosel Valley, with a riverside promenade to rival any along the Rhine. It's especially lively during the wine festivals in June and late August. If time permits, savor the landscape from the deck of a boat—many excursions are available, lasting from one hour to an entire day. From the **Enderttor** (Endert Town Gate) you can see the entrance to one of Germany's longest railroad tunnels, the Kaiser-Wilhelm, an astonishing example of 19th-century engineering. The 4-km (2½-mile) tunnel saves travelers a 21-km (13-mile) detour along one of the Mosel's great loops.

ESSENTIALS

Visitor Information Cochem Tourist-Information. ⊠ *Endertpl. 1* ☎ *02671/60040* ⊕ *www.cochem.de.*

EXPLORING

Cochemer Sesselbahn (*Cochem Chairlift*). A ride on the chairlift to the Pinner Kreuz provides great vistas. ✉ *Endertstr. 44* ☎ *02671/989–063* 🌐 *www.cochemer-sesselbahn.de* 🎟 *€6.30 round-trip* 🕒 *Late Mar.–early July, daily 10–6; early July–Aug., daily 9:30–7; Sept., daily 10–6:30; Oct., daily 10–4; early Nov.–mid-Nov., daily 11–4.*

Historische Senfmühle. Wolfgang Steffens conducts daily tours at 11, 2, 3, and 4, showing how he produces the gourmet mustard at his 200-year-old mill. Garlic, cayenne, honey, curry, and Riesling wine are among the flavors you can sample and buy in the shop. From the Old Town, walk across the bridge toward Cond. The mill is to the left of the bridgehead. ✉ *Stadionstr. 1* ☎ *02671/607–665* 🌐 *www.senfmuehle.net* 🎟 *Tours €2.50* 🕒 *Daily 10–6.*

Reichsburg (*Imperial Fortress*). The 15-minute walk to this 1,000-year-old castle overlooking the town will reward you with great views of the area. In a tie-in with the fortress's past, falconry demonstrations are put on Tuesday to Sunday at 11, 1, 2:30, and 4. With advance reservations, you can also get a taste of the Middle Ages at a medieval banquet, complete with costumes, music, and entertainment. Banquets take place on Friday (7 pm) and Saturday (6 pm) and last four hours; the price (€49) includes a castle tour. During the *Burgfest* (castle festival) the first weekend of August, there's a medieval market and colorful tournaments. ✉ *Schlossstr. 36* ☎ *02671/255* 🌐 *www.reichsburg-cochem.de* 🎟 *€6, including 40-min tour; falconry €4* 🕒 *Mid-Mar.–early Nov., daily 9–5.*

WHERE TO EAT

$ GERMAN

🍴 **Alte Gutsschänke.** Locals and tourists mingle naturally here, near the open fireplace and antique wine-making equipment. The food is local and fortifying: sausages, cheeses, ham, and homemade soups served with the wines from host Arthur Schmitz's own estate. As the night progresses, locals might unpack their musical instruments and start playing. Note that this place doesn't serve beer. [$] *Average main: €8* ✉ *Schlossstr. 6* ☎ *02671/8950* 💳 *No credit cards* 🕒 *No lunch weekdays.*

$$$ GERMAN FAMILY

🍴 **Restaurant Müllerstube.** The rustic family inn Moselromantik Hotel Weissmühle is set amid the forested hills of the Enderttal (Endert Valley) on the site of a historic mill that belonged to the current proprietor's great-great-grandfather. Lined with photos and memorabilia from the original mill, it's an oasis from traffic and crowds yet only 2½ km (1½ miles) from Cochem. Beneath the exposed beams and painted ceiling of Restaurant Müllerstube, trout from the hotel's own fish farm will grace your table. German and French wines are served. The inn's underground bar, originally built to become a swimming pool, opens around 9 pm and is a bit of a time capsule with lots of 1970s German kitsch. [$] *Average main: €25* ✉ *Wilde Endert 2* ☎ *02671/8955* 🌐 *www.hotel-weissmuehle.de.*

EDIGER-ELLER

61 km (38 miles) southwest of Koblenz.

Ediger-Eller, once two separate hamlets, is another photogenic wine village with well-preserved houses and remnants of a medieval town wall. It's particularly romantic at night, when the narrow alleys and half-timber buildings are illuminated by historic streetlights.

EXPLORING

Martinskirche (*St. Martin's Church*). The church is a remarkable amalgamation of art and architectural styles, inside and out. Take a moment to admire the 117 carved bosses in the star-vaulted ceiling of the nave. Among the many fine sculptures throughout the church and the chapel is the town's treasure: a Renaissance stone relief, *Christ in the Winepress.* ✉ *Kirchstr.*

WHERE TO STAY

$$ HOTEL 🏨 **Zum Löwen.** This simply furnished hotel comes with friendly service and a splendid terrace overlooking the Mosel. **Pros:** fine view of the Mosel. **Cons:** on a busy street; no elevator. [$] *Rooms from: €110* ✉ *Moselweinstr. 23* ☎ *02675/208* 🌐 *www.mosel-hotel-loewen.de* 🕓 *Closed late Dec.–Mar.* 🛏 *20 rooms* 🍴 *Breakfast.*

EN ROUTE

Calmont. As you continue along the winding course of the Mosel, you'll pass Europe's steepest vineyard site, Calmont, just before the loop at Bremm. Opposite Calmont are the romantic ruins of a 12th-century Augustinian convent. **Zell.** This popular village is full of pubs and wineshops that ply the crowds with Zeller Schwarze Katz, "Black Cat" wine, a commercially successful product and the focal point of a large wine festival in late June. Some 6 million vines hug the slopes around Zell, making it one of Germany's largest wine-growing communities. The area between Zell and Schweich (near Trier), known as the Middle Mosel, is home to some of the world's finest Riesling.

TRABEN-TRARBACH

30 km (19 miles) south of Cochem.

The Mosel divides Traben-Trarbach, which has pleasant promenades on both sides of the river. Its wine festivals are held the second and last weekends in July. Traben's art nouveau buildings are worth seeing, including the Hotel Bellevue, the gateway on the Mosel bridge, the post office, the train station, and the town hall.

EXPLORING

Mittelmosel Museum. For a look at fine period rooms and exhibits on the historical development of the area, visit the Mittelmosel Museum, in the Haus Böcking (1750). ✉ *Casino Str. 2* ☎ *06541/9480* 🎟 *€2.50* 🕓 *Easter–Oct., Tues.–Sun. 10–5.*

EN ROUTE

During the next 24 km (15 miles) of your drive down the Mosel from Traben-Trarbach you'll pass by world-famous vineyards, such as Erdener Treppchen, Ürziger Würzgarten, the *Sonnenuhr* (sundial) sites of Zeltingen and Wehlen, and Graacher Himmelreich, before reaching Bernkastel-Kues.

BERNKASTEL-KUES

22 km (14 miles) southwest of Traben-Trarbach, 100 km (62 miles) southwest of Koblenz.

Bernkastel and Kues straddle the Mosel, on the east and west banks, respectively. Bernkastel is home to famed Bernkasteler Doctor, a small, especially steep vineyard that makes one of Europe's most expensive wines. Early German humanist Nikolaus Cusanus (1401–64) was from Kues; today his birthplace and St.-Nikolaus-Hospital are popular attractions.

GETTING HERE AND AROUND

By car, Bernkastel-Kues is about 45 minutes northeast of Trier and 90 minutes southwest of Koblenz. The closest train station (Regionalbahn) is in Wittlich, about a 20-minute taxi ride away.

ESSENTIALS

Visitor Information Bernkastel-Kues Tourist-Information. ⊠ *Gestade 6* ☎ *06531/500–190* ⊕ *www.bernkastel.de.*

EXPLORING

Burg Landshut. From the hilltop ruins of this 13th-century castle there are splendid views. It was here that Trier's Archbishop Boemund II is said to have recovered from an illness by drinking the local wine. This legendary vineyard, still known as "the Doctor," soars up from Hinterm Graben street near the town gate, Graacher Tor. You can purchase these well-regarded wines at some of the shops around town. ⊠ *Bernkastel-Kues.*

Jewish cemetery. Bernkastel's former Jewish population was well assimilated into town society until the Nazis took power. You can ask at the tourist center to borrow a key to the town's Jewish cemetery, reachable by a scenic half-hour hike through the vineyards in the direction of Traben-Trarbach. Opened in the mid-19th century, it contains a few headstones from a destroyed 17th-century graveyard. ⊠ *Old Town* ✚ *About 1 km (½ mile) from Graacher Tor.*

Market square. Elaborately carved half-timber houses (16th–17th century) and a Renaissance town hall (1608) frame St. Michael's Fountain (1606) on Bernkastel's photogenic market square. In early September the square and riverbank are lined with wine stands for one of the region's largest wine festivals, the Weinfest der Mittelmosel. ⊠ *Bernkastel-Kues.*

St.-Nikolaus-Hospital. The Renaissance philosopher and theologian Nikolaus Cusanus (1401–64) was born in Kues. The St.-Nikolaus-Hospital is a charitable *Stiftung* (foundation) he established in 1458, and it still operates a home for the elderly and a wine estate. ⊠ *Cusanusstr. 2* ☎ *06531/2260* ⊕ *www.cusanus.de* ▨ *Tours €5* ⊙ *Tours: Tues. at 10:30, Fri. at 3.*

Mosel-Weinmuseum (*Wine museum*). Within St.-Nikolaus-Hospital is a wine museum as well as a bistro. There's also a Vinothek (wineshop) in the vaulted cellar, where you can sample more than 150 wines from the entire Mosel-Saar-Ruwer region. ⊠ *St.-Nikolaus-Hospital, Cusanusstr. 2* ⊕ *www.moselweinmuseum.de* ▨ *Museum €5; Vinothek free, or €15 with wine tasting* ⊙ *Mid-Apr.–Oct., daily 10–6; Nov.–mid-Apr., daily 2–5.*

Continued on page 508

In the heart of the Mosel Valley lies the Mittelmosel (Middle Mosel), where vineyards tumble down steep slate slopes to riverside villages full of half-timbered, baroque, and belle époque architecture. Famed for its warm climate and 2,000-year-old wine-making tradition, it produces some of the best Rieslings in the world. The Middle Mosel's many wineries and tasting rooms are concentrated along a meandering 75-mile stretch of lush river valley, picturesque towns, and rural estates between the ancient town of Trier and the village of Zell, allowing for multiple sips in a short amount of time.

By Jeff Kavanagh

Above, Dr Pauly-Bergweiler bottle.
Left, Vineyards in the Mosel Valley.

Wine Tasting *in the* Mosel Valley

TWO DAYS IN THE MIDDLE MOSEL

DAY 1

Traben-Trarbach

Small, family-run wineries that have been producing high-quality wines for generations dominate the Middle Mosel. Starting in Trier, just across the border from Luxembourg, the tour follows the B-53 and the Mosel River as it flows northwest through a succession of pretty wine villages and steep-sloped estates.

🍷 **Bischöfliche Weingüter**
Drop down into a labyrinth of cellars beneath Trier's streets or visit the estate's elegant *vinothek* (wine store) to sample fine Rieslings built upon almost two millennia of priestly tradition. **Try:** fruity and elegant Scharzhofberger Riesling.
✉ Gervasiusstrasse 1, Trier
☎ 0651/145–760
🌐 www.bischoeflicheweingueter.de

Mosel grape harvest

🍷 **Sektgut St. Laurentius**
Whether in the spacious tasting room, on the outdoor terrace, or in the modern little wine bar near the river, there are plenty of places to taste this winery's *sekt* (sparkling wine), considered some of the best in the region. **Try:** fruity, creamy, and yeasty Crémant.
✉ Laurentiusstrasse 4, Leiwen
☎ 06507/3836
🌐 www.st-laurentius-sekt.de

🍷 **Weingut Lehnert-Veit**
In addition to Riesling, visitors can sample Merlot, Pinot Noir, and Chardonnay in this winery's Mediterranean-style garden on the banks of the Mosel. **Try:** playfully fruity Felsenwingert Goldtröpfchen Riesling.

✉ In der Dur 6–10, Piesport
☎ 06507/2123
🌐 www.weingut-lv.net

🍷 **Weingut Karp-Schreiber**
This welcoming winery's varietals include Riesling and Weissburgunder; it also produces a nice Rotling, a *cuvée* (blend) of Müller-Thurgau and Regent. When the sun's shining, the best place to taste them is on the winery's little trellised veranda. **Try:** fresh, elegant "my karp" Riesling.
✉ Moselweinstrasse 186, Brauneberg
☎ 06534/236
🌐 www.karp-schreiber.de

🍷 **Weingut Bauer**
An extension of the family home, where four generations reside beneath the same roof, the Bauer's simple, modern tasting room is a good place to sample award-winning still and sparkling white wines presented with old-fashioned hospitality. **Try:** fruity, refreshing Winzersekt Riesling Brut.
✉ Moselstrasse 3, Mülheim
☎ 06534/571
🌐 www.weingut-bauer.de

Wine barrels at Kerpen

Weingut Karp-Schreiber

Vineyards in the Mosel Valley

11

IN FOCUS WINE TASTING IN THE MOSEL VALLEY

DAY 2

From the quiet village of Mülheim, the Mosel makes a couple
of sweeping loops up the valley, passing through the towns
of Bernkastel-Kues and Traben-
Trarbach as it winds along.

Dr. Pauly-Bergweiler

This winery's presence in
the Mosel includes vineyards
in seven different villages and
a grand villa in the center
of Bernkastel, where its cozy
vinothek finds space within the
mansion's vaulted cellars. **Try:**
racy, flinty Alte Badstube am
Doctorberg Riesling.

✉ Gestade 15, Bernkastel
☎ 06531/3002
🌐 www.pauly-bergweiler.com

Kerpen

A friendly husband-and-wife-
run winery, Kerpen has eight
generations of winemaking tradition, a special collection of
Rieslings with labels designed
by visiting artists, and an unpretentious tasting room within
a stone's throw of the river.
Try: dry Graacher Himmelreich
Riesling Kabinett Feinherb.

✉ Uferallee 6, Bernkastel-
Wehlen
☎ 06531/6868
🌐 www.weingut-kerpen.de

Rebenhof

You'll find only Rieslings in
Rebenhof's stylish, contemporary tasting room, which shares
space with stainless-steel
fermentation tanks. **Try:** flinty,

old-vine Ürziger Würtgarten
Riesling Spätlese.

✉ Hüwel 2-3, Ürzig
☎ 06532/4546
🌐 www.rebenhof.de

Schmitges

Located on an unassuming
village lane, Schmitges specializes in the production of
high-quality dry whites that,
along with the modern, wine-
bar style of their vinothek,
distinguishes them from many
other local establishments.
Try: light, summery Rivaner.

✉ Hauptstrasse 4, Erden
☎ 06532/2743
🌐 www.schmitges-weine.de

Weingut Martin Müllen

Established in 1991, this
winery is a mere infant compared to many others here,
but its success has its roots
in modern and traditional
winemaking principles, and
one of the best *Grand Cru*
(great growth) vineyards in
the region. **Try:** light but complex Trarbacher Hühnerberg
Riesling Spätlese.

✉ Alte Marktstrasse 2, Traben-
Trarbach
☎ 06541/9470
🌐 www.muellen.de

STOP FOR A BITE

✗ Weinstube Kesselstatt

Sitting beneath vines in the
shadow of the Liebfrauen-
kirche and the Trier Dom you
can sip Kesselstatt estate
wines and snack on wild boar
and locally produced cheese.

✉ Liebfrauenstrasse 10, Trier
☎ 0651/41178
🌐 weinstube-kesselstatt.de

✗ Weinromantik Richters-
hof Hotel

An ideal place for lovers of
the grape, this stately hotel
has a bistro that serves
seasonal dishes such as
white asparagus and ham, a
gourmet restaurant offering
contemporary cuisine, and
a wine list that runs to 350
bottles, 150 of which are
from the Mosel.

✉ Hauptstrasse 81-83, Mülheim
☎ 06534/9480
🌐 www.weinromantikhotel.de

✗ Der Ratskeller

Just off Bernkastel's main
square, Der Ratskeller's uncomplicated regional fare
can be enjoyed at an outside
table with a view of the
action or inside cozily surrounded by dark wood and
leadlight windows.

✉ Markt 30, Bernkastel-Kues
☎ 06531/973–000

✗ Jugendstilhotel Bellevue

Traben-Trarbach's premier
hotel has a first-class reputation that derives from its
belle époque architecture,
fine cuisine, professional,
knowledgeable staff, and superb wine list.

✉ An der Mosel 11, Traben-
Trarbach
☎ 06541/7030
🌐 www.bellevue-hotel.de

WINE TOURING AND TASTING

WHEN TO GO

The best time to visit the region is between May and September, when a lightly chilled glass or two of wine is the perfect complement to a sunny spring day or a warm summer evening. This coincides with high season in the valley, when roads and cycle paths swell with tourists, particularly in the warmer months, and in September during the wine harvest. Fortunately, the next wine village is never far along the Mosel River. If you arrive and find a tasting room that's too busy, there's invariably another just around the corner.

IN THE TASTING ROOM

While varietals such as Müller-Thurgau, Weissburgunder, and Pinot Noir are produced in the Middle Mosel, the staple of most estates is Riesling. Given that the wineries are predominantly small, family-owned operations, there tends to be an emphasis on the production of high-quality, low-quantity wines. Their tasting rooms, when not part of the winery itself, are frequently extensions of family homes, affording visitors intimate contact with the winemakers. Naturally, German is the dominant language spoken by local tourists and many of the Dutch, Belgians, and Luxembourgers who pop across the border for a visit, but most winemakers speak English at least well enough to describe their wines. Opening hours vary, and although you can drop into most tasting rooms outside of these times, there may not always be someone around to serve you. To avoid disappointment it's worth checking websites for opening times first.

BOTTLE PRICES AND TASTING FEES

Once the most expensive wines in the world, Mosel Valley Rieslings have come down significantly in price since their heyday in the early 20th century, yet they remain world class. Quality bottles of Riesling start at about €10; each winery's price list is generally detailed in brochures found in its tasting room. Most wineries won't charge to taste a couple of their wines, but will expect you to purchase a bottle or two if you try more. Those that do have tasting fees, which are commonly between €5 and €15, will often waive them if you purchase a bottle.

Left, Romantic wine village on the Mosel River. Right, Bottle display from Mosel-Weinmuseum in Bernkastel-Kues

WINE TASTING PRIMER

Ordering and tasting wine—whether at a winery, bar, or restaurant—is easy once you master a few simple steps.

LOOK AND NOTE

Hold your glass by the stem and look at the wine in the glass. Note its color, depth, and clarity.

For whites, is it greenish, yellow, or gold? For reds, is it purplish, ruby, or garnet? Is the wine's color pale or deep? Is the liquid clear or cloudy?

SWIRL AND SNIFF

Swirl the wine gently in the glass to intensify the scents, then sniff over the rim of the glass. What do you smell? Try to identify aromas like:

- **Fruits**—citrus, peaches, berries, figs, melon

- **Flowers**—orange blossoms, honey, perfume

- **Spices**—baking spices, pungent, herbal notes

- **Vegetables**—fresh or cooked, herbal notes

- **Minerals**—earth, steely notes, wet stones

- **Dairy**—butter, cream, cheese, yogurt

- **Oak**—toast, vanilla, coconut, tobacco

- **Animal**—leathery, meaty notes

Are there any unpleasant notes, like mildew or wet dog, that might indicate that the wine is "off?"

SIP AND SAVOR

Prime your palate with a sip, swishing the wine in your mouth. Then spit in a bucket or swallow.

Take another sip and think about the wine's attributes. Sweetness is detected on the tip of the tongue, acidity on the sides of the tongue, and tannins (a mouth-drying sensation) on the gums. Consider the body—does the wine feel light in the mouth, or is there a rich sensation? Are the flavors consistent with the aromas? If you like the wine, try to pinpoint what you like about it, and vice versa if you don't like it.

Take time to savor the wine as you're sipping it—the tasting experience may seem a bit scientific, but the end goal is your enjoyment.

WHERE TO EAT

$$ ✕ **Rotisserie Royale.** The fish menu, vegetarian selection, and fancy twists
FRENCH   on traditional and regional dishes are what set this initially unassuming
restaurant apart from the crowd. It's in one of Burgstrasse's charming
half-timber houses. $ *Average main: €17* ✉ *Burgstr. 19* ☎ *06531/6572*
⊕ *www.rotisserie-royale.de* ⊟ *No credit cards* ⊘ *Closed Wed.*

$$$$ ✕ **Waldhotel Sonnora.** At their elegant country inn in the forested Eifel
FRENCH   Hills, Helmut and Ulrike Thieltges offer guests one of Germany's
Fodor'sChoice   absolute finest dining experiences. Helmut is an extraordinary chef,
★   renowned for transforming truffles, foie gras, and Persian caviar into
masterful dishes. Challans duck in an orange-ginger sauce is his spe-
cialty. The wine list is equally superb. The dining room, with gilded
and white-wood furnishings and plush red carpets, has a Parisian look,
and the pretty gardens add to a memorable visit. Sonnora can prepare a
vegetarian menu, but call ahead. $ *Average main: €60* ✉ *Dreis* ⊹ *Auf'm
Eichelfeld, 8 km (5 miles) southwest of Wittlich, which is 18 km (11
miles) west of Kues via B-50; from A-1, exit Salmtal* ☎ *06578/98220*
⊕ *www.hotel-sonnora.de* ⊘ *Closed Mon. and Tues., Jan., and 1st 2 wks
in July* ⬦ *Reservations essential.*

$$$ ✕ **Weinhotel St. Stephanus.** Rita and Hermann Saxler operate a comfort-
EUROPEAN   able, modern hotel and upscale restaurant in a 19th-century manor
house on the Ufer (riverbank) at Zeltingen. Whether you opt for the
handsome dining room or the terrace overlooking the Mosel, Saxler's
Restaurant is a good destination for refined regional cooking with a
Mediterranean touch. The spa offers vinotherapy—treatments using
grape-based products, such as grapeseed oil. $ *Average main: €22*
✉ *Uferallee 9, Zeltingen-Rachtig* ☎ *06532/680* ⊕ *www.hotel-stephanus.
de* ⊘ *No lunch Mon.–Thurs. in Jan.–Mar.*

WHERE TO STAY

$$ ⌂ **Wein- & Landhaus S. A. Prüm.** The traditional wine estate S.A. Prüm has
B&B/INN   state-of-the-art cellars and an attractive Vinothek for cellar tours and
tastings, as well as a stunning dining room and an idyllic patio facing the
Mosel and the vineyards. **Pros:** good rooms, some of which have vine-
yard and Mosel views. **Cons:** no elevator. $ *Rooms from: €110* ✉ *Ufer-
allee 25* ⊹ *About 4 km (2½ miles) north, at Wehlen* ☎ *06531/3110*
⊕ *www.sapruem.com* ⊘ *Closed mid-Dec.–Feb.* ⤶ *8 rooms, 2 apart-
ments* ⦉⊙⦊ *Breakfast.*

$$ ⌂ **Weinromantikhotel Richtershof.** This renovated 17th-century manor in
HOTEL   a shady park offers comfortable rooms and first-class friendly service.
Fodor'sChoice   **Pros:** garden terrace; wheelchair-accessible rooms; 24-hour room ser-
★   vice. **Cons:** thin walls. $ *Rooms from: €160* ✉ *Hauptstr. 81–83, Mül-
heim* ⊹ *5 km (3 miles) south of Bernkastel via B-53* ☎ *06534/9480*
⊕ *www.weinromantikhotel.de* ⤶ *38 rooms, 5 suites* ⦉⊙⦊ *Breakfast.*

**EN
ROUTE**   **Paulinshof.** The 55-km (34-mile) drive from Bernkastel to Trier takes in
another series of outstanding hillside vineyards, including the Braune-
berg, 10 km (6 miles) upstream from Bernkastel. On the opposite side of
the river is the Paulinshof, where Thomas Jefferson was impressed by a
1783 Brauneberger Kammer Auslese during his visit here in 1788. You
can sample contemporary vintages of this wine in the beautiful chapel

on the estate grounds. ⊠ *Paulinsstr. 14, Kesten* ☏ *06535/544* ⊕ *www. paulinshof.de* ⊙ *Weekdays 8–6, Sat. 9–4.*

EN
ROUTE

Piesport. On a magnificent loop 12 km (7½ miles) southwest of Braune-berg stands the famous village of Piesport, whose steep, slate cliff is known as the Loreley of the Mosel. The village puts on a fireworks display for its Loreleyfest the first weekend in July. Wines from its 35 vineyards are collectively known as Piesporter Michelsberg. The finest individual vineyard site, and one of Germany's very best, is the Gold-tröpfchen ("little droplets of gold").

TRIER

55 km (34 miles) southwest of Bernkastel-Kues, 150 km (93 miles) southwest of Koblenz.

Thanks to its deep history, the Trier of today holds a wealth of ancient sites. It's also an important university town, and accordingly boasts a surprisingly rich modern cultural landscape for a city of its size (just over 100,000 residents).

Its roots reach back to at least 400 BC, by which time a Celtic tribe, the Treveri, had settled the Trier Valley. Eventually Julius Caesar's legions arrived at this strategic point on the river, and Augusta Treverorum ("the town of [Emperor] Augustus in the land of the Treveri") was founded in 16 BC. It was described as an opulent city, as beautiful as any outside Rome.

Around AD 275 an Alemannic tribe stormed Augusta Treverorum and reduced it to rubble. But it was rebuilt in even grander style and renamed Treveris. Eventually it evolved into one of the leading cities of the empire, and was promoted to "Roma secunda" (a second Rome) north of the Alps. As a powerful administrative capital it was adorned with all the noble civic buildings of a major Roman settlement, as well as public baths, palaces, barracks, an amphitheater, and temples. The Roman emperors Diocletian (who made it one of the four joint capitals of the empire) and Constantine both lived in Trier for years at a time.

Trier survived the collapse of Ancient Rome and became an important center of Christianity and, ultimately, one of the most powerful arch-bishoprics in the Holy Roman Empire. The city thrived throughout the Renaissance and baroque periods, taking full advantage of its location at the meeting point of major east–west and north–south trade routes and growing fat on the commerce that passed through.

GETTING HERE AND AROUND
The area is excellent for biking. Rentals are available at the bicycle garage (*Fahrradgarage*) directly next to the Porta Nigra in the city cen-ter, or near track 11 of the main train station. Cyclists can follow the marked route of the *Radroute Nahe-Hunsrück-Mosel* between Trier and Bingen.

FESTIVALS
Altstadtfest. In late June, more than 100,000 people come out for this music festival in the Old Town, which also features a city run, mar-kets, and a parade. Major venues include the Trier Arena and Trier

Europahalle, hosting the likes of André Rieu, James Last, and Deep Purple. ⊠ *Trier* ⊕ *www.altstadtfest-trier.de.*

Moselfest Zurlauben. Wine, sparkling wine, beer, and fireworks fill this annual July celebration along the riverbank in Zurlauben district. ⊠ *Trier* ⊕ *www.zurlaubener-heimatfest.de.*

Weinfest (*Wine Festival*). This popular wine-focused event happens over a four-day weekend in early August in the Olewig district. ⊠ *Trier.*

Weihnachtsmarkt. This Christmas market and festival features nearly a hundred booths, and takes place on the market square and in front of the cathedral. ⊠ *Trier* ⊕ *www.trierer-weihnachtsmarkt.de.*

TOURS

Römer-Express. You can circumnavigate the town with the multilingual narrated tours of the Römer-Express trolley. It departs from Porta Nigra, near the tourist office. ⊠ *An der Porta Nigra* 🎫 *€9.*

Toga Tours. Actors dressed in Roman costume bring the history of the amphitheater, the Kaiserthermen (Imperial Baths), and the old town gate to life in these 2½-hour tours. They are conducted in German, but the guide or someone else in the group probably speaks some English and can translate the basic points. Reservations are essential, and tickets are available from the tourist office. ⊠ *Trier* 🎫 *€10.50.*

Tourist Office Bus Tour. The tourist office runs a bus tour of the town, departing from near their building at the Porta Nigra, but the narration is only in German. ⊠ *An der Porta Nigra* 🎫 *€12.50.*

Tourist Office Walking Tours. Various walking tours are offered by the tourist office, including one conducted in English which is available on Saturday at 1, May through October. ⊠ *An der Porta Nigra* 🎫 *€6.50.*

TIMING

To do justice to Trier, consider staying for at least two full days. A walk around Trier will take a good two hours, and you will need extra time to climb the tower of the Porta Nigra, walk through the vast interior of the Dom and its treasury, visit the underground passageways of the Kaiserthermen, and examine the cellars of the Amphitheater. Allow at least another half hour each for the Museum am Dom Trier (formerly known as the Bischöfliches Museum) and Viehmarktthermen, as well as an additional hour for the Rheinisches Landesmuseum.

DISCOUNTS AND DEALS

The **Trier Card,** available from the visitor center's website or at the center in Porta Nigra, entitles the holder to free public transportation and discounts on tours and admission fees to Roman sights, museums, and sports and cultural venues. It costs €9.90 and is valid for three successive days. The **Antiquity Card** (€10) grants admission to the Landesmuseum and two Roman structures, and is available at those locations and the tourist office.

ESSENTIALS

Visitor Information Trier Tourist-Information. ⊠ *An der Porta Nigra* ☎ *0651/978–080* ⊕ *www.trier-info.de.*

EXPLORING
TOP ATTRACTIONS

Fodor's Choice ★ **Amphitheater.** The sheer size of Trier's oldest Roman structure (circa AD 100) is impressive; in its heyday it seated 20,000 spectators. You can climb down to the cellars beneath the arena—animals were kept in cells here before being unleashed to do battle with gladiators. ⊠ *Olewiger Str.* ⚏ *€3* ⊘ *Apr.–Sept., daily 9–6; Oct. and Mar., daily 9–5; Nov.–Feb., daily 9–4.*

Fodor's Choice ★ **Dom** (*Cathedral*). The oldest Christian church north of the Alps, the Dom stands on the site of the Palace of Helen. Constantine tore the palace down in AD 330 and put up a large church in its place. The church burned down in 336, and a second, even larger one was built. Parts of the foundations of this third building can be seen in the east end of the present structure (begun in about 1035). The cathedral you see today is a weighty and sturdy edifice with small round-head windows, rough stonework, and asymmetrical towers, as much a fortress as a church. Inside, Gothic styles predominate—the result of remodeling in the 13th century—although there are also many baroque tombs, altars, and confessionals. ⊠ *Domfreihof* ☎ *0651/979–0792* ⊕ *www.dominformation.de* ⚏ *Free; tours €4.50* ⊘ *Apr.–Oct., daily 6:30–6, tours at 2; Nov.–Mar., daily 6:30–5:30.*

Domschatzkammer (*Cathedral Treasure Chamber*). The highlight of the cathedral's museum is the 10th-century Andreas Tragaltar (St. Andrew's Portable Altar), constructed of oak and covered with gold leaf, enamel, and ivory by local craftsmen. It's a reliquary for the soles of St. Andrew's sandals, as signaled by the gilded, life-size foot on the top of the altar. ⊠ *Dom, Domfreihof* ⚏ *€1.50; €4 for combined ticket with Museum am Dom Trier* ⊘ *Mid-Mar.–Oct. and Dec., Mon.–Sat. 10–5, Sun. 12:30–5; Nov. and Jan.–mid-Mar., Tues.–Sat. 11–4, Sun. 12:30–4.*

Fodor's Choice ★ **Kaiserthermen** (*Imperial Baths*). This enormous 4th-century bathing palace once housed cold- and hot-water baths and a sports field. Although only the masonry of the Calderium (hot baths) and the vast basements remain, they are enough to give a fair idea of the original splendor and size of the complex. Originally 98 feet high, the walls you see today are just 62 feet high. ⊠ *Weimarer-Allee and Kaiserstr.* ☎ *0651/436–2550* ⚏ *€3* ⊘ *Apr.–Sept., daily 9–6; Oct. and Mar., daily 9–5; Nov.–Feb., daily 9–4.*

Konstantin Basilika (*Constantine Basilica*). An impressive reminder of Trier's Roman past, this edifice, now the city's major Protestant church, was built by the emperor Constantine around AD 310 as the imperial throne room of the palace. At 239 feet long, 93 feet wide, and 108 feet high, it demonstrates the astounding ambition of its Roman builders and the sophistication of their building techniques. The basilica is one of the two largest Roman interiors in existence (the other is the Pantheon in Rome). Look up at the deeply coffered ceiling; more than any other part of the building, it conveys the opulence of the original structure. An ornate rococo garden now separates the basilica from the Landesmuseum. ⊠ *Konstantinpl.* ☎ *0651/42570* ⊘ *Apr.–Oct., Mon.–Sat. 10–6, Sun. 1–4; Nov.–Mar., Mon.–Sat. 10–noon and 2–4, Sun. 1–4.*

Museum am Dom Trier (*Museum at the Trier Cathedral*). This collection, just behind the Dom, focuses on medieval sacred art, and there are also fascinating models of the cathedral as it looked in Roman times. Look for 15 Roman frescoes, discovered in 1946, that may have adorned the Emperor Constantine's palace. ✉ *Bischof-Stein-Pl. 1* ☎ *0651/710–5255* ⊕ *www.bistum-trier.de/museum* ☜ *€3.50; €4 for combined ticket with Domschatzkammer* ⊙ *Tues.–Sat. 9–5; Sun. 1–5.*

Fodor'sChoice **Porta Nigra** (*Black Gate*). The best-preserved Roman structure in Trier
★ was originally a city gate, built in the 2nd century (look for holes left by the iron clamps that held the structure together). The gate served as part of Trier's defenses and was proof of the sophistication of Roman military might and its ruthlessness. Attackers were often lured into the two innocent-looking arches of the Porta Nigra, only to find themselves enclosed in a courtyard. In the 11th century the upper stories were converted into two churches, in use until the 18th century. The tourist office is next door. ✉ *Porta-Nigra-Pl.* ☎ *0651/718–2451* ☜ *€3* ⊙ *Apr.–Sept., daily 9–6; Oct. and Mar., daily 9–5; Nov.–Feb., daily 9–4.*

Fodor'sChoice **Rheinisches Landesmuseum** (*Rhenish State Museum*). The largest collec-
★ tion of Roman antiquities in Germany is housed here. The highlight is the 4th-century stone relief of a Roman ship transporting barrels of wine up the river. This tombstone of a Roman wine merchant was discovered in 1874, when Constantine's citadel in Neumagen was excavated. Have a look at the 108-square-foot model of the city as it looked in the 4th century—it provides a sense of perspective to many of the sights you can still visit today. ✉ *Weimarer-Allee 1* ☎ *0651/97740* ⊕ *www.landesmuseum-trier.de* ☜ *€6* ⊙ *Tues.–Sun. 10–5.*

WORTH NOTING

Hauptmarkt. The main market square of Old Trier—lined with gabled houses from several ages—is easily reached via Simeonstrasse. The market cross (958) and richly ornate St. Peter's Fountain (1595), dedicated to the town's patron saint, stand in the square. A flower and vegetable market is held here every weekday, while a farmers' market can be found at nearby Viehmarktplatz on Tuesday and Friday 8–2. ✉ *Trier.*

Karl-Marx-Haus. Marx was born on May 5, 1818, in this bourgeois house built in 1727. Visitors with a serious interest in social history will be fascinated by its small museum. Some of Marx's personal effects, as well as first-edition manifestos are on display. Audio guides are available in English, and English-language tours can be arranged on request. ✉ *Brückenstr. 10* ☎ *0651/970–680* ⊕ *www.fes.de/karl-marx-haus* ☜ *€4* ⊙ *Apr.–Oct., daily 10–6; Nov.–Mar., Mon. 2–5, Tues.–Sun. 11–5.*

Stadtmuseum Simeonstift Trier (*Simeon Foundation City Museum*). Built around the remains of the Romanesque Simeonskirche, this church is now a museum. It was constructed in the 11th century by Archbishop Poppo in honor of the early medieval hermit Simeon, who for seven years shut himself up in the east tower of the Porta Nigra. Collections include art and artifacts produced in Trier from the Middle Ages to the 19th century. ✉ *Simeonstr. 60* ☎ *0651/718–1459* ⊕ *www.museum-trier. de* ☜ *€5.50, €1 on 1st Sun. of month* ⊙ *Tues.–Sun. 10–5.*

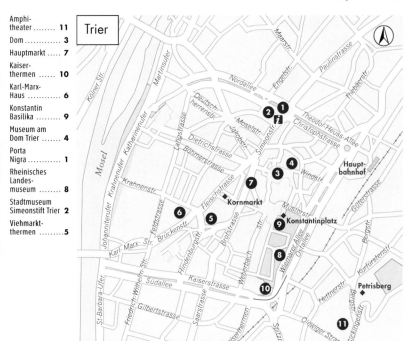

Amphitheater 11
Dom 3
Hauptmarkt 7
Kaiserthermen 10
Karl-Marx-Haus 6
Konstantin Basilika 9
Museum am Dom Trier 4
Porta Nigra 1
Rheinisches Landesmuseum 8
Stadtmuseum Simeonstift Trier 2
Viehmarktthermen 5

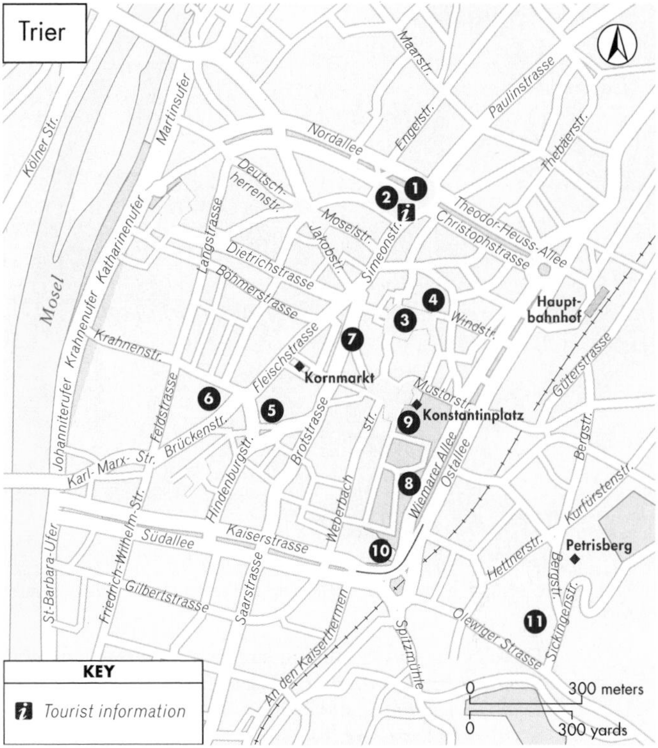

Viehmarktthermen. Trier's third Roman bath (early 1st century) was discovered when ground was broken for a parking garage. Finds of the excavations from 1987 to 1994 are now beneath a protective glass structure. You can visit the baths and see the cellar of a baroque Capuchin monastery. ✉ *Viehmarktpl.* ☎ *0651/994–1057* 🎫 *€3* 🕘 *Tues.–Sun. 9–5.*

WHERE TO EAT

$$$$ GERMAN 🍴 **Becker's Hotel.** This wine estate in the peaceful suburb of Olewig features a gourmet restaurant with prix-fixe menus, a Weinhaus serving regional cuisine, and a casual Weinstube. Dining alfresco is a nice option in summer. Bordeaux and Burgundy wines are available in addition to the estate's own wines, and wine tastings, cellar visits, and guided tours on the wine path can be arranged. [$] *Average main: €29* ✉ *Olewiger Str. 206* ☎ *0651/938–080* 🌐 *www.beckers-trier.de* 🕘 *Restaurant closed Sun. and Mon.*

$$$$ GERMAN 🍴 **Schlemmereule.** The name means "gourmet owl," and, indeed, the chef caters to gourmets in the 19th-century Palais Walderdorff complex opposite the cathedral. Truffles are a specialty, and the fish is always excellent. Wines from top German estates, particularly from the Mosel, and an extensive selection of red wines are available. Lots of windows lend a light, airy look to the restaurant, and a replica of one of Michelangelo's Sistine Chapel paintings is on the ceiling.

Trier's Porta Nigra (Black Gate), a city gate dating from the 2nd century, is the largest Roman structure north of the Alps.

There's courtyard seating in summer. $\boxed{\$}$ *Average main: €29* ⊠ *Palais Walderdorff, Domfreihof 1B* ☎ *0651/73616* ⊕ *www.schlemmereule. de* ⊗ *Closed Sun.* ⊿ *Reservations essential.*

$$ ✕ **Weinstube Kesselstatt.** Two soups daily, hearty fare, and fresh, regional
GERMAN cuisine are served with wines from the Reichsgraf von Kesselstatt estate. The *Tagesgericht* (daily special) and *Aktionsmenü* (prix-fixe menu) are a good bet. *Das Beste der Region* (the region's best) is an ample selection of local hams, cheeses, fish, and breads, served on a wooden board for two. The interior has exposed beams and polished wood tables, and the shady terrace is popular in summer. $\boxed{\$}$ *Average main: €15* ⊠ *Liebfrauenstr. 10* ☎ *0651/41178* ⊕ *www.weinstube-kesselstatt.de.*

$ ✕ **Zum Domstein.** Whether you dine inside or out, don't miss the col-
GERMAN lection of Roman artifacts displayed in the cellar. In addition to the German dishes on the regular menu, you can order from à la carte or prix-fixe menus based on recipes attributed to the Roman gourmet Marcus Gavius Apicius in the evening. $\boxed{\$}$ *Average main: €14* ⊠ *Hauptmarkt 5* ☎ *0651/74490* ⊕ *www.domstein.de.*

WHERE TO STAY

$$ ☗ **Hotel Ambiente.** Markus and Monika Stemper—a passionate cook
B&B/INN and a gracious hostess—bring modern style to their country inn near the Luxembourg border. **Pros:** country atmosphere; legendary garden. **Cons:** removed from city center. $\boxed{\$}$ *Rooms from: €109* ⊠ *In der Acht 1–2* ✛ *7 km (4½ miles) southwest of Trier via B-49* ☎ *0651/827–280* ⊕ *www.ambiente-trier.de* ⇱ *12 rooms* ⦿*Breakfast.*

$$ ☗ **Hotel Petrisberg.** The Pantenburgs' friendly, family-run hotel is high
HOTEL on Petrisberg hill overlooking Trier, not far from the amphitheater and

a 20-minute walk to the Old Town. **Pros:** fine view of Trier. **Cons:** somewhat removed from the city center. [$] *Rooms from: €110* ✉ *Sickingenstr. 11–13* ☎ *0651/4640* 🌐 *www.hotelpetrisberg.de* 🛏 *24 rooms, 2 apartments* 🍴 *Breakfast.*

$$ HOTEL 🏨 **Römischer Kaiser.** Centrally located near the Porta Nigra, this handsome patrician manor from 1885 offers well-appointed rooms with attractive baths. **Pros:** near the Porta Nigra; free Wi-Fi. **Cons:** some rooms are dark due to a neighboring building. [$] *Rooms from: €116* ✉ *Porta-Nigra-Pl. 6* ☎ *0651/977–0100* 🌐 *www.friedrich-hotels.de* 🛏 *43 rooms* 🍴 *Breakfast.*

NIGHTLIFE AND PERFORMING ARTS

Most of the town's pubs and cafés are on Viehmarktplatz and Stockplatz in the Old Town. ■ **TIP→ For up-to-the-minute information on performances, concerts, and events all over town, visit** 🌐 *www.trier-today.de.*

Metropolis. This popular Trier dance club features international DJs, theme parties, and live music. ✉ *Hindenburgstr. 4* ☎ *0651/9949–6603* 🌐 *www.metropolis-trier.de.*

Theater Trier. Opera, theater, and ballet performances are staged here, as well as concerts. ✉ *Am Augustinerhof* ☎ *0651/718–1818* 🌐 *www.theater-trier.de.*

TUFA–Tuchfabrik. Concerts, theater, and other cultural events are staged here. ✉ *Wechselstr. 4, at Weberstr.* ☎ *0651/718–2412* 🌐 *www.tufa-trier.de.*

BONN AND THE KÖLN (COLOGNE) LOWLANDS

Bonn, the former capital of West Germany, and of reunified Germany until 1999, is the next major stop after Koblenz on the Rhine. It's close to the legendary Siebengebirge (Seven Hills), a national park and site of western Germany's northernmost vineyards. According to German mythology, Siegfried (hero of the Nibelungen saga) killed a dragon here and bathed in its blood to make himself invincible. The lowland, a region of gently rolling hills north of Bonn, lacks the drama of the Rhine Gorge upstream but offers the urban pleasures of Köln (Cologne), an ancient cathedral town, and Düsseldorf, an elegant city of art and fashion. Although not geographically in the Rhineland proper, Aachen is an important side trip for anyone visiting the region. Its stunning cathedral and treasury are the greatest storehouses of Carolingian art and architecture in Europe.

BONN

61 km (38 miles) north of Koblenz, 28 km (17 miles) south of Köln.

Bonn was the postwar seat of the federal government and parliament until Berlin became its capital again in 1999. Aptly described by the title of John le Carré's spy novel *A Small Town in Germany*, the quiet university town was chosen as a stopgap measure to prevent such weightier

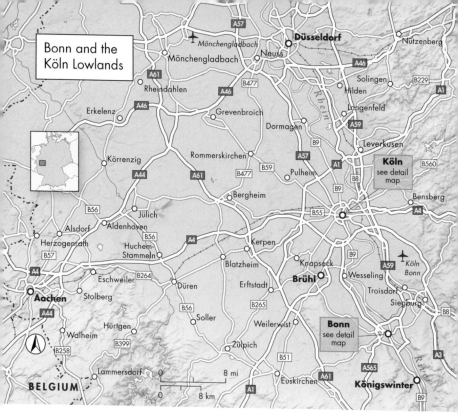

Bonn and the Köln Lowlands

contenders as Frankfurt from becoming the capital, a move that would have lessened Berlin's chances of regaining its former status. With the exodus of the government from Bonn, the city has become a bit less cosmopolitan. Still, Bonn thrives as the headquarters of two of Germany's largest multinational corporations (Deutsche Telekom and Deutsche Post/DHL), and the UN has expanded its presence in the city as well. The fine museums and other cultural institutions that once served the diplomatic elite are still here to be enjoyed.

GETTING HERE AND AROUND

The town center is a car-free zone; an inner ring road circles it with parking garages on the perimeter. A convenient parking lot is just across from the train station and within 50 yards of the tourist office, which is on Windeckstrasse near the Hauptbahnhof. Bonn has extensive bike paths downtown; these are designated paths (often demarcated with blue-and-white bicycle symbols) on the edges of roads or sidewalks. ■ TIP→ Pedestrians, beware: anyone walking on a bike path risks getting mowed down. Bicyclists are expected to follow the same traffic rules as cars. In Bonn the Radstation, at the main train station, will not only rent you a bike and provide maps, but will also fill your water bottle and check the pressure in your tires for free.

Bilingual bus tours of Bonn cost €16 and start from the tourist office. They're conducted daily at 2 from Easter to October, and Saturday only November to March. A variety of walking tours are also available, including the "Bonn zu Fuss" city tour (€9), offered Saturday at 11 am from late April to October.

Bus Tours. Bilingual bus tours of Bonn start from the tourist office daily at 2, Easter through October and on Saturday in March and November. ⊠ *Bonn* 🚌 *€16.*

FESTIVALS

Beethoven-Festival. Concerts are held at numerous indoor and outdoor venues during September's monthlong Beethoven-Festival. ⊠ *Bonn* ☎ *0228/201–0345* ⊕ *www.beethovenfest.de.*

DISCOUNTS AND DEALS

Bonn's tourism office sells the **Bonn Regio Welcome Card,** which offers an array of reductions, plus free entry into most museums, in combination with low- or no-cost transportation; the card costs €9 per 24-hour period.

ESSENTIALS

Bicycle Contact Radstation. ⊠ *Quantiusstr. (opposite Nos. 4–6)* ☎ *0228/981–4636* ⊕ *www.radstationbonn.de.*

Visitor Information Bonn Information. ⊠ *Windeckstr. 1, on Münsterpl.* ☎ *0228/775–000* ⊕ *www.bonn.de.*

EXPLORING

TOP ATTRACTIONS

Beethoven-Haus (*Beethoven House*). Beethoven was born in Bonn in 1770 and, except for a short stay in Vienna, lived here until the age of 22. You'll find scores, paintings, a grand piano (his last, in fact), and an ear trumpet or two. Thanks to the modern age, there's now a "Stage for Music Visualization," an interactive exhibit involving 3-D glasses that shows Beethoven's best-loved works. The museum shop carries everything from kitsch to elegant Beethoven memorabilia. ⊠ *Bonng. 20* ☎ *0228/981–7525* ⊕ *www.beethoven-haus-bonn.de* 🎟 *€6* ☉ *Apr.–Oct., daily 10–6; Nov.–Mar., Mon.–Sat. 10–5, Sun. 11–5.*

Bundesviertel (*Federal Government District*). Walking through the pleasant area that was once the government district is like taking a trip back in time, to an era when Bonn was still the sleepy capital of West Germany. Bordered by Adenauerallee, Kaiser-Friedrich-Strasse, Franz-Josef-Strasse, and the Rhine, the quarter boasts sights such as the **Bundeshaus**, which includes the Plenarsaal (plenary hall). Designed to serve as the new Federal Parliament, the Bundeshaus was completed only seven years before the capital was relocated to Berlin in 1999. A few steps away, you'll find the historic **Villa Hammerschmidt,** the German equivalent of the White House. This stylish neoclassical mansion began serving as the Federal president's permanent residence in 1950, and is still his home when he stays in Bonn. Equally impressive is the **Palais Schaumburg,** another fine example of the Rhein Riveria estates that once housed the Federal Chancellery (1949–76). It became the center of Cold War politics during the Adenauer administration. Tours of the quarter,

Bonn is the city of Beethoven: he was born here, you can tour his home, there is a concert hall named after him, and a monument to him on Münsterplatz.

including a visit to the Villa Hammerschmidt, are offered by the Bonn Tourist Office. ⊠ *U-Bahn Heussallee.*

Kunstmuseum Bonn (*Art Museum*). Changing exhibits are generally excellent at this large museum that focuses on Rhenish expressionists and German art since 1945 (Beuys, Baselitz, and Kiefer, for example). The museum's airy and inexpensive café is better than the stuffier version across the plaza at the Kunst- und Ausstellungshalle. ⊠ *Friedrich-Ebert-Allee 2* ☎ *0228/776–260* ⊕ *www.kunstmuseum-bonn.de* ✉€7 ⊙ *Tues.–Sun. 11–6 (until 9 pm Wed.).*

Kurfürstliches Schloss (*Prince-Electors' Palace*). Built in the 18th century by the prince-electors of Köln, this grand palace now houses Bonn's university. If the weather is good, stroll through Hofgarten park in front of it. When Bonn was a capital, this patch of grass drew tens of thousands to antinuclear demonstrations. Today it's mostly used for games of pickup soccer and ultimate Frisbee. ⊠ *Am Hofgarten.*

Münster (*Minster*). The 900-year-old church is vintage late Romanesque, with a massive octagonal main tower and a soaring spire. It stands on a site where two Roman soldiers were executed in the 3rd century for being Christian. It saw the coronations of two Holy Roman Emperors (in 1314 and 1346) and was one of the Rhineland's most important ecclesiastical centers in the Middle Ages. The 17th-century bronze figure of St. Helen and the ornate rococo pulpit are highlights of the interior; outside you'll find two giant stone heads: those of Cassius and Florentius, the martyred soldiers. ⊠ *Münsterpl.* ☎ *0228/985–880* ⊕ *www.bonner-muenster.de* ✉ *Free* ⊙ *Weekends 7–7.*

WORTH NOTING

Alter Friedhof (*Old Cemetery*). This ornate, leafy cemetery is the resting place of many of the country's most celebrated sons and daughters. Look for the tomb of composer Robert Schumann (1810–56) and his wife, Clara, also a composer and accomplished pianist. ✉ *Bornheimerstr.* ✥ *From the main train station, follow Quantiusstr. west, parallel to the tracks until it becomes Herwarthstr.; before the street curves to the left, turning into Endenicherstr., take the underpass below the railroad track. You'll then be on Thomastr., which borders the cemetery* ⊗ *Mar.–Oct., daily 7 am–8 pm; Nov.–Feb. daily 8–5.*

Altes Rathaus (*Old Town Hall*). This 18th-century rococo town hall looks somewhat like a pink dollhouse. Its elegant steps and stair entry have seen a great many historic figures, including French president Charles de Gaulle and U.S. president John F. Kennedy. It's now the seat of the Lord Mayor of Bonn and can only be admired from the outside. ✉ *Am Markt.*

Bundeskunsthalle (*Art and Exhibition Hall of the German Federal Republic*). This is one of the Rhineland's most important venues for major temporary exhibitions about art, culture, and archaeology. Its modern design, by Viennese architect Gustave Peichl, is as interesting as anything on exhibit in the museum. It employs three enormous blue cones situated on a lawnlike rooftop garden. ✉ *Friedrich-Ebert-Allee 4* ☎ *0228/91710* ⊕ *www.bundeskunsthalle.de* 🎫 *One exhibit €10, all exhibits €15 (reduced to €6.50 2 hrs before closing)* ⊗ *Tues. and Wed. 10–9, Thurs.–Sun. 10–7.*

Haus der Geschichte (*House of History*). German history since World War II is the subject of this museum, which begins with "hour zero," as the Germans call the unconditional surrender of 1945. The museum displays an overwhelming amount of documentary material organized on five levels and engages various types of media. It's not all heavy either—temporary exhibits have featured political cartoonists, Cold War–era sporting contests pitting East Germany versus West Germany, and an in-depth examination of the song "Lili Marleen," sung by troops of every nation during World War II. An audio guide in English is available. ✉ *Willy-Brandt-Allee 14* ☎ *0228/91650* ⊕ *www.hdg.de* 🎫 *Free* ⊗ *Tues.–Fri. 9–7, weekends 10–6.*

Poppelsdorfer Schloss (*Poppelsdorf Palace*). This former electors' palace, built in the baroque style between 1715 and 1753, now houses the university's mineralogical collection. Its botanical gardens are home to 12,000 species, among the largest variety in Germany. ✉ *Meckenheimer Allee 171* ☎ *0228/732–764* ⊕ *www.steinmann.uni-bonn.de/museen; www.botgart.uni-bonn.de* 🎫 *Mineralogical collection €2.50; botanical garden free weekdays, Sun. €3* ⊗ *Mineralogical collection: Wed. and Fri. 3–6, Sun. 10–5. Botanical garden: Apr.–Oct., daily 10–6 (until 8 Thurs.); Nov.–Mar., weekdays 10–4.*

WHERE TO EAT

$$

GERMAN

✕ **Em Höttche.** Beethoven was a regular at this tavern, which has been around since the late 14th century. Today it offers one of the best-value lunches in town, and the kitchen stays open until 1 am. The interior is

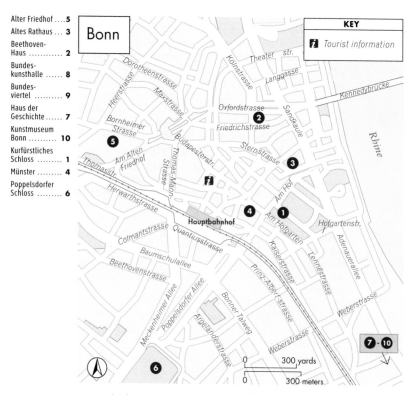

rustic, the food hearty and non-fussy. $ *Average main: €16* ⊠ *Markt 4* ☎ *0228/690–009* ⊕ *www.em-hoettche.de.*

$$$
ITALIAN

✕ **Ristorante Sassella.** When the Bundestag was still in town, this Bonn institution used to be cited in the press as frequently for its backroom political dealings as for its Lombardy-influenced food. Locals, prominent and otherwise, still flock to the restaurant, in an 18th-century house in the suburb of Kessenich. The style is pure Italian farmhouse, with stone walls and exposed beams, but the handmade pastas often stray from the typical, as in the salmon-filled black-and-white pasta pockets in shrimp sauce. $ *Average main: €25* ⊠ *Karthäuserpl. 21* ☎ *0228/530–815* ⊕ *www.ristorante-sassella.de* ۞ *Closed Mon. No lunch Sat., no dinner Sun.* ⌂ *Reservations essential.*

$$$$
EUROPEAN
Fodor'sChoice
★

✕ **Strandhaus.** On a quiet residential street, and hidden from view in summer by an ivy-covered patio, this restaurant feels like a true escape—befitting its laid-back name ("beach house"). The chef insists on local produce, and presents her delicate, innovatively spiced food with elegance, but no fuss. A carefully compiled wine list long on Geman bottles, along with a frequently changing menu, means locals come here often. $ *Average main: €27* ⊠ *Georgstr. 28* ☎ *0228/369–4949* ⊕ *www. strandhaus-bonn.de* ۞ *Closed Sun. and Mon. No lunch.*

WHERE TO STAY

$$$ **Best Western Domicil.** A group of
HOTEL buildings around a quiet, central courtyard has been converted into a charming and comfortable hotel, with rooms individually furnished and decorated in styles ranging from fin de siècle romantic to Italian modern. **Pros:** quiet courtyard; handy to the train station. **Cons:** plain exterior. $ *Rooms from: €195* ✉ *Thomas-Mann-Str. 24–26* ☎ *0228/729–090* ⊕ *domicil-bonn. bestwestern.de* ⤳ *43 rooms, 1 apartment* ⟨○⟩ *Breakfast.*

$$ **Hotel Mozart.** Elegant on the outside and simple on the inside, this
HOTEL small, attractive hotel is often recommended to friends by locals. **Pros:** quiet tree-lined street; close to the train station. **Cons:** thin walls. $ *Rooms from: €105* ✉ *Mozartstr. 1* ☎ *0228/659–071* ⊕ *www.hotel-mozart-bonn.com* ⤳ *38 rooms* ⟨○⟩ *Breakfast.*

$$$ **Sternhotel.** For solid comfort and a picturesque, central location, the
HOTEL Sternhotel is tops—and their weekend rates are a bargain. **Pros:** in the center of town; partnership with gym across the square, allowing guests free entry. **Cons:** market square location can be noisy in the morning; expensive for the area. $ *Rooms from: €185* ✉ *Markt 8* ☎ *0228/72670* ⊕ *www.sternhotel-bonn.de* ⤳ *80 rooms* ⟨○⟩ *Breakfast.*

PERFORMING ARTS

Beethovenhalle. The Bonn Beethoven Orchestra opens its season in grand style every year in late summer as part of Beethovenfest Bonn. Many of its concerts are held in the Beethovenhalle. ✉ *Wachsbleiche 16* ☎ *0228/72220* ⊕ *www.beethovenhalle.de.*

Beethoven-Haus. In the Beethoven-Haus, recitals are sometimes given on a 19th-century grand piano, and concerts take place regularly in the chamber music hall. ✉ *Bonng. 20* ☎ *0228/981–750* ⊕ *www.beethoven-haus-bonn.de.*

Pantheon Theater. This is a major venue for comedy and cabaret. ✉ *Bundeskanzlerpl. 2–10* ☎ *0228/212–521* ⊕ *www.pantheon.de.*

Schumannhaus. Chamber-music concerts are given regularly at the Schumannhaus, where composer Robert Schumann spent his final years. ✉ *Sebastianstr. 182* ☎ *0228/773–656* ⊕ *www.schumannhaus-bonn.de.*

Theater Bonn. Operas are staged regularly at the Theater Bonn, which also hosts musicals and performances by world-renowned dance companies, including ballet. ✉ *Am Boeselagerhof 1* ☎ *0228/778–000* ⊕ *www.theater-bonn.de.*

CLASSICAL MUSIC

Few regions in Europe rival the quality of classical music performances and venues on the Rhine. Beethoven was born in Bonn, and the city hosts a Beethoven festival every year in mid- to late September. Düsseldorf, once home to Mendelssohn, Schumann, and Brahms, has the finest concert hall in Germany after Berlin's Philharmonie: the Tonhalle, in a former planetarium. Köln also has one of Germany's best concert halls, and its opera company is known for exciting classical and contemporary productions. The cathedrals of Aachen, Köln, and Trier are magnificent settings for concerts and organ recitals.

SHOPPING

There are plenty of department stores and boutiques in the pedestrian shopping zone around the Markt and the Münster.

Flohmarkt (*Flea Market*). Bargain hunters search for secondhand goods and knickknacks at the city's renowned—and huge—flea market. It's held in Rheinaue south of the Konrad-Adenauer-Brücke on the third Saturday of each month from March through October. ⊠ *Rheinaue* ⊕ *www.flohmarkt-rheinaue.de*.

Wochenmarkt (*Weekly Market*). Bonn's Wochenmarkt is open every day but Sunday, filling the Markt with vendors of produce and various edibles. Things get really busy in springtime, when the locals flock to find the best asparagus. ⊠ *Markt*.

BIER AM RHEIN

When it's warm out, most Germans like nothing better than to sit outside with a beer in hand. In Bonn, the best beer gardens are right on the River Rhine, which runs through the city. On the Bonn city center side, there's the **Alter Zoll** (*Brassertufer 1*) and **Schänzchen** (*Rosental 105*). Across the Kennedy Bridge in Beuel, however, is where the late-afternoon sun shines best. On either side of the bridge are **Rheinlust** (*Rheinaustr. 134*) and **Bahnhöfchen** (*Rheinaustr. 116*).

KÖNIGSWINTER

12 km (7 miles) southeast of Bonn.

Home to one of Germany's most popular castles, Drachenfels, Königswinter is also the gateway to the 30 large and small hills that make up the Siebengebirge, the country's oldest nature reserve. In early May, festivities and fireworks light up the town as part of the "Rhine in Flames" fireworks display.

GETTING HERE AND AROUND

Königswinter is 15 minutes south of Bonn by car. It can also be reached by a 40-minute train ride (via Regionalbahn) from Köln.

Visitor Information Siebengebirge Tourist Office. ⊠ *Drachenfelsstr. 51* ☎ *02223/917–711* ⊕ *www.siebengebirge.com*.

EXPLORING

Drachenfels. The town of Königswinter has one of the most visited castles on the Rhine, the **Drachenfels**. Its ruins crown one of the highest hills in the Siebengebirge, with a spectacular view of the Rhine. It's also part of Germany's oldest nature reserve, with more than 100 km (62 miles) of hiking trails. The castle was built in the 12th century by the archbishop of Köln, and takes its name from a dragon said to have lived in a nearby cave. (The dragon was slain by Siegfried, hero of the epic *Nibelungenlied*.)

The castle ruins can be reached via two different hikes, each of about 45 minutes. One route begins at the Drachenfelsbahn station, and passes the Nibelungenhalle reptile zoo along the way. The other route starts at Rhöndorf on the other side of the hill. The Siebengebirge Tourist Office at Drachenfelsstrasse 51 in Königswinter can provide a map that includes these and other local hiking trails. ⊠ *Königswinter* 🎫 *Free* ⊙ *Always accessible*.

Drachenfelsbahn. If hiking to Drachenfels isn't for you, you can also reach the castle ruins by taking the Drachenfelsbahn, a steep, narrow-gauge train that makes trips to the summit every half hour March through October, and hourly in January and February. ✉ *Drachenfelsstr. 53* ☎ *02223/92090* ⊕ *www.drachenfelsbahn-koenigswinter.de* 💰 *€10 round-trip* ⊗ *Mar. and Oct., daily 10–6; Apr., daily 10–7; May–Sept., daily 9–7; early Nov., Jan., and Feb., weekdays noon–5, weekends 11–6.*

FAMILY **Sea Life.** Königswinter's huge aquarium features 2,000 creatures from the sea. The biggest pool has a glass tunnel that enables you to walk on the "bottom of the sea." ✉ *Rheinallee 8* ☎ *0180/6666–90101 tickets; €0.20–€0.60 per call* ⊕ *www.visitsealife.com* 💰 *€14.95* ⊗ *Late Mar.–Oct., daily 10–6; Nov.–late Mar., weekdays 10–5, weekends 10–6.*

BRÜHL

20 km (12 miles) northwest of Bonn.

In the center of Brühl stands the Rhineland's most important baroque palace, the Augustusburg. Brühl is also home to one of Germany's most popular theme parks, Phantasialand.

EXPLORING

Jagdschloss Falkenlust. This small castle, at the end of an avenue leading under the tracks across from Schloss Augustusburg's grounds, was built as a getaway where the prince could indulge his passion for falconry. ✉ *Otto-Wels-Str.* ☎ *02232/44000* ⊕ *www.schlossbruehl.de* 💰 *€6* ⊗ *Feb.–Nov., Tues.–Fri. 9–noon and 1:30–4, weekends 10–5.*

Schloss Augustusburg. This castle and the magnificent pleasure park that surrounds it were created in the time of Prince Clemens August, between 1725 and 1768. The palace contains one of the most famous achievements of rococo architecture, a staircase by Balthasar Neumann. The castle can be visited only on guided tours, which leave the reception area every hour or so. An English-language recorded tour is available. ✉ *Max-Ernst-Allee* ☎ *02232/44000* ⊕ *www.schlossbruehl.de* 💰 *€8* ⊗ *Feb.–Nov., Tues.–Fri. 9–noon and 1:30–4, weekends 10–5.*

KÖLN (COLOGNE)

28 km (17 miles) north of Bonn, 47 km (29 miles) south of Düsseldorf, 70 km (43 miles) southeast of Aachen.

Köln (Cologne in English) is the largest city on the Rhine (the fourth largest in Germany) and one of the most interesting. The city is vibrant and bustling, with a lightness and cheerfulness that's typical of the Rhineland. At its heart is tradition, manifested in the abundance of bars and brew houses serving the local Kölsch beer and old Rhine cuisine. These are good meeting places to start a night on the town. Tradition, however, is mixed with the contemporary, found in a host of elegant shops, sophisticated restaurants, modern bars and dance clubs, and a contemporary-art scene that's now just hanging on against unstoppable competition from Berlin.

Although not as old as Trier, Köln has been a dominant power in the Rhineland since Roman times, and it remains a major commercial, intellectual, and ecclesiastical center. Köln was first settled in 38 BC. For nearly a century it grew slowly, in the shadow of imperial Trier, until a locally born noblewoman, Julia Agrippina, daughter of the Roman general Germanicus, married the Roman emperor Claudius. Her hometown was elevated to the rank of a Roman city and given the name Colonia Claudia Ara Agrippinensium (Claudius Colony at the Altar of Agrippina). For the next 300 years Colonia (hence Cologne, or Köln) flourished. Evidence of the Roman city's wealth resides in the Römisch-Germanisches Museum. In the 9th century Charlemagne,

> ### KÖLN, GERMANY'S GAY CAPITAL
>
> Köln is widely considered to be Germany's gay capital—despite what Berliners may say. Every summer, up to 1 million visitors come for two weeks to attend **Cologne Pride** (⊕ *www.colognepride.de*), transforming Köln into an international LGBT hot spot. The festivities begin in mid-June and culminate in early July with the citywide **Christopher Street Day Parade.** The city's gay nightlife centers on what locals call the "Bermuda Triangle"—the city's biggest concentration of gay bars, on Schaafenstrasse.

the towering figure who united the sprawling German lands (and ruled much of present-day France) as the first Holy Roman Emperor, restored Köln's fortunes and elevated it to its preeminent role in the Rhineland by appointing the first archbishop of Köln. The city's ecclesiastical heritage is one of its most striking features; it has a full dozen Romanesque churches and one of the world's largest and finest Gothic cathedrals. In the Middle Ages it was a member of the powerful Hanseatic League, occupying a position of greater importance in European commerce than either London or Paris.

Köln was a thriving modern city until World War II, when bombings destroyed 90% of it. Only the cathedral remained relatively unscathed. Like many other German cities that rebounded during the "Economic Miracle" of the 1950s, Köln is a mishmash of old and new, sometimes awkwardly juxtaposed. A good part of the former Old Town along the Hohe Strasse (old Roman High Road) was turned into a remarkably charmless pedestrian shopping mall. It's all framed by six-lane expressways winding along the rim of the city center—barely yards from the cathedral—illustrating the problems of postwar reconstruction. However, much of the Altstadt, ringed by streets that follow the line of the medieval city walls, is closed to traffic. Most major sights are within this area and are easily reached on foot. Here, too, you'll find the best shops.

GETTING HERE AND AROUND

As one of Germany's most important railroad hubs, Köln is connected by fast trains to cities throughout northwestern Europe, including Paris, Brussels, and Frankfurt. The German railroad network links Köln to the entire nation. You can reach Köln from Bonn in about 20 minutes, and Brühl in about 15.

FESTIVALS

Weihnachtsmarkt am Kölner Dom. Of Cologne's four main Christmas markets the Weihnachtsmarkt am Kölner Dom, in the shadow of the city's famed cathedral, is the most impressive. Set against the backdrop of the church's magnificent twin spires, a giant Christmas tree stands proudly in the middle of the market's 160 festively adorned stalls, which sell mulled wine, roasted chestnuts, and many other German yuletide treats. ⊕ *www.koelnerweihnachtsmarkt.com* ☉ *Late Nov.–Dec. 23, Sun.–Wed. 11–9, Thurs. and Fri. 11–10, Sat. 10–10.*

TOURS

Bus trips into the countryside (to the Eifel Hills, the Ahr Valley, and the Westerwald) are organized by several city travel agencies.

City Bus Tours. The 90-minute tours, conducted in English and German, leave year-round from the tourist office next to the cathedral. There are departures every half hour between 10 am and 4 pm, from Wednesday to Sunday, and once every two hours on Monday and Tuesday. ⊠ *Köln* 🎫*€12–€15.*

Radstation Köln Bike Tours. In addition to their bike rentals, Radstation Köln conduct three-hour bike tours of the city, departing daily at 1:30 pm. ⊠ *Köln Hauptbahnhof (Cologne Central Station) or Markmannsg. next to Deutzer Brücke, Köln* ☎ *0221/139–7190* ⊕ *www.radstationkoeln.de* 🎫*€17.50.*

Walking Tours. From mid-June to September, a 90-minute English-language walking tour leaves from the tourist office every Saturday at 3 pm. Additional walking tours in English are often available by arrangement with the tourist office. ⊠ *Köln* 🎫*€11.*

DISCOUNTS AND DEALS

Most central hotels sell the **Köln Card** (€9 for one day, €18 for two days), which entitles you to discounts on sightseeing tours, admissions to all the city's museums, free city bus and tram travel, and other reductions.

ESSENTIALS

Visitor Information Köln Tourismus Office. ⊠ *Kardinal-Höffner-Pl. 1, Köln* ☎ *0221/346–430* ⊕ *www.cologne-tourism.com.*

EXPLORING

TOP ATTRACTIONS

Fodor'sChoice
★

Dom (*Cathedral*). Köln's landmark embodies one of the purest expressions of the Gothic spirit in Europe. The cathedral, meant to be a tangible expression of God's kingdom on Earth, was conceived with such immense dimensions that construction, begun in 1248, was not completed until 1880, after the original plan was rediscovered. At 515 feet high, the two west towers of the cathedral were briefly the tallest structures in the world when they were finished (before being eclipsed by the Washington Monument). The cathedral was built to house what are believed to be the relics of the Magi, the three kings who paid homage to the infant Jesus (the trade in holy mementos was big business in the Middle Ages—and not always scrupulous). The size of the building was not simply an example of self-aggrandizement on the part of the people of Köln, however; it was a response to the vast numbers of pilgrims who arrived to see the relics. The ambulatory, the passage that curves around the back of the altar, is unusually large, allowing cathedral authorities to funnel large numbers of visitors up to the crossing (where the nave and transepts meet and where the relics were originally displayed), around the back of the altar, and out again.

Today the relics are kept just behind the altar, in the original, enormous gold-and-silver **reliquary.** The other great treasure of the cathedral, in the last chapel on the left as you face the altar, is the **Gero Cross,** a monumental oak crucifix dating from 971. The Altar of the City Patrons (1440), a triptych by Stephan Lochner, Köln's most famous medieval painter, is to the right. Other highlights are the stained-glass windows, some dating from the 13th century and another, designed by Gerhard Richter with help from a computer program, from the 21st; the 15th-century altarpiece; and the early-14th-century high altar, with its glistening white figures and intricate choir screens. If you're up to it, climb to the top of the bell tower to get the complete vertical experience (but be aware that viewing Köln from the Dom itself removes the skyline's most interesting feature). The treasury includes the silver shrine of Archbishop Engelbert, who was stabbed to death in 1225. Allow at least an hour for the whole tour of the interior, treasury, and tower climb. ⊠ *Dompl., Altstadt* ☎ *0221/9258–4730* ⊕ *www.koelner-dom. de* ⌨ *Tower €4, cathedral treasury €6, guided tours €7* ⊙ *May–Oct., Mon.–Sat. 6 am–9 pm, Sun. 1–4:30; Nov.–Apr., Mon.–Sat. 6 am–7:30 pm, Sun. 1–4:30. Tower and stairwell: May–Sept., daily 9–6; Mar., Apr., and Oct., daily 9–5; Nov.–Feb., daily 9–4. Treasury: daily 10–6. Guided tours in English Mon.–Sat. at 10:30 and 2:30, Sun. at 2:30.*

Museum Ludwig. This museum is dedicated to art from the beginning of the 20th century to the present day. Its American pop-art collection (including Andy Warhol, Jasper Johns, Robert Rauschenberg, Claes Oldenburg, and Roy Lichtenstein) rivals that of most American museums. ⊠ *Heinrich-Böll-Pl., Innenstadt* ☎ *0221/2212–6165* ⊕ *www.museum-ludwig.de* ⌨ *€11* ⊙ *Tues.–Sun. 10–6; 1st Thurs. of every month 10–10. Closed 1 wk during Karneval, mid-Feb.–early Mar.*

Fodor's Choice **Römisch-Germanisches Museum** (*Roman-Germanic Museum*). This cultural landmark was built in the early 1970s around the famous Dionysius mosaic discovered here during the construction of an air-raid shelter in 1941. The huge mosaic, more than 800 square feet, once formed the dining-room floor of a wealthy Roman trader's villa. Its millions of tiny earthenware and glass tiles depict some of the adventures of Dionysius, the Greek god of wine. The pillared 1st-century tomb of Lucius Publicius (a prominent Roman officer), some stone Roman coffins, and everyday objects of Roman life are among the museum's other exhibits. Bordering the museum on the south is a restored 90-yard stretch of the old Roman harbor road. ⊠ *Roncallipl. 4, Altstadt* ☎ *0221/2212–4438* ⊕ *www.roemisch-germanisches-museum.de* ⌨ *€9* ⊙ *Tues.–Sun. 10–5, 1st Thurs. of every month 10–10.*

Wallraf-Richartz-Museum. This museum contains paintings spanning the years 1300 to 1900. The Dutch and Flemish schools are particularly

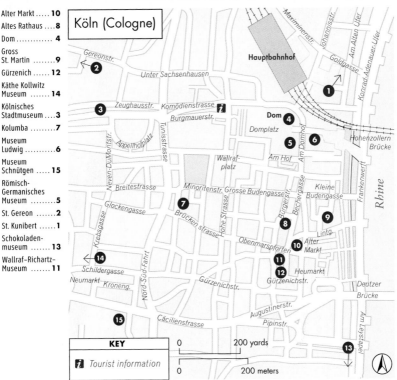

well represented, as is the 15th- to 16th-century Köln school of German painting. Its two most famous artists are the Master of the St. Veronica (whose actual name is unknown) and Stefan Lochner, represented by two luminous works, *The Last Judgment* and *The Madonna in the Rose Bower*. Large canvases by Rubens, who spent his youth in Köln, hang prominently on the second floor. There are also outstanding works by Rembrandt, Van Dyck, and Frans Hals, and the largest collection of French impressionism in Germany. ✉ *Obenmarspforten, Altstadt* ☎ *0221/2212–1119* ⊕ *www.wallraf.museum* 🎫 *€8* ⊘ *Daily 10–6 (to 9 Thurs.).*

WORTH NOTING

Alter Markt (*Old Market*). The square has an eclectic assembly of buildings, most of them postwar. However, two 16th-century houses survived the war intact—Nos. 20 and 22, which are today a Kölsch brewpub. The oldest structure dates from 1135. In late November and December, Alter Markt is the site of one of the city's prettiest Christmas markets. ✉ *Altstadt.*

Altes Rathaus (*Old Town Hall*). The Rathaus is worth a look, even from the outside. (Tours of the interior, for groups only, must be booked at the tourist office.) It's the oldest town hall in Germany, with elements remaining from the 14th century. The famous bell tower rings

its bells daily at 9 am, noon, 3 pm, and 6 pm. Standing on pedestals at one end of the town hall are figures of prophets made in the early 15th century. Ranging along the south wall are nine additional statues, the so-called *Nine Good Heroes,* carved in 1360. Charlemagne, Alexander the Great, and King David are among them. Sculptures of 124 later Cologne heroes, up through the 20th century, have been added outside at the Town Hall Tower. ✉ *Rathauspl. 2, Altstadt* ☎ *0221/2212–3332.*

Gross St. Martin (*Great St. Martin*). This remarkable Romanesque parish church was rebuilt after being flattened in World War II. Its massive 13th-century tower, with distinctive corner turrets and an imposing central spire, is another

> ## EAU DE COLOGNE
>
> The original "eau de Cologne" was first produced here in the early 18th century from an Italian formula. It's made from a secret formula and aged in oak barrels. The most famous cologne is 4711, which derives its name from the firm's address at 4711 Glockengasse. The building itself is equipped with a carillon, a museum, and (naturally) a gift shop. The light scent, primarily derived from citrus, rosemary, and lavender, may seem a little old-fashioned to some, but it comes in an elegant bottle with a turquoise-and-gilt label, and makes a nice souvenir.

Köln landmark. The church was built on the site of a Roman granary. ✉ *Martinspförtchen 8, Altstadt* ☎ *0221/2779–4747* ⊕ *www. romanische-kirchen-koeln.de* ◷ *Sept.–July, Tues.–Fri. 9–7:30; weekends 10–7:30; Aug., Tues.–Sun. 2–6.*

Gürzenich. This Gothic structure at the south end of Martinsviertel was all but demolished in World War II, but carefully reconstructed afterward. It's named after a medieval knight from whom the city acquired valuable real estate in 1437. The official reception and festival hall here has played a central role in civic life through the centuries. At one end of the complex are the remains of the 10th-century Gothic church of **St. Alban,** which were left ruined after the war as a memorial. On what's left of the church floor you can see a sculpture of a couple kneeling in prayer, *Mourning Parents,* by Käthe Kollwitz, a memorial to the ravages of war. ✉ *Martinstr. 29–37, Altstadt* ⊕ *www.koelnkongress.de.*

Käthe Kollwitz Museum. The works of Käthe Kollwitz (1867–1945), the most important German female artist of the 20th century, focus on social themes like the plight of the poor and the atrocities of war. This is the larger of the country's two Kollwitz collections and comprises all of her woodcuts, as well as paintings, etchings, lithographs, and sculptures. There are also changing exhibits of other modern artists. ✉ *Neumarkt 18–24, in Neumarkt Passage, Innenstadt* ☎ *0221/227–2899* ⊕ *www.kollwitz.de* ⊡ *€4* ◷ *Tues.–Fri. 10–6, weekends 11–6.*

Kölnisches Stadtmuseum (*Cologne City Museum*). The triumphs and tragedies of Köln's rich past are packed into this museum at the historic *Zeughaus,* the city's former arsenal. Here you'll find an in-depth chronicle of Köln's history—including information about the lives of ordinary people and high-profile politicians, the industrial revolution

KARNEVAL IN KÖLN

As the biggest city in the tradition-ally Catholic Rhineland, Köln puts on Germany's most exciting and rowdy carnival. The Kölsch starts flowing on November 11 at 11:11 am with screams of the famous motto *Kölle alaaf!* ("Köln is alive!"). Karneval then calms down for a few months, only to reach a fever pitch in February for the last five days before Lent. On Fat Thursday, known as *Weiberfast-nacht,* women roam the streets with scissors and exercise merciless preci-sion in cutting off the ties of any men foolish enough to wear them. Starting then, bands, parades, and parties go all night, and people of all ages don silly costumes, including the customary red clown nose. It's a good time to meet new people; in fact, it is practically impossible not to, as kissing strangers is considered par for the course. ■TIP➡ During this time, visitors who are claus-trophobic or who don't want to risk having beer spilled on them should avoid the Heumarkt area in the Old Town, and possibly the whole city. The festivities come to an end Tuesday at midnight with the ritual burning of the "Nubbel"—a dummy that acts as the scapegoat for everyone's drunken, embarrassing behavior. Note: Many museums are closed during Karneval.

(car manufacturer Henry Ford headquartered his European operations here), and the destruction incurred during World War II. For those who've always wanted to be privy to the inside stories surrounding local words such as *Klüngel, Kölsch,* and *Karneval,* the answers are waiting to be discovered within the museum's walls. ⊠ *Zeughausstr. 1–3, Alt-stadt* ☎ *0221/2212–5789* ⊕ *www.museenkoeln.de* ⊠ *€5* ⊙ *Wed.–Sun. 10–5, Tues. 10–8, first Thurs. of every month 10–10.*

Kolumba. The origins of the official art museum of the Archdiocese of Cologne stretch back to 1853, but the institution received a big boost in 2007, with the opening of a unique new home atop—and masterfully incorporating— the ruins of the Gothic parish church of St. Kolumba. Designed by the Swiss architect Peter Zumthor, the new building pays homage to the site's Roman, Gothic, and medieval heritage, while unstuffily presenting a collection of art spanning from late antiquity to the present. ⊠ *Kolumbastr. 4, Innenstadt* ☎ *0221/933–1930* ⊕ *www. kolumba.de* ⊠ *€5* ⊙ *Wed.–Mon. noon–5.*

Museum Schnütgen. A treasure house of medieval art from the Rhine region, the museum has an ideal setting in a 12th-century basilica. Don't miss the crucifix from the St. Georg Kirche or the original stained-glass windows and carved figures from the Dom. Other exhibits include intri-cately carved ivory book covers, rock-crystal reliquaries, and illumi-nated manuscripts. ⊠ *Cäcilienstr. 29, Innenstadt* ☎ *0221/2213–1355* ⊕ *www.museum-schnuetgen.de* ⊠ *€6* ⊙ *Tues.–Sun. 10–6 (to 8 Thurs.), 1st Thurs. of every month 10–10.*

St. Gereon. This exquisite Romanesque basilica stands on the site of an old Roman burial ground six blocks west of the train station. An enor-mous dome rests on walls that were once clad in gold mosaics. Roman masonry forms part of the medieval structure, which is believed to have been built over the grave of its namesake, the 4th-century martyr and Köln's patron. ✉ *Gereonskloster 2–4, Altstadt* ☎ *0221/474–5070* 🌐 *www.stgereon.de* 🎟 *Free* 🕒 *Weekdays 10–6, Sat. 10–5:30, Sun. 1–6.*

St. Kunibert. The most lavish of the churches from the late-Romanesque period is by the Rhine, three blocks north of the train station. The apse's precious stained-glass windows have filtered light for more than 750 years (they were put in protective storage during World War II). Consecrated in 1247, the church contains an unusual room, concealed under the altar, which gives access to a pre-Christian well once believed to promote fertility in women. ✉ *Kunibertsklosterg. 2, Altstadt* ☎ *0221/121–214* 🌐 *www.basilika-st-kunibert.de* 🎟 *Free* 🕒 *Mon.–Sat. 10–1 and 3–6, Sun. 3–6.*

FAMILY **Schokoladenmuseum** (*Chocolate Museum*). This riverside museum south of the cathedral is a real hit, and so crowded on weekends that it can be unpleasant. It recounts 3,000 years of civilization's production and enjoyment of chocolate, from the Central American Maya to the colonizing and industrializing Europeans. It's also a real factory, with lava flows of chocolate and a conveyer belt jostling thousands of truffles, but that's not open to view. The museum shop, with a huge variety of chocolate items, does a brisk business, and the riverside panorama café serves some of the best cake in town. ✉ *Am Schockoladenmuseum 1a, Rheinufer* ☎ *0221/931–8880* 🌐 *www.schokoladenmuseum.de* 🎟 *€9* 🕒 *Tues.–Fri. 10–6, weekends 11–7.*

WHERE TO EAT

$ EUROPEAN

🍴 **Café Elefant.** For three decades, writers and artists from Köln's elegant Agnesviertel neighborhood have been meeting at this cosy locale on a quiet, tree-lined street. Inside, the ambience—like a little corner of Montmartre—is just right for thinking deep thoughts, or simply chatting over a slice of chocolate cake. Even when the cake's all gone, night owls can enjoy the café's delicious Camembert and lingonberry blintzes. [$] *Average main: €7* ✉ *Weissenburgstr. 50, Köln* ☎ *0221/734–520* 💳 *No credit cards.*

$$$ FRENCH Fodor's Choice ★

🍴 **Capricorn i Aries.** This corner brasserie—part neighborhood bistro, part upscale restaurant—serves the staples of French rural cuisine with a Rhineland twist, whether it's a simple soup or a five-course dinner. The owners' highly regarded four-table restaurant across the street is also available for special events. Those aiming to improve their own skills can participate in a Sunday cooking class, in which students prepare and then eat four courses. [$] *Average main: €22* ✉ *Alteburger Str. 31, Neustadt-Süd* ☎ *0221/397–5710* 🌐 *www.capricorniaries.com* 💳 *No credit cards* 🕒 *Closed Wed. and Sun. No lunch Sat.* ✍ *Reservations essential.*

$$$$ ITALIAN Fodor's Choice ★

🍴 **Casa di Biase.** The sophisticated Italian cuisine is served here in a warm, elegant setting on the city's southwest side. The seasonally changing menu focuses on fish and game, and the wine list is interesting and extensive—although sometimes pricey. [$] *Average main: €26* ✉ *Eifelpl. 4, Südstadt* ☎ *0221/322–433* 🌐 *www.casadibiase.de* 🕒 *Closed Sun. No lunch Sat.*

$ GERMAN

🍴 **Früh am Dom.** For real down-home German cooking, few places in Köln compare to this time-honored former brewery in the shadow of the Dom. It's often crowded, but the mood's fantastic. Bold frescoes on the vaulted ceilings establish that mood, and the authentically Teutonic experience is completed by such dishes as *Hämmchen* (pork knuckle). The beer garden is perfect for summer dining. $ *Average main: €14* ⊠ *Am Hof 12–18, Altstadt* ☎ *0221/261–3215* ⊕ *www.frueh-am-dom.de* 🖃 *No credit cards.*

$$$ ✕ **Heising & Adelmann.** A young
ECLECTIC crowd gathers here to do what people along the Rhine have done for centuries—talk, drink, and enjoy good company. There's a party every Friday and Saturday with a DJ. Consistently voted one of the best deals in town, this restaurant offers good German beer, tangy cocktails, and a creative mixture of German and French food. $ *Average main: €22* ⊠ *Friesenstr. 58–60, Neustadt-Nord* ☎ *0221/130–9424* ⊕ *www.heising-und-adelmann.de* ☽ *Closed Sun. and Mon. No lunch.*

$ ✕ **Päffgen.** There's no better Bräuhaus in Köln for drinking Kölsch,
GERMAN the city's home brew. You won't sit long in front of an empty glass before a blue-aproned waiter sweeps by and places another one before you. With its worn wooden interior, colorful clientele, and typical Rhenish fare (sauerbraten, pork knuckle, and potato pancakes), Päffgen sums up local tradition. The brewery is the family business of the late singer-actress Nico, née Christa Päffgen, who became famous in the '60s through her collaborations with Andy Warhol and the Velvet Underground. $ *Average main: €11* ⊠ *Friesenstr. 64–66, Friesenviertel* ☎ *0221/135–461* ⊕ *www.paeffgen-koelsch.de* 🖃 *No credit cards.*

WHERE TO STAY

The tourist office, across from the cathedral, can make hotel bookings for you for the same night, at a cost of €3 per booking. If you plan to be in town for Karneval, be sure to reserve a room well in advance.

$$$$ 🏨 **Excelsior Hotel Ernst.** Old-master paintings, including a Van Dyck, grace
HOTEL this 1863 hotel's sumptuous Empire-style lobby, while Gobelins tapestries hang in the ballroom; the rooms are spacious, and the deluxe category of rooms melds old-world elegance with modern sophistication. **Pros:** Van Dyck paintings and Gobelins tapestries; steps from both the train station and Dom. **Cons:** expensive. $ *Rooms from: €270* ⊠ *Domplatz, Trankg. 1, Altstadt* ☎ *0221/2701* ⊕ *www.excelsiorhotelernst.de* ⤴ *114 rooms, 26 suites* ⦿ *No meals.*

$$ 🏨 **Hopper Hotel et cetera.** The rooms in this former monastery in the
HOTEL Belgian Quarter are spare but not spartan, though a startlingly realistic sculpture of a bishop, sitting in the reception area, serves as a constant reminder of the building's ecclesiastic origins. **Pros:** chic renovation;

EHRENFELD: THE WORLD IN KÖLN

If you ever needed proof of Köln's multiethnic mix, head to Ehrenfeld, just beyond the city center's western edge, for a meal and let your taste buds be convinced. Within a square mile you'll find restaurants serving home-style versions of a host of world cuisines. Two of the best are **Yadaary-Orienthaus** (*Sömmerlingstr. 48*), which serves flavorful Arab dishes in an intimate atmosphere, and **Saudade** (*Wahlenstr. 2*), a Portuguese wine bar and café where the *vinho verde* comes fresh from the cask. Ehrenfeld is also home to Köln's most exclusive sauna and spa, **Neptunbad** (*Neptunpl. 1*).

attractive neighborhood. **Cons:** not centrally located; showers tricky for older guests. $ *Rooms from: €130* ✉ *Brüsselerstr. 26, Belgisches Viertel* ☎ *0221/924–400* ⊕ *www.hopper.de* 🛏 *48 rooms, 1 suite, 1 apartment* ⦿ *Breakfast.*

$ ⌂ **Hotel Chelsea.** This designer hotel with classic modern furnishings has
HOTEL a strong following among artists and art dealers, as well as with the musicians who come to play at the nearby Stadtgarten jazz club. **Pros:** an artsy clientele and neighborhood. **Cons:** some rooms need freshening up; a few rooms don't have their own bathroom. $ *Rooms from: €98* ✉ *Jülicherstr. 1, Belgisches Viertel* ☎ *0221/207–150* ⊕ *www.hotel-chelsea.de* 🛏 *35 rooms, 3 suites, 1 apartment* ⦿ *No meals.*

$ ⌂ **Hotel im Kupferkessel.** The best things about this small, unassuming,
HOTEL family-run hotel are its immaculate housekeeping—the very model of German fastidiousness—and the price (small single rooms with shared bath can be had for as little as €45). **Pros:** inexpensive, and breakfast is included. **Cons:** no elevator and four stories; some rooms don't have their own bathroom. $ *Rooms from: €82* ✉ *Probsteig. 6, Altstadt* ☎ *0221/270–7960* ⊕ *www.im-kupferkessel.de* 🛏 *12 rooms* ⦿ *Breakfast.*

$$ ⌂ **Hotel im Wasserturm.** What used to be Europe's tallest water tower is
HOTEL now an independent, 11-story luxury hotel that's welcomed guests like Brad Pitt and fashion mogul Wolfgang Joop. **Pros:** modern luxury at its finest. **Cons:** expensive breakfast. $ *Rooms from: €174* ✉ *Kayg. 2, Altstadt* ☎ *0221/20080* ⊕ *www.hotel-im-wasserturm.de* 🛏 *45 rooms, 33 suites* ⦿ *No meals.*

$$ ⌂ **Hotel Pullman Cologne.** One of the city's favorite business hotels, the
HOTEL 12-story Pullman Cologne draws tourists from around the world too with its welcoming vibe and unexpectedly lighthearted flair. **Pros:** great location; 90 rooms with Dom views; very helpful and friendly staff. **Cons:** standard rooms are small. $ *Rooms from: €148* ✉ *Helenenstr. 14, Altstadt* ☎ *0221/275–2200* ⊕ *www.pullmanhotels.com* 🛏 *265 rooms, 10 suites* ⦿ *No meals.*

NIGHTLIFE AND PERFORMING ARTS

Kölnticket. Tickets to most arts events can be purchased through Köln-ticket. ☎ *0221/2801* ⊕ *www.koelnticket.de.*

NIGHTLIFE

Köln's nightlife is centered on three distinct areas: along the river in the Old Town, which seems to be one big party on weekends; on Zulpicherstrasse near the university; and around the Friesenplatz U-bahn station. Many streets off the Hohenzollernring and Hohenstaufenring, particularly Roonstrasse and Aachenerstrasse, also provide a broad range of nightlife. In summer the Martinsviertel, a part of the Altstadt around the Gross St. Martin church, which is full of restaurants, brew houses, and *Kneipen* (pubs), is a good place to go around sunset.

Papa Joe's Em Streckstrump. For live jazz, head to the tiny Papa Joe's Jazzlokale, where there's never a cover charge. ✉ *Buttermarkt 37, Altstadt* ☎ *0221/257–7931* ⊕ *www.papajoes.de.*

Papa Joe's Klimperkasten. This classic, kitschy, roaring twenties–style Altstadt *biersalon* plays oldies from Piaf to Porter. ✉ *Alter Markt*

50–52, Altstadt ☎ *0221/258–2132* ⊕ *www.papajoes.de.*

Stadtgarten. In summer, head straight for the Stadtgarten and sit in the Biergarten for some good outdoor *Gemütlichkeit* (coziness). At other times of the year it's still worth a visit for its excellent jazz club. Stadtgarten also runs a beer garden with cheap, tasty eats in the shaded Rathenauplatz park, by Köln's synagogue. ✉ *Venloerstr. 40, Altstadt* ☎ *0221/952–9940* ⊕ *www.stadtgarten.de.*

PERFORMING ARTS

Antoniterkirche. Organ recitals and chamber concerts are presented in many of the Romanesque churches around town, and in the Gothic Antoniterkirche. ✉ *Schilderg. 57, Innenstadt* ☎ *0221/9258–4615* ⊕ *www.antonitercitykirche.de.*

KÖLSCH, BITTE!
It is said that the city's beloved beer can only be called Kölsch if it's brewed within sight of the cathedral. The beverage is served in traditional *Kölschkneipen*. Your waiter, called a *Köbes*, is likely to tease you (that's the Rhenish humor) and will replace your empty glass with a full one whether you order it or not. (If you want to avoid this, leave a swallow in the nearly empty glass or cover it with a coaster.) This automatic replacement is justified by the fact that the glass, called a *stange* (pole), is quite small due to the belief that Kölsch doesn't stay fresh for long after it has been poured.

Oper der Stadt Köln. Köln's opera company is known for exciting classical and contemporary productions, including collaborative efforts with the French fashion designer Christian Lacroix. The opera house on Offenbachplatz, originally scheduled to reopen in the fall of 2015 after a major multiyear renovation, is now expected to return in 2016. ✉ *Offenbachpl., Innenstadt* ☎ *0221/2212–8400* ⊕ *www.oper.koeln.*

Philharmonie. Köln's WDR Sinfonieorchester performs regularly in the city's excellent concert hall. ✉ *Bischofsgartenstr. 1, Altstadt* ☎ *0221/204–080* ⊕ *www.koelner-philharmonie.de.*

Schauspielhaus. Köln's principal theater is the Schauspielhaus, home to the 20 or so private theater companies in the city. Until its main space on Offenbachplatz reopens in 2016 after a major renovation, Schauspielhaus productions take place at an industrial space (Carlswerk, Schanzenstrasse 6–20) in the Mülheim neighborhood. ✉ *Offenbachpl., Innenstadt* ☎ *0221/2212–8400* ⊕ *www.schauspielkoeln.de.*

SHOPPING

A good shopping loop begins at the **Neumarkt Galerie**. From there, head down the charmless but practical pedestrian shopping zone of the Schildergasse. From Schildergasse, go north on Herzogstrasse to arrive at **Glockengasse**. A block north is Breite Strasse, another pedestrian shopping street. At the end of Breite Strasse is Ehrenstrasse, where the young and young-at-heart can shop for hip fashions and trendy housewares. After a poke around here, explore the small boutiques on Benesisstrasse, which will lead you to Mittelstrasse, best known for high-tone German fashions and luxury goods. Follow Mittelstrasse to the end to return to the Neumarkt. For some of the city's coolest shopping, head a few blocks farther west to the Belgian Quarter, where you'll find a hodgepodge of indie fashion designers, concept shops, and secondhand stores.

Glockengasse. Köln's most celebrated product, Eau de Cologne No. 4711, was first concocted here by the 18th-century Italian chemist Johann Maria Farina. At the company's flagship store there's a small exhibition of historical 4711 bottles, as well as a perfume fountain in which you can dip your fingers. ⊠ *House of 4711, Glockeng. 4, Innenstadt* ☏ *0221/2709–9910* ⊕ *www.4711.com.*

> ## GO BELGIAN
>
> Among Köln's most enticing areas for a drink or light meal is the leafy and attractive Belgian Quarter. German soap stars and media power brokers flock to eateries like Pepe (*Antwerpener-str. 63*). There's a hipper crowd at cafés like **Hallmackenreuther** (*Brüsselerpl. 9*) and **Salon Schmitz** (*Aachenerstr. 30*)—a place to see and be seen.

Neumarkt Galerie. This bright, modern indoor shopping arcade has a web of shops and cafés (including the city's only Primark) surrounding an airy atrium. Just look for the huge sculpture of an upside-down ice cream cone above the entrance. ⊠ *Richmodstr. 8, Köln* ⊕ *www. neumarktgalerie.com* ⊙ *Closed Sun.*

Peek & Cloppenburg. This big clothing store is a highlight of Shildergasse. Designed by the architect Renzo Piano, the building looks like a spaceship, and its selection of fashions—for men and women, from budget to couture—is out of this world. ⊠ *Schilderg. 65–67, Innenstadt* ☏ *0221/453–900* ⊕ *www.peek-cloppenburg.com.*

AACHEN

70 km (43 miles) west of Köln.

At the center of Aachen, the characteristic three-window-wide facades give way to buildings dating from the days when Charlemagne made Aix-la-Chapelle (as it was then called) the great center of the Holy Roman Empire. Thirty-two German emperors were crowned here, gracing Aachen with the proud nickname "Kaiserstadt" (Emperors' City). Roman legions had been drawn here for the healing properties of the sulfur springs emanating from the nearby Eifel Mountains. (The name "Aachen," based on an old Frankish word for "water," alludes to this.) Charlemagne's father, Pepin the Short, also settled here to enjoy the waters, and to this day the city is also known as Bad Aachen and is still drawing visitors in search of a cure. One-and-a-half-hour walking tours (€7) of the Altstadt depart from the tourist office throughout the year at 11 on weekends, as well as at 2 on weekdays from April to December. The Saturday tours are conducted in English (€9) as well as German.

ESSENTIALS

Visitor Information Aachen Tourist-Information. ⊠ *Friedrich-Wilhelm-Pl.* ☏ *0241/180–2960* ⊕ *www.aachen.de.*

EXPLORING
TOP ATTRACTIONS

Centre Charlemagne. Despite its name, this museum, which opened in 2014, doesn't just pay homage to Charlemagne, the man who put Aachen on the map in the 8th century. It also reveals Aachen's much broader history, from Neolithic times to the present, including its Celto-Roman and baroque-era stints as a spa town, and its centuries as Holy Roman imperial coronation city. Multimedia stations help bring the past to life, and the interactive audio guide is highly recommended. ⊠ *Katschhof 1* ☎ *0241/432–4998* ⊕ *www.centre-charlemagne.eu* 🖃 *€5* ⊙ *Tues.–Sun. 10–6.*

Fodor's Choice **Dom** (*Cathedral*). Aachen's stunning cathedral, the "Chapelle" of the ★ town's earlier name of Aix-la-Chapelle, remains the single greatest storehouse of Carolingian architecture in Europe, and it was the first place in Germany to be named a UNESCO World Heritage Site. Though it was built over the course of 1,000 years and reflects architectural styles from the Middle Ages to the 19th century, its commanding image remains the magnificent octagonal royal chapel, rising up two arched stories to end in the cap of the dome. It was this section, the heart of the church, that Charlemagne saw completed in AD 800. His bones now lie in the Gothic choir, in a golden shrine surrounded by wonderful carvings of saints. Another treasure is his marble throne. Charlemagne had to journey all the way to Rome for his coronation, but the next 32 Holy Roman emperors were crowned here in Aachen, and each marked the occasion by presenting a lavish gift to the cathedral. In the 12th century Emperor Frederick I (aka Barbarossa) donated the great chandelier now hanging in the center of the Palatine chapel; his grandson, Friedrich II, donated Charlemagne's shrine. English-language guided tours of the cathedral (€4) are offered daily at 2. ⊠ *Münsterpl., Domhof 1* ☎ *0241/477–090* ⊕ *www.aachendom.de* 🖃 *Free* ⊙ *Apr.–Dec., daily 7–7; Jan.–Mar., daily 7–6.*

Domschatzkammer (*The Cathedral Treasury*). The cathedral houses sacred art from late antiquity and the Carolingian, Ottonian, and Hohenstaufen eras. A bust of Charlemagne on view here was commissioned in the late 14th century by Emperor Karl IV, who traveled here from Prague for the sole reason of having it made. The bust incorporates a piece of Charlemagne's skull. Other highlights include the Cross of Lothair and the Persephone Sarcophagus. ⊠ *Klosterpl. 2* ☎ *0241/4770–9127* ⊕ *www.aachendom.de/schatzkammer.html* 🖃 *€5* ⊙ *Jan.–Mar., Mon. 10–1, Tues.–Sun. 10–5; Apr.–Dec., Mon. 10–1, Tues.–Sun. 10–6.*

Elisenbrunnen (*Elisa Fountain*). Southeast of the cathedral and the site of the city's tourist-information center is an arcaded, neoclassical structure built in 1822. The central pavilion contains two fountains with thermal water—the hottest north of the Alps—that is reputed to help cure a wide range of ailments in those who drink it. If you can brave a gulp of the sulfurous water, you'll be emulating the likes of Dürer, Frederick the Great, and Charlemagne. ⊠ *Friedrich-Wilhelm-Pl.*

Rathaus (*Town Hall*). Aachen's town hall sits behind the Dom, across Katschhof Square. It was built in the early 14th century on the site of the *Aula Regia,* or "great hall," of Charlemagne's palace. Its first major official function was the coronation banquet of Emperor Karl IV in 1349, held in the great Gothic hall you can still see today (though this was largely rebuilt after World War II). On the north wall of the building are statues of 50 emperors of the Holy Roman Empire. The greatest of them all, Charlemagne, stands in bronze atop the Karlsbrunnen in the center of the market square. ✉ *Marktpl.* ☎ *0241/432–7310* 🌐 *rathaus-aachen.de* 🎟 *€5* 🕑 *Daily 10–6.*

WORTH NOTING

Ludwig Forum für Internationale Kunst. One of the world's most important art collectors, chocolate magnate Peter Ludwig, endowed two museums in the town he called home. The Forum, the larger of the two, holds a portion of Ludwig's enormous collection of contemporary art and hosts traveling exhibits. ✉ *Jülicher Str. 97–109* ☎ *0241/180–7104* 🌐 *www.ludwigforum.de* 🎟 *€5* 🕑 *Tues.–Fri. noon–6 (to 8 Thurs.), weekends 11–6.*

Suermondt-Ludwig Museum. The smaller of the two Ludwig art institutions in town (the Ludwig Forum is the larger one) has a collection that concentrates paintings from the 12th to the early 20th century, including a sizable holding of 17th-century Dutch and Flemish works by the likes of Anthony Van Dyck and Frans Hals. It's also home to one of Germany's largest sculpture collections. ✉ *Wilhelmstr. 18* ☎ *0241/479–8040* 🌐 *www.suermondt-ludwig-museum.de* 🎟 *€5* 🕑 *Tues.–Fri. noon–6 (to 8 Wed.), weekends 11–6.*

WHERE TO EAT

$$ GERMAN

🍴 **Am Knipp.** At this Bierstube dating from 1698, you can dig into regional dishes like *Zwiebelrahmrostbraten* (onion meat loaf) at low wooden tables next to the tile stove. Pewter plates and beer mugs line the walls. [$] *Average main: €16* ✉ *Bergdriesch 3* ☎ *0241/33168* 🌐 *www.amknipp.de* 🕑 *Closed Tues. Closed Dec. 24–Jan. 2, and 2 wks in Apr. and Oct. No lunch.*

$$ GERMAN Fodor's Choice ★

🍴 **Der Postwagen.** This annex of the more upscale Ratskeller is worth a stop for the building alone, a half-timber medieval edifice at one corner of the old Rathaus. You'll be impressed by the food as well, which also comes from the kitchen of the Ratskeller's chef. Sitting at one of the low wooden tables, surveying the marketplace through the wavy old glass, you can dine well on solid German fare. If you really want to go local, try *Himmel en Erd* (mashed potatoes and apple sauce topped by panfried slices of blood sausage and onions). [$] *Average main: €15* ✉ *Markt 40* ☎ *0241/35001* 🌐 *www.ratskeller-aachen.de.*

$$$$ FRENCH

🍴 **La Becasse.** The sophisticated French nouvelle cuisine and attentive staff here are a hit with upscale locals. The restaurant, which is named for the woodcock, has been in operation just outside the Old Town by the Westpark since 1981. Try the distinctively light veal kidney or the Wagyu steak. The five-course lunch menu (€36.50) changes daily. [$] *Average main: €37* ✉ *Hanbrucherstr. 1* ☎ *0241/74444* 🌐 *www.labecasse.de* 🕑 *Closed Sun. No lunch Sat. and Mon.* ✍ *Reservations essential.*

WHERE TO STAY

$ ⊡ **ibis Styles Aachen City.** A 15-minute walk from the Dom, this colorfully
HOTEL furnished modern budget hotel is a good value, especially for families
FAMILY with children. **Pros:** kids under 16 get their own room at half price.
Cons: on a busy street somewhat removed from the center. *$ Rooms
from: €89 ⊠ Jülicherstr. 10–12* ☎ *0241/51060* ⊕ *www.ibis.com* ⤵ *102
rooms* ⦿ *Breakfast.*

$$ ⊡ **Pullmann Aachen Quellenhof.** This old-fashioned and grand hotel has
HOTEL rooms with high ceilings, a Roman-style spa area, and an inviting pool.
Pros: spacious; elegant; formal. **Cons:** on a busy street. *$ Rooms from:
€173 ⊠ Monheimsallee 52* ☎ *0241/91320* ⊕ *www.pullmanhotels.com*
⤵ *180 rooms, 3 suites* ⦿ *Breakfast.*

NIGHTLIFE AND PERFORMING ARTS

Most activity in town is concentrated around the market square and
Pontstrasse, a pedestrian street that radiates off the square.

NIGHTLIFE

Domkeller. Aachen's most popular bar is a good place to mingle with
locals of all ages at old wooden tables, enjoying an impressive selec-
tion of Belgian beers in a historic building from 1658. There are free
concerts every Monday, apart from a short break in summer. ⊠ *Hof 1*
☎ *0241/34265* ⊕ *www.domkeller.de.*

Wild Rover. This Irish pub has Murphy's Stout on tap and on most
nights, there's live music starting at 8:30. It's closed Sunday and Mon-
day, except for special occasions. ⊠ *Hirschgraben 13* ☎ *0241/35453.*

PERFORMING ARTS

Eurogress Aachen. The Aachen Symphony, along with touring bands
and orchestras from across Europe, give regular concerts in Aachen's
Eurogress convention center. ⊠ *Monheimsallee 48* ☎ *0241/91310*
⊕ *www.eurogress-aachen.de.*

SHOPPING

Don't leave Aachen without stocking up on the traditional local ginger-
bread, *Aachener Printen.* Each bakery in town offers its own varieties
(topped with whole or crushed nuts, milk or dark chocolate, etc.), and
guards its recipe like a state secret.

Café Van den Daele. Some of the best Aachener Printen (gingerbread) can
be found here, at one of Aachen's most beloved cafés, as can another
tasty Aachen specialty, *Reisfladen* (a sort of tart filled with milk rice
and often topped with fruit—pears, apricots, or cherries). Also known
as Alt Aachener Kaffeestuben, the café is worth a visit if for nothing
more than its atmosphere and tempting aromas. They can also mail
their goods to you (or others) back home. ⊠ *Büchel 18* ☎ *0241/35724*
⊕ *www.van-den-daele.de.*

DÜSSELDORF

47 km (29 miles) north of Köln.

Düsseldorf, the state capital of North Rhine–Westphalia, may suffer by
comparison to Köln's remarkable skyline, but the elegant city has more
than enough charm—and money—to keeps its own self-esteem high.

By contrast to Cologne's boisterous, working-class charm, Düsseldorf is known as one of the country's richest cities, with an extravagant lifestyle that epitomizes the economic success of postwar Germany. Because 80% of Düsseldorf was destroyed in World War II, the city has since been more or less rebuilt from the ground up—and that includes re-creating landmarks of long ago and restoring a medieval riverside quarter.

At the confluence of the Rhine and Düssel rivers, this dynamic city started as a small fishing town. The name means "village on the Düssel," but obviously this Dorf is a village no more. Raised expressways speed traffic past towering glass-and-steel structures; within them, glass-enclosed shopping malls showcase the finest clothes, furs, jewelry, and other goods that money can buy.

GETTING HERE AND AROUND

Trains connect Düsseldorf to the Rhineland region's main cities; a trip from Köln takes under 25 minutes. The impressive Flughafen Düsseldorf, Germany's third-largest airport, serves more than 180 destinations.

TOURS

Düsseldorf Bus Tours. Hop-on, hop-off bus tours of Düsseldorf depart from the main train station at 10 and every half hour thereafter (until 4 on weekdays, 5 weekends) from late March to early November; hourly 10 to 4 from early November to late December; and at 11, 1, and 3 from late December to late March. Tickets can be purchased on the bus or at the information center ⊠ *Düsseldorf* 🖾 *€15.*

Old Town Walking Tour. A walking tour of the Old Town leaves from the Altstadt tourist-info center (Marktstrasse/Rheinstrasse corner) daily from April to October, Sunday to Thursday at 3, Friday at 3 and 4, and Saturday at 2. From November to March, tours are on Friday and Saturday at 3, and Sunday at 11. ⊠ *Düsseldorf* 🖾 *€11.*

DISCOUNTS AND DEALS

The **DüsseldorfCard** costs €9 for 24 hours, €14 for 48 hours, and €19 for 72 hours, and allows free public transportation and reduced admission to museums, theaters, and even boat tours on the Rhine.

ESSENTIALS

Visitor Information Düsseldorf Tourist-Information. ⊠ *Marktstr. 6* ☎ *0211/172–020* ⊕ *www.duesseldorf-tourismus.de.*

EXPLORING

TOP ATTRACTIONS

Altstadt (*Old Town*). This party-hearty district has been dubbed "the longest bar in the word" by locals. Narrow alleys thread their way to some 300 restaurants and taverns. All crowd into the 1-square-km (½-square-mile) area between the Rhine and Heinrich-Heine-Allee. When the weather cooperates, the area really does seem like one big sidewalk café. ⊠ *Düsseldorf.*

Fodor'sChoice
★
Königsallee. Düsseldorf's main shopping avenue epitomizes the city's affluence, lined as it is with designer boutiques and stores. Known as the Kö, this wide, double boulevard is divided by an ornamental waterway fed by the River Düssel. Rows of chestnut trees line the Kö, shading a string of sidewalk cafés. Beyond the Triton Fountain, at the

Düsseldorf's elegant high-end malls are great for window-shopping.

street's north end, begins a series of parks and gardens. In these patches of green you can sense a joie de vivre that might be surprising in a city devoted to big business. ⊠ *Düsseldorf.*

Kunstsammlung Nordrhein-Westfalen (*Art Collection of North Rhine–Westphalia*). This important fixture on Düsseldorf's art scene is split into two parts, plus an installation space. Behind the sleek, polished black stone facade of **K20** is a treasure trove of art (*kunst*, hence the K) of the 20th century, including works from masters like Picasso, Klee, and Richter. Within the more conservative 19th-century architecture of **K21** is edgier fare—international art since about 1980, including the works of Thomas Ruff and Nam June Paik. Rounding things off is the quirky, modern **Schmela Haus** (1967), a former commercial gallery, which the museum uses as a space for special events and exhibitions. ⊠ *K20, Grabbepl. 5* ☎ *0211/838–1204* ⊕ *www.kunstsammlung. de* ⊠ *K20: €12; K21: €12; or €18 for both (prices vary); free entry 1st Wed. of month, 6–10; Schmela Haus: free* ☉ *Tues.–Fri. 10–6, weekends 11–6; 1st Wed. of each month 10–10* ⊠ *K21, Ständehausstr. 1.*

Neanderthal Museum. Just outside Düsseldorf, the Düssel River forms a valley, called the Neanderthal, where the bones of a Stone Age relative of modern man were found. The impressive museum, built at the site of the discovery in the suburb of Mettmann, includes models of the original discovery, replicas of cave drawings, and life-size models of Neanderthal Man. Many scientists think he was a different species of human; short, stocky, and with a sloping forehead. The bones were found in 1856 by workers quarrying the limestone cliffs to get flux for blast furnaces. ⊠ *Talstr. 300, Mettmann* ☎ *02104/97970* ⊕ *www.*

neanderthal.de ⌨ Permanent exhibition €9, special exhibitions €7, both €11 ⊙ Tues.–Sun. 10–6.

Rhine Promenade. Traffic is routed away from the river and underneath this pedestrian strip, which is lined by chic shopping arcades and cafés. Joggers, rollerbladers, and folks out for a stroll make much use of the promenade as well. ⊠ *Düsseldorf.*

WORTH NOTING

Heinrich-Heine-Institut. This museum and archive houses significant manuscripts of the German poet and man of letters, Heinrich Heine. Part of the complex was once the residence of the composer Robert Schumann. ⊠ *Bilkerstr. 12–14* ☎ *0211/899–5571* ⊕ *www.duesseldorf. de/heineinstitut* ⌨ *€4* ⊙ *Tues.–Fri. and Sun. 11–5, Sat. 1–5.*

Hofgarten Park. The oldest remaining parts of the Hofgarten date back to 1769, when it was transformed into Germany's first public park. The promenade leading to what was once a hunting palace, Schloss Jägerhof, was all the rage in late-18th-century Düsseldorf before the park was largely destroyed by Napoléon's troops. Today it's an oasis of greenery at the heart of downtown. ⊠ *Düsseldorf.*

MedienHafen. This stylish, revamped district is a mix of late-19th-century warehouses and ultramodern restaurants, bars, and shops: it's one of Europe's masterpieces in urban redevelopment. Surrounding the historic commercial harbor, now occupied by yachts and leisure boats, are the many media companies that have made this area their home. On the riverbank you'll find Frank Gehry's **Neuer Zollhof,** a particularly striking ensemble of three organic-looking high-rises. The best way to tackle the buzzing architecture is to take a stroll down the promenade. ⊠ *Düsseldorf.*

Museum Kunst Palast. This impressive art museum lies at the northern extremity of the Hofgarten, close to the Rhine. Its excellent German expressionist collection (Beckmann, Kirchner, Nolde, Macke, among others) makes it worth a trip, as does its collection of glass art—one of the largest in Europe. ⊠ *Ehrenhof 4–5* ☎ *0211/899–2460* ⊕ *www.smkp. de* ⌨ *Permanent collection €5, special exhibition prices vary* ⊙ *Tues.– Sun. 11–6 (to 9 Thurs.).*

St. Lambertus. This Gothic church is near the palace tower on Burgplatz. Its spire became distorted because unseasoned wood was used in its construction. The Vatican elevated the 14th-century brick church to a basilica minor (small cathedral) in 1974 in recognition of its role in church history. Built in the 13th century, with additions from 1394, St. Lambertus contains the tomb of William the Rich and a graceful late-Gothic tabernacle. ⊠ *Stiftspl. 7* ⊕ *www.lambertuspfarre.de* ⌨ *Free.*

Schloss Jägerhof. At the far-east edge of the Hofgarten, this baroque structure is more a combination town house and country lodge than a palace. It houses the **Goethe-Museum,** featuring original manuscripts, first editions, personal correspondence, and other memorabilia of Germany's greatest writer. A collection of Meissen porcelain, the Sammlung Ernst Schneider Collection, is also here . ⊠ *Jacobistr. 2* ☎ *0211/899–6262* ⊕ *www.goethe-museum.com* ⌨ *€4* ⊙ *Tues.–Fri. and Sun. 11–5, Sat. 1–5.*

Schlossturm (*Palace Tower*). A squat tower is all that remains of the palace built by the Berg family, which ruled Düsseldorf for more than five centuries. The tower also houses the **SchifffahrtMuseum,** which charts 2,000 years of Rhine boatbuilding and navigation. ⊠ *Burgpl. 30* ☎ *0211/899–4195* ⊕ *www.freunde-schifffahrtmuseum.de* ₪ *€3* ☉ *Tues.–Sun. 11–6.*

WHERE TO EAT

$$$$
FRENCH

✕ **Berens am Kai.** Set in the redeveloped Düsseldorf harbor, this glass-and-steel building with ceiling-to-floor windows looks more like a modern office complex than the sleek restaurant it is. Head here for creative French recipes, a wine list with vintages from around the world, and tempting desserts—it's a good option if you're hankering for a change from old-style German cooking. The steep, expense-account-ready prices are warranted by exquisite cuisine, refined service, and the great setting with magnificent views of the harbor and the city, which are particularly stunning at night. $ *Average main: €40* ⊠ *Kaistr. 16* ☎ *0211/300–6750* ⊕ *www.berensamkai.de* ☉ *Closed Sun. No lunch Sat.* ⌕ *Reservations essential.*

$
FRENCH

✕ **Bistro Zicke.** Weekend brunch (served until 4 pm) can get busy at this French-inspired artists' café on a quiet square one block from the riverfront. Otherwise, the bistro—with its big windows and walls plastered with old movie and museum posters—is an oasis from the hustle and bustle of the busy Altstadt. The word *Zicke* ("nanny goat") is a common insult for a moody woman, but whatever your feelings, this is a friendly place to stop in for a drink or to try the simple French-Italian cooking. $ *Average main: €14* ⊠ *Bäckerstr. 5a* ☎ *0211/327–800* ⊕ *www.bistro-zicke.de* ▭ *No credit cards.*

$
GERMAN

✕ **Brauerei Zur Uel.** A nontraditional brew house, the Uel is the popular hangout for Düsseldorf's students. The basic menu consists of soups, salads, and pastas; the ingredients are fresh and the portions are generous. What seems like every cultural and political event in the city is advertised in the entry hall. $ *Average main: €13* ⊠ *Ratingerstr. 16* ☎ *0211/325–369* ⊕ *www.zuruel.de* ▭ *No credit cards.*

$$$$
FRENCH
Fodor's Choice
★

✕ **Im Schiffchen.** Although Im Schiffchen is out of the way, it's also one of Germany's best restaurants and more than worth the trip. This is grande luxe, with cooking turned into fine art through the skills of chef Jean-Claude Bourgueil and his staff. The restaurant Enzo im Schiffchen on the ground floor features lighter Continental fare created by the same chef but at lower prices. There are more than 1,100 wines in the cellar, many available by the glass. $ *Average main: €48* ⊠ *Kaiserswerther*

Markt 9 ☎ *0211/401–050* 🌐 *www.im-schiffchen.de* 🕒 *Closed Sun. and Mon. No lunch.* ✍ *Reservations essential.*

$ GERMAN 🍴 **Zum Uerige.** Among beer buffs, Düsseldorf is famous for its *Altbier,* so called because of the old-fashioned brewing method. The mellow and malty copper-color brew is produced by eight breweries in town. This tavern, which brews its own beer, provides the perfect atmosphere for drinking it. The beer is poured straight out of polished oak barrels and served with hearty local food by busy waiters in long blue aprons. The food offered is mainly snacks, with a small selection of entrées. After dinner, try the bar's tasty house liquor, called "Stickum"—a sort of beer brandy. [$] *Average main: €13* ✉ *Bergerstr. 1* ☎ *0211/866–990* 🌐 *www.uerige.de* 💳 *No credit cards.*

WHERE TO STAY

$$$$ HOTEL 🏨 **Breidenbacher Hof.** The original, two-centuries-old Breidenbacher Hof was rebuilt from the ground up in 2008 to create this opulent, high-tech establishment, which added a luxurious new 6,500-square-foot spa to its basement in 2014. **Pros:** luxurious; very indulgent staff; great location on the Kö. **Cons:** expensive. [$] *Rooms from: €360* ✉ *Königsallee 11* ☎ *0211/1609–0909* 🌐 *www.capellahotels.com/dusseldorf* 🛏 *85 rooms, 21 suites* 🍽 *Breakfast.*

$$ HOTEL 🏨 **carathotel Düsseldorf.** Besides bright, good-size rooms, the true strength of this modern hotel is its location, near the market in the Altstadt. **Pros:** right in the Altstadt; free Wi-Fi. **Cons:** style is a bit dated. [$] *Rooms from: €129* ✉ *Benratherstr. 7a* ☎ *0211/13050* 🌐 *www.carathotel-duesseldorf.de* 🛏 *71 rooms, 2 suites* 🍽 *Breakfast.*

$$ HOTEL 🏨 **Hotel Orangerie.** Steps away from Altstadt action and the Rhine, this small hotel on a cobblestone road offers simple comfort and a surprising amount of quiet. **Pros:** unbeatable location; free Wi-Fi. **Cons:** small rooms; no parking at the hotel; caters to business travelers. [$] *Rooms from: €130* ✉ *Bäckerg. 1* ☎ *0211/866–800* 🌐 *www.hotel-orangerie-mcs.de* 💳 *No credit cards* 🛏 *27 rooms* 🍽 *Breakfast.*

$$$ RENTAL 🏨 **Steigenberger Parkhotel.** Miraculously quiet despite its central location on the edge of the Hofgarten and at the beginning of the Königsallee, this old hotel is anything but stodgy, especially after its €10 million facelift in 2013. **Pros:** central but quiet. **Cons:** expensive. [$] *Rooms from: €225* ✉ *Königsallee 1a* ☎ *0211/13810* 🌐 *www.steigenberger.de* 🛏 *119 rooms, 11 suites* 🍽 *Breakfast.*

NIGHTLIFE AND PERFORMING ARTS

The **Altstadt** is a landscape of pubs, dance clubs, ancient brewery houses, and jazz clubs in the vicinity of the Marktplatz and along cobblestone streets named Bolker, Kurze, Flinger, and Mühlen. These places may be crowded, but some are very atmospheric. The local favorite for nightlife is the **Hafen** neighborhood. Its restaurants and bars cater to the youngish professionals who work and party there.

Fodor's Choice ★ **Deutsche Oper am Rhein.** The city's highly regarded opera company and ballet troupe are showcased here. ✉ *Heinrich-Heine-Allee 16a* ☎ *0211/892–5211* 🌐 *www.operamrhein.de.*

Robert-Schumann-Saal. Classical and pop concerts, symposia, film, and international theater are presented at the Robert-Schumann-Saal. ⊠ *Ehrenhof 4–5* ☎ *0211/899–0200* ⊕ *www.smkp.de.*

Tonhalle. The finest concert hall in Germany after Berlin's Philharmonie is a former planetarium on the edge of the Hofgarten. It's the home of the Düsseldorfer Symphoniker, which plays from September to June. ⊠ *Ehrenhof 1* ☎ *0211/899–6123* ⊕ *www.tonhalle-duesseldorf.de.*

SHOPPING

For antiques, go to the area around Hohe Strasse. The east side of the **Königsallee** is lined with some of Germany's trendiest boutiques, grandest jewelers, and most extravagant furriers.

Kö Center. This shopping arcade houses clothing stores like Eickhoff, a Düsseldorf institution with more than 10,000 square feet of very high-end goods, many straight from the runways of Paris and Milan. ⊠ *Königsallee 28–30.*

Kö Galerie. High-end boutiques and half a dozen restaurants line this luxurious two-story mall. ⊠ *Königsallee 60* ⊕ *www.koe-galerie.com.*

Schadow Arkaden. At one end of Kö Galerie, this mall caters to normal budgets, with stores such as H&M and Habitat. ⊠ *Schadowstr. 11* ⊕ *www.schadow-arkaden.com.*

THE FAIRY-TALE ROAD

WELCOME TO
THE FAIRY-TALE ROAD

TOP REASONS
TO GO

★ **Valley Road:** Drive or bike the scenic highway between Hannoversch-Münden and Hameln (Hamelin)—it's a landscape of green hills, Weser Renaissance towns, and inviting riverside taverns.

★ **Marburg:** Staircase streets cover the steep hillsides of this half-timber university town; sit outdoors and soak up the atmosphere.

★ **Bremen:** Browse the shops and galleries lining the picturesque Böttcherstrasse and Schnoorviertel, then savor the city's rich coffee tradition.

★ **Dornröschenschloss Sababurg:** With its spiral staircases, imposing turrets, and fairy-tale setting, this castle was said to have been the Grimm brothers' inspiration for Sleeping Beauty's castle.

★ **Schlosspark Wilhelmshöhe:** Home to a stunning, crescent-moon palace and a fairy-tale castle, the park's trees, ponds, and wide-open spaces offer a dramatic contrast to the urbanity below.

1 Hesse. Though well-populated in the south of the state, with cities like Frankfurt and Wiesbaden, the northern part of Hesse is a place of forests and castles, which inspired the tales recorded by the Grimm brothers.

2 Lower Saxony. Germany's second-largest state after Bavaria, Lower Saxony (Niedersachsen) has a diverse landscape, including the Weser River, which forms a picturesque part of the Fairy-Tale Road, and the Lüneburg Heath. Its capital and largest city is Hannover.

GETTING ORIENTED

The Fairy-Tale Road begins 20 minutes east of Frankfurt in the city of Hanau, and follows the Fulda and Weser rivers as it heads north 700 km (about 430 miles) to the North Sea port of Bremerhaven. Traversing through the states of Hesse and Lower Saxony, the road cuts through countryside as beguiling as any other in northern Europe. It may not have the glamour of the Romantic Road, but it doesn't have the crowds and commercialism either.

DRIVING THE FAIRY-TALE ROAD

Weaving its way through rolling hills and a gentle river valley, between whispering woods and past stone castles, this drive along the Fairy-Tale Road connects Göttingen, a vibrant university town, with tranquil riverside villages and the modern state capital of Hannover along the way.

(above) Hannover's impressive Altes Rathaus illuminates a foggy night. (upper right) A kayaker paddles the flat Weser River.

Beginning in the south of Lower Saxony and ending in the heart of the state, with a brief excursion into Hesse, this two-day drive is best enjoyed in early spring, when cherry and apple blossoms dot the countryside. Late summer is another good time to go—the weather is at its best and the roads are no longer cluttered with peak-season traffic. Avoiding the high-speed stress of the autobahns, the drive keeps mainly to country roads, which allow time to take in the surroundings between stops. Gazing out at the landscape, it's not difficult to conjure images of wicked witches lurking among the trees, kind woodsmen, and fair maidens trapped in distant towers.

—Jeff Kavanagh

PADDLE THE WESER

Flowing placidly between Hannoversch Münden and Hameln, and on to the North Sea, the Weser passes through many towns offering canoe and boating equipment for rent. If time and weather permit, swap the car for a canoe and paddle the river's glassy waters. Check out ⊕ www.weserbergland-tourismus.de for details on canoe operators.

A German breakfast at **Bullerjahn** in the lively town square in front of **Göttingen's** Altes Rathaus is a great way to start your trip. Once sated, jump in the car and drive 29 km (18 miles) west through the **Hannoversch-Münden** nature reserve to the town itself. Here, you can stroll among its delightful Renaissance architecture and watch the Fulda and Werra rivers converge to form the Weser River. Half an hour up the road is the town of **Sababurg,** and perhaps the Fairy-Tale Road's most famous landmark, the **Dornröschen-schloss,** Sleeping Beauty's castle. Spend some time wandering the castle's rose gardens and contemplating the princess's enchanted 100-year slumber. From the castle it's an easy 20-minute drive across the border to Hesse and the baroque spa town of **Bad Karlshafen,** where you can soothe whatever ails you with a long soak in a thermal, saltwater spring at **Weser-Therme.** Suitably relaxed, head to the peaceful riverside town of **Bodenweder,** which lies just over 50 km (31 miles) to the north along winding country roads. Stay overnight here, and visit the small but fun **Münchhausen Museum** in the morning, which has artifacts from Baron von Münchhausen's tall tales, and enjoy the gentle murmur of the Weser as it flows its way past. Before lunch, travel 25 minutes north to **Hameln** (Hamelin) and the home of the *Rattenfänger,* the Pied Piper, where you can experience rat-themed dining at the **Rattenfängerhaus.** Afterward, drive the 47 km (29 miles) up to **Hannover** for an afternoon of culture in one of the city's impressive museums and a predinner drink on the terrace of the stunning **Neues Rathaus.**

12

QUICK BITES

Back und Naschwerk. Delicious breads are baked in the back of this little bakery, using only natural ingredients and real butter. Their maple syrup and walnut or poppy-seed-and-nougat muffins are worth a visit alone. ✉ *Kramerstr. 14, Hannover* ☎ *0511/7003–5221* ⊕ *www.back-und-naschwerk.de* ☰ *No credit cards.*

Bullerjahn. For a hearty breakfast at this cellar-level restaurant, order the enormous "Ratsfrühstück," which consists of bread rolls, jams, honey, Gouda, cold cuts, salmon, yogurt and fruit, orange juice, coffee, sparkling wine, and a boiled egg. ✉ *Markt 9, Göttingen* ☎ *0551/307–0100* ⊕ *www.bullerjahn. info* ☰ *No credit cards.*

Museums Café. Afternoon coffee and cake is as strong a culinary tradition in Germany as tea and scones are in England. This elegant café in Hamelin has cakes and tortes that'll have you embracing the custom like a local in no time. ✉ *Osterstr. 8, Hameln* ☎ *05151/21553* ⊕ *www. museumscafe.de* ☰ *No credit cards.*

Updated by
Courtney Tenz

With a name evocative of magic and adventure, the Fairy-Tale Road (Märchenstrasse) takes its travelers on a path through the land of the Brothers Grimm and a rolling countryside of farmland and forests that inspired tales of sleeping princesses, hungry wolves, and gingerbread houses. Flowing through the heart of western Germany to its North Sea coast, the Märchenstrasse stops along the way at towns and villages where the brothers spent much of their lives two centuries ago.

It was here among medieval castles and witch towers that the brothers, first as young boys, and then later as students and academics, listened to legends told by local storytellers, and adapted them into the fairy tales that continue to be read around the world today; enchanted and frequently dark tales that include "Sleeping Beauty," "Little Red Riding Hood," and "Hansel and Gretel."

Following the Grimms' footsteps through a landscape of river valleys and wide-open skies, or down cobblestone streets flanked by half-timber houses and baroque palaces, it's possible to imagine things haven't changed that much since the brothers' time. Traditional taverns serving strong German beers and thick slabs of beef and pork dot the way, and storytelling continues to be a major attraction along the Fairy-Tale Road, though nowadays more commonly in the form of guided tours and interactive museum displays.

The Fairy-Tale Road, of course, is also a modern route, and its wide, smooth roads pass through larger urban areas, such as Kassel and Bremen, full of contemporary hotels, eateries, and stores. Like large parts of the rest of the country, many of these towns and cities were greatly damaged during World War II, and their hurried reconstruction often favored functionality over form, so that many buildings are much more stark than those they replaced. This contrast, however, often only serves to emphasize the beauty of what remained.

Not every town on the road can lay claim to a connection to the Brothers Grimm or the inspiration for a specific tale, but many continue to celebrate the region's fairy-tale heritage with theme museums, summer festivals, and outdoor plays.

It's this heritage, the natural appeal of the countryside, and the tradition and culture found in its towns and cities that attract travelers along the Märchenstrasse; that, mixed with the promise of adventure and the opportunity to create some tales of their own.

12

PLANNING

WHEN TO GO

Summer is the ideal time to travel through this varied landscape, although in spring you'll find the river valleys carpeted in the season's first flowers, and in fall the sleepy Weser is often blanketed in mist. Keep in mind that retail stores and shops in the smaller towns in this area often close for two to three hours at lunchtime.

GETTING HERE AND AROUND

AIR TRAVEL

The closest international airports to this region are in Frankfurt, Hannover, and Hamburg. Frankfurt is less than a half hour from Hanau, and Hamburg is less than an hour from Bremen.

Airport Information City Airport Bremen. ⊠ *Flughafenallee 20, Bremen* ☎ *0421/55950* ⊕ *www.airport-bremen.de.* **Hannover-Langenhagen Airport.** ⊠ *Petzelstr. 84, Hannover* ☎ *0511/9770* ⊕ *www.hannover-airport.de.*

BIKE TRAVEL

The Fulda and Werra rivers have 190 km (118 miles) of bike paths, and you can cycle the whole length of the Weser River from Hannoversch-Münden to the North Sea at Cuxhaven without making too many detours from the river valley. Five- and seven-day cycle tours of the Fulda and Werra river valleys are available. These typically include bike rentals, overnight accommodations, and luggage transport between stops.

BIKE TOURS **SRJ.** This bike-tour company offers a number of packages for those interested in cycling north along the Weser River. A five-day package along the 84-mile (136-km) route from Hannoversche-Munden to Hamil costs €349; the 235-mile (377-km) route to Bremen over nine days starts at €610. ⊠ *Hermannstr 46, Minden* ☎ *0571/889–1900* ⊕ *www.srj.de* 💺 *From €349.*

BUS TRAVEL

Eurolines. Eurolines offers bus service across Europe and has stations in Bremen, Kassel, Göttingen, Fulda, and Hanau. ☎ *069/7903–501* ⊕ *www.eurolines.de* 💺 *From €9.*

CRUISE TRAVEL

Flotte Weser. The eight boats of Flotte Weser operate short summer excursions along a considerable stretch of the Weser River between Bremen and Bad Karlshafen. The trip between Corvey and Bad Karlshafen, for example, takes slightly less than three hours and costs €15.

✉ *Am Stockhof 2, Hameln* ☎ *05151/939–999* ⊕ *www.flotte-weser.de* 🖃 *From €15.*

Personenschiffahrt K. & K. Söllner. The excursion boat has a 2½-hour round-trip between Kassel and the reservoir at Wahnhausen for €10 in the summer. ✉ *Die Schlagd, Kassel* ✛ *Along the river between the Karl Branner and Fulda bridges* ☎ *0561/774–670* ⊕ *www.personenschiffahrt. com/kassel/route.html* 🖃 *From €10.*

Rehbein-Linie Kassel. There are a number of short cruises, such as a Sunday brunch tour and a three-hour trip from Kassel to Bad Karlshafen available from two main ports of operation in Kassel and Hannoversch-Münden. The company also prides itself on the only "three-river tour" in the area, where in a single trip you travel on the Fulda and Werra rivers as well as the Weser, where these two rivers meet at the tour's starting point of Hannoversch-Münden. ✉ *Ostpreussenstr. 8, Fuldatal* ☎ *0561/18505* ⊕ *www.fahrgastschiffahrt.com* 🖃 *From €17.*

CAR TRAVEL
The best way to travel is by car. The A-1 and A-7 autobahn network connects most major stops on the route, including Hanau, Fulda, Kassel, Göttingen, and Bremen, but you can't savor the fairy-tale country from this high-speed superhighway. Bremen is 60 km (35 miles) northwest of Hannover.

The Fairy-Tale Road incorporates one of Germany's loveliest scenic drives, the Wesertalstrasse, or Weser Valley Road (B-80 and B-83), between Hannoversch-Münden and Hameln; the total distance is approximately 103 km (64 miles).

TRAIN TRAVEL
Hanau, Fulda, Kassel, Göttingen, Hannover, and Bremen are reachable via InterCity Express (ICE) trains from Frankfurt and Hamburg. Rail service, but not ICE service, is available to Hannoversch-Münden, Marburg, and Hameln.

Train Information Deutsche Bahn. ☎ *0800/150–7090* ⊕ *www.bahn.de.*

RESTAURANTS
In this largely rural area many restaurants serve hot meals only between 11:30 am and 2 pm, and 6 pm and 9 pm. You rarely need a reservation here, and casual clothing is generally acceptable.

Prices in the reviews are the average cost of a main course at dinner, or if dinner is not served, at lunch.

HOTELS
Make hotel reservations in advance if you plan to visit in summer. Though it's one of the less-traveled tourist routes in Germany, the main destinations on the Fairy-Tale Road are popular. Hannover is particularly busy during trade-fair times.

Prices in the reviews are the lowest cost of a standard double room in high season. For expanded reviews, facilities, and current deals, visit Fodors.com.

WHAT IT COSTS IN EUROS			
	$	**$$**	**$$$**	**$$$$**
Restaurants	under €15	€15–€20	€21–€25	over €25
Hotels	under €100	€100–€175	€176–€225	over €225

12

PLANNING YOUR TIME

The Fairy-Tale Road isn't really for the traveler in a hurry. If you only have a day or two to savor it, concentrate on a short stretch. A good suggestion is the Weser River route between Hannoversch-Münden and Hameln (Hamelin). The landscape is lovely, and the towns are romantic. If you have more time, but not enough to travel the whole route, focus on the southern half of the road. It's more in character with the fairy tales.

DISCOUNTS AND DEALS

Free summer weekend performances along the Fairy-Tale Road include Münchhausen plays in Bodenwerder, the Dr. Eisenbart reenactments in Hannoversch-Münden, the Town Musicians shows in Bremen, and especially the Pied Piper spectacle at Hameln (Hamelin). Kassel, Hannover, and Bremen also sell visitor cards that let you ride free on public transportation, grant reduced admissions at museums, and give other perks.

VISITOR INFORMATION

Deutsche Märchenstrasse. The official tourist planning office for the Fairy-Tale Road is where you can book tours and hotels and take a look at the area's event calendar, which is packed through 2019 as the cities and towns celebrate 200 years of Grimms' Fairy Tales. ⊠ *Kurfürstenstr. 9, Kassel* ☎ *0561/9204–7911* ⊕ *www.deutsche-maerchenstrasse.de.*

HESSE

The first portion of the Fairy-Tale Road, from Hanau to Bad Karlshafen, lies within the state of Hesse. Much of the state's population is concentrated in the south, in such cities as Frankfurt, Darmstadt, and Wiesbaden; here in the northern part it is quieter, with a pretty, rural, hilly, and forested landscapes. Here you'll find Steinau, the almost vertical city of Marburg, and Kassel, all of which have associations with the Grimm brothers.

HANAU

16 km (10 miles) east of Frankfurt.

The Fairy-Tale Road begins in Hanau, the town where the Brothers Grimm were born. Although Grimm fans will want to start their pilgrimage here, Hanau is now a traffic-congested suburb of Frankfurt, with post–World War II buildings that are not particularly attractive.

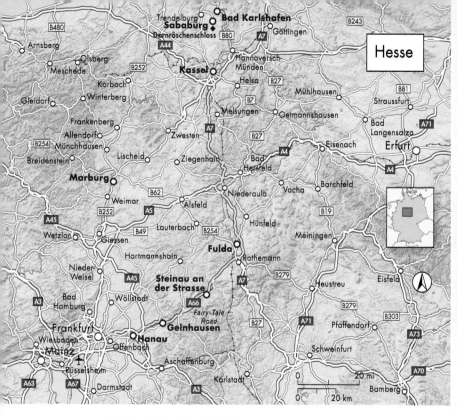

Hesse

GETTING HERE AND AROUND

Less than a 50-minute S-bahn (Line No. 9) journey from Frankfurt Airport, Hanau is also reachable by high-speed ICE trains from Berlin and Munich, or a combination of ICE and regional trains from Hannover, Bremen, and Hamburg.

ESSENTIALS

VISITOR INFORMATION

Tourist Information Hanau. This small tourist office in the town hall can help with hotel and restaurant recommendations as well as city maps and information about local landmarks; they're only open Monday through Thursday 9 to 1 and 1:30 to 4:30, Friday 9 to 1 and Saturday 9 to noon. ⊠ *Am Markt 14–18* ☎ *06181/295–950* ⊕ *www.hanau.de*.

EXPLORING

Nationaldenkmal Brüder Grimm (*Brothers Grimm Memorial*). Hanau's main attraction can be reached only on foot. The bronze memorial, erected in 1898, is a larger-than-life-size statue of the brothers, one seated, the other leaning on his chair, the two of them pondering an open book. ⊠ *Marktpl.* ☜ *Free.*

Schloss Philippsruhe. Completed in 1880, this palace mixes a bit of rococo, neo-Renaissance, and neoclassism in its design; a museum inside has a small Grimm exhibit that includes clothing, artifacts, and writings. It's on the bank of the Main in the suburb of Kesselstadt

(Bus 5 will take you there in 10 minutes). Historical Hanau treasures, including a priceless collection of faience, are also on display here. ☒ *Philippsruher Allée 45* ☎ *06181/295–564* ⊕ *www.museen-hanau.de* 🎫 *€2.50* ☉ *Tues.–Sun. 11–6.*

Rathaus (*Town Hall*). The solid bulk of Hanau's 18th-century Rathaus stands behind the Grimm brothers statue. Every day at noon its bells play tribute to another of the city's famous sons, the composer Paul Hindemith (1895–1963), by chiming out one of his canons. ☒ *Marktpl. 14.*

GELNHAUSEN

20 km (12 miles) northeast of Hanau, 35 km (21 miles) northeast of Frankfurt.

Perched elegantly on the side of a hill above the Kinzig River, Gelnhausen's picturesque Altstadt (Old Town) offers the first taste of the half-timber houses and cobblestone streets that lie in abundance farther north. In spring and summer, school children dressed in traditional garb are guided down its winding streets and through lively little squares flanked by ice-cream parlors and outdoor cafés, to listen to tales of Red Beard, and the fate of those poor townswomen suspected of being witches.

GETTING HERE AND AROUND

If you're flying into Frankfurt, Gelnhausen is an ideal spot for your first night on the Fairy-Tale Road. It's smaller and more charming than Hanau, and is still less than an hour's drive from Frankfurt's main airport. Trains to Gelnhausen leave from Frankfurt's main station every half hour and take approximately 35 minutes, with frequent connections to and from Hanau. Once here, the historic Old Town is hilly, but small enough to walk around. April through October, a walking tour leaves from the town hall at 2 on Sunday.

ESSENTIALS

VISITOR
INFORMATION
Gelnhausen. Though small, this tourist office coordinates a number of themed walking tours and events year-round for visitors young and old and can recommend accommodations. Inside, kids will enjoy climbing on a larger-than-life sculpture of a human ear. ☒ *Tourist-Information, Obermarkt 7* ⊹ *House to the rear (Hinterhaus No. 24)* ☎ *06051/830– 300* ⊕ *www.gelnhausen.de.*

EXPLORING

Hexenturm (*Witches' Tower*). The Hexenturm was originally constructed in the 15th century as a watchtower to protect the town from invaders. What remains today is an imposing 9 meters in diameter and 24-meter-high tower which was used as a grim prison during the time when Gelnhausen was the center of a witch hunt in the late 16th century. Dozens of women were either burned at the stake or bound hand and foot and then thrown into the Kinzig River after being held prisoner here. ☒ *Am Fratzenstein* ☎ *06051/830–300* 🎫 *Free.*

Kaiserpfalz. On an island in the gentle little Kinzig River you'll find the remains of the Kaiserpfalz. Emperor Friedrich I—known as Barbarossa, or Red Beard—built the castle in this idyllic spot in the 12th century; in 1180 it was the scene of the first all-German Imperial Diet, a gathering of princes and ecclesiastical leaders. Today only parts of the russet walls and colonnaded entrance remain. Still, you can stroll beneath the castle's ruined ramparts and you'll get a tangible impression of the medieval importance of the court of Barbarossa. ⊠ *Burgstr. 14* ☎ *06051/3805* 🖼 *€3* ⏲ *Mar.–Oct., Tues.–Sun. 10–5; Nov. and Dec., Tues.–Sun. 10–4.*

WHERE TO STAY

$
HOTEL
🏨 **Romantisches Hotel Burg Mühle.** This peaceful hotel, a few steps from the Kaiserpfalz and within an easy walk of the Altstadt, was once the castle's mill (*Mühle*) and sawmill. **Pros:** large rooms (many with balconies). **Cons:** showing a little wear. 💲 *Rooms from: €77* ⊠ *Burgstr. 2* ☎ *06051/82050* ⊕ *www.burgmuehle.de* 🛏 *40 rooms* 🍽 *Breakfast.*

STEINAU AN DER STRASSE

30 km (18 miles) northeast of Gelnhausen, 65 km (40 miles) northeast of Frankfurt.

The little town of Steinau—full name Steinau an der Strasse (Steinau "on the road," referring to an old trade route between Frankfurt and Leipzig)—had a formative influence on the Brothers Grimm as they arrived in the town as preschoolers and stayed until they were aged 10 and 11, when they left after their father's death.

Steinau dates from the 13th century, and is typical of villages in the region. Marvelously preserved half-timber houses are set along cobblestone streets; an imposing castle bristles with towers and turrets. In its woodsy surroundings you can well imagine encountering Little Red Riding Hood, Snow White, or Hansel and Gretel. A major street is named after the brothers; the building where they lived is now named after them.

GETTING HERE AND AROUND

Regional trains leave hourly from Gelnhausen and take about 15 minutes to reach Steinau an der Strasse. The train station is just over a kilometer (½ mile) from the Old Town's center and, should the walk be too far, the MKK90 bus goes into the town, albeit at irregular and sometimes lengthy intervals (get off at Ringstrasse). Or you can take a taxi. A city walking tour takes place April to October, the first Sunday of the month, leaving at 2 from the Märchenbrunnen (fountain).

ESSENTIALS

VISITOR
INFORMATION
Steinau an der Strasse. Though small, the tourist office will work to coordinate tours of the city specialized for children, or with topics such as the half-timber houses or Steinau during the Middle Ages. ⊠ *Verkehrsbüro, Brüder-Grimm-Str. 70* ☎ *06663/96310* ⊕ *www.steinau.eu.*

EXPLORING

FAMILY
Brüder Grimm Haus and Museum Steinau. Occupying both the house where the Brothers Grimm lived for much of their childhoods as well as the house's old barn, the Brüder Grimm Haus and Museum Steinau are fun and engaging museums. Featuring a reconstruction of the family's old kitchen, the brothers' former house also displays old personal

possessions such as letters and reading glasses, and has an upper floor divided into nine rooms with interactive displays that celebrate the Grimms' stories and other fairy tales from around Europe. Across a small courtyard, the town's museum documents what life was like on the old trade route that ran through Steinau, incorporating into its exhibits a coach, inn signs, milestones, and the type of pistols travelers used to defend themselves from bandits. ✉ *Brüder-Grimm-Str. 80* ☎ *06663/7605* 🌐 *www.museum-steinau.de* 🎟 *€6* 🕘 *Jan.–mid-Dec., daily 10–5.*

Schloss Steinau (*Steinau Castle*). Schloss Steinau is straight out of a Grimm fairy tale. It stands at the top of the town, with a "Fairy-tale Fountain" in front of it. Originally an early-medieval fortress, it was rebuilt in Renaissance style between 1525 and 1558 and first used by the counts of Hanau as their summer residence. Later it was used to guard the increasingly important trade route between Frankfurt and Leipzig. It's not difficult to imagine the young Grimm boys playing in the shadow of its great gray walls or venturing into the encircling dry moat.

The castle houses a **Grimm Museum,** one of two in Steinau, which exhibits the family's personal effects, including portraits of the Grimm relatives, the family Bible, an original copy of the Grimms' dictionary (the German equivalent of the *Oxford English Dictionary*), and all sorts of mundane things such as spoons and drinking glasses. Climb the tower for a breathtaking view of Steinau and the countryside. ✉ *Schloss an der Steinau* ☎ *06663/6843* 🎟 *Museum €2.50, tower €1, tour of castle and museum €8* 🕘 *Mar.–Oct., Tues.–Sun. 10–5; Nov.–mid-Dec., Tues.–Sun. 10–4.*

FAMILY **Steinauer Marionettentheater.** Located in what was once the stables at Schloss Steinau, this marionette theater portrays Grimm fairy tales and other children's classics. Performances are held most weekends at 3. ✉ *Schloss Steinau, Am Kumpen 2* ☎ *06663/245* 🌐 *www.die-holzkoeppe.de* 🎟 *€7.50.*

WHERE TO EAT AND STAY

$ GERMAN 🍴 **Brathähnchenfarm.** This cheery hotel-restaurant is a long, long way from the center of Steinau, uphill all the way. But it's worth it. As your nose will tell you immediately, just about everything on the menu is charcoal-grilled. The name ("Roast Chicken Farm") sets the theme, though other grilled meats are available. It's also good for peace and quiet and has several single and double rooms in the attached guesthouse (from €70). [$] *Average main: €14* ✉ *Im Ohl 1* ☎ *06663/228* 🌐 *www.brathaehnchenfarm.de* 💳 *No credit cards* 🕘 *Closed Mon. and late Dec.–mid-Feb.*

$ B&B/INN 🏨 **Burgmannenhaus.** Previously a 16th-century customs house, sitting on 1,000-year-old foundations and a secret tunnel that runs to the nearby Schloss and church, this friendly travelers' inn is the type of place made for history buffs. **Pros:** in the middle of Steinau; tasty regional beer on tap. **Cons:** restaurant ($) serves solid, if unspectacular German food. [$] *Rooms from: €78* ✉ *Brüder Grimm Str. 49* ☎ *06663/911–2602* 🌐 *www.burgmannenhaus-steinau.de* 💳 *No credit cards* 🛏 *5 rooms* 🍽 *No meals.*

To begin your tour of the Grimm brothers' fairy-tale landscape, head to the Nationaldenkmal Brüder Grimm (Brothers' Grimm Memorial) in Hanau.

EN ROUTE **Deutsche Fachwerkstrasse.** In case you don't get enough half-timber on the Fairy-Tale Road there is also the German Half-Timber Road (Deutsche Fachwerkstrasse), with lots more storybook architecture. A map and brochure can be obtained from the Deutsche Fachwerkstrasse. ⊠ *Propstei Johannesberg, Fulda* ☎ *0661/43680, 0661/9425–0366* ⊕ *www.fachwerkstrasse.de.*

FULDA

32 km (20 miles) northeast of Steinau an der Strasse, 100 km (62 miles) northeast of Frankfurt.

The cathedral city of Fulda is worth a brief detour off the Fairy-Tale Road. There are two distinct parts to its downtown area. One is a stunning display of baroque architecture, with the cathedral, orangery, and formal garden, which grew up around the palace. The other is the Old Town, where the incredibly narrow and twisty streets are lined with boutiques, bistros, and a medieval tower. ■TIP→ **You'll find Kanalstrasse and Karlstrasse in the Old Town lined with good, inexpensive cafés and restaurants, serving German, Mediterranean, and other dishes.**

GETTING HERE AND AROUND

InterCity Express trains connect Fulda with Frankfurt, Hannover, and Hamburg, while regional trains link the city with many other Fairy-Tale Road destinations. Within Fulda itself, the Old Town and the city's other main attractions are all in walking distance of each other.

The Brothers Grimm

The Grimm fairy tales originated in the southern part of the Märchenstrasse. This area, mainly in the state of Hesse, was the home region of the brothers Jacob (1785–1863) and Wilhelm (1786–1859) Grimm. They didn't create the stories they are famous for. Their feat was to mine the great folklore tradition that was already deeply ingrained in local culture.

COLLECTING THE STORIES

For generations, eager children had been gathering at dusk around the village storyteller to hear wondrous tales of fairies, witches, and gnomes, tales passed down from storytellers who had gone before. The Grimms sought out these storytellers and recorded their tales.

The result was the two volumes of their work *Kinder- und Hausmärchen* (*Children's and Household Tales*), published in 1812 and 1814 and revised and expanded six times during their lifetimes. The last edition, published in 1857, is the basis for the stories we know today. Earlier versions contained more violence and cruelty than was deemed suitable for children.

That is how the world got the stories of Cinderella, Sleeping Beauty, Hansel and Gretel, Little Red Riding Hood, Snow White and the Seven Dwarfs, Rumpelstiltskin, Puss-in-Boots, Mother Holle, Rapunzel, and some 200 others, many of which remain unfamiliar.

THE BROTHERS' OTHER WORK

Both Jacob and Wilhelm Grimm had distinguished careers as librarians and scholars, and probably would be unhappy to know that they are best remembered for the fairy tales. Among other things, they began what would become the most comprehensive dictionary of the German language and produced an analysis of German grammar.

The brothers were born in Hanau, near Frankfurt, which has a statue memorializing them as well as a Grimm exhibit at Schloss Philippsruhe. They spent their childhood in Steinau, 30 km (18 miles) to the north, where their father was magistrate. There are two Grimm museums there, one in their home. On their father's untimely death they moved to their mother's home city of Kassel, where they found the best of their stories. Kassel has an important Grimm museum, the GRIMMWELT, which opened in 2015 and is dedicated to promoting the brothers' role in enhancing the German language as we know it today. Although they attended the university at Marburg from 1802 to 1805, they later returned to Kassel to work as librarians before they went on to work in the university town of Göttingen; the brothers spent their last years as academics in Berlin.

ESSENTIALS

VISITOR INFORMATION **Tourismus und Kongressmanagement Fulda.** Located in the heart of the city, the tourist office coordinates group tours in addition to the award-winning hour-long daily tours that take place at 11:30 and 3 pm and which can be combined with an hour-long tour of the city's castle. ⊠ *Bonifatiuspl. 1* ☏ *0661/102–1813* ⊕ *www.tourismus-fulda.de.*

EXPLORING

Dom zu Fulda. Fulda's 18th-century cathedral, an impressive baroque building with an ornate interior, has two tall spires and stands on the other side of the broad boulevard that borders the palace park. The basilica accommodated the ever-growing number of pilgrims who converged on Fulda to pray at the grave of the martyred St. Boniface, the "Apostle of the Germans." A black alabaster bas-relief depicting his death marks the martyr's grave in the crypt. ⊠ *Dompl. 1* ⊕ *www. bistum-fulda.de/bistum_fulda* ⊗ *Apr.–Oct., weekdays 10–6, Sat. 10–3, Sun. 1–6; Nov.–Mar., weekdays 10–5, Sat. 10–3, Sun. 1–6.*

Cathedral Museum. The Cathedral treasury contains a document bearing St. Boniface's writing, along with several other treasures, including Lucas Cranach the Elder's fine 16th-century painting *Christ and the Adulteress.* ⊠ *Dompl. 2* ☎ *0661/87207* ⊕ *www.bistum-fulda.de/ bistum_fulda/* ⊠ *€2.10* ⊗ *Apr.–Oct., Tues.–Sat. 10–5:30, Sun. 12:30– 5:30; Nov., Dec.–mid-Jan., and mid-Feb.–Mar., Tues.–Sat. 10–12:30 and 1:30–4, Sun. 12:30–4.*

FAMILY **Kinder-Akademie-Fulda.** Germany's first children's museum has interactive exhibits to help explain science and technology, including a walk-through heart. ⊠ *Mehlerstr. 4* ☎ *0661/902–730* ⊕ *www.kaf.de* ⊠ *€9* ⊗ *Weekdays 10–5:30, Sun. 1–5:30, and Apr.–Oct., Sat. 1–5.30.*

Michaeliskirche. Dating back to 819 AD, this is one of Germany's oldest churches. Formerly a part of the Benedictine order, the church's interior is bare bones and yet impressive with its domed ceiling and arched cupola. ⊠ *Fulda* ⊠ *Free* ⊗ *Apr.–Oct., Tues.–Sun. 10–6; Nov.–Mar., Tues.–Sun. 10–noon and 2–5.*

Fodor'sChoice **Stadtschloss** (*City Palace*). The city's grandest example of baroque design
★ is the immense Stadtschloss, formerly the residence of the prince-bishops. The **Fürstensaal** (Princes' Hall), on the second floor, provides a breathtaking display of baroque decorative artistry, with ceiling paintings by the 18th-century Bavarian artist Melchior Steidl, and fabric-clad walls. The palace also has permanent displays of fine Fulda porcelain.

Also worth seeing is the **Spiegelsaal**, with its many tastefully arranged mirrors. Pause at the windows of the Grünes Zimmer (Green Chamber) to take in the view across the palace park to the **Orangery**, a large garden with summer-flowering shrubs and plants. ⊠ *Schlossstr. 1* ☎ *0661/1020* ⊕ *www.fulda.de/kultur/stadtschloss-fulda.html* ⊠ *€3.50* ⊗ *Tues.–Sun. 10–5; tours Nov.–Mar., Tues.–Fri. at 2, weekends 10:30 and 2; Apr.– Oct., Tues.–Thurs. and Sat. 10:30 and 2, Fri. 2.*

FAMILY **Vonderau Museum.** The Vonderau Museum is housed in a former Jesuit seminary. Its exhibits chart the cultural and natural history of Fulda and eastern Hesse. A popular section of the museum is its **planetarium**, which has a variety of shows, including one for children. Since it has only 35 seats, an early reservation is advisable. Shows take place Friday at 7, and on weekends at 2:30 and 3:30. ⊠ *Jesuitenpl. 2* ☎ *0661/928–350* ⊕ *www.museum-fulda.de* ⊠ *Museum €3.50, planetarium €4* ⊗ *Tues.–Sun. 10–5.*

EATING WELL ON THE FAIRY-TALE ROAD

A specialty of northern Hesse is sausages with *Beulches,* made from potato balls, leeks, and black pudding. *Weck,* which is local dialect for "heavily spiced pork," appears either as *Musterweck,* served on a roll, or as *Weckewerk,* a frying-pan concoction with white bread. Heading north into Lower Saxony, you'll encounter the ever-popular *Speckkuchen,* a heavy and filling onion tart. Another favorite main course is *Pfefferpothast,* a sort of heavily browned goulash with lots of pepper. Trout and eels are common in the rivers and streams around

Hameln, and by the time you reach Bremen, North German cuisine has taken over the menu. *Aalsuppe grün,* eel soup seasoned with dozens of herbs, is a must in summer, and the hearty *Grünkohl mit Pinkel,* a cabbage dish with sausage, bacon, and cured pork, appears in winter. Be sure to try the coffee. Fifty percent of the coffee served in Germany comes from beans roasted in Bremen. The city has been producing the stuff since 1673, and knows just how to serve it in pleasantly cozy or, as locals say, *gemütlich* surroundings.

WHERE TO EAT AND STAY

$
GERMAN

✕ **Dachsbau.** An intimate atmosphere in a 350-year-old house near the city's baroque quarter complements the gourmet menu, which focuses on using regional, in-season ingredients in its traditional German dishes. An extensive wine list ensures you'll always have the right glass to go with your locally caught trout or grilled pork loin. Arrive early on warm summer days to grab a seat on the sunny terrace. $ *Average main: €14* ✉ *Pfandhausstr. 8* ☎ *0661/74112* ⊕ *www.dachsbau-fulda.de* ☾ *Closed Mon. and Tues.* ▬ *No credit cards.*

$
B&B/INN

🏨 **Hotel zum Ritter.** Centrally located but tucked away on a side alley, this charming hotel and restaurant has quiet, comfortable rooms and very friendly staff, making it a great base for city exploring or for business travelers. **Pros:** friendly staff; great location. **Cons:** rooms are charmlessly modern. $ *Rooms from: €99* ✉ *Kanalstr. 18–20* ☎ *0661/250–800* ⊕ *www.hotel-ritter.de* ⤺ *33 rooms* ⦿ *Breakfast.*

$$
HOTEL

🏨 **Maritim Hotel am Schlossgarten.** At the luxurious showpiece of the Maritim chain, guests can breakfast beneath frescoed ceilings and enormous chandeliers in a stunning 18th-century orangery overlooking Fulda Palace Park. **Pros:** large, comfortable rooms; lovely terrace with views of park and nearby cathedral. **Cons:** no air-conditioning. $ *Rooms from: €175* ✉ *Pauluspromenade 2* ☎ *0661/2820* ⊕ *www.maritim.de* ⤺ *111 rooms, 1 suite* ⦿ *No meals.*

$$
HOTEL
Fodor'sChoice
★

🏨 **Romantik Hotel Goldener Karpfen.** An institution in Fulda for more than 100 years, the Goldener Karpfen has remained family owned and run, with an elegant disposition and engaging hosts that have brought singers, actors, and archbishops through its doors. **Pros:** luxury lodging; a short stroll to the town's major attractions; excellent breakfast buffet. **Cons:** public spaces can feel cluttered with knickknacks. $ *Rooms from: €165* ✉ *Simpliziusbrunnen 1* ☎ *0661/86800* ⊕ *www.hotel-goldener-karpfen.de* ⤺ *46 rooms, 4 suites* ⦿ *Breakfast.*

EN ROUTE Marburg is the next major stop on the road. Take B-254 to **Alsfeld** (34 km [21 miles] northwest of Fulda), where you can make a short stop to admire its half-timber houses and narrow streets; then take B-62 into Marburg.

MARBURG

60 km (35 miles) northwest of Fulda.

Fodor's Choice ★ "I think there are more steps in the streets than in the houses." That is how Jacob Grimm described the half-timber hillside town of Marburg, which rises steeply from the Lahn River to the spectacular castle that crowns the hill. Many of the winding, crooked "streets" are indeed stone staircases, and several of the hillside houses have back doors five stories above the front doors. The town's famous university and its students are the main influence on its social life, which pulses through the many cafés, restaurants, and hangouts around the marketplace. The Grimms themselves studied here from 1802 to 1805.

Many of the streets are closed to traffic, and are filled with outdoor tables when the weather cooperates. There is a free elevator near the tourist-information office on Pilgrimstein that can transport you from the level of the river to the Old Town.

GETTING HERE AND AROUND

Two hours from Fulda by train, the cheapest way to get here is by taking a regional train to the town of Giessen, and changing there; and every two hours a regional train runs between Marburg and Kassel. By car, take the B-254 and then B-62 from Fulda.

ESSENTIALS

VISITOR INFORMATION **Marburg Tourismus und Marketing.** Located in the heart of the city, the tourist office sells souvenirs and event tickets as well as organizing public tours, including a two-hour tour (€6) every Saturday at 3 pm, which meets at Elisabethkirche, and an English-language hour-long tour of the Altstadt that meets at the fountain on the Market Square on the first Monday of each month from May to October at 6:30 pm. ⊠ *Pilgrimstein 26* ☎ *06421/99120* ⊕ *www.marburg.de.*

EXPLORING

Elisabethkirche (*St. Elizabeth Church*). Marburg's most important building is the Elisabethkirche, which marks the burial site of St. Elizabeth (1207–31), the town's favorite daughter. She was a Hungarian princess, betrothed at age 4 and married at 14 to a member of the nobility, Ludwig IV of Thuringia. In 1228, when her husband died in the Sixth Crusade, she gave up all worldly pursuits. She moved to Marburg, founded a hospital, gave her wealth to the poor, and spent the rest of her very short life (she died at the age of 24) in poverty, caring for the sick and the aged. She is largely responsible for what Marburg became. Because of her selflessness she was made a saint four years after her death. The Teutonic Knights built the Elisabethkirche, which quickly became a pilgrimage site, enabling the city to prosper. You can visit the shrine in the sacristy that once contained her bones, a masterpiece of the goldsmith's art. The church is a veritable museum of religious art, full of statues and

Many of Marburg's cobblestone streets are pedestrian-only zones, perfect for strolling and people-watching.

frescoes. Walking tours of Marburg begin at the church on Saturday at 3, year-round. Tours inside the church are held Monday to Friday at 3 from April to October (€3.50) and Sunday shortly after Mass (around 11:15). ✉ *Elisabethstr. 1* 🌐 *www.elisabethkirche.de* 🎟 *Free* ⏲ *Nov.–Mar., Mon.–Sat. 10–4, Sun. 11–4; Apr.–Oct., Mon.–Sat. 9–5, Sun. 11–5.*

Landgrafenschloss. Sitting at the highest point in the town, this castle was finished in 1500 and survived the war unscathed. It offers panoramic views of Marburg below and a small museum with displays of weaponry, pottery, religious art, and local history. ✉ *Landgrafenschloss* ☎ *06421/282–5871* 🌐 *www.uni-marburg.de/uni-museum* 🎟 *€4* ⏲ *Apr.–Oct., daily 10–6; Nov.–Mar., daily 10–4; tours (in German) Apr.–Oct., Sun. at 3.*

Wendelgasse. Fascinating narrow lanes, crooked steps, superbly restored half-timber houses, and venerable old churches abound in the old town of Marburg; the narrow Wendelgasse takes you up 175 stairs through the city, surrounded by old timber-framed houses. ✉ *Wendelg.* 🎟 *Free.*

WHERE TO EAT AND STAY

$ CAFÉ 🍴 **Cafe Vetter.** This café has the most spectacular view in town—and Marburg is famous for its panoramas. Both an outdoor terrace and a glassed-in terrace take full advantage of the site. It's all very "Viennese coffeehouse traditional" here, and the homemade cakes and chocolate creams are hard to resist. This institution, four generations in the same family, has piano music on weekend afternoons. [$] *Average main: €7* ✉ *Reitg. 4* ☎ *06421/25888* 🌐 *www.cafe-vetter-marburg.de* 💳 *No credit cards* ⏲ *No dinner.*

$ WINE BAR 🍴 **Weinlädele.** If you've tired of the big glasses of beer and plates of enormous schnitzel on offer in traditional eating establishments, this half-timbered wine bar's fine selection of German wines, and light, crispy *Flammkuchen* (a flambéed tart) is a welcome break. Just up the street from the Old Town's main marketplace, it's a busy spot, popular with patrons of all ages. When the weather is good, get there early, grab a table on its little terrace for a view down the hill, order a cheese platter and glass of white, and watch the world idle by. [$] *Average main: €9* ✉ *Schlosstreppe 1* ☎ *06421/14244* 🌐 *www.weinlaedele.com* 💳 *No credit cards.*

$$ HOTEL 🏨 **Welcome Hotel Marburg.** While the plain facade of this large, modern hotel may suffer in comparison with much of Marburg's traditional architecture, its generous rooms, comfy beds, and excellent breakfast buffet draw guests back. **Pros:** across from the elevator to the Altstadt. **Cons:** no real views from many of the rooms. [$] *Rooms from: €131* ✉ *Pilgrimstein 29* ☎ *06421/9180* 🌐 *www.welcome-hotels.com* 🛏 *147 rooms, 3 suites* 🍽 *Breakfast.*

KASSEL

100 km (62 miles) northeast of Marburg.

The Brothers Grimm lived in Kassel, their mother's hometown, as teenagers, and also worked there as librarians at the court of the king of Westphalia, Jerome Bonaparte (Napoléon's youngest brother), and for the elector of Kassel. In researching their stories and legends, their best source was not books but storyteller Dorothea Viehmann, who was born in the Knallhütte tavern, which is still in business in nearby Baunatal.

Much of Kassel was destroyed in World War II, and the city was rebuilt with little regard for its architectural past. The city's museums and the beautiful Schloss Wilhelmshöhe and Schlosspark, however, are well worth a day or two of exploration.

GETTING HERE AND AROUND

On a main InterCity Express line between Munich and Hamburg, you can also travel to Kassel-Wilhelmshöhe from Hannover and Bremen by high-speed train. By car, travel northeast from Marburg on the B-3 to Borken, then take autobahn A-49 into Kassel.

TOURS

Guided bus tours of Kassel set off from the Stadttheater on Saturday at 11.

DISCOUNTS AND DEALS

When you arrive, you may want to buy a **Kassel Card,** which gives you a reduced rate for the city bus tour, free travel on the local transportation system, and reduced admission to the museums and the local casino. It's available at the tourist office for €9 for 24 hours and €12 for 72 hours, for two people per card.

ESSENTIALS

VISITOR INFORMATION **Kassel Marketing GmbH.** Though small, the "documenta" city—a reference to the 100-day-long outdoor art exhibition that takes place there every five years—knows how to show visitors its good side. Every Friday at 4, the tourist office organizes a walking tour of the major sites for €7 and in summer months, adds themed guided tours highlighting the Grimm brothers' time in the city. ✉ *Wilhelmsstr. 23* ☎ *0561/707–707* ⊕ *www.kassel-marketing.de.*

FESTIVALS

documenta. Every five years, a 100-day contemporary and modern art show takes over the city of Kassel. Begun in 1955, the next exhibit will occur in 2017. ⊕ *www.documenta.de.*

EXPLORING

GRIMMWELT (*Grimm's World*). Opened in 2015, this museum and exhibition space brings the world of the Grimm brothers to life with a combination of artifacts from their time in Kassel and interactive exhibitions devoted to furthering awareness of their important role in the development of the German language. Temporary exhibits include video art installations focusing on language or take a playful view of the brothers' fairy tales. ✉ *Weinbergstr. 21* ☎ *0561/598–6190* ⊕ *www.grimmwelt.de* 🎫 *Museum €8, presentation €5, combined museum and presentation €10* ⊙ *Tues.–Thurs. and weekends 10–6, Fri. 10–8.*

Fodor's Choice ★ **Schloss und Bergpark Wilhelmshöhe** (*Wilhelmshöhe Palace and Palace Park*). The magnificent grounds of the 18th-century Schloss and the Bergpark Wilhelmshöhe, at the western edge of Kassel, are said to be Europe's largest hill park. If you have time, plan to spend an entire day at this UNESCO World Heritage Site, exploring its wonderful gardens, water features, museums, and castle. Wear good walking shoes and bring some water if you want to hike all the way up to the giant statue of Hercules that crowns the hilltop.

The Wilhelmshöher Park was laid out as a baroque park in the early 18th century, its elegant lawns separating the city from the thick woods of the Habichtswald (Hawk Forest). Schloss Wilhelmshöhe was added between 1786 and 1798. The great palace stands at the end of the 5-km-long (3-mile-long) Wilhelmshöher Allée, an avenue that runs straight as an arrow from one side of the city to the other.

Kassel's leading art gallery and the state art collection lie within Schloss Wilhelmshöhe as part of the **Museumslandschaft Hessen Kassel**. Its collection includes 11 Rembrandts, as well as outstanding works by Rubens, Hals, Jordaens, Van Dyck, Dürer, Altdorfer, Cranach, and Baldung Grien.

The giant 18th-century statue of Hercules that crowns the Wilhelmshöhe heights is an astonishing sight. You can climb the stairs of the statue's castlelike base—and the statue itself—for a rewarding look over the entire city. At 2:30 pm on Sunday and Wednesday from mid-May through September, water gushes from a fountain beneath the statue, rushes down a series of cascades to the foot of the hill, and ends its precipitous journey in a 175-foot-high jet of water. A café lies a short walk from the statue. ✉ *Schloss Wilhelmshöhe, Schlosspark 1* ☎ *0561/316–800* ⊕ *www.wilhelmshoehe.de* 🎫 *Museum Schloss Wilhelmshöhe €6; Hercules Octagon €3* ⊙ *Tues., Thurs., and Fri.–Sun. 10–5, Wed. 10–8.*

Löwenburg (*Lion Fortress*). Amid the thick trees of the Wilhelmshöher Park, it comes as something of a surprise to see the turrets of a medieval castle breaking the harmony. There are more surprises at the Löwenburg, for this is not a true medieval castle but a fanciful, stylized copy of a Scottish castle, built in 1793 (70 years after the Hercules statue that towers above it). The Löwenburg contains a collection of medieval armor and weapons, tapestries, and furniture. ✉ *Schlosspark 9* ☎ *0561/3168–0244* 🌐 *www.museum-kassel.de* 🎟 *€4 including tour* ⏲ *Mar.–Oct., Tues.–Sun. 10–5; Nov.–Feb., Fri.–Sun. 10–4.*

WHERE TO EAT AND STAY

$ GERMAN 🍴 **Brauhaus Knallhütte.** This brewery and inn, established in 1752, was the home of the village storyteller Dorothea Viehmann, who supplied the Grimms with some of their best stories, including "Little Red Riding Hood," "Hansel and Gretel," and "Rumpelstiltskin." To this day "Dorothea" tells her stories here (in German only) every first and third Saturday of the month at 5:30. Once a wayside inn on the road to Frankfurt, the Knallhütte now sits alongside a busy highway. However, this hasn't diminished its popularity, and if you're planning on visiting on the weekend, it's best to book ahead. Those that arrive hungry can tour the brewery and then eat and drink as much as they want for €24.90. [$] *Average main: €14* ✉ *Rengershausen, Knallhütte. 1, Baunatal* ☎ *0561/492–076* 🌐 *www.knallhuette.de.*

$$ HOTEL Fodor's Choice ★ 🏨 **Hotel Gude.** It may be 10 minutes by tram away from the city center, but this modern, friendly hotel and its spacious rooms, sauna, and excellent restaurant ($$$) justify the journey. **Pros:** close to the autobahn; easy parking; comfortable beds. **Cons:** removed from the city center; on a busy street. [$] *Rooms from: €119* ✉ *Frankfurter Str. 299* ☎ *0561/48050* 🌐 *www.hotel-gude.de* 🛏 *84 rooms, 1 suite* 🍽 *Breakfast.*

$$ HOTEL 🏨 **Schlosshotel Wilhelmshöhe.** Positioned beside the lovely baroque gardens and woodland paths of the hilltop Wilhelmshöhe Park, this comfortable, modern hotel and its rooms take in views on the park grounds on one side and stunning vistas over Kassel on the other. **Pros:** tranquil atmosphere; historic setting; views. **Cons:** no mini-refrigerator/minibar in "classic" rooms; a modern-looking hotel, despite its romantic name. [$] *Rooms from: €129* ✉ *Am Schlosspark 8* ☎ *0561/30880* 🌐 *www.schlosshotel-kassel.de* 🛏 *120 rooms, 2 suites* 🍽 *Breakfast.*

BAD KARLSHAFEN

50 km (31 miles) north of Kassel.

Popular with holidaymakers in mobile homes and trailers, who park up on the banks of the Weser directly across from its historic center, Bad Karlshafen's a pretty little spa town with baroque architecture that is best viewed from the campsite side of the river, as the town is surrounded by hills covered in dense forest. Its elevation and rural location provide fresh air, and there are salt springs that the locals believe can cure just about whatever ails you.

GETTING HERE AND AROUND

Regional trains run here from Göttingen, but only infrequently, so check train timetables well ahead of any visit.

Climb to the top of the Schloss und Bergpark Wilhelmshöhe, where a giant statue of Hercules and a fantastic view of Kassel await.

ESSENTIALS

VISITOR
INFORMATION **Bad Karlshafen.** Tours of the town leave from the Tourist Office at the Rathaus on Sunday at 3 pm from May to October (€4) and follow the trail of the Protestant Huguenots responsible for much of the baroque architecture. ⊠ *Kur- und Touristik-Information, Hafenpl. 8* ☎ *05672/999–922* ⊕ *www.bad-karlshafen.de.*

EXPLORING

Rathaus. Bad Karlshafen's baroque beauty, the town's best example of the stunning architectural style, stands in surprising contrast to the abundance of half-timber houses found along the rest of the Weser. Inside, the building is still used for administrative purposes so it is not accessible to the public. ⊠ *Hafenpl. 8.*

FAMILY **Weser Therme.** This huge spa facility sitting on the banks of the Weser River has whirlpools, sauna and steam baths, thermal saltwater pools, and an outdoor pool that is said to be as salty as the Dead Sea. The spa's waters are famed for their therapeutic benefits, and a couple of hours bathing in them often helps relieve aches and stress. Massages are available to further aid the relaxation process. ⊠ *Kurpromenade 1* ☎ *05672/92110* ⊕ *www.wesertherme.de* ⊠ *Pools €12.50 for 3 hrs, €16 with sauna; €17/€20 for full day* ⏱ *Sun.–Thurs. 9 am–10 pm, Fri. and Sat. 9 am–11 pm.*

WHERE TO STAY

$ **Hotel zum Weserdampfschiff.** From the snug riverside rooms of this HOTEL popular hotel-tavern, guests can watch passengers step directly off Weser pleasure boats and into the hotel's welcoming beer garden below.

Pros: river view; low rates; near spa and city center. **Cons:** no wireless Internet; no credit cards accepted. $ *Rooms from: €90* ✉ *Weserstr. 25* ☎ *05672/2425* ⊕ *www.zumweserdampfschiff.de* ▬ *No credit cards* ⛵ *14 rooms* ⏐◉⏐ *Breakfast.*

█ EN
ROUTE

Fürstenberg Porcelain factory. Germany's second-oldest porcelain factory is at Fürstenberg, 24 km (14 miles) north of Bad Karlshafen and 8 km (5 miles) south of Höxter, in a Weser Renaissance castle high above the Weser River. The crowned Gothic letter *F*, which serves as its trademark, is known worldwide. You'll find Fürstenberg porcelain in Bad Karlshafen and Höxter, but it's more fun to journey to the 18th-century castle itself, where production first began in 1747, and buy directly from the manufacturer. Fürstenberg and most dealers will take care of shipping arrangements and any tax refunds. Porcelain workshops can be booked ahead of time, and there's also a sales outlet, museum, and café. The view from the castle is a pastoral idyll, with the Weser snaking through the immaculately tended fields and woods. You can also spot cyclists on the riverside paths. ✉ *Schloss Fürstenberg, Meinbrexener Str. 2, Fürstenberg* ☎ *05271/401–161* ⊕ *www.fuerstenberg-porzellan. com* 🎫 *Museum is free through 2017 due to renovations* ☉ *Museum: Apr.–Oct., Tues.–Sun. 10–5; Nov.–Mar., weekends 10–5 (closed Dec. 20–Jan. 8); Shop: mid-Jan.–Oct., Tues.–Sun. 10–6.*

SABABURG

50 km (31 miles) west of Göttingen, 100 km (62 miles) south of Hannover.

Sababurg's not really a village as such, but it is the location of an enchanting, 700-year-old Renaissance castle, an impressive animal park, and Germany's oldest forest nature reserve, all of which lie within the peaceful, wooded surrounds of the Reinhardswald. The castle, which sits proudly on the crest of a hill in the forest, is also known as Dornröschenschloss, widely believed to be the source of inspiration for the Grimms Brothers' tale of "Sleeping Beauty."

GETTING HERE AND AROUND

Removed from the main highway and with no rail connection, Sababurg, Dornröschenschloss, and the nearby Sababurg Tierpark are best visited by car.

EXPLORING

Fodor'sChoice
★

Dornröschenschloss (*Sleeping Beauty's Castle*). The story goes that after Sleeping Beauty had slumbered for 100 years, the thick thorn hedge surrounding her castle suddenly burst into blossom, thereby enabling a daring prince to find a way in to lay a kiss upon her lips and reawaken her. Nowadays home to a handsome hotel, the stony exterior of Dornröschenschloss continues to be clad in colorful roses, and its walled garden is home to an impressive collection of the flowers. Even if you don't stay the night, a drive here is scenic, and there are ruins as well as the garden to explore, and a pleasant outdoor terrace with views over forest-covered hills to enjoy afterward. ✉ *Sababurg 12* ⊕ *www. sababurg.de* 🎫 *Free.*

FAMILY **Tierpark Sababurg.** The Tierpark Sababurg is one of Europe's oldest wildlife refuges. Bison, red deer, wild horses, and all sorts of waterfowl populate the park. There's also a petting zoo for children. ✉ *Sababurg 1* ☎ *05671/766–4990* 🌐 *www.tierpark-sababurg.de* 🎟 *€8* 🕒 *Apr.–Sept., daily 8–7; Oct., daily 9–6; Nov.–Feb., daily 10–4; Mar., daily 9–5.*

WHERE TO STAY

$$ HOTEL 🏨 **Dornröschenschloss Sababurg.** The medieval fortress thought to have inspired the tale of "Sleeping Beauty" is today a small luxury hotel, complete with domed turrets, spiral staircases, and tower rooms with four-poster beds and spa baths. **Pros:** sylvan setting; incredibly romantic. **Cons:** some dated rooms; takes some effort to find the place. [$] *Rooms from: €165* ✉ *Sababurg 12, Hofgeismar* ☎ *05671/8080* 🌐 *www.sababurg.de* 🛏 *17 rooms* 🍴 *Breakfast.*

$$ HOTEL Fodor's Choice ★ 🏨 **Hotel Burg Trendelburg.** Ivy-bedecked towers, a shadowy foyer decorated with suits of armor and swords, and guest rooms with four-poster beds and little bathrooms hidden behind cupboard doors endow this fine establishment with an atmosphere of fairy-tale adventure. **Pros:** great views; authentic castle experience. **Cons:** some rooms small; in a otherwise uninspiring village. [$] *Rooms from: €155* ✉ *Steinweg 1, Trendelburg* ☎ *05675/9090* 🌐 *www.burg-hotel-trendelburg.com* 🛏 *22 rooms, 2 suites* 🍴 *Breakfast.*

LOWER SAXONY

Lower Saxony (Niedersachsen) was formed from an amalgamation of smaller states in 1946. Its picturesque landscape includes one of Germany's most haunting river roads, along the Weser River between Hannoversch-Münden and Hameln (Hamelin). This road, part of the Fairy-Tale Road, follows green banks where it's hard to see where the water ends and the land begins. Standing sentinel are superb little towns whose half-timber architecture gave rise to the term "Weser Renaissance." The Lower Saxon landscape also includes the juniper bushes and flowering heather of the Lüneburg Heath.

HANNOVERSCH-MÜNDEN

24 km (15 miles) north of Kassel, 150 km (93 miles) south of Hannover.

You'll have to travel a long way through Germany to find a grouping of half-timber houses as harmonious as those in this delightful town, seemingly untouched by the modern age—there are some 700 of them. Hannoversch-Münden is surrounded by forests and the Fulda and Werra rivers, which join here and flow northward as the Weser River.

GETTING HERE AND AROUND

Regional trains linking Hannoversch Münden to both Kassel and Göttingen run every hour.

ESSENTIALS

VISITOR INFORMATION **Hannoversch-Münden.** The tourist office has maps to the surrounding national park and coordinates walking tours, including a daily tour that takes place May to October at 10:30 and 2:30, leaving from the town hall (€5.50). ✉ *Touristik Naturpark Münden, Lotzestr. 2, Hannoversch Münden* ☎ *05541/75313* ⊕ *www.hann.muenden-tourismus.de.*

EXPLORING

Johann Andreas Eisenbart. Much is made of the fact that the quack doctor to end all quacks died in Hannoversch-Münden. Dr. Johann Andreas Eisenbart (1663–1727) would be forgotten today if a ribald 19th-century drinking song ("Ich bin der Doktor Eisenbart, widda, widda, wit, boom! boom!") hadn't had him shooting out aching teeth with a pistol, anesthetizing with a sledgehammer, and removing boulders from kidneys. He was, as the song has it, a man who could make "the blind walk and the lame see." This is terribly exaggerated, of course, but the town takes advantage of it.

The good Dr. Eisenbart has "office hours" in the town hall at 1:30 on Saturday from May through December; and a glockenspiel on the town hall depicts Eisenbart's feats, to the tune of the Eisenbart song, daily throughout the year at noon, 3 pm, and 5 pm. There's a statue of the doctor in front of his home at Langestrasse 79, and his grave is outside the St. Ägidien Church. ✉ *Lotzestr. 2* ☎ *05541/75313* ⊕ *www.hann. muenden-tourismus.de.*

GÖTTINGEN

30 km (19 miles) northeast of Hannoversch-Münden, 110 km (68 miles) south of Hannover.

Distinguished by its famous university, where the Brothers Grimm served as professors and librarians between 1830 and 1837, the fetching town of Göttingen buzzes with student life. Young people on bikes zip past bookshops and secondhand boutiques; when night falls, the town's cozy bars and cafés swell with students making the most of the drinks specials and free Wi-Fi on offer.

In the streets around the Rathaus you'll find magnificent examples of Renaissance architecture. Many of these half-timber, low-gable buildings house businesses that have been here for centuries. It's also a large and modern place and boasts the shiny stores, chain coffee shops, and other trappings you'd expect of a 21st-century German town. Though not strictly on the Fairy-Tale Road (despite its association with the Grimms), Göttingen is still well worth visiting.

GETTING HERE AND AROUND

Göttingen is a stop on the same InterCity Express line between Munich and Hamburg as Kassel-Wilhelmshöhe, and is also easily reached from Bremen.

ESSENTIALS

VISITOR INFORMATION **Göttingen Tourist Information.** Göttingen offers walking tours in English on the first and third Saturday of the month, April to October at 11 from the Old Town Hall. ✉ *Altes Rathaus, Markt 9* ☎ *0551/499–800* ⊕ *www.goettingen-tourismus.de.*

EXPLORING

Altes Rathaus. The Old Town Hall was begun in the 13th century and houses a completely preserved Gothic heating system in the part-medieval, part-Renaissance building. The tourist-information office is on the first floor. ☒ *Markt 9* ☎ *0551/499–800* ⊕ *www.goettingen.de* ☒ *Free* ☉ *Weekdays 9:30–6, Sat. 10–6, Sun. 10–4.*

Gänseliesel. The statue of Gänseliesel, the little Goose Girl of German folklore, stands in Göttingen's central market square, symbolizing the strong link between the students and their university city. The girl, according to the story, was a princess who was forced to trade places with a peasant, and the statue shows her carrying her geese and smiling shyly into the waters of a fountain. The students of Göttingen gave her a ceremonial role: traditionally, graduates who earn a doctorate bestow a kiss of thanks upon Gänseliesel. Göttingen's citizens say she's the most kissed girl in the world.

WHERE TO EAT AND STAY

$$$

MEDITERRANEAN

✕ **Gaudi.** In a town rich with cozy taverns and hearty local food, the appearance of this Mediterranean restaurant, with its terra-cotta-and-blue color scheme, arty chandeliers, and light, airy spaces, stands out as much as its cuisine. Right in the middle of Göttingen's historic Börner Viertel, the restaurant is a favorite with staff from the university, who

The virgin forests of Sababurg, where Sleeping Beauty slumbered for 100 years, are still wild and dense.

feast on its fine consommés, tapas, pasta, and fish and meat dishes. The food and excellent service are worth the extra cost here. $\boxed{\text{S}}$ *Average main: €24* ✉ *Rote Str. 16* ☎ *0551/531–3001* ⊕ *www.restaurant-gaudi. de* ⊘ *Closed Sun. No lunch Mon.*

$$ ✕ **Landgasthaus Lockemann.** If you like to walk and hike, consider head-
GERMAN ing to the Stadtwald (city forest) and then eating a hearty meal at this half-timber lodge. Take Bus 10 from the Busbahnhof, direction Herbershausen, to the last stop; then walk left on Im Beeke. The trip will take 20 minutes. $\boxed{\text{S}}$ *Average main: €16* ✉ *Im Beeke 1* ☎ *0551/209–020* ⊕ *www.landgasthaus-lockemann.de* ▭ *No credit cards* ⊘ *Closed Mon. No lunch weekdays.*

$$$ 🏨 **Romantik Hotel Gebhards.** Though within walking distance to the main
HOTEL train station, this family-run hotel stands aloof and serene on its own grounds, a modernized 18th-century building that's something of a local landmark. **Pros:** across from the train station. **Cons:** on a busy street; expensive. $\boxed{\text{S}}$ *Rooms from: €208* ✉ *Goethe-Allée 22–23* ☎ *0551/49680* ⊕ *www.gebhardshotel.de* ⇱ *45 rooms, 5 suites* ⦿ *Breakfast.*

NIGHTLIFE

Among the delights of Göttingen are the ancient taverns where generations of students have lifted their steins. Among the best known are the Kleiner Ratskeller and Trou. Don't be shy about stepping into either of these taverns or any of the others that catch your eye; the food and drink are inexpensive, and the welcome is invariably warm and friendly.

HÖXTER

24 km (14 miles) north of Bad Karl-shafen, 100 km (62 miles) south of Hannover.

Höxter is not actually in Lower Saxony, but just over the border in North Rhine-Westphalia. The town's appeal lies in its Rathaus, a perfect example of the Weser Renaissance style, and its proximity to the impressive Reichsabtei Corvey, an abbey that's a short drive away. There's not much Grimm here; overshadowed by Sababurg's claim to Sleeping Beauty's castle and Bodenwerder's Baron von Münchhausen, Höxter's connection to a fairy tale is limited to a small Hansel and Gretel fountain in the middle of town.

HIKING AND WALKING

Two protected nature parks—the Weserbergland and the Lüneburg Heath—are in or near the Fairy-Tale Road. You can hike the banks of the Weser, stopping at ancient waterside inns, from Hannoversch-Münden, in the south, to Porta-Westfalica, where the Weser River breaks through the last range of North German hills and into the plain of Lower Saxony. The Lüneburg Heath is flat, and hiking is particularly pleasant in late summer, when the heather is in bloom. The tourist offices can tell you where to find nearby trails.

GETTING HERE AND AROUND

Every couple of hours buses and regional trains run from Bad Karl-shafen to Höxter Rathaus and take about 45 minutes, or you can take a combination of regional trains from Göttingen that take from 90 minutes to 2½ hours.

ESSENTIALS

VISITOR INFORMATION **Höxter.** Located in the historical Rathaus, the tourist office coordinates walking tours of the city every Wednesday at 3 and Saturday at 11 from May to September (€4). ⊠ *Tourist-Info, Weserstr. 11* ☎ *05271/963–431* ⊕ *www.hoexter-tourismus.de.*

EXPLORING

Fodor's Choice **Reichsabtei Corvey** (*Imperial Abbey of Corvey*). The impressive Reichsab-
★ tei Corvey, or Schloss Corvey, is idyllically set between the wooded heights of the Solling region and the Weser River. During its 1,200-year history it has provided lodging for several Holy Roman emperors. Heinrich Hoffmann von Fallersleben (1798–1874), author of the poem "Deutschland, Deutschland über Alles," worked as librarian here in the 1820s. The poem, set to music by Joseph Haydn, became the German national anthem in 1922. A music festival is held in the church and great hall, the Kaisersaal, in May and June of every even-numbered year. Corvey is reached on an unnumbered road heading east from Höxter (3 km [2 miles]) toward the Weser. There are signposts to "Schloss Corvey." ⊠ *Schloss Corvey* ☎ *05271/68120* ⊕ *www.schloss-corvey.de* 🎫 *€6, abbey church €0.80, tour €3* ⊗ *Apr.–Oct., Tues.–Sun. 10–6.*

WHERE TO EAT

$ ╳ **Schlossrestaurant.** In summer you can dine on flambéed tart and salad
GERMAN under centuries-old trees. When it's cooler, slip inside the Reichsab-tei Corvey's excellent and elegant restaurant for a hot coffee and a

piece of one its delicious cakes. With advance notice, a *Fürstenbankett,* or princely banquet, can be arranged for groups in the vaulted cellars. $ *Average main: €12* ⊠ *Schloss Corvey* ☎ *05271/8323* ⊗ *Closed Nov.–Mar.*

BODENWERDER

34 km (21 miles) north of Höxter, 70 km (43 miles) south of Hannover.

The charming Weser town of Bodenwerder is the home of the Lügenbaron (Lying Baron) von Münchhausen (1720–97), who was known as a teller of whoppers and whose fantastical tales included a story about riding a cannonball toward an enemy fortress but then, having second thoughts, returning to where he started by leaping onto a cannonball heading the other way. Stretched out along a peaceful valley, the nicest part of the town is around the Baron's old home, now the town hall, its half-timber architecture set against a backdrop of the river and surrounding hills. A regular stop for cyclists on the Wesertal route, the town also attracts canoeists, and anglers who can tell their own whoppers about the one that got away.

GETTING HERE AND AROUND

Reachable from Höxter by a combination of bus and regional train, or by bus from Hameln (Hamelin), changes are required along the way and any visits requiring public transport should be planned in advance.

ESSENTIALS

VISITOR INFORMATION **Bodenwerder Tourist-Information.** The regional tourist office can organize tours for Bodenwerder as well as Münchhausen, including a special tour featuring the literary figure Baron von Münchhausen. ⊠ *Münchausenpl. 3* ☎ *05533/40542* ⊕ *www.muenchhausenland.de.*

EXPLORING

Münchhausen Museum. Housed in an old, renovated farm building right next to the imposing family home in which Baron von Münchhausen grew up (it's now the Rathaus), the Münchhausen Museum is crammed with mementos of his adventurous life, including his cannonball. A fountain in front of the house represents another story. The baron, it seems, was puzzled when his horse kept drinking insatiably at a trough. Investigating, he discovered that the horse had been cut in two by a closing castle gate and that the water ran out as fast as the horse drank. The water in the fountain, of course, flows from the rear of a half-horse. At 3 on the first, second, and fourth Sundays of the month from May through October, townspeople retell von Münchhausen's life story with performances in front of the Rathaus. ⊠ *Münchhausenpl. 1* ☎ *05533/409–147* ⊠ *Museum €2.50* ⊗ *Apr.–Oct., daily 10–5.*

WHERE TO STAY

$ HOTEL ⌨ **Hotel Goldener Anker.** The riverside rooms of this friendly, family-owned and -run hotel on the banks of the Weser river come with the best view in town. **Pros:** directly beside the river; friendly staff. **Cons:** standard rooms are very simple; close to the town's main bridge. $ *Rooms from: €84* ⊠ *Brückenstr. 5* ☎ *05533/400–730* ⊕ *www.goldeneranker. com* ⇱ *19 rooms* ⫿⊙⫿ *Breakfast.*

$ HOTEL **Parkhotel Deutsches Haus.** Clean, comfortable, and friendly, this country hotel combines a traditional half-timber facade with uncomplicated, if a little dated, interior styling. **Pros:** elevator; rooms get plenty of natural light. **Cons:** on a busy street; plain furnishings. [$] *Rooms from: €97* ✉ *Münchhausenpl. 4* ☎ *05533/400–780* 🌐 *www.parkhotel-bodenwerder.de* 🛏 *39 rooms* 🍴 *Breakfast.*

$$$ HOTEL Fodor's Choice ★ **Schlosshotel Münchhausen.** This 17th-century castle was converted into a top-class luxury hotel in a manner that retains much of the original charm and decoration without sacrificing modern amenities, including a spa and swimming area. **Pros:** accommodations in a real castle; gorgeous park surroundings; pool. **Cons:** several rooms are in the Zehntscheune (former barn) out back; a/c not in all rooms. [$] *Rooms from: €200* ✉ *Schwöbber 9, Aerzen bei Hameln* ☎ *05154/70600* 🌐 *www.schlosshotel-muenchhausen.com* 🛏 *68 rooms* 🍴 *Breakfast.*

HAMELN (HAMELIN)

24 km (15 miles) north of Bodenwerder, 47 km (29 miles) southwest of Hannover.

Given their relationship with one of the most famous fairy-tale characters of all time, it's unsurprising that Hameln's townsfolk continue to take advantage of the Pied Piper. Known locally as the *Rattenfänger,* or "rat-catcher," these days he tends to be celebrated more than exploited (even if his name does adorn everything from coffee mugs to restaurants), and regular costumed tours through the town relive his deeds, while a bronze statue of him stands proudly in the town's lovely pedestrian zone. Not as exciting as Hannover to the north or as relaxing as Bodenwerder to the south, Hameln is still one of the top places to visit along the Fairy-Tale Road thanks to its fairy-tale legacy, elegantly painted and inscribed half-timber buildings, and laid-back atmosphere.

GETTING HERE AND AROUND

At 45 minutes away from Hannover by S-bahn (Line No. 5), Hameln is within easy reach of the Lower Saxon capital.

ESSENTIALS

VISITOR INFORMATION **Hameln Marketing und Tourismus.** Walking tours of Hameln are held year-round, leaving from the tourist office (April to October, daily at 10:30 and 2:30; November and January to March, Saturday at 2:30, Sunday at 10:30; December, daily at 10:30). ✉ *Deisterallee 1* ☎ *05151/957–823* 🌐 *www.hameln.de.*

EXPLORING

Hochzeitshaus (*Wedding House*). On central Osterstrasse you'll see several examples of Weser Renaissance architecture, including the Rattenfängerhaus (Rat-Catcher's House) and the Hochzeitshaus, a beautiful 17th-century sandstone building now used for city offices. From mid-May to mid-September the Hochzeitshaus terrace is the scene of two free open-air events commemorating the Pied Piper legend. From May to September, local actors and children present a half-hour reenactment each Sunday at noon, and there is also a 40-minute musical, *Rats,* each Wednesday at 4:30 during the same months. The carillon of the

Hochzeitshaus plays tunes every day at 9:35 and 11:35, and mechanical figures enact the piper story on the west gable of the building at 1:05, 3:35, and 5:35. ✉ *Osterstr. 2.*

FAMILY **Museum Hameln.** The story of the city of Hameln comes to life in this museum, which contains the **Rattenfänger Theater,** a unique mechanical theater that shows the Pied Piper in action with a sound-and-light show that lasts 12 minutes and occurs hourly from 11:30 to 5:30 each day. ✉ *Osterstr. 8–9* ☎ *05151/202–1215* ⊕ *www.museum-hameln.de* 💶 *€5* ⊙ *Tues.–Sun. 11–6.*

WHERE TO EAT AND STAY

$ ✕ **Rattenfängerhaus.** This brilliant example of Weser Renaissance architecture is Hameln's most famous building, where the Pied Piper supposedly stayed during his rat-extermination assignment (it wasn't actually built until centuries after his supposed exploits). A plaque in front of it fixes the date of the incident at June 26, 1284. "Rats" are all over the menu, from the "rat-killer liqueur" to a "rat-tail flambé." But don't be put off by the names: the traditional dishes are excellent. $ *Average main: €13* ✉ *Osterstr. 28* ☎ *05151/3888* ⊕ *www.rattenfaengerhaus.de.*

GERMAN

$ 🏨 **Hotel zur Börse.** A few paces off Hameln's picturesque pedestrian shopping zone, this pleasant, modern hotel is also within easy walking distance of the rest of the town's main attractions. **Pros:** in the pedestrian zone. **Cons:** modern look seems out of place; bathrooms on the small side. $ *Rooms from: €93* ✉ *Osterstr. 41a, entrance on Kopmanshof* ☎ *05151/7080* ⊕ *www.hotel-zur-boerse.de* ⤴ *31 rooms, 2 apartments* ⦿| *Breakfast.*

HOTEL

$$ 🏨 **Hotel zur Krone.** On the Old Town's pedestrian zone, Hotel zur Krone has a terrace that lets you watch locals coming and going, and afternoon coffee here is a summer delight. **Pros:** a half-timber marvel; lovely terrace. **Cons:** modern annex lacks charm; some guest rooms a little small. $ *Rooms from: €102* ✉ *Osterstr. 30* ☎ *05151/9070* ⊕ *www.hotelzurkrone.de* ⤴ *32 rooms* ⦿| *Breakfast.*

HOTEL

HANNOVER

47 km (29 miles) northeast of Hameln.

A little off the Fairy-Tale Road, and better known internationally as a trade-fair center than a tourist destination, the Lower Saxon capital holds an attractive mix of culture, arts, and nature. With several leading museums, an opera house of international repute, and the finest baroque park in the country, it's a place that packs a surprising amount into a city of only half a million people. Conveniently centered between the city's main train station and its pleasant inner city lake, most of Hannover's major attractions, including its fine New and Old Town Halls, are within an easy walk of one another. In spring and summer the city's parks fill with picnicking families, while fall and winter are celebrated first with the second-biggest Oktoberfest in the world and then cheery Christmas markets.

GETTING HERE AND AROUND

Travel northeast from Hameln on autobahn A-33 to Hannover in under an hour. There is also frequent direct rail service from Hameln and InterCity Express (ICE) trains run to and from larger cities nearby. Hannover has an airport and is served by Eurolines buses.

DISCOUNTS AND DEALS

A **Hannover Card** entitles you to free travel on local transportation, reduced admission to seven museums, and discounts on certain sightseeing events and performances at the theater and opera. It's available through the tourist office for €9.50 per day (€18 for three days).

ESSENTIALS

VISITOR **Hannover Tourismus.** Directly across from the central station, the tourist
INFORMATION office can assist with package arrangements or sell a one- to three-day Hannover Card that will get you discounts and a free travel pass on public transportation. From mid-April through the end of October, hop-on, hop-off city bus tours of Hannover leave from here daily at 10:30, 12:30, and 2:30 (and 11:30, 1:30, 3:30, and 4:30 on Saturday). ⊠ *Hannover Tourismus, Ernst-August-Pl. 8* ☎ *0511/1684–9700* ⊕ *www.visit-hannover.com.*

EXPLORING

TOP ATTRACTIONS

Altes Rathaus (*Old Town Hall*). It took nearly 100 years, starting in 1410, to build this gabled brick edifice that once contained a merchants' hall and an apothecary. In 1844 it was restored to the style of about 1500, with its exceptional Gothic gables and the ornamental frieze. The facade's fired-clay frieze depicts coats of arms and representations of princes, and a medieval game similar to arm wrestling using only the fingers. This marvellous picture above the outer right arched window in the Schmiedestrasse can only be seen by following the "red line" around the Old Town Hall. Inside is a modern interior with boutiques and a restaurant. ⊠ *Karmarschstr. 42* 🎫 *Free.*

Fodor'sChoice **Herrenhausen Palace and Gardens.** The gardens of the former Hannoverian
★ royal summer residence are the city's showpiece, unmatched in Germany for its formal precision, with patterned walks, gardens, hedges, and chestnut trees framed by a placid moat. There is a fig garden with a collapsible shelter to protect it in winter and dining facilities behind a grotto. The mausoleum in the Berggarten houses the remains of local royalty, including those of King George I of Britain. From Easter until October there are fireworks displays and fountains play for a few hours daily (weekdays 10–noon and 3–5, weekends 10–noon and 2–5). The 17th-century palace on the grounds was completely destroyed in 1943, leaving only the fountains and stairs remaining. In 2013, a relatively faithful reconstruction replaced the castle, which now houses a museum dedicated to its history and is used frequently as an event location. Herrenhausen is outside the city, a short ride on Tramline 4 or 5. ⊠ *Herrenhauserstr. 5* 🎫 *0511/1684–4543* ⊕ *www.hannover.de/herrenhausen* 🎫 *Museum tour €5; Gardens Apr.–Oct. €8, Nov.–Mar. €6* ☉ *Museum: Apr.–Oct., daily 11–6; Nov.–Mar., Thurs.–Sun. 11–4; Gardens: daily 9–7.*

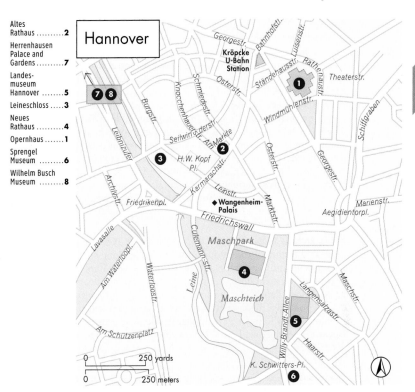

12

Landesmuseum Hannover. The priceless art collection of this regional museum includes works by Tilman Riemenschneider, Veit Stoss, Hans Holbein the Younger, Claude Monet, and Lucas Cranach. There are also historical and natural history sections. ✉ *Willy-Brandt-Allée 5* ☎ *0511/980–7686* ⊕ *www.landesmuseum-hannover.niedersachsen.de* 💳 *€4* ⊘ *Tues., Wed., and Fri.–Sun. 10–5, Thurs. 10–7.*

Leineschloss. The former royal palace of the Hanovers—whose members sat on the British throne from 1714 to 1837 as kings George I–IV—stands grandly beside the River Leine, and is now home to the Lower Saxony State Parliament. Although the interior of the palace is largely closed to the public, its imposing Corinthian columns and river setting provide some excellent photo ops. At this writing, it is under renovation through 2017 and hidden behind scaffolding. ✉ *Hinrich-Wilhelm-Kopf-Pl. 1.*

Sprengel Museum. An important museum of modern art, the Sprengel holds major works by Max Beckmann, Max Ernst, Paul Klee, Emil Nolde, Oscar Schlemmer, Hans Arp, and Pablo Picasso. A recent addition to the museum known as Ten Rooms, Three Loggias and a Hall, added space to feature contemporary artists reflecting on space, light, and perception. The street where it's located is named after Kurt Schwitters, a native son and prominent Dadaist, whose works are also exhibited. ⊠ *Kurt-Schwitters-Pl. 1* ☎ *0511/1684–3875* ⊕ *www. sprengel-museum.de* 🎫 *€7* ⊙ *Tues. 10–8, Wed.–Sun. 10–6.*

Fodor's Choice
★
Wilhelm Busch Museum. This section of the Georgenpalais, near Herrenhausen, is devoted to the works of cartoonists and caricaturists through the centuries. The emphasis is on Wilhelm Busch, the "godfather of the comic strip," whose original drawings and effects are on display. More than a century ago, Busch (1832–1908) wrote and illustrated a very popular children's book, still in print, called *Max und Moritz*. The story tells of two boys who mixed gunpowder into the village tailor's pipe tobacco and, with fishing lines down the chimney, filched roasting chickens off the fire. The first American comic strip, *The Katzenjammer Kids* (1897), drew not only on Busch's naughty boys (they even spoke with a German accent) but also on his loose cartoon style. ⊠ *Georgengarten 1* ☎ *0511/1699–9916* ⊕ *www.karikatur-museum.de* 🎫 *€6* ⊙ *Tues.–Sun. 11–6.*

WORTH NOTING

Neues Rathaus (*New Town Hall*). The massive New Town Hall was built at the start of the 20th century in Wilhelmine style (named for Kaiser Wilhelm). The pomp and circumstance were important ingredients of the German bureaucracy of the time. Four scale models on the ground floor depict Hannover in various stages of development and destruction: as a medieval walled city, in the years before World War II, immediately following World War II, and in its present-day form. An elevator rises diagonally to the dome for a splendid view. ⊠ *Trammpl. 2* ☎ *0511/1684–5333* 🎫 *Dome €3* ⊙ *Mar.–Oct., weekdays 9:30–6, weekends 10–6.*

Opernhaus (*Staatsoper Hannover*). Hannover's neoclassical opera house, completed in 1852, has two large wings and a covered, colonnaded portico adorned with statues of great composers and poets. The building originally served as the court theater, but now is used almost exclusively for opera. It was gutted by fire in a 1943 air raid and restored in 1948. Unless you have tickets to a performance, the only part of the interior you can visit is the foyer (official tours are held on a near-monthly basis). ⊠ *Opernpl. 1* ☎ *0511/9999–1111* ⊕ *www.staatstheater-hannover.de/oper.*

WHERE TO EAT

$$$
ECLECTIC
✕ **Basil.** Constructed in 1867 as a riding hall for the Royal Prussian military, this upmarket restaurant's home is as striking as the menu. Cast-iron pillars support the vaulted brick ceiling, and two-story drapes hang in the huge windows. The menu, which changes every few weeks, includes dishes from the Mediterranean to Asia. Game, fish, and white *Spargel* (asparagus) are served in season. 🅢 *Average main: €22* ⊠ *Dragonerstr. 30* ☎ *0511/622–636* ⊕ *www.basil.de* ⊙ *Closed Sun. No lunch.*

$
GERMAN
✕ **Brauhaus Ernst August.** This brewery has so much artificial greenery that you could imagine yourself in a beer garden. Hannoverian pilsner is brewed on the premises, and regional specialties are the menu's focus. Besides beer paraphernalia such as mugs and coasters, you can also buy, empty or full, a huge old-fashioned beer bottle with a wired porcelain stopper. There's also live music and DJs on Friday nights and

weekends. $ *Average main: €13* ✉ *Schmiedstr. 13* ☎ *0511/365–950* ⊕ *www.brauhaus.net.*

$$ ✕ **Broyhan Haus.** The claim of "Hannoverian hospitality over three
GERMAN floors" written on the exterior of this half-timber tavern in the middle of town isn't made frivolously. Convivial waitstaff ferry plates loaded with standard brew-house fare like rump steak (sirloin) and sauerkraut and pork, along with large glasses of the local, crisp-tasting Einbecker beer to diners in the tavern's upstairs room, and to tables outside on the pedestrian zone in summer. On the ground floor there's a well-stocked bar to pull up a seat at, and downstairs the cellar can be booked for private parties and events. $ *Average main: €16* ✉ *Kramerstr. 24* ☎ *0511/323–919* ⊕ *www.broyhanhaus.de* ▭ *No credit cards.*

WHERE TO STAY

$$ ☷ **Concorde Hotel am Leineschloss.** Near the elegant Altes Rathaus and the
HOTEL stately Leineschloss, and only a leisurely stroll from the Neues Rathaus, Opernhaus, and the city's main museums, this simple, modern hotel has easily one of the best locations in the city. **Pros:** in the middle of the shopping district; close to the U-bahn (U3, 7, and 9); every double room has a bath. **Cons:** no restaurant; not much character. $ *Rooms from: €136* ✉ *Am Markte 12* ☎ *0511/357–910* ⊕ *www.concordehotel-am-leineschloss.de* ⇗ *81 rooms (30 of which are singles)* ⦿❘*Breakfast.*

$$ ☷ **Kastens Hotel Luisenhof.** Antiques are everywhere in this elegant hotel,
HOTEL which is traditional both in appearance and service; tapestries adorn
Fodor'sChoice the lobby walls, oil paintings hang in the foyer, and copper engravings
★ enliven the bar. **Pros:** near the train station; helpful staff; elegant. **Cons:** expensive; on a narrow, ordinary street. $ *Rooms from: €169* ✉ *Luisenstr. 1–3* ☎ *0511/30440* ⊕ *www.kastens-luisenhof.de* ⇗ *131 rooms, 11 suites, 4 apartments* ⦿❘*No meals.*

NIGHTLIFE AND PERFORMING ARTS

Hannover's nightlife is centered on the Bahnhof and the Steintor red-light district.

Casino. Play in the town's elegant casino is divided over two floors, with roulette and blackjack on one, slots and other automated games on the other. Open daily from 10 am to 3 am, there's also a substantial bar and a business dress code to keep the atmosphere classy. ✉ *Leistermeile 2* ☎ *0511/980–6641* ⊕ *www.spielbanken-niedersachsen.de/index.php/casinos/hannover.*

FAMILY **Opera.** Hannover's opera company is internationally known, with productions staged in one of Germany's finest 19th-century classical opera houses. The rotating program includes a number of classics as well as special shows for children above the age of four. ✉ *Opernpl. 1* ☎ *0511/9999–1111* ⊕ *www.staatstheater-hannover.de/oper.*

BERGEN-BELSEN

58 km (36 miles) northeast of Hannover.

A visit to the site of the infamous prisoner of war and concentration camp where Anne Frank, along with tens of thousands of others, perished isn't an easy undertaking. All that remains are foundations and burial mounds, but the interpretive center helps to contextualize what you'll see.

GETTING HERE AND AROUND

Although it's possible to get here via public transport, it requires traveling first to the town of Celle by train, and then taking an hour-long bus journey. Buses run every two hours and require multiple changes. By car, take autobahn exits Mellendorf or Solltau Süd and follow the signposts to the memorial.

EXPLORING

Gedenkstätte Bergen-Belsen (*Bergen-Belsen Memorial*). The site of the infamous POW and concentration camp is now a memorial to the victims of World War II and the Holocaust. Anne Frank was among the more than 70,000 Jews, prisoners of war, homosexuals, Roma, and others who died here.

A place of immense suffering, the camp was burned to the ground by British soldiers, who liberated it in April 1945, arriving to find thousands of unburied corpses and typhus, typhoid, tuberculosis, and other diseases spreading rapidly among the survivors. Today, all that physically remains of the camp, which is inside a nature preserve, are the foundations of some of its prisoner barracks and a number of burial mounds overgrown with heather and grass and bearing stark inscriptions such as "Here lie 1,000 dead."

The history of the camp and its victims is explained further through a series of moving video, audio, photo, and text exhibits within the slender, minimalist structure of the 200-meter-long (656-foot-long), 18-meter-wide (59-foot-long) Documentation Center. Built almost entirely of plain concrete panels, the center is softly lit and peaceful inside, its floor sloping gently upward from the entrance and beyond the exhibits to windows that let in light and views of the trees outside.

Visitors to the Memorial should plan to stay at least two or three hours. Free 90-minute tours of the site in German and English leave the Documentation Center information desk at 2:30 on Thursday and Friday and at 11:30 and 2:30 on weekends, from March to September. Don't try to see everything when visiting the memorial, but do take some time to walk around outside, visiting the site of the barracks to gain a better understanding of the atrocious living conditions inmates of the camp were forced to suffer.

Bear in mind that the memorial is not recommended for children under the age of 14. Older children should be in the company of an adult. ⊠ *Anne-Frank-Pl., Lohheide* ☎ *05051/47590* ⊕ *www.bergenbelsen.de* 🖾 *Free* ☉ *Apr.–Sept., daily 10–6; Oct.–Mar., daily 10–5.*

BREMEN

110 km (68 miles) northwest of Hannover.

Germany's smallest city-state, Bremen, is also Germany's oldest and second-largest port (only Hamburg is larger). Together with Hamburg and Lübeck, Bremen was an early member of the merchant-run Hanseatic League, and its rivalry with the larger port on the Elbe River is still tangible. Though Hamburg may still claim its title as Germany's "gateway to the world," Bremen likes to boast, "But we have the key." Bremen's symbol is, in fact, a golden key, which you will see displayed on flags and signs throughout the city.

GETTING HERE AND AROUND
Bremen's international airport is a gate to many European destinations, and Intercity (IC) and Intercity Express (ICE) trains connect the city with much of the rest of Germany, including Hamburg and Hannover in just one hour.

ESSENTIALS
VISITOR
INFORMATION

Bremen Tourist Information. Bremen offers both bus and walking tours in English organized by the Tourist Information Center on Oberstrasse. The walking tours in German/English begin daily at 2 from there (€6.90); bus tours depart daily at 11 and 12:30 (€13.90) from the central bus station on Breiteweg. ⊠ *Obernstr. 1* ☎ *0421/308–0010* ⊕ *www. bremen-tourism.de.*

DISCOUNTS AND DEALS
Bremen has an **ErlebnisCARD,** which lets you ride free on the public transportation, gets you into museums and other cultural facilities at half price, and gets you a reduction on tours. It costs €8.90 for one day and €11.50 for two days. You can buy it at tourist-information centers.

EXPLORING
TOP ATTRACTIONS
Böttcherstrasse (*Barrel Makers' Street*). Don't leave Bremen's Altstadt without strolling down this street, at one time inhabited by coopers. Between 1924 and 1931 the houses were torn down and reconstructed, in a style at once historically sensitive and modern, by the Bremen coffee millionaire Ludwig Roselius. (He was the inventor of decaffeinated coffee, and held the patent for decades.) Many of the restored houses are used as galleries for local artists. ⊠ *Bremen.*

Marktplatz. Bremen's impressive market square sits in the charming Altstadt. It's bordered by the St. Petri Dom, an imposing 900-year-old Gothic cathedral; an ancient Rathaus; a 16th-century guildhall; and a modern glass-and-steel state parliament building, with gabled town houses finishing the panorama. Alongside the northwest corner of the Rathaus is the famous bronze statue of the four **Bremen Town Musicians,** one atop the other in a sort of pyramid. Their feats are reenacted in a free, open-air play at the Neptune Fountain near the cathedral, at noon each Sunday, from May to September. Another well-known figure on the square is the stone statue of **Roland,** a knight in service to Charlemagne, erected in 1404. Three times larger than life, the statue serves as Bremen's good-luck piece and a symbol of freedom and independence. It is said that as long as Roland stands, Bremen will remain a free and independent state. ⊠ *Bremen.*

Fodor'sChoice ★

Schnoorviertel. Stroll through the narrow streets of this idyllic district, a jumble of houses, taverns, and shops. This is Bremen's oldest district, dating back to the 15th and 16th centuries. The neighborhood is fashionable among artists and craftspeople, who have restored the tiny cottages to serve as galleries and workshops. Other buildings have been

converted into popular antiques shops, cafés, and pubs. The area's definitely a great source for souvenirs, with incredibly specialized stores selling porcelain dolls, teddy bears, African jewelry, and smoking pipes, among many other things. There's even an all-year-round Christmas store. ⊠ *Bremen*.

WORTH NOTING

Museen Böttcherstraße. Two separate museums are housed in this 17th-century building that stands at one end of Böttcherstrasse. **Ludwig Roselius-Haus** showcases late-medieval art and a silver treasury, and a unique collection of German and Dutch art. These pieces contrast with the paintings of **Paula Modersohn-Becker**, a noted early expressionist of the Worpswede art colony whose work is housed

> ### BREMEN TOWN MUSICIANS
>
> In this folktale adapted by the Brothers Grimm, a donkey, dog, cat, and rooster ran away because they had become old and their masters were going to dispose of them. In order to support themselves they headed toward Bremen. After some adventures, they came upon a cottage occupied by robbers. The menagerie managed to scare the miscreants away by standing on each other's backs and singing. The robbers fled, and the animals lived in their new house happily ever after. Their statues are found throughout the city.

in the same building. Notice also the arch of Meissen bells at the rooftop. Except when freezing weather makes them dangerously brittle, the bells chime daily on the hour from noon to 6 from May to December (and only at noon, 3, and 6 January–April). ⊠ *Böttcherstr. 6–10* ☎ *0421/336–5077* ⊕ *www.pmbm.de* ✑ *€6* ⊙ *Tues.–Sun. 11–6.*

Rathaus. A 15th-century statue of Charlemagne, together with seven princes, adorns the Gothic town hall, the only European town hall built in the late Middle Ages that has not been destroyed or altered, managing to survive in its original form over the centuries. It was Charlemagne who established a diocese here in the 9th century. The Rathaus acquired a Weser Renaissance facade during the early 17th century. Tours, given when no official functions are taking place, are in German and English and take you into the upper hall as well as the Golden Chamber, a magnificent plenary hall. Inside, the model ships that hang from the ceiling bear witness to the importance of commerce and maritime trade for the city. Their miniature cannons can even be fired if the occasion demands. ⊠ *Am Markt 21* ✑ *Tour €5* ⊙ *Tours Mon.–Sat. at 11, noon, 3, and 4, Sun. at 11 and noon.*

St. Petri Dom (*St. Peter's Cathedral*). Construction of the cathedral began in the mid-11th century. Its two prominent towers, one of which can be climbed, are Gothic, but in the late 1800s the cathedral was restored in the Romanesque style. It served as the seat of an archbishop until the Reformation turned the cathedral Protestant. It has a small museum and five functioning organs. ⊠ *Sandstr. 10–12* ☎ *0421/365–0447* ✑ *Free; Tower €1* ⊙ *Weekdays 10–5, Sat. 10–2, Sun. 2–5; Tower: Apr.–Oct., weekdays 10–4:30, Sat. 10–1:30, Sun. 2–4:30.*

WHERE TO EAT AND STAY

$$$$
FRENCH
Fodor's Choice
★

✕ **Grashoffs Bistro.** An enthusiastic crowd, willing to put up with cramped conditions, descends at lunchtime on this restaurant and deli. The room is so small that there's little room between the square tables; a table has to be pulled out for anyone who has a seat next to the wall. The menu has a French touch, with an emphasis on fresh fish from the Bremerhaven market. The deli has a whole wall of teas, another of cheeses, and a huge assortment of wines. $ *Average main: €27* ✉ *Contrescarpe 80* ☎ *0421/178–8952* ⊕ *www.grashoff.de* ⊙ *Closed Sun. and Mon. No dinner Sat.* ⟡ *Reservations essential.*

$$
GERMAN

✕ **Ratskeller.** This cavernous cellar with vaulted ceilings is said to be Germany's oldest and most renowned town-hall restaurant—it's been here for 600 years. Its walls are lined with wine casks, and there are small alcoves with sliding wooden doors, once shut tight by merchants as they closed their deals. The food's solid traditional northern German fare and the menu is limited outside of the standard meal times. By long tradition only German wines are served here, and the only beer you can get is Beck's and Franziskaner from the barrel. $ *Average main: €15* ✉ *Am Markt 1* ☎ *0421/321–676* ⊕ *www.ratskeller-bremen.de.*

$$$$
HOTEL
Fodor's Choice
★

🛏 **Dorint Park Hotel Bremen.** This palatial hotel comes with an enviable location between a small lake and an extensive area of park and forest not far from the main train station. **Pros:** traditional luxury; on a lake. **Cons:** expensive; outside the city. $ *Rooms from: €239* ✉ *Im Bürgerpark* ☎ *0421/340–800* ⊕ *www.parkhotel-bremen.de* ⇆ *160 rooms, 15 suites* ⦿ *No meals.*

$
HOTEL

🛏 **Hotel Pension Weidmann.** There are only five rooms in this small and friendly family-run pension in one of the brick buildings so characteristic of Bremen. **Pros:** English-speaking staff; welcomes dogs (even large ones). **Cons:** no restaurant; shared bathroom; minimal decor. $ *Rooms from: €50* ✉ *Am Schwarzen Meer 35* ☎ *0421/498–4455* ⊕ *www.pension-weidmann.de* ▭ *No credit cards* ⇆ *5 rooms* ⦿ *No meals.*

NIGHTLIFE

Bremen may be Germany's oldest seaport, but it can't match Hamburg for racy nightlife. Nevertheless, the streets around the central Marktplatz and in the historic Schnoor District are filled with all sorts of taverns and cafés. The Bremen coffee tradition will be evident when you have your coffee and cake at a café in a charming old building with plush sofas, huge mirrors, and chandeliers.

Bremen casino. Try your luck at American roulette, poker, slot machines, and blackjack at the Bremen casino, open for play daily 3 pm–3 am; slots open at noon. Dress code includes closed shoes (no sandals or sneakers) and a collared shirt for men. ✉ *An der Schlachte 26* ☎ *0421/329–000.*

BREMERHAVEN

66 km (41 miles) north of Bremen.

This busy port city, where the Weser empties into the North Sea, is technically part of Bremen, which is an hour to the south. You can take in the enormity of the port from a promenade that runs its length. In addition to being a major port for merchant ships, it is the biggest fishery pier in Europe, and its promenade is lined with excellent sea-food restaurants.

GETTING HERE AND AROUND
Regional trains run every hour from Bremen to this North Sea port, and take 35 minutes to get here. Reederei HaRuFa offers a one-hour trip around the Bremerhaven harbor for €10. If you'd like to go farther afield and view Schnoorviertel and the stark, red-cliff island of Helgoland from the sky, OFD has a daily round-trip flight for €187 per person.

ESSENTIALS
Visitor Information Bremerhaven Tourism. ⊠ *H.-H.-Meierstr. 6* ☎ *0471/8093–6100* ⊕ *www.bremerhaven-touristik.de.* **OFD Airlines.** ⊠ *Flughafen, Am Luneort 15* ☎ *0471/77188* ⊕ *www.fliegofd.de.* **Reederei HaRuFa.** ⊠ *H.-H.-Meierstr. 4* ☎ *0471/415–850* ⊕ *www.hafenrundfahrt-bremerhaven.de.*

EXPLORING
FodorśChoice ★ **Deutsches Auswandererhaus** (*German Emigration Center*). Located at the point where 7 million Europeans set sail for the New World, the Deutsches Auswandererhaus is made to order for history buffs and those wanting to trace their German ancestry. "Passengers" get boarding passes; wait on dimly lit docks with costumed mannequins and piles of luggage; and once on board navigate their way through cramped and creaky sleeping and dining cabins. After being processed at Ellis Island, visitors can then research their genealogy using the museum's emigration database and its extensive collection of passenger lists. Further on, there is a section of the museum dedicated to immigrants to Germany, complete with an impressive 1970s-era shopping mall, and a retro movie theater screens short films about German emigrants and their families. ⊠ *Columbusstr. 65* ☎ *0471/902–200* ⊕ *www.dah-bremerhaven.de* 💶 *€12.80* ⏱ *Mar.–Oct., daily 10–6; Nov.–Feb., daily 10–5.*

Deutsches Schifffahrtsmuseum (*German Maritime Museum*). The country's largest and most fascinating maritime museum, the Deutsches Schifffahrtsmuseum, includes a harbor, open from April through October, that shelters seven old trading ships. ⊠ *Hans-Scharoun-Pl. 1, from Bremen take A–27 to exit for Bremerhaven-Mitte* ☎ *0471/482–070* ⊕ *www.dsm.museum* 💶 *€6* ⏱ *Nov.–Mar., Tues.–Sun. 10–6; Apr.–Oct., daily 10–6.*

Klimahaus Bremerhaven 8° Ost. This unique interactive museum takes visitors through nine stations covering the various climatic regions of the Earth. The history of the climate, ranging from the origins of the Earth 3.9 thousand million years ago and looking forward to the year 2050 is on display in this museum dedicated to helping visitors understand what factors determine the weather and the climate. Located directly on the seafront, it also has information about an offshore wind farm that will put the city's relationship to the sea and the changing climate into perspective. ⊠ *Hermann-Henrich-Meier-Str.* ☎ *0471/902–0300* ⊕ *www.klimahaus-bremerhaven.de* 💶 *€15* ⏱ *Apr.–Aug., weekdays 9–7, weekends 10–7; Sept.–Mar., daily 10–6.*

WHERE TO STAY

$$ ⊞ **Atlantic Hotel SailCity.** Designed in the shape of a sail catching the
HOTEL   wind, this glass skyscraper located directly on the harbor and within
walking distance to all the major sights is popular with travelers hoping
to catch a glimpse of the Atlantic—which they can from most rooms.
Pros: friendly staff; great location with sea views. **Cons:** can fill up
with business and convention travelers. $ *Rooms from: €134* ⊠ *Am
Strom 1* ☎ *0471/309–900* ⊕ *www.atlantic-hotels.de/sailcity/de/Start.
html* ⇆ *120 rooms* ⦿| *Breakfast.*

$$ ⊞ **Hotel Haverkamp.** Not far from Bremerhaven's harbor and world-class
HOTEL   museums, this modern hotel may not look like much from the outside,
but its enviable reputation is built on excellent service, a fine restaurant,
and quiet, tidy guest rooms with modern furnishings. **Pros:** convenient
location; quiet area; good restaurant. **Cons:** plain exterior; pool is very
small; no views. $ *Rooms from: €129* ⊠ *Pragerstr. 34* ☎ *0471/48330*
⊕ *www.hotel-haverkamp.de* ⇆ *85 rooms* ⦿| *Breakfast.*

HAMBURG

WELCOME TO HAMBURG

TOP REASONS TO GO

★ **Alster cruises:** Marvel at the luxurious villas gracing the shores of the Alster lakes and its canals while relaxing with a *Glühwein* (mulled wine) or cool beer and listening to tidbits of trivia about the city.

★ **Hamburger Kunsthalle and the Deichtorhallen:** Spend an afternoon admiring the fantastic art collections at two of Germany's leading galleries of modern art.

★ **Historic harbor district:** Travel back in time and walk the quaint cobblestone alleys around Deichstrasse and the Speicherstadt.

★ **Retail therapy:** Indulge your inner shopper as you weave your way through the streets behind the elegant Jungfernstieg, amble up and down Mönckebergstrasse, stroll through Altona and the Schanzenviertel, and end the afternoon at one of the quarters' funky cafés.

★ **Sin City:** Adventure along the Reeperbahn, browse its quirky sex shops, and dive into the nightlife of Europe's biggest party district.

1 Altstadt and Neustadt. Together, the "Old Town" and "New Town" make up the *Innenstadt*, or inner city. Humming with locals and tourists on Saturday afternoons and public holidays, the center of town is the place to come for shopping, culture, and snaps in front of the Inner Alster lake and town hall.

2 St.Pauli and Schanzenviertel. An entertainment district since the 17th century, St. Pauli continues to draw fun seekers and night owls to its massive red-light and party district. Just down the road, the Schanzenviertel is filled with little shops and chilled-out cafés.

3 St. Georg. The center of Hamburg's gay and lesbian scene and also home to a large

S DAMMTOR

Aussenalster

Alster Lakes

U STEPHANS-PLATZ

Esplanade

Alsterglacis
Warburgstr.
Alsterufer

Kennedybrücke

An der Alster

Lombardsbrücke

Colonnaden

Neuer Jungfernstieg

Binnenalster

ST. GEORG

Holzdamm

U 3

Grosse Bleichen

Jungfernstieg

U JUNGFERN-STIEG **S**

Ballindamm

Ferdinandstr.

Brandsende

Hamburger
Kunsthalle

Glockengiesser wall

Ernst-Merck-Str.

Kirchen Allee

U HBF.-NORD

i

NEUSTADT

Adolfstr.
Alter Wall

Hermannstr.

Raboisen

Gerh.
Hauptm
Pl.

Kurze
Mühren

Lange
Mühren

Steintor-wall

U MÖNKEBERGSTR.

Mönckebergstr.

Johannis-Wall

Steinlor-wall

Kurt-Schumacher-Allee

Klosterwall

1

RATHAUS **U**

Gr.
Johannisstr.

Pelzerstr.

Schmiedtstr.

Speer sort

Burchardstr.

Steinstr.

Burchard-pl.

STEINSTR **U**

Mönkedamm
Gr.
Burstah

ALTSTADT

Domstrasse

Kl. Reichenstr.

Deichtor
Pl.

Willy-Brandt-Strasse

MESSBERG **U**

Dovenfleet

Alter Wandrahm

Oberbaumbrücke

Deichtorstr.

Burstah

B.D.
Mühren

Zippelhaus

Neuer Wandrahm

Zollkanal

SPEICHERSTADT

4

HAFENCITY

KEY

S   S-Bahn

i   Tourist information

U   U-Bahn

GETTING ORIENTED

13

The second-largest city in Germany after Berlin, Hamburg sits on northern Germany's fertile lowlands, within easy reach of the North and Baltic seas. A city-state of 1.8 million inhabitants, Hamburg covers an area of 755 square km (291 square miles), making it one of the least densely populated cities to have more than a million inhabitants. Taking up much of that space are its many parks and trees; it's also centered on two major bodies of water. The Elbe River is the site of the city's busy port, and it's near some of its most colorful quarters. The inner and outer Alster lakes, meanwhile, are encircled by Hamburg's downtown, and a cluster of upscale neighborhoods. It's here, somewhere between the commerce of the river and the tranquility of the lakes, that visitors to the city tend to spend most of their time.

Turkish community, St. Georg is an intriguing mix of affluence, relaxed attitudes, and cultures. It's also full of many nice little shops and cafés.

4 Speicherstadt and HafenCity. The old and the new are both part of Hamburg's inner city port, with formidable 19th-century redbrick warehouses at the UNESCO-listed Speicherstadt

and state-of-the-art riverside apartment and office complexes at HafenCity.

5 Altona and Ottensen. These former working-class areas are now particularly desirable places to live and visit. Many of the old buildings and factories have been refurbished to accommodate fancy restaurants, art-house movie theaters, and design hotels.

6 Blankenese and Beyond. Many of Hamburg's outlying suburbs have their own distinct atmosphere and feel—none more so than the elegant riverside neighborhood of Blankenese, which some locals compare to the French and Italian rivieras.

COFFEE AND CAKE

When the afternoon rolls around, it's time for *Kaffee und Kuchen,* one of Germany's most beloved traditions. In villages and cities alike, patrons still stroll into their favorite *Konditorei* (pastry shop) for a leisurely cup of coffee and slice of cake.

(above) Cake is serious business in Germany, and you'll have your pick of many at any Konditorei worth its salt. (upper right) Mohnkuchen. (lower right) Gugelhupf.

The tradition stretches back hundreds of years, when coffee beans were first imported to Germany in the 17th century. Coffee quickly became the preferred hot drink of the aristocracy, who paired it with cake, their other favorite indulgence. In time, the afternoon practice trickled down to the bourgeoisie, and was heartily embraced. Now everyone can partake in the tradition.

There are hundreds of German cakes, many of which are regional and seasonal with an emphasis on fresh fruits in summer, and spiced cakes in winter. Due to modern work schedules, not as many Germans take a daily coffee and cake break anymore. Families will have theirs at home on the weekend, and it's often an occasion for a starched tablecloth, the best china, and candles.

—Tania Ralli

VISITING THE KONDITOREI

Seek out the most old-fashioned shops, as these tend to have the best cakes. Check out what's in the glass case, since most Konditorein don't have printed menus. Don't worry about a language barrier—when it comes time to order, just point to the cake of your choice.

BEST CAKES TO TRY

FRANKFURTER KRANZ

The *Frankfurter Kranz,* or Frankfurt wreath, is a butter cake flavored with lemon zest and a touch of rum. It's then split into three layers and spread with fillings of buttercream and red preserves. The cake's exterior is generously coated with crunchy cookie crumbs or toasted nuts, and each slice is graced with a swirl of buttercream frosting and a bright red cherry.

GUGELHUPF

Of all cakes, the *Gugelhupf* has the most distinctive shape, one that you'll likely recognize as a bundt cake. It tends to be more popular in southern Germany. Gugelhupf had its start as a bready yeast cake, studded with raisins and citrus peel, but today you're just as likely to have it as a marble cake. During the Biedermeier period, in the early 19th century, the wealthy middle class regarded the Gugelhupf as a status symbol.

HERRENTORTE

A layer cake of dark chocolate, *Herrentorte* means "gentleman's cake." It's not as sweet or creamy as most layer cakes, and thus meant to appeal to a man's palate. A *Torte* refers to a fancier layered cake, as opposed to the more humble *Kuchen,* which is more rustic. The Herrentorte has a rich and refined taste—in Germany, all chocolate is required to

13

have a high cocoa content, improving its overall taste and texture.

MOHNKUCHEN

Mohnkuchen is a poppy seed cake—in fact, this is a cake so completely brimming with poppy seeds you could mistake it for a piece of chocolate cake. You'll come across it as a tall wedge, sprinkled with powdered sugar, or a fat square glazed with a lick of icing. The poppy seeds are mixed with sugar, butter, and sometimes milk. Lightly crushed they make for a very moist filling.

STREUSELKUCHEN

This cake became especially popular in the 19th century, in Prussia. Owing to its versatility, you'll find it today all over Germany. The simple, buttery yeast cake's selling point is its sugary, crunchy topping of pebbled *Streusel,* which can stand on its own or be combined with rhubarb, apricots, cherries, apples, or other fruit. *Streuselkuchen* is baked on large sheet pans and cut into generous squares

Updated by
Jeff Kavanagh

Frequently described as "the gateway to the world" by its proud citizens, the handsome port city of Hamburg has for centuries welcomed merchants, traders, and sailors to a rich assortment of grand hotels, fine restaurants, and, yes, seedy bars and brothels.

This vibrant, affluent city's success began with its role as a founding member of the Hanseatic League, a medieval alliance of northern European cities that once dominated the shipping trade in the North and Baltic Seas. To this day, the city is known as "the Free and Hanseatic City of Hamburg," reflecting both its association with the league and its status as an independent city-state.

Shipping continues to be a major industry. Straddling the mighty Elbe River, more than 100 km (62 miles) inland from the North Sea, Hamburg's inner city harbor is the third-biggest port in Europe. The city is now also one of Germany's major media hubs, serving as headquarters for the publishing giants Axel Springer, Grüner + Jahr, and Bau Verlag; and for such influential publications as *Die Zeit, Der Spiegel,* and *Stern.*

The profits of these endeavors are apparent throughout Hamburg, from its imposing neo-Renaissance town hall, to the multitude of luxury boutiques studding the adjacent Neuerwall, to the Elbchaussee, a long, leafy stretch of road lined with Hollywood-like mansions and overlooking the Elbe. Hamburg has more millionaires per capita than any other German city.

Like many other of the country's urban centers, however, the city has suffered a tumultuous history. Since its founding as "Hammaburg" in 811, Hamburg has been destroyed by Vikings, burned down by Poles, and occupied by Danish and French armies. The Great Fire of 1842 devastated much of its commercial center, and in 1943 the Allied Forces' Operation Gomorrah bombing raids and the resulting firestorms left 40,000 people dead and large swaths of Hamburg in ruins.

Scars from World War II still remain, and you need only walk down a residential street to see the plain, functional apartment buildings that were built to replace those destroyed by bombs. There are also frequent reminders of the terrible fate suffered by Hamburg's Jews, and others considered enemies of the state during this time. Memorials in Hafen-City and near Dammtor train station mark where those persecuted by Nazis were deported to concentration camps. As part of a Germany-wide project, small brass plaques set into sidewalks outside apartment buildings commemorate former residents executed by the regime.

Modern-day Hamburg is a progressive city endowed with attractive architecture, cultural diversity, and liberal attitudes. It's notable for its parks and trees and a pair of beautiful inner city lakes, but it's famous for its enormous red-light party district, which fans off from the seamy, neon-lit Reeperbahn. Shabby but chic quarters such as St. Pauli and the Schanzenviertel are as beloved by locals as the affluent Blankenese and Eppendorf, and the city's annual schedule of spring and summer festivals has enough room for a huge gay-pride parade in the middle of town, as well as a celebration of *Hafengeburtstag*—the harbor's birthday.

As you'd expect in such a wealthy city, Hamburg has more than its share of world-class museums and art galleries, as well as an assortment of grand theaters and music venues, an opera company, and an internationally renowned ballet company. Not content to rest on its laurels, the city is also steaming ahead with the ambitious HafenCity, an urban-renewal project that has transformed a significant section of the city's port front. The Elbphilharmonie—a futuristic concert hall that the city hopes will become as iconic as the Sydney Opera House—is to be its centerpiece.

PLANNING

WHEN TO GO

Known for its long, gray winters, Hamburg is frequently treated to a pleasant spring come late March or early April. Once the weather warms, the city's mood visibly improves. One of the highlights of the season is Hafengeburtstag, in early May, when the Elbe comes alive with a long parade of ships and riverside festivities.

Summer may be the best time of the year to visit. Temperatures rarely exceed the mid-80s, and the days are long, with the sun rising at around 5 am and light still in the sky till after 10 pm. Tables outside cafés and bars fill up with alfresco diners and drinkers; plumes of smoke rise from grills in parks and beaches along the Elbe. From mid-June to August, the *Schlemmersommer* (Gourmet Summer) comes to tempt food lovers. During this time, more than 100 restaurants throughout the city, including a number of award winners, offer multicourse dinners for two for €64.

September and October are usually good months to visit, despite the fact that October can often be quite cold and wet. September's Reeperbahn Festival is great for music fans hoping to see the next big thing, and Hamburg's small but popular film festival (held the same month) usually attracts one or two of the leading lights of European and world cinema.

The mercury drops quickly once the clocks go back an hour at the end of October. Happily, Christmas markets selling Glühwein begin to spring up on street corners and in public squares around the last week of November, and many continue on to *Silvester* (New Year's Eve). December, despite temperatures frequently dropping below zero, is a fun time to visit the city. January and February, however, are quiet and fairly uneventful.

FESTIVALS

Historischer Weihnachtsmarkt. Hamburg's Historischer Weihnachtsmarkt enjoys a spectacular backdrop—the city's Gothic town hall. The market's stalls are filled with rows of candy apples, chocolates, and doughnuts. Woodcarvers from Tyrol, bakers from Aachen, and gingerbread makers from Nürnberg (Nuremberg) come to sell their wares. And in an appearance arranged by the circus company Roncalli, Santa Claus ho-ho-hos his way along a tightwire high above the market every evening at 4, 6, and 8. ⊠ *Rathausmarkt 1, Altstadt* ⊕ *www.hamburger-weihnachtsmarkt.com* ⊘ *Nov. 23–Dec. 23, Sun.–Thurs. 11–9, Fri. and Sat. 11–10* Ⓜ *Rathaus (U-bahn).*

GETTING HERE AND AROUND

AIR TRAVEL

Hamburg Airport is 8 km (5 miles) northwest of the city. S-bahn line No. 1 runs about every 10 minutes from the airport to Hamburg's main station (*Hauptbahnhof*) on its way to Altona. The trip takes 25 minutes, and tickets are €3.10. A taxi to the center of the city (Alstadt and Neustadt) will cost about €25. If you're driving a rental car from the airport, follow the signs to "Zentrum" (Center). ∎TIP➔ There is an Edeka supermarket on the arrivals level between Terminal 1 and 2. It's a bit smaller than a full-size German supermarket and the prices are a bit higher than they would be in town. However, it is a great place to pick up some snacks or drinks for your hotel room or some food for an extended journey.

Airport Information Hamburg Airport. ⊠ *Flughafenstr. 1–3* ☎ *040/50750* ⊕ *www.hamburg-airport.de.*

BUS AND SUBWAY TRAVEL

The HVV, Hamburg's public transportation system, includes the U-bahn (subway), the S-bahn (commuter train), ferries, buses, and express buses (which cost an additional €1.90). Distance determines fares; a single trip costs €3.10 for longer journeys (such as the airport into Hamburg's main station); €2.10 for shorter distances (for instance, from St. Pauli or Altona into the center of town); and €1.50 if you're only traveling a couple of stops. If you're planning to make multiple trips about the city, then you may want to get the Tageskarte, or day pass, which for an adult and three children under 15 costs €7.50 when purchased before 9 am and €6 after that. An €11.20 Gruppenkarte is the best option for those traveling in a group. A group of five adults can use this card after 9 am on weekdays and all day on weekends.

Tickets and passes are available on all buses and from vending machines in every U- or S-bahn station. HVV is partially based on the honor system. You only need to show a ticket to the bus driver after 9 pm and all day on Sunday, but not on trains or ferries unless asked by a ticket inspector during random checks. Those caught without a ticket are fined €60 on the spot. Subway and commuter trains run throughout the night on weekends, but stop running around 12:30 am during the week. After that, night buses (Nos. 600–688) take over.

Information is available in English on the HVV website. The trip planner function gives the times, prices, walking directions, and maps for each journey. If you don't know the address of a site, you can simply type in the name of the popular destination, such as "Hamburg airport." Prepared commuters can buy tickets and passes from the website and print them out, or use HVV's smart-phone app

Don't be afraid to take the bus. Buses have dedicated traffic lanes, and most of their stops aren't too close together, so travel tends to be fast. It's a good way to see more of this beautiful city.

Hamburg's intercity bus station, the Zentral-Omnibus-Bahnhof (ZOB), is located diagonally across from the south exit of the main train station.

Contacts HVV (*Hamburg Transportation Association*). ⊠ *Johanniswall 2, Altstadt* ☎ *040/19449* ⊕ *www.hvv.de/en* Ⓜ *Steinstrasse (U-bahn).* **Zentral-Omnibus-Bahnhof** (*ZOB*). ⊠ *Adenauerallee 78, St. Georg* ☎ *040/247–576* ⊕ *www. zob-hamburg.de.*

CAR TRAVEL

With its popular public transportation system, Hamburg is easier to negotiate by car than many other German cities, and traffic here is relatively free-flowing outside of rush hours. Several autobahns (A-1, A-7, A-23, A-24, and A-250) connect with Hamburg's three beltways, which then lead to the downtown area. Follow the "Zentrum" (Center) signs.

TAXI TRAVEL

Taxi meters start at €3.20, then add €2.35 per km for the first 4 km (2½ miles); €2.10 per km for the next 5 km (3 miles); and €1.45 per km after that. You can hail taxis on the street, outside subway and train stations, and at popular locations (like along Mönckebergstrasse). You can also order one by phone or online.

Taxi Information Hansa-Taxi. ⊠ *Hamburg* ☎ *040/211–211* ⊕ *www.taxi211211.de.*

TRAIN TRAVEL

Hamburg Hauptbahnhof (Hamburg Main Station) is the city's central hub for local, regional, long-distance, and international trains. InterCity Express (ICE) trains going to and from Basel, Stuttgart, and Munich all start and terminate in Hamburg-Altona, and pass through Hauptbahnhof and Dammtor stations on the way.

Train Information Deutsche Bahn. ⊠ *Hamburg* ☎ *0180/699–6633* ⊕ *www.bahn.de.*

VISITOR INFORMATION

Hamburg Tourismus (Hamburg Tourism Office) has several outlets around the city. The main office is in the Hauptbahnhof and is open Monday to Saturday 9–7, Sunday 10–6. The airport branch is open from 6:30 am to 11 pm daily and sits on the departure level between Terminals 1 and 2. At the harbor there's an office at the St. Pauli Landungsbrücken, between Piers 4 and 5, open 9–6 Sunday to Wednesday, and 9–7 Thursday to Saturday. All tourist offices can help with accommodations, and there's a central call-in booking office for hotel and ticket reservations and general information, the Hamburg-Hotline.

Visitor Information Hamburg Tourismus Main Office. ⊠ *Hamburg Hauptbahnhof, Hachmannpl. 16, Altstadt* ☎ *040/3005–1701 hotline* ⊕ *www.hamburg-travel.com* Ⓜ *Hauptbahnhof (U-Bahn and S-Bahn).*

TOURS
BOAT TOURS

There are few better ways to get to know the city than by taking a trip on its waters. Alster Touristik, Rainer Abicht, Kapitän Prüsse, and Maritime Circle Line offer a wide variety of tour options, or you can simply take the HADAG ferry for great harbor views.

■ TIP→ **An HVV public transport day pass is valid for trips on the No. 62 HADAG ferry between Landungsbrücken Pier 1 and Finkenwerder, a suburb on the south side of the Elbe river. There's no commentary on the ferry, but on a fine day the top deck's a great spot to watch ships sailing in and out of the harbor, and for superb views of the city from the river.**

Alster Touristik. This company operates a variety of picturesque boat trips around the Alster lakes and through the canals, leaving from a small dock at the Jungfernstieg. The one-hour round-trip Alster cruise leaves every half hour, daily 10–6 April–early October and at 10 and 5, plus every half hour 11–4 until the end of October. The Winter Warmer Trip, November through March, offers hot chocolate and Glühwein (for an additional charge) several times a day. You can also get a two-hour twilight tour through the canals from Jungfernstieg to the bucolic Harvestehude neighborhood May through August, and also into the waters around the historic warehouse district in September. The tour starts at 8 pm. A two-hour Speicherstadt canal tour runs April–October daily at 10:45, 1:45, and 4:45. Audio guides in English are available for all tours. ☎ *040/357–4240* ⊕ *www.alstertouristik.de* ✉ *€15 for Alster cruise; €21 for twilight and Speicherstadt canal tours* Ⓜ *Jungfernstieg (U-bahn and S-bahn).*

HADAG. Harbor ferries offer an inexpensive way to get out on the water. Either take one of the scheduled ferries, or opt for the harbor tour or one of the hop-on, hop-off cruises. ☎ *040/311–7070* ⊕ *www.hadag. de* ✉ *From €1.50.*

Kapitän Prüsse. Every day of the year, Kapitän Prüsse offers cruises around the Elbe harbor that last 60–90 minutes. These include a night cruise that leaves between 6 and 9 pm (depending on the time of year) from Pier 3. ☎ *040/313–130* ⊕ *www.kapitaen-pruesse.de* ✉ *From €18* Ⓜ *Hamburg Landungsbrücken (S-bahn).*

Maritime Circle Line. The Maritime Circle Line tours major attractions on the Elbe. Passengers embark at St Pauli Landungsbrücken Pier 10 and can hop on and hop off at a number of stops including BallinStadt, Hamburg Harbor Museum, HafenCity, and the historic ship MV *Cap San Diego*. The tours run every two hours daily from 11 to 3, April through October, and every two hours from 11 to 3 on weekends, November to March. Tickets, which can be bought at the pier or online,

Hamburg's Speicherstadt, its historic warehouse district, was awarded a UNESCO World Heritage Site. It's best seen from a cruise.

include discounts at all the venues. ✉ *Landungsbrücke 10, St. Pauli* ☎ *040/2849–3963* ⊕ *www.maritime-circle-line.de* ✉ *€16* Ⓜ *Hamburg Landungsbrücken (S-bahn).*

Rainer Abicht. One-hour tours of the harbor with commentary in English are offered aboard one of Rainer Abicht's small fleet of boats, which include its famous *Louisiana Star* riverboat. The tours leave every day at midday from April until October from Landungsbrücken Pier 4. ☎ *040/317–8220* ⊕ *www.abicht.de* ✉ *€18* Ⓜ *Hamburg Landungsbrücken (S-bahn).*

ORIENTATION TOURS

Hamburger Stadtrundfahrt. Sightseeing bus tours of the city, all with guides, who rapidly narrate in both English and German, leave from Kirchenallee by the main train station. A 90-minute bus tour sets off at varying times daily and one of the bus tours can be combined with a one-hour boat trip on the harbor. Departure times for tours vary according to season. There's also a hop-on, hop-off service that runs daily, every 20 or 30 minutes, from 9:30 to 5, April through October; hourly Monday to Thursday 10–4, every half hour Friday to Sunday, 9:30–4, November through March. ☎ *040/792–8979* ⊕ *www.die-roten-doppeldecker.de* ✉ *€17.50; €30 for combined bus and boat trip; €30 day pass for hop-on, hop-off service* Ⓜ *Hauptbahnhof Sud (U-bahn).*

WALKING TOURS

A great way to learn more about the city while also getting some exercise is on a walking tour. There are plenty of tours to choose from, although many only run from April through November. In addition to guided walks of the Altstadt and Neustadt, the harbor district,

HafenCity, and St. Pauli, there are also themed excursions, such as Beatles tours and a red-light walking tour of the Reeperbahn. To find a guided walk in English, contact Hamburg Tourismus, the tourist office (⊕ *www.hamburg-travel.com*).

PLANNING YOUR TIME

Hamburg's almost custom-made for a long-weekend visit. Its airport is less than half an hour by train or taxi from the city center; it has an efficient and extensive public transportation system; taxis are reasonably priced and plentiful; and the city's flat terrain is perfectly suited to walking and cycling. Exploring the Altstadt and Neustadt areas, where Hamburg's Rathaus (Town Hall), the Alster lakes, the Kunsthalle and Deichtorhallen galleries, and a number of the city's churches are all within a short stroll of one another, can easily fill a day and night—particularly if you throw in some shopping, and then dinner in nearby St. Georg. Another day can be spent wandering the harbor, taking a cruise, and perhaps bicycling around the Speicherstadt and HafenCity, followed by a night out in St. Pauli or the Schanzenviertel. A less vigorous day's activities might include brunch in a café in Altona, lunch and a riverside walk in Blankenese, and some dinner back in Ottensen.

DISCOUNTS AND DEALS

Hamburg is one of Germany's most expensive cities, but the several citywide deals can make attractions more affordable.

The **Hamburg Card** allows unlimited travel on all public transportation (including express buses) within Hamburg and more than 150 discounts at many of the city's museums, cruises, restaurants, and stores. A one-day card, which is valid until 6 am the following day, costs €9.50 for one adult and up to three children under 15. The three-day card will set you back €24.50. A *Gruppenkarte* costs €16.50 for one day, €41.50 for three days, and covers five people. The Hamburg Card is available from HVV buses, vending machines, and service centers; tourist offices; and many hotels and hostels; as well as online at ⊕ *www.hvv.de* and ⊕ *www.hamburg-travel.com*.

EXPLORING HAMBURG

Despite being a large, sprawling city that covers almost as much ground as Berlin, Hamburg feels a lot more compact. The bulk of its major attractions and sights are between the Alster lakes to the north and the city's harbor and the Elbe River to the south. At the center of the city are the Altstadt and Neustadt—the city's historical core. East of the Altstadt is St. Georg, a major gay neighborhood. To the west of the Neustadt lie the nightlife district of St. Pauli and its neighbor the Schanzenviertel, while farther down the river are the more multicultural areas of Altona and Ottensen, and the quaint settlement of Blankenese. Just south of the Altstadt are the port-side districts of the Speicherstadt and the HafenCity.

ALTSTADT AND NEUSTADT

Divided by the *Binnenalster* (inner Alster lake) and the Kleine Alster canal, the Altstadt (Old Town) and Neustadt (New Town) form the heart of Hamburg's Innenstadt (Inner City).

ALTSTADT

Stretching from Hauptbahnhof to Hamburg's town hall and down to the canals of the Speicherstadt and the Elbe, the Altstadt was heavily bombed during World War II (as was the Neustadt). Much of its splendor was restored during the postwar reconstruction of the city. Sprinkled between its office blocks and modern department stores are a number of majestic churches, handsome museums, and stately government buildings.

> ### TOURING TIPS
>
> **Information:** Before you start your walk, stock up on maps and brochures at the tourist office inside the Hauptbahnhof.
>
> **Scenic spot:** Wander around the Binnenalster to the Lombards-brücke for lovely views of the lake and the grand office buildings, department stores, and hotels that frame it.
>
> **Snacks:** There are many inexpensive restaurants in and around the Hauptbahnhof, as well as on Mönckebergstrasse. You can easily get a filling snack and soft drink for under €6.

13

GETTING HERE AND AROUND

The best way to get to the center of the Altstadt is to take the U-bahn or S-bahn to the Hauptbahnhof or the U-bahn stations of Mönckeberg-strasse and Rathaus. Once here, most of the sights and attractions are within an easy walk of each other.

TIMING

If you plan four hours for visits to the museums and the Rathaus and two more hours for a boat tour on the Alster lakes, you'll comfortably end up spending a full day here.

TOP ATTRACTIONS

Fodor's Choice ★ **Alster Lakes.** The twin lakes of the Binnenalster (Inner Alster) and Aussenalster (Outer Alster) provide Hamburg with some of its most celebrated vistas. The two lakes meet at the Lombardsbrücke and Ken-nedybrücke (Lombard and Kennedy bridges). The boat landing at the Jungfernstieg, below the Alsterpavillon, is the starting point for lake and canal cruises. Small sailboats and rowboats, rented from yards on the shores of the Alster, are very much a part of the summer scene.

Every Hamburger dreams of living within sight of the Alster, but only the wealthiest can afford it. Those that can't still have plenty of opportunities to enjoy the waterfront, however, and the outer Alster is ringed by 7 km (4½ miles) of tree-lined public pathways. ■TIP→ **Popular among joggers, these paths are also a lovely place for a stroll.** ⊠ *Altstadt* Ⓜ *Jungfernstieg (U-bahn).*

Fodor's Choice ★ **Chilehaus** (*Chile House*). Almost 5 million bricks went into the construction of this marvelous building at the heart of the Kontorhausviertel, a collection of handsome office buildings that were built in the 1920–40s and now, together with the nearby Speicherstadt, form a UNESCO

World Heritage site. Built in a brick expressionist style in 1924 for expat Brit Henry Brarens Sloman, who emigrated to Chile from Hamburg as a young man, made a considerable fortune trading saltpeter and returned to the city to make his mark, the Chilehaus stands 10 stories high, its impressive, jutting tip resembling the prow of a ship. Still a home to business offices, it also counts a number of small cafés and shops, and a bar as residents, and is well worth a visit, particularly at night when illuminated. ⊠ *Fischertwiete 2, Altstadt* Ⓜ *Messberg (U-bahn), Mönckebergstrasse (U-Bahn).*

HARBOR TOURS

A cruise of Germany's "gateway to the world" is a must. The energy from the continuous ebb and flow of huge cargo vessels and container ships, the harbor's prosperity, and its international flavor best symbolize the city's spirit. The surrounding older parts of town, with their narrow cobblestone streets and late-medieval warehouses, testify to Hamburg's powerful Hanseatic past.

QUICK BITES

Alt Hamburger Aalspeicher. The Alt Hamburger Aalspeicher specializes in fish dishes, including Hamburg's famous *Aalsuppe* (a clear broth with a variety of vegetables, seafood, and meat—basically everything that is leftover). Over time the Low German word for everything—*all*—became mistaken for the word for eel (*aal*), so some restaurants make eel the focus, while others stick with creating their own versions of the soup. ⊠ *Deichstr. 43, Altstadt* ☎ *040/362–990* ⊕ *www.aalspeicher.de* Ⓜ *Rödingsmarkt (U-bahn).*

Fodor's Choice ★

Deichstrasse. The oldest residential area in the Old Town of Hamburg now consists of lavishly restored houses from the 17th through the 19th century. Many of the original, 14th-century houses on Deichstrasse were destroyed in the Great Fire of 1842, which broke out in No. 38 and left approximately 20,000 people homeless; only a few of the early dwellings escaped its ravages. These days the narrow cobblestone street is flanked by a number of lovely little restaurants specializing in fish or German cuisine, which have taken residence inside its historic buildings. ⊠ *Altstadt* Ⓜ *Rödingsmarkt (U-bahn).*

Hamburger Kunsthalle. One of the most important art museums in Germany, the Kunsthalle has 3,500 paintings, 650 sculptures, and a coin and medal collection that includes exhibits from the ancient Roman era. In the postmodern, cube-shaped building designed by Berlin architect O. M. Ungers, the **Galerie der Gegenwart** has housed a collection of international modern art since 1960, including works by Andy Warhol, Joseph Beuys, Georg Baselitz, and David Hockney. With 1,200 drawings and other works, graphic art is well represented, including works by Pablo Picasso and Horst Janssen, a Hamburg artist famous for his satirical worldview. In the other areas of the museum, you can view works by local artists dating from the 16th century. The outstanding collection of German Romantic paintings includes pieces by Caspar David Friedrich. Paintings by Holbein, Rembrandt, Van Dyck, Tiepolo, and Canaletto are also on view, while late-19th-century impressionism is represented by works by Leibl, Liebermann, Manet, Monet, and

Renoir. ⊠ *Glockengiesserwall, Altstadt* ☎ *040/4281–31200* ⊕ *www. hamburger-kunsthalle.de* 🖃 *€12* ⊗ *Tues., Wed., and Fri.–Sun. 10–6, Thurs. 10–9* Ⓜ *Hauptbahnhof (U-bahn and S-bahn).*

Mönckebergstrasse. This broad street of shops, which cuts through the city's Altstadt, is Hamburg's major thoroughfare. Built between 1908 and 1911 to connect the main train station to the town hall, but only open to taxis and buses, the street is perfect for a stroll. Home to the Karstadt and Galeria Kaufhof department stores, electronics megastore Saturn, as well as a host of global brand stores from Adidas to Zara, it swells with local and out-of-town shoppers on Saturday and public holidays. The best cafés and restaurants tend to be found on side streets off Mönckebergstrasse, where the rents for shop space are generally not as high. ⊠ *Altstadt* Ⓜ *Mönckebergstrasse (U-bahn), Hauptbahnhof (U-bahn and S-bahn), Jungfernstieg (U-bahn).*

Fodor's Choice ★ **Rathaus** (*Town Hall*). To most Hamburgers this impressive neo-Renaissance building is the symbolic heart of the city. The seat of the city's Senate (state government) and Bürgerschaft (parliament), it was constructed between 1886 and 1897, with 647 rooms and an imposing clock tower. Along with much of the city center, the Rathaus was heavily damaged during World War II, but was faithfully restored to its original beauty in the postwar years, and it's now one of the most photographed sights in Hamburg. The 40-minute tours of the building begin in the ground floor Rathausdiele, a vast pillared hall. Although visitors are only shown the state rooms, their tapestries, glittering chandeliers, coffered ceilings, and grand portraits give you a sense of the city's great wealth in the 19th century and the Town Hall's status as an object of civic pride. Outside, the Rathausmarkt (Town Hall Square) is the site of regular festivals and events, including the annual Stuttgarter Wine Festival and the city's biggest Christmas market. ⊠ *Rathausmarkt, Altstadt* ☎ *040/42831–2064* ⊕ *www.hamburgische-buergerschaft.de* 🖃 *€4* ⊗ *Daily tours in English at 10:15, 1:15, and 3:15* Ⓜ *Rathaus (U-bahn), Jungfernstieg (U-bahn and S-bahn).*

St. Jacobi Kirche (*St. James's Church*). This 15th-century church was almost completely destroyed during World War II. Only the interiors survived, and reconstruction was completed in 1963. The interior is not to be missed—it houses such treasures as a massive baroque organ and three Gothic altars from the 15th and 16th centuries. ⊠ *Jacobikirchhof 22 at Steinstr., Altstadt* ☎ *040/303–7370* ⊕ *www.jacobus.de* ⊗ *Apr.– Sept., Mon.–Sat. 10–5, Sun. after service; Oct.–Mar., Mon.–Sat. 11–5, Sun. after service. German guided tours: 1st Tues. of month at 12:45; 1st Sat. at 2 and 3; 3rd Fri. at 12:30. English guided tours available on request by emailing ahead of time* Ⓜ *Rathaus (U-bahn), Jungfernstieg (U-bahn and S-bahn).*

St. Petri Kirche (*St. Peter's Church*). This church was created in 1195 and has been in continuous use since then. St. Petri is the only one of the five main churches in Hamburg that came out of World War II relatively undamaged. The current building was built in 1849, after the previous building burned down in the Great Fire of 1842. Every Wednesday at 5:15 pm is the *Stunde der Kirchenmusik*, an hour of liturgical organ

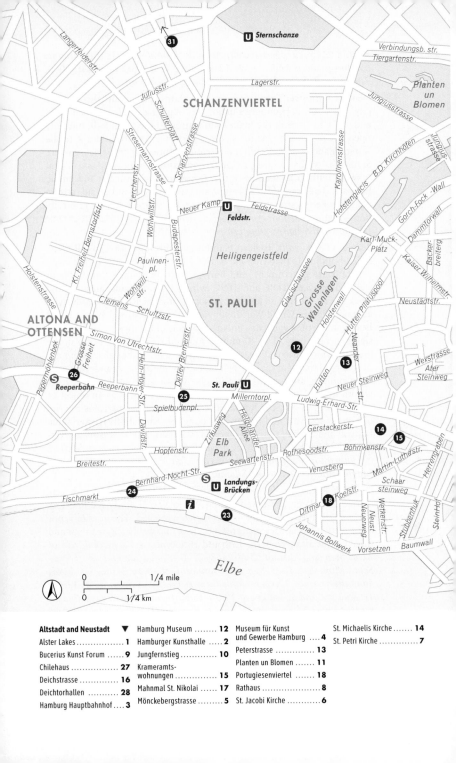

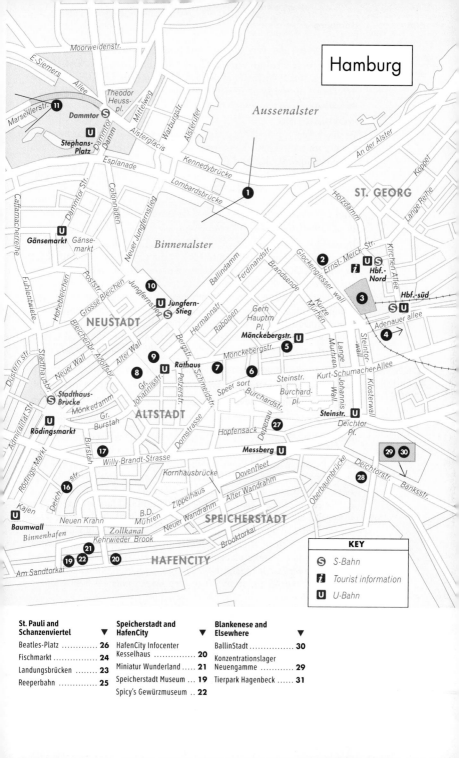

Hamburg

Aussenalster

Moorweidenstr.

E.-Siemers Allee

Marseiller str.

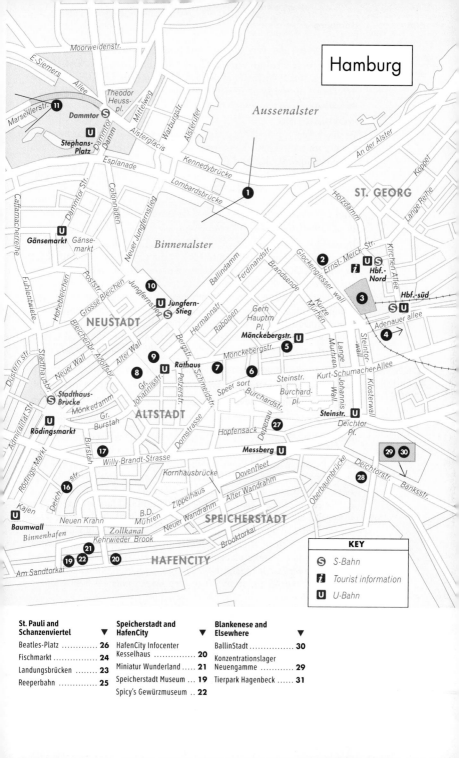 **11**

Dammtor Ⓢ

Theodor Heuss-pl.

Stephans-Platz Ⓤ

Mittelweg

Warburgstr.

Alsterglacis

Alsterufer

Kennedybrücke

An der Alster

Koppel

ST. GEORG

Lange Reihe

Esplanade

Lombardsbrücke

❶

Holzdamm

Caffamacherreihe

Gänsemarkt Ⓤ

Gänse-markt

Dammtor Str.

Colonnaden

Neuer Jungfernstieg

Binnenalster

Ballindamm

Ferdinandstr.

Brandsende

Glockengiesser wall

Ernst-Merck-Str.

Kirchen-Allee

❷

🛈 Ⓤ Ⓢ **Hbf.-Nord**

Hbf.-süd

Ⓢ Ⓤ

Fuhlentwiete

Postistr.

Hohe Bleichen

Grosse Bleichen

Jungfernstieg

❿

NEUSTADT

Ⓤ **Jungfern-Stieg** Ⓢ

Hermannstr.

Raboisen

Gerh Hauptm Pl.

Kurze Mühren

Lange Mühren

Steintor-wall

Adenauer allee

❸

❹

Duststr.

Stadthausbr.

Neuer Wall

Bleichenbr.

Adolfsbr.

Alter Wall

Bergstr.

❾

Ⓤ **Rathaus**

❽

Pelzerstr.

❼

❻

Schmiedstr.

Mönckebergstr. Ⓤ

❺

Mönckebergstr.

Steinstr.

Burchard-pl.

Kurt-Schumacher-Allee

Johannis Wall

Klosterwall

Admiralität Str.

Stadthausstr.

Stadthaus-Brücke Ⓢ

Mönkedamm

Gr. Johannisstr.

Gr. Burstah

ALTSTADT

Domstrasse

Speer sort

Burchardstr.

Steinstr.

27

Depenau

Steinstr. Ⓤ

Deichtor Pl.

Rödings-Markt

Rödingsmarkt Ⓤ

Burstah

17

Deich str.

Willy-Brandt-Strasse

Hopfensack

Messberg Ⓤ

29 **30**

28

Kajen

16

Kornhausbrücke

Dovenfleet

Alter Wandrahm

Oberbaumbrücke

Deichtorstr.

Banksstr.

Ⓤ **Baumwall**

Neuen Krahn

B.D. Mühren

Zippelhaus

Neuer Wandrahm

SPEICHERSTADT

Binnenhafen

19 **22** **21**

20

Zollkanal

Kehrwieder Brook

HAFENCITY

Brooktorkai

Am Sandtorkai

KEY

Ⓢ S-Bahn

🛈 Tourist information

Ⓤ U-Bahn

music . ⊠ *Bei der Petrikirche 2, Altstadt* ☎ *040/325–7400* ⊕ *www. sankt-petri.de* ⊙ *Mon., Tues., Thurs., and Fri. 10–6:30, Wed. 10–7, Sat. 10–5, Sun. 9–8. Tower Mon.–Sat. 11–4:30, Sun. 11:30–4:30. Tours 1st Thurs. of month at 12:30; 3rd Thurs. at 3; and 1st Sun. at 11:30* Ⓜ *Rathaus (U-bahn), Jungfernstieg (U-bahn and S-bahn).*

WORTH NOTING

Deichtorhallen. A pair of large markets built in 1911–12, not far from the main train station, now house two of Germany's largest exhibition halls for contemporary art and photography. One of the Deichtorhallen's modern, airy interiors resembles an oversized loft space, and its changing exhibits have presented the works of such artists as Andy Warhol, Roy Lichtenstein, and Miró. The halls also accommodate the Fillet of Soul restaurant. ⊠ *Deichtorstr. 1–2, Altstadt* ☎ *040/321–030* ⊕ *www. deichtorhallen.de* ⬚*€10* ⊙ *Tues.–Sun. 11–6* Ⓜ *Steinstrasse (U-bahn).*

Hamburg Hauptbahnhof (*Main Train Station*). This central train station's cast-iron-and-glass architecture evokes the grandiose self-confidence of imperial Germany. The chief feature of the enormous 680-foot-long structure is its 446-foot-wide glazed roof. One of the largest structures of its kind in Europe, it's remarkably spacious and bright inside. Though completed in 1906 and having gone through many modernizations, it continues to have tremendous architectural impact. Today it sees a heavy volume of international, national, and suburban rail traffic. ⊠ *Hachmannpl. 16, Altstadt* Ⓜ *Hauptbahnhof (U-bahn and S-bahn).*

▎**QUICK BITES**

Das Kontor. Seasonal dishes such as plaice in spring and game in winter are served at this inviting Hamburg tavern. You could also head here for some of the city's best fried potatoes and traditional desserts. ⊠ *Deichstr. 32, Altstadt* ☎ 040/371–471 ⊕ www.das-kontor-hamburg.de Ⓜ *Rödingsmarkt (U-bahn).*

Mahnmal St. Nikolai (*St. Nicholas Memorial*). Originally erected in 1195 and destroyed by fire in 1842, the church was rebuilt in neo-Gothic style, before it burned down again during the air raids of World War II. Today, the remains of the church serve as a memorial for the victims of war and persecution from 1933 to 1945. The memorial features an exhibition on the air raids and the destruction of Hamburg and other European cities. A glass elevator on the outside of the building takes visitors 250 feet up to the steeple, which offers magnificent views of the surrounding historic streets. Lectures, film screenings, panel discussions, and concerts also take place at the memorial. ⊠ *Willy-Brandt-Str. 60 at Hopfenmarkt, Altstadt* ☎ *040/371–125* ⊕ *www.mahnmal-st-nikolai. de* ⬚*€5* ⊙ *Apr.–Sept., daily 10–6; Oct.–Mar., daily 10–5* Ⓜ *Rödings-markt (U-bahn).*

Museum für Kunst und Gewerbe Hamburg (*Arts and Crafts Museum*). The museum houses a wide range of exhibits, from 15th- to 18th-century scientific instruments to an art nouveau interior complete with ornaments and furnishings. It was built in 1876 as a combination museum and school. Its founder, Justus Brinckmann, intended it to be a bastion of the applied arts that would counter what he saw as a decline in taste owing to industrial mass production. A keen collector, Brinckmann amassed a wealth of unusual objects, including ceramics from around

Hamburg's neo-Renaissance Rathaus is worth a peek inside for its opulent interiors.

the world. ✉ *Steintorpl., Altstadt* ☎ *040/4281–34880* ⊕ *www.mkg-hamburg.de* 🖾 *€10; €7 Thurs. after 5* ⊙ *Tues., Wed., and Fri.–Sun. 11–6, Thurs. 11–9* Ⓜ *Hauptbahnhof (U-bahn and S-bahn).*

NEUSTADT

To the west of the Altstadt, and bordered by the *Aussenalster* (outer Alster) to the north and the Elbe to the south, lies the Neustadt. The area dates back to the 17th century, when a second wall was built to protect the city during the Thirty Years' War. These days, the Neustadt is more or less indistinguishable from its older neighbor. Similarly blessed with a number of stunning buildings, including those that line the pretty lakeside promenade of Jungfernstieg, the Neustadt is also famed for its wealth of shopping opportunities.

GETTING HERE AND AROUND

The Neustadt is served by a number of U-bahn stops, but Gänsemarkt or Jungfernstieg are the most central. Hamburg's downtown area isn't particularly large, and strolling to Jungfernstieg from the main train station via Mönckebergstrasse won't take much more than 10 minutes, assuming it's not a Saturday or during the school holidays.

TIMING

Shoppers could easily while away a day here, perusing the boutiques of Neuerwall and the Alsterhaus department store, with stops for refreshments along the way. For those more interested in sightseeing, a visit to the Hamburg Museum, followed by a look around St. Michaelis church and the Krameramtswohnungen, and then a wander down the hill to the Portugiesenviertel for something to eat could also take the best part of a day.

TOP ATTRACTIONS

Jungfernstieg. This wide promenade looking out over the Alster lakes is the beginning of the city's premier shopping district. Laid out in 1665, it used to be part of a muddy mill-race that channeled water into the Elbe. Hidden from view behind the sedate facade of Jungfernstieg is a network of several small shopping centers that together account for almost a mile of shops selling everything from souvenirs to haute couture. Many of these passages have sprung up in the past two decades, but some have been here since the 19th century; the first glass-covered arcade, called Sillem's Bazaar, was built in 1845. ⊠ *Neustadt* Ⓜ *Jungfernstieg (U-bahn and S-bahn).*

Peterstrasse. This elegant street lies steps away from the site of the former city wall, and is of great historical interest. At No. 35–39, for example, is a replica of the baroque facade of the Beylingstift complex, built in 1751. The composer Johannes Brahms's former home, now a museum in his honor, is at No. 39. All the buildings in the area have been painstakingly designed to follow the style of the original buildings, thanks largely to nonprofit foundations. ⊠ *Neustadt* Ⓜ *St. Pauli (U-bahn).*

Fodor's Choice
★

St. Michaelis Kirche (*St. Michael's Church*). The Michel, as it's called locally, is Hamburg's principal church and northern Germany's finest baroque-style ecclesiastical building. Its first incarnation, built between 1649 and 1661 (the tower followed in 1669), was razed after lightning struck almost a century later. It was rebuilt between 1750 and 1786 in the decorative Nordic baroque style, but was gutted by a terrible fire in 1906. The replica, completed in 1912, was demolished during World War II and the present church is a reconstruction.

The distinctive 436-foot brick-and-iron tower bears the largest tower clock in Germany, 26 feet in diameter. Just above the clock is a viewing platform (accessible by elevator or stairs) that affords a magnificent panorama of the city, the Elbe River, and the Alster lakes. Twice a day, at 10 am and 9 pm (Sunday at noon), a watchman plays a trumpet solo from the tower platform. In the crypt a 30-minute movie about the 1,000-year history of Hamburg and its churches is shown.

For a great view of Hamburg's skyline, head to the clock tower at night. In the evenings you can sip a complimentary soft drink while listening to classical music in a room just below the tower. This is usually held from 5:30 to 11 pm: check *www.nachtmichel.de* to confirm times. ⊠ *Englische Planke 1, Neustadt* ☎ *040/376–780* ⊕ *www.st-michaelis. de* 🎫 *Tower €5; crypt and movie €4; combined ticket €7* ⊗ *May–Oct., daily 9–7:30; Nov.–Apr., daily 10–5:30* Ⓜ *Rödingsmarkt (U-bahn), Stadthausbrücke (S-bahn).*

QUICK BITES

Old Commercial Room. Just opposite St. Michaelis Kirche, this is one of Hamburg's most traditional and best-loved restaurants. Book a table in one of its cozy booths to sample a local specialty such as *Labskaus* **(a curious mixture of potato, corned beef, beet, and herring). If you don't make it to the restaurant, you can buy cans of the stuff in Hamburg supermarkets and department stores.** ✉ *Englische Planke 10, Neustadt* ☎ *040/366–319* ⊕ *www.oldcommercialroom.de* Ⓜ *Rödingsmarkt (U-bahn), Stadthausbrücke (S-bahn).*

13

WORTH NOTING

Bucerius Kunst Forum. This independent art gallery, considered one of the leading exhibition houses in northern Germany, has staged four major exhibitions a year since opening in 2002 inside a historic Reichsbank building next door to the Rathaus. The gallery commissions guest curators from around the world to create shows, collectively covering every art period and style. ✉ *Rathausmarkt 2, Neustadt* ☎ *040/360–9960* ⊕ *www.buceriuskunstforum.de* ⬛€8, €5 Mon. ⏱ Fri.–Wed. 11–7, Thurs. 11–9 Ⓜ Rathaus (U-bahn).

NEED A BREAK?

Alex im Alsterpavillon. Perhaps Hamburg's best-known café, the Alex im Alsterpavillon sits on the edge of the Binnenalster at Jungfernstieg. Its curving terrace and high-windowed dining room make ideal spots for observing the near-constant activity of the lake's little tour boats while imbibing a refreshment or two between bouts of shopping and sightseeing. ✉ *Jungfernstieg 54, Neustadt* ☎ *040/350–1870* ⊕ *www.dein-alex.de/ dein-alex-hamburg* Ⓜ *Jungfernstieg (U-bahn and S-bahn).*

FAMILY **Hamburg Museum** (*Museum of Hamburg History*). The museum's vast and comprehensive collection of artifacts gives you an excellent overview of Hamburg's development, from its origins in the 9th century to the present. Pictures and models portray the history of the port and shipping here, from 1650 onward. ✉ *Holstenwall 24, Neustadt* ☎ *040/4281–32100* ⊕ *www.hamburgmuseum.de* ⬛€9 ⏱ Tues.–Sat. 10–5, Sun. 10–6 Ⓜ St. Pauli (U-bahn).

Krameramtswohnungen (*Shopkeepers' Houses*). The shopkeepers' guild built this tightly packed group of courtyard houses between 1620 and 1626 for members' widows. The houses became homes for the elderly after 1866. The half-timber, two-story dwellings, with unusual twisted chimneys and decorative brick facades, were restored in the 1970s. A visit inside the Kramer-Witwen-Wohnung—one of the old apartments that has been turned into a little museum—gives you a sense of what life was like in these 17th-century dwellings. ✉ *Historic House C, Krayenkamp 10, Neustadt* ☎ *040/3750–1988* ⬛€2.50 ⏱ Tues.–Sun. 10–5 Ⓜ Rödingsmarkt (U-bahn), Stadtbahnstrasse (S-bahn).

FAMILY **Planten un Blomen** (*Plants and Flowers Park*). In 1821, a botanist planted a sycamore tree in a park near Dammtor train station. From this tree, a sanctuary for birds and plants evolved and a botanical garden that resembles the current park opened in 1930. This 116-acre inner-city oasis features a grand Japanese garden, a mini-golf course, an outdoor roller-skating and ice-skating rink, trampolines, and water features.

The original sycamore tree still stands near an entrance. If you visit on a summer evening, you'll see the *Wasserlichtkonzerte*, the play of an illuminated fountain set to organ music. Make sure you get to the lake in plenty of time for the nightly show, which begins at 10 pm from May through August and at 9 pm in September. ⊠ *Stephanspl., Neustadt* ☎ *040/4285–44723* ⊕ *www.plantenunblomen.hamburg.de* ⊠ *Free* ◷ *Apr., daily 7 am–10 pm; May–Sept., daily 7 am–11 pm; Oct.–Mar., daily 7 am–8 pm* Ⓜ *Dammtor-Bahnhof or St. Pauli (S-bahn), Messehallen (U-bahn).*

Portugiesenviertel (*Portuguese Quarter*). On the edge of the harbor, tucked in between Landungsbrücken and Baumwall, lies a small slice of Iberia in Hamburg. Famed for its cluster of tapas restaurants and little cafés on and around Ditmar-Koel-Strasse, the Portugiesenviertel is a great place to go to feast on a plate of grilled sardines or have a creamy *galão* (espresso with foamed milk). Head here in summer, when the streets are flooded with tables and diners making the most of the good weather. ⊠ *Ditmar-Koel-Str., Neustadt* Ⓜ *Landungsbrücken (U-bahn and S-bahn), Baumwall (U-bahn).*

ST. PAULI AND SCHANZENVIERTEL

The harborside quarter of St. Pauli is perhaps the city's best-known neighborhood, its web of narrow streets branching off the bright neon vein of the Reeperbahn. Named after the rope makers that once worked here, the long street runs the length of St Pauli's extensive red-light district—one of the largest in Europe. The broad sidewalks here are lined with strip joints, sex shops, and bars. In the early 1960s, the Beatles famously cut their teeth in clubs just off the street, playing 12-hour-long gigs in front of drunken revelers. These days St. Pauli's all-night bars, nightclubs, and pubs continue to be a big draw. Despite the seediness of its sex industry, however, the area has undergone some serious gentrification over the years, and those dive bars and flophouses now rub shoulders with trendy eateries and design hotels.

The neighboring Schanzenviertel has also experienced a significant makeover in the last decade. Once filled with artists, punks, and students, and infused with an antiestablishment culture, the "Schanze" remains a neighborhood where the most recognizable building is the Rote Flora, an old theater occupied by squatters who use it for concerts and cultural events. Now, however, it's also a place where cool young Hamburgers go to browse through clothing boutiques and then drink and dine in laid-back, reasonably priced bars and restaurants. Germany's answer to Jamie Oliver, Tim Mälzer, has a hugely popular café and restaurant here, and global labels such as Adidas and American Apparel have also set up shop. Ten minutes from the center of town by S-bahn, Schanzenviertel has elegant old apartment buildings that have found favor with Hamburg's media and finance professionals. This has driven the rents up, and forced out many of the same tenants who once imbued the Schanzenviertel with its original edginess.

GETTING HERE AND AROUND

The harbor can be reached by taking a U-bahn or S-bahn train to Landungsbrücken. The mile-long Reeperbahn is bookended by the Reeperbahn S-bahn and St. Pauli U-bahn stations. The Schanzenviertel is served by the Sternschanze U-bahn and S-bahn station.

TIMING

You can easily spend a full day and a long night here, starting with breakfast and shopping in the Schanzenviertel, then lunch and a river cruise at the harbor, and a night on the Reeperbahn after dinner.

13

TOP ATTRACTIONS

Fischmarkt (*Fish Market*). A trip to the Altona Fischmarkt is definitely worth getting out of bed early—or staying up all night—for. The Sunday markets hark back to the 18th century, when fishermen sold their catch before church services. Today, freshly caught fish sold to the locals by salty auctioneers from little stalls is only a part of the scene. You can find almost anything here: live parrots and palm trees, armloads of flowers and bananas, valuable antiques, and fourth-hand junk. Those keen to continue partying from the night before can get down to live bands rocking the historic Fischauktionshalle. ⊠ *Grosse Elbestr. 9, St. Pauli* ⏲ *Apr.–Oct., Sun. 5 am–9:30 am; Nov.–Mar., Sun. 7 am–9:30 am* Ⓜ *Reeperbahn (S-Bahn).*

FAMILY **Landungsbrücken** (*Piers*). Hamburgers and tourists flock to the city's impressive port (Germany's largest) to marvel at the huge container and cruise ships gliding past, pick up maritime-themed gifts from souvenir stores, and treat themselves to something from the many snack and ice-cream stands. It's best to take a tour to get a complete idea of the massive scale of the place, which is one of the most modern and efficient harbors in the world. Barge tours leave from the main passenger terminal, along with a whole range of ferries and boats heading to other destinations on the Elbe and in the North Sea. There's frequently a breeze here, so it's worth packing something warm, particularly if you're planning on taking an open-top harbor tour. ⊠ *Bei den St. Pauli Landungsbrücken, St. Pauli* Ⓜ *Landungsbrücken (U-bahn and S-bahn).*

Rickmer Rickmers. This majestic 19th-century sailing ship once traveled as far as Cape Town. Now it's permanently docked at Hamburg's piers, where it serves as a museum and site for painting and photography exhibitons. ⊠ *St. Pauli Landungsbrücken Ponton 1a, St. Pauli* ☎ *040/319–5959* ⊕ *www.rickmer-rickmers.de* 💶 *€4* ⏲ *Daily 10–6* Ⓜ *Landungsbrücken (U-bahn and S-bahn).*

Cap San Diego. Close to the *Rickmer Rickmers* ship at Hamburg's piers sits the handsome 1960s freighter *Cap San Diego*, nowadays a seaworthy museum and hotel. Before it docked at Hamburg permanently, it regularly sailed between Germany and South America. ⊠ *Überseebrücke, Landungsbrücken, St. Pauli* ☎ *040/364–209* ⊕ *www.capsandiego.de* 💶 *€7* ⏲ *Daily 10–6* Ⓜ *Landungsbrücken (U-bahn and S-bahn).*

Fodor'sChoice ★ **Reeperbahn.** The hottest nightspots in town are concentrated on and around St. Pauli's pulsating thoroughfare, the Reeperbahn, and a buzzing little side street known as Grosse Freiheit ("Great Freedom"). It was there, in the early 1960s, that a then-obscure band called the

Beatles polished their live act. The Kiez, as the area is known colloquially, is a part of town that never sleeps—literally, in the case of at least a couple of bars that claim to never close their doors. It has long been famed for its music halls and drinking holes, but also for its strip clubs, sex shops, and brothels. The first brothel was registered here in the 15th century, and although the love-hungry sailors that the area became famous for no longer roam the streets, streetwalkers still line Davidstrasse; around the corner, on Herbertstrasse, skimpily dressed women sit in windows and offer their services to passersby.

The Kiez is about more than just its red-light activities, however, and the Reeperbahn swells on evenings and weekends with bar hoppers and nightclubbers, concert- and theatergoers, and locals and out-of-towners out for dinner and a few drinks. And maybe a walk on— or at least through—the wild side afterward. ⊠ *St. Pauli* Ⓜ *St. Pauli (U-bahn), Reeperbahn (S-bahn)*.

TOURING TIPS

Scenic spot: A great way to experience harbor life is to visit St. Pauli Landungsbrücken, where cruise boats and ferries chug in and out and a couple of handsome museum ships are permanently moored. The best cluster of souvenir shops in Hamburg call these piers home.

Snacks: If you are an early riser stop by the Fischmarkt Sunday morning for a *Fischbrötchen* (a bread roll filled with fried, smoked, or pickled fish), or grab a snack from one of the many stands along St. Pauli Landungsbrücken later in the day.

WORTH NOTING

Beatles-Platz. At the entrance to Grosse Freiheit stand life-size steel silhouettes commemorating the five original Beatles—John Lennon, Paul McCartney, George Harrison, Pete Best, and Stuart Sutcliffe. In the summer of 1960, they played in the area while seeking fame and fortune. Although the statues are rather ordinary looking during the day, they make for a good photo op when they're lit up at night. ⊠ *Reeperbahn end of Grosse Freiheit, St. Pauli* Ⓜ *Reeperbahn (S-bahn)*.

ST. GEORG

First-time visitors to Hamburg may have some trouble, at least initially, getting their heads around this vibrant quarter. Fanning out to the northeast of the Altstadt, St. Georg is a place whose rich diversity is best understood by trips down its three main streets: Steindamm, Lange Reihe, and An der Alster. Just across the main station, Steindamm begins as a one-way street full of sex shops and prostitutes lurking in doorways and turns into a busy road lined with Middle Eastern restaurants and minimarkets and a large mosque. A few blocks over, in the middle of the three, is Lange Reihe, a long, narrow thoroughfare brimming with gay and lesbian bars and cafés and some of the best places to drink and eat in town. Lastly, a short walk from Lange Reihe to the outer Alster lake's edge, sits An der Alster and a row of luxury hotels and penthouse apartments that come with million-euro views.

Grosse Freiheit, a side street off the Reeperbahn, comes alive at night with crowds looking for a good time.

GETTING HERE AND AROUND

The closest station for U-bahn and S-bahn trains is Hauptbahnhof, and the No. 6 bus runs the length of Lange Reihe. St. Georg is compact, making it easy enough to stroll around.

TIMING

With all its cafés and little restaurants, St. Georg is an ideal spot for a lazy breakfast or an afternoon coffee or two. Factor in a stroll along the lake, and a few hours here can soon slip by.

SPEICHERSTADT AND HAFENCITY

No two places in Hamburg embody the changing commerce of the city and its love affair with the Elbe as vividly as the harbor districts of the Speicherstadt and the HafenCity. Built around a series of narrow canals, the stunning redbrick, Gothic architecture of the former's warehouses (which make up the largest complex of integrated warehouses in the world and have recently been named a UNESCO World Heritage site) sits next to the gleaming glass and steel of Europe's largest urban renewal development project. The Speicherstadt's 100-year-old warehouses continue to store and trade in everything from coffee to Oriental carpets, but now count restaurants, museums, and the world's largest model railway amongst their tenants. The HafenCity, meanwhile, has become a popular site for the headquarters of many of the city's largest firms, as well as home to a number of new apartment blocks, hotels and restaurants, a university, and the jewel in its crown, the hugely ambitious Elbphilarmonie concert hall, which is scheduled to open in 2017.

The Beatles in Hamburg

It was on the mean streets of St. Pauli, and specifically Grosse Freiheit, that four young lads from Liverpool cut their teeth playing to frequently hostile crowds of sailors, prostitutes, and thugs before going on to become the biggest band in the world. Signed by Bruno Koschmider, a nightclub owner and entrepreneur of dubious character, the Beatles first arrived in Hamburg in August 1960. Their first gig was at Koschmider's Indra Club, a seedy joint that doubled as a strip club, and their first lodgings consisted of a couple of windowless rooms in the back of a movie theater, the Bambi Kino. Over the next two-and-a-half years, the young Beatles would visit Hamburg five times and play almost 300 concerts in the city. During one stint in 1961, they performed 98 nights in a row, often starting at 8:30 at night and playing their last song around the same time the next morning.

Perhaps surprisingly, some of the venues where the Beatles strutted their stuff remain. The Star Club, the site of their last Hamburg concert, on New Year's Eve 1962, may be gone, but the **Indra Club** is still at Grosse Freiheit 64. Down the road, at No. 36, is the **Kaiserkeller**, where the boys moved after the Indra was closed down for being too rowdy. In addition to hitting the clubs, fans of the Fab Four can pose beside the life-size, metal sculptures of the five original Beatles on the **Beatles-Platz**, and also retrace the band's steps on a number of walking tours, which take in the **Bambi Kino** and other venues they played at, along with the **Gretel und Alfons** pub, a favorite haunt.

GETTING HERE AND AROUND

To get to the Speicherstadt, take the U-bahn to Messberg or Baumwall stations, or walk or bike over from the Altstadt. The HafenCity is served by the city's U4 train line, which stops at the U-bahn stations of Überseequartier and HafenCity Universität. Both areas are close enough to each other to walk between.

TIMING

This part of town is a popular spot for Sunday strollers, and ambling along its canals, taking snaps of the area's impressive riverside edifices, combined with a visit to a museum or the Miniatur Wunderland can happily fill half a day.

HafenCity Infocenter Kesselhaus (*HafenCity Information Center*). In an old 19th-century boiler house, this popular information center documents the HafenCity urban development project. In addition to changing photographic and architectural exhibitions, the center also has an impressive 1:500 scale model of the HafenCity. Free two-hour walking and cycling tours of the HafenCity are also available. Tours in English are offered for groups of 10 people or more and can be booked ahead of time on the center's website. ✉ *Am Sandtorkai 30, HafenCity* ☎ *040/3690–1799* ⊕ *www.hafencity.com* ✉ *Free* ☉ *May–Sept., Tues., Wed., and Fri.–Sun. 10–6, Thurs. 10–8; Oct.–Apr., Tues.–Sun. 10–6* Ⓜ *Baumwall (U-bahn), Überseequartier (U-bahn).*

13

FAMILY

Fodor's Choice

★

Miniatur Wunderland. You don't need to be a model-railroad enthusiast or a 10-year-old to be blown away by the sheer scale and attention to detail of the Miniatur Wunderland. The largest model railroad in the world features more than 14,000 square feet of little trains click-clacking their way through wonderfully faithful miniature replicas of Hamburg itself as well as foreign towns in Switzerland, Austria, the United States, and elsewhere. Planes land at a little airport; every 15 minutes, day turns into night and hundreds of thousands of LED lights illuminate the trains, buildings, and streets. Unsurprisingly, it's one of Hamburg's most popular attractions, so it's best to book ahead, particularly on weekends and school holidays, when waiting times for entry can stretch to a couple of hours. If you do have to wait, free drinks and ice cream for children, and videos to watch ease the pain. ⊠ *Kehrwieder 2–4, Block D, Speicherstadt* ☎ *040/300–6800* ⊕ *www.miniatur-wunderland.com* ⛁ *€13* ⏱ *Mon. and Wed.–Fri. 9:30–6, Tues. 9:30–9, Sat. 8 am–9 pm, Sun. 8:30–8. Hrs vary; call or check website before setting out* Ⓜ *Baumwall (U-bahn), Messberg (U-bahn).*

Speicherstadtmuseum. An excursion to this little museum, inside an original, 19th-century warehouse, gives you a sense of the trade that flowed through the Speicherstadt in its heyday. Sacks of coffee and spices, chests of tea, and scales and mills are scattered throughout the museum and there is information detailing the history and architecture of the district as well as historical photographs and diagrams. ⊠ *Am Sandtorkai 36, Speicherstadt* ☎ *040/321–191* ⊕ *www.speicherstadtmuseum. de* ⛁ *€4.20* ⏱ *Apr.–Oct., weekdays 10–5, weekends 10–6; Nov.–Mar., Tues.–Sun. 10–5* Ⓜ *Baumwall (U-bahn).*

Spicy's Gewürzmuseum. Hamburg's proud past as Europe's gateway to the world comes to life at the tiny but fascinating Spicy's Gewürzmuseum, where you can smell and touch more than 50 spices. Nearly 1,000 objects chronicle five centuries of the once-prosperous spice trade in Hamburg. ⊠ *Am Sandtorkai 34, Speicherstadt* ☎ *040/367–989* ⊕ *www. spicys.de* ⛁ *€5* ⏱ *Nov.–June, Tues.–Sun. 10–5; July–Oct., daily 10–5* Ⓜ *Baumwall (U-bahn).*

ALTONA AND OTTENSEN

Generally the closer an area is to water in Hamburg, the more desirable a place it is to live. This is particularly true of the borough of Altona and Ottensen, an upscale neighborhood. Bordered by the Elbe, where Altona forms part of the port, and centered on a large domestic and international train station, the area has an allure heightened by a lively shopping boulevard and narrow side streets with bakeries, boutiques, and bars.

Much of this predominantly working-class area has been transformed over the last few decades. Nineteenth-century factories and industrial plants now accommodate cultural centers, movie theaters, offices, and hotels. Despite its increasingly middle-class makeup the quarter remains multicultural, and a large Turkish population continues to live and run all sorts of businesses here. It's a part of Hamburg that in many ways feels separate from the city surrounding it, which is unsurprising given

Check out HafenCity for a look at the Hamburg of the future, a planned development with offices, apartments, restaurants, museums, and entertainment spaces all in one neighborhood.

its history. Part of Denmark until 1864, Altona was an independent city as late as 1937, and its stately town hall above the river is a reminder of its distinguished past.

GETTING HERE AND AROUND

The Altona train station, 15 minutes from Hauptbahnhof, is the starting and finishing point for all domestic and international InterCity Express trains that pass through the main station. It's also a stop on a number of local S-bahn lines. The main shopping area surrounds the station.

TIMING

The area is a good place to while away an afternoon people-watching and browsing through shops, perhaps followed by a drink or two in one the area's many fine cafés.

QUICK BITES

Strandperle. While it may not conform to everyone's definition of a "beach"—in this case a long stretch of trucked-in sand on the north bank of the Elbe, directly across from the giant cranes and container terminals of the city's port—there's little doubting the popularity of the Elbstrand (Elbe beach) among locals. Whenever the sun's out, you'll find them out here in force, walking dogs and sipping beers and white-wine spritzers from a couple of little beach bars. Strandperle also does a decent chili con carne as well as curry sausages and fish rolls to keep hunger pangs at bay. ⊠ *Oevelgönne 60, Altona* ⊹ *About 700 yards from bus and ferry stops* ⊕ *www.strandperle-hamburg.de* Ⓜ *Neumühlen/Övelgönne (Bus No. 112), Neumühlen (Ferry No. 62).*

BLANKENESE AND ELSEWHERE

Twenty or so minutes along the Elbe by car or by S-bahn from the middle of the city lies the lovely riverside suburb of Blankenese. It's nicely situated on the side of a hill, with steep flights of narrow steps that snake between its handsome villas. It makes a popular destination for weekend walks and coffee and cake afterward.

Other parts of town within easy reach of the main station, and worth a visit, include the upscale neighborhood of Eppendorf, its more modest, less self-conscious neighbor Eimsbüttel, and the lakeside suburbs of Harvestehude, Winterhude, and Uhlenhorst.

Farther afield are the BallinStadt emigration museum in Veddel and the Neuengamme Concentration Camp.

Other than driving, the best way to get to Blankenese and Veddel is to take the S-bahn to their respective stations. Neuengamme is reachable by a combination of S-bahn and bus. The other suburbs are no more than 15 minutes away from the center of town by U-bahn.

TIMING

Given that a major selling point of Blankenese is that it's far from the hustle and bustle of the city, and the fact that you'll need an hour to get there and back, it's best to give yourself half a day to visit. Excursions to Ballinstadt and Neuengamme shouldn't be rushed either.

BallinStadt. This museum and family-research center tells the story of European emigration to the United States and elsewhere. The complex on the peninsula here, completed in 1901, was built by the HAPAG shipping line for its passengers, which came from all across Europe to sail across the Atlantic.

When the immigrants landed in the United States, they were subjected to thorough physical examinations. Those who were deemed sick were quarantined for weeks or returned to their home country. To reduce the likelihood of trouble, HAPAG began examining passengers before they left Hamburg for new shores. During the first 34 years of the 20th century, about 1.7 million people passed through emigration halls. Processing this many people took a long time, and Hamburg officials did not want foreigners roaming the city. To accommodate visitors for several days or months, the shipping company built a town, complete with a hospital, church, music hall, housing, and hotels. The emigrant experience comes to life with artifacts; interactive displays; detailed reproductions of the buildings (all but one was demolished); and first-hand accounts of oppression in Europe, life in the "city," conditions during the 60-day ocean crossing, and life in their new home.

As compelling as the exhibits are, the main draw is the research booths, where you can search the complete passenger lists of all ships that left the harbor. Research assistants are available to help locate and track your ancestors. From St. Pauli, the museum can be reached by S-bahn or Maritime Circle Line at St. Pauli Landungsbrücken No. 10. ⊠ *Veddeler Bogen 2, Veddel* ☎ *040/3197–9160* ⊕ *www.ballinstadt.de* 🎫 *€12.50* 🕐 *Apr.–Oct., daily 10–6; Nov.–Mar., daily 10–4:30* Ⓜ *Veddel (S-bahn).*

Konzentrationslager Neuengamme (*Neuengamme Concentration Camp*). Hamburg is a city of great beauty but also tragedy. On the southeastern edge of the city, between 104,000 and 106,000 people, including children, were held at Neuengamme concentration camp in its years of operation from 1938 to 1945. It was primarily a slave-labor camp, not an area focused on extermination, where bricks and weapons were the main products. German political prisoners and Europeans pushed into servitude composed most of the population. Neuengamme held gays, Roma (gypsies), and Jews. Jewish children were the subjects of cruel medical experiments; others worked with their parents or simply grew up in prison. To keep people in line, there were random acts of violence, including executions, and atrocious living conditions. Officials estimate that as many as 50,000 people died at Neuengamme before it ceased operation in May 1945.

A memorial opened on the site in 2005. Where the dormitories, dining hall, and hospital once sat, there are low pens filled with large rocks. With so much open space, the camp has an eerie silence. There is still a gate at the entrance. The camp has several areas; the main area has exhibits describing working conditions in an actual factory as well as a museum with interactive displays about the prisoner experience. Firsthand accounts, photographs from prisoners, furniture, clothing, and possessions make the experience even more affecting. ⊠ *Jean-Dolidier-Weg 75, Neuengamme* ☏ *040/4281–31500* ⊕ *www. kz-gedenkstaette-neuengamme.de* ✉ *Free* ☾ *Grounds always accessible; exhibits Apr.–Sept., weekdays 9:30–4, weekends noon–7; Oct.–Mar., weekdays 9:30–4, weekends noon–5* Ⓜ *KZ-Gedenkstätte, Mahnmal (Bus 227 or 327 from Bergedorf station [S-bahn])*.

FAMILY **Tierpark Hagenbeck** (*Hagenbeck Zoo*). One of the country's oldest and most popular zoos, the Tierpark Hagenbeck was founded in 1907 and is family owned. It was the world's first zoo to let wild animals such as lions, elephants, chimpanzees, and others roam freely in vast, open-air corrals. In summer, you can ride a pony.

The Tropen-Aquarium, on the same property as the zoo, is like a trip around the world. Sea life, insects, curious reptiles, marvelous birds, and exotic mammals live in replicas of their natural habitat. Detailed recreations of deserts, oceans, rain forests, and jungles are home to birds, fish, mammals, insects, and reptiles from almost every continent, including black-tailed lemurs living in a "Madagascar" village. ⊠ *Lokstedter Grenzstr. 2, Stellingen* ☏ *040/530–0330* ⊕ *www.hagenbeck.de* ✉ *Zoo €20, aquarium €14, combination ticket €30* ☾ *Zoo: Mar.–June, Sept., and Oct., daily 9–6; July and Aug., daily 9–7; Nov.–Feb., daily 9–4:30. Aquarium: daily 9–6* Ⓜ *Hagenbecks Tierpark (U-bahn)*.

WHERE TO EAT

Hamburg has plenty of chic restaurants to satisfy the fashion-conscious local professionals, as well as the authentically salty taverns typical of a harbor town. There may not be a huge range of restaurants, but what they serve is delicious.

Prices in the reviews are the average cost of a main course at dinner, or if dinner is not served, at lunch. Use the coordinates (✥ B2) at the end of each listing to locate a site on the corresponding map.

WHAT IT COSTS IN EUROS				
	$	$$	$$$	$$$$
AT DINNER	under €15	€15–€20	€21–€25	over €25

ALTSTADT AND NEUSTADT

$$ FRENCH 🍴 **Café Paris.** A slice of Paris in the heart of Hamburg, this turn-of-the-19th-century café's unfailing popularity derives from its superb traditional French fare, which naturally includes steak frites and beef tartare, served by crisply polite staff beneath a tiled art nouveau ceiling. Tables may be hard to secure without a reservation at usual dining times late in the week and on weekends, but the café's bar is an ideal spot to take in the atmosphere and sample something off the superb wine list until one becomes free. [$] *Average main: €20* ✉ *Rathausstr. 4, Altstadt* ☎ *040/3252–7777* 🌐 *www.cafeparis.net* [M] *Rathaus (U-bahn)* ✥ *F5.*

$$$ GERMAN 🍴 **Deichgraf.** This small and elegant fish restaurant in the heart of the historic district is a Hamburg classic. It's one of the best places to get traditional dishes such as *Hamburger Pannfisch* (fried pieces of the day's catch in a wine-and-mustard sauce) at a very reasonable price. The restaurant is in an old merchant house, and oil paintings in the dining room feature ships from the 19th century. Reservations are essential on weekends. [$] *Average main: €22* ✉ *Deichstr. 23, Altstadt* ☎ *040/364–208* 🌐 *www.deichgraf-hamburg.de* 🕒 *Closed Mon.* [M] *Rödingsmarkt (U-bahn)* ✥ *E6.*

$$$$ FRENCH 🍴 **Die Bank.** Venture beyond the grand exterior of this 19th-century bank building and you'll find yourself in an elegant bar and brasserie lighted by opulent chandeliers set in a ceiling supported by handsome black columns. Diners can feast on steaks, goose, and sashimi at white-clothed tables or out on the restaurant's spacious, sunny terrace. [$] *Average main: €28* ✉ *Hohe Bleichen 17, Neustadt* ☎ *040/238–0030* 🌐 *www.diebank-brasserie.de* 🕒 *Closed Sun.* [M] *Gänsemarkt (U-bahn)* ✥ *E5.*

$$$ GERMAN Fodor's Choice ★ 🍴 **Fillet of Soul.** The art of fine contemporary European cuisine is on display at this hip, yet casual restaurant set among the modern art exhibits of the Deichtorhallen. The minimalist dining room fills rapidly for lunch and dinner every day, its guests drawn to dishes that combine fresh, organic produce such as apricot-and-ginger-glazed ling with yellow turnips or grilled chicken breast with mushroom risotto and hollandaise sauce. Although it's not as sophisticated as the evening's offerings, the lunch menu here is still very good—and with most dishes hovering around €10, it's also a great value for money. [$] *Average main: €23* ✉ *Deichtorstr. 2, Altstadt* ☎ *040/7070–5800* 🌐 *www.fillet-of-soul.de* 🕒 *No dinner Sun. and Mon.* [M] *Steinstrasse (U-bahn)* ✥ *G6.*

$$ GERMAN 🍴 **Parlament.** Snugly sited beneath vaulted ceilings in the cellar of the city's town hall, this elegant old pub turned restaurant and cocktail bar

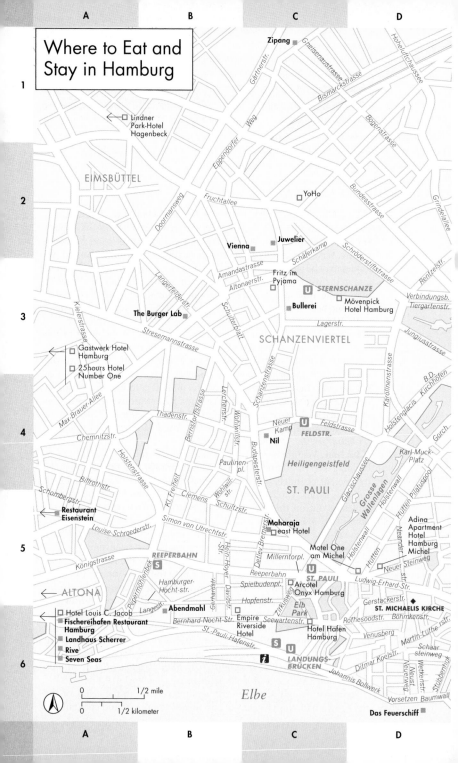

Where to Eat and Stay in Hamburg

A   **B**   **C**   **D**

1

Zipang

Gneisenaustrasse
Gartnerstr.
Weg
Eppendorfer
Bismarckstrasse
Hoheluftchaussee
Bogenstrasse

Lindner
Park-Hotel
Hagenbeck

2

EIMSBÜTTEL
Doormansweg
Fruchtallee
YoHo
Bundesstrasse
Grindelallee

Juwelier
Vienna
Schäferkamp
Schröderstiftstrasse
Rentzelstr.

Amandastrasse
Altonaerstr.
Fritz im
Pyjama
U STERNSCHANZE
Verbindungsbe.
Tiergartenstr.

3

Langenfelderstr.
Kielerstrasse
The Burger Lab
Schulterblatt
Stresemannstrasse
Bullerei
Mövenpick
Hotel Hamburg
SCHANZENVIERTEL
Lagerstr.
Junggiusstrasse

Gastwerk Hotel
Hamburg
25hours Hotel
Number One
Schanzenstrasse
Karolinenstrasse
Holstenglacis
B.D.
Kirchhöfen

4

Max-Brauer-Allee
Chemnitzstr.
Thadenstr.
Bernstorffstrasse
Lerchenstr.
Wohlwillstr.
Budapesterstr.
Neuer
Kamp
U FELDSTR.
Feldstrasse
Nil
Heiligengeistfeld
Karl-Muck-Platz
Gorch

5

Biltrothstr.
Schombergstr.
Holstenstrasse
Kr. Freiheit
Clemens
Wohlwill-str.
Schultzstr.
Paulinen-pl.
Simon von Utrechtstr.
Detlev Bremerstr.
Maharaja
east Hotel
Motel One
am Michel
ST. PAULI
Glacischaussee
Grosse
Wallanlagen
Holstenwall
Hütten Plataspool
Adina
Apartment
Hotel
Hamburg
Michel

Restaurant
Eisenstein
Louise-Schroederstr.
Königstrasse
REEPERBAHN
S
Hamburger-
Hocht-str.
Hein-Hoyer-Str.
Millerntorpl.
Reeperbahn
Spielbudenpl.
Hopfenstr.
U ST. PAULI
Arcotel
Onyx Hamburg
Ludwig-Erhard-Str.
Holstenwall
Hütten
Neuer Steinweg

6

ALTONA
Pepermöhlenbek
Langestr.
Abendmahl
Bernhard-Nocht-Str.
St.-Pauli-Hafenstr.
Empire
Riverside
Hotel
Seewartenstr.
Elb
Park
Zirkusweg
Hotel Hafen
Hamburg
Venusberg
Gerstackerstr.
ST. MICHAELIS KIRCHE
Rothesoodstr.
Böhmkenstr.
Martin-Luther-Str.
Schaar
steinweg
Ditmar Koelstr.
Neust.
Neuerweg
Wetkenstr.
Vorsetzen Baumwall
Stubbenhuk

Hotel Louis C. Jacob
Fischereihafen Restaurant
Hamburg
Landhaus Scherrer
Rive
Seven Seas
S U LANDUNGS-
BRÜCKEN
i
Johannis Bollwerk
Das Feuerschiff

Elbe

0   1/2 mile
0   1/2 kilometer

A   **B**   **C**   **D**

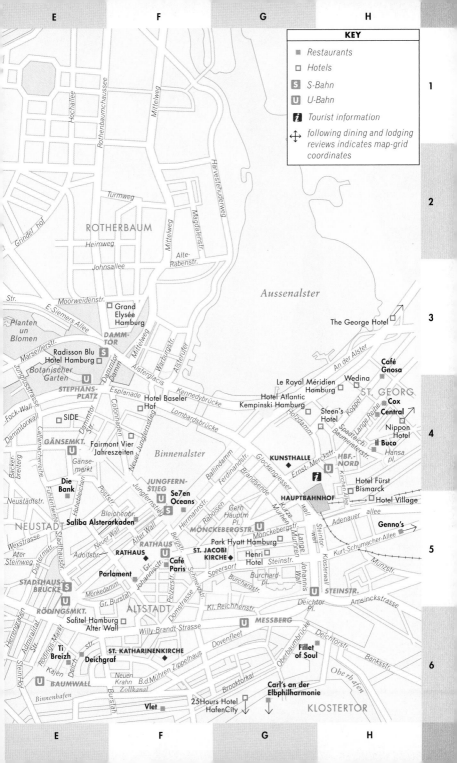

serves no-nonsense meat and fish meals, including shrimp fresh from the North Sea, with a light touch of German nouvelle cuisine. Popular with local businesspeople during and after work, it's also a nice spot for a frothy beer and some *Flammkuchen*, Alsace's take on pizza, between traipsing around the nearby sights. $ *Average main: €20* ✉ *Rathausmarkt 1, Altstadt* ☎ *040/7038–3399* ⊕ *www.parlament-hamburg.de* ☾ *Closed Sun.* Ⓜ *Rathaus (U-Bahn)* ✛ *F5.*

$$$
MIDDLE EASTERN

✕ **Saliba Alsterarkaden.** On the edge of a canal and beneath the arches of the elegant Alster arcade, this popular Syrian meze restaurant enjoys superb views of Hamburg's town hall. Naturally, the best tables in the house are actually outside and fill up quickly when the sun shines. While it specializes in lamb dishes, including homemade sausages, Saliba's menu also caters to vegetarian and vegan diners with offerings of falafels in harissa sauce and eggplant with dates and almonds. Wines to wash down the small plates of meze include whites from Germany and reds from Lebanon. $ *Average main: €21* ✉ *Neuer Wall 13, Neustadt* ☎ *040/345–021* ⊕ *www.saliba.de* Ⓜ *Jungfernstieg (U-bahn and S-bahn)* ✛ *F5.*

$$$$
ECLECTIC

✕ **Se7en Oceans.** It may not have the best location, inside a busy shopping mall, but this intriguing combination of a Michelin-starred restaurant, sushi bar, bistro, and cigar lounge is worth a visit nonetheless. On the upper floor (OG2) of the large Europa Passage mall, Se7ven Oceans has a wall of windows to provide amazing views of the inner Alster lake and Jungfernstieg. Promoting itself as a "multidimensional" culinary experience, the restaurant aims to cater to every size of wallet and appetite, with foie gras and lobster in the Gourmet Restaurant, sashimi and sake in the Sushi Bar, or cocktails and chicken wings at the Oceans Bar. The sushi bar is a great option for lunch. It's reasonably priced and rarely crowded. $ *Average main: €30* ✉ *Europa Passage, Ballindamm 40, Altstadt* ☎ *40/3250–7944* ⊕ *www.se7en-oceans.de* ▭ *No credit cards* ☾ *Gourmet Restaurant closed Sun. and Tues. Sushi Bar closed Sun.* ⌂ *Reservations essential* Ⓜ *Jungfernstieg (U-bahn and S-bahn)* ✛ *F5.*

$
FRENCH
Fodor'sChoice
★

✕ **Ti Breizh.** Stepping into this 18th-century merchant's house turned Breton crêpe restaurant, with its elegant white walls and sky-blue window frames, is a little like being transported to a seaside eatery in northern France. Waitstaff in striped fishermen's shirts and speaking with heavy French accents take orders for fantastically good galettes (buckwheat crêpes) topped with ham, cheese, mushrooms, and fried eggs, and uncork bottles of cider to wash them down. French chansons emanate from the sound system, and through the windows the Nikolaifleet canal can be seen. An unfailingly popular slice of Brittany in Hamburg, Ti Breizh's caramelized apple, banana, almond, and vanilla ice-cream crêpe is worth a visit alone. $ *Average main: €9* ✉ *Deichstr. 39, Altstadt* ☎ *040/3751–7815* ⊕ *www.tibreizh.de* Ⓜ *Rödingsmarkt (U-bahn), Baumwall (U-bahn)* ✛ *E6.*

ST. PAULI AND SCHANZENVIERTEL

$$
MEDITERRANEAN

✕**Abendmahl.** On a quiet square off the Reeperbahn, Abendmahl is a great launching point for a night out on the town. Candlelight, wooden tables, and a deep red interior set the tone. Relaxed yet romantic, it's the type of place where you can show up in everything from jeans and a T-shirt to a suit, and still get the same attentive service. In addition to a small selection of primarily Mediterranean and northern German dishes on the à la carte menu, there's also a four-course menu that changes daily. $ *Average main: €19* ✉ *Hein-Köllisch-Pl. 6, St. Pauli* ☎ *040/312–758* ⊕ *www.restaurantabendmahl.de* ▭ *No credit cards* Ⓜ *Reeperbahn (S-bahn)* ✛ *B6.*

> ### CAFÉ CULTURE
>
> The area around the Alster lakes and the canals is dotted with small restaurants with outside dining and an excellent selection of wine. They make good places to discover a refreshing *Grauburgunder* (Pinot Gris) while watching swans glide on the canal waters, sample classic French fare, or sip a perfect cup of coffee at one of the cafés sprinkled throughout central Hamburg.

$$$
STEAKHOUSE

✕**Bullerei.** The success of this extremely popular café and restaurant derives from its celebrity-chef ownership—Tim Mälzer, an old friend of Jamie Oliver, is a regular TV presence—its location in a former livestock hall in the heart of the Schanze, and its heavy emphasis on quality cuts of meat. Every night, the busy but friendly waitstaff ferries large plates of steak and pork through an interior of exposed brickwork and pipes, while diners dig into bowls of lamb, pork, and veal Bolognese in the white-tiled "deli" next door. If you can't get a table, grab a place at the busy bar and eat there instead. $ *Average main: €25* ✉ *Lagerstr. 34 B, Schanzenviertel* ☎ *040/3344–2100* ⊕ *www.bullerei.com* ☉ *No lunch at restaurant* ⌂ *Reservations essential* Ⓜ *Sternschanze (U-bahn and S-bahn)* ✛ *C3.*

$$$
MODERN
EUROPEAN

✕**Juwelier.** Despite its luxurious name (which means "Jeweler"), this excellent little restaurant not far from Schanzenpark is anything but ostentatious. Its wood tables are covered in white tablecloths, and the cream-color walls are gently lit by art deco lamp shades. Featuring a small number of starters and desserts and single vegetarian, fish, and meat options, the menu is similarly austere, but in terms of choice rather than the quality of contemporary European cuisine prepared from seasonal and regional produce. Dishes such as flat-headed mullet with ratatouille and risotto or leg of lamb with cassoulet and baby potatoes can be ordered individually or in three- to five-course variations. $ *Average main: €21* ✉ *Weidenallee 27, Schanzenviertel* ☎ *040/2548–1678* ⊕ *www.juwelier-restaurant.de* ▭ *No credit cards* ☉ *Closed Sun. and Mon. No lunch* Ⓜ *Christuskirche (U-bahn), Sternschanze (U-bahn and S-bahn)* ✛ *C2.*

$
INDIAN

✕**Maharaja.** Such is the popularity of this occasionally hectic little Indian restaurant in the heart of St. Pauli, a table booking doesn't always mean you'll be seated at the time you booked, especially if it's the weekend. The high quality of its vegetable and meat dishes—Himalayan *kofta* (vegetables and cheese mixed into balls and served with a tomato, cashew nut, and fruit sauce) and *rogan josh* (lamb cooked with red onions, peppers, and *paneer*) among them—combined with the coziness of its shabby-chic styling is enough to forgive the inconvenience, however. [$] *Average main: €14* ✉ *Detlev-Bremer-Str. 25–27, St. Pauli* ☎ *040/3009–3466* 🌐 *www.maharaja-hamburg.de* 🕒 *No lunch weekends* ✍ *Reservations essential* [M] *St. Pauli (U-bahn)* ✥ *C5.*

$$$ GERMAN 🍴 **Nil.** The simple but cool style, excellent service, and high-quality food at this busy bistro keep the locals coming back. The focus is on seafood and modern German dishes, with seasonal variations using local produce. Inventive four-course menus merge typical German cuisine with international flavors. [$] *Average main: €21* ✉ *Neuer Pferdemarkt 5, St. Pauli* ☎ *040/439–7823* 🌐 *www.restaurant-nil.de* 💳 *No credit cards* 🕒 *Closed Tues. No lunch* ✍ *Reservations essential* [M] *Feldstrasse (U-bahn)* ✥ *C4.*

ST. GEORG

$ GERMAN 🍴 **Café Gnosa.** A stalwart of Hamburg's gay and lesbian neighborhood, this local favorite is probably best known for its friendly service and outrageously good cakes—spiced apple; rhubarb; and Black Forest gâteau among them—that are baked on-site in the café's own Konditorei. Beyond its sweet treats, the café whips up solid German breakfasts of bread rolls with smoked salmon and herring or cold cuts and cheeses, and has a dependable if somewhat unexciting menu featuring pasta, schnitzel, and salads for lunch and dinner. [$] *Average main: €9* ✉ *Lange Reihe 93, St. Georg* ☎ *040/243–034* 🌐 *www.gnosa.de* 💳 *No credit cards* [M] *Lohmühlenstrasse (U-bahn), Gurlittstrasse (Bus No. M6)* ✥ *H3.*

$$ MODERN EUROPEAN 🍴 **Central.** Aptly situated in the middle of St. Georg's main drag, this trendy yet friendly eatery justifies a visit for its good-sized yet varied menu that includes the likes of teriyaki steak and wasabi burgers and house-made gnocchi with mushrooms, sage butter, and apple chutney. All the meat and fish served here is organic, and the Mediterranean-style vegetarian dishes are prepared with seasonal produce. Styling itself as a classic yet modern dining experience, Central's narrow, minimally decorated dining room can feel a little overcrowded on busy nights, and the use of projections to create a mood will feel a little dated to some. [$] *Average main: €20* ✉ *Lange Reihe 50, St. Georg* ☎ *040/2805–3704* 🌐 *www.central-hamburg.de* 🕒 *No lunch weekends* [M] *Gurlittstrasse (Bus M6), Hauptbahnhof (U-bahn and S-Bahn)* ✥ *H4.*

$$ GERMAN 🍴 **Cox.** Cox has delighted guests with its nouvelle German cuisine for years, and with a cool, dark interior and red-leather banquettes reminiscent of a French brasserie, it remains one of the hippest places around. Friday and Saturday nights see its two large rooms swell with diners, and consequently service can slow a little, but dishes such as red fish with miso and coriander or grilled chicken breast with spicy papaya relish, and a friendly, knowledgeable staff, easily compensate. [$] *Average main: €20* ✉ *Lange Reihe 68 at Greifswalder Str. 43, St. Georg* ☎ *040/249–422* 🌐 *www.restaurant-cox.de* 🕒 *No lunch weekends* [M] *Gurlittstrasse (Bus M6), Hauptbahnhof (U-bahn and S-Bahn)* ✥ *H4.*

$$ ITALIAN 🍴 **Il Buco.** Hidden down a side street off Hansaplatz, this neighborhood favorite is easily missed, but it's worth seeking out for its excellent plates

of *vitello tonnato* (cold sliced veal with a creamy sauce), *saltimbocca* (marinated veal with prosciutto and herbs), and truffle pasta. Down a few steps from the street, diners find themselves in a narrow, yet cozy, dining room that's more grandmother's living room than downtown trattoria. This intimacy extends beyond the candlelight and banquette seating to the restaurant's amicable staff and spoken menu, which features many of the filling and comforting pasta, meat, and fish dishes typical of rustic Italian cuisine. $ *Average main: €18* ⊠ *Zimmerpforte 5, St. Georg* ☎ *040/247–310* ⊙ *Closed Sun. No lunch* Ⓜ *Hauptbahnhof (U-bahn and S-bahn)* ✛ *H4.*

SPEICHERSTADT AND HAFENCITY

$$$ ✕ **Carl's an der Elbphilharmonie.** This extension of the Hotel Louis C.
FRENCH   Jacob, at the edge of the Elbe and next to the site of the Elbphilharmonie, is a pleasure on many levels. The relaxed Bistro restaurant serves quiche, tartines, and other small dishes. The more formal Brasserie looks like typically Parisian brasserie and features a large bay window with excellent views of ships gliding up the Elbe. The French menu has touches of German flavors and local fish dishes, and service here is warm and knowledgeable. Below the two restaurants sits an elegant bar and the Kultur Salon, with live classical music concerts and jazz performances. $ *Average main: €25* ⊠ *Am Kaiserkai 69, HafenCity* ☎ *40/3003–22400* ⊕ *www.carls-brasserie.de* ⌂ *Reservations essential* Ⓜ *Baumwall (U-bahn)* ✛ *G6.*

$$$ ✕ **Das Feuerschiff.** This bright-red lightship served in the English Chan-
EUROPEAN   nel before it retired to the city harbor in 1989 and became a landmark restaurant, guesthouse, and pub. Local favorites such as Hamburger Pannfisch (panfried fish with mustard sauce) and Labskaus (a mixture of corned beef, potato, onion, beet, and, if you're brave, herring) are on the ship's extensive menu, along with Argentinean steaks and rack of lamb. Head along on a Monday night to listen to live jazz. $ *Average main: €22* ⊠ *City Sporthafen, Vorsetzen, Speicherstadt* ☎ *040/362–553* ⊕ *www.das-feuerschiff.de* Ⓜ *Baumwall (U-bahn)* ✛ *D6.*

$$$ ✕ **Vlet.** Much like its setting inside a Speicherstadt warehouse, where
GERMAN   exposed bricks and beams are offset by sleek furniture and lighting, Vlet's menu blends traditional German methods with new techniques. The restaurant's Labskaus, for example, is a twist on the old Hamburg favorite of beef, potato, and beet and made as a clear soup instead of a stew. The kitchen also offers diverse à la carte menus, including a tasting menu that can be accompanied by corresponding glasses of wine, and the permanent "Durable" menu, which includes beef tartare prepared at the table. Although service is formal, the dining room is relaxed. $ *Average main: €24* ⊠ *Am Sandtorkai 23/24, entrance at Kibbelstegbrücke, Speicherstadt* ☎ *040/3347–53750* ⊕ *www.vlet.de* ⊙ *Closed Sun. No lunch Sat.* Ⓜ *Überseequartier (U-bahn)* ✛ *F6.*

ALTONA AND OTTENSEN

$ BURGER Fodor's Choice ★ 🍴 **The Burger Lab.** Somewhat ironically, for a long time it was very hard to find a decent hamburger in Hamburg. The last few years, however, have seen a number of very good hamburger joints sprout up around the city and this small restaurant sandwiched between the Schanzenviertel and Altona is perhaps the pick of the bunch. Set up by two Germans and a Kiwi, The Burger Lab grinds the beef for its gourmet burgers as well as whipping up their own excellent sauces, which include chipotle aioli and grilled onion. They don't take reservations, so if you're hankering for a lamb burger and some sweet-potato fries, it's worth getting there early to secure a table, particularly if you want to sit outside in summer. [$] *Average main: €9* ✉ *Max-Brauer-Allee 251, Altona* ☎ *040/4149–4529* 🌐 *www.theburgerlab.de* ✍ *Reservations not accepted* 💳 *No credit cards* [M] *Schulterblatt (Bus No. M15)* ✥ *B3.*

$$$$ SEAFOOD 🍴 **Fischereihafen Restaurant Hamburg.** For some of the best fish in Hamburg, book a table at this splendid port-side restaurant. Plain from the outside, the restaurant feels like a dining room aboard a luxury liner inside, with oil paintings of nautical scenes hanging on the walls and white linen on the tables. The menu changes daily according to what's available in the fish market that morning; the elegant oyster bar here is a favorite with the city's beau monde. In summer, try to get a table on the sun terrace for a great view of the Elbe. [$] *Average main: €29* ✉ *Grosse Elbstr. 143, Altona* ☎ *040/381–816* 🌐 *www.fischereihafenrestaurant.de* ✍ *Reservations essential* [M] *Altona (S-bahn), Dockland (Fischereihafen) (Bus No. 111), Königstrasse (S-bahn)* ✥ *A6.*

$$$$ GERMAN Fodor's Choice ★ 🍴 **Landhaus Scherrer.** A proud owner of a Michelin star since it opened its doors in 1978, Landhaus Scherrer continues to be one of the city's best-known and most celebrated restaurants. The focus is on the use of organic, sustainable ingredients to produce classic and modern German cuisine with international touches. Wood-panel walls and soft lighting create a low-key mood in the main building, which was once a brewery. Unsurprisingly, the accompanying wine list is exceptional. There's also a small bistro here, where diners can feast on similar fare at lower prices. For delicious German comfort food (currywurst and potato salad), try the sister property, Ö1. [$] *Average main: €40* ✉ *Elbchaussee 130, Ottensen* ☎ *040/8830–70030* 🌐 *www.landhausscherrer.de* ⏲ *Closed Sun.* ✍ *Reservations essential* [M] *Hohenzollernring (Bus Nos. M15 and 36)* ✥ *A6.*

$ ITALIAN 🍴 **Restaurant Eisenstein.** A long-time neighborhood favorite, Eisenstein sits inside a handsome 19th-century industrial complex turned art center and serves fantastic Italian and Mediterranean cuisine at affordable prices. Sharing space with a movie theater, the restaurant is popular with pre- and post-movie crowds and though it offers dishes such as herb-crusted veal steaks and fried gilthead sea bream, it's probably best known for its gourmet wood-fired pizzas. Well worth trying are the Pizza Helsinki (salmon, crème fraîche, and onions) and the Blöde Ziege (Stupid Goat) with rosemary-tomato sauce, crispy bacon, and goat cheese. [$] *Average main: €14* ✉ *Friedensallee 9, Ottensen* ☎ *040/390–4606* 🌐 *www.restaurant-eisenstein.de* 💳 *No credit cards* ✍ *Reservations essential* [M] *Altona (S-bahn)* ✥ *A5.*

13

$$$ SEAFOOD 🍴 **Rive.** It would be difficult to find a better spot in town than this handsome fish restaurant to watch big boats cruise by while satisfying your appetite for fresh lobster and oysters. Its ample sun terrace sits just above the Elbe, while the large open-plan dining room has ceiling-high windows facing downstream toward the city and the soon-to-be-completed Elbe Philharmonic Hall. With golden palms and sash curtains, it feels a bit like dining on a cruise ship. In addition to crustaceans and shellfish, diners can choose from a fairly extensive menu featuring sashimi, bouillabaisse, Scottish salmon, and Dover sole, as well as at least a couple of meat dishes. [$] *Average main: €25* ✉ *Kreuzfahrt-Center, Van-der-Smissen Str. 1, Altona* ☎ *040/380–5919* 🌐 *www.rive.de* ✍ *Reservations essential* [M] *Königstrasse (S-bahn), Dockland (Fischereihafen) (Bus No. 111)* ✥ *A6.*

BLANKENESE AND ELSEWHERE

$$$$ EUROPEAN Fodor's Choice ★ 🍴 **Seven Seas.** With a couple of Michelin stars, Karlheinz Hauser, one of Europe's premier chefs at the helm, and a spot high on a hill overlooking the Elbe, this restaurant of the Süllberg Hotel literally and figuratively is a cut above the competition. Naturally, with this lofty position come correspondingly high prices. Dishes can only be ordered in three- to eight-course set menus, and the full degustation menu, featuring scallops with Jerusalem artichokes and Iberian pork with corn and horseradish and accompanying glasses of wine, will set you back just over €300 per person. [$] *Average main: €36* ✉ *Süllbergsterrasse 12, Blankenese* ☎ *040/866–2520* 🌐 *www.suellberg-hamburg.de* 🕒 *Closed Mon. and Tues. No lunch Wed.–Fri.* ✍ *Reservations essential* [M] *Blankenese (S-bahn), Kahlkamp (Bus No. 48)* ✥ *A6.*

$$ EUROPEAN Fodor's Choice ★ 🍴 **Vienna.** The trick to getting a table at this much-loved little bistro in Eimsbüttel is to get there early. The kitchen officially opens for business at 7 pm, but Vienna opens its doors early in the afternoon for those wanting an espresso or apertif from their tiny bar. Early arrivers might still be asked to share a table in the dining room or outside in the courtyard but, given the lovingly prepared schnitzels, fresh fish dishes, and hearty desserts coming out of the kitchen, it will matter little to most. [$] *Average main: €17* ✉ *Fettstr. 2, Eimsbüttel* ☎ *040/439–9182* 🌐 *www.vienna-hamburg.de* 💳 *No credit cards* 🕒 *Closed Mon. No lunch* ✍ *Reservations not accepted* [M] *Christuskirche (U-bahn)* ✥ *C2.*

$$$ JAPANESE 🍴 **Zipang.** Hamburg may not have many good Japanese restaurants, but this modern bistro-style restaurant is undoubtedly a gem. On a long suburban artery of little eateries and clothes shops between Eppendorf and Eimsbüttel, Zipang has developed a loyal clientele of locals and Japanese expats through its warm service and modern interpretation of Japanese haute cuisine. As well as the typical offerings of sushi and tempura udon, the menu here features such treats as Wagyu beef with dipping sauces and duck and eggplant in red miso sauce. The restaurant also has a lunch special with a small miso soup and a dessert for around €10. [$] *Average main: €25* ✉ *Eppendorfer Weg 171, Eppendorf* ☎ *040/4328–0032* 🌐 *www.zipang.de* 🕒 *Closed Mon. No lunch Sun.–Wed.* [M] *Hoheluftbrücke (U-bahn)* ✥ *C1.*

WHERE TO STAY

Hamburg has simple pensions as well as five-star luxury enterprises. Nearly year-round conference and convention business keeps most rooms booked well in advance, and the rates are high. But many of the more expensive hotels lower their rates on weekends, when business-people have gone home. The tourist office can help with reservations if you arrive with nowhere to stay. In Hamburg, independent hotels may not have coffeemakers or an information book in the guest rooms, but, in general, you will find generously sized rooms and staff willing to answer questions about the hotel. Hotels without business centers will fax and copy for you. At hotels without concierges, front-desk staff will whip out a map and give recommendations.

All accommodations offer no-smoking rooms. Although breakfast is not generally included, those who opt for the meal are usually greeted with an all-you-can-eat masterpiece with hot food options that sometimes includes an omelet station.

Keep in mind that you'll probably encounter nudity in coed saunas at most hotels. Also, most double beds are made of two single beds on a large platform and an individual blanket for each mattress.

Prices in the reviews are the lowest cost of a standard double room in high season. For expanded reviews, facilities, and current deals, visit Fodors.com. Use the coordinates (⊕ B3) at the end of each listing to locate a site on the corresponding map.

WHAT IT COSTS IN EUROS				
	$	$$	$$$	$$$$
FOR TWO PEOPLE	under €100	€100–€175	€176–€225	over €225

ALTSTADT AND NEUSTADT

$$
HOTEL
FAMILY
Adina Apartment Hotel Hamburg Michel. With its position on a quiet backstreet and handsome apartments equipped with kitchenettes and fridges, the Adina will appeal to those who appreciate a few home comforts when they travel. **Pros:** excellent location; huge guest rooms with many amenities. **Cons:** indoor pool area is small; no real views. $ *Rooms from: €149* ⊠ *Neuer Steinweg 26, Altstadt* ☎ *040/226–3500* ⊕ *www.adina.eu* ⌁ *128 apartments* ❖ *No meals* Ⓜ *Stadhausbrücke (S-bahn)* ⊕ *D5.*

$$$$
HOTEL
Fodor's Choice
★
Fairmont Vier Jahreszeiten. Some claim that this beautiful 19th-century town house on the edge of the Binnenalster is the best hotel in Germany. **Pros:** luxury hotel with great view of Alster lakes; close to shopping on Jungfernstieg; large, charming rooms. **Cons:** high prices even in off-season; not much in way of nightlife outside of the hotel. $ *Rooms from: €495* ⊠ *Neuer Jungfernstieg 9–14, Neustadt* ☎ *040/34940* ⊕ *www. fairmont-hvj.de* ⌁ *123 rooms, 33 suites* ❖ *No meals* Ⓜ *Jungfernstieg (U-bahn and S-bahn)* ⊕ *F4.*

$$$ HOTEL **Grand Elysée Hamburg.** The "grand" here refers to its size, from the nearly 11,000-square-foot spa area and five restaurants to the 511 guest rooms and extra-wide beds. **Pros:** large, quiet guest rooms; close to tourist sites; diverse art throughout hotel. **Cons:** rooms' tasteful beiges won't set many hearts racing; public spaces can feel a little cold. [$] *Rooms from: €200* ✉ *Rothenbaumchaussee 10, Altstadt* ☎ *040/414–120* 🌐 *www.grand-elysee.com* 🛏 *494 rooms, 17 suites* 🍴 *No meals* [M] *Dammtor (S-bahn)* ✥ *F3.*

$$ HOTEL **Henri Hotel.** Concealed down a side street not far from the main station, this small boutique hotel, with its retro-styled rooms, furniture, and phones, will undoubtedly please fans of film noir and *Mad Men*. **Pros:** intimate, friendly service; very quiet; excellent house cocktail; stylish black-and-white-tiled bathrooms. **Cons:** may seem a little masculine for some tastes; on an otherwise uninspiring side street; limited nightlife in the area. [$] *Rooms from: €118* ✉ *Bugenhagenstr. 21, Altstadt* ☎ *040/554–3570* 🌐 *www.henri-hotel.com* 🛏 *65 rooms* 🍴 *No meals* [M] *Hauptbahnhof (U-bahn and S-bahn), Mönckebergstrasse (U-bahn)* ✥ *G5.*

$$ HOTEL **Hotel Baseler Hof.** It's hard to find fault with this handsome central hotel near the Binnenalster and the opera house; the service is friendly and efficient, the rooms are neatly albeit plainly furnished, and the prices are reasonable for such an expensive city. **Pros:** directly across from the casino; walking distance from Dammtor train station. **Cons:** small rooms; rooms at the front of the hotel face onto a busy street. [$] *Rooms from: €155* ✉ *Esplanade 11, Neustadt* ☎ *040/359–060* 🌐 *www.baselerhof.de* 🛏 *163 rooms, 9 suites* 🍴 *Breakfast* [M] *Stephansplatz (U-bahn)* ✥ *F4.*

$$ HOTEL **Hotel Fürst Bismarck.** Despite its slightly sketchy location on a busy street opposite the Hauptbahnhof, the Fürst Bismarck is a surprisingly attractive hotel that feels homey yet contemporary. **Pros:** centrally located; competitive prices; free pass for public transportation. **Cons:** basic bathrooms; small rooms; small additional fee for Wi-Fi. [$] *Rooms from: €133* ✉ *Kirchenallee 49, Altstadt* ☎ *040/7902–51640* 🌐 *www.fuerstbismarck.de* 🛏 *102 rooms* 🍴 *No meals* [M] *Hauptbahnhof (U-bahn and S-bahn)* ✥ *H4.*

$ HOTEL **Motel One Am Michel.** Perched at the end of the Reeperbahn, this branch of the Motel One chain is ideal for those looking for a trendy, design-minded, central yet inexpensive base. **Pros:** close to the best nightlife in town; bar open 24 hours; hard to beat value for money. **Cons:** no amenities; no restaurant; small rooms. [$] *Rooms from: €94* ✉ *Ludwig-Erhard-Str. 26, Altstadt* ☎ *040/3571–8900* 🌐 *www.motel-one.com* 🛏 *437 rooms* 🍴 *No meals* [M] *St. Pauli (U-bahn), Landungsbrücken (U-bahn and S-bahn)* ✥ *D5.*

$$$$ HOTEL Fodor's Choice ★ **Park Hyatt Hamburg.** Housed within the historic Levantehaus, a luxury mall on the city's main shopping drag, the Park Hyatt Hamburg delivers the hospitality and comfort expected of one of Germany's best hotels, with plush beds, marble bathrooms, and peace and quiet. **Pros:** close to museums; warm interior design; large, quiet rooms with all modern amenities; friendly and helpful service. **Cons:** area can feel dead on Sunday, when all the stores are closed; far from most nightlife. [$] *Rooms*

from: €235 ⊠ *Bugenhagenstr. 8, Neustadt* ☎ *040/3332–1234* ⊕ *www. hamburg.park.hyatt.com* ↪ *176 rooms, 21 suites, 31 apartments* ⫿⊙⫿ *No meals* Ⓜ *Mönckebergstrasse (U-bahn)* ✛ *G5.*

$$ 🛏 **Radisson Blu Hotel, Hamburg.** There's no missing the black glass and
HOTEL gray concrete form of the Radisson Blu, which towers 330 feet above
Dammtor train station, with sweeping views of Planten un Blomen and
the city. **Pros:** some of the best views in town; award-winning nightclub;
next to a major train station; super-fast Internet. **Cons:** small gym;
lower-floor rooms have no real view; few good restaurants in immediate
area. ⑧ *Rooms from: €175* ⊠ *Marseiller Str. 2, Neustadt* ☎ *040/35020*
⊕ *www.radissonblu.de* ↪ *547 rooms, 9 suites* ⫿⊙⫿ *No meals* Ⓜ *Dammtor (S-bahn)* ✛ *E3.*

$$ 🛏 **SIDE.** Futuristic, minimalistic—call it what you like, but this hip five-
HOTEL star hotel has been a byword for inner city cool since its opening in
2001. **Pros:** within a short wander of many major sights and attractions;
convenient but quiet location. **Cons:** some might find interior design
sterile; most guest rooms lack views. ⑧ *Rooms from: €160* ⊠ *Drehbahn
49, Neustadt* ☎ *040/309–990* ⊕ *www.side-hamburg.de* ↪ *168 rooms,
10 suites* ⫿⊙⫿ *No meals* Ⓜ *Gänsemarkt (U-bahn)* ✛ *E4.*

$$$ 🛏 **Sofitel Hamburg Alter Wall.** Behind the facade of a centrally located, for-
HOTEL mer Deutsche Post building hides the sleek style and famously comfort-
able beds of one of the city's finest business hotels. **Pros:** in the historic
downtown area; close to luxury shops; large rooms. **Cons:** somewhat
cold design; no real nightlife within walking distance. ⑧ *Rooms from:
€215* ⊠ *Alter Wall 40, Altstadt* ☎ *040/369–500* ⊕ *www.sofitel.com*
↪ *223 rooms, 18 suites* ⫿⊙⫿ *No meals* Ⓜ *Rödingsmarkt (U-bahn)* ✛ *F6.*

ST. PAULI AND SCHANZENVIERTEL

$$ 🛏 **Arcotel Onyx Hamburg.** Moored at the start of the Reeperbahn, like
HOTEL a giant spaceship that's just touched down, this black-glass monolith
houses a welcoming design hotel ideal for those who want to just dip
their toes into the waters of the red-light district. **Pros:** close to a number
of attractions, including St. Michaelis and the harbor; just across from
St. Pauli U-bahn; unique experience; exciting part of town. **Cons:** no
real views, even from upper floors; buffet area in breakfast room can get
overcrowded; designer furniture and carpets won't be to eveyone's taste.
⑧ *Rooms from: €120* ⊠ *Reeperbahn 1 A, St. Pauli* ☎ *040/209–4090*
⊕ *www.arcotelhotels.com* ↪ *204 rooms, 9 suites, 2 apartments* ⫿⊙⫿ *No
meals* Ⓜ *St. Pauli (U-bahn)* ✛ *C5.*

$$$ 🛏 **east Hotel.** Not content to limit itself to merely being a place to sleep,
HOTEL this chic landmark hotel combines a buzzing cocktail bar with a simi-
Fodor'sChoice larly trendy sushi and steak restaurant to create one of the hottest
★ spots in town. **Pros:** unique design and atmosphere; popular nightclub
on fourth floor (Friday and Saturday only); excellent service. **Cons:**
area around the hotel can be frenetic on weekends; parking garage is
removed from main building; open bathrooms not for those who prefer
privacy. ⑧ *Rooms from: €190* ⊠ *Simon-von-Utrecht-Str. 31, St. Pauli*
☎ *040/309–930* ⊕ *www.east-hamburg.de* ↪ *122 rooms, 6 suites* ⫿⊙⫿ *No
meals* Ⓜ *St Pauli (U-bahn)* ✛ *C5.*

13

$$ HOTEL Fodor's Choice ★ 🏨 **Empire Riverside Hotel.** The prime location between the Reeperbahn and the harbor, the clever use of space and light, and a top-floor cocktail joint that attracts thousands every weekend make this a favorite with locals and out-of-towners alike. **Pros:** close to nightlife; excellent view of the city and river; bright rooms; free Wi-Fi. **Cons:** a steep hill separates the hotel from the harbor; top-floor bar gets crowded after 9 pm on weekends. [$] *Rooms from: €159* ✉ *Bernhard-Nocht-Str. 97, St. Pauli* ☎ *040/311–190* 🌐 *www.empire-riverside.de* 🛏 *315 rooms, 12 suites* 🍴 *No meals* [M] *Reeperbahn (S-bahn)* ⊕ *B6.*

$$ HOTEL 🏨 **Fritz im Pyjama.** Previously just a convenient spot to lay your head, this little hotel squeezed into an old apartment building in the center of the Schanzenviertel has been transformed by new ownership into fun, swinging-'60s-style accommodations. **Pros:** unique, funky accommodations; S- and U-bahn stations directly across the street; myriad eating and drinking options nearby. **Cons:** noise from nearby train tracks; area crowded on weekend nights; difficult to find parking. [$] *Rooms from: €115* ✉ *Schanzenstr. 101–103, Schanzenviertel* ☎ *040/8222–2830* 🌐 *www.fritz-im-pyjama.de* 🛏 *17 rooms* 🍴 *No meals* [M] *Sternschanze (U-bahn and S-bahn)* ⊕ *C3.*

$$ HOTEL 🏨 **Hotel Hafen Hamburg.** This harbor landmark, just across from the famous St. Pauli Landungsbrücken and a few streets back from the Reeperbahn, is a good value considering its four-star status. **Pros:** top location for harbor and St. Pauli sightseeing; in the heart of the city's best nightlife; Port restaurant serves good-quality Hanseatic fare. **Cons:** hotel spread between three separate buildings; a bit of a climb to reach hotel from the pier. [$] *Rooms from: €140* ✉ *Seewartenstr. 7–9, St. Pauli* ☎ *040/311–130* 🌐 *www.hotel-hafen-hamburg.de* 🛏 *380 rooms* 🍴 *No meals* [M] *Landungsbrücken (U-bahn and S-bahn)* ⊕ *C6.*

$$ HOTEL 🏨 **Mövenpick Hotel Hamburg.** For its Hamburg outpost, the Mövenpick chain transformed a 19th-century water tower on a hill in the middle of the leafy Schanzenpark into a state-of-the-art hotel. **Pros:** in the middle of a quiet park; unique building; amazing views from upper floors; English-language newspaper available in restaurant. **Cons:** modern styling will feel a little sterile to some; some lower-level rooms have ordinary views. [$] *Rooms from: €139* ✉ *Sternschanze 6, Schanzenviertel* ☎ *040/334–4110* 🌐 *www.movenpick.com* 🛏 *226 rooms, 10 suites* 🍴 *No meals* [M] *Sternschanze (U-bahn and S-bahn)* ⊕ *C3.*

ST. GEORG

$$$ HOTEL 🏨 **The George Hotel.** At the end of a strip of funky cafés and bars that stretches down from the central station, the George, with its groovy New British styling and renowned gin and whisky bar, fits right in. **Pros:** bar serves some of the best G&Ts in town; DJs play in the hotel on weekends; a stone's throw from the Alster. **Cons:** can be noisy, particularly for guests on the first floor; rooftop bar's lounge music won't be to everyone's taste; no gym. [$] *Rooms from: €185* ✉ *Barcastr. 3, St. Georg* ☎ *040/280–0300* 🌐 *www.thegeorge-hotel.de* 🛏 *118 rooms, 7 suites* 🍴 *No meals* [M] *Hauptbahnhof (U-bahn and S-bahn), AK St. Georg (Bus No. 6)* ⊕ *H3.*

$$$$ ▥ **Hotel Atlantic Kempinski Hamburg.** There are few hotels in Germany
HOTEL more sumptuous than this gracious Edwardian palace facing the Aussenalster, which draws both celebrities and the not-so-famous searching
for a luxe retreat. **Pros:** large rooms; great views of lakeside skyline;
impeccable service; historic flair. **Cons:** public areas can be crowded;
faces onto a busy thoroughfare. $ *Rooms from: €229* ⊠ *An der Alster
72–79, St. Georg* ☎ *040/28880* ⊕ *www.kempinski.com* ⤶ *188 rooms,
33 suites* ⦿ *No meals* Ⓜ *Hauptbahnhof (U-bahn and S-bahn)* ✛ *G4.*

$ ▥ **Hotel Village.** Near the central train station and once a thriving
HOTEL brothel, this hotel and its red-and-black carpets, glossy wallpaper, and
dinky chandeliers still exudes lasciviousness. **Pros:** in the heart of downtown; individually designed rooms; fun interior design; free coffee at
reception. **Cons:** sometimes casual service; although it's slowly being
gentrified, the neighborhood remains a little seedy. $ *Rooms from:
€90* ⊠ *Steindamm 4, St. Georg* ☎ *040/480–6490* ⊕ *www.hotel-village.
de* ⤶ *20 rooms, 3 suites, 4 apartments* ⦿ *No meals* Ⓜ *Hauptbahnhof
(U-bahn/S-bahn)* ✛ *H5.*

$$$ ▥ **Le Royal Méridien Hamburg.** This luxury hotel along the Alster oozes
HOTEL beauty inside and out, with contemporary art on view throughout—
including the elevator. **Pros:** great location with views of the Alster;
smartly designed, large rooms; more than 650 art works decorate the
hotel. **Cons:** basic gym facilities; top-floor bar and restaurant can be
crowded. $ *Rooms from: €189* ⊠ *An der Alster 52–56, St. Georg*
☎ *040/21000* ⊕ *www.leroyalmeridienhamburg.com* ⤶ *265 rooms, 19
suites* ⦿ *No meals* Ⓜ *Hauptbahnhof (U-bahn and S-bahn)* ✛ *H4.*

$ ▥ **Steen's Hotel.** This small, family-run hotel in a four-story town house
HOTEL near the central train station provides modest but congenial service.
Pros: highly competitive prices; good breakfast; friendly service.
Cons: rooms fairly plain; few amenities and hotel services; no eleva-
tor. $ *Rooms from: €95* ⊠ *Holzdamm 43, St. Georg* ☎ *040/244–642*
⊕ *www.steens-hotel.com* ⤶ *15 rooms* ⦿ *Breakfast* Ⓜ *Hauptbahnhof
(U-bahn and S-bahn)* ✛ *H4.*

$$ ▥ **Wedina.** A laid-back oasis in the bustling neighborhood of St. Georg,
HOTEL this unique small hotel is spread over four different buildings a short
Fodor'sChoice amble from the outer Alster. **Pros:** cozy, comfortable, and quiet rooms;
★ very accommodating; knowledgeable staff; great breakfast. **Cons:** hotel
spread over several buildings; smallish rooms. $ *Rooms from: €145*
⊠ *Gurlittstr. 23, St. Georg* ☎ *040/280–8900* ⊕ *www.hotelwedina.com*
⤶ *46 rooms, 13 apartments* ⦿ *Breakfast* Ⓜ *Hauptbahnhof (U-bahn
and S-bahn), Gurlittstrasse (Bus No. 6)* ✛ *H4.*

SPEICHERSTADT AND HAFENCITY

$$ ▥ **25Hours Hotel HafenCity.** Despite its bland, modern office block exte-
HOTEL rior, this trendy HafenCity hotel is full of fun, from guest rooms that
Fodor'sChoice resemble designer ship cabins to a chill-out room with retro couches
★ and a record player for guests to use. **Pros:** has a little shop selling
magazines and souvenirs; up-and-coming part of town; something
outside the norm. **Cons:** quiet, but directly across from a construc-
tion site; not a lot of other nightlife options within walking distance.

13

$ Rooms from: €135 ⊠ Überseeallee 5, Speicherstadt ☎ 040/257–7770 ⊕ www.25hours-hotels.com ⟿ 170 rooms ○ No meals M Übersee-quartier (U-bahn) ✛ G6.

ALTONA AND OTTENSEN

$$ **Gastwerk Hotel Hamburg.** Proudly dubbing itself Hamburg's first
HOTEL design hotel, the Gastwerk, named after the 120-year-old gasworks it's housed inside, is certainly one of the most stylish places to stay in town. **Pros:** free English-language newspapers; free use of a MINI car. **Cons:** removed from downtown area and most sightseeing spots; breakfast room, bar, and other public spaces can get crowded. $ Rooms from: €160 ⊠ Beim Alten Gaswerk 3, Altona ☎ 040/890–620 ⊕ www.gastwerk.com ⟿ 127 rooms, 14 suites ○ No meals M Bahrenfeld (S-bahn) ✛ A3.

$$ **25hours Hotel Number One.** Packing fun and retro design into a relaxed
HOTEL package that includes beanbag chairs, shag carpets, and bold wallpapers, this is the type of place for travelers seeking something a bit different. **Pros:** '60s and '70s retro style sets it apart; shopping center and supermarket nearby. **Cons:** removed from the city center; a 10-minute walk to the nearest train station. $ Rooms from: €135 ⊠ 2 Paul-Dessau-Str., Altona ☎ 040/855–070 ⊕ www.25hours-hotels.com ⟿ 128 rooms ○ No meals M Bahrenfeld (S-bahn) ✛ A3.

BLANKENESE AND ELSEWHERE

$$$$ **Hotel Louis C. Jacob.** Those who make the effort to travel 20 minutes
HOTEL from the center of town to this small yet luxurious hotel perched above
Fodor's Choice Elbe will gain a mixture of sophistication, Michelin-starred dining,
★ and fine Hanseatic hospitality. **Pros:** outstanding service with attention to personal requests; quiet, serene setting; historic building; extremely comfortable beds. **Cons:** lounge is a little stuffy; away from downtown area and most nightlife, restaurants, and shopping; expensive. $ Rooms from: €275 ⊠ Elbchaussee 401–403, Blankenese ☎ 040/822–550 ⊕ www.hotel-jacob.de ⟿ 66 rooms, 19 suites ○ No meals M Hochkamp (S-bahn) ✛ A6.

$$ **Lindner Park-Hotel Hagenbeck.** Everything at this hotel is aimed at
HOTEL transporting you from metropolitan Hamburg to the wilds of Asia and
FAMILY Africa. **Pros:** smartly designed Africa and Asia theme carried throughout hotel; a/c in guest rooms; good restaurant. **Cons:** removed from the city center; not much else going on in the immediate area. $ Rooms from: €149 ⊠ Hagenbeckstr. 150, Stellingen ☎ 040/8008–08100 ⊕ www.lindner.de ⟿ 151 rooms, 7 suites ○ No meals M Hagenbecks Tierpark (U-bahn) ✛ A1.

$$ **Nippon Hotel.** You'll be asked to remove your shoes before entering
HOTEL your room at this small but welcoming Japanese-style hotel, where tatami mats line the floor and shoji blinds cover the windows. **Pros:** quiet, residential neighborhood; a/c in guest rooms; unique experience. **Cons:** location removed from major sightseeing attractions; limited parking. $ Rooms from: €138 ⊠ Hofweg 75, Uhlenhorst ☎ 040/227–1140

⊕ *www.nipponhotel.de* ⤙41 *rooms, 1 suite* ◯◯ *No meals* Ⓜ *Munds-burg (U-bahn), Zimmerstrasse (Bus No. M6)* ✛ *H4.*

$ Ⓣ **YoHo.** Housed in a historic villa that's an easy walk from the Schan-
HOTEL zenviertel, this friendly, modern little hotel was originally designed and
priced to attract a young, cosmopolitan crowd, but has also found
favor among families and business travelers. **Pros:** quiet neighborhood;
reasonable prices without skimping on quality; free parking. **Cons:**
sometimes noisy due to young travelers; removed from all major sights.
$ *Rooms from: €99* ✉ *Moorkamp 5, Eimsbüttel* ☎ *040/284–1910*
⊕ *www.yoho-hamburg.de* ⤙30 *rooms* ◯◯ *No meals* Ⓜ *Christuskirche
(U-bahn), Schlump (U-bahn)* ✛ *C2.*

13

NIGHTLIFE AND PERFORMING ARTS

NIGHTLIFE

ALTSTADT AND NEUSTADT
JAZZ AND LIVE MUSIC
Cotton Club. A visit to the Cotton Club, Hamburg's oldest jazz club, is
worth it for the house beer alone. Throw in the club's relaxed vibe and
nights devoted to jazz, blues, soul, and Dixieland, and it's not difficult to
find a reason to drop in. ✉ *Alter Steinweg 10, Neustadt* ☎ *040/343–878*
⊕ *www.cotton-club.de* Ⓜ *Stadthausbrücke (S-bahn).*

ST. PAULI AND SCHANZENVIERTEL
Whether you think it sexy or seedy, the Reeperbahn and its nightlife
defines Hamburg as much as as the upscale department stores and boutiques on Jungfernstiegasse. St Pauli's main drag is peppered with bars
and clubs, while its most famous side street, Grosse Freiheit, heaves
with dance clubs every night of the week. Hans-Elber-Platz also has a
cluster of bars, some with live music.

BARS
Unsurprisingly for an area known as an entertainment district, St.
Pauli has an enormous spectrum of places to get a drink, from cheap
beer-and-shots dive bars to high-rise cocktail joints and everything in
between.

Christiansen's. Discreetly positioned on a quiet corner an easy meander
down from the Reeperbahn is one of St Pauli's coziest cocktail bars.
Inside, red leather stools flank an enormously well-stocked bar staffed
by knowledgeable and friendly bartenders. ✉ *Pinnasberg 60, St. Pauli*
☎ *040/317–2863* ⊕ *www.christiansens.de* ☽ *Closed Sun.* Ⓜ *Reeperbahn (S-bahn).*

Mandalay. With its fancy cocktails and "reservations recommended"
exclusivitiy, the Mandalay verges on being out of place among the
shabby-chic pubs and bars typical of the Schanzenviertel, but its sleek
styling and eclectic mix of swing, ambient, and disco nights ensures
its enduring popularity. ✉ *Neuer Pferdemarkt 13, Schanzenviertel*
☎ *040/4321–4922* ⊕ *www.mandalay-hamburg.de* ☽ *Closed Sun.–Tues.*
Ⓜ *Feldstrasse (U-bahn).*

Tower Bar at Hotel Hafen Hamburg. Facing stiff competition from a number of newly opened and similarly loftily perched cocktail joints, the Tower Bar may have aged a tad since its opening in 1987, but its service, reasonably priced drinks, and views over the harbor and city all remain good reasons to reserve a window table for a sundowner or two. ✉ *Seewartenstr. 9, St. Pauli* ☎ *040/31113–70450* ⊕ *www.hotel-hafen-hamburg.de* Ⓜ *Landungsbrücken (U-bahn and S-bahn).*

20up at the Empire Riverside Hotel. For a smooth cocktail, cool lounge music, and jaw-droppingly good views over the city and harbor, try this bar, which is one of the most popular nightspots in town. It's best to book ahead, particularly on weekends. ✉ *Bernhard-Nocht-Str. 97, St. Pauli* ☎ *040/31119–70470* ⊕ *www.empire-riverside.de* Ⓜ *Reeperbahn (S-bahn).*

Yakshi's Bar at the east Hotel. With its combination of exposed brickwork, soft lighting, and soothing, curvy shapes—not to mention a drinks menu that runs to more than 250 different drinks, shots, and cocktails—it's little wonder that this popular cocktail bar draws fashionable people of all ages. ✉ *Simon-von-Utrecht-Str. 31, St. Pauli* ☎ *040/309–930* ⊕ *www.east-hamburg.de* Ⓜ *St. Pauli (U-bahn).*

CABARET THEATER

Schmidts Theater and Schmidts Tivoli. The quirky Schmidt Theater and Schmidts Tivoli has become Germany's most popular variety theater, presenting a classy repertoire of live music, vaudeville, and cabaret. ✉ *Spielbudenpl. 24–28, St. Pauli* ☎ *040/3177–8899* ⊕ *www.tivoli.de* Ⓜ *Reeperbahn (S-bahn), St. Pauli (U-bahn).*

DANCE CLUBS

Mojo Club. After changing locations, the storied Mojo Club has been reborn and is now located beneath a spaceship-like hatch, which rises out of the sidewalk to allow in revelers who come to see live local and international acts, as well as DJs spinning jazz, funk, soul, and electronic beats. ✉ *Reeperbahn 1, St. Pauli* ☎ *040/319–1999* ⊕ *www.mojo.de* Ⓜ *St. Pauli (U-bahn), Reeperbahn (S-bahn).*

Stage Club. On the first floor of the Theater Neue Flora, the Stage Club is a popular spot with a mostly older crowd, who turn up to see acts as diverse as Adele, Nigel Kennedy, and Right Said Fred, and dance to Latin and '80s sounds. ✉ *Stresemannstr. 163, Schanzenviertel* ☎ *040/4316–5460* ⊕ *www.stageclub.de* Ⓜ *Holstenstr. (S-bahn).*

JAZZ AND LIVE MUSIC

Docks. There's a stylish bar here, as well as one of Hamburg's largest venues for live music acts from around the world. Once the stage has been cleared, techno and house parties keep Docks rocking late into the night. ✉ *Spielbudenpl. 19, St. Pauli* ☎ *040/317–8830* ⊕ *www.docks-prinzenbar.de* Ⓜ *St. Pauli (U-bahn), Reeperbahn (S-bahn).*

Grosse Freiheit 36. One of the best-known nightspots in town, Grosse Freiheit 36 has made its name as both a popular venue for big names from around the world and as the location of the Kaiserkeller, a nightclub where the Beatles once played that's still going strong. ✉ *Grosse Freiheit 36, St. Pauli* ☎ *040/317–7780* ⊕ *www.grossefreiheit36.de* Ⓜ *Reeperbahn (S-bahn), St. Pauli (U-bahn).*

HIP AND HAPPENING NIGHTLIFE

People flock to Hamburg for shopping, but there's much more to experience come nightfall. The city has plenty of places where you can hop from bar to bar or lounge to lounge. Here are some of the most fun streets in Hamburg:

Grindelallee and side streets in the Univiertel: Home to the Universität der Hamburg, the quarter, with its mix of affordable cafés and Asian and Middle Eastern restaurants, is popular with students and townies alike.

Grosse Elbstrasse in Altona: This is the home of the Altona Fischmarkt and a variety of popular riverside restaurants and bars.

Grossneumarkt: This square is packed with comfortable, relaxing pubs and German restaurants. In summer it's a popular meeting point for Hamburgers who want to sit outside and eat and drink in relaxed surroundings.

Reeperbahn, Grosse Freiheit, and the streets around Spielbuden-platz in St. Pauli: This sinful mile has everything—strip clubs, pubs, live music, dive bars, and nightclubs. It's loud and crazy and fun just to walk up and down the streets.

Schanzenstrasse in Sternschanze: Hipsters flock to this compact row of buzzing bars and laid-back lounges that pour onto the sidewalk when the weather is warm.

Indra Club. The Beatles' first stop on the road to fame was the Indra Club. The club's owner, Bruno Koschmider, asked for one thing, and that was a wild show. These days, the Indra is still a nightclub, with live music acts nearly every night. ⊠ *Grosse Freiheit 64, St. Pauli* ⊕ *www. indramusikclub.com* Ⓜ *Reeperbahn (S-bahn), St. Pauli (U-bahn).*

PUBS

Altes Mädchen. Beer fans will be hard-pressed to find a better spot in town to sample that amber nectar. With a number of local beers on tap and more than 60 craft beers to order from, plus a decent selection of German pub food, it's unsurprising that this gastropub has maintained a glowing reputation since opening in early 2013. ⊠ *Lagerstr. 28b, Schanzenviertel* ☎ *040/8000–77750* ⊕ *www.altes-maedchen.com* Ⓜ *Sternschanze (U-bahn and S-bahn).*

Gretel und Alfons. Northern Germans are not best known for mingling, but at this small pub in the middle of Grosse Freiheit, you can strike up a conversation with the person sitting next to you. Perhaps that's why it was a firm favorite with the Beatles, who could often be found here when not performing at a number of clubs on the street. ⊠ *Grosse Freiheit 29, St. Pauli* ☎ *040/313–491* ⊕ *www.gretelundalfons.de* Ⓜ *Reeperbahn (S-bahn), St. Pauli (U-bahn).*

ST. GEORG

BARS

Bar DaCaio at the George Hotel. This bar has a black-on-black design, good looks all over, great service, and endless drink options. It's also within one of the hottest hotels in town. ⊠ *Barcastr. 3, St. Georg*

☎ *040/280–0300* ⊕ *www.thegeorge-hotel.de* Ⓜ *Hauptbahnhof (U-bahn and S-bahn), AK St. Georg (Bus No. 6).*

DANCE CLUBS

Golden Cut. Just across from the main train station, this place swells on weekends with a fairly chic crowd who party to DJs pumping out house, hip-hop, and electronic sounds. ⊠ *Holzdamm 61, St. Georg* ☎ *040/8510–3532* ⊕ *www.goldencut.org* Ⓜ *Hauptbahnhof (U-bahn).*

PERFORMING ARTS

The arts flourish in this cosmopolitan city. Hamburg's ballet company is one of the finest in Europe, and the Hamburger Ballett-Tage, its annual festival, brings the best from around the world to the city.

At the end of September, the city comes alive with movie showings. The Hamburg Film Festival features the best feature films, documentaries, short films, and children's movies. About 80% of the films are in English or have English subtitles. For two weeks, thousands of people watch mainstream and quirky films in various theaters around town.

Information on all major events is available on the Hamburg Tourism Office website. ■TIP➡ **The best way to order tickets for all major Hamburg theaters, musicals, and most cultural events is through the Hamburg-Hotline (040/3005–1300).**

TICKETS

Funke Konzertkassen. Hamburg's largest ticket seller has box offices throughout Hamburg, including one at Dammtor train station with English-speaking agents. The website is only in German, but a ticket hotline will connect you with English-speaking representatives. ⊠ *Dammtorbahnhof, Dag-Hammarskjöldpl. 15, Neustadt* ☎ *040/4501–18676* ⊕ *www.funke-ticket.de* Ⓜ *Stephansplatz (U-bahn).*

Hamburg.de. The city's official website is a good source for information about cultural and arts events in the city. Just click on the "What's on" tab. ⊠ *Hamburg* ⊕ *www.english.hamburg.de.*

Landungsbrücken. A number of agencies, including the Hamburg tourist office at Landungsbrücken, sell tickets for plays, concerts, and the ballet. Tickets can also be booked online or via the hotline in English. ⊠ *Between Brücke (Piers) 4 and 5, St. Pauli* ☎ *040/3005–1701* ⊕ *www.hamburg-travel.com* Ⓜ *Landungsbrücken (S-bahn).*

Stage Entertainment. Tickets and information about musicals currently running in Hamburg are available online or by calling the pay-per-minute hotline. ☎ *01805/4444* ⊕ *www.stage-entertainment.de/.*

BALLET AND OPERA

Hamburgische Staatsoper. One of the most beautiful theaters in the country, the Hamburgische Staatsoper is the leading northern German venue for opera and ballet. The Hamburg Ballet has been directed by the renowned American choreographer John Neumeier since 1973. ⊠ *Grosse Theaterstr. 25, Neustadt* ☎ *040/356–868* ⊕ *www.hamburgische-staatsoper.de* Ⓜ *Stephansplatz (U-bahn), Gänsemarkt (U-bahn).*

Stage Operettenhaus. The Stage Operettenhaus stages productions of top musicals including the musical adaptation of *Rocky*, and *Love Never Die s*, the follow-up to *The Phantom of the Opera*. Tours of the theater are also available. ✉ *Spielbudenpl. 1, St. Pauli* ☎ *01805/4444 ticket hotline (pay per minute), 040/311–170 theater* ⊕ *www.stage-entertainment.de* Ⓜ *St. Pauli (U-bahn), Reeperbahn (S-bahn).*

CONCERTS

Laeiszhalle. Both the Philharmoniker Hamburg (Hamburg Philharmonic) and the Hamburger Symphoniker (Hamburg Symphony) appear regularly in the magnificent neo-baroque interior of the Laeiszhalle, which also hosts international orchestras and some of the biggest names in contemporary music. ✉ *Johannes-Brahms-Pl., Neustadt* ☎ *040/3576–6666* ⊕ *www.elbphilharmonie.de* Ⓜ *Messehallen (U-bahn), Gänsemarkt (U-bahn).*

FILM

Abaton. Both dubbed into German and in the original language with subtitles, mainstream, art-house, and independent films are shown at this comfy, three-screen movie theater next to the University of Hamburg. ✉ *Allendepl. 3, Neustadt* ☎ *040/320–320* ⊕ *www.abaton.de* Ⓜ *Hallerstrasse (U-bahn).*

Savoy Filmtheater. The Savoy's a fantastic, old-school movie theater with impressive modern features that include high-quality sound and enormous, reclinable leather seats. It shows mainstream and independent movies in English. ✉ *Steindamm 54, St. Georg* ☎ *040/2840–93628* ⊕ *www.savoy-filmtheater.de* Ⓜ *Lohmühlenstrasse (U-bahn), Hauptbahnhof Sud (U-bahn and S-bahn).*

THEATER

Deutsches Schauspielhaus. One of Germany's leading drama stages, Deutsches Schauspielhaus has been lavishly restored to its full 19th-century opulence. It's the most important venue in town for classical and modern theater. ✉ *Kirchenallee 39, St. Georg* ☎ *040/248–710* ⊕ *www.schauspielhaus.de* Ⓜ *Huptbahnhof (U-bahn).*

English Theatre of Hamburg. The name says it all: the English Theatre, first opened in 1976, is the city's premier theater for works in English. Actors from near and far bring contemporary and classic drama to life on the small stage of this historic building. ✉ *Lerchenfeld 14, Uhlenhorst* ☎ *040/227–7089* ⊕ *www.englishtheatre.de* Ⓜ *Mundsburg (U-bahn).*

Neue Flora Theater. Handily located just across the street from the Holstenstrasse S-bahn, the 2,000-seat Neue Flora attracts big crowds, who come for popular, long-running musicals such as *Tarzan* and *The Phantom of the Opera*. ✉ *Stresemannstr. 159a at Alsenstr., Schanzenviertel* ☎ *01805/4444 ticket hotline (pay per minute), 040/4316–5133 theater* ⊕ *www.stage-entertainment.de* Ⓜ *Holstenstrasse (S-bahn).*

FAMILY **Theater im Hamburger Hafen.** Theater im Hamburger Hafen is home to *Der König der Löwen*, a German version of the hit musical *The Lion King*. The easiest way to reach the theater, which is on the south side of the Elbe, is by ferry from St. Pauli Landungsbrücken. ✉ *Rohrweg 13, St. Pauli* ☎ *01805/4444 (pay-per-minute hotline)* ⊕ *www.stage-entertainment.de* Ⓜ *Landungsbrücken (U-bahn), then ferry.*

13

SPORTS AND THE OUTDOORS

BICYCLING

More or less flat as a pancake, and with dedicated cycle paths running parallel to sidewalks throughout the city, Hamburg's an incredibly bike-friendly place. A number of hotels let their guests borrow bikes, but perhaps the most convenient option is to hire a "Stadtrad"—a city bike. Chunky and red framed, and outfitted with locks and lights, they can be picked up and dropped off at a multitude of locations around the city, including at the Hauptbahnhof, at larger U-bahn and S-bahn stations, and near popular tourist spots. Bikes are free for the first 30 minutes, and then cost 8¢ per minute up to a maximum daily rate of €12. For more information and to register, visit ⊕ *www.stadtradhamburg.de.*

Hamburg City Cycles. From a central location, this friendly little outfit rents bikes and also offers guided tours around the city and day trips to destinations that are farther afield, such as Lüneburg and Kiel. ✉ *Bernhard-Nocht-Str. 89–91, St. Pauli* ☎ *040/7421–4420* ⊕ *www. hhcitycycles.de* Ⓜ *Landungsbrücken (U-bahn).*

SAILING

A lovely way to see Hamburg is from the water, and visitors to the city can rent paddleboats, canoes, rowboats, and sailboats on the Outer Alster in summer between 10 am and 9 pm. Rowboats cost around €18 an hour, and sailboats about €26 an hour assuming you have a sailing license. A list of various operators around the lake and farther afield can be found on the Hamburg Tourismus website (⊕ *www.hamburg-travel.com*).

SHOPPING

Although not appearing as rich or sumptuous as Düsseldorf or Munich, Hamburg is nevertheless expensive, and ranks first among Germany's shopping experiences. Some of the country's premier designers, such as Karl Lagerfeld, Jil Sander, and Wolfgang Joop, are native Hamburgers, or at least worked here for quite some time. Hamburg has the greatest number of shopping malls in the country—they're mostly small, elegant downtown arcades offering entertainment, fashion, and fine food.

All the big luxury names—Chanel, Versace, Armani, Prada, Louis Vuitton, Cartier, Tiffany—are found in the warren of streets bounded by Jungferstieg, the Rathaus, and Neue ABC-Strasse. International chain stores, like Fossil, Adidas, and MAC, and European chains, such as Görtz shoe stores, Zara clothing stores, and Christ jewelry stores, and German department stores mingle on Mönckebergstrasse. Independent boutiques sell primarily distinguished and somewhat conservative fashion; understatement is the style here. Eppendorf offers miles of unique shops for shoes, clothes, home design, and housewares with quaint cafés sprinkled among them. Sternschanze offers a funky mix of stores selling cool home accessories and fashion, with dive bars and small restaurants for pit stops.

SHOPPING DISTRICTS

Hamburg's shopping districts are among the most elegant on the continent, and the city has Europe's largest expanse of covered shopping arcades, most of them packed with small, exclusive boutiques. The streets **Grosse Bleichen** and **Neuer Wall,** which lead off Jungfernstieg, are a big-ticket zone. The Grosse Bleichen holds four malls with the most sought-after labels, and several of these shopping centers are connected. The marble-clad **Galleria** is reminiscent of London's Burlington Arcade. Daylight streams through the immense glass ceilings of the **Hanse-Viertel,** an otherwise ordinary reddish-brown brick building. At 101, **Kaufmannshaus** is one of the oldest malls in Hamburg. Steps away from these retail giants are the fashionable **Hamburger Hof,** the historic Alte Post with a beautiful, waterfront promenade, the posh Bleichenhof, and the stunningly designed, larger **Europa Passage** mall.

In the fashionable Rotherbaum district, take a look at Milchstrasse and Mittelweg. Both are filled with small boutiques, restaurants, and cafés.

Walk down Susannenstrasse and Schanzestrasse in Sternschanze to find unique clothes, things for the home, and even LPs. Eppendorfer Landstrasse and Eppendorfer Weg are brimming with stores that sell clothing in every flavor—high-end labels, casual wear, sportswear, German designers—and elegant and fun home decor.

Running from the main train station to Gerhard-Hauptmann-Platz, the boulevard Spitalerstrasse is a pedestrian-only street lined with stores. ■TIP→ **Prices here are noticeably lower than those on Jungfernstieg.**

ALTSTADT AND NEUSTADT

ANTIQUES

Neustadt and St. Georg. ABC-Strasse in the Neustadt is a happy hunting ground for antiques lovers, as are the shops in the St. Georg district behind the train station, especially those along Lange Reihe and Koppel. You'll find a mixture of genuine antiques (*Antiquitäten*) and junk (*Trödel*) there. You'll also be lucky if you find many bargains, however. ⊠ *Hamburg.*

DEPARTMENT STORES AND SHOPPING MALLS

Alsterhaus. Hamburg's large and high-end department store is a favorite with locals, as well as an elegant landmark. A food hall and a champagne bar on the top level are both worth a stop. ⊠ *Jungfernstieg 16–20, Neustadt* ☎ *040/3590–1218* ⊕ *www.alsterhaus.de* Ⓜ *Jungfernstieg (U-bahn).*

Europa Passage. With 120 shops over five stories, a food hall, an icecream stand and even a Michelin-star restaurant, this shopping mall slap-bang in the middle of town almost literally has something for everyone. ⊠ *Ballindamm 40, Altstadt* ☎ *040/3009–2640* ⊕ *www. europa-passage.de* Ⓜ *Jungfernstieg (U-bahn).*

Hamburger Hof. The historic Hamburger Hof is one of the most beautiful, upscale shopping complexes in town, with a wide variety of designer clothing, jewelry, and gift stores that cater primarily to women. ⊠ *Jungfernstieg 26–30/Grosse Bleichen, Neustadt* ⊕ *www.hhof-passage.de* Ⓜ *Jungfernstieg (U-bahn and S-bahn).*

Karstadt. Germany's leading department-store chain isn't as posh as the Alsterhaus, but it still has a good and varied selection of clothing, perfume, watches, household goods, and food. Hamburg's downtown Karstadt Sports, which is up the street from the main store at Lange Mührn 14, is the city's best place to shop for sports clothing and gear. ⊠ *Mönckebergstr. 16, Altstadt* ☎ *040/30940* ⊕ *www.karstadt.de* Ⓜ *Mönckebergstrasse (U-bahn), Rathaus (U-bahn).*

JEWELRY

Wempe. Germany's largest seller of fine jewelry has two locations in Hamburg, and this is its flagship. The selection of watches here is particularly outstanding. ⊠ *Jungfernstieg 8, Neustadt* ☎ *040/3344–8824* ⊕ *www.wempe.com* Ⓜ *Jungfernstieg (U-bahn and S-bahn).*

MEN'S CLOTHING

Thomas-I-Punkt. Occupying the entire five floors of a handsome Dutch Renaissance building in the middle of town, Thomas-I-Punkt has long been supplying the fashion-conscious with trendy brand and private label clothes and shoes. ⊠ *Mönckebergstr. 21, Altstadt* ☎ *040/327–172* ⊕ *www.thomasipunkt.de* Ⓜ *Rathaus (U-bahn), Mönckebergstrasse (U-bahn).*

Wormland. The Hamburg outlet of the chain store is the city's largest store for men's clothes. Wormland offers both affordable yet very fashionable clothes, as well as (much more expensive) top designer wear. ⊠ *Europa Passage, Ballindamm 40, Altstadt* ☎ *040/4689–92700* ⊕ *www.wormland.de* Ⓜ *Jungfernstieg (U-bahn and S-bahn).*

WOMEN'S CLOTHING

& other stories. A part of the ever-expanding H&M empire, this recent addition to Neuer Wall specializes in premium brand yet alternative clothes, bags, jewelry, and cosmetics, designed to be mixed and matched. ⊠ *Neuer Wall 20, Neustadt* ☎ *040/5003–2251* ⊕ *www. stories.com* Ⓜ *Jungfernstieg (U-bahn and S-bahn).*

ST. PAULI AND SCHANZENVIERTEL

ANTIQUES

Flohschanze. Germans in search of a great deal love a good *Flohmarkt* (Flea market). These markets unfold every weekend throughout Hamburg, and the best of the lot may be the one at Flohschanze. With acres of clothes, furniture, books, CDs, records, home accessories, jewelry, and art, the market attracts both collectors and bargain hunters every Saturday from 8 until 4. ⊠ *Neuer Kamp 30, Schanzenviertel* ☎ *040/270–2766* ⊕ *www.marktkultur-hamburg.de* Ⓜ *Feldstrasse (U-bahn).*

GIFTS

Baqu. The two storefronts here are filled with wacky knickknacks, useful home appliances, and modern home accessories, all at reasonable prices. ⊠ *Susannenstr. 39, Schanzenviertel* ☎ *040/433–814* Ⓜ *Sternschanze (U-bahn and S-bahn).*

Captain's Cabin. Don't miss this Hamburg institution, which is the best place for all of the city's specialty maritime goods, including elaborate model ships and brass telescopes. ⊠ *Landungsbrücken 3, St. Pauli* ☎ *040/316–373* ⊕ *www.captains-cabin.de* Ⓜ *Landungsbrücken (U-bahn and S-bahn).*

Yokozuna. At this funky little shop, many of the quirky notebooks, earrings, handbags, and postcards are made by local designers, who rent shelves in the shop to sell their products. It's a great place for creative gift ideas. ⊠ *Weidenallee 17, Schanzenviertel* ☎ *040/3199–3729* ⊕ *www.yokozuna.de* Ⓜ *Schlump (U-bahn), Sternschanze (U-bahn and S-bahn), Christuskirche (U-bahn).*

MEN'S CLOTHING

Herr von Eden. Fine tailored suits and everything else you need to look like a true gentleman are sold at this elegant and ultrahip store on the vintage-clothing paradise of Marktstrasse. ⊠ *Marktstr. 33, Schanzenviertel* ☎ *040/439–0057* ⊕ *www.herrvoneden.com* Ⓜ *Feldstrasse (U-bahn).*

PERFUME AND COSMETICS

Mimulus Naturkosmetik. The all-natural cosmetics and toiletries here, as well as the facial and body treatments, are available at surprisingly reasonable prices. ⊠ *Schanzenstr. 39a, Schanzenviertel* ☎ *040/430–8037* ⊕ *www.mimulus-kosmetik.de* Ⓜ *Sternschanze (U-bahn and S-bahn).*

WOMEN'S CLOTHING

Fräuleinwunder. This small emporium sells trendy sportswear, shoes, accessories, and jewelry for women. There's also a small selection of casual clothing for men. ⊠ *Susannenstr. 13, Schanzenviertel* ☎ *40/3619–3329* Ⓜ *Sternschanze (U-bahn and S-bahn).*

Kauf dich glücklich. With a name that translates to "Shop yourself happy," this inviting store—one of two in the Schanzenviertel—sells clothes and shoes for men and women, as well as sunglasses, jewelry, scarves, hats, and other accessories. ⊠ *Susannenstr. 4, Schanzenviertel* ☎ *040/4922–2221* ⊕ *www.kaufdichgluecklich-shop.de* Ⓜ *Sternschanze (U-bahn and S-bahn).*

Lille/Stor. Head here for a mix of casual clothes, shoes, colorful items for the home, and small jewelry. ⊠ *Schanzenstr. 97, Schanzenviertel* ☎ *040/343–741* ⊕ *www.lille-stor.de* Ⓜ *Sternschanze (U-bahn and S-bahn).*

Purple Pink. The tiny shop sells a good selection of cool Scandinavian labels, such as Stine Goya, Carin Wester, and Minimarket. It's also great for jewelry and bags. ⊠ *Weidenallee 21, Schanzenviertel* ☎ *040/4321–5379* ⊕ *www.purple-pink.de* Ⓜ *Schlump (U-bahn), Sternschanze (U-bahn and S-bahn), Christuskirche (U-bahn).*

13

Weide. Primarily known for its funky wallpapers, handmade lamps, and retro-style furniture, this great little design store on the increasingly trendy Weidenallee also sells stylish modern clothes and accessories. ⊠ *Weidenallee 23, Schanzenviertel* ☎ *040/2878–1227* ⊕ *www.weide-hamburg.de* Ⓜ *Schlump (U-bahn), Sternschanze (U-bahn and S-bahn), Christuskirche (U-bahn).*

ALTONA AND OTTENSEN

VINTAGE CLOTHING

Pick N Weight. The concept here is fairly simple: paying for vintage clothes and accessories by how much they weigh rather than a fixed price per item. The store has a huge collection of pre-loved jeans, jackets, bags, and belts, which cost between €25 and €85 per kilo, depending on their label and quality. ⊠ *Grosse Bergstr. 167, Altona* ☎ *040/4319–3334* ⊕ *www.picknweight.de* Ⓜ *Altona (S-bahn).*

BLANKENESE AND ELSEWHERE

FOOD MARKETS

Wochenmarkt Blankenese. This small but top-class food market in the heart of Blankenese manages to preserve the charm of a small village. It sells only fresh produce from what it considers environmentally-friendly farms. ⊠ *Blankeneser Bahnhofstr., Blankenese* ☉ *Tues. 8–2, Fri. 8–6, Sat. 8–1* Ⓜ *Blankenese (S-bahn).*

GIFTS

WohnDesign Cosi. The most interesting pieces of contemporary design from around the world are on view at this home-furnishings store. ⊠ *Eppendorfer Landstr. 48, Eppendorf* ☎ *040/470–670* ⊕ *www.wohndesign-cosi.de* Ⓜ *Kellinghusenstrasse (U-bahn), Eppendorfer Baum (U-bahn).*

WOMEN'S CLOTHING

Anita Hass. This impressive store covers several storefronts and carries the newest apparel, shoes, jewelry, handbags, and accessories, such as iPhone covers. It's a Hamburg classic that carries both international brands and several German designers. ⊠ *Eppendorfer Landstr. 60, Eppendorf* ☎ *040/465–909* ⊕ *www.anitahass.com* Ⓜ *Kellinghusenstrasse (U-bahn).*

Kaufrausch. The upscale shop on the handsome suburban thoroughfare of Isestrasse carries mostly clothing and accessories for women. ⊠ *Isestr. 74, Harvestehude* ☎ *040/477–154* ⊕ *www.kaufrausch-hamburg.de* Ⓜ *Eppendorfer Baum (U-bahn).*

SCHLESWIG-HOLSTEIN AND THE BALTIC COAST

14

Visit Fodors.com for advice, updates, and bookings

WELCOME TO SCHLESWIG-HOLSTEIN AND THE BALTIC COAST

TOP REASONS TO GO

★ **Brick Gothic architecture:** The historic towns of Lübeck, Wismar, and Stralsund have some of the finest redbrick Gothic architecture in northern Europe. A walk through medieval Stralsund, in particular, is like a trip into the proud past of the powerful Hansetic League.

★ **Rügen:** One of the most secluded islands of northern Europe, Rügen is a dreamy Baltic oasis where endless beaches, soaring chalk cliffs, and a quiet pace of life have charmed painters, writers, and artists for centuries.

★ **Schwerin:** Nestled in a romantic landscape of lakes, rivers, forests, and marshland, the Mecklenburg state capital and its grand water palace make a great place to relax.

★ **Sylt:** A windswept outpost in the rough North Sea, Sylt is home to Germany's jet set, who come here for the tranquility, the white beaches, the gourmet dining, and the superb hotels throughout the year.

1 Schleswig-Holstein. Rural Schleswig-Holstein is accented by laid-back, medieval towns and villages famed for their fresh seafood and great local beers (such as Asgaard in Schleswig), and the bustling island of Sylt, a summer playground for wealthy Hamburgers.

2 Western Mecklenburg. Lakes, rivers, and seemingly endless fields of wheat, sunflowers, and yellow rape characterize this rural landscape. Although the area is extremely popular with Germans, only a few foreign tourists or day-trippers from nearby Berlin venture here to visit beautiful Schwerin or enjoy the serenity. The area is famous for its many wellness and spa hotels, making it a year-round destination.

GETTING ORIENTED

The Baltic Sea Coast is convieniently broken down into three major areas of interest: the western coastline of Schleswig-Holstein; the lakes inland in Western Mecklenburg; and Vorpommern's secluded, tundralike landscape of sandy heath and dunes. If you only have three days, slow down to the area's pace and focus on one area. In five days you could easily cross the region. Berlin is the natural approach from the east; Hamburg is a launching point from the west.

3 Vorpommern. Remote and sparsely populated, Vorpommern is one of Europe's quietest corners. Compared to the coast and islands in the west, sleepy Vorpommern sea resorts on the islands of Usedom and Hidensee have preserved a distinct, old-fashioned charm worth exploring. Bismarck popularized the area by saying that it was like going back 20 years in time.

BALTIC COAST BEACHES

Although Germany may not be the first place on your list of beach destinations, a shore vacation on the Baltic never disappoints. The coast here ranges from the remote bucolic shores of Usedom to the chic beaches of Sylt.

(above) You can rent one of the colorful Strandkorb on Usedom Island's beaches. (upper right) Stroll along Ahlbeck's beach and pier. (lower right) The "it" crowd hangs out on Sylt.

Be sure to rent a *Strandkorb*, a kind of beach chair in a wicker basket, which gives you all of the sun, but protects you from the wind and flying sand. You can rent these chairs by the hour, half day, or day. There is usually an office near the chairs; look for the kiosk that sells sundries and beach toys nearest the chair you want.

A blue flag on the beach indicates that the water is safe for swimming. But, be aware that water temperatures even in August rarely exceed 20°C (65°F). There's a *Kurtaxe* (a tax that goes to the upkeep of the beaches) of €1.50–€5 for most resort areas; the fees on Sylt average €3 per day. Fees are usually covered by your hotel; you should get a card indicating that you've paid the tax. You can use the card for discounted services, but don't need to present it to visit the beach.

BALTIC AMBER

It is believed that about 40 million years ago a pine forest grew in the area that is now the Baltic Sea. Fossilized resin from these trees, aka amber, lies beneath the surface. In fact, this area has the largest known amber deposit—about 80% of the world's known accessible deposits. The best time for amber "fishing," dipping a net into the surf, is at low tide after a storm when pieces of amber dislodge from the seabed.

BALTIC COAST BEST BEACHES

HIDDENSEE ISLAND
If you're partial to the bucolic and tranquil, head to the car-free island of **Hiddensee,** Rügen's neighbor to the west. With a mere 1,300 inhabitants, Hiddensee is the perfect place to look for washed-up amber.

RÜGEN ISLAND
Germany's largest island, Rügen has picture-perfect beaches, chalk cliffs, and pristine nature. It also served as the stomping ground for the likes of Albert Einstein, Christopher Isherwood, and Caspar David Friedrich. An easy day trip from Berlin, the town of **Binz** is the perfect Rügen getaway. Binz has a nice boardwalk, a pretty beach dotted with Strandkörbe, and fine mansions.

You'll find a wonderful white-sand beach at **Prora** and a smattering of artists' studios; the hulking abandoned resort here was designed by the Nazis to house 20,000 vacationers in the *Kraft durch Freude* (Strength Through Joy) program.

SYLT
Germany's northernmost island is the granddaddy of all beach resorts and by far the most popular seaside destination in Germany. Sylt is chic and trendy, but, despite being overrun by tourists, it is still possible to find your own romantic abandoned stretch of beach. **Westerland** is the most popular beach, with its long

promenade and sun-drenched sand. The "Fun-Beach Brandenburg" bursts at the seams with family-friendly activities, volleyball, and other sporting contests. Farther afield, the red cliffs of **Kampen** are the perfect backdrop for a little mellow sun and schmoozing with the locals. It's a lovely place for a walk along the shore and up the cliffs, where the view is spectacular. The best beach for families is at **Hörnum,** where a picture-perfect red-and-white lighthouse protects the entrance to the bay.

USEDOM ISLAND
The towns of **Ahlbeck** and **Herringsdorf** are the most popular on Usedom Island, with pristine 19th-century villas and mansions paired with long boardwalks extending into the sea. For the true and unspoiled experience, head west to **Ückeritz,** where the beach feels abandoned.

WARNEMÜNDE
A resort town popular with German tourists and local day-trippers from Rostock, the 20 km (12 miles) of windswept white-sand beach can't be beat. A fun promenade stretches the length of the beach and features daily music performances and restaurants ranging from high-end dining to fish shacks where you can get a paper bag filled with fried mussels.

Updated by
Lee A. Evans

Germany's true north is a quiet and peaceful region that belies, but takes a great deal of pride in, its past status as one of the most powerful trading centers in Europe. The salty air and lush, green landscape of marshlands, endless beaches, fishing villages, and lakes are the main pleasures here, not sightseeing. The Baltic coast is one of the most visited parts of Germany, but because most visitors are German, you'll feel like you have discovered Germany's best-kept secret. On foggy November evenings, or during the hard winter storms that sometimes strand islanders from the mainland, you can well imagine the fairy tales spun by the Vikings who once lived here.

In Schleswig-Holstein, Germany's most northern state, the Danish-German heritage is the result of centuries of land disputes, flexible borders, and intermarriage between the two nations—you could call this area southern Scandinavia. Since the early 20th century its shores and islands have become popular weekend and summer retreats for the well-to-do from Hamburg. The island of Sylt, in particular, is known throughout Germany for its rich and beautiful sunbathers.

The rest of Schleswig-Holstein, though equally appealing in its green and mostly serene landscape, is far from rich and worldly. Most people farm or fish, and often speak Plattdütsch, or Low German, which is difficult for outsiders to understand. Cities such as Flensburg, Husum, Schleswig, Kiel (the state capital), and even Lübeck all exude a laid-back, small-town charm.

The neighboring state of Mecklenburg-Vorpommern includes the Baltic Coast and is even more rural. On the resort islands of Hiddensee and Usedom, the clock appears to have stopped before World War II. Though it has long been a popular summer destination for families and city-weary Berliners, few foreign tourists venture here.

PLANNING

WHEN TO GO

The region's climate is at its best when the two states are most crowded with vacationers—in July and August. Winter can be harsh in this area, and even spring and fall are rather windy, chilly, and rainy. ■ TIP➔ **To avoid the crowds, schedule your trip for June or September. But don't expect tolerable water temperatures or hot days on the beach.**

GETTING HERE AND AROUND

AIR TRAVEL

The international airport closest to Schleswig-Holstein is in Hamburg. For an eastern approach to the Baltic Coast tour, use Berlin's Tegel or Schönefeld Airports.

BOAT AND FERRY TRAVEL

The Weisse Flotte (White Fleet) line operates ferries linking the Baltic ports, as well as running short harbor and coastal cruises. Boats depart from Warnemünde, Zingst (to Hiddensee), Sassnitz, and Stralsund. In addition, Scandlines ferries run from Stralsund and Sassnitz to destinations in Sweden, Denmark, Poland, and Finland.

Scandlines also operates ferries between Rostock/Warnemünde and the Danish island of Bornholm, as well as Sweden. Almost all Baltic Sea cruises dock in Warnemünde.

Contacts Scandlines. ☎ 01805/116–688 ⊕ www.scandlines.de. **Weisse Flotte.** ☎ 0180/321–2120 for Warnemünde and Stralsund, 0385/557–770 for Schwerin ⊕ www.weisseflotte.de.

BUS TRAVEL

Local buses link the main train stations with outlying towns and villages, especially the coastal resorts. Buses operate throughout Sylt, Rügen, and Usedom islands.

CAR TRAVEL

The two-lane roads (*Bundesstrassen*) along the coast can be full of traffic in summer. The ones leading to Usedom Island can be extremely log-jammed, as the causeway bridges have scheduled closings to let ships pass. Using the Bundesstrassen takes more time, but these often tree-lined roads are by far more scenic than the autobahn.

Sylt island is 196 km (122 miles) from Hamburg via autobahn A-7 and bundesstrasse B-199 and is ultimately reached via train. B-199 cuts through some nice countryside, and instead of A-7 or B-76 between Schleswig and Kiel you could take the slow route through the coastal hinterland (B-199, B-203, or B-503). Lübeck, the gateway to Mecklenburg-Vorpommern, is 56 km (35 miles) from Hamburg via A-1. B-105 leads to all sightseeing spots in Mecklenburg-Vorpommern. A faster route is the A-20, connecting Lübeck and Rostock. From Stralsund, B-96 cuts straight across Rügen Island, a distance of 51 km (32 miles). From Berlin, take A-11 and head toward Prenzlau for B-109 all the way to Usedom Island, a distance of 162 km (100 miles). A causeway connects the mainland town of Anklam to the town of Peenemünde, on Usedom Island; coming from the west, use the causeway at Wolgast.

14

TRAIN TRAVEL

Trains connect almost every notable city in the area and it's much more convenient than bus travel. Sylt, Kiel, Lübeck, Schwerin, and Rostock have InterCity train connections to either Hamburg or Berlin, or both.

A north–south train line links Schwerin and Rostock. An east–west route connects Kiel, Hamburg, Lübeck, and Rostock, and some trains continue through to Stralsund and Sassnitz, on Rügen Island.

TOURS

Although tourist offices and museums have worked to improve the English-language literature about this area, English-speaking tours are infrequent and must be requested ahead of time through the local tourist office. Because most tours are designed for groups, there's usually a flat fee of €20–€30. Towns currently offering tours are Lübeck, Stralsund, and Rostock. Schwerin has two-hour boat tours of its lakes. Many of the former fishermen in these towns give sunset tours of the harbors, shuttle visitors between neighboring towns, or take visitors fishing in the Baltic Sea, which is a unique opportunity to ride on an authentic fishing boat. In Kiel, Rostock, and on Sylt, cruise lines make short trips through the respective bays and/or islands off the coast, sailing even as far as Denmark and Sweden. Inquire at the local tourist office about companies and times, as well as about fishing-boat tours.

RESTAURANTS

Don't count on eating a meal at odd hours or after 10 pm in this largely rural area. Many restaurants serve hot meals only between 11:30 am and 2 pm, and from 6 to 9 pm. You rarely need a reservation here, and casual clothing is generally acceptable.

Prices in the reviews are the average cost of a main course at dinner, or if dinner is not served, at lunch.

HOTELS

In northern Germany you'll find both small *Hotelpensionen* and fully equipped large hotels; along the eastern Baltic Coast, some hotels are renovated high-rises dating from GDR (German Democratic Republic, or East Germany) times. Many of the small hotels and pensions in towns such as Kühlungsborn and Binz have been restored to the romantic, quaint splendor of German *Bäderarchitektur* (spa architecture) from the early 20th century. In high season all accommodations, especially on the islands, are in great demand. ■ TIP➔ **If you can't book well in advance, inquire at the local tourist office, which will also have information on the 150 campsites along the Baltic Coast and on the islands.**

Prices in the reviews are the lowest cost of a standard double room in high season. For expanded reviews, facilities, and current deals, visit Fodors.com.

WHAT IT COSTS IN EUROS			
	$	$$	$$$	$$$$
Restaurants	under €15	€15–€20	€21–€25	over €25
Hotels	under €100	€100–€175	€176–€225	over €225

PLANNING YOUR TIME

The bigger coastal former Hanseatic League cities make for a good start before exploring smaller towns. Lübeck is a natural base for exploring Schleswig-Holstein, particularly if you arrive from Hamburg. From here it's easy to venture out into the countryside or explore the coastline and towns such as Schleswig, Flensburg, or Husum. The island of Sylt is a one- or two-day trip from Lübeck, though.

If you have more time, you can also travel east from Lübeck into Mecklenburg-Vorpommern: Some of the must-see destinations on an itinerary include Schwerin and the surrounding lakes, the island of Rügen, and the cities Wismar and Rostock.

DISCOUNTS AND DEALS

Larger cities such as Kiel, Lübeck, Wismar, Schwerin, and Rostock offer tourism "welcome" cards, which include sometimes-considerable discounts and special deals for attractions and tours as well as local public transportation. Ask about these at the visitor-information bureaus.

VISITOR INFORMATION

Tourismusverband Mecklenburg-Vorpommern. ⌧ *Pl. der Freundschaft 1, Rostock* ☎ *0381/403–0500* ⊕ *www.tmv.de.*

SCHLESWIG-HOLSTEIN

This region once thrived, thanks to the Hanseatic League (a trading confederation of Baltic towns and cities) and the Salzstrasse (Salt Route), a merchant route connecting northern Germany's cities. The kings of Denmark warred with the dukes of Schleswig and, later, the German Empire over the prized northern territory of Schleswig-Holstein. The northernmost strip of land surrounding Flensburg became German in 1864. The quiet, contemplative spirit of the region's people, the marshland's special light, and the ever-changing face of the sea are inspiring. Today the world-famous Schleswig-Holstein-Musikfestival ushers in classical concerts to farmhouses, palaces, and churches.

HUSUM

158 km (98 miles) northwest of Hamburg.

The town of Husum is the epitome of northern German lifestyle and culture. Immortalized in a poem as the "gray city upon the sea" by its famous son, Theodor Storm, Husum is actually a popular vacation spot in summer.

The central **Marktplatz** (Market Square) is bordered by 17th- and 18th-century buildings, including the historic Rathaus (Town Hall), which houses the tourist-information office. The best impression of Husum's beginnings in the mid-13th century is found south of the Marktplatz, along **Krämerstrasse;** the **Wasserreihe,** a narrow and tortuous alley; and **Hafenstrasse,** right next to the narrow **Binnenhafen** (city harbor).

ESSENTIALS

Visitor Information Husum Tourist Office. ✉ *Grossstr. 27* ☎ *04841/89870* ⊕ *www.husum.de.*

EXPLORING

Schloss vor Husum (*Husum Castle*). Despite Husum's remoteness, surrounded by the stormy sea, wide marshes, and dunes, the city used to be a major seaport and administrative center. The Husum Castle, which was originally built as a Renaissance mansion in the late 16th century, was transformed in 1752 by the dukes of Gottorf into a redbrick baroque country palace. ✉ *König-Friedrich V.-Allee* ☎ *04841/897–3130* 🖼 *€5* ⊙ *Mar.–Oct., Tues.–Sun. 11–5.*

Theodor-Storm-Haus. This is the most famous house on Wasserreihe, where writer Theodor Storm (1817–88) lived between 1866 and 1880. It's a must if you're interested in German literature or if you want to gain insight into the life of the few well-to-do people in this region during the 19th century. The small museum includes the poet's living room and a small *Poetenstübchen* (poets' parlor), where he wrote many of his novels. ✉ *Wasserreihe 31* ☎ *04841/803–8630* 🖼 *€3.50* ⊙ *Apr.–Oct., Tues.–Fri. 10–5, Mon. and Sun. 2–5, Sat. 11–5; Nov.–Mar., Tues., Thurs., and Sat. 2–5.*

WHERE TO STAY

$$$ HOTEL Fodor's Choice ★ **Geniesser Hotel Altes Gymnasium.** In a former redbrick high school behind a pear orchard, you'll find a surprisingly elegant country-style hotel. **Pros:** stylish and quiet setting; a perfect overnight stop on the way to Sylt. **Cons:** far from any other sights. [$] *Rooms from: €195* ✉ *Süderstr. 2–10* ☎ *04841/8330* 🌐 *www.altes-gymnasium.de* 🛏 *66 rooms, 6 suites* 🍴 *Breakfast.*

SYLT

44 km (27 miles) northwest of Husum, 196 km (122 miles) northwest of Hamburg.

Fodor's Choice ★ Sylt (pronounced ts-oo-LT) is a long, narrow island (38 km [24 miles] by as little as 220 yards) of unspoiled beaches and marshland off the western coast of Schleswig-Holstein and Denmark. Famous for its clean air and white beaches, Sylt is the hideaway for Germany's rich and famous.

A popular activity here is *Wattwanderungen* (walking in the Watt, the shoreline tidelands), whether on self-guided or guided tours. The small villages with their thatch-roof houses, the beaches, and the nature conservation areas make Sylt one of the most enchanting German islands.

GETTING HERE AND AROUND

Trains are the *only* way to access Sylt (other than flying from Hamburg or Berlin). The island is connected to the mainland via the train causeway Hindenburgdamm, and Deutsche Bahn will transport you and your car from central train stations at Dortmund, Düsseldorf, Hamburg, Stuttgart, and Frankfurt directly to the Westerland station on the island. In addition, a daily shuttle car train leaves Niebüll roughly every 30 minutes from 5:10 am to 10:10 pm (Friday and Sunday 5:10 am to 9:40 pm). There are no reservations on this train.

ESSENTIALS

Visitor Information **Tourismus-Service Kampen.** ✉ *Hauptstr. 12, Kampen* ☎ *04651/46980* 🌐 *www.kampen.de.* **Sylt Marketing GmbH.** ✉ *Stephanstr. 6, Rantum* ☎ *04651/82020* 🌐 *www.sylt.de.* **Westerland.** ✉ *Strandstr. 35, Westerland* ☎ *04651/9988* 🌐 *www.westerland.de.*

EXPLORING

TOP ATTRACTIONS

Kampen. The Sylt island's unofficial capital is the main destination for the wealthier crowd and lies 9 km (6 miles) northeast of Westerland. Redbrick buildings and shining white thatch-roof houses spread along the coastline. The real draw—aside from the fancy restaurants and chic nightclubs—is the beaches. ✉ *Kampen* 🌐 *www.kampen.de.*

Rotes Kliff (*Red Cliff*). One of the island's best-known features is this dune cliff on the northern end of the Kampen beaches, which turns an eerie dark red when the sun sets. ✉ *Kampen.*

WORTH NOTING

Altfriesisches Haus (*Old Frisian House*). For a glimpse of the rugged lives of 19th-century fishermen, visit the small village of **Keitum** to the south, and drop in on the Old Frisian House, which preserves an old-world peacefulness in a lush garden setting. The house also documents a time when most seamen thrived on extensive whale hunting. ⊠ *Am Kliff 13, Keitum* 🕾 *04651/31101* 🖃*€3.50* ☉ *Easter–Oct., weekdays 10–5, weekends 11–5; Nov.–Easter, Tues.–Fri. 1–4.*

FAMILY **Naturschutzgebiet Kampener Vogelkoje** (*Birds' Nest Nature Conservation Area*). From the mid-17th century, this area served as a mass trap for

AWAY FROM THE CROWDS

If you're looking for privacy on Sylt, detour to the village of **List**, on the northern tip of the island, or to **Archsum** or **Hörnum**. The last is on the southernmost point of the island and, like List, has a little harbor and lighthouse.

wild geese, but today it's a nature preserve for wild birds. ⊠ *Lister Str., Kampen* 🕾 *04651/871–077* 🖃*€3* ☉ *Apr.–Oct., weekdays 10–5, weekends 11–5.*

St. Severin Church. The 800-year-old church was built on the highest elevation in the region. Its tower once served the island's fishermen as a beacon. Strangely enough, the tower also served as a prison until 1806. Now a Lutheran church, it is a popular site for weddings. ⊠ *Pröstwai 20, Keitum* 🕾 *04651/31713* ⊕ *www.st-severin.de* 🖃 *Free* ☉ *Daily 9–6. Tours Apr.–Oct., Sun. at 10; Nov.–Mar., Sun. at 4.*

Sylter Heimatmuseum (*Sylt Island Museum*). This small museum tells the centuries-long history of the island's seafaring people. It presents traditional costumes, tools, and other gear from fishing boats and relates stories of islanders who fought for Sylt's independence. ⊠ *Am Kliff 19, Keitum* 🕾 *04651/31669* 🖃*€3.50* ☉ *Easter–Oct., weekdays 10–5, weekends 11–5; Nov.–Easter, Tues.–Fri. 1–4.*

FAMILY **Westerland.** The island's major town is not quite as expensive as Kampen, but it's more crowded. An ugly assortment of modern hotels lines an undeniably clean and broad beach. Each September windsurfers meet for the Surf Cup competition off the **Brandenburger Strand,** the best surfing spot. ⊠ *Westerland.*

BEACHES

FAMILY **Buhne 16 and Roter Kliff.** Kampen's beach—divided into the **Buhne 16** and the **Roter Kliff**—is the place where the rich and famous meet average joes. Bunhe 16 is Germany's most popular nudist beach and Germans call this section the great equalizer, as social inequalities disappear with the clothing. The Red Cliff section is less crowded than Buhne 16 and clothing is required. The beach access point offers one of the best views of the Cliffs and North Sea; the viewing platform is wheelchair accessible. The beaches are surrounded by a ring of dunes that beg for exploration. **Amenities:** food and drink; lifeguards; parking; showers; toilets; water sports. **Best for:** partiers; sunset; swimming; walking. ⊠ *Kurstr. 33, Kampen.*

FAMILY **Fun-Beach Brandenburg.** Westerland's beach bursts at the seams in the summer months. More than 6 kilometers (4 miles) of pristine white sand is filled with more than 4,000 Strandkörbe, a kind of beach chair in a wicker basket, which are all for rent. There's also volleyball, soccer, darts, and other beach sports, and everyone is invited to participate in

The beach at Westerland on Sylt is clean and wide.

the Beach Olympics, which are held every Friday at 2 pm in the summer months. Despite its popularity, it is easy to find some privacy on the many secluded bike and footpaths. **Amenities:** food and drink; lifeguards; parking; showers; toilets; water sports. **Best for:** partiers; snorkeling; walking; windsurfing. ✉ *Kurpromenade, Westerland.*

FAMILY **Hornum Beach.** The town of Hornum is bordered on three sides by a rock-free, fine-white-sand beach that is perfect for paddling, quick dips in the sea, or simply lounging in one of the ever-present Strandkörbe beach chairs. The main beach is one of the most family-friendly on the island and it's easily accessible from the promenade. A magnificent red-and-white lighthouse looms over the beach. Hornum is the best place to take long walks along the Wattenmeer. **Amenities:** food and drink; lifeguards; parking; showers; toilets; water sports. **Best for:** surfing; swimming; walking; windsurfing. ✉ *An Der Dune, Hornum.*

WHERE TO EAT

$$$$ SEAFOOD Fodor's Choice ★ 🍴 **Hotelrestaurant Jörg Müller.** Owner Jörg Müller, considered by many to be the island's leading chef, serves haute cuisine in the gracious and friendly setting of an old thatch-roof farmhouse, which doubles as a small hotel. Müller even makes his own salt from the North Sea water. Of the two restaurants, the Pesel serves local fish dishes, whereas the formal Jörg Müller offers a high-quality blend of international cuisines, where any of the four- to six-course menus are a nice option. [$] *Average main: €48* ✉ *Süderstr. 8, Westerland* ☎ *04651/27788* 🌐 *www.hotel-joerg-mueller.de* 🕓 *No lunch* ✍ *Reservations essential.*

$$$$ ╳ **Sansibar.** Sansibar is the island's most popular restaurant, and more
ECLECTIC   a way of life than a place to eat. It's the longtime favorite of a diverse
clientele—basically everyone ever on Sylt—who often make it a ram-
bunctious night out by imbibing drinks with no regard for the morning
after under the bar's maverick logo of crossed pirates' sabers. The cuisine includes seafood and fondue, and more than 800 wines are on offer.
The Sunday brunch is incredible. To get a table even in the afternoon,
you must reserve at least six weeks in advance. $ *Average main: €30*
✉ *Strand, Rantum-Süd, Hörnumer Str. 80, Rantum* ☎ *04651/964–546*
⊕ *www.sansibar.de* ⚓ *Reservations essential.*

WHERE TO STAY

$$$$ ⊡ **Dorint Söl'ring Hof.** This luxurious resort is set *on* the dunes in a white,
RESORT   thatch-roof country house, and the view from most of the rooms is
Fodor'sChoice   magnificent—with some luck you may even spot frolicking harbor por-
★   poises. **Pros:** one of the few luxury hotels on the island with perfect
service and a top-notch restaurant; right on the beach. **Cons:** remote
location; often fully booked; rooms tend to be small. $ *Rooms from:*
€395 ✉ *Am Sandwall 1, Rantum* ☎ *04651/836–200* ⊕ *www.soelring-
hof.de* ⌇ *11 rooms, 4 suites* ⍾ *Breakfast.*

$$$ ⊡ **Ulenhof Wenningstedt.** One of Sylt's loveliest old thatch-roof apartment
B&B/INN   houses, this is a quiet alternative to the busier main resorts in Kampen
and Westerland. **Pros:** a great, but small, spa. **Cons:** off the beaten track
and away from the main action in Kampen and Westerland; credit
cards are not accepted. $ *Rooms from: €180* ✉ *Friesenring 14, Wen-
ningstedt* ☎ *04651/94540* ⊕ *www.ulenhof.de* ▬ *No credit cards* ⌇ *35
apartments* ⍾ *Breakfast.*

NIGHTLIFE

Club Rotes Kliff. The nightspots in Kampen are generally more upscale
and more expensive than the pubs and clubs of Westerland. This is one
of the most classic clubs on Sylt—a bar and dance club that attracts a
hip crowd of all ages. ✉ *Braderuper Weg 3, Kampen* ☎ *04651/43400.*

Compass. The Compass is not as trendy as the typical Sylt nightclub.
The mostly young patrons, however, create a cheerful party atmosphere
on weekend nights. ✉ *Friedrichstr. 40, Westerland* ☎ *04651/23513.*

SCHLESWIG

82 km (51 miles) southeast of Sylt, 114 km (71 miles) north of Hamburg.

Schleswig-Holstein's oldest city is also one of its best-preserved exam-
ples of a typical north German town. Once the seat of the dukes of
Schleswig-Holstein, it has not only their palace but also ruins left by
the area's first rulers, the Vikings. The Norse conquerors, legendary and
fierce warriors from Scandinavia, ruled northern Germany between 800
and 1100. Although they brought terror and domination to the region,
they also contributed commerce and a highly developed social structure.
Under a wide sky, Schleswig lies on the Schlei River in a landscape of
freshwater marshland and lakes, making it a good departure point for
bike or canoe tours.

EATING WELL IN SCHLESWIG-HOLSTEIN

The German coastline is known for fresh and superb seafood, particularly in summer. A few of the region's top restaurants are on Sylt and in Lübeck. Eating choices along the Baltic Coast tend to be more down-to-earth. However, restaurants in both coastal states serve mostly seafood such as *Scholle* (flounder) or North Sea *Krabben* (shrimp), often with fried potatoes, eggs, and bacon. Mecklenburg specialties to look for

are *Mecklenburger Griebenroller*, a custardy casserole of grated potatoes, eggs, herbs, and chopped bacon; *Mecklenburger Fischsuppe*, a hearty fish soup with vegetables, tomatoes, and sour cream; *Gefüllte Ente* (duck with bread stuffing); and *Pannfisch* (fish patty). A favorite local nightcap since the 17th century is *Grog*, a strong blend of rum, hot water, and local fruits.

14

GETTING HERE AND AROUND
Schleswig's train station is 3 km (2 miles) from the city center. It's easiest to take Bus No. 1501, 1505, or 1506 into town. You'll find the buses across the street from the front of the train station, and all stop at Schloss Gottorf.

EXPLORING
The Holm. The fishing village comes alive in the Holm neighborhood, an old settlement with tiny and colorful houses. The windblown buildings give a good impression of what villages in northern Germany looked like 150 years ago. ⊠ *Süderholmstr.*

Schloss Gottorf. The impressive baroque Schloss Gottorf, dating from 1703, once housed the ruling family. It has been transformed into the **Schleswig-Holsteinisches Landesmuseum** (State Museum of Schleswig-Holstein) and holds a collection of art and handicrafts of northern Germany from the Middle Ages to the present, including paintings by Lucas Cranach the Elder. ⊠ *Schlossinsel 1* ☎ *04621/8130* ⊕ *www. schloss-gottorf.de* ⦿*€9* ⊘ *Apr.–Oct., daily 10–6; Nov.–Mar., Tues.–Fri. 10–4, weekends 10–5.*

FAMILY **Wikinger-Museum Haithabu** (*Haithabu Viking Museum*). The most thrilling museum in Schleswig is at the site of an ancient Viking settlement. This was the Vikings' most important German port, and the boats, gold jewelry, and graves they left behind are displayed in the museum. Be sure to walk along the trail to the Viking village, to see how the Vikings really lived. The best way to get there is to take the ferry across the Schlei from Schleswig's main fishing port. ⊠ *Haddeby, Am Haddebyer Noor 2, Busdorf* ☎ *04621/813–222* ⊕ *www.schloss-gottorf.de/ haithabu* ⦿*€7* ⊘ *Apr.–Oct., daily 9–5; Nov.–Mar., Tues.–Sun. 10–4* ☞ *Free parking.*

WHERE TO EAT AND STAY
$ ╳**Asgaard Brauerei.** Taste the "Divine beer of the Vikings" at Schleswig's GERMAN only brewery. While the Luzifer Restaurant offers typical brewpub fare, it is the small Viking twists, like roast meat served only with a knife and horned glasses that make this place worth a visit. The Divine beer is a

malty cold-fermented amber lager that can be highly addictive. [$] *Average main: €12* ✉ *Königstr. 27* ☎ *04621/29206* 🌐 *www.asgaard.de.*

$ GERMAN 🍴 **Stadt Flensburg.** This small restaurant in a city mansion dating back to 1699 serves mostly fish from the Schlei River. The food is solid regional fare such as *Zanderfilet* (pike-perch fillets) or *Gebratene Ente* (roast duck). The familial, warm atmosphere and the local dark tap beers more than make up for the simplicity of the setting. Reservations are advised. [$] *Average main: €13* ✉ *Lollfuss 102* ☎ *04621/23984* 🕓 *Closed Wed. No lunch.*

$$ HOTEL 🏨 **Ringhotel Strandhalle Schleswig.** A modern hotel overlooking the small yacht harbor, this establishment has surprisingly low rates. **Pros:** central spot in the heart of Schleswig; great views. **Cons:** lack of flair; rather bland rooms. [$] *Rooms from: €100* ✉ *Strandweg 2* ☎ *04621/9090* 🌐 *www.hotel-strandhalle.de* 🛏 *30 rooms* 🍽 *Breakfast.*

SHOPPING

Keramik-Stube. The tiny Keramik-Stube offers craft work and beautiful traditional handmade pottery. ✉ *Rathausmarkt 14* ☎ *04621/24757.*

Teekontor Hansen. Northern Germans are devout tea drinkers, and the best place to buy tea is Teekontor Hansen. Try the *Schliekieker,* a strong blend, or the *Ostfriesenmischung,* the traditional daily tea. ✉ *Kornmarkt 3* ☎ *04621/23385.*

KIEL

53 km (33 miles) southeast of Schleswig, 130 km (81 miles) north of Hamburg.

The state capital of Schleswig-Holstein, Kiel, is known throughout Europe for the annual Kieler Woche, a regatta that attracts hundreds of boats from around the world. Despite the many wharves and industries concentrated in Kiel, the **Kieler Föhrde** (Bay of Kiel) has remained mostly unspoiled. Unfortunately, this cannot be said about the city itself. Because of Kiel's strategic significance during World War II—it served as the main German submarine base—the historic city, founded more than 750 years ago, was completely destroyed. Sadly, due to the modern reconstruction of the city, there is no real reason to spend more than half a day in Kiel.

ESSENTIALS

Visitor Information Kiel Tourist Office. ✉ *Andreas-Gayk-Str. 31* ☎ *0431/679–100* 🌐 *www.kiel.de.*

EXPLORING

FAMILY **Kieler Hafen** (*Kiel Harbor*). At Germany's largest passenger-shipping harbor, you can always catch a glimpse of one of the many ferries leaving for Scandinavia from the **Oslokai** (Oslo Quay). ✉ *Oslokai.*

Kunsthalle zu Kiel (*Kiel Art Gallery*). One of northern Germany's best collections of modern art can be found here. Russian art of the 19th and early 20th centuries, German expressionism, and contemporary international art are on display. ✉ *Düsternbrooker Weg 1* ☎ *0431/880–5756* 🌐 *www.kunsthalle-kiel.de* 🎟 *€7* 🕓 *Tues.–Sun. 10–6 (to 8 pm Wed.).*

FAMILY **Schifffahrtsmuseum** (*Maritime Museum*). Housed in a hall of the old fish market, this museum pays tribute to Kiel's impressive maritime history. The exhibit includes two antique fishing boats and an impressive collection of multimedia workstations that detail Kiel's role as a center of the fishing industry. ✉ *Wall 65* ☎ *0431/901–3428* 🌐 *www.kiel.de* 🎫 *€3* 🕑 *Apr.–Oct., daily 10–6; Nov.–Mar., Tues.–Sun. 10–5.*

U-Boot-Museum (*Submarine Museum*). A grim reminder of one aspect of Kiel's marine past is exhibited at this museum in Kiel-Laboe. The vessels of the much-feared German submarine fleet in both World Wars were mostly built and stationed in Kiel before leaving for the Atlantic, where they attacked American and British supply convoys. Today the submarine U995, built in 1943, serves as a public-viewing model of a typical World War II German submarine. The 280-foot-high **Marineehrenmal** (Marine Honor Memorial), in Laboe, was built in 1927–36. You can reach Laboe via ferry from the Kiel harbor or take B-502 north. ✉ *Strandstr. 92, Laboe* ☎ *04343/42700* 🎫 *Memorial €6, museum €4.50, or €9.50 for both* 🕑 *Apr.–Oct., daily 9:30–6; Nov.–Mar., daily 9:30–4.*

14

WHERE TO EAT AND STAY

$ GERMAN 🍴 **Kieler Brauerei.** Kiel has been a center of German brewing since the Middle Ages, when industrious citizens brewed around the clock for export and visiting merchant seamen. Although this brauhaus is relatively new, beer has been brewed in this house since medieval times. You can try the *Naturtrübes Kieler* and other north German beers in pitchers, or order a small barrel for your table and tap it yourself (other patrons will cheer you). The hearty food—mostly fish, pork, and potato dishes—does not earn awards, but it certainly helps get down just one more beer. [$] *Average main: €11* ✉ *Alter Markt 9* ☎ *0431/906–290* 🌐 *www.kieler-brauerei.de.*

$$ ECLECTIC 🍴 **Quam.** Because modern locals aren't interested in anything old-fashioned, there are no traditional fish restaurants in Kiel—instead, the dining scene looks for new and innovative seafood from all over the world. The stylish Quam, its yellow walls and dimmed lights paying homage to Tuscany, serves specialties from Germany, Italy, France, and Japan to a mostly young, very chic crowd. [$] *Average main: €15* ✉ *Düppelstr. 60* ☎ *0431/85195* 🕑 *Closed Sun. No lunch* ✍ *Reservations essential.*

$$$ HOTEL 🏨 **Hotel Kieler Yachtclub.** This traditional hotel overlooking the Kieler Föhrde provides standard yet elegant refurbished rooms in the main building and completely new, bright accommodations in the Villentrakt. **Pros:** central location in the heart of Kiel; nice views. **Cons:** service and attitude can feel a bit too formal at times. [$] *Rooms from: €197* ✉ *Hindenburgufer 70* ☎ *0431/88130* 🌐 *www.hotel-kyc.de* 🛏 *19 rooms, 2 suites* 🍽 *Breakfast.*

NIGHTLIFE

Hemingway. This is one of the many chic and hip bars in Kiel. ✉ *Alter Markt 19* ☎ *0431/96812.*

Traumfabrik. A college crowd goes to Traumfabrik to eat pizza, watch a movie, or dance (Friday is best for dancing). ✉ *Grasweg 19* ☎ *0431/544–450.*

LÜBECK

60 km (37 miles) southeast of Kiel, 56 km (35 miles) northeast of Hamburg.

Fodor's Choice ★ The ancient island core of Lübeck, dating from the 12th century, was a chief stronghold of the Hanseatic merchant princes, until its almost complete destruction in 1942. It was the roving Heinrich der Löwe (King Henry the Lion) who established the town and, in 1173, laid the foundation stone of the redbrick Gothic cathedral. The town's famous landmark gate, the **Holstentor,** built between 1464 and 1478, is flanked by two round squat towers and serves as a solid symbol of Lübeck's prosperity as a trading center.

GETTING HERE AND AROUND

Lübeck is accessible from Hamburg in 45 minutes either by InterCity trains or by car via the A-24 and A-1, which almost takes you from one city center to the other. Lübeck is also well connected by autobahns and train service to Kiel, Flensburg, and the neighboring eastern coastline. The city, however, should be explored on foot or by bike, as the many tiny, medieval alleys in the center cannot be accessed by car. Tours of Old Lübeck depart daily from the tourist Welcome Center on Holstentorplatz (€7, *June–Aug., Sat. at 11:30*).

FESTIVALS

Schleswig-Holstein Music Festival. In summer, try to catch a few performances at this annual music festival (mid-July–late August), which features orchestras composed of young musicians from more than 25 countries. Some concerts are held in the Lübecker Dom or the Marienkirche; some are staged in barns in small towns and villages. For exact dates and tickets, contact Schleswig-Holstein Konzertorganisation. ⊠ *Lübeck* ☎ *0431/570–470 information, 0431/237–070 ticket hotline* ⊕ *www.shmf.de.*

ESSENTIALS

Visitor Information Lübeck Tourist Office. ⊠ *Holstentorpl. 1* ☎ *00451/889–9700* ⊕ *www.luebeck.de.*

EXPLORING

TOP ATTRACTIONS

Fodor's Choice ★ **Altstadt** (*Old Town*). Proof of Lübeck's former position as the golden queen of the Hanseatic League is found at every step in the Altstadt, which contains more 13th- to 15th-century buildings than all other large northern German cities combined. This fact has earned the Altstadt a place on UNESCO's register of the world's greatest cultural and natural treasures. ⊠ *Lübeck.*

Fodor's Choice ★ **Holstentor** (*Holsten Gate*). Lübeck's famous gate was part of the medieval fortifications of the city. It has two faces: one it shows the world and one it shows the city. The "field side," which faces away, appears as if it is made of two defensive towers connected by a middle gate. The "city side" looks like one smooth building and has more windows, arcades, and friezes. The inscription on the field side, added in 1871, reads, "Concordia domi foris pax," an abbreviated version of the statement, "Harmony within and peace outside are indeed the greatest good of all." It houses a museum with ship models, suits of armor, and other artifacts from Lübeck's heyday. ✉ *Holstentorpl.* ☎ *0451/1224129 museum ⊕ www. museum-holstentor.de* 🎫 *Museum €6 ⊗ Museum: Jan.–Mar., Tues.–Sun. 11–5; Apr.–Dec., daily 10–6.*

Lübecker Dom (*Lübeck Cathedral*). Construction of this, the city's oldest building, began in 1173. ✉ *Dom-kirchhof* ☎ *0451/74704* 🎫 *Free ⊗ Apr.–Oct., daily 10–6; Nov.–Mar., daily 10–4.*

Rathaus. Dating from 1240, the Rathaus is among the buildings lining the arcaded Marktplatz, one of Europe's most striking medieval market squares. ✉ *Breitestr. 64* ☎ *0451/122–1005* 🎫 *Guided tour in German €4 ⊗ Tour weekdays at 11, noon, and 3; Sat. at 1:30.*

NEARBY KIEL

Two attractive beach towns close to Kiel, **Laboe** and **Strande,** are crowded with sun-loving Kielers on summer weekends. Both retain their fishing-village appeal, and you can buy fresh fish directly from the boats in the harbor, such as famous *Kieler Sprotten,* a small, salty fish somewhat like a sardine. Though you can get to Laboe and Strande by car, it's more fun to catch a ferry leaving from Kiel.

14

WORTH NOTING

Buddenbrookhaus. Two highly respectable-looking mansions are devoted to two of Germany's most prominent writers, Thomas Mann (1875–1955) and Günter Grass (born 1927). The older mansion is named after Mann's saga *Buddenbrooks.* Mann's family once lived here, and it's now home to the **Heinrich und Thomas Mann Zentrum,** a museum documenting the brothers' lives. A tour and video in English are offered. ✉ *Mengstr. 4* ☎ *0451/122–4240 ⊕ www.buddenbrookhaus.de* 🎫 *€6 ⊗ Jan.–Mar., Tues.–Sun. 11–5; Apr.–Dec., daily 10–5.*

Günter Grass-Haus. This mansion contains a museum devoted to wide-ranging exhibits on literature and visual arts, including the work of Germany's most famous postwar writer and winner of the Nobel Prize for Literature (1999), Günter Grass. ✉ *Glockengiesserstr. 21* ☎ *0451/122–4230 ⊕ grass-haus.de* 🎫 *€6 ⊗ Jan.–Mar., Tues.–Sun. 11–5; Apr.–Dec., daily 10–5.*

Heilig-Geist-Hospital (*Hospital of the Holy Ghost*). Take a look inside the entrance hall of this Gothic building. It was built in the 14th century by the town's rich merchants and was one of the country's first hospitals. It still cares for the sick and elderly. ✉ *Am Koberg 11* ☎ *0451/790–7841* 🎫 *Free ⊗ Apr.–Sept., Tues.–Sun. 10–5; Oct.–Mar., Tues.–Sun. 10–4.*

Marienkirche (*St. Mary's Church*). The impressive redbrick Gothic structure, which has the highest brick nave in the world, looms behind the Rathaus. Look for the old bells, as they are still in the spot where they fell during the bombing of Lübeck. ✉ *Marienkirchhof* ☎ *0451/397–700 ⊕ www.st-marien-luebeck.de ⊗ Apr.–Sept., daily 10–6; Mar. and Oct., daily 10–5; Nov.–Feb., daily 10–4.*

1477. S.P.Q.L. 1871.

WHERE TO EAT

$$
GERMAN
Fodor's Choice
★

✕ **Schiffergesellschaft.** This dark, wood-paneled restaurant dating back to 1535 is the city's old Mariners' Society house, which was off-limits to women until 1870. Today locals and visitors alike enjoy freshly brewed beer and great seafood in church-style pews at long 400-year-old oak tables. Above are a bizarre collection of low-hanging old ship models. A good meal here is the *Ostseescholle* (plaice), fried with bacon and served with potatoes and cucumber salad. $ *Average main: €19* ⊠ *Breitestr. 2* ☎ *0451/76776* ⊕ *schiffergesellschaft.com* ⌂ *Reservations essential.*

$$$$
GERMAN

✕ **Wullenwever.** This restaurant has set a new standard of dining sophistication for Lübeck. Committed to the city's maritime heritage, Wullenwever serves fish such as bass, halibut, plaice, pike, and trout, which is fried or sautéed according to local country cooking. It's certainly one of the most attractive establishments in town, with dark furniture, chandeliers, and oil paintings on pale pastel walls. In summer, tables fill a quiet flower-strewn courtyard. Don't order à la carte here. Instead choose one of the three- to seven-course menus, paired with wine. $ *Average main: €50* ⊠ *Beckergrube 71* ☎ *0451/704–333* ⊕ *www.wullenwever.de* ☽ *Closed Sun. and Mon. No lunch* ⌂ *Reservations essential.*

WHERE TO STAY

$$
B&B/INN

▦ **Hotel zur Alten Stadtmauer.** This historic town house in the heart of the city is Lübeck's most charming hotel with small, modest, well-kept guest rooms on two floors. **Pros:** cozy hotel with personal, friendly service; great location. **Cons:** rather simply furnished rooms; when it's full, the hotel feels cramped. $ *Rooms from: €109* ⊠ *An der Mauer 57* ☎ *0451/73702* ⊕ *www.hotelstadtmauer.de* ⇱ *22 rooms* ⦿ *Breakfast.*

$$
HOTEL

▦ **Ringhotel Friederikenhof.** A lovely country hotel set in 19th-century, redbrick farmhouses 10 minutes outside Lübeck, the family-run Friederikenhof is a perfect hideaway with a soothing garden and great view of the city's skyline. **Pros:** charming, old-style farmhouse typical of the region; personal and very friendly service. **Cons:** outside Lübeck. $ *Rooms from: €110* ⊠ *Langjohrd 15–19* ☎ *0451/800–880* ⊕ *www. friederikenhof.de* ⇱ *30 rooms* ⦿ *Breakfast.*

$
HOTEL

▦ **Ringhotel Jensen.** Only a stone's throw from the Holstentor, this hotel is close to all the main attractions and faces the moat surrounding the Old Town. **Pros:** perfect location in the heart of Lübeck's downtown area; major sights are all within walking distance. **Cons:** small pensionlike hotel without many of the amenities of larger hotels; bland decoration in rooms. $ *Rooms from: €93* ⊠ *An der Obertrave 4–5* ☎ *0451/702–490* ⊕ *www.hotel-jensen.de* ⇱ *41 rooms, 1 suite* ⦿ *Breakfast.*

$$
HOTEL

▦ **SAS Radisson Senator Hotel Lübeck.** Close to the famous Holstentor, this ultramodern hotel, with its daring architecture, still reveals a north German heritage: the redbrick building, with its oversize windows and generous, open lobby, mimics an old Lübeck warehouse. **Pros:** luxury hotel in a central location; some rooms with river views. **Cons:** lacks the historic charm typical of medieval Lübeck. $ *Rooms from: €134* ⊠ *Willy-Brandt-Allee 6* ☎ *0451/1420* ⊕ *www.senatorhotel.de* ⇱ *217 rooms, 7 suites* ⦿ *Breakfast; Some meals.*

14

PERFORMING ARTS

Musik und Kongresshallen Lübeck. Myriad concerts, operas, and theater performances take place at this major venue in Lübeck. ⊠ *Willy-Brandt-Allee 10* ☎ *0451/79040* ⊕ *www.muk.de.*

SHOPPING

Local legend has it that marzipan was invented in Lübeck during the great medieval famine. According to the story, a local baker ran out of grain for bread and, in desperation, began experimenting with the only four ingredients he had: almonds, sugar, rose water, and eggs. The result was a sweet almond paste known today as marzipan. The story is more fiction than fact; it is generally agreed that marzipan's true origins lie in the Middle East. ■**TIP→** **Lübecker Marzipan, an appellation that has been trademarked, is now considered among the best in the world. Any marzipan that uses the appellation Lübecker must be made within the city limits.**

Holstentor-Passage. The city's largest downtown shopping mall is next to the Holstentor and is filled with stores selling clothing or home accessories. ⊠ *An der Untertrave 111* ☎ *0451/75292.*

Konditorei-Café Niederegger. Lübeck's most famous marzipan maker, Niederegger, sells the delicacy molded into a multitude of imaginative forms at its Konditorei-Café flagship store. ⊠ *Breitestr. 89* ☎ *0451/530–1127* ⊕ *www.niederegger.de.*

WESTERN MECKLENBURG

This long-forgotten Baltic Coast region, pinned between two sprawling urban areas—the state capital of Schwerin, in the west, and Rostock, in the east—is thriving with trade, industry, and tourism. Though the region is close to the sea, it's made up largely of seemingly endless fields of wheat and yellow rape and a hundred or so wonderful lakes. "When the Lord made the Earth, He started with Mecklenburg," wrote native novelist Fritz Reuter.

WISMAR

60 km (37 miles) east of Lübeck.

The old city of Wismar was one of the original three sea-trading towns, along with Lübeck and Rostock, which banded together in 1259 to combat Baltic pirates. From this mutual defense pact grew the great and powerful private-trading bloc, the Hanseatic League (the *Hanse* in German), which dominated the Baltic for centuries. The wealth generated by the Hanseatic merchants can still be seen in Wismar's ornate architecture.

ESSENTIALS

Visitor Information Wismar Tourist Office. ⊠ *Stadthaus, Am Markt 11* ☎ *03841/19433* ⊕ *www.wismar.de.*

The Baltic Coast

FERRY TO
COPENHAGEN,
DENMARK

FERRY TO
YSTAD,
SWEDEN

FERRY TO
RØNNE,
DENMARK

FERRY TO
TRELLEBORG,
SWEDEN

FERRY TO
TRELLEBORG,
SWEDEN

DENMARK

Baltic Sea

Sakskøbing

A9

Nykøbing
Falster

E55

Rødbyhavn

Gedser

Puttgarden

0   20 mi

0   20 km

*Mecklenburger
Bucht*

Heiligendamm

Kühlungsborn

Neubukow

Wismar

WESTERN
MECKLENBURG

Güstrow

A14

A20

Schwerin

B104

Sternberg

Karow

Waren

Kap
Arkona

Hiddensee
Island

Schaprode

**Rügen
Island**

129 Sassnitz

Prora

Bergen

Binz

Prerow

Wustrow

Barth

B96

Putbus

Göhren

Deutsches ♦
Bernsteinmuseum

Ribnitz-
Damgarten

B105

Stralsund

*Greifswalder
Bodden*

B105

B194

Peenemünde

**Usedom
Island**

Warnemünde

**Bad
Doberan**

Rostock

A20

Greifswald

Wolgast

B111

Ückeritz

Bansin

Heringsdorf

Ahlbeck

Loitz

Bandelin

Swinoujscie

A20   A19   Laage

B110

Demmin

A20

Anklam

PL

Teterow

Reuterstadt
Stavenhagen

B197

B109

A19

B104

Neubrandenburg

A20

Pasewalk

B192

VORPOMMERN

EXPLORING

TOP ATTRACTIONS

Marktplatz (*Market Square*). One of the largest and best-preserved squares in Germany is framed by patrician gabled houses. Their style ranges from redbrick late Gothic through Dutch Renaissance to 19th-century neoclassical. The square's **Wasserkunst**, the ornate pumping station built in Dutch Renaissance style, was constructed between 1580 and 1602 by the Dutch master Philipp Brandin. ⊠ *Wismar*.

St. Georgen zu Wismar. One of northern Germany's biggest Gothic churches, built between 1315 and 1404, St. Georgen zu Wismar stands next to the Fürstenhof. It was a victim of the war, but has been almost completely restored. ⊠ *St.-Georgen-Kirchhof 6.*

NEED A BREAK?

To'n Zägenkrog. While wandering among the medieval and modern jetties and quays of the port, you might feel the need for a snack. This seamen's haven, decorated with sharks' teeth, stuffed seagulls, and maritime gear, is a good pit stop along the harbor. ⊠ *Ziegenmarkt 10* ☎ *03841/282–716.*

If the weather is fine, take a stroll along Wismar's historic harbor.

WORTH NOTING

Fürstenhof (*Princes' Court*). The home of the former dukes of Mecklenburg stands next to the Marienkirche. It's an early-16th-century Italian Renaissance palace with touches of late Gothic. The facade is a series of fussy friezes depicting scenes from the Trojan War. ✉ *Fürstenhof 1.*

Marienkirche (*St. Mary's Church*). All that remains of the oldest sacral building in Wismar is the 250-foot tower. Although only partialy damaged in the war, the East German government demolished the hall of the church in 1960. Just behind the Marktplatz; the church is still undergoing restoration. At noon, 3, and 5, listen for one of 14 hymns played on its carillon. ✉ *St.-Marien-Kirchhof.*

St. Nikolaikirche (*St. Nicholas's Church*). The late-Gothic church, with a 120-foot-high nave, was built between 1381 and 1487. A remnant of the town's long domination by Sweden is the additional altar built for Swedish sailors. ✉ *St.-Nikolai-Kirchhof 15* ☎ *03841/210–143* 🎟 *Free* 🕓 *May–Sept., daily 8–8; Apr. and Oct., daily 10–6; Nov.–Mar., daily 11–4.*

WHERE TO EAT

$$ GERMAN 🍴 **Alter Schwede.** Regarded as one of the most attractive, authentic taverns on the Baltic—and correspondingly busy—this eatery focuses on Mecklenburg's game and poultry dishes, such as the traditional *Mecklenburger Ente* (Mecklenburg duck). This filling dish is filled with baked plums, apples, and raisins, and served with red cabbage and potatoes. [$] *Average main: €15* ✉ *Am Markt 19* ☎ *03841/283–552* 🌐 *www.alter-schwede-wismar.de.*

$ GERMAN 🍴 **Brauhaus am Lohberg.** Wismar's first brewery (1452) is the only place that still brews *Wismarer Mumme,* a dark beer with enough alcohol to keep it fresh for export as far away as St. Petersburg. The restaurant serves good-value typical pub food in an old half-timber house near the harbor. $ *Average main: €13* ⊠ *Kleine Hohe Str. 15* ☎ *03841/250–238.*

WHERE TO STAY

$$ ⚏ **Citypartner Hotel Alter Speicher.**

B&B/INN This small and personable family-owned hotel lies behind the facade of an old merchant house in the downtown area. **Pros:** good location in easy walking distance to medieval Wismar. **Cons:** rooms have outdated furnishings and style; rooms tend to be small. $ *Rooms from: €119* ⊠ *Bohrstr. 12–12a* ☎ *03841/211–746* ⊕ *www.hotel-alter-speicher.de* ⤳ *70 rooms, 3 suites, 2 apartments* ⍾⦶ *Breakfast.*

$$ ⚏ **Seehotel Neuklostersee.** Set at the dreamy Naun Lake, this country hotel

B&B/INN is a hidden gem 15 km (9 miles) east of Wismar. **Pros:** great rural setting in quaint surroundings. **Cons:** outside Wismar; many day-trip visitors. $ *Rooms from: €175* ⊠ *Seestr. 1, Nakenstorf* ☎ *038422/4570* ⊕ *www.seehotel-neuklostersee.de* ⤳ *10 suites, 3 apartments* ⍾⦶ *Breakfast.*

$ ⚏ **Steigenberger–Hotel Stadt Hamburg.** This first-class hotel hides behind

HOTEL a rigid gray facade dating back to the early 19th century, but the interior is surprisingly open and airy, with skylights and a posh lobby. **Pros:** the only upscale hotel in town; great package deals available; appealing interior design. **Cons:** lacks atmosphere and personal touches. $ *Rooms from: €95* ⊠ *Am Markt 24* ☎ *03841/2390* ⊕ *www.wismar.steigenberger.de* ⤳ *102 rooms, 2 suites* ⍾⦶ *Breakfast.*

> **DID YOU KNOW?**
>
> In 1922 filmmaker Friedrich Wilhelm Murnau used the tortuous streets of Wismar's Old Town in his expressionist horror-film classic, *Nosferatu.*

14

SCHWERIN

32 km (20 miles) south of Wismar on Rte. 106.

Schwerin, the second-largest town in the region after Rostock and the capital of the state of Mecklenburg-Vorpommern, is worth a trip just to visit its giant island castle.

TOURS

FAMILY **Weisse Flotte.** The quintessential experience in Schwerin is one of the Weiss Flotte boat tours of the lakes—there are seven in the area. A trip to the island of Kaninchenwerder, a small sanctuary for more than 100 species of waterbirds, is an unforgettable experience. Boats for this 1½-hour standard tour depart from the pier adjacent to the Schweriner Schloss. ⊠ *Anlegestelle Schlosspier* ☎ *0385/557–770* ⊕ *www.weisseflotteschwerin.de* ⍿ *€12.50.*

ESSENTIALS

Visitor Information Schwerin. ⊠ *Rathaus, Am Markt 14* ☎ *0385/592–5212* ⊕ *www.schwerin.de.*

EXPLORING

Alter Garten (*Old Garden*). The town's showpiece square was the setting for military parades during the years of Communist rule. It's dominated by two buildings: the ornate neo-Renaissance state theater, constructed in 1883–86; and the Kunstsammlungen Schwerin (Schwerin Art Collection). ⊠ *Schwerin.*

Kunstsammlungen Schwerin (*Schwerin Art Collection*). This gallery houses an interesting collection of paintings by Max Liebermann and Lovis Corinth, along with Dutch and Flemish works and sculpture. There are also exhibitions of contemporary art. ⊠ *Alter Garten 3* ☎ *0385/595–8119* ⊕ *www.museum-schwerin.de* 🖃 *€8; temporary exhibitions €5; combined ticket for two museums €9, three museums €11, four museums €13* ⊙ *Mid-Apr.–mid-Oct., Tues.–Sun. 10–6; mid-Oct.–mid-Apr., Tues.–Sun. 10–5.*

Schlossmuseum. North of the castle's main tower is the **Neue Lange Haus** (New Long House), built between 1553 and 1555 and now used as the Schlossmuseum. The Communist government restored and maintained the fantastic opulence of this rambling, 80-room reminder of an absolutist monarchy—and then used it to board kindergarten teachers in training. Antique furniture, objets d'art, silk tapestries, and paintings are sprinkled throughout the salons (the throne room is particularly extravagant), but of special interest are the ornately patterned and highly burnished inlaid wooden floors and wall panels. ⊠ *Lennéstr. 1* ☎ *0385/525–2920* ⊕ *www.museum-schwerin.de* 🖃 *€6; combined ticket for two museums €9, three museums €11, four museums €13* ⊙ *Mid-Apr.–mid-Oct., daily 10–6; mid-Oct.–mid-Apr., Tues.–Sun. 10–5.*

Schweriner Dom (*Schwerin Cathedral*). This Gothic cathedral is the oldest building (built 1222–48) in the city. The bronze baptismal font is from the 14th century; the altar was built in 1440. Religious scenes painted on its walls date from the late Middle Ages. Sweeping views of the Old Town and lake await those with the energy to climb the 219 steps to the top of the 320-foot-high cathedral tower. ⊠ *Am Dom 4* ☎ *0385/565–014* 🖃 *Free* ⊙ *Tower and nave May–Oct., Mon.–Sat. 10–5, Sun. noon–5; Nov.–Apr., Mon.–Sat. 11–4, Sun. noon–4.*

Schweriner Schloss. On an island near the edge of Lake Schwerin, this meticulously restored palace once housed the Mecklenburg royal family. The original palace dates from 1018, but was enlarged by Henry the Lion when he founded Schwerin in 1160. Portions of it were later modeled on Chambord, in the Loire Valley. As it stands now, the palace is surmounted by 15 turrets, large and small, and is reminiscent of a French château. The portions that are neo-Renaissance in style are its many ducal staterooms, which date from between 1845 and 1857. ⊠ *Lennéstr. 1* 🖃 *€6; combined ticket for two museums €9, three museums €11, four museums €13* ⊙ *Mid-Apr.–mid-Oct., Tues.–Sun. 10–6; mid-Oct.–mid-Apr., Tues.–Sun. and public holidays 10–5.*

WHERE TO EAT

$ ✕ **Alt-Schweriner Schankstuben.** A small family-owned restaurant and
GERMAN   hotel with 16 guest rooms, the Schankstuben emphasizes Mecklenburg tradition. Its inviting restaurant is perfect for sampling local recipes such as *Rollbraten von Spanferkel* (roast suckling pig) or *Maisscholle* (corn-fed plaice). $ *Average main: €12* ⊠ *Am Schlachtermarkt 9–13* ☎ *0385/592–530* ⊕ *www.alt-schweriner-schankstuben.de* ⊙ *No lunch.*

$ ✕ **Weinhaus Krömer.** One of the most traditional and popular eateries
GERMAN in Schwerin, this restaurant has a long history of serving good wines
that dates from 1740. The *Weinbistro* offers primarily German wine
tasting and a small menu (mostly cheese plates or soups such as lobster
bisque). Regional and international specialties are served in the modern restaurant, while in summer the Weingarten courtyard is one of
the city's most secluded spots to enjoy a good glass of wine. $ *Average
main: €13* ✉ *Grosser Moor 56* ☎ *0385/562–956.*

$ ✕ **Zum Stadtkrug-Altstadtbrauhaus.** Don't be fooled by the prefab exterior:
GERMAN Schwerin's only brewery is an oasis of great beer and down-to-earth
regional and brauhaus specialties like the *Malzsack* (a pork schnitzel
breaded with brewing malt) or Mecklenburger lamb. There are also
barbecued steaks and some vegetarian options. Wash it down with
the house-brewed unfiltered light or dark beer. $ *Average main: €13*
✉ *Wismarsche Str. 126* ☎ *0385/593–6693* ⊕ *www.altstadtbrauhaus.
de* ▭ *No credit cards.*

WHERE TO STAY

$$ ☖ **Hotel Niederländischer Hof.** The city's most elegant hotel has a 4½-star
HOTEL rating in view of its luxurious interior, decorated in a classic style,
its romantic, airy rooms, and the impeccable service. **Pros:** interesting
packages include tours, dinner, and more; great location right off a
pond; within walking distance of the Schloss, boat docks, and down-
town museums. **Cons:** formal atmosphere. $ *Rooms from: €150* ✉ *Al-
exandrinenstr. 12–13* ☎ *0385/591–100* ⊕ *www.niederlaendischer-hof.
de* ⮌ *27 rooms, 6 suites* ❙○❙ *Breakfast.*

$$ ☖ **Sorat-Hotel Speicher am Ziegelsee.** Towering seven stories above the old
HOTEL harbor, the Speicher am Ziegelsee was once a grain warehouse. **Pros:**
unbeatable location on a lovely lake; very friendly and professional
service; lakeside dining. **Cons:** old-style warehouse building; rooms may
seem cramped for some travelers; a bit far from the action. $ *Rooms
from: €110* ✉ *Speicherstr. 11* ☎ *0385/50030* ⊕ *www.speicher-hotel.com*
⮌ *59 rooms, 20 apartments* ❙○❙ *Breakfast.*

NIGHTLIFE AND PERFORMING ARTS

Mecklenburgisches Staatstheater. German drama and opera are staged in
this fine historic theater. ✉ *Am Alten Garten* ☎ *0385/53000* ⊕ *www.
theater-schwerin.de.*

Mexxclub. This is the city's hottest dance club. It features house and soul DJs
who attract a stylish young crowd every Saturday night. ✉ *Klöresgang 2.*

Schlossfestspiele. Started in 1993, this annual summertime festival features open-air drama or comedy performances, which are heald at various venues around Schwerin including the Mecklenburg State Theatre,
the castle garden, the National Theatre, and the National Museum.
✉ *Schlossstr. 1.*

SHOPPING

Antiques and bric-a-brac that have languished in cellars and attics since
World War II are still surfacing throughout eastern Germany, and the
occasional bargain can be found. The best places to look in Schwerin are
on and around Schmiedestrasse, Schlossstrasse, and Mecklenburgstrasse.

14

BAD DOBERAN

60 km (37 miles) east of Wismar on Rte. 105, 90 km (56 miles) northeast of Schwerin.

Mostly famous for its cathedral, Bad Doberan is a quaint town that also has Germany's oldest sea resort, Heiligendamm. The city is a popular weekend and summer getaway for people from Rostock and Berlin, but it's managed to maintain its laid-back charm.

ESSENTIALS

Visitor Information Bad Doberan Tourist Office. ✉ *Severinstr. 6* ☎ *038203/62154* 🌐 *www.bad-doberan.de.*

EXPLORING

Doberaner Münster (*Monastery Church*). Bad Doberan is home to this meticulously restored redbrick church, one of the finest of its kind in Germany. It was built by Cistercian monks between 1294 and 1368 in the northern German brick Gothic style, with a central nave and transept. The main altar dates from the early 14th century. ✉ *Klosterstr. 2* ☎ *038203/62716* 🌐 *www.doberanermuenster.de* 🎫 *€3* 🕒 *May–Sept., Mon.–Sat. 9–6, Sun. 11–6; Mar., Apr., and Oct., Mon.–Sat. 10–5, Sun. 11–5; Nov.–Feb., Mon.–Sat. 10–4, Sun. 11–4. Tours May–Oct., Mon.–Sat. at noon and 3; Nov.–Apr., Mon.–Sat. at 11 and 1.*

FAMILY ***Molli.*** No visit to this part of the country would be complete without a ride on this narrow-gauge steam train that has been chugging its 16-km (10-mile) route through the streets of Bad Doberan to the nearby beach resorts of **Heiligendamm** and **Kühlungsborn** since 1886. The train was nicknamed after a little local dog that barked its approval every time the smoking iron horse passed by. In summer *Molli* runs 13 times daily between Bad Doberan and Kühlungsborn. ✉ *Am Bahnhof* ☎ *038203/4150* 🌐 *www.molli-bahn.de* 🎫 *Same-day round-trip €9.50–€13.50* 🕒 *May–Sept., daily 8:35–6:45 (last return from Heiligendamm at 7:02); Oct.–Apr., daily 8:35–4:40 (last return from Heiligendamm at 5).*

WHERE TO EAT AND STAY

$ GERMAN 🍴 **Weisser Pavillon.** Here's a mixed setting for you: a 19th-century Chinese-pagoda-type structure in an English-style park. Come for lunch or high tea; regional specialties are featured. In summer the café stays open until 10 pm. [$] *Average main: €10* ✉ *Auf dem Kamp* ☎ *038203/62326* 💳 *No credit cards.*

$$$$ HOTEL FAMILY Fodor's Choice ★ 🏨 **Grand Hotel Heiligendamm.** Nestled in five meticulously restored, gleaming white structures on a secluded beach, the hotel displays an almost Californian Bel Air charm and offers timelessly furnished rooms decorated in soft colors. **Pros:** the only real first-class hotel on the Baltic Coast; wide range of sports and activities; wonderful amenities for children up to age 11. **Cons:** very large hotel spread out over somewhat long distances; service is formal and stiff at times; books up quickly in high season. [$] *Rooms from: €245* ✉ *Prof.-Dr.-Vogel-Str. 16–18, Heiligendamm* ☎ *038203/7400* 🌐 *www.grandhotel-heiligendamm.de* 🛏 *118 rooms, 107 suites* 🍽 *Breakfast.*

ROSTOCK

14 km (9 miles) east of Bad Doberan on Rte. 105.

The biggest port and shipbuilding center of the former East Germany, Rostock was founded around 1200. Of all the Hanseatic cities, this once-thriving city suffered the most from the dissolution of the League in 1669. The GDR reestablished Rostock as a major port, but after reunification, shipbuilding all but disappeared. Nevertheless, the city set its sights to the future, retooled its factories and is now a major producer of wind turbines. Ferries from Gedser (Denmark) and Trelleborg (Sweden) come here. The population doubles in the summer due to Baltic cruise ships that dock in Warnemünde. ■ TIP➡ **The biggest local annual attraction is Hanse Sail, a week of yacht racing held in August.**

14

ESSENTIALS

Visitor Information Rostock Tourist Office. ⊠ *Universitätspl. 6* ☎ *0381/32222* ⊕ *www.rostock.de.*

EXPLORING

TOP ATTRACTIONS

Kröpelinerstrasse. This pedestrian-only shopping street stretches from the Kröpeliner Tor (the old western gate) to the Neuer Markt. Here you'll find the finest examples of late-Gothic and Renaissance houses of rich Hanse merchants. ⊠ *Kröpelinerstr.*

St. Marienkirche (*St. Mary's Church*). This eight-centuries-old church, Rostock's greatest example of Gothic architecture, contains a bronze baptismal font from 1290 and some interesting baroque features, notably the oak altar (1720) and organ (1770). The huge astronomical clock, dating from 1472, has a calendar extending to 2017. ⊠ *Am Ziegenmarkt 4* ☎ *0381/492–3396* 🎟 *Free* 🕐 *May–Sept., Mon.–Sat. 10–6, Sun. 11:15–5; Oct.–Apr., Mon.–Sat. 10–12:15 and 2–4, Sun. 11–12:15.*

Universitätsplatz (*University Square*). The triangular University Square, commemorating the founding of one of northern Europe's oldest universities here in 1419, is home to Rostock University's Italian Renaissance–style main building, finished in 1867. ⊠ *Rostock.*

WORTH NOTING

Neuer Markt (*Town Square*). Here, you'll immediately notice the architectural potpourri of the **Rathaus.** The pink baroque facade from the 18th century hides a wonderful 13th-century Gothic building underneath. The Town Hall spouts seven slender, decorative towers that look like candles on a peculiar birthday cake. Walk around the back to see more of the Gothic elements. Historic gabled houses surround the rest of the square. ⊠ *Rostock.*

FAMILY **Schifffahrtsmuseum** (*Maritime Museum*). Tracing the history of shipping on the Baltic, this museum displays models of ships, which especially intrigue children. It's just beyond the city wall, at the old city gateway, Steintor. ⊠ *August-Bebel-Str. 1* ☎ *0381/492–2697* ⊕ *www. schifffahrtsmuseum-rostock.de* 🎟 *€4* 🕐 *Tues.–Sun. 11–6.*

FAMILY **Zoologischer Garten** (*Zoological Garden*). Here you'll find one of the largest collections of exotic animals and birds in northern Germany. This zoo is particularly noted for its polar bears, some of which were bred in Rostock. If you're traveling with children, a visit is a must. ✉ *Rennbahnallee 21* ☎ *0381/20820* 🌐 *www.zoo-rostock.de* 🎟 *€16* 🕘 *Apr.–Oct., daily 9–7; Nov.–Mar., daily 9–5.*

WHERE TO EAT

$$ GERMAN 🍴 **Petrikeller.** Once you've crossed the threshold of the Petrikeller, you'll find yourself in the medieval world of Hanseatic merchants, seamen, and wild pirates such as Klaus Störtebecker. The restaurant's motto, "Wer nicht liebt Wein, Weib und Gesang bleibt ein Narr sein Leben lang" (He who doth not love wine, woman and song will be a fool his whole life long), a quote from reformer Martin Luther no less, sets the right tone. The largely meat-centric menu reflects the cuisine of the Middle Ages, when meat and roots were the common daily ration. Try duck roasted over an open fire with braised red cabbage, or a host of other delights that can easily be eaten with your hands or from the back of a dagger. [$] *Average main: €16* ✉ *Harte Str. 27* ☎ *0381/455–855* 🌐 *www.petrikeller.de* 💳 *No credit cards* 🕘 *Closed Mon. No lunch.*

$$$ ASIAN 🍴 **Restaurant & Bar Silo 4.** This restaurant provides proof that eastern Germany can do sleek and modern. At the top of a waterfront office tower, this innovative restaurant offers spectacular views of the river and a fun and interesting approach to Asian-fusion cuisine. The menu consists of a list of ingredients and seasonings. Guests choose what they like and then leave it to the experts in the show kitchen to work their magic. [$] *Average main: €25* ✉ *Am Strande 3d* ☎ *0381/458–5800* 🌐 *www.silo4.de* 🕘 *Closed Mon. No lunch.*

$ SEAFOOD 🍴 **Zur Kogge.** Looking like the cabin of a Kogge (a Hanseatic sailing vessel), the oldest sailors' beer tavern in town serves mostly fish. Order the *Mecklenburger Fischsuppe* (fish soup) if it's on the menu. The *Grosser Fischteller,* consisting of three kinds of fish—depending on the day's catch—served with vegetables, lobster and shrimp sauce, and potatoes, is also a popular choice. Meals are served from 4:30 pm, but it's open for unremarkable snacks from 11:30. [$] *Average main: €13* ✉ *Wokrenterstr. 27* ☎ *0381/493–4493* 🌐 *www.zur-kogge.de* ✍ *Reservations essential.*

WHERE TO STAY

$ HOTEL 🏨 **Pental Hotel.** A 19th-century mansion, this hotel is a genuine part of Rostock's historic Old Town. **Pros:** good location; very quiet backstreet. **Cons:** restaurant isn't very good; uninspired room design. [$] *Rooms from: €99* ✉ *Schwaansche Str. 6* ☎ *0381/49700* 🌐 *www.pentahotels.com* 🛏 *150 rooms, 2 suites* 🍽 *Breakfast.*

$$ HOTEL 🏨 **Steigenberger–Hotel zur Sonne Rostock.** With more than 200 years of history behind it, the "Sun," within the Old Town, is one of the nicest hotels in Rostock. **Pros:** nice view and near many sights; good restaurants, cafés, and bars nearby. **Cons:** rooms get direct sunlight in summer, and therefore are very warm; a room with open setting of bed in the middle of the room may be unsettling for some. [$] *Rooms from: €102* ✉ *Neuer Markt 2* ☎ *0381/49730* 🌐 *www.rostock.steigenberger.de* 🛏 *90 rooms, 21 suites* 🍽 *Breakfast.*

NIGHTLIFE AND PERFORMING ARTS

The summer season brings with it a plethora of special concerts, sailing regattas, and parties on the beach.

Volkstheater. The Volkstheater presents plays, from the classics to more contemporary works, and concerts. ⊠ *Patriotischer Weg 33* ☎ *0381/4600* ⊕ *www.volkstheater-rostock.de.*

SHOPPING

Echter Rostocker Doppel-Kümmel und -Korn, a kind of schnapps made from various grains and flavored with cumin, is a traditional liquor of the area around Rostock. Fishermen have numbed themselves to the cold for centuries with this 80-proof beverage. A bottle costs €8–€11; Lehmmet is the best brand of this local moonshine.

14

WARNEMÜNDE

14 km (9 miles) north of Rostock on Rte. 103.

Warnemünde, officially a suburb of Rostock, is a quaint seaside resort town with the best hotels and restaurants in the area, as well as 20 km (12 miles) of beautiful white-sand beach. It's been a popular summer getaway for families in eastern Germany for years.

There is little to do in Warnemünde except relax, and the town excels brilliantly at that. However, Warnemünde is a major cruise-ship terminal. Whenever there is more than one ship at dock, the town explodes with a county fair–like atmosphere, and shops and restaurants stay open until the ships leave at midnight. The city celebrates the *dreifache Anlauf,* when three ships dock simultaneously, with fireworks.

GETTING HERE AND AROUND

Thanks to its proximity to Rostock and the A-20, Warnemünde is easily accessible from any major city in the region. Traffic between the seaside district of Rostock and the downtown area can be heavy on summer weekends. The best way to explore the city is by riding a bike or walking.

ESSENTIALS

Visitor Information Warnemünde Tourist Office. ⊠ *Am Strom 59, Ecke Kirchenstr., Rostock* ☎ *0381/381–2222* ⊕ *www.rostock.de.*

EXPLORING

Alter Strom (*Old Stream*). Inland from the lighthouse is this yacht marina. Once the entry into the port of Warnemünde, it now has bars, plenty of good restaurants, and touristy shops. The fishing boats lining the Strom sell the day's catch, smoked fish, and bags of fried mussels. ⊠ *Rostock.*

FAMILY **Leuchtturm.** Children enjoy climbing to the top of the town landmark, a 115-foot-high lighthouse, dating from 1898; on clear days it offers views of the coast and Rostock Harbor. In summer, adults can enjoy a cold beer from the Marlower Brauhaus trailer at the base of the lighthouse. ⊠ *Seepromenade, Rostock.*

BEACHES

FAMILY **Warnemünde.** The beach fronting the resort town of Warnemünde is one of Germany's most popular and it can get fairly crowded in summer. The expansive beach, with its soft, clean sand, is fabulous for sunbathing, relaxing, or walking. The pleasant sea breeze invites kite flyers and you can purchase different kinds of kites from the open-air market along the promenade. Food and drinks are available from many vendors and at several supermarkets in the town itself. **Amenities:** food and drink; parking; showers; toilets; water sports. **Best for:** sunrise; sunset; swimming; walking. ✉ *Seepromende 1, Rostock.*

WHERE TO EAT AND STAY

$ SEAFOOD 🍴 **Fischerklause.** Sailors have stopped in at this restaurant's bar for more than a century. The smoked fish sampler, served on a lazy Susan, is delicious, and the house specialty of fish soup is best washed down with some Rostocker Doppel-Kümmel schnapps. An accordionist entertains the crowd on weekends. [$] *Average main: €11* ✉ *Am Strom 123, Rostock* ☎ *0381/52516* ✍ *Reservations essential.*

$ RESORT 🏨 **Landhotel Ostseetraum.** This family-owned hotel, in a thatch-roof farmhouse outside Warnemünde, blends contemporary style with rural architecture. **Pros:** quiet; green setting not far away from the sea; friendly and personalized service; very private apartments. **Cons:** old-fashioned interior design in need of updating in some rooms and public areas; outside Warnemünde proper. [$] *Rooms from: €95* ✉ *Stolteraerweg 34b, Rostock* ☎ *0381/519–1848* 🌐 *www.ostseetraum.de* 🛏 *18 rooms* 🍽 *Breakfast.*

$$$ RESORT 🏨 **Yachthafenresidenz Hohe Düne.** The star on the Baltic Coast is this huge, modern resort, comfortably residing on a peninsula between the yacht harbor, a sandy beach, and the port entrance. **Pros:** very well run; stylish hotel with a great ambience and amenities; impressive wellness and spa area. **Cons:** outside Warnemünde; accessible only by ferry from the town center and not along the central promenade; only a few attractions and restaurants in walking distance; pretentious staff. [$] *Rooms from: €215* ✉ *Am Yachthafen 1–8, Rostock* ☎ *0381/5040* 🌐 *www.yhd.de* 🛏 *345 rooms, 23 suites* 🍽 *Breakfast.*

NIGHTLIFE

The pubs in the marina **Alter Strom** are fun gathering places.

Skybar. This bar is open until 3 am Friday and Saturday. Roof access gives you the chance to sit under the stars and watch ship lights twinkle on the sea. ✉ *Neptun Hotel, Seestr. 19, 19th fl., Rostock* ☎ *0381/7770* 🌐 *www.hotel-neptun.de/sky-bar.html.*

EN ROUTE **Ribnitz-Damgarten.** Ribnitz-Damgarten, 30 km (19 miles) northeast of Warnemünde, is the center of the amber (in German, *Bernstein*) business, unique to the Baltic Coast. Amber is a yellow-brown fossil formed from the sap of ancient conifers and is millions of years old. Head for a beach and join the locals in the perennial quest for amber stones washed up among the seaweed. ✉ *Ribnitz-Damgarten.*

Deutsches Bernsteinmuseum (*German Amber Museum*). In the Deutsches Bernsteinmuseum, which adjoins the main factory, you can see a fascinating exhibit of how this precious "Baltic gold" is collected from the sea and refined to make jewelry. The museum has pieces of amber that are between 35 and 50 million years old. ⊠ *Im Kloster 1–3, Rib-nitz-Damgarten* ☎ *03821/2931* ⊕ *www.deutsches-bernsteinmuseum.de* 🎫*€8.50* ⊘ *Mar.–Oct., daily 9:30–6; Nov.–Feb., Tues.–Sun. 9:30–5; last entry 30 mins before closing.*

VORPOMMERN

The best description of this region is found in its name, which simply means "before Pomerania." This area, indeed, seems trapped between Mecklenburg and the authentic, old Pomerania farther east, now part of Poland. Its remoteness ensures an unforgettable view of unspoiled nature, primarily attracting families and younger travelers.

14

STRALSUND

68 km (42 miles) east of Rostock on Rte. 105.

This jewel of the Baltic has retained its historic city center and parts of its 13th-century defensive wall. The wall was built following an attack by the Lübeck fleet in 1249. In 1815 the Congress of Vienna awarded the city, which had been under Swedish control, to the Prussians.

GETTING HERE AND AROUND

Stralsund is well linked to both Rostock and Berlin by A-20 and A-19. The city is an ideal base for exploring the coast via the well-developed network of Bundesstrassen around it. Inside the city, walking or biking are better options, though, as the dense, historic downtown area makes it difficult to drive.

ESSENTIALS

Visitor Information Stralsund Tourist Office. ⊠ *Alter Markt 9* ☎ *03831/24690* ⊕ *www.stralsund.de.*

EXPLORING

TOP ATTRACTIONS

Alter Markt (*Old Market Square*). The Alter Markt has the best local architecture, ranging from Gothic to Renaissance to baroque. Most homes belonged to rich merchants, notably the late-Gothic **Wulflam-haus,** with 17 ornate, steeply stepped gables. Stralsund's architectural masterpiece, however, is the 14th-century **Rathaus,** considered by many to be the finest secular example of redbrick Gothic. The Rathaus is a mirror image of its counterpart in Lübeck, Stralsund's main rival in the Hanseatic League ⊠ *Stralsund.*

FAMILY **Deutsches Meeresmuseum** (*German Sea Museum*). The Stralsund aquar-ium of Baltic Sea life is part of this three-floor museum, which also displays the skeletons of a giant whale and a hammerhead shark, and a 25-foot-high chunk of coral. ⊠ *Katharinenberg 14–20, entrance on Mönchstr.* ☎ *03831/265–021* ⊕ *www.meeresmuseum.de* 🎫 *€9* ⊘ *June–Sept., daily 10–6; Oct.–May, daily 10–5.*

St. Marienkirche (*St. Mary's Church*). This enormous church is the largest of Stralsund's three redbrick Gothic churches. With 4,000 pipes and intricate decorative figures, the magnificent 17th-century Stellwagen organ (played only during Sunday services) is a delight to see and hear. The view from the church tower of Stralsund's old city center is well worth climbing the 349 steps. ✉ *Neuer Markt, Marienstr., entrance at Bleistr.* ☎ *03831/293–529* 🎫 *Tour of church tower €4* 🕘 *May–Oct., weekdays 9–6, weekends 10–noon; Nov.–Apr., weekdays 10–noon and 2–6, weekends 10–noon.*

WORTH NOTING

Katherinenkloster (*St. Catherine's Monastery*). In this former cloister, 40 rooms now house two museums: the famed Deutsches Meeresmuseum, and the Kulturhistorisches Museum. ✉ *Bielkenhagen.*

Kulturhistorisches Museum (*Cultural History Museum*). This museum exhibits diverse artifacts from more than 10,000 years of this coastal region's history. Highlights include a toy collection and 10th-century Viking gold jewelry found on Hiddensee. You reach the museum by walking along Ossenreyerstrasse through the Apollonienmarkt on Mönchstrasse. ✉ *Mönchstr. 25–27* ☎ *03831/28790* 🎫 *€6* 🕘 *Tues.–Sun. 10–5.*

St. Nikolaikirche (*St. Nicholas's Church*). The treasures of the 13th-century Gothic church include a 15-foot-high crucifix from the 14th century, an astronomical clock from 1394, and a famous baroque altar. ✉ *Alter Markt* ☎ *03831/297–199* 🎫 *Free* 🕘 *Apr.–Sept., Mon.–Sat. 10–6, Sun. 11–noon and 2–4; Oct.–Mar., Mon.–Sat. 10–noon and 2–4, Sun. 11–noon and 2–4.*

WHERE TO EAT AND STAY

$$ SEAFOOD 🍴 **Wulflamstuben.** This restaurant is on the ground floor of the Wulflamhaus, a 14th-century gabled house on the old market square. Steaks and fish are the specialties; in late spring or early summer, get the light and tasty *Ostseescholle* (grilled plaice), fresh from the Baltic Sea. In winter the hearty *Stralsunder Aalsuppe* (Stralsund eel soup) is a must. [$] *Average main: €16* ✉ *Alter Markt 5* ☎ *03831/291–533* 🌐 *www.wulflamstuben.de* 🕘 *No lunch* ✍ *Reservations essential.*

$ GERMAN 🍴 **Zum Alten Fritz.** It's worth the trip here just to see the rustic interior and copper brewing equipment. Since the restaurant is owned by the Stralsunder Brewery, all Stralsunder and several Störtebecker beers are on tap, including the rare Störtebecker Roggen-Weizen, a wheat beer made with rye, and Germany's first India Pale Ale. In summer the beer garden gets somewhat rambunctious. [$] *Average main: €13* ✉ *Greifswalder Chaussee 84–85, at B-96a* ☎ *03831/25550* 🌐 *www.alter-fritz.de.*

$$ HOTEL 🏨 **Hotel zur Post.** This redbrick hotel is a great deal for travelers looking for a homey yet first-class ambience. **Pros:** very good location in the heart of historic downtown; good deals offered on hotel website. **Cons:** very small rooms with too much furniture; some rooms in need of updating. [$] *Rooms from: €122* ✉ *Am Neuen Markt, Tribseerstr. 22* ☎ *03831/200–500* 🌐 *www.hotel-zur-post-stralsund.de* 🛏 *104 rooms, 2 suites, 8 apartments* 🍽 *Breakfast.*

$$ HOTEL 🏨 **Wyndham Stralsund HanseDom Hotel.** This hotel, part of the Wyndham brand, is a modern property with winning amenities and great hospitality at an unbeatable price. **Pros:** top spa; solid and reliable services and amenities; breakfast until 11 am. **Cons:** for Stralsund, this is a

large, busy hotel; far away from city center (15 minutes). [$] *Rooms from: €129* ✉ *Grünhofer Bogen 18–20* ☎ *030/9780–8888* 🌐 *www.wyndhamstralsund.com* 🛏 *109 rooms, 5 suites* 🍴 *Breakfast.*

NIGHTLIFE

Bar Hemingway. Bar Hemingway lures a clientele mostly in their thirties with the best cocktails in town. ✉ *Tribseerstr. 22* ☎ *03831/200–500.*

Fun und Lollipop. A young crowd dances here. ✉ *Grünhofer Bogen 11* ☎ *03834/399–039.*

Störtebeker-Keller. For a genuine old harbor *Kneipe* (tavern), head to the Störtebeker-Keller, named for an infamous pirate. ✉ *Ossenreyerstr. 49* ☎ *03831/292–758.*

SHOPPING

Buddelschiffe (ships in a bottle) are a symbol of the magnificent sailing history of this region. They look easy to build, but they aren't, and they're quite delicate. Expect to pay more than €70 for a 1-liter bottle. Also look for *Fischerteppiche* (fishermen's carpets). Eleven square feet of these traditional carpets take 150 hours to create, which explains why they're meant only to be hung on the wall—and why they cost from €260 to €1,200. They're decorated with traditional symbols of the region, such as the mythical griffin.

RÜGEN ISLAND

4 km (2½ miles) northeast of Stralsund on B-96.

Fodor's Choice ★ Rügen's diverse and breathtaking landscapes have inspired poets and painters for more than a century. Railways in the mid-19th century brought the first vacationers from Berlin and many of the grand mansions and villas on the island date from this period. The island's main route runs between the **Grosser Jasmunder Bodden** (Big Jasmund Inlet), a giant sea inlet, and a smaller expanse of water, the **Kleiner Jasmunder Bodden** (Little Jasmund Inlet Lake), to the port of Sassnitz. You're best off staying at any of the island's four main vacation centers—Sassnitz, Binz, Sellin, and Göhren.

GETTING HERE AND AROUND

Rügen is an easy two-hour drive from Rostock and a 15-minute drive from Stralsund via the B-96. As there is only one bridge connecting the island to the mainland, the road can get clogged occasionally in summer. On the island, a car is highly recommended to reach the more-remote beaches, but watch out for island teenagers and their infatuation with muscle cars; give them a wide berth.

ESSENTIALS

Visitor Information **Sassnitz Tourist Office.** ✉ *Bahnhofstr. 19a, Sassnitz* ☎ *038392/6490* 🌐 *www.insassnitz.de.* **Tourismusverband Rügen.** ✉ *Bahnhofstr. 15, Bergen auf Rügen* ☎ *03838/807–780* 🌐 *www.ruegen.de.*

EXPLORING
TOP ATTRACTIONS

Binz. The largest resort town on Rügen's east coast, it has white villas and a beach promenade. Four kilometers (2½ miles) north of Binz are five massive facist resorts of **Bad Prora,** where the Nazis once planned to provide vacation quarters for up to 20,000 German workers. The complex was never used, except by the East German army. Redevelopment of the site began in 2003 and by 2014 refurbished apartments were available for purchase; there's also a youth hostel. Museums and galleries here today do their best to document the history of the site. ⊠ *Strandpromenade 1, Binz.*

Jagdschloss Granitz. Standing on the highest point of East Rügen, 2 km (1 mile) south of Binz, is the Jagdschloss Granitz, a hunting lodge built in 1836. It offers a splendid view in all directions from its lookout tower and has an excellent hunting exhibit. ⊠ *Binz* ☎ *038393/663–814* ⊕ *www.jagdschloss-granitz.de* ⊠ *€6* ⊙ *May–Sept., daily 9–6; Oct.–Apr., Tues.–Sun. 10–4.*

Kap Arkona. Marking the northernmost point in eastern Germany is the lighthouse at Kap Arkona, a nature lover's paradise filled with blustery sand dunes. The redbrick lighthouse was designed by Karl Friedrich Schinkel, the Prussian court-architect responsible for so many of today's landmarks in Berlin. ⊠ *Putgarten.*

Sassnitz. This small fishing town is the island's harbor for ferries to Sweden. Sassnitz is surrounded by some of the most pristine nature to be found along the Baltic Coast. Ten kilometers (6 miles) north of Sassnitz are the twin chalk cliffs of Rügen's main attraction, the **Stubbenkammer** headland. From here you can best see the much-photographed whitechalk cliffs called the **Königstuhl,** rising 350 feet from the sea. A steep trail leads down to a beach. ⊠ *Sassnitz.*

Jasmund Nationalpark. From Sassnitz, it is an easy walk to the Jasmund Nationalpark, where you can explore the marshes, lush pine forests, and towering chalk cliffs. ⊠ *Johanniskirchstr., Sassnitz* ⊕ *www. nationalpark-jasmund.de.*

WORTH NOTING

Bergen. This small town is the island's administrative capital, founded as a Slavic settlement some 900 years ago. The **Marienkirche** (St. Mary's Church) has geometric murals dating back to the late 1100s and painted brick octagonal pillars. The pulpit and altar are baroque. Outside the front door and built into the church facade is a gravestone from the 1200s. ⊠ *Bergen.*

Putbus. The heart of this town, 28 km (17 miles) southwest of Binz, is the Circus, a round central plaza dating back to the early 19th century. The immaculate white buildings surrounding the Circus give the city its nickname, "Weisse Stadt" (White City). In summer the blooming roses in front of the houses (once a requirement by the ruling noble family of Putbus) are truly spectacular. ✉ *Putbus*.

Rügenschen BäderBahn - Rasender Roland (*Racing Roland*). From Putbus you can take a ride on the 90-year-old narrow-gauge steam train, which runs 24 km (16 miles) to Göhren, at the southeast corner of Rügen. Trains leave hourly from Göhren to Binz and every two hours from Binz to Putbus; the ride takes 70 minutes each way. ✉ *Binzer Str. 12, Putbus* ☎ *038301/8010* ⊕ *www.rasender-roland.de* ✉ *Day ticket €22* ◷ *Apr.– Oct., daily 7:48 am–7:46 pm, with two departures per hr from Putbus; Nov.–Mar., daily 7:48 am–5:44 pm, with departures every 2 hrs.*

OFF THE BEATEN PATH

Hiddensee. Just 5 km (3 miles) off the northwest corner of Rügen is a smaller island called Hiddensee. The undisturbed solitude of this sticklike island has attracted such visitors as Albert Einstein, Thomas Mann, Rainer Maria Rilke, and Sigmund Freud. As Hiddensee is an auto-free zone, leave your car in Schaprode, 21 km (13 miles) west of Bergen, and take a ferry. Reederei Hiddensee *(03831/268–116; www. reederei-hiddensee.de)* makes the 45-minute trip from Schapröde on Rugen to Vitte on Hiddensee eight times a day, with other departures from Stralsund. They also serve the towns of Kloster and Neuendorf on Hiddensee. Fares start at €15.50. Vacation cottages and restaurants are on the island.

BEACHES

FAMILY **Binz.** The rule of the Baltics' most exclusive beach is "see and be seen." The 5-km-long (3-mile-long) and 54-yard-wide beach is the perfect place to sunbathe and swim, as well as stroll—there's a 150-year-old beach path promenade. The somewhat rocky beach is punctuated by the *Seebrücke*, a boardwalk that extends into the sea, and the nearby Smart Beach Tour Stadium, which regularly hosts parties, beach volleyball tournaments, and other events. **Amenities:** food and drink; lifeguards; parking; showers; toilets; water sports. **Best for:** partiers; surfing; swimming; walking. ✉ *Strandpromenade, Binz*.

Prora. This is one of the finest beaches on Rügen, and there's probably not another place like it in the world—think fine white beach bordered by a dense pine forest sitting in the shadow of the ruins of a monstrous Nazi beach resort. Prora actually sits in the Prorer Wiek, a pleasant cove with shallow water and plentiful sandbanks. **Amenities:** food and drink; lifeguards; parking; showers; toilets; water sports. **Best for:** nudists; sunset; swimming; walking. ✉ *Binz*.

Vitte. Tucked away on the west coast of Hiddensee near Vitte, is a 5-km-long (3-mile-long) beach with shimmering turquoise waters and sand so fine that you might mistake it for the Caribbean. The 50-yard-wide beach is ideal for families with children, but is only accessible by bicycle. The water is quite shallow and it's easy to walk out to the sandbanks. Vitte is divided between a nudist section to the south and a "textile" section to the north. Locals decorate the beach with baskets of flowers in summer. **Amenities:** showers; toilets; water sports. **Best for:** partiers; nudists; swimming; walking. ✉ *Süderende, Vitte*.

14

WHERE TO EAT

$$ GERMAN 🍴 **Panoramahotel Lohme.** Dinner at this restaurant dubbed "Rügen's balcony" offers some of the most beautiful views on the island. While enjoying fresh fish from local waters, prepared with a light Italian touch, you can watch the sunset over the cliffs of Kap Arkona. Fresh produce comes from local farmers, and the superb vintages are from small private wineries. Make a reservation, and insist on a table in the *Fontane-Veranda* (in winter) or the *Arkonablick-Terrasse* (in summer). [$] *Average main: €17* ✉ *An der Steilküste 8, Lohme* ☎ *038302/9110* 🌐 *www.panorama-hotel-lohme.de* 💳 *No credit cards* 🕒 *No lunch.*

WHERE TO STAY

$$ B&B/INN 🏨 **Hotel Godewind.** This small hotel offers food and lodging at very reasonable prices. **Pros:** quiet setting; very cozy rooms with nice furniture. **Cons:** almost no amenities or services offered. [$] *Rooms from: €105* ✉ *Süderende 53, Vitte* ☎ *038300/6600* 🌐 *www.hotelgodewind.de* 💳 *No credit cards* 🛏 *23 rooms, 19 cottages* 🍽 *Breakfast.*

$ RENTAL 🏨 **Hotel Villa Granitz.** This mostly wooden mansion is a small and quiet retreat for those who want to avoid the masses. **Pros:** cozy hotel in traditional style of the area; very competitive prices for the size and comfort of rooms. **Cons:** off the beaten track at the outskirts of the city; a distance from the beach. [$] *Rooms from: €84* ✉ *Birkenallee 17, Baabe* ☎ *038303/1410* 🌐 *www.villa-granitz.de* 💳 *No credit cards* 🛏 *44 rooms, 6 suites, 8 apartments* 🍽 *Breakfast.*

$$$$ HOTEL 🏨 **Travel Charme Hotel Kurhaus Binz.** The grand old lady of the Baltic Sea, the neoclassical 19th-century Kurhaus Binz is reviving the splendor of times past, when Binz was called the Nice of the North. **Pros:** great breakfast buffet; extremely clean; highly trained and friendly personnel; all the amenities. **Cons:** lacks the feel of a typical Rügen hotel; not very personal or intimate. [$] *Rooms from: €228* ✉ *Strandpromenade 27, Binz* ☎ *038393/6650* 🌐 *www.travelcharme.com* 🛏 *106 rooms, 20 suites* 🍽 *Breakfast.*

$$ HOTEL 🏨 **Vier Jahreszeiten.** This first-class beach resort in Binz is a sophisticated blend of historic seaside architecture and modern elegance. **Pros:** varied cultural and entertainment programs; stylish spa with great massages. **Cons:** small rooms; few places to relax in the hotel; aged shuttle service to the train station. [$] *Rooms from: €149* ✉ *Zeppelinstr. 8, Binz* ☎ *038393/500* 🌐 *www.vier-jahreszeiten.de* 🛏 *69 rooms, 7 suites, 50 apartments* 🍽 *Breakfast.*

USEDOM ISLAND

67 km (42 miles) to Wolgast bridge from Stralsund.

Fodor's Choice ★ Usedom Island has almost 32 km (20 miles) of sandy shoreline and a string of resorts. Much of the island's untouched landscape is a nature preserve that provides refuge for a number of rare birds, including the giant sea eagle, which has a wingspan of up to 8 feet. Even in summer this island feels more or less deserted, and is ready to be explored by bicycle. Due to a fluke in the postwar division of Germany, about one-fifth of the island is actually in Poland.

Vacationers sunbathe in Strandkörbe, or on a towel on Ahlbeck's beach.

GETTING HERE AND AROUND

From the west, Usedom is accessed via the causeway at **Wolgast.** The bridge closes to traffic at times to allow boats to pass through. From the south, the B-110 leads from Anklam to Usedom. In summer, particularly before and after weekends, traffic can be very heavy on both roads. Trains of the Usedomer-Baderbahn traverse the island every 30 minutes; the company also runs an extensive bus network.

ESSENTIALS

Bus and Train Contact Usedomer Bäderbahn. ⊠ *Am Bahnhof 1, Heringsdorf* ☎ *38378/27132* ⊕ *www.ubb-online.com.*

Visitor Information Usedom Island Tourismus. ⊠ *Waldstr. 1, Seebad Bansin* ☎ *038378/47710* ⊕ *www.usedom.de.*

EXPLORING

Ahlbeck. The island's main town is also one of its best resorts. The tidy and elegant resort is one of the three *Kaiserbäder* (imperial baths)—the two others are Heringsdorf and Bansin—where the Emperor Wilhelm II liked to spend his summers in the early 20th century. Noble families and rich citizens followed the emperor, turning Ahlbeck into one of the prettiest summer retreats on the Baltic Coast. Ahlbeck's landmark is the 19th-century wooden pier with four towers. Stroll the beach to the right of the pier and you'll arrive at the Polish border. ⊠ *1 Kurstr., Ahlbeck.*

Peenemünde. At the northwest tip of Usedom, 16 km (10 miles) from land-side Wolgast, is the launch site of the world's first ballistic missiles, the V-1 and V-2, developed by Germany during World War II. You can view these rockets as well as models of early airplanes and ships at the extensive Historical-Technical Museum Peenemünde. ✉ *Fährstr. 10, Peenemünde.*

Das Historisch-Technische Museum Peenemünde (*Historical-Technical Museum Peenemünde*). At this museum housed in the former factory power plant, one exhibit in particular covers the moral responsibility of scientists who develop new technology by focusing on the secret plants where most of the rocket parts were assembled, and where thousands of slave laborers died. Explanations of the exhibits in English are available. ✉ *Im Kraftwerk, Peenemünde* ☎ *038371/5050* 🌐 *www.peenemuende.de* 🎫 *€8* 🕒 *Apr.–Sept., daily 10–6; Oct., daily 10–4; Nov.–Mar., Tues.–Sun. 10–4.*

BEACHES

FAMILY **Kaiserbäder.** The Kaiserbäder Strand stretches for more than 12 km (7½ miles) along Usedom Island's northeast coast from Bansin to Heringsdorf to Ahlbeck. A promenade connects the three towns and the Imperial Bathing Beaches are a mix of 19th-century beach architecture on one side and beach-chair relaxation on the other. A stroll through the windy sea air is said to have magical recuperative powers and locals claim that when the conditions are right, the sand actually sings when the grains rub together. The wide beach bustles with weekend Berliners and long-term visitors in summer. **Amenities:** food and drink; lifeguards; parking; showers; toilets; water sports. **Best for:** partiers; sunrise; swimming; walking. ✉ *Strandpromenade, Heringsdorf.*

Ückeritz. One of the best-kept secrets on Usedom, this 12-km-long (7½-mile-long) beach is quite busy in the north but almost deserted farther south. The area is quite rustic and it's the perfect place to feel like you have the beach to yourself. **Amenities:** food and drink; parking **Best for:** solitude; nudists; sunrise; sunset. ✉ *Uferpromenade, Ückeritz.*

WHERE TO STAY

$$$ HOTEL 🏨 **Romantik Seehotel Ahlbecker Hof.** The grande dame of Ahlbeck, this four-star hotel calls to mind the island's past as a getaway for Prussian nobility in the 19th century. **Pros:** has one of the area's best spas; two gourmet restaurants; near beach. **Cons:** no elevator. [$] *Rooms from: €201* ✉ *Dünenstr. 47, Ahlbeck* ☎ *038378/620* 🌐 *www.seetel.de* 🛏 *70 rooms* 🍴 *Breakfast.*

BERLIN

WELCOME TO BERLIN

TOP REASONS TO GO

★ **Affordability:** Of the European capitals, Berlin is the best bargain. It's a city of high culture and low prices—tickets for the opera, theater, and museums tend to hover around €10.

★ **Long, creative nights:** The only European city without official closing hours, Berlin's young artists put on installations, performance events, and parties to keep you up all night.

★ **Museum Island (Museuminsel):** The architectural monuments and art treasures here will take you from an ancient Greek altar to Egyptian busts and a Roman market town to 18th-century Berlin and back.

★ **The Reichstag's cupola:** Reserve a coveted spot on a tour of Berlin's seat of parliament to admire the spectacular glass cupola, and to enjoy great views of Berlin.

★ **Trace history's path:** The division of Berlin was a major historical event and an anomaly in urban history. Follow the cobblestone markers of the Wall's path.

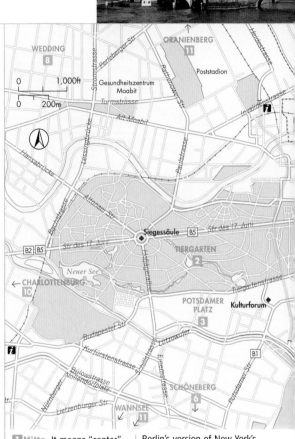

1 Mitte. It means "center" or "middle" in German, and it's at the center of the city. Once home to the city's Jewish quarters, after the war Mitte was part of East Berlin. Today, it's the center of the city once again, packed with monuments, museums, and shops.

2 Tiergarten. The Tiergarten neighborhood extends around the Tiergarten ("animal garden"), which is Berlin's version of New York's Central Park.

3 Potsdamer Platz. One of the busiest squares in prewar Europe, Potsdamer Platz is still the center of commercial action.

4 Friedrichshain. In the former East, Friedrichshain's offbeat bars, restaurants, and clubs attract creative types.

5 Kreuzberg. When Berlin was divided, West Berlin's Kreuzberg was right alongside the wall.

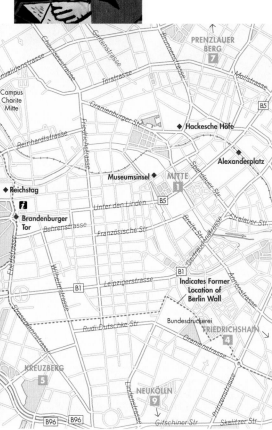

GETTING ORIENTED

In eastern Germany, almost halfway between Paris and Moscow, Berlin is Germany's largest city. When the city-state of Berlin was incorporated in 1920, it swallowed towns and villages far beyond what had been the downtown area around the two main rivers, the Spree and the Havel. After World War II, Berlin was divided among the conquering powers, and in 1961 the East German government built a wall through the middle of the city, more or less overnight. For the next decades, the city was divided. In November 1989, the wall fell, and a peaceful revolution put an end to the Communist East German regime. In 1999, Berlin became the capital of a reunified Germany, once again.

15

The neighborhood drew punks, artists, and anarchists, as well as a large Turkish population. It's still edgy and artsy.

6 Schöneberg. Historically Berlin's gay neighborhood, Schöneberg mixes the alternative vibe of Kreuzberg with the residential feel of West Berlin.

7 Prenzlauer Berg. Once a working-class neighborhood, it's now one of the city's most gentrified areas, perfect for

strolling leafy streets, past sidewalk cafés.

8 Wedding. A working-class neighborhood in the former West, this is where Berlin's artists are heading, as rents rise elsewhere.

9 Neukölln. Neukölln has gone from bleak to chic. Abandoned storefronts have turned into DIY art galleries, homemade fashion shops, and funky wine bars.

10 Charlottenburg. Lovely Charlottenburg is as elegant as Berlin gets. This beautifully sedate West Berlin neighborhood hasn't changed as much as much of the rest of the city.

11 Wannsee and Oranienburg. The concentration camp in Oranienburg is a somber excursion; Wannsee also has a dark past but there are also parks and lakes to explore.

Updated
by Adam
Groffman

Since the fall of the Iron Curtain, no other city in Europe has seen more change than Berlin, the German capital. The two Berlins that had been physically separated for almost 30 years have become one, and the reunited city has become a cutting-edge destination for architecture, culture, entertainment, nightlife, and shopping.

After successfully uniting its own East and West, Berlin now plays a pivotal role in the European Union. But even as the capital thinks and moves forward, history is always tugging at its sleeve. Between the wealth of neoclassical and 21st-century buildings there are constant reminders, both subtle and stark, of the events of the 20th century.

Berlin is quite young by European standards, beginning as two separate entities in 1237 on two islands in the Spree River: Cölln and Berlin. By the 1300s, Berlin was prospering, thanks to its location at the intersection of important trade routes, and rose to power as the seat of the Hohenzollern dynasty. The Great Elector Friedrich Wilhelm, in the nearly 50 years of his reign (1640–88), touched off a cultural renaissance. Later, Frederick the Great (1712–86) made Berlin and Potsdam glorious centers of his enlightened yet autocratic Prussian monarchy.

In 1871, Prussia, ruled by the "Iron Chancellor" Count Otto von Bismarck, unified the many independent German states into the German Empire. Berlin maintained its status as capital for the duration of that Second Reich (1871–1918), through the post–World War I Weimar Republic (1919–33), and also through Hitler's so-called Third Reich (1933–45). The city's golden years were the Roaring Twenties, when Berlin evolved as the energetic center for the era's cultural avant-garde. World-famous writers, painters, and artists met here while the impoverished bulk of its 4 million inhabitants lived in heavily overpopulated quarters. This "dance on the volcano," as those years of political and economic upheaval have been called, came to a grisly and bloody end after January 1933, when Adolf Hitler became chancellor. The Nazis made Berlin their capital but ultimately failed to remake the city into a monument to their power, as they had planned. By World War II's end, 70% of the city lay in ruins, with more rubble than in all other German cities combined.

Along with the division of Germany after World War II, Berlin was partitioned into American, British, and French zones in the West and a Soviet zone in the East. The three western-occupied zones became West Berlin, while the Soviets, who controlled not only Berlin's eastern zone but also all of the east German land surrounding it tried to blockade West Berlin out of existence. (They failed thanks to the year-long Berlin Airlift [1948–49], during which American airplanes known in German as "raisin bombers," dropped supplies until the blockade lifted.) In 1949 the Soviet Union established East Berlin as the capital of its new satellite state, the German Democratic Republic (GDR). The division of the city was cruelly finalized in concrete in August 1961, when the GDR erected the Berlin Wall, the only border fortification in history built to keep people from leaving rather than to protect them.

For nearly 30 years, the two Berlins served as competing visions of the new world order: Capitalist on one side, Communist on the other. West Berlin, an island of democracy in the Eastern bloc, was surrounded by guards and checkpoints. Nonetheless, thanks in part to being heavily subsidized by Western powers, the city became a haven for artists and freethinkers. Today, with the Wall long relegated to history (most of it was recycled as street gravel), visitors can appreciate the whole city and the anything-goes atmosphere that still pervades.

15

PLANNING

WHEN TO GO

Berlin tends to be gray and cold; it can be warm and beautiful in summer but there's no guarantee, so it's best to always pack a jacket. The best time to visit is from May to early September, though late July and early August can get hot—in which case, everyone heads to one of the city's many lakes. Many open-air events are staged in summer, when the exceedingly green city is at its most beautiful. October and November can be overcast and rainy, though the city occasionally sees crisp blue autumn skies. If you want to get a real feel for Berlin, come during the long winter months, when a host of indoor cultural events combat perpetually gray skies, but bring a heavy winter coat to combat the sleet, icy rain, strong winds, and freezing temperatures.

DISCOUNTS AND DEALS

The **Berlin WelcomeCard** (⊕ *www.visitberlin.de*) entitles one adult and three children up to age six to unlimited travel in Berlin and includes discounted admission at museums and theaters (it does not include state museums); if you're using public transportation to get to or from the airport and also plan to go to Potsdam, get the card for Zones A, B, and C (€21.50, €28.70, or €39.50 for two, three, or five days; less for just Zones A and B). Similarly, the **CityTourCard** (⊕ *www.citytourcard. com*) good for two, three, or five days of unlimited travel in the A and B zones, costs €17.40, €24.50, and €31.90, respectively, and includes many entertainment discounts; up to three children under age six can accompany an adult. The cost is slightly higher to include Zone C. The difference between the two types of cards are the attractions that are discounted so it's worth doing some research.

Many of the 17 Staatliche Museen zu Berlin (state museums of Berlin) offer several ticket options (children up to 18 are welcomed free of charge). A single ticket ranges €8–€12. A three-day pass (*Tageskarte* or *SchauLust Museen Ticket*) to all state museums costs €24. This ticket allows entrance to all state museums plus many others for three consecutive days.

GETTING HERE AND AROUND

AIRPORT TRANSFERS

Tegel Airport is 6 km (4 miles) from the downtown area. The express X9 airport bus runs at 10-minute intervals between Tegel and Bahnhof Zoologischer Garten (Zoo Station), the center of west Berlin. From here you can connect to bus, train, or subway. The trip takes about 20 minutes; the fare is €2.70. The express bus TXL runs at 10-minute intervals between Tegel and Alexanderplatz via Hauptbahnhof and takes about 30 minutes. Alternatively, you can take Bus No. 128 to Kurt Schumacher Platz or Bus No. 109 to Jakob-Kaiser-Platz and change to the U-bahn, where your bus ticket is also valid. Expect to pay between €30 or €30 for a taxi from the airport to most destinations in central Berlin. If you rent a car at the airport, follow the signs for the Stadtautobahn into Berlin. The exit to Kurfürstendamm is clearly marked.

At Schönefeld, which is quite a bit farther out, buy an Einzelfahrschein or single ride ticket (€3.30) for the ABC zone from the DB (Deutsche Bahn) office or from an S-bahn platform vending machine (no credit cards) to get you into town. This ticket is good for both the S-bahn and the Airport Express train, which runs about every half hour from a track that has no vending machine. To take the Airport Express, look for a small dark-blue sign at the foot of the stairs leading to its platform. Bus 171 also leaves Schönefeld every 20 minutes for the Rudow U-bahn station. A taxi ride from Schönefeld Airport takes about 40 minutes and will cost around €35. By car, follow the signs for Stadtzentrum Berlin.

AIR TRAVEL

Major airlines will continue to serve western Berlin's Tegel Airport (TXL), usually after a stop at a major European hub (such as Frankfurt or London), until eastern Berlin's Schönefeld Airport, about 24 km (15 miles) outside the center, has been expanded into BBI "Berlin-Brandenburg International," otherwise known as "Willy Brandt"—the international airport is expected to open in late 2017. Until then, Schönefeld is mostly used by charter and low-budget airlines.

BICYCLE TRAVEL

Berlin is a great city for biking. Particularly in summer, you can get just about anywhere you want by bike. An extensive network of bike paths are generally marked by red pavement or white markings on the sidewalks (when you're walking, try to avoid walking on bike paths if you don't want to have cyclists ring their bells at you). Many stores that rent or sell bikes carry the Berlin biker's atlas, and several places offer terrific bike tours of the city.

Bicycle Information **Fahrradstation.** ✉ *Dorotheenstr. 30, Mitte* ☏ *0180/510–8000* ⊕ *www.fahrradstation.de.*

CAR TRAVEL

Rush hour is relatively mild in Berlin, but the public transit system is so efficient here that it's best to leave your car at the hotel altogether (or refrain from renting one in the first place). All cars entering downtown Berlin inside the S-bahn ring need to have an environmental certificate. All major rental cars will have these—if in doubt, ask the rental-car agent, as without one you can be fined €40. Daily parking fees at hotels can run up to €18 per day. Vending machines in the city center dispense timed tickets to display on your dashboard. Thirty minutes costs €0.50.

PUBLIC TRANSIT

The city has an efficient public-transportation system, a smoothly integrated network of subway (U-bahn) and suburban (S-bahn) train lines, buses, and trams (almost exclusively in eastern Berlin). Get a map from any information booth. ■ TIP→ **Don't be afraid to try buses and trams—in addition to being well marked, they often cut the most direct path to your destination.**

15

From Sunday through Thursday, U-bahn trains stop around 12:45 am and S-bahn trains stop by 1:30 am. All-night bus and tram service operates seven nights a week (indicated by the letter *N* next to bus route numbers). On Friday and Saturday nights some S-bahn and all U-bahn lines except U4 run all night. Buses and trams marked with an *M* for Metro mostly serve destinations without an S-bahn or U-bahn link.

Most visitor destinations are in the broad reach of the fare zones A and B. The €2.70 ticket (fare zones A and B) and the €3 ticket (fare zones A, B, and C) allow you to make a one-way trip with an unlimited number of changes between trains, buses, and trams. Buy a Kurzstreckentarif ticket (€1.60) for short rides of up to six bus or tram stops or three U-bahn or S-bahn stops. The best deal if you plan to travel around the city extensively is the Tageskarte (day card for Zones A and B), for €6.90, good on all transportation until 3 am (added cost for A, B, and C zones). A *7-Tage-Karte* (seven-day ticket) costs €29.50, and allows unlimited travel for fare zones A and B (added cost for A, B, and C zones).

Tickets are available from vending machines at U-bahn and S-bahn stations. After you purchase a ticket, you are responsible for validating it when you board the train or bus. Both Einzelfahrt and Kurzstreckentarif tickets are good for 120 minutes after validation. If you're caught without a ticket or with an unvalidated one, the fine is €40.

■ TIP→ **The BVG website (www.bvg.de) makes planning any trip on public transportation easier. Enter your origin and destination point into their "Journey Planner" to see a list of your best routes, and a schedule of the next three departure times. If you're not sure which station is your closest, simply type in your current address and the system will tell you (along with the time it takes to walk there).**

Most major S-bahn and U-bahn stations have elevators, and most buses have hydraulic lifts. Check the public transportation maps or call the Berliner Verkehrsbetriebe. The Deutscher Service-Ring-Berlin e.V. runs a special bus service for travelers with physical disabilities, and is a good information source on all travel necessities, that is, wheelchair rental and other issues.

Public Transit Information **Berliner Verkehrsbetriebe** (*BVG*). ☏ *030/19449* ⊕ *www.bvg.de.* **S-Bahn Berlin GmbH.** ☏ *030/2974–3333* ⊕ *www.s-bahn-berlin.de.*

TAXI TRAVEL

The base rate is €3.90, after which prices vary according to a complex tariff system. Figure on paying around €8–€10 for a ride the length of the Ku'damm. ■TIP→ **If you've hailed a cab on the street and are taking a short ride of up to 2 km (1 mile), ask the driver as soon as you start off for a special fare (€5) called "Kurzstreckentarif."** You can also get cabs at taxi stands or order one by calling; there's no additional fee if you call a cab by phone. U-bahn employees will call a taxi for passengers after 8 pm.

BikeTaxi, rickshawlike bicycle taxis, pedal along Kurfürstendamm, Friedrichstrasse, Unter den Linden, and in Tiergarten. Just hail a cab on the street along the boulevards mentioned. The fare is €5 for up to 1 km (½ mile) and €3 for each additional kilometer, and €22.50 to €30 for longer tours. Velotaxis operate April–October, daily noon–7. ■TIP→ **Despite these fixed prices, make sure to negotiate the fare before starting the tour.**

Taxi Information **Taxis.** ☏ *030/210–101, 030/443–322, 030/261–026.*

TRAIN TRAVEL

All long-distance trains stop at the huge and modern central station, Hauptbahnhof, which lies at the northern edge of the government district in central Berlin. Regional trains also stop at the two former "main" stations of the past years: Bahnhof Zoo (in the West) and Ostbahnhof (in the East), as well as at the central eastern stations Friedrichstrasse and Alexanderplatz.

VISITOR INFORMATION

The main information office of Berlin Tourismus Marketing is in the Neues Kranzler Eck, a short walk from Zoo Station. There are branches in the south wing of the Brandenburg Gate, at Hauptbahnhof (Level 0), and in a pavilion opposite the Reichstag that are open daily 10–6. The tourist-information centers have longer hours April–October. The tourist office and Berlin's larger transportation offices (BVG) sell the **Berlin WelcomeCard**. Some *Staatliche* (state) museums are closed Monday. A free audio guide is included at all state museums.

Visitor Information **Visit Berlin** (*Berlin Tourist Info*). ✉ *Berlin* ☏ *030/250– 025* ⊕ *www.visitberlin.de.* **Staatliche Museen zu Berlin.** ✉ *Charlottenburg* ☏ *030/2664–24242 operator* ⊕ *www.smb.museum.* **Tourist-Information Center in Prenzlauer Berg.** ✉ *Kulturbrauerei, Schönhauser Allee 36, Prenzlauer Berg* ✛ *Other entrances on Knaackstr. or Sredzkistr.* ☏ *030/4435–2170* ⊕ *www. tic-berlin.de.*

A boat tour along the Spree River is a lovely way to take in the sights.

TOURS

BOAT TOURS

Tours of central Berlin's Spree and the canals give you up-close views of sights such as Museum Island, Charlottenburg Palace, the Reichstag, and the Berliner Dom. Tours usually depart twice a day from several bridges and piers in Berlin, such as Schlossbrücke in Charlottenburg; Hansabrücke and Haus der Kulturen der Welt in Tiergarten; Friedrichstrasse, Museum Island, and Nikolaiviertel in Mitte; and near the Jannowitzbrücke S-bahn and U-bahn station. Drinks, snacks, and *wurst* are available during the narrated trips.

BWSG. General city tours and specialized options, like architectural tours, are offered from March to November by this company. ✉ *Berlin* ⊕ *www.bwsg-berlin.de* 🖼 *From €12.*

Reederei Riedel. One-hour city tours along the Spree take visitors past key city sights, including Museuminsel. ✉ *Berlin* ☎ *030/6796–1470* ⊕ *www.reederei-riedel.de* 🖼 *From €12.*

BUS TOURS

Several companies, including Berliner Bären Stadtrundfahrten and BEX, offer city tours that run every 15 or 30 minutes, depending on the season. The full circuit takes two hours, as does the recorded narration listened to through headphones. For €20 you can jump on and off at between 13 and 20 stops, depending on the company. The bus driver sells tickets. Most companies have tours to Potsdam.

BBS Berliner Bären Stadtrundfahrt (*BBS*). These bright yellow hop-on, hop-off buses tour the city, past the major sights. It's a great way to get an overview if you have limited time. They also include trips to the East

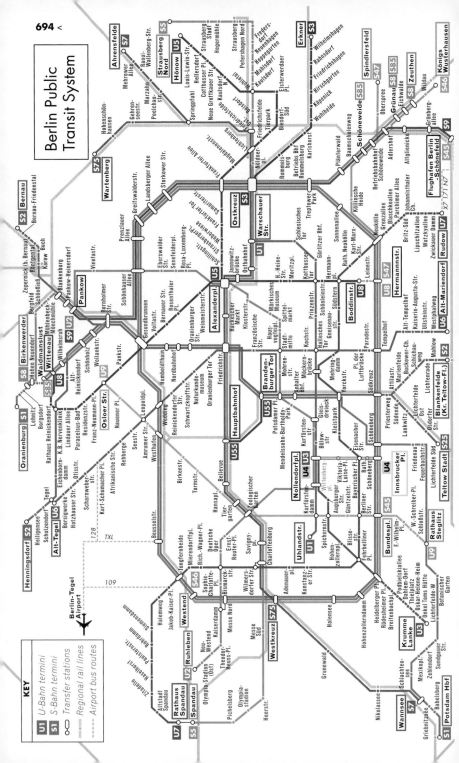

694 <

Berlin Public Transit System

Side Gallery and trendier parts of town. ⊠ *Berlin* ☎ *030/3519–5270* ⊕ *www.bbsberlin.de* 🖃 *From €15.*

BEX Sightseeing. Hop-on, hop-off tours, as well as themed excursions, are offered by this company. ⊠ *Mannheimer Str. 33/34, Wilmersdorf* ☎ *030/880–4190* ⊕ *www.bex.de* 🖃 *From €20.*

WALKING AND BIKE TOURS

Getting oriented through a walking tour is a great way to start a Berlin visit. In addition to daily city highlight tours, companies have themed tours such as Third Reich Berlin, Potsdam, and pub crawls. Printable discount coupons may be available on the tour operators' websites; some companies grant discounts to WelcomeCard and City-Card holders.

Berliner Unterwelten. For a truly memorable experience, check out Berliner Unterwelten, which translates as "Berlin Underworlds." The company offers access to several of Berlin's best-preserved WWII bunkers that are normally closed to the public on intriguing yet eerie tours that take you literally underground. ⊠ *Berlin* ⊕ *berliner-unterwelten. de* 🖃 *From €11.*

Brewer's Berlin Tours. Brit Terry Brewer's firsthand accounts of divided and reunified Berlin are a highlight of the all-day "Brewer's Best of Berlin" tour. ⊠ *Berlin* ☎ *0177/388–1537* ⊕ *www.brewersberlintours. com* 🖃 *From €15.*

Fat Tire Bike Tours. Fat Tire Bike Tours rides through Berlin daily early March–November and has a Berlin Wall tour; the 4½-hour city tour includes the bike rental. ⊠ *Panoramastr. 1a, base of TV tower, Mitte* ☎ *030/2404–7991* ⊕ *www.fattirebiketoursberlin.com* 🖃 *From €24.*

Insider Tour. Insider Tours has a "Cold War" Berlin tour about the Soviet era and a bike tour as well as a Cruise'n'Walk tour, a combination of boating and walking. ⊠ *Bahnhof Zoologischer Garten, outside McDonalds, Charlottenburg* ☎ *030/692–3149* ⊕ *www.insidertour. com* 🖃 *From €12.*

Original Berlin Walks. Themed walks including a Monday "Jewish Life" tour, a Potsdam tour on Thursday and Sunday, and visits to the Sachsenhausen concentration camp, are just a few of the offerings on the roster here. ⊠ *Berlin* ☎ *030/301–9194* ⊕ *www.berlinwalks.com* 🖃 *From €12.*

MAKING THE MOST OF YOUR TIME

With so much to see, a good place to start your visit is in Mitte. You can walk around the Scheunenviertel, which used to be the city's Jewish quarter and is now a center for art galleries and upscale shops, punctuated by memorials to the Holocaust.

For culture buffs, great antique, medieval, Renaissance, and modern art can be found at the Kulturforum in the Tiergarten, and on Museum Island in Mitte—both cultural centers are a must, and either will occupy at least a half day. On your way to the Tiergarten, visit the emotionally moving Memorial to the Murdered Jews of Europe (referred to by many as simply the Holocaust Memorial), the Brandenburg Gate, and the Reichstag with its astonishing cupola. Most of the historic sights of German and Prussian history line the city's other

15

grand boulevard, Unter den Linden, in Mitte. Unter den Linden can be strolled in a leisurely two hours, with stops. Other spots not to miss are Potsdamer Platz and the Kulturforum in Tiergarten, and the hip and edgy neighborhoods of Wedding and Neukölln. Walk along the East Side Gallery in Freidrichshain, then head to Simon-DachStrasse or cross the bridge over the Spree to Kreuzberg for something to eat. Head over to Charlottenburg for an elegant, old-fashioned afternoon of coffee and cake.

The nearby town of Potsdam has the fabulous palace, Schloss Sanssouci, as well as extensive parks and lakes. To the north, in Oranienburg, is the Gedenkstätte und Museum Sachsenhausen concentration camp.

EXPLORING

MITTE

After the fall of the wall, Mitte, which had been in East Germany, once again became the geographic center of Berlin. The area comprises several minidistricts, each with its own distinctive history and flair. Alexanderplatz, home of the iconic TV Tower, was the center of East Berlin. With its Communist architecture, you can still get a feel for the GDR aesthetic here. The nearby Nikolaiviertel is part of the medieval heart of Berlin. The Scheunenviertel, part of the Spandauer Vorstadt, was home to many of the city's Jewish citizens. Today, the narrow streets that saw so much tragedy house art galleries, increasingly excellent restaurants, and upscale shops popular with tourists. Treasures once split between East and West Berlin museums are reunited on Museuminsel, the stunning Museum Island, a UNESCO World Heritage Site. Bordering Tiergarten and the government district are the meticulously restored Brandenburger Tor (Brandenburg Gate), the unofficial symbol of the city, and the Memorial to the Murdered Jews of Europe, whose design and scope engendered many debates.

The historic boulevard Unter den Linden proudly rolls out Prussian architecture and world-class museums—now the site of increased construction related to the extension of U-bahn U5 line, slated for completion in 2019. Its major cross street is Friedrichstrasse, revitalized in the mid-1990s with car showrooms (including Bentley, Bugatti, and Volkswagen) and upscale malls.

TOP ATTRACTIONS

Altes Museum (*Old Museum*). This red-marble, neoclassical building abutting the green Lustgarten was Prussia's first structure purpose-built to serve as a museum. Designed by Karl Friedrich Schinkel, it was completed in 1830. The permanent collection consists of everyday utensils from ancient Greece as well as vases and sculptures from the 6th to 4th century BC. Etruscan art is the highlight here, and there are also a few examples of Roman art. Antique sculptures, clay figurines, and bronze art of the Antikensammlung (Antiquities Collection) are also here (the other part of the collection is in the **Pergamonmuseum**). ✉ *Museuminsel, Am Lustgarten, Mitte* ☎ *30/2664–24242* ⊕ *www.smb.*

Berliner Dom (Berlin's Cathedral) is one of the city's landmark buildings, and the vast lawn across from it is a popular gathering spot in nice weather.

museum ✉ *€10 (combined ticket for all Museumsinsel €18)* ⊘ *Tues., Wed., and Fri.–Sun. 10–6, Thurs. 10–8* Ⓜ *Hackescher Markt (S-bahn).*

Fodor's Choice **Alte Nationalgalerie** (*Old National Gallery*). The permanent exhibit here
★ is home to an outstanding collection of 18th-, 19th-, and early-20th-century paintings and sculpture, by the likes of Cézanne, Rodin, Degas, and one of Germany's most famous portrait artists, Max Liebermann. Its Galerie der Romantik (Gallery of Romanticism) collection has masterpieces from such 19th-century German painters as Karl Friedrich Schinkel and Caspar David Friedrich, the leading members of the German Romantic school. ✉ *Museumsinsel, Bodestrasse 1-3, Mitte* ☎ *30/2664–24242* ⊕ *www.smb.museum* ✉ *€10 (combined ticket for all Museumsinsel €18)* ⊘ *Tues., Wed., and Fri.–Sun. 10–6, Thurs. 10–8.* Ⓜ *Hackescher Markt (S-bahn).*

Bebelplatz. After he became ruler in 1740, Frederick the Great personally planned the buildings surrounding this square (which has a huge parking garage cleverly hidden beneath the pavement). The area received the nickname "Forum Fridericianum," or Frederick's Forum. On May 10, 1933, Joseph Goebbels, the Nazi minister for propaganda and "public enlightenment," organized one of the nationwide book burnings here. The books, thrown on a pyre by Nazi officials and students, included works by Jews, pacifists, and Communists. In the center of Bebelplatz, a modern and subtle memorial (built underground but viewable through a window in the cobblestone pavement) marks where 20,000 books went up in flames. The **Staatsoper Unter den Linden** (State Opera) is on the east side of the square. **St. Hedwigskathedrale** is on the south

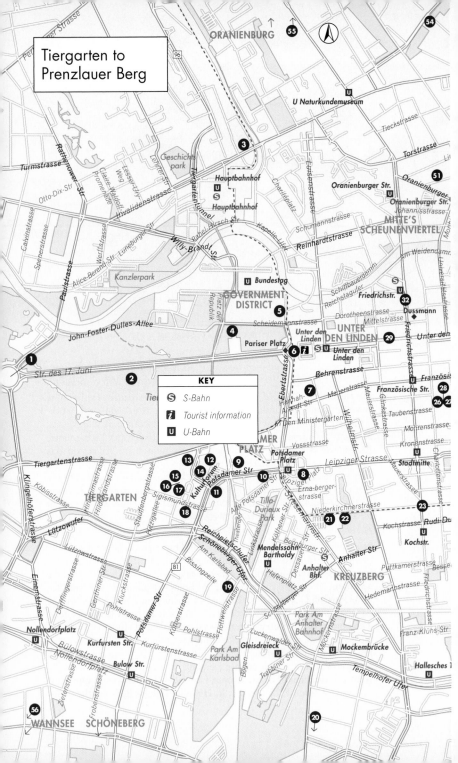

15

side of the square. The **Humboldt-Universität** is to the west. ✉ *Mitte* Ⓜ *Französische Strasse (U-bahn), Bhf Hausvogteiplatz (U-bahn).*

Berliner Dom (*Berlin Cathedral*). A church has stood here since 1536, but this enormous version dates from 1905, making it the largest 20th-century Protestant church in Germany. The royal Hohenzollerns worshipped here until 1918, when Kaiser Wilhelm II abdicated and left Berlin for Holland. The massive dome wasn't restored from World War II damage until 1982; the interior was completed in 1993. The climb to the dome's outer balcony is made easier by a wide stairwell, plenty of landings with historic photos and models, and even a couple of chairs. The 94 sarcophagi of Prussian royals in the crypt are significant, but to less-trained eyes can seem uniformly dull. Sunday services include communion. ✉ *Am Lustgarten 1, Mitte* ☎ *030/2026–9136* ⊕ *www.berlinerdom.de* 🎫 *€7, audio guide €3* ⊙ *Mon.–Sat. 9–8, Sun. noon–8* Ⓜ *Hackescher Markt (S-bahn).*

FAMILY **Berliner Fernsehturm** (*TV Tower*). Finding Alexanderplatz is no problem: just head toward the 1,207-foot-high tower piercing the sky. Built in 1969 as a signal to the West (clearly visible over the Wall, no less) that the East German economy was thriving, it is deliberately higher than both western Berlin's broadcasting tower and the Eiffel Tower in Paris. You can get the best view of Berlin from within the tower's disco ball–like observation level; on a clear day you can see for 40 km (25 miles). One floor above, the city's highest restaurant rotates for your panoramic pleasure. During the summer season, order VIP tickets online to avoid a long wait. ✉ *Panoramastr. 1a, Mitte* ☎ *030/247–5750 for restaurant* ⊕ *www.tv-turm.de* 🎫 *€13* ⊙ *Nov.–Feb., daily 10 am–midnight; Mar.–Oct., daily 9 am–midnight; last admission ½ hr before closing* Ⓜ *Alexanderplatz (U-bahn and S-bahn).*

Bode-Museum. At the northern tip of Museum Island is this somber-looking gray edifice graced with elegant columns. The museum is home to the state museums' stunning collection of German and Italian sculptures since the Middle Ages, as well as the Museum of Byzantine Art, and a huge coin collection. ✉ *Museuminsel, Am Kupfergraben, Mitte* ☎ *030/2664–24242* ⊕ *www.smb.museum* 🎫 *€10 (combined ticket for all Museumsinsel €18)* ⊙ *Tues., Wed., and Fri.–Sun. 10–6, Thurs. 10–8* Ⓜ *Hackescher Markt (S-bahn).*

Fodor'sChoice ★ **Brandenburger Tor** (*Brandenburg Gate*). Once the pride of Prussian Berlin and the city's premier landmark, the Brandenburger Tor was left in a desolate no-man's-land when the Wall was built. Since the Wall's dismantling, the sandstone gateway has become the scene of the city's Unification Day and New Year's Eve parties. This is the sole remaining gate of 14 built by Carl Langhans in 1788–91, designed as a triumphal arch for King Frederick Wilhelm II. Its virile classical style pays tribute to Athens's Acropolis. The quadriga, a chariot drawn by four horses and driven by the Goddess of Victory, was added in 1794. Troops paraded through the gate after successful campaigns—the last time in 1945, when victorious Red Army troops took Berlin. The upper part of the gate, together with its chariot and Goddess of Victory, was destroyed in the war. In 1957 the original molds were discovered in

The Brandenburg Gate is one of the most famous landmarks in Germany.

West Berlin, and a new quadriga was cast in copper and presented as a gift to the people of East Berlin. A tourist information center is in the south part of the gate.

The gate faces one of Europe's most famous historic squares, **Pariser Platz,** with bank headquarters, the ultramodern French embassy, and the offices of the federal parliament. On the southern side, Berlin's sleek Academy of Arts, integrating the ruins of its historic predecessor, and the DZ Bank, designed by star architect Frank Gehry, stand next to the new American embassy, rebuilt on its prewar location and reopened on July 4, 2008. The legendary Hotel Adlon (now the Adlon Kempinski) looks on from its historic home at the southeast edge of the square. ⊠ *Pariser Pl., Mitte* Ⓜ *Unter den Linden (S-bahn).*

Fodor's Choice
★

DDR Museum. Half museum, half theme park, the DDR Museum is an interactive and highly entertaining exhibit about life during socialism. It's difficult to say just how much the museum benefits from its prime location beside the Spree, right across from the Berliner Dom, but it's always packed, filled with tourists, families, and student groups trying to get a hands-on feel for what the East German experience was really like. Exhibitions include a re-creation of an East German kitchen, all mustard yellows and bilious greens; a simulated drive in a Trabi, the only car the average East German was allowed to own; and a walk inside a very narrow, very claustrophobic interrogation cell. ⊠ *Karl-Liebknecht-Str. 1, at the Spree opposite the Berliner Dom, Mitte* ☎ *030/8471–23731* ⊕ *www.ddr-museum.de* ✉ *€7* ⊙ *Sun.–Fri. 10-8, Sat. 10–10* Ⓜ *Alexanderplatz (U-bahn and S-bahn), Hackescher Markt (S-bahn).*

Fodor's Choice
★ **Denkmal für die Ermordeten Juden Europas** (*Memorial to the Murdered Jews of Europe*). An expansive and unusual memorial dedicated to the 6 million Jews who were killed in the Holocaust, the monument was designed by American architect Peter Eisenman. The stunning place of remembrance consists of a grid of more than 2,700 concrete stelae, planted into undulating ground. The abstract memorial can be entered from all sides and offers no prescribed path. An information center that goes into specifics about the Holocaust lies underground at the southeast corner. Just across Eberstrasse, inside the Tiergarten, is the **Memorial to the Homosexuals Persecuted under the National Socialist Regime**: a large concrete block with a window through which visitors can see a short film depicting a kiss. ✉ *Cora-Berliner-Str. 1, Mitte* ☎ *030/2639–4336* ⊕ *www.stiftung-denkmal.de* ⬚ *Free* ⊙ *Daily 24 hrs; information center: Oct.–Mar., Tues.–Sun. 10–7; Apr.–Sept., Tues.–Sun. 10–8 (last admission 45 mins before closing)* Ⓜ *Unter den Linden (S-bahn).*

Deutsches Historisches Museum (*German History Museum*). The museum is composed of two buildings. The magnificent pink, baroque Prussian arsenal (Zeughaus) was constructed between 1695 and 1730, and is the oldest building on Unter den Linden. It also houses a theater, the Zeughaus Kino, which regularly presents a variety of films, both German and international, historic and modern. The new permanent exhibits, reopened after much debate in mid-2006, offer a modern and fascinating view of German history since the early Middle Ages. Behind the arsenal, the granite-and-glass Pei-Bau building by I. M. Pei holds often stunning and politically controversial changing exhibits, such as 2010's unprecedented blockbuster "Hitler und die Deutschen" ("Hitler and the Germans"), which explored the methods of propaganda used by Hitler and the Nazis to gain power, and 2013's "Zerstörte Vielfalt" or "destroyed diversity," which documents the multifaceted societal, ethnic, and political ruination of Berlin in the years leading up to WWII. The museum's Café im Zueghaus is a great place to stop and restore your energy. ✉ *Unter den Linden 2, Mitte* ☎ *030/203–040* ⊕ *www. dhm.de* ⬚ *€8* ⊙ *Daily 10–6* Ⓜ *Französische Strasse (U-bahn), Friedrichstrasse (S-bahn and U-bahn), Hackesher Markt (S-bahn).*

Fodor's Choice
★ **Ehemalige Jüdische Mädchenschule.** This boxy brick building in central Berlin, which formerly served as a Jewish girls' school and then a military hospital during WWII, sat neglected until recently. Now it is one of the city's newest star attractions: a renovated multiplex with art galleries, restaurants, and a bar. The former gymnasium is now the restaurant Pauly Saal; upstairs, art galleries share space with the newly relocated Kennedys museum. Berlin's now-thriving Jewish community still owns the building and leases it out to the current management. Both Jewish and non-Jewish visitors will rejoice at the inclusion of Mogg & Melzer, a deli dedicated to Jewish delicacies like matzo ball soup, pastrami, and *shakshuka.* ✉ *Auguststr. 11–13, Mitte* ⊕ *www.maedchenschule. org/* ⊙ *Hrs vary by business* Ⓜ *Oranienburger Strasse (S-bahn).*

Friedrichstrasse. The once-bustling street of cafés and theaters of prewar Berlin has risen from the rubble of war and Communist neglect to reclaim the crowds with shopping emporiums. Heading south from the Friedrichstrasse train station, you'll pass hotels and various stores (including the sprawling, comprehensive bookstore **Dussmann** and its large but cozy new English-language bookshop around the corner). After crossing Unter den Linden, you'll come upon the Berlin outpost of the Parisian department store **Galeries Lafayette** on your left. North of the train station you will see the rejuvenated heart of the entertainment center of Berlin's Roaring Twenties, including the **Admiralspalast** and the somewhat kitschy **Friedrichstadt Palast.** ⊠ *Berlin* Ⓜ *Französische Strasse (U-bahn), Friedrichstrasse (S-bahn and U-bahn).*

Gendarmenmarkt. This is without a doubt the most elegant square in former East Berlin. Anchored by the beautifully reconstructed 1818 **Konzerthaus** and the **Deutscher Dom** and **Französischer Dom** (German and French cathedrals) and lined with some of the city's best restaurants, it also hosts one of Berlin's classiest annual Christmas markets. ⊠ *Berlin* Ⓜ *Stadtmitte (U-bahn), Hausvogteiplatz (U-bahn).*

Hackesche Höfe (*Hacke Courtyards*). Built in 1905–07, this series of eight connected courtyards is the finest example of art nouveau industrial architecture in Berlin. Most buildings are covered with glazed white tiles, and additional Moorish mosaic designs decorate the main courtyard off Rosenthaler Strasse. Shops (including one dedicated to Berlin's beloved street-crossing signal, the "Ampelmann"), restaurants, the variety theater Chamäleon Varieté, and a movie theater populate the spaces once occupied by ballrooms, a poets' society, and a Jewish girls' club. ⊠ *Rosenthaler Str. 40–41, and Sophienstr. 6, Mitte* ☎ *030/2809–8010* ⊕ *www.hackesche-hoefe.com* Ⓜ *Hackescher Markt (S-bahn).*

Hugenottenmuseum. Inside the Französischer Dom (French Cathedral), built by Kaiser Friedrich II for the Protestant Huguenots who fled France and settled in Berlin, is the Hugenottenmuseum, with exhibits charting their history and art. The Huguenots were expelled from France at the end of the 17th century by King Louis XIV. Their energy and commercial expertise contributed much to Berlin. ⊠ *Französischer Dom, Gendarmenmarkt 5, Mitte* ⚓ *Entrance is along Markgrafenstr., on the side of the cathedral* ☎ *030/229–1760* ☑ *€3.50* ⊙ *Tues.–Sun. noon–5* Ⓜ *Stadtmitte (U-bahn), Hausvogteiplatz (U-bahn).*

OFF THE BEATEN PATH

The Kennedys. In West Berlin in 1963, John F. Kennedy surveyed the recently erected Berlin Wall, and said "Ich bin ein Berliner"—I am one with the people of Berlin. And with that, he secured his fame throughout Germany. He's honored in this small but intriguing museum, which used to reside opposite the American embassy on Pariser Platz, but has since found a new home in the Ehemalige Jüdische Mädchenschule. With photographs, personal memorabilia, documents, and films, the collection traces the fascination JFK and the Kennedy clan evoked in Berlin and elsewhere. ⊠ *Auguststr. 11-13, in the Ehemalige Jüdische Mädchenschule, Mitte* ☎ *030/2065–3570* ⊕ *www.thekennedys.de* ☑ *€5* ⊙ *Tues.–Sun. 11–7* Ⓜ *Oranienburger Strasse (S-bahn).*

Fodor's Choice ★ **Museumsinsel** (*Museum Island*). On the site of one of Berlin's two original settlements, this unique complex of five state museums is a UNESCO World Heritage Site and a must-visit in Berlin. The museums are the **Alte Nationalgalerie**, the **Altes Museum** (Old Museum),

15

The Pergamonmuseum, on Museumsinsel (Museum Island), is where you'll find a wealth of artifacts from the ancient world, including the Ishtar Gate.

the **Bode-Museum**, the **Pergamonmuseum**, and the the **Neues Museum** (New Museum). If you get tired of antiques and paintings, drop by any of the museums' cafés. ⊠ *Museumsinsel, Mitte* ☎ *030/2664–24242* ⊕ *www.smb.museum* ✉ *€18 combined ticket to all Museum Island museums* Ⓜ *Hackescher Markt (S-bahn).*

Neue Synagoge (*New Synagogue*). This meticulously restored landmark, built between 1859 and 1866, is an exotic amalgam of styles, the whole faintly Middle Eastern. Its bulbous, gilded cupola stands out in the skyline. When its doors opened, it was the largest synagogue in Europe, with 3,200 seats. The synagogue was damaged on November 9, 1938 (*Kristallnacht*—Night of the Broken Glass), when Nazi looters rampaged across Germany, burning synagogues and smashing the few Jewish shops and homes left in the country. It was destroyed by Allied bombing in 1943, and it wasn't until the mid-1980s that the East German government restored it. The effective exhibit on the history of the building and its congregants includes fragments of the original architecture and furnishings. Sabbath services are held in a modern addition. ⊠ *Oranienburger Str. 28–30, Mitte* ☎ *030/8802–8300* ⊕ *www.centrumjudaicum.de* ✉ *€5; English/Hebrew audio guides €3* ☉ *Apr.–Sept., weekdays 10–6, Sun. 10–7; Oct.–Mar., Sun.–Thurs. 10–6, Fri. 10–3* Ⓜ *Oranienburger Tor (U-bahn), Oranienburger Strasse (S-bahn).*

Fodor'sChoice
★ **Neues Museum** (*New Museum*). Originally designed by Friedrich August Stüler in 1843–55, the building housing the Neues Museum was badly damaged in World War II and was only in the last decade been elaborately redeveloped by British star architect David Chipperfield, who has been overseeing the complete restoration of Museum Island. Instead

of completely restoring the Neues Museum, the architect decided to integrate modern elements into the historic landmark, while leaving many of its heavily bombed and dilapidated areas untouched. The result is a stunning experience, considered by many to be one of the world's greatest museums. Home to the Egyptian Museum, including the famous bust of Nefertiti (who, after some 70 years, has returned to her first museum location in Berlin), it also features the Papyrus Collection and the Museum of Prehistory and Early History. ⊠ *Museumsinsel, Bodestrasse 1-3, Mitte* ☎ *030/2664–24242* ⊕ *www.smb.museum* 🎟 *€12 (combined ticket for all Museumsinsel €18)* ⊘ *Fri.–Wed. 10–6, Thurs. 10–8* Ⓜ *Hackescher Markt (S-bahn).*

Nikolaiviertel (*Nicholas Quarter*). Renovated in the 1980s and a tad concrete-heavy as a result, this tiny quarter grew up around Berlin's oldest parish church, the medieval, twin-spire **St. Nikolaikirche** (St. Nicholas's Church), now a museum, dating from 1230. The adjacent Fischerinsel (Fisherman's Island) area was the heart of Berlin almost 800 years ago, and retains a bit of its medieval character. At Breite Strasse you'll find two of Berlin's oldest buildings: No. 35 is the **Ribbeckhaus**, the city's only surviving Renaissance structure, dating from 1624, and No. 36 is the early-baroque **Marstall**, built by Michael Matthais between 1666 and 1669. The area feels rather artificial, but draws tourists to its gift stores, cafés, and restaurants. ⊠ *Church: Nikolaikirchpl., Mitte* ☎ *030/2400–2162* ⊕ *www.stadtmuseum.de* Ⓜ *Alexanderplatz (U-bahn and S-bahn).*

Fodor's Choice
★
Pergamonmuseum. The Pergamonmuseum is one of the world's greatest museums and its name is derived from its principal display, the Pergamon Altar, a monumental Greek temple discovered in what is now Turkey and dating from 180 BC. The altar was shipped to Berlin in the late 19th century. Equally impressive are the gateway to the Roman town of Miletus, the Ishtar Gate, and the Babylonian processional way. At the end of 2014, the hall with the Pergamon Altar closed for refurbishment and is not expected to reopen until 2019. The rest of the Pergamonmuseum continues to be open to the public, though, and it still very much worth a visit. ⊠ *Museumsinsel, Bodestrasse 1-3, Mitte* ☎ *030/2664–24242* ⊕ *www.smb.museum* 🎟 *€12 (combined ticket for all Museumsinsel €18)* ⊘ *Fri.–Wed. 10–6, Thurs. 10–8* Ⓜ *Hackescher Markt (S-bahn).*

Fodor's Choice
★
Reichstag (*Parliament Building*). After last meeting here in 1933, the Bundestag, Germany's federal parliament, returned to its traditional seat in the spring of 1999. British architect Sir Norman Foster lightened up the gray monolith with a glass dome, which quickly became one of the city's main attractions: you can circle up a gently rising ramp while taking in the rooftops of Berlin and the parliamentary chamber below. At the base of the dome is an exhibit on the Reichstag's history, in German and English. Completed in 1894, the Reichstag housed the imperial German parliament and later served a similar function during the ill-fated Weimar Republic. On the night of February 27, 1933, the Reichstag burned down in an act of arson, a pivotal event in Third Reich history. The fire led to state protection laws that gave the Nazis a pretext to arrest their political opponents. The Reichstag was rebuilt but again

The dome atop the Reichstag is one of the city's top attractions, and a walk inside it offers superb views.

badly damaged in 1945. The graffiti of the victorious Russian soldiers can still be seen on some of the walls in the hallways. After terrorism warnings at the end of 2010, the Reichstag tightened its door policy, asking all visitors to register their names and birthdates in advance and reserve a place on a guided tour. Since then, the crowds that used to snake around the outside of the building have subsided, and a visit is worth the planning. As always, a reservation at the pricey rooftop Käfer restaurant (*030/2262–9933*) will also get you in. Those with reservations can use the doorway to the right of the Reichstag's main staircase. The building is surrounded by ultramodern federal government offices, such as the boxy, concrete **Bundeskanzleramt** (Federal Chancellery), which also has a nickname, of course: the "Washing Machine." Built by Axel Schultes, it's one of the few new buildings in the government district by a Berlin architect. Participating in a guided tour of the Chancellery is possible if you apply in writing several weeks prior to a visit. A riverwalk with great views of the government buildings begins behind the Reichstag. ⊠ *Pl. der Republik 1, Mitte* ☎ *030/2273–2152 Reichstag, 030/2273–0027 Reichstag, 030/4000–1881 Bundeskanzleramt* ⊕ *www. bundestag.de* ✉ *Free with prior registration online* ⊙ *Daily 8 am–midnight* Ⓜ *Unter den Linden (S-bahn), Bundestag (U-bahn).*

Unter den Linden. The name of this historic Berlin thoroughfare, between the Brandenburg Gate and Schlossplatz, means "under the linden trees," and it was indeed lined with fragrant and beloved lindens until the 1930s. Imagine Berliners' shock when Hitler decided to fell the trees in order to make the street more parade-friendly. The grand boulevard began as a riding path that the royals used to get from their palace to their hunting grounds (now the central Berlin park called Tiergarten). It is once again lined with linden trees planted after World War II. ⊠ *Mitte.*

WORTH NOTING

Alexanderplatz. This bleak square, bordered by the train station, the Galeria Kaufhof department store, and the 37-story Park Inn Berlin-Alexanderplatz hotel, once formed the hub of East Berlin and was originally named in 1805 for Czar Alexander I. German writer Alfred Döblin dubbed it the "heart of a world metropolis" (a quote from his 1929 novel *Berlin Alexanderplatz* is written on a building at the northeastern end of the square). Today it's a basic center of commerce and the occasional festival. The unattractive modern buildings are a reminder not just of the results of Allied bombing but also of the ruthlessness practiced by East Germans when they demolished what remained. A famous meeting point in the south corner is the World Time Clock (1969), which even keeps tabs on Tijuana. ⊠ *Mitte.*

Berliner Rathaus (*Berlin Town Hall*). Nicknamed the "Rotes Rathaus" (Red Town Hall) for its redbrick design, the town hall was completed in 1869. Its most distinguishing features are its neo-Renaissance clock tower and frieze that depicts Berlin's history up to 1879 in 36 terra-cotta plaques, each 20 feet long. Climb the grand stairwell to view the coat-of-arms hall and a few exhibits. The Rathaus has a very inexpensive, cafeteria-style canteen offering budget lunches. The entrance is inside the inner courtyard. ⊠ *Rathausstr. 15, Mitte* ☏ *030/90260* 🎟 *Free* ⊙ *Weekdays 9–6* Ⓜ *Alexanderplatz (U-bahn and S-bahn).*

Deutscher Dom. The Deutscher Dom holds an extensive exhibition on the emergence of the democratic parliamentary system in Germany since the late 1800s, including the 1848 revolution. The free museum is sponsored by the German parliament. Leadership and opposition in East Germany are also documented. An English-language audio guide covers a portion of the exhibits on the first three floors. Floors four and five have temporary exhibitions with no English text or audio. ⊠ *Gendarmenmarkt 1, Mitte* ☏ *030/2273–0431* 🎟 *Free* ⊙ *Oct.–Apr., Tues.–Sun. 10–6; May–Sept., Tues.–Sun. 10–7* Ⓜ *Hausvogteiplatz (U-bahn), Stadtmitte (U-bahn).*

Hamburger Bahnhof - Museum für Gegenwart (*Museum of Contemporary Art*). This light-filled, remodeled train station is home to a rich survey of post-1960 Western art. The permanent collection includes installations by German artists Joseph Beuys and Anselm Kiefer, as well as paintings by Andy Warhol, Cy Twombly, Robert Rauschenberg, and Robert Morris. An annex presents the hotly debated Friedrich Christian Flick Collection, the largest and most valuable collection of the latest in the world's contemporary art. The 2,000 works rotate, but you're bound to see some by Bruce Naumann, Rodney Graham, and Pipilotti Rist. ⊠ *Invalidenstr. 50–51, Mitte* ☏ *030/3978–3411* ⊕ *www.smb.museum* 🎟 *€14* ⊙ *Tues., Wed., and Fri. 10–6, Thurs. 10–8, weekends 11–6* Ⓜ *Naturkundemuseum (U-bahn), Hauptbahnhof (S-bahn).*

Märkisches Museum (*Brandenburg Museum*). This redbrick museum includes exhibits on the city's theatrical past, its guilds, and its newspapers. A permanent exhibit, "Here is Berlin!," tells the story of Berlin's history through its different neighorhoods. Paintings capture the look of the city before it crumbled during World War II. On Sunday at 3 pm, fascinating mechanical musical instruments from the collection are played. ⊠ *Am Köllnischen Park 5, Mitte* ☎ *030/2400–2162* ⊕ *www.stadtmuseum.de* ⊡ *€5* ⊙ *Tues.–Sun. 10–6* Ⓜ *Märkisches Museum (U-bahn).*

Siegessäule (*Victory Column*). The 227-foot granite, sandstone, and bronze column is topped by a winged, golden goddess and has a splendid view of Berlin. It was erected in front of the Reichstag in 1873 to commemorate Prussia's military successes and then moved to the Tiergarten in 1938–39. You have to climb 270 steps up through the column to reach the observation platform, but the view is rewarding. The gold-tipped cannons surrounding the column are those the Prussians captured from the French in the Franco-Prussian War. ⊠ *Str. des 17. Juni/Am Grossen Stern, Mitte* ☎ *030/391–2961* ⊡ *€3* ⊙ *Nov.–Mar., daily 9:30–5:30; Apr.–Oct., weekdays 9:30–6:30, weekends 9:30–7; last admission ½ hr before closing* Ⓜ *Tiergarten (S-bahn), Bellevue (S-bahn).*

Staatsoper Unter den Linden (*State Opera*). Frederick the Great was a music lover and he made the Staatsoper Unter den Linden, on the east side of Bebelplatz, his first priority. The lavish opera house was completed in 1743 by the same architect who built Sanssouci in Potsdam, Georg Wenzeslaus von Knobelsdorff. The house is currently undergoing a complete makeover, expected to be completed in 2017, when the historic interior will be replaced with a modern design. The show goes on at the Schiller Theater across town, where maestro Daniel Barenboim continues to oversee a diverse repertoire. ⊠ *Unter den Linden 7, Mitte* ☎ *030/2035–4555* ⊕ *www.staatsoper-berlin.de* ⊙ *Box office Mon.–Sat. 10–8, Sun. noon–8* Ⓜ *Französische Strasse (U-bahn).*

TIERGARTEN

The Tiergarten, a bucolic 630-acre park with lakes, meadows, and wide paths, is the "green heart" of Berlin. In the 17th century it served as the hunting grounds of the Great Elector (its name translates into "animal garden"). Now it's the Berliners' backyard for sunbathing and summer strolls.

The government district, Potsdamer Platz, and the embassy district ring the park from its eastern to southern edges. A leisurely walk from Zoo Station through the Tiergarten to the Brandenburger Tor and the Reichstag takes about 90 minutes.

TOP ATTRACTIONS

Sowjetisches Ehrenmal Tiergarten (*Soviet Memorial*). Built immediately after World War II, this monument stands as a reminder of the Soviet victory over the shattered German army in Berlin in May 1945. The Battle of Berlin was one of the deadliest on the European front. A hulking bronze statue of a soldier stands atop a marble plinth taken from Hitler's former Reichkanzlei (headquarters). The memorial is flanked by what are said to be the first two T-34 tanks to have fought their way into the city. ⊠ *Str. des 17. Juni, Tiergarten* Ⓜ *Unter den Linden (S-bahn).*

Tiergarten (*Animal Garden*). The quiet greenery of the 520-acre Tiergarten is a beloved oasis, with some 23 km (14 miles) of footpaths, meadows, and two beer gardens, making it the third-largest green space in Germany. The inner park's 6½ acres of lakes and ponds were landscaped by garden architect Peter Joseph Lenné in the mid-1800s. ⊠ *Tiergarten* Ⓜ *Zoologischer Garten (S-bahn and U-bhan), Bellevue (S-bahn), Hansaplatz (U-bahn), Potsdamer Platz (U-bahn).*

POTSDAMER PLATZ

The once-divided Berlin is rejoined at Potsdamer Platz, which now links Kreuzberg with the former East once again. Potsdamer Platz was Berlin's inner-city center and Europe's busiest plaza before World War II. Bombings and the Wall left this area a sprawling, desolate lot, where tourists in West Berlin could climb a wooden platform to peek into East Berlin's death strip. After the Wall fell, various international companies made a rush to build their German headquarters on this prime real estate. In the mid-1990s, Potsdamer Platz became Europe's largest construction site. Today's modern complexes of red sandstone, terracotta tiles, steel, and glass have made it a city within a city.

A few narrow streets cut between the hulking modern architecture, which includes two high-rise office towers owned by Daimler, one of which was designed by star architect Renzo Piano. The round atrium of the Sony Center comes closest to a traditional square used as a public meeting point. Farther down Potsdamer Strasse are the state museums and cultural institutes of the Kulturforum.

TOP ATTRACTIONS

Gemäldegalerie (*Picture Gallery*). The Kulturforum's Gemäldegalerie reunites formerly separated collections from East and West Berlin. It's one of Germany's finest art galleries, and has an extensive selection of European paintings from the 13th to 18th century. Seven rooms are reserved for paintings by German masters, among them Dürer, Cranach the Elder, and Holbein. A special collection has works of the Italian masters—Botticelli, Titian, Giotto, Lippi, and Raphael—as well as paintings by Dutch and Flemish masters of the 15th and 16th centuries: Van Eyck, Bosch, Bruegel the Elder, and van der Weyden. The museum also holds the world's second-largest Rembrandt collection. ⊠ *Kulturforum, Matthäikirchpl., Potsdamer Platz* ☎ *030/2664–24242* ⊕ *www. smb.museum* 🎟 *€10* 🕙 *Tues., Wed., and Fri. 10–6, Thurs. 10–8, weekends 11–6* Ⓜ *Potsdamer Platz (U-bahn and S-bahn).*

Fodor's Choice ★ **Kulturforum** (*Cultural Forum*). This unique ensemble of museums, galleries, and the Philharmonic Hall was long in the making. The first designs were submitted in the 1960s and the last building completed in 1998. Now it forms a welcome modern counterpoint to the thoroughly restored Prussian splendor of Museum Island, although Berliners and tourists alike hold drastically differing opinions on the area's architectural aesthetics. Whatever your opinion, Kulturforum's artistic holdings are unparalleled and worth at least a day of your time, if not more. The Kulturforum includes the **Gemäldegalerie** (Picture Gallery), the **Kunstbibliothek** (Art Library), the **Kupferstichkabinett** (Print Cabinet), the **Kunstgewerbemuseum** (Museum of Decorative Arts), the **Philharmonie**, the **Musikinstrumenten-Museum** (Musical Instruments Museum), and the **Staatsbibliothek** (National Library). ⊠ *Potsdamer Platz* Ⓜ *Potsdamer Platz (U-bahn and S-bahn).*

Kunstbibliothek (*Art Library*). With more than 400,000 volumes on the history of European art, the Kunstbibliothek (art library), in the Kulturforum, is one of Germany's most important institutions on the subject. It contains art posters and advertisements, examples of graphic design and book design, ornamental engravings, prints and drawings, and a costume library. Visitors can view items in the reading rooms, but many samples from the collections are also shown in rotating special exhibitions. ⊠ *Kulturforum, Matthäikirchpl., Potsdamer Platz* ☎ *030/2664–24242* ⊕ *www.smb.museum* ✉ *Varies according to exhibition* ⓧ *Tues.–Fri. 10–6, weekends 11–6; reading room weekdays 9–8* Ⓜ *Potsdamer Platz (U-bahn and S-bahn).*

Kunstgewerbemuseum (*Museum of Decorative Arts*). Inside the Kulturforum's recently renovated Kunstgewerbemuseum are European arts and crafts from the Middle Ages to the present. Among the notable exhibits are the Welfenschatz (Welfen Treasure), a collection of 16th-century gold and silver plates from Nürnberg; a floor dedicated to design and furniture; and extensive holdings of ceramics and porcelain. Though there is a free English-language audio guide, the mazelike museum is difficult to navigate and most signage is in German. ⊠ *Kulturforum, Herbert-von-Karajan-Str. 10, Potsdamer Platz* ☎ *030/266–2902* ⊕ *www. smb.museum* ✉ *€8* ⓧ *Tues.–Fri. 10–6, weekends 11–6* Ⓜ *Potsdamer Platz (U-bahn and S-bahn).*

Kupferstichkabinett (*Drawings and Prints Collection*). One of the Kulturforum's smaller museums, Kupferstichkabinett has occasional exhibits, which include European woodcuts, engravings, and illustrated books from the 15th century to the present (highlights of its holdings are pen-and-ink drawings by Dürer and drawings by Rembrandt). You can request to see one or two drawings in the study room. Another building displays paintings dating from the late Middle Ages to 1800. ⊠ *Kulturforum, Matthäikirchpl. 4, Potsdamer Platz* ☎ *030/2664–24242* ⊕ *www. smb.museum* ✉ *€6* ⓧ *Tues.–Fri. 10–6, weekends 11–6* Ⓜ *Potsdamer Platz (U-bahn and S-bahn).*

Musikinstrumenten-Museum (*Musical Instruments Museum*). Across the parking lot from the Philharmonie, the Kulturforum's Musikinstrumenten-Museum has a fascinating collection of keyboard, string, wind, and percussion instruments. These are demonstrated during a noon tour on Saturday, which closes with a 35-minute Wurlitzer organ concert for an extra €3. ⊠ *Kulturforum, Ben-Gurion-Str. 1, Potsdamer Platz* ☎ *030/2548–1178* ⊕ *www.sim.spk-berlin.de* ✉ *€6* ⓧ *Tues., Wed., and Fri. 9–5, Thurs. 9–8, weekends 10–5* Ⓜ *Potsdamer Platz (U-bahn and S-bahn).*

Neue Nationalgalerie (*New National Gallery*). Bauhaus member Mies van der Rohe originally designed this glass-box structure for Bacardi Rum in Cuba, but Berlin became the site of its realization in 1968.

The main exhibits are below ground. Highlights of the collection of 20th-century paintings, sculptures, and drawings include works by expressionists Otto Dix, Ernst Ludwig Kirchner, and Georg Grosz. Special exhibits often take precedence over the permanent collection, though the entire museum is closed during the next several years for renovations. ⊠ *Potsdamer Str. 50, Potsdamer Platz* ☏ *030/2664–24242* ⊕ *www.smb.museum* 🖾 *Varies according to exhibition* ☉ *Tues., Wed., and Fri. 10–6, Thurs. 10–8, weekends 11–6* Ⓜ *Potsdamer Platz (U-bahn and S-bahn).*

Panoramapunkt. Located 300 feet above Potsdamer Platz at the top of one of its tallest towers, the new Panoramapunkt (Panoramic Viewing Point) not only features the world's highest-standing original piece of the Berlin wall, but also a fascinating, multimedia exhibit about the dramatic history of Berlin's former urban center. A café and a sun terrace facing west make this open-air viewing platform one of the city's most romantic. ⊠ *Potsdamer Pl. 1, Potsdamer Platz* ☏ *030/2593–7080* ⊕ *www.panoramapunkt.de* 🖾 *€6.50* ☉ *Summer, daily 10–8; winter, daily 10–5; last entrance 30 mins before closing* Ⓜ *Potsdamer Platz (U-bahn and S-bahn).*

Fodor's Choice ★ **Spy Museum.** Some 25 years after the end of the Cold War, a new museum dedicated to the world of espionage opened in September 2015. The museum features interactive exhibits from the time of the Bible to the present day, covering topics that include military interrogation techniques and the world of secret services. The museum even touches on celebrated fictional spies, James Bond among them. An exhibit on the Enigma machine and the history of code breaking is one of the museum's most buzzed-about draws. ⊠ *Leipziger Pl. 9, Potsdamer Platz* ☏ *030/206–2019* ⊕ *www.spymuseumberlin.com* 🖾 *€18* ☉ *Daily 10–8* Ⓜ *Potsdamer Platz (U-bahn and S-bahn).*

WORTH NOTING

Sony Center. This glass-and-steel construction wraps around a spectacular circular forum. Topping it off is a tentlike structure meant to emulate Mt. Fuji. The architectural jewel, designed by German-American architect Helmut Jahn, is one of the most stunning public spaces of Berlin's new center, filled with restaurants, cafés, movie theaters, and apartments. A faint reminder of glorious days gone by is the old **Kaisersaal** (Emperor's Hall), held within a very modern glass enclosure, and today a pricey restaurant. The hall originally stood 75 yards away in the Grand Hotel Esplanade (built in 1907) but was moved here lock, stock, and barrel. Red-carpet glamour returns every February with the Berlinale Film Festival, which has screenings at the commercial cinema within the center. ⊠ *Potsdamer Platz* Ⓜ *Potsdamer Platz (U-bahn and S-bahn).*

Staatsbibliothek (*National Library*). The Kulturforum's Staatsbibliothek is one of the largest libraries in Europe, and was one of the Berlin settings in Wim Wenders's 1987 film *Wings of Desire*. ⊠ *Kulturforum, Potsdamer Str. 33, Potsdamer Platz* ☏ *030/2664–32333* ⊕ *staatsbibliothek-berlin.de* ☉ *Weekdays 9–9, Sat. 10–7* Ⓜ *Potsdamer Platz (U-bahn and S-bahn).*

15

FRIEDRICHSHAIN

The cobblestone streets of Friedrichshain, bustling with bars, cafés, and shops, give it a Greenwich Village feel. There's plenty to see here, including Karl-Marx-Allee, a long, monumental boulevard lined by grand Stalinist apartment buildings (conceived of as "palaces for the people" that would show the superiority of the Communist system over the capitalist one); the area's funky parks; the East Side Gallery; and lively Simon-Dach-Strasse. It's cool, it's hip, it's historical. If you're into street art, this is a good place to wander.

TOP ATTRACTIONS

Fodor's Choice ★ **East Side Gallery.** This 1-km (½-mi) stretch of concrete went from guarded border to open-air gallery within three months. East Berliners breached the Wall on November 9, 1989, and between February and June of 1990, 118 artists from around the globe created unique works of art on its longest remaining section. Restoration in 2010 renewed the old images with a fresh coat of paint, but while the colors of the artworks now look like new, the gallery has lost a bit of its charm. One of the best-known works, by Russian artist Dmitri Vrubel, depicts Brezhnev and Honecker (the former East German leader) kissing, with the caption "My God. Help me survive this deadly love." The stretch along the Spree Canal runs between the Warschauer Strasse S- and U-bahn station and Ostbahnhof. The redbrick Oberbaumbrücke (an 1896 bridge) at Warschauer Strasse makes that end more scenic. ⊠ *Mühlenstr., Friedrichshain* Ⓜ *Warschauer Strasse (U-bahn and S-bahn), Ostbahnhof (S-bahn).*

KREUZBERG

Hip Kreuzberg, stretching from the West Berlin side of the border crossing at Checkpoint Charlie all the way to the banks of the Spree next to Friedrichshain, is home base for much of Berlin's famed nightclub scene and a great place to get a feel for young Berlin. A large Turkish population shares the residential streets with a variegated assortment of political radicals and bohemians of all nationalities. In the minds of most Berliners, it is split into two even smaller sections: Kreuzberg 61 is a little more upscale, and contains a variety of small and elegant shops and restaurants, while Kreuzberg 36 has stayed grittier, as exemplified by the garbage-strewn, drug-infested, but much-beloved Görlitzer Park. Oranienstrasse, the spine of life in the Kreuzberg 36 district, has mellowed from hard core to funky since reunification. When Kreuzberg literally had its back against the Wall, West German social outcasts, punks, and the radical left made this old working-class street their territory. Since the 1970s the population has also been largely Turkish, and many of yesterday's outsiders have turned into successful owners of shops and cafés. The most vibrant stretch is between Skalitzer Strasse and Oranienplatz. Use Bus M29 or the Görlitzer Bahnhof or Kottbusser Tor U-bahn stations to reach it.

CLOSE UP

Berlin Wall Walk

The East German government, in an attempt to keep its beleaguered citizens from fleeing, built the Berlin Wall practically overnight in August 1961. On November 9, 1989, it was torn down, signaling the dawning of a new era. Most of the Wall has been demolished but you can still walk the trail where it used to stand and visualize the 12-foot-tall border that once divided the city.

FOLLOW THE COBBLESTONES

These days, it's hard to believe that Potsdamer Platz used to be a no-man's-land. But in front of the gleaming skyscrapers, next to the S-bahn station, a tiny stretch of the Berlin Wall stands as a reminder of the place's history. Just over on Erna-Berger-Strasse is the last of the hundreds of watchtowers that stood along the Wall.

Today, you can follow the rows of cobblestones on the ground that mark where the Wall used to stand. The path illuminates the effects the Wall had on the city, cutting through streets, neighborhoods, and even through buildings, which were then abandoned.

GO EAST

Walk south along Stresemanstrasse from Potsdamer Platz, then head east along Niederkirchnerstrasse two blocks to Checkpoint Charlie, a border crossing that foreign nationals used to cross between the American and Soviet zones. Niederkirchnerstrasse turns into Zimmerstrasse. Continue east along that to the modest column engraved "He only wanted freedom," in German, at Zimmerstrasse 15, commemorating Peter Fechter, an 18-year-old who was shot and killed while trying to escape to the West.

Follow Zimmerstrasse and turn left on Axel-Springer-Strasse, then right, onto Kommandantenstrasse. Keep walking past Sebastian and Waldemar streets and you'll reach Engelbecken Pond. This is a good place to rest or have lunch at one of the cafés in Kreuzberg.

A DIFFERENT WALL WALK

Potsdamer Platz, Checkpoint Charlie, and the surrounding areas are not the only places to see remnants of the Wall. For another glimpse into the past, head to the border between Mitte and Wedding, just north of Nordbahnhof train station. Starting there, you can follow Bernauer Strasse to the Berlin Wall Memorial (Gedenkstätte Berliner Mauer), in the former "death strip," where a church was once blown up by the East because it was a possible hiding place for those trying to flee.

Follow Bernauer Strasse until you reach the corner of Schwedter Strasse, then take the path that cuts through Mauer Park. The park is now home to one of the city's hippest flea markets but it used to be the dangerous no-man's-land between East and West Berlin. At its northern end, Schwedter Strasse turns into the Schwedter Steg, a footbridge over an impressive chasm of connecting train tracks and S-bahn lines. Turn around for a spectacular view of the TV tower, then descend the steps on your left and continue along Norwegerstrasse. When the path goes under an imposing brick bridge, take the steps that lead up the bridge instead. This is the famous Bornholmer Brücke, where East Berliners overwhelmed the Wall checkpoint and became the first to push through to West Berlin.

15

TOP ATTRACTIONS

Fodor's Choice
★
Mauermuseum-Museum Haus am Checkpoint Charlie. Just steps from the famous crossing point between the two Berlins, the Wall Museum–House at Checkpoint Charlie presents visitors with the story of the Wall and, even more riveting, the stories of those who escaped through, under, and over it. An infamous hot spot during the Cold War, this border crossing for non-Germans was manned by the Soviet military in East Berlin's Mitte district and, several yards south, by the U.S. military in West Berlin's Kreuzberg district. Tension between the superpowers in October 1961 led to an uneasy standoff between Soviet and American tanks. Today the touristy intersection consists of a replica of an American guardhouse and signage, plus cobblestones that mark the old border.

The homespun museum reviews the events leading up to the Wall's construction and, with original tools and devices, plus recordings and photographs, shows how East Germans escaped to the West (one of the most ingenious contraptions was a miniature submarine). Exhibits about human rights and paintings interpreting the Wall round out the experience. Come early or late in the day to avoid the multitudes dropped off by tour buses. Monday can be particularly crowded because the state museums are closed on Mondays. ⊠ *Friedrichstr. 43–45, Kreuzberg* ☎ *030/253–7250* ⊕ *www.mauermuseum.com* ☜ *€12.50* ☉ *Daily 9 am–10 pm* Ⓜ *Kochstrasse (U-bahn).*

Fodor's Choice
★
Topographie des Terrors (*Topography of Terror*). Before 2010, Topographie des Terrors was an open-air exhibit, fully exposed to the elements. Now, in a stunning new indoor exhibition center at the same location, you can view photos and documents explaining the secret state police and intelligence organizations that planned and executed Nazi crimes against humanity. The fates of both victims and perpetrators are given equal attention here. The cellar remains of the Nazis' Reich Security Main Office (composed of the SS, SD, and Gestapo), where the main exhibit used to be, are still open to the public and now contain other exhibitions, which typically run from April to October as the remains are outdoors. ⊠ *Niederkirchnerstr. 8, Kreuzberg* ☎ *030/2545–0950* ⊕ *www.topographie.de* ☜ *Free* ☉ *Daily 10–8.*

WORTH NOTING

Berlinische Galerie. Talk about site-specific art: all the modern art, photography, and architecture models and plans here, created between 1870 and the present, were made in Berlin (or in the case of architecture competition models, intended for the city). Russians, secessionists, Dadaists, and expressionists all had their day in Berlin, and individual works by Otto Dix, George Grosz, and Georg Baselitz, as well as artists' archives such as the Dadaist Hannah Höch's, are highlights. There's a set price for the permanent collection, but rates vary for special exhibitions, which are usually well attended and quite worthwhile. Bus M29 to Waldeckpark/Oranienstrasse is the closest transportation stop. ⊠ *Alte Jakobstr. 124–128, Kreuzberg* ☎ *030/7890–2600* ⊕ *www.berlinischegalerie.de* ☜ *€8* ☉ *Wed.–Mon. 10–6* Ⓜ *Kochstrasse (U-bahn).*

The East Side Gallery, the largest surviving section of the Berlin Wall, displays graffiti from artists around the world.

FAMILY **Deutsches Technikmuseum** (*German Museum of Technology*). A must if you're traveling with children, this musem will enchant anyone who's interested in technology or fascinated with trains, planes, and automobiles. Set in the remains of Anhalter Bahnhof's industrial yard and enhanced with a newer, glass-enclosed wing, the museum has several floors of machinery, including two airplane rooms on the upper floors crowned with a "Rosinenbomber," one of the beloved airplanes that delivered supplies to Tempelhof Airport during the Berlin Airlift of 1948. Don't miss the train sheds, which are like three-dimensional, walkable timelines of trains throughout history, and the historical brewery, which has a great rooftop view of today's trains, U-bahn lines U1 and U2, converging at the neighboring Gleisdreieck station. Berlin's quirky Sugar Museum, which relates the history of this ubiquitous and profoundly important commodity, is slated to have relocated by the end of 2015. ⊠ *Trebbiner Str. 9, Kreuzberg* ☎ *030/902–540* ⊕ *www. sdtb.de/Home.623.0.html* 🎫 *€8* ⏰ *Tues.–Fri. 9–5:30, weekends 10–6* Ⓜ *Gleisdreieck (U-bahn), Anhalter Bahnhof (S-bahn).*

Golgatha. This beloved local watering hole has taken up space in Viktoriapark since 1928. Open all day long and late into the night, it's the perfect place to while away the hours with a cup of coffee during the day, or sip a cocktail or beer during the evening, when a DJ is spinning. It's also a reliable lunch spot, with salads, grilled meats, and the "German pizzas" known as *Flammkuchen* on the menu. ⊠ *Dudenstr. 40–64, in Viktoriapark, closest entrance at Katzbachstr., Kreuzberg* ☎ *030/785–2453* ⊕ *www.golgatha-berlin.de* ⏰ *Apr.–Oct., 9 am–late* Ⓜ *Yorckstrasse (S-bahn and U-bahn).*

Jüdisches Museum Berlin (*Jewish Museum*). The history of Germany's Jews from the Middle Ages through today is chronicled here, from prominent historical figures to the evolution of laws regarding Jews' participation in civil society. A few of the exhibits document the Holocaust itself, but this museum celebrates Jewish life and history far more than it focuses on the atrocities committed during WWII. An attraction in itself is the highly conceptual building, designed by Daniel Libeskind, where various physical "voids" in the oddly constructed and intensely personal modern wing of the building represent the idea that some things can and should never be exhibited when it comes to the Holocaust. Libeskind also directed the construction of the recently opened "Akademie" of the museum just across the street, which offers a library and temporary exhibitions, as well as space for workshops and lectures. Reserve at least three hours for the museum and devote more time to the second floor if you're already familiar with basic aspects of Judaica, which are the focus of the third floor. ⊠ *Lindenstr. 9–14, Kreuzberg* ☎ *030/2599–3300* ⊕ *www.jmberlin.de* ⌂ *€7* ⊙ *Mon. 10–10, Tues.– Sun. 10–8* Ⓜ *Hallesches Tor (U-bahn).*

Martin-Gropius-Bau. This magnificent palazzo-like exhibition hall first opened in 1881, and once housed Berlin's Arts and Crafts Museum. Its architect, Martin Gropius, was the great-uncle of Walter Gropius, the Bauhaus architect who also worked in Berlin. The international, changing exhibits on art and culture have recently included Aztec sculptures, Henri Cartier-Bresson's photographs, an expansive Frida Kahlo retrospective, and works from Anish Kapoor and Meret Oppenheim. ⊠ *Niederkirchnerstr. 7, Kreuzberg* ☎ *030/254–860* ⊕ *www.gropiusbau. de* ⌂ *Varies with exhibit* ⊙ *Wed.–Mon. 10–7* Ⓜ *Kochstrasse (U-bahn), Potsdamer Platz (U-bahn and S-bahn).*

SCHÖNEBERG

Long known as Berlin's gay neighborhood, these days Schöneberg is yet another burgeoning hipster area, attracting artists and creative types and young families. You'll find many stylish shops and cafés in and around Nollendorfplatz, steps away from Winterfeldtplatz, where a weekly food and flea market takes place Wednesdays and Saturdays.

PRENZLAUER BERG

Once a spot for edgy art spaces, squats, and all manner of alternative lifestyles, Prenzlauer Berg has morphed into an oasis of artisanal bakeries, cute kids' clothing stores (where the prices could knock your socks off), and genteel couples with baby strollers. That said, it's a beautiful area, with gorgeous, perfectly renovated buildings shaded by giant plantain and chestnut trees. If you're in the mood for an upscale, locally made snack and a nice stroll, this is the place to be. You'll find a denser concentration of locals and long-settled expats in Prenzlauer Berg than in other parts of the city like the Scheunenviertel.

15

WORTH NOTING

Jüdischer Friedhof Weissensee (*Jewish Cemetery*). More than 150,000 graves make up Europe's largest Jewish cemetery, in Berlin's Weissensee district, near Prenzlauer Berg. The grounds and tombstones are in excellent condition—a seeming impossibility, given its location in the heart of the Third Reich—and wandering through them is like taking an extremely moving trip back in time through the history of Jewish Berlin. To reach the cemetery, take the M4 tram from Hackescher Markt to Albertinenstrasse and head south on Herbert-Baum-Strasse. At the gate you can get a map from the attendant. The guidebook is in German only. ⊠ *Herbert-Baum-Str. 45, Prenzlauer Berg* ☎ *030/925–3330* ⊙ *Summer, Sun.–Thurs. 8–5, Fri. 8–2:30; winter, Sun.–Thurs. 8–4, Fri. 8–2:30. Last entry 30 mins before closing.*

Kulturbrauerei (*Culture Brewery*). The redbrick buildings of the old Schultheiss brewery are typical of late-19th-century industrial architecture. Parts of the brewery were built in 1842, and at the turn of the 20th century the complex expanded to include the main brewery of Berlin's famous Schultheiss beer, then the world's largest brewery. Today, the multiplex cinema, pubs, clubs, and a concert venue that occupy it make up an arts and entertainment nexus (sadly, without a brewery). Pick up information at the Prenzlauer Berg tourist office here, and come Christmastime, visit the Scandinavian-themed market, which includes children's rides. ⊠ *Schönhauser Allee 36, entry at Sredzkistr. 1 and Knaackstr. 97, Prenzlauer Berg* ☎ ⊕ *www.kulturbrauerei.de* Ⓜ *Eberswalder Strasse (U-bahn).*

WEDDING

While much of Berlin has gentrified rapidly in recent years, Wedding, north of Mitte, is still an old-fashioned, working-class district. Because rents are still relatively low, it will probably be the next hot spot for artists and other creative types looking for cheap studios and work places. If you want to be on the cutting edge, ferret out an underground show or two in this ethnically diverse neighborhood.

For a historical perspective on the years of Berlin's division, head to the excellent Berlin Wall Memorial Site. This illuminating museum (some of which is open-air) is located along one of the few remaining stretches of the wall, and chronicles the sorrows of the era.

Gedenkstätte Berliner Mauer (*Berlin Wall Memorial Site*). This site combines memorials and a museum and research center on the Berlin Wall. The division of Berlin was particularly heart-wrenching on Bernauer Strasse, where neighbors and families on opposite sides of the street were separated overnight. The Reconciliation Chapel, completed in 2000, replaced the community church dynamited by the Communists in 1985. The church had been walled into the "death strip," and was seen as a hindrance to patrolling it. A portion of the Wall remains on Bernauer Strasse, along with an installation meant to serve as a memorial, which can be viewed 24/7. ⊠ *Bernauer Str. 111, Wedding* ☎ *030/4679–86666* ⊕ *www.berliner-mauer-gedenkstaette.de* 🗌 *Free, tours €3* ⊙ *Visitor center: Tues.–Sun. 10–6* Ⓜ *Bernauer Strasse (U-bahn), Nordbahnhof (S-bahn).*

NEUKÖLLN

If you missed Prenzlauer Berg's heyday, you can still get a good feel for its raw charm and creative flair if you head to ultrahip Neukölln. Just southeast of Kreuzberg below the Landwehrkanal, Neukölln was an impoverished, gritty West Berlin neighborhood until the hip crowd discovered it a few years ago. It's since been almost completely transformed. Makeshift bars-galleries brighten up semi-abandoned storefronts, and vintage café or breakfast spots put a new twist on old concepts. Everything has a salvaged feel, and the crowds are young and savvy. If you're looking for nightlife, there are bars galore.

TOP ATTRACTIONS

Fodor's Choice
★

Tempelhofer Park. Of all Berlin's many transformations, this one—from airport to park—might be the quickest. The iconic airport (it was the site of the 1948–49 Berlin airlift) had its last flight in 2008. Only two years later, it opened as a park, complete with untouched runways. It has quickly become one of the city's most beloved and impressive outdoor spots, where bikers, skaters, kite flyers, urban gardeners, picnickers, and grillers all gather. Although the Nazi-era airport buildings are not open for wandering, you can explore them on a two-hour tour (book online at berlinkompakt.net). ⊠ *Bordered by Columbiadamm and Tempelhoferdamm, Neukölln* ☎ *030/2000–37400* ⊕ *www.thf-berlin.de* ☉ *Daily sunrise–sunset* Ⓜ *Tempelhof (S-bahn and U-bahn).*

CHARLOTTENBURG

An important part of former West Berlin but now a western district of the united city, Charlottenburg has retained its old-world charm. Elegance is the keyword here. Whether you're strolling and shopping around Savignyplatz or pausing for a refreshment at the LiteraturHaus, you'll be impressed with the dignity of both the neighborhood's architecture and its inhabitants. Kurfürstendamm (or Ku'damm, as the locals call it) is the central shopping mile, where you'll find an international clientele browsing brand-name designers, or drinking coffee at sidewalk cafés.

TOP ATTRACTIONS

Kaiser-Wilhelm-Gedächtnis-Kirche (*Kaiser Wilhelm Memorial Church*). A dramatic reminder of World War II's destruction, the ruined bell tower is all that remains of this once massive church, which was completed in 1895 and dedicated to the emperor, Kaiser Wilhelm I. The Hohenzollern dynasty is depicted inside in a gilded mosaic whose damage, like that of the building, will not be repaired. The exhibition revisits World War II's devastation throughout Europe. On the hour, the tower chimes out a melody composed by the last emperor's great-grandson, the late Prince Louis Ferdinand von Hohenzollern. In stark contrast to the old bell tower (dubbed the "Hollow Tooth"), which is in sore need of restoration now, are the adjoining Memorial Church and Tower, designed by the noted German architect Egon Eiermann and finished in 1961. These ultramodern octagonal structures, with their myriad honeycomb windows, have nicknames as well: the "Lipstick" and the

Jewish Berlin Today

As Berlin continues to grapple with the past, important steps toward celebrating Jewish history and welcoming a new generation of Jews to Berlin are in the making.

Somber monuments have been built in memory of victims of the Holocaust and National Socialism. An especially poignant but soft-spoken tribute is the collection of **Stolpersteine** (stumbling blocks) found all over Berlin, imbedded into sidewalks in front of the pre-Holocaust homes of Berlin Jews, commemorating former residents simply with names and dates. German artist Gunter Demnig has personally installed these tiny memorials in big cities and small towns across Germany and Austria, and continues to do so as requests come in from communities across Europe.

The **Ronald S. Lauder Foundation** has gone a step further. Along with **Lauder Yeshurun**, Berlin's Jewish communities have been further strengthened by building housing for Jews in the city center, founding a Yeshiva, a rabbinical school, and offering special services for returning Jews.

It's difficult to say how many Jews live in Berlin today, but an official estimate puts the number at 22,000–27,000.

About 12,000 members of the Jewish community are practicing Jews, mostly from the former Soviet Union, who belong to one of several synagogues. Berlin is also gaining in popularity among young Israelis, and today, some estimates say there may be as many as 20,000 Israelis who call Berlin home. These numbers don't include the secular and religious Jews who wish to remain anonymous in the German capital.

The government supports Jewish businesses and organizations with funding, keeps close ties with important members of the community, and, perhaps most visibly, provides 24-hour police protection in front of any Jewish establishment that requests it. Two recent events proved that Jewish Berlin is thriving once again. On November 4, 2010, three young rabbis were ordained at the Pestalozzi Strasse synagogue, the first ceremony of its kind to occur in Berlin since before the Holocaust. Also in 2010, Charlotte Knobloch, a Holocaust survivor and the president of the German Jewish Council at the time, showed the ultimate faith in Germany's recovery and reparation efforts by declaring the country "once again a homeland for Jews."

"Powder Box." Brilliant, blue stained glass designed by Gabriel Loire of Chartres, France, dominates the interiors. Church music and organ concerts are presented in the church regularly, which is slated for restoration in the near future. ⊠ *Breitscheidpl., Charlottenburg* ⊕ *www. gedaechtniskirche-berlin.de* ☐ *Free* ⊙ *Memorial church daily 9–7* Ⓜ *Zoologischer Garten (U-bahn and S-bahn).*

Käthe-Kollwitz-Museum. Right next door to the Literaturhaus, this small but lovingly curated museum in a formerly private home pays homage to one of Berlin's favorite artists, the female sculptor, printmaker, and painter Käthe Kollwitz. Perhaps best known for her harrowing sculpture of a mother mourning a dead child inside the Neue Wache on Unter den Linden, she also lent her name to one of the city's most beautiful squares, the posh, leafy Kollwitzplatz, which contains a sculpture of her. ⊠ *Fasanenstr. 24, Charlottenburg* ☎ *030/882–5210* ⊕ *www.kaethe-kollwitz.de* ☞ *€6* ⊙ *Daily 10–6* Ⓜ *Uhlandstrasse (U-bahn)*.

Kurfürstendamm. This busy thoroughfare began as a riding path in the 16th century. The elector Joachim II of Brandenburg used it to travel between his palace on the Spree River and his hunting lodge in the Grunewald. The Kurfürstendamm (Elector's Causeway) was transformed into a major route in the late 19th century, thanks to the initiative of Bismarck, Prussia's Iron Chancellor.

Even in the 1920s, the Ku'damm was still relatively new and by no means elegant; it was fairly far removed from the old heart of the city, Unter den Linden in Mitte. The Ku'damm's prewar fame was due mainly to its rowdy bars and dance halls, as well as the cafés where the cultural avant-garde of Europe gathered. Almost half of its 245 late-19th-century buildings were completely destroyed in the 1940s, and the remaining buildings were damaged to varying degrees. As in most of western Berlin, what you see today is either restored or newly constructed. Many of the 1950s buildings have been replaced by high-rises, in particular at the corner of Joachimstaler Strasse. Although Ku'damm is still known as the best shopping street in Berlin, its establishments have declined in elegance and prestige over the years. Nowadays you'll want to visit just to check it off your list, but few of the many downmarket chain stores will impress you with their luxury. ⊠ *Charlottenburg* Ⓜ *Kurfürstendamm (U-bahn)*.

Literaturhaus Berlin. This grand, 19th-century villa on one of West Berlin's prettiest streets, is best known for its café, which approximates a Viennese coffeehouse in both food and atmosphere. It also serves as an intellectual meeting place for high-minded and well-to-do Berliners. The house hosts readings, literary symposia, exhibitions, and writing workshops year-round, and has a cozy and comprehensive bookstore (one of the city's best) on the lower level. ⊠ *Fasanenstr. 23, Charlottenburg* ☎ *030/887–2860* ⊕ *www.literaturhaus-berlin.de/* ⊙ *Bookshop weekdays 10:30–7:30, Sat. 10:30–6; café daily 9–midnight* Ⓜ *Uhlandstrasse (U-bahn)*.

Museum Berggruen. This small modern-art museum holds works by Matisse, Klee, Giacometti, and Picasso, who is particularly well represented with more than 100 works. Heinz Berggruen (1914–2007), a businessman who left Berlin in the 1930s, collected the excellent paintings. He narrates portions of the free audio guide, sharing anecdotes about how he came to acquire pieces directly from the artists, as well as his opinions of the women portrayed in Picasso's portraits. ⊠ *Schlossstr. 1, Charlottenburg* ☎ *030/2664–24242* ⊕ *www.smb.museum* ☞ *€10* ⊙ *Tues.–Fri. 10–6, weekends 11–6* Ⓜ *Sophie-Charlotte-Platz (U-bahn), Richard-Wagner-Platz (U-bahn)*.

Schloss Charlottenburg (*Charlottenburg Palace*). A grand reminder of imperial days, this showplace served as a city residence for the Prussian rulers. The gorgeous palace started as a modest royal summer residence in 1695, built on the orders of King Friedrich I for his wife, Sophie-Charlotte. In the 18th century Frederick the Great made a

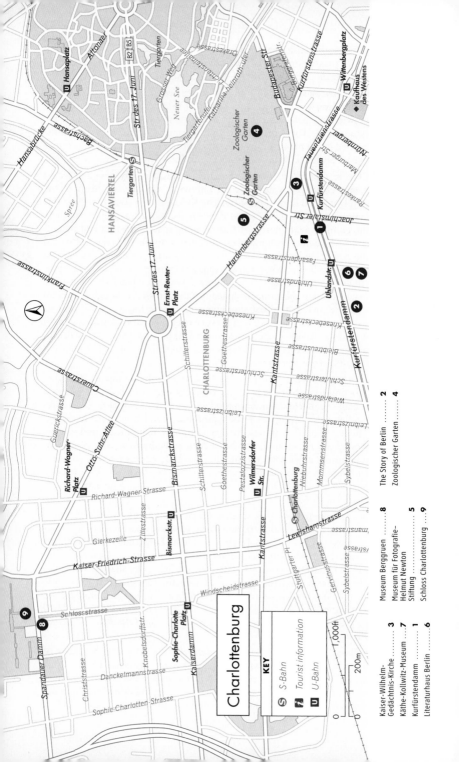

Charlottenburg

KEY

- Ⓢ S-Bahn
- 🅸 Tourist information
- Ⓤ U-Bahn

0	200m
0	1,000ft

Kaiser-Wilhelm-
Gedächtnis-Kirche **3**
Käthe-Kollwitz-Museum **7**
Kurfürstendamm **1**
Literaturhaus Berlin **6**

Museum Berggruen **8**
Museum für Fotografie–
Helmut Newton
Stiftung **5**
Schloss Charlottenburg **9**

The Story of Berlin **2**
Zoologischer Garten **4**

number of additions, such as the dome and several wings designed in the rococo style. By 1790 the complex had evolved into a massive royal domain that could take a whole day to explore. Behind heavy iron gates, the Court of Honor—the front courtyard—is dominated by a baroque statue of the Great Elector on horseback. Buildings can be visited separately for different admission prices, or altogether as part of a €19 Tageskarte (day card).

The **Altes Schloss** is the main building of the Schloss Charlottenburg complex, with the ground-floor suites of Friedrich I and Sophie-Charlotte. Paintings include royal portraits by Antoine Pesne, a noted court painter of the 18th century. A guided tour visits the Oak Gallery, the early-18th-century palace chapel, and the suites of Friedrich Wilhelm II and Friedrich Wilhelm III, furnished in the Biedermeier style. Tours leave hourly from 9 to 5. The upper floor has the apartments of Friedrich Wilhelm IV, a silver treasury, and Berlin and Meissen porcelain and can be seen on its own.

The **Neuer Flügel** (New Building), where Frederick the Great once lived, was designed by Knobbelsdorff, who also built Sanssouci. The 138-foot-long Goldene Galerie (Golden Gallery) was the palace's ballroom. West of the staircase are Frederick's rooms, in which parts of his extravagant collection of works by Watteau, Chardin, and Pesne are displayed. An audio guide is included in the separate €6 admission fee.

The Schlosspark Charlottenburg behind the palace was laid out in the French baroque style beginning in 1697, and was transformed into an English garden in the early 19th century. In it are the Neuer Pavillon by Karl Friedrich Schinkel and Carl Langhan's **Belvedere Pavillon** (€3, Apr.–Oct., Tues.–Sun. 10–6; winter hrs vary) which overlooks the lake and the Spree River and holds a collection of Berlin porcelain. ✉ *Spandauer Damm 20–24, Charlottenburg* ☎ *030/3319–694200* ⊕ *www.spsg.de* 💶 *€19 Tageskarte (day card) for all buildings, excluding tour of Altes Schloss baroque apartments* ⊘ *Palaces closed Mon., except New Palace and Charlottenburg Palace New Wing, which are closed Tues.* Ⓜ *Richard-Wagner-Platz (U-bahn).*

FAMILY **Zoologischer Garten** (*Zoological Gardens*). Even though Knut, the polar bear cub who captured the heart of the city, is sadly no longer with us, there are 14,000 other animals to see here, many of whom may be happy to have their time in the spotlight once again. There are 1,500 different species (more than any other zoo in Europe), including those rare and endangered, which the zoo has been successful at breeding. New arrivals in the past years include a baby rhinoceros. The animals' enclosures are designed to resemble their natural habitats, though some structures are ornate, such as the 1910 Arabian-style Zebra House. Pythons, frogs, turtles, invertebrates, Komodo dragons, and an amazing array of strange and colorful fish are part of the three-floor aquarium. Check the feeding times posted to watch creatures such as seals, apes, hippos, penguins, and pelicans during their favorite time of day. ✉ *Hardenbergpl. 8 and Budapester Str. 32, Tiergarten* ☎ *030/254–010* ⊕ *www. zoo-berlin.de* 💶 *Zoo or aquarium €13, combined ticket €20* ⊘ *Zoo:*

The modern sculpture on Breitscheidplatz frames the Kaiser-Wilhelm-Gedächtnis-Kirche in the background.

mid-Mar.–Oct., daily 9–6:30; Nov.–mid-Mar., daily 9–5; Aquarium: daily 9–6 Ⓜ *Zoologischer Garten (U-bahn and S-bahn).*

WORTH NOTING

Museum für Fotografie–Helmut Newton Stiftung. Native son Helmut Newton (1920–2004) pledged this collection of 1,000 photographs to Berlin months before his unexpected death. The man who defined fashion photography in the 1960s through the 1980s was an apprentice to Yva, a Jewish fashion photographer in Berlin in the 1930s. Newton fled Berlin with his family in 1938, and his mentor was killed in a concentration camp. The photographs, now part of the state museum collection, are shown on a rotating basis in the huge Wilhelmine building behind the train station Zoologischer Garten. You'll see anything from racy portraits of models to serene landscapes. ⊠ *Jebensstr. 2, Charlottenburg* ☎ *030/6642–4242* ⊕ *www.helmutnewton.com* 🎟 *€10* 🕑 *Tues.–Fri. 10–6 (Thurs. until 8), weekends 11–6* Ⓜ *Zoologischer Garten (U-bahn and S-bahn).*

FAMILY **The Story of Berlin.** You can't miss this multimedia museum—just look for the airplane wing exhibited in front. It was once part of a "Raisin bomber," a U.S. Air Force DC-3 that supplied Berlin during the Berlin Airlift in 1948 and 1949. Eight hundred years of the city's history, from the first settlers casting their fishing lines to Berliners heaving sledgehammers at the Wall, are conveyed through hands-on exhibits, film footage, and multimedia devices in this unusual venue. The sound of footsteps over broken glass follows your path through the exhibit on the *Kristallnacht* pogrom, and to pass through the section on the Nazis' book-burning on Bebelplatz, you must walk over book bindings.

Many original artifacts are on display, such as the stretch Volvo that served as Erich Honecker's state carriage in East Germany. The eeriest relic is the 1974 nuclear shelter, which you can visit by guided tour on the hour. Museum placards are also in English. ⊠ *Ku'damm Karree, Kurfürstendamm 207–208, Charlottenburg* ☏ *030/8872–0100* ⊕ *www. story-of-berlin.de* ☞ *€12* ◷ *Daily 10–8; last entry at 6* Ⓜ *Uhlandstrasse (U-bahn).*

WANNSEE

Most tourists come to leafy, upscale Wannsee to see the House of the Wannsee Conference, where the Third Reich's top officials met to plan the "final solution." Beyond this dark historical site, however, there are parks, lakes, and islands to explore. Leave a day for a trip here, especially in warm weather: the Wannsee lake is a favorite spot for a summer dip.

TOP ATTRACTIONS

Gedenkstätte Haus der Wannsee-Konferenz (*Wannsee Conference Memorial Site*). The lovely lakeside setting of this Berlin villa belies the unimaginable Holocaust atrocities planned here. This elegant edifice hosted the fateful conference held on January 20, 1942, at which Nazi leaders and German bureaucrats, under SS leader Reinhard Heydrich, planned the systematic deportation and mass extinction of Europe's Jewish population. Today this so-called "Endlösung der Judenfrage" ("final solution of the Jewish question") is illustrated with a chilling exhibition that documents the conference and, more extensively, the escalation of persecution against Jews and the Holocaust itself. A reference library offers source materials in English. ⊠ *Am Grossen Wannsee 56–58, from the Wannsee S-bahn station, take Bus 114, Wannsee* ☏ *030/805–0010* ⊕ *www.ghwk.de* ☞ *Free, tour €3* ◷ *Daily 10–6; library weekdays 10–6* Ⓜ *Wannsee (S-bahn).*

ORANIENBURG

In this little village a short drive north of Berlin, the Nazis built one of the first concentration camps (neighbors claimed not to notice what was happening there). After the war, the Soviets continued to use it. Only later did the GDR regime turn it into a memorial site. If you feel like you've covered all the main sites in Berlin, this is worth a day trip.

Gedenkstätte und Museum Sachsenhausen (*Sachsenhausen Memorial and Museum*). This concentration camp was established in 1936 and held 200,000 prisoners from every nation in Europe, including British officers and Joseph Stalin's son. It is estimated that tens of thousands died here, among them more than 12,000 Soviet prisoners of war.

Between 1945 and 1950 the Soviets used the site as a prison, and malnutrition and disease claimed the lives of 20% of the inmates. The East German government made the site a concentration camp memorial in April 1961. Many original facilities remain; the barracks and other buildings now hold exhibits.

To reach Sachsenhausen, take the S-bahn 1 to Oranienburg, the last stop. The ride from the Friedrichstrasse Station will take 50 minutes. Alternatively, take the Regional 5 train, direction north, from one of Berlin's main stations. From the Oranienburg Station it's a 25-minute walk (follow signs), or you can take a taxi or Bus 804 (a seven-minute ride, but with infrequent service) in the direction of Malz. An ABC zone ticket will suffice for any type of train travel and bus transfer. Allow three hours at the memorial, whose exhibits and sites are spread apart. Oranienburg is 35 km (22 miles) north of Berlin's center. ⊠ *Str. der Nationen 22, Oranienburg* ☎ *03301/200–200* ⊕ *www.stiftung-bg.de* ▨ *Free, audio guide €3* ☉ *Visitor center and grounds: Mid-Mar.–mid-Oct., daily 8:30–6; mid-Oct.–mid-Mar., daily 8:30–4:30; last admission ½ hr before closing. Museum closed Mon., all other days same hrs as above* Ⓜ *Oranienburg (S-bahn).*

WHERE TO EAT

Updated by
Giulia Pines

Berlin has plenty of unassuming neighborhood restaurants serving old-fashioned German food; but happily, the dining scene in this thriving city has expanded to incorporate all sorts of international cuisine. Italian food is abundant, from relatively mundane "red sauce" pizza and pasta establishments to restaurants offering specific regional Italian delicacies. Asian food, in particular, has made a big entrance, with Charlottenburg's Kantstrasse leading the way as Berlin's unofficial "Asiatown." Turkish food continues to be popular, too, especially *döner kebab* shops that sell pressed lamb or chicken in flatbread pockets with a variety of sauces and salads, which are great for a quick meal. Wurst, especially *currywurst*—pork sausage served with a mildly curried ketchup—is also popular if you're looking for a quick meal on the go.

And as in other big cities around the world, eating local is more and more the rage in Berlin. Restaurants are beginning to understand that although they could import ingredients from other European countries, fresh farm resources are closer to home. Surrounding the city is the rural state of Brandenburg, whose name often comes before *Ente* (duck) on a menu. In spring, *Spargel*, white asparagus from Beelitz, is all the rage, showing up in soups and side dishes.

It's worth noting that Berlin is known for curt or slow service, except at high-end restaurants. And keep in mind that many of the top restaurants are closed Sunday.

If you want to experience that old-fashioned German cuisine, Berlin's most traditional four-part meal is *Eisbein* (pork knuckle), always served with sauerkraut, pureed peas, and boiled potatoes. Other old-fashioned Berlin dishes include *Rouladen* (rolled stuffed beef), *Spanferkel* (suckling pig), *Berliner Schüsselsülze* (potted meat in aspic), and *Hackepeter* (ground beef).

Use the coordinates (⊕ 1:B3) at the end of each listing to locate a site on the corresponding map.

WHAT IT COSTS IN EUROS				
	$	$$	$$$	$$$$
AT DINNER	under €15	€15–€20	€21–€25	over €25

Restaurant prices are per person for a main course at dinner.

MITTE

$
GERMAN

✕ Altes Europa. By day, this is a quiet café reminiscent of a classic Viennese coffeehouse (the name means "Old Europe"), with shabby but trendy decor, and fashionable Mitte-ites chatting and intellectuals paging through newspapers and magazines. At night, it turns into a comfortable but bustling neighborhood pub, just crowded enough to look like a scene, but never too packed. The daily menu includes six or seven tasty dishes like classic German *Knödel* (dumplings) baked with mushrooms and spinach or *Tafelspitz* (boiled beef) with potatoes. The food is inventively prepared and served in record time (for notoriously slow Berlin). Ⓢ *Average main: €8 ⊠ Gipsstr. 11, Mitte* ☎ *030/2809–3840* ⊕ *www.alteseuropa.com* ▭ *No credit cards* Ⓜ *Hackescher Markt (S-bahn)* ✛ *1:A6.*

$$$$
FRENCH

✕ Bandol sur Mer. This tiny, 20-seat eatery serves inspired French cuisine in rotating five-course (or more) menus celebrating what's regional and seasonal—you can order à la carte but the menus are better value, and more fun. The entrecôte is a standout, if it's available. Wine pairings are well chosen. This is a magnet for the hip and fashionable so it's worth dressing up a bit. If you can't get a reservation here, try the sister restaurant next door: the larger and slightly more casual 3 Minutes Sur Mer, which is also open for lunch. Ⓢ *Average main: €32 ⊠ Torstr. 167, Mitte* ☎ *030/6730–2051* ⊕ *www.bandolsurmer.de* ☉ *Closed Sun. No lunch* ⚎ *Reservations essential* Ⓜ *Rosenthaler Platz (U-bahn)* ✛ *1:F1.*

$
JAPANESE
Fodor's Choice
★

✕ Cocolo. The most surprising thing about this very authentic-seeming ramen joint is the fact that the owner and chef is German, not Japanese. When it comes to the narrow, blink-and-you-miss-it Cocolo, Oliver Prestele has obviously got it right; the noodle kitchen is packed almost every night of the week and has gained a devoted following. Soups come with a variety of pork-based broths, like creamy *tonkotsu*, salty *shio*, or soy-based *shoyu*, along with flavorful toppings like tender pork or chicken, vegetables, bonito flakes, and an egg. The ramen is served in nubby clay bowls made by Prestele himself in his Wedding workshop. If you can't get a table at this tiny original location, there's a newer and larger outpost in Kreuzberg, at Paul-Linke-Ufer 39/40, which is also open for lunch. Ⓢ *Average main: €9 ⊠ Gipsstr. 3, Mitte* ☎ *0172/304–7584* ⊕ *www.oliverprestele.de* ▭ *No credit cards* ⚎ *Reservations not accepted* Ⓜ *Rosenthaler Platz, Weinmeisterstrasse (U-bahn), Hackescher Markt (S-bahn)* ✛ *1:A6.*

$
CAFÉ

✕ Confiserie Orientale. If you think the döner kebab is the pinnacle of Turkish food in Berlin, a visit to this exquisite sweets boutique will make you rethink your priorities. The gleaming, all-white interior mimics the nearby art galleries, and all the better to show off jewel-like

15

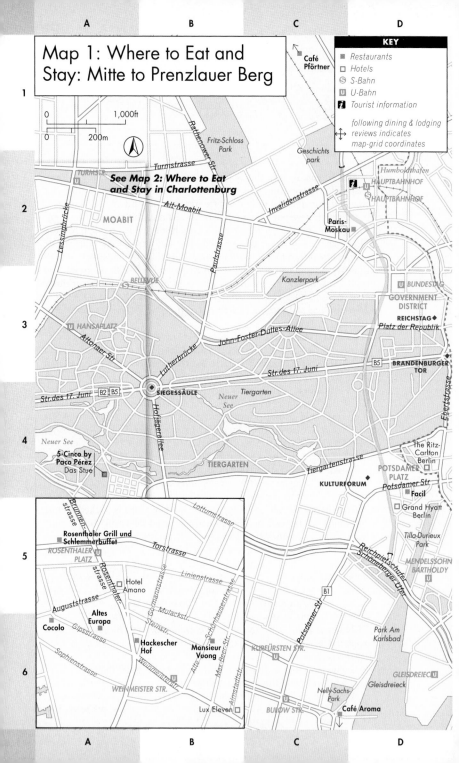

Map 1: Where to Eat and Stay: Mitte to Prenzlauer Berg

See Map 2: Where to Eat and Stay in Charlottenburg

KEY
- ■ Restaurants
- □ Hotels
- Ⓢ S-Bahn
- Ⓤ U-Bahn
- 🛈 Tourist information

following dining & lodging reviews indicates map-grid coordinates

0 — 1,000ft
0 — 200m

Café Pförtner

Fritz-Schloss Park

Geschichts park

Humboldthafen
HAUPTBAHNHOF
HAUPTBAHNHOF

TURMSTR. Ⓤ
Turmstrasse
Alt-Moabit
Invalidenstrasse
Paris-Moskau ■

MOABIT

Lessingbrücke
Paulstrasse
Rathenower Str.

BELLEVUE Ⓢ

Kanzlerpark
BUNDESTAG Ⓤ

GOVERNMENT DISTRICT
REICHSTAG ◆
Platz der Republik

HANSAPLATZ Ⓤ
Altonaer Str.
John-Foster-Dulles-Allee
Lutherbrücke
Str. des 17. Juni
B5
BRANDENBURGER TOR

Str. des 17. Juni B2 B5
SIEGESSÄULE
Tiergarten
Neuer See
Hofjägerallee
Ebertstrasse

Neuer See
5-Cinco by Paco Pérez ■
Das Stue

TIERGARTEN
Tiergartenstrasse
KULTURFORUM ◆

The Ritz-Carlton Berlin □
POTSDAMER PLATZ ◆
Potsdamer Str
Facil ■
Grand Hyatt Berlin □

Tilla-Durieux Park

Reichpietschufer
Schöneberger Ufer
MENDELSSOHN BARTHOLDY

B1
Potsdamer Str.

Park Am Karlsbad

KURFÜRSTEN STR. Ⓤ

Inset map

Brunnenstrasse
Lottumstrasse
Torstrasse

Rosenthaler Grill und ■ Schlemmerbuffet
ROSENTHALER PLATZ Ⓤ
Rosenthaler Strasse
Linienstrasse
Gormannstrasse
Steinstr.
Mulackstr.
Schönhauser strasse

Hotel Amano □

Auguststrasse
Altes Europa ■
Gipsstrasse
Cocolo ■
Sophienstrasse

Hackescher Hof ■
Monsieur Vuong ■
Max-Beer-Str.
Alte Schönhauser Str.
Weinmeisterstr.

WEINMEISTER STR. Ⓤ

Lux Eleven □

GLEISDREIECK Ⓤ
Gleisdreieck

Nelly-Sachs-Park

BÜLOW STR. Ⓤ
Café Aroma ■

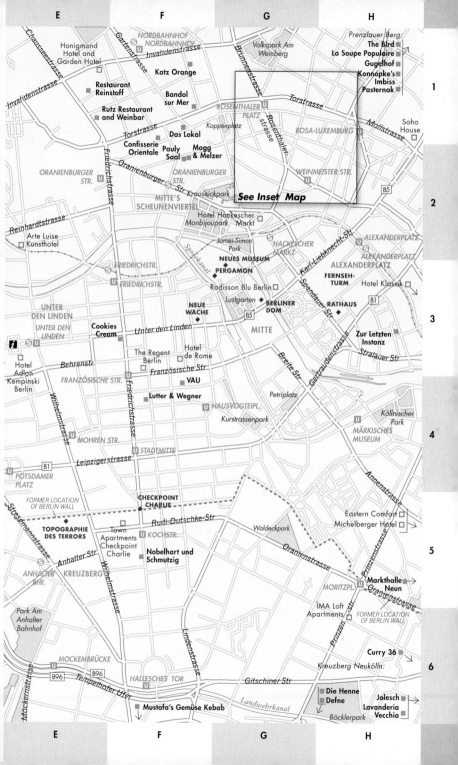

Locals line up for currywurst at Curry 36.

offerings: multicolor and multiflavored marzipan and *lokum* (Turkish delight), made with the highest quality ingredients. Dine in on the homemade cakes and pastries, best accompanied with a samovar of tea or a tiny cup of Turkish coffee—and get a beautifully wrapped and beribboned box of treats to go. $ *Average main: €3* ✉ *Linienstr. 113, Mitte* ☎ *030/6092–5957* ⊕ *www.confiserie-orientale-berlin.com* ▭ *No credit cards* Ⓜ *Oranienburger Tor (U-bahn), Oranienburger Strasse (S-bahn)* ✛ *1:F1.*

$$ ✕ **Cookies Cream.** The name might have you thinking something different, but this is actually a vegetarian fine-dining restaurant that serves some of the best food in Berlin (it's above what used to be a club called Cookies, owned by a nightlife mogul by the same moniker). The entrance, too, is misleading: the only access is via a dingy alley between the Westin Grand Hotel and the Komische Oper next door, which seems designed to deter would-be visitors, but once you're through the door the service is friendly and casual, and the vibe not at all intimidating. The chef steers away from "easy" vegetarian dishes like pasta and stir-fries and instead focuses on innovative preparations like kohlrabi turned into ravioli-esque pockets filled with lentils, or celery that's wrapped cannelloni-style around potato puree and chanterelle mushrooms. $ *Average main: €18* ✉ *Behrenstr. 55, Mitte* ☎ *030/2749–2940* ⊕ *www.cookiescream.com* ▭ *No credit cards* ☾ *Closed Sun. and Mon. No lunch* ◇ *Reservations essential* Ⓜ *Friedrichstrasse (S-bahn and U-bahn), Französische Strasse (U-bahn), Brandenburger Tor (S-bahn)* ✛ *1:E3.*

VEGETARIAN

Fodor's Choice

★

$$ ✕**Das Lokal.** This popular restaurant, located on the corner of one of
GERMAN Berlin's prettiest streets, serves locally sourced dishes like Brandenburg
Fodor'sChoice wild boar, lake trout, or venison on stylish long wooden tables to an
★ equally stylish crowd. The unfussy German standards have become fast
favorites with local gallerists and shop owners, and on warm weekend
nights the place opens up to the street, beckoning passersby with the
cozy sound of clinking glasses and the low hum of conversation. This
is a neighborhood eatery of the highest order. $ *Average main: €18*
⊠ *Linienstr. 160, Mitte* ☎ *030/2844–9500* ⊕ *www.lokal-berlinmitte.*
de ▭ *No credit cards* ☉ *No lunch Sat.–Mon.* Ⓜ *Oranienburger Tor*
(U-bahn), Oranienburger Strasse (S-bahn) ✛ *1:F1.*

$$ ✕**Hackescher Hof.** This beautiful, wood-paneled restaurant is spacious
GERMAN but almost always crowded, and usually smoke-filled as well, but it's
right in the middle of the action at bustling Hackesche Höfe, and one of
the best places to eat German food while doing some excellent people-
watching. Opt for regional country dishes like Brandenburg wild boar
if it's available. The clientele is a fun mix of tourists and local artists
and intellectuals, which gives the place a vibrant, lively atmosphere.
When the weather is good there are tables outside in the courtyard,
too. $ *Average main: €16* ⊠ *Rosenthalerstr. 40–41, inside Hackesche*
Höfe, Mitte ☎ *030/283–5293* ⊕ *www.hackescher-hof.de* Ⓜ *Hackescher*
Markt (S-bahn) ✛ *1:A6.*

$$$ ✕**Katz Orange.** This lovely restaurant, hidden in a courtyard off a quiet,
CONTEMPORARY residential street, is both elegant enough for a special occasion and
Fodor'sChoice homey enough to be a favorite local haunt. Local ingredients are used
★ whenever possible on the inventive menu; perhaps artichoke stuffed
with quinoa, watercress, and smoked pepper, or a halibut ceviche.
The restaurant is known, however, for its slow-cooked meats for two:
choose pork, short ribs, or lamb shoulder, along with fresh side dishes
like grilled eggplant, creamy polenta, or asparagus ragout. The desserts
are excellent. $ *Average main: €23* ⊠ *Bergstr. 22, Mitte* ☎ *030/9832–*
08430 ⊕ *www.katzorange.com* ▭ *No credit cards* ☉ *Closed Sun.*
Ⓜ *Nordbahnhof (S-bahn)* ✛ *1:F1.*

$$$ ✕**Lutter & Wegner.** The dark-wood-panel walls, parquet floor, and mul-
GERMAN tiple rooms of this bustling restaurant across from Gendarmenmarkt
have an air of 19th-century Vienna, and the food, too, is mostly German
and Austrian, with superb game dishes in winter and, of course, the
classic Wiener schnitzel with potato and cucumber salad. The *Sauerbra-*
ten (marinated pot roast) with red cabbage is a national prizewinner.
In the Weinhandlung, a cozy room lined with wine shelves, meat and
cheese plates are served until 1 am. There are several other locations
around Berlin but this one is widely considered the best. $ *Average*
main: €23 ⊠ *Charlottenstr. 56, Mitte* ☎ *030/2029–5415* ⊕ *www.l-w-*
berlin.de Ⓜ *Französische Strasse (U-bahn), Stadtmitte (U-bahn)* ✛ *1:F4.*

$ ✕**Mogg & Melzer.** In the renovated Ehemalige Jüdische Mädchenschule
CAFÉ (Old Jewish Girls' School), this deli-style café serves delicious versions
of Jewish deli standards like matzo-ball soup, pastrami on rye, a Reu-
ben sandwich, and New York cheesecake. Breakfast dishes include an
excellent version of the Israeli dish shakshuka (tomato stew with eggs).
The space, with wood floors and tables, blue walls, and low, deep

15

purple banquettes is trendier than any traditional deli. $ *Average main: €10* ⊠ *Ehemalige Jüdische Mädchenschule, Auguststr. 11–13, Mitte* ☏ *030/3300–60770* ⊕ *www.moggandmelzer.com* ▭ *No credit cards* Ⓜ *Tucholskystrasse (S-bahn)* ✛ *1:F2.*

$ ✕ **Monsieur Vuong.** This hip Vietnamese eatery is a convenient place to

VIETNAMESE   meet before hitting Mitte's galleries or clubs, or for a light lunch after browsing the area's popular boutiques. The atmosphere is always lively, and the clientele is an entertaining mix of tech geeks on their lunch breaks from the area's many start-ups, fashionistas with multiple shopping bags, tourists lured in by the crowd, and students from the nearby Goethe Institut, Germany's most prestigious language school. There are only five items and two specials to choose from, but the delicious *goi bo* (spicy beef salad) and *pho ga* (chicken noodle soup) keep the regulars coming back. The teas and shakes are also excellent. $ *Average main: €7* ⊠ *Alte Schönhauserstr. 46, Mitte* ☏ *030/9929–6924* ⊕ *www. monsieurvuong.de* ⌦ *Reservations not accepted* Ⓜ *Weinmeisterstrasse (U-bahn), Rosa-Luxemburg-Platz (U-bahn)* ✛ *1:B6.*

$$$$ ✕ **Nobelhart und Schmutzig.** The locavore obsession is taken seriously at

GERMAN   this trendy spot that uses only the most local ingredients in the simple

Fodor'sChoice   but sublime preparations that come from the open kitchen. One menu

★   is served each evening (dietary restrictions can usually be accommodated) and everything from the bread and butter through several vegetable, meat, and fish courses is gorgeously presented and delicious. Unusual herbs and plants like rapeseed blossom or lovage might make you want to head straight to Berlin's outskirts for foraging. The careful attention of renowned sommelier Billy Wagner guarantees that each simple but stunning dish finds its ideal partner in wine or beer. $ *Average main: €80* ⊠ *Friedrichstr. 218, Mitte* ☏ *030/2594–0610* ⊕ *www. nobelhartundschmutzig.com* ◷ *Closed Sun. and Mon.* ⌦ *Reservations essential* Ⓜ *Kochstrasse (U-bahn)* ✛ *1:F5.*

$$$$ ✕ **Pauly Saal.** With an airy, high-windowed space in what used to be the

GERMAN   school gym of the converted Ehemalige Jüdische Mädchenschule (Old Jewish Girls' School), and outdoor tables taking over the building's expansive courtyard, the setting here alone is a draw, but the food is also some of the most exquisite in this part of Mitte. The menu focuses on artful presentation and local ingredients, like meat from Brandenburg, prawns from Pomerania, and cheese from Bad Tölz. The lunch prix fixe is a great way to sample the restaurant's best dishes. Quirky artworks, excellent service, and an extensive wine list all add to the experience. $ *Average main: €34* ⊠ *Ehemalige Jüdische Mädchenschule, Auguststr. 11–13, Mitte* ☏ *030/3300–6070* ⊕ *www.paulysaal.com* ◷ *Closed Sun.* Ⓜ *Tucholskystrasse (S-bahn)* ✛ *1:F2.*

$$$$ ✕ **Restaurant Reinstoff.** The perfectly crafted and creative haute cuisine

CONTEMPORARY   at the Michelin-starred Reinstoff, prepared by renowned chef Daniel

GERMAN   Achilles, focuses on both rare and traditional German ingredients but

Fodor'sChoice   gives them an avant-garde twist and often playful presentations. Din-

★   ers choose either five-, six-, seven-, eight-, or nine-course menus (à la carte is only by special request), either with or without wine pairings, and the relaxed but professional service and quietly refined atmosphere make this one of the most enjoyable dining experiences in the city. It's expensive but worth it. The wine selection is heavy on European wines. $ *Average main: €50* ⊠ *Schlegelstr. 26c, in Edison Höfe, Mitte* ☎ *030/3088–1214* ⊕ *www.reinstoff.eu* ☉ *Closed Sun. and Mon.* ☎ *Reservations essential* Ⓜ *Nordbahnhof (S-bahn)* ✛ *1:E1.*

$ ✗**Rosenthaler Grill und Schlemmerbuffet.** Döner kebab aficionados love
TURKISH   this bright, casual spot for the delicious food—the fact that it's in the middle of the city and open 24 hours a day is an added bonus. The friendly staff expertly carve paper-thin slices of perfectly cooked meat from the enormous, revolving spit. If you like things spicy, ask for the red sauce. The rotisserie chicken is also good, but most people come for the döner, either as a meal with salad and fries, or as a sandwich. $ *Average main: €5* ⊠ *Torstr. 125, Mitte* ☎ *030/283–2153* ⊟ *No credit cards* Ⓜ *Rosenthaler Platz (U-bahn)* ✛ *1:A5.*

$$$$ ✗**Rutz Restaurant and Weinbar.** The narrow, unassuming facade of
GERMAN   this Michelin-starred restaurant, tucked away on a sleepy stretch of
Fodor's Choice   Chausseestrasse, belies the the elegant interior and stellar food you'll
★   find inside. "Inspiration" tasting menus of 4, 6, 8, or 10 courses (here called "experiences" and starting at €98) make the most of ingredients like goose liver and Wagyu beef and combine unusual items like black radishes and mushrooms, or asparagus and wild violets. For a more casual affair, and more à la carte choices, head to the separate Weinbar downstairs. $ *Average main: €60* ⊠ *Chausseestr. 8, Mitte* ☎ *030/2462–8760* ⊕ *www.weinbar-rutz.de* ☉ *Closed Sun. and Mon.* Ⓜ *Oranienburger Tor (S-bahn)* ✛ *1:E1.*

$$$$ ✗**VAU.** Exemplary and innovative food served in a refined atmosphere
GERMAN   defines the experience at VAU. Much-lauded chef Kolja Kleeberg is a stalwart on the Berlin dining scene, and his Michelin-starred pan-European menu might include duck with red cabbage, quince, and sweet chestnuts, or turbot with veal sweetbread and shallots in red wine. The four- to eight-course dinner menus are €120 to €160; some dishes can be ordered à la carte. Lunch might be the best time to visit, when entrées are a bargain at €18. The cool interior was designed by Meinhard von Gerkan, one of Germany's leading industrial architects. $ *Average main: €40* ⊠ *Jägerstr. 54/55, Mitte* ☎ *030/202–9730* ⊕ *www. vau-berlin.de* ☉ *Closed Sun.* ☎ *Reservations essential* Ⓜ *Französische Strasse (U-bahn), Stadtmitte (U-bahn)* ✛ *1:F4.*

$ ✗**Zur Letzten Instanz.** Berlin's oldest restaurant (established in 1621) is
GERMAN   half hidden in a maze of medieval streets, though it's welcomed some illustrious diners over the centuries: Napoléon is said to have sat by the tile stove, Mikhail Gorbachev sipped a beer here in 1989, and Chancellor Gerhard Schröder treated French president Jacques Chirac to a meal here in 2003. The small, well-priced menu focuses on some of Berlin's most traditional specialties, including Eisbein (pork knuckle), and takes its whimsical dish titles from classic legal jargon—the national courthouse is around the corner, and the restaurant's name is a rough equivalent of the term "at the 11th hour." Inside, the restaurant is cozy and casual, and while the service is always friendly it can sometimes feel a bit erratic. $ *Average main: €11* ⊠ *Waisenstr. 14–16, Mitte* ☎ *030/242–5528* ⊕ *www.zurletzteninstanz.de* ☉ *Closed Sun.* ☎ *Reservations essential* Ⓜ *Klosterstrasse (U-bahn)* ✛ *1:H3.*

15

TIERGARTEN

$$$$ SPANISH Fodor's Choice ★ 🍴 **5 - Cinco by Paco Pérez.** It was only a matter of time before someone connected to Spain's legendary el Bulli came to Berlin. Enter Catalan chef Paco Pérez, offering an "experience" menu of 25 to 30 courses that unfolds over a leisurely two and a half to three hours. Dishes are what you'd expect from a disciple of Ferran Adrià—i.e., expect the unexpected. The food is colorful and playful, highlighting the maximum flavor of each ingredient, and containing some fun surprises. It truly is an experience. The contemporary interior stands in stark contrast to Berlin's vintage-obsessed establishments: walls mix slick tile with dark wood, and the ceiling is hung with a jumble of bronze pots, pans, and jugs. You can also order à la carte. Note that Casual by Paco Pérez, next door, offers a less expensive sampling of Pérez's food; it's open for all three meals. [$] *Average main: €40* ✉ *Drakestr. 1, Das Stue hotel, Tiergarten* ☎ *030/311–7220* 🌐 *www.5-cinco.com* 🕒 *Closed Sun. and Mon.* ✍ *Reservations essential* [M] *Zoologischer Garten (S-bahn and U-bahn)* ✥ *1:A4.*

$$$$ ECLECTIC Fodor's Choice ★ 🍴 **Facil.** One of Germany's top restaurants, Facil is also one of the more relaxed of its class. The elegant, minimalist setting—it's in the fifth-floor courtyard of the Mandala Hotel, with exquisite wall panels and a glass roof that opens in summer—and impeccable service make this feel like something of an oasis in the busy city. Diners can count on a careful combination of German classics and Asian inspiration; you can choose from the four- to eight-course set meals, or order à la carte. Seasonal dishes include goose liver with celery and hazelnuts, char with an elderflower emulsion sauce, or roasted regional squab. The wine list is extensive but the staff can provide helpful advice. [$] *Average main: €40* ✉ *The Mandala Hotel, Potsdamer Str. 3, Tiergarten* ☎ *030/5900–51234* 🌐 *www.facil.de* 🕒 *Closed weekends* [M] *Potsdamer Platz (U-bahn and S-bahn)* ✥ *1:D4.*

$$$ ECLECTIC 🍴 **Paris-Moskau.** If you're looking for a one-of-a-kind dining experience, head to this half-timber house that stands dwarfed by a government complex and the hotels and office buildings around Hauptbahnhof. The restaurant Paris-Moskau was built more than 100 years ago as a pub and guesthouse along the Paris–Moscow railway. Today, it serves dishes so intricately prepared they look like works of art, with unique flavor combinations such as smoked eel with pork belly, or guinea hen with beetroots and dates. In addition to the à la carte menu, there are a variety of set menus in the evening—you can choose four, five, or six courses. The well-chosen wine list and attentive service make this restaurant a standout. [$] *Average main: €25* ✉ *Alt-Moabit 141, Tiergarten* ☎ *030/394–2081* 🌐 *www.paris-moskau.de* 🕒 *No lunch weekends* ✍ *Reservations essential* [M] *Berlin Hbf (S-bahn)* ✥ *1:D2.*

KREUZBERG

$ FAST FOOD Fodor's Choice ★ 🍴 **Curry 36.** This currywurst stand in Kreuzberg has a cult following and just about any time of day or night you'll find yourself amid a crowd of cab drivers, students, and lawyers munching on currywurst *mit Darm* (with skin) or *ohne Darm* (without skin). Go local

Hackesche Höfe's eight connected courtyards are an always-buzzing, hip place to hang out in the city.

and order your sausage with a big pile of crispy fries served *rot-weiss* (red and white)—with curry ketchup and mayonnaise. Curry 36 stays open until 5 in the morning. [$] *Average main: €3* ✉ *Mehringdamm 36, Kreuzberg* ☎ *030/251–7368* 💳 *No credit cards* [M] *Mehringdamm (U-bahn)* ✣ *1:H6.*

$ TURKISH

🍴 **Defne.** In a city full of Turkish restaurants, Defne stands out for its exquisitely prepared food, friendly service, and pleasant setting. Beyond simple kebabs, the fresh and healthy menu here includes a selection of hard-to-find fish dishes from the Bosphorus, such as *acili ahtapot* (spicy octopus served with mushrooms and olives in a white-wine-and-tomato sauce), as well as delicious mezes and typical Turkish dishes like "the Imam Fainted," one of many eggplant preparations. All the vegetable dishes are popular. Defne is by the Maybachufer, on the bank of the Landwehrkanal, near the Turkish market. [$] *Average main: €11* ✉ *Planufer 92c, Kreuzberg* ☎ *030/8179–7111* 🌐 *www.defne-restaurant.de* 💳 *No credit cards* ⏲ *No lunch* [M] *Kottbusser Tor (U-bahn)* ✣ *1:H6.*

$ GERMAN Fodor's Choice ★

🍴 **Die Henne.** This 100-plus-year-old Kreuzberg stalwart has survived a lot. After two world wars, it found itself quite literally with its back against the wall: the Berlin Wall was built right next to the front door, forcing it to close its front-yard beer garden. But Die Henne (it means "the hen") has managed to stick around thanks in part to its most famous dish, which is still just about all it serves: a crispy, half fried chicken. The rest of the menu is short: coleslaw, potato salad, a few *boulette* (meat patty) options, and several beers on tap. For "dessert," look to the impressive selection of locally sourced brandies and fruit schnapps. The small front-yard beer garden, reopened after the wall came down in 1989, is once again a lovely and lively place to sit in summer. Make reservations a few of days in advance. $ *Average main: €8* ⊠ *Leuschnerdamm 25, Kreuzberg* ☎ *030/614–7730* ⊕ *www.henne-berlin.de* ⊟ *No credit cards* ⊘ *Closed Mon.* Ⓜ *Moritzplatz (U-bahn), Kottbusser Tor (U-bahn)* ✛ *1:H6.*

$$ ✕ **Jolesch.** The front bar area and a cozy dining room are usually filled
AUSTRIAN with chattering locals and the occasional dog peeking out from under the table (pets are allowed in unexpected places in Berlin, including many restaurants). The house specialties include Viennese classics like Wiener schnitzel and apple strudel, but look for surprises, too, on the seasonal daily menu, which is full of interesting ingredients and unusual combinations like grilled octopus with saffron sorbet in spring, or a trio of duck, including silky foie gras, in fall. In late April and May, during "Spargelzeit," the white asparagus season, there is a special menu featuring the delicacy. $ *Average main: €15* ⊠ *Muskauerstr. 1, Kreuzberg* ☎ *030/612–3581* ⊕ *www.jolesch.de* Ⓜ *Görlitzer Bahnhof (U-bahn)* ✛ *1:H6.*

$ ✕ **Markthalle Neun.** Thanks to the efforts of local activists, this century-
INTERNATIONAL old market hall (sometimes spelled Markthalle IX) was saved from
Fodor$Choice becoming a chain supermarket and instead turned into a center for
★ local food vendors, chefs, wine dealers, and brewers. Tuesday to Saturday, popular Big Stuff Smoked BBQ sells scrumptious meat samplers and pulled pork sandwiches next to Glut & Späne, where you can find smoked fish platters and ceviche. The Italian bakery is open every day except Sunday and sells wonderful foccacias, huge loaves of bread, and pastries. In one ocorner is the craft beer producer Heiden-peters, which brews unusual beers like Thirsty Lady and Spiced Ale in the basement. The space also hosts a dazzling array of rotating events like the popular Street Food Thursday or the bimonthly, sweets-only Naschmarkt, so it's best to check what's on before heading there. $ *Average main: €8* ⊠ *Eisenbahnstr. 42/43, Kreuzberg* ☎ *030/5770–94661* ⊕ *www.markthalleneun.de* ⊟ *No credit cards* ⊘ *Closed Sun.* Ⓜ *Görlitzer Bahnhof (U-bahn)* ✛ *1:H5.*

$ ✕ **Mustafa's Gemüse Kebab.** For a twist on the traditional döner kebab,
MEDITERRANEAN head to to Mustafa's for mouthwateringly delicious vegetable kebabs (it's also available with chicken for those who can't resist a bit of protein, but the vegetarian is what people rave about). The specialty is toasted pita bread stuffed full of roasted veggies—carrots, potatoes, zucchini—along with fresh tomato, lettuce, cucumber, and cabbage. The sandwich is topped with sauce, a generous squeeze of fresh lemon juice, and sprinkling of feta cheese. The line can sometimes stretch down the block, but it's well worth the wait. This is a traditional street stand, so no seating. $ *Average main: €3* ⊠ *Mehringdamm 32, Kreuzberg* ☎ *283/2153* ⊕ *www.mustafas.de* ⊟ *No credit cards* Ⓜ *Mehringdamm (U-bahn)* ✛ *1:F6.*

SCHÖNEBERG

$ ITALIAN 🍴 **Café Aroma.** On a small winding street in an area between Kreuzberg and Schöneberg known as *Rote Insel* or "red island" because of its location between two S-bahn tracks and its socialist, working-class history, this neighborhood institution was an early advocate of the Slow Food movement. The food is Italian and focuses on high quality, locally sourced ingredients and everything, whether it's an innovative prepartion of artichokes or beef fillet with green peppercorns, is delicious. Brunch is extremely popular: pile your plate high with Italian delicacies like stuffed mushrooms, meatballs in homemade tomato sauce, and bean salads, but leave room for the fluffy tiramisu, which, of course, they'll bring out the moment you declare yourself stuffed. [$] *Average main: €13* ✉ *Hochkirchstr. 8, Schöneberg* ☎ *030/782–5821* 🌐 *www.cafe-aroma.de* 🕒 *No lunch weekdays* [M] *Yorckstrasse (S-bahn and U-bahn)* ✥ *1:C6.*

$$ AUSTRIAN Fodor's Choice ★ 🍴 **Café Einstein Stammhaus.** In the historic grand villa of silent movie star Henny Porten, the Einstein is one of the leading coffeehouses in town and it charmingly recalls the elegant days of the Austrian-Hungarian empire, complete with slightly snobbish waiters gliding across the parquet floors. Order Austrian delicacies such as goulash or schnitzel (the half order is plenty large), coffee, and, of course, some cake: the fresh strawberry cake is outstanding—and best enjoyed in summer, in the shady garden behind the villa. Up one flight of stairs is the cocktail bar Lebensstern, from the same owners, which also has a sumptuous, old-world feel. [$] *Average main: €18* ✉ *Kurfürstenstr. 58, Schöneberg* ☎ *030/2639–1918* 🌐 *www.cafeeinstein.com* [M] *Kurfürstenstrasse (U-bahn), Nollendorfplatz (U-bahn)* ✥ *2:C6.*

$ TURKISH 🍴 **Hisar.** The lines here are often long, but they move fast and the combination of seasoned, salty meat with crunchy salad and warm bread is unbeatable. Most people come here for a quick döner kebab, line up outside on the sidewalk, and order from the window. If you prefer a more leisurely sit-down meal, head into the more upscale, adjoining Turkish restaurant for the *Dönerteller* (döner plate), heaped with succulent meat, rice, potatoes, and salad; there is also an extensive list of other Turkish specialties. [$] *Average main: €3* ✉ *Yorckstr. 49, Schöneberg* ☎ *030/216–5125* 💳 *No credit cards* [M] *Yorckstrasse (U-bahn and S-bahn)* ✥ *2:C6.*

$$ GERMAN Fodor's Choice ★ 🍴 **Renger-Patzsch.** Black-and-white photographs by the German landscape photographer Albert Renger-Patzsch, the restaurant's namesake, decorate the darkwood-paneled dining room at this beloved local gathering place where chef Hannes Behrmann focuses on top-notch ingredients, respecting the classics while also reinventing them. The menu changes daily but might feature blood sausage with lentils or perhaps venison with choucroute. Lighter bites like a selection of Flammkuchen (Alsatian flatbread pizzas) are perfect for sharing. The attentive and good-humored service makes this a relaxing dining experience, even on the busiest nights. [$] *Average main: €16* ✉ *Wartburgstr. 54, Schöneberg* ☎ *030/784–2059* 🌐 *www.renger-patzsch.com* 💳 *No credit cards* [M] *U Eisenacher Str. (U-bahn)* ✥ *2:D5.*

PRENZLAUER BERG

$ ✕ **Gugelhof.** Although far from Alsatian France and the Mosel and Saar
ECLECTIC   regions of Germany's southwest that inspire the hearty fare here, a visit
to this busy but homey Kollwitzplatz restaurant will leave you pleasantly surprised at the authenticity of the food—and deliciously full. The
raclette for two and the "pate de canard" (Alsation duck paté) are the
best you're likely to get this side of the Rhine, and classic choucroute
comes with *Blutwurst* (blood sausage) provided by an award-winning
Berlin butcher. The vegetarian Tarte Flambée, a crispy crust topped with
cheese and grilled vegetables, holds its own on the meat-centric menu.
$ *Average main: €14* ✉ *Knaackstr. 37, Prenzlauer Berg* ☏ *030/442–
9229* ⊕ *www.gugelhof.de* 🖃 *No credit cards* ☻ *No lunch weekdays*
🍴 *Reservations essential* Ⓜ *Senefelder Platz (U-bahn)* ✛ *1:H1.*

$ ✕ **Konnopke's Imbiss.** Under the tracks of the elevated U2 subway line is
GERMAN   Berlin's most beloved sausage stand. Konnopke's is a family business
Fodor'sChoice   that's been around for more than 70 years and though there are several
★   options on the menu, this place is famous for its currywurst, which is
served on a paper tray with a plastic prong that can be used to spear
the sauce-covered sausage slices. With french fries and a pilsner, this is
one of the quintessential Berlin meals. The location, in the center of one
of Berlin's trendiest neighborhoods, is extremely convenient. $ *Average
main: €5* ✉ *Schönhauser Allee 44b, Prenzlauer Berg* ☏ *030/442–7765*
⊕ *www.konnopke-imbiss.de* 🖃 *No credit cards* Ⓜ *Eberswalderstrasse
(U-bahn)* ✛ *1:H1.*

$$ ✕ **La Soupe Populaire.** Berliners love glamorous ruins, and Bötzow Brau-
GERMAN   erei, the old brewery complex that houses this restaurant, is one of the
Fodor'sChoice   most evocative settings around. Local chef Tim Raue serves reinter-
★   preted Berlin classics in the soaring industrial space, where culinary art
and fine art come together—the ground floor houses a gallery of work
by rotating artists-in-residence. Upstairs in the airy open restaurant,
decorated with vintage furniture, highlights on the menu include the
Königsberger Klöpse—meatballs served with potato mash, which Raue
served President Barack Obama on his visit to the German capital. Fin-
ish with the Bienenstich (literally "bee sting") cake, a classic German
dessert with a crisp honey-almond topping. Here, it comes with a little
chocolate bee perched on the plate. $ *Average main: €17* ✉ *Prenzlauer
Allee 242, in Bötzow Brauerei, Prenzlauer Berg* ☏ *030/4431–9680*
⊕ *www.lasoupepopulaire.de* 🖃 *No credit cards* ☻ *Closed Sun.–Wed.*
🍴 *Reservations essential* Ⓜ *Senefelderplatz (U-bahn)* ✛ *1:H1.*

$ ✕ **Pasternak.** Russian treats such as dumplings, borscht, deviled eggs
RUSSIAN   topped with salmon roe, blini with sour cream and dill, pierogi, and
much more are the mainstays at this casually refined restaurant with
a lovely outdoor terrace for when the weather is nice. Lunch and din-
ner are popular, and there are several set menus available, but if you
come for the weekend brunch buffet, you can try just about all of the
delicous dishes, as well as dessert. $ *Average main: €13* ✉ *Knaackstr.
22/24, Prenzlauer Berg* ☏ *030/441–3399* ⊕ *www.restaurant-pasternak.
de* 🖃 *No credit cards* Ⓜ *Senefelder Platz (U-bahn)* ✛ *1:H1.*

WEDDING

$ 🍴 **Café Pförtner.** There are plenty of places in Wedding for a quick falafel or döner but if you're looking for something different, head to Café Pförtner, at the entrance to the Uferhallen on the Panke canal. The squat, brick café space may be small, but Pförtner makes good use of what there is, adding long tables out front in good weather and, in a nod to the Uferhallen's previous incarnation as a BVG garage, turning a brightly painted bus into a dining area next door. Order at the counter from choices that include several vegetarian and meat dishes at lunch, and an expanded dinner menu that includes fresh, house-made pasta. [$] *Average main: €9* ✉ *Uferstr. 8–11, Wedding* ☎ *030/5036–9854* 🌐 *www.pfoertner.co* 💳 *No credit cards* 🕑 *Closed Sun.* [M] *Pankstrasse (U-bahn)* ✥ *1:C1.*

GERMAN ITALIAN

NEUKÖLLN

$$$$ 🍴 **Lavanderia Vecchia.** Hidden away in a courtyard off a busy Neukölln street, in a space that used to contain an old laundrette (hence the name, which means "old laundrette" in Italian) Lavanderia Vecchia offers a prix-fixe-only menu that includes at least 10 appetizers, a pasta "primo," a meat or fish "secondo," and dessert, followed by coffee and a digestif. The open kitchen allows diners to watch as the chef makes classics like Insalata di Polpo (octopus and potato salad) or homemade tagliatelle with eggplant. The white-painted industrial space is decorated with vintage kerchiefs strung along old wash lines. In the front of the building, the more casual sister café Lava serves an à la carte menu of antipasti and panini at lunch and dinner, as well as a good selection of Italian wines. [$] *Average main: €45* ✉ *Flughafenstr. 46, Neukölln* ☎ *030/6272–2152* 🌐 *www.lavanderiavecchia.de* 🕑 *Closed Sun. and Mon.* ✍ *Reservations essential* [M] *Boddinstrasse (U-bahn), Rathaus Neukölln (U-bahn)* ✥ *1:H6.*

ITALIAN

CHARLOTTENBURG

$$ 🍴 **Engelbecken.** The beer coasters are trading cards of the Wittelsbach dynasty at this relaxed, seemingly always busy restaurant that focuses on food from Bavaria and the Alps. Excellent renditions of classics like Wiener schnitzel and grilled saddle steak use organic meats and vegetables, and the selection of beer—by the bottle and on tap—is small but includes a range of varieties and regions. The corner location facing a park on Lake Lietzensee makes this a particularly lovely spot for open-air dining in the summer; in the winter, the interior feels festive and cozy. [$] *Average main: €17* ✉ *Witzlebenstr. 31, Charlottenburg* ☎ *030/615–2810* 🌐 *www.engelbecken.de* 🕑 *No lunch Mon.–Sat.* [M] *Sophie-Charlotte-Platz (U-bahn)* ✥ *2:B1.*

GERMAN

$$ 🍴 **Florian.** The handwritten menu is just one page, but everything on it is fresh and delicious at this popular restaurant in the heart of the buzzing nightlife scene around Savignyplatz. *Steinbeisser,* a white, flaky fish, might be served with a salsa of rhubarb, chili, coriander, and ginger, or you can opt for some Franconian comfort cuisine such

GERMAN

15

as *Kirchweihbraten* (marinated pork with baked apples and plums) or their legendary *Nürnberger Rostbratwurst* (small pork sausages) served as late-night snacks. The kitchen is open until midnight, and smaller dishes are available until 1 am. Ⓢ *Average main: €18* ✉ *Grolmanstr. 52, Charlottenburg* ☎ *030/313–9184* ⊕ *www.restaurant-florian.de* ⊘ *No lunch* ⌕ *Reservations essential* Ⓜ *Savignyplatz (S-bahn)* ✛ *2:B3.*

$$$ ✕ **Francucci's.** This upscale restaurant on the far western end of
ITALIAN Kurfürstendamm is one of the best-kept Italian secrets in Berlin. You won't find many tourists here, but the posh neighborhood's residents pack the cheerful, rustic dining room. The high-quality, straightforward cooking means incredibly fresh salads and appetizers (the bruschetta is excellent), as well as homemade bread and exquisite pasta dishes. More-refined Tuscan and Umbrian creations might include meat options like wild boar and there is usually a Mediterranean fish dish on the menu as well, such as grilled *loup de mer* or dorade. In warm weather there are tables on the sidewalk. Ⓢ *Average main: €24* ✉ *Kurfürstendamm 90, at Lehniner Pl., Charlottenburg* ☎ *030/323–3318* ⊕ *www.francucci. de* Ⓜ *Adenauerplatz (U-bahn)* ✛ *2:C1.*

$ ✕ **Hot Spot.** In a city that's unfortunately full of mediocre pseudo-Asian
CHINESE restaurants that serve bland, tasteless versions of curries, noodles, and rice dishes, Hot Spot stands out for its daring and authenticity. The menu features recipes from the provinces of Sichuan, Jiangsu, and Shanghai, and the freshest ingredients are guaranteed—with no MSG. *Mala* (numbing and spicy) dishes are a specialty here, and the mostly cold appetizers, like the beef in chili sauce, can't be found anywhere else in Berlin. The selection of German wines goes well with the spicy food. In summer, try to reserve one of the tables on the sidewalk. Ⓢ *Average main: €14* ✉ *Eisenzahnstr. 66, Charlottenburg* ☎ *030/8900–6878* ⊕ *www.restaurant-hotspot.de* Ⓜ *Adenauerplatz (U-bahn)* ✛ *2:C1.*

$ ✕ **Lubitsch.** One of the few traditional, artsy restaurants left in bohe-
GERMAN mian Charlottenburg, the Lubitsch—named after the famous Berlin film director Ernst Lubitsch—exudes an air of faded elegance and serves hearty local fare (and lighter international options) that's hard to find these days. Dishes like Königsberger Klopse (cooked dumplings in a creamy caper sauce) and *Kassler Nacken mit Sauerkraut* (salted, boiled pork knuckle) are examples of the home-style German cooking. The local clientele don't mind the dingy seating or good-humored, but some-times cheeky service. In summer the outdoor tables are perfect for peo-ple-watching on one of Berlin's most beautiful streets. The three-course lunch is a great bargain at €10. Ⓢ *Average main: €13* ✉ *Bleibtreustr. 47, Charlottenburg* ☎ *030/882–3756* ⊕ *www.restaurant-lubitsch.de* ⊘ *No lunch Sun.* Ⓜ *Savignyplatz (S-bahn)* ✛ *2:C3.*

$$ ✕ **Ottenthal.** This intimate restaurant with white tablecloths is owned by
AUSTRIAN Austrians from the small village of Ottenthal, and serves as an homage to their hometown—the wines, pumpkinseed oil, and organic ingredi-ents on the menu all come from there. Interesting and delicious combi-nations might include pike perch with lobster sauce and pepper-pine-nut risotto, or venison medallions with vegetable-potato strudel, red cab-bage, and rowanberry sauce. The huge Wiener schnitzel extends past the plate's rim, and the pastas and strudel are homemade. Ottenthal

opens at 5 pm, which makes it a good option for a leisurely meal before catching a show at Theater des Westens around the corner. This is also a good choice on Sunday evening, when many of Berlin's fine restaurants are closed. $ *Average main: €16* ⊠ *Kantstr. 153, Charlottenburg* ☎ *030/313–3162* ⊕ *www.ottenthal.com* ☉ *No lunch* Ⓜ *Zoologischer Garten (U-bahn and S-bahn)* ✢ *2:B4.*

WHERE TO STAY

Updated
by Juergen
Scheunemann

Tourism is on the upswing in Berlin. Though prices in midrange to luxury hotels have increased, Berlin's first-class hotels still tend to be cheaper than their counterparts in Paris, London, or Rome. Many are housed in beautiful historic buildings and, compared to other European cities, most hotel rooms in Berlin are large, though many are part of chains that allow for less individual character.

Hotels listed here as $$$$ often come down to a $$ level on weekdays or when there is low demand. You often have the option to decline the inclusion of breakfast, which can save you anywhere from €8 to €30 per person per day.

For expanded hotel reviews, visit Fodors.com.

Use the coordinate (✢ 1:B3) at the end of each listing to locate a site on the corresponding map.

15

WHAT IT COSTS (IN EUROS)			
$	$$	$$$	$$$$
FOR TWO PEOPLE			
Under €100	€100–€175	€176–€225	over €225

MITTE

$
HOTEL

⬚ Arte Luise Kunsthotel. The Luise is one of Berlin's most original boutique hotels, with each fantastically creative room in the 1825 building or 2003 built-on wing—facing the Reichstag—styled by a different artist. **Pros:** central location; historic flair; individually designed rooms. **Cons:** simple rooms with limited amenities and hotel facilities; can be noisy because of the nearby rail station. $ *Rooms from: €80* ⊠ *Luisenstr. 19, Mitte* ☎ *030/284–480* ⊕ *www.luise-berlin.com* ⇌ *54 rooms, 36 with bath* ⦿ *No meals* Ⓜ *Friedrichstrasse (U-bahn and S-bahn)* ✢ *1:E2.*

$$$
HOTEL
Fodor's Choice
★

⬚ Grand Hyatt Berlin. Stylish guests feel at home at Europe's first Grand Hyatt, which has a feng shui–approved design that combines inspirations from tropical decor, thought-provoking modern art, and the city's history with Bauhaus photographs. **Pros:** large rooms; excellent service; stylish spa; large pool area. **Cons:** hotel can be very busy, particularly in February; location is very touristy and crowded; in-room Wi-Fi is only free for the first 30 minutes. $ *Rooms from: €216* ⊠ *Marlene-Dietrich-Pl. 2, Mitte* ☎ *030/2553–1234* ⊕ *www.berlin.grand.hyatt.de* ⇌ *326 rooms, 16 suites* ⦿ *Breakfast* Ⓜ *Potsdamer Platz (U-bahn and S-bahn)* ✢ *1:D5.*

$$ HOTEL
Honigmond Hotel and Garden Hotel. These two hotels are charming, quaint oases only a few steps away from the buzzing neighborhoods of Mitte. **Pros:** individually designed rooms; warm, welcoming service; quiet courtyard rooms. **Cons:** front rooms can be noisy due to busy street; restaurant is expensive relative to the area's budget choices. [$] *Rooms from: €159* ✉ *Tieckstr. 12 and Invalidenstr. 122, Mitte* ☎ *030/284–4550* 🌐 *www.honigmond.de* 🛏 *50 rooms* 🍴 *Breakfast* [M] *Nordbahnhof (S-bahn)* ✚ *1:E1.*

$$$$ HOTEL Fodor's Choice ★
Hotel Adlon Kempinski Berlin. The first Adlon was considered Europe's ultimate luxury resort until it was destroyed in World War II. **Pros:** top-notch luxury hotel; surprisingly large rooms; excellent in-house restaurants. **Cons:** sometimes stiff service with an attitude; rooms off Linden are noisy with the windows open; inviting lobby often crowded. [$] *Rooms from: €280* ✉ *Unter den Linden 77, Mitte* ☎ *030/22610* 🌐 *www.kempinski.com/adlon* 🛏 *304 rooms, 78 suites* 🍴 *No meals* [M] *Brandenburger Tor (U-bahn and S-bahn)* ✚ *1:E3.*

$$ HOTEL
Hotel Amano. Built as a "budget design hotel," the basic rooms of the Amano are fairly small, and there is no real restaurant or room service, but stay here and you'll be in the center of the action. **Pros:** excellent location; happening bar scene; popular, hip roof deck and garden. **Cons:** no room service; too trendy for some. [$] *Rooms from: €150* ✉ *Auguststr. 43, Mitte* ☎ *030/809–4150* 🌐 *www.hotel-amano.com* 🛏 *71 rooms, 46 apartments* 🍴 *Breakfast* [M] *Rosenthaler Platz (U-bahn)* ✚ *1:A5.*

$$$$ HOTEL Fodor's Choice ★
Hotel de Rome. Discreet service and a subdued but boutiquey atmosphere make the Hotel de Rome a major draw for the Hollywood jet set. **Pros:** great location; large rooms. **Cons:** design may be over the top for some guests; expensive even for five-star hotel; can be dark during the day due to low lighting. [$] *Rooms from: €350* ✉ *Behrenstr. 37, Mitte* ☎ *030/460–6090* 🌐 *www.hotelderome.com* 🛏 *109 rooms, 37 suites* 🍴 *No meals* [M] *Französische Strasse (U-bahn)* ✚ *1:F3.*

$ HOTEL
Hotel Hackescher Markt. Amid the nightlife around Hackescher Markt, this hotel provides discreet and inexpensive top service. **Pros:** great location for shops, restaurants, and nightlife; large rooms. **Cons:** some rooms may be noisy due to tram stop; rooms in need of an update. [$] *Rooms from: €84* ✉ *Grosse Präsidentenstr. 8, Mitte* ☎ *030/280–030* 🌐 *www.hotel-hackescher-markt.com* 🛏 *27 rooms, 5 suites* 🍴 *No meals* [M] *Hackescher Markt (S-bahn)* ✚ *1:G2.*

$$ HOTEL
Radisson Blu Berlin. This hotel has an ideal location in the heart of Berlin near the Berlin Cathedral, Nikolai Church, and Unter den Linden, but you may prefer a view into the courtyard, where the world's largest cylindrical aquarium is located. **Pros:** central location; discounted entry to the adjacent Sea Life Berlin. **Cons:** location can be very busy; hotel is fairly big and lacks atmosphere. [$] *Rooms from: €168* ✉ *Karl-Liebknecht-Str. 3, Mitte* ☎ *030/238–280* 🌐 *www.radissonblu.com/hotel-berlin* 🛏 *403 rooms, 24 suites* 🍴 *Breakfast* [M] *Hackescher Markt (S-bahn)* ✚ *1:G3.*

$$$$ HOTEL
The Regent Berlin. One of Berlin's most esteemed hotels, the Regent pairs the opulence of gilt furniture, thick carpets, marble floors, tasseled settees, and crystal chandeliers with such modern conveniences as flat-screen TVs. **Pros:** Berlin's most hushed five-star hotel; unobtrusive

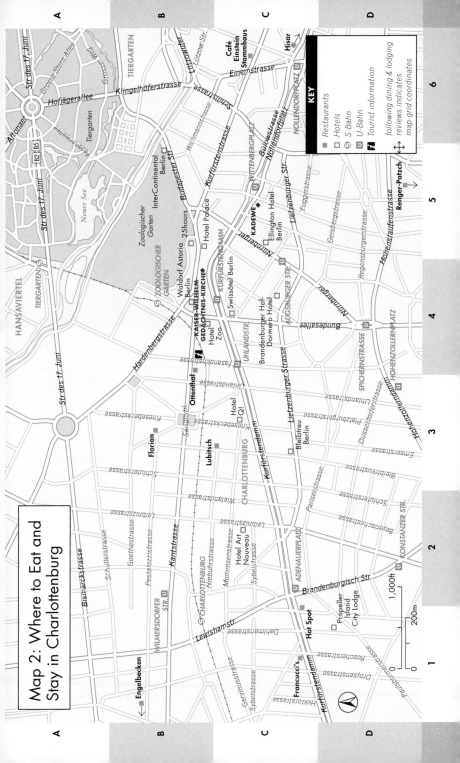

Map 2: Where to Eat and Stay in Charlottenburg

KEY

- Restaurants
- Hotels
- Ⓢ S-Bahn
- Ⓤ U-Bahn
- 🛈 Tourist information

⊕ following dining & lodging reviews indicates map-grid coordinates

Labels on map

TIERGARTEN

HANSAVIERTEL

Str. des 17. Juni

Grosse Stern Allee

Hofjägerallee

Altonaer Str.

B2 B5

Neuer See

Zoologischer Garten

Ⓢ ZOOLOGISCHER GARTEN

TIERGARTEN Ⓢ

Klingelhöferstrasse

Lützowufer

Lützow-Str.

Café Einstein Stammhaus

Hisar

Einemstrasse

NOLLENDORFPLATZ Ⓤ

Schillstrasse

Wichmannstrasse

Kurfürstenstrasse

Budapester Str.

InterContinental Berlin

25hours

Waldorf Astoria Berlin

Hotel Palace

WITTENBERGPLATZ Ⓤ

Bülowstrasse

Bülowstrasse

Nollendorfpl.

Hardenbergstrasse

KAISER-WILHELM-GEDÄCHTNIS-KIRCHE ◆

Ⓢ KURFÜRSTENDAMM Ⓤ

Hotel Zoo

Swissôtel Berlin

KADEWE ◆

Ellington Hotel Berlin

Nürnberg Ⓤ

Nürnberger Str.

Lietzenburger Str.

Fuggerstrasse

Geisbergstrasse

Regensburgerstrasse

Renger-Patzch →

Hohenstaufenstrasse

Fasanenstrasse

Oftenhof

UHLANDSTR. Ⓤ

Uhlandstrasse

Brandenburger Hof

Dormero Hotel

AUGSBURGER STR.

Bundesallee

SPICHERNSTRASSE Ⓤ

HOHENZOLLERNPLATZ Ⓤ

Schlüterstrasse

Savignyplatz

Florian

Lubitsch

Knesebeckstrasse

Leibnizstrasse

Wielandstrasse

Hotel Q!

Bleibtreu Berlin

Lietzenburger Strasse

Platzdülgerstrasse

Düsseldorferstrasse

Uhlandstrasse

Nürnberger

CHARLOTTENBURG

Kurfürstendamm

Kantstrasse

Goethestrasse

Pestalozzistrasse

Bismarckstrasse

Schutterstrasse

WILMERSDORFER STR. Ⓤ

Ⓢ CHARLOTTENBURG

Leibnizstrasse

Niebuhrstrasse

Mommsenstrasse

Sybelstrasse

Hotel Art Nouveau

Paristerstrasse

Schlüterstrasse

Bleibtreustrasse

Emserstrasse

Beyerischestrasse

KONSTANZER STR. Ⓤ

ADENAUERPLATZ Ⓤ

Brandenburgisch Str.

Propeller Island City Lodge

Hot Spot

Lewishamstr.

Dahlmannstrasse

Roscherstrasse

Sybelstrasse

Francucci's

Kurfürstendamm

Gervinusstrasse

Droysenstrasse

Pariserstrasse

Hektorstrasse

Engelbecken ←

1,000ft

200m

0

Berliners look forward to the first warm day of the year to sunbathe in deck chairs on the banks of the Spree River.

service; very large rooms and top location off Gendarmenmarkt. **Cons:** some public areas and rooms in need of update; the primary hotel restaurant specializes in fish only; cleaning service can be spotty at times. [$] *Rooms from: €234* ✉ *Charlottenstr. 49, Mitte* ☎ *030/20338* 🌐 *www.regenthotels.com* 🛏 *156 rooms, 39 suites* 🍴 *No meals* ⊕ *1:F3.*

$$$$ HOTEL 🏨 **The Ritz-Carlton Berlin.** Judging from the outside of this gray, high-rise hotel that soars above Potsdamer Platz, you would never guess that inside it's all luxurious, 19th-century grandeur. **Pros:** stylish and luxurious interior design; great views; elegant setting yet informal service. **Cons:** rooms surprisingly small for a luxury hotel; not family-friendly (business-oriented atmosphere). [$] *Rooms from: €226* ✉ *Potsdamer Pl. 3, Mitte* ☎ *030/337–777* 🌐 *www.ritzcarlton.com* 🛏 *264 rooms, 39 suites* 🍴 *Breakfast* [M] *Potsdamer Platz (U-bahn and S-bahn)* ⊕ *1:D4.*

FRIEDRICHSHAIN

$ B&B/INN 🏨 **Eastern Comfort.** The Spree River is one of Berlin's best assets, and this unique hotel is moored right next to a stretch of the Berlin Wall called the East Side Gallery, which you'll get to enjoy aboard the two three-level ships that make up Eastern Comfort. **Pros:** unique accommodation on a boat; friendly staff; perfect location for nightclubbing in Kreuzberg and Friedrichshain. **Cons:** insects may be a bother in summer; smallish rooms not pleasant in rainy or stormy weather; can be fairly noisy due to partying groups. [$] *Rooms from: €62* ✉ *Mühlenstr. 73–77, Friedrichshain* ☎ *030/6676–3806* 🌐 *www.eastern-comfort.com* 🛏 *26 cabins* 🍴 *No meals* [M] *Warschauer Strasse (U-bahn and S-bahn)* ⊕ *1:H5.*

$ HOTEL **Hotel Klassik.** One of the best things about the Hotel Klassik is its central location, walking distance to Friedrichshain's countless eating, drinking, and shopping hot spots. **Pros:** excellent location for neighborhood vibe and access to transportation; plentiful, fresh breakfast buffet; knowledgable and helpful staff. **Cons:** located on a loud and busy corner; neigborhood can be unsafe at night; location is far from most tourist sights. [$] *Rooms from: €89* ✉ *Revaler Str. 6, Friedrichshain* ☎ *030/319–8860* 🌐 *www.hotelklassik-berlin.com* 🛏 *57 rooms, 2 suites* 🍴 *Breakfast* [M] *Warschauer Strasse (U-bahn and S-bahn)* ✥ *1:H3.*

$ HOTEL **Michelberger Hotel.** Started by a group of young Berliners who dreamed of a uniquely designed, artsy space, the Michelberger Hotel is part budget hotel, part clubhouse, and part bar and restaurant. **Pros:** located at the epicenter of eastern Berlin nightlife; great design and fun atmosphere; affordable prices. **Cons:** busy thoroughfare and transit hub, so front rooms can be noisy; small rooms; no phone in rooms. [$] *Rooms from: €84* ✉ *Warschauer Str. 39–40, Friedrichshain* ☎ *030/2977–8590* 🌐 *www.michelbergerhotel.com* 🛏 *113 rooms* 🍴 *Breakfast* [M] *Warschauer Strasse (S-bahn and U-bahn)* ✥ *1:H5.*

15

KREUZBERG

$ RENTAL FAMILY **ÏMA Loft Apartments.** A comfortable cross between apartment rental and hotel, ÏMA's aim is to throw its guests into the fray of Kreuzberg's hectic, artistic, multicultural scene. **Pros:** maximum privacy (a separate entrance means you never have to interact with hotel staff and other guests unless you want to); great central location. **Cons:** minimal amenities and services; level of noise in courtyard can be bothersome. [$] *Rooms from: €79* ✉ *Ritterstr. 12–14, Kreuzberg* ☎ *030/6162–8913* 🌐 *www.imalofts.com* 🛏 *20 apartments* 🍴 *No meals* [M] *Moritzplatz (U-bahn)* ✥ *1:H6.*

$$ RENTAL FAMILY **Town Apartments Checkpoint Charlie.** This apartment-only hotel is right around the corner from Checkpoint Charlie, thus combining a typical (but quiet) Kreuzberg ambience with a perfect location for visiting the historic sights and museums in Mitte. **Pros:** large and quiet apartments; offers a distintive Kreuzberg feeling, yet close to all historic sights in Mitte. **Cons:** no meals or room service; location can be very busy and seem touristy at times. [$] *Rooms from: €120* ✉ *Kochstr. 16-25, Kreuzberg* ☎ *030/6449–5000* 🌐 *www.town-apartments.com* 🛏 *25 apartments* 🍴 *No meals* [M] *Kochstrasse (U-bahn)* ✥ *1:F5.*

SCHÖNEBERG

$$ HOTEL Fodor's Choice ★ **Ellington Hotel Berlin.** Tucked away behind the beautiful, historic facade of a grand Bauhaus-style office building, this sleek, modern hotel has small but stylish rooms, accentuated with modern art. **Pros:** stylish interior design with alluring 1920s touches; perfect location off Tauentzienstrasse and great for shopping sprees; nice bar; great, green courtyard. **Cons:** small rooms; no spa. [$] *Rooms from: €124* ✉ *Nürnbergerstr. 50–55, Schöneberg* ☎ *030/683–150* 🌐 *www.ellington-hotel.com* 🛏 *285 rooms* 🍴 *Some meals* [M] *Wittenbergplatz (U-bahn)* ✥ *2:C5.*

PRENZLAUER BERG

$$$ ⟨⟩ **Soho House.** The Berlin branch of this luxury hotel–club brings the
HOTEL   chic atmosphere of London and New York's Soho to the German capi-
Fodor'sChoice   tal. **Pros:** great staff; perfect location for club- and bar-hopping; roof-
★   top pool. **Cons:** may seem too clubby; club areas can be crowded on
weekends; hotel is on a very busy and noisy street corner. $ *Rooms*
from: €180 ✉ *Torstr. 1, Prenzlauer Berg* ☎ *030/405–0440* ⊕ *www.*
sohohouseberlin.com ⟲ *89 rooms* ⟨⟩*Breakfast* Ⓜ *Rosa-Luxemburg-*
Platz (U-bahn) ✛ *1:H1.*

CHARLOTTENBURG

$$ ⟨⟩ **25hours.** Opened in 2014, this stylish hotel is currently the symbol of
HOTEL   West Berlin's dynamic revitalization. **Pros:** great central location; trendy
on-site restaurant and bar; rooms facing the zoo are very quiet. **Cons:**
rooms fairly small by Berlin standards; ambience might be too lively
and clubby for some guests; rooms facing city can be noisy if windows
are opened. $ *Rooms from: €150* ✉ *Budapester Str. 40, Charlotten-*
burg ☎ *030/1202–21255* ⊕ *www.25hours-hotels.com* ⟲ *149 rooms*
⟨⟩*Breakfast* Ⓜ *Zoologischer Garten (U-bahn and S-bahn)* ✛ *2:B5.*

$ ⟨⟩ **Bleibtreu Berlin.** Opened in 1995, Berlin's first design hotel is relatively
HOTEL   unassuming, with simple and serene rooms decorated with untreated
oak, polished stone, and neutral shades. **Pros:** warm, welcoming service;
top location on one of Ku'damm's most beautiful side streets; international clientele. **Cons:** design somewhat dated; rooms not overly comfortable for price; few amenities. $ *Rooms from: €86* ✉ *Bleibtreustr.*
31, Charlottenburg ☎ *030/884–740* ⊕ *www.bleibtreu.com* ⟲ *60 rooms*
⟨⟩*No meals* Ⓜ *Uhlandstrasse (U-bahn)* ✛ *2:C3.*

$$$ ⟨⟩ **Brandenburger Hof - Dormero Hotel.** On a quiet residential street this
HOTEL   turn-of-the-20th-century mansion feels like a hideaway even though
Ku'damm is a short walk away. **Pros:** great mansion; quiet location only
steps away from the Ku'damm; large rooms. **Cons:** stuffy atmosphere;
extras are expensive; no pool or fitness club on-site. $ *Rooms from:*
€215 ✉ *Eislebenerstr. 14, Charlottenburg* ☎ *030/214–050* ⊕ *www.*
brandenburger-hof.com ⟲ *58 rooms, 14 suites* ⟨⟩*No meals* Ⓜ *Augs-*
burger Strasse (U-bahn) ✛ *2:C4.*

$$ ⟨⟩ **Hotel Art Nouveau.** The English-speaking owners' discerning taste in
B&B/INN   antiques, color combinations, and even televisions (a few designed by
Philippe Starck) makes this B&B-like pension a great place to stay.
Pros: stylish ambience; friendly and personal service; great B&B feeling despite being a hotel. **Cons:** front rooms can be noisy due to heavy
traffic on Leibnizstrasse; few amenities for a hotel of this price category;
downtown location, yet longer walks to all major sights in the area.
$ *Rooms from: €126* ✉ *Leibnizstr. 59, Charlottenburg* ☎ *030/327–*
7440 ⊕ *www.hotelartnouveau.de* ⟲ *16 rooms, 6 suites* ⟨⟩*Breakfast*
Ⓜ *Adenauerplatz (U-bahn)* ✛ *2:C2.*

$$ ⟨⟩ **Hotel Palace.** This is one of the only non-chain first-class hotels in
HOTEL   the heart of western downtown, and although it may not look like
much from the outside, inside, the friendly staff and spacious rooms
make it a popular choice. **Pros:** large rooms; central location close to

Kurfürstendamm; impeccable service. **Cons:** interior design outdated in some areas; nearby area of Europa-Center and Breitscheidplatz a little seedy. Ⓢ *Rooms from: €128* ✉ *Europa-Center, Budapesterstr. 45, Charlottenburg* ☎ *030/25020* ⊕ *www.palace.de* ⟲ *238 rooms, 40 suites* ⦿ *Breakfast* Ⓜ *Zoologischer Garten (U-bahn and S-bahn)* ✛ *2:B5.*

$$
HOTEL
🏨 **Hotel Q!** The Q! has received several international design awards, and it's easy to see how the gently sloping, sweeping interior of the hotel could charm any judge. **Pros:** beautiful design; affordable rates; great location for exploring western downtown. **Cons:** not for families; nightlife makes hotel noisy at times. Ⓢ *Rooms from: €110* ✉ *Knesebeckstr. 67, Charlottenburg* ☎ *030/810–0660* ⊕ *www.loock-hotels.com* ⟲ *73 rooms, 4 suites* ⦿ *No meals* Ⓜ *Uhlandstrasse (U-bahn), Savignyplatz (S-bahn)* ✛ *2:C3.*

$$
HOTEL
🏨 **Hotel Zoo.** Tucked inside one of the city's oldest grand hotels, this recently remodeled hotel is an eclectic clash of New York City design meets Berlin tradition with bare redbrick walls and a cutting-edge interior design employing objets d'art and oversize mirrors and lamps. **Pros:** excellent service; quiet rooms despite central location right on Ku'damm; great design and trendy location. **Cons:** attitude of some guests and staff might be an issue for some visitors; design might be over the top for some; rooms are fairly small by Berlin standards. Ⓢ *Rooms from: €170* ✉ *Kurfürstendamm 25, Charlottenburg* ☎ *30/884–370* ⊕ *www. zoohotel.de* ⟲ *131 rooms, 14 suites* ⦿ *Breakfast* Ⓜ *Kurfürstendamm (U-bahn)* ✛ *2:B4.*

$$
B&B/INN
🏨 **Propeller Island City Lodge.** At this wildly eccentric accommodation, you can choose from 27 Wonderlands, each with one-of-a-kind design by multi-talented artist Lars Stroschen. **Pros:** individually designed rooms; personal and friendly atmosphere; quiet location on Ku'damm side street. **Cons:** designer art rooms can be overwhelming; few amenities; slow service. Ⓢ *Rooms from: €130* ✉ *Albrecht-Achilles-Str. 58, Charlottenburg* ☎ *030/891–9016* ⊕ *www.propeller-island.de* ⟲ *25 rooms, 20 with bath; 2 suites* Ⓜ *Adenauerplatz (U-bahn)* ✛ *2:D1.*

$$
HOTEL
🏨 **Swissôtel Berlin.** At the bustling corner of Ku'damm and Joachimsthaler Strasse, this hotel excels with its reputable Swiss hospitality—from accompanying guests to their floor after check-in to equipping each room with an iron, an umbrella, and a Nespresso coffee machine that preheats the cups. **Pros:** large rooms; unobtrusive service; great location. **Cons:** the lobby is on the third floor, with shops on the lower levels; mostly for business travelers. Ⓢ *Rooms from: €135* ✉ *Augsburger Str. 44, Charlottenburg* ☎ *030/220–100* ⊕ *www.swissotel.com* ⟲ *296 rooms, 20 suites* ⦿ *No meals* Ⓜ *Kurfürstendamm (U-bahn)* ✛ *2:C4.*

$$$$
HOTEL
🏨 **Waldorf Astoria Berlin.** This impressive skyscraper, a nod to the Waldorf's original New York location, has a chic art deco look and unparalleled service. **Pros:** ideal location near Ku'damm; large, luxurious rooms and bathrooms; breathtaking views of the Memorial Church and West Berlin. **Cons:** limited amenities for the price; nearby construction may bother some travelers. Ⓢ *Rooms from: €230* ✉ *Hardenbergst. 28, Charlottenburg* ☎ *030/814–0000* ⊕ *www.waldorfastoriaberlin.com* ⟲ *152 rooms, 50 suites* ⦿ *No meals* Ⓜ *Zoologischer Garten (U-bahn and S-bahn)* ✛ *2:B4.*

NIGHTLIFE AND PERFORMING ARTS

NIGHTLIFE

Updated
by Adam
Groffman

Clubs often switch the music they play from night to night, so crowds and popularity can vary widely.

Clubs and bars in Charlottenburg and in Mitte tend to be dressier and more conservative; the scene in Kreuzberg, Prenzlauer Berg, the Scheunenviertel, and Friedrichshain is laid-back and alternative. For the latest information on Berlin's house, electro, and hip-hop club scene, pick up *(030)*, a free weekly. Dance clubs don't get going until about 12:30 am, but parties labeled "after-work" start as early as 8 pm for professionals looking to socialize during the week.

Note that Berlin's nightspots are open to the wee hours of the morning, but if you stay out after 12:45 Sunday–Thursday, you'll have to find a night bus (designated by "N" before the number, which often corresponds to the subway line it is replacing) or catch the last S-bahn home. On Friday and Saturday nights all subway lines (except U-bahn Line No. 4) run every 15 to 20 minutes throughout the night.

MITTE

BARS AND LOUNGES

La Banca. Just off the luxurious Hotel de Rome's main reception area, this sumptuous bar and lounge, one of the city's most upscale evening spots, has deep leather sofas, high ceilings, and an impressive collection of spirits. Cocktails range from the classic to the inventive, with ingredients like arugula, oregano, balsamic vinegar, and rose syrup. Prices are high for Berlin but worth every penny. In warm weather, the bar opens up on the hotel's roof terrace, which offers one of the few great city views you can enjoy without waiting in line or paying admission. ✉ *Behrenstr. 37, Mitte* ☎ *030/460–6090* ⊕ *www.roccofortehotels.com.*

Neue Odessa Bar. Many patrons of this cocktail bar come to see and be seen; there are also a number of first-time visitors who stumble in from nearby Rosenthaler Platz, a central party destination in Mitte. Given this crowd, it's easy to forget just how good the drinks are here. While other cocktail bars in Berlin are content to regenerate the classics, Neue Odessa takes it a step further, with delicious, original concoctions using ingredients like lavender, lychee, and ginger. ✉ *Torstr. 89, Mitte* ⊕ *www. neueodessabar.de/.*

Newton Bar. This posh bar in Mitte has been around for ages. Helmut Newton's larger-than-life photos of nude women decorate the walls. ✉ *Charlottenstr. 57, Mitte* ☎ *030/2029–5421* ⊕ *www.newton-bar.de.*

Redwood. Run by a California native, this simple, solid cocktail bar serves near-perfect concoctions that belie the bare wood surroundings. If loud crowds and smoky rooms aren't your thing, this is the place for you—the cocktails are excellent and you'll be able to carry on a conversation in a normal voice. The menu is helpfully arranged according to "dry" or "sweet and sour" but if you're still unsure whether to go for a Dark and Stormy or a Blood and Sand, ask the friendly young bartenders—everyone speaks English here. ✉ *Bergstr. 25, Mitte* ☎ *030/7024–8813* ⊕ *www. redwoodbar.de* ⊗ *Closed Sun. and Mon.* Ⓜ *Nordbahhof (S-bahn).*

CLUBS

Fodor's Choice
★
Clärchen's Ballhaus. A night out at Clärchen's Ballhaus (Little Clara's Ballroom) is like a trip back in time. Opened in 1913, the club is an impressive sight on Mitte's now-upscale Auguststrasse. On summer nights, lines often stretch out the door, while the front courtyard comes alive with patrons dining alfresco on brick-oven pizzas (lunch and dinner are served daily). The main ballroom features a different style of music every night and there are often dance lessons before the party starts. One of the best things about this place, though, is the variety of people of different ages, nationalities, and social backgrounds. The upstairs Spiegelsaal ("mirror hall") has intimate, salon-type concerts on Sunday. ✉ *Auguststr. 24, Mitte* ☎ *030/282–9295* ⊕ *www.ballhaus.de.*

Felix. The over-the-top Felix greatly benefits from its location behind the famous Adlon Kempinski Hotel—Hollywood stars drop by when they're in town, or during the frenzied weeks of the Berlinale. The door policy can be tough, but dress in your finest and hope for the best. ✉ *Behrenstr. 72, Mitte* ☎ *030/3011–17152* ⊕ *www.felix-clubrestaurant.de/.*

Kaffee Burger. More of a neighborhood clubhouse than a bar, there's always something going on at Kaffee Burger. The original home of writer Wladimir Kaminer's popular Russendisko ("Russian disco") nights, this spot has a cozy dance floor and a separate smoking room. On any given night, you might encounter electro, rock, funk, swing, or Balkan beats; live bands play frequently. ✉ *Torstr. 58/60, Mitte* ☎ *030/2804–6495* ⊕ *www.kaffeeburger.de.*

Sage Club. Affiliated with nearby Sage Restaurant, this eclectic club is open only on Thursdays. Different floors play different music, from rock to electro, so expect to see diverse crowds depending on the vibe (check the program on the website). ✉ *Köpenicker Str. 76, Mitte* ☎ *030/278–9830* ⊕ *www.sage-club.de.*

JAZZ CLUBS

b-flat. Young German artists perform most nights at b-flat. The club has some of the best sight lines in town, as well as a magnificent floor-to-ceiling front window that captures the attention of passersby. The well-known and well-attended Wednesday jam sessions focus on free and experimental jazz, and once a month on Thursday the Berlin Big Band takes over the small stage with up to 17 players. Snacks are available. ✉ *Rosenthalerstr. 13, Mitte* ☎ *030/283–3123* ⊕ *www.b-flat-berlin.de.*

Kunstfabrik Schlot. Schlot hosts Berlin jazz scenesters, aspiring musicians playing Monday-night free jazz sessions, and local heavy-hitters. It's a bit hard to find—it's in the cellar of the Edison Höfe—but enter the courtyard via Schlegelstrasse and follow the music. ✉ *Invalidenstr. 117, entrance at Schlegelstr. 26, Mitte* ☎ *030/448–2160* Ⓜ *Nordbahnhof (S-bahn), Naturkundemuseum (U-bahn).*

15

In hip Kreuzberg, you can sip drinks canalside at Freischwimmer

FRIEDRICHSHAIN

GAY AND LESBIAN BARS

Fodor'sChoice
★

Berghain. In an imposing power station in a barren stretch of land between Kreuzberg and Friedrichshain (the name borrows from both neighborhoods), Berghain has achieved international fame as the hedonistic heart of techno music—it was originally a '90s techno club called Ostgut. Although it's also a well-respected center of gay nightlife, the club welcomes all. It's only open as a club on weekends (for 48-plus hours straight, from midnight on Friday to early Monday), though many international music acts pass through for concert performances during the week. It's become something of a local tradition to arrive on Sunday morning or afternoon and dance until closing. Upstairs, the slightly smaller (but by no means intimate) Panorama Bar opens on Friday at midnight and offers different beats before the main club opens at midnight on Saturday. ⊠ *Am Wriezener Bahnhof, Friedrichshain* ✥ *Exit north from Ostbahnhof and follow Str. der Pariser Kommune, then make a right on badly marked Am Wriezener Bahnhof and look for the line of clubbers* ☎ *030/2936–0210* ⊕ *www.berghain.de* Ⓜ *Ostbahnhof (S-bahn).*

KREUZBERG

BARS

Bellmann Bar. The candle-lit, rough wood tables, water-stained walls, and frequent appearances by local musicians just dropping by for a few tunes gives this cozy cocktail bar an artsty old-world feel. Lovingly nicknamed "the gramophone bar" for the old gramophone that sits in its window,

Bellmann is a place to linger and chat over a glass of wine or a whiskey from the outstanding collection. ✉ *Reichenbergerstr. 103, Kreuzberg.*

Freischwimmer. When it's warm out, the canal-side deck chairs at Freischwimmer are the perfect place to be, though heat lamps and an enclosed area make this a cozy setting for cool nights, too. To get here, walk five minutes east of the elevated Schlesisches Tor U-bahn station and turn left down a path after the 1920s Aral gas station, the oldest in Berlin. ✉ *Vor dem Schlesischen Tor 2a, Kreuzberg* ☎ *030/6107–4309* ⊕ *www.freischwimmer-berlin.com.*

Würgeengel. Named after a 1962 surrealist film by Luis Buñuel (known as *The Exterminating Angel* in English), this classy joint has offered an elaborate cocktail menu in a well-designed space off Kottbusser Tor since 1992—long before this part of Kreuzberg was hip, or even safe. Today, the bar's loyal fans spill out onto the streets on busy nights, and an evening tapas menu comes from the neighboring restaurant Gorgonzola Club. The team behind the restaurant Renger-Patzsch run Würgeengel and the Gorgonzola Club. ✉ *Dresdenerstr. 122, Kreuzberg* ✛ *Dresdener Str. is reachable through passageway under buildings at Kottbusser Tor, next to Adalbertstr.* ☎ *030/615–5560* ⊕ *www.wuergeengel.de.*

CLUBS

Watergate. The elegant Watergate is a club for people who usually don't like clubbing. It sits languidly at the base of the Oberbaumbrücke, on the Kreuzberg side, and has two dance floors with bars. The terrace extending over the River Spree is one of the city's best chill-out spaces. In addition to hosting internationally renowned DJs, the club is the beautiful and intimate setting for infrequent but popular classical music nights. ✉ *Falckensteinstr. 49, Kreuzberg* ☎ *030/6128–0396* ⊕ *www.water-gate.de* Ⓜ *Schlesisches Tor (U-bahn), Warschauer Strasse (U-bahn and S-bahn).*

GAY AND LESBIAN BARS

Roses. If you don't find any eye candy at tiny Roses there are always the furry red walls and kitschy paraphernalia to admire. It opens at 10 pm and keeps going until very late. ✉ *Oranienstr. 187, Kreuzberg* ☎ *030/615–6570.*

SCHÖNEBERG

BARS

Green Door. A grown-up crowd focused on conversation and appreciating outstanding cocktails heads to Green Door, a Schöneberg classic. The decor is 1960s retro style, with gingham walls and stand-alone lamps. Although the expertly crafted drinks are not cheap by Berlin standards, the Green Door has long offered wallet-friendly happy hour deals. ✉ *Winterfeldstr. 50, Schöneberg* ☎ *030/215–2515* ⊕ *www.greendoor.de.*

CLUBS

Havanna Club. Berlin's multiculti crowd frequents the Havanna Club, where you can dance to soul, R&B, or hip-hop on four different dance floors. The week's highlights are the wild salsa and merengue nights (Wednesday at 9 pm, Friday and Saturday at 10 pm). If your Latin steps are weak, come an hour early for a lesson. Friday and Saturday are "ladies free" nights until 11. ⊠ *Hauptstr. 30, Schöneberg* ☎ *030/784–8565* ⊕ *www.havanna-berlin.de.*

GAY AND LESBIAN BARS

Connection Club. Just south of Wittenbergplatz, the dance club Connection is known for heavy house music and lots of dark corners. ⊠ *Fuggerstr. 33, Schöneberg* ☎ *030/218–1432* ⊕ *www.connection-berlin.de.*

Hafen. The stylish decor and the energetic crowd at Hafen make it a popular singles hangout. The first Monday of every month there's an English-language quiz night popular with locals, expats, and tourists. ⊠ *Motzstr. 19, Schöneberg* ☎ *030/211–4118* ⊕ *www.hafen-berlin.de.*

TREPTOW

CLUBS

Fodor'sChoice
★
Club der Visionaere. It may not be much more than a series of wooden rafts and a few shoddily constructed shacks, but this club is one of the most beloved outdoor venues in town. The place is packed at all hours, either with clubbers on their last stop of the evening, or with students soaking up the sunshine on a Sunday morning. Since it shares a narrow canal with Freischwimmer, which hosts a massive brunch on Sunday, an easy hop across the water (by bridge, of course) will get you coffee and breakfast at dawn. ⊠ *Am Flutgraben 1, Treptow* ⊹ *Follow Schlesische Str. east from the U-bahn station until you cross two small canals. After the second bridge, look left* ☎ ⊕ *www.clubdervisionaere. com* Ⓜ *Schlesisches Tor (U-bahn).*

CHARLOTTENBURG

BARS

Monkey Bar. On the rooftop of the 25hours Hotel Bikini Berlin, this often-packed watering hole affords scenic views over Tiergarten Park and an impressive range of well-crafted cocktails. Expect a crowd at the ground-floor entrance (no matter what day of the week)—this place is worth the wait. ⊠ *Budapester Str. 40, Charlottenburg* ☎ *030/1202–21210* ⊕ *www.25hours-hotels.com.*

JAZZ CLUBS

A-Trane. A-Trane in West Berlin has hosted countless greats throughout the years, including Herbie Hancock and Wynton Marsalis. Weekly free jam nights on Saturday in winter and numerous other free events make it a good place to see jazz on a budget. ⊠ *Bleibtreustr. 1, Charlottenburg* ☎ *030/313–2550* ⊕ *www.a-trane.de* Ⓜ *Savignyplatz (S-bahn).*

Quasimodo. To get to Quasimodo, the most established and popular jazz venue in the city, you'll need to descend a small staircase to the basement of the Theater des Westens. Despite its college-town pub feel, the club has hosted many Berlin and international greats. Seats are few, but there's plenty of standing room in the front. ⊠ *Kantstr. 12a, Charlottenburg* ☎ *030/3180–4560* ⊕ *www.quasimodo.de.*

PERFORMING ARTS

Detailed information about events is covered in the *Berlin Programm,* a monthly tourist guide to Berlin arts, museums, and theaters. The magazines *Tip* and *Zitty,* which appear every two weeks, provide full arts listings (in German), although the free weekly *(030)* is the best source for club and music events. For listings in English, consult the monthly *Ex-Berliner,* or their website (⊕ *www.exberliner.com*), which is updated regularly.

Hekticket offices. The Hekticket offices offer discounted and last-minute tickets, including half-price, same-day tickets daily at 2 pm. ✉ *Karl-Liebknecht-Str. 13, off Alexanderpl., Mitte* ☎ *030/230–9930* ⊕ *www. hekticket.de.*

Showtime Konzert und Theaterkassen. If your hotel can't book a seat for you or you can't make it to a box office directly, go to a ticket agency. Surcharges are 10%–18% of the ticket price. Showtime Konzert und Theaterkassen has offices within the major department stores, including KaDeWe. ✉ *KaDeWe, Tauentzienstr. 21, Charlottenburg* ☎ *030/8060–2929* ⊕ *www.showtimetickets.de.*

CONCERTS

Berliner Philharmonie. The Berlin Philharmonic Orchestra is one of the world's best and their resident venue is the Philharmonie, comprising the Grosser Saal, or large main hall, and the smaller Kammermusiksaal, dedicated to chamber music. Tickets sell out in advance for the nights when star maestros conduct, but other orchestras and artists appear here as well. Tuesday's free Lunchtime Concerts fill the foyer with eager listeners of all ages at 1 pm. Show up early as these concerts can get very crowded. Daily guided tours (€5) also take place at 1:30 pm. ✉ *Herbert-von-Karajan-Str. 1, Tiergarten* ☎ *030/2548–8134* ⊕ *www. berliner-philharmoniker.de.*

Konzerthaus Berlin. The beautifully restored hall at Konzerthaus Berlin is a prime venue for classical music concerts. The box office is open from noon to curtain time. ✉ *Gendarmenmarkt, Mitte* ☎ *030/2030–92101* ⊕ *www.konzerthaus.de.*

DANCE, MUSICALS, AND OPERA

Berlin's three opera houses also host guest productions and companies from around the world. Vladimir Malakhov, a principal guest dancer with New York's American Ballet Theatre, is a principal in the Staatsballett Berlin as well as its director. The company performs its classic and modern productions at the Deutsche Oper and the Schiller Theater while the famed Staatsoper on Unter den Linden undergoes renovations *(See the Staatsoper listing in Exploring for more about the building).*

Deutsche Oper Berlin. Of the many composers represented in the repertoire of Deutsche Oper Berlin, Verdi and Wagner are the most frequently presented. ✉ *Bismarckstr. 35, Charlottenburg* ☎ *030/343–8401* ⊕ *www.deutscheoperberlin.de.*

Komische Oper. The operas performed here are sung in their original language (often with English subtitles), but the lavish and at times over-the-top and kitschy staging and costumes make for a fun night even if you

15

don't speak the language. ⊠ *Behrenstr. 55–57, Mitte* ☎ *030/4799–7400* ⊕ *www.komische-oper-berlin.de.*

Neuköllner Oper. The small and alternative Neuköllner Oper puts on fun, showy performances of long-forgotten operas as well as humorous musical productions. It also is more likely than other Berlin opera houses to stage productions offering modern social commentary and individual takes on the immigrant experience—which is fitting for this international neighborhood. ⊠ *Karl-Marx-Str. 131–133, Neukölln* ☎ *030/6889–0777* ⊕ *www.neukoellneroper.de.*

Schiller Theater. Currently serving as interim stage for the Staatsoper, until renovations are finished in 2017, the Schiller Theater is also known for light musical and theater fare. ⊠ *Bismarckstr. 110, Charlottenburg* ☎ *030/2035–4555.*

Tanzfabrik. The Tanzfabrik is Berlin's best venue to see young dance talent and the latest from Europe's avant-garde. Additionally, contemporary artists come to learn and practice here in dance classes and workshops. ⊠ *Studio, Möckernstr. 68, Kreuzberg* ☎ *030/786–5861* ⊕ *www.tanzfabrik-berlin.de.*

FESTIVALS

Berliner Festspiele. This annual Berlin festival, held from late August through September or early October, unites all the major performance halls (especially the Haus der Berliner Festspiele and the Martin-Gropius-Bau) as well as some smaller venues for concerts, opera, ballet, theater, and art exhibitions. It also sponsors some smaller-scale events throughout the year. ⊠ *Ticket office, Schaperstr. 24* ☎ *030/2548–9100* ⊕ *www.berlinerfestspiele.de.*

FILM

International and German movies are shown in the big theaters on Potsdamer Platz and around the Ku'damm. If a film isn't marked "OF" or "OV" (*Originalfassung,* or "original version") or "OmU" ("original with subtitles"), it's dubbed. Many Berlin theaters let customers reserve seats in advance when purchasing tickets, so buy them early to nab those coveted center spots. ■TIP→ **Previews and commercials often run for 25 minutes, so don't worry if you walk in late.**

Freiluftkinos. When warm weather hits the city and Berliners come out of hibernation, they often head to the Freiluftkinos (open-air cinemas). These outdoor viewing areas are in just about every park in town, offer food and drinks, and screen a good balance of German and international films, many of them new releases. Check the website for schedules from three of the city's best, in Volkspark Friedrichshain, Mariannenplatz Kreuzberg, and Volkspark Rehberge in Wedding. ⊠ *Berlin* ⊕ *www.freiluftkino-berlin.de* 🎟 €7.

Hackesche Höfe Kino. Documentary films, international films in their original language, and German art-house films are shown at the Hackesche Höfe Kino, or cinema. There's no elevator to this top-floor movie house, but you can recover on the wide banquettes in the lounge. ⊠ *Rosenthaler Str. 40–41, Mitte* ☎ *030/283–5293* ⊕ *www.hoefekino.de.*

VARIETY SHOWS, COMEDY, AND CABARET

Berlin's variety shows can include magicians, circus performers, musicians, and classic cabaret stand-ups. Be aware that in order to understand and enjoy traditional cabaret, which involves a lot of political humor, your German has to be up to snuff.

Admiralspalast. The completely restored 1920s entertainment emporium Admiralspalast draws on its glitzy Jazz Age glamour, and houses several stages and a restaurant. The main theater features everything from large-scale shows to theater, comedy, and concerts. ⊠ *Friedrichstr. 101, Mitte* ☎ *030/4799–7499* ⊕ *www.admiralspalast.de.*

Bar Jeder Vernunft. The intimate Bar Jeder Vernunft is inside a glamorous tent and usually showcases intriguing solo entertainers as well as concerts and comedy shows. Note that the venue is set back from the street and is hard to find. Just to the left of Haus der Berliner Festspiele, look for a lighted path next to a parking lot and follow it until you reach the tent. ⊠ *Schaperstr. 24, Wilmersdorf* ☎ *030/883–1582* ⊕ *www. bar-jeder-vernunft.de.*

BKA–Berliner Kabarett Anstalt. Social and political satire has a long tradition in cabaret theaters and the BKA–Berliner Kabarett Anstalt is known for performances by Germany's leading young comedy talents as well as chanson vocalists. ⊠ *Mehringdamm 34, Kreuzberg* ☎ *030/202–2007* ⊕ *www.bka-theater.de.*

Chamäleon Varieté. Within the Hackesche Höfe, the Chamäleon Varieté is the most affordable and offbeat variety venue in town. German isn't required to enjoy most of the productions. ⊠ *Rosenthaler Str. 40–41, Mitte* ☎ *030/400–0590* ⊕ *www.chamaeleonberlin.com.*

Grüner Salon. This is one of Berlin's hippest venues for live music, cabaret, dancing, and drinks. The programs change almost daily. ⊠ *Freie Volksbühne, Rosa-Luxemburg-Pl., side door of the Volksbühne, Mitte* ☎ *030/2859–8936* ⊕ *www.gruener-salon.de.*

Tipi am Kanzleramt (*Tipi am Kanzleramt*). Tipi is a tent venue between the Kanzleramt (Chancellor's Office) and Haus der Kulturen der Welt. Artists featured are well suited for an international audience, and you can opt to dine here before the show. Even the back-row seats are good. ⊠ *Grosse QueralLee, Tiergarten* ☎ *030/3906–6550* ⊕ *www.tipi-am-kanzleramt.de.*

15

SHOPPING

Updated by
Yasha Wallin

What's fashionable in Berlin is creative, bohemian style, so designer labels have less appeal here than in Hamburg, Düsseldorf, or Munich. For the young and trendy, it is bad form to be seen wearing clothes that appear to have cost much more than a *Brötchen* (bread roll), so most step out in vintage and secondhand threads.

MITTE

The finest shops in historic Berlin are along Friedrichstrasse, including the French department store Galeries Lafayette and the international luxury department store Departmentstore Quartier 206. Nearby, Unter den Linden offers a few souvenir shops and a Meissen ceramic showroom, while the area surrounding the picturesque Gendarmenmarkt is home to top fashion designers and many international brands.

The charming side streets of Mitte's Scheunenviertel area have turned into a true destination for serious fashion aficionados. The area between Hackescher Markt, Weinmeister Strasse, and Rosa-Luxemburg-Platz alternate pricey independent designers with groovy secondhand shops, and a string of ultrahip flagship stores by the big sports and fashion designer brands. Neue Schönhauser Strasse meets up with Rosenthaler Strasse on one end and curves into Alte Schönhauser Strasse on the other. All three streets are full of stylish and original casual wear. Galleries along Gipsstrasse and Sophienstrasse round out the mix.

ACCESSORIES

Hecking. Designer Luisa Hecking opened this accessories boutique in 2007 as a showcase for her timeless collection of HeckingHandermann bags, sunglasses, and jewelry. It's one of the best places for scarves in the city, with a wide selection of designs, at a variety of price points. ✉ *Gormannstr. 8–9, entrance Mulackstr., Mitte* ☎ *030/2804–7528* ⊕ *www.hecking-shop.com* ۞ *Closed Tues. and Sun.* Ⓜ *Weinmeisterstrasse (U-bahn), Rosa-Luxemburg-Platz (U-bahn).*

BOOK STORES

Fodor's Choice ★ **Do You Read Me?** Whether you're looking for something to read on the plane or a special present, this charming bookstore is guaranteed to have something to pique your literary interests. The wide selection of magazines and literature—many of the titles are in English—comes from around the world and spans fashion, photography, architecture, interior design, and cultural topics. ✉ *Auguststr. 28, Mitte* ☎ *030/6954–9695* ⊕ *www.doyoureadme.de* ۞ *Closed Sun.* Ⓜ *Weinmeisterstrasse (U-bahn), Rosa-Luxemburg-Platz (U-bahn).*

soda. BERLIN. Opened in early 2015, this branch of the Munich bookstore started by Isabell Hummel and Sebastian Steinacker gives the many mainstream and DIY magazines and books carried here plenty of room to breathe. Hummel and Steinacker's goal for their spaces is to offer "curious publications for curious people." Here you'll find plenty of both. ✉ *Weinbergsweg 1, Mitte* ☎ *030/4373–3700* ⊕ *www.sodabooks.com* ۞ *Closed Sun.* Ⓜ *Rosenthaler Platz (U-bahn).*

CLOTHING

14 oz. Inside a beautiful old building in the heart of Mitte's Hackescher Markt shopping district, 14 oz. sells high-end denim (Denham the Jeanmaker, Momotaro Jeans, Edwin), along with sneakers, accessories, knitwear, and outerwear. For true VIP treatment, a private shopping area is available on the second floor. Shoppers on a budget will also love 14 oz.'s outlet store, also in Mitte on Memhardstrasse. ✉ *Neue Schönhauserstr.*

13, Mitte ☎ *030/2804–0514* ⊕ *www.14oz-berlin.com/berlin* ☉ *Closed Sun.* Ⓜ *Weinmeisterstrasse (U-bahn), Hackescher Markt (S-bahn).*

A.D. Deertz. This tiny shop on Torstrasse is the flagship outlet for designer Wibke Deertz, who uses fabrics and inspirations from her travels around the world to create a collection of handmade, limited-edition pieces, including pants, shirts, jackets, and accessories. ✉ *Torstr. 106, Mitte* ☎ *030/9120–6630* ⊕ *www.addeertz.com/* ☉ *Closed Sun.* Ⓜ *Rosenthaler Platz (U-bahn).*

Apartment. Don't be deterred when you arrive at this seemingly empty storefront: the real treasure lies at the bottom of the black spiral staircase. On the basement level you'll find one of Berlin's favorite shops for local designs and wardrobe staples for both men and women. Think distressed tops, shoes, leather jackets, and skinny jeans. ✉ *Memhardstr. 8, Mitte* ☎ *030/2804–2251* ⊕ *www.apartmentberlin.de* ☉ *Closed Sun.* Ⓜ *Weinmeisterstrasse (U-bahn), Alexanderplatz (U-bahn and S-bahn).*

Fodor'sChoice **Baerck.** Baerck artfully displays its mix of European and Berlin men's
★ and women's wear on wheeled structures, allowing them to be rearranged in the store whenever necessary. Along with designers like Stine Goya, Henrik Vibskov, and Hope, you'll find the store's eponymous accessories line of handbags and scarves, as well as their clothing label NIA for blouses and trousers, and their product line llot llov—a play on the German word "toll" meaning great or cool. A changing display of lifestyle and interior decor items like lamps, mirrors, and handmade furniture invite you in, while the basement level always has great sale pieces. ✉ *Mulackstr. 12, Mitte* ☎ *030/2404–8994* ⊕ *www.baerck.net* ☉ *Closed Sun.* Ⓜ *Weinmeisterstrasse (U-bahn).*

Claudia Skoda. One of Berlin's top avant-garde designers, Claudia Skoda's creations are mostly for women, but there's also a selection of men's knitwear. ✉ *Mulackstr. 8, Mitte* ☎ *030/4004–1884* ⊕ *www.claudiaskoda.com* ☉ *Closed Sun.* Ⓜ *Weinmeisterstrasse (U-bahn), Rosa-Luxemburg-Platz (U-bahn).*

The Corner Berlin. In the heart of the stunning Gendarmenmarkt, this luxury concept store sells a contemporary collection of new and vintage clothing from high-end designers like Yves Saint Laurent and Chloé, as well as cosmetics, home furnishings, and art books. The shop is also a popular venue for exclusive fashion events and is home to a gallery and café. ✉ *Französischstr. 40, Mitte* ☎ *030/2067–0940* ⊕ *www.thecornerberlin.de* ☉ *Closed Sun.* Ⓜ *Französische Strasse (U-bahn).*

Fodor'sChoice **Das Neue Schwarz.** Whether you want a new little black dress or a cool
★ vintage bag to carry around this season, a peek into Das Neue Schwarz (The New Black) is guaranteed to result in some special finds. In the midst of Mitte's fashionista neighborhood of avant-garde designers and exclusive boutiques, this shop holds its own with a collection of secondhand items, many never worn, from big name designers including Vivienne Westwood, Helmut Lang, and Yves Saint Laurent. ✉ *Mulackstr. 38, Mitte* ☎ *030/2787–4467* ⊕ *www.dasneueschwarz.de* ☉ *Closed Sun.* Ⓜ *Weinmeisterstrasse (U-bahn), Rosa-Luxemburg-Platz (U-bahn).*

Esther Perbant. An avant-garde pioneer with a penchant for black, Esther Perbant's buzzed-about runway shows during Berlin Fashion Week are

15

as adventurous as the designs sold in her shop. Expect androgynous silhouettes for men and women including tailored trousers, blazers, wrap dresses with generous, draping fabric and her signature, military-inspired hats. A visit here is a must to get a sense of how real Berliners dress. ⊠ *Almstadtstr. 3, Mitte* ☎ *030/8853–6791* ⊕ *estherperbandt.com* ⊗ *Closed Sun.* Ⓜ *Weinmeisterstrasse (U-bahn), Alexanderplatz (U-bahn and S-bahn).*

Konk. Since 2003, this Mitte hot spot has nurtured Berlin independent designers who are as visionary in their aesthetics as they are in their production mode: most items are handmade and sustainably sourced. Look for local favorite NCA for hats, and elegant gold earrings and rings by Savoir Joaillerie. ⊠ *Kleine Hamburger Str. 15, Mitte* ☎ *030/2809–7839* ⊕ *www.konk-berlin.de* ⊗ *Closed Sun.* Ⓜ *Oranienburger Strasse (S-bahn), Rosenthaler Platz (U-bahn).*

Fodor's Choice ★ **Lala Berlin.** Originally from Tehran, former MTV editor Lelya Piedayesh is one of Berlin's top design talents. Her popular boutique relocated and expanded in 2014 to make room for even more of her high-quality fabric scarves, sweaters, and accessories that use the reinterpreted Palestinian keffiyeh pattern she's become known for. ⊠ *Alte Schonhauser Str. 3, Mitte* ☎ *030/2576–2924* ⊕ *www.lalaberlin.com* ⊗ *Closed Sun.* Ⓜ *Weinmeisterstrasse (U-bahn), Rosa-Luxemburg-Platz (U-bahn).*

Made in Berlin. One of the more established secondhand shops in Berlin, this outpost is always crowded with trendsetting locals and discerning visitors looking for hidden gems. The selection is more curated-thrift look than high-end designs, and includes an extensive range of 1980s wear as well as a broad selection of shoes. Make sure to pop in for the shop's happy hour, where you'll get 20% off on purchases (Tuesday noon–3). ⊠ *Neue Schönhauser Str. 19, Mitte* ☎ *030/2123–0601* ⊗ *Closed Sun.* Ⓜ *Weinmeisterstrasse (U-bahn), Hackescher Markt (S-bahn).*

Oukan. This demure boutique originally began as a fund-raising project during Berlin's Fashion Week in response to the 2011 Japanese tsunami. Along with two floors of avant-garde Japanese and international designs for men and women (expect to find plenty in black and white, and a lot of angular silhouettes), lifestyle products, and interior decor, the space is also home to Avan, an in-house teahouse serving a variety of Asian-fusion dishes like *banh mi* sandwiches, dumplings, and curries. ⊠ *Kronenstr. 71, Mitte* ☎ *030/2062–6700* ⊕ *www.oukan.de/* ⊗ *Closed Sun.* Ⓜ *Stadtmitte (U-bahn).*

Fodor's Choice ★ **SOTO.** SOTO is the name of the hip, fashion-forward area of Mitte, south of Torstrasse, filled with charming side streets and numerous fashion boutiques. So, it's appropriate that it's also the name of this boutique where you'll find a mix of timeless and trendsetting menswear including the house label, Le Berlinois, along with brands like Band of Outsiders, Norse Projects, and Our Legacy, grooming products, and accessories ranging from cameras to lanyards. ⊠ *Torstr. 72, Mitte* ☎ *030/2576–2070* ⊕ *www.sotostore.com* ⊗ *Closed Sun.* Ⓜ *Rosa-Luxemburg-Platz (U-bahn).*

Thone Negron. From the back of her Linienstrasse atelier, Ettina Berrios-Negron creates some of the most elegant dresses and silk blouses seen in the city. Her intimate shop also accommodates made-to-measure services, and bridal fittings are available by appointment. ✉ *Linienstr. 71, Mitte* ☎ *030/5316–1116* ⊕ *www.thonenegron.com* ⊗ *Closed Sun.* Ⓜ *Rosenthaler Platz (U-bahn).*

Wood Wood Annex. The avant-garde street-wear brand out of Copenhagen stocks its Berlin annex with its eponymous line of bags, shoes, and clothing for men and women. Also in-store are contemporary labels like Comme des Garçons, Opening Ceremony, and Kenzo. ✉ *Rochstr. 3, Mitte* ☎ *030/2759–59770* ⊕ *www.woodwood.dk* ⊗ *Closed Sun.* Ⓜ *Weinmeisterstrasse (U-bahn), Alexanderplatz (U-bahn and S-bahn).*

DEPARTMENT STORES

Fodor'sChoice ★ **DepartmentStore Quartier 206.** The smallest, and often considered the most luxurious, department store in town, DepartmentStore Quartier 206 has a wide range of women's and men's international designers from the likes of Prada, Givenchy, and Tom Ford. Much of the store's inventory is hand-picked by founder Anne Maria Jagdfeld on travels around the world, and the store also carries a variety of cosmetics, perfumes, home accessories, art, and books. ✉ *Friedrichstr. 71, Mitte* ☎ *030/2094–6500* ⊕ *www.dsq206.com* ⊗ *Closed Sun.* Ⓜ *Französische Strasse (U-bahn), Stadtmitte (U-bahn).*

Fodor'sChoice ★ **Galeries Lafayette.** At the corner of Französische Strasse (it means "French Street" and is named for the nearby French Huguenot cathedral) is the French department store Galeries Lafayette. French architect Jean Nouvel included an impressive steel-and-glass funnel at the center of the building, and it's surrounded by four floors of expensive clothing and luxuries as well as an excellent food department with counters offering French cuisine, and a market with some of the best produce in the area. Intimate and elegant, Galeries Lafayette carries almost exclusively French products. ✉ *Friedrichstr. 76–78, Mitte* ☎ *030/209–480* ⊕ *www.galerieslafayette.de* ⊗ *Closed Sun.* Ⓜ *Französische Strasse (U-bahn).*

GIFTS

Ampelmann. This gallery shop opened in the mall-like Hackesche Höfe shopping area in 2001, promoting the red and green Ampelmännchen, the charming symbol used on the former East traffic lights. The brand now operates six shops in Berlin, and you can find the logo on everything from T-shirts and umbrellas to ice cube trays and candy. ■TIP→ It's a perfect stop for souvenirs. ✉ *Hackesche Höfe, Hof 5, Rosenthalerstr. 40–41, Mitte* ☎ *030/4472–6438* ⊕ *ampelmann.de/* Ⓜ *Weinmeisterstrasse (U-bahn), Hackescher Markt (S-bahn).*

ausberlin. This shop near Alexanderplatz provides a wide range of Berlin memories, all designed and manufactured in the city. There is everything from Berlin-themed emergency candy bars and tote bags with city landmark designs to Berlin-produced liquors. ✉ *Karl-Liebknechtstr. 9, Mitte* ☎ *030/9700–5640* ⊕ *www.ausberlin.de* Ⓜ *Alexanderplatz (U-bahn and S-bahn).*

Berlin Story. More than 5,000 different books, maps, and souvenirs about the city of Berlin can be found at this shop, which is, unlike

15

many, open on Sunday. The company also runs a translation and publishing house and a small museum, as well as a web shop for those still looking for souvenirs after the trip is over. ☒ *Unter den Linden 40, Mitte* ☎ *030/2045–3842* ⊕ *www.berlinstory.de* Ⓜ *Brandenburger Tor (S-bahn), Französische Strasse (U-bahn).*

Bonbonmacherei. Tucked into a small courtyard near the New Synagogue, this charming candy store has been making and selling handmade sweets for the past 100 years. The brightly colored sugar bonbons are pressed on vintage molds into leaf, raspberry, and diamond shapes, and more than 30 different varieties are available. For a real insider's peek at candy production, join one of the store's twice-daily tours, which walk customers step-by-step through the candy production. ☒ *Oranienburgerstr. 32, Mitte* ☎ *030/4405–5243* ⊕ *www.bonbonmacherei. de* ⊙ *Closed July and Aug., and Sun.–Tues.* Ⓜ *Oranienburger Strasse (U-bahn and S-bahn).*

JEWELRY

Fodor'sChoice
★

Sabrina Dehoff. The flagship store of German jewelry designer Sabrina Dehoff balances bling and minimalism—bright crystals are paired with chunky metals. ☒ *Torstr. 175, Mitte* ☎ *030/9362–4680* ⊕ *www. sabrinadehoff.com* ⊙ *Closed Sun.* Ⓜ *Rosenthaler Strasse (U-bahn).*

POTSDAMER PLATZ

On the border between the city's former east and west regions, this touristy area is popular thanks to the towering Sony Center, which offers an English-language movie theater as well as restaurants and bars. The main shopping arcade here, also named Potsdamer Platz, offers a wide selection of chain shops, but you'll find a few original shops tucked on the side streets.

CLOTHING

Fodor'sChoice
★

Andreas Murkudis. Andreas Murkudis moved his successful concept shop from Mitte to the former Taggespiegel newspaper office space near Potsdamer Platz in 2011. Inside the stark white room you'll find hand-picked mens, women's, and children's clothing, including designs by brother Kostas Murkudis, Dries van Noten, and Christian Haas, as well as accessories, and contemporary home ware. ☒ *Potsdamer Str. 81e, Potsdamer Platz* ☎ *030/6807–98306* ⊕ *www.andreasmurkudis. com* ⊙ *Closed Sun.* Ⓜ *Kurfürstenstrasse (U-bahn).*

GIFTS

Fodor'sChoice
★

Frau Tonis Parfum. This elegant perfumery will help you create a completely personal scent; choose from vials filled with perfumes like acacia, linden tree blossoms, cedarwood, or pink peppercorns. All the perfumes are produced locally in Berlin, creating a really one-of-a kind gift. ☒ *Zimmerstr. 13, Potsdamer Platz* ☎ *030/2021–5310* ⊕ *www.frau-tonis-parfum.com* ⊙ *Closed Sun.* Ⓜ *Kochstrasse/Checkpoint Charlie (U-bahn).*

FRIEDRICHSHAIN

The cobblestone streets and densely packed neighborhoods of cafés, shops, and boutiques make the area between Frankfurter Allee and Warschauer Strasse an ideal shopping stretch. Both Boxhagener Platz and Simon-Dach Strasse are home to fashionable shops, and the neighborhood holds shopping nights on select Saturdays.

CLOTHING

Prachtmädchen. Near Boxhagener Platz, this is great shop to find a piece of Berlin's young, colorful style. Prachtmädchen specializes in trendy T-shirts, coats, sustainable pieces from Scandinavian and Japanese brands, and accessories from their own line. There is also a small inventory of menswear. ✉ *Wühlischst. 28, Friedrichshain* ☎ *030/9700–2780* ⊕ *www.prachtmaedchen.de/* ⊙ *Closed Sun.* Ⓜ *Warschauer Strasse (U-bahn and S-bahn).*

Something Coloured. This Friedrichshain boutique looks like a trendy concept shop at first glance, but inside you'll find a selection of stylish secondhand pieces. Among their advertised "1,000 pieces paired with rationality," expect to find jeans from Paige and J brand, bags from Chanel, and pieces from COS, Comptoir des Cotonniers, and Zoe Karssen. ✉ *Grünberger Str. 90, Friedrichshain* ☎ *030/2935–2075* ⊙ *Closed Sun. and Mon.* Ⓜ *Samariterstrasse (U-bahn).*

GIFTS

Workaholic Fashion. This showroom puts Berlin's music culture front and center, with fashion inspired by the DJ and club scene. Selling a range of shoes, bags, accessories, clothing, and vinyl, the store is as high energy as one of the city's late-night parties: you may be offered a vodka shot to round out your shopping experience. ✉ *Kopernikusstr. 12, Friedrichshain* ☎ *030/8411–8358* ⊕ *www.workaholicfashion.net* ⊙ *Closed Sun.* Ⓜ *Warschauer Strasse (U-bahn and S-bahn).*

HOME DECOR

Victoria Met Albert. You could easily spend hours in this charming household, gift, and clothing concept shop in the heart of the bustling Boxhagener Platz. They've stocked their large Friedrichshain emporium with a huge range of decorative lifestyle items from furniture paint to welcome mats and light fixtures. In their second, smaller Prenzlauer Berg shop, you'll find similar, enviable items. ✉ *Krossener Str. 9–10, Friedrichshain* ☎ *030/2977–4366* ⊕ *www.victoriametalbert. com* ⊙ *Closed Sun.* Ⓜ *Samariterstrasse (U-bahn), Warschauer Strasse (U-bahn and S-bahn).*

KREUZBERG

Locals love Kreuzberg for its grittier landscape, and the fashion style here is more urban as well. The lively Bergmannstrasse is home to several worthy destinations, as is Mehringdamm. This, along with neighboring Neukölln, is the place to score a unique Berlin find.

CLOTHING

Michael Sontag. Berlin-based Michael Sontag's new, architecturally striking boutique is a welcome neighbor in an increasingly lively part of Kreuzberg. Often celebrated by the German fashion press, Sontag thinks in terms of timeless garments rather than seasonally, so you'll see a lot of versatile silk shirts and draping dresses to be worn year-round. ⊠ *Muskauerstr. 41, Kreuzberg* ☏ *0179/971–5932* ⊕ *www.michaelsontag.com* ⊗ *Closed Sun. and Mon.* Ⓜ *Görlitzer Bahnhof (U-bahn).*

Fodor's Choice ★ **Voo.** This "super boutique" in a former locksmith's workshop is a Berlin favorite for women's and men's separates, shoes, accessories, and outerwear, often from rare collections around the world. It's also home to Companion Coffee, for when you need a shopping pick-me-up. ⊠ *Oranienstr. 24, Kreuzberg* ☏ *030/6165–1119* ⊕ *www.vooberlin.com* ⊗ *Closed Sun.* Ⓜ *Kottbusser Tor (U-bahn).*

GIFT IDEAS

Hardwax. This iconic record store is run by music veteran Mark Ernestus, who hand-picks all the vinyl and CDs with a heavy focus on techno, electronic, and dubstep. On the third floor of a heavily graffitied building, it's the true essence of Berlin grunge and totally worth a visit for music lovers. ⊠ *Paul-Lincke-Ufer 44a, Kreuzberg* ☏ *030/6113–0111* ⊕ *www.hardwax.com* ⊗ *Closed Sun.* Ⓜ *Kottbusser Tor (U-bahn).*

Fodor's Choice ★ **Süper Store.** Located in the charming neighborhood of Kreuzberg known as the Graefekiez, this cute little shop supplies a variety of lovely odds and ends, sourced from all over the world, including Turkey, Italy, and Switzerland, as well as locally produced items. Inside you'll find linens, housewares, pantry items, and jewelry. ⊠ *Dieffenbachstr. 12, Kreuzberg* ☏ *030/9832–7944* ⊕ *www.sueper-store.de/* ⊗ *Closed Sun. and Mon.* Ⓜ *Schönleinstrasse (U-bahn).*

HOME DECOR

Fodor's Choice ★ **Hallesches Haus.** Part playfully curated general store, part café, and soon-to-be outdoor cinema, Hallesches Haus is the brainchild of three ex-Fab and Monoqi staffers. Shop terrariums, artfully designed gardening tools, Pendelton blankets, housewares, and gifts with a sense of humor like matches to "scent your beard like the wilderness," and gum that "erases past mistakes." ⊠ *Tempelhofer Ufer 1, Kreuzberg* ☏ *176/8413–8777* ⊕ *www.hallescheshaus.com/* ⊗ *Closed Sun.* Ⓜ *Hallesches Tor (U-bahn).*

PRENZLAUER BERG

Stretching east of Mitte's Rosenthaler Platz, the fashionable boutiques continue into Prenzlauer Berg. This area is well-known for its own collection of designer boutiques, secondhand shops, and original designs. The busy Kastanienallee is packed with shops and boutiques, as is the more quiet area around Hemholzpatz.

CLOTHING

Dear. A secondhand shop for men is an anomaly in Berlin. Yet this laid-back storefront, on one of Prenzlauer Berg's most charming streets, more than makes up for that fact. You'll find stylish labels like Acne and Nike for him, and there's also a small women's selection of shoes and wardrobe staples. ⊠ *Stargarder Str. 9, Prenzlauer Berg* ☎ *030/4908–1169* ⊗ *Closed Sun.* Ⓜ *Schönhauser Allee (U-bahn and S-bahn).*

Fodor'sChoice
★

Garments. This chic store offers Prenzlauer Berg's fashion lovers an excellent selection of vintage and secondhand clothing, costume jewelry, and accessories. There is also a branch in Mitte, at Linienstrasse 204–205. ⊠ *Stargarderstr. 12 A, Prenzlauer Berg* ☎ *030/7477–9919* ⊕ *www.garments-vintage.de* ⊗ *Closed Sun.* Ⓜ *Schönhauser Allee (U-bahn and S-bahn).*

Isobel Gowdie. Friendly staffers aren't always a given in Germany's capital, so the extra attention you'll get at Isobel Gowdie is a welcome treat while you're browsing the vintage, second-season, and new garments by Dries van Noten, Chloé, and more. There's a second location on Alte Schönhauser Strasse in Mitte. ⊠ *Kastanienallee 40, Prenzlauer Berg* ⊕ *www.isobelgowdie-berlin.com* ⊗ *Closed Sun.* Ⓜ *Senefelderplatz (U-bahn).*

Kauf Dich Glücklich. With an odd assortment of retro furnishings, this ice-cream café and waffle shop takes over the entire corner of a Prenzlauer Berg sidewalk, especially on sunny days. Head to the second story and you'll find a shop that captures young Berliner style, with vintage pieces, bold prints, and skinny fits, as well as shoes and jewelry. The collection focuses on women's wear, although there is also a small offering of men's clothing. The newly opened Mitte outpost on Rosenthaler Strasse boasts even more menswear options as well as home accessories, and there's also an outlet shop in Wedding. ⊠ *Kastanien Allee 54, Prenzlauer Berg* ☎ *030/4172–5651* ⊕ *www.kaufdichgluecklich-shop.de/* Ⓜ *Rosenthaler Platz (U-bahn).*

NO WÓDKA. This minimal showroom is offset by a playfully curated selection of Polish art, fashion, and design items. The store's name hints at irony, and indeed, no vodka can be found here, but rather covetable contemporary products that reinterpret the meaning of "made in Poland." ⊠ *Pappelallee 10, Prenzlauer Berg* ☎ *030/4862–3086* ⊕ *nowodka.com* ⊗ *Closed Sun.* Ⓜ *Eberswalder Strasse (U-bahn).*

GIFT IDEAS

Fodor'sChoice
★

Dr. Kochan Schapskultur. This small shop embodies traditional German liquor culture; there are schnapps and fruit brandies from family farms and independent distilleries for sale, among other items to pique a tippler's interest. ⊠ *Immanuelkirchstr. 4, Prenzlauer Berg* ☎ *030/3462–4076* ⊕ *www.schnapskultur.de* ⊗ *Closed Sun.* Ⓜ *Senefelderplatz (U-bahn).*

MARKETS

Markt am Kollwitzplatz. One of the city's best farmers' markets sits on the pretty Kollwitzplatz square in Prenzlauer Berg. During its smaller Thursday and bustling Saturday markets, you'll not only find a superb selection of organic produce, meats, cheeses, and pantry items, but also an array of prepared foods and sellers offering handmade home goods and gifts. ⊠ *Kollwitzplatz, Prenzlauer Berg* ⊗ *Closed Mon.–Wed., Fri., and Sun.* Ⓜ *Senefelderplatz (U-bahn).*

NEUKÖLLN

Just over the canal from Kreuzberg, the neighborhood of Neukölln is home to a large Turkish population, and brims with Turkish shops, cafés, and restaurants, as well as a lovely weekly market. More and more of the city's young creatives are moving into this area, and it caters to their bohemian lifestyle with a number of secondhand and vintage shops.

CLOTHING

Let Them Eat Cake. A favorite of the vintage shoppers in Neukölln, this delightful shop offers a mixture of handmade pieces and high-quality secondhand clothing for him and her. ✉ *Weserstr. 164, Neukölln* ☎ *030/6096–5095* ⊕ *letthemeatcake-berlin.tumblr.com/* ⊙ *Closed Sun.* Ⓜ *Rathaus Neukölln (U-bahn).*

Sing Blackbird. This Kreuzkölln shop, located on the border between Kreuzberg and Neukölln, has become popular for its carefully edited collection of vintage finds, dating back to the 1960s and '70s. The shop also holds a monthly flea market, as well as occasional movie nights, and is home to a popular café, where a menu of homemade cakes and weekend vegan brunch is served on mismatched vintage china. ✉ *Sanderstr. 11, Neukölln* ☎ *030/5484–5051* Ⓜ *Schönleinstrasse (U-bahn).*

Vintage Galore. Imagine bringing the midcentury European look home with a walk through this shop, which features a collection of Scandinavian furniture and lamps. The shop also has a limited selection of clothing, bags, and accessories, as well as small housewares like teapots and ceramics, which should all fit more comfortably inside a suitcase. ✉ *Sanderstr. 12, Neukölln* ☎ *030/6396–3338* ⊕ *www.vintagegalore.de/* ⊙ *Closed Sun. and Mon.* Ⓜ *Schönleinstrasse (U-bahn).*

CHARLOTTENBURG

Although Ku'damm is still touted as the shopping mile of Berlin, many shops are ho-hum retailers. The best stretch for exclusive fashions, such as Louis Vuitton, Hermès, and Jil Sander, are the three blocks between Leibnizstrasse and Bleibtreustrasse. For home furnishings, gift items, and unusual clothing boutiques, follow this route off Ku'damm: Leibnizstrasse to Mommsenstrasse to Bleibtreustrasse, then on to the ring around Savignyplatz. Fasanenstrasse, Knesebeckstrasse, Schlüterstrasse, and Uhlandstrasse are also fun places to browse.

Ku'damm ends at Breitscheidplatz, but the door-to-door shopping continues along Tauentzienstrasse, which, in addition to international retail stores, offers continental Europe's largest department store, the upscale Kaufhaus des Westens, or KaDeWe.

BOOKSTORES

Fodor'sChoice ★ **Bucherbogen.** Peek under the rails of Charlottenburg's Savignyplatz and you'll find this much-loved bookstore. The large selection of books, many of them special editions or out of print, include numerous titles on art, design, and architecture, and the international offerings are extensive. ✉ *Stadtbahnbogen 593, Charlottenburg* ☎ *303/186–9511* ⊕ *www.buecherbogen.com* ⊙ *Closed Sun.* Ⓜ *Savignyplatz (S-bahn).*

CLOTHING

Cos. For wardrobe staples with a twist, this Swedish chain has something for everyone, from accessories, shoes, clothing, and even a section for the little ones. Their Charlottenburg location is just one of their many stores in Berlin. ⊠ *Kurfürstendamm 217, Charlottenburg* ☏ *030/8800–1987* ⊕ *www.cosstores.com* ⊙ *Closed Sun.* Ⓜ *Uhlandstrasse (U-bahn).*

Jil Sander. The flagship store of German designer Jil Sander carries the newest collections from this iconic, understated brand, including fashions for men. ⊠ *Kurfürstendamm 185, Charlottenburg* ☏ *030/886–7020* ⊕ *www.jilsander.com* ⊙ *Closed Sun.* Ⓜ *Adenauerplatz (U-bahn), Savignyplatz (S-bahn).*

Wunderkind. Potsdam's hometown hero, fashion designer Wolfgang Joop, brings his vibrant designs to Berlin at this Charlottenburg atelier. ⊠ *Kurfürstendamm 46, Charlottenburg* ☏ *030/2804–1817* ⊕ *wunderkind.com/* ⊙ *Closed Sun.* Ⓜ *Savignyplatz (S-bahn), Uhlandstrasse (U-bahn).*

DEPARTMENT STORES

Fodor'sChoice ★ **Kaufhaus des Westens** (*KaDeWe*). The largest department store in continental Europe, classy Kaufhaus des Westens (KaDeWe) has a grand selection of goods, spread over seven floors, as well as food and deli counters, champagne bars, beer bars, a beautiful art deco–style atrium café, and for men, a newly opened "sneaker hall"—a 2,000-square-foot space offering the latest in urban footwear. The wealth of services offered here includes luxury gift basket arrangements, exclusive travel guides, and an international box office. ⊠ *Tauentzienstr. 21–24, Charlottenburg* ☏ *030/21210* ⊕ *www.kadewe.de* ⊙ *Closed Sun.* Ⓜ *Wittenbergplatz (U-bahn).*

FOOD

Fodor'sChoice ★ **Paper & Tea.** Enter this serene shop just off Kantstrasse and you'll be stepping into a world of high-quality loose-leaf teas. Rather than bulk up on inventory, the stylish store has a restrained selection of 70 teas, all displayed in museumlike cases, where you can smell the wares. There are two tasting areas, where expert attendants brew and explain the teas. There is also a newly opened Mitte shop on Alte Schönhauser Strasse. ⊠ *Bleibtreust. 4, Charlottenburg* ☏ *030/9561–5468* ⊕ *www. paperandtea.com* ⊙ *Closed Sun.* Ⓜ *Savignyplatz (S-bahn).*

Fodor'sChoice ★ **Wald Königsberger Marzipan.** This third-generation artisan shop offers a taste of the old-world treat marzipan, using a family recipe that dates back to the turn of the 20th century. The vintage-style shop features candy-striped wall paper, vintage tools, and rows of handmade marzipan, all wrapped in delicate packaging. ⊠ *Pestalozzistr. 54a, Charlottenburg* ☏ *030/323–8254* ⊕ *www.wald-koenigsberger-marzipan.de* ⊙ *Closed Sun.* Ⓜ *Sophie-Charlotte-Platz (U-bahn).*

GIFTS AND SOUVENIRS

Harry Lehmann. If you want a taste—or rather, a smell—of old Berlin, head to Harry Lehmann on Kantstrasse in Charlottenburg. The shopkeeper will greet you in a white lab coat, helpfully explaining the origin and inspiration of the expertly mixed perfumes, which fill large apothecary jars along a mirrored wall. This is definitely old-school—the shop

15

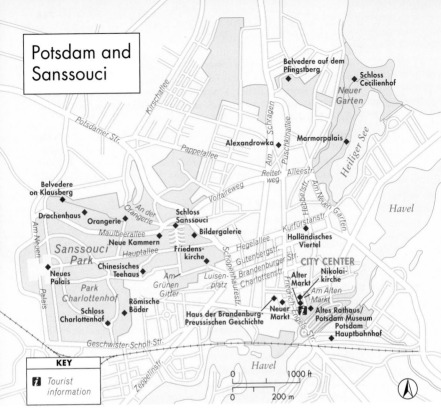

Potsdam and Sanssouci

KEY

ℹ Tourist information

---

was opened in 1926. Scents are fresh, simple, and clean, and a 30 ml bottle (€15.50) makes for a reasonably priced gift or souvenir. ✉ *Kant-str. 106, Charlottenburg* ☎ *030/324–3582* ⊕ *www.parfum-individual. de* ⊗ *Closed Sun.* Ⓜ *Wilmersdorfer Strasse (U-bahn), Berlin-Charlottenburg (S-bahn).*

Königliche Porzellan Manufaktur. Fine porcelain is still produced by Königliche Porzellan Manufaktur, the former Royal Porcelain Manufactory for the Prussians, also called KPM. You can buy this delicate handmade, hand-painted china at KPM's manufactory, where you can learn about the brand's rich history, as well as purchase products directly, with the option to find seconds at reduced prices. ✉ *Wegelystr. 1, Tiergarten* ☎ *030/3900–9215* ⊕ *de-de.kpm-berlin.com/* ⊗ *Closed Sun.* Ⓜ *Tiergarten (S-bahn).*

MALLS

Bikini Berlin. At this experimental "concept mall," which opened in 2014, you can shop well-known international brands or browse through the rotating roster of young labels in the center's pop-up "boxes." The building used to have an open-air middle floor separating the top and ground levels, giving the appearance of a bikini, hence the name. ✉ *Budapester Str. 38–50, Charlottenburg* ☎ *030/5549–6454* ⊕ *www.bikiniberlin.de* ⊗ *Closed Sun.* Ⓜ *Zoologischer Garten (S-bahn and U-bahn).*

SIDE TRIP TO POTSDAM

Updated by
Giulia Pines

A trip to Berlin wouldn't be complete without paying a visit to Potsdam and its park, which surrounds the important Prussian palaces Neues Palais and Sanssouci. This separate city, the state capital of Brandenburg (the state surrounding Berlin), can be reached within a half hour from Berlin's Zoo Station and most major Berlin S-bahn stations.

Potsdam still retains the imperial character it earned during the many years it served as a royal residence and garrison quarters. The Alter Markt and Neuer Markt show off stately Prussian architecture, and both are easily reached from the main train station by any tram heading into the town center.

GETTING HERE AND AROUND

Potsdam is 20 km (12 miles) southwest of Berlin's center and a half-hour journey by car or bus. From Zoo Station to Potsdam's main train station, the regional train RE-1 takes 17 minutes, and the S-bahn Line No. 7 takes about 30 minutes; use an ABC zone ticket for either service. City traffic is heavy, so a train journey is recommended. Several Berlin tour operators have Potsdam trips.

15

There are several tours that include Potsdam (most are two or six hours). They leave from the landing across from Berlin's Wannsee S-bahn station between late March and early October. Depending on the various tours on offer, a round-trip ticket costs €7.50–€23.

ESSENTIALS

Visitor Information Potsdam Tourist Office. ⊠ *Touristenzentrum Potsdam, Brandenburgerstr. 3, at Brandenburger Tor Potsdam* ☎ *0331/275–580* ⊕ *www. potsdamtourismus.de.*

EXPLORING

CITY CENTER

Most visitors to Potsdam come for the castles, but the town itself is picturesque, elegant, and compact enough to be explored in an hour or two. It contains both Alter Markt (Old Market) and Neuer Markt (New Market) squares, which show off stately Prussian architecture, while the Holländisches Viertel (Dutch Quarter) is home to a collection of redbrick, gable-roofed buildings, many of which now house popular restaurants, boutiques, and cafés. Friedrich-Ebert-Strasse, the town's main thoroughfare, is full of coffee shops and restaurants, and Brandenburger Strasse, the pedestrian walking street, often has outdoor café seating and street musicians. Leafy Hegelallee, to the north, with its tree-lined central pedestrian strip, is where you will find Potsdam's historic gates. Potsdam's city center is easily reached by foot or tram from the main train station.

Alter Markt (*Old Market Square*). The "Old Market" square is the hub of Potsdam's historical center and was home to the city's baroque palace for three centuries. The area was heavily damaged by Allied bombing in World War II and then further destroyed by the East German regime in 1960. After reunification, Potsdam decided to rebuild its palace, and the re-created structure, with a combination of modern and historic elements, has housed the state parliament since 2013. Thanks to private donors, a magnificent replica of the Fortunaportal, or Fortune's Gate, now stands proudly at the center of the square.

A gilded figure of Atlas tops the tower of the **Altes Rathaus** (Old City Hall), built in 1755 in the model of an Italian palazzo, its dome meant to mimic the Pantheon's in Rome. A modern structure joins the Altes Rathaus with a neighboring building designed by Sanssouci architect Georg Wenzeslaus von Knobelsdorff, simply referred to as the Knobelsdorffhaus. Together, the one new and two old structures house the **Potsdam Museum**, with its large collection of paintings, photographs, and historical objects, and the Potsdam Forum, a cultural center.

Karl Friedrich Schinkel designed the Alter Markt's domed **Nikolaikirche** (St. Nicholas Church), which was also heavily damaged in the war and only reopened in 1981 after extensive renovations. In front of it stands an Egyptian obelisk also erected by von Knobelsdorff. ⊠ *Alter Markt.*

Holländisches Viertel. The center of the small Holländisches Viertel—the Dutch Quarter—is an easy walk north along Friedrich-Ebert-Strasse to Mittelstrasse. Friedrich Wilhelm I built the settlement in the 1730s to entice Dutch artisans who would be able to support the city's rapid growth. The 134 gabled, mansard-roof brick houses make up the largest Dutch housing development outside of the Netherlands today. Antiques shops, boutiques, and restaurants fill the buildings now, and the area is one of Potsdam's most visited. ⊠ *Potsdam.*

Neuer Markt (*New Market Square*). Neuer Markt (New Market) square has baroque-style architecture similar to that of the Alter Markt square and a handful of the city's best-preserved buildings, some of which date back to the 18th century. In the former royal stables at the west side of the square, the **Haus der Brandenburg-Preussischen Geschichte** (House of Brandenburg-Prussian History), is both a museum and a cultural center, with exhibitions that delve into the past and present of both the city and the region (€4.50, Tues.–Thurs. 10–5, Fri.–Sun. 10–6; 0331/620–8550; www.hbpg.de). At the center of the square is a squat, pink structure built on the site of a **grain weighing station** in the 18th century: the newer incarnation was built in the 19th century, and today houses a restaurant, fittingly named Waage or "Scales." ⊠ *Am Neuen Markt 9* 🏠.

NEED A BREAK?

Wiener Restaurant. Fine coffee blends and rich cakes are available at Wiener Restaurant, an old-style European coffeehouse on Luisenplatz, steps from the Grünes Gitter entrance to Sanssouci. ⊠ *Luisenpl. 4* ☎ *0331/6014–9904* ⊕ *www.wiener-potsdam.de.*

OFF THE BEATEN PATH

Alexandrowka. If you take Tram 92 to Neuer Garten, you'll pass by an unusual sight: a cluster of intricately carved wooden houses that look like something out of *Dr. Zhivago*. This is the so-called "Russian Colony," built by Frederick Wilhelm III to commemorate the death of his close friend, Czar Alexander I and to house Russian singers who were sent over to be part of the First Prussian Regiment of the Guards. It was modeled after St. Petersburg's Glasovo artist village, and today is a UNESCO World Heritage site. The park, which consists of 13 wooden houses laid out along a diagonal cross, was designed by Peter Joseph Lenné, who is also responsible for some of the most beautiful landscaped parks in and around Berlin. There is also a small museum that tells the history of the settlement. Stop in at Alexandrowka on your way to, or from, Neuer Garten. ⊠ *Russische Kolonie 2* ☎ *49/331 8170203* ⌨ *Museum €3.50* ☉ *Museum Mar.–Dec., Tues.–Sun. 10–6.*

SANSSOUCI PARK

Fodor'sChoice
★

The main attraction for Potsdam visitors, the sprawling Sanssouci Park has been a World Heritage Site since 1990. The former summer residence of the Prussian royals, the park is home to numerous palaces, landscaped gardens, and eye-catching architecture. Your best bet is to hop on Bus 695, which stops right outside the train station and will get you to the park in 10 minutes. Otherwise it's about a half-hour walk.

Neues Palais (*New Palace*). The **Neues Palais**, a larger and grander palace than Sanssouci, stands at the end of the long avenue that runs through Sanssouci Park. It was built after the Seven Years' War (1756–63), when Frederick loosened his purse strings. It is said he wanted to demonstrate that the state coffers hadn't been depleted too severely by the long conflict. Impressive interiors include the Grotto Hall with walls and columns set with shells, coral, and other aquatic decorations. The royals' upper apartments have paintings by 17th-century Italian masters. You can tour the palace yourself, with an audio guide, from April through October; the rest of the year you must be accompanied by a tour guide; the cost is €8 for either option.

If you reach the Neues Palais by foot from Sanssouci, you'll pass some other ornate structures on the way: The **Chinesisches Teehaus** (Chinese Teahouse, €2) was erected in 1754 in a Chinese style that was all the rage at the time. It houses porcelain from Meissen and Asia. The curious **Drachenhaus** or "Dragonhouse" was modeled in 1770 after the Pagoda at London's Kew Gardens and named for the gargoyles ornamenting the roof corners. It now houses a popular restaurant and café. The two-story **Belvedere on Klausberg** (€2) is impressively situated at the top of a hill, at the end of a tree-lined boulevard which starts at the Orangerie near Sanssouci and then juts northwest. There's not much to see inside but the lookout over the park is lovely. ⊠ *Sanssouci Park* ☎ *0331/969–4200* ⊕ *www.spsg.de.*

Schloss Charlottenhof. After Frederick the Great died in 1786, the ambitious Sanssouci building program ground to a halt, and the park fell into neglect. It was 50 years before another Prussian king, Friedrich Wilhelm IV, restored Sanssouci's earlier glory, engaging the great Berlin architect Karl Friedrich Schinkel to build the small Schloss Charlottenhof for the crown prince. Schinkel's demure interiors are preserved, and the most fanciful room is the bedroom, decorated like a Roman tent, with walls and ceiling draped in striped canvas.

15

Friedrich Wilhelm IV also commissioned the Römische Bäder (Roman Baths), about a five-minute walk north of Schloss Charlottenhof. It was also designed by Schinkel, and built between 1829 and 1840. Like many other structures in Potsdam, this one is more romantic than authentic. Half Italian villa, half Greek temple, it is nevertheless a charming addition to the park. ⊠ *Geschwister-Scholl-Str. 34a* ☎ *0331/969–4228* 🖃 *Schloss Charlottenhof €4 with guided tour; Roman Baths €5; combination ticket €8.*

Fodor's Choice
★

Schloss Sanssouci. Prussia's most famous king, Friedrich II—Frederick the Great—spent more time at his summer residence, **Schloss Sanssouci**, than in the capital of Berlin. Its name means "without a care" in French, the language Frederick cultivated in his own private circle and within the court. Some experts believe that Frederick actually named the palace "Sans, Souci," which they translate as "with and without a care," a more apt name, since its construction caused him a lot of trouble and expense, and sparked furious rows with his master builder, Georg Wenzeslaus von Knobelsdorff. His creation nevertheless became one of Germany's greatest tourist attractions.

Executed according to Frederick's impeccable French-influenced taste, the palace, which lies on the northeastern edge of Sanssouci Park, was built between 1745 and 1747. It is extravagantly rococo, with scarcely a patch of wall left unadorned. Be advised that during peak tourist months, timed tickets for Schloss Sanssouci tours (€12) can sell out before noon. Combined tickets for all park sights cost €19 and can be booked in advance online.

Just east of the palace sits the **Bildergalerie** or "Picture Gallery" (€6), which displays Frederick II's collection of 17th-century Italian and Dutch paintings, including works by Caravaggio, Rubens, and Van Dyck. The main cupola contains expensive marble from Siena. To the west of the palace are the **Neue Kammern** or "New Chambers," which began as a greenhouse and then hosted guests of the king's family (€4 with guided tour only).

Farther west, the **Orangerie** was completed in 1864; its two massive towers linked by a colonnade evoke an Italian Renaissance palace. Today it houses more than 50 copies of paintings by Raphael, (€4 with guided tour, €2 tower only).

From Schloss Sanssouci, you can wander down the extravagant terraced gardens, filled with climbing grapevines, trellises, and fountains to reach the Italianate **Friedenskirche** or "Peace Church," which was completed in 1854, and houses a 13th-century Byzantine mosaic taken from an island near Venice. ⊠ *Park Sanssouci* ☎ *0331/969–4200* ⊕ *www.spsg.de.*

NEUER GARTEN

Just north of the city center, the Neuer Garten (New Garden) is along the west shore of the Heiliger See (Holy Lake), with beautiful views. The park is home to the Marmorpalais (Marble Palace) and Schloss Cecilienhof, the last palace built by the Prussian Hohenzollern family.

To get here from the Potsdam train station, take Tram 92 and then walk 10 to 15 minutes; another option is to take a taxi.

Belvedere auf dem Pfingstberg. Commissioned by King Friedrich Wilhelm IV, the Belvedere on Pfingstberg was built in the Italian Renaissance style with grand staircases, colonnades, and perfect symmetry. It served as a pleasure palace and lofty observation platform for the royals, and the towers still offer one of the best views of Potsdam. Nearby is the Pomona Temple, the first work of the soon-to-be-famous architect Karl Friedrich Schinkel, who built it at the tender age of 19. ⊠ *Am Pfingstberg* ☎ *0331/2005–7930* ⊕ *www.pfingstberg.de* ⊠ *€4* ☉ *Belvedere towers Apr., May, Sept., and Oct., daily 10–6; June–Aug., daily 10–8; Mar. and Nov., weekends 10–4.*

Schloss Cecilienhof (*Cecilienhof Palace*). Resembling a rambling Tudor manor house, Schloss Cecilienhof was built for Crown Prince Wilhelm in 1913, on what was then the newly laid-out stretch of park called the Neuer Garten. It was here, in the last palace built by the Hohenzollerns, that the leaders of the allied forces—Stalin, Truman, and Churchill (later Attlee)—hammered out the fate of postwar Germany at the 1945 Potsdam Conference. From Potsdam's main train station, take Tram 92 to Reiterweg/Alleestrasse, then transfer to Bus 603 to Schloss Cecilienhof, or walk 15 minutes. ⊠ *Im Neuen Garten 11* ☎ *0331/969–4244, 0331/969–4200* ⊕ *www.spsg.de* ⊠ *€6 with tour (Nov.–Mar. tour is mandatory), €4 tour of royal couple's private apartments* ☉ *Apr.–Oct., Tues.–Sun. 10–6; Nov.–Mar., Tues.–Sun. 10–5. Tours of the private apartments at 10, noon, 2, 4.*

WHERE TO EAT

$$
GERMAN
✕ **Der Butt.** Potsdam is surrounded by lakes and rivers so the fish served here is almost always local—try the rainbow trout or the eel, fresh from the Havel River; the house beer is brewed in Potsdam. It's just a block from the busy pedestrian shopping area, and has a casual, friendly atmosphere that makes this an excellent spot for a light meal. $ *Average main: €17* ⊠ *Gutenbergstr. 25* ☎ *0331/200–6066* ⊕ *www.der-butt. de* ▭ *No credit cards.*

$$
FRENCH
✕ **Restaurant Juliette.** Potsdam is proud of its past French influences, and the highly praised French food at this intimate restaurant on the edge of the Dutch Quarter is served in a lovely space, with brick walls and a fireplace. The menu offers small portions of dishes such as rack of lamb, quail with roasted chanterelles, and a starter plate of seasonal foie-gras preparations. The wine list of 120 French vintages is unique for the Berlin area. Chef Ralph Junick has cornered the market in Potsdam, with four other French restaurants, including a creperie and a café. $ *Average main: €20* ⊠ *Jägerstr. 39* ☎ *0331/270–1791* ⊕ *www. restaurant-juliette.de* ☉ *Closed Tues.*

$$$
GERMAN
✕ **Speckers Landhaus.** This restored Tudor-style cottage is a 10-minute walk from the town center, and well worth a visit for its charming historic architecture and relaxing, farmhouse-style dining room. The menu is unfailingly local, emphasizing produce like white asparagus

in spring and pumpkin in fall. Daily dishes include house-made pastas, local game, and German specialties. The three-course lunch for €18 is a great deal. There are also three spacious guest rooms, each of which accommodates up to four people, decorated in a simple, country-home style. [$] *Average main: €25* ✉ *Jägerallee 13* ☎ *0331/280–4311* 🌐 *www.speckers.de.*

SAXONY,
SAXONY-ANHALT,
AND THURINGIA

WELCOME TO SAXONY, SAXONY-ANHALT, AND THURINGIA

TOP REASONS TO GO

★ **Following Martin Luther:** Trace the path of the ultimate medieval rebel in Wittenberg, Erfurt, Eisenach, and the Wartburg, and gain valuable insight into the mind and culture of a person whose ideas helped change the world. Germany will celebrate 500 years of the Reformation in 2017; look out for special events.

★ **Frauenkirche in Dresden:** Rising like a majestic baroque phoenix, the church is a worthy symbol of a city destroyed and rebuilt from its ashes.

★ **Görlitz:** This architectural gem is relatively undiscovered; you'll feel as if you have the whole town to yourself.

★ **Weimar:** The history of Germany seems to revolve around this small town, whose past residents include Goethe, Schiller, Bach, Liszt, and Gropius.

★ **Wine tasting in the Salle-Unstrut:** The castle-topped, rolling hills covered in terraced vineyards are perfect for biking, hiking, and horseback riding.

1 Saxony. The pearl of eastern Germany, Saxony's countryside is dotted with beautifully renovated castles and fortresses, and the people are charming and full of energy. (They also speak in an almost incomprehensible local dialect.) Dresden and Leipzig are cosmopolitan centers that combine the energy of the avant-garde with a distinct respect for tradition.

2 Saxony-Anhalt. Although long ignored by travelers, Saxony-Anhalt has more UNESCO World Heritage sites than any other region in Europe. The

GETTING ORIENTED

These three states cover the southeastern part of the former East Germany, and the area holds Germany's most historical and beautiful cities. It is increasingly difficult to find the dirty, depressing towns of the Communist past. Over 25 years of reconstruction programs and almost €3 trillion transformed the area, restoring its former glory. Dresden revels in its reputation as "the Florence on the Elbe," and just downstream Meissen has undergone an impressive face-lift. Weimar, one of the continent's old cultural centers, and Leipzig, in particular, are thriving cultural magnets, bustling with sparkling historic city centers. Görlitz, Germany's easternmost city, benefited from an infusion of cash and is consistently lauded as one of the country's 10 most beautiful cities.

16

city of Naumburg is famed for its cathedral and for the wines produced in the surrounding vineyards.

3 Thuringia. Of all the eastern German states, Thuringia has the best travel infrastructure. Visitors to the classical jewel of Weimar and those interested

in outdoor sports in the lush Thuringian Forest flock to the area, much as they have for centuries. Thuringia offers unparalleled natural sights as well as classical culture at reasonable prices.

FOLLOWING MARTIN LUTHER

Saxony-Anhalt and Thuringia are currently celebrating the "Luther decade," preparing to mark the Protestant Reformation's 500th anniversary in 2017. A drive between the *Lutherstädte* (Luther Cities) allows for a deeper understanding of Martin Luther and the Reformation.

(above) Lutherhaus in Eisenach, where he lived as a student. (upper right) Martin Luther. (lower right) Memorial for Martin Luther in Eisleben.

Dissatisfaction was already brewing, but Martin Luther (1483–1546) was the first German to speak out against the Catholic Church. His 95 Theses, which he brashly nailed to a church door, called for a return to faith in the Bible's teachings over papal decrees, and an end to the sale of indulgences (letters from the pope purchased by wealthy Christians to absolve them of sins). Luther's greatest feat was translating the Bible into German, making it accessible to everyone who could read. His translation united the German dialects into the High German that almost everyone speaks today. Despite such so-called heretical beginnings, Luther overcame condemnation by the pope and other authorities. He continued to preach, building a family with Katharina von Bora, a former nun he married after "rescuing" her from a convent. After his death, Lutheranism spread across Europe as an accepted branch of Christianity.

LUTHER QUOTES

"I am more afraid of my own heart than of the pope and all his cardinals. I have within me the great pope, Self."

"When the Devil...sees men use violence to propagate the gospel, he...says with malignant looks and frightful grin: 'Ah, how wise these madmen are to play my game! Let them go on; I shall reap the benefit...'"

ON THE TRAIL OF MARTIN LUTHER

Start in the town of Wittenberg, the unofficial capital of the Reformation. The comprehensive **Lutherhaus** museum is in the Augustinian monastery where Luther lived twice, first as a monk and later with his family. This multilevel, bilingual museum will convince the skeptics that Luther is worth remembering. From the museum, it's a short walk down the main thoroughfare Collegienstrasse to two churches that felt the influence of his teachings. The first is **Stadtkirche St. Marien** (Parish Church of St. Mary), where Luther often preached. The second, **Schlosskirche** (Castle Church), is where Luther changed history by posting his 95 Theses. The original wooden doors were destroyed in a 1760 fire, now replaced by bronze doors with the Latin text of the 95 Theses. On the way from one church to the other, stop to admire the statues of Luther and his friend and collaborator Philipp Melanchthon—they are buried next to each other in Schlosskirche.

In the nearby town of Eisleben, the houses where Luther was born, the **Luthers Geburtshaus**, and died, **Luthers Sterbehaus,** lie 10 minutes from each other. From there, it's easy to spot the steeples of two churches: **St. Petri-Pauli-Kirche** (*Church of Sts. Peter and Paul*) and **St. Andreaskirche** (*St. Andrew's Church*). The first was Luther's place of baptism, while the second houses the pulpit where Luther gave his last four sermons. His funeral was also held here before his body was taken back to Wittenberg.

Continuing southwest the stunning medieval castle **Wartburg** is in the hills high above the town of Eisenach. Luther took refuge here after he was excommunicated by the pope and outlawed by a general assembly called the Diet of Worms, famously translating the New Testament from the original Greek into German.

REFORMATION TIMELINE

1517: Luther nails his 95 Theses to Wittenberg's Schlosskirche.

1521: Refusing to recant, Luther is excommunicated.

1537: Denmark's Christian III declares Lutheranism the state religion, leading to its spread in Scandinavia.

1555: Charles V signs Peace of Augsburg, ending open hostilities between Catholicism and Lutheranism and granting the latter official status. Due to the rise of Calvinism, conflict bubbles under the surface.

1558: Queen Elizabeth I of England supports the establishment of the English Protestant Church.

1577: The Formula of Concord ends disputes between sects, strengthening and preserving Lutheranism.

1618: Religious tensions explode in Bohemia, thrusting Europe into the Thirty Years' War. At war's end, much of Central Europe is in ruins, with 40%–70% of people dead.

1650s and beyond: Lutheran explorers and settlers bring their beliefs to the New World.

16

BAUHAUS IN WEIMAR

(above) Bauhaus Museum in Weimar. (upper right) Bauhaus Building in Dessau.

Begun in Weimar, the Bauhaus movement's futuristic design, "form from function" mentality, and revolutionary spirit have inspired artists worldwide.

Founded in 1919 by architect Walter Gropius, the Bauhaus movement had roots in the past but was also unabashedly modern. Based on the principles of William Morris and the Arts and Crafts movement, Bauhaus promoted the idea of creation as a service to society: art should permeate daily life, and the Bauhaus transformed practical objects such as a chair, teapot, or lamp into true works of art. Its style was art deco but less ornate, machine age but not industrial, its goal to put both spaces and materials to their most natural and economical uses. Although the Bauhaus school was shut down by the Nazis in the early 1930s, many former Bauhaus students left Germany and went to work in other parts of the world. Today, their influence can even be seen as far away as Tel Aviv, where Jewish architects fleeing Europe came to build their vision of a modern city.

—Giulia Pines

BAUHAUS IN DESSAU

If you have an extra day, take the train to Dessau, Bauhaus's second city, to see the iconic **Bauhaus Building,** adorned on one side with vertical block lettering spelling out "Bauhaus." Still an architecture school, it now houses the Bauhaus Dessau Foundation, and a multilevel Bauhaus Museum. You can even stay in the monastic Bauhaus studio flats here.

A BAUHAUS WALK IN WEIMAR

Start with the **Bauhaus Museum** in Weimar's central Theaterplatz, which offers a film about the history of Bauhaus and rotating exhibitions covering much of what there is to see in Weimar. Head south along Schützengasse and continue down Amalienstrasse to catch a glimpse of the Henry van de Velde–designed main building of **Bauhaus University**, formerly the Grand Ducal School of Arts and Crafts. A faithful reconstruction of Gropius's office can be found here as well. The **Bauhaus Atelier** at the university is a central meeting place for students. It contains a café and shop offering books about the movement as well as Bauhaus-designed souvenirs, and also marks the starting point for university-run Bauhaus walks. Head just south for the Gropius-designed **Monument to the March Dead** in Weimar's **Historischer Friedhof** (Historical Cemetery). This jagged expressionist structure, built in 1921, commemorates those who died in the Kapp Putsch, an attempt to overthrow the Weimar Republic a year earlier. Follow the signs for **Goethes Gartenhaus** (perhaps the most visited historical structure in Weimar) through the Park on the Ilm, and look just beyond it for the **Haus am Horn**. This modest, cubical structure designed by Georg Muche for the 1923 Bauhaus exhibition was meant to be a model of Bauhaus's functional philosophy. It was fully restored in 1999 to mark the 80th anniversary of the founding of Bauhaus.

STYLE ELEMENTS

According to the standards of Bauhaus, good design should be accompanied by good engineering. That's why so many Bauhaus buildings still look strikingly modern, even industrial, even though they may have been designed as early as the 1920s. Bauhaus's timelessness results from its use of three basic shapes—square, circle, and triangle—and three basic colors—red, blue, and yellow. To spot its influence, look for unadorned, **boxlike structures** with repeating parallel lines, **flat roofs,** and rectangular windowpanes. Furniture and household objects feature strong lines, retro-futuristic shapes, and the abundant use of **metals.** Bauhaus designers also revolutionized typography: the sign on the Bauhaus Building in Dessau is a prime example: look for **clear, boxy typefaces,** often combined collagelike with photographs and **colorful graphics** and shapes to create bold messages. The Swedish furniture chain IKEA owes a lot to Bauhaus.

16

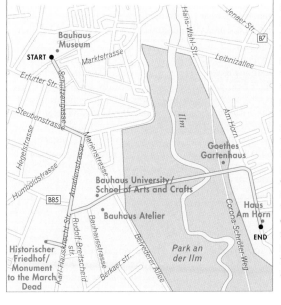

Updated by
Lee A. Evans

Germany's traditional charm is most evident in the eastern states of Saxony, Saxony-Anhalt, and Thuringia. Although the area formed the cultural core of the former East Germany, rolling hills, terraced vinyards, and wonderfully restored cities speak to an area reborn and reestablished as the German heartland. The region can be a little gritty at times, but a uniquely unspoiled German state of mind predominates.

Eastern Germans resolutely cling to their German heritage. They proudly preserve their connections with such national heroes as Luther, Goethe, Schiller, Bach, Handel, Wagner, and the Hungarian-born Liszt. Towns in the regions of the Thüringer Wald (Thuringian Forest) or the Harz Mountains—long considered the haunt of witches—are drenched in history and medieval legend. The area hides a fantastic collection of rural villages and castles unparalleled in other parts of the country.

Many cities, such as Erfurt, escaped World War II relatively unscathed, and the East Germans extensively rebuilt towns damaged by bombing. Although historical city centers were faithfully restored to their past glory, there are also plenty of eyesores of industrialization and stupendously bland housing projects, which the Germans refer to as *Bausünden* (architectural sins). Famous palaces and cultural wonders—the rebuilt historical center of Dresden, the Wartburg at Eisenach, the Schiller and Goethe houses in Weimar, Luther's Wittenberg, as well as the wonderfully preserved city of Görlitz—are waiting to have their subtle and extravagant charms discovered.

PLANNING

WHEN TO GO

Winters in this part of Germany can be cold, wet, and dismal, so unless you plan to ski in the Harz Mountains or the Thüringer Wald, visit in late spring, summer, or early autumn. Avoid Leipzig at trade-fair times, particularly in March and April. In summer every city, town, and village has a festival, with streets blocked and local culture spilling out into every open space.

GETTING HERE AND AROUND

AIR TRAVEL

It's easiest, and usually cheapest, to fly into Berlin or Frankfurt and rent a car from there. Dresden and Leipzig both have international airports that are primarily operated by budget carriers serving European destinations. Dresden Flughafen is about 10 km (6 miles) north of Dresden, and Leipzig's Flughafen Leipzig-Halle is 12 km (8 miles) northwest of the city.

Airport Contacts Dresden Flughafen. ⊠ *Flughafenstr., Dresden* ☎ *0351/881– 3360* ⊕ *www.dresden-airport.de.* **Flughafen Leipzig-Halle.** ⊠ *Termanalring 11, Schkeuditz* ☎ *0341/224–1155* ⊕ *www.leipzig-halle-airport.de.*

BUS TRAVEL

Long-distance buses travel to Dresden and Leipzig. Bus service within the area is infrequent and mainly connects with rail lines. Check schedules carefully at central train stations or call the service phone number of Deutsche Bahn (German Railway) at local railway stations.

CAR TRAVEL

Expressways connect Berlin with Dresden (A-13) and Leipzig (A-9). Both journeys take about two hours. The A-4 stretches east–west across the southern portion of Thuringia and Saxony.

A road-construction program in eastern Germany is ongoing, and you should expect traffic delays on any journey of more than 300 km (186 miles). The Bundesstrassen throughout eastern Germany are narrow, tree-lined country roads, often jammed with traffic. Roads in the western part of the Harz Mountains are better and wider.

Cars can be rented at the Dresden and Leipzig airports, at train stations, and through all major hotels. Be aware that you are not allowed to take rentals into Poland or the Czech Republic.

TRAIN TRAVEL

The fastest and least expensive way to explore the region is by train. East Germany's rail infrastructure is exceptional; trains serve even the most remote destinations with astonishing frequency. Slower S, RB, and RE trains link smaller towns, while Leipzig, Dresden, Weimar, Erfurt, Naumburg, and Wittenberg are all on major InterCity Express (ICE) lines. Some cities—Dresden and Meissen, for example—are linked by commuter trains.

From Dresden a round-trip ticket to Leipzig costs about €43 (a 1½-hour journey one way); to Görlitz it's about €38 (a 1½-hour ride). Trains connect Leipzig with Halle (a 30-minute ride, €10), Erfurt (a 1-hour ride, €28), and Eisenach (a 1½-hour journey, €28). The train ride between Dresden and Eisenach (2½ hours) costs €56 one way.

■TIP➡ Consider using a Länder-Ticket: a €23 (plus €4 per person up to five people) regional day ticket from the German Railroad that covers local train travel in the respective state (for example, within Saxony, Saxony-Anhalt, or Thuringia).

16

Train Contacts **German Railroad (Deutsche Bahn).** ☎ *0180/599–6633* ⊕ *www.bahn.de.*

TOURS

With two luxury ships, Viking K–D operates a full program of cruises on the Elbe River, from Hamburg as far as Prague. They run up to eight days from mid-April until late October. All the historic cities of Saxony and Thuringia are ports of call—including Dresden, Meissen, Wittenberg, and Dessau. There are also popular narrow-gauge train tours.

Harzer Schmalspurbahnen GmbH. The famous steam locomotive *Harzquerbahn* connects Nordhausen-Nord with Wernigerode and Gernerode in the Harz Mountains. The most popular track of this line is the *Brockenbahn*, a special narrow-gauge train transporting tourists to the top of northern Germany's highest mountain. See website for schedule and further information. ⊠ *Friedrichstr. 151, Wernigerode* ☎ *03943/5580* ⊕ *www.hsb-wr.de.*

Lössnitzgrundbahn. In Saxony, historic narrow-gauge trains still operate on a regular schedule. The *Lössnitzgrundbahn*, which connects Ost-Radebeul-Ost and Radeburg is perfect for taking in some of Saxony's romantic countryside. A round-trip ticket is between about €7 and €11, depending on the length of the ride. For schedule and information, contact Deutsche Bahn's regional Dresden office. ⊠ *Geyersdorfer Str. 32, Annaberg-Buchholz* ☎ *0351/46165–63684* ⊕ *www. loessnitzgrundbahn.de* ☑ *From €7.*

Sächsische Dampfschiffahrt. Weisse Flotte's historic paddle-steam tours depart from and stop in Dresden, Meissen, Pirna, Pillnitz, Königsstein, and Bad Schandau. Besides tours in the Dresden area, boats also go into the Czech Republic. ⊠ *Hertha-Lindner-Str. 10, Dresden* ☎ *0351/866–090* ⊕ *www.saechsische-dampfschiffahrt.de* ☑ *From €16.*

Weiseritztalbahn. These tours are perfect for railway enthusiasts: take a tour on this historic narrow-gauge railroad. ⊠ *Dresdner Str. 280, Freital* ☎ *0351/641–2701* ⊕ *www.weiseritztalbahn.de* ☑ *From €7.*

RESTAURANTS

Enterprising young managers and chefs are well established in the East, so look for new, usually small, trendy restaurants. People in the region are extremely particular about their traditional food (rumor has it that one can be deported for roasting Mützbraten over anything other than birch). Some new creative chefs successfully blend contemporary regional German with international influences. Medieval-theme restaurants and "experience dining," complete with entertainment, are all the rage in the East, and, despite being often quite kitschy, warrant at least one try. As the region slowly rediscovers its tremendous beer heritage, microbreweries and brewpubs have sprouted up in almost every city. Pubs are a good bet for meeting locals.

Prices in the reviews are the average cost of a main course at dinner, or if dinner is not served, at lunch.

HOTELS

Hotels in eastern Germany are up to international standards and, due to economic subsidies in the 1990s, often far outshine their West German counterparts. In the East it's quite normal to have a major international hotel in a 1,000-year-old house or restored mansion. Smaller and family-run hotels are more charming local options, and often include a good restaurant. Most big hotels offer special weekend or activity-oriented packages that aren't found in the western part of the country. All hotels include breakfast, unless indicated otherwise.

During the trade fairs and shows of the **Leipziger Messe,** particularly in March and April, most Leipzig hotels increase their prices.

Prices in the reviews are the lowest cost of a standard double room in high season. For expanded reviews, facilities, and current deals, visit Fodors.com.

WHAT IT COSTS IN EUROS			
$	$$	$$$	$$$$
Restaurants	under €15	€15–€20	€21–€25	over €25
Hotels	under €100	€100–€175	€176–€225	over €225

16

PLANNING YOUR TIME

Eastern Germany is a small, well-connected region that's well suited for day trips. Dresden and Leipzig are the largest cities with the most facilities, making them good bases from which to explore the surrounding countryside, either by car or train. Both are well connected with Berlin, Munich, and Frankfurt. Leipzig, Dresden, Lutherstadt-Wittenberg, and Dessau can be explored as day trips from Berlin. Dresden is also a perfect stop for the day on the train from Berlin to Prague. Any of the smaller towns offer a quieter, possibly more authentic look at the area. A trip into the Salle-Unstrut wine region is well worth the time, using Naumburg as a base.

DISCOUNTS AND DEALS

Most of the region's larger cities offer special tourist exploring cards, such as the **Dresdencard, Hallecard, Leipzigcard,** and **Weimarcard,** which include discounts at museums, concerts, hotels, and restaurants or special sightseeing packages for up to three days. For details, check with the local visitor-information office.

SAXONY

The people of Saxony identify themselves more as Saxon than German. Their hardworking and rustic attitudes, their somewhat peripheral location on the border with the Czech Republic and Poland, and their almost incomprehensible dialect are the targets of endless jokes and puns. However, Saxon pride rebuilt three cities magnificently: Dresden and Leipzig—the showcase cities of eastern Germany—and the smaller town of Görlitz, on the Neisse River.

LEIPZIG

184 km (114 miles) southwest of Berlin.

Leipzig is one of the coolest cities in Europe—but not so cool as to be pretentious. With its world-renowned links to Bach, Schubert, Mendelssohn, Martin Luther, Goethe, Schiller, and the fantastic Neue-Leipziger-Schule art movement, Leipzig is one of the great German cultural centers. It has impressive art nouveau architecture, an incredibly clean city center, meandering narrow streets, and the temptations of coffee and cake on every corner. In *Faust*, Goethe describes Leipzig as "a little Paris"; in reality it's more reminiscent of Vienna, while remaining a distinctly energetic Saxon town.

> ### THE FIVE KS
>
> A long-standing joke is that the priorities of the people of Saxony, Saxony-Anhalt, and Thuringia can be summed up in five Ks: Kaffee, Kuchen, Klösse, Kartoffeln, and Kirche (coffee, cake, dumplings, potatoes, and church)—in that order.

Leipzig's musical past includes Johann Sebastian Bach (1685–1750), who was organist and choir director at Leipzig's Thomaskirche, and the 19th-century composer Richard Wagner, who was born in the city in 1813. Today's Leipzig continues the cultural focus with extraordinary offerings of music, theater, and opera, not to mention fantastic nightlife.

Wartime bombs destroyed much of Leipzig's city center, but reconstruction efforts have uncovered one of Europe's most vibrant cities. Leipzig's art nouveau flair is best discovered by exploring the countless alleys, covered courtyards, and passageways. Some unattractive buildings from the postwar period remain, but only reinforce Leipzig's position on the line between modernity and antiquity.

With a population of about 535,000, Leipzig is the third-largest city in eastern Germany (after Berlin and Dresden) and has long been a center of printing and bookselling. Astride major trade routes, it was an important market town in the Middle Ages, and it continues to be a trading center, thanks to the *Leipziger Messe* (trade and fair shows) throughout the year that bring together buyers from East and West.

Unfortunately, Leipzig has a tendency to underwhelm first-time visitors. If you take Leipzig slow and have some cake, its subtle, hidden charms may surprise you.

GETTING HERE AND AROUND

Leipzig is an hour from Berlin by train. Leipzig-Halle airport serves many European destinations, but no North American ones.

FESTIVALS

Music Days. Leipzig's annual music festival is in June. ⊠ *Augustuspl.*

TIMING

Leipzig can easily be explored in one day; it's possible to walk around the downtown area in just about three hours. The churches can be inspected in less than 20 minutes each. But if you're interested in German history and art, plan for two full days, so you can spend one

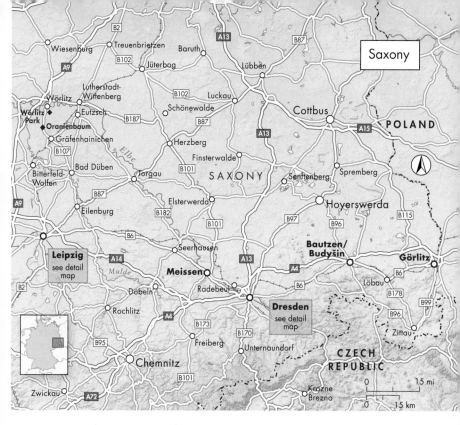

Saxony

SAXONY

POLAND

CZECH REPUBLIC

day just visiting the museums and go to the symphony. The Völkerschlachtdenkmal is perfect for a three-hour side trip.

ESSENTIALS

Visitor Information Leipzig Tourismus und Marketing. ✉ *Augustuspl. 9* ☎ *0341/710–4260, 0341/710–4301* ⊕ *www.leipzig.travel.*

EXPLORING

TOP ATTRACTIONS

Grassimuseum. British "starchitect" David Chipperfield restored and modernized this fine example of German art deco in 2003–05. The building, which opened in 1929, houses three important museums. ✉ *Johannispl. 5–11* ⊕ *www.grassimuseum.de* 🎟 *€8* ⊙ *Tues.–Sun. 10–6.*

Museum für Angewandte Kunst (*Museum of Applied Art*). This museum showcases 2,000 years of works from Leipzig's and eastern Germany's proud tradition of handicrafts, such as exquisite porcelain, fine tapestry art, and modern Bauhaus design. ✉ *Johannispl. 5–11* ☎ *0341/222–9100* ⊕ *www.grassimuseum.de* 🎟 *€8* ⊙ *Tues.–Sun. 10–6.*

Museum für Völkerkunde (*Ethnological Museum*). Presenting arts and crafts from all continents and various eras, this museum includes a thrilling collection of Southeast Asian antique art and the world's only Kurile Ainu feather costume, in the Northeast Asia collection.

✉ *Johannispl. 5–11* ☎ *0341/973–1300* ⊕ *www.grassimuseum.de* 🖅 *€8* ⊙ *Tues.–Sun. 10–6.*

Museum für Musikinstrumente (*Musical Instruments Museum*). Historical musical instruments, mostly from the Renaissance, include the world's oldest clavichord, constructed in 1543 in Italy. There are also spinets, flutes, and lutes. Recordings of the instruments can be heard at the exhibits. ✉ *Johannispl. 5–11* ☎ *0341/973–0750* 🖅 *€6* ⊙ *Tues.–Sun. 10–6.*

Mädlerpassage (*Mädler Mall*). The ghost of Goethe's Faust lurks in every marble corner of Leipzig's finest shopping arcade. One of the scenes in *Faust* is set in the famous Auerbachs Keller restaurant, at No. 2. A bronze group of characters from the play, sculpted in 1913, beckons you down the stone staircase to the restaurant. Touching the statues' feet is said to bring good luck. A few yards away is a delightful art nouveau bar called Mephisto. ✉ *Grimmaische Str.*

Markt. Leipzig's showpiece is its huge, old market square. One side is completely occupied by the Renaissance town hall, the **Altes Rathaus.** ✉ *Marktpl., Böttchergässchen 3.*

Museum der Bildenden Künste (*Museum of Fine Arts*). The city's leading art gallery is modernist minimalism incarnate, set in a huge concrete cube encased in green glass in the middle of Sachsenplatz Square. The museum's collection of more than 2,700 paintings and sculptures represents everything from the German Middle Ages to the modern Neue Leipziger Schule. Especially notable are the collections focusing on Lucas Cranach the Elder and Caspar David Friedrich. Be sure to start at the top and work your way down. Don't miss Max Klinger's Beethoven as Zeus statue. ✉ *Katharinenstr. 10* ☎ *0341/216–990* ⊕ *www.mdbk.de* 🖅 *€5, special exhibits €6–€8* ⊙ *Tues. and Thurs.– Sun. 10–6, Wed. noon–8.*

Nikolaikirche (*St. Nicholas Church*). This church with its rough undistinguished facade was center stage during the demonstrations that helped bring down the Communist regime. Every Monday for months before the government collapsed, thousands of citizens gathered in front of the church chanting "Wir sind das Volk" ("We are the people"). Inside are a soaring Gothic choir and nave. Note the unusual patterned ceiling supported by classical pillars that end in palm-tree-like flourishes. Martin Luther is said to have preached from the ornate 16th-century pulpit. The prayers for peace that began in 1989 are still held on Monday at 5 pm. ✉ *Nikolaikirchhof* ☎ *0341/960–5270* 🖅 *Free* ⊙ *Mon.–Sat. 10–6; Sun. services at 9:30, 11:15, and 5.*

Stadtgeschichtliches Museum. Inside the Altes Rathaus, this museum documents Leipzig's past. The entrance is behind the Rathaus. The museum is expanding its exhibition space behind the Museum for Applied Arts. ✉ *Böttchergässchen 3* ☎ *0341/965–130* ⊕ *www.stadtgeschichtliches- museum-leipzig.de* 🖅 *€6* ⊙ *Tues.–Sun. 10–6.*

Fodor'sChoice
★ **Thomaskirche** (*St. Thomas's Church*). Bach served as choirmaster at this Gothic church for 27 years, and Martin Luther preached here on Whitsunday 1539, signaling the arrival of Protestantism in Leipzig. Originally the center of a 13th-century monastery, the tall church (rebuilt in

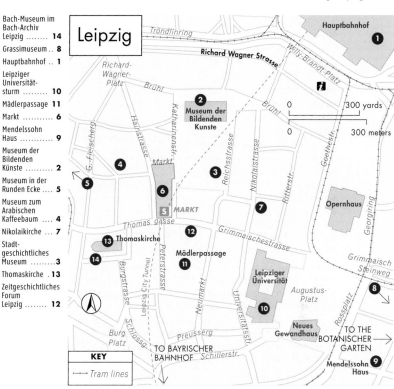

the 15th century) now stands by itself. Bach wrote most of his cantatas for the church's famous boys' choir, the Thomanerchor, which was founded in the 13th century. Today, the church continues to serve as the choir's home as well as a center of Bach tradition.

The great music Bach wrote during his Leipzig years commanded little attention in his lifetime, and when he died he was given a simple grave, without a headstone, in the city's Johannisfriedhof (St. John Cemetery). It wasn't until 1894 that an effort was made to find where the great composer lay buried, and after a thorough, macabre search, his coffin was removed to the Johanniskirche. That church was destroyed by Allied bombs in December 1943, and Bach subsequently found his final resting place in the church he would have selected: the Thomaskirche. You can listen to the famous boys' choir during the *Motette,* a service with a special emphasis on choral music.

Bach's 12 children and the infant Richard Wagner were baptized in the early-17th-century font; Karl Marx and Friedrich Engels also stood before this same font, godfathers to Karl Liebknecht, who grew up to be a revolutionary as well.

In front of the church is a memorial to Felix Mendelssohn, rebuilt with funds collected by the Leipzig Citizens Initiative. The Nazis destroyed the original in front of the Gewandhaus. ⊠ *Thomaskirchhof* ☏ *0341/222–240*

⊕ www.thomaskirche.org ⊠ Free, Motette €2 ⊙ Daily 9–6; Motette Fri. at 6 pm, Sat. at 3; no Motette during Saxony summer vacation (usually mid-July–Aug.).

WORTH NOTING

Bach-Museum im Bach-Archiv Leipzig (*Bach Museum at the Bach Archives Leipzig*). The Bach family home, the old Bosehaus, stands opposite the Thomaskirche, and is now a museum devoted to the composer's life and work. The exhibition offers several interactive displays; arranging the instrumental parts of Bach's hymns is by far the most entertaining. ⊠ *Thomaskirchhof 16* ☎ *0341/913–7200* ⊕ *www.bach-leipzig.de* ⊠*€8; free 1st Thurs. of month* ⊙ *Tues.–Sun. 10–6.*

> ## TOURING TIPS
>
> **Information:** The friendly tourist-information office is at Augustusplatz 1. If you plan to visit any museums, consider the **Leipzigcard.**
>
> **People-watching:** Take a seat upstairs—above the elephant heads—at the coffeehouse Riquet and watch the world go by.
>
> **Typically Leipzig:** Drink a Gose and try the "Meadowlark" pastry.

Hauptbahnhof. With 26 platforms, Leipzig's main train station is Europe's largest railhead. It was built in 1915 and is now a protected monument, but modern commerce rules in its bi-level shopping mall (the Promenaden). The only thing the complex is missing is a pub. Many of the shops and restaurants stay open until 10 pm and are open on Sunday. Thanks to the historic backdrop, this is one of the most beautiful shopping experiences in Saxony. ⊠ *Willy-Brandt-Pl.* ☎ *0341/141–270 for mall, 0341/9968–3275 for train station.*

Leipziger Universitätsturm (*Leipzig University Tower*). Towering over Leipzig's city center is this 470-foot-high structure, which houses administrative offices and lecture rooms. Dubbed the "jagged tooth" or "wisdom tooth" by some University of Leipzig students, it supposedly represents an open book. Students were also largely responsible for changing the university's name, replacing its postwar title, Karl Marx University, with the original one. The **Augustusplatz** spreads out below the university tower like a space-age campus. ⊠ *Augustuspl. 9.*

Mendelssohn Haus (*Mendelssohn House*). The only surviving residence of the composer Felix Mendelssohn-Bartholdy is now Germany's only museum dedicated to him. Mendelssohn's last residence and the place of his death has been preserved in its original 19th-century state. Concerts are held every Sunday at 11. ⊠ *Goldschmidtstr. 12* ☎ *0341/127–0294* ⊕ *www.mendelssohn-stiftung.de* ⊠*€4.50, concert €15* ⊙ *Daily 10–6.*

Museum in der Runden Ecke (*Museum in the Round Corner*). This building once served as the headquarters of the city's detachment of the Communist secret police, the dreaded *Staatssicherheitsdienst*. The exhibition *Stasi—Macht und Banalität* (Stasi—Power and Banality) presents not only the Stasi's offices and surveillance work, but also hundreds of documents revealing the magnitude of its interests in citizens' private lives. Though the material is in German, the items and atmosphere convey an impression of what life under the regime might have been like. The exhibit about the death penalty in the GDR is particularly chilling. For

Bach was choirmaster at the Thomaskirche and is buried here. Bach wrote cantatas for the boys' choir, which you can still hear performed.

a detailed tour of the Revolutions of 1989, be sure to download the museum's app. ⊠ *Dittrichring 24* ☎ *0341/961–2443* ⊕ *www.runde-ecke-leipzig.de* ✉ *Free; tour in English, by appointment, €4* ☉ *Daily 10–6.*

Museum zum Arabischen Kaffeebaum (*Arabic Coffee Tree Museum*). This museum and café-restaurant tells the fascinating history of coffee culture in Europe, particularly in Saxony. The café is one of the oldest on the continent, and once proudly served coffee to such luminaries as Gotthold Lessing, Schumann, Goethe, and Liszt. The museum features many paintings, Arabian coffee vessels, and coffeehouse games. It also explains the basic principles of roasting coffee. The café is divided into traditional Viennese, French, and Arabian coffeehouses, but no coffee is served in the Arabian section, which is only a display. The cake is better and the seating more comfortable in the Viennese part. ⊠ *Kleine Fleischerg. 4* ☎ *0341/960–2632* ⊕ *www.coffe-baum.de* ✉ *Free* ☉ *Tues.–Sun. 11–5.*

Zeitgeschichtliches Forum Leipzig (*Museum of Contemporary History Leipzig*). This excellent history museum focuses on issues surrounding the division and reunification of Germany after World War II. ⊠ *Grimmaische Str. 6* ☎ *0341/225–0500* ⊕ *www.hdg.de* ✉ *Free* ☉ *Tues.–Sun. 10–6.*

WHERE TO EAT

$$
GERMAN
Fodor'sChoice
★

✕ **Auerbachs Keller.** The most famous of Leipzig's restaurants is actually two restaurants: one that's upscale, international, and gourmet (down the stairs to the right) and a rowdy beer cellar (to the left) specializing in hearty Saxon fare, mostly roasted meat dishes. The fine-dining section's seven-course menus (€89) are worth a splurge, and it also has a good wine list. The beer cellar has been around since 1530, making it one of the oldest continually running restaurants on the continent. Goethe immortalized one of the vaulted historic rooms in his *Faust,* and Bach was a regular here because of the location halfway between the Thomaskirche and the Nikolaikirche. [$] *Average main: €20* ✉ *Mädlerpassage, Grimmaische Str. 2–4* ☎ *0341/216–100* 🌐 *www.auerbachs-keller-leipzig.de* 🕒 *Closed Mon.* ✍ *Reservations essential.*

$ GERMAN 🍴 **Barthels Hof.** The English-language menu at this restaurant explains not only the cuisine but the history of Leipzig. Waitresses wear traditional *Trachten* dresses, but the rooms are quite modern. With a prominent location on the Markt, the restaurant is popular with locals, especially for the incredible breakfast buffet. Barthels has managed to elevate the local *Leipziger Allerlei* (vegetables and crayfish in beef bouillon) to an art form. Enjoy a meal here with a fresh Bauer Gose. [$] *Average main: €14* ✉ *Hainstr. 1* ☎ *0341/141–310.*

$ GERMAN 🍴 **Gasthaus & Gosebrauerei Bayrischer Bahnhof.** Hidden on the far southeast edge of the city center, the Bayrischer Bahnhof was the terminus of the first rail link between Saxony and Bavaria. The brewery here is at the heart of a cultural renaissance, and is the only place currently brewing Gose in Leipzig. The restaurant is well worth a visit for its solid Saxon and German cuisine. Brewery accents surface in dishes such as rump steak with black-beer sauce, and the onion rings can't be beat. If the Gose is too sour for your taste, order it with one of the sweet syrups—raspberry is the best. Groups of four or more can try dinner prepared in a *Römertopf* (a terra-cotta baking dish; the first was brought to Germany by the Romans, centuries ago). In summer the beer garden is a pleasant place to get away from the bustle of the city center. [$] *Average main: €13* ✉ *Bayrischer Pl. 1* ☎ *0341/124–5760* 🌐 *www.bayrischer-bahnhof.de* 💳 *No credit cards.*

$ CAFÉ 🍴 **Kaffeehaus Riquet.** The restored art nouveau house dates from 1908. Riquet is a company that has had dealings in the coffee trade in Africa and East Asia since 1745, as is indicated by the large elephant heads adorning the facade of the building. The upstairs section houses a pleasant Viennese-style coffeehouse—the best views are had from up here—while downstairs is noisier and more active. Afternoon coffee and cake are one of Leipzig's special pleasures (in a country obsessed with coffee and cake), and Riquet is the best place in the city to satisfy the urge. Enjoy Leipzig Medowlark pastry for €2.50. [$] *Average main: €4* ✉ *Schulmachergässchen 1* ☎ *0341/961–0000* 💳 *No credit cards* 🕒 *No dinner.*

$$ GERMAN 🍴 **Thüringer Hof.** One of Germany's oldest restaurants and pubs (dating back to 1454) served its hearty Thuringian and Saxon fare to Martin Luther and the like—who certainly had more than a mere pint of the beers on tap. The menu in the reconstructed, cavernous, and always buzzing dining hall doesn't exactly offer gourmet cuisine, but rather an impressively enormous variety of game, fish, and bratwurst dishes. The Thuringian sausages (served with either sauerkraut and boiled potatoes or onions and mashed potatoes) and the famous Thuringian *Sauerbraten* (beef marinated in a sour essence) are musts. [$] *Average main: €15* ✉ *Burgstr. 19* ☎ *0341/994–4999* 🌐 *www.thueringer-hof.de.*

$$
GERMAN
✕ **Zill's Tunnel.** The "tunnel" refers to the barrel-ceiling ground-floor restaurant, where foaming glasses of excellent Gose beer are served with a smile. The friendly staff will also help you decipher the Old Saxon descriptions of the menu's traditional dishes. Upstairs there's a larger wine restaurant with an open fireplace. Try some of the best pan-seared *Rinderroulladen*, a filled beef roll, in the city. Ⓢ *Average main: €15* ✉ *Barfussgässchen 9* ☎ *0341/960–2078* ⊕ *www.zillstunnel.de.*

16

WHERE TO STAY

$$$
HOTEL
Fodor's Choice
★
🏨 **Hotel Fürstenhof Leipzig.** The city's grandest hotel—part of Starwood's Luxury Collection—is inside the renowned Löhr-Haus, a revered old mansion 500 yards from the main train station on the ring road surrounding the city center. **Pros:** an elegant full-service hotel with stunning rooms; safes big enough for a laptop are a nice touch. **Cons:** the ring road can be noisy at night, especially on Friday and Saturday. Ⓢ *Rooms from: €179* ✉ *Tröndlinring 8* ☎ *0341/140–370* ⊕ *www.hotelfuerstenhofleipzig.com/* 🛏 *80 rooms, 12 suites* ⊗ *No meals.*

$
HOTEL
🏨 **Ringhotel Adagio Leipzig.** The quiet Adagio, tucked away behind the facade of a 19th-century city mansion, is centrally located between the Grassimuseum and the Neues Gewandhaus. **Pros:** large rooms with luxurious bathrooms; breakfast available all day. **Cons:** room decor is slightly bland; hotel not built to accommodate guests with disabilities. Ⓢ *Rooms from: €77* ✉ *Seeburgstr. 96* ☎ *0341/216–690* ⊕ *www.hotel-adagio.de* 🛏 *30 rooms, 2 suites, 1 apartment* ⊗ *Breakfast.*

NIGHTLIFE AND PERFORMING ARTS

NIGHTLIFE

With a vast assortment of restaurants, cafés, and clubs to match the city's exceptional musical and literary offerings, Leipzig is a fun city at night. The *Kneipenszene* (pub scene) is centered on the **Drallewatsch** (a Saxon slang word for "going out"), the small streets and alleys around Grosse and Kleine Fleischergasse and the Barfussgässchen.

Moritzbastei. A magnet for young people, this is reputedly Europe's largest student club, with bars, a disco, a café, a theater, and a cinema. Nonstudents are welcome . . . if you're cool enough. ✉ *Universitätsstr. 9* ☎ *0341/702–590.*

Schauhaus. A favorite hangout among the city's business elite, this stylish bar serves great cocktails. ✉ *Bosestr. 1* ☎ *0341/960–0596.*

EATING WELL IN SAXONY

The cuisine of the region is hearty and seasonal, and almost every town has a unique specialty unavailable outside the immediate area. Look for *Sächsische Sauerbraten* (marinated sour beef roast), spicy *Thüringer Bratwurst* (sausage), *Schlesische Himmelreich* (ham and pork roast smothered in baked fruit and white sauce, served with dumplings), *Teichlmauke* (mashed potato in broth), *Blauer Karpfe* (blue carp, marinated in vinegar), and *Raacher Maad* (grated and boiled potatoes fried in butter and served with blueberries). Venison and wild boar are standards in forest and mountainous areas, and lamb from Saxony-Anhalt is particularly good. In Thuringia, *Klösse* (potato dumplings) are virtually a religion.

Eastern Germany is experiencing a renaissance in the art of northern German brewing. The first stop for any beer lover should be the Bayrische Bahnhof in Leipzig, to give Gose a try. Dresden's Brauhaus Watzke, Quedlinburg's Lüddebräu, and even the Landskron Brauerei in Görlitz are bringing craft brewing back to a region inundated with mass-produced brew.

Saxony has cultivated vineyards for more than 800 years, and is known for its dry red and white wines, among them Müller-Thurgau, Weissburgunder, Ruländer, and the spicy Traminer. The Sächsische Weinstrasse (Saxon Wine Route) follows the course of the Elbe River from Diesbar-Seusslitz (north of Meissen) to Pirna (southeast of Dresden). Meissen, Radebeul, and Dresden have upscale wine restaurants, and wherever you see a green seal with the letter S and grapes depicted, good local wine is being served. One of the best-kept secrets in German wine making is the Salle-Unstrut region, which produces spicy Silvaner and Rieslings.

Spizz Keller. This hip place is one of the city's top dance clubs. ⊠ *Markt 9* ☎ *0341/960–8043.*

Tanzpalast. In the august setting of the *Schauspielhaus* (city theater), the Tanzpalast attracts a thirtysomething crowd. This was *the* place to be seen in GDR Leipzig. ⊠ *Bosestr. 1* ☎ *0341/960–0596.*

Weinstock. This upscale bar, pub, and restaurant in a Renaissance building offers a huge selection of good wines. ⊠ *Markt 7* ☎ *0341/1406–0606.*

PERFORMING ARTS

Krystallpalast. This variety theater features a blend of circus, vaudeville, and comedy that is fairly accessible for non-German speakers. ⊠ *Magazing. 4* ☎ *0341/140–660* ⊕ *www.krystallpalast.de.*

Leipziger Pfeffermühle. One of Germany's most famous cabarets has a lively bar off a courtyard opposite the Thomaskirche. On pleasant evenings the courtyard fills with benches and tables, and the scene rivals the indoor performance for entertainment. ⊠ *Katharinenstr. 17* ☎ *0341/960–3196* ⊕ *www.kabarett-leipziger-pfeffermuehle.de.*

Neues Gewandhaus. This uninspired touch of socialist architecture is home to an undeniably splendid orchestra. Tickets to concerts are difficult to obtain unless you reserve well in advance. Sometimes spare tickets are available at the box office a half hour before the evening performance. ⊠ *Augustuspl. 8* ☎ *0341/127–0280* ⊕ *www.gewandhaus.de.*

Opernhaus (*Opera House*). Leipzig's stage for operas was the first post-war theater to be built in Communist East Germany. Its solid, boxy style is the subject of ongoing local discussion. ⊠ *Augustuspl.*

SHOPPING

Small streets leading off the Markt attest to Leipzig's rich trading past. Tucked in among them are glass-roof arcades of surprising beauty and elegance, including the wonderfully restored **Specks Hof, Barthels Hof, Jägerhof,** and the **Passage zum Sachsenplatz.** Invent a headache and step into the *Apotheke* (pharmacy)

LEIPZIGER LERCHE

As far back as the 18th century, Leipzig was known for a bizarre culinary specialty: roast meadowlark in crust. The dish was so popular that Leipzig consumed more than 400,000 meadowlarks every month. When the king of Saxony banned lark hunting in 1876, Leipzig's industrious bakers came up with a substitute: a baked short-crust pastry filled with almonds, nuts, and strawberries. Today, the substitute Meadowlark, when prepared correctly, is a delicious treat—found only in Leipzig.

16

at Hainstrasse 9—it is spectacularly art nouveau, with finely etched and stained glass and rich mahogany. For more glimpses into the past, check out the antiquarian bookstores of the nearby **Neumarkt Passage.**

Hauptbahnhof. Leipzig's main train station has more than 150 shops, restaurants, and cafés, all open Monday through Saturday 9:30 am–10 pm; many are also open on Sunday, with the same hours. ⊠ *Willy-Brandt-Pl.*

DRESDEN

25 km (16 miles) southeast of Meissen, 140 km (87 miles) southeast of Leipzig, 193 km (120 miles) south of Berlin.

Sitting in baroque splendor on a wide sweep of the Elbe River, Dresden has been the capital of Saxony since the 15th century, although most of its architectural masterpieces date from the enlightenment of the 18th century and the reigns of Augustus the Strong and his son, Frederick Augustus II. Today the city's yellow and pale-green facades are enormously appealing, and their mere presence is even more overwhelming when you compare what you see with photographs of Dresden from February 1945. That's when Allied bombing destroyed almost all of the Altstadt (Old City). Today, Dresden has risen from these ashes, regaining its reputation as "the Florence on the Elbe."

Although parts of the city center still look stuck between demolition and construction, the city's rebuilding is an enormous tribute to Dresdeners' skill, dedication, and thoroughness. The resemblance of today's riverside to Dresden cityscapes painted by Canaletto in the mid-1700s is remarkable. Unfortunately, war-inflicted gaps in other parts of the city are far too massive to be reconstructed anytime soon. Main sights are contained within the Altstadt. On the other side of the river, the

Neustadt (New City), which escaped wartime destruction, is the place to go out at night.

GETTING HERE AND AROUND

Dresden is two hours from Berlin on the Hamburg-Berlin-Prague-Vienna train line. The city's international airport serves mostly European destinations with budget airlines. The newly completed Norman Foster train station is a short walk along the Prager Strasse from the city center. Streetcars are cheap and efficient.

Dresden bus tours (in German and English, run by the Dresdner Verkehrsbetriebe) leave from Postplatz daily at 10, 11:30, and 3; the Stadtrundfahrt Dresden bus tours (also in German and English) leave from Theaterplatz/Augustusbrücke (April–October, daily 9:30–5, every 30 minutes; November–March, daily 10–3, every hour) and stop at most sights.

FESTIVALS

Filmnächte am Elbufer (*Elbe Riverside Film Nights*). In addition to the annual film festival in April, open-air Filmnächte am Elbufer take place on the bank of the Elbe from late June to late August. ⊠ *Am Königsufer, next to State Ministry of Finance* ☎ *0351/899–320.*

Jazz. May brings an annual international Dixieland-style jazz festival, and the Jazz Autumn festival follows in October. ⊠ *Altmarkt.*

TIMING

A long full day is sufficient for a quick tour of historic Dresden with a brief visit to one of the museums. The focus of your day should be a visit to the Grünes Gewölbe. If you plan to explore any of the museums at length, such as the Zwinger, or take a guided tour of the Semperoper, you'll need more time. One of the best ways to see Dresden is as a stop between Berlin and Prague.

ESSENTIALS

Tour Information Dresdner Verkehrsbetriebe AG. ⊠ *Service Center, Postpl. 1* ☎ *0351/857–2201.* **Stadtrundfahrt Dresden.** ⊠ *Theaterpl.* ☎ *0351/899–5650.*

Visitor Information Dresden Tourist. ⊠ *Schlossstr. 1, inside the Kulturpalast* ☎ *0351/491–920* ⊕ *www.dresden.de.*

EXPLORING

TOP ATTRACTIONS

Fodor'sChoice ★ **Frauenkirche** (*Church of Our Lady*). This masterpiece of baroque church architecture was completed in 1743. The huge dome set on a smaller square base, known as the Stone Bell, was the inspiration of George Bähr, who designed the church to be built "as if it was a single stone from the base to the top." On February 15, 1945, two days after the bombing of Dresden, the burned-out shell of the magnificent Stone Bell collapsed. For the following five decades the remains of the church, a pile of rubble, remained a gripping memorial to the horrors of war. In a move shocking to the East German authorities, who organized all public demonstrations, a group of young people spontaneously met here on February 13, 1982, for a candlelight vigil for peace.

Although the will to rebuild the church was strong, the political and economic situation in the GDR prevented it. It wasn't until the reunification

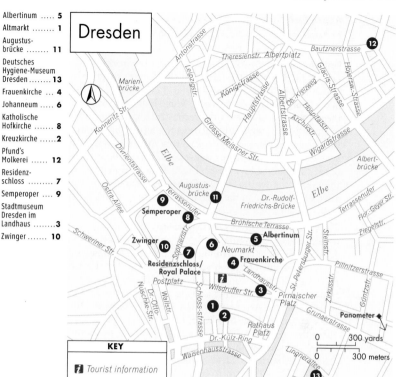

of Germany that Dresden began to seriously consider reconstruction. In the early 1990s a citizens' initiative, joined by the Lutheran Church of Saxony and the city of Dresden, decided to rebuild the church using the original stones. The goal of completing the church by 2006, Dresden's 800th anniversary, seemed insurmountable. Money soon started pouring in from around the globe, however, and work began. The rubble was cleared away, and the size and shape of each stone were cataloged. Computer-imaging technology helped place each recovered stone in its original location.

During construction, guided tours and Frauenkirche concerts brought in donations. The biggest supporter of the project in the United Kingdom, the Dresden Trust, is centered in the city of Coventry, itself bombed mercilessly by the German *Luftwaffe* during the war. The Dresden Trust raised more than €600,000, and donated the gold pinnacle cross that now graces the church dome.

On Sunday, October 30, 2005 (almost a year ahead of schedule), Dresden's skyline became a little more complete with the consecration of the Frauenkirche. Leading the service was the bishop of Coventry. Although the church is usually open to all, it closes frequently for concerts and other events. Check the English-language schedule next to Entrance D. ⊠ *An der Frauenkirche* ☎ *0351/498–1131* ⊕ *www.*

frauenkirche-dresden.org ✉️ *Free; cupola and tower €8; audio guides in English €2.50* ⊘ *Weekdays 10–noon and 1–6, cupola and tower daily 10–6.*

Residenzschloss (*Royal Palace*). Restoration work is still under way behind the Renaissance facade of this former royal palace, much of which was built between 1709 and 1722. Some of the finished rooms in the **Georgenbau** (Count George Wing) hold historical exhibits, among them an excellent one on the reconstruction of the palace itself. The palace's main gateway, the Georgentor, has an enormous statue of the fully armed Saxon count George. From April through October, the palace's old Hausmannsturm (Hausmann Tower) offers a wonderful view of the city and the Elbe River. The main attraction in the Royal Palace, though, is the world-famous **Grünes Gewölbe** (Green Vault). Named after a green room in the palace of Augustus the Strong, the collection is divided into two sections.

The palace also houses the **Münzkabinett** (Coin Museum) and the **Kupferstichkabinett** (Museum of Prints and Drawings), with more than 500,000 pieces of art spanning several centuries. Changing exhibits at the Kupferstichkabinett have presented masterworks by Albrecht Dürer, Peter Paul Rubens, and Jan van Eyck; 20th-century art by Otto Dix, Edvard Munch, and Ernst Ludwig Kirchner; East European art; and some Southeast Asian prints. The **Türckische Cammer** (Turkish Chamber) comprises a huge number of Ottoman artifacts collected by Saxon dukes over centuries. It's worth going just to see the six carved Arabian horses, bedecked with jeweled armor. ✉️ *Schlosspl.* ☎️ *0351/491–4619* ⊕ *www.skd.museum* ✉️ *All museums and collections except Historic Green Vault €12; Historic Green Vault €12; combination ticket €21* ⊘ *Wed.–Mon. 10–6; Historic Green Vault by appointment.*

Historisches Grünes Gewölbe (*Historic Green Vault*). This section of the castle most reflects Augustus the Strong's obsession with art as a symbol of power. The intricately restored baroque interior is an integral part of the presentation, highlighting the objects in the collection. The last section of the museum houses the Jewel Room, which displays the ceremonial crown jewels of Augustus the Strong and his son. Access to the Historic Green Vault is limited to 100 visitors per hour and is by appointment only, reserved by phone or online. ✉️ *Taschenberg 2* ☎️ *0351/4919–2285 for tours* ⊕ *www.skd.museum* ✉️ *€12* ⊘ *By appointment.*

Neues Grünes Gewölbe (*New Green Vault*). The exquisite collection here consists of objets d'art fashioned from gold, silver, ivory, amber, and other precious and semiprecious materials. Among the crown jewels are the world's largest "green" diamond, 41 carats in weight, and a dazzling group of tiny gem-studded figures called *Hofstaat zu Delhi am Geburtstag des Grossmoguls Aureng-Zeb* (the Court at Delhi during the Birthday of the Great Mogul Aureng-Zeb). The unwieldy name gives a false idea of the size of the work, dating from 1708; some parts of the tableau are so small they can be admired only through a magnifying glass. Somewhat larger and less delicate is the drinking bowl of Ivan the Terrible, perhaps the most sensational artifact in this extraordinary museum. ✉️ *Taschenberg 2* ⊕ *www.skd.museum* ✉️ *€12* ⊘ *Wed.–Mon. 10–6.*

The Frauenkirche was painstakingly rebuilt after it was reduced to rubble in the bombing of Dresden.

Semperoper (*Semper Opera House*). One of Germany's best-known and most popular theaters, this magnificent opera house saw the premieres of Richard Wagner's *Rienzi, Der Fliegende Holländer,* and *Tannhäuser* and Richard Strauss's *Salome, Elektra,* and *Der Rosenkavalier.* The Dresden architect Gottfried Semper built the house in 1838–41 in Italian Renaissance style, then saw his work destroyed in a fire caused by a careless lamplighter. Semper had to flee Dresden after participating in a democratic uprising, but his son Manfred rebuilt the theater in the neo-Renaissance style you see today, though even Manfred Semper's version had to be rebuilt after the devastating bombing raid of February 1945. On the 40th anniversary of that raid—February 13, 1985—the Semperoper reopened with a performance of *Der Freischütz,* by Carl Maria von Weber, the last opera performed in the building before its destruction. There is a statue of Weber, another artist who did much to make Dresden a leading center of German music and culture, outside the opera house in the shadow of the Zwinger. Even if you're no opera buff, the Semper's lavish interior can't fail to impress. Velvet, brocade, and well-crafted imitation marble create an atmosphere of intimate luxury (it seats 1,323). Guided tours (must be reserved in advance) of the building are offered throughout the day, depending on the opera's rehearsal schedule. Check the website for schedules. Tours begin at the entrance to your right as you face the Elbe River. ⊠ *Theaterpl. 2* ☎ *0351/491–1496* ⊕ *www.semperoper-erleben.de* 🎫 *Tour €10.*

Fodor's Choice ★ **Zwinger** (*Bailey*). Dresden's magnificent baroque showpiece is entered by way of the mighty Kronentor (Crown Gate), off Ostra-Allee. Augustus the Strong hired a small army of artists and artisans to create a

"pleasure ground" worthy of the Saxon court on the site of the former bailey, part of the city fortifications. The artisans worked under the direction of the architect Matthäus Daniel Pöppelmann, who came reluctantly out of retirement to design what would be his greatest work, begun in 1707 and completed in 1728. Completely enclosing a central courtyard filled with lawns, pools, and fountains, the complex is made up of six linked pavilions, one of which boasts a carillon of Meissen bells, hence its name: Glockenspielpavillon.

The Zwinger is quite a scene—a riot of garlands, nymphs, and other baroque ornamentation and sculpture. Wide staircases beckon to galleried walks and to the romantic Nymphenbad, a coyly hidden courtyard where statues of nude women perch in alcoves to protect themselves from a fountain that spits unexpectedly. The Zwinger once had an open view of the riverbank, but the Semper Opera House now occupies that side. Stand in the center of this quiet oasis, where the city's roar is kept at bay by the outer wings of the structure, and imagine the court festivities once held here. ⊠ *Zwinger entrance, Ostra–Allee* ⊕ *www.skd. museum* ☎ *€10* ⊗ *Tues.–Sun. 10–6.*

Gemäldegalerie Alte Meister (*Gallery of Old Masters*). This museum, in the northwestern corner of the complex, was built to house portions of the royal art collections. Among the priceless paintings are works by Dürer, Holbein, Jan Van Eyck, Rembrandt, Rubens, van Dyck, Hals, Vermeer, Raphael, Titian, Giorgione, Veronese, Velázquez, Murillo, Canaletto, and Watteau. On the wall of the entrance archway you'll see an inscription in Russian, one of the few amusing reminders of World War II in Dresden. It rhymes in Russian: "Museum checked. No mines. Chanutin did the checking." Chanutin, presumably, was the Russian soldier responsible for checking one of Germany's greatest art galleries for anything more explosive than a Rubens nude. The highlight of the collection is Raphael's *Sistine Madonna*, whose mournful look is slightly less famous than the two cherubs who were added by Raphael after the painting was completed, in order to fill an empty space at the bottom. ⊠ *Dresden* ☎ *0351/491–4679* ☎ *€10: Zwingerticket for all museums in the Zwinger* ⊗ *Tues.–Sun. 10–6.*

Porzellansammlung (*Porcelain Collection*). Stretching from the curved gallery that adjoins the Glockenspielpavillon to the long gallery on the east side, this collection is considered one of the best of its kind in the world. The focus, naturally, is on Dresden and Meissen china, but there are also outstanding examples of Japanese, Chinese, and Korean porcelain. ⊠ *Dresden* ☎ *0351/491–4619* ☎ *€6, Zwingerticket €10* ⊗ *Tues.–Sun. 10–6.*

Rüstkammer (*Armory*). Holding medieval and Renaissance suits of armor and weapons, the Rüstkammer is in two parts: the main exhibitt and the Türckische Cammer, both in the Residenzschloss. ⊠ *Dresden* ☎ *0351/491–4619* ☎ *€12* ⊗ *Tues.–Sun. 10–6.*

WORTH NOTING

Albertinum. Named after Saxony's King Albert, who between 1884 and 1887 converted a royal arsenal into a suitable setting for the treasures he and his forebears had collected, this massive, imperial-style

16

building houses one of the world's great galleries featuring works from the romantic period to the modern. The Galerie Neue Meister (New Masters Gallery) has an extensive collection ranging from Caspar David Friedrich and Gauguin to Ernst Kirchner and Georg Baselitz. ✉ *Am Neumarkt, Brühlsche Terrasse* ☎ *0351/49849–14973* ⊕ *www.skd. museum* 🎟 *€10* ⊙ *Wed.–Mon. 10–6.*

Altmarkt (*Old Market Square*). Although dominated by the nearby unappealing Kulturpalast (Palace of Culture), the Altmarkt is a fascinating concrete leftover from the 1970s (check out the "workers and peasants" GDR mosaic), and the broad square and its surrounding streets are the true center of Dresden. The colonnaded beauty (from the Stalinist-era architecture of the early 1950s) survived the efforts of city planners to turn it into a huge outdoor parking lot. The rebuilt **Rathaus** (Town Hall) is here (go around the front to see bullet holes in the statuary), as is the yellow-stucco, 18th-century Landhaus, which contains the Stadtmuseum Dresden im Landhaus. Dresdeners joke that you should never park your car here because the square is under almost constant construction and you might never find it again. ✉ *Dresden.*

Augustusbrücke (*Augustus Bridge*). This bridge, which spans the river in front of the Katholische Hofkirche, is the reconstruction of a 17th-century baroque bridge blown up by the SS shortly before the end of World War II. It was restored and renamed for Georgi Dimitroff, one of the Bulgarian communists accused by the Nazis of instigating the Reichstag fire and first communist leader of postwar Bulgaria. After the fall of Communism the original name, honoring Augustus the Strong, was reinstated. ✉ *Dresden.*

OFF THE BEATEN PATH

Deutsches Hygiene-Museum Dresden. This unique (even in a country with a national tendency for excessive cleanliness) and unfortunately named museum relates the history of public health and science. The permanent exhibit offers lots of hands-on activities. The building itself housed the Nazi eugenics program, and the special exhibit on this period is not recommended for children under 12. ✉ *Lingnerpl. 1* ☎ *0351/48460* ⊕ *www.dhmd.de* 🎟 *€7* ⊙ *Tues.–Sun. 10–6.*

Johanneum. At one time the royal stables, this 16th-century building now houses the **Verkehrsmuseum** (Transportation Museum), a collection of historic conveyances, including vintage automobiles and engines. The former **stable exercise yard**, behind the Johanneum and enclosed by elegant Renaissance arcades, was used during the 16th century as an open-air festival ground. A ramp leading up from the courtyard made it possible for royalty to reach the upper story to view the jousting below without having to dismount. More popular even than jousting in those days was *Ringelstechen*, a risky pursuit in which riders at full gallop had to catch small rings on their lances. Horses and riders often came to grief in the narrow confines of the stable yard.

On the outside wall of the Johanneum (behind the building on the Augustrasse) is a remarkable example of porcelain art: a 336-foot-long Meissen tile mural of a royal procession. More than 100 members of the royal Saxon house of Wettin, half of them on horseback, are represented on the giant mosaic, known as the **"Procession of Princes,"** which is made of 25,000 porcelain tiles, painted in 1904–07 after a design by Wilhelm Walther. The representations are in chronological order: at 1694, Augustus the Strong's horse is trampling a rose, the symbol of Martin Luther and the Protestant Reformation. The Johanneum is reached by steps leading down from the Brühlsche Terrasse. ⊠ *Am Neumarkt at Augustusstr. 1* 📞 *0351/86440* ⊕ *www.verkehrsmuseum-dresden.de* 🎫 *€9* 🕐 *Tues.–Sun. 10–6.*

Katholische Hofkirche (*Catholic Court Church*). The largest Catholic church in Saxony is also known as the Cathedral of St. Trinitatis. Frederick Augustus II (who reigned 1733–63) brought architects and builders from Italy to construct a Catholic church in a city that had been the first large center of Lutheran Protestantism (like his father, Frederick Augustus II had to convert to Catholicism to be eligible to wear the Polish crown). Inside, the treasures include a beautiful stone pulpit by the royal sculptor Balthasar Permoser and a painstakingly restored 250-year-old organ, said to be one of the finest ever to come from the mountain workshops of the famous Silbermann family. In the cathedral's crypt are the tombs of 49 Saxon rulers and a reliquary containing the heart of Augustus the Strong, which is rumored to start beating if a beautiful woman comes near. ⊠ *Schlosspl.* 📞 *0351/484–4712* 🎫 *Free* 🕐 *Mon.–Thurs. 9–5, Fri. 1–5, Sat. 10–5, Sun. noon–4:30.*

Kreuzkirche (*Cross Church*). Soaring high above the Altmarkt, the richly decorated tower of the baroque Kreuzkirche dates back to 1792, but Dresden's main Protestant church has graced this spot for more than 800 years. The church's massive exterior is punctuated by a very simple and dignified nave. It was here that Lutherans celebrated their first mass in Saxony in 1539. A famous boys' choir, the Kreuzchor, performs here regularly (check website or call for times). ⊠ *Altmarkt* 📞 *0351/439–390* 🎫 *Tower €1.50* 🕐 *Nov.–Mar., weekdays 10–4, Sun. 11–4; Apr.–Oct., daily 10–6.*

Pfund's Molkerei (*Pfund's Dairy Shop*). This decorative 19th-century shop has been a Dresden institution since 1880, and offers a wide assortment of cheese and other goods. The shop is renowned for its intricate tile mosaics on the floor and walls. Pfund's is also famous for introducing pasteurized milk to the industry; it invented milk soap and specially treated milk for infants as early as 1900. ⊠ *Bautzener Str. 79* 📞 *0351/808–080* ⊕ *www.pfunds.de* 🕐 *Mon.–Sat. 10–6, Sun. 10–3.*

Stadtmuseum Dresden im Landhaus (*Dresden City Museum at the Landhaus*). The city's small but fascinating municipal museum tells the ups and downs of Dresden's turbulent past—from the dark Middle Ages to the bombing of Dresden in February 1945. There are many peculiar exhibits on display, such as an American 250-kilogram bomb and a stove made from an Allied bomb casing. The building has the most interesting fire escape in the city. ⊠ *Wilsdruffer Str. 2* 📞 *0351/656–480* ⊕ *www.stmd.de* 🎫 *€5* 🕐 *Tues.–Sun. 10–6 (Fri. until 8).*

WHERE TO EAT

$$

GERMAN

✕ **Alte Meister.** Set in the historic mansion of the architect who rebuilt the Zwinger, and named after the school of medieval painters that includes Dürer, Holbein, and Rembrandt, the Alte Meister has a sophisticated old-world flair that charms locals and tourists alike. The food is very current, despite the decor, and the light German nouvelle cuisine with careful touches of Asian spices and ingredients has earned chef Dirk Wende critical praise. In summer this is one of the city's premier dining spots, offering a grand view of the Semperoper from a shaded terrace. [$] *Average main: €20* ✉ *Theaterpl. 1a* ☎ *0351/481–0426.*

$ GERMAN 🍴 **Ball und Brauhaus Watzke.** One of the city's oldest microbreweries, the Watzke offers a great reprieve from Dresden's mass-produced Radeberger. Several different homemade beers are on tap—you can even help brew one. Tours of the brewery cost €5 with a tasting, or €12.50 with a meal, and you can get your beer to go in a 1- or 2-liter jug called a *Siphon*. The food is hearty, contemporary Saxon. When the weather is nice, enjoy the fantastic panoramic view of Dresden from the beer garden. [$] *Average main: €14* ✉ *Koetzschenbroderstr. 1* ☎ *0351/852–920.*

$ GERMAN 🍴 **Sophienkeller.** One of the liveliest restaurants in town re-creates an 18th-century beer cellar in the basement of the Taschenberg Palace. The furniture and porcelain are as rustic as the food is traditional, including the typically Saxon *Gesindeessen* (rye bread, panfried with mustard, slices of pork, and mushrooms, baked with cheese). The Sophienkeller is popular with larger groups; you might have to wait if you're a party of three or fewer. During the wait, check out the bread baker near the entrance. [$] *Average main: €14* ✉ *Taschenbergpalais, Taschenberg 3* ☎ *0351/497–260.*

$ GERMAN 🍴 **Watzke Brauereiausschank am Goldenen Reiter.** The Ball und Brauhaus Watzke microbrewery operates this smaller restaurant with the same beer and hearty menu, directly across from the Goldene Reiter statue of Augustus the Strong. [$] *Average main: €14* ✉ *Hauptstr. 11* ☎ *0351/810–6820.*

WHERE TO STAY

$ HOTEL 🏨 **art'otel Dresden.** This hotel keeps the promise of its name: it's all modern, designed by Italian interior architect Denis Santachiara, and decorated with more than 600 works of art by Dresden-born painter and sculptor A. R. **Pros:** art elements make the hotel fun. **Cons:** bathrooms have an opaque window into the room; decor is not for everyone. [$] *Rooms from: €75* ✉ *Ostra-Allee 33* ☎ *0351/49220* 🌐 *www.artotels.com* 🛏 *155 rooms, 19 suites* 🍽 *Breakfast.*

$ HOTEL 🏨 **Hotel Bülow-Residenz.** One of the most intimate first-class hotels in eastern Germany, the Bülow-Residenz is in a baroque palace built in 1730 by a wealthy Dresden city official. **Pros:** extremely helpful staff. **Cons:** air-conditioning can be noisy; hotel is located in Neustadt, a 10-minute walk across the river to the city center. [$] *Rooms from: €69* ✉ *Rähnitzg. 19* ☎ *0351/80030* 🌐 *www.buelow-residenz.de* 🛏 *25 rooms, 5 suites* 🍽 *No meals.*

$ HOTEL 🏨 **Hotel Elbflorenz.** This centrally located hotel with Dresden's somewhat presumptuous nickname ("Florence on the Elbe") contains Italian-designed rooms bathed in red and yellow and arranged alongside a garden courtyard. **Pros:** extraordinary breakfast buffet. **Cons:** in need of renovation; located at edge of city center. [$] *Rooms from: €71* ✉ *Rosenstr. 36* ☎ *0351/86400* 🌐 *www.hotel-elbflorenz.de* 🛏 *212 rooms, 15 suites* 🍽 *Breakfast.*

$$$ HOTEL **Kempinski Hotel Taschenbergpalais Dresden.** Rebuilt after wartime bombing, the historic Taschenberg Palace—the work of Zwinger architect Matthäus Daniel Pöppelmann—is Dresden's premier address and the last word in luxury, as befits the former residence of the Saxon crown princes. **Pros:** ice-skating in the courtyard in winter; concierge knows absolutely everything about Dresden. **Cons:** expensive extra charges for breakfast and Internet. [$] *Rooms from: €179* ✉ *Taschenberg 3* ☎ *0351/49120* 🌐 *www.kempinski-dresden.de* 🛏 *188 rooms, 25 suites* 🍴 *No meals.*

$ HOTEL **Rothenburger Hof.** One of Dresden's smallest and oldest luxury hotels, the historic Rothenburger Hof opened in 1865, and is only a few steps away from the city's sightseeing spots. **Pros:** nice garden and indoor pool. **Cons:** across the river in Neustadt, about 20 minutes from the city center; street can be noisy in summer. [$] *Rooms from: €99* ✉ *Rothenburger Str. 15–17* ☎ *0351/81260* 🌐 *www.dresden-hotel.de* 🛏 *26 rooms, 13 apartments* 🍴 *Breakfast.*

NIGHTLIFE AND PERFORMING ARTS

NIGHTLIFE

Dresdeners are known for their industriousness and efficient way of doing business, but they also know how to spend a night out. Most of Dresden's pubs and *Kneipen* (bars) are in the **Neustadt** district, across the river from most sights, and along the buzzing **Münzgasse** (between the Frauenkirche and the Brühlsche Terrasse).

Aqualounge. This groovy and hip place is one of the best bars in town. ✉ *Louisenstr. 56* ☎ *0351/810–6116* 🌐 *www.aqualounge.de.*

Bärenzwinger. Folk and rock music are regularly featured here. ✉ *Brühlscher Garten* ☎ *0351/495–1409* 🌐 *www.baerenzwinger.de.*

Motown Club. Hot African rhythms attract a young and stylish crowd. ✉ *St. Petersburger Str. 9* ☎ *0351/487–4150.*

Planwirtschaft. The name ironically refers to the planned socialist economic system; it attracts an alternative crowd. ✉ *Louisenstr. 20* ☎ *0351/801–3187.*

Tonne Jazz Club. Jazz musicians perform most nights of the week at this friendly, laid-back club. ✉ *Waldschlösschen, Am Brauhaus 3* ☎ *0351/802–6017.*

PERFORMING ARTS

Philharmonie Dresden (*Philharmonic Orchestra Dresden*). Dresden's fine orchestra takes center stage in the city's annual music festival, from mid-May to early June. ✉ *Kulturpalast am Altmarkt* ☎ *0351/486–6286* 🌐 *en.dresdnerphilharmonie.de.*

Semperoper Dresden (*Semper Opera House*). The opera in Dresden holds an international reputation largely due to its opera house. Destroyed during the war, the building has been meticulously rebuilt and renovated. Tickets are reasonably priced but also hard to come by; they're often included in package tours. Try reserving tickets on the website, or stop by the box office (just left of the main entrance) about a half hour before the performance. If that doesn't work, take one of the opera-house

The Semperoper Dresden (Semper Opera House) saw the openings of several of Richard Wagner's and Richard Strauss's best-loved operas. Its plush interiors are rich with velvet and brocade.

tours, a nice consolation that gets you into the building. ⊠ *Theaterpl.* ☎ *0351/491–1705 Evening box office* ⊕ *www.semperoper.de.*

SHOPPING

Dresden's Striezelmarkt. Dating to 1434, this market was named after the city's famous Stollen, a buttery Christmas fruitcake often made with marzipan and sprinkled with powdered sugar. The market hosts a festival in its honor, complete with a 9,000-pound cake, on the Saturday of the second weekend of Advent. Traditional wooden toys produced in the nearby Erzgebirge mountains are the other major draw. ⊠ *Altmarkt* ⊕ *www.dresden-striezelmarkt.de* ☉ *Nov. 24–Dec. 23, daily 10–9; Dec. 24, 10–2.*

MEISSEN

25 km (15 miles) northwest of Dresden.

This romantic city with its imposing castle looming over the Elbe River is known the world over for Europe's finest porcelain, emblazoned with its trademarked crossed blue swords. The first European porcelain was made in this area in 1708, and in 1710 the Royal Porcelain Workshop was established in Meissen, close to the local raw materials.

The story of how porcelain came to be produced here reads like a German fairy tale: the Saxon elector Augustus the Strong, who ruled from 1694 to 1733, urged his court alchemists to find the secret of making gold, something he badly needed to refill a state treasury depleted by his extravagant lifestyle. The alchemists failed to produce gold, but one of them, Johann Friedrich Böttger, discovered a method for making something almost as precious: fine hard-paste porcelain. Already a rapacious collector of Oriental porcelains, the prince put Böttger and a team of craftsmen up in a hilltop castle—Albrechtsburg—and set them to work.

GETTING HERE AND AROUND

Meissen is an easy 45-minute train ride from Dresden. On arrival, exit the station and walk to the left; as you turn the corner there is a beautiful view of Meissen across the river. Trains run about every 30 minutes.

ESSENTIALS

Visitor Information Tourist-Information Meissen. ⊠ *Markt 3* ☎ *03521/41940, 03521/419–419* ⊕ *www.touristinfo-meissen.de.*

EXPLORING

Albrechtsburg. The story of Meissen porcelain actually began high above Old Meissen. Towering over the Elbe River, this 15th-century castle is Germany's first truly residential one, a complete break with the earlier style of fortified bastions. In the central *Schutzhof,* a typical Gothic courtyard protected on three sides by high rough-stone walls, is an exterior spiral staircase, the **Wendelstein,** a masterpiece of early masonry hewn in 1525 from a single massive stone block. The ceilings of the castle halls are richly decorated, although many date only from a restoration in 1870. Adjacent to the castle is an early Gothic cathedral. It's a bit of a climb up Burgstrasse and Amtsstrasse to the castle, but a bus runs regularly up the hill from the Marktplatz. ⊠ *Meissen* ☎ *03521/47070* ⊕ *www.albrechtsburg-meissen.de* ✉ *€8* ☉ *Mar.–Oct., daily 10–6; Nov.–Feb., daily 10–5.*

Altes Brauhaus (*Old Brewery*). Near the Frauenkirche, the Altes Brauhaus dates to 1460 and is graced by a Renaissance gable. It now houses city offices. ⊠ *An der Frauenkirche 3.*

Franziskanerkirche (*St. Francis Church*). The city's medieval past is recounted in the museum of this former monastery. ⊠ *Heinrichspl. 3* ☎ *03521/458–857* ✉ *€3* ☉ *Daily 11–5.*

Frauenkirche (*Church of Our Lady*). A set of porcelain bells at the late-Gothic Frauenkirche, on the central Marktplatz, was the first of its kind anywhere when installed in 1929. ⊠ *An der Frauenkirche.*

Nikolaikirche (*St. Nicholas Church*). Near the porcelain works, this church holds the largest set of porcelain figures ever crafted (8¼ feet tall) as well as the remains of early Gothic frescoes. ⊠ *Neumarkt 29.*

Staatliche Porzellan–Manufaktur Meissen (*Meissen Porcelain Works*). Outgrowing its castle workshop in the mid-19th century, today's porcelain factory is on the southern outskirts of town. One of its buildings has a demonstration workshop and a museum whose Meissen collection rivals that of Dresden's Porzellansammlung. ⊠ *Talstr. 9* ☎ *03521/468–208* ⊕ *www.meissen.de* ✉ *€9 including workshop and museum* ☉ *May–Oct., daily 9–6; Nov.–Apr., daily 9–5.*

WHERE TO EAT AND STAY

$ ╳**Domkeller.** Part of the centuries-old complex of buildings ringing
GERMAN the town castle, this ancient and popular hostelry is a great place to enjoy fine wines and hearty German dishes. It's also worth a visit for

16

the sensational view of the Elbe River valley from the large dining room and tree-shaded terrace. $ *Average main: €14* ⊠ *Dompl. 9* ☎ *03521/457–676.*

$$
GERMAN
✕ **Restaurant Vincenz Richter.** Tucked away in a yellow wooden-beam house, this historic restaurant has been painstakingly maintained by the Richter family since 1873. The dining room is adorned with rare antiques, documents, and medieval weapons, as well as copper and tin tableware. Guests can savor the exquisite dishes on the Saxon-German menu while sampling the restaurant's own personally produced white wine; a bottle of the Riesling is a real pleasure. Try the delicious wild rabbit with bacon-wrapped plums, paired with a glass of Kerner Meissener Kapitelberg , and cleanse your palate between courses with an inspiring Riesling sorbet $ *Average main: €15* ⊠ *An der Frauenkirche 12* ☎ *03521/453–285* ⊘ *Closed Mon. No dinner Sun.*

> ### THE ORIGINS OF THE MEISSEN FUMMEL
>
> At the beginning of the 18th century, the Great Elector of Saxony routinely sent proclamations by messenger to his subjects in Meissen. The messengers were known to chase women and behave poorly, often drinking so much of the famous Meissen wine that their horses were the only ones who remembered the way back to Dresden. To curb this behavior, the elector charged the bakers of Meissen with creating an extremely fragile cake, which the messengers would have to remain sober enough to deliver to the elector intact. Today, the Meissner Fummel remains a local specialty.

$
HOTEL
☷ **Welcome Parkhotel Meissen.** Most of the luxuriously furnished and appointed rooms are in newly built annexes, but for turn-of-the-century charm, opt for a room in the art nouveau villa, which sits on the bank of the Elbe across from the hilltop castle. **Pros:** gorgeous views; elegant rooms; fine dining. **Cons:** villa rooms are not as newly furnished; international chain hotel. $ *Rooms from: €74* ⊠ *Hafenstr. 27–31* ☎ *03521/72250* ⊕ *www.welcome-hotel-meissen.de* ⤵ *92 rooms, 5 suites* ⦿ *Breakfast.*

PERFORMING ARTS

Concerts. Regular concerts are held at the Albrechtsburg castle, and in early September the *Burgfestspiele*—open-air evening performances—are staged in the castle's romantic courtyard. ⊠ *Meissen* ☎ *03521/47070.*

Dom. Meissen's cathedral, the Dom, has a yearlong music program, with organ and choral concerts every Saturday in summer. ⊠ *Dompl. 7* ☎ *03521/452–490.*

SHOPPING

Sächsische Winzergenossenschaft Meissen. To wine connoisseurs, the name "Meissen" is associated with vineyards producing top-quality white wines much in demand throughout Germany. Müller-Thurgau, Weissburgunder, and Goldriesling are worthy choices and can be bought directly from the producer, Sächsische Winzergenossenschaft Meissen. ⊠ *Bennoweg 9* ☎ *03521/780–970* ⊕ *www.winzer-meissen.de.*

Staatliche Porzellan–Manufaktur Meissen. Meissen porcelain is available directly from the porcelain works as well as in every china and gift shop in town. ⊠ *Talstr. 9* ☎ *03521/468–700.*

BAUTZEN/BUDYŠIN

53 km (33 miles) east of Dresden.

Bautzen has perched high above a deep granite valley formed by the River Spree for more than 1,000 years. Its almost-intact city walls hide a remarkably well-preserved city with wandering back alleyways and fountain-graced squares. Bautzen is definitely a German city, but it is also the administrative center of Germany's only indigenous ethnic minority, the Sorbs.

In the area, the Sorb language enjoys equal standing with German in government and education, and Sorbs are known for their colorful folk traditions. As in all Slavic cultures, Easter Sunday is the highlight of the calendar, when ornately decorated eggs are hung from trees and when the traditional *Osterreiten,* a procession of Catholic men on horseback who carry religious symbols and sing Sorbian hymns, takes place.

> ### BAUTZEN CUTS THE MUSTARD
>
> Bautzen is famous for mustard, which has been ground here since 1866. Mustard is Germany's favorite condiment, and East Germans consume an average of 5 pounds of the stuff annually. It's so deeply ingrained that here one "gives his mustard" in the same way English speakers would their "two cents." The most popular Bautzen mustard, Bautz'ner Senf, is one of the rare East German products that sells well in the West. Available at almost every supermarket, a 200-milliliter (7-ounce) tub costs approximately €0.30, making it a great present for those at home.

16

GETTING HERE AND AROUND

Bautzen is halfway between Dresden and Görlitz. Trains leave both cities once every hour; travel time is about an hour.

ESSENTIALS

Visitor Information Tourist-Information Bautzen-Budyšin. ⊠ *Tourist-Information Bautzen-Budyšin, Hauptmarkt 1, Bautzen* ☎ *03591/42016, 03591/327–629* ⊕ *www.bautzen.de.*

EXPLORING

Alte Wasserkunst (*Old Waterworks*). Erected in 1558, the Alte Wasserkunst served as part of the town's defensive fortifications, but its true purpose was to pump water from the Spree into 86 cisterns spread throughout the city. It proved so efficient that it provided the city's water supply until 1965. It is now a technical museum. ⊠ *Wendischer Kirchhof 7, Bautzen* ☎ *03591/41588* ₪ *€3* ⊙ *Daily 10–5.*

Dom St. Petri (*St. Peter's Cathedral*). Behind the Rathaus is one of Bautzen's most interesting sights: Dom St. Petri is Germany's only *Simultankirche,* or "simultaneous" church. In order to avoid the violence that often occurred during the Reformation, St. Peter's has a Protestant side and a Roman Catholic side in the same church. A short fence, which once reached a height of 13 feet, separates the two congregations. The church was built in 1213 on the sight of a Milzener (the forerunners of the Sorbs) parish church. ✉ *An der Petrikirche 6, Bautzen* ☎ *03591/31180* 🌐 *www.dompfarrei-bautzen.de* 🎫 *Free* ⏱ *May–Oct., Mon.–Sat. 10–3, Sun. 1–4; Nov.–Apr., daily 11–noon.*

Hexenhäuser (*Witches' Houses*). Below the waterworks and outside the walls, these three reddish houses were the only structures to survive all the city's fires—leading Bautzeners to conclude that they could only be occupied by witches. ✉ *Fischergasse, Bautzen.*

Rathaus. Bautzen's main market square is actually two squares, the **Hauptmarkt** (Main Market) and the **Fleischmarkt** (Meat Market), separated by the yellow, baroque Rathaus. The current town hall dates from 1705, but there has been a town hall in this location since 1213. Bautzen's friendly tourist-information center, next door, has a great Bautzen-in-two-hours walking-tour map and an MP3 guide to the city. ✉ *Fleischmarkt 1, Bautzen.*

Reichenturm (*Rich Tower*). Bautzen's city walls have a number of gates and towers. This one, at the end of Reichenstrasse, is the most impressive. Although the tower base dates from 1490, it was damaged in four city fires (in 1620, 1639, 1686, and 1747) and rebuilt, hence its baroque cupola. The reconstruction caused the tower to lean, however, and its foundation was further damaged in 1837. The "Leaning Tower of Bautzen" currently sits about 5 feet off center. The view from the top is a spectacular vista of Bautzen and the surrounding countryside. ✉ *Reichenstr. 1, Bautzen* ☎ *03591/460–431* 🎫 *€2* ⏱ *Daily 10–5.*

WHERE TO EAT AND STAY

$ EASTERN EUROPEAN 🍴 **Wjelbik.** The name of Bautzen's best Sorbian restaurant means "pantry." Very popular on Sorb holidays, Wjelbik uses exclusively regional produce in such offerings as the *Sorbisches Hochzeitsmenu* (Sorb wedding feast)—a vegetable and meatball soup followed by beef in creamed horseradish. The restaurant is in a 600-year-old building near the cathedral. [$] *Average main: €14* ✉ *Kornstr. 7, Bautzen* ☎ *03591/42060* 🌐 *www.wjelbik.de.*

$$ HOTEL 🏨 **Hotel Goldener Adler.** This pleasant hotel occupies a 450-year-old building on the main market square, and great effort has been made to incorporate traditional building elements into the modern and spacious rooms. **Pros:** a complete package: comfortable historical hotel, good restaurant, and yummy fondue. **Cons:** a little too modern for a historical town. [$] *Rooms from: €120* ✉ *Hauptmarkt 4, Bautzen* ☎ *03591/48660* 🌐 *www.goldeneradler.de* 🛏 *30 rooms* 🍽 *No meals.*

GÖRLITZ

48 km (30 miles) east of Bautzen, 60 km (38 miles) northeast of Dresden.

Tucked away in the country's easternmost corner (bordering Poland), Görlitz's quiet, narrow cobblestone alleys and exquisite architecture make it one of Germany's most beautiful cities. It emerged from the destruction of World War II relatively unscathed. As a result it has more than 4,000 historic houses in styles including Gothic, Renaissance,

Görlitz's Untermarkt contains the Rathaus and also building No. 14, where all goods coming into the city were weighed and taxed.

baroque, rococo, Wilhelminian, and art nouveau. Although the city has impressive museums, theater, and music, it's the ambience created by the casual dignity of these buildings, in their jumble of styles, that makes Görlitz so attractive. Notably absent are the typical socialist eyesores and the glass-and-steel modernism found in many eastern German towns.

The Gothic Dicker Turm (Fat Tower) guards the entrance to the city; it's the oldest tower in Görlitz, and its walls are 5 meters (6½ feet) thick.

GETTING HERE AND AROUND

Görlitz can be reached by hourly trains from Dresden (1½ hours) and from Berlin (3 hours, with a change in Cottbus). Görlitz's train station (a wonderful neoclassical building with an art nouveau interior) is a short tram ride outside town.

ESSENTIALS

Visitor Information Görlitz-Information und Tourist-Service. ⊠ *Bruderstr. 1* ☎ *03581/47570, 03581/475–727* ⊕ *www.goerlitz.de.*

EXPLORING

Biblical House. This house is interesting for its Renaissance facade decorated with sandstone reliefs depicting biblical stories. The Catholic Church banned religious depictions on secular buildings, but by the time the house was rebuilt after a fire in 1526, the Reformation had Görlitz firmly in its grip. ⊠ *Neissestr. 29.*

Dreifaltigkeitskirche (*Church of the Holy Trinity*). On the southeast side of the market lies this pleasant Romanesque church with a Gothic interior, built in 1245. The interior houses an impressive Gothic triptych altarpiece. The clock on the thin tower is set seven minutes fast in remembrance of a trick played by the city guards on the leaders of a rebellion. In 1527 the city's disenfranchised cloth makers secretly met to plan a rebellion against the city council and the powerful guilds. Their plans were uncovered, and by setting the clock ahead the guards fooled the rebels into thinking it was safe to sneak into the city. As a result they were caught and hanged. ⊠ *Obermarkt* ☎ €4.

Karstadt. Dating from 1912–13, Germany's only original art nouveau department store has a main hall with a colorful glass cupola and several stunning freestanding staircases. The store dominates the Marienplatz, a small square outside the city center that serves as Görlitz's transportation hub. It's next to the 15th-century Frauenkirche, the parish church for the nearby hospital and the poor condemned to live outside the city walls. Though the department store is closed (the city is trying to open it to the public), you can peek inside through the perfume shop. ⊠ *An der Frauenkirche 5–7* ☎ *03581/4600*.

Kirche St. Peter und Paul (*St. Peter and Paul Church*). Perched high above the river is one of Saxony's largest late-Gothic churches, dating to 1423. The real draw is the church's famous one-of-a-kind organ, built in 1703 by Eugenio Casparini. The Sun Organ gets its name from the circularly arranged pipes and not from the golden sun at the center. Its full and deep sound, as well as its birdcalls, can be heard on Sunday and Wednesday afternoons. ⊠ *Bei der Peterkirche 5* ☎ *03581/409–590* ☎ *Free* ☉ *Mon.–Sat. 10:30–4, Sun. 11:30–4; guided tours Thurs. and Sun. at noon.*

OFF THE BEATEN PATH

Landskron Braumanufaktur (*Landskron Brewery*). Germany's easternmost Brauhaus is one of the few breweries left that gives tours. Founded in 1869, Landskron isn't very old by German standards, but it's unique in that it hasn't been gobbled up by a huge brewing conglomerate. *Görlitzer* are understandably proud of their own Premium Pilsner, but the brewery also produces good dark, Silesian, and winter beers. Landskron Hefeweizen is one of the best in the country. ⊠ *An der Landskronbrauerei* ☎ *03581/465–121* ⊕ *www.landskron.de* ☎ *Tours €8–€25* ☉ *Sun.–Thurs., tours by appointment.*

Obermarkt (*Upper Market*). The richly decorated Renaissance homes and warehouses on the Obermarkt are a vivid legacy of the city's wealthy past. During the late Middle Ages the most common merchandise here was cloth, which was bought and sold from covered wagons and on the

---

GÖRLITZ'S SECRET ADMIRER

After German unification, Görlitz was a run-down border town, but renovations costing upward of €400 million returned the city to much of its former splendor. In 1995 it got an additional boost when an anonymous philanthropist pledged to the city a yearly sum of 1 million marks. Every March, Görlitz celebrates the arrival in its coffers of the mysterious Altstadt-Million (albeit, with the change in currency, now €511,000).

ground floors of many buildings. Napoléon addressed his troops from the balcony of the house at No. 29. ⊠ *Görlitz.*

Schlesisches Museum (*Silesian Museum*). Exploring 900 years of Silesian culture, this is a meeting place for Silesians from Germany, Poland, and the Czech Republic. The museum is housed in the magnificent Schönhof building, one of Germany's oldest Renaissance *Patrizierhäuser* (grand mansions of the city's ruling business and political elite). ⊠ *Brüderstr. 8* ☎ *03581/87910* ⊕ *www.schlesisches-museum.de* 🎫 *€6* ⊗ *Tues.–Sun. 10–5.*

Untermarkt (*Lower Market*). One of Europe's most impressive squares, this market is a testament to the prosperity brought by the cloth trade. It's built up in the middle, and the most important building is No. 14, which formerly housed the city scales. The duty of the city scale masters, whose busts adorn the Renaissance facade of the Gothic building, was to weigh every ounce of merchandise entering the city and to determine the taxes due.

The square's most prominent building is the Rathaus. Its winding staircase is as peculiar as its statue of the goddess of justice, whose eyes—contrary to European tradition—are not covered. The corner house on the square, the Alte Ratsapotheke (Old Council Pharmacy), has two intricate sundials on the facade, painted in 1550. ⊠ *Görlitz.*

Verrätergasse (*Traitors' Alley*). On Verrätergasse, across the Obermarkt square from the church, is the **Peter-Liebig-Haus**, where the initials of the first four words of the rebels' meeting place, *Der verräterischen Rotte Tor* (the treacherous gang's gate), are inscribed above the door. The Obermarkt is dominated by the **Reichenbach Turm**, a tower built in the 13th century, with additions in 1485 and 1782. Until 1904 the tower housed the city watchmen and their families. The apartments and armory are now a museum. There are great views of the city from the tiny windows at the top. The massive **Kaisertrutz** (Emperor's Fortress) once protected the western city gates, and now houses late-Gothic and Renaissance art from the area around Görlitz, as well as some impressive historical models of the city. Both buildings are part of the Kulturhistorisches Museum. ⊠ *Görlitz* ☎ *03581/671–355* ⊕ *www. museum-goerlitz.de* 🎫 *€7, ticket valid 2 consecutive days* ⊗ *Tues.– Thurs. and weekends 10–5.*

WHERE TO EAT AND STAY

$
GERMAN

✕ **Die Destille.** This small family-run establishment overlooks the Nikolaiturm, one of the towers of the city's wall. The restaurant offers good solid Silesian fare and absolutely the best *Schlesische Himmelreich* (ham and pork roast smothered in baked fruit and white sauce, served with dumplings) in town. There are also eight inexpensive, spartan guest rooms where you can spend the night. 🅂 *Average main: €12* ⊠ *Nikolaistr. 6* ☎ *03581/405–302* ▭ *No credit cards* ⊗ *Sometimes closed in Sept.*

$
HOTEL

▦ **Hotel Bon-Apart.** The name says it all: this hotel is an homage to Napoléon, whose troops occupied Görlitz, and it's a splendid departure from a "normal" hotel. **Pros:** large rooms with kitchens and artistically decorated bathrooms; huge breakfast buffet. **Cons:** eclectic design may not appeal to everyone; neighboring market can be noisy

16

in the morning; no elevator. $ *Rooms from: €95* ⊠ *Elisabethstr. 41* ☎ *03581/48080* ⊕ *www.bon-apart.de* ⇘ *20 rooms* ⧀ *Breakfast.*

SAXONY-ANHALT

The central state of Saxony-Anhalt is a region rich in history and natural beauty, almost completely undiscovered by modern visitors. In the Altmark, on the edge of the Harz Mountains, fields of grain and sugar beets stretch to the horizon. In the mountains themselves are the deep gorge of the Bode River and the stalactite-filled caves of Rubeland. The songbirds of the Harz are renowned, and though pollution has taken its toll, both the flora and the fauna of the Harz National Park (which encompasses much of the region) are coming back. Atop the Brocken, the Harz's highest point, legend has it that witches convene on Walpurgis Night (the night between April 30 and May 1).

Saxony-Anhalt's Letzlinger Heide (Letzling Heath), another home to rare birds and animals, is one of Germany's largest tracts of uninhabited land. The Dübener Heide (Düben Heath), south of Wittenberg, has endless woods of oaks, beeches, and evergreens that are wonderful to explore by bike or on foot. In and around Dessau are magnificent parks and gardens. Architecturally, Saxony-Anhalt abounds in half-timber towns and Romanesque churches. Quedlinburg has both the oldest half-timber house in Germany and the tomb of Germany's first king, 10th-century Henry I. In Dessau the Bauhaus School pointed the world to modern architecture and design just before the start of World War II. Music has thrived in Saxony-Anhalt as well. Among its favorite sons are the composers Georg Philipp Telemann, of Magdeburg; George Frideric Handel, of Halle; and in modern times Kurt Weill, of Dessau. And it was in Wittenberg that Martin Luther nailed his 95 Theses to a church door.

LUTHERSTADT-WITTENBERG

107 km (62 miles) southwest of Berlin, 67 km (40 miles) north of Leipzig.

Protestantism was born in the little town of Wittenberg (officially called Lutherstadt-Wittenberg). In 1508 the fervently idealistic young Martin Luther, who had become a priest only a year earlier, arrived to study and teach at the new university founded by Elector Frederick the Wise. Nine years later, enraged that the Roman Catholic Church was pardoning sins through the sale of indulgences, Luther attacked the policy by posting his 95 Theses on the door of the Schlosskirche (Castle Church).

Martin Luther is still the center of attention in Wittenberg, and sites associated with him are marked with plaques and signs. You can see virtually all of historic Wittenberg on a 2-km (1-mile) stretch of Collegienstrasse and Schlossstrasse that begins at the railroad tracks and ends at the Schlosskirche.

In preparation for the 500th anniversary of the Reformation, much of the city will be under massive reconstruction until the summer of 2017.

The Lutherhaus and the Schlosskirche are only accessible on special occasions during construction.

GETTING HERE AND AROUND
Lutherstadt-Wittenberg is approximately halfway between Berlin and Leipzig, and is served by regional and ICE trains. The station is slightly outside the city center, a pleasant walking distance away.

ESSENTIALS
Visitor Information Tourist-Information Lutherstadt Wittenberg. ⊠ *Schlosspl. 2, Wittenberg* ☎ *03491/498–610, 03491/498–611* ⊕ *www. wittenberg.de.* **Wittenberg District Rural Information Office.** ⊠ *Neustr. 13, Wittenberg* ☎ *03491/402–610, 03491/405–857.*

FESTIVALS
Luthers Hochzeit (*Luther's Wedding*). The best time to visit Wittenberg is during this citywide festival that commemorates (and reenacts) Martin Luther's marriage to Katharina von Bora. On the second weekend in June the city center goes back in time to 1525, with period costumes and entertainment. ⊕ *www.lutherhochzeit.de.*

EXPLORING

TOP ATTRACTIONS

Luther Melanchthon Gymnasium (*Luther Melanchthon High School*). In 1975 the city erected a typical East German prefab building to house the Luther Melanchthon Gymnasium, but in the early 1990s, art students contacted Friedensreich Hundertwasser, the famous Austrian architect and avant-garde artist who designed the Hundertwasserhaus in Vienna. Hundertwasser, who argued that there are no universal straight lines or completely flat surfaces in nature, agreed to transform the school, and renovations were completed in 1998. The school is one of only three Hundertwasser buildings in eastern Germany and an interesting contrast to the medieval architecture in the rest of the city. Although the building is a school, the students operate a small office that distributes information about the school and Hundertwasser's art. ⊠ *Str. der Völkerfreundschaft 130, Wittenberg* ☎ *03491/881–131* ⊕ *www. hundertwasserschule.de* ⊡ *€2* ⊙ *Tues.–Fri. 2:30–4, weekends 10–4.*

Fodor's Choice ★ **Lutherhaus** (*Luther's House*). Within Lutherhhaus is the Augustinian monastery where Martin Luther lived both as a teacher-monk and later, after the monastery was dissolved, as a married man. Today it's a museum dedicated to Luther and the Reformation. Visitors enter through a garden and an elegant door with a carved stone frame; it was a gift to Luther from his wife, Katharina von Bora. Be sure to visit the monks' refectory, where works by the painter Lucas Cranach the Elder, Luther's contemporary, are displayed. The room that remains closest to the original is the dark, wood-panel Lutherstube. The Luthers and their six children used it as a living room, study, and meeting place for friends and students. Prints, engravings, paintings, manuscripts, coins, and medals relating to the Reformation and Luther's translation of the Bible into the German vernacular are displayed throughout the house. ⊠ *Collegienstr. 54, Wittenberg* ☎ *03491/42030* ⊕ *www.martinluther.de* ⊡ *€6* ⊙ *Apr.–Oct., daily 9–6; Nov.–Mar., Tues.–Sun. 10–5.*

Fodor's Choice ★ **Schlosskirche** (*Castle Church*). In 1517 an indignant Martin Luther nailed his 95 Theses, which attacked the Roman Catholic Church's policy of selling indulgences, to this church's doors. Written in Latin, the theses might have gone unnoticed had not someone—without Luther's knowledge—translated them into German and distributed them. In 1521 the Holy Roman Emperor Charles V summoned Luther to Worms when Luther refused to retract his position. On the way home from his confrontation with the emperor, Luther was "captured" by his protector, Elector Frederick the Wise, and hidden from papal authorities in Eisenach for the better part of a year. Today the theses hang in bronze on the door, while inside, simple bronze plaques mark the burial places of Luther and his contemporary, Philipp Melanchthon. ⊠ *Schlosspl. 1, Wittenberg* ☎ *03491/402–585* ⊡ *Free, tower €2* ⊙ *Church interior closed until summer 2017. May–Oct., Mon.–Sat. 10–5, Sun. 11:30–5; Nov.–Apr., Mon.–Sat. 10–4, Sun. 11:30–4.*

Stadtkirche St. Marien (*Parish Church of St. Mary*). From 1514 until his death in 1546, Martin Luther preached two sermons a week in the twin-tower Stadtkirche St. Marien. He and Katharina von Bora were married here (Luther broke with monasticism in 1525 and married the

Martin Luther taught in the Lecture Hall within Lutherhaus, which is now a museum dedicated to Martin Luther and the Reformation.

former nun). The altar triptych by Lucas Cranach the Elder includes a self-portrait, as well as portraits of Luther wearing the knight's disguise he adopted when hidden at the Wartburg; Luther preaching; Luther's wife and one of his sons; Melanchthon; and Lucas Cranach the Younger. Also notable is the 1457 bronze baptismal font by Herman Vischer the Elder. On the church's southeast corner is a discomforting juxtaposition of the two **monuments** dedicated to Wittenberg's Jews; a 1304 mocking caricature called the Jewish Pig, erected at the time of the expulsion of the town's Jews, and, on the cobblestone pavement, a contemporary memorial to the the city's Jews murdered by the Nazis. ⊠ *Kirchpl., Wittenberg* ☎ *03491/404–415* ⊠ *€1.50, including tour* ⊗ *May–Oct., daily 10–5; Nov.–Apr., daily 10–4.*

WORTH NOTING

Cranachhaus (*First Cranach House*). Lucas Cranach the Elder—court painter, printer, mayor, pharmacist, friend of Luther's, and probably the wealthiest man in Wittenberg—lived in two houses during his years in town. This Cranachhaus is believed to have been the first one. His son, the painter Lucas Cranach the Younger, was born here. Some of the interior has been restored to its 17th-century condition. It's now a gallery with exhibits about Cranach's life and work. Check out the goldsmith and potter that are occasionally on hand demonstrating their crafts in the courtyard. ⊠ *Markt 4, Wittenberg* ☎ *03491/420–190* ⊠ *€6* ⊗ *Mon.–Sat. 10–5, Sun. 1–5.*

Cranachhaus (*Second Cranach House*). In the second Wittenberg home of Cranach the Elder, the Renaissance man not only lived and painted but also operated a print shop, which has been restored, and an apothecary.

The courtyard, where it's thought he did much of his painting, remains much as it was in his day. Children attend the *Malschule* (painting school) here. ⊠ *Schlossstr. 1, Wittenberg* ☎ *03491/410–912* 💳 *Free* 🕙 *Mon.–Thurs. 8–4, Fri. 8–3.*

Haus der Geschichte (*House of History*). This museum makes a valiant attempt to evaluate the history of the GDR. It provides fascinating insight into the day-to-day culture of East Germans through the re-creation of a typical East German apartment, and a display of more than 20,000 objects, including detergent packaging and kitchen appliances. A special section deals with Germans and Russians in the Wittenberg region. ⊠ *Schlossstr. 6, Wittenberg* ☎ *03491/409–004* ⊕ *www.pflug-ev. de* 💳 *€6* 🕙 *Weekdays 10–5, weekends 11–6.*

Luthereiche (*Luther Oak*). In a small park, the Luthereiche marks the spot where, in 1520, Luther burned the papal bull excommunicating him for his criticism of the Church. The present oak was planted in the 19th century. ⊠ *Weserstr. and Collegienstr., Wittenberg.*

Marktplatz (*Market Square*). Two statues are the centerpiece here: an 1821 statue of Luther by Johann Gottfried Schadow, designer of the quadriga and Victory atop Berlin's Brandenburg Gate, and an 1866 statue of Melanchthon by Frederick Drake. Gabled Renaissance houses containing shops line part of the square. ⊠ *Wittenberg.*

Rathaus. The handsome, white High Renaissance town hall forms the backdrop for the Marktplatz's two statues. ⊠ *Markt 26, Wittenberg* ☎ *03491/421–720* 🕙 *Daily 10–5.*

Melanchthonhaus (*Melanchthon House*). In this elegantly gabled Renaissance home, the humanist teacher and scholar Philipp Melanchthon corrected Luther's translation of the New Testament from Greek into German. Luther was hiding in the Wartburg in Eisenach at the time, and as each section of his manuscript was completed it was sent to Melanchthon for approval. (Melanchthon is a Greek translation of the man's real name, Schwarzerdt, which means "black earth"; humanists routinely adopted such classical pseudonyms.) The second-floor furnishings have been painstakingly re-created after period etchings. ⊠ *Collegienstr. 60, Wittenberg* ☎ *03491/403–279* ⊕ *www.martinluther. de* 💳 *€4* 🕙 *Apr.–Oct., daily 10–6; Nov.–Mar., Tues.–Sun. 10–5.*

Wittenberg English Ministry. English-speaking visitors can worship in the churches where Martin Luther conducted his ministry thanks to *this* ministry. During the summer months it brings English-speaking pastors from the United States to provide Lutheran worship services in the Schlosskirche and Stadtkirche St. Marien. Services follow German Protestant tradition (albeit in English) and conclude with singing Luther's "A Mighty Fortress Is Our God," accompanied on the organ. Tours of Wittenberg and other Luther sites are also offered. Despite the reconstruction of the Castle Church, services are being held as scheduled. ⊠ *Schlosspl. 2, Wittenberg* ☎ *03491/498–610* ⊕ *www.wittenberg-english-ministry.com* 🕙 *May–Oct., Sat. at 5, other times by request.*

WHERE TO EAT

$ 🍴 **Brauhaus Wittenberg.** This historic brewery-cum-restaurant is the perfect stop for a cold beer after a long day of sightseeing. Set in the Old Town's magnificent Beyerhof courtyard, the Brauhaus still produces local beer such as Wittenberger Kuckucksbier. In the medieval restaurant with its huge beer kettles, you can sample local and south German cuisine; a specialty is the smoked fish—such as eel, trout, and halibut—from the Brauhaus smokery. In summer, try to get a table in the courtyard. [$] *Average main: €12* ✉ *Markt 6, Wittenberg* ☎ *03491/433–130* 🌐 *www.brauhaus-wittenberg.de.*

GERMAN

$ 🍴 **Schlosskeller.** At the back of the Schlosskirche, this restaurant's four dining rooms are tucked away in a basement with 16th-century stone walls and barrel-vaulted ceilings. The kitchen specializes in German dishes, such as *Kümmelfleisch mit Senfgurken* (caraway beef with mustard-seed pickles). [$] *Average main: €12* ✉ *Schlosspl. 1, Wittenberg* ☎ *03491/480–805.*

GERMAN

DESSAU

35 km (22 miles) southwest of Wittenberg.

The name "Dessau" is known to students of modern architecture as the epicenter of architect Walter Gropius's highly influential Bauhaus school of design. During the 1920s, Gropius hoped to replace the dark and inhumane tenement architecture of the 1800s with standardized yet spacious and bright apartments. His ideas and methods were used in building 316 villas in the city's Törten neighborhood in the 1920s.

GETTING HERE AND AROUND

Dessau makes an excellent day trip from Berlin and the Bauhaus is really the only reason to make the journey. The direct Regional Express train leaves Berlin every hour, and the trip takes 90 minutes.

ESSENTIALS

Visitor Information Tourist-Information Dessau. ✉ *Zerbster Str. 2c* ☎ *0340/204–1442, 0340/220–3003* 🌐 *www.dessau-rosslau-tourismus.de.*

EXPLORING

Bauhaus Building. The architecture school is still operating in this building, where artists conceived styles that influenced the appearance of such cities as New York, Chicago, and San Francisco. Other structures designed by Gropius and the Bauhaus architects, among them the Meisterhäuser, are also open for inspection off Ebertallee and Elballee. ✉ *Gropiusallee 38* ☎ *0340/650–8251* 🌐 *www.bauhaus-dessau.de* 🎫 *€22, includes all Bauhaus sites* 🕒 *Daily 10–6; Meisterhäuser: mid-Feb.–Oct., Tues.–Sun. 10–6; Nov.–mid-Feb., Tues.–Sun. 10–5.*

Georgkirche (*St. George's Church*). Like other older buildings in downtown Dessau, this Dutch-baroque church, built in 1712, is quite a contrast to the no-nonsense Bauhaus architecture. ✉ *Georgenstr. 15.*

Technikmuseum Hugo Junkers (*Hugo Junkers Technical Museum*). The Bauhaus isn't the only show in town. Professor Hugo Junkers, one of the most famous engineers-cum-inventors of the 20th century, was at the forefront of innovation in aircraft and industrial design until his inventions were expropriated by the Nazis in 1933. The star of the museum is a completely restored JU-52/3—the ubiquitous German passenger airplane transformed into military transport. The museum also houses a fascinating collection of industrial equipment, machinery, engines, and the original Junkers wind tunnel. ☒ *Kühnauerstr. 161a* ☎ *0340/661–1982* ⊕ *www.technikmuseum-dessau.de* ☜ *€5* ⊗ *Apr.– Oct., daily 10–5; Nov.–Mar., Tues.–Sun. 10–5.*

HALLE

52 km (32 miles) south of Dessau.

This city deserves a second look. The first impression produced by an ever-under-construction train station and dismal tram ride into town is pleasantly swept away by the pretty 1,000-year-old city built on the salt trade. The name Halle comes from the Celtic word for salt, while the Saale, the name of the river the city straddles, is derived from the German word for salt. Halle has suffered from the shortfalls of Communist urban planning, yet the Old Town has an unusual beauty, particularly in its spacious central marketplace, the **Markt**, with its five distinctive sharp-steeple towers.

GETTING HERE AND AROUND
Frequent S-bahn trains connect Halle with Leipzig (30 minutes) and with Naumburg (20 minutes).

FESTIVALS
Handel Festival. This annual festival takes place in the first half of June, and two youth-choir festivals occur in May and October. ☒ *Halle* ☎ *0345/5009–0222.*

ESSENTIALS
Visitor Information Stadtmarketing Halle. ☒ *Marktpl. 1360* ☎ *0345/122– 9984* ⊕ *www.halle.de.*

EXPLORING
Dom (*Cathedral*). Halle's only early-Gothic church, the Dom stands about 200 yards southeast of the Moritzburg. Its nave and side aisles are of equal height, a common characteristic of Gothic church design in this part of Germany. ☒ *Dompl. 3* ☎ *0345/202–1379* ☜ *Free* ⊗ *June– Oct., Mon.–Sat. 2–4.*

OFF THE BEATEN PATH

Halloren Schokoladenfabrik. Germany's oldest chocolate factory was founded in 1804 and has changed hands several times (including a brief period when it was used to manufacture airplane wings during the war). Its Schokoladenmuseum explores 200 years of chocolate production and contains a 27-square-meter (290-square-foot) room made entirely from chocolate. Entrance to the museum also allows entrance to the glass-enclosed production line, where you can watch almost all aspects of chocolate making. The factory is on the other side of the train station from the main town. To get here, take Tram 7 to Fiete-Schultze-Strasse and walk back about 200 yards. ☒ *Delitzscherstr. 70* ☎ *0345/564–2192* ⊕ *www.halloren.de* ☜ *€4, includes samples* ⊗ *Mon.–Sat. 9–4.*

Händelhaus (*Handel House*). Handel's birthplace is now a museum devoted to the composer. The entrance hall displays glass harmonicas and curious musical instruments perfected by Benjamin Franklin in the 1760s. Be sure to look for the small courtyard where Handel played as a child. ☒ *Grosse Nikolaistr. 5* ☏ *0345/500–900* ☒ *Free* ⊙ *Tues., Wed., and Fri.–Sun. 9:30–5:30, Thurs. 9:30–7.*

Marienkirche (*St. Mary's Church*). Of the four towers belonging to the late-Gothic Marienkirche, two are connected by a vertiginous catwalk bridge. Martin Luther preached in the church, and George Frideric Handel (Händel in German), born in Halle in 1685, was baptized at its font. He went on to learn to play the organ beneath its high, vaulted ceiling. ☒ *An der Marienkirche 2.*

Marktschlösschen (*Market Palace*). This late-Renaissance building just off the market square houses an interesting collection of historical musical instruments, some of which could have been played by Handel and his contemporaries. ☒ *Marktpl. 13* ☏ *0345/202–9141* ☒ *Free* ⊙ *Tues.–Fri. 10–7, weekends 10–6.*

> ### SALT AND CHOCOLATE
>
> In Halle the salt trade was controlled by the *Halloren* (members of the brotherhood of salt workers), who cooked brine into salt on the banks of the Saale River. All that remains of the once incredibly powerful Halloren are the tasty *Halloren-Kügel*, a praline made by the Halloren Schokoladenfabrik, Germany's oldest chocolate factory. The candy is modeled after the silver buttons worn by the Halloren. Very popular in eastern Germany, the chocolates can be purchased just about anywhere in town—there is an outlet store in the train station.

16

Moritzburg (*Moritz Castle*). The Archbishop of Magdeburg built the Moritzburg in the late 15th century, after he claimed the city for his archdiocese. The typical late-Gothic fortress, with a dry moat and a sturdy round tower at each of its four corners, is a testament to Halle's early might, which vanished with the Thirty Years' War (1618–48). Prior to World War II the castle contained a leading gallery of German expressionist paintings, which were ripped from the walls by the Nazis and condemned as "degenerate." Some of the works are back in place at the **Staatliche Galerie Moritzburg,** together with some outstanding late-19th- and early-20th-century art. You'll find Rodin's famous sculpture *The Kiss* here. ☒ *Friedemann-Bach-Pl. 5* ☏ *0345/212–590* ⊕ *stiftung-moritzburg.de* ☒ *€6, special exhibits €11* ⊙ *Tues. 11–8:30, Wed.–Sun. 10–6.*

Roter Turm (*Red Tower*). The Markt's fifth tower is Halle's celebrated Roter Turm, built between 1418 and 1506 as an expression of the city's power and wealth. The carillon inside is played on special occasions. ☒ *Markt.*

FAMILY **Technisches Halloren- und Salinemuseum** (*Technical Saline Extraction Museum*). The salt trade on which Halle built its prosperity is documented in this museum. A replica brine mill shows the salt-extraction process, and the exquisite silver-goblet collection of the Salt Workers' Guild (the Halloren) is on display. The old method of evaporating brine from local springs is sometimes demonstrated. The museum is on the south side of the Saale River (across the Schiefer Bridge). ☒ *Mansfelderstr. 52* ☏ *0345/202–5034* ⊕ *www.salinemuseum.de* ☒ *€3.80* ⊙ *Tues.–Sun. 10–5.*

DID YOU KNOW?

George Frideric Handel was baptized and learned to play the organ at Halle's Marienkirche.

WHERE TO EAT AND STAY

Halle's café scene spreads out along the Kleine Ullrichstrasse. It's a good area for searching out an affordable meal and lively conversation.

$ ✕**Hallesches Brauhaus Kühler Brunnen.** Halle's first and best brewpub
GERMAN serves traditional brewery fare in huge portions at reasonable prices. The Brauhaus is most famous for its large selection of *Flammkuchen,* a kind of thin-crust flatbread originating from the Alsace region of France. The best beer is the brewery's own Hallsch, an amber top-fermented ale served in funky glasses. $ *Average main: €12 ⌧ Grosse Nikolaistr. 2 ☏ 0345/212–570 ⊕ www.halleschesbrauhaus.de ▭ No credit cards.*

$ ✕**Restaurant Mönchshof.** Hearty German fare in heartier portions is
GERMAN served in high-ceiling, dark-wood surroundings. Lamb from Saxony-
FAMILY Anhalt's Wettin region and venison are specialties in season, but there are always fish and crisp roast pork on the menu. The wine list is extensive, with international vintages. The restaurant is popular with locals, and the staff are particularly accommodating with children. If you're not picky, the fair selection of vegetarian dishes make the Mönchhof the best vegetarian option in the city $ *Average main: €13 ⌧ Talamtstr. 6 ☏ 0345/202–1726.*

$$ ⊡**Ankerhof Hotel.** In an old warehouse, this reflection on Halle's salt-
HOTEL strewn past contains individually decorated rooms, most with wooden ceiling beams, bare stone walls, and heavy furniture made from exquisite wood. **Pros:** casual elegance worked into a traditional setting. **Cons:** building creaks and groans when it is windy; can be cold in winter. $ *Rooms from: €110 ⌧ Ankerstr. 2a ☏ 0345/232–3200 ⊕ www. ankerhof.de ⤳ 49 rooms, 1 suite ❍ Breakfast.*

PERFORMING ARTS

The city of Handel's birth is, not surprisingly, an important music center. Halle is famous for its opera productions, its orchestral concerts, and particularly its choirs.

Opernhaus (*Opera House*). Both Halle's opera and its venue are renowned. ⌧ *Universitätsring 24 ☏ 0345/5110–0355.*

Philharmonisches Staatsorchester Halle (*State Philharmonic Orchestra*). The city's main orchestra performs at the Konzerthalle. ⌧ *Grosse Gosenstr. 12 ☏ 0345/523–3141 for concert information and tickets ⊕ www. staatskapelle.halle.de.*

EN
ROUTE **Eisleben.** To reach Quedlinburg in the Harz, you can take E-49 directly, or take a somewhat longer route via E-80, stopping in Eisleben first. Martin Luther came into and out of the world here: both the square Franconian house with the high-pitched roof that was his birthplace (**Luthers Geburtshaus**) and the Gothic patrician house where he died (**Luthers Sterbehaus**) are open to the public, as are, on request, the **St. Petri-Pauli Kirche** (Church of Sts. Peter and Paul), where he was baptized, and the **St. Andreaskirche** (St. Andrew's Church), where his funeral was held. From Eisleben take B-180 north to join E-49 to Quedlinburg. ⌧ *Eisleben.*

NAUMBURG

60 km (65 miles) south of Halle.

Once a powerful trading and ecclesiastical city, 1,000-year-old Naumburg is the cultural center of the Salle-Unstrut. Although the city is most famous for its Romanesque/Gothic cathedral, it hides a well-preserved collection of patrician houses, winding back alleys, and a marketplace so distinctive that it warrants the appellation "Naumburger Renaissance."

GETTING HERE AND AROUND

From the train station the fun way to get into the city is to take the Naumburger Historical Tram, which runs every 30 minutes. A single ride on Europe's smallest tramway, in antique streetcars, costs €1.50.

ESSENTIALS

Visitor Information Tourist und Tagungsservice Naumburg. ⊠ *Markt 12* ☎ *03445/273–125, 03445/273–128* ⊕ *www.naumburg-tourismus.de.*

EXPLORING

Dom St. Peter und Paul (*St. Peter and Paul Cathedral*). Perched high above the city and dominating the skyline, this cathedral is the symbol of Naumburg. For the most part constructed during the latter half of the 13th century, it's considered one of the masterpieces of the late Romanesque period. What makes the cathedral unique, however, is the addition of a second choir in the Gothic style less than 100 years later. The Gothic choir is decorated with statues of the cathedral's benefactors from the workshop of the Naumburger Meister. Be sure to find Neo Rauch's red triptych windows in the St. Elisabeth Chapel. The most famous statues are of Uta and Ekkehard, the city's most powerful patrons. Uta's tranquil face is everywhere, from postcards to city maps. ⊠ *Dompl. 16* ☎ *03445/23010* 🎫 *€6.50* ◷ *Mon.–Sat. 10–4, Sun. noon–4; guided tours by appointment.*

Marientor. Naumburg was once ringed by a defensive city wall with five gates. The only remaining one, the Marientor, is a rare surviving example of a dual-portal gate, called a *barbican*, from the 14th century. The museum inside the gate provides a brief history of the city's defenses. A pleasant walk along the remaining city walls from Marienplatz to the Weingarten is the easiest way to explore the last intact section of Naumburg's wall, moat, and defensive battlements. ⊠ *Marienpl.* 🎫 *€0.50, automated turnstile at the entrance* ◷ *Daily 10–4:30.*

Marktplatz. Naumburg's historic market square lies strategically at the intersection of two medieval trade routes. Although the market burned in 1517, it was painstakingly rebuilt in Renaissance and baroque styles. ⊠ *Naumburg.*

Kaysersches Haus (*Imperial House*). Supported by seven Gothic gables, the Kaysersches Haus has a carved oak doorway from the Renaissance. ⊠ *Markt 10.*

Rathaus. Naumburg's town hall, rebuilt in 1523, incorporates the remnants of the original building destroyed by fire. ⊠ *Markt 1.*

Schlösschen (*Little Castle*). The Schlösschen houses the offices of Naumburg's first and only Protestant bishop, Nikolaus von Amsdorf, who was consecrated by Martin Luther in 1542. ⊠ *Markt 2.*

Naumburger Wein und Sekt Manufaktur (*Naumburg Wine and Sparkling Wine*). Producing fine still and sparkling wines on the bank of the Salle River, this winery in a 200-year-old monastery is a pleasant 2-km (1-mile) walk or bike ride from Naumburg's city center. Tours of the production rooms and the vaulted cellar, with wine tastings, take place whenever a group forms and last about an hour. The wine garden is a pleasant place to relax on the bank of the river and the restaurant serves small snacks. Larger appetites find relief across the street

SALLE-UNSTRUT: WINE COUNTRY

The Salle-Unstrut is Europe's northernmost wine-producing region, and with more than 30 different grape varieties one of the most diverse. The region stretches from Halle to Eisleben, and has more than 700 vintners operating on a mere 1,600 acres. Grapes are grown on the terraced slopes of rolling hills, guarded by numerous castles and fortresses. The area is easy to explore by the regional train that meanders through the Unstrut Valley once every hour or the bicycle path that stretches along the banks of both rivers.

16

at the Gasthaus Henne. ⊠ *Blütengrund 35* ☎ *03445/202–042* ⊕ *www.naumburger.com* 🍷 *Tours with tasting €6* ⊗ *Daily 11–6; tours Apr.–Oct., Mon., Wed., Fri., and Sat. at 2.*

Nietzsche Haus Museum. The philosopher Friedrich Nietzsche's family lived in Naumburg from 1858 to 1897, in a small classical house in the Weingarten. The Nietzsche Haus Museum documents the life and times of one of Naumburg's most controversial residents. The exhibition does not delve too deeply into Nietzsche's philosophy, but focuses a great deal on his bizarre relationship with his sister and her manipulation of his manuscripts. ⊠ *Weingarten 18* ☎ *03445/703–503* ⊕ *www.mv-naumburg.de* 🍷 *€3* ⊗ *Tues.–Fri. 2–5, weekends 10–4.*

St. Wenceslas. The parish church of St. Wenceslas dominates the southern end of the Markt. A church has stood on this spot since 1218, but the current incarnation dates from 1426, with interior renovations in 1726. The church is most famous for its huge Hildebrandt Organ, which was tested and tuned by J. S. Bach in 1746. Fans of Lucas Cranach the Elder get their due with two of his paintings, *Suffer the Little Children Come Unto Me* and the *Adoration of the Three Magi*. The 240-foot-tall tower belongs to the city, *not* the church, and was used as a watchtower for the city guards, who lived there until 1994. ⊠ *Topfmarkt* ☎ *03445/208–401* 🍷 *Free, tower €2* ⊗ *Mon.–Sat. 10–noon and 2–5, tower daily 10–5.*

WHERE TO EAT AND STAY

$ ✕ **Alt-Naumburg.** Enjoy simple but tasty regional specialties directly
GERMAN   in front of the Marientor. The beer garden is a good place to relax away from the action of the city center. The three-room pension is

often booked far in advance. $\boxed{\text{S}}$ *Average main: €12* ⊠ *Marienpl. 13* ☏ *03445/234–425* ⊟ *No credit cards.*

$ 🛏 **Hotel Stadt Aachen.** Many of the simply decorated rooms overlook the
HOTEL central market at this pleasant hotel in a medieval house. **Pros:** comfortable hotel in the middle of the action; helpful staff. **Cons:** location by the market is sometimes noisy. $\boxed{\text{S}}$ *Rooms from: €85* ⊠ *Markt 11* ☏ *03445/2470* ⊕ *www.hotel-stadt-aachen.de* ⇨ *38 rooms* ⦸ *No meals.*

FREYBURG

10 km (6 miles) north of Naumburg.

Stepping off the train in the sleepy town of Freyburg, it is not difficult to see why locals call the area "the Tuscany of the North." With clean, wandering streets, whitewashed buildings, and a huge castle perched on a vine-terraced hill, Freyburg is a little out of place. The town owes its existence to Schloss Neuenburg, which was built by the same Thuringian count who built the Wartburg. Although most visitors head straight for the wine, the historic Old Town and castle certainly warrant a visit.

Freyburg is surrounded by a ¾-mile-long, almost completely intact city wall. The **Ekstädter Tor** was the most important gate into the city and dates from the 14th century. The gate is dominated by one of the few remaining barbicans in central Germany.

GETTING HERE AND AROUND

Hourly trains connect Naumburg and Freyburg in nine minutes. Bike paths along the Unstrut River are a pleasure to cycle. The most serene way to reach Freyburg is to take a small steamboat.

ESSENTIALS

Visitor Information Freyburger Fremdenverkehrsverein. ⊠ *Markt 2* ☏ *034464/27260, 034464/273–760* ⊕ *www.freyburg-info.de.*

TOURS

Saale-Unstrut Schiffahrtsgesellschaft mbH. Three times per day, in the summer, the *Fröhliche Dörte* (Happy Dorothy) steams from Naumburg to Freyburg and back. The trip takes about an hour and is the most pleasant way to reach Freyburg from Naumburg. ⊠ *Steinweg 33, Naumburg* ⊕ *www.froehliche-doerte.de/* 🎫 *€10 one way, €16 round-trip.*

EXPLORING

Rotkäppchen Sektkellerei (*Little Red Riding Hood Sparkling Wine*). Freyburg is the home of one of Europe's largest producers of sparkling wine, a rare eastern German product with a significant market share in the West. Hour-long tours of the production facility include the world's largest wooden wine barrel. ⊠ *Sektkellereistr. 5* ☏ *034464/340* ⊕ *www.rotkaeppchen.de* 🎫 *€5* ⊙ *Daily 10–6; tours weekdays at 11 and 2, weekends at 11, 12:30, 2, and 3:30.*

St. Marien Kirche (*St. Mary's Church*). In 1225 the Thuringian count Ludwig IV erected the St. Marien Kirche as a triple-naved basilica and the only church within the city walls. The coquina limestone building, which resembles the cathedral in Naumburg, was renovated in the

15th century into its current form as a single-hall structure. The great carved altarpiece also dates from the 15th century and the baptistery from 1592. ✉ *Markt 2.*

Schloss Neuenburg (*Neuenburg Castle*). Since its foundation was laid in 1090 by the Thuringian Ludwig I, this castle has loomed protectively over Freyburg. The spacious residential area and huge towers date from the 13th century, when Neuenburg was a part of Thuringia's eastern defenses. The spartan Gothic double-vaulted chapel from 1190 is one of the few rooms that evoke an early medieval past, since most of the castle was renovated in the 15th century. ✉ *Schloss 1* ☎ *34464/35530* 🌐 *www.schloss-neuenburg.de* 🎟 *€7* 🕐 *Tues.–Sun. 10–5.*

Winzervereinigung-Freyburg (*Freyburg Vintner's Association*). The best way to try Salle-Unstrut wine is with this trade group. Its 500 members produce some of Germany's finest wines, both white and red, mostly pure varietals, with some limited blends. (A wonderful light red from a hybrid of the Blauer Zweigelt and St. James grape, called Andre, may change how you think about German red wine.) Tastings and tours must be arranged in advance—with options ranging from a simple tour of one of Germany's largest barrel cellars to the grand tasting (€16)—or you can simply show up on Fridays at 1 (€12). The association goes out of its way to cater to the tastes of its guests, and bread, cheese, and water are always in plentiful supply. ✉ *Querfurter Str. 10* ☎ *034464/30623* 🌐 *www.winzervereinigung-freyburg.de* 🕐 *Mon.–Sat. 10–6, Sun. 10–4.*

16

WHERE TO EAT

$ GERMAN 🍴 **Burgwirtschaft.** Where better than a castle serenely overlooking the village of Freyburg for a medieval restaurant? Everything is prepared according to historical recipes with ingredients from the region. Try the roast chicken with honey or any of the grilled meats. Most menu items are available in the spacious beer garden. [$] *Average main: €10* ✉ *Schloss 1* ☎ *034464/66200* 🌐 *www.burgwirtschaft.de.*

QUEDLINBURG

79 km (49 miles) northwest of Halle.

This medieval Harz town has more half-timber houses than any other town in Germany: more than 1,600 of them line the narrow cobblestone streets and squares. The town escaped destruction during World War II and was treasured in GDR days, though not very well preserved. Today the nicely restored town is a UNESCO World Heritage Site.

For nearly 200 years Quedlinburg was a favorite imperial residence and site of imperial diets, beginning with the election in 919 of Henry the Fowler (Henry I) as the first Saxon king of Germany. It became a major trading city and a member of the Hanseatic League, equal in stature to Köln.

Quedlinburg lies on a spur rail line between Magdeburg and Thale. Despite being difficult to reach by train, it is still well worth the trouble. The train station is 1 km (½ mile) from the city center. Quedlinburg is an easy drive, 80 km (50 miles), from both Dessau (along the B-71) or from Halle (following the B-80).

ESSENTIALS

Visitor Information Quedlinburg Tourismus-Marketing GmbH. ⊠ *Markt 2* ☎ *03946/905–624, 03946/905–629* ⊕ *www.quedlinburg.de.*

EXPLORING

Lyonel Feininger Gallery. This sophisticated, modern gallery is placed behind half-timber houses so as not to affect the town's medieval feel. When the art of American-born painter Lyonel Feininger, a Bauhaus teacher in both Weimar and Dessau, was declared "decadent" by the Hitler regime in 1938, the artist returned to America. Left behind with a friend were engravings, lithographs, etchings, and paintings. The most comprehensive Feininger print collection in the world is displayed here. ⊠ *Finkenherd 5a* ☎ *03946/2238* ⊕ *www.feininger-galerie.de* ⊡ *€6* ⊙ *Apr.–Oct., Wed.–Mon. 10–6; Nov.–Mar., Wed.–Mon. 10–5.*

Marktplatz. The Altstadt (Old Town) is full of richly decorated half-timber houses, particularly along Mühlgraben, Schuhof, the Hölle, Breitestrasse, and Schmalstrasse. Notable on the Marktplatz are the Renaissance **Rathaus**, with a 14th-century statue of Roland signifying the town's independence, and the baroque 1701 Haus Grünhagen. Street and hiking maps and guidebooks (almost all in German) are available in the information office at the Rathaus. ⊠ *Markt 2* ☎ *03946/90550* ⊡ *Free* ⊙ *Mon.–Sat. 9–3.*

Schlossmuseum (*Castle Museum*). Quedlinburg's largely Renaissance castle buildings perch on top of the Schlossberg (Castle Hill), with a terrace overlooking woods and valley. The grounds include the Schlossmuseum, which has exhibits on the history of the town and castle, artifacts of the Bronze Age, and the wooden cage in which a captured 14th-century robber baron was put on public view. Restored 17th- and 18th-century rooms give an impression of castle life at that time. ⊠ *Schlossberg 1* ☎ *03946/2730* ⊡ *€4.50* ⊙ *Apr.–Oct., Tues.–Sun. 10–6; Nov.–Mar., Tues.–Sun. 10–5.*

Ständerbau Fachwerkmuseum (*Half-Timber House*). The oldest half-timber house in Quedlinburg, built about 1310, is now a museum. ⊠ *Wordg. 3* ☎ *03946/3828* ⊡ *€3* ⊙ *Apr.–Oct., Fri.–Wed. 10–5; Nov.–Mar., Fri.–Wed. 10–4.*

Stiftskirche St. Servatius (*Collegiate Church of St. Servatius*). This simple, graceful church is one of the most important and best-preserved 12th-century Romanesque structures in Germany. Henry I and his wife Mathilde are buried in its crypt. The renowned Quedlinburg Treasure of 10th-, 11th-, and 12th-century gold and silver and bejeweled manuscripts is also kept here (what's left of it). Nazi SS leader Heinrich Himmler made the church into a shrine dedicated to the SS, insisting that it was only appropriate, since Henry I was the founder of the first German Reich. ⊠ *Schlossberg 1* ☎ *03946/709–900* ⊡ *€4.50* ⊙ *Nov.–Mar., Tues.–Sun. 10–4; Apr.–Oct., Tues.–Sun. 10–6.*

Adorable Quedlinburg has 1,600 half-timber houses: that's more than any other town in Germany.

WHERE TO EAT AND STAY

$ GERMAN 🍴 **Lüdde Bräu.** Brewing *Braunbier* (a hoppy, top-fermented beer) has been a Quedlinburg tradition for several centuries. The Lüdde brewery traces its history to 1807, when Braunbier breweries dotted the Harz Mountains, and it was the last surviving brewery when it closed its doors in 1966. After German reunification, Georg Lüdde's niece reopened the business, and it remains the only Braunbier brewery in Quedlinburg. Sampling the reemergence of an almost lost German tradition as well as some incredible beer-based game dishes, makes the restaurant well worth a visit—the top-fermented Braunbier is called *Pubarschknall.* [$] *Average main: €12* ✉ *Carl-Ritter-Str. 1* ☎ *03946/901–481* 🌐 *www.hotel-brauhaus-luedde.de.*

$ HOTEL 🏨 **Hotel Zum Brauhaus.** In a beautifully restored half-timber house, many of the rooms incorporate the bare load-bearing timbers and have pleasant views of the castle. **Pros:** friendly staff; location next to Lüdde brewery. **Cons:** a little rough around the edges; upper rooms get hot in summer. [$] *Rooms from: €89* ✉ *Carl-Ritter-Str. 1* ☎ *03946/901–481* 🌐 *www.hotel-brauhaus-luedde.de* 🛏 *50 rooms, 1 suite* 🍽 *Breakfast.*

$ HOTEL 🏨 **Hotel Zur Goldenen Sonne.** Rooms in this baroque half-timber inn are furnished in a pleasing, rustic fashion. **Pros:** beautiful half-timber house with modern conveniences; reasonable rates. **Cons:** the clock on the square strikes every 15 minutes; rooms in the modern section not quite as nice as the ones in the half-timber house. [$] *Rooms from: €79* ✉ *Steinweg 11* ☎ *03946/96250* 🌐 *www.hotelzurgoldenensonne.de* 🛏 *27 rooms* 🍽 *Breakfast.*

THURINGIA

Unlike other eastern states, unassuming Thuringia was not taken from the Slavs by wandering Germanic tribes but has been German since before the Middle Ages. The hilly countryside is mostly rural and forested, and it preserves a rich cultural past in countless small villages, medieval cities, and country palaces. In the 14th century traders used the 168-km (104-mile) Rennsteig ("fast trail") through the dark depths of the Thuringian Forest, and cities such as Erfurt and Eisenach evolved as major commercial hubs. Today the forests and the Erzgebirge Mountains are a remote paradise for hiking and fishing. The city of Weimar is one of Europe's old cultural centers, where Germany attempted its first go at a true democracy in 1918. Thuringia is the land of Goethe and Schiller, but it is also marked by the ominous presence of one of the Third Reich's most notorious concentration camps: Buchenwald.

EISENACH

140 km (90 miles) southwest of Quedlinburg, 95 km (59 miles) northeast of Fulda.

When you stand in Eisenach's ancient market square it's difficult to imagine this half-timber town as an important center of the East German automobile industry. Yet this is where Wartburgs (very tiny, noisy, and cheaply produced cars, which are now collector's items) were made. The cars were named after the Wartburg, the famous castle that broods over Eisenach from atop one of the foothills of the Thuringian Forest. Today West German automaker Opel continues the tradition by building one of Europe's most modern car-assembly lines on the outskirts of town. Eisenach will be one of the focal points of the 500th anniversary celebrations of the Reformation in 2017.

GETTING HERE AND AROUND

Hourly trains connect Eisenach with Leipzig (two hours) and Dresden (three hours). There are frequent connections to Weimar and Erfurt. Eisenach is about 160 km (100 miles) south of Goslar

ESSENTIALS

Visitor Information Eisenach-Information. ⊠ *Markt 24* ☎ *03691/79230, 03691/792–320* ⊕ *www.eisenach.de.*

EXPLORING

Bachhaus. Johann Sebastian Bach was born in Eisenach in 1685. The Bachhaus has exhibits devoted to the entire lineage of the musical Bach family and includes a collection of historical musical instruments. It is the largest collection of Bach memorabilia in the world, and displays a bust of the composer built using forensic science from a cast of his skull. The price of admission includes a 20-minute recital using historical instruments, held once per hour. ⊠ *Frauenplan 21* ☎ *03691/79340* ⊕ *www.bachhaus.de* ⊑ *€8.50* ⊗ *Daily 10–6.*

Lutherhaus. This downtown house has many fascinating exhibits illustrating the life of Martin Luther, who lived here as a student. ⊠ *Lutherpl. 8* ☎ *03691/29830* ⊕ *www.lutherhaus-eisenach.de* ⊑ *€8* ⊗ *Tues.–Sun. 10–5.*

Narrowest house. Built in 1890, this is said to be the narrowest house in eastern Germany. Its width is just over 6 feet, 8 inches; its height, 24½ feet; and its depth, 34 feet. ✉ *Johannespl. 9.*

Reuter-Wagner-Museum. Composer Richard Wagner gets his due at this museum, which has the most comprehensive exhibition on Wagner's life and work outside Bayreuth. Monthly concerts take place in the old **Teezimmer** (tearoom), a hall with wonderfully restored French wallpaper. The Erard piano, dating from the late 19th century, is occasionally rolled out. ✉ *Reuterweg 2* ☎ *03691/743–293* 🎟 *€4* 🕓 *Tues., Wed., and Fri.–Sun. 11–5, Thurs. 3–8.*

Fodor's Choice ★ **Wartburg Castle.** Begun in 1067 (and expanded through the centuries), this mighty castle has hosted a parade of German celebrities. Hermann I (1156–1217), count of Thuringia and count palatine of Saxony, was a patron of the wandering poets Walther von der Vogelweide (1170–1230) and Wolfram von Eschenbach (1170–1220). Legend has it that this is where Walther von der Vogelweide, the greatest lyric poet of medieval Germany, prevailed in the celebrated *Minnesängerstreit* (minnesinger contest), which is featured in Richard Wagner's *Tannhäuser.*

Within the castle's stout walls, Frederick the Wise (1463–1525) shielded Martin Luther from papal proscription from May 1521 until March 1522, even though Frederick did not share the reformer's beliefs. Luther completed the first translation of the New Testament from Greek into German while in hiding, an act that paved the way for the Protestant Reformation. You can peek into the simple study in which Luther worked. Be sure to check out the place where Luther supposedly saw the devil and threw an inkwell at him. Pilgrims have picked away at the spot for centuries, forcing the curators to "reapply" the ink.

Frederick was also a patron of the arts. Lucas Cranach the Elder's portraits of Luther and his wife are on view in the castle, as is a very moving sculpture, the *Leuchterengelpaar* (Candlestick Angel Group), by the great 15th-century artist Tilman Riemenschneider. The 13th-century great hall is breathtaking; it's here that the minstrels sang for courtly favors. Don't leave without climbing the belvedere for a panoramic view of the Harz Mountains and the Thuringian Forest. You can wander the grounds of the Wartburg for free, but the only way into the interior of the castle is to take a guided tour. The English tour takes place every day at 1:30 ✉ *Auf der Wartburg 1* ☎ *03691/2500* 🌐 *www.wartburg-eisenach.de* 🎟 *€9, including guided tour; family ticket €21* 🕓 *Mar.–Oct., daily 8:30–5; Nov.–Feb., daily 9–3:30.*

16

WHERE TO STAY

$$$$ HOTEL 🏨 **Hotel auf der Wartburg.** In this castle hotel, where Martin Luther, Johann Sebastian Bach, and Richard Wagner were guests, you'll get a splendid view over the town and the countryside. **Pros:** medieval music and fireplaces in the lobby. **Cons:** it's a hike to and from the city center. [$] *Rooms from: €300* ✉ *Wartburg* ☎ *03691/7970* 🌐 *www.wartburghotel.de* 🛏 *35 rooms* 🍴 *Breakfast.*

$ HOTEL 🏨 **Hotel Glockenhof.** At the base of Wartburg Castle, this former church-run hostel has blossomed into a handsome hotel, cleverly incorporating the original half-timber city mansion into a modern extension. **Pros:** out of the hustle and bustle of the downtown; plenty of parking; an incredible breakfast buffet. **Cons:** uphill walk from the station is strenuous; location is a bit far from the city center. $ *Rooms from: €99* ⊠ *Grimmelg. 4* ☎ *03691/2340* ⊕ *www.glockenhof.de* 🏷 *38 rooms, 2 suites* ❑ *Breakfast.*

ERFURT

55 km (34 miles) east of Eisenach.

The city of Erfurt emerged from World War II relatively unscathed, with most of its innumerable towers intact. Of all the cities in the region, Erfurt is the most evocative of its prewar self, and it's easy to imagine that many of the towns in northern Germany would look like this had they not been destroyed. The city's highly decorative and colorful facades are easy to admire on a walking tour. ■ **TIP→ Downtown Erfurt is a photographer's delight, with narrow, busy, ancient streets dominated by a magnificent 14th-century Gothic cathedral, the Mariendom.**

GETTING HERE AND AROUND

Hourly trains connect Erfurt with Leipzig (two hours) and Dresden (three hours). There are frequent connections to Weimar (twice per hour, 15 minutes) and Eisenach (hourly, 50 minutes). Erfurt is easily walkable from the train station and the streetcar is easy to use.

ESSENTIALS

Visitor Information Erfurt Tourist-Information. ⊠ *Benediktspl. 1* ☎ *0361/66400, 0361/664–0290* ⊕ *www.erfurt-tourist-info.de.*

EXPLORING

TOP ATTRACTIONS

Fodor'sChoice ★ **Krämerbrücke** (*Merchant's Bridge*). Behind the predominantly neo-Gothic Rathaus, Erfurt's most outstanding attraction spans the Gera River. This Renaissance bridge, similar to the Ponte Vecchio in Florence, is the longest of its kind in Europe and the only one north of the Alps. Built in 1325 and restored in 1967–73, the bridge served for centuries as an important trading center. Today antiques shops fill the majority of the timber-frame houses built into the bridge, some dating from the 16th century. The bridge comes alive on the third weekend of June for the Krämerbrückenfest. ⊠ *Erfurt.*

Mariendom (*St. Mary's Cathedral*). This cathedral's Romanesque origins (foundations can be seen in the crypt) are best preserved in the choir's glorious stained-glass windows and beautifully carved stalls, and its biggest bell, the Gloriosa, is the largest free-swinging bell in the world. Cast in 1497, it took three years to install in the tallest of the three sharply pointed towers, painstakingly lifted inch by inch with wooden wedges. No chances are taken with this 2-ton treasure; its deep boom resonates only on special occasions, such as Christmas and New Year's. The Mariendom is reached by way of a broad staircase from the expansive Cathedral Square. ⊠ *Dompl.* ☎ *0361/646–1265* 🏷 *Free; tour €5.50* ⊗ *May–Oct., Mon.–Sat. 9–5, Sun. 1–4; Nov.–Apr., Mon.–Sat. 10–11:30 and 12:30–4, Sun. 1–4.*

WORTH NOTING

The Anger. Erfurt's main transportation hub and pedestrian zone, the Anger developed as a result of urban expansion due to the growth of the railroad in Thuringia in the early 19th century. With some exceptions, the houses are all architecturally historicized, making them look much older than they really are. The **Hauptpostgebäude** was erected in 1892 in a mock Gothic style. ✉ *Erfurt.*

Domplatz (*Cathedral Square*). This square is bordered by houses dating from the 16th century. ✉ *Erfurt.*

Klein Venedig (*Little Venice*). The area around the bridge, crisscrossed with old streets lined with picturesque and often crumbling homes, is known as Little Venice because of the recurrent flooding it endures ✉ *Erfurt.*

St. Augustin Kloster (*St. Augustine Monastery*). The young Martin Luther studied the liberal arts as well as law and theology at Erfurt University from 1501 to 1505. After a personal revelation, Luther asked to become a monk in the St. Augustin Kloster on July 17, 1505. He became an ordained priest here in 1507, and remained at the Kloster until 1511. Today the Kloster is a seminary and retreat hotel. ✉ *Augustinerstr. 10* ☎ *0361/576–600* 🌐 *www.augustinerkloster.de* 🕓 *Mon.–Sat. 10–noon and 2–4, Sun. irregular hrs.*

16

St. Severus. This Gothic church has an extraordinary font, a masterpiece of intricately carved sandstone that reaches practically to the ceiling. It's linked to the cathedral by a 70-step open staircase. ✉ *Dompl.*

Zum Stockfisch. Erfurt's interesting local-history museum is in a late-Renaissance house. ✉ *Johannesstr. 169* ☎ *0361/655–5644* 🎟 *Museum €6* 🕓 *Tues.–Sun. 10–6.*

WHERE TO EAT

$$$$ GERMAN 🍴 **Clara.** This restaurant in the historic, elegant Kaisersaal edifice is the jewel in Erfurt's small gourmet crown. Thuringia native chef Maria Gross has worked in top restaurants around Germany and developed her own minimalist style. Here she is pursuing her vision of a gourmet restaurant: a cozy, service-oriented oasis in which to enjoy delicious international dishes with a Thuringian accent. Using local producers, Clara serves delicious four- to seven-course menus from a list of 10 dishes. Even though you can order à la carte, the menus are a tasty splurge for between €107 and €167 with paired wine. The wine list is one of the best in eastern Germany, offering more than 300 vintages from around the world. [$] *Average main: €30* ✉ *Futterstr. 1, 15–16* ☎ *0361/568–8207* 🌐 *www.restaurant-clara.de* 🕓 *Closed Sun. and Mon. No lunch.*

$$ GERMAN 🍴 **Faustus Restaurant.** In the heart of historic Erfurt the stylish Faustus defines fine Thuringian dining. This restaurant is in an old mansion, with both an inviting summer terrace and a bright, airy dining room. An after-dinner drink at the superb bar is a must. [$] *Average main: €15* ✉ *Wenigermarkt 5* ☎ *0361/540–0954* 💳 *No credit cards.*

$ ✕ **Luther Keller.** Head down the straw-covered stairs in front of Clara
GERMAN   restaurant, and you'll find yourself transported to the Middle Ages.
FAMILY   The Luther Keller offers simple but tasty medieval cuisine in a candlelit vaulted cellar. Magicians, minnesingers, jugglers, and other players round out the enjoyable experience. Sure, it's pure kitsch, but it is entertaining, and the roast wild boar is delicious. The staff will get angry if you don't throw your peanut shells on the floor. $ *Average main: €14* ⊠ *Futterstr. 15* ☎ *0361/568–8205* ⊘ *Closed Sun. and Mon. No lunch.*

$ ✕ **Zum Goldenen Schwan.** Beer lovers rejoice: in addition to the Braugold
GERMAN   brewery, Erfurt has six brewpubs, among which the Golden Swan is by far the best. The house beer is a pleasant unfiltered *Kellerbier,* and other beers are brewed according to the season. The constantly changing seasonal menu is a step above normal brewpub fare, and the sauerbraten defines how the dish should be made. $ *Average main: €12* ⊠ *Michaelisstr. 9* ☎ *0361/262–3742.*

WHERE TO STAY

$$ ☆ **Radisson Blu Hotel Erfurt.** Since the SAS group gave the ugly high-
HOTEL   rise Kosmos a face-lift, the socialist-realist look of the GDR years no longer intrudes on Hotel Erfurt. **Pros:** a safe, clean option in the city center; good restaurant. **Cons:** rather characterless business hotel. $ *Rooms from: €105* ⊠ *Juri-Gagarin-Ring 127* ☎ *0361/55100* ⊕ *www. radissonblu.com* ⤺ *282 rooms, 3 suites* �ㅣ◯ㅣ *Breakfast.*

WEIMAR

21 km (13 miles) east of Erfurt.

Sitting prettily in the geographical center of Thuringia, Weimar occupies a place in German political and cultural history completely disproportionate to its size (population 63,000). It's not even particularly old by German standards, with a civic history that started as late as 1410. Yet by the early 19th century the city had become one of Europe's most important cultural centers, where poets Goethe and Schiller wrote, Johann Sebastian Bach played the organ for his Saxon patrons, Carl Maria von Weber composed some of his best music, and Franz Liszt was director of music, presenting the first performance of *Lohengrin* here. In 1919 Walter Gropius founded his Staatliches Bauhaus here, and behind the classical pillars of the National Theater the German National Assembly drew up the constitution of the Weimar Republic, the first German democracy. As the Weimar Republic began to collapse in 1926, Hitler chose the little city as the site for the second national congress of his Nazi party, where he founded the Hitler Youth. On the outskirts of Weimar the Nazis built—or forced prisoners to build for them—the infamous Buchenwald concentration camp.

GETTING HERE AND AROUND

Weimar is on the ICE line between Dresden/Leipzig and Frankfurt. IC trains link the city with Berlin. Weimar has an efficient bus system, but most sights are within walking distance in the compact city center. If you plan on visiting four or more of Weimar's fine collection of museums and cultural sites, consider using the 48-hour WeimarCard (€28) which is valid for the city buses as well.

ESSENTIALS

Visitor Information Tourist-Information Weimar. ⊠ *Markt 10* ☎ *03643/7450, 03643/745–420* ⊕ *www.weimar.de.*

EXPLORING

TOP ATTRACTIONS

Bauhaus Museum. Walter Gropius founded the Staatliches Bauhaus (Bauhaus design school) in Weimar in 1919. It was Germany's most influential and avant-garde design school, and it ushered in the era of modern architecture and design just before the start of World War II. Although the school moved to Dessau in 1925, Weimar's Bauhaus Museum is a modest, yet superb collection of the works of Gropius, Johannes Itten, and Henry van de Velde. ⊠ *Theaterpl.* ☎ *03643/545–961* ⊕ *www. klassik-stiftung.de* 🖾 *€4* ⊙ *Apr.–Oct., Tues.–Sun. 10–6; Nov.–Mar., Tues.–Sun. 10–4.*

Fodor'sChoice
★

Goethe Nationalmuseum (*Goethe National Museum*). Goethe spent 57 years in Weimar, 47 of them in a house two blocks south of Theaterplatz that has since become a shrine attracting millions of visitors. The Goethe Nationalmuseum consists of several houses, including the **Goethehaus,** where Goethe lived. It shows an exhibit about life in Weimar around 1750 and contains writings that illustrate not only the great man's literary might but also his interest in the sciences, particularly medicine, and his administrative skills (and frustrations) as minister of state and Weimar's exchequer. You'll see the desk at which Goethe stood to write (he liked to work standing up) and the modest bed in which he died. The rooms are dark and often cramped, but an almost palpable intellectual intensity seems to illuminate them. ⊠ *Frauenplan 1* ☎ *03643/545–320* ⊕ *www.klassik-stiftung.de/en/institutions/goethe-national-museum/* 🖾 *€12* ⊙ *Apr.–Oct., Tues.–Sun. 9–6; Nov.–Mar., Tues.–Fri. and Sun. 9–4, Sat. 9–7.*

Goethes Gartenhaus (*Garden House*). Goethe's beloved Gartenhaus is a modest country cottage where he spent many happy hours, wrote much poetry, and began his masterly classical drama *Iphigenie.* The house is set amid meadowlike parkland on the bank of the River Ilm. Goethe is said to have felt very close to nature here, and you can soak up the same rural atmosphere on footpaths along the peaceful little river. ⊠ *Im Park an der Ilm, Hans-Wahl-Str. 4* ☎ *03643/545–375* ⊕ *www.klassik-stiftung.de/index.php?id=90* 🖾 *Cottage €6* ⊙ *Apr.–Oct., Wed.–Mon. 9–6; Nov.–Mar., Wed.–Mon. 10–4.*

Neues Museum Weimar (*New Museum Weimar*). The city is proud of eastern Germany's first museum exclusively devoted to contemporary art. The building, dating from 1869, was carefully restored and converted to hold collections of American minimalist and conceptual art and works by German installation-artist Anselm Kiefer and American painter Keith Haring. In addition, it regularly presents international modern-art exhibitions. ⊠ *Weimarpl. 5* ☎ *03643/545–930* 🖾 *€4* ⊙ *Apr.–Oct., Tues.–Sun. 11–6; Nov.–Mar., Tues.–Sun. 11–4.*

16

Take a carriage ride through Weimar to absorb the city's impressive history.

WORTH NOTING

OFF THE
BEATEN
PATH

Gedenkstätte Buchenwald (*Buchenwald Memorial*). Just north of Weimar, amid the natural beauty of the Ettersberg hills that once served as Goethe's inspiration, sits the blight of Buchenwald, one of the most infamous Nazi concentration camps. Fifty-six thousand men, women, and children from 35 countries met their deaths here through forced labor, starvation, disease, and gruesome medical experiments. Each is commemorated by a small stone placed on the outlines of the barracks, which have long since disappeared from the site, and by a massive memorial tower. In an especially cruel twist of fate, many liberated inmates returned to the camp as political prisoners of the Soviet occupation; they are remembered in the exhibit *Soviet Special Camp #2*. Besides exhibits, tours are available. To reach Buchenwald by public transportation, take Bus 6 (in the direction of Buchenwald, not Ettersburg), which leaves every 10 minutes from Goetheplatz in downtown Weimar. The one-way fare is €1.90. ⊠ *Weimar* ☎ *03643/4300* ⊕ *www.buchenwald.de* 🖃 *Free* ⊘ *May–Sept., Tues.–Sun. 10–5:30; Oct.–Apr., Tues.–Sun. 9–4:30.*

Herderkirche (*Herder Church*). The Marktplatz's late-Gothic church has a large winged altar started by Lucas Cranach the Elder and finished by his son in 1555. The elder Cranach lived in a nearby house (two blocks east of Theaterplatz) during his last years, 1552–53. Its wide, imposing facade is richly decorated and bears the coat of arms of the Cranach family. It now houses a modern art gallery. ⊠ *Herderpl. 8.*

Historischer Friedhof (*Historic Cemetery*). Goethe and Schiller are buried in this leafy cemetery, where virtually every gravestone commemorates a famous citizen of Weimar. Their tombs are in the vault of the classical-style chapel. The cemetery is a short walk past Goethehaus and Wieland Platz. ⊠ *Am Poseckschen Garten* ☎ *03643/545–400* ⚰ *Goethe-Schiller vault €4* ⊙ *Apr.–Oct., Wed.–Mon. 9–1 and 2–6; Nov.–Mar., Wed.–Mon. 10–1 and 2–4.*

Schillerhaus. This green-shuttered residence, part of the Goethe National Museum, is on a tree-shaded square not far from Goethe's house. Schiller and his family spent a happy, all-too-brief three years here (he died here in 1805). Schiller's study is tucked underneath the mansard roof, a cozy room dominated by his desk, where he probably completed *Wilhelm Tell*. Much of the remaining furniture and the collection of books were added later, although they all date from around Schiller's time. ⊠ *Schillerstr. 17* ☎ *03643/545–350* ⊕ *www.klassik-stiftung.de* ⚰ *€7.50* ⊙ *Apr.–Oct., Tues.–Sun. 9–6; Nov.–Mar., Tues.–Sun. 9–4.*

Stadtschloss (*City Castle*). Around the corner from the Herderkirche, this 16th-century castle has a finely restored classical staircase, a festival hall, and a falcon gallery. The tower on the southwest projection dates from the Middle Ages but received its baroque overlay circa 1730. The **Kunstsammlung** (art collection) here includes several works by Cranach the Elder and many early-20th-century pieces by such artists as Böcklin, Liebermann, and Beckmann. ⊠ *Burgpl. 4* ☎ *03643/545–930* ⊕ *www. klassik-stiftung.de* ⚰ *€7.50* ⊙ *Apr.–Oct., Tues.–Sun. 10–6; Nov.–Mar., Tues.–Sun. 10–4.*

Theaterplatz. A statue on this square, in front of the National Theater, shows Goethe placing a paternal hand on the shoulder of the younger Schiller. ⊠ *Weimar.*

Wittumspalais (*Wittum Mansion*). Much of Weimar's greatness is owed to its patron, the widowed countess Anna Amalia, whose home, the Wittumspalais, is surprisingly modest. In the late 18th century the countess went talent hunting for cultural figures to decorate the glittering court her Saxon forebears had established. She discovered Goethe, and he served the countess as a counselor, advising her on financial matters and town design. Schiller followed, and he and Goethe became valued visitors to the countess's home. Within this exquisite baroque house you can see the drawing room in which she held soirées, complete with the original cherrywood table at which the company sat. The east wing of the house contains a small museum that's a fascinating memorial to those cultural gatherings. ⊠ *Am Theaterpl.* ☎ *03643/545–377* ⚰ *€6* ⊙ *Apr.–Oct., Tues.–Sun. 9–6; Nov.–Mar., Tues.–Sun. 10–4.*

WHERE TO EAT

$ ✕ **Felsenkeller.** When Ludwig Deinhard purchased the Weimar Stadt-
GERMAN brauerei in 1875, Felsenkeller was already 100 years old. Beer has been brewed here in small batches ever since. Although the brewpub is outside the city center, it's worth a trip to sample the brews and the inventive seasonal selections. The pub serves standard fare at reasonable prices. $ *Average main: €11* ⊠ *Humboldtstr. 37* ☎ *03643/414–741* ▭ *No credit cards* ⊙ *Closed Mon.*

$ ✕ **Ratskeller.** This is one of the region's most authentic town hall–cel-
GERMAN lar restaurants. Its whitewashed, barrel-vaulted ceiling has witnessed

centuries of tradition. At the side is a cozy bar, where you can enjoy a preprandial drink beneath a spectacular art nouveau skylight. The delicious sauerbraten and the famous bratwurst (with sauerkraut and mashed potatoes) are the highlights of the Thuringian menu. If venison is in season, try it—likewise the wild duck or wild boar in red-wine sauce. $ *Average main: €12* ⊠ *Am Markt 10* ☎ *03643/850–573.*

$ ✕ **Scharfe Ecke.** If *Klösse* (dumplings) are a Thuringia religion, this res-
GERMAN taurant is their cathedral. Thuringia's traditional Klösse are at their best
FAMILY here, but be patient—they're made to order and can take up to 20 min-
utes. The dumplings come with just about every dish, from roast pork to venison stew, and the wait is well worth it. The ideal accompaniment to anything on the menu is one of the three locally brewed beers on tap or the fine selection of Salle-Unstrut wines. Since the Klösse are the best in the province, the restaurant fills quickly; reservations are essential. $ *Average main: €11* ⊠ *Eisfeld 2* ☎ *03643/202–430* ▭ *No credit cards* ☉ *Closed Mon.* ⚞ *Reservations essential.*

$ ✕ **Sommer's Weinstuben und Restaurant.** The city's oldest pub and restau-
GERMAN rant, a 130-year-old landmark in the center of Weimar, is still going strong. The authentic Thuringian specialties and huge *Kartoffelpfan-nen* (potato pans), with fried potatoes and various kinds of meat, are prepared by the fifth generation of the Sommer family, and are as tasty as ever. Added attractions are a romantic courtyard and a superb wine list with some rare vintages from local vineyards. $ *Average main: €11* ⊠ *Humboldtstr. 2* ☎ *03643/400–691* ▭ *No credit cards* ☉ *Closed Sun. No lunch.*

WHERE TO STAY

$ ☷ **Amalienhof VCH Hotel.** Book far ahead to secure a room at this friendly
HOTEL little hotel central to Weimar's attractions. **Pros:** surprisingly good value; rooms are often upgraded to the highest available category at check-in. **Cons:** street noise can be bothersome. $ *Rooms from: €95* ⊠ *Amalienstr. 2* ☎ *03643/5490* ⊕ *www.amalienhof-weimar.de* ⇴ *23 rooms, 9 apartments* ⦿ *Breakfast.*

$$ ☷ **Grand Hotel Russischer Hof.** This historic, classical hotel, once the haunt
HOTEL of European nobility and intellectual society, continues to be a luxurious
Fodor'sChoice gem in the heart of Weimar—it's one of Germany's finest hotels. **Pros:**
★ a quiet hotel in the city center. **Cons:** rooms are on the small side, with thin walls; some overlook an unsightly back courtyard. $ *Rooms from: €135* ⊠ *Goethepl. 2* ☎ *03643/7740* ⊕ *www.russischerhof.com* ⇴ *119 rooms, 6 suites* ⦿ *No meals.*

$$ ☷ **Hotel Elephant.** The historic Elephant, dating from 1696, has long
HOTEL been famous for its charm—even through the Communist years. **Pros:**
Fodor'sChoice a beautiful historical building right in the city center. **Cons:** no air-con-
★ ditioning; rooms in the front are sometimes bothered by the town clock if windows are open. $ *Rooms from: €150* ⊠ *Markt 19* ☎ *03643/8020* ⊕ *www.hotelelephantweimar.com* ⇴ *94 rooms, 5 suites* ⦿ *Breakfast.*

UNDERSTANDING GERMANY

CHRONOLOGY

GERMAN VOCABULARY

MENU GUIDE

CHRONOLOGY

ca. 5000 BC Indo-Germanic tribes settle in the Rhine and Danube valleys.

ca. 2000–800 BC Distinctive German Bronze Age culture emerges, with settlements ranging from coastal farms to lakeside villages.

ca. 450–50 BC Salzkammergut people, whose prosperity is based on abundant salt deposits (in the area of upper Austria), trade with Greeks and Etruscans; Salzkammerguts spread as far as Belgium and have first contact with the Romans.

9 BC –AD 9 Roman attempts to conquer the "Germans"—the tribes of the Cibri, the Franks, the Goths, and the Vandals—are only partly successful; the Rhine becomes the northeastern border of the Roman Empire (and remains so for 300 years).

212 Roman citizenship is granted to all free inhabitants of the empire.

ca. 400 Pressed forward by Huns from Asia, such German tribes as the Franks, the Vandals, and the Lombards migrate to Gaul (France), Spain, Italy, and North Africa, scattering the empire's populace and eventually leading to the disintegration of central Roman authority.

486 The Frankish kingdom is founded by Clovis; his court is in Paris.

497 The Franks convert to Christianity.

Early Middle Ages
776 Charlemagne becomes king of the Franks.

800 Charlemagne is declared Holy Roman Emperor; he makes Aachen capital of his realm, which stretches from the Bay of Biscay to the Adriatic and from the Mediterranean to the Baltic. Under his enlightened patronage there is an upsurge in art and architecture—the Carolingian renaissance.

843 The Treaty of Verdun divides Charlemagne's empire among his three sons: West Francia becomes France; Lotharingia becomes Lorraine (territory to be disputed by France and Germany into the 20th century); and East Francia takes on, roughly, the shape of modern Germany.

911 Five powerful German dukes (of Bavaria, Lorraine, Franconia, Saxony, and Swabia) establish the first German monarchy by electing King Conrad I. Henry I (the Fowler) succeeds Conrad in 919.

962 Otto I is crowned Holy Roman Emperor by the pope; he establishes Austria—the East Mark. The Ottonian renaissance is marked especially by the development of Romanesque architecture.

Middle Ages
1024–1125 The Salian dynasty is characterized by a struggle between emperors and the Church that leaves the empire weak and disorganized; the great Romanesque cathedrals of Speyer, Trier, and Mainz are built.

1138–1254 Frederick Barbarossa leads the Hohenstaufen dynasty; there is temporary recentralization of power, underpinned by strong trade and Church relations.

1158 Munich, capital of Bavaria, is founded by Duke Henry the Lion. He is deposed by Emperor Barbarossa, and Munich is presented to the House of Wittelsbach, which rules it until 1918.

1241 The Hanseatic League is founded to protect trade; Bremen, Hamburg, Köln, and Lübeck are early members. Agencies are soon established in London, Antwerp, Venice, and along the Baltic and North seas; a complex banking and finance system results.

mid-1200s The Gothic style, exemplified by the grand Köln Cathedral, flourishes.

1349 The Black Death plague kills one-quarter of the German population.

Renaissance and Reformation
1456 Johannes Gutenberg (1400–68) prints the first book in Europe.

1471–1553 The Renaissance flowers under influence of painter and engraver Albrecht Dürer (1471–1528); Dutch-born philosopher and scholar Erasmus (1466–1536); Lucas Cranach the Elder (1472–1553), who originates Protestant religious painting; portrait and historical painter Hans Holbein the Younger (1497–1543); and landscape-painting pioneer Albrecht Altdorfer (1480–1538). Increasing wealth among the merchant classes leads to strong patronage of the revived arts.

1517 The Protestant Reformation begins in Germany when Martin Luther (1483–1546) nails his 95 Theses to a church door in Wittenberg, contending that the Roman Church has forfeited divine authority through its corrupt sale of indulgences. Luther is outlawed, and his revolutionary doctrine splits the Church; much of north Germany embraces Protestantism.

1524–30 The (Catholic) Habsburgs rise to power; their empire spreads throughout Europe (and as far as North Africa, the Americas, and the Philippines). Erasmus breaks with Luther and supports reform within the Roman Catholic Church. In 1530 Charles V—a Habsburg—is crowned Holy Roman Emperor; he brutally crushes the Peasants' War, one in a series of populist uprisings in Europe.

1545 The Council of Trent marks the beginning of the Counter-Reformation. Through diplomacy and coercion, most Austrians, Bavarians, and Bohemians are won back to Catholicism, but the majority of Germans remain Lutheran; persecution of religious minorities grows.

Thirty Years' War

1618–48 Germany is the main theater for the Thirty Years' War. The powerful Catholic Habsburgs are defeated by Protestant forces, swelled by disgruntled Habsburg subjects and the armies of King Gustav Adolphus of Sweden. The bloody conflict ends with the Peace of Westphalia (1648); Habsburg and papal authority are severely diminished.

Absolutism and Enlightenment

1689 Louis XIV of France invades the Rhineland Palatinate and sacks Heidelberg. At the end of the 17th century, Germany consolidates its role as a center of scientific thought.

1708 Johann Sebastian Bach (1685–1750) becomes court organist at Weimar and launches his career; he and Georg Friederic Handel (1685–1759) fortify the great tradition of German music. Baroque and, later, rococo art and architecture flourish.

1740–86 Reign of Frederick the Great of Prussia; his rule sees both the expansion of Prussia (it becomes the dominant military force in Germany) and the spread of Enlightenment thought.

ca. 1790 The great age of European orchestral music is raised to new heights with the works of Joseph Haydn (1732–1809), Wolfgang Amadeus Mozart (1756–91), and Ludwig van Beethoven (1770–1827).

early 1800s Johann Wolfgang von Goethe (1749–1832) is part of the Sturm und Drang movement, which leads to Romanticism. Painter Caspar David Friedrich (1774–1840) leads early German Romanticism. Other luminary cultural figures include writers Friedrich Schiller (1759–1805) and Heinrich von Kleist (1777–1811); and composers Robert Schumann (1810–56), Hungarian-born Franz Liszt (1811–86), Richard Wagner (1813–83), and Johannes Brahms (1833–97). In architecture, the severe lines of neoclassicism become popular.

Road to Nationhood

1806 Napoléon's armies invade Prussia; it briefly becomes part of the French Empire.

1807 The Prussian prime minister Baron vom und zum Stein frees the serfs, creating a new spirit of patriotism; the Prussian army is rebuilt.

1813 The Prussians defeat Napoléon at Leipzig.

1815 Britain and Prussia defeat Napoléon at Waterloo. At the Congress of Vienna the German Confederation is created as a loose union of 39 independent states, reduced from more than 300 principalities. The Bundestag (national assembly) is established at Frankfurt. Already powerful Prussia increases its territory, gaining the Rhineland, Westphalia, and most of Saxony.

1848 The "Year of the Revolutions" is marked by uprisings across the fragmented German Confederation; Prussia expands. A national parliament is elected, taking the power of the Bundestag to prepare a constitution for a united Germany.

1862 Otto von Bismarck (1815–98) becomes prime minister of Prussia; he is determined to wrest German-populated provinces from Austro-Hungarian (Habsburg) control.

1866 Austria-Hungary is defeated by the Prussians at Sadowa; Bismarck sets up the Northern German Confederation in 1867. A key figure in Bismarck's plans is Ludwig II of Bavaria. Ludwig—a political simpleton—lacks successors, making it easy for Prussia to seize his lands.

1867 Karl Marx (1818–83) publishes *Das Kapital.*

1870–71 The Franco-Prussian War: Prussia lays siege to Paris. Victorious Prussia seizes Alsace-Lorraine but eventually withdraws from all other occupied French territories.

1871 The four South German states agree to join the Northern Confederation; Wilhelm I is proclaimed first kaiser of the united empire.

Modernism

1882 The Triple Alliance is forged between Germany, Austria-Hungary, and Italy. Germany's industrial revolution blossoms, enabling it to catch up with the other great powers of Europe. Germany establishes colonies in Africa and the Pacific.

ca. 1885 Daimler and Benz pioneer the automobile.

1890 Kaiser Wilhelm II (rules 1888–1918) dismisses Bismarck and begins a new, more aggressive course of foreign policy; he oversees the expansion of the navy.

1890s A new school of writers, including Rainer Maria Rilke (1875–1926), emerges. Rilke's *Sonnets to Orpheus* gives German poetry new lyricism.

1905 Albert Einstein (1879–1955) announces his theory of relativity.

1906 Painter Ernst Ludwig Kirchner (1880–1938) helps organize *Die Brücke,* a group of artists who, along with *Der Blaue Reiter,* create the avant-garde art movement expressionism.

1907 Great Britain, Russia, and France form the Triple Entente, which, set against the Triple Alliance, divides Europe into two armed camps.

1914–18 Austrian archduke Franz-Ferdinand is assassinated in Sarajevo. The attempted German invasion of France sparks World War I; Italy and Russia join the Allies, and four years of pitched battle ensue. By 1918 the Central Powers are encircled and must capitulate.

Weimar Republic

1918 Germany is compelled by the Versailles Treaty to give up its overseas colonies and much European territory (including Alsace-Lorraine to France) and to pay huge reparations to the Allies; Kaiser Wilhelm II repudiates the throne and goes into exile in Holland. The tough terms leave the new democracy, called the Weimar Republic, shaky.

1919 The Bauhaus school of art and design, the brainchild of Walter Gropius (1883–1969), is born. Thomas Mann (1875–1955) and Hermann Hesse (1877–1962) forge a new style of visionary intellectual writing.

1923 Germany suffers runaway inflation. Adolf Hitler's Beer Hall Putsch, a rightist revolt, fails; leftist revolts are frequent.

1925 Hitler publishes *Mein Kampf* (*My Struggle*)

1932 The Nazi party gains the majority in the Reichstag (parliament).

1933 Hitler becomes chancellor; the Nazi "revolution" begins. In Berlin, Nazi students stage the burning of more than 25,000 books by Jewish and other politically undesirable authors.

Nazi Germany

1934 President Paul von Hindenburg dies; Hitler declares himself Führer (leader) of the Third Reich. Nazification of all German social institutions begins, spreading a policy that is virulently racist and anticommunist. Germany recovers industrial might and re-arms.

1936 Germany signs anticommunist agreements with Italy and Japan, forming the Axis; Hitler reoccupies the Rhineland.

1938 The *Anschluss* (annexation): Hitler occupies Austria. Germany occupies the Sudetenland in Czechoslovakia. *Kristallnacht* (Night of Broken Glass), in November, marks the Nazis' first open and direct terrorism against German Jews. Synagogues and Jewish-owned businesses are burned, looted, and destroyed in a night of violence.

1939-40 In August Hitler signs a pact with the Soviet Union; in September he invades Poland. War is declared by the Allies. Over the next three years there are Nazi invasions of Denmark, Norway, the Low Countries, France, Yugoslavia, and Greece. Alliances form between Germany and the Baltic states.

1941-45 Hitler launches his anticommunist crusade against the Soviet Union, reaching Leningrad in the north and Stalingrad and the Caucasus in the south. In 1944 the Allies land in France; their combined might brings the Axis to its knees. In addition to the millions killed in the fighting, more than 6 million Jews and other victims die in Hitler's concentration camps. Germany is again in ruins. Hitler kills himself in April 1945. East Berlin and what becomes East Germany are occupied by the Soviet Union.

The Cold War

1945 At the Yalta Conference, France, the United States, Britain, and the Soviet Union divide Germany into four zones; each country occupies a sector of Berlin. The Potsdam Agreement expresses the determination to rebuild Germany as a democracy.

1946 East Germany's Social Democratic Party merges with the Communist Party, forming the SED, which would rule East Germany for the next 40 years.

1948 The Soviet Union tears up the Potsdam Agreement and attempts, by blockade, to exclude the three other Allies from their agreed zones in Berlin. Stalin is frustrated by a massive airlift of supplies to West Berlin.

1949 The three western zones are combined to form the Federal Republic of Germany; the new West German parliament elects Konrad Adenauer as chancellor (a post he held until his retirement in 1963). Soviet-held East Germany becomes the Communist German Democratic Republic (GDR).

1950s West Germany, aided by the financial impetus provided by the Marshall Plan, rebuilds its devastated cities and economy—the *Wirtschaftswunder* (economic miracle) gathers speed. The writers Heinrich Böll, Wolfgang Koeppen, and Günter Grass emerge.

1957 The Treaty of Rome heralds the formation of the European Economic Community (EEC); West Germany is a founding member.

1961 Communists build the Berlin Wall to stem the outward tide of refugees.

1969-74 The vigorous chancellorship of Willy Brandt pursues *Ostpolitik*, improving relations with Eastern Europe and the Soviet Union and acknowledging East Germany's sovereignty.

mid-1980s The powerful German Green Party emerges as the leading environmentalist voice in Europe.

Reunification

1989 Discontent in East Germany leads to a flood of refugees westward and to mass demonstrations. Communist power collapses across Eastern Europe; the Berlin Wall falls.

1990 In March the first free elections in East Germany bring a center-right government to power. The Communists, faced with corruption scandals, suffer a big defeat but are represented (as Democratic Socialists) in the new, democratic parliament. The World War II victors hold talks with the two German governments, and the Soviet Union gives its support for reunification. Economic union takes place on July 1, with full political unity on October 3. In December, in the first democratic national German elections in 58 years, Chancellor Helmut Kohl's three-party coalition is reelected.

1991 Nine months of emotional debate end on June 20, when parliamentary representatives vote to move the capital from Bonn—seat of the West German government since 1949—to Berlin, the capital of Germany until the end of World War II.

1998 Helmut Kohl's record 16-year-long chancellorship of Germany ends with the election of Gerhard Schröder. Schröder's Social Democratic Party (SPD) pursues a coalition with the Greens in order to replace the three-party coalition of the Christian Democratic Union (CDU), Christian Social Union (CSU), and Free Democratic Party (FDP).

1999 The Bundestag, the German parliament, returns to the restored Reichstag in Berlin on April 19. The German federal government also leaves Bonn for Berlin, making Berlin capital of Germany again.

1999–2003 For the first time since 1945, the German army (the *Bundeswehr*) is deployed in combat missions in the former Yugoslavia and Afghanistan.

Today

2000 Hannover hosts Germany's first world's exposition, expo 2000, the largest ever staged in the 150-year history of the event.

2005 Chancellor Schröder asks for a vote of confidence in parliament and fails. After a new election in September, Angela Merkel (CDU) becomes the new chancellor with a "grand coalition" of CDU/CSU and SPD.

2005 Joseph Cardinal Ratzinger, the oldest person to be elected pope and the first German since 1523, becomes Pope Benedict XVI.

2006 Germany hosts the 2006 FIFA World Cup, the world's soccer championship.

2007 Angela Merkel as German chancellor and also in her role as the then President of the Council of the European Union hosts the G-8 summit in Heiligendamm, Germany.

2008 Chancellor Merkel (CDU) together with her minister of Finance Steinbrück (SPD) announce at a specially called nationwide TV press conference the safety of all private savings accounts.

2009 In Bundestag elections the alliance of the CDU/CSU and FDP receive an outright majority of seats, ensuring that Angela Merkel continues as chancellor.

2013 In December, Angela Merkel begins her third term as chancellor. She forms a grand coalition government with the center-left Social Democrats (SPD). The right-wing Populist Party AFD (Alternative für Deutschland), founded in the same year, fails to enter the Bundestag.

2014 For the first time, Germany adopts a minimum wage of €8.50 an hour.

2015 The German government insists on draconian conditions at EU talks that give Greece a third bailout package and prevents its exit from the eurozone.

2015 As thousands of Syrian war refugees enter Germany, Angela Merkel reminds Germans of their moral responsibility to offer protection to the persecuted.

2015 Volkswagen admits to deceiving U.S. consumers and the EPA with software that cheated emissions testing.

GERMAN VOCABULARY

ENGLISH	GERMAN	PRONUNCIATION

BASICS

Yes/no	Ja/nein	yah/nine
Please	Bitte	**bit**-uh
Thank you (very much)	Danke (vielen Dank)	**dahn**-kuh (**fee**-lun-dahnk)
Excuse me	Entschuldigen Sie	ent- **shool**-de-gen zee
I'm sorry	Es tut mir leid	es toot meer lite
Good day	Guten Tag	**goo**-ten tahk
Good-bye	Auf Wiedersehen	auf **vee**-der-zane
Mr./Mrs.	Herr/Frau	hair/frau
Miss	Fräulein	**froy**-line

NUMBERS

1	Ein(s)	ein(ts)
2	Zwei	tsvai
3	Drei	dry
4	Vier	fear
5	Fünf	funph
6	Sechs	zex
7	Sieben	**zee**-ben
8	Acht	ahkt
9	Neun	noyn
10	Zehn	tsane

DAYS OF THE WEEK

Sunday	Sonntag	**zone**-tahk
Monday	Montag	**moan**-tahk
Tuesday	Dienstag	**deens**-tahk
Wednesday	Mittwoch	**mit**-voah
Thursday	Donnerstag	**doe**-ners-tahk
Friday	Freitag	**fry**-tahk
Saturday	Samstag/Sonnabend	**zahm**-stakh/ **zonn**-a-bent

ENGLISH	GERMAN	PRONUNCIATION

USEFUL PHRASES

ENGLISH	GERMAN	PRONUNCIATION
Do you speak	Sprechen Sie	**shprek**-hun zee
English?	Englisch?	**eng**-glish
I don't speak	Ich spreche kein	ich **shprek**-uh kine
German.	Deutsch.	Doych
Please speak	Bitte sprechen Sie	**bit**-uh **shprek**-en-
slowly.	langsam.	zee **lahng**-zahm
I am	Ich bin	ich bin
American/	Amerikaner(in)/	A-mer-i- **kahn**-er(in)/
British	Engländer(in)	**Eng**-glan-der(in)
My name is . . .	Ich heisse . . .	ich **hi**-suh
Where are the	Wo ist die	vo ist dee
restrooms?	Toilette?	twah- **let**-uh
Left/right	links/rechts	links/rekts
Open/closed	offen/geschlossen	**O**-fen/geh- **shloss**-en
Where is . . .	Wo ist . . .	**vo** ist
the train station?	der Bahnhof?	dare **bahn**-hof
the bus stop?	die Bushaltestelle?	dee **booss**-hahlt-uh-shtel-uh
the subway	die U-bahn-	dee oo-bahn- **staht**-
station?	Station?	Sion
the airport?	der Flughafen?	dare **floog**-plats
the post office?	die Post?	dee **post**
the bank?	die Bank?	dee **banhk**
the police station?	die Polizeistation?	dee po-lee-tsai-**staht**-sion
the hospital?	das Krankenhaus?	dahs **krahnk**-en-house
the telephone?	das Telefon?	dahs te-le- **fone**
I'd like . . .	Ich hätte gerne . . .	ich **het**-uh gairn-uh
a room	ein Zimmer	ein **tsim**-er
the key	der Schlüssel	den **shlooh**-sul

ENGLISH	GERMAN	PRONUNCIATION
a map	eine Stadtplan	I-nuh **staht**-plahn
a ticket	eine Karte	I-nuh **cart**-uh
How much is it?	Wie viel kostet das?	**vee-feel cost**-et dahs
I am ill/sick.	Ich bin krank.	ich bin krahnk
I need . . .	Ich brauche . . .	ich **brow**-khuh
a doctor	einen Arzt	I-nen artst
the police	die Polizei	dee po-li- **tsai**
help	Hilfe	**hilf-uh**
Stop!	Halt!	Hahlt
Fire!	Feuer!	**foy**-er
Look out/Caution!	Achtung!/Vorsicht!	**ahk**-tung/ **for**-zicht

DINING OUT

A bottle of . . .	eine Flasche . . .	I-nuh **flash**-uh
A cup of . . .	eine Tasse . . .	I-nuh **tahs**-uh
A glass of . . .	ein Glas . . .	ein glahss
Ashtray	der Aschenbecher	dare **Ahsh**-en-bekh-er
Bill/check	die Rechnung	dee **rekh**-nung
Do you have . . .?	Haben Sie . . .?	**hah**-ben zee
I am a vegetarian.	Ich bin Vegetarier(in)	ich bin ve-guh-**tah**- re-er
I'd like to order . . .	Ich möchte . . . bestellen	ich **mohr**-shtuh . . . buh- **shtel**-en
Menu	die Speisekarte	dee **shpie**-zeh-car-tuh
Napkin	die Serviette	dee zair-vee- **eh**-tuh
Knife	das Messer	das **mess**-ehr
Fork	die Gabel	dee **gah**-bell
Spoon	die Löffel	der **luf**-fell

MENU GUIDE

ENGLISH	GERMAN
GENERAL DINING	
Side dishes	Beilagen
Extra charge	Extraaufschlag
When available	Falls verfügbar
Entrées	Hauptspeisen
.. (not) included	. . . (nicht) inbegriffen
Depending on the season	je nach Saison
Lunch menu	Mittagskarte
Desserts	Nachspeisen
.. at your choice	. . . nach Wahl
.. at your request	. . . nach Wunsch
Prices are . . .	Preise sind . . .
Waiter/Waitress	die Bedienung
Service included	inklusive Bedienung
Value added tax included	inklusive Mehrwertsteuer (Mwst.)
Specialty of the house	Spezialität des Hauses
Soup of the day	Tagessuppe
Appetizers	Vorspeisen
Is served from . . . to . . .	Wird von . . . bis . . . serviert
BREAKFAST	
Bread	das Brot
Roll(s)	die Brötchen
Egg/Eggs	das Ei/die Eier
Hot	Heiss
Cold	Kalt
Jam	die Konfitüre
Milk	die Milch
Orange juice	der Orangensaft
Scrambled eggs	die Rühreier
Bacon	der Speck

ENGLISH	GERMAN
Fried eggs	die Spiegeleier
Lemon	die Zitrone
Sugar	der Zucker

SOUPS

Stew	der Eintopf
Chicken soup	die Hühnersuppe
Potato soup	die Kartoffelsuppe
Liver dumpling soup	die Leberknödelsuppe
Onion soup	die Zwiebelsuppe

METHODS OF PREPARATION

Blue (boiled in salt and vinegar)	Blau
Baked	Gebacken
Fried	Gebraten
Steamed	Gedämpft
Grilled (broiled)	Gegrillt
Boiled	Gekocht
Sautéed	In Butter geschwenkt
Breaded	Paniert
Raw	Roh

When ordering steak, the English words "rare, medium, (well) done" are used and understood in German.

GAME AND POULTRY

Duck	die Ente
Pheasant	der Fasan
Chicken	das Hähnchen (das Huhn)
Deer	der Hirsch
Rabbit	das Kaninchen
Venison	das Rehfleisch
Pigeon	die Taube
Turkey	die Truthahn
Quail	die Wachtel

ENGLISH	GERMAN

FISH AND SEAFOOD

Eel	der Aal
Oysters	die Austern
Trout	die Forelle
Flounder	die Flunder
Prawns	die Garnelen
Halibut	der Heilbutt
Herring	der Hering
Lobster	der Hummer
Scallops	die Jakobsmuscheln
Cod	der Kabeljau
Crab	die Krabbe
Salmon	der Lachs
Mackerel	die Makrele
Mussels	die Muscheln
Squid	der Tintenfisch
Tuna	der Thunfisch

MEATS

Veal	das Kalb
Lamb	das Lamm
Beef	das Rind
Pork	das Schwein

CUTS OF MEAT

Example: For "Lammkeule" see "Lamm" (above) + ". . . keule" (below)

Breast	die . . brust
Leg	die. . . keule
Liver	die. . . leber
Tenderloin	die. . . lende
Kidney	die. . . niere
Rib	die. . . rippe

ENGLISH	GERMAN
Meat patty	die Frikadelle
Meat loaf	der Hackbraten
Ham	der Schinken

VEGETABLES

Eggplant	die Aubergine
Cauliflower	der Blumenkohl
Beans	die Bohnen
Green	Grüne
White	Weisse
Peas	die Erbsen
Cucumber	die Gurke
Cabbage	der Kohl
Lettuce	der Kopfsalat
Mix of asparagus, peas, and carrots	die Leipziger Allerlei
Corn	der Mais
Carrots	die Karotte/die Mohrrüben
Peppers	der Paprika
Mushrooms	der Pilze/der Champignon
Celery	der Sellerie
Asparagus (tips)	der Spargel(spitzen)
Tomatoes	die Tomaten
Onions	die Zwiebeln

CONDIMENTS

Vinegar	der Essig
Garlic	der Knoblauch
Horseradish	der Meerettich
Oil	das Öl
Mustard	der Senf
Artificial sweetener	der Süssstoff
Cinnamon	der Zimt

ENGLISH	GERMAN
Sugar	der Zucker
Salt	das Salz

FRUITS

Apple	der Apfel
Orange	das Orange/die Apfelsine
Apricot	die Aprikose
Blueberry	die Blaubeere
Strawberry	die Erdbeere
Raspberry	die Himbeere
Cherry	die Kirsche
Grapefruit	die Pampelmuse
Raisin	die Rosine
Grape	die Weintraube
Banana	die Banane
Pear	die Birne

DRINKS

Water	das Wasser
With/without carbonation	mit/ohne Gas
Juice	der Saft
Beer	das Bier
White Wine/Red Wine	der Weisswein/der Rotwein
Sparkling Wine	der Sekt
Coffee	der Kaffee
Tea	der Tee
Hot Chocolate	die heisse Schokolade
with/without ice	mit/ohne Eis
with/without water	mit/ohne Wasser
straight	pur
mulled claret	der Glühwein
caraway-flavored liquor	der Kümmel
fruit brandy	der Obstler

TRAVEL SMART
GERMANY

GETTING HERE AND AROUND

Germany's transportation infrastructure is extremely well developed, so all areas of the country are well connected to each other by road, rail, and air. The autobahns are an efficient system of highways, although they can get crowded during holidays. In winter you may have to contend with closed passes in the Alps or difficult driving on smaller roads in the Black Forest and the Saarland region. High-speed trains are perhaps the most comfortable way of traveling. Munich to Hamburg, for example, a trip of around 966 km (600 miles), takes 5½ hours. Many airlines offer extremely cheap last-minute flights, but you have to be fairly flexible.

■ AIR TRAVEL

The least-expensive airfares on major carriers to Germany are often priced for round-trip travel and usually must be purchased in advance. Budget airline tickets are always priced one way. Airlines generally allow you to change your return date for a fee; most low-fare tickets, however, are nonrefundable. Fares between the British Isles and Germany on "no-frills" airlines such as Air Berlin and EasyJet can range from €15 to €70. ■TIP➜ **Although a budget airfare may not be refundable, new EU regulations require that all other supplemental fees and taxes are. That means that when the €1 fare from Berlin to Munich turns out to cost €70 with fuel surcharges and the like, you only lose €1. Refund procedures vary between airlines.**

Flying time to Frankfurt is 1½ hours from London, 7½ hours from New York, 10 hours from Chicago, and 12 hours from Los Angeles.

Lufthansa is Germany's leading carrier and has shared mileage plans and flights with Air Canada and United, as well as all members of the Star Alliance.

Germany's internal air network is excellent, with flights linking all major cities

in, at most, little more than an hour. Germany's second-largest airline, Air Berlin, is a low-cost, full-service operator flying domestic and international routes from its hubs in Berlin, Stuttgart, Düsseldorf, and Hamburg. It is almost always a cheaper and more comfortable option than a flag carrier. Air Berlin is a member of the OneWorld Alliance and shares frequent-flyer programs with British Airways and American Airlines. A handful of smaller airlines—Germanwings, EasyJet, and TUIfly—compete with low-fare flights within Germany and to other European cities. These companies are reliable, do business almost exclusively over the Internet, as talking to an actual person drives the price of the ticket up astronomically, and often beat the German rail fares. The earlier you book, the cheaper the fare.

AIRPORTS

Frankfurt is Germany's air hub. The large airport has the convenience of its own long-distance train station, but if you're transferring between flights, don't dawdle or you could miss your connection.

Munich is Germany's second air hub, with many services to North America and Asia. The airport is like a minicity, with plenty of activities to keep you entertained during a long layover. Experience a true German tradition and have a beer from the world's first airport brewery at the *Hofbräuhaus* here. For a more active layover, play miniature golf, beach volleyball, or soccer, or ice-skate in winter. There's also a playground. Live concerts and 150 shops with downtown prices draw locals to the airport as well. If you're an airplane aficionado (and German speaker), you can take advantage of a small cinema showing movies on aviation themes or take a bus tour of the airport's facilities, including maintenance hangars and engine-testing facilities. Looking for some R&R? The airport offers massages at the gate, relaxation zones, and napcabs (soundproof minirooms to nap in). Munich's S-bahn railway connects the airport with the city center; trips take about 40 minutes, and trains leave every 10 minutes.

United and Air Berlin have nonstop service between New York and Berlin-Tegel. Air Berlin also flies from Berlin-Tegel to Chicago, Miami, and Los Angeles. Major airlines, like Lufthansa, fly in and out of Berlin-Tegel, while most budget airlines use Berlin-Schönefeld. Once the Berlin Brandenburg airport finally opens—it was originally slated to open in 2011, but it likely won't open until late 2017—both Tegel and Schönefeld will close.

United also has nonstop service between New York and Hamburg. There are a few nonstop services from North America to Düsseldorf. Stuttgart is convenient to the Black Forest. Also convenient to the Black Forest is the EuroAirport Freiburg-Basel-Mulhouse, which is used by many airlines for European destinations and as a stopover.

AIRPORT INFORMATION

Berlin Flughafen Berlin Schönefeld (*SXF*). ☎ *030/000–186 €0.14 per min* ⊕ *www. berlin-airport.de.* **Flughafen Berlin Tegel** (*TXL*). ✉ *Berlin* ☎ *030/000–186 €0.14 per min* ⊕ *www.berlin-airport.de.*

Düsseldorf Flughafen Düsseldorf (*DUS*). ☎ *0211/4210* ⊕ *www.duesseldorf-international.de.*

Frankfurt Flughafen Frankfurt Main (*FRA*). ✉ *Frankfurt* ☎ *01805/372–4636, 069/6900 from outside Germany* ⊕ *www.frankfurt-airport.de.*

Freiburg EuroAirport Freiburg-Basel-Mulhouse (*MLH*). ☎ *0033/3899–03111 French number—airport is across the border in France* ⊕ *www.euroairport.com.*

Hamburg Hamburg International Airport (*HAM*). ☎ *040/50750* ⊕ *www.ham.airport.de.*

Köln Flughafen Köln/Bonn (*CGN*). ☎ *02203/404–001* ⊕ *www.koeln-bonn-airport.de.*

Munich Flughafen München (*MUC*). ✉ *Munich* ☎ *089/97500* ⊕ *www.munich-airport.de.*

Stuttgart Flughafen Stuttgart (*STR*). ☎ *0711/9480* ⊕ *www.stuttgart-airport.de.*

■ BOAT TRAVEL

Eurailpasses and German Rail Passes are honored by KD Rhine Line on the Rhine River and on the Mosel River between Trier and Koblenz. (If you use the fast hydrofoil, a supplementary fee is required.) The rail lines follow the Rhine and Mosel rivers most of their length, meaning you can go one way by ship and return by train. Cruises generally operate between April and October. If you are planning to visit Denmark or Sweden after Germany, note that Scandlines ferries offer discounts for Eurailpass owners.

The MS *Duchess of Scandinavia* carries passengers and cars three times a week for the 19½-hour run between Cuxhaven, Germany, and Harwich, England.

Information KD Rhine Line. ☎ *0221/208–8318* ⊕ *www.k-d.com.* **Scandlines.** ☎ *0381/54350* ⊕ *www.scandlines.de.*

■ BUS TRAVEL

Germany has good local and long-distance bus service. Many cities are served by Ber-linLinien Bus or MeinFernBus. Deutsche Touring, a subsidiary of the Deutsche Bahn, has offices and agents countrywide, and travels from Germany to cities elsewhere in Europe. It offers one-day tours along the Castle Road and the Romantic Road. The Romantic Road route is between Würzburg (with connections to and from Frankfurt) and Füssen (with connections to and from Munich, Augsburg, and Garmisch-Partenkirchen). With a Eurailpass or German Rail Pass you get a 20% discount on this route. Buses, with an attendant on board, travel in each direction between April and October.

All towns of any size have local buses, which often link up with trams (streetcars) and electric railway (S-bahn) and subway (U-bahn) services. Fares sometimes vary according to distance, but a ticket usually allows you to transfer freely between the various forms of transportation.

Bus Information Deutsche Touring.
☏ 069/790–3501 ⊕ www.touring-travel.eu.
MeinFernBus. ☏ 0180/ 515–9915 ⊕ www.meinfernbus.de.

CAR TRAVEL

Entry formalities for motorists are few: all you need is proof of insurance; an international car-registration document; and a U.S., Canadian, Australian, or New Zealand driver's license. If you or your car is from an EU country, Norway, or Switzerland, all you need is your domestic license and proof of insurance. *All* foreign cars must have a country sticker. There are no toll roads in Germany, except for a few Alpine mountain passes, although the autobahn may change to a toll system in 2017. Many large German cities require an environmental sticker on the front windshield. If your rental car doesn't have one, it's likely you'll be required to pay the fine.

CAR RENTAL

It is easy to rent a car in Germany, but not always cheap. You will need an International Driving Permit (IDP); it's available from the American Automobile Association (AAA) and the National Automobile Club. These international permits are universally recognized, and having one in your wallet may save you problems with the local authorities. In Germany you usually must be 21 to rent a car. Nearly all agencies allow you to drive into Germany's neighboring countries. It's frequently possible to return the car in another West European country, but not in Poland or the Czech Republic, for example.

Rates with the major car-rental companies begin at about €55 per day and €300 per week for an economy car with a manual transmission and unlimited mileage. It is invariably cheaper to rent a car in advance from home than to do it on the fly in Germany. Most rentals are manual, so if you want an automatic, be sure to

request one in advance. If you're traveling with children, don't forget to ask for a car seat when you reserve. Note that in some major cities, even automobile-producing Stuttgart, rental firms are prohibited from placing signs at major pickup and drop-off locations, such as the main train station. If dropping a car off in an unfamiliar city, you might have to guess your way to the station's underground parking garage; once there, look for a generic sign such as *Mietwagen* (rental cars). The German railway system, Deutsche Bahn, offers discounts on rental cars.

Depending on what you would like to see, you may or may not need a car for all or part of your stay. Most parts of Germany are connected by reliable rail service, so it might be a better plan to take a train to the region you plan to visit and rent a car only for side trips to out-of-the-way destinations.

Major Rental Agencies Avis. ☏ 800/331–1212 ⊕ www.avis.com. **Budget.** ☏ 800/472–3325 ⊕ www.budget.com. **Europecar.** ⊕ www.europecar.com. **Hertz.** ☏ 800/654–3001 ⊕ www.hertz.com.

Car Rental Comparison Sites Auto Europe. ☏ 888/223–5555 ⊕ www.autoeurope.com. **Europe by Car.** ☏ 212/581–3040 in New York, 800/223–1516 ⊕ www.europebycar.com. **Eurovacations.** ☏ 877/471–3876 ⊕ www.eurovacations.com. **Kemwel.** ☏ 877/820–0668 ⊕ www.kemwel.com.

GASOLINE

Gasoline costs are around €1.30 per liter—which is higher than in the United States. Some cars use diesel fuel, which is about €0.20 cheaper. If you're renting a car, find out which fuel the car takes. German filling stations are highly competitive, and bargains are often available if you shop around, but *not* at autobahn filling stations. Self-service, or *SB-Tanken,* stations are cheapest. Pumps marked *Bleifrei* contain unleaded gas.

PARKING

Daytime parking in cities and small, historic towns is difficult to find. Restrictions are not always clearly marked and can be hard to understand even when they are. Rental cars come with a "time wheel," which you can leave on your dashboard when parking signs indicate free, limited-time allowances. Larger parking lots have parking meters (*Parkautomaten*). After depositing enough change in a meter, you will be issued a timed ticket to display on your dashboard. Parking-meter spaces are free at night. In German garages you must pay immediately on returning to retrieve your car, not when driving into out. Put the ticket you got on arrival into the machine and pay the amount displayed. Retrieve the ticket, and upon exiting the garage, insert the ticket in a slot to raise the barrier. ■ TIP→ **You must lock your car when it is parked. Failure to do so risks a €25 fine and liability for anything that happens if the car is stolen.**

ROAD CONDITIONS

Roads are generally excellent. *Bundesstrassen* are two-lane state highways, abbreviated "B," as in B-38. Autobahns are high-speed thruways abbreviated with "A," as in A-7. If the autobahn should be blocked for any reason, you can take an exit and follow little signs bearing a "U" followed by a number. These are official detours.

ROAD MAPS

The best-known road maps of Germany are put out by the automobile club ADAC, by Shell, and by the Falk Verlag. They're available at gas stations and bookstores.

ROADSIDE EMERGENCIES

The German automobile clubs ADAC and AvD operate tow trucks on all autobahns. "Notruf" signs every 2 km (1 mile) on autobahns (and country roads) indicate emergency telephones. By picking up the phone, you'll be connected to an operator who can determine your exact location and get you the services you need. Help is free (with the exception of materials).

Emergency Services **Roadside assistance.**
☎ *01802/222–222.*

RULES OF THE ROAD

In Germany, road signs give distances in kilometers. There *are* posted speed limits on most of the autobahns, and they advise drivers to keep below 130 kph (80 mph) or 110 kph (65 mph). A sign saying *Richtgeschwindigkeit* and the speed indicates this. Slower traffic should stay in the right lane of the autobahn, but speeds under 80 kph (50 mph) are not permitted. Speed limits on country roads vary from 70 kph to 100 kph (43 mph to 62 mph) and are usually 50 kph (30 mph) through small towns.

Don't enter a street with a signpost bearing a red circle with a white horizontal stripe—it's a one-way street. Blue "Einbahnstrasse" signs indicate you're headed the correct way down a one-way street. The blood-alcohol limit for driving in Germany is very low (.05%), and passengers, but not the driver, are allowed to consume alcoholic beverages in the car. Note that seatbelts must be worn at all times by front- *and* back-seat passengers.

German drivers tend to drive fast and aggressively. There is no right turn at a red light in Germany. Though prohibited, tailgating is the national pastime on German roads. Do not react by braking for no reason: this is equally prohibited.

You may not use a handheld mobile phone while driving.

SCENIC ROUTES

Germany has many specially designated tourist roads that serve as promotional tools for towns along their routes. The longest is the Deutsche Ferienstrasse, the German Holiday Road, which runs from the Baltic Sea to the Alps, a distance of around 1,720 km (1,070 miles). The most famous, however, is the Romantische Strasse (⇨ *See Romantic Road Chapter 4*), which runs from Würzburg to Füssen, in the Alps, covering around 355 km (220 miles).

Among other notable touring routes are the Strasse der Kaiser und Könige (Route of Emperors and Kings), running from Frankfurt to Passau (and on to Vienna and Budapest); the Burgenstrasse (Castle Road), running from Mannheim to Bayreuth; the Deutsche Weinstrasse (⇨ *See German Wine Road in Chapter 10*), running through the Palatinate wine country; and the Deutsche Alpenstrasse, running the length of the country's Alpine southern border from near Berchtesgaden to the Bodensee. Less well-known routes are the Märchenstrasse (⇨ *See Fairy-Tale Road Chapter 12*), the Weser Renaissance Strasse, and the Deutsche Fachwerkstrasse (German Half-Timber Road).

▌ CRUISE SHIP TRAVEL

The American-owned Viking River Cruises company tours the Rhine, Main, Elbe, and Danube rivers, with four- to eight-day itineraries that include walking tours at ports of call. The longer cruises (up to 18 days) on the Danube (Donau, in German), which go to the Black Sea and back, are in great demand, so reserve six months in advance. The company normally books American passengers on ships that cater exclusively to Americans. If you prefer to travel on a European ship, specify so when booking. Köln–Düsseldorfer Deutsche Rheinschiffahrt (KD Rhine Line) offers trips of one day or less on the Rhine and Mosel. Between Easter and October there's Rhine service between Köln and Mainz, and between May and October, Mosel service between Koblenz and Cochem. Check the website for special winter tours. You'll get a free trip on your birthday if you bring a document verifying your date of birth.

Cruise Lines KD Rhine Line. ☎ *0221/208–8318* ⊕ *www.k-d.com.* **Viking River Cruises.** ☎ *0800/258–4666, 800/1887–10033 in Germany, 800/319–6660 in U.K.* ⊕ *www.vikingrivercruises.com.*

▌ TRAIN TRAVEL

Deutsche Bahn (DB—German Rail) is a very efficient, semi-privatized railway. Its high-speed InterCity Express (ICE), InterCity (IC), and EuroCity (EC) trains make journeys between the centers of many cities—Munich–Frankfurt, for example—faster by rail than by air. All InterCity and InterCity Express trains have restaurant cars and trolley service. RE, RB, and IRE trains are regional trains. It's also possible to sleep on the train and save a day of your trip: a decreasing number of CityNightLine (CNL) trains serving domestic destinations and neighboring countries have sleepers, couches, and recliners.

Once on your platform or *Bahnsteig*—the area between two tracks—you can check the notice boards that give details of the layout of trains (*Wagenstandanzeiger*) arriving on that track (*Gleis*). They show the locations of first- and second-class cars and the restaurant car, as well as where they will stop, relative to the lettered sectors, along the platform. Large railroad stations have English-speaking staff handling information inquiries.

For fare and schedule information, the Deutsche Bahn information line connects you to a live operator; you may have to wait a few moments before someone can help you in English. The automated number is toll-free and gives schedule information. Deutsche Bahn has an excellent website (⊕ *www.bahn.de*), available in English. To calculate the fare, enter your departure and arrival points, any town you wish to pass through, and whether you have a bike. The fare finder will tell you which type of train you'll be riding on—which could be important if you suffer from motion sickness. The ICE, the French TGV, the Swiss ICN, and the Italian Cisalpino all use "tilt technology" for a less jerky ride. One side effect, however, is that some passengers might feel queasy, especially if the track is curvy. An over-the-counter drug for motion sickness should help.

BAGGAGE

Most major train stations have luggage lockers (in four sizes). By inserting exact change into a storage unit, you release the unit's key. Prices range from €2 for a small locker to €5 for a "jumbo" one. Smaller towns' train stations may not have any storage options.

Throughout Germany, Deutsche Bahn can deliver your baggage from a private residence or hotel to another or even to one of six airports: Berlin, Frankfurt, Leipzig-Halle, Munich, Hamburg, or Hannover. You must have a valid rail ticket. Buy a *Kuriergepäck* ticket at any DB ticket counter, at which time you must schedule a pickup three workdays before your flight. The service costs €38 for a medium suitcase up to 31 kg (68 pounds).

DISCOUNTS

Deutsche Bahn offers many discount options with specific conditions, so do your homework on its website or ask about options at the counter before paying for a full-price ticket. For round-trip travel you can save 25% if you book at least three days in advance, 50% if you stay over a Saturday night and book at least three to seven days in advance. However, there's a limited number of seats sold at any of these discount prices, so book as early as possible, at least a week in advance, to get the savings. A discounted rate is called a *Sparpreis*. If you change your travel plans after booking, you will have to pay a fee. The surcharge for tickets bought on board is 10% of the ticket cost, or a minimum of €5. Most local, RE, and RB services do not allow purchasing tickets on board. Not having a ticket is considered *Schwarzfahren* (riding black) and is usually subject to a €60 fine. Tickets booked at a counter always cost more than over the Internet or from an automated ticket machine.

Children under 15 travel free when accompanied by a parent or relative on normal, discounted, and some, but not all, special-fare tickets. However, you must indicate the number of children traveling with you when you purchase the ticket; to ride free, the child (or children) must be listed on the ticket. If you have a ticket with 25% or 50% off, a *Mitfahrer-Rabatt* allows a second person to travel with you for a 50% discount (minimum of €15 for a second-class ticket). The *Schönes Wochenend Ticket* (Happy Weekend Ticket) provides unlimited travel on regional trains on weekends for up to five persons for €42 (€40 if purchased online or at a vending machine). Groups of six or more should inquire about *Gruppen & Spar* (group) savings. Each German state, or *Land,* has its own *Länder-Ticket,* which lets up to five people travel from 9 am to 3 am for around €25.

If you plan to travel by train within a day after your flight arrives, purchase a heavily discounted "Rail and Fly" ticket for DB trains at the same time you book your flight. Trains connect with 14 German airports and two airports outside Germany, Basel and Amsterdam.

FARES

A first-class seat is approximately 55% more than a second-class seat. For this premium you get a bit more legroom and the convenience of having meals (not included) delivered directly to your seat. Most people find second class entirely adequate and first class not worth the cost. Many regional trains offer an upgrade to first class for as little as €4. This is especially helpful on weekends when local trains are stuffed with cyclists and day-tripping locals. ICs and the later-generation ICE trains are equipped with electrical outlets for laptops and other gadgets.

Tickets purchased through Deutsche Bahn's website can be retrieved from station vending machines. Always check that your ticket is valid for the type of train you are planning to take, not just for the destination served. If you have the wrong type of ticket, you will have to pay the difference on the train, in cash or by credit card. If you book an online ticket and print it yourself, you must present the credit card used to pay for the ticket to the conductor for the ticket to be valid.

The ReisePacket service is for travelers who are inexperienced, elderly, disabled, or just appreciative of extra help. It costs €11 and provides, among other things, help boarding, disembarking, and transferring on certain trains that serve major cities and vacation areas. It also includes a seat reservation and a voucher for an onboard snack. Purchase the service at least one day before travel.

PASSES

If Germany is your only destination in Europe, consider purchasing a German Rail Pass, which allows 3 to 10 days of unlimited first- or second-class travel within a one-month period on any DB train, up to and including the ICE. A Twin Pass saves two people traveling together 50% off one person's fare. A Youth Pass, sold to those 12–25, is much the same but for second-class travel only. You can also use these passes aboard KD Rhine Line (see *Cruise Ship Travel*) along certain sections of the Rhine and Mosel rivers. Prices begin at $304 per person in second class. Twin Passes begin at $338 for two people in second class, and Youth Passes begin at $180. Additional days may be added to either pass, but only at the time of purchase and not once the pass has been issued. Extensions of the German Rail Pass to Brussels, Venice, Verona, Prague, and Innsbrück are also available.

Germany is one of 21 countries in which you can use a Eurailpass, which provides unlimited first-class rail travel in all participating countries for the duration of the pass. Two adults traveling together can pay either €580 each for 15 consecutive days of travel or €746 each for 21 consecutive days of travel. The youth fare is €379 for 15 consecutive days and €446 for 10 days within two months. Eurailpasses are available from most travel agents and directly from ⊕ *www.eurail.com*.

Eurailpasses and some of the German Rail Passes should be purchased before you leave for Europe. You can purchase a Eurailpass and 5- or 10-day German Rail Passes at the Frankfurt airport and at some major German train stations, but the cost will be higher (a youth ticket for five days of travel is just under €149). When you buy your pass, consider purchasing rail-pass insurance in case you lose it during your travels.

In order to comply with the strict rules about validating tickets before you begin travel, read the instructions carefully. Some tickets require that a train official validate your pass, while others require you to write in the first date of travel.

Many travelers assume that rail passes guarantee them seats on the trains they wish to ride. Not so. You need to book seats ahead even if you are using a rail pass; seat reservations are required on some European trains, particularly high-speed trains, and are a good idea in summer, on national holidays, and on popular routes. If you board the train without a reserved seat, you risk having to stand. You'll also need a reservation if you purchase sleeping accommodations. Seat reservations on InterCity trains cost €6, and a reservation is absolutely necessary for the ICE-Sprinter trains (€12 for second class). There are no reservations on regional trains.

TRAVEL FROM GREAT BRITAIN

There are several ways to reach Germany from London on British Rail. Travelers coming from the United Kingdom should take the Channel Tunnel to save time, the ferry to save money. Fastest and most expensive is the route via the Channel Tunnel on Eurostar trains. They leave at two-hour intervals from St. Pancras International and require a change of trains in Brussels, from which ICE trains reach Köln in 2½ hours and Frankfurt in 3½ hours. Prices for one-way tickets from London to Köln begin at €100–€129. Cheapest and slowest are the 8 to 10 departures daily from Victoria using the Ramsgate–Ostend ferry, jetfoil, or SeaCat catamaran service.

Channel Tunnel Car Transport Eurotunnel. ☎ *0870/535–3535 in the U.K., 070/223–210 in Belgium, 0810/630–304 in France* ⊕ *www. eurotunnel.com.* **Rail Europe.** ☎ *0870/241–5415* ⊕ *www.raileurope.co.uk.*

Channel Tunnel Passenger Service Eurostar. ☎ *08432/186–186 in the U.K., 1233/617–575 outside the U.K.* ⊕ *www. eurostar.co.uk.* **Rail Europe.** ☎ *888/382–7245 in U.S., 0870/584–8848 in U.K., inquiries and credit-card bookings* ⊕ *www.raileurope.com.*

Train Information Deutsche Bahn (*German Rail*). ☎ *0800/150–7090 for automated schedule information, 11861 for 24-hr hotline €0.39 per min, 491805/996–633 from outside Germany €0.12 per min* ⊕ *www. bahn.de.* **Eurail.** ⊕ *www.eurail.com.* **Eurostar.** ☎ *0870/518–6186* ⊕ *www.eurostar.com.*

ESSENTIALS

■ ACCOMMODATIONS

The standards of German hotels, down to the humblest inn, are very high. You can nearly always expect courteous and polite service and clean and comfortable rooms. In addition to hotels proper, the country has numerous *Gasthöfe* or *Gasthäuser* (country inns that serve food and also have rooms). At the lowest end of the scale are *Fremdenzimmer*, meaning simply "rooms," normally in private houses. Look for the sign reading "Zimmer frei" (room available) or "zu vermieten" (to rent) on a green background; a red sign reading "besetzt" means there are no vacancies.

If you are looking for a very down-to-earth experience, try an *Urlaub auf dem Bauernhof*, a farm that has rooms for travelers. This can be especially exciting for children. You can also opt to stay at a winery's *Winzerhof*.

Room rates are by no means inflexible and depend very much on supply and demand. You can save money by inquiring about deals: many resort hotels offer substantial discounts in winter, for example. Likewise, many $$$$ and $$$ hotels in cities cut their prices dramatically on weekends and when business is quiet. Major events like Munich's Oktoberfest and the Frankfurt Book Fair will drive prices through the roof.

Tourist offices will make bookings for a nominal fee, but they may have difficulty doing so after 4 pm in high season and on weekends, so don't wait until too late in the day to begin looking for your accommodations. If you do get stuck, ask someone—like a mail carrier, police officer, or waiter, for example—for directions to a house renting a Fremdenzimmer or to a Gasthof.

Most hotels and other lodgings require you to give your credit-card details before they will confirm your reservation. If you don't feel comfortable emailing this information, ask if you can fax it (some places even prefer faxes). However you book, get confirmation in writing and have a copy of it handy when you check in.

Be sure you understand the hotel's cancellation policy. Some places allow you to cancel without any kind of penalty—even if you prepaid to secure a discounted rate—if you cancel at least 24 hours in advance. Others require you to cancel a week in advance or penalize you the cost of one night. Small inns and B&Bs are most likely to require you to cancel far in advance. Most hotels allow children under a certain age to stay in their parents' room at no extra charge, but others charge for them as extra adults; find out the cutoff age for discounts.

APARTMENT AND HOUSE RENTALS

If you are staying in one region, renting an apartment is an affordable alternative to a hotel or B&B. *Ferienwohnungen*, or vacation apartments, are especially popular in more rural areas. They range from simple rooms with just the basics to luxury apartments with all the trimmings. Some even include breakfast. It may seem low tech, but the best way to find an apartment is through the local tourist office or the website of the town or village where you would like to stay. Be aware, though, that in some cities like Berlin there are draconian rules limiting vacation apartments (which are seen as accelerating gentrification).

International Agencies AirBnB. ⊕ *www.airbnb.com.* **At Home Abroad.** ☎ *212/421–9165* ⊕ *www.athomeabroadinc.com.* **Barclay International Group.** ☎ *516/364-0064, 800/845-6636* ⊕ *www.barclayweb.com.* **Forgetaway.** ⊕ *www.forgetaway.com.* **Home Away.** ☎ *512/493-0382* ⊕ *www.homeaway.com.* **Interhome.** ☎ *954/791-8282, 800/882-6864* ⊕ *www.interhomeusa.com.* **Suzanne B. Cohen & Associates.** ☎ *207/200-2255* ⊕ *www.villaeurope.com.*

Vacation Home Rentals Worldwide.
☎ 201/767–9393, 800/633–3284 ⊕ www.
vhrww.com. **Villanet.** ☎ 206/417–3444,
800/964–1891 ⊕ www.vhrww.com. **Villas
& Apartments Abroad.** ☎ 212/213–6435,
800/433–3020 ⊕ www.vaanyc.com. **Villas
International.** ☎ 415/499–9490, 800/221–
2260 ⊕ www.villasintl.com. **Villas of Distinc-
tion.** ☎ 707/778–1800, 800/289–0900
⊕ www.villasofdistinction.com. **Wimco.**
☎ 800/449–1553 ⊕ www.wimco.com.

BED-AND-BREAKFASTS

B&Bs remain one of the most popular
options for traveling in Germany. They
are often inexpensive, although the price
depends on the amenities. For breakfast,
expect some muesli, cheese, cold cuts,
jam, butter, and hard-boiled eggs at the
very least. Some B&Bs also supply lunch
baskets if you intend to go hiking, or
arrange an evening meal for a very affordable price.

Reservation Services Bed & Breakfast.com.
☎ 512/322–2710, 800/462–2632 ⊕ www.
bedandbreakfast.com. **Bed & Breakfast Inns
Online.** ☎ 615/868–1946, 800/215–7365
⊕ www.bbonline.com. **BnB Finder.com.**
☎ 212/432–7693, 888/469–6663 ⊕ www.
bnbfinder.com.

CASTLE-HOTELS

Staying in a historic castle, or *Schloss,* is
a great experience. The simpler ones may
lack character, but most combine four-
star luxury with antique furnishings,
four-poster beds, and a baronial atmosphere. Some offer all the facilities of a
resort. Euro-Connection can advise you
on castle-hotel packages, including four-
to six-night tours.

Contacts Euro-Connection. ☎ 800/645–
3876 ⊕ www.euro-connection.com.

FARM VACATIONS

Almost every regional tourist office has
a brochure listing farms that offer bed-
and-breakfasts, apartments, and entire
farmhouses to rent (*Ferienhöfe*). The German Agricultural Association provides
an illustrated brochure, *Urlaub auf dem*

Bauernhof (*Vacation Down on the Farm*),
that covers more than 2,000 inspected
and graded farms, from the Alps to the
North Sea. It costs €9.90 and is also sold
in bookstores.

**German Agricultural Association DLG
Reisedienst, Agratour** (*German Agricultural Association*). ☎ 069/247–880 ⊕ www.
landtourismus.de.

HOME EXCHANGES

With a direct home exchange you stay in
someone else's home while they stay in
yours. Some outfits also deal with vacation homes, so you're not actually staying
in someone's full-time residence, just their
vacant weekend place.

EXCHANGE CLUBS

Home Exchange.com. $150 for a one-year
online listing. ☎ 800/877–8723 ⊕ www.
homeexchange.com.

HomeLink International. €120 yearly for Web
membership. ☎ 800/638–3841 ⊕ www.
homelink.org.

Intervac U.S. $99 for annual member-
ship. ☎ 800/756–4663 ⊕ us.intervac-
homeexchange.com.

HOTELS

Most hotels in Germany do not have air-
conditioning, nor do they need it, given
the climate and the German style of building construction that uses thick walls and
recessed windows to help keep the heat
out. Smaller hotels do not provide much
in terms of bathroom amenities. Except in
four- and five-star hotels, you won't find a
washcloth. Hotels often have nonsmoking
rooms or even nonsmoking floors, so it's
always worth asking for one when you
reserve. Beds in double rooms often consist of two twin mattresses placed side by
side within a frame. When you arrive, if
you don't like the room you're offered,
ask to see another.

Among the most delightful places to
stay—and eat—in Germany are the aptly
named Romantik Hotels and Restaurants.
The Romantik group has over 100 members in Germany. All are in atmospheric

and historic buildings—a condition for membership—and are run by the owners with the emphasis on excellent amenities and service. Prices vary considerably, but in general they are a good value.

Contacts Romantik Hotels and Restaurants. ☎ 800/650–8018, 817/678–0038 *from the U.S., 069/661–2340 in Germany* ⊕ *www. romantikhotels.com.*

SPAS

Taking the waters in Germany, whether for curing the body or merely pampering, has been popular since Roman times. More than 300 health resorts, mostly equipped for thermal or mineral-water, mud, or brine treatments, are set within pleasant country areas or historic communities. The word *Bad* before or within the name of a town means it's a spa destination, where many patients reside in health clinics for two to three weeks of doctor-prescribed treatments.

Saunas, steam baths, and other hot-room facilities are often used "without textiles" in Germany—in other words, nude. Wearing a bathing suit is sometimes even prohibited in saunas, but sitting on a towel is always required. (You may need to bring your own towels.) The Deutsche Heilbäderverband has information, but it is in German only.

Contacts Deutsche Heilbäderverband (*German Health Resort and Spa Association*). ☎ 0228/201–200 ⊕ *www.deutscher-heilbaederverband.de.*

▮ COMMUNICATIONS

INTERNET

Many hotels have in-room data ports, but you may have to purchase, or borrow from the front desk, a cable with an end that matches German phone jacks. If you're plugging into a phone line, you'll need a local access number for a connection. Wireless Internet (called WLAN in Germany) is more and more common in even the most average hotel. The service is not always free, however. Sometimes you

must purchase blocks of time from the front desk or online using a credit card. The cost is fairly high, usually around €4 for 30 minutes.

There are alternatives. Some hotels have an Internet room for guests needing to check their email. Otherwise, Internet cafés are common, and many bars and restaurants let you surf the Web.

PHONES

The good news is that you can make a direct-dial telephone call from Germany to virtually any point on Earth. The bad news? You can't always do so cheaply. Calling from a hotel is almost always the most expensive option; hotels usually add huge surcharges to all calls, particularly international ones. In some countries you can phone from call centers or even the post office. Calling cards usually keep costs to a minimum, but only if you purchase them locally. Because most Germans own mobile phones, finding a telephone booth is becoming increasingly difficult. As expensive as mobile phone calls can be, they are still usually a much cheaper option than calling from your hotel.

The country code for Germany is 49. When dialing a German number from abroad, drop the initial "0" from the local area code.

Many companies have service lines beginning with 0180. The cost of these calls averages €0.28 per call. Numbers that begin with 0190 can cost €1.85 per minute and more.

CALLING WITHIN GERMANY

The German telephone system is very efficient, so it's unlikely you'll have to use an operator unless you're seeking information. For information in English, dial ☎ 11837 for numbers within Germany and ☎ 11834 for numbers elsewhere. But first look for the number in the phone book or online (⊕ *www.teleauskunft.de*), because directory assistance is costly. Calls to 11837 and 11834 cost at least €0.50, more if the call lasts more than 30 seconds.

A local call from a telephone booth costs €0.10 per minute. Dial the "0" before the area code when making a long-distance call within Germany. When dialing within a local area code, drop the "0" and the area code.

Telephone booths are no longer a common feature on the streets, so be prepared to walk out of your way to find one. Phone booths have instructions in English as well as German. Most telephone booths in Germany are card-operated, so buy a phone card. Coin-operated phones, which take €0.10, €0.20, €0.50, €1, and €2 coins, don't make change.

CALLING OUTSIDE GERMANY

The country code for the United States is 1.

International calls can be made from any telephone booth in Germany. It costs only €0.13 per minute to call the United States, day or night, no matter how long the call lasts. Use a phone card. If you don't have a good deal with a calling card, there are many stores that offer international calls at rates well below what you will pay from a phone booth. At a hotel, rates will be at least double the regular charge.

Access Codes AT&T Direct. ☎ 0800/225-5288. **MCI WorldPhone.** ☎ 0800/955-0925. **Sprint International Access.** ☎ 0800/888-0013.

CALLING CARDS

Post offices, newsstands, and exchange places sell cards with €5, €10, or €20 worth of credit to use at public pay phones. An advantage of a card: it charges only what the call costs. A €5 card with a good rate for calls to the United States, United Kingdom, and Canada is Go Bananas!

MOBILE PHONES

You can buy an inexpensive unlocked mobile phone and a SIM card at almost every corner shop and even at the supermarket. Most shops require identification to purchase a SIM card, but you can avoid this by purchasing a card at any number of phone centers or call shops, usually located near train stations. This is the best option if you just want to make local calls.

If you bring a phone from abroad, your provider may have to unlock it for you to use a different SIM card and a prepaid service plan in the destination. You'll then have a local number and can make local calls at local rates. If your trip is extensive, you could also simply buy a new cell phone in your destination, as the initial cost will be offset over time.

Many prepaid plans, like Blau World, offer calling plans to the United States and other countries, starting at €0.03 per minute. Many Germans use these SIM cards to call abroad, as the rates are much cheaper than from landlines.

If you have a multiband phone (some countries use different frequencies from what's used in the United States) and your service provider uses the world-standard GSM network (as do T-Mobile, AT&T, and Verizon), you can probably use your phone abroad. Roaming fees can be steep, however: 99¢ a minute is considered reasonable. And overseas you normally pay the toll charges for incoming calls. It's almost always cheaper to send a text message than to make a call, because text messages have a very low set fee (often less than 5¢).

Cellular Abroad rents and sells GMS phones and sells SIM cards that work in many countries. Mobal rents mobiles and sells GSM phones (starting at $49) that will operate in 140 countries. Planet Fone rents cell phones, but the per-minute rates are expensive.

■**TIP→** If you travel internationally frequently, save one of your old mobile phones or buy a cheap one on the Internet; ask your cell phone company to unlock it for you, and take it with you as a travel phone, buying a new SIM card with pay-as-you-go service in each destination.

Contacts Cellular Abroad. ☎ 800/287-5072 ⊕ www.cellularabroad.com. **Mobal.** ☎ 888/888-9162 ⊕ www.mobalrental.com. **Planet Fone.** ☎ 888/988-4777 ⊕ www.planetfone.com.

■ CUSTOMS AND DUTIES

German Customs and Border Control is fairly simple and straightforward. The system works efficiently and professionally, and 99% of all travelers will have no real cause to interact with them.

You're always allowed to bring goods of a certain value back home without having to pay any duty or import tax. But there's a limit on the amount of tobacco and liquor you can bring back duty-free, and some countries have separate limits for perfumes; for exact figures, check with your customs department. The values of so-called duty-free goods are included in these amounts. When you shop abroad, save all your receipts, as customs inspectors may ask to see them as well as the items you purchased. If the total value of your goods is more than the duty-free limit, you'll have to pay a tax (most often a flat percentage) on the value of everything beyond that limit.

For anyone entering Germany from outside the EU, the following limitations apply: (1) 200 cigarettes or 100 cigarillos or 50 cigars or 250 grams of tobacco; (2) 2 liters of still table wine; (3) 1 liter of spirits over 22% alcohol by volume (ABV) or 2 liters of spirits under 22% ABV (fortified and sparkling wines) or 2 more liters of table wine; (4) 50 grams of perfume and 250 milliliters of eau de toilette; (5) 500 grams of roasted coffee or 200 grams of instant coffee; (6) other goods to the value of €175.

If you have questions regarding customs or bringing a pet into the country, contact the Zoll-Infocenter.

Information in Germany Zoll-Infocenter.
☎ *0351/4483–4510* ⊕ *www.zoll.de.*

U.S. Information U.S. Customs and Border Protection. ⊕ *www.cbp.gov.*

■ EATING OUT

Almost every street in Germany has its *Gaststätte,* a sort of combination restaurant and pub, and every village its *Gasthof,* or inn. The emphasis in either is on simple food at reasonable prices. A *Bierstube* (pub) or *Weinstube* (wine cellar) may also serve light snacks or meals.

Service can be slow, but you'll never be rushed out of your seat. Something else that may seem jarring at first: people can, and do, join other parties at a table in a casual restaurant if seating is tight. It's common courtesy to ask first, though.

Since Germans don't generally drink from the tap, water always costs extra and comes as still or sparkling mineral water.

BUDGET EATING TIPS

Imbiss (snack) stands can be found in almost every busy shopping street, in parking lots, train stations, and near markets. They serve *Würste* (sausages), grilled, roasted, or boiled, and rolls filled with cheese, cold meat, or fish. Many stands sell Turkish-style wraps called *döner kebab.* Prices range from €1.50 to €2.50 per portion. It's acceptable to bring sandwich fixings to a beer garden so long as you order a beer there; just be sure not to sit at a table with a tablecloth.

Butcher shops, known as *Metzgereien,* often serve warm snacks or very good sandwiches. Try *warmer Leberkäs mit Kartoffelsalat,* a typical Bavarian specialty, which is a sort of baked meat loaf with mustard and potato salad. In northern Germany try *Bouletten,* small meatballs, or *Currywurst,* sausages in a piquant curry sauce. Thuringia has a reputation for its bratwurst, which is usually broken in two and packed into a roll with mustard. Up north, the specialty snack is a herring sandwich with onions.

Restaurants in department stores are especially recommended for appetizing and inexpensive lunches. Kaufhof, Karstadt, Wertheim, and Horton are names to note. Germany's vast numbers of Turkish,

Italian, Greek, Chinese, and Balkan restaurants are often inexpensive.

MEALS AND MEALTIMES

Most hotels serve a buffet-style breakfast (*Frühstück*) of rolls, cheese, cold cuts, eggs, cereals, yogurt, and spreads, which is often included in the price of a room. Cafés, especially the more trendy ones, offer breakfast menus sometimes including pancakes, omelets, muesli, or even Thai rice soup. By American standards, a cup (*Tasse*) of coffee in Germany is very petite, and you don't get free refills. Order a *Pot* or *Kännchen* if you want a larger portion.

For lunch (*Mittagessen*), you can get sandwiches from most cafés and bakeries, and many fine restaurants have special lunch menus that make the gourmet experience much more affordable. Dinner (*Abendessen*) is usually accompanied by a potato or spätzle side dish. A salad sometimes comes with the main dish.

Gaststätten normally serve hot meals from 11:30 am to 9 pm; many places stop serving hot meals between 2 pm and 6 pm, although you can still order cold dishes. If you feel like a hot meal, look for a restaurant advertising *durchgehend geöffnet*, or look for a pizza parlor.

Once most restaurants have closed, your options are limited. Take-out pizza parlors and Turkish eateries often stay open later. Failing that, your best option is a train station or a gas station with a convenience store. Many bars serve snacks.

Unless otherwise noted, the restaurants listed are open daily for lunch and dinner.

PAYING

Credit cards are generally accepted only in moderate to expensive restaurants, so check before sitting down. You will need to ask for the bill (say "Die Rechnung, bitte.") in order to get it from the waiter, the idea being that the table is yours for the evening. Round up the bill 5% to 10% and pay the waiter directly rather than leaving any money or tip on the table. The waiter will likely wait at the table for you to pay after he has brought the check. He will also wear a money pouch and make change out of it at the table. If you don't need change, say "Stimmt so." ("Keep the change."), otherwise tell the waiter how much change you want back, adding in the tip. Meals are subject to 19% tax (abbreviated as "MwSt" on your bill). *For guidelines on tipping see Tipping, below.*

RESERVATIONS AND DRESS

Regardless of where you are, it's a good idea to make a reservation if you can. In most fine-dining establishments it's expected. We only mention them specifically when reservations are essential (there's no other way you'll ever get a table) or when they are not accepted. For popular restaurants, book as far ahead as you can (often 30 days), and reconfirm as soon as you arrive. (Parties of more than four should always call ahead to check the reservations policy.) We mention dress only when men are required to wear a jacket or a jacket and tie.

Note that even when Germans dress casually, their look is generally crisp and neat. Jeans are acceptable for most social occasions, unless you're meeting the president.

SMOKING

For such an otherwise health-conscious nation, Germans do smoke. A lot. New anti-smoking laws came into effect in 2008, effectively banning smoking in all restaurants and many pubs, but many Germans, particularly in Berlin and Hamburg, tend to ignore them. Many hotels have nonsmoking rooms and even nonsmoking floors. However, a smoker will find it intrusive if you ask him or her to refrain.

WINES, BEER, AND SPIRITS

Wines of Germany promotes the wines of all 13 German wine regions and can supply you with information on wine festivals and visitor-friendly wineries. It also arranges six-day guided winery tours in spring and fall in conjunction with the German Wine Academy.

It's legal to drink beer from open containers in public (even in the passenger seat of a car), and having a beer at one's midday break is nothing to raise an eyebrow at. Bavaria is not the only place to try beer. While Munich's beers have achieved world fame—Löwenbräu and Paulaner, for example—beer connoisseurs will really want to travel to places farther north like Alpirsbach, Bamberg, Erfurt, Cologne, or Görlitz, where smaller breweries produce top-notch brews. Berlin is at the center of a beer revolution that makes it one of the most interesting beer cities in Germany.

Wine Information German Wine Academy. ☎ 06131/28290 ⊕ www.germanwines.de. **Wines of Germany.** ☎ 212/994–7523 ⊕ www.germanwineusa.org.

▌ ELECTRICITY

The electrical current in Germany is 220 volts, 50 cycles alternating current (AC); wall outlets take Continental-type plugs, with two round prongs.

Consider making a small investment in a universal adapter, which has several types of plugs in one lightweight, compact unit. Most laptops and mobile phone chargers are dual voltage (i.e., they operate equally well on 110 and 220 volts) so require only an adapter. These days the same is true of small appliances such as hair dryers. Always check labels and manufacturer instructions to be sure. Don't use 110-volt outlets marked "for shavers only" for high-wattage appliances such as hair dryers. Walkabout Travel Gear has good coverage of electricity under "adapters."

Contacts Walkabout Travel Gear. ⊕ www.walkabouttravelgear.com.

▌ EMERGENCIES

Throughout Germany call ☎ 110 for police, ☎ 112 for an ambulance or the fire department.

Foreign Embassies U.S. Embassy. ✉ Pariser Pl. 2, Berlin ☎ 030/83050, 030/8305–1200 ⊕ www.usembassy.de.

▌ ETIQUETTE

CUSTOMS OF THE COUNTRY

Being on time for appointments, even casual social ones, is very important. There is no "fashionably late" in Germany. Germans are more formal in addressing each other than Americans. Always address acquaintances as Herr (Mr.) or Frau (Mrs.) plus their last name; do not call them by their first name unless invited to do so. The German language has informal and formal pronouns for "you": formal is *Sie*, and informal is *du*. Even if adults are on a first-name basis with one another, they may still keep to the *Sie* form.

Germans are less formal when it comes to nudity: a sign that reads "freikörper" or "fkk" indicates a park or beach that allows nude sunbathing. At a sauna or steam bath, you will often be asked to remove all clothing.

GREETINGS

The standard "Guten Tag" is the way to greet people throughout the country. When you depart, say "Auf Wiedersehen." "Hallo" is also used frequently, as is "Hi" among the younger crowd. A less formal leave-taking is "Tschüss" or "ciao." You will also hear regional differences in greetings.

LANGUAGE

English is spoken in most hotels, restaurants, airports, museums, and other places of interest. However, English is not widely spoken in rural areas or by people over 40; this is especially true of the eastern part of Germany. Learning the basics before going is always a good idea, especially *bitte* (please) and *danke* (thank you). Apologizing for your poor German before asking a question in English will make locals feel respected and begins all communication on the right foot.

A phrase book and language-tape set can help get you started.

■ TIP➡ Under no circumstances use profanity or pejoratives. Germans take these very seriously, and a slip of the tongue can result in expensive criminal and civil penalties. Calling a police officer a "Nazi" or using vulgar finger gestures can cost you up to €10,000 and two years in jail.

HEALTH

Warm winters have recently caused an explosion in the summertime tick population, which often causes outbreaks of Lyme disease. If you intend to do a lot of hiking, especially in the southern half of the country, be aware of the danger of ticks spreading Lyme disease. There is no vaccination against them, so prevention is important. Wear high shoes or boots, long pants, and light-color clothing. Use a good insect repellent, and check yourself for ticks after outdoor activities, especially if you've walked through high grass.

OVER-THE-COUNTER REMEDIES

All over-the-counter medicines, even aspirin, are only available at an *Apotheke* (pharmacy): the German term *Drogerie*, or drugstore, refers to a shop for sundry items.

Apotheken are open during normal business hours, with those in train stations or airports open later and on weekends. Apotheken are plentiful, and there is invariably one within a few blocks. Every district has an emergency pharmacy that is open after hours. These are listed as *Apotheken Notdienst* or *Apotheken-Bereitschaftsdienst* on the window of every other pharmacy in town, often with directions for how to get there. Pharmacies will have a bell you must ring to enter. Most pharmacists in larger cities speak enough English to help. Some drugs have different names: acetaminophen—or Tylenol—is called *paracetomol*.

SHOTS AND MEDICATIONS

Germany is by and large a healthy place. There are occasional outbreaks of measles—including one in North Rhine–Westfalia—so be sure you have been vaccinated.

HOURS OF OPERATION

Business hours are inconsistent throughout the country and vary from state to state and even from city to city. Banks are generally open weekdays from 8:30 or 9 am to 3 or 4 pm (5 or 6 pm on Thursday), sometimes with a lunch break of about an hour at smaller branches. Some banks close by 2:30 on Friday afternoon. Banks at airports and main train stations open as early as 6:30 am and close as late as 10:30 pm.

Most museums are open from Tuesday to Sunday 10–6. Some close for an hour or more at lunch. Many stay open until 8 pm or later one day a week, usually Thursday. In smaller towns or in rural areas, museums may be open only on weekends or just a few hours a day.

All stores are closed Sunday, with the exception of those in or near train stations. Larger stores are generally open from 9:30 or 10 am to 8 or 9 pm on weekdays and close between 6 and 8 pm on Saturday. Smaller shops and some department stores in smaller towns close at 6 or 6:30 on weekdays and as early as 4 on Saturday. German shop owners take their closing times seriously. If you come in five minutes before closing, you may not be treated like royalty. Apologizing profusely and making a speedy purchase will help.

Along the autobahn and major highways, as well as in larger cities, gas stations and their small convenience shops are often open late, if not around the clock.

HOLIDAYS

The following national holidays are observed in Germany: January 1; January 6 (Epiphany—Bavaria, Saxony-Anhalt, and Baden-Württemberg only); Good Friday; Easter Monday; May 1 (Workers' Day); Ascension; Pentecost Monday; Corpus Christi (southern Germany only); Assumption Day (Bavaria and Saarland only); October 3 (German Unity Day); November 1 (All Saints' Day—Baden-Württemberg, Bavaria, North

Rhine-Westphalia, Rhineland-Pfalz, and Saarland); December 24–26 (Christmas).

Pre-Lenten celebrations in Cologne and the Rhineland are known as Karneval, and for several days before Ash Wednesday work grinds to a halt as people celebrate with parades, banquets, and general debauchery. Farther south, in the state of Baden-Württenburg, the festivities are called Fasching, and tend to be more traditional. In either area, expect businesses to be closed both before and after "Fat Tuesday."

▌MAIL

A post office in Germany (*Postamt*) is recognizable by the postal symbol, a black bugle on a yellow background. In some villages you will find one in the local supermarket. Stamps (*Briefmarken*) can also be bought at some news agencies and souvenir shops. Post offices are generally open weekdays 8–6, Saturday 8–noon.

Airmail letters and postcards to anywhere outside Germany, even to the United Kingdom and within Europe cost €0.80. These rates apply to standard-size envelopes and postcards. Letters take approximately 3–4 days to reach the United Kingdom, 5–7 days to the United States, and 7–10 days to Australia and New Zealand.

You can arrange to have mail (letters only) sent to you in care of any German post office; have the envelope marked "Postlagernd." This service is free, and the mail will be held for seven days. Or you can have mail sent to any American Express office in Germany. There's no charge to cardholders, holders of American Express traveler's checks, or anyone who has booked a vacation with American Express.

SHIPPING PACKAGES

Most major stores that cater to tourists will also ship your purchases home. You should check your insurance for coverage of possible damage.

The Deutsche Post has an express international service that will deliver your letter or package the next day to countries within the EU, within one to two days to the United States, and slightly longer to Australia. A letter or package to the United States weighing less than 5 kg costs €99. You can drop off your mail at any post office, or it can be picked up for an extra fee. Deutsche Post works in cooperation with DHL. International carriers tend to be slightly cheaper (€35–€45 for the same letter) and provide more services.

Express Services Deutsche Post.
☎ *0228/1820* ⊕ *www.deutschepost.de.*
DHL. ☎ *0800/225–5345* ⊕ *www.dhl.de.*
FedEx. ☎ *0800/123–0800* ⊕ *www.fedex.com.*
UPS. ☎ *0800/882–6630* ⊕ *www.ups.com.*

▌MONEY

Credit cards are not usually accepted by most businesses, but you probably won't have to use cash for payment in high-end hotels and restaurants. Many businesses on the other end of the spectrum don't accept them, however. It's a good idea to check in advance if you're staying in a budget lodging or eating in a simple country inn.

Prices throughout *this guide* are given for adults. Substantially reduced fees are almost always available for children, students, and senior citizens.

▌TIP→ **Banks almost never have every foreign currency on hand, and it may take as long as a week to order. If you're planning to exchange funds before leaving home, don't wait until the last minute.**

ATMS AND BANKS

Twenty-four-hour ATMs (*Geldautomaten*) can be accessed with Plus or Cirrus credit and banking cards. Your own bank will probably charge a fee for using ATMs abroad, and some German banks exact €3–€5 fees for use of their ATMs. Nevertheless, you'll usually get a better rate of exchange via an ATM than you will at a currency-exchange office or even when changing money in a bank. And extracting funds as you need them is a safer option than carrying around a large amount of cash. Since some ATM keypads show no letters, know the numeric equivalent of your password. Always use ATMs inside the bank.

■ TIP➔ PINs with more than four digits are not recognized at ATMs in many countries. If yours has five or more, remember to change it before you leave.

CREDIT CARDS

Most credit cards issued in Europe are now so-called "chip-and-PIN" credit cards that store user information on a computer chip embedded in the card. In the United States, all credit cards switched to "chip-and-signature" cards in fall 2015. While European cardholders are expected to know and use their PIN number for all transactions rather than signing a charge slip, U.S. chip-and-signature cards usually still require users to sign the charge slip. (Very few U.S. issuers offer a PIN along with their cards, except for cash withdrawals at an ATM, though this is expected to change in the future.) The good news: unlike the old magnetic-strip cards that gave American travelers in Europe so much trouble, the new chip-and-signature cards are accepted at many more locations, including in many cases at machines that sell train tickets, machines that process automated motorway tolls at unmanned booths, and automated gas stations—even without a signature or PIN. The bad news: not all European locations will accept the chip-and-signature cards, and you won't know until you try, so it's a good idea to carry enough cash to cover small purchases.

All major U.S. credit cards are accepted in Germany. The most frequently used are MasterCard and Visa. American Express is used less frequently, and Diners Club even less. Since the credit-card companies demand fairly substantial fees, some businesses will not accept credit cards for small purchases. Cheaper restaurants and lodgings often do not accept credit cards.

Many credit-card companies charge substantial foreign transaction fees—typically about 3% on every transaction. You can save money by applying for a no-fee credit card well ahead of your departure.

It's a good idea to inform your credit-card company before you travel, especially if you're going abroad and don't travel internationally very often. Otherwise, the credit-card company might put a hold on your card owing to unusual activity—not a good thing halfway through your trip. Record all your credit-card numbers—as well as the phone numbers to call if your cards are lost or stolen—in a safe place, via email, or in the Cloud, so you're prepared should something go wrong.

If you plan to use your credit card for cash advances, you'll need to apply for a PIN at least two weeks before your trip. Although it's usually cheaper (and safer) to use a credit card abroad for large purchases (so you can cancel payments or be reimbursed if there's a problem), note that some credit-card companies *and* the banks that issue them add substantial percentages to all foreign transactions, whether they're in a foreign currency or not. Check on these fees before leaving home, so there won't be any surprises when you get the bill.

■ TIP➔ Before you charge something, ask the merchant whether he or she plans to do a dynamic currency conversion (DCC). In such a transaction the credit-card processor (shop, restaurant, or hotel, not Visa or MasterCard) converts the currency and charges you in dollars. In most cases you'll pay the merchant a 3% fee for this service in addition to any credit-card company and issuing-bank foreign-transaction surcharges.

Dynamic currency conversion programs are becoming increasingly widespread. Merchants who participate in them are supposed to ask whether you want to be charged in dollars or the local currency, but they don't always do so. And even if they do offer you a choice, they may well avoid mentioning the additional surcharges. The good news is that you *do* have a choice. And if this practice really gets your goat, you can avoid it entirely thanks to American Express; with its cards, DCC simply isn't an option.

Reporting Lost Cards American Express.
☎ *800/333–2639 in U.S., 715/343–7977 collect from abroad* ⊕ *www.americanexpress. com.* **Diners Club.** ☎ *800/234–6377 in U.S., 303/799–1504 collect from abroad* ⊕ *www. dinersclub.com.* **MasterCard.** ☎ *800/627–8372 in U.S., 636/722–7111 collect from abroad* ⊕ *www.mastercard.com.* **Visa.** ☎ *800/847– 2911 in U.S., 410/581–9994 collect from abroad* ⊕ *www.visa.com.*

CURRENCY AND EXCHANGE

Germany shares a common currency, the euro (€), with 18 other countries: Austria, Belgium, Cyprus, Estonia, Finland, France, Greece, Ireland, Italy, Latvia, Lithuania, Luxembourg, Malta, the Netherlands, Portugal, Slovakia, Slovenia, and Spain. The euro is divided into 100 cents. There are bills of 5, 10, 20, 50, 100, and 500 euros and coins of €1 and €2, and 1, 2, 5, 10, 20, and 50 cents. Many businesses and restaurants do not accept €200 and €500 notes. It is virtually impossible to pay for anything in U.S. dollars, but you should have no problem exchanging currency. The large number of banks and exchange services means that you can shop around for the best rate, if you're so inclined. But the cheapest and easiest way to go is using your ATM card.

At this writing, the exchange rate was €0.88 for a U.S. dollar. But the exchange rate changes daily.

■ TIP➔ Even if a currency-exchange booth has a sign promising no commission, rest assured that there's some kind of huge, hidden fee. (Oh . . . that's right. The sign didn't say no fee.) And as for rates, you're almost always better off getting foreign currency at an ATM or exchanging money at a bank.

▌ PACKING

For visits to German cities, pack as you would for an American city: dressy outfits for formal restaurants and nightclubs, casual clothes elsewhere. Jeans are as popular in Germany as anywhere else, and are perfectly acceptable for sightseeing and informal dining. In the evening, men will probably feel more comfortable wearing a jacket in more expensive restaurants, although it's almost never required. Many German women wear stylish outfits to restaurants and the theater, especially in the larger cities.

Winters can be bitterly cold; summers are warm but with days that suddenly turn cool and rainy. In summer, take a warm jacket or heavy sweater if you are visiting the Bavarian Alps or the Black Forest, where the nights can be chilly even after hot days. In Berlin and on the Baltic, it is windy, which can be quite pleasant in summer but a complete bear in winter. To discourage purse snatchers and pickpockets, carry a handbag with long straps that you can sling across your body bandolier style and with a zippered compartment for money and other valuables.

For stays in budget hotels, pack your own soap. Many provide no soap at all or only a small bar.

▌ PASSPORTS AND VISAS

Visitors from the United States and Canada, including children, are required to have a passport to enter the EU for a period of up to 90 days. There are no official passport controls at any of Germany's land borders, although random spot checks and customs checks are becoming more frequent. Most travelers will only show their documents on entering and leaving the EU. Your passport should be valid for up to six months after your trip ends or this will raise questions at the border. EU citizens can enter Germany with a national identity card or passport. Traveling with children can be problematic. Single parents traveling with their own children rarely face any hassle, but overzealous border guards have been known to ask children about their relationship with the other parent. If you are a parent or grandparent traveling with a child, it helps to have a signed and notarized power of attorney in order to dispel any questions.

▌ RESTROOMS

Public restrooms are found in large cities, although you are not guaranteed to find one in an emergency. If you are in need, there are several options. You can enter the next café or restaurant and ask very politely to use the facilities. You can find a department store and look for the "WC" sign. Museums are also a good place to find facilities.

Train stations are increasingly turning to McClean, a privately run enterprise that demands €0.60 to €1.10 for admission to its restrooms. These facilities, staffed by attendants who clean almost constantly, sparkle. You won't find them in smaller stations, however. Their restrooms are usually adequate.

On the highways, the vast majority of gas stations have public restrooms, though you may have to ask for a key—we won't vouch for their cleanliness. You might want to wait until you see a sign for a restaurant.

Restrooms almost always cost money. It's customary to pay €0.20–€0.70 to the bathroom attendant.

▌ SAFETY

Germany has one of the lowest crime rates in Europe. There are some areas, such as the neighborhoods around train stations and the streets surrounding red-light districts, where you should keep an eye out for potential dangers. The best advice is to take the usual precautions. Secure your valuables in the hotel safe. Don't wear flashy jewelry, and keep expensive electronics out of sight when you are not using them. Carry shoulder bags or purses so that they can't be easily snatched, and never leave them hanging on the back of a chair at a café or restaurant. Avoid walking alone at night, even in relatively safe neighborhoods. Due to increasing incidents of violence in Berlin, Hamburg, and Munich, use caution late at night in the subway.

When withdrawing cash, don't use an ATM in a deserted area or one that is outside. It is best to avoid freestanding ATMs in subway stations and other locations away from a bank. Make sure that no one is looking over your shoulder when you enter your PIN. And never use a machine that appears to have been tampered with.

▌TIP→ **Distribute your cash, credit cards, IDs, and other valuables between a deep front pocket, an inside jacket or vest pocket, and a hidden money pouch. Don't reach for the money pouch once you're in public.**

Contacts **Transportation Security Administration** (*TSA*). ⊕ *www.tsa.gov.*

▌ TAXES

Most prices you see on items already include Germany's 19% value-added tax (V.A.T.). Some goods, such as food, books, and antiquities, carry a 7% V.A.T. as a percentage of the purchase price. A physical item must cost at least €25 to qualify for a V.A.T. refund.

When making a purchase, ask for a V.A.T. refund form and find out whether the merchant gives refunds—not all stores do, nor are they required to. Have the form stamped like any customs form by customs officials when you leave the country or, if you're visiting several European Union countries, when you leave the EU. After you're through passport control, take the form to a refund-service counter for an on-the-spot refund (which is usually the quickest and easiest option), or mail it to the address on the form (or the envelope with it) after you arrive home. You receive the total refund stated on the form, but the processing time can be long, especially if you request a credit-card adjustment.

Global Refund is a Europe-wide service with 225,000 affiliated stores and more than 700 refund counters at major airports and border crossings. Its refund form, called a Tax Free Check, is the most common across the European continent. The service issues refunds in the form of cash, check, or credit-card adjustment.

V.A.T. REFUNDS AT THE AIRPORT

If you're departing from Terminal 1 at Frankfurt Airport, where you bring your purchases to claim your tax back depends on how you've packed the goods. If the items are in your checked luggage, check in as normal, but let the ticket counter know you have yet to claim your tax refund. They will give you your luggage back to bring to the customs office in Departure Hall B, Level 2. For goods you are carrying on the plane with you, go to the customs office on the way to your gate. After you pass through passport control, there is a Global Refund office.

If you're departing from Terminal 2, bring goods in luggage to be checked to the customs office in Hall D, Level 2 (opposite the Delta Airlines check-in counters). For goods you are carrying on the plane with you, see the customs office in Hall E, Level 3 (near security control).

At Munich's airport, the Terminal 2 customs area is on the same level as check-in. If your V.A.T. refund items are in your luggage, check in first, and then bring your bags to the customs office on Level 04. From here your bags will be sent to your flight, and you can go to the Global Refund counter around the corner. If your refund items are in your carry-on, go to the Global Refund office in the customs area on Level 05 south. Terminal 1 has customs areas in modules C and D, Level 04.

V.A.T. Refunds Global Refund. ☎ *800/566–9828* ⊕ *www.globalblue.com.*

∎ TIME

All of Germany is on Central European Time, which is six hours ahead of Eastern Standard Time and nine hours ahead of Pacific Standard Time. Daylight Saving Time begins on the last Sunday in March and ends on the last Sunday in October. Timeanddate.com can help you figure out the correct time anywhere.

Germans use the 24-hour clock, or "military time" (1 pm is indicated as 13:00), and write the date before the month, so October 3 will appear as 03.10.

Time Zones Timeanddate.com. ⊕ *www. timeanddate.com/worldclock.*

∎ TIPPING

Tipping is done at your own discretion. Theater ushers do not necessarily expect a tip, while waiters, tour guides, bartenders, and taxi drivers do. Rounding off bills to the next highest sum is customary for bills under €10. Above that sum you should add a little more.

Service charges are included in all restaurant checks (listed as *Bedienung*), as is tax (listed as *MwSt*). Nonetheless, it is customary to round up the bill to the nearest euro or to leave about 5%–10%. Give it to the waitstaff as you pay the bill; don't leave it on the table, as that's considered rude.

TIPPING GUIDELINES FOR GERMANY

Bartender	Round up the bill for small purchases. For rounds of drinks, around 10% is appropriate.
Bellhop	€1 per item.
Hotel Concierge	€3–€5 if the concierge performs a special service for you.
Hotel Doorman	€1–€2 if he helps you get a cab.
Hotel Maid	€1 per day.
Hotel Room-Service Waiter	€1 per delivery.
Taxi Driver	Round up the fare if the ride is short. For longer trips, about €1 is appropriate.
Tour Guide	€5–€10 per person, or a bit more if the tour was especially good.
Valet Parking Attendant	€1–€2, but only when you retrieve your car.
Waiter	Round off the bill, giving 5% to 10% for very good service.

▮ TRIP INSURANCE

Comprehensive trip insurance is valuable if you're booking a very expensive or complicated trip (particularly to an isolated region) or if you're booking far in advance. Comprehensive policies typically cover trip-cancellation and interruption, letting you cancel or cut your trip short because of illness, or, in some cases, acts of terrorism in your destination. Such policies might also cover evacuation and medical care. Some cover you for trip delays because of bad weather or mechanical problems as well as for lost or delayed luggage.

Another type of coverage to consider is financial default—that is, when your trip is disrupted because a tour operator, airline, or cruise line goes out of business. Generally you must buy this when you book your trip or shortly thereafter, and it's available to you only if your operator isn't on a list of excluded companies.

Always read the fine print of your policy to make sure that you're covered for the risks that most concern you. Compare several policies to be sure you're getting the best price and range of coverage available.

Comprehensive Insurers AIG Travel Guard. ☎ *800/826–4919* ⊕ *www.travelguard.com.* **Allianz Global Assistance.** ☎ *866/284–8300* ⊕ *www.allianztravelinsurance.com.* **CSA Travel Protection.** ☎ *800/873–9855* ⊕ *www. csatravelprotection.com.* **Travelex Insurance.** ☎ *888/228–9792* ⊕ *www.travelexinsurance. com.* **Travel Insured International.** ☎ *800/243–3174* ⊕ *www.travelinsured.com.*

Insurance Comparison Information Insure My Trip. ☎ *800/487–4722* ⊕ *www. insuremytrip.com.* **Square Mouth.** ☎ *800/240–0369* ⊕ *www.squaremouth.com.*

▮ VISITOR INFORMATION

⇨ *Local tourist offices are listed in the individual chapters.* Staff at the smaller visitor information offices might not speak English. Many offices keep shorter hours than normal businesses, and you can expect some to close during weekday lunch hours and as early as noon on Friday. Almost all German cities and towns have an Internet presence under ⊕ *www. cityname.de,* for example ⊕ *www.berlin. de.* The Internet portal Deutschland.de has lots of information about the country's best-known sights, as well as those that are often overlooked.

Contacts Deutschland.de. ⊕ *www. deutschland.de.* **German National Tourist Office.** ✉ *New York* ☎ *212/661–7200* ⊕ *www. germany.travel.*

INDEX

PHOTO CREDITS

Front cover: sack/iStockphoto [Description: Historic half-timbered houses in the Weissgerbergasse in Nuremberg, Germany]. 1, Massimiliano Pieraccini/Shutterstock. 2-3, Wolfgang Kaehler / age fotostock. 5, Marco Maccarini/iStockphoto. Chapter 1: Experience Germany: 10-11, BerlinPictures/Shutterstock. 20 (left), linerpics/Shutterstock. 20 (top center), Nilsz | Dreamstime.com. 20 (top right), Scirocco340 / Shutterstock. 20 (bottom right), anweber/Shutterstock. 21 (left), Image Focus/Shutterstock. 21 (top center), Andrei Dimofte/Shutterstock. 21 (bottom center), Maugli/Shutterstock. 21 (top right), Semmickphoto | Dreamstime.com. 21 (bottom right), robert paul van beets/Shutterstock. 24, Ingolf Pompe / age fotostock. 25, Tilo G/Shutterstock. Chapter 2: Munich: 45, Scanrail | Dreamstime.com. 48, Viktualienmarkt Munich by zen-foto http://www.flickr.com/photos/wygiwys/2263622792/ Attribution-ShareAlike License. 49 (top), L. Kaster/Munich Tourist Office. 49 (bottom), Viktualienmarkt by Katie Homan http://www.flickr.com/photos/86507982@N00/2321029179/ Attribution-ShareAlike License. 50, B. Roemmelt/Munich Tourist Office. 51 (top), IMG_8676.jpg by Jay Tong http://www.flickr.com/photos/jaytong/543554848/Attribution-ShareAlike License. 51 (bottom), IMG_8692.jpg by Jay Tong http://www.flickr.com/photos/jaytong/543557406/ Attribution-ShareAlike License. 52, Munich Tourist Office. 54-55, Noppasinw | Dreamstime.com. 67, Manfred Bail / age fotostock. 77, Deutsches Museum. 79, BORGESE Maurizio / age fotostock. 82, McPHOTO PWI / age fotostock. 83, Pierre Adenis/GNTB. 84, Mirenska Olga/Shutterstock. 85 (top left), Fabian von Poser / age fotostock. 85 (bottom left), sebastian-julian/iStockphoto. 85 (right), chirapbogdan/Shutterstock. 86, Pierre Adenis/GNTB. 87, Marco Maccarini / iStockphoto. 88, Abhijeet Rane / Flickr, [CC BY 2.0]. 89, Oktoberfest München 2008 -Karussell by digital cat http://www.flickr.com/photos/14646075@N03/2909792955/ Attribution License. 92, gary718/Shutterstock. 122, Tory Marie / 500px. Chapter 3: The Bavarian Alps: 131, Charles Bowman / age fotostock. 132, Christina Hanck/iStockphoto. 133 (top), Manfred Steinbach/Shutterstock. 133 (bottom), filmfoto / Shutterstock. 134, Andreas Strauss / age fotostock. 135 (top), Kaster, Andreas/GNTB. 135 (bottom), Andreas Strauss / age fotostock. 136, Alexander Mertz/iStockphoto. 139, St. Nick/Shutterstock. 147, Manfred Bail / age fotostock. 149, St. Nick/Shutterstock. 159, Alpabob GmbH & Co. KG. 164, juergen2008/iStockphoto. 171, Priyendu Subashchandran/iStockphoto. Chapter 4: The Romantic Road: 173, Cowin, Andrew/GNTB. 174, Yuri Yavnik/Shutterstock. 175 (top), Konstantin Mironov/Shutterstock. 175 (bottom), Cowin, Andrew/GNTB. 176, Adrian Zenz/Shutterstock. 184, Thonig / age fotostock. 185 (top), bilwissedition com / age fotostock. 185 (bottom), yannick luthy / Alamy. 186, jean-pierre lescourre / age fotostock.187 (top), McPHOTO PWI / age fotostock. 187 (bottom), Neues Schloss Herrenchiemsee by digital cat http://www.flickr.com/photos/14646075@N03/3092981895/ Attribution License. 188, Schloss Neuschwan-stein by Ashutosh Garg http://www.flickr.com/photos/ashugarg/2570002062/ Attribution License. 189 (top), Public domain. 189 (bottom), Neuschwanstein interior by Tim Schapker http:// www.flickr.com/photos/albany_tim/2912135255/ Attribution License. 190, Werner Otto / age fotostock. 191 (top), Dainis Derics/Shutterstock. 191 (bottom), AYArktos/Wikimedia Commons. 197, Hubertus Blume / age fotostock. 200, STELLA / age fotostock. 209, Martin Siepmann / age fotostock. 214, Martin Moxter / age fotostock. Chapter 5: Franconia and the German Danube: 217, Walter Bibikow / age fotostock. 218, Arpad Benedek/iStockphoto. 219 (top), Heiko Stahl/Nuernberg Messe. 219 (bottom), Cowin, Andrew/Deutsche Zentrale für Tourismus e.V./GNTB. 220, Cowin, Andrew/GNTB. 221 (top), hsvrs/iStockphoto. 221 (bottom), Congress & Tourismus Zentrale Nürnberg/GNTB. 222, Cowin, Andrew/Deutsche Zentrale für Tourismus e.V./GNTB. 231, Martin Siepmann / age fotostock. 238, Sunny Celeste / age fotostock. 245, Germanisches Nationalmuseum, Nuremberg. 246, Cowin, Andrew/GNTB. 253, Spectral-Design/Shutterstock. 255, Rudi1976 | Dreamstime.com. 262, Walter Bibikow / age fotostock. Chapter 6: The Bodensee: 265, Dr. Heinz Linke/iStockphoto. 266, Gregory Perkins/iStockphoto. 267 (top), Frank Vincentz/Wikimedia Commons. 267 (bottom), Weingarten Basilica and Abbey by Clemens v. Vogelsang http://www.flickr.com/photos/vauvau/4402345694/ Attribution License. 268, Bodensee-Radweg Service. 269 (top), Photodesign, Tourist-Information Wasserburg. 270, Mainau GmbH/GNTB. 284, xyno/iStockphoto. 287, Bildagentur RM / age fotostock. 290, Clemens v. Vogelsang/Wikimedia Commons. 295, Ralf Brunner/GNTB. 298, parasola / age fotostock. Chapter 7: The Black Forest: 301, Juergen Stumpe / age fotostock. 302 (top), Yuriy Davats/Shutterstock. 303 (top), ZKM | Center for Art and Media Karlsruhe Photo: Fabry. 303 (bottom), lullabi/Shutterstock. 304, Bad Saarow Kur GmbH/GNTB. 305, Baden-Baden Kur und Tourismus. 306, Elke Wetzig (Elya)/Wikimedia Commons. 317, Cowin, Andrew/GNTB. 330, Blaine Harrington / age fotostock. 333, Europa-Park Rust/GNTB. Chapter 8: Heidelberg and the Neckar Valley: 335, Esbin-Anderson / age fotostock. 336, Kyle Lagatol/iStockphoto. 337 (top left), Mercedes-Benz Museum. 337 (top right), Dipl. Fotograf, Ralf/Deutsche Zentrale für Tourismus/GNTB. 337 (bottom), Patrick Poendl/iStockphoto. 338, Cowin, Andrew/GNTB. 346, Marschall H / age fotostock. 357, Kai Koehler/iStockphoto. 363, Michael Weber

NOTES

NOTES

ABOUT OUR WRITERS

Dan Allen is a veteran travel and entertainment writer who has covered Germany far and wide for numerous global publications and websites. He is a regular contributor to TravelChannel.com, Yahoo.com, Westways, and the New York Post, and his collected work can be seen on ⊕ *danallenism.com*. A former Berlin expat, he now splits his time between New York and Los Angeles, but his lifelong love affair with Germany—and the irresistible annual pull of the Berlin International Film Festival—keep him constantly coming back for more. He updated the Rhineland chapter for this edition.

Having lived in the U.K. and France and traveled extensively around the globe, **Christie Dietz** moved from London to Wiesbaden in 2010 to join her German husband. A food and travel writer, she has since busied herself exploring Riesling country and learned to cook all manner of traditional German dishes. She has written for various online publications and documents her culinary adventures at ⊕ *www.asausagehastwo.com*. For this edition, Christie updated the chapter on her favorite region for food and drink, the Pfalz and Rhine Terrace.

Lee A. Evans left his secluded eastern Washington home on a Congress-Bundestag youth exchange in 1986 and witnessed firsthand the revolutions that swept the Eastern bloc in 1989. Since then, he's had a front-row seat as his favorite city, Berlin, has transformed into one of the cultural epicenters of Europe. He has worked extensively as a travel writer and tour manager. He managed the German Railroad's EuRail Aid office, helping thousands of travelers discover the secrets of Berlin and East Germany. Over the last 20 years, he established himself as one of the best and most sought after guides in

Berlin. He is the President of the Berlin Guide Federation and serves on the board of the Berlin Historical Association. He lives happily with his wife and daughter in a quiet, bucolic Charlottenburg neighborhood and is a closet currywurst aficionado. Visit his website at ⊕ *www.berlinandbeyond.de*. He updated the Franconia and the German Danube; Schleswig-Holstein and the Baltic Coast; Saxony, Saxony-Anhalt, and Thuringia; and Travel Smart chapters this edition.

Evelyn Kanter is a NYC-based travel and automotive journalist who visits Germany often, where she succumbs to what she describes as her "wurst eating habits," prowls car museums, and sees relatives in her parents' hometowns of Munich and Frankfurt. A former on-air consumer reporter for ABC News and CBS News in New York, she now writes for publications including airline in-flights and AAA magazines, and online for Fodors.com. Evelyn also writes two websites—NYC on the Cheap, which is also a smartphone app, and ecoXplorer, about green travel and green cars. She updated the Frankfurt and Heidelberg and the Neckar Valley chapters this edition, and has contributed in the past to Fodor's New York City, Canada, and Bahamas guidebooks.

Jeff Kavanagh is a freelance writer from New Zealand based in Hamburg. Having left his hometown, Dunedin, in the South Island of the country in 1997, he lived in Korea, Japan, and England before settling in Germany in 2002. Since moving to the Hanseatic port city he has developed an enhanced appreciation for German food, wine, sports, and culture. His work has appeared in a number of publications and websites worldwide including Germany's *The Local*, *NZ Adventure Magazine*, and the *Listener* in New Zealand. He updated Hamburg this edition.

Clare Richardson is a journalist based in Berlin, where she works for Germany's international broadcaster Deutsche Welle TV. Previously she was the World Editor of Reuters.com and The Huffington Post in New York City. Samples of her work in video and print, as well as musings on expat life in Berlin, are at ⊕ *www. whereisclare.com.*

Leonie Schaumann once convinced a German boy visiting her native New Zealand to introduce her to his homeland. She's been there ever since, and is now married to him. Based in Munich, she misses the New Zealand seaside, but consoles herself with the excellent food, beer, and storybook scenery of her German backyard: Upper Bavaria. When she's not writing, editing, and translating things for international organizations, she sometimes blogs about her gustatory German adventures at ⊕ *www.eatdrinkgermany. wordpress.com.* Leonie updated the Bodensee chapter for this edition.

Courtney Tenz came to Germany in 2005 as a Fulbright recipient and has lived in Cologne, Germany ever since. She is a culture editor at *Deutsche Welle* and writes frequently about German culture and the arts. For this edition, she toured Bavaria to update the Bavarian Alps and Romantic Road chapters as well as those on the Black Forest and Fairy-Tale Road.

After several years living in South America, Canadian freelance writer Elizabeth Willoughby made Bavaria her home in 2004. Once she adjusted to the little things, like looking out for cyclists before crossing the sidewalk and standing to the right on escalators, Munich's prettiness in both nature and architecture, its German-style efficiency, charming traditions, and small town feel quickly won her over. The quality of life in Munich is unbeatable. She updated the Munich chapter.

BERLIN UPDATERS

Adam Groffman is a travel writer and blogger who has been based in Berlin since 2011. His work has been featured in *Vanity Fair*, *AFAR*, *Condé Nast Traveler*, *DETAILS*, *Pink News*, and many online publications. When he's not out exploring the coolest bars and clubs, he's usually in a museum or gallery. Find more on his blog, ⊕ *travelsofadam.com.*

Giulia Pines spent her first 23 years in New York and is now proud to call Berlin home. She is a writer, photographer, and avid traveler who has contributed to numerous online and print publications both in Germany and internationally, including *Kinfolk*, *Serious Eats*, *Roads & Kingdoms*, *Thrillist*, *The Atlantic CityLab*, NPR Berlin, and *Slow Travel Berlin*. She updated the Where to Eat and Potsdam sections of our Berlin chapter.

Juergen Scheunemann, a native German, has been living in Berlin for almost 30 years. He has published and translated several history and travel books on U.S. and German cities. He has been an editor at Berlin's leading daily, *Der Tagesspiegel*, and an associate producer for the BBC. Today, his award-winning articles are also published travel magazines. He updated the Where to Stay and Getting Here and Around sections of our Berlin chapter.

Yasha Wallin is an award-winning editor and writer based in Berlin. She writes about travel, fashion, and sustainability for *Interview Magazine*, *GOOD*, *Guardian UK*, *A Hotel Life*, and others. She is co-founder of *The Usual*, a seasonal surf publication and creative agency, collaborating with clients as diverse as EDITION Hotels, Patagonia, Metallica, and The Surf Lodge. Visit ⊕ *theusualmontauk.*

com and ⊕ *yashawallin.com* for more. Wallin has lived in Berlin for three years, enjoying the city's plentiful cultural activities, spacious apartments, abundant bike lanes, and killer schnitzel. She updated the Shopping section of our Berlin chapter.